P9-DDY-765

Wadsworth Introductory Psychology Transparencies
(ISBN: 0-534-13013-5)

This set of 95 full-color transparencies from other sources complements the text-specific transparencies available with Kalat's text.

The Wadsworth Film and Video Library for Introductory Psychology
(ISBN: 0-534-48474-3)

Instructors can choose from a variety of programs from Films for the Humanities and Sciences and the Annenberg/CPB Discovering Psychology Series. Also, an exclusive CNN introductory psychology video will be available in early 1999.

Integrator Online™ for Introductory Psychology (Instructor's Edition)
by Arthur J. Kohn and Wendy Kohn (ISBN 0-534-36590-6)

You can deliver your course over the Web quickly and easily. Ideal for use in any teaching and learning situation—from standard lecture to full Internet delivery—Integrator Online is designed for use with this text and is directly linked to the content of each chapter. The instructor's edition of Integrator Online includes CourseWeaver Online™, which allows you to deliver course materials via local lecture, individual computers, or the Internet. Using CourseWeaver Online, you can deliver individual lessons or an entire course with embedded Internet links, interactive activities, study sessions, and simulations. Alternately, students can use the CD-ROM on their own to explore activities, complete homework, or practice for quizzes.

FOR STUDENTS

Integrator Online™ for Introductory Psychology (Student Edition)
by Arthur J. Kohn and Wendy Kohn (ISBN 0-534-35746-6)

For each chapter of this text, students can interact with linked review and testing modules: the Glossary Module, the Study Module, and the Quiz Module (which provides randomized quizzes on any topic). With a click of the mouse, students can call up interactive experiments, animations, homework assignments, video clips, transparencies, audio clips, dynamic images, demonstrations, study pages, and more.

InfoTrac® College Edition

When you adopt this text, your students receive four full months' access to InfoTrac College Edition, a fully searchable online university library with access to full articles from over 600 periodicals. InfoTrac gives your students access to full-length articles from over 700 scholarly and popular periodicals, updated daily, and dating back as much as four years. Your students will be able to print complete articles right from InfoTrac, whenever it's convenient for them. These articles are available to you and your students through this exclusive offer, and include readings from American Journal of Psychology, U.S. News & World Report, and Journal of Social Psychology. Visit: http://www.infotrac-college.com.

PsychNow!™: Interactive Experiences in Psychology CD-ROM
by Joel Morgovsky, Lonnie Yandell, Elizabeth Lynch, and project consultant Dennis Coon
(ISBN: 0-314-07220-9)

This CD-ROM for Macintosh and Windows provides students with a dynamic multimedia experience that goes beyond the boundaries of the classroom to let students explore the concepts of psychology like never before. Stunning graphics and animations, interesting video clips, and interactive exercises bring the theories of psychology to life. With PsychNow!, students can do more than just read about a topic—they can read, watch, listen, and react to it.

(continued inside back cover)

Let me hear from you...

A teacher or textbook writer is like someone who plants seeds and hopes they will grow. I would like to hear from you about the results. Did your interest in psychology blossom and flourish? What did you like best or least? Frequently students, having a fresh approach to the field, suggest excellent new ideas or notice contradictions and problems that even their professors have overlooked.

You may tear out this form, fold it, and mail it.

School: _____ Your instructor's name: _____

1. How did this book affect you? Was it interesting, useful, thought-provoking?

    _____

    _____

    _____

    _____

2. Do you have suggestions for what I should add or change in the next edition? (For example, did you find any particular section difficult or confusing?)

    _____

    _____

    _____

    _____

3. Here is a place for any additional comments:

    _____

    _____

    _____

    _____

Optional:

Your name: _____

Address: _____

Email address: _____

Date: _____

May the publisher quote you in publicity for the text?   _____ yes   _____ no

Thanks!

James W. Kalat

FOLD HERE

NO POSTAGE
NECESSARY
IF MAILED
IN THE
UNITED STATES

BUSINESS REPLY MAIL
FIRST CLASS   PERMIT NO. 358   PACIFIC GROVE, CA

POSTAGE WILL BE PAID BY ADDRESSEE

ATT: *James W. Kalat*

Wadsworth Publishing Company
10 Davis Drive
Belmont, California 94002

FOLD HERE

INTRODUCTION TO
Psychology

INTRODUCTION TO
Psychology

5TH EDITION

JAMES W. KALAT

North Carolina State University

Brooks/Cole · Wadsworth

ITP® An International Thomson Publishing Company

Pacific Grove · Albany · Belmont · Bonn · Boston · Cincinnati · Detroit · Johannesburg · London
Madrid · Melbourne · Mexico City · New York · Paris · Singapore · Tokyo · Toronto · Washington

Sponsoring Editor: *Jim Brace-Thompson, Stacey Purviance*
Project Development Editor: *Penelope Sky*
Editorial Assistants: *Bryon Granmo, Erin Conlon*
Production Coordinator: *Kirk Bomont*
Manuscript Editor: *Jan de Prosse*
Permissions Editor: *The Permissions Group*
Production: *Hespenheide Design*
Typesetting: *GTS Graphics, Inc.*

Interior and Cover Design: *E. Kelly Shoemaker*
Interior Illustration: *Beck Visual Communications, Deborah Cowder, GTS Graphics, Inc., Darwen Hennings, Hespenheide Design, Joel Ito, Carlyn Iverson, Sandra McMahan, Randy Miyake, Jeanne Schreiber, Mark Stearney, Alexander Teshin Associates, John and Judy Waller*
Art Coordinator: *Gary Hespenheide*
Photo Researcher: *Leslie Shapiro*
Printing and Binding: *Von Hoffman Press*

COPYRIGHT © 1999 by Wadsworth Publishing Company
A division of International Thomson Publishing Inc.
I(T)P The ITP logo is a registered trademark under license.

For more information, contact:

WADSWORTH PUBLISHING COMPANY
10 Davis Drive
Belmont, CA 94002
USA

International Thomson Publishing Europe
Berkshire House 168-173
High Holborn
London WC1V 7AA
England

Thomas Nelson Australia
102 Dodds Street
South Melbourne, 3205
Victoria, Australia

Nelson Canada
1120 Birchmount Road
Scarborough, Ontario
Canada M1K 5G4

International Thomson Editores
Seneca 53
Col. Polanco
11560 México, D. F., México

International Thomson Publishing GmbH
Königswinterer Strasse 418
53227 Bonn
Germany

International Thomson Publishing Asia
60 Albert Street
#15-01 Albert Complex
Singapore 189969

International Thomson Publishing Japan
Hirakawacho Kyowa Building, 3F
2-2-1 Hirakawacho
Chiyoda-ku, Tokyo 102
Japan

All rights reserved. No part of this work may be reproduced, stored in a retrieval system, or transcribed, in any form or by any means—electronic, mechanical, photocopying, recording, or otherwise—without the prior written permission of the publisher, Wadsworth Publishing Company, Belmont, California 94002.

Printed in the United States of America

10 9 8 7 6 5 4 3 2 1

Library of Congress Cataloging-in-Publication Data
Kalat, James W.
    Introduction to psychology / James W. Kalat.—5th ed.
      p. cm.
    Includes bibliographical references and indexes.
    ISBN 0-534-35578-1 (alk. paper)
    1. Psychology.   I. Title.
BF121.K26 1999
150—dc21   98-37394
                        CIP

To Sam, Robin, Sheila, Julie, Ann, and David

About the Author

Jim Kalat (rhymes with ballot) has been teaching the introductory psychology course at North Carolina State University since 1977. He received a bachelor's degree *summa cum laude* from Duke University in 1968 and a Ph.D. in psychology from the University of Pennsylvania in 1971. Recipient of Duke's Alumni Outstanding Teacher Award and North Carolina State University's Outstanding Teacher Award, Kalat is a Fellow of the American Association for the Advancement of Science, the American Psychological Association, and the American Psychological Society, for which he was the program committee chair in 1991. The author of the bestselling *Biological Psychology* (sixth edition published by Brooks/Cole in 1998), Kalat has also published many articles in psychological journals.

Brief Contents

Contents

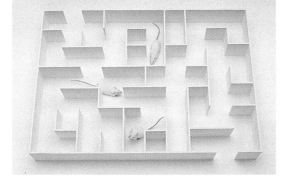

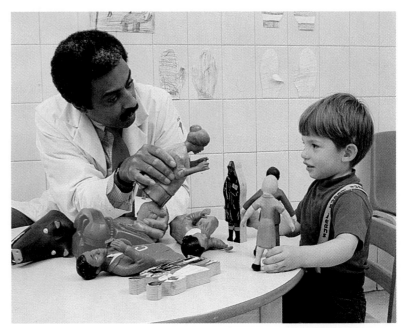

Scientific Methods in Psychology

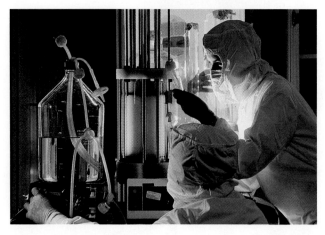

Biological Psychology 3

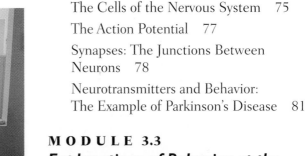

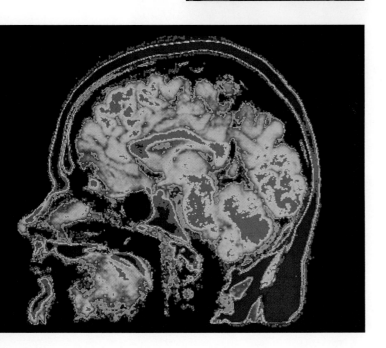

Sensation and Perception 4

Altered States 5

Learning 6

Memory **7**

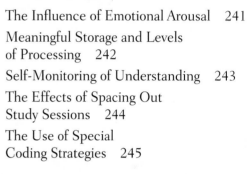

Cognition and Language

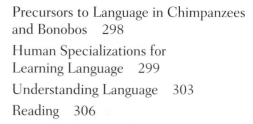

Intelligence and Its Measurement 9

Development 10

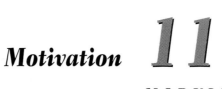

Emotions, Health Psychology, and Stress

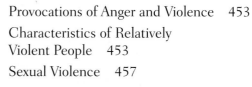

12

Personality 13

Social Psychology 14

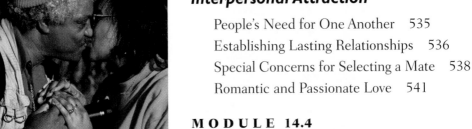

Abnormalities and Therapies I: General Principles 15

Abnormalities and Therapies II: Explorations of Specific Disorders

16

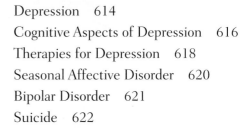

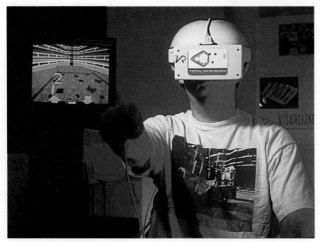

Preface to the Instructor

Teaching psychology means more than just adding to what students know: It should change how they think. It should ensure that something worthwhile remains long after they have forgotten the details.

When students leave my classroom, I certainly want them to know important theories and research. But, more importantly, they should be ready to learn more on their own. They should have the habit of questioning assertions, of asking for evidence and knowing how to evaluate it.

I do not believe that a textbook can instill the habit of questioning assertions merely through boxes labeled "Critical Thinking." I have tried to model that habit throughout the text by interweaving material that challenges students to examine the evidence (or lack of it) behind some common assertions. This textbook can help students ask their own questions, look for more than pat answers, and, ultimately, learn to appreciate the excitement of psychological inquiry.

WHAT'S NEW IN THE FIFTH EDITION

The first and second editions of this text were published by Wadsworth Publishing Company; the third and fourth by Brooks/Cole Publishing Company; this edition is again published by Wadsworth. The changes in publisher reflect reorganizations by the parent organization, International Thomson Publishing.

The fifth edition includes almost 500 new references, most from 1996 to 1998. Every chapter has been reorganized with new material; retained material has been clarified. Many figures and photographs have been revised or replaced. Major changes include the following:

* The definitions of all boldfaced terms appear in text; they are italicized for clarity and easy reference.
* Icons call attention to "Try It Yourself" demonstrations throughout the text that allow students to experience (at least on a small scale) the phenomenon under discussion, and thereby to understand the research better.
* Each module closes with a section titled "The Message," which puts the main themes into a broader context.
* The contents of "Applied Psychology" (the final module in the previous edition) have been integrated into relevant parts of other chapters, especially the introductory chapter and the chapters on cognition, intelligence, and motivation. This reorganization actually increases the emphasis on applied psychology. A module at the end of the book could easily be omitted; including the material in other chapters shows the connections of applied psychology to other topics.
* "What's the Evidence?" sections have been added for insomnia (Chapter 5) and object permanence (Chapter 10), and revised for false memories (Chapter 7) and alcoholism (Chapter 16).
* The emphasis on evaluating evidence and questioning assertions is stronger than ever. For example, in Chapter 7, "Memory," new examples of how people exaggerate and distort old memories are the Indian rope trick and the rumors of a flying saucer crash near Roswell, New Mexico. Chapter 13, "Personality," includes new, highly critical scholarship about Freud, and critiques of handwriting analysis and doll play as projective techniques.
* The order of the last three chapters has been changed. Social psychology has been moved from the 16th to the 14th chapter. Abnormal psychology and therapy, previously the 14th and 15th chapters, are now the 15th and 16th.
* In previous editions, all the psychological disorders were covered before all the therapies. The problem with this structure is that a certain therapy may be used only for a particular disorder; for example, systematic desensitization for phobia and antidepressant drugs and ECT for depression. In this edition, general principles of abnormalities and therapies are surveyed in Chapter 15, and anxiety disorders, substance abuse disorders, mood disorders, and schizophrenia are discussed in Chapter 16. Therapeutic approaches are included in the discussion of the disorders.
* Chapter 11, "Motivation," contains a new module on anger and violent behavior.
* Chapter 13, "Personality," contains a new module about major approaches to the study of personality.
* Chapter 1 includes a new section, "What Are My Prospects If I Major in Psychology?"
* In Chapter 6, "Learning," the third module has been changed from "Social Learning" to "Other Kinds of Learning," and includes social learning, conditioned taste aversions, and birdsong learning.
* In Chapter 8, "Cognition," the section on attention has been revised and expanded to include material about

attentive and preattentive processes that was previously in the chapter on sensation and perception.

* The language module in Chapter 8 is extensively revised, and now covers language development (previously in the developmental chapter), bilingualism, language and the brain, and controversies about language evolution.

* Chapter 10, "Development," contains new material on infant cognition and attachment.

* Chapter 11, "Motivation," includes new material about obesity and the hormone leptin.

* Chapter 14, "Social Psychology," now starts with the module on social perception and cognition, in which the discussion of stereotypes and prejudice is heavily revised. The module on attitudes now includes discussion of rigid, ill-informed attitudes toward the death penalty. The module on attraction is also substantially revised.

* Chapters 15 and 16, "Abnormal Behavior and Therapies," include a new section on criticisms of DSM–IV, an expanded and updated discussion of research on therapy effectiveness, new material on the neurodevelopmental and glutamate hypotheses of schizophrenia, and new discussion of the role of expressed emotion.

TEACHING AND LEARNING SUPPLEMENTS

A number of important supplements accompany the text. Greg and Bridget Robinson-Riegler prepared a very thorough and creative Instructor's Resource Guide (also available electronically) that includes suggestions for class demonstrations and lecture material; it also contains possible answers to the "Something to Think About" questions. The Study Guide, by Ruth and William S. Maki, provides various study aids and practice test items as well as an ESL component by Sally Gearhart. Additional supplements include test items by Leonard W. Hamilton and C. Robin Timmons (also available on disc), videos, an electronic study guide, PsychLab II (interactive software with psychology demonstrations and simulations), and one generic and one book-specific set of transparencies. John Nichols researched and annotated the Web sites.

In addition, you and your students will also have access to the *Kalat Fifth Edition* section of the Psychology Study Center at http://psychstudy.wadsworth.com/. This Web site is a convenient place to communicate with students and other instructors, pick up pedagogical tips, lecture ideas, and other instruction aids, and find pertinent Web resources among annotated lists of Internet links, organized by the subject areas covered in the book. Students can use the *Kalat Fifth Edition* site to test and enhance their understanding of the text through chapter-by-chapter interactive tutorial quizzes and practice tests.

ACKNOWLEDGMENTS

A potential author needs self-confidence bordering on arrogance just to begin the job of writing a textbook and, to complete it, the humility to accept criticism of favorite ideas and carefully written prose. A great many people provided helpful suggestions that made this a far better text than it would have been without them.

In preparing this edition, I was fortunate to work with very skilled and dedicated people. Jim Brace-Thompson, my acquisitions editor until the final stages, provided consistent encouragement, friendship, support, and good advice. Penelope Sky, my developmental editor, was the guiding force behind the illustrations, from identifying what needed to be depicted to selecting photos and revising drawings. Kirk Bomont did an excellent job of supervising the production, a most complicated task with a book such as this. Gary Hespenheide, who managed the art development, and Kelly Shoemaker, who designed the interior and the cover, had the patience and artistic judgment to counterbalance their very nonartistic author. Jan de Prosse, the copyeditor, was skillful, efficient, and very pleasant. Faith Stoddard did a marvelous job of coordinating all the supplementary and ancillary materials. May Clark and Cheryl Besenjak accomplished the nearly impossible task of managing all the permissions requests. Lauren Harp planned and executed the marketing strategies. To each of these, my thanks and congratulations.

My sincere thanks also to the staff of Hespenheide Design, the company that produced the book. Gary Hespenheide did a remarkable job of taking a late manuscript and meeting an early publication date. Leslie Shapiro, the photo researcher, found an amazing variety of photographs.

Art Kohn is the source of a number of creative ideas on how to approach certain topics; he is also a stimulating person to talk to and a good friend. My colleagues at North Carolina State University provided me with encouragement, ideas, and free advice. I thank Larry Upton particularly for his extensive and insightful comments.

I thank the following people for their helpful reviews of all or part of the book: Bob Arkin, Ohio State University; Susan Baillet, University of Portland; Joe Bean, Shorter College; Mark Bodamer, John Carroll University; Gordon Brown, Pasadena City College; James Calhoun, University of Georgia; Bernardo Carducci, Indiana University Southeast; Mark Casteel, Pennsylvania State University, York Campus; Patricia Deldin, Harvard University; Janet Dizinno, St. Mary's University; Gabriel Frommer, Indiana University; Robert Gehring, University of Southern Indiana; Judy Gentry, Columbus State Community College; Joel Grace, Mansfield University; Richard Hanson, Fresno City College; W. Bruce Haslam, Weber State University; James Johnson, Illinois State University; Craig Jones, Arkansas State University; Dale Jorgenson, California State University, Long Beach; Peter Kaplan, University of Colorado, Denver; Cindy J. Lahar, University of Calgary; Cynthia Ann Lease, Virginia Polytechnic Institute and State University; John Lindsay, Georgia College and State University; Mary Livingston, Louisiana Technical University; Sanford Lopater, Christopher Newport University; Michael McCall, Ithaca College; Dianne Mello-Goldner, Pine Manor College; Rowland Miller, Sam Houston State University; Gloria Mitchell, De Anza College; Jeffrey

Nagelbush, Ferris State University; Bethany Neal-Beliveau, Indiana University Purdue University-Indianapolis; Jan Ochman, Inver Hills Community College; David Reitman, Louisiana State University; Thomas Rieg, Winona State University; Jeffrey Rudski, Muhlenberg College; Richard Russell, Santa Monica College; Kim Sawrey, University of North Carolina at Wilmington; Noam Shpancer, Purdue University; James Spencer, West Virginia State College; Douglas Wallen, Mankato State University; Fred Whitford, Montana State University; Don Wilson, Lane Community College; and David Woehr, Texas A & M University.

I also thank the following for their helpful comments and suggestions: G. William Domhoff, University of California, Santa Cruz; Janet Gebelt, University of Portland; Edward Pollak, West Chester University; and Anthony Wagner, Harvard and Stanford Universities. A great many students who read the previous edition sent me letters with helpful comments and suggestions. I especially thank Kenneth Gahagan, N.C. State University; Timothy Gorrill, SUNY Buffalo; and Lisa Solberg, Santa Monica College.

James Kalat

Preface to the Student

Welcome to introductory psychology! I hope you will enjoy reading this text as much as I enjoyed writing it. When you finish, I hope you will write your comments on the comments page, cut the page out, and mail it to the publisher, who will pass it along to me. Please include a return address.

The first time I taught introductory psychology, several students complained that the book we were using was interesting to read but impossible to study. What they meant was that they had trouble finding and remembering the main points. I have made this book easy to study in many ways. I have tried to select interesting material and to present it as clearly as possible.

I have also included some special features to help you study. Each chapter begins with an outline and a brief introduction to the main topic and is divided into two or more major sections, or modules. Each module begins with one or more questions—the fundamental questions that psychologists are trying to answer, the questions that motivate research. In some cases you will be able to answer the questions after you read the section; but in some cases psychologists themselves are not sure about the answers. At least you will come to understand the questions better. At the end of each module is a summary of some important points, with page references. If a point is unfamiliar you should reread the appropriate section.

Throughout the text certain words are highlighted in **boldface.** These are important terms whose meaning you should understand. Their definitions are in *italics.* All the boldface terms reappear with their definitions at the end of the chapter and in the Glossary/Subject Index at the end of the book. You might want to find the Glossary/Subject Index right now and familiarize yourself with it. Note that for each term there is both a definition and a page reference. Note also the Theme Index, which directs you to places in the text where general issues are discussed, such as the influences of gender and culture on behavior.

I sometimes meet students who think they have mastered the course because they have memorized all the definitions. They are making a mistake. You do need to understand the defined words, so that you can understand discussions that use them. You should be able to recognize what is an example of the term and what is not. But don't waste time memorizing definitions word for word.

At various points in the text are "Concept Checks," questions that do not ask you simply to repeat what you have read, but to use or apply the information in some way. Try to answer each of these questions, and then turn to the indicated page to check your answer. If your answer is incorrect, you probably have not been reading carefully enough, and you might want to reread the section that the Concept Check refers to.

You will also find an occasional text passage marked "Something to Think About." Here you are required to go beyond what is discussed in the text. In some cases there may be a number of reasonable ways to approach the question. I hope you will think about these questions, perhaps talk about them with fellow students, and maybe ask your instructor what he or she thinks.

Now I'll answer a few of the questions often asked by students.

Do you have any useful suggestions for improving study habits? Whenever students ask me why they did badly on the last test, I ask, "When did you read the assignment?" Some answer, "Well, I didn't exactly read *all* of the assignment," or "I read it the night before the test." To learn the material well, read each assignment *before the lecture.* Within 24 hours after the lecture, review your lecture notes. Then, before you take the test, reread both the textbook assignment and your lecture notes. If you do not have time to reread everything, at least skim the text and reread the material you need to refresh in your memory. As a rule, if you are not satisfied with your test scores you need to spend more time studying, and the best way to study is to spread it out over several days.

Some students, however, spend enough time studying without spending that time effectively. If you read the material but don't remember it, perhaps you are not thinking about what you're reading. As you read this book, try to think actively about what you are learning. One way to improve your studying is to read by the SPAR method: **S**urvey, **P**rocess meaningfully, **A**sk questions, **R**eview.

Survey: Know what to expect so that you can focus on the main points. When you start a chapter, first look over the outline to get a preview of the contents. When you start a new module, turn to the end and read the summary.

Process meaningfully: Read the chapter carefully, stopping to think from time to time. Tell your roommate some of the interesting things you learn. Think about how you might apply a certain concept to a real-life situation. Pause when you come to the Concept Checks and try to answer them. Good readers read quickly through unimportant or familiar material, but slowly through difficult or unfamiliar material.

Ask questions: When you finish the chapter, try to anticipate what you might be asked later. You can use questions in the Study Guide or compose your own. Write out the questions and think about them, but do not answer them yet.

Review: Pause for a while—at least several hours or, better yet, a day or more. If you first read a chapter before class, come back to it the evening after class. Now write the answers to the questions you prepared earlier. Check your answers against the text or against the answers in the Study Guide. Reinforcing your memory a day or two after you first read the chapter will help you retain the material longer and with deeper understanding. If you study the same material several times at lengthy intervals, you increase your chance of remembering it long after the course is over.

Is it worthwhile to buy and use the Study Guide? The Study Guide is designed to help students who would like help studying, remembering the material, or answering multiple-choice questions. It is most likely to be helpful to freshmen and to students who have had trouble with similar courses in the past. The multiple-choice questions include not only the correct answers but also explanations of why they are correct. You can work through each chapter of the Study Guide in one or two hours. The Study Guide can help if you are willing to spend enough time with it in addition to reading the text.

Does it help to underline or highlight key sentences while reading? Maybe, but don't overdo it. I have seen books in which students underlined or highlighted more than half the sentences. What good that does, I have no idea.

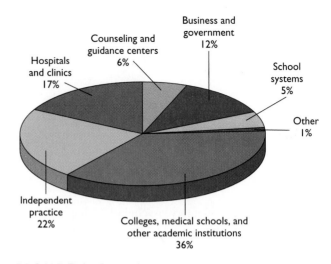

FIGURE I   Pie graph

What do those parentheses mean, as in "(Maki & Serra, 1992)"? Am I supposed to remember the names and dates? Psychologists generally cite references not in footnotes but in parentheses. "(Maki & Serra, 1992)" refers to an article written by Maki and Serra, published in 1992. All the references cited in the text are listed in alphabetical order (by the author's last name) in the References section at the back of the book.

You will also notice a few citations that include two dates separated by a slash, such as "(Wundt, 1862/1961)." This means that Wundt's document was originally published in 1862 and was republished in 1961.

No one expects you to memorize the parenthetical source citations. They are provided so you can look up the source of a statement and check for further information. A few names *are* worth remembering, however. For instance, you will read about the research and theories of such famous psychologists as B. F. Skinner, Jean Piaget, and Sigmund Freud. You should certainly remember those names and a

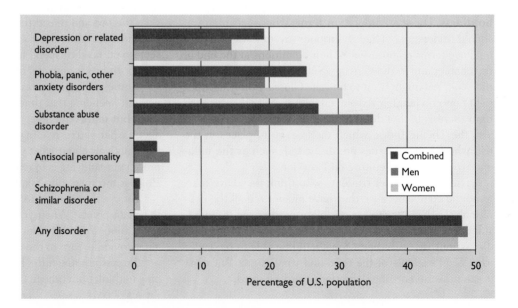

FIGURE 2   Bar graph

few others. But names that are important to remember are emphasized in the discussion, not enclosed in parentheses.

Can you help me read and understand graphs? The graphs in this book are easy to follow. Just take a minute or so to study them carefully. You will encounter four kinds: pie graphs, bar graphs, line graphs, and scatter plots. Let's look at each kind.

Pie graphs show how a whole is divided into parts. Figure 1 shows that more than one-third of all psychologists take a starting job with a college or some other educational institution. Another one-fifth to one-fourth of psychologists work in independent practice. The total circle represents 100% of all psychologists.

Bar graphs show how often events fall into one category or another. Figure 2 shows how many adults in the United States suffer from certain psychological disorders. The length of the bars indicates the frequency of particular disorders.

Line graphs show how one variable is related to another variable. In Figure 3, you see that 80% of people correctly remembered a set of letters—such as HOZDF—after a 3-second delay. As the delay time increased, the percentage of people remembering the letters declined sharply.

Scatter plots are similar to line graphs, with this difference: A line graph shows averages, whereas a scatter plot shows individual data points. By looking at a scatter plot, we can see how much variation occurs among individuals.

To prepare a scatter plot, we make two observations about each individual. In Figure 4, each student is represented by one point. If you take that point and scan down to the *x*-axis, you find that student's SAT score. If you then scan across to the *y*-axis, you find that student's grade average for the freshman year. A scatter plot shows whether two variables are closely or only loosely related.

We may have to take multiple-choice tests on this material. How can I do better on those tests?

1. Read each choice carefully. Do not choose the first answer that looks correct; first make sure that the other

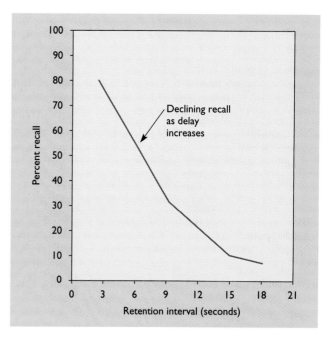

FIGURE 3   Line graph

answers are wrong. If two answers seem reasonable, decide which of the two is better.

2. If you don't know the correct answer, make an educated guess. Start by eliminating any answer that you know cannot be right. An answer that includes absolute words such as *always* or *never* is probably wrong. Also eliminate any answer that includes unfamiliar terms. (Correct choices use only terms that you should know; incorrect choices may include obscure terms or even outright nonsense.)

3. After you finish a test, go back and check your answers and rethink them. You have probably heard the advice, "Don't change your answers; stick with your first impulse." No matter how often you have heard that advice, it is wrong. J. J. Johnston (1975) tested it by looking through the answer sheets of a number of classes that had taken a multiple-choice test. He found that of all the

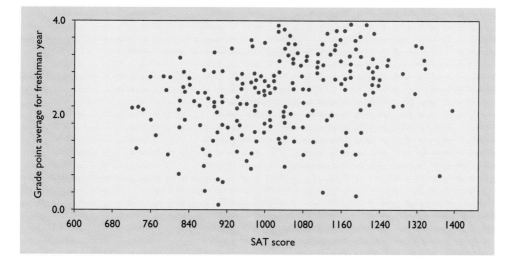

FIGURE 4   Scatter plot

students who changed one or more answers, 71 students improved their scores by doing so and only 31 lowered their scores. Similar results have been reported in a number of other studies. I do not mean that you should make changes just for the sake of making changes. But there are many reasons why your reconsidered answer might be better than the first. Sometimes when you read the questions that appear later in a test, one of them may remind you of something that helps you correct an earlier answer. Sometimes you reread a question and realize that you misunderstood it the first time.

Why, then, do so many students (and professors) believe that it is a mistake to change an answer? Think of what happens when you get a test paper back. When you look it over, which items do you examine most carefully? The ones you got wrong, of course. You may notice three items that you originally answered correctly and then changed. You never notice the five other items you changed from incorrect to correct.

If you want to practice your multiple-choice skills, you can try your hand at the interactive tutorial quizzes available at the *Kalat Fifth Edition* Web site (http://psychstudy.wadsworth.com/). These quizzes go hand-in-hand with the material in this book, with one quiz per chapter. Each quiz is designed to help you find out whether you understand a chapter's main points; if you answer a question incorrectly, you get immediate feedback guiding you to a better understanding of the topic. The *Kalat Fifth Edition* site also includes practice tests, discussion boards where you can exchange ideas with instructors and other students, and Internet links where you can go to learn more about the topics in the book.

James Kalat

A Guide Through the Book

A NOTE FROM THE PUBLISHER

The scientific method is the most powerful tool in the psychologist's and, indeed, the student's intellectual armory. In this book, students learn that questioning assertions, challenging evidence, and evaluating results—all components of the scientific method—are second nature to the study of psychology itself. Jim Kalat introduces students to psychology in a way that will remain with them long after they may have forgotten specific theories, experiments, and results.

The material that follows demonstrates how Kalat encourages students to experience for themselves the excitement of psychological discovery and how he uses the scientific method throughout the book. His carefully integrated learning tools clarify important theories and research.

Kalat's remarkable skill in getting students involved in using the scientific method to question assertions is what distinguishes *Introduction to Psychology, Fifth Edition*. Most books present the research and facts and expect students to memorize what's been discovered. Kalat encourages students to open the doors to further exploration: He helps them become more intelligent consumers of psychological research.

A BOOK STUDENTS TRULY LOVE

Throughout the text, Jim Kalat does more than tell students what they ought to know—he engages their desire to learn. He speaks directly to his readers, drawing them into psychological concepts and information in a way that actually changes the way they look at assertions and facts. Kalat's engaging writing style includes humor and personal anecdotes, and helps make the Fifth Edition an exceptional learning tool that your students will truly enjoy using.

AN INTRODUCTION TO THE POWER OF QUESTIONING ASSERTIONS

Chapter 2 is the most important chapter in the book. It not only deals with the procedures for conducting research but also provides a conceptual guide to how psychologists evaluate evidence and theories and, in general, to how they think. For example, Kalat highlights the importance of replicability, the criterion of falsifiability, and the principle of parsimony.

Early in Chapter 2, Kalat presents an overview of the research process. He introduces the *four steps* in gathering and evaluating evidence—**1** Hypothesis, **2** Method, **3** Results, and **4** Interpretation. This critical material—the heart of the scientific method—is then reinforced throughout the text.

---

30   Chapter 2   Scientific Methods in Psychology

watch one set of programs and another group to watch a different set of programs, and then record behavioral differences between the groups.

3 *Results*   Fundamental to any research is good measurement, and a phenomenon such as "violent behavior" can be especially tricky to measure. (How do we decide what is *real* violence and what is just playfulness? Do threats count? verbal abuse?) It is important for an investigator to adopt clear rules for making measurements and then use these rules consistently. Depending on the nature of the study, the investigator calculates appropriate statistics for expressing the results and evaluating whether these probably indicate a meaningful trend or just a random fluctuation.

4 *Interpretation*   The final task is to determine the significance of the results. If the results clearly contradict the hypothesis, researchers should either abandon or modify the original hypothesis. (Maybe it applies only to certain kinds of people or only under certain circumstances.) If the results *match* the prediction, investigators may gain confidence in their hypothesis but they should not necessarily accept it. Even though the results fit the hypothesis, they might also fit other hypotheses or explanations as well. Because almost any study has limitations, the ultimate conclusion can come only from a pattern of results derived from many studies.

Replicability

Years ago, investigators trained rats to respond in a certain way, then ground up the rats' brains, injected an extract of the trained rats' brains into other rats, and reported that the new rats remembered what the old rats had learned (Babich, Jacobson, Bubash, & Jacobson, 1965). Many other experimenters tried to replicate this surprising result. A few reported results somewhat similar to those of the first experimenters, but most investigators could not (Gaito, 1976; L. T. Smith, 1975). That is, these results were not replicable. **Replicable results** are *those that anyone can obtain, at least approximately, by following the same procedures.*

What should we do when results are not replicable? First, we determine whether the different investigators really used the same procedures. Sometimes, what appears to be a minor change in procedure yields a major difference in results. Did the researchers use different kinds of rats, or different methods of training, or different ways of extracting brain chemicals? In the research on transfer of training by brain extracts, psychologists found no consistent relationship between the results and any aspect of the procedure. In fact, most laboratories found no evidence that the brain extracts had any influence on other rats under any conditions. So, then what? The rule is that, if researchers cannot find conditions under which they dependably get a particular result, then they do not accept that result. This rule may

seem unduly har[...]
If scientists can[...]
claiming to have[...]

Sometimes, [...] ample, many stud[...] behavior in men a[...] men are substan[...] men to be slightly[...] difference or a di[...] this variation, we [...] sive behavior to b[...] is that the sex dif[...] many other influ[...] bine the results o[...] measure of the s[...] *bines the results [...] though they were all one very large study.* For example, one meta-analysis found that men are indeed more likely than women to engage in unprovoked violence (Bettencourt & Miller, 1996). In most cases, a meta-analysis will also determine which variations in procedure are associated with the largest effects.

Criteria for Evaluating Scientific Theories

Up to now, I have alluded to research in psychology without using much detail. We shall consider the details of research methods later. Here, let's look at the big picture: After investigators collect mounds of evidence, what do they do with it?

One goal of scientific research is to establish **theories**, *comprehensive explanations of observable events*. A good theory predicts many observations in terms of a few assumptions and thus reduces the amount of information we must keep available for reference. For example, according to the *law of effect* (to be discussed in Chapter 6), if a human or any other animal makes a response that is consistently followed by a reinforcer (such as food to a hungry person or water to a thirsty one), then the future probability of that response will increase. This law summarizes results achieved for many species, many responses, and many reinforcers.

When we are confronted with several competing theories, we must evaluate them to decide which is the most acceptable (Figure 2.2). To illustrate, let's consider some unsatisfactory theories. First, consider what is wrong with this theory: "Karl is stingy, so he must have had a fixation in the anal period of psychosocial development." The theory fits the data (Karl is stingy), but we already knew those data before the theorist said anything. No one had any other reason to believe that Karl had an anal fixation, except that he became stingy. So the theory does not really make any predictions. One important criterion for any theory is that it *should predict new observations*. If it accurately predicts ob-

---

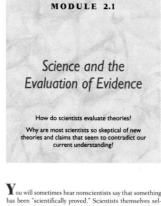

MODULE 2.1

Science and the Evaluation of Evidence

How do scientists evaluate theories?

Why are most scientists so skeptical of new theories and claims that seem to contradict our current understanding?

You will sometimes hear nonscientists say that something has been "scientifically proved." Scientists themselves seldom use the word *proved*, except when they are talking about a mathematical proof. As scientists collect more and better evidence, they may become confident about a given conclusion, but the word *prove* sounds a little too final.

One distinguishing characteristic of science is that scientists generally agree on how to evaluate competing theories. Even when they disagree about which theory is best, they can usually agree on what kinds of evidence they will accept. Most psychologists are quick to concede that our knowledge of psychology is less complete and less systematic than our knowledge of physics, chemistry, and biology. But like physicists, chemists, and biologists, psychologists do generally agree on what constitutes good evidence and what does not. They try to rely on the best available evidence and draw no conclusion at all if the evidence is weak.

SOMETHING TO THINK ABOUT

If people interested in ethics agreed with one another about how to evaluate theories, could they make progress comparable to that of scientists? Could theologians? ✷

Steps for Gathering and Evaluating Evidence

Above all, scientists want to know the evidence behind a given claim. In psychology, as in other fields, students should learn to question assertions, to ask for the evidence behind a given claim.

The word *science* derives from a Latin word meaning *knowledge*, and there are many routes to scientific knowledge. The simplest is just careful observation, and much of science consists of recording observations. We also gain scientific knowledge by testing **hypotheses**, which are *testable predictions of what will happen under certain conditions*. Research designed to test hypotheses goes through the series of steps described in the following four paragraphs (see also Figure 2.1). Articles in scientific publications generally follow this sequence, too. In each of the following chapters of this book, you will find an example of a psychological study, described in a section entitled "What's the Evidence?"

1 **Hypothesis**   A hypothesis can be based on a larger theory. For example, "if our understanding of social influence is correct, then children who watch a great deal of violence will themselves become more violent." In other cases, the hypothesis is the product of preliminary observations. For example, a psychologist might notice that several children who have outbursts of violent behavior have a habit of watching violent television programs and therefore suggest the hypothesis that watching violent programs leads to violent behavior.

2 **Method**   Researchers have many methods for testing hypotheses. To test the effects of violent television shows, one possibility would be to measure how much time various children watch violence on television and relate that amount to a measure of their violent behavior. However, even if the correlation appeared strong, the results would not demonstrate cause and effect. (Maybe watching violence provokes violence, but it is also possible that children who are predisposed to violence like to watch it on TV.) Another approach would be to ask one group of children to

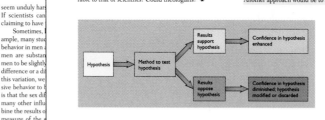

FIGURE 2.1 A hypothesis leads to predictions. An experimental method tests those predictions; a confirmation of a prediction supports the hypothesis; a disconfirmation indicates a need to revise or discard the hypothesis. Conclusions remain tentative, especially after only one experiment. Most scientists avoid saying that their results "prove" a conclusion.

29

WHAT'S THE EVIDENCE?

Appearing in each chapter from Chapter 2 on, each *What's the Evidence?* section presents an interesting problem and then examines one or more experiments in some detail. The format reinforces the steps of the scientific method, until it becomes part of the way students think.

These sections illustrate how scientific research is set into motion by posing a question. Then, using the scientific method of Hypothesis–Method–Results–Interpretation, Kalat walks students through one or two studies that explore the question. Where appropriate, he points out limitations in the research, ethical considerations in the methods, and alternative interpretations of the results so that students have a model of how psychologists evaluate evidence.

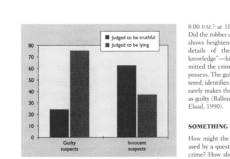

FIGURE 12.8 Polygraph examiners correctly identified 76% of guilty suspects as lying. However, they also identified 37% of innocent suspects as lying. (Based on data of Kleinmuntz & Szucko, 1984.)

free than to convict innocent people, these polygraph results are disturbing.

* * *

The results of this study are typical of similar research; in fact, this study may have even underestimated the tendency of polygraph administrators to call innocent people liars. In some studies, polygraph administrators have called half or more of the innocent people liars (Forman & Mc-Cauley, 1986; Horvath, 1977; Patrick & Iacono, 1989).

Imagine the consequences: Suppose we give polygraph tests to ten suspects, one of whom is guilty. The test would have about a 76% chance of identifying the guilty person as lying, but it would also identify several of the innocent people as liars. Or imagine giving a polygraph to all the people who work for a company, asking whether they have ever stolen from the company. Even if every employee is loyal and innocent, the test may identify almost half of them as liars. Because of the low accuracy of polygraph tests, the U.S. Congress passed a law in 1988 prohibiting private employers from giving polygraph tests to employees or job applicants, except under special circumstances (Camara, 1988). Polygraph results are only rarely admissible as evidence in a court of law.

An Alternative: The Guilty-Knowledge Test

The **guilty-knowledge test,** *a modified version of the polygraph test,* produces more accurate results by *asking questions that should be threatening only to someone who knows the facts of a crime that have not been publicized* (Lykken, 1979). Instead of asking, "Did you rob the gas station?" the interrogator asks, "Was the gas station robbed at

---

440 Chapter 12 Emotions, Health Psychology, and Stress

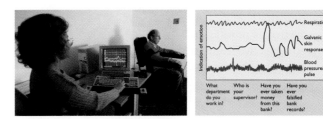

FIGURE 12.7 The polygraph, a method for detecting nervous arousal, is the basis for the so-called lie detector test. The polygraph operator asks a series of nonthreatening questions to establish baseline readings of the subject's autonomic responses, then asks questions relevant to an investigation. The underlying assumption is that an increase in arousal indicates nervousness, which in turn indicates lying. Unfortunately, a large percentage of innocent people also become nervous and therefore appear to be lying.

WHAT'S THE EVIDENCE?
The Effectiveness of a Polygraph in Detecting Lies

Hypothesis Polygraph administrators will identify guilty suspects as liars more often than they identify innocent suspects as liars.

Method To test this hypothesis, the investigators need a sample of people who are known to be guilty and another sample who are known to be innocent but who are otherwise similar to the guilty people. In one study, the investigators selected 50 criminal cases where two suspects had taken a polygraph test, and one suspect had later confessed to the crime (Kleinmuntz & Szucko, 1984). Thus, the investigators knew which 50 suspects were guilty, and they knew that the 50 innocent people were similar enough to have been plausible suspects. It is important to note that all suspects had denied their guilt at the time of the polygraph test.

During the administration of the polygraph, suspects were asked two kinds of questions: *Relevant* questions pertained to the crime itself; for example, "Did you steal $125 from the convenience store last Tuesday?" *Control* questions took the following form: "Have you ever taken anything of value that was not yours?" Theoretically, someone who robbed the convenience store should be more nervous about the first question; anyone else should be, if anything, more nervous about the second.

Six professional polygraph administrators examined all the polygraph results and judged which suspects were lying and which were telling the truth.

Results Figure 12.8 shows the results. The polygraph administrators did manage to identify 76% of the guilty suspects as liars; however, they also classified 37% of the innocent suspects as liars.

Interpretation Recall from the discussion of signal detection in Chapter 4 that, when a person is trying to determine whether something is present or absent, there are two possible correct decisions (green in the following diagram) and two possible errors (red).

	Stimulus actually present	Stimulus actually absent
Report stimulus present	Hit	False alarm
Report stimulus absent	Miss	Correct rejection

Polygraph administrators can also make two kinds of correct decisions and two kinds of errors:

	Actually lying	Actually telling truth
Polygraph says lying	Hit	False alarm
Polygraph says telling the truth	Miss	Correct rejection

A polygraph user obtains more "hits" than most people do on their own. However, most of the errors made by polygraph users are "false alarms" (also known as "false positives")—falsely identifying innocent people as lying. Given the usual belief that we would prefer to let guilty people go

---

8:00 P.M.? at 10:[...]
Did the robber c[...]
shows heightened[...]
details of the [...]
knowledge"—kn[...]
mitted the crime[...]
possess. The guil[...]
tered, identifies a[...]
rarely makes the [...]
as guilty (Ballou[...]
Elaad, 1990).

SOMETHING T[...]

How might the r[...]
ased by a questio[...]
crime? How should the test be administered to minimize
that bias? ✷

Pencil-and-Paper Integrity Tests

Suppose you are an employer who wants to know whether someone applying for a job at your company is likely to be an honest worker. Giving a polygraph test is illegal and would not be very accurate anyway, and you can't give a guilty-knowledge test, because no one can have guilty knowledge about a crime that has not yet occurred. So what do you do?

One approach is to administer pencil-and-paper "integrity tests" that ask such questions as these:

• Have you ever stolen money or property from a previous employer?
• Do you think that most employees occasionally steal from their employers?
• On previous jobs, have you ever left work early while claiming to work a full day?
• Have you sometimes come to work while under the influence of illegal drugs?
• If you were sure you wouldn't get caught, would you ever make personal long-distance phone calls and charge them to your employer?

You might imagine that anyone who has a history of dishonest dealings with previous employers would lie about it. Amazingly, many people fill out the questionnaire honestly, admitting a long history of past dishonesty. (Perhaps they assume the new employer will find out about this history anyway by checking with previous employers.) Research on such tests is limited, but it suggests that these tests manage to identify a good percentage of dishonest people (Camara & Schneider, 1994).

However, the integrity tests have two major problems: First, they misidentify some extremely ethical and scrupulous people who "confess" to being imperfect (Lilienfeld, Alliger, & Mitchell, 1995). For example, someone may read the question, "Have you ever stolen property from a previous employer?" and think, "Well, there was that one time

TRY IT YOURSELF

New to the Fifth Edition are unique *Try It Yourself* activities that appear in each chapter. These activities provide students with fun, interesting, active learning experiences that they can try themselves.

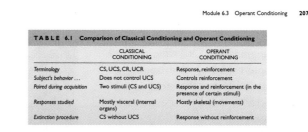

TABLE 6.1	Comparison of Classical Conditioning and Operant Conditioning	
	CLASSICAL CONDITIONING	OPERANT CONDITIONING
Terminology	CS, UCS, CR, UCR	Response, reinforcement
Subject's behavior . . .	Does not control UCS	Controls reinforcement
Paired during acquisition	Two stimuli (CS and UCS)	Response and reinforcement (in the presence of certain stimuli)
Responses studied	Mostly visceral (internal organs)	Mostly skeletal (movements)
Extinction procedure	CS without UCS	Response without reinforcement

You will recall the phenomena of stimulus generalization and discrimination in classical conditioning. Similar phenomena occur in operant conditioning. An individual who receives reinforcement for a particular response to a certain stimulus will probably make the same response to a similar stimulus. *The more similar a new stimulus is to the original reinforced stimulus, the more strongly the subject is likely to respond.* This phenomenon is known as **stimulus generalization.** For example, you might reach for the turn signal in a rented car in the same place where you would find it in your own car.

An individual who is *reinforced for responding to one stimulus and not for responding to another stimulus* will come to **discriminate** between them and *will respond more vigorously to one than to the other.* For example, you walk toward a parked car that you think is yours but then you realize it is not. After several such experiences, you learn to identify your own car from a distance.

A *stimulus that indicates which response is appropriate or inappropriate* is called a **discriminative stimulus.** A great deal of our behavior is governed by discriminative stimuli. For example, your professor standing at the front of the class is a discriminative stimulus to stop talking and get ready to take notes. When class is about over, the hands on the clock provide a discriminative stimulus to get ready to leave the room. A scowl on your roommate's face is a discriminative stimulus for you to keep quiet. Road signs provide discriminative stimuli to tell you when to speed up, slow down, or change lanes. Throughout your day, one stimulus after another signals which behaviors are likely to be reinforced and which ones are not.

Why Are Certain Responses Learned More Easily Than Others?

Thorndike's cats quickly learned to push and pull various devices in their efforts to escape from his puzzle boxes. But when Thorndike tried to teach them to scratch or lick themselves to receive the same reinforcement, they learned slowly and performed inconsistently. Why?

One possible reason is **belongingness,** the *concept that certain stimuli "belong" together or that a given response is more readily associated with certain outcomes*

than with others. Belongingness is an idea that Thorndike himself suggested, although psychologists neglected it for decades, preferring to believe that animals could just as easily associate almost any stimulus with any response. Eventually, psychologists revived the concept of belongingness, also sometimes known as "preparedness" (Seligman, 1970). For example, dogs can readily learn that a sound coming from one location means "raise your left leg," and a sound coming from another location means "raise your right leg." But it takes them virtually forever to learn that a ticking metronome means raise the left leg and a buzzer means raise the right leg (Dobrzecka, Szwejkowska, & Konorski, 1966). (See Figure 6.14.)

Presumably, Thorndike's cats were slow to associate scratching themselves with escaping from a box because the two activities do not "belong" together. (Cats evolved the ability to learn "what leads to what" in the real world, and scratching oneself is very unlikely to open doors in the real world.) But there is another possible explanation for why cats have trouble learning to scratch themselves for reinforcement: Perhaps a cat will scratch itself only when it itches (Charlton, 1983). Consider what would happen if you knew that you could win a large prize if you finished first in a rapid swallowing contest. (Why not? People compete at everything else.) You quickly swallow once, twice, maybe three times, but each successive swallow gets harder and harder. (Go ahead and try it.) Some behaviors are just not easy to produce in large quantities.

TRY IT YOURSELF

B. F. Skinner and the Shaping of Responses

The most influential radical behaviorist, B. F. Skinner (1904–1990), demonstrated many uses of operant conditioning. Skinner was an ardent practitioner of parsimony, always seeking simple explanations in terms of reinforcement histories rather than more complex explanations in terms of mental states.

One problem confronting any student of behavior is how to define a response. For example, imagine watching a group of children and trying to count "aggressive behaviors."

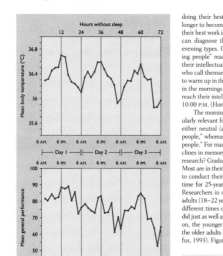

FIGURE 5.2 Cumulative effects of 3 nights without sleep: Both body temperature and logical reasoning decrease each night and increase the next morning. They also deteriorate from one day to the next. (From Babkoff, Caspy, Mikulincer, & Sing, 1991.)

second and third nights, temperature and reasoning decreased more than they had the first night, but they again improved the following morning (Figure 5.2). Thus, sleep deprivation produces a pattern of progressive deterioration that is superimposed on the normal circadian cycle of rising and falling body temperature and alertness (Babkoff, Caspy, Mikulincer, & Sing, 1991). In short, sleepiness apparently depends partly on how long one has gone without sleep and partly on the time of day (that is, where one is within the circadian rhythm).

Morning People and Evening People

Our circadian rhythms do not affect us all in exactly the same way. "Morning people" awaken early and full of energy,

doing their best [...] longer to become [...] their best work in [...] can diagnose th[...] evening types. O[...] ing people" reac[...] their intellectual [...] who call themsel[...] to warm up in [...] in the mornings [...] reach their intell[...] 10:00 P.M. (Hor[...]

The morning[...] ularly relevant fo[...] either neutral (a[...] people," whereas [...] people." For many years, researchers reported substantial declines in memory with older people. But who did most of this research? Graduate students. How old are graduate students? Most are in their 20s. What time do graduate students choose to conduct their research? Late afternoon or evening, a fine time for 25-year-olds but a miserable time for 65-year-olds. Researchers in one study compared the memories of young adults (18–22 years old) and older adults (66–78 years old) at different times of day. Early in the morning, the older adults did just as well as the younger ones. However, as the day went on, the younger adults either remained steady or improved; the older adults deteriorated steadily (May, Hasher, & Stoltzfus, 1993). Figure 5.3 shows the results of this study.

SOMETHING TO THINK ABOUT

Are most college classes offered in the early morning or late afternoon? Is that because *you* want to take them at that time, or because your aging professors want to schedule them then? ✳

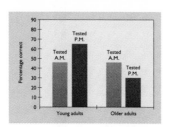

FIGURE 5.3 If tested early in the morning, older people perform as well as younger people on memory tasks. As the day progresses, young people improve and older people deteriorate.

SOMETHING TO THINK ABOUT

Something to Think About questions, found throughout the text, raise provocative issues relevant to the preceding material, and often ask students to use the scientific method as a means of exploring the issues in new and different ways.

These brief segments can be used to trigger class discussion. Many are designed to extend psychology beyond the classroom to real life.

CONCEPT CHECKS

Almost 200 *Concept Checks*, strategically placed at the ends of sections, get students to think about, manipulate, and apply the preceding material rather than just repeat what they read. Students go beyond remembering facts to understanding main ideas.

To further enhance continuity and clarity, these checks are presented within the main text, not set off in boxes. Answers are given at the end of each module.

Module 3.3   Explanations of Behavior at the Level of the Nervous System   **95**

no fear or anxiety (LaBar, LeDoux, Spencer, & Phelps, 1995). Most people remember emotionally distressing events better than neutral events, but those with damage to the amygdala do not, presumably because they do not feel the emotional distress (Cahill, Babinsky, Markowitsch, & McGaugh, 1995). These people can neither recognize facial expressions of fear in others nor imagine what a frightened face would look like (Adolphs, Tranel, Damasio, & Damasio, 1994).

The **frontal lobe**, *at the anterior (forward) pole of the brain*, includes the **primary motor cortex** (Figure 3.38), *a structure that is important for the control of fine movements*, such as moving one finger at a time. As with the primary somatosensory cortex, each area of the primary motor cortex controls a different part of the body, and larger areas are devoted to precise movements of the tongue and fingers than to, say, the shoulder and elbow muscles. The *anterior sections of the frontal lobe*, called the **prefrontal cortex**, contribute to the organization and planning of movements and to certain aspects of memory. Indeed, planning a movement depends on memory. Recall, for example, the delayed response task (page 92): The individual must remember a signal during a delay and then make the appropriate movement.

Certain areas in the left frontal lobe are essential for human language production. People with extensive damage to the left frontal lobe have trouble speaking, writing, or gesturing in sign language (Bellugi, Poizner, & Klima, 1983; Geschwind, 1970). What they say still makes sense, although they generally omit prepositions, conjunctions, and word endings.

How do we know that these brain areas have the functions that I have described? For many years, nearly all the evidence came from observations of brain damage. Researchers can now supplement such evidence with modern techniques that measure activity in an unanesthetized brain (see Figure 3.39). For example, **functional magnetic resonance imaging (fMRI)** *uses magnetic detectors outside the head to measure the amounts of hemoglobin, with and without oxygen, in different parts of the brain* (Cohen, Noll, & Schneider, 1993). Brain areas that are highly active use much oxygen and therefore decrease the amount of oxygen bound to hemoglobin in the blood. The fMRI technique therefore provides a way of inferring which brain areas are currently more active than others. Figure 3.40 gives an example of an fMRI scan.

CONCEPT CHECK

12. The following five people are known to have suffered damage to the cerebral cortex. From their behavioral symptoms, determine the probable location of the damage for each person: (a) impaired perception of the left half of the body and a tendency to ignore the left half of the body and the left half of the world; (b) impaired hearing and some changes in emotional experience; (c) inability to make fine movements with the right hand; (d) loss of vision in the left visual field; and (e) poor performance on a delayed response task, indicating difficulty remembering what has just happened. (Check your answers on page 101.)

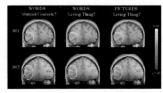

FIGURE 3.40 This brain scan was made with functional magnetic resonance imaging (fMRI). Participants looked at words or pictures and judged whether each item was abstract or concrete, living or nonliving. Yellow shows the areas most activated by this judgment; red shows areas less strongly activated. (From Wagner, Desmond, Demb, Glover, & Gabrieli, 1997. Photo courtesy of Anthony D. Wagner.)

FIGURE 3.39 Devices such as this computerized axial tomography (CAT) scanner produce detailed views of a living human brain.

---

98   Chapter 3   Biological Psychology

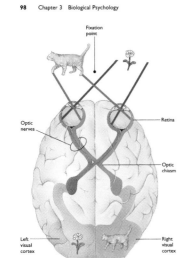

FIGURE 3.42 In the human visual system (viewed here from above), light from either half of the world crosses through the pupils to strike the opposite side of each retina. Axons from the left half of each retina travel to the left hemisphere of the brain; axons from the right half of each retina travel to the right hemisphere of the brain.

corpus callosum to your left hemisphere, so you can talk about anything that reaches any receptor in your body.

But what happens when the corpus callosum is severed? When a woman with a severed corpus callosum touches something with her right hand without looking at it, she can say what it is, because the touch information reaches her left hemisphere (Nebes, 1974; Sperry, 1967). However, if she feels something with her left hand, then she cannot say what it is, because the information reaches only her right hemisphere. If she is given several choices and is asked to point to what her left hand has just felt, she can point to it correctly—but only with her left hand. In fact, she will sometimes point to the correct object with her left hand while saying, "I have no idea what it was. I didn't feel anything." Evidently, the right hemisphere can understand the instructions and answer with the hand it controls, but it cannot talk. Roger Sperry won a Nobel Prize in physiology and medicine in 1981 for these pioneering discoveries.

Now consid[...] woman looks at [...] conditions, when [...] almost the same [...] tory, however, it [...] side of the brain [...] faster than the e[...] focuses her eyes [...] investigator flash[...] for only a split s[...] enough time to m[...] she replies, "ban[...] (Information fro[...] recall, goes to the [...] the left hemisphere [...] of band it might [...] band? rubber band?" However, if she is asked to point with the left hand at what she saw, the left hand points to a hat (what the right hemisphere saw).

Split-brain people get along reasonably well in everyday life. Walking, for example, is no problem; it is largely controlled by subcortical areas of the brain that exchange information through connections below the corpus callosum.

In special circumstances, the two hemispheres find clever ways to cooperate. In one experiment, a split-brain person was looking at pictures flashed on a screen, as in Figure 3.43a. He could not name most of the objects flashed in the left visual field, but after some delay, he could name such simple shapes as round, square, or triangular. Here is how he did it: After seeing the object (with the right hemisphere), he let his eyes move around the room. (Both hemispheres have control of the eye muscles.) When the right hemisphere saw something with the same shape as the object it had seen on the screen, it would stop moving the eyes. The left hemisphere just waited for the eyes to stop moving and then called out the shape of the object it saw.

CONCEPT CHECKS

13. Information coming to the left hemisphere of the brain comes from which part of the retinas?
14. After damage to the corpus callosum, a person can describe some of what he or she sees, but not all. Where must the person see something in order to describe it in words? one eye or the other? one half of the retina? one visual field or the other? (Check your answers on page 101.)

Split-brain surgery is extremely rare. We study such patients not because you are likely to encounter one but because they can teach us something about the organization of the brain: Although we cannot fully explain our experience of a unified consciousness, we do see that it depends on communication across brain areas. If communication between the two hemispheres is lost, then each hemisphere begins to act and experience independently of the other.

HABITUALLY QUESTIONING ASSERTIONS

The theme of questioning assertions permeates the text, sometimes appearing as a sentence or two in the middle of a discussion, sometimes as a paragraph, a full page, or more. This best-selling book is known for the way it encourages students to question the information before them and ask themselves, *How was a given conclusion reached? Does the evidence really support that conclusion?*

Kalat helps students learn to separate what sounds plausible from what can be substantiated scientifically, and how to tell the difference between sound and flawed evidence. The result is a book that challenges students to think carefully about each topic as they read.

Here are some of the assertions students are challenged to reconsider:

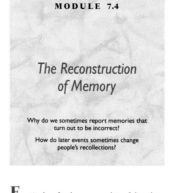

MODULE 7.4

The Reconstruction of Memory

Why do we sometimes report memories that turn out to be incorrect?

How do later events sometimes change people's recollections?

Forgetting has often been compared to a fading photograph, but in one important way it is very different: As we start to forget, we don't just lose the facts; we sometimes exaggerate or distort them. For example, many people who have visited India report seeing an amazing feat in which a magician throws one end of a rope into the air, where it becomes stiff long enough for a boy to climb it (Figure 7.23). Climbing an unsupported rope would be magical enough, but some people claim to have seen even more amazing feats. Researchers located 21 people who had seen the Indian rope trick and others with second-hand reports. They compared the reports to how recently the witnesses claimed to have seen the trick (Wiseman & Lamont, 1996). Here are the results:

Reported event	When seen (mean)
Saw a boy climb a rope and then climb down, but admittedly it might have been a bamboo pole instead of a rope.	4 years ago
Saw a boy start to climb a rope, then seem to vanish, then reappear at the top of the rope.	12.67 years ago
Saw a boy climb a rope, reach the top, then vanish and reappear behind the crowd.	32.5 years ago
Saw a boy climb a rope, reach the top, then vanish and reappear in a basket that had been in plain view of the audience.	41.75 years ago
Still more amazing reports...	Didn't actually see it, but heard about it from someone else.

One possible interpretation of these results is that, over the years, Indian boys have become less magical. The more parsimonious interpretation is that, over the years, the witnesses' memories have become distorted.

Another example: You have probably heard claims that a UFO crashed near Roswell, New Mexico, in 1947, and that the U.S. government hid the spacecraft and the aliens' bodies. However, according to Kal Korff (1997), one of the most serious UFO investigators, the facts are these:

In 1947, a Roswell man reported that he might have found the remains of a flying saucer. The local Air Force commander sent Major Jesse Marcel to retrieve the wreckage. The next day, the commander announced, with Marcel present, that it was nothing but a weather balloon. (Much later, the government admitted it had actually been the remains of an experimental spying device.) No one said anything more about it until 1978—more than 30 years later—when Marcel met a UFO enthusiast and told him a version of the "wrecked saucer" story. Marcel, whose military file indicates that he had a long history of exaggerating to impress people, apparently continued that habit. For example, he bragged to the *National Enquirer* that he had shot down five enemy aircraft during the war, although his military file indicates that he was never even a pilot.

UFO enthusiasts nevertheless believed Marcel's report and boast that they then interviewed "more than ninety witnesses." However, of those, only seven claim to

257

FIGURE 7.23 Some visitors to India report seeing a boy climb a rope (or maybe a bamboo pole). Some claim they also saw him disappear and later reappear. Generally, the more spectacular the account, the less recent the event.

---

258 Chapter 7 Memory

have actually seen anything; the other "witnesses" had just heard about it from someone else. Since then, some of those seven have changed their stories several times, contradicting themselves and one another. Some of them are apparently confusing events that they remember from the 1950s or later with the original 1947 event. In short, the parsimonious interpretation is that the memories are as distorted as those of the Indian rope trick.

Distortions of memory over time, even fairly short times, are common. They tell us about how memory normally works and how skeptical we should be of eyewitness reports of long-ago events.

Reconstruction of the Past

If you try to recall what you did three nights ago, you will start with the details that you remember clearly and **reconstruct** the rest to fill in the gaps: *During an original experience, we construct a memory. When we try to retrieve that memory, we reconstruct an account based partly on surviving memories and partly on our expectations of what must have happened.* For example, suppose you recall that you studied in the library three nights ago. With a little effort, you may remember where you sat, what you were reading, who sat next to you, and where you went for a snack afterward. As time passes, you will probably forget that evening altogether, unless you happen to fall in love with the person who sat down next to you. If so, you will long remember that chance meeting and perhaps even where you went for a snack, but probably not which book you were reading. If you wanted to recall the book, you might reconstruct the event: "Let's see, that semester I was taking a chemistry course that took a

lot of study, so m[...]
wait, I remember [...]
about politics. So[...]
ence text."

We also dep[...]
of various memor[...]
adults who consis[...]
watched the tele[...]
each participant [...]
ous news events [...]
results: People c[...]
news events, but [...]
utes episodes wh[...]
aired during the [...]
locher, 1997). (See Figure 7.24.) The reason for this difference is that news stories have a logical order and connections to other events in one's life. ("Oh, yeah, I remember what I did when I heard about . . .") With *60 Minutes* episodes, however, we have few links to any other experience. The important conclusion of this study is that, except for very recent events, we cannot attach a date to a memory based on its freshness or sharpness. Our attempts to date a memory involve mostly reconstructions and logical inferences.

Reconstruction and Inference in List Memory

TRY IT YOURSELF Try this demonstration: Read the words in list A, then turn away from the list and pause for a few seconds, and then write as many of the words as you can remember. Then repeat the same procedure for lists B and C. (*Please do this now, before reading the following paragraph.*)

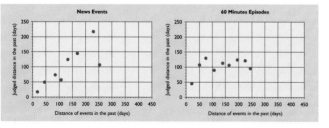

FIGURE 7.24 People who followed the news and regularly watched the television program *60 Minutes* could estimate the time of various news events but guessed almost randomly about when they saw various *60 Minutes* episodes, except those from the most recent two months. (From Friedman & Huttenlocher, 1997.)

---

* On a multiple-choice test, you should stick with your first impulse.
* We use only 10% of our brains.
* Subliminal messages can control people's behavior in powerful ways.
* Under hypnosis people will not do anything they would refuse to do otherwise.
* Psychotherapists can help people recall long-repressed memories.
* Lie-detector tests can determine accurately who is telling the truth.
* Hypnosis can enable us to remember forgotten materials, including some from early childhood.
* The Rorschach inkblot technique provides information about a person's thoughts and motivations.
* If you want to change people's behavior, you must first change their attitudes.

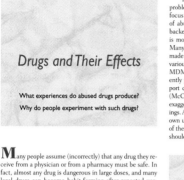

MODULE 5.3

Drugs and Their Effects

What experiences do abused drugs produce?

Why do people experiment with such drugs?

The abuse of alcohol and other drugs is a widespread problem, which we shall consider in Chapter 16. Here, our focus is on the experiences associated with common drugs of abuse. I have tried to present only information that is backed by solid evidence, but in the study of drug effects, it is more difficult than usual to separate fact from fiction. Many people who are trying to discourage drug use have made strong claims about the harms that result from using various drugs. For example, although some drugs—such as MDMA ("ecstasy") and PCP ("angel dust")—can apparently produce brain damage, there is little evidence to support claims of permanent damage from using other drugs (McCann, Lowe, & Ricaurte, 1997). The risk of presenting exaggerated claims is that people stop believing the warnings. At the opposite extreme, many people who defend their own use of drugs have minimized the dangers; again, many of their claims go beyond the facts. As with other topics, we should be skeptical of claims that go beyond the evidence.

Many people assume (incorrectly) that any drug they receive from a physician or from a pharmacy must be safe. In fact, almost any drug is dangerous in large doses, and many legal drugs can become habit-forming after repeated use. Furthermore, many abused drugs—including amphetamines, morphine, and even cocaine—have legitimate medical uses. The dividing line between "good drugs" and "bad drugs" is a blurry one; it depends more on the quantities used and the reasons for their use than it does on the chemistry of the drugs themselves.

A Survey of Abused Drugs and Their Effects

Some abused drugs, such as alcohol and opiates, have predominantly calming effects. Others, such as amphetamines and cocaine, are known for their stimulating effects. Still others, such as LSD, produce hallucinations. Table 5.2 lists some of the commonly abused drugs and their

TABLE 5.2 Commonly Abused Drugs and Their Effects

DRUG CATEGORY	EFFECTS ON BEHAVIOR	EFFECTS ON CENTRAL NERVOUS SYSTEM AND ORGANS
Depressants Alcohol	Relaxant; relieve inhibitions; impair memory and judgment	Widespread effects on membranes of neurons; facilitate activity at GABA synapses
Tranquilizers Barbiturates; benzodiazepines (Valium, Xanax)	Relieve anxiety; relax muscles; induce sleep	Facilitate activity at GABA synapses
Opiates Morphine, heroin	Decrease pain; decrease attention to real world; unpleasant withdrawal effects as drug leaves synapses	
Stimulants Caffeine	Increase energy, alertness	
Amphetamines Cocaine	Increase energy, alertness	
Mixed Stimulant-Depressants Nicotine	Stimulate brain activity, but most smokers say cigarettes relax them	
Distortion of Experience Marijuana (THC)	Intensifies sensory experiences; distorts perception of time; can relieve glaucoma, nausea; sometimes impairs learning, memory	
Hallucinogens LSD; mescaline	Cause hallucinations, sensory distortions, and occasionally panic	

A MODULAR APPROACH

The hallmark of any book by Jim Kalat is the way he organizes the material for students' comprehension. Each chapter is divided into two to five freestanding modules, providing logical breaks that help students manage the material easily.

Each module begins with one or more *key questions* that are important in motivating research. New in the Fifth Edition, Kalat closes each module with a section called "The Message," which puts the main themes in a broader context.

Each module also has its own *introduction, summary, review of terms,* and *answers.* This enables instructors to select or rearrange assigned readings or to omit sections. Each module ends with *recommended additional readings* and *Web resources.*

CONCEPT CHECK

6. People who use stimulant drugs as appetite suppressants ordinarily develop a tolerance. How could they prevent the development of this tolerance? (Check your answer later on this page.)

THE MESSAGE
Drugs and Awareness

If you were to change a few of a computer's connections at random, you could produce an "altered state," which would almost certainly not be an improvement. Giving drugs to a human brain is a little like changing the connections of a computer, and almost any drug at least temporarily impairs brain functioning somehow, even if the drug is used under medical supervision and accomplishes some good along with the bad. By examining both the desirable and undesirable effects of drugs on the brain, we can gain greater insight into the brain's normal processes and functions.

SUMMARY

* *Alcohol.* Alcohol, the most widely abused drug in our society, relaxes people and relieves their inhibitions. It can also impair judgment and reasoning. (page 182)
* *Tranquilizers.* Benzodiazepine tranquilizers are widely used to relieve anxiety; they are sometimes also used to relax muscles or to promote sleep. (page 183)
* *Opiates.* Opiate drugs bind to endorphin receptors in the nervous system. The immediate effect of opiates is pleasure and relief from pain. (page 183)
* *Marijuana.* Marijuana's active compound, THC, acts on abundant receptors, found mostly in the hippocampus and certain brain areas important for the control of movement. Because the medulla has few THC receptors, a large dose of marijuana is seldom fatal. (page 183)
* *Stimulants.* Stimulant drugs such as amphetamines and cocaine increase activity levels and pleasure. Compared to other forms of cocaine, crack produces more rapid effects on behavior, greater risk of addiction, and greater risk of damage to the heart and other organs. (page 184)
* *Hallucinogens.* Hallucinogens induce sensory distortions. LSD acts at one type of serotonin synapse; we do not yet know why activity at that type of synapse should produce these effects. (page 185)
* *Withdrawal.* After using a drug, the user enters a rebound state known as withdrawal. Drug users often crave drugs as a way of decreasing their withdrawal symptoms. (page 186)
* *Tolerance.* People who use certain drugs repeatedly become less and less sensitive to them over time. (page 186)

Suggestion for Further Reading

Rivers, P. C. (1994). *Alcohol and human behavior.* Englewood Cliffs, NJ: Prentice-Hall. Covers all aspects of alcohol use from its effects on physiology to its role in society and culture.

Terms

alcohol a class of molecules that includes methanol, ethanol, propyl alcohol (rubbing alcohol), and others (page 182)

tranquilizers drugs that help people to relax (page 183)

opiates either drugs derived from the opium poppy or synthetic drugs that produce effects similar to those of opium derivatives (page 183)

endorphins chemicals produced by the brain that have effects resembling those of opiates (page 183)

stimulants drugs that boost energy, heighten alertness, increase activity, and produce a pleasant feeling (page 184)

hallucinogens drugs that induce sensory distortions (page 185)

withdrawal effects experiences that occur as a result of the removal of a drug from the brain (page 186)

tolerance the weakened effect of a drug after repeated use (page 186)

physical dependence a condition whereby a habitual drug user is driven to seek the drug to escape or avoid the unpleasant withdrawal effects that occur during abstention from the drug (page 186)

psychological dependence a strong repetitive desire for something without any physical symptoms of withdrawal (page 186)

Answer to Concept Check

6. Instead of taking a pill just before a meal, people should take it between meals, when they are not planning to eat right away or when they plan to skip a meal altogether. If they eat right after taking a pill, they soon develop a tolerance to its appetite-suppressing effects. However, even if they follow the advice to take the pills between meals, most people are not likely to lose weight in the long run. After their appetite is suppressed for a while, they are likely to experience increased appetite later. (page 187)

Web Resources

Web of Addictions
www.well.com/user/woa/
Andrew L. Homer and Dick Dillon provide factual information about alcohol and other abused drugs. Fact sheets and other material are arranged by drug, with links to net resources related to addictions, in-depth information on special topics, and a list of places to get help with addictions.

National Clearinghouse for Alcohol and Drug Information
www.health.org/survey.htm
Dozens of research and statistical reports about alcohol and drug use. Backtrack to Prevention Online's front page to access even more information, searchable databases, forums, and links.

FIGURE 10.36 One of many poorly understood differences between the sexes: Beyond the age of puberty, most males carry packages at their side, whereas females carry them in an elevated position.

could say that women are more conformist or more flexible and that men are more independent or more stubborn.) Males and females also differ in helping behavior. It is not a simple case of one sex being more helpful than the other; men and women tend to help in different ways. For example, men are generally more likely to help a stranger change a flat tire; women are more likely to help people who need long-term nurturing support (Eagly & Crowley, 1986).

Sex Differences in Social Situations   It is now clear that certain important differences between males and females emerge only in a social context (Maccoby, 1990). Psychologists ordinarily test people in isolation. When tested one at a time, boys and girls tend to behave about the same in most regards. However, in a group setting, boys usually get together with other boys and girls get together with other girls; suddenly, the two groups act very differently (Figure 10.37).

Girls sometimes play competitive games, but they are more likely than boys to spend long times at quiet, cooperative play. They take turns; they present their desires as "suggestions" instead of demands; they exchange compliments; and they generally try to avoid hurting each other's feelings.

Meanwhile, boys are almost always competing with each other. They compete even when they are just talking: They shout orders, they interrupt, they make threats and boasts, and they exchange insults. Their play is often rough and aggressive and almost always competitive. When a group of elementary-school boys play a game, sooner or later they will have a dispute about the rules; invariably, they work out a compromise and continue playing, but they may continue screaming "you cheater!" or "you liar!" while they play. Still, when the game is over, they almost always part as friends.

When boys grow up, do they change their ways of interacting with one another? Not entirely. Deborah Tannen (1990) reports one episode at a college basketball game: At the University of Michigan, student tickets have seat numbers on them, but students generally ignore those assignments and take seats on a first-come, first-served basis. One night, several men from the visiting team, Michigan State, tried to go to the seats listed on their tickets, only to find some University of Michigan students, both men and women, already seated there. The Michigan State students

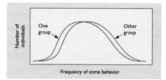

FIGURE 10.37 One girl tested alone behaves about the same as one boy tested alone. But when boys play together, they "show off" to one another and to other observers; girls play more cooperatively.

MULTICULTURAL AND GENDER-RELATED CONTENT

Where appropriate and relevant, Kalat includes discussions of how culture, ethnicity, and gender influence behavior. (To make the book more convenient for both instructors and students, a special thematic index helps locate related material.) By studying this diversity, psychologists can investigate the generality of psychological findings more thoroughly.

asked the others to get out of their seats; the men in those seats then replied rudely, and the dispute quickly grew loud, heated, and insulting. The women were mortified with embarrassment.

Within a few minutes, however, the Michigan State men settled into seats next to the University of Michigan students, and before long the two groups of men were happily discussing basketball strategies. The women didn't understand why the men had screamed insults in the first place or why they had made friends so quickly afterward.

Male-Female Relationships in Childhood and Adulthood   What do you suppose happens when boys and girls play together? If they are working on a task that requires cooperation, few sex differences are evident (Powlishta & Maccoby, 1990). However, in an unsupervised situation with no need to cooperate, the boys often dominate and intimidate the girls. In some cases, the boys take control and the girls simply watch (Maccoby, 1990).

When boys and girls become young men and women, romantic interests may draw them together, but both are ill prepared to deal with the other sex. Men are used to demanding what they want; women are used to a cooperative give-and-take. Men worry about their status in relation to other men; women often fail to understand these status contests. When women discuss their problems, they expect their listeners to express sympathy; men often fail to understand this need. Here are some examples of the resultant misunderstanding (Tannen, 1990):

- A man invites an out-of-town friend to spend the night in the guest bedroom. The man's wife is upset that her husband did not check with her before inviting his friend. He replies that he would feel embarrassed to say, "I have to ask my wife first."
- A woman asks her husband to get their VCR to record a TV movie. The husband says this particular kind of VCR plays tapes but cannot record. The woman then asks their next-door neighbor to check the VCR. He too tells her the VCR cannot record. The husband feels resentful about this episode for years, because his wife implied that he was too incompetent to understand their VCR.
- A woman who has had breast surgery tells her husband she is unhappy about the scar left by the surgery. Instead of expressing sympathy, he replies, "You can have plastic surgery. . . ." She is upset by the implication that he doesn't like the way she looks. He replies that he doesn't care about the scar; he was trying to help because *she* said she was unhappy.

Are male-female relationships always like this? Of course not. There are many differences *on the average* between men and women, just as there are between 25-year-olds and 20-year-olds or between Northerners and Southerners, or between almost any other identifiable groups. The distributions may overlap completely; therefore, the discussion of averages may not tell us what to expect from a given individual.

Many immigrants are bicultural, having reasonable familiarity with two sets of customs. These Asian immigrants to Australia adopt some Australian customs while maintaining some of their own.

Ethnic and Cultural Influences

Membership in a minority group molds a child's development in two major ways: First, the customs of the minority group may in fact differ from those of other groups. For example, many Japanese parents put great emphasis on educational achievement and bringing honor to one's family (Yamamoto & Kubota, 1983). Secondly, members of a minority group are affected by the attitudes of other people, who may treat them differently or expect certain behaviors from them simply because they are members of that minority group.

Immigrants to the United States or any other country undergo a period of **acculturation,** *a transition from feeling part of the culture of their original country to the culture of the country they enter.* Acculturation is gradual; people sometimes require a generation or more before they or their descendants feel fully comfortable in a new culture.

In many cases, a person may have to function as a member of two or more cultures or subcultures. For example,

INTRODUCTION TO
Psychology

What Is Psychology?

If you are like most students, you start off assuming that just about everything you read in your textbooks and everything your professors tell you must be true. But what if it isn't? Just suppose that a group of impostors has replaced the faculty of your college. They pretend to know what they are talking about and they all vouch for one another's competence, but in fact they are all totally unqualified. They have managed to find textbooks that support their own prejudices, but the information in the textbooks is just as nonsensical as their own opinions. If that happened, how would you know?

As long as we are entertaining such skeptical thoughts, let's consider that there may be other impostors too. When you read an advice column in the newspaper, or read a book about how to invest money, or listen to a political commentator, how do you know who has the real answers and who is just an impostor?

The answer is that *all* of us are impostors—you, me, everybody—at least some of the time. Sometimes we act more confident of our conclusions than we really ought to. Sometimes we just quote each other: "They say we only use ten percent of our brain," or "They say you should always stick with your first impulse on a multiple-choice test,"
without even pausing to find out who "they" are or why they say such things.

The problem is that anybody—even a professor or a textbook author—has strong reasons for some conclusions, weak ones for others, and absolute certainty for only a few. I don't mean to imply that you should shift from indiscriminately believing everything you read and hear to completely disbelieving everything. But you should insist that people who draw a conclusion should also tell you why they arrived at that conclusion. Don't be satisfied if someone suggests, "Take my word for it." Ask for the evidence. Then you can draw your own conclusions. You still might not be right, but if you make a mistake, at least it will be your own mistake and not someone else's.

You have just encountered the theme of this book: Ask for the evidence. You have heard and you will continue to hear all sorts of claims concerning psychology. Some of these are valid, some are wrong, some are partly valid under certain conditions, and some are so vague that we cannot even evaluate them. When you finish this book, you will be in a better position to evaluate evidence and to judge for yourself which claims are reasonable and which ones are not.

Who has the correct answers? None of us do, at least not always. Even when people we trust seem very confident of their opinions, we should ask for their evidence or reasoning.

MODULE 1.1

The Goals of Psychologists

What do the various kinds of psychologists do?

What are their guiding assumptions about the causes of behavior, the relation of brain activity to experience, and the roles of nature (heredity) and nurture (environment)?

Years ago, one of my students asked me, "When will we get to the kind of psychology we can 'use' on people?" Another student asked me whether I, as a psychologist, had any tips to offer him on how to seduce his girlfriend. (I don't. If I did, I wouldn't tell him, for ethical reasons. If I did know powerful tricks to control people's behavior and had no ethics, I would probably have a different job than college professor!) Psychologists do not seek techniques for manipulating or tricking people. They *do* try to understand why people act the way they do, to help people to better understand themselves, and also to help people change their behavior to achieve their own goals.

Broadly defined, **psychology** is *the systematic study of behavior and experience.* The term *psychology* derives from the Greek roots *psyche,* meaning "soul" or "mind," and *logos,* meaning "word"; thus, psychology is literally the study of the mind or soul. Every culture has developed a "folk psychology" to try to explain people's feelings and actions. As an example, the *Illongot* people of the Philippines believe in a concept called *rinawa* (roughly, a "life force") that is responsible for a person's energy and health. They believe that *rinawa* gradually leaves the body throughout life, so even by age 20 one has much less *rinawa* than a child has. During dreams, *rinawa* leaves the body and travels around. If the *rinawa* happens to eat with a dead person during a dream, then it will start to feel comfortable among the dead, and the person will in fact begin to die (Lillard, 1997).

These assumptions seem very natural to the Illongot, less so to most other people. But we also make assumptions that we take for granted. Some suggest that psychology is nothing more than common sense. Well, if so, psychologists need not be ashamed. Most people spend a great deal of time trying to understand their own and other people's behavior, and common sense is much more accurate about

psychology than it is about, say, physics. But your common sense is probably not the same as that of the Illongot. Every culture, and I suppose even every individual, has different notions of common sense, and we all need to evaluate those ideas. When we do, we find that some of our common sense ideas are correct and some are not.

In this text, I shall be much more concerned with evaluating the ideas that are common among the probable readers of this book than exposing the possible weaknesses of, for example, Illongot folk psychology. Here we shall be concerned primarily with psychological issues as they relate to life in a technological society and as they relate to the philosophical concerns that have traditionally interested people in Western cultures. Psychologists in other societies, such as the rural parts of India, for example, have different concerns (Gergen, Gulerce, Lock, & Misra, 1996). It is completely natural for each society to focus on different issues, although at times it is helpful to compare notes. Sometimes people from a different culture raise questions and challenge ideas that we might otherwise take for granted.

Major Philosophical Issues in Psychology

Many psychological concerns date back to the philosophers of ancient Greece. Although psychology has moved away from philosophy in its methods, it continues to be motivated by some of the same issues. Three of the most profound questions are free will versus determinism, the mind-brain problem, and the nature-nurture issue.

Free Will Versus Determinism

Beginning with the Renaissance period in Europe, people began to look for scientific explanations for the phenomena they observed. One of the key points of this scientific revolution was a shift toward seeking the *immediate* causes of an event (what led to what) instead of the *final* causes (the ultimate purpose of the event in an overall plan). Scientists analyzed the motion of objects in terms of pushes and pulls and other laws of nature (White, 1990). That is, they made an assumption called **determinism,** *the assumption that everything that happens has a cause, or determinant, in the observable world.*

Is the same true for human behavior? Each of us is, after all, part of the physical world. Your brain is made of chemical compounds that are subject to the same laws of nature as anything else. According to the *determinist* assumption of human behavior, everything we do has a cause (Figure 1.1).

Clearly, at least some of these causes lie within us. A person walking down a mountainside is not the same as a rock that rolls or bounces down the same mountainside. The claim of psychological determinism is that, even when

FIGURE 1.1   Behavior is guided by external forces, such as waves, and by forces within the individual. According to the determinist view, even those internal forces follow physical laws.

you make complicated decisions about how to get down a mountain safely, your decision is a product of the combined influence of your genetics, your past experiences, and the current environment (Sappington, 1990). Just as an engineer can design a robot to consider information and make appropriate decisions, your genes and your experience have programmed you to make appropriate decisions. (You did not design or program yourself.)

Logically, the opposite of determinism should be *indeterminism,* the idea that events happen randomly with no cause at all. In psychology, however, few people argue that behavior is random or indeterminate. Opponents of determinism instead defend **free will,** generally defined as the ***belief that behavior is caused by a person's independent decisions, not by external determinants.*** But what are "independent decisions"? If we are talking about an "internal" decision made by the individual, then there may be no difference between the determinist and free will positions; determinism agrees that the individual makes decisions but points out that a robot does too. To be really different from determinism, the free will position must hold that a person's "independent decision" is independent from the physics and chemistry of the body.

The test of determinism is ultimately empirical: If everything we do has a cause, our behavior should be predictable. To some extent, it is. For example, suppose that students studying in various rooms of a campus building hear an announcement: "A fire has broken out in this building. By the time we bring the fire under control, the smoke and fumes may become hazardous. We therefore request that everyone calmly leave the building." We can predict that almost everyone will promptly leave the building. We can make an even more accurate prediction if we know something about the individual students: Everyone will leave the building *except* those who could not hear the announcement, those who do not understand English, and those who have been advised by a friend "every year at about this time someone says to leave the building because

of a fire, but it's just a silly exercise to show that psychologists can predict your behavior, so ignore the warning."

In other situations, however, you might object that no one could possibly predict your behavior, no matter how much they knew about you. For example, no one could accurately predict what you will choose to eat for lunch tomorrow or which color sweater you will buy or how many pages of this book you will read before you quit to do something else.

You are right; psychologists will probably never be able to predict every detail of your behavior; however, this unpredictability does not imply an absence of causes. Physicists and mathematicians today talk about *chaos,* the complex effects that result from many small influences. For example, imagine that I drop a golf ball at the top of a hilly road and measure the exact point at which it eventually comes to rest. Then I take the ball back to the same location at the top of the hill and drop it again the same way—or as close to the same way as I can. Will the ball eventually land in the same place as it did the first time? No, the first bounce or two will land in nearly the same place as before, but with each succeeding bounce, the ball will veer further and further from its original route, reflecting the cumulative effect of an enormous number of tiny influences. Similarly, when you are deciding what to eat for lunch or which sweater to buy, your behavior is subject to so many tiny influences that your choice may be no more predictable than the final bounce of that golf ball. This unpredictability stems from a great number of small causes, not from a lack of causes.

Let me concede an important point, however. In the introduction to this chapter I said that we all sometimes state something with confidence that is really only an assumption. This is such a case. Researchers assume that every behavior has a natural cause, because that assumption seems to work and because the only way to test the assumption is to see how far we can go with it before we find some limits. Still, to be honest, it is merely an assumption, not a certainty.

SOMETHING TO THINK ABOUT

What kind of evidence, if any, would support the concept of free will? Demonstrating that a particular theory makes incorrect predictions about behavior under given circumstances would not refute determinism. To support the concept of free will, one would need to demonstrate that no conceivable theory could make correct predictions. Should a psychologist who believes in free will conduct the same kind of research that determinists conduct, or a different kind of research, or no research at all? ✳

The Mind-Brain Problem

Every movement we make depends on muscle activity controlled by the nervous system, and every sensory experience depends on the activity of the nervous system. All activities of the nervous system follow the laws of physics and chemistry. What, then, is the role of the mind? *The philosophical question of how experience is related to the brain* is the **mind-brain problem** (or mind-body problem). Does the brain produce the mind? If so, how and why? Or does the mind control the brain? If so, how can a nonphysical entity control a physical substance? Or are the mind and the brain just two names for the same thing? If so, what does it mean to say that they are the same?

Although the mind-brain problem is a particularly difficult philosophical issue, it does lend itself to research. Research can determine links between brain activity, on the one hand, and behavior and experience, on the other hand. For example, consider Figure 1.2. A technique called positron-emission tomography enables investigators to measure the amount of activity in different parts of the brain at various times. The photos in Figure 1.2 show brain activity while a person is engaged in nine different tasks. Red indicates the highest degree of brain activity, followed by yellow, green, and blue. As you can see, the various tasks tend to activate different areas of the brain, although all areas show at least some activity at all times (Phelps & Mazziotta, 1985).

Data such as these show a very close relationship between brain activity and psychological events. You might well ask: Does this mean that brain activity caused the associated thoughts, or did those thoughts cause that pattern of brain activity? Many brain researchers would reply that neither brain activity nor mental activity "causes" the other; rather, brain activity and mental activity are the same. (See Dennett, 1991.)

Even if we accept this position, we are still far from understanding the mind-brain relationship fully. Is mental activity associated with all brain activity or just certain types? Why is there such a thing as conscious experience at all? Could a brain get along without it?

Research studies are not about to resolve the mind-brain problem and put philosophers out of business. But research results do constrain the types of philosophical answers that we can seriously consider. The hope of learning more about the mind-brain relationship is one of the ultimate goals for many psychologists, especially those whose work we shall study in Chapters 3 and 4.

SOMETHING TO THINK ABOUT

One way to think about the mind-brain relationship is to ask whether something other than a brain—a computer, for example—could have a mind. How would we know?

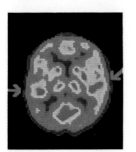
Resting state

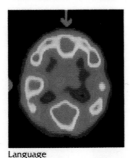
Music

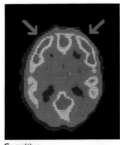
Cognitive

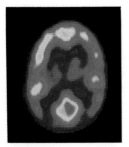
Visual

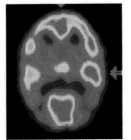
Language

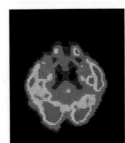
Memory

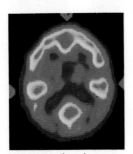
Auditory

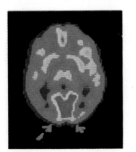
Language and music

Motor

F I G U R E 1.2 PET scans show the brain activity of normal people engaged in different activities. Left column: Brain activity with no special stimulation, while passively watching something or listening to something. Center column: Brain activity while listening to music, language, or both. Right column: Brain activity during performance of a cognitive task, an auditory memory task, and the task of moving the fingers of the right hand. Red indicates the highest activity, followed by yellow, green, and blue. Arrows indicate the most active areas. (Courtesy of Michael E. Phelps and John C. Mazziotta, University of California, Los Angeles, School of Medicine.)

What if we built a computer that could perform all the intellectual functions that humans perform? Could we then decide that the computer is conscious, as human beings are? ✳

The Nature-Nurture Issue

Why do most little boys spend more time than little girls do with toy guns and trucks and less time playing with dolls? Are such behavioral differences mostly the result of genetic differences between boys and girls, or are they mostly the result of differences in how society treats boys and girls?

In many countries, alcoholism is a serious problem. In other countries—Turkey, for example—alcohol abuse is rare. Are these differences entirely a matter of social custom, or do certain genes influence how much alcohol people consume?

Certain psychological disorders are more common in large cities than in small towns and in the countryside. Does life in crowded cities somehow cause psychological disorders? Or do people develop such disorders because of a genetic predisposition and then move to a big city because that is the best place to find jobs, housing, and welfare services?

Each of these questions is related to the **nature-nurture issue** (Figure 1.3): *What are the roles of heredity and environment in the development of various behaviors?* Obviously, people need both heredity and environment to develop at all. However, the *differences* between one person and another may depend mostly on differences in heredity or differences in environment. The nature-nurture issue shows up from time to time in practically all fields of psychology, and it seldom has a simple answer.

SOMETHING TO THINK ABOUT

Suppose researchers found that the difference in the rate of alcohol abuse between Turkey and most other countries is due to environmental causes (the strict legal sanctions against alcohol in Turkey). Should we then assume that the differences in alcohol use among other countries is also due to environmental causes? ✳

What Psychologists Do

We have presented some major philosophical issues related to the entire field of psychology. However, few psychologists are ambitious enough to attempt to answer these ultimate questions; they usually deal with more specific or more detailed issues.

Psychology is an academic, nonmedical discipline that includes many branches and specialties, ranging from the helping professions to research on learning, memory, brain functions, and so forth. The educational requirements for becoming a psychologist vary from one country to another (Newstead & Makinen, 1997). In the United States and Canada, a psychology student gets a bachelor's degree (usually after four years of college) and then probably a Ph.D. degree (at least another four or five years, sometimes much more). Some people practice psychology with a master's degree (intermediate between a bachelor's and a doctorate), and others have a Psy.D. (Doctor of Psychology) degree, which generally requires less research experience than a Ph.D. Any psychologist specializes in a particular branch of psychology, such as experimental, developmental, clinical, or industrial.

FIGURE 1.3 Why do different children develop different interests? They may have had different hereditary tendencies, but they have also experienced different environmental influences. Separating the roles of nature and nurture can be difficult.

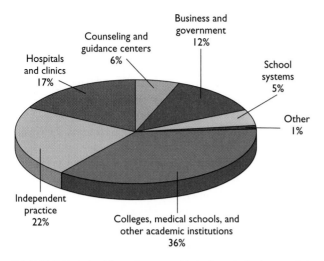

Counseling and guidance centers 6%

Business and government 12%

Hospitals and clinics 17%

School systems 5%

Other 1%

Independent practice 22%

Colleges, medical schools, and other academic institutions 36%

FIGURE 1.4 More than one third of psychologists work in academic institutions; the remainder find positions in a variety of settings.

Psychologists work in many occupational settings, as shown in Figure 1.4. A little more than a third work in academic institutions—colleges, universities, and medical schools. Almost 40% work in health-provider settings—independent practices, hospitals, and clinics. Others work in business, government, guidance and counseling centers, and public school systems.

Psychologists in Teaching and Research

Many psychologists who are not clinical psychologists have positions in colleges and universities where they teach and do research that will, they hope, lead to a greater understanding of behavior and experience and perhaps have useful applications. A small percentage of psychologists work in full-time research institutions. Here, we preview a few major categories of psychological research.

Biological Psychology A **biopsychologist** (or **behavioral neuroscientist**) *tries to explain behavior in terms of biological factors, such as electrical and chemical activities in the nervous system, the effects of drugs and hormones, genetics, and evolutionary pressures.* For example, the evidence suggests that certain genes influence the probability that someone will develop schizophrenia, depression, or alcoholism. These genes do not completely control the outcome; the final results depend on experience as well as genes.

Biopsychologists also study the effects of brain damage. Brain damage can result from such things as a sharp blow to the head, a ruptured blood vessel in the brain, an interruption of oxygen supply, prolonged malnutrition, or exposure to toxic chemicals. The effects of brain damage on behavior vary enormously, depending on the location and extent of the damage.

People have long known that various drugs can alter behavior. For example, opiates (such as heroin or morphine)

generally make people quiet, passive, and insensitive to pain. Amphetamines and cocaine stimulate increased activity in most people. Biopsychologists try to understand how drugs affect the brain. They have found that most drugs that affect behavior do so by altering the chemical communication between one neuron and another at junctions called *synapses*.

So, according to biopsychologists, why are people different from each other? There are many reasons: People are born with different genes; they develop slightly different brains and different hormonal patterns. Some have suffered brain damage; some are under the influence of drugs or of nutritional deficiencies that affect the brain. Anything that affects the body, especially the brain, will also affect behavior.

Learning and motivation The research field of **learning and motivation** studies *how behavior depends on the outcomes of past behaviors and on current motivations.*

How often we engage in any particular behavior depends on the results of engaging in that behavior in the past. For example, you undoubtedly have a friend whose interests differ from yours. One of you likes dancing; the other likes painting. Or one likes to play the guitar, and the other is active in political activities. The one who likes dancing may have received praise for dancing, or may experience some good bodily sensations while dancing. The one who enjoys painting may once have tripped while dancing. The details vary from one person to another, but our current behavior depends on our past learning.

Behaviorists do research to determine how the consequences of an action modify future behavior. For example, do frequent payoffs (money, praise, etc.) produce the same results as less frequent or less predictable rewards? If someone were expecting a large payoff and instead got a smaller payoff, what would be the effect, compared to someone who was used to a smaller payoff? What are the effects of punishment? Notice the theoretical orientation: The behaviorist studies what the person *does* as a result of the consequences of past actions, not what the person *thinks*. Because of this emphasis on actions instead of thoughts, behaviorists can conduct many of their studies on nonhuman animals.

Cognitive Psychology **Cognition** refers to *thinking and acquiring knowledge.* A **cognitive psychologist** *studies those processes.* (The root *cogn-* also shows up in the word *recognize*, which literally means "to know again.") As a rule cognitive psychologists do not simply ask people to describe their thought processes. (If people understood their own thoughts that well, there would be less need for psychologists.) Cognitive psychologists conduct experiments to infer what people know, how they came to know it, and how they use their knowledge to solve new problems. Some cognitive psychologists develop and test computer models of how people think.

One typical question for a cognitive psychologist: What do experts know or do that sets them apart from other people? One possible distinction is simply that the expert knows more facts. Consider a subject on which you are an expert: how to find your way around your college campus. A fellow student asks you, "How do I get from here to the biology building?" To answer, you can draw on the knowledge you share with the other student: "Go over toward the library. Then cut behind the library, between the library and the math building. The biology building will be right in front of you." Now, suppose that a visitor who has never been on campus before asks you the same question. You say, "Go over toward the library . . ." "Wait, where's the library?" "Well, go out this door, make a right, go to the next street . . ." Someone with little or no previous knowledge will need detailed and extensive instructions (Isaacs & Clark, 1987).

Another distinction between the expert and the nonexpert is that the expert can identify more categories. For example, someone might look at a group of birds on a beach and say, "Hey, look at all the seagulls." An expert birdwatcher might reply, "There are three gull species and two tern species." Moreover, the expert can identify the *right* categories. The inexperienced bird-watcher might say, sheepishly, "Oh, I see. Some of them have darker feathers than others." The expert would reply, "No, the ones with darker feathers are just younger. To tell one species from the other you have to check the color of the beak, the color of the legs, the size of the bird, the color of the eyes . . ." The expert knows what to look for—what is relevant and what is not (Murphy & Medin, 1985).

Developmental Psychology
Developmental psychologists *study the behavioral capacities typical of different ages and how behavior changes with age,* "from womb to tomb." In a typical study, developmental psychologists examine a particular behavior across a certain age span, such as language from age 2 to age 4, or the speed of solving intellectual tasks from age 60 to age 80. The first

question is: What do people do at one age that they do *not* do at another age? The second question is: Why? Was the change due to a biological process, or to changes in experience, or to a complex combination of both? Developmental psychologists frequently need to address the nature-nurture issue that we mentioned earlier.

Social Psychology
Social psychologists *study how an individual influences other people and is influenced by others.* When we are with other people, we tend to take our cues from them about what we should do. Suppose you arrive at a party and notice that the other guests are walking around, talking, and helping themselves to snacks. You do the same. When you go to a religious service or an art museum, you notice how other people are acting and, again, conform your behavior to theirs.

Certainly, if you had grown up in a different country, you would have developed vastly different customs. Even within a given culture, though, people acquire different behaviors because of the people around them. If you had made friends with a different set of people in high school, you might be a much different person today. According to social psychologists, people are also heavily influenced by other people's expectations. For example, parents often intentionally or unintentionally convey expectations that boys will be more competitive and girls will be more cooperative, or that teenagers will be immature and that 25-year-olds will be responsible. At least to some extent, people's behavior tends to live up to—or down to—the expectations of others. Social psychologists study such influences.

CONCEPT CHECK

1. **(a)** Of the kinds of psychological research just described—biological psychology, learning and motivation, cognitive psychology, developmental psychology, and social psychology—which field concentrates most on children? **(b)** Which is most concerned with how people behave in groups? **(c)** Which concentrates most on thought and knowledge? **(d)** Which would be most interested in the effects of brain damage? **(e)** Which is most concerned with studying the effect of a reward on future behavior? (Check your answers on page 16).

Clinical Psychologists and Other Psychotherapists

When most people hear the term *psychologist,* they first think of *clinical psychologists,* who constitute one type of **psychotherapist,** *specialists in helping people with psychological problems* ranging from depression or other serious disorders to marriage conflicts, difficulties making decisions, or even the mere feeling that "I should be getting more out of life." Some clinical psychologists are college professors and researchers, but most are full-time private practitioners.

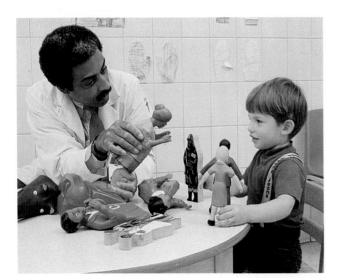

Developmental psychologists study the behavioral differences among people of different ages.

It is important to distinguish between clinical psychologists and psychiatrists. **Clinical psychologists** *have an advanced degree in psychology, with a specialty in understanding and helping people with psychological problems.* As part of their training, they undergo at least one year of supervised clinical work called an *internship.* Clinical psychologists can base their work on any of various theoretical viewpoints, which we shall explore in later chapters. They try, in one way or another, to understand why a person is having difficulties and then to help that person to become more successful and to make better choices.

Psychiatry is a *branch of medicine that deals with emotional disturbances.* To become a psychiatrist, a student first earns an M.D. degree and then takes an additional four years of residency training in psychiatry. Psychiatrists and clinical psychologists provide similar services for most clients: They listen, ask questions, and try to help. Psychiatrists, however, are medical doctors and can therefore prescribe drugs, such as tranquilizers and antidepressants, whereas psychologists cannot.

Does psychiatrists' ability to prescribe drugs give them an advantage over psychologists? Sometimes, but not always. Ours is an overmedicated society. Some psychiatrists habitually treat anxiety and depression with drugs, whereas a psychologist tries to treat problems by changing the person's way of living. Some psychologists favor a change in the law that would permit them to take some extra training to gain the right to prescribe drugs. Others fear that gaining prescription privileges would mean losing psychologists' distinctive focus on talking extensively with their clients (Hayes & Helby, 1996). Prescription privileges will probably remain a controversial topic.

Several other kinds of professionals also provide help and counsel. Psychiatric nurses and psychiatric social workers have an undergraduate or master's degree in nursing or social work plus additional training in the care of emotionally troubled people. **Psychoanalysts** are *psychotherapists who rely heavily on the theories and methods of the early 20th-century Viennese physician Sigmund Freud.* There is some question about who may rightly call themselves psychoanalysts. Some people apply the term to any psychotherapist who relies heavily on Freud's methods; others apply the term only to graduates of a six- to eight-year program at an institute of psychoanalysis. Those institutes admit only people who are already either psychiatrists or clinical psychologists. Thus, people completing psychoanalytic training will be at least in their late 30s.

Table 1.1 compares various types of psychotherapists.

CONCEPT CHECK

2. Can psychoanalysts prescribe drugs? (Check your answer on page 16.)

Nonclinical Fields of Applied Psychology

Psychologists also work in business, industry, and school systems in some capacities that might be unfamiliar to you, doing things you might not think of as psychology. The job prospects in these fields have been quite good, however, and you might find these fields interesting. Let's explore these fields in detail here, because they do not have whole chapters devoted to them later, as do areas such as developmental and social psychology.

Industrial/Organizational Psychology   **Industrial/organizational psychology** is *the study of people at work.* It deals with such issues as how to match the

---

TABLE 1.1   Clinical Psychologists and Other Psychotherapists

TYPE OF THERAPIST	EDUCATION	NUMBER ACTIVELY PRACTICING IN U.S.*
Clinical psychologist	Ph.D. with clinical emphasis, or Psy.D., plus internship. Total of generally 5+ years after undergraduate degree.	42,000
Psychiatrist	M.D. plus psychiatric residency. Total of 8 years after undergraduate degree.	33,000
Psychoanalyst	Psychiatry or clinical psychology plus 6–8 years in a psychoanalytic institute. Others who rely on Freud's methods also call themselves psychoanalysts.	9,000
Psychiatric nurse	From 2-year (A.A.) degree to master's degree, plus supervised experience.	16,000
Clinical social worker	Master's degree plus 2 years of supervised experience. Total of at least 4 years after undergraduate degree.	45,000

*Based on data from Howard et al. (1996) and estimates provided by the American Psychoanalytic Association, the American Psychiatric Nurses Association, and the National Association of Social Workers.

right person with the right job, how to train people for jobs, how best to determine salaries, and how to organize the workplace so that workers will be both productive and satisfied. Industrial/organizational psychologists call upon their knowledge of social psychology, cognitive psychology, and standardized testing.

Here's one example of a typical concern for industrial/organizational (I-O) psychologists (Campion & Thayer, 1989): A company that manufactures complex electronic equipment needed to publish reference and repair manuals for its products. The engineers who designed the devices could not devote the necessary time to write the manuals, and none of them were skilled writers anyway. So the company hired a technical writer to prepare the manuals, but after a year she received an unsatisfactory performance rating. The manuals she wrote contained too many technical errors; besides that, she was constantly complaining.

The writer countered that, when she asked various engineers in the company to check her manuals or to explain technical details to her, they were always too busy. She found her job complicated and frustrating; her office was badly lit, noisy, and overheated, and her chair was uncomfortable. Whenever she mentioned any of these problems, however, she was told that she "complained too much."

In a situation like this, an industrial/organizational psychologist can help the company to evaluate the possible solutions. First, the problem might be employee selection; maybe the company hired the wrong person for this job. If so, they should fire the current writer and hire someone who is an expert on electrical engineering, who is also an outstanding writer, and who *likes* a badly lit, noisy, overheated, uncomfortable office. However, if the company cannot find or afford such a person, then the company needs to improve the working conditions and provide the current employee with more training or more help with the technical aspects of the job.

Here is another example of what an industrial/organizational psychologist does: A plywood plant required workers to align strips of wood on a moving belt (Campion & Thayer, 1985). They had to bend over and reach out to move the strips while balancing on one leg and operating a foot pedal with the other. The supervisor was dissatisfied with their performance and grumbled that "workers today are lazy and inefficient." In fact, given how the task was designed, no one could have performed it comfortably. After I-O psychologists helped the company to redesign the equipment, workers were able to perform the task more effectively and to do so with fewer complaints.

As these two examples show, when a company blames its workers for doing a poor job, I-O psychologists often discover that the real problem lies with the job itself. In some cases, however, the problem does lie with the workers. In such cases, the I-O psychologist would try to improve the company's method of selecting employees, such as identify-

ing useful cognitive tests (similar to the tests students take in school), personality tests, improved interviews, biographical inventories, and so forth.

SOMETHING TO THINK ABOUT

I-O psychologists usually consult with business and industry, but suppose they were called upon to help a university where certain professors had complained that "the students are too lazy and stupid to understand the lectures." How might the I-O psychologists react? ✳

Ergonomics   Several years ago, my son Sam, who was then about 16 years old, turned to me as he was rushing out the door and asked me to turn off his stereo. I went to the stereo in his room and tried to find an "on-off" switch or a power switch. No such luck. I looked in vain for the manual. Finally, in desperation, I simply unplugged the stereo.

Learning to operate our increasingly complex machinery is one of the perennial struggles of modern life. Sometimes, the consequences can be serious. Imagine an airplane

Ergonomists help redesign machines to make them easier and safer to use. An ergonomist uses principles of both engineering and psychology.

pilot who intends to lower the landing wheels and instead raises the wing flaps. Or a worker in a nuclear power plant who fails to notice a warning signal.

In one specialized field of psychology, an **ergonomist,** or **human factors specialist,** *attempts to facilitate the operation of machinery so that the average user can use it as efficiently and as safely as possible.* The term *ergonomics* is derived from Greek roots meaning "laws of work." Ergonomics was first used in military settings, where complex technologies sometimes required soldiers to spot nearly invisible targets, to understand speech through deafening noise, to track objects in three dimensions while using two hands, and to make life-or-death decisions in a split second (Taylor, 1957). The military turned to psychologists to determine what skills their personnel could master and to redesign the tasks to fit those skills.

Ergonomists soon applied their experience not only to business and industry, but also to everyday devices. As Donald Norman (1988) pointed out, many intelligent and educated people find themselves unable to use all the features on a camera, a microwave oven, or a videocassette recorder; some even have trouble setting the time on a digital watch.

When designing machinery, ergonomists emphasize the **principle of compatibility,** *the concept that people's built-in or learned expectations enable them to learn certain procedures more easily than others.* For example, it is easier for us to learn that a burst of loud noise means danger than to learn that a particular melody means danger. Also, we are accustomed to turning a knob clockwise to increase the volume on a radio or television, so we expect to turn the knob clockwise on any new machine to increase almost anything. Similarly, we expect to turn the knob clockwise to move something to the right and counterclockwise to move something to the left (as we do when steering a car). These examples may seem obvious, but in many cases ergonomists must do trial-and-error research to find the best way to set up the controls for a new device.

At some universities, the ergonomics program is part of the psychology department; at others it is part of engineering; at still others, it is administered jointly by both departments. Regardless of who administers the program, ergonomics necessarily combines features of psychology, engineering, and computer science.

School Psychology   A great many children have academic problems at one time or another. Some children simply have trouble sitting still or paying attention. Others get into trouble for misbehavior. Others have specialized problems with reading, spelling, arithmetic, or other academic skills. Some have distractions in their home life that prevent them from concentrating on their studies. Other children, because of their special gifts or talents, master their schoolwork faster than most children and become bored. They, too, need special attention.

School psychologists are *specialists in the psychological condition of students,* usually in kindergarten through 12th grade. The role of school psychologists varies substantially, depending on the psychologists themselves, their education, and the school system for which they work. Broadly speaking, school psychologists identify the educational needs of children, devise a plan to meet those needs, and then either implement the plan themselves or advise teachers how to implement it. As of 1992, there were an estimated 87,000 active school psychologists worldwide (Oakland & Cunningham, 1992).

School psychology can be taught in a psychology department, a branch of the department of education, or a special department of educational psychology. In some countries, it is possible to practice school psychology with only a bachelor's degree. In the United States, the minimum is usually a master's degree, but job opportunities are much greater for people with a doctorate degree, and in the future, a doctorate may become necessary. The number of people employed as school psychologists has been growing sharply, and job opportunities are expected to continue to be plentiful. Most school psychologists work for a school system; others work for mental health clinics, guidance centers, and other institutions.

Table 1.2 summarizes some of the major fields of psychology, including several not discussed in the previous sections.

Should You Major in Psychology?

Can you get a job if you major in psychology? Psychology is one of the most popular majors in the United States, Canada, and Europe. So, if psychology majors cannot get jobs, a huge number of people are going to be in trouble!

The bad news is that very few jobs specifically advertise for college graduates with a bachelor's degree in psychology. The good news is that an enormous variety of jobs are available for graduates with a bachelor's degree, not specifying any major. Therefore, if you get a degree in psychology, you will compete with history majors, English majors, astronomy majors, phys ed majors, and lots of others for jobs in government, business, and industry. Some of those jobs do have direct relevance to psychology, particularly in personnel work or social services. Even if you get a job that seems remote from psychology, your psychology courses will have taught you a good deal about how to evaluate evidence, organize and write papers, handle statistics, listen carefully to what people say, understand and respect cultural differences, and so forth. In short, a psychology major can provide a useful background for a variety of jobs.

Psychology also provides a good background for people entering professional schools. Many students major in psychology and then apply to medical school, law school, divinity school, or other programs. Find out what course work is expected for the professional program of your choice, and

TABLE 1.2   Some Major Specializations in Psychology

SPECIALIZATION	GENERAL INTEREST	EXAMPLE OF SPECIFIC INTEREST OR RESEARCH TOPIC
Clinical psychologist	Emotional difficulties	How can people be helped to overcome severe anxiety?
Community psychologist	Organizations and social structures	Would improved job opportunities decrease certain types of psychological distress?
Counseling psychologist	Helping people to make important decisions and to achieve their potential	Should this person consider changing careers?
Developmental psychologist	Changes in behavior as people grow older	At what age can a child first distinguish between appearance and reality?
Educational psychologist	Improvement of learning in school	What is the best way to test a student's knowledge?
Environmental psychologist	The influence of noise, heat, crowding, and other environmental conditions on human behavior	How can a building be designed to maximize the comfort and productivity of the people who use it?
Ergonomist	Communication between person and machine	How can an airplane cockpit be redesigned to increase safety?
Experimental psychologist	Sensation, perception, learning, thinking, memory	Do people have several kinds of learning? Do they have several kinds of memory?
Industrial and organizational psychologist	People at work, production efficiency	Should jobs be made simple and foolproof or interesting and challenging?
Personality researcher	Personality differences	Why are certain people shy and others gregarious?
Biopsychologist	Relationship between brain and behavior	What body signals indicate hunger and satiety?
Psychometrician	Measurement of intelligence, personality, and interests	How fair are current IQ tests? Can we devise better tests?
School psychologist	Problems that affect schoolchildren	How should the school handle a child who regularly disrupts the classroom?
Social psychologist	Group behavior, social influences	What methods of persuasion are most effective for changing attitudes?

then compare the course work required for a psychology major. You will probably find considerable overlap.

If you want a career in psychology, you can greatly increase your options with an advanced degree, especially a doctorate. A doctorate will qualify you to apply for positions as a college professor or, depending on your area of specialization, jobs in hospitals, clinics, private practice, school systems, business and industry. If you are a first- or second-year college student now, it would probably take you at least eight years and probably longer, to get a doctorate, and no one can accurately predict the job market that far into the future. Learn as much as you can, both inside and outside the field of psychology, and keep your options open.

The types of people majoring in psychology have become more diverse over the years. For a long time, academic psychology, like most other academic disciplines, was dominated by men. Women students were not encouraged to seek a Ph.D. degree; those who did were rarely offered professorships at the most prestigious colleges or universities. Since the early 1970s, though, women have received a greatly increasing percentage of the advanced degrees in almost all academic fields. Figure 1.5 shows the growing percentage of women in psychology and several other fields (Pion et al., 1996). Women now receive more than half of the new doctorates in psychology, not only in the United States but in all European countries as well (Newstead & Makinen, 1997), and women dominate psychology more than most other academic and professional fields. Figure 1.6 shows the increasing representation of women separately in several subdivisions of psychology. Note the strong dominance in developmental psychology.

Minorities also constitute a growing percentage of psychologists, although the total number is still small. According to a 1988 survey in the United States, African-Americans, Hispanics, Asian-Americans, and other ethnic minorities combined received 11.4% of the doctorates awarded in clinical psychology. That percentage is low compared to many other academic fields. Many graduate schools now actively seek applications from minority students who would like to become psychologists (Hammond & Yung, 1993).

THE MESSAGE
Types of Psychologists

An experimental psychology researcher, a clinical psychologist, an ergonomist, and an industrial/organizational psychologist are all psychologists, even though their daily

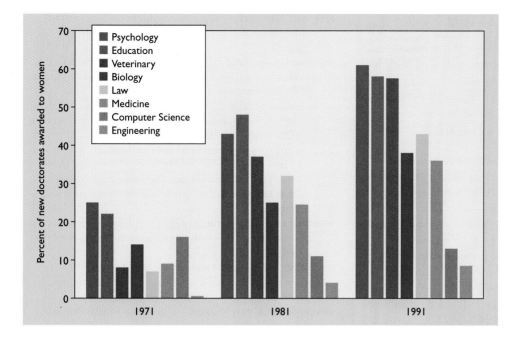

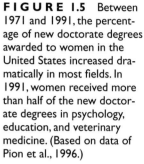

FIGURE 1.5 Between 1971 and 1991, the percentage of new doctorate degrees awarded to women in the United States increased dramatically in most fields. In 1991, women received more than half of the new doctorate degrees in psychology, education, and veterinary medicine. (Based on data of Pion et al., 1996.)

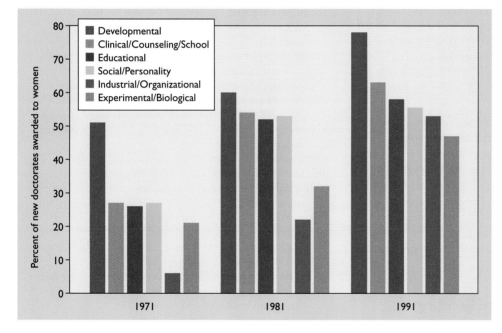

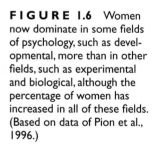

FIGURE 1.6 Women now dominate in some fields of psychology, such as developmental, more than in other fields, such as experimental and biological, although the percentage of women has increased in all of these fields. (Based on data of Pion et al., 1996.)

activities have little in common. What does unite psychologists is a dedication to psychological progress through research.

I have oversimplified this discussion of the various psychological approaches in several ways. First, it is only partly correct to refer to biological psychology, cognitive psychology, social psychology, and other fields as approaches. True, each constitutes one way of approaching certain phenomena of interest to all psychologists. But each is also a separate field of study with its own special phenomena. Biological psychologists ask questions about how the brain works; social psychologists ask questions about group behavior. Furthermore, the various approaches overlap significantly.

Nearly all psychologists combine insights and information gained from a variety of approaches. To understand why one person differs from another, most psychologists are interested in their biology, their past learning experiences, the social influences that have affected them, and much more.

As we proceed through this book, we shall consider one type of behavior at a time and, generally, one approach at a time. That is simply a necessity; we cannot talk intelligently about all kinds of psychological processes at once. But bear in mind that all these processes do ultimately fit together; what you do at any given moment depends on your biology, your past experiences, your social setting, your emotions, and a great deal more.

S U M M A R Y*

✳ *What is psychology?* Psychology is the systematic study of behavior and experience. Psychologists deal with both theoretical and practical questions. (page 5)

✳ *Determinism/free will.* Determinism is the view that everything that occurs, including human behavior, has a physical cause. That view is difficult to reconcile with the conviction that humans have free will—that we deliberately, consciously decide what to do. (page 5)

✳ *Mind-brain.* The mind-brain problem is the question of how conscious experience is related to the activity of the brain. (page 6)

✳ *Nature-nurture.* Behavior depends on both nature (heredity) and nurture (environment). Psychologists try to determine the influence of those two factors on differences in behavior. The relative contributions of nature and nurture vary from one behavior to another. (page 8)

✳ *Research fields in psychology.* Psychology is an academic field with many subfields, including biological psychology, learning and motivation, cognitive psychology, developmental psychology, and social psychology. (page 9)

✳ *Psychology versus psychiatry.* Clinical psychologists have either a Ph.D., Psy.D., or master's degree; psychiatrists are medical doctors. Both clinical psychologists and psychiatrists treat people with emotional problems, but only psychiatrists can prescribe drugs and other medical treatments. (page 11)

✳ *Nonclinical applied psychology.* Nonclinical fields of application include industrial/organizational psychology, ergonomics, and school psychology. (page 11)

✳ *Job prospects.* People with a bachelor's degree in psychology enter a wide variety of careers or continue their education in professional schools. Those with a doctorate in psychology have additional possibilities, depending on their area of specialization. In psychology, as in any other field, job prospects can change between the start and finish of one's education. (page 13)

Suggestion for Further Reading

Sechenov, I. (1965). *Reflexes of the brain.* Cambridge, MA: MIT Press. (Original work published 1863.) One of the first attempts to deal with behavior scientifically and still one of the clearest and most stimulating statements of the argument for determinism in human behavior.

Terms

psychology   the systematic study of behavior and experience (page 5)

determinism   the assumption that all behavior has a cause, or *determinant,* in the observable world (page 5)

free will   the doctrine that behavior is caused by a person's independent decisions, not by external determinants (page 7)

mind-brain problem   the philosophical question of how the conscious mind is related to the physical nervous system, including the brain (page 8)

nature-nurture issue   the question of the relative roles played by heredity (nature) and environment (nurture) in determining differences in behavior (page 9)

biopsychologist (or **behavioral neuroscientist**)   a specialist who tries to explain behavior in terms of biological factors, such as electrical and chemical activities in the nervous system, the effects of drugs and hormones, genetics, and evolutionary pressures (page 9)

learning and motivation   study of how behavior depends on the outcomes of past behaviors and on current motivations (page 9)

cognition   thinking and acquiring knowledge (page 9)

cognitive psychologist   a specialist who studies thought processes and the acquisition of knowledge (page 9)

developmental psychologist   a specialist who studies the behavioral capacities of different ages and how behavior changes with age (page 10)

social psychologist   a specialist who studies how an individual influences others and is influenced by other people (page 10)

psychotherapist   a specialist who provides help for people with psychological problems (page 10)

clinical psychologist   someone with an advanced degree in psychology, with a specialization in understanding and helping people with psychological problems (page 11)

psychiatry   a branch of medicine that deals with emotional disturbances (page 11)

psychoanalyst   a psychotherapist who relies heavily on the theories of Sigmund Freud (page 11)

industrial/organizational psychology   the study of people at work (page 11)

ergonomist or **human factors specialist**   a psychologist with engineering skills who works to facilitate the operation of machinery so that the average user can use it as efficiently and as safely as possible (page 13)

principle of compatibility   the concept that people's built-in or learned expectations enable them to learn certain procedures more easily than others (page 13)

school psychologist   a specialist in the psychological condition of students (page 13)

Answers to Concept Checks

1. **a.** Developmental psychology. **b.** Social psychology. **c.** Cognitive psychology. **d.** Biological psychology. **e.** Learning and motivation. (page 10)

2. Most psychoanalysts can prescribe drugs, because most are psychiatrists, and psychiatrists are medical doctors. However, psychoanalysts who are psychologists are not medical doctors and therefore cannot prescribe drugs. (page 11)

---

*The page numbers following each item indicate where you can review a topic.

Web Resources

What Is Psychology?

www.kean.edu/~psych/What_is.html

The Psychology Department at Kean University offers information about the discipline of psychology, some of the major subfields of psychology, and careers available to holders of undergraduate, master's, and doctoral degrees.

Psychological Science Agenda

www.apa.org/psa/

Psychological Science Agenda, the newsletter of the American Psychological Association Science Directorate, carried a series of articles written by people working in interesting and unusual nonacademic careers. Among the careers: Research in the Public Sector, Highway Safety Research, Market Research and Consulting, Acquisition and Sponsoring Editor, Director of Education and Research, Human Factors and User Interface Design, Trial Consultant, and Executive Search Consultant. The APA Science Directorate now sponsors a Personal Stories of Nonacademic Careers Web page (www.apa.org/science/psa.html) that lists most of these, and others.

MODULE 1.2
Psychology Then and Now

How did psychology originate?

How is it different now from what it was in its earliest era?

I magine yourself as a young scholar in about 1880. Enthusiastic about the new scientific approach in psychology, you have decided to become a psychologist yourself. Like other early psychologists, you have a background in either biology or philosophy. You are determined to apply the scientific methods of biology to the problems of philosophy.

So far, so good. But what questions will you address? A good, worthwhile research question is both important and answerable. In 1880, how would you decide which questions are important? You cannot get research ideas from a psychological journal, because the first issue won't be published until next year. You cannot follow in the tradition of previous researchers, because there haven't *been* any previous researchers. You are on your own.

Furthermore, in the late 1800s and early 1900s, psychologists were not yet sure which questions were answerable. Sometimes they are still unsure: Should we try to study the nature of human consciousness, or should we skip conscious experience and instead concentrate on describing what people actually do? Many of the changes that have occurred during the history of psychology have been changes in investigators' decisions about what constitutes a good research question.

In the next several pages, we shall explore some of these changes in psychological research questions, featuring a few projects that dominated psychology for a while and then faded from interest. I shall not mention Sigmund Freud or several other early pioneers whose contributions will be discussed in later chapters.

Psychology in the Early Era (1879 to about 1920)

At least since Aristotle (384–322 B.C.), philosophers have been debating why people act the way they do, why they have the experiences they do, and why one person is different from another. Writers such as Chaucer, Dostoyevsky, and Goethe have also made profound observations on human behavior.

Without discounting the importance of these great thinkers, several 19th-century scholars wondered whether a scientific approach would be fruitful. They were impressed by the great strides made in physics, chemistry, and biology; they believed that similar progress could be made in psychology if evidence were collected and evaluated scientifically.

Wilhelm Wundt and the First Psychological Laboratory

The origin of psychology, as we now know it, is generally dated to 1879, when a medical doctor and sensory researcher named Wilhelm Wundt (pronounced "voont") set up the first psychology laboratory, in Leipzig, Germany. Wundt and others had conducted psychological experiments before, but this was the first time anyone had established a laboratory exclusively for psychological research.

Wundt's fundamental question was: What are the components of experience, or mind? He proposed that psychological experience is composed of compounds, just as chemistry has compounds. Psychology, he maintained, has two kinds of elements—sensations and feelings (Wundt, 1896/1902)[1]. So, at any particular moment you might experience the taste of a fine meal, the sound of good music, and a certain degree of pleasure. These would merge together into a single experience, but that experience would still include the separate elements. Furthermore, Wundt maintained, your experience is partly under your control; even when the physical situation stays the same, you can shift your attention from one element to another and get a different experience.

Wundt's question about the components of experience was a philosophical one, and some of his opinions about the elements of the mind resembled the writings of philosophers before him. But Wundt, unlike these philosophers, tried to test his statements by collecting data. He presented various kinds of lights, textures, and sounds and asked subjects to report the intensity and quality of their sensations. He measured the changes in people's experiences as he changed the stimuli.

Wundt also demonstrated that it was possible to conduct meaningful psychological experiments. For example, in one of Wundt's earliest studies, he set up a pendulum that struck metal balls and made a sound at two points on its swing (points b and d in Figure 1.7). He or another subject would watch the pendulum and determine where it appeared to be when they heard the sound. In some cases, the pendulum appeared to be slightly in front of the ball and, in other cases, slightly behind the ball. The apparent position of the pendulum at the time of the sound differed from its actual position by an average of $\frac{1}{8}$ of a second (Wundt, 1862/1961). Apparently, we can be slightly wrong about the time that we see or hear something. Wundt's interpretation

---

[1]A reference containing a slash, such as this one, refers to a book originally published in the first year (1896) and reprinted in the second year (1902).

FIGURE 1.7 (Left) In one of Wilhelm Wundt's earliest experiments, the pendulum struck the metal balls (b and d), making a sound each time. To an observer, however, the ball appeared to be somewhere else at the time of the sound, generally the distance that it would travel in about ⅛ of a second. Wundt inferred that a person needs about ⅛ of a second to shift attention from one stimulus to another. (Right) The Walt Disney studios rediscovered Wundt's observation decades later: The character's mouth movements seem to be in synchrony with the sounds if the movements precede the sounds by ⅛ to ⅙ of a second.

was that a person needs about ⅛ second to shift attention from one stimulus to another.

Wundt and his students were prolific investigators; the brief treatment here does not do him justice. He contributed a great deal (writing more than 50,000 pages), but his most lasting impact on the field of psychology came from setting the precedent of studying psychological questions by collecting scientific data.

Edward Titchener and Structuralism

For years, most of the world's scientific psychologists received their education from Wilhelm Wundt himself. One of Wundt's students, Edward Titchener, came to the United States in 1892 as a psychology professor at Cornell University. Like Wundt, Titchener believed that the main question of psychology was the nature of mental experiences.

Titchener (1910) typically presented a stimulus and asked his subject to analyze it into its separate features— for example, to look at an apple and describe its redness, its brightness, its shape, and so forth. He called his approach **structuralism,** *an attempt to describe the structures that compose the mind.* He was less interested in what those elements *do* (their functions).

If you asked psychologists today whether they thought Titchener had correctly described the structures of the mind, you would probably get blank looks or shrugs of the shoulders. After Titchener died in 1927, psychologists virtually abandoned his research methods and even the questions he asked. Why? Remember that a good scientific question is both important and answerable. Regardless of whether Titchener's question about the elements of the mind was important, after all of his efforts, the question

seemed less and less answerable. The main reason was that, when observers described their experiences, Titchener could not check the accuracy of their descriptions.

For example, suppose you are the psychologist: I look at a lemon and tell you I have an experience of brightness that is totally separate from my experience of yellowness. How do you know whether I am lying to you, telling you what I think you want me to say, or even deceiving myself? You must take my word for it, unless you have another way of seeing into my mind. Other psychologists' frustration with this approach eventually turned many of them against studying the mind and toward studying observable behaviors.

William James and Functionalism

Almost simultaneously with the work of Wundt and overlapping the work of Titchener, Harvard University's William James articulated some of the major issues of psychology and won eventual recognition as the founder of American psychology. James's book *The Principles of Psychology* (James, 1890) defined the questions that dominated psychology for years afterward, and even to some extent today.

James had little patience for either Wundt's or Titchener's search for the elements of the mind. He focused concern on the actions that the mind *performs,* rather than the ideas that the mind *has.* That is, he did not care to isolate the elements of consciousness; he preferred *to learn how the mind produces useful behaviors.* For this reason, we call his approach **functionalism.** He suggested the following examples of good psychological questions (James, 1890):

- How can people strengthen good habits?
- How many objects can a person attend to at once?

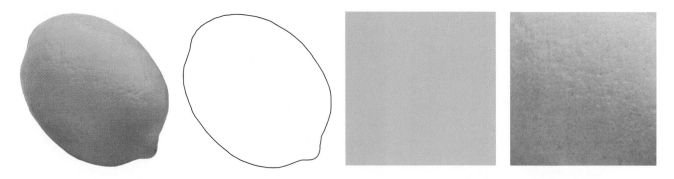

Edward Titchener asked subjects to describe their sensations. For example, they might describe their sensation of shape, their sensation of color, and their sensation of texture while looking at a lemon. Titchener had no way to check the accuracy of these reports, however, so later psychologists abandoned his methods.

- How do people recognize that they have seen something before?
- How does an intention lead to an action?

James proposed some possible answers, but did little research of his own to address these questions. His main contribution was to inspire later researchers to address the questions that he posed.

Studies of Sensation

For many early psychologists, the most important question was the relationship between physical stimuli and psychological sensations. To a large extent, the study of sensation *was* psychology. The first English-language textbook of the "new," scientifically based psychology devoted almost half of its pages to a discussion of the senses and the related topic of attention (Scripture, 1907). By the 1930s, standard psychology textbooks devoted less than 20% of their pages to these topics (Woodworth, 1934); today, the coverage of this topic constitutes about 5–10%.

Why were early psychologists so interested in sensation? One reason was philosophical: They wanted to understand mental experience, and experience is composed mostly if not entirely of sensations. The other reason was strategic: If psychologists were to demonstrate the possibil-

ity of a scientific psychology, they needed to begin with questions that were answerable, and many questions about sensation are indeed answerable.

Early psychologists discovered that what we see, hear, and otherwise sense is not the same as what is actually there. For example, the *perceived* intensity of a stimulus is not directly proportional to the *actual* physical intensity of the stimulus: For example, a light that is twice as intense as another light does not look twice as bright. Figure 1.8 shows the actual relationship between the intensity of light and its perceived brightness. *The mathematical description of the relationship between the physical properties of a stimulus and its perceived properties* is called the **psychophysical function,** because it relates psychology to physics. Such research demonstrated that, at least in the study of sensation, scientific methods can provide nonobvious answers to psychological questions.

The Influence of Darwin and the Study of Animal Intelligence

Charles Darwin's theory of evolution by natural selection (Darwin, 1859, 1871) had an enormous impact not only on biology but also on psychology. Darwin argued that humans and other species share a remote common ancestor. This

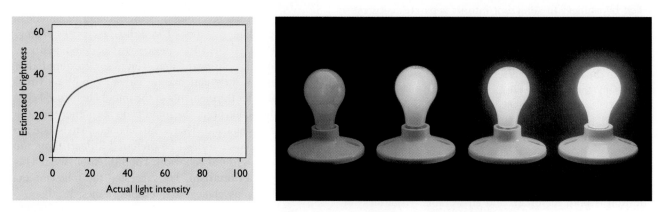

FIGURE 1.8   This graph of a psychophysical event shows the perceived intensity of light versus its physical intensity. When a light becomes twice as intense physically, it does not seem twice as bright. (Adapted from Stevens, 1961.)

proposal implied that each species had evolved specializations adapted to different ways of life, but it also implied that all vertebrate species had certain basic features in common. It implied also that nonhuman animals should exhibit varying degrees of human characteristics, including intelligence similar to human intelligence.

Presuming that we accept this last implication, what should psychologists do about it? Some early **comparative psychologists,** *specialists who compare different animal species,* did something that seemed reasonable at first, though it later seemed less and less fruitful: They set out to measure animal intelligence. They apparently imagined that they would be able to rank-order all animals from the smartest to the dullest. Toward that goal, they set various species to such tasks as the delayed-response problem and the detour problem. In the *delayed-response problem,* an animal was given a signal indicating where it could find food. Then the animal was delayed in its movement toward the food (Figure 1.9), to find out how long each species could remember the signal. In the *detour problem,* an animal was separated from food by a barrier (Figure 1.10), to find out which species would take a detour away from the food at first in order to get to it later.

Comparative psychologists set their animals to other tasks as well (Maier & Schneirla, 1964). But measuring animal intelligence turned out to be much more difficult than it sounded. Too often a species that seemed dull-witted with one task seemed highly capable on a very similar one. For example, zebras are generally slow to learn to approach one pattern instead of another for food, unless the patterns happen to be narrow stripes versus wide stripes, in which case zebras become geniuses (Giebel, 1958). (See Figure 1.11.) Rats perform very poorly when they have to find an object that looks different from the others but very well when they have to find an object that smells different (Langworthy & Jennings, 1972).

Eventually, psychologists realized that the relative intelligence of nonhuman animals was a complicated and perhaps meaningless question. Some researchers today even hesitate to say that monkeys are more intelligent than frogs (Macphail, 1985), preferring instead to talk about which particular sensory or learning functions are better developed in one species or another.

The Measurement of Human Intelligence

Some psychologists studied animal intelligence, but most had an even greater interest in human intelligence. Francis Galton, a first cousin of Charles Darwin, was among the

FIGURE 1.10 Another task popular among early comparative psychologists was the detour problem. An animal needed to first go away from the food in order to move toward it.

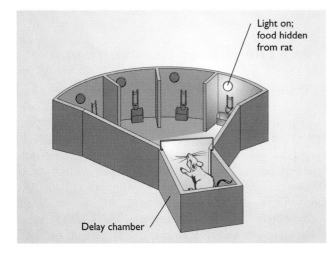

FIGURE 1.9 One of the tasks used by early comparative psychologists to assess animal intelligence tested the delayed-response problem. A stimulus was presented, and a delay ensued; then the animal was expected to respond to the remembered stimulus. Variations on this delayed-response task are still used today.

FIGURE 1.11 Zebras learn rapidly when they have to compare stripe patterns (Giebel, 1958). How "smart" a species is perceived to be depends in part on what ability or skill is being tested.

first to try to measure intelligence and to ask whether intellectual variations were based on heredity. Galton was fascinated with the measurement of almost anything and pioneered many new methods of measurements (Hergenhahn, 1992). For example, he invented the weather map, measured degrees of boredom during lectures, suggested the use of fingerprints to identify individuals, and—presumably, in the name of science—attempted to measure the degree of beauty of women in different countries.

In an effort to determine the role of heredity in human achievement, Galton (1869/1978) examined whether the sons of famous and accomplished men were likely to become equally eminent themselves. (He paid little attention to women, on the grounds that women in 19th-century England had little prospect of attaining eminence.) Galton found that the sons of judges, writers, politicians, and other noted men had a high probability of reaching high levels of accomplishment themselves. He attributed this edge to heredity, although today we would hardly consider his evidence persuasive: Sons of eminent men clearly had a favorable environment, not just favorable genes. Furthermore, he suggested that eminence is partly due to intelligence; thus, he believed that a tendency toward high or low intelligence was heritable.

Galton, however, had no valid test of intelligence. He attempted to measure intelligence using simple tests of sensory capacities and motor coordination, but none of these tests proved satisfactory. In 1905 a French researcher, Alfred Binet, devised the first useful intelligence test, which we shall discuss further in Chapter 9. At this point, we will just note that the idea of testing intelligence quickly captured a great deal of interest in the United States and other Western countries. Psychologists, perhaps inspired by the popularity of intelligence tests, later developed tests of personality, interests, and other psychological characteristics.

The Role of Women in the Early Days of Psychology

In the late 1800s and early 1900s, most U.S. colleges provided very limited opportunities for women, either as students or as faculty. Psychology was not much different from other fields in this regard, but a few women did make major contributions and achieved prominence.

One of the first to do so was Mary Calkins (Scarborough & Furomoto, 1987). When Henry Durant founded Wellesley College in 1870, he decided to hire only women to teach the all-female student body, but he could find no women with an advanced degree in psychology. Finally, in 1890, he hired a bright young woman, Mary Calkins (Figure 1.12), who had a B.A. degree in classics, to teach psychology, promising to pay for her graduate education in psychology. Then, he needed to find a graduate program that would accept a female student. After much debate and resistance, nearby Harvard University finally agreed to let her attend graduate classes. In 1895, when she passed the final examination for the Ph.D. degree, one of her professors re-

FIGURE 1.12 Mary Calkins, one of the first prominent women in U.S. psychology.

marked that she had performed better on the exam than had any other student in the history of the department.

The Harvard administration, however, was still unwilling to grant a Ph.D. degree to a woman and suggested a compromise instead: Calkins would receive a Ph.D. degree from Radcliffe College, the recently established women's undergraduate college associated with Harvard. Calkins refused, declaring that to accept the compromise would violate the high ideals of education. She never gave in, and neither did Harvard. Although Mary Calkins never did receive a Ph.D. degree, she became a pioneer in psychological research, served as president of the American Psychological Association, and invented a technique for studying memory, known as the paired-associates method, that is still used today.

The first woman to receive a Ph.D. degree in psychology was Margaret Washburn, who received her degree from Cornell University in 1894. She later wrote *The Animal Mind* (1908), the first textbook on that topic; she also served as president of the American Psychological Association. Christine Ladd-Franklin, another early psychologist, did outstanding research on vision, beginning in 1887.

The Rise of Behaviorism

Earlier in this chapter, I casually defined psychology as "the systematic study of behavior and experience." Most psychologists today would probably offer a similar definition, but for a substantial period of psychology's history, most experimental psychologists would have objected to the words "and experience." Some psychologists still object today, a little less strenuously. From about 1920 to 1960 or 1970, most laboratory researchers described psychology as simply the study of behavior, period. These researchers had little to say about minds, experiences, or anything of the sort. (According to one quip, psychologists had "lost their minds.")

How did psychologists reach this conclusion? Recall that Titchener's effort to analyze experience into its components had failed. Most psychologists then concluded that questions about the mind were unanswerable. The comparative psychologists had also failed in their efforts to measure animal intelligence, but in the process they had developed techniques for studying animal learning. Many psychologists discarded the question about animal intelligence but kept the research methods. The research questions they addressed were broad and simple: What do people and other animals do? And how do changes in the environment or in their experience change what they do? These questions were clearly meaningful, although no one knew yet whether the answers would consist of long lists of details or a short list of general laws.

John B. Watson and the Origin of Behaviorism

We can regard John B. Watson as the founder of **behaviorism,** *a field of psychology that concentrates on observable, measurable behaviors and not on mental processes.* Watson was not the first behaviorist—actually, it is difficult to say who was the first—but he systematized the approach, popularized it, and stated its goals and assumptions (Watson, 1919, 1925). Here are two quotes from Watson:

> Psychology as the behaviorist views it is a purely objective experimental branch of natural science. Its theoretical goal is the prediction and control of behavior. (Watson, 1913, p. 158)

> The goal of psychological study is the ascertaining of such data and laws that, given the stimulus, psychology can predict what the response will be; or, on the other hand, given the response, it can specify the nature of the effective stimulus. (Watson, 1919, p. 10)

Studies of Learning

Inspired by Watson, many researchers set out to study animal behavior, especially animal learning. Many optimistically expected to discover simple, basic laws of behavior

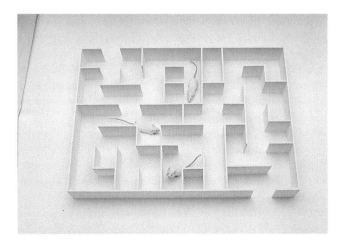

Early behaviorists studied rats in mazes, hoping to find general laws of behavior. As they discovered that this apparently simple behavior was very complicated, their interest declined and they turned to other topics.

comparable to Newton's laws of physics. Many experimenters believed that behavioral laws would be more or less the same from one species to another, so they studied animals, especially rats. By 1950, one psychologist found that well over half of all psychological studies on animals used rats as subjects (Beach, 1950).

Researchers simplified their task by not only concentrating on a few convenient species, but also by focusing on a few convenient examples of learning, such as maze learning. One highly influential Yale psychologist, Clark Hull, was very explicit about what he considered an important psychological question: "One of the most persistently baffling problems which confronts modern psychologists is the finding of an adequate explanation of the phenomena of maze learning" (Hull, 1932). Would you list that topic today as one of the most important things you would like to understand in psychology?

As research progressed, however, psychologists found that even the behavior of a rat in a maze was far more complicated than they had expected. As a result, they largely lost interest in maze studies, so the kinds of maze studies that were popular in the 1950s are a rarity today. Just as psychologists of the 1920s decided that Titchener's structuralist approach was unlikely to answer his questions within a reasonable period of time, psychologists of a later era abandoned the hope of discovering everything important about psychology by studying a few simple learning situations.

The Current Era in Psychology

The rest of this book will focus on the current era in psychology, with occasional flashbacks to the history of particular subfields. Psychology today is an extremely diverse field. Some researchers are trying to isolate simple mechanisms of behavior; others are attempting to understand highly complex processes; still others engage in a wide variety of practical applications.

Psychologists today have also broadened their scope to include more of human diversity. In an earlier era, psychological researchers who were seeking general laws or principles of behavior often assumed that they could discover these by studying rats, pigeons, or any other convenient species. When they studied humans, they generally limited themselves to convenient samples, such as college students. That strategy is justifiable for certain purposes—such as understanding how the eyes work—including characteristics that do not vary from one group of people (or animals) to another. For other purposes, the differences among people may be more important than the similarities, however. For example, when studying child-rearing practices, the growth of self-esteem, or marriage customs, psychologists compare the results from different cultures throughout the world and of various ethnic groups within a

Social psychologists study how our behavior depends on cultural influences, the expectations of others, and what we observe in other people's behavior.

given country. **Cross-cultural studies,** *research that compares people from various cultures,* have become increasingly influential in psychology.

Another noteworthy change in psychology is the explosive growth of neuroscience (the study of the brain). At one time, most psychologists thought they could safely ignore brain research, but no more. A theoretical understanding of behavior requires an understanding of the brain mechanisms behind it, and you will find references to biology in many sections of this text.

THE MESSAGE
Psychology Through the Years

Throughout the early years of psychology, many psychologists went down blind alleys, devoting enormous efforts to projects that produced disappointing results. Not all the efforts of early psychologists were fruitless, though; in later chapters, you will encounter some classic studies that have withstood the test of time. Still, if psychologists of the past spent countless years on fashionable projects, only to decide later that their efforts were misguided, how do we know that many psychologists aren't on the wrong track right now?

The answer is that we don't. Thousands of psychologists are engaged in various kinds of research, and chances are, many of them are working on projects that will never accomplish much. As you read through later chapters, you are welcome to entertain doubts. Maybe some psychologists' questions are not so simple as they seem; perhaps some of their answers are not very solid; perhaps you can think of a better way to approach certain topics.

In short, psychologists do not have all the answers. But that is not a reason for despair. Much like a rat in a maze, researchers make progress by trial and error. They pose a question, try a particular research method, and find out what happens. Sometimes the results are fascinating and rich in practical consequences; sometimes they turn out to be puzzling or inconclusive. If one study after another proves disappointing, psychologists either look for a new method or else they change the question they are asking. By abandoning unsuccessful approaches, they eventually find the way to better questions and better answers.

SUMMARY

✳ *Choice of research questions.* During the history of psychology, researchers have several times changed their opinions about what constitutes an interesting, important, answerable question. (page 18)

✳ *First experiments.* In 1879 Wilhelm Wundt established the first laboratory devoted to psychological research. He demonstrated the possibility of psychological experimentation. (page 18)

✳ *Limits of self-observation.* One of Wundt's students, Edward Titchener, attempted to analyze the elements of mental experience, relying on people's own observations. Other psychologists became discouraged with this approach. (page 19)

✳ *The founding of American psychology.* William James, generally considered the founder of American psychology, focused attention on how the mind guides useful behavior, rather than on the contents of the mind. By doing so, James paved the way for the rise of behaviorism. (page 19)

✳ *Early sensory research.* In the early days of psychology, many researchers concentrated on studies of the senses, partly because they were more likely to find definite answers on this topic than on other topics. (page 20)

✳ *Darwin's influence.* Charles Darwin's theory of evolution by natural selection influenced psychology in many ways; it prompted some prominent early psychologists to compare the intelligence of different species. That question turned out to be more complicated than anyone had expected. (page 20)

✳ *Intelligence testing.* The measurement of human intelligence was one concern of early psychologists that has persisted through the years. (page 21)

✳ *Women in the early days of psychology.* In spite of an environment that discouraged women from pursuing academic careers, several women (including Mary Calkins and Margaret Washburn) became leaders during the early days of psychology. (page 22)

✳ *The era of behaviorist dominance.* As psychologists became discouraged with their attempts to analyze the mind, they turned to behaviorism. For many years, psychological researchers concentrated on behavior, especially animal learning, to the virtual exclusion of mental experience. (page 22)

✳ *Maze learning.* Clark Hull exerted great influence for a number of years. Eventually, his approach became less popular because rats in mazes did not seem to generate simple or general answers to major questions. (page 23)

✳ *Psychological research today.* Today, psychologists study a wide variety of topics. Still, we cannot be certain that we are not currently going down some blind alleys, just as many psychologists did before us. (page 23)

Suggestion for Further Reading

Scarborough, E., & Furomoto, L. (1987). *Untold lives: The first generation of American women psychologists.* New York: Columbia University Press. A rich account of history and biography.

Terms

structuralism an attempt to describe the structures that compose the mind (page 19)

functionalism an attempt to understand how mental processes produce useful behaviors (page 19)

psychophysical function the mathematical description of the relationship between the physical properties of a stimulus and its perceived properties (page 20)

comparative psychologist a specialist who compares different animal species (page 21)

behaviorism a field of psychology that concentrates on observable, measurable behaviors and not on mental processes (page 23)

cross-cultural studies research studies that compare people from various cultures (page 24)

Web Resources

HistPsyc Headlines Pages

www.unb.ca/web/units/psych/likely/headlines/

David Likely, at the University of New Brunswick, produced the HistPsyc Headlines Pages, which provide a history of important events related to psychology from 1650 to 1959, plus links to related sites. He has also developed several on-line study aids for students interested in the history of psychology that are available from his home page at www.unb.ca /web/units/psych/likely/psyc4053.htm.

Today in the History of Psychology

www.cwu.edu/~warren/today.html

Warren Street, at Central Washington University, offers a sample of events in the history of psychology for every day of the year. Pick a date, any date (as they say), from the History of Psychology Calendar and see what happened on that date. APA sponsors this site, which is based on Street's book, *A Chronology of Noteworthy Events in American Psychology.*

Scientific Methods in Psychology

2

Every year spectacular claims are published about human behavior and related matters, even if little or no evidence exists to support the claims. Some examples:

• *Alien abductions*. Some people claim that they have been abducted by alien invaders, examined aboard a spacecraft, and then returned to Earth. To the question of why other people have not seen or photographed these aliens or their spacecraft, some of the "abductees" reply that the invaders and their craft are invisible, and so are the abductees during the period of their abduction.

• *Age regression*. Some people claim that, under hypnosis and using similar techniques, a person can recall in great detail what it was like to be a young child, a baby, an embryo, or even a sperm cell (Sadger, 1941). (One man said that he and his fellow sperm cells had resented their father because they knew he did not want them to fertilize the egg!)

• *Buried treasures*. According to one group of believers, a vault buried beneath Bruton Parish Church in Williamsburg, Virginia, contains "the missing crown jewels of England," Francis Bacon's birth certificate, the original manuscripts of Shakespeare's plays, and some documents that can establish world peace (Sheaffer, 1992). Leaders of this church had to get a legal restraining order to make these people stop digging under their church. One point that the believers cite as "evidence" for their claims: Look at the flag of the state of Virginia. It shows the Greek goddess Athena pointing a spear. And where is the spear pointed? *At the ground! Where the vault is buried!*

Most of us quickly dismiss such preposterous claims. Even if we do not dismiss them immediately, we are likely to ask the correct skeptical questions: What is the evidence? How good is that evidence? Can we find another, more reasonable explanation?

It is more difficult to discipline ourselves to ask these same questions about more plausible claims. When someone announces a "new scientific finding" that agrees with what we already believe or want to believe, we may find it very tempting to accept this new finding without subjecting it to careful scrutiny. It is a good idea to habitually check the evidence carefully for every claim, so far as possible; occasionally, the evidence will force us to change our opinions. This chapter concerns the kinds of evidence that psychologists use and the methods that they use to evaluate theoretical claims.

Science and the Evaluation of Evidence

How do scientists evaluate theories?

Why are most scientists so skeptical of new theories and claims that seem to contradict our current understanding?

You will sometimes hear nonscientists say that something has been "scientifically proved." Scientists themselves seldom use the word *proved*, except when they are talking about a mathematical proof. As scientists collect more and better evidence, they may become confident about a given conclusion, but the word *prove* sounds a little too final.

One distinguishing characteristic of science is that scientists generally agree on how to evaluate competing theories. Even when they disagree about which theory is best, they can usually agree on what kinds of evidence they will accept. Most psychologists are quick to concede that our knowledge of psychology is less complete and less systematic than our knowledge of physics, chemistry, and biology. But like physicists, chemists, and biologists, psychologists do generally agree on what constitutes good evidence and what does not. They try to rely on the best available evidence and draw no conclusion at all if the evidence is weak.

SOMETHING TO THINK ABOUT

If people interested in ethics agreed with one another about how to evaluate theories, could they make progress comparable to that of scientists? Could theologians? ✳

Steps for Gathering and Evaluating Evidence

Above all, scientists want to know the evidence behind a given claim. In psychology, as in other fields, students should learn to question assertions, to ask for the evidence behind a given claim.

The word *science* derives from a Latin word meaning *knowledge,* and there are many routes to scientific knowledge. The simplest is just careful observation, and much of science consists of recording observations. We also gain scientific knowledge by testing **hypotheses,** which are *testable predictions of what will happen under certain conditions.* Research designed to test hypotheses goes through the series of steps described in the following four paragraphs (see also Figure 2.1). Articles in scientific publications generally follow this sequence, too. In each of the following chapters of this book, you will find an example of a psychological study, described in a section entitled "What's the Evidence?"

Hypothesis A hypothesis can be based on a larger theory. For example, "if our understanding of social influence is correct, then children who watch a great deal of violence will themselves become more violent." In other cases, the hypothesis is the product of preliminary observations. For example, a psychologist might notice that several children who have outbursts of violent behavior have a habit of watching violent television programs and therefore suggest the hypothesis that watching violent programs leads to violent behavior.

Method Researchers have many methods for testing hypotheses. To test the effects of violent television shows, one possibility would be to measure how much time various children watch violence on television and relate that amount of time to a measure of their violent behavior. However, even if the correlation appeared strong, the results would not demonstrate cause and effect. (Maybe watching violence provokes violence, but it is also possible that children who are predisposed to violence like to watch it on TV.) Another approach would be to ask one group of children to

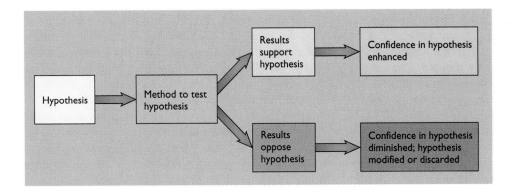

FIGURE 2.1 A hypothesis leads to predictions. An experimental method tests those predictions; a confirmation of a prediction supports the hypothesis; a disconfirmation indicates a need to revise or discard the hypothesis. Conclusions remain tentative, especially after only one experiment. Most scientists avoid saying that their results "prove" a conclusion.

watch one set of programs and another group to watch a different set of programs, and then record behavioral differences between the groups.

Results   Fundamental to any research is good measurement, and a phenomenon such as "violent behavior" can be especially tricky to measure. (How do we decide what is *real* violence and what is just playfulness? Do threats count? verbal abuse?) It is important for an investigator to adopt clear rules for making measurements and then use these rules consistently. Depending on the nature of the study, the investigator calculates appropriate statistics for expressing the results and evaluating whether these probably indicate a meaningful trend or just a random fluctuation.

Interpretation   The final task is to determine the significance of the results. If the results clearly contradict the hypothesis, researchers should either abandon or modify the original hypothesis. (Maybe it applies only to certain kinds of people or only under certain circumstances.) If the results *match* the prediction, investigators may gain confidence in their hypothesis but they should not necessarily accept it. Even though the results fit the hypothesis, they might also fit other hypotheses or explanations as well. Because almost any study has limitations, the ultimate conclusion can come only from a pattern of results derived from many studies.

Replicability

Years ago, investigators trained rats to respond in a certain way, then ground up the rats' brains, injected an extract of the trained rats' brains into other rats, and reported that the new rats remembered what the old rats had learned (Babich, Jacobson, Bubash, & Jacobson, 1965). Many other experimenters tried to replicate this surprising result. A few reported results somewhat similar to those of the first experimenters, but most investigators could not (Gaito, 1976; L. T. Smith, 1975). That is, these results were not replicable. **Replicable results** are *those that anyone can obtain, at least approximately, by following the same procedures.*

What should we do when results are not replicable? First, we determine whether the different investigators really used the same procedures. Sometimes, what appears to be a minor change in procedure yields a major difference in results. Did the researchers use different kinds of rats, or different methods of training, or different ways of extracting brain chemicals? In the research on transfer of training by brain extracts, psychologists found no consistent relationship between the results and any aspect of the procedure. In fact, most laboratories found no evidence that the brain extracts had any influence on other rats under any conditions. So, then what? The rule is that, if researchers cannot find conditions under which they dependably get a particular result, then they do not accept that result. This rule may

seem unduly harsh, but it is our best defense against error. If scientists cannot replicate a result, then the studies claiming to have that result may have hidden flaws.

Sometimes, however, an effect is small but real. For example, many studies have compared unprovoked aggressive behavior in men and women. Some studies have found that men are substantially more aggressive; some have found men to be slightly more aggressive; and a few have found no difference or a difference in the opposite direction. Despite this variation, we do not regard the sex difference in aggressive behavior to be unreplicable. Rather, our interpretation is that the sex difference is small and that it competes with many other influences on aggressive behavior. If we combine the results of many studies, we can get an approximate measure of the size of the effect. A **meta-analysis** *combines the results of many studies and analyzes them as though they were all one very large study.* For example, one meta-analysis found that men are indeed more likely than women to engage in unprovoked violence (Bettencourt & Miller, 1996). In most cases, a meta-analysis will also determine which variations in procedure are associated with the largest effects.

Criteria for Evaluating Scientific Theories

Up to now, I have alluded to research in psychology without using much detail. We shall consider the details of research methods later. Here, let's look at the big picture: After investigators collect mounds of evidence, what do they do with it?

One goal of scientific research is to establish **theories,** *comprehensive explanations of observable events.* A good theory predicts many observations in terms of a few assumptions and thus reduces the amount of information we must keep available for reference. For example, according to the *law of effect* (to be discussed in Chapter 6), if a human or any other animal makes a response that is consistently followed by a reinforcer (such as food to a hungry person or water to a thirsty one), then the future probability of that response will increase. This law summarizes results achieved for many species, many responses, and many reinforcers.

When we are confronted with several competing theories, we must evaluate them to decide which is the most acceptable (Figure 2.2). To illustrate, let's consider some unsatisfactory theories. First, consider what is wrong with this theory: "Karl is stingy, so he must have had a fixation in the anal period of psychosocial development." The theory fits the data (Karl is stingy), but we already knew those data before the theorist said anything. No one had any other reason to believe that Karl had an anal fixation, except that he became stingy. So the theory does not really make any predictions. One important criterion for any theory is that it *should predict new observations.* If it accurately predicts ob-

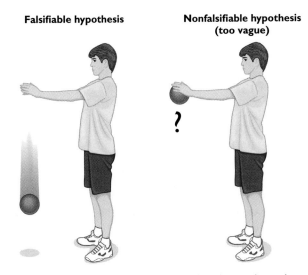

Falsifiable hypothesis

**Nonfalsifiable hypothesis
(too vague)**

?

An object dropped near the Earth's surface will fall at a rate of 980.665 cm/sec², slowed slightly by air resistance.

If an object is dropped, something interesting will happen.

FIGURE 2.2 A good theory makes precise (falsifiable) predictions.

servations that no one had previously expected, then we have reason to be impressed with the theory.

Second, consider what is wrong with this theory: "People who are under too much stress will fail to achieve their full potential." The statement is probably true, but it is too vague to be useful. We do not know how much stress is "too much" for a given individual, and there is no way to measure a person's "full potential." The more precise a theory's predictions, the better. One way of saying this is that a theory should be **falsifiable.** What scientists mean by *falsifiable* is that *the theory makes sufficiently precise predictions that we can at least imagine evidence that would contradict the theory (if we in fact obtained such evidence).* Of course, if someone actually obtained evidence that contradicted the predictions, then the theory would be falsifi-*ed.* Falsified is not good. Falsifi-*able* is different; it does not mean that the theory has been shown to be wrong, just that, if it *were* wrong, we could demonstrate it to be wrong. "Too much stress prevents someone from reaching full potential" is not falsifiable, because no conceivable result would contradict it. "Vision occurs after light stimulates the eyes" is falsifiable; vision experienced by an eyeless person or vision in complete darkness would contradict the theory. Therefore, we are impressed that no one has ever found such results.

Now, consider what is wrong with this theory: "I did not wake up on time today, so I must have been kidnapped by aliens." The problem here is that we can easily conceive of a simpler explanation for the fact that someone overslept. Given a choice between an exciting, surprising explanation and a commonplace, boring explanation that fits the same results, scientists favor the commonplace explanation. This preference for simple explanations, known as the *principle of parsimony (literally, stinginess),* is central to scientific thinking, so we shall examine it in detail on the following pages.

CONCEPT CHECK

1. Identify each of the following theories as either falsifiable or not falsifiable:
    a. An object dropped in a vacuum at a low altitude above the Earth will fall with an acceleration of 9.8 m/s^2, where m = meters and s = seconds.
    b. Some people have supernatural powers that science cannot explain.
    c. Children who suffer any kind of frustration during the first year of life will eventually develop emotional difficulties. (Check your answers on page 36.)

SOMETHING TO THINK ABOUT

Is the theory that "there is intelligent life elsewhere in the universe" falsifiable? Is the theory that "there is *no* intelligent life elsewhere in the universe" falsifiable? When it is impractical to test a theory or its converse, should we compromise our usual rules about replicable evidence and falsifiability? ✱

The Principle of Parsimony and Degrees of Open-Mindedness

According to the principle of **parsimony,** *scientists prefer the theory that explains the results using the simplest assumptions.* In other words, scientists prefer a new theory that is consistent with other theories that they have already accepted. A theory that makes radically new assumptions is acceptable only after we have made every attempt to explain the results in a simpler way.

Parsimony is a conservative tendency: It tells us to adhere as much as possible to what we already believe. You might protest: "Shouldn't we remain open-minded to new possibilities?"

Yes, if open-mindedness means a willingness to consider proper evidence, but not if it means the assumption that "anything has as much chance of being true as anything else." That is, the degree of our open-mindedness should depend on the strength of the evidence or logic supporting our current opinion. Consider two examples:

Visitors from outer space. I personally do not believe that visitors from other planets have ever landed on Earth, and I regard the prospect of travel between one solar system and another as unlikely. Still, the technology and the biology of alien life could be very different from ours. If I saw nonhuman pilots stepping out of an odd-looking spacecraft, I would quickly change my opinion about long-distance space travel.

Perpetual motion machines. A "perpetual motion machine" is one that generates more energy than it uses. For centuries, people have attempted and failed to develop such a machine. (Figure 2.3 shows one example.) The U.S. Patent Office is officially closed-minded on this issue, refusing even to consider patent applications for such machines, because a perpetual motion machine violates the second law of thermodynamics. (According to that law, within a closed system, entropy—disorganization—can never decrease. Any work will increase the entropy, and therefore waste some energy.) The second law of thermodynamics is more than just a summary of careful observations; it is a logical necessity, equivalent to stating that a more probable state is more probable than a less probable state. If someone shows you what appears to be a perpetual motion machine, you should not be easily persuaded; look for a hidden battery or other power source. The more extraordinary someone's claim is, the more extraordinary the evidence must be before you should accept their claim.

But what does all this discussion have to do with psychology? Sometimes, people claim spectacular results that would seem to be impossible according to everything else we know or think we know. Although it is only fair to examine the evidence behind such claims, it is also reasonable to maintain a skeptical attitude and to look as hard as possible for a simple, parsimonious explanation of the results. Let us consider two examples.

An Example of Applying Parsimony: Clever Hans, the Amazing Horse

Early in the 20th century, Mr. von Osten, a German mathematics teacher, set out to prove that his horse, Hans, had great intellectual abilities, particularly in arithmetic (Figure 2.4). To teach Hans arithmetic, he first showed him a single object, said "One," and lifted Hans's foot once. Then he raised Hans's foot twice for two ob-

jects, and so on. Eventually, when von Osten presented a group of objects, Hans learned to tap his foot by himself, and with practice he managed to tap the correct number of times. With more practice, it was no longer necessary for Hans to see the objects. Von Osten would just call out a number, and Hans would tap the appropriate number of times.

Mr. von Osten moved on to addition and then to subtraction, multiplication, and division. Hans caught on quickly, soon responding with 90–95% accuracy. Then von Osten began touring Germany to exhibit Hans's abilities. He would ask Hans a question, and Hans would tap out the answer. As time passed, Hans's abilities grew, until he could add fractions, convert fractions to decimals or vice versa, do simple algebra, tell time to the minute, and give the values of all German coins. Using a letter-to-number code, he could spell out the names of objects and even identify musical notes such as D or B-flat. (Hans, it seems, had perfect pitch.) He responded correctly even when questions were put to him by persons other than von Osten, in unfamiliar places, with von Osten nowhere in sight.

Given this evidence, many people were ready to assume that Hans had great intellectual prowess. But others sought a more parsimonious explanation. Enter Oskar Pfungst. Pfungst (1911) discovered that Hans could not answer a question correctly unless the questioner had calculated the answer first. Evidently, the horse was somehow getting the answers from the questioner. Next Pfungst learned that, when the experimenter stood in plain sight, Hans's accuracy was 90% or better, but when he could not see the experimenter, his answers were almost always wrong.

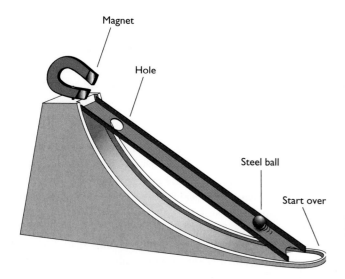

FIGURE 2.3 A proposed "perpetual motion machine": The magnet pulls the metal ball up the inclined plane. When the ball reaches the top, it falls through the hole and returns to its starting point, from which the magnet will again pull it up. Can you see why this device is sure to fail? (See Answer A on page 36.)

FIGURE 2.4 Clever Hans and his owner, Mr. von Osten, demonstrated that the horse could answer complex mathematical questions with great accuracy. The question was "how?" (After Pfungst, 1911, in Fernald, 1984.)

Eventually, Pfungst observed that any questioner who asked Hans a question would lean forward to watch Hans's foot. Hans had simply learned to start tapping whenever someone stood next to his right forefoot and leaned forward. As soon as Hans had given the correct number of taps, the experimenter would give a slight upward jerk of the head and change facial expression in anticipation that this might be the last tap. (Even skeptical scientists who tested Hans did this involuntarily.) Hans simply continued tapping until he received that cue.

In short, Hans was indeed a clever horse. However, his feats could be explained in simple terms. We now prefer the explanation in terms of facial expressions because it is more parsimonious.

SOMETHING TO THINK ABOUT

If Clever Hans had died before Pfungst had discovered his secret, we would never have known for sure how the horse was making his "calculations." Would we be obliged to believe forever that this one horse could understand spoken language and solve complex mathematical problems? How could we have evaluated such a hypothesis years later? (Hint: Would we have needed to discover how Hans answered the questions? Or would it be enough just to determine how he *could* have answered them?) ✳

Another Example of Applying Parsimony: Extrasensory Perception

One highly controversial topic in psychology is **extrasensory perception.** Supporters of extrasensory perception (ESP) *claim that certain people can acquire information without using any sense organ and without receiving any form of physical energy.* These people claim, for instance, that a person gifted with ESP can identify another person's thoughts (via telepathy) even when the two are separated by a thick lead barrier that would block the transmission of almost any form of energy. They also claim that people with telepathic powers can identify thoughts just as accurately from a distance of a thousand kilometers as from an adjacent room, in apparent violation of the inverse-square law of physics.

Some ESP supporters also claim that certain people can perceive inanimate objects that are hidden from sight (clairvoyance), predict the future (precognition), and influence such physical events as a roll of dice by sheer mental concentration (psychokinesis). In other words, they claim it is possible to gain information or to influence physical events without receiving or transmitting any physical energy. A conclusive demonstration of any of these claims would require us not only to overhaul some major concepts in psychology, but also to discard some of the most fundamental tenets of physics.

What evidence is there for ESP?

Master magician Lance Burton can make people and animals seem to suddenly appear, disappear, float in the air, or do other things that we know are impossible. Even if we don't know how he accomplishes these feats, we take it for granted that they are magic tricks, based on methods of misleading the audience. Other performers claim their amazing results depend on psychic powers. A more parsimonious explanation is that their feats, like Burton's, depend on misleading the audience.

Anecdotes

One kind of evidence consists of anecdotes—people's reports of isolated events. Someone has a dream or a hunch that comes true or says something and someone else says, "I was just thinking exactly the same thing!" Such experiences may seem impressive when they occur, but they are meaningless as scientific evidence for several reasons: First, consider the possibility of coincidence. Of all the hunches and dreams that people have, some are bound to come true eventually by pure chance. Second, people tend to remember and talk about the hunches and dreams that *do* come true and to forget those that do not. They hardly ever say, "Strangest thing! I had a dream, but then nothing like it actually happened!" Third, people tend to exaggerate the coincidences that occur, both in their own memories and in the retelling. We could evaluate anecdotal evidence only if people recorded their hunches and dreams before the predicted events and then determined how many unlikely predictions actually came to pass.

You may have heard of the "prophet Nostradamus," a 16th-century French writer who allegedly predicted many events in later centuries. Figure 2.5 presents four samples of his writings. No one knows what his predictions mean until after the predicted events happen. After something happens, people imaginatively reinterpret his writings to fit the event. (His predictions are not falsifiable.)

1. The great man will be struck down in the day by a thunderbolt. An evil deed, foretold by the bearer of a petition. According to the prediction another falls at night time. Conflict at Reims, London, and pestilence in Tuscany.

2. When the fish that travels over both land and sea is cast up on to the shore by a great wave, its shape foreign, smooth, and frightful. From the sea the enemies soon reach the walls.

3. The bird of prey flying to the left, before battle is joined with the French, he makes preparations. Some will regard him as good, others bad or uncertain. The weaker party will regard him as a good omen.

4. Shortly afterwards, not a very long interval, a great tumult will be raised by land and sea. The naval battles will be greater than ever. Fires, creatures which will make more tumult.

FIGURE 2.5 According to the followers of Nostradamus, each of these statements is a specific prophecy of a 20th-century event (Cheetham, 1973). Can you figure out what the prophecies mean? Compare your answers to Answer B on page 36. The prophecies of Nostradamus are so vague that no one knows what they mean until after the predicted event. Consequently, they are not really predictions and also not testable.

CONCEPT CHECK

2. How could someone scientifically evaluate the accuracy of Nostradamus's predictions? (Check your answer on page 36.)

Professional Psychics Several stage performers claim to read other people's minds and to perform other psychic feats. Two of the most famous are Uri Geller and the Amazing Kreskin. Actually, Kreskin has consistently denied doing anything supernatural; he prefers to talk of his "extremely sensitive," rather than "extrasensory" perception (Kreskin, 1991). Still, part of Kreskin's success as a performer comes from allowing people to believe he has mental powers that defy explanation, and his performances are similar to those of people who do call themselves psychics.

 After carefully observing Geller, Kreskin, and others, David Marks and Richard Kammann (1980) concluded that these performers exhibited the same kinds of deception commonly employed in magic shows. For example, Kreskin sometimes begins his act by asking the audience to read his mind. Let's try to duplicate this trick right now: Try to read my mind. I am thinking of a number between 1 and 50. Both digits are odd numbers, but they are not the same. That is, it could be 15 but it could not be 11. (These are the instructions Kreskin gives.) Have you chosen a number? Please do.

All right, my number was 37. Did you think of 37? If not, how about 35? You see, I started to think 35 and then changed my mind, so you might have got 35.

Probably about half of my readers successfully "read my mind." If you were one of them, are you impressed? Don't be. There are not many numbers that you could have chosen. The first digit had to be 1 or 3, and the second had to be 1, 3, 5, 7, or 9. You had to eliminate 11 and 33 because

both digits are the same, and you probably eliminated 15 because I cited it as a possible example. That leaves only seven possibilities. Most people like to stay far away from the example given and tend to avoid the highest and lowest possible choices. That leaves 37 as the most likely choice and 35 as the second most likely.

Second act: Kreskin asks the audience to write down something they are thinking about while he walks along the aisles talking. Then, back on stage, he "reads people's minds." He might say something like, "Someone is thinking about their mother . . ." In any large crowd, someone is bound to stand up and shout, "Yes, that's me, you read my mind!" On occasion he describes something that someone has written out in great detail. That person generally turns out to be someone sitting along the aisle where Kreskin was walking.

After a variety of other tricks (see Marks & Kammann, 1980), Kreskin goes backstage while the local mayor or some other dignitary hides Kreskin's paycheck somewhere in the audience. Then Kreskin comes back, walks up and down the aisles and across the rows, and eventually shouts, "The check is here!" The rule is that if he guesses wrong, then he does not get paid. (He hardly ever misses.)

How does he do this trick? Think for a moment before reading on. Very simply, it is a Clever Hans trick. Kreskin studies people's faces. Most of the people are silently cheering for him to find the check. Their facial expression changes subtly as he comes close to the check and then moves away. In effect, they are saying, "Now you're getting closer" and "Now you're moving away." At last he closes in on the check. That is, Kreskin has trained himself to use his senses very well; he does not need an "extra" sense.

We can also explain the performances of many other stage performers in terms of simple tricks and illusions. Of course, someone always objects, "Well, maybe so. But there's this other guy you haven't investigated yet. Maybe he really does possess psychic powers." Until there is solid evidence to the contrary, it is simpler (more parsimonious) to assume that other performers are also using illusion and deception.

Experiments

Because stage performances and anecdotal events always take place under uncontrolled conditions, we cannot determine the probability of coincidence or the possibility of deception. Laboratory experiments provide the only evidence about ESP worth serious consideration.

For example, consider the *ganzfeld* procedure (from German words meaning "the entire field"). A "sender" is given a photo or film, selected at random from four possibilities, and a "receiver" in another room is asked to describe the sender's thoughts and images. Typically, the receiver wears half Ping-Pong balls over the eyes and listens to static noise over earphones to minimize normal stimuli that might overpower the presumably weaker extrasensory stimuli (Figure 2.6). Later, a judge examines a transcript of what the receiver said and compares it to the four photos or films, determining which one it matches most closely. On the average, it should match the target about one out of four times. If a subject "hits" more often than one in four, we can calculate the probability of accidentally doing that well. (ESP researchers, or parapsychologists, use a variety of other experimental procedures, but in each case the goal is to determine whether someone can gain more information than could be explained by chance without using their senses.)

We can summarize the results of ESP experiments as follows: Over the decades we have gone through many cycles. First, ESP researchers announce that they have good evidence for a given phenomenon. Then, critics find flaws in the procedure or report failures to replicate. Then ESP researchers admit that the previous research was inconclusive but claim that they now have a better procedure and better evidence (Hyman, 1994). Currently, ESP researchers seem most enthusiastic about the ganzfeld method described above. According to one review, six of the ten laboratories that have used this method have reported positive results (Bem & Honorton, 1994); believers claim that researchers have finally found a replicable experiment.

Perhaps, and certainly the best way to test this claim is for more investigators to conduct more research. However, most psychologists remain skeptical—I would say justifiably so. Why? First, they are aware of the long history of flawed procedures, weak evidence, and nonreplicable results in this field of study. With the *ganzfeld* procedures, half of the published research has come from just two laboratories, and one of those laboratories has been strongly criticized for using faulty research methods (Blackmore, 1994). Under the circumstances, it would be premature (at least) to call the latest results "replicable."

Second, psychologists generally look for the most parsimonious explanation for any phenomenon. If someone

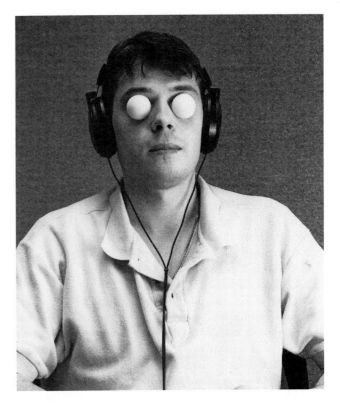

FIGURE 2.6 In the *ganzfeld* procedure, a "receiver," who is deprived of most normal sensory information, tries to describe the photo or film that a "sender" is examining.

claims to have a horse that does mathematics or a person claims to be able to read the mind of a person in another room, we should search thoroughly for a simpler explanation and adopt a radically new explanation only if the evidence absolutely and consistently forces us to do so. (Even then, we cannot accept a new explanation until someone specifies it clearly. Saying that some result demonstrates "an amazing ability that science cannot explain" does not constitute an explanation.)

THE MESSAGE
Scientific Thinking in Psychology

What have we learned about science in general? Science does not deal with proof or certainty. All scientific conclusions are tentative and are subject to revision. The history of any scientific field contains examples of theories that were once widely accepted and were later revised. Nevertheless, this tentativeness does not imply a willingness to abandon well-established theories in the face of any apparently contradictory evidence.

Scientists always prefer the most parsimonious theory. They abandon accepted theories and assumptions only when better theories and assumptions become available. Scientists closely scrutinize any claim that violates the rule of parsimony. Before they will accept any such claim, they insist that it be supported by replicable experiments that rule out simpler explanations.

SUMMARY

✳ *Scientific approach to psychology.* Although psychology does not possess the same wealth of knowledge as other sciences, it shares with other scientific fields a commitment to scientific methods, including a set of criteria for evaluating theories. (page 29)

✳ *Steps in a scientific study.* A scientific study goes through the following sequence of steps: hypothesis, methods, results, interpretation. Because almost any study is subject to more than one possible interpretation, we base our conclusions on a pattern of results from many studies. The results of a given study are taken seriously only if other investigators can replicate them. (page 29)

✳ *Criteria for evaluating theories.* A good theory agrees with observations and leads to correct predictions of new information. It leads to predictions precise enough that we can state what results would or would not contradict them. All else being equal, scientists prefer the theory that relies on simpler assumptions. (page 30)

✳ *Skepticism about extrasensory perception.* Claims of the existence of extrasensory perception are scrutinized very cautiously, because the evidence reported so far has been unreplicable and because the scientific approach includes a search for parsimonious explanations. (page 33)

Suggestion for Further Reading

Carey, S. S. (1994). *A beginner's guide to scientific method.* Belmont, CA: Wadsworth. A description of scientific methods, particularly in their application to extraordinary (nonparsimonious) claims.

Terms

hypothesis   a testable prediction of what will happen under certain conditions (page 29)

replicable result   a result that can be repeated (at least approximately) by any competent investigator who follows the same procedures used in the original study (page 30)

meta-analysis   a procedure that combines the results of many studies and analyzes them as though they were all one very large study (page 30)

theory   a comprehensive explanation of observable events (page 30)

falsifiable   (with reference to a theory) making sufficiently precise predictions that we can at least imagine evidence that would contradict the theory (if anyone had obtained such evidence) (page 31)

parsimony   (literally, stinginess)   scientists' preference for the theory that explains the results using the simplest assumptions (page 31)

extrasensory perception (ESP)   the alleged ability of certain people to acquire information without using any sense organ and without receiving any form of energy (page 33)

Answers to Concept Checks

1.   **a.** Falsifiable. Anyone who found an object that had fallen with a different rate of acceleration could contradict the theory, but no one has ever found such an object. This is a good theory because it is *falsifiable* (in principle) and because it has never been *falsified* (by actual data). **b.** Not falsifiable. Even if researchers could scientifically explain every action of every person they had ever tested, the possibility would remain that some untested people have unexplainable powers. (Can you restate the theory so that it is falsifiable?) **c.** Probably not falsifiable, unless someone can specify a reliable method to determine whether a child has suffered "frustration" and a reliable way to determine whether someone has emotional difficulties. As stated, the theory is too vague to be scientifically useful. (page 31)

2.   To evaluate Nostradamus's predictions, we would need to ask someone to tell us precisely what his predictions mean before the events they supposedly predict had transpired. Then, we would ask someone else to estimate the likelihood of those events. Eventually, we would compare the accuracy of the predictions to the advance estimates of their probability. That is, we should be impressed with seemingly correct predictions only if our observers had rated these events "unlikely" before they occurred. (page 33)

Answers to Other Questions in the Text

A.   Any magnet strong enough to pull the metal ball up the inclined plane would not release the ball when it reached the hole at the top. (page 32)

B.   The prophecies of Nostradamus (see page 34), as interpreted by Cheetham (1973), refer to the following: (1) the assassinations of John F. Kennedy and Robert F. Kennedy, (2) Polaris ballistic missiles shot from submarines, (3) Hitler's invasion of France, and (4) World War II.

Web Resources

Center for Social Research Methods

trochim.human.cornell.edu/

Bill Trochim of Cornell University offers Knowledge Base, an interactive on-line textbook for an introductory course in research methods. The site includes links to other Web sites devoted to social research and research methods; an on-line statistical advisor to help you select the appropriate statistical test for your data; common research design exercises; several full-length research papers; and more for the budding researcher.

MODULE 2.2

Methods of Investigation in Psychology

How do psychological researchers study processes that are difficult to define?

How do they design their research, and what special problems can arise?

How do researchers confront the ethical problems of conducting research using both human and nonhuman species?

A radio talk show once featured two psychologists as guests. The first argued that day care was bad for children, because she had seen in her clinical practice many clients who had been left in day care as children and grew up to be sadly disturbed adults. The second psychologist, researcher Sandra Scarr (1997), pointed out that the clinician had no way of knowing about the children left in day care who had become healthy, well-adjusted adults. (Such people have no reason to consult a therapist.) Scarr then described the eight best research studies on this question, which included thousands of children in four countries and found no evidence that day care, even with multiple caregivers, produced any long-term emotional consequences.

What conclusion would you draw? I hope you would conclude that day care is okay for children. To Scarr's dismay, however, the people who called in to the program seemed just as convinced by the anecdotes of disturbed people as by the extensive research studies, and several callers described anecdotes of their own.

Psychology, like any other field, can make progress only by distinguishing between good evidence and weak evidence. Furthermore, psychological research can be tricky; sometimes even a careful investigation runs into unexpected difficulties. In this module we shall consider some of the special problems encountered when applying scientific methods to psychological phenomena.

General Principles for Conducting Psychological Research

The primary goal of this module is not to prepare you to conduct psychological research, although I hope that at least a few readers will eventually do just that. The primary goal is to prepare you to be an intelligent interpreter of psychological research. When you hear about a new study in psychology or a related field, you should be able to ask a few pertinent questions to decide how good the evidence is and what conclusion (if any) it justifies.

Definitions of Psychological Terms

Suppose a physicist asks a student to measure the effect of temperature on the length of an iron bar. The student asks, "What do we really mean by temperature and length?" The physicist might reply, "Don't worry about it. Just measure the length with this ruler and measure the temperature with this thermometer. What I mean by length is the measurement you get with the ruler, and what I mean by temperature is the reading on the thermometer."

We need to use the same strategy for research in psychology. If we wanted to measure the effect of hunger on students' ability to concentrate, we could spend hours attempting to define what hunger and concentration really are, or we could say, "Let's measure hunger by the hours since the last meal and concentration by the length of time that the student continues reading without looking away or doing something else."

By doing so, we would be relying on an **operational definition,** *a definition that specifies the operations (or procedures) used to produce or measure something, a way to give it a numerical value.* An operational definition is not the same as a dictionary definition. You might object that "time since the last meal" is not what you really mean by *hunger.* True, but an operational definition offers a precision that enables one researcher to copy the procedures of another. Later we can worry about what hunger or concentration *really* is.

Suppose that someone wishes to investigate whether children who watch violence on television are likely to behave aggressively themselves. In this case, the investigator needs operational definitions for *televised violence* and *aggressive behavior.* For example, the investigator might define *televised violence* as "the number of acts shown or described in which one person injures another." According to this definition, a 20-minute stalking scene would count as much as a quick attack, and a murder shown on screen would be equivalent to one that the characters just talk about. An unsuccessful attempt to injure someone would not count as violence at all. Also, it is unclear from this definition whether we should count verbal insults. In many ways, this definition might prove to be unsatisfactory, but at least it states how one investigator measures violence. If the results collected on the basis of this definition were confusing, we might try changing the definition.

Similarly, the investigator needs an operational definition of *aggressive behavior.* To define it as "the number of acts of assault or murder committed within 24 hours after watching a particular television program" would be an operational definition but not a very useful one. A better operational definition of *aggressive behavior* specifies less extreme, more likely acts. For example, the experimenter might place a large plastic doll in front of a young child and record how often the child punches it.

Let's take one more example: What is love? Never mind what it *really* is. If we want to measure how it affects another behavior, or how something else affects love, we need an operational definition. One possibility would be "how many hours you are willing to spend with another person who asked you to stay nearby."

CONCEPT CHECK

3. Which of the following is an operational definition of intelligence? **(a)** the ability to comprehend relationships, **(b)** a score on an IQ test, **(c)** the ability to survive in the real world, or **(d)** the product of the cerebral cortex of the brain? What would you propose as an operational definition of friendliness? (Check your answers on page 52.)

Samples of the Population

Researchers generally wish to draw conclusions that apply to a large population, such as all 3-year-olds, or all people with depression, or even all human beings. Because it is not practical to examine everyone in the target population, researchers study a small number of people, a *sample,* and hope that what is true of the sample applies to the whole population.

Finding an appropriate sample is easy when you are studying general mechanisms. For example, early investigators established that the eyes, ears, and other sense organs operate on the same principles for all people (with obvious exceptions such as those with visual or hearing impairments). Indeed, many of these principles are the same even in other animal species. Similarly, many of the principles of learning, memory, hunger, thirst, sleep, and so forth are similar enough among all people that an investigator can explore those principles further with almost any group—students in an introductory psychology class, for example. We refer to *a group chosen because of its ease of study* as a **convenience sample.**

Even with fairly simple behaviors, we can add to our understanding by studying a more diverse sample, however. For example, we can establish general principles about sleep by studying college students, or even a group of laboratory rats, but those studies will not tell us how age differences affect sleep or about the effects of depression on sleep. With many issues, a convenience sample is obviously inappropriate. Imagine that we wanted to determine the frequencies of various political attitudes within a certain country. Obviously, we should not draw generalizations from a study of the students at one college.

To conduct a meaningful study of a behavior that varies significantly among people, we need either a representative sample or a random sample of the relevant population. A **representative sample** *closely resembles the entire popu-*

lation in its percentage of males and females, blacks and whites, young and old, city dwellers and farmers, or whatever other characteristics are likely to affect the results. To get a representative sample of the people in a given region, an investigator would first determine what percentage of the residents belong to each category and then select people to match those percentages. The disadvantage of this method is that a sample that is representative with regard to one set of characteristics might not be representative of something the investigators did not consider, such as religion or education.

In a **random sample,** *every individual in the population has an equal chance of being selected.* To produce a random sample of city residents, an investigator might select a certain number of city blocks at random from a map of the city, randomly select one house from each of those blocks, and then randomly choose one person from each of those households. A random sample of a thousand people or so is likely to resemble the whole population, but it is difficult to get a truly random sample. We can choose people randomly, but not everyone we choose will agree to participate. Using surveys, we can usually get fairly close to a random sample; with experiments, however, researchers almost always use volunteers. Imagine that I advertise a study on the effects of marijuana on behavior. What kind of people are most likely to volunteer to participate? Probably not a random sample of the population. What if I advertised a study on hypnosis? I would expect to get mostly volunteers who are curious to experience hypnosis, people who might turn out to be easily hypnotized.

Such limitations are not a cause for despair, but certainly a reason to exercise caution. Any researcher who cannot get a random or representative sample should at least state the conclusions cautiously, making it clear that these results may not apply to a broader population.

What if we want to draw generalizations about all humans, not just those in one country? If you imagine trying to get a random or representative sample of all the people on the planet, you will quickly realize the impracticalities. Nevertheless, although we cannot expect to study people from all cultures, it can be very useful to study **cross-cultural samples,** groups of people from at least two cultures, preferably more, and preferably cultures as different as possible. For example, consider some important theoretical issues concerning courtship and marriage: Are certain aspects of male and female behavior predictable consequences of human nature? Or are they all more or less arbitrary customs that a society could readily change? One good way to investigate this question is to compare customs in different societies. Similarly, cross-cultural samples are helpful for studying many other issues: Do people learn facial expressions of emotions? Or is there a fixed relationship between each expression and an emotion? Is a financially prosperous society necessarily a happy society? Do the same psychological disorders occur throughout the world, or are some of them limited to a particular location? And so forth.

A psychological researcher can test generalizations about human behavior by comparing people from different cultures.

Cross-cultural sampling is difficult, however (Matsumoto, 1994). Obvious problems include language barriers and convincing members of another culture to answer personal questions and cooperate with psychological tests that may seem very strange to them. Additional problems arise with behaviors that vary as much within one culture as between cultures. Imagine trying to compare "typical" sexual behaviors between two countries. There may be so much diversity within each country that the comparison between the two countries becomes almost meaningless.

CONCEPT CHECK

4. Suppose I compare the interests and abilities of male and female students at my university. If I find a consistent difference, can I assume that it represents a difference between men in general and women in general? (Obviously the answer is no, or else I would not have asked the question.) Why not? (Check your answer on page 52.)

Experimenter Bias and Blind Studies

When experimenters record their data, sometimes they have trouble separating what they really see from what they expect to see. Here is a class demonstration to illustrate the point: Students in one psychology class were told that they would watch a person engage in a difficult hand-eye coordination task before and after drinking alcohol. That person was in fact drinking only apple juice and performed equally well before and after drinking. Nevertheless, most of the students observing the performance described it as sharply

deteriorating (Goldstein, Hopkins, & Strube, 1994). They saw what they had expected to see.

Experimenter bias is *the tendency of an experimenter unintentionally to distort the procedures or results of an experiment based on the expected outcome of the study.* The experimenter does not intend this distortion and may even be trying to avoid it. Imagine that you, as a psychological investigator, are testing the hypothesis that left-handed children are more creative than right-handed children. (I don't know why you would be testing this silly hypothesis, but just suppose you are.) If the results support your hypothesis, you can expect to get your results published and you will be well on your way to becoming a famous psychologist. Now, a left-handed child does something slightly creative. You are not sure whether to count it or not. You want to be fair. You don't want your hypothesis to influence your decision about whether to consider this act creative. Just try to ignore your hypothesis.

To overcome the potential source of error in an investigator's bias, psychologists prefer to use a **blind observer**—that is, *an observer who can record data without knowing what the researcher has predicted.* For example, we might ask someone to record creative acts by a group of children, without any hint that we are interested in the effects of handedness. Because blind observers do not know what hypothesis is being tested, they can record their observations as fairly as possible.

Ideally, the experimenter will conceal the procedure from the subjects as well. For example, suppose experimenters gave one group of children a pill that was supposed to increase their creativity. If those children knew the prediction, maybe they would act more creatively just because

TABLE 2.1 Single-Blind and Double-Blind Studies

Who is aware of which subjects are in which group?

	OBSERVER	SUBJECTS	EXPERIMENTER WHO ORGANIZED THE STUDY
Single-blind	aware	unaware	aware
Single-blind	unaware	aware	aware
Double-blind	unaware	unaware	aware

they knew they were expected to do so. Or maybe the children not taking the pill would pout about not getting it and therefore not do much. The best solution therefore is to give the drug to one group and a **placebo** (*a pill with no known pharmacological effects*) to another group, without telling the children which pill they are taking or what results the experimenter expects. The advantage of this kind of study is that the two groups will not be influenced to behave differently because of their expectations.

A study in which either the observer or the subjects are unaware of which subjects received which treatment is called a **single-blind study** (Table 2.1). *A study in which both the observer and the subjects are unaware* is known as a **double-blind study.** Of course, the experimenter who organized the study would need to keep records of which subjects received which procedure. (A study in which everyone loses track of the procedure is jokingly known as "triple blind.")

Observational Research Designs

The general principles that we just discussed apply to many kinds of research. Psychologists use various methods of investigation, and each has its own advantages and disadvantages. Most research in any field starts with description: What happens, when, and under what circumstances? Astronomers deal almost entirely with observational data; most other scientific fields, including psychology, start with observational data and proceed, when possible, to experiments. Let's start with a description of several kinds of observational studies. Later, we shall consider experiments, which have a much greater ability to illuminate cause-and-effect relationships.

Naturalistic Observations

A **naturalistic observation** is *a careful examination of what many people or nonhuman animals do under more or less natural conditions.* For example, biologist Jane Goodall (1971) spent years observing chimpanzees in the wild, recording their food habits, their social interactions, their gestures, and their whole way of life (Figure 2.7).

Similarly, psychologists sometimes try to observe human behavior "as an outsider." A psychologist might observe what happens when two unacquainted people get on an elevator together: Do they stand close or far apart? Do they speak? Do they look toward each other or away? Does it matter whether the people are two men, two women, or a man and a woman? Do Japanese people act the same as British or Brazilians? A psychologist might also record the behaviors of 6-month-old children, expert crossword puzzle solvers, depressed patients, or any other type of people. After all, the first step toward understanding people is to know in detail what they do.

Case Histories

Psychologists are sometimes interested in rare conditions. For example, some people have amazingly good memories, whereas others have equally amazingly poor memories. People with Williams syndrome have normal or above-average language abilities, but in other regards they are mentally retarded (Bellugi, Wang, & Jernigan, 1994). (Some cannot

FIGURE 2.7 In a naturalistic study, observers record the behavior of people or other species in their natural settings. Here, noted biologist Jane Goodall records her observations on chimpanzees. By patiently staying with the chimps, Goodall gradually won their trust and learned to recognize individual animals. In this manner she was able to add enormously to our understanding of chimpanzees' natural way of life.

even learn to dress themselves.) A psychologist who encounters someone with a rare condition may report a **case history,** *a thorough description of the unusual person.* A case history often relies on naturalistic observation; we distinguish it because it focuses on a single individual.

A case history may include information about the person's medical condition, family background, unusual experiences, current behavior, and a description of the tasks that person can and cannot perform—in short, anything that the investigator thinks might be interesting or important.

A case history is more than just an anecdote. An anecdote is a report of an experience that was not necessarily carefully recorded, such as "I had a hunch and it came true," or "I think I saw Elvis at the pizza parlor." An anecdote is virtually worthless as evidence, because no one can determine whether the person misunderstood or misreported the experience. A case history is potentially replicable by anyone who has the chance to study the same individual or a similar individual again.

A case history is well suited to exploring an unusual behavioral condition; however, the case history does not tell us whether the described individual is typical of others with the same condition. Ideally, a series of case histories can either reveal a pattern or encourage investigators to conduct other kinds of follow-up research.

Surveys

A **survey** is *a study of the prevalence of certain beliefs, attitudes, or behaviors, based on people's responses to specific questions.* A survey is a very common research method. In fact, no matter what your occupation, at some time you will probably conduct a survey yourself, either of your employees, your customers, your students, your neighbors, or fellow members of an organization you have joined. You will also frequently read survey results in the newspaper or hear them reported on television. Thus, you should be aware of some of the difficulties of survey research and understand that survey results can be misleading.

Sampling Getting a truly random or representative sample is a prerequisite for any kind of serious research—and particularly with surveys. Consider what happens with a distorted sample: In 1936, the *Literary Digest* mailed 10 million postcards, asking people their choice for president of the United States. Of the 2 million responses, 57% preferred the Republican candidate, Alfred Landon. Landon was later soundly defeated by the Democratic candidate, Franklin Roosevelt. The problem with this survey was that the *Literary Digest* had selected names from the telephone book and automobile registration lists. In 1936, at the end of the Great Depression, most poor people were Democrats, and very few of them owned telephones or cars.

The Competence of Those Being Interviewed

People will often respond to a survey with answers that have not been well thought out. In one 1997 survey, 55% of the respondents said they did not believe in the existence of intelligent life on other planets. However, 82% said they believed the U. S. government was "hiding evidence of intelligent life in space" (Emery, 1997). Granted, it is possible to hide evidence of something that doesn't exist, but more likely some of these people didn't give a lot of thought to their answers.

 Here's another example: Which of the following programs would you most like to see on television reruns? Rate your choices from highest (1) to lowest (10). (Please fill in your answers, either in the text or on a separate sheet of paper, before continuing to the next paragraph.)

____ Bonanza	____ Jack Benny
____ Car 54	____ My Three Sons
____ Dallas	____ Smothers Brothers
____ Honeymooners	____ Space Doctor
____ I Love Lucy	____ You Bet Your Life

When I conducted this survey at North Carolina State University in 1997, a few of my students refused to answer because they were unfamiliar with most of the listings, but most students ranked all ten programs—including *Space Doctor,* a program that never existed. In fact, 34% of the students ranked this program above average of the 10 programs, and 5% ranked it as their first choice.

Certainly these students did nothing wrong. I asked them to rank all of the programs, and they did. We could only criticize someone who interpreted these results as if they represented informed opinions. This exercise demonstrates that most people will express opinions even when they have no idea what they are talking about.

The Wording of the Questions

If a survey includes unclear, ambiguous questions, the results will also be unclear. For example, several years ago, just after basketball star Magic Johnson revealed that he was infected with the HIV virus, one survey asked, "Has the publicity concerning Magic Johnson made you more likely than before to practice safe sex?" A "yes" answer had a reasonably clear meaning. But what did a "no" answer mean? It might mean, "I plan to continue having unsafe sex," or "I was already practicing safe sex, so I did not become more likely to have safe sex." It might even mean, "I was previously having no sex and I expect, unfortunately, to continue not having sex."

Here is another example: Early in 1997, television and other news media briefly mentioned a survey of noted scientists that found that 40% said they believed in God. Some people found this to be an interesting statistic, because it was either higher or lower than they had expected. But unless you know how the question was worded, you won't know what the results mean, and I think some of the write-in answers were far more interesting than the 40% who answered yes. This yes-or-no question was phrased like this:

I believe in a God in intellectual and affective communication with humankind, i.e., a God to whom one may pray in expectation of receiving an answer. By "answer" I mean more than the subjective, psychological effect of prayer.

Some of the scientists objected that they had religious or spiritual beliefs, even though they could not answer yes to the question as it was worded. One wrote, "When backed into a corner, as it were, by questions such as those on the survey I have to come down on the side of nonbelief. . . . This result for me, however (and possibly for others), is an unduly harsh picture. I try frequently to open my mind to an influence of what is good, and the 'subjective and psychological' effects of this can be quite profound, such that I am happy to make contact with the religious tradition by saying that I am praying to God."

In short, for many people, scientists or not, the issue of religious faith is not a simple yes-or-no question (Larson & Witham, 1997). Similarly, any other survey question that forces people to provide a yes-or-no answer may thereby overlook a wide range of interesting shades of opinion.

Surveyor Biases Sometimes a survey is sponsored by an organization that is hoping the results will come out in

their favor, and therefore words the questions to encourage the desired outcome. Here is an example: According to a 1993 survey, 92% of high school boys and 98% of high school girls claimed to have been victims of sexual harassment (Shogren, 1993). According to the sponsors of the survey, these results show that sexual harassment has reached "epidemic" proportions. Maybe it has, but the wording of the survey *defined* sexual harassment into an epidemic by specifying that sexual harassment included any of a long list of acts, which ranged from very serious offenses (such as having someone rip your clothes off) to a variety of minor annoyances. For example, if someone wrote sexually explicit graffiti on the rest room wall and you read it and found it offensive, then you could consider yourself sexually harassed. If you tried to make yourself look sexually attractive (as most teenagers do, right?) and then attracted a suggestive stare from someone you *didn't* want to attract, that look would count as sexual harassment.

Sexual harassment is indeed a serious problem, but a survey that lumps the major offenses together with the minor ones fails to provide useful information. Figure 2.8 shows a

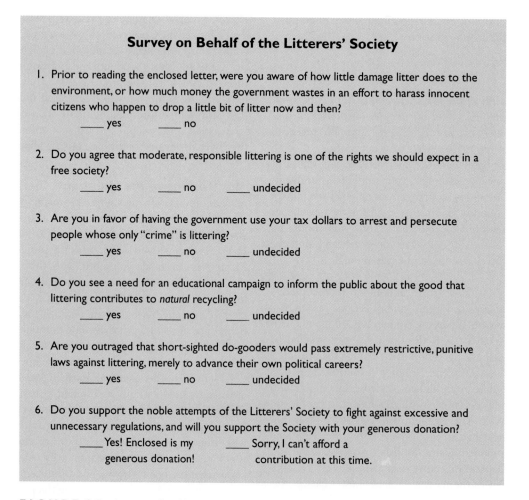

Survey on Behalf of the Litterers' Society

1. Prior to reading the enclosed letter, were you aware of how little damage litter does to the environment, or how much money the government wastes in an effort to harass innocent citizens who happen to drop a little bit of litter now and then?
   ____ yes   ____ no

2. Do you agree that moderate, responsible littering is one of the rights we should expect in a free society?
   ____ yes   ____ no   ____ undecided

3. Are you in favor of having the government use your tax dollars to arrest and persecute people whose only "crime" is littering?
   ____ yes   ____ no   ____ undecided

4. Do you see a need for an educational campaign to inform the public about the good that littering contributes to *natural* recycling?
   ____ yes   ____ no   ____ undecided

5. Are you outraged that short-sighted do-gooders would pass extremely restrictive, punitive laws against littering, merely to advance their own political careers?
   ____ yes   ____ no   ____ undecided

6. Do you support the noble attempts of the Litterers' Society to fight against excessive and unnecessary regulations, and will you support the Society with your generous donation?
   ____ Yes! Enclosed is my   ____ Sorry, I can't afford a
         generous donation!   contribution at this time.

F I G U R E 2.8 An example of how to bias a survey: This imaginary survey for an imaginary society has a style of questions similar to those found in many surveys sponsored by actual political and social organizations. The request for a donation is a reliable clue that the organization is not really seeking your opinion and will probably not even bother to tabulate the results.

fictional survey very similar to those you probably receive occasionally from various organizations. Whenever the questions are written to suggest one "correct" answer, you can safely assume that the organization is much more interested in soliciting money than in knowing your honest opinions.

Correlational Studies

Another type of study is a correlational study. A **correlation** is *a measure of the relationship between two variables, which are both outside the investigator's control.* (A variable is a measurable item that can vary in magnitude. Height and weight are variables; so are years of education and reading speed.) For example, investigators have observed that students who attend class regularly generally receive better test scores than do students who frequently miss class (Cavell & Woehr, 1994). This statement highlights a relationship between two variables—class attendance and test scores. The investigator simply measured these variables, without attempting to influence anything.

A survey can be considered a correlational study if the interviewers compare two or more groups. For example, the interviewers might compare the beliefs of men and women or those of young people and old people. The interviewer could thereby measure a relationship between one variable (sex or age) and another (beliefs).

The Correlation Coefficient

Some correlations are strong; others are weak. For example, we would probably find a strong positive correlation between hours per week spent reading novels and scores on a vocabulary test. We would observe a lower correlation between hours spent reading novels and scores on a chemistry test.

It is often helpful to have a method for measuring the direction and strength of a correlation. The standard method is known as a **correlation coefficient,** *a mathematical estimate of the relationship between two variables. The coefficient can range mathematically from +1 to −1.* A correlation coefficient indicates how accurately we can use a measurement or one variable to predict another. A correlation coefficient of +1, for example, means that, as one variable increases, the other increases also. A correlation coefficient of −1 means that as one variable increases, the other decreases. A correlation of either +1 or −1 would enable us to make perfect predictions of either variable whenever we know the other one. (In real life, psychologists seldom encounter a perfect +1 or −1 correlation coefficient.) The closer the correlation coefficient is to +1 or to −1, the stronger the relationship between the two variables and the more accurately we can use one variable to predict the other. For example, the more people practice a video game, the higher their scores tend to be; this is a positive correlation. The more that people practice golf, the lower their golf scores; this is a negative correlation. (Low golf scores are better.) A negative correlation is just as useful as a positive correlation and can indicate just as strong a relationship.

Figure 2.9 shows hypothetical (fictitious) data demonstrating how grades on a final exam in psychology might correlate with five other variables. (This kind of graph is called a scatterplot; each dot represents the measurements of two variables for one person.) Grades on a psychology final exam correlate very strongly with grades on the previous tests in psychology, less strongly with grades on the French final exam, not at all with the person's weight, and negatively with the amount of time spent watching television and the number of times the student was absent from class. Note that a correlation of +0.9 is almost a straight line ascending; a correlation of −0.9 is close to a straight line descending.

Here are three examples of findings from correlational studies:

- The most crowded areas of a city are generally the most impoverished. (Positive correlation between crowdedness and poverty.)

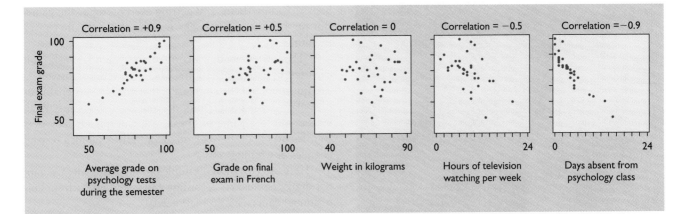

FIGURE 2.9 In a scatterplot, each dot represents data for one person; for example, each point in the center graph tells us one person's weight and that person's grade on the psychology final exam, in this case using hypothetical data. A positive correlation indicates that, as one variable increases, the other generally does also. A negative correlation indicates that, as one variable increases, the other generally decreases. The closer a correlation coefficient is to +1 or −1, the stronger the relationship.

- People's IQ scores have no relationship to their telephone numbers. (Zero correlation between the two.)
- People who trust others are unlikely to cheat other people. (Negative correlation between trusting and cheating.)

CONCEPT CHECK

5. Which indicates a stronger relationship between two variables, a +0.50 correlation or a −0.75 correlation? (Check your answer on page 52.)

Illusory Correlations   It is difficult to identify a correlation between two variables solely on the basis of casual observation. For example, years ago, a drug company marketed the drug Bendectin to relieve morning sickness in pregnant women. After a few women who had taken the drug had babies with birth defects, widespread publicity blamed the drug. Thereafter, women who took the drug and had babies with birth defects blamed the drug. Actually, only 2–3% of the women taking the drug had babies with birth defects—the same as the percentage among women not taking the drug! When people expect to see a connection between two events (such as Bendectin and birth defects), they remember the cases that support the connection and disregard the exceptions, thus perceiving an **illusory correlation,** *an apparent relationship based on casual observations of unrelated or weakly related events.* Many social stereotypes are examples of illusory correlations.

As another example of an illusory correlation, consider the widely held belief that a full moon affects human behavior. For hundreds of years, many people have believed that crime and various kinds of mental disturbance are more common under a full moon than at other times. In fact, the term *lunacy* (from the Latin word *luna,* meaning "moon") originally meant mental illness caused by the full moon. Some police officers report that they receive more

People's expectations and faulty memories produce illusory correlations, such as between the full moon and abnormal behavior.

calls on nights with a full moon, and hospital workers report more emergency cases on such nights. Those reports, however, are based on what people recall rather than on carefully analyzed data. James Rotton and I. W. Kelly (1985) examined all available data relating crime, mental illness, and other phenomena to the phases of the moon. They concluded that the phase of the moon has either no effect at all on human behavior or so little effect that it is almost impossible to measure.

Why then does this belief persist? We do not know when or how it first arose. (It may have been true many years ago, before the widespread use of artificial lights.) But we can guess why it persists. Suppose, for example, you are working at a hospital. You expect to handle more emergencies on a night with a full moon than at other times. Sooner or later, on a full-moon night, you encounter an unusually high number of accidents, assaults, and suicide attempts. You say, "See? There was a full moon and people just went crazy!" You will remember that night for a long time and disregard all the other full-moon nights when nothing special happened and all the other nights when there was no full moon and yet you were swamped with emergency cases.

Correlation and Causation

A correlational study tells us whether two variables are related to each other and, if so, how strongly. It does not tell us *why* they are related, and a correlation does not justify a cause-and-effect conclusion. For example, there is a very strong positive correlation between the number of books someone owns about chess and how good that person is at playing chess. Does owning chess books cause someone to become a good chess player? Of course not; if it did, I could go buy 50 chess books and suddenly become a great player. Does being a good chess player cause someone to buy chess books? Not necessarily. The real pattern is more complicated: People who start to like chess buy chess books, which help them improve their game. As they get better, they become even more interested, buying more books, reading them, and getting even better at the game. But neither the chess books nor the skill actually causes the other.

"Then, what good is a correlation," you might ask, "if it can't tell us about causation?" There are various answers to this question, but the simplest is that correlations enable us to make useful predictions. If your friend has just challenged you to a game of chess, you can quickly look over your friend's bookshelves and get a fairly good idea of your chances of winning.

Here are two more examples to illustrate why we cannot draw conclusions regarding cause and effect from correlational data (see also Figure 2.10):

- *Unmarried men are more likely than married men to wind up in a mental hospital or prison.* That is, for men, marriage is negatively correlated with mental illness and criminal activity. Does the correlation mean that marriage leads

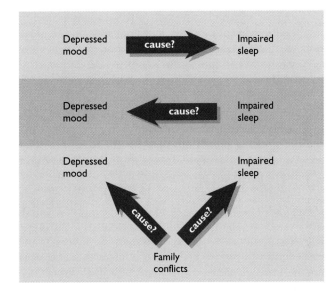

F I G U R E 2.10 A strong correlation between depression and impaired sleep does not tell us whether depression interferes with sleep, poor sleep leads to depression, or whether another problem leads to both depression and sleep problems.

to mental health and good social adjustment? Or does it mean that men who are confined to mental hospitals or prisons are unlikely to marry? (Both explanations could, of course, be valid.)

• *People who engage in regular exercise tend to have high self-esteem and tend not to feel depressed.* This correlation could indicate that exercise helps to raise self-esteem and to decrease the chance of depression. It could also mean that nondepressed people with high self-esteem are likely to get some exercise. (Very depressed people seldom do much of anything.) The correlation could also reflect that being young, healthy, and employed increases the chances that a person will find time to exercise and also (independently) improves self-esteem and guards against depression.

To repeat: A correlation does not tell us about causation. To determine causation, an investigator needs to manipulate one of the variables directly, through a research design known as an *experiment*. When an investigator manipulates

one variable and then observes corresponding changes in another variable, causation is clear.

CONCEPT CHECK

6. Suppose someone demonstrates a 0.8 correlation between students' reported interest in psychology and their grades on a psychology test. What conclusion can we draw? (Check your answer on page 52.)

Experiments

An **experiment** is *a study in which the investigator manipulates at least one variable while measuring at least one other variable.* The logic behind the simplest possible experiment is as follows: The investigator assembles a suitable sample of people (or animals), divides them randomly into two groups, and then conducts some procedure with one group and not the other. Someone, preferably a blind observer, records the behavior of the two groups. If the behavior of the two groups differs in some consistent way, then the difference is probably the result of the experimental procedure. Table 2.2 contrasts experiments with observational studies.

I shall describe psychological experiments and some of their special difficulties. To illustrate, let's use the example of experiments conducted to determine whether watching violent television programs leads to an increase in aggressive behavior.

Independent Variables and Dependent Variables

An experiment is an attempt to measure the effect of changes in one variable on one or more other variable(s). The **independent variable** is *the item that an experimenter changes or controls—for example, the amount of violent television that the subjects are permitted to watch. The* **dependent variable** is *the item that an ex-*

TABLE 2.2 Comparison of Five Methods of Research	
OBSERVATIONAL STUDIES	
Case Study	Detailed description of a single individual; suitable for studying rare conditions.
Naturalistic Observation	Description of behavior under natural conditions; particularly valuable method when it is unethical or impractical to conduct laboratory investigations.
Survey	Study of attitudes, beliefs, or behaviors based on answers to questions.
Correlation	Description of the relationship between two variables that the investigator measures but does not control; determines whether two variables are closely related but does not address questions of cause and effect.
Experiment	Determination of the effect of an independent variable (controlled by the investigator) on the dependent variable (that being measured); the only method that can inform us about cause and effect.

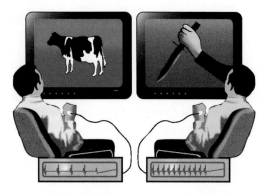

FIGURE 2.11 An experimenter manipulates the independent variable (in this case, the films people watch) so that two or more groups experience different treatments. Then the experimenter measures the dependent variable (in this case, pulse rate) to see how the independent variable affected it.

perimenter measures to determine how it was affected. In our example, the experimenter measures the amount of aggressive behavior that the subjects exhibit. You can think of the independent variable as the influence and the dependent variable as the result (see Figure 2.11).

CONCEPT CHECK

7.   An instructor wants to find out whether the frequency of testing in an introductory psychology class has any effect on students' final exam performance. The instructor gives weekly tests in one class, just three tests in a second class, and only a single midterm exam in the third class. All three classes are given the same final exam, and the instructor then compares their performances. Identify the independent variable and the dependent variable. (Check your answers on page 52.)

Experimental Group, Control Group, and Random Assignment

An **experimental group** *receives the treatment that an experiment is designed to test.* In our example, the experimental group would watch televised violence. The **control group** *is a set of individuals treated in the same way as the experimental group except for the procedure that the experiment is designed to test.* People in the control group would watch only nonviolent television programs (Figure 2.12). (The type of television program is the independent variable; the resulting behavior is the dependent variable.)

In principle, this procedure sounds easy, although difficulties can arise in practice. For example, if we are studying a group of teenagers who have a history of violent behavior, it may be difficult to find nonviolent television programs that can hold their attention. As their attention wanders, they might start picking fights with one another, and suddenly the results of the experiment look very odd indeed.

Suppose we conduct a study inviting young people to watch either violent or nonviolent programs, and then we discover that those who watched violent programs act more aggressively. What conclusion could we draw? None, of course. Those who chose to watch violence were probably different from those who chose the nonviolent programs. Any good experiment has **random assignment** of subjects to groups: *The experimenter uses a chance procedure, such as drawing names out of a hat, to make sure that every subject has the same probability as any other subject of being assigned to a given group.*

Consider another example: We set up a rack of cages and put each of several rats in a cage by itself. The rack has five rows of six cages each, numbered from 1 in the upper left-hand corner to 30 in the lower right. Regardless of the procedures we use, we find that the rats with higher cage numbers are more aggressive than those with lower cage numbers. Why?

We might first guess that the difference has to do with location. The rats in the cages with high numbers are farthest from the lights and closest to the floor. They get fed last each day. To test the influence of these factors, we move some of the cages to different positions in the rack, leaving each rat in its own cage. To our surprise, the rats in cages 26–30 are still more aggressive than those in cages 1–5. Why? (How could they possibly know which number is on their cage, and even if they did know, why would they care?)

The answer concerns how rats get assigned to cages. When an investigator buys a shipment of rats, which one goes into cage 1? The one that is easiest to catch! Which ones go into the last few cages? The vicious, ornery little critters that put up the greatest resistance. The rats in the last few cages were already aggressive before they were put into those cages.

The point is that, even when using rats, an experimenter must assign individuals at random to the experimental group and the control group. It would not be random to assign the

Even rats must be assigned to groups randomly.

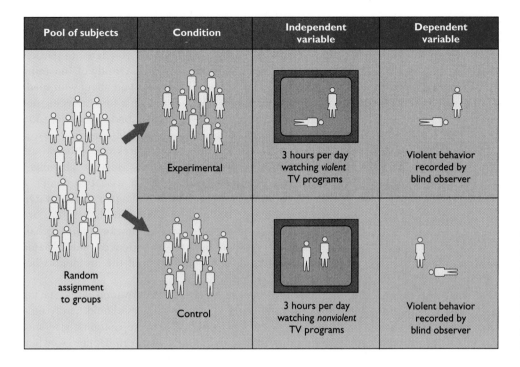

Pool of subjects	Condition	Independent variable	Dependent variable
Random assignment to groups	Experimental	3 hours per day watching *violent* TV programs	Violent behavior recorded by blind observer
	Control	3 hours per day watching *nonviolent* TV programs	Violent behavior recorded by blind observer

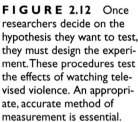

F I G U R E 2.12 Once researchers decide on the hypothesis they want to test, they must design the experiment. These procedures test the effects of watching televised violence. An appropriate, accurate method of measurement is essential.

first 15 rats to one group and the second 15 to another group. This advice is even more important with experiments involving humans.

W H A T ' S   T H E   E V I D E N C E ?
Studies of the Effects of Televised Violence on Aggressive Behavior

We have talked in general terms about experiments on the effects of televised violence. Now let's consider some actual examples.

Some of the evidence regarding the effects of televised violence comes from correlational studies. Several such studies have found that people who watch a great deal of televised violence are more likely to engage in aggressive behavior than people who do not (National Institute of Mental Health, 1982). These results are suggestive but inconclusive. They do not tell us whether watching violence leads to aggressive behavior or whether people prone to aggressive behavior like to watch violence on television. To examine a possible cause-and-effect relationship, we must conduct experiments.

Hypothesis   Children who watch violent television programs will engage in more acts of aggression than will children who spend the same amount of time watching nonviolent programs.

Method   One set of experimenters chose to study male juvenile delinquents in an institution (Parke, Berkowitz,

Leyens, West, & Sebastian, 1977). The disadvantage of the study was that the conclusions might apply to only a limited group. The advantage was that the experimenters could control the choice of television programs (the independent variable) much better in a detention center than they could with youngsters living at home.

The boys in the study were randomly assigned to two cottages. Those in one cottage watched violent films on five consecutive nights; those in the other cottage watched nonviolent films. Throughout the study period, blind observers recorded incidents of aggressive behavior by each boy. On the sixth day, each boy was put into an experimental setting where he was given the opportunity at certain times to press a button that, he thought, would deliver an electric shock to another boy. (In fact, no shocks were given.) The experimenters recorded the frequency and intensity of shocks that each boy chose to deliver (the dependent variable).

Results   Compared to the boys who had watched nonviolent films, those who had watched the violent films engaged in more acts of aggression and pressed the button to deliver more frequent and more intense electric shocks.

Interpretation   At least in this study, watching violent films did lead to increased violence. As with most studies, however, this one had limitations. The boys in this experiment were not representative of boys in general, much less of people in general. Moreover, we cannot assume that we would get similar results with different violent films or different methods of measuring aggressive behavior.

The only way to get around the limitations of a given experiment is to conduct additional experiments, using different samples of people, different films, and different measures of aggressive behavior. Several such experiments have been conducted. Although the results vary considerably, most psychologists have concluded that watching televised violence does indeed increase aggressive behavior, at least temporarily (Comstock & Strasburger, 1990). However, we have little information about the cumulative effects of years of watching violence on television.

✳ ✳ ✳

How Experiments Can Go Wrong: Demand Characteristics

Research on human behavior poses some thorny problems, because people who know they are part of an experiment figure out, or think they have figured out, what is going to happen in the experiment. Their expectations can influence behavior enough to overwhelm the effects of whatever the experimenter is actually doing.

To illustrate: In some well-known studies on sensory deprivation that were popular many years ago, subjects were placed in an apparatus that minimizes vision, hearing, touch, and other forms of sensory stimulation. After several hours, many subjects reported hallucinations, anxiety, and difficulty concentrating. Now, suppose you have heard about these studies, and you agree to participate in an experiment described as a study of "meaning deprivation." The experimenter asks you about your medical history and then asks you to sign a form agreeing not to sue the institution if you have a bad experience. You see an "emergency tray" containing medicines and instruments, which the experimenter assures you is there "just as a precaution." Now you enter an "isolation chamber," which is actually an ordinary room with two chairs, a desk, a window, a mirror, a sandwich, and a glass of water. You are going to be left there for four hours. You are shown a microphone which you can use to report any hallucinations or other distorted experiences and a "panic button" you could press for escape if the discomfort becomes unbearable.

In fact, this is not a study of deprivation at all. Staying in a room by yourself for a few hours should hardly be a traumatic experience. But all the preparations have suggested that terrible things were about to happen, so when this study was actually conducted, several students reported that they were hallucinating "multicolored spots on the wall," or that "the walls of the room are starting to waver," or that "the objects on the desk are becoming animated and moving about" (Figure 2.13). Some complained

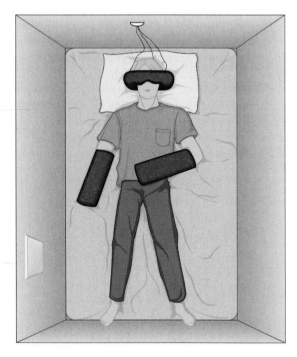

a

b

F I G U R E 2.13 (a) In experiments on sensory deprivation, a person who is deprived of most sensory stimulation becomes disoriented, loses track of time, and reports hallucinations. But do these results partly reflect the person's expectation of having distorted experiences? (b) In one experiment, students were placed in a normal room after undergoing various procedures designed to make them expect a dreadful experience. Many reported hallucinations and distress.

of anxiety, restlessness, difficulty concentrating, and spatial disorientation. One pressed the panic button to demand release (Orne & Scheibe, 1964).

Students in a control group were led to the same room, but they were not shown the "emergency tray," they were not asked to sign a release form, and were given no other indication that they were expected to have any unpleasant experiences. And they, in fact, reported no unusual experiences.

Sensory deprivation may very well have significant effects on behavior. But as this experiment illustrates, we must carefully distinguish between the effects of the independent variable and the effects of what the subjects expect from the experiment. Martin Orne (1969) defined **demand characteristics** as *cues that tell a subject what is expected of him or her and what the experimenter hopes to find.* In a sense, demand characteristics set up *self-fulfilling prophecies.* That is, when designing an experiment, the experimenter has a certain expectation in mind and may then inadvertently convey that expectation to the subjects, thereby influencing them to behave as expected. Many experimenters take elaborate steps to conceal the purpose of the experiment from the subjects to eliminate demand characteristics. A double-blind study serves the purpose: If two groups share the same expectations but behave differently because of the treatment they receive, then the differences in behavior are presumably not the result of their expectations.

CONCEPT CHECK

8. Which of the following would an experimenter try to minimize or avoid?
   a. falsifiability
   b. independent variables
   c. dependent variables
   d. blind observers
   e. demand characteristics
   (Check your answers on page 52.)

Ethical Considerations in Experimentation

In any experiment, psychologists manipulate a variable to determine how it affects behavior. Perhaps the concept of someone trying to alter your behavior sounds objectionable. If so, consider that every time you talk to other people you are trying to alter their behavior at least slightly. Most experiments in psychology produce effects that are no more disruptive than the effects of a conversation.

Still, some experiments do raise ethical issues. Psychologists are seriously concerned about the ethical issues that arise both in the experiments they conduct with humans and in those they conduct with animals.

Ethical Concerns in Experiments on Humans

Earlier in this chapter, I discussed experiments on the effects of televised violence. If psychologists believed that watching violent programs on television would really transform viewers into murderers, then it would be unethical for them to conduct an experiment to find out for sure. It would also be unethical to perform any experimental procedure likely to cause people significant pain or embarrassment or to exert any long-lasting, undesirable effects on their lives.

One important ethical principle is that experiments should include only procedures that people would agree to experience. No one should leave a study muttering, "If I had known what was going to happen, I never would have agreed to participate." To maintain high ethical standards for the conduct of experiments, psychologists ask prospective participants to give their **informed consent** before proceeding, *a statement that they have been told what to expect and that they agree to continue.* When experimenters post a sign-up sheet asking for volunteers, or at the start of the experiment itself, they explain what will happen—that the participants will receive electric shocks, or they will be asked to drink concentrated sugar water, or whatever. Any prospective participant who objects to the procedure can simply withdraw. Informed consent sounds like a simple principle, and usually it is. However, special problems arise with research on retarded or otherwise impaired people who may not understand the proposed procedure (Bonnie, 1997) and with severely depressed people, who sometimes agree to very risky experiments, partly because they have lost interest in their own well-being (Elliott, 1997). In such cases, it is sometimes necessary to consult the person's guardian or nearest relative, and sometimes wise investigators themselves decide not to proceed.

Experiments conducted at a college or at any other reputable institution must first be approved by a Human Subjects Committee at that institution. Such a committee judges whether the proposed studies include procedures for informed consent and whether they safeguard each participant's confidentiality. The committee also tries to prevent procedures that might expose participants to any serious risk. For example, the committee would not approve an experiment that called for administering large doses of cocaine, even if some of the subjects were eager to give their informed consent. The committee also judges procedures in which the investigators want to hide the purpose of the study. For example, suppose that a researcher is testing a method for changing people's attitudes. If the people knew that the researcher was trying to change their attitudes, they might resist strongly. It is also possible that they might pretend to change their attitudes, just to help the researcher. In either case, the results would be invalid. So the investigator might ask permission to conceal certain procedures, or even to mislead the participants temporarily, and the Human Subjects Committee would decide whether to permit the study under these conditions.

Finally, the American Psychological Association, or APA (1982), publishes a booklet detailing the proper ethical treatment of volunteers in experiments. Any member who disregards these principles may be censured or expelled from membership in the APA.

Ethical Concerns in Experiments on Animals

Much psychological research requires the use of human subjects—for example, research on reading or television viewing. However, animal research can help us understand basic processes, such as how nerves work, how the eyes and ears work, the functions of sleep, and the effects of rewards and punishments on the rates of behaviors (Figure 2.14). Researchers are especially likely to turn to animals if they want to control aspects of life that people will not let them control (such as who mates with whom), or if they want to study behavior continuously over months or years (longer than people are willing to stay in a laboratory), or if the research poses possible health risks. Animal research has long been essential for preliminary testing of most new drugs, surgical procedures, and methods of relieving pain. People with untreatable illnesses argue that they have the right "to hope for cures or relief from suffering through research using animals" (Feeney, 1987). Even outside the medical field, much of our current knowledge in psychology either began with animal research or made use of animal studies at some point.

Nevertheless, some people oppose much or all of animal research. Animals, after all, are unable to give informed consent. Some animal rights supporters insist that animals should have the same rights as humans, that keeping animals (even pets) in cages is nothing short of slavery, and that killing any animal is murder. Others oppose some kinds of research but are willing to compromise about others. Psychologists,

too, vary in their attitudes. Most support animal research in general, but most would draw a line somewhere separating acceptable research from unacceptable (Plous, 1996). Naturally, psychologists draw that line at different places.

In this debate, as in so many other political controversies, one common tactic is for each side to criticize the most extreme actions of their opponents. For example, animal-rights advocates point to studies that exposed monkeys or puppies to painful procedures that seem hard to justify. On the other hand, researchers point to protesters who have distorted facts, vandalized laboratories, and even threatened to kill researchers and their children. Some protesters have even stated that they would oppose the use of any AIDS medication if its discovery came out of research with animals.

Unfortunately, when both sides concentrate on criticizing their most extreme opponents, they trivialize the real issues and make points of agreement more difficult to find. One fairly thorough study by a relatively unbiased outsider concluded that the truth is messy: Some research is painful or harmful to animals *and* nevertheless valuable for advancing our understanding of important scientific or medical issues in ways that we could not otherwise achieve (Blum, 1994). In other words, we cannot remain innocent of harming animals and still make the scientific and medical progress that we value.

If we cannot simply choose between progress and protecting animals, we must find a compromise. Professional organizations such as the Neuroscience Society and the American Psychological Association publish guidelines for the proper use of animals in research. Colleges and other research institutions maintain laboratory animal care committees to ensure that laboratory animals are treated humanely, that their pain and discomfort are kept to a minimum, and that experimenters consider alternatives before they impose potentially painful procedures on animals. Because such committees must deal with competing values, their decisions are never beyond dispute. How can we determine in advance whether the value of the expected

FIGURE 2.14 A mirror mounted on a young owl's head enables investigators to track the owl's head movements and thereby to discover how it localizes sounds with one ear plugged. The findings may help researchers understand how blind people use their hearing to compensate for visual loss. An experiment such as this subjects the animal to only a minor inconvenience. Some experiments, however, inflict pain or discomfort and are therefore more likely to raise ethical objections.

experimental results (which are hard to predict) will outweigh the pain the animals will endure (which is hard to measure)? As is so often the case with ethical decisions, reasonable arguments can be raised on both sides of the question, and no compromise is fully satisfactory.

THE MESSAGE
Psychological Research

I mentioned at the beginning of this chapter that scientists avoid the word *prove*. Psychologists certainly do. (The joke is that psychology courses do not have true-false tests, just maybe-perhaps tests.) The most complex, and therefore most interesting, aspects of human behavior are products of genetics, a lifetime of experiences, and countless current influences. Given the practical and ethical limitations, it might seem that the whole idea of psychological research is doomed from the start. However, largely because of these difficulties, many psychologists have been highly inventive in designing complex ways to isolate the effects of certain influences. A single study rarely answers a question decisively, but many studies can converge to increase our total understanding.

SUMMARY

* *Operational definitions.* For many purposes, psychologists prefer operational definitions, which state how to measure a given phenomenon or how to produce it. (page 37)
* *Sampling.* Psychologists hope to draw conclusions that apply to a large population and not just to the small sample they have studied, so they try to select a sample that resembles the total population. They may select either a representative sample or a random sample. To apply the results to people worldwide, they need a cross-cultural sample. (page 38)
* *Experimenter bias and blind observers.* An experimenter's expectations can influence the interpretations of behavior and the recording of data. To ensure objectivity, investigators use blind observers, who do not know what results are expected. In a double-blind study, neither the observer nor the subjects know the researcher's predictions. (page 39)
* *Naturalistic observations.* Naturalistic observations provide descriptions of humans or other species under natural conditions. (page 40)
* *Case histories.* A case history is a detailed research study of a single individual, generally someone with unusual characteristics. (page 40)
* *Surveys.* A survey is a report of people's answers on a questionnaire. It is fairly easy to conduct a survey and, unfortunately, very easy to conduct a survey badly. (page 41)
* *Correlations.* A correlational study is a study of the relationship between variables that are outside the investigator's control. The strength of this relationship is mea-

sured by a correlation coefficient, which ranges from 0 (no relationship) to plus or minus 1 (a perfect relationship). (page 43)
* *Illusory correlations.* Beware of illusory correlations—relationships that people think they observe between variables after mere casual observation. (page 44)
* *Inferring causation.* A correlational study will not uncover cause-and-effect relationships, but an experiment can. (page 44)
* *Experiments.* Experiments are studies in which the investigator manipulates one variable to determine its effect on another variable. The manipulated variable is the independent variable. Changes in the independent variable may lead to changes in the dependent variable, the one the experimenter measures. (page 45)
* *Random assignment.* An experimenter should randomly assign individuals to form experimental and control groups. That is, all individuals should have an equal probability of being chosen for the experimental group. (page 46)
* *Demand characteristics.* Cues that inform participants of the expected results are called demand characteristics. Skillful experimenters try to minimize demand characteristics. (page 48)
* *Ethics of experimentation.* Experimentation on either humans or animals raises ethical questions. Psychologists try to minimize risk to their subjects, but they cannot avoid making difficult ethical decisions. (page 49)

Suggestion for Further Reading

Stanovich, K. E. (1998). *How to think straight about psychology* (5th ed.). Reading, MA: Addison-Wesley. An excellent discussion of how to evaluate evidence in psychology and how to avoid pitfalls.

Terms

operational definition   a definition that specifies the operations (or procedures) used to produce or measure something, a way to give it a numerical value (page 37)

convenience sample   a group chosen because of its ease of study (page 38)

representative sample   a selection of the population chosen to match the entire population with regard to specific variables (page 38)

random sample   a group of people picked in random fashion, so that every individual in the population has an equal chance of being selected (page 38)

cross-cultural samples   groups of people from at least two cultures (page 38)

experimenter bias   the tendency of an experimenter to unintentionally distort procedures or results, based on the experimenter's own expectations of the outcome of the study (page 39)

blind observer   an observer who can record data without knowing what the researcher has predicted (page 39)

placebo   an inactive pill that has no known pharmacological effect on the subjects in an experiment (page 40)

single-blind study   a study in which either the observer or the subjects are unaware of which subjects received which treatment (page 40)

double-blind study   a study in which neither the observer nor the subjects know which subjects received which treatment (page 40)

naturalistic observation   a careful examination of what many people or nonhuman animals do under natural conditions (page 40)

case history   a thorough description of a single individual, including information on both past experiences and current behavior (page 41)

survey   a study of the prevalence of certain beliefs, attitudes, or behaviors, based on people's responses to specific questions (page 41)

correlation   a measure of the relationship between two variables, which are both outside the investigator's control (page 43)

correlation coefficient   a mathematical estimate of the relationship between two variables, ranging from +1 (perfect positive relationship) to 0 (no linear relationship) to −1 (perfect negative relationship) (page 43)

illusory correlation   an apparent relationship based on casual observations of unrelated or weakly related events (page 44)

experiment   a study in which the investigator manipulates at least one variable while measuring at least one other variable (page 45)

independent variable   in an experiment, the item that an experimenter manipulates to determine how it affects the dependent variable (page 45)

dependent variable   the item that an experimenter measures to determine how changes in the independent variable affect it (page 45)

experimental group   the group that receives the treatment that an experiment is designed to test (page 46)

control group   a group treated in the same way as the experimental group except for the procedure that the experiment is designed to test (page 46)

random assignment   a chance procedure for assigning subjects to groups so that every subject has the same probability as any other subject of being assigned to a particular group (page 46)

demand characteristics   cues that tell a subject what is expected of him or her and what the experimenter hopes to find (page 49)

informed consent   a subject's agreement to take part in an experiment after being told what to expect (page 49)

Answers to Concept Checks

3.   A score on an IQ test is an operational definition of intelligence. (Whether it is a particularly good definition is another question.) None of the other definitions tells us how to measure or produce intelligence. Many operational definitions are possible for "friendliness," such as "the number of people that someone speaks to within 24 hours." You can probably think of a better operational definition. Remember, that an operational definition specifies a clear method of measurement. (page 38)

4.   Clearly not. It is unlikely that the men at a given college are typical of men in general or that the women are typical of women in general. Moreover, at some colleges the men are atypical in some respects and the women atypical in different ways. (page 39)

5.   The −0.75 correlation indicates a stronger relationship—that is, a greater accuracy of predicting one variable based on measurements of the other. A negative correlation is just as useful as a positive one. (page 44)

6.   We can conclude only that, if we know either someone's interest level or test score, we can predict the other with reasonably high accuracy. We *cannot* conclude that an interest in psychology will help someone to learn the material or that doing well on psychology tests increases someone's interest in the material. Both conclusions may well be true, but a correlational study cannot demonstrate a cause-and-effect relationship. (page 45)

7.   The independent variable is the frequency of tests during the semester. The dependent variable is the students' performance on the final exam. (page 46)

8.   Of these, only demand characteristics are to be avoided. If you did not remember that falsifiability is a good feature of a theory, check page 31. Every experiment must have at least one independent variable (what the experimenter controls) and at least one dependent variable (what the experimenter measures). Blind observers provide an advantage. (page 49)

Web Resources

HyperText Psychology—BASICS

www.science.wayne.edu/~wpoff/basics.html

This site walks you through the basics of research: social science methods; field studies, surveys, and experiments; and the use of statistics in interpreting results.

MODULE 2.3

Measuring and Analyzing Results

How can the "average" results in a study be described?

How can we describe the variations among individuals?

How can a researcher determine whether the results reflect a consistent trend, or whether these results could have arisen just by chance?

Some years ago, a television program about the alleged dangers of playing the game Dungeons and Dragons reported 28 known cases of D&D players who had committed suicide. Alarming, right?

Not necessarily. At that time at least 3 million young people played the game regularly. The reported suicide rate among D&D players—28 per 3 million—was considerably *less* than the suicide rate among teenagers in general.

So, do these results mean that playing D&D *prevents* suicide? Hardly. The 28 reported cases are probably an incomplete count of all suicides by D&D players. Besides, the correlation between playing D&D and committing suicide,

regardless of its direction and magnitude, could not possibly tell us about cause and effect. Maybe the kinds of young people who play D&D are simply different from those who do not.

Then, what conclusion should we draw from these data? *None at all.* Sometimes, as in this case, the data are meaningless because of how they were collected. Even when the data are potentially meaningful, people sometimes present them in a confusing or misleading manner (Figure 2.15). Let's consider some proper ways of analyzing and interpreting results.

Descriptive Statistics

To explain the meaning of a study, an investigator must summarize the results in an orderly fashion. When a researcher observes the behavior of 100 people, we have no interest in hearing all the details about every person observed. We want to know what the researcher found in general, on the average. We might also want to know whether most people were similar to the average or whether they varied a great deal. An investigator presents the answers to those questions through **descriptive statistics,** which are *mathematical summaries of results,* such as measures of the average and the amount of variation. The correlation coefficient, discussed earlier in this chapter, is one kind of descriptive statistic.

Measurements of the Central Score: Mean, Median, and Mode

There are three ways of representing the central score: mean, median, and mode. The **mean** is *the sum of all the scores divided by the total number of scores.* (Generally,

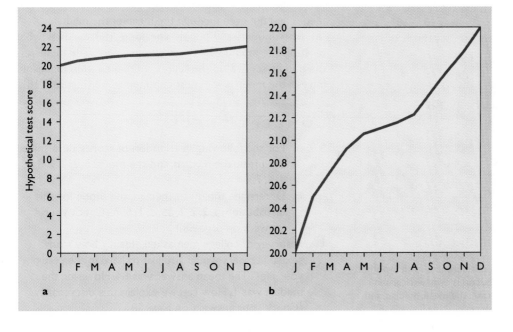

FIGURE 2.15 Why statistics can be misleading: Both of these graphs present the same data, an increase from 20 to 22 over one year's time. But by ranging only from 20 to 22 (rather than from 0 to 22), graph (b) makes that increase look much more dramatic. (After Huff, 1954.)

when people say "average," they refer to the mean.) For example, the mean of 2, 10, and 3 is 5 (15 ÷ 3). The mean is especially useful if the scores approximate the **normal distribution** (or normal curve), *a symmetrical frequency of scores clustered around the mean.* A normal distribution is sometimes described as a bell-shaped curve. For example, if we measure how long it takes 30 students to memorize a poem, these times will probably follow a pattern similar to the normal distribution.

The mean can be misleading, however, if the distribution is far from normal. Suppose, for example, we want to find out whether an article published in 1998 relied on up-to-date information. We check the dates of the references cited in the article and find the distribution shown in Figure 2.16. Here, the scores follow an approximately normal distribution, and the mean of 1994 adequately represents the results. However, suppose the author had added three quotes—one from Shakespeare (published in 1610), one from Aristotle (324 B.C.), and one from *Genesis* (4000? B.C.). The addition of those three references would lower the mean date from 1994 to 1841, giving the very misleading impression that the article had relied on out-of-date information.

The addition of these three old references would have much less effect on the median, however. To determine the **median,** *we arrange all the scores in order from the highest score to the lowest score. The middle score is the median.* For example, if the scores are 2, 10, and 3, the median is 3. In Figure 2.16 the median date of the references is 1994. After adding three very old references, the median is still 1994. If the author had added eight more old references, the median would fall to 1993. In short, a few extreme scores have less effect on the median than they do on the mean.

The third way to represent the central score is the **mode,** *the score that occurs most frequently.* For example, in the distribution of scores 2, 2, 3, 4, and 10, the mode is 2.

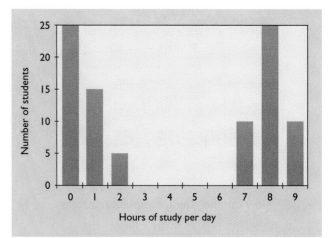

FIGURE 2.17   Results of an imaginary survey of study habits at one college. This college apparently has two groups of students—those who study as hard as they can, and those who find other things to do. In this case, both the mean and the median are misleading. This distribution is bimodal; its two modes are 0 and 8.

The mode is less useful than the mean or median, except under special circumstances. Suppose we surveyed a sample of students at a college about how much they study and gathered the results shown in Figure 2.17. Half of the students study a great deal, and half of them study very little. The mean for this distribution is 4.28 hours per day, a very misleading figure because all the students study either much more or much less than that. In this case, the median is no better as a representation of the results: Because we have an even number of students, there is no middle score. We could take a figure midway between the two scores nearest the middle, but in this case those scores are 2 and 7, so we would compute a median of 4.5, again a very misleading figure. A distribution like this is called a *bimodal distribution* (one with two modes); the researcher might simply describe the two modes and not even mention the mean or the median.

To summarize: Roughly speaking, the mean is what most people intend when they say "average." The median is the middle score after the scores are ranked from highest to lowest; the mode is the most common score (Figure 2.18).

CONCEPT CHECK

9. **a.** For the following distribution of scores, determine the mean, the median, and the mode: 5, 2, 2, 2, 8, 3, 1, 6, 7.
    b. Determine the mean, median, and mode for this distribution: 5, 2, 2, 2, 35, 3, 1, 6, 7. (Check your answers on page 58.)
10. A survey of college men asked, "Ideally, how many sexual partners would you like to have in the rest of your life?" The mean answer was 64. However, the median was 1. How can we explain this discrepancy? (Check your answers on page 58.)

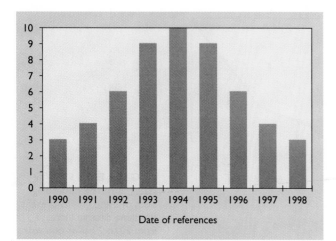

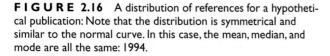

FIGURE 2.16   A distribution of references for a hypothetical publication: Note that the distribution is symmetrical and similar to the normal curve. In this case, the mean, median, and mode are all the same: 1994.

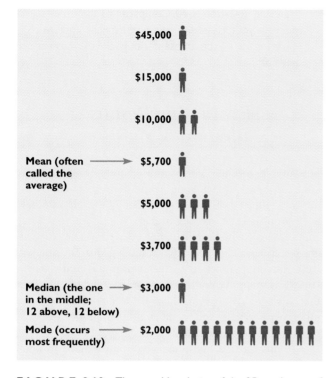

FIGURE 2.18 The monthly salaries of the 25 employees of company X, showing the mean, median, and mode. (After Huff, 1954.)

Measures of Variation

Figure 2.19 shows two distributions of test scores. Suppose that these represent scores on two introductory psychology tests. Both tests have the same mean, 70, but different distributions. If you had a score of 80, you would beat only three fourths of the other students on the first test, but with the same score you would beat 95% on the second test.

To describe the difference between Figure 2.20a and b, we need a measurement of the variation (or spread) around the mean. The simplest such measurement is the **range** of a distribution, *a statement of the highest and lowest scores.* The range in Figure 2.20a is 39 to 100, and in Figure 2.20b it is 58 to 92.

The range is a simple calculation, but it is not very useful, because it reflects only the extremes. Statisticians need to know whether most of the scores are clustered close to the mean or scattered widely. The most useful measure is the **standard deviation (SD),** *a measurement of the amount of variation among scores in a normal distribution.* In the appendix to this chapter, you will find a formula for calculating the standard deviation. For present purposes, you can simply remember that when the scores are closely clustered near the mean, the standard deviation is small; when the scores are more widely scattered, the standard deviation is large.

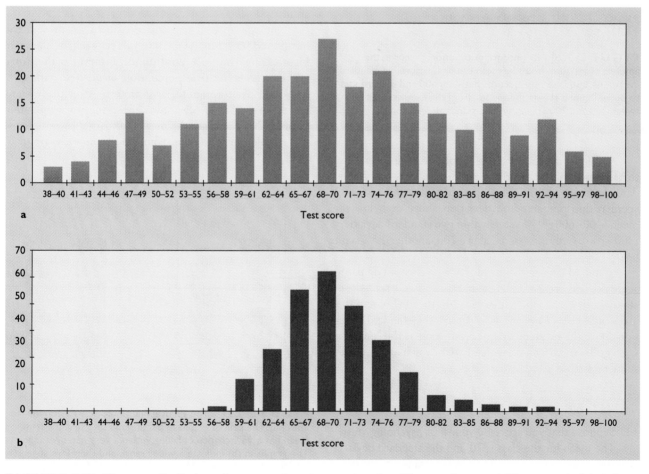

FIGURE 2.19 These two distributions of test scores have the same mean but different variances and different standard deviations.

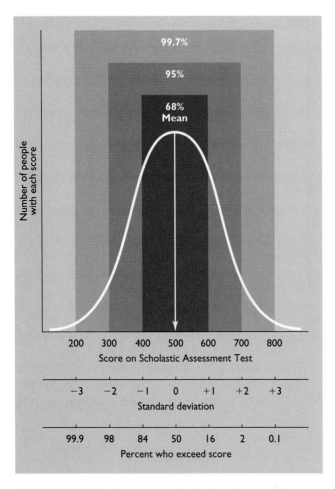

FIGURE 2.20 In a normal distribution of scores, the amount of variation from the mean can be measured in standard deviations. In this example, scores between 400 and 600 are said to be within one standard deviation from the mean; scores between 300 and 700 are within two standard deviations.

As Figure 2.20 shows, the Scholastic Assessment Test (SAT) was designed to produce a mean of 500 and a standard deviation of 100. Of all people taking the test, 68% score within one standard deviation above or below the mean (400–600); 95% score within two standard deviations (300–700). Only 2.5% score above 700; another 2.5% score below 300.

Standard deviations provide a useful way of comparing scores on different tests. For example, if you scored one standard deviation above the mean on the SAT, you tested about as well as someone who scored one standard deviation above the mean on another test, such as the American College Test. We would say that both of you had a deviation score of +1.

CONCEPT CHECK

11. Suppose that you score 80 your first psychology test. The mean for the class is 70, and the standard deviation is 5. On the second test, you receive a score of 90. This time the mean for the class is also 70, but the standard deviation is 20. Compared to the other students in your class, did your performance improve, deteriorate, or stay the same? (Check your answer on page 58.)

Evaluating Results: Inferential Statistics

Suppose researchers conducted a study comparing two kinds of therapy for helping people to quit smoking cigarettes. At the end of six weeks of therapy, people who have been punished for smoking average 7.5 cigarettes per day, whereas those who have been rewarded for *not* smoking average 6.5 cigarettes per day. Presuming that the smokers were randomly assigned to the two groups and that the study was properly conducted, is this the kind of difference that might easily arise by chance? Or should we take this difference seriously and recommend that all therapists use rewards and not punishment?

To answer this question, we obviously need to know more than just the numbers 7.5 and 6.5. How many smokers were in the study? (10 in each group? a hundred? a thousand?) And how much variation occurred within each group? Are most people's behaviors close to the group means, or are there a few extreme scores that distort the averages?

One way to deal with these issues is to present the means and 95% confidence intervals for each, as shown in Figure 2.21. The **95% confidence interval** is *the range within which the true population mean lies, with 95% certainty.* "Wait a minute," you protest. "We already know the means: 7.5 and 6.5. Aren't those the *true* population means?" No, those are the means for particular samples of the population. Someone who studies another group of

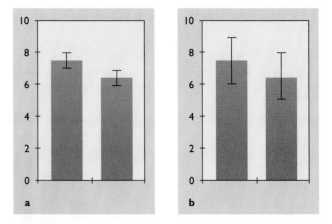

FIGURE 2.21 The vertical lines indicate 95% confidence intervals. The pair of graphs in part (a) indicate that the true mean has a 95% chance of falling within a very narrow range. The graphs in (b) indicate a wider range and therefore suggest less certainty that reward is a more effective therapy than punishment.

smokers may not get quite the same results. What we care about is the mean for all smokers. It is impractical to measure that mean, but if we know the sample mean, the size of the sample, and the standard deviation, we can estimate whether the sample mean is likely to be close to the population mean. Figure 2.21 presents two possibilities. In part (a), the 95% confidence intervals are small; in other words, the standard deviations were small, the samples were large, and the sample means are almost certainly close to the true population means. In part (b), the confidence intervals are larger, so the numbers 7.5 and 6.5 are just rough approximations of the true population means. Presenting data with confidence intervals can enable readers to decide for themselves how large and impressive the difference is between two groups (Hunter, 1997; Loftus, 1996).

A 95% confidence interval is one kind of **inferential statistic,** which is a *statement about a large population based on an inference from a small sample.* One alternative to the 95% confidence interval is a test that determines the probability of achieving a difference as large as the observed one by purely chance variation. For example, if we compared two groups of smokers who were actually undergoing the same therapy, what would be the chance that the difference between the two groups would be at least as large as the difference between 7.5 and 6.5? The result is summarized by a *p* (as in *probability*) value. For example, **$p < .05$** indicates that *the probability that randomly generated results would resemble the observed results is less than 5%.* The smaller the *p* value, the more impressive the results. The usual convention is that, if *p* is less than 0.05, researchers consider the results to be **statistically significant** or **statistically reliable**—that is, *unlikely to have arisen by chance.* A more cautious researcher might consider the results to be significant or reliable only if *p* were less than 0.01 or even 0.001. The appendix at the end of this chapter gives an example of a statistical test that can be used to determine a *p* value. Statistical significance depends on three factors: the size of the difference between the groups, the number of research participants in each group, and the amount of variation among individuals within each group (Figure 2.22).

CONCEPT CHECK

12. Should we be more impressed with results when the 95% confidence intervals are large or small? Should we be more impressed if the *p* value is large or small? (Check your answer on page 58.)

Examining the statistics is only the first step toward drawing a conclusion. To say that an experiment has statistically reliable results means only that we would be unlikely to get such results merely by chance. If not by chance, then how? At that point, psychologists use their knowledge to try to determine the most likely interpretation of the results.

THE MESSAGE
Statistics and Drawing Conclusions

Sometimes psychological researchers get consistent, dependable effects, and they do not even have to consider statistics: Turn out the lights in a sealed room; people will no longer be able to see. Add sugar to your iced tea; it tastes sweet. The bigger the effect, the less we need to rely on complicated statistical tests. We pay more attention to statistics when we measure smaller effects: Does a change in the wording alter people's responses to a survey? Does the use of an electronic study guide improve students' test scores? Does family therapy provide better results than individual therapy to treat alcohol and drug abuse? Psychologists frequently deal with small, fragile effects and therefore need a solid understanding of statistics.

SUMMARY

✳ *Mean, median, and mode.* One way of presenting the central score of a distribution is via the mean, determined by adding all the scores and dividing by the number of individuals. Another way is the median, which is the middle score, after all the scores have been arranged from highest to lowest. The mode is the score that occurs most frequently. (page 53)

✳ *Standard deviation (SD).* To indicate whether most scores are clustered close to the mean or whether they are spread out, psychologists report the range of scores, called the standard deviation. If we know that a given score is a certain number of standard deviations above or below the

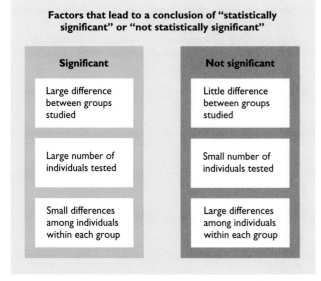

FIGURE 2.22 Researchers say that results are *statistically significant* if they calculate that chance variations in data would be unlikely to produce a difference between groups as large as the one that the researchers actually observed.

mean, then we can determine what percentage of other scores it exceeds. (page 55)

✳ *Inferential statistics.* Inferential statistics are attempts to deduce the properties of a large population based on the results from a small sample of that population. (page 56)

✳ *Probability of chance results.* The most common use of inferential statistics is to calculate the probability that a given research result could have arisen by chance. That probability is low if the difference between the two groups is large, if the variability within each group is small, and if the number of individuals in each group is large. (page 57)

✳ *Statistical significance.* When psychologists say p < .05, they mean that the probability that accidental fluctuations could produce the kind of results they obtained is less than 5%. They generally set a standard of 5% or less. If the results meet that standard, they are then said to be statistically significant or reliable. (page 57)

Suggestion for Further Reading

Martin, D. (1996). *Doing psychology experiments* (4th ed.). Pacific Grove, CA: Brooks/Cole. A discussion of all aspects of research, including methods of conducting research and statistical analyses of results.

Terms

descriptive statistics   mathematical summaries of results, such as measures of the average and the amount of variation (page 53)

mean   the sum of all the scores reported in a study divided by the number of scores (page 53)

normal distribution (or **normal curve**)   a symmetrical frequency of scores clustered around the mean (page 54)

median   the middle score in a list of scores arranged from highest to lowest (page 54)

mode   the score that occurs most frequently in a distribution of scores (page 54)

range   a statement of the highest and lowest scores in a distribution of scores (page 55)

standard deviation (SD)   a measurement of the amount of variation among scores in a normal distribution (page 55)

95% confidence interval   the range within which the true population mean lies, with 95% certainty (page 56)

inferential statistics   statements about large populations based on inferences from small samples (page 57)

p < .05   an expression meaning that the probability of accidentally achieving results similar to the reported results is less than 5% (page 57)

statistically significant or **statistically reliable results**   effects that have a low probability of having arisen by chance (page 57)

Answers to Concept Checks

9.   **a.** Mean = 4; median = 3; mode = 2. **b.** Mean = 7; median = 3; mode = 2. Note that changing just one number in the distribution from 8 to 35 greatly altered the mean without affecting the median or the mode. (page 54)

10.   Most of the men replied "1," indicating a preference for a monogamous relationship. However, some specified much higher numbers (perhaps even in the thousands), raising the mean. (page 54)

11.   Even though your score rose from 80 on the first test to 90 on the second, your performance actually deteriorated in comparison to other students' scores. A score of 80 on the first test was two standard deviations above the mean, better than 98% of all other students. A 90 on the second test was only one standard deviation above the mean, a score that beats only 84% of the other students. (page 56)

12.   In both cases, smaller. A small 95% confidence interval indicates high confidence in the results. A small *p* value indicates a low probability of getting such a large difference merely by chance. (page 57)

Web Resources

Statistical Assessment Service (STATS)

www.stats.org/

Here you'll learn how statistical and quantitative information and research are represented (and misrepresented) by the media, and how journalists can learn to convey such material more accurately and effectively. The *Vital STATS* newsletter and STATS Spotlight include many interesting articles; Dubious Data Awards provide hilarious reading about the misuse of statistics; Newsclips are more serious examples of mangled and misunderstood data.

Statistical Calculations

This appendix shows you how to calculate a few of the statistics mentioned in Chapter 2. It is intended primarily to satisfy your curiosity. Ask your instructor whether you should use this appendix for any other purpose.

Standard Deviation

To determine the standard deviation (SD):

1. Determine the mean of the scores.
2. Subtract each of the individual scores from the mean.
3. Square each of those results, add the square roots together, and divide by the total number of scores.

The result is called the *variance*. The standard deviation is the square root of the variance. See Table 2.3 for examples.

A Typical Statistical Test: The t-test

Several statistical tests are available to suit different kinds of data and different kinds of experiments. For the simple purpose of comparing two groups, both of which show results that approximate the normal distribution, one of the most popular tests is the *t-test*. Assume that for two populations the means are $x1$ and $x2$, the numbers of individuals measured are n_1 and n_2, and the standard deviations are s_1 and s_2.

TABLE 2.3

INDIVIDUAL SCORES	MEAN MINUS THE INDIVIDUAL SCORES	DIFFERENCES SQUARED
12.5	2.5	6.25
17.0	−2.0	4.00
11.0	4.0	16.00
14.5	0.5	0.25
16.0	−1.0	1.00
16.5	−1.5	2.25
17.5	−2.5	6.25
		36.00

Mean = 15.0
Variance = 36/7 = 5.143
Standard deviation = 2.268

We calculate t by this formula:

$$t = \frac{(\bar{x}_2 - \bar{x}_1)\sqrt{n_1 \cdot n_2 \cdot (n_1 + n_2 - 2)}}{\sqrt{n_1 \cdot s_1^2 + n_2 + s_2^2} \cdot \sqrt{n_1 + n_2}}$$

The larger the value of t, the less likely that the difference between the two groups is due to chance. The value of t will be high if the difference between the two means $(x_2 - x_1)$ is large, if the standard deviations $(s_1$ and $s_2)$ are small relative to the means, and if the number of individuals is large. For example, if a group of 50 people has a mean of 81 and a standard deviation of 7, and a group of 150 people has a mean of 73 and a standard deviation of 9; then

$$t = \frac{(81 - 73)\sqrt{150 \cdot 50 \cdot 198}}{\sqrt{(150 \cdot 81 + 50 \cdot 49)}\sqrt{(200)}} = \frac{9748.8}{120.83 \times 14.14} = 5.71$$

The larger the value of t, the less likely that the results have arisen by accident. Statistics books contain tables to show the likelihood of a given t value. In this case, with 2 hundred people in the two groups combined, a t value of 5.71 is significant ($p < 0.001$).

Correlation Coefficients

To determine the correlation coefficient, we designate one of the variables x and the other one y. We obtain pairs of measures, x_i and y_i. Then we use the following formula:

$$= \frac{[(\Sigma x_i y_i) - n \cdot \bar{x} \cdot \bar{y}]}{n \cdot sx \cdot sy}$$

In this formula, $(\Sigma x_i y_i)$ is the sum of the products of x and y. For each pair of observations (x, y), we multiply x times y and then add together all the products. The term $n \cdot \bar{x} \cdot \bar{y}$ means n (the number of pairs) times the mean of x times the mean of y. The denominator, $n \cdot sx \cdot sy$ means n times the standard deviation of x times the standard deviation of y.

Web Resources

Introductory Statistics: Concepts, Models, and Applications
www.psychstat.smsu.edu/introbook/sbk00.htm
You can read an entire statistics textbook by David W. Stockburger, Southwest Missouri State University, on the Web or download it, free!

Biological Psychology

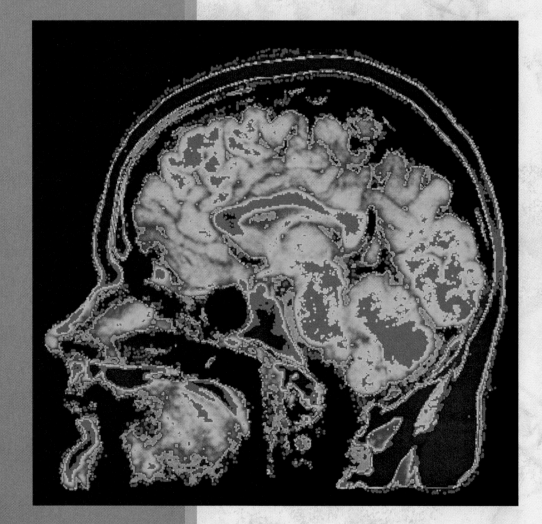

3

It is easy to look at a human brain, which weighs only 1.2 to 1.4 kg (2 ½ to 3 pounds), and marvel at its amazing abilities. But let's contemplate some even more compact brains. A bee has a brain (if you want to call it that) so small that one needs a microscope to find it. And yet a bee's behavior is remarkably complex. A bee flies around until it locates flowers, finds the food in the flower, evades predators, finds its way back to the hive, and then does a dance that tells other bees where it found the food. When necessary, it also takes care of the queen bee, protects the hive against intruders, and so forth. The bee's very tiny brain can do some incredible tasks.

What does it feel like to be a bee? In fact, does it feel like anything, or does a bee have no more consciousness than an automobile? We don't know; we cannot get inside the brain of a bee to find out. In fact, you and I cannot get inside each other's heads, either. When we speak of "experiences like yours and mine," we are really just inferring each other's experiences. We do not know them directly.

Researchers necessarily proceed piecemeal, first answering the questions that are easiest to answer. We now know a great deal about how nerves work, how brains record sensory experiences, and how various kinds of brain damage interfere with behavior and experience. What we understand least is why brain activity produces experience at all. We have much evidence indicating genetic influences on behavior, but in most cases we still know little about how these genes exert their effects. Progress in brain research has been enormous, and yet we can be just as easily awed by how much we have learned or how much we do not yet know.

Will we someday understand nerves well enough to "read the mind" of a bee? or even to decide whether a bee has experiences at all? We cannot say, but the fascination of the mind-brain question attracts a great many people to research in this area and motivates them to make tireless efforts.

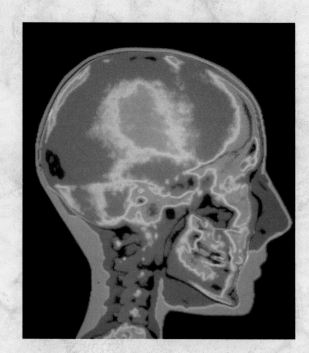

"I think, therefore I am"—René Descartes' declaration points to the mind–body problem facing psychologists: How and why does the brain's activity produce conscious experience?

Psychological Explanations at the Level of the Gene

How do heredity and evolution influence behavior?

The nature-nurture question shows up throughout the field of psychology in one form or another. Why do little boys get into fights more often than little girls do? Is it because of some genetic difference, or is it because other people intentionally or unintentionally encourage boys and girls to act differently? Why do some people develop drug and alcohol-related problems, yet others do not? Why do some people become depressed and others not? We should not expect any of the causes to be entirely genetic or entirely environmental, but it is pointless to say simply "both are important." Ideally, we would like to know exactly how certain genes influence development, which aspects of environment are most crucial, and how genes and environment combine and interact.

Let's first take a quick survey of genes and what they do. Then we shall explore in more detail the application of genetics to human behavior. At the end of this module we shall attend to the evolution of behavior.

Principles of Genetics

If you have already studied genetics in a biology class, much of this discussion will be a review. Skim it if you already know this material; read more carefully if it is unfamiliar to you.

Nearly every plant or animal cell (with a few exceptions, such as red blood cells) contains a nucleus, which includes *strands of hereditary material* called **chromosomes** (Figure 3.1). Chromosomes provide the chemical basis of heredity. Humans have 23 pairs of chromosomes in each cell of the body, except egg or sperm cells which have 23 unpaired chromosomes. At fertilization, the 23 chromosomes in the egg cell combine with the 23 in the sperm to form the 23 pairs that will characterize the new person (Figure 3.2).

Sections along each chromosome are known as **genes,** *these control the chemical reactions that direct the individual's development,* for example, determining whether

one becomes a tall dark-haired woman or a short blond man. Genes exert these effects by controlling the body's chemistry: Genes are composed of a chemical called DNA, which controls the production of another chemical called RNA, which in turn controls the production of proteins. These proteins either become part of the body's structure or control the rates of chemical reactions in the body. So, genes exert their effects by a long, complex route (Figure 3.3).

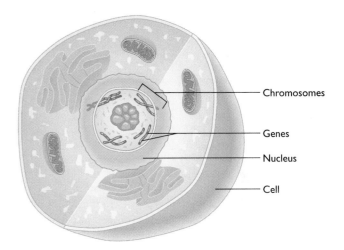

FIGURE 3.1 Genes are sections of chromosomes in the nuclei of cells. (Scale is exaggerated for illustration purposes.)

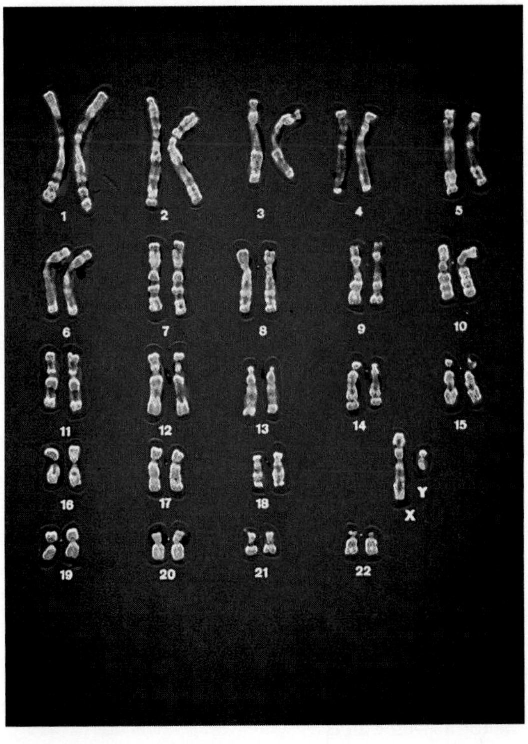

FIGURE 3.2 The nucleus of each human cell contains 46 chromosomes, 23 from the sperm and 23 from the ovum, united in pairs.

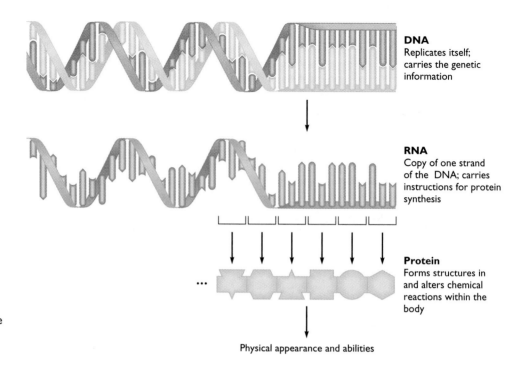

FIGURE 3.3 The genes, composed of DNA, control the production of RNA, which in turn controls the production of proteins. Proteins form many structures of the body (such as muscles); they also control the rate of many chemical reactions (such as digestion).

DNA
Replicates itself; carries the genetic information

RNA
Copy of one strand of the DNA; carries instructions for protein synthesis

Protein
Forms structures in and alters chemical reactions within the body

Physical appearance and abilities

All body cells that contain pairs of chromosomes have pairs of genes, one on each chromosome. You have two genes for eye color, two for hair color, and so forth. (The exception: Men have one X chromosome and one Y chromosome and therefore have unpaired genes on their X and Y chromosomes.) *If both genes of a pair are the same,* you are **homozygous** (HO-mo-ZI-gus) for that gene. *If the two genes are different,* you are **heterozygous** (HET-er-o-ZI-gus) for that gene (Figure 3.4). (A *zygote* is a fertilized egg.

Homozygous means that the egg—or other cell—has the same gene on both chromosomes.)

If you have one gene for brown eyes and one for blue eyes, you will have brown eyes. The gene for brown eyes is considered a **dominant gene** because *it exerts evident effects even if someone is heterozygous for that gene;* a **recessive gene** *shows its effects only in the homozygous condition.* Very few behavioral differences in humans depend on a single gene. One example, admittedly not a very

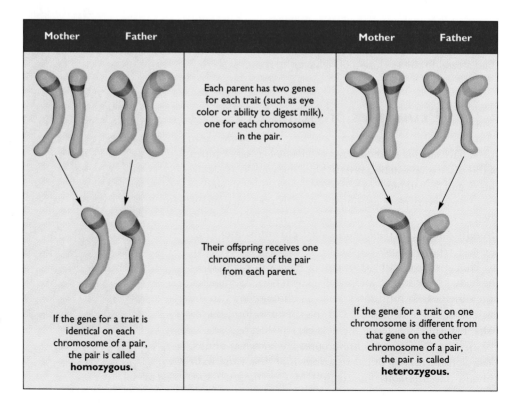

FIGURE 3.4 In a pair of homozygous chromosomes, the gene for a given trait is identical on both chromosomes. In a heterozygous pair, the chromosomes contain different genes for a trait.

Mother   Father

Each parent has two genes for each trait (such as eye color or ability to digest milk), one for each chromosome in the pair.

Their offspring receives one chromosome of the pair from each parent.

If the gene for a trait is identical on each chromosome of a pair, the pair is called **homozygous.**

Mother   Father

If the gene for a trait on one chromosome is different from that gene on the other chromosome of a pair, the pair is called **heterozygous.**

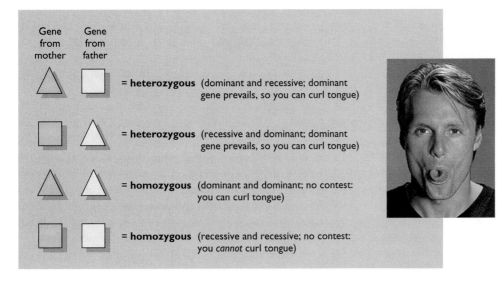

Gene from mother   Gene from father

= **heterozygous** (dominant and recessive; dominant gene prevails, so you can curl tongue)

= **heterozygous** (recessive and dominant; dominant gene prevails, so you can curl tongue)

= **homozygous** (dominant and dominant; no contest: you can curl tongue)

= **homozygous** (recessive and recessive; no contest: you *cannot* curl tongue)

FIGURE 3.5 This figure depicts the ability to curl the tongue lengthwise as an example of a behavior that depends on a single gene. The gene that enables you to curl your tongue is a dominant gene, indicated by a triangle here. The square refers to a recessive gene for the inability to curl the tongue.

important one, is the ability to curl the tongue lengthwise (Figure 3.5). The gene enabling tongue-curling is dominant, so if you have this gene, you can curl your tongue. If you are homozygous for the noncurling gene, you will have to get through life without this ability.

A person who is heterozygous for a particular gene will show the effects of the dominant gene but can still pass on the recessive gene to a son or daughter. For example, two parents who are heterozygous for the tongue-curling gene will both be able to curl their tongues, but they could each pass a recessive gene to their child, who would then lack this ability.

CONCEPT CHECKS

1. Suppose you can curl your tongue but your sister cannot. Are you homozygous or heterozygous for the tongue-curling gene, or is it impossible to say? What about your sister?
2. If two parents cannot curl their tongues, what can you predict about their children? (Check your answers on page 74.)

Sex-Linked and Sex-Limited Genes

One pair of human chromosomes is known as **sex chromosomes,** because they *determine whether an individual will develop as a male or as a female.* There are two types of sex chromosomes, known as X and Y (Figure 3.6). *A female has two* **X chromosomes** *in each cell; a male has one*

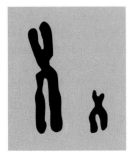

FIGURE 3.6 An electron micrograph of X and Y chromosomes shows the difference in length. (From Ruch, 1984.)

X chromosome and one **Y chromosome.** The mother contributes one X chromosome to each child, and the father contributes either an X or a Y chromosome.

Genes located on the X chromosome are known as X-linked or **sex-linked genes.** An X-linked recessive gene shows its effects more often in men than in women. For example, the most common type of colorblindness depends on an X-linked recessive gene and is therefore more common in men than in women. A man with that gene on his X chromosome will definitely be colorblind, because he has no other X chromosome. He has a Y chromosome, but that Y chromosome contains neither the gene for colorblindness nor the gene for normal color vision. A woman who has the colorblindness gene has a second X chromosome, which probably contains a dominant gene for normal color vision. If so, she will have normal color vision herself but could transmit the colorblindness gene to any of her children (Figure 3.7).

Genetically controlled differences between the sexes do not necessarily depend on sex-linked genes. For example, adult men generally have deeper voices and more facial hair than women do. Those characteristics are controlled by genes that are present in both sexes but activated by men's hormones. Similarly, the genes controlling breast development are present in both sexes but activated by women's hormones. **Sex-limited genes** are *those that affect one sex more strongly than the other, even though both sexes have the genes.*

Why do most boys fight more than girls do? We don't know, but if genes are responsible, they are probably *sex-limited* genes rather than sex-linked genes. Male hormones may activate certain genes that promote aggressive behavior; we have no evidence suggesting an X-linked or Y-linked gene for aggressive behavior.

CONCEPT CHECK

3. Suppose a colorblind man marries a woman who is homozygous for normal color vision. What sort of color vision will their children have? (Check your answer on page 74.)

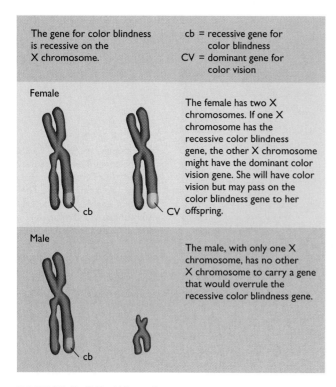

The gene for color blindness is recessive on the X chromosome.

cb = recessive gene for color blindness

CV = dominant gene for color vision

Female

The female has two X chromosomes. If one X chromosome has the recessive color blindness gene, the other X chromosome might have the dominant color vision gene. She will have color vision but may pass on the color blindness gene to her offspring.

Male

The male, with only one X chromosome, has no other X chromosome to carry a gene that would overrule the recessive color blindness gene.

FIGURE 3.7 Why males are more likely than females to be colorblind.

Identifying and Localizing Genes

Modern technology enables researchers to identify and localize the genes responsible for certain conditions. For example, researchers have located several genes that increase the risk of Alzheimer's disease (a condition associated with progressive memory loss), one gene strongly linked with Huntington's disease (associated with loss of muscle control) and genes that lead to several other diseases. You could (for a price) have someone examine your genes today and tell you which diseases you are likely to get, which ones you will not get, and in some cases even an estimate of how soon you will contract a particular disease. As research progresses, perhaps a chromosomal test will someday be able to tell you about your risks for depression, alcoholism, schizophrenia, and other behavioral disorders.

How much would you want to know? For most of us, the answer depends on what we could do with the information. For example, if you learned that you were predisposed to alcoholism, you might take some precautions to prevent it. At a minimum, you might decide not to join a fraternity or sorority with a reputation for heavy drinking. On the other hand, learning that you were likely to develop Alzheimer's disease at age 70 would do you less good, because no one knows yet how to prevent Alzheimer's. Still, identifying the genes that predispose one to Alzheimer's disease may lead researchers to a better understanding of the disease and ultimately to methods of prevention or treatment.

Identifying risk genes poses some possible harms as well. Conceivably, employers or insurance companies could someday require genetic tests of all job applicants and then discriminate against anyone whose test indicated a likelihood of developing a serious disease or psychological disorder. At present, no employers or insurance companies seem inclined to institute such a policy, but society will certainly face a serious ethical issue.

Measuring Heritability in Humans

The ability to curl your tongue lengthwise is an oddity; it apparently depends entirely on a single gene. Huntington's disease (a condition marked by tremors, loss of muscle control, and eventual deficits in memory and judgment) is a disorder also associated with a single gene: If you have that gene, you will almost certainly get the disease (unless you die of something else first), and if you don't have the gene, you cannot get the disease, as far as we know. We could name a few other examples of single-gene determinants of behavior, but not many.

For the most part, in psychology, we deal with behaviors that develop through complex influences of many genes and many environmental influences. You will occasionally hear someone ask whether a behavior, alcoholism for example, depends on heredity or on environment. That question is meaningless as stated. Obviously, you need both heredity and environment. However, after a small change in wording, the question becomes more meaningful and potentially answerable: Does a given *difference* in behavior (such as that one person becomes an alcoholic and another doesn't) depend more on *differences* in heredity or *differences* in environment? That is, if we want to predict whether more people in group A or group B will become alcoholics, how well could we succeed if we knew their heredity, and how well if we knew their environment?

The answer to a question like this is summarized by the term **heritability,** *an estimate of the variance within a population that is due to heredity.* Heritability ranges from 1, indicating that all variance is due to heredity, to 0, indicating that none of it is. For example, tongue curling has a heritability of almost 1. (It would be exactly 1 except that it is possible to suffer an injury to the tongue muscles that prevents tongue curling.)

For an example of a condition with zero heritability, consider the language that someone speaks. If you want to predict whether a child will speak English, Greek, or Bengali, you should ask which language is spoken by the child's parents and others around the child. An examination of the child's genes will not help at all.

Most behaviors have a heritability somewhere between zero and one. To estimate the heritability of any behavior, researchers rely on the following types of evidence (Segal, 1993):

• Do **monozygotic** (*identical; literally, "one-egg"*) **twins** resemble each other more closely than **dizygotic** (*fraternal; literally, "two-egg"*) **twins** do (Figure 3.8)? Monozygotic twins have identical heredities; dizygotic twins resemble each other genetically only as much as a brother and sister do. A greater resemblance between monozygotic twins is suggestive but not conclusive evidence for a genetic influence. A *lack* of such resemblance would argue strongly against a genetic influence.

• Do twins who are adopted by separate families and reared apart resemble each other more closely than we would expect for unrelated people? If so, genetic similarity is a likely explanation, although it is not the only possibility. Twins also share a *prenatal* (before-birth) environment; they share influences from the mother's eating, drinking, and smoking habits, her age, and so forth, and those prenatal influences can have a major influence on brain development (Devlin, Daniels, & Roeder, 1997).

• To what extent do adopted children resemble their adoptive parents and their biological parents? If children who are adopted in infancy closely resemble their biological parents in some regard, that resemblance probably reflects a genetic influence.

SOMETHING TO THINK ABOUT

A greater resemblance between a pair of monozygotic twins than between a pair of dizygotic twins is not considered conclusive evidence for a genetic influence. Why not? ✱

CONCEPT CHECK

4. If our society changed so that an equally good environment was provided for all children, would the heritability of behaviors increase or decrease? (See page 74.)

Whenever possible, researchers try to examine data from both twins and adopted children. Almost any kind of evidence has possible flaws and alternative explanations for its results, but if two or three kinds of studies all indicate a probable genetic influence, the conclusion becomes stronger.

Based on studies of twins and adopted children, researchers have found at least moderate heritability for a wide variety of behaviors and conditions, including schizophrenia, depression, and alcohol abuse (Loehlin, Willerman, & Horn, 1988), as well as a range of personality traits (Nigg & Goldsmith, 1994) and attitudes (Tesser, 1993). Adopted children have been shown to resemble their birth parents more than they do their adopting parents with regard to how much time they spend watching television (Plomin, Corley, DeFries, & Fulker, 1990). Monozygotic twins reared apart resemble each other in their religious devoutness (Waller, Kojetin, Bouchard, Lykken, & Tellegen, 1990). (Their religious affiliation, however, depends on the adoptive family. There is no gene for Presbyterian.)

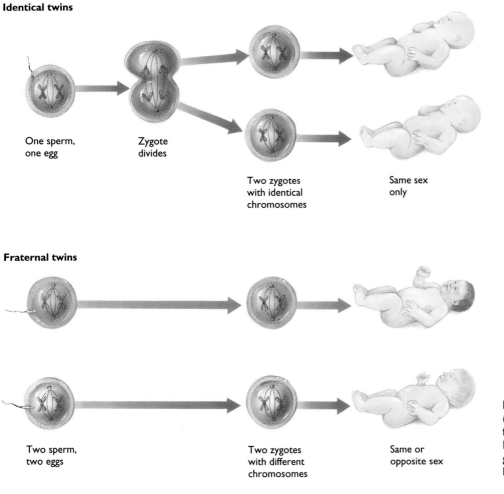

Identical twins

One sperm, one egg → Zygote divides → Two zygotes with identical chromosomes → Same sex only

Fraternal twins

Two sperm, two eggs → Two zygotes with different chromosomes → Same or opposite sex

FIGURE 3.8 Identical (monozygotic) twins develop from the same fertilized egg. Fraternal (dizygotic) twins grow from two eggs fertilized by two different sperm.

Monozygotic twins reared apart also resemble each other, sometimes to an amazing degree, in their interests (such as hunting, fishing, or arts and crafts), an optimistic or pessimistic outlook on life, and even their hobbies (Lykken, McGue, Tellegen, & Bouchard, 1992). One pair of twins who were separated at birth, reared in different western Ohio cities, and reunited in adulthood discovered that they had a great deal in common: Both had been named Jim by their adoptive parents. Each liked carpentry and drafting, had built a bench around a tree in his yard, worked as a deputy sheriff, drove a Chevrolet, took his vacations in western Florida, had gained weight at the same age, had married a woman named Linda, had divorced her and married a woman named Betty, and had a son named James Alan (or James Allen) and a pet dog named Toy (Figure 3.9). Surely, some of these similarities are mere coincidences. (Lots of people drive Chevrolets, for example.) And clearly the environment was not irrelevant. If either twin had been adopted by a family in Afghanistan, he would have had a hard time finding a woman named Linda or Betty and he probably would not have taken his vacations in Florida. Nevertheless, so many twins separated from birth have such striking similarities that it is hard to deny that at least part of the similarity reflects genetic influences.

Why might monozygotic twins resemble each other so closely? One possible answer is that many behavioral traits depend on the combined influences of many genes. For example, genes A, B, C, and D might together produce an

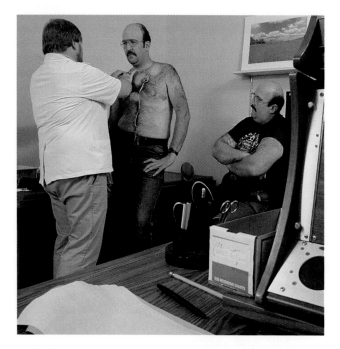

FIGURE 3.9 Identical twins Jim Lewis and Jim Springer were separated at birth, reared in separate cities of western Ohio, and reunited in adulthood. Like many identical twins who were reunited after growing up separately, they discovered that they shared a long list of detailed similarities.

effect that we would never suspect from any one of the genes separately, much as the effects of mixing four ingredients might produce a cake that one could never approximate from only three of the ingredients. Because monozygotic twins share all their genes in common, they will share these combinations or configuration results; other people in the same family will not.

The Route from Genes to Behavior

Some years ago, when researchers announced an apparent link between one gene and a predisposition to alcoholism, several psychologists said that this link was impossible, because no mere gene could explain something so complicated as alcoholism. Similar reactions have greeted announcements of genes linked to many other behaviors and personality traits.

Perhaps the problem is that, from the first time we are introduced to genetics, we are given examples such as eye color, in which a single gene has almost complete control of the outcome and environmental variations have almost no effect. With alcoholism and many other behaviors, it is obvious that no one gene can have such tight control. Furthermore, it is more difficult in some cases than others to imagine a route from gene to behavior. Certain genetic variations in humans are known to affect the microscopic structure of certain parts of the brain, in ways that probably affect behavior (Benjamin et al., 1996; Blum, Cull, Braverman, & Comings, 1996; Zuckerman, 1995). But how could genes affect a complicated behavior like television viewing? or religious devoutness? or alcoholism?

Probably no one gene has any direct effects on these behaviors, although genes can influence a behavior by influencing other characteristics that are either associated with it or antagonistic to it. For example, a gene that tends to make someone active and restless will probably interfere with any behavior that requires sitting for long periods—such as watching television or attending religious services.

Or consider dietary choices: Most Asian adults, including Americans of Asian ancestry, seldom drink milk. Within other ethnic groups, some adults enjoy milk, but others do not. Part of the variations in dairy consumption are under genetic control, but the genes do not affect taste or motivation; rather, they control the body's ability to digest *lactose,* the sugar in milk (Figure 3.10).

Almost all infants of any ethnic group can digest lactose. As they grow older, most Asian children and a large number of non-Asian children lose the ability to digest it. (They lose that ability even if they drink milk frequently. The loss depends on genes.) They can still eat and enjoy small amounts of milk, but larger amounts will cause gas and stomach cramps (Flatz, 1987; Rozin & Pelchat, 1988).

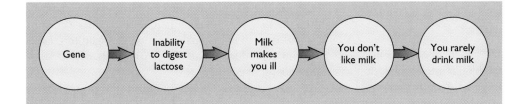

FIGURE 3.10 Genes don't control behavior directly but instead through many indirect routes. They control chemical reactions in the body, which in turn influence behavior.

Figure 3.11 shows how the ability to digest dairy products varies from one part of the world to another. The main point is that one gene can affect a behavior by altering chemical reactions outside the brain itself.

Consider another result: A study of thousands of Australian twins found that monozygotic twins resembled each other more closely than dizygotic twins did with regard to age of first sexual intercourse (Dunne et al., 1997). It is always hazardous to put too much trust in any one study, but for the sake of illustration, let's accept the conclusion that genes influence the age at which one first has sexual intercourse, and then let's ask how a gene could possibly do so. First, obviously one gene does not directly control that behavior, nor does it override the environment. If some of these twins had been adopted into a Bedouin Arab society, their sexual behavior would have been severely constrained. In Bedouin Arab culture, boys and girls are not permitted to play together or to intermingle in any way before marriage. A girl who managed nevertheless to have premarital intercourse would not be permitted to marry—a disaster in a society with hardly any jobs for women. Whatever genes influenced behavior in the Australian study had effects that depended on a culture that tolerates premarital sex.

So, how could a gene influence age at first sexual intercourse? We can imagine several possibilities:

- Genes influence rate of maturation: Those who begin puberty at 12 or 13 are more likely to have early sexual experiences than those who start puberty at 16 or 17.
- Genes influence secretion of sex hormones: Young people with higher hormonal levels probably have a stronger sex drive.
- Genes influence physical appearance: A very attractive individual will probably have more opportunities for sexual activity than someone less appealing.

Note that this third possibility implies that a gene can affect your behavior by influencing how other people react to you. That example underscores the difficulty of separating genetic influences from environmental influences. If you have a gene that affects your appearance and your appearance influences the way other people treat you, then the gene has influenced your behavior. If you had an identical twin who was reared in a separate environment, both of you would no doubt share some similar behaviors, and those similarities would count as evidence for heritability of the behavior; however, demonstrating heritability (even high heritability) for a behavior does not tell us how the genes exert their effects and does not deny that a change in the environment might drastically change the behavior.

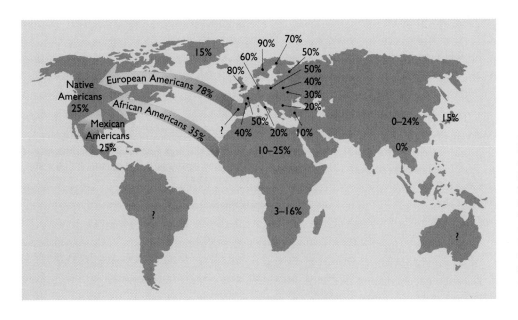

FIGURE 3.11 Adult humans vary in their ability to digest lactose, the main sugar in milk. The numbers in this figure refer to the percentage of each population's adults that can easily digest lactose. In Asian countries and other locations where most adults cannot digest lactose, cooks seldom use dairy products. (Based on Flatz, 1987, and Rozin & Pelchat, 1988.)

How Heredity Interacts with Environment

You might sometimes hear someone say, "I hope researchers never conclude that . . . [fill in the blank: intelligence, depression, alcoholism, etc.] is under genetic control, because if it is, that means that we can't do anything about it." That statement is nonsense. The fact that genetic differences have a major influence says nothing about whether some environmental intervention might change the results. For example, even if you have genes for straight hair, your health, your diet, and your grooming habits might cause you to have straight hair, curly hair, or no hair at all.

Here is another example: **Phenylketonuria (PKU)** is *an inherited condition that, if untreated, leads to mental retardation.* (The condition depends on a recessive gene. About 2% of people of European or Asian ancestry are heterozygous carriers for this gene; the gene is absent in African populations.) People who are homozygous for PKU lack the chemical reactions that break down a substance called *phenylalanine,* a common constituent of proteins, into other chemicals. On an ordinary diet, an affected child will accumulate phenylalanine in the brain and become mentally retarded; however, an affected child who observes a diet low in phenylalanine for at least the first 12 to 15 years of life will not become mentally retarded. Thus, an environmental intervention (here, a controlled diet) can greatly influence a condition that is known to be under genetic control.

Evolution

Our genes are a product of evolution. Given what we know about genes, we can infer that evolution *must* occur and must have been occurring for as long as genetics and reproduction have been as they are today. The argument, based on the ideas of English naturalist Charles Darwin (1859) is as follows:

1. The genes that an organism inherits from its parents strongly influence its characteristics. In short, like begets like. Children generally look somewhat like their parents, for example.

2. On occasion, genetic variations will cause an organism to differ from its parents. Such variations may arise from recombinations of genes (some from one parent and some from the other) or from **mutations,** *random changes in the structure of genes.* Recombinations and mutations alter the appearance or activity of the organism. Most mutations are disadvantageous, although an occasional mutation will give an individual an advantage in coping with some situations.

3. If individuals with a certain gene or gene combination reproduce more successfully than others do, the genes that confer an advantage will spread. Over many generations, the frequency of those genes will increase while the frequency of others will decrease (Weiner, 1994). Such

changes in the gene frequencies of a species constitute **evolution.** We know that mutations sometimes occur in genes and that an occasional mutation can lead to greater success in reproduction, so we can logically deduce that evolution *must* occur.

This argument does not tell us, however, whether all forms of life evolved from a single common ancestor. To deal with that question, we need other kinds of evidence, such as the fossil record.[1]

Animal and plant breeders discovered a long time ago that they could develop new strains through **artificial selection,** or *selective breeding.* By purposefully breeding only animals with certain traits, breeders developed cocker spaniels, thoroughbred racehorses, and chickens that lay enormous numbers of eggs. Darwin's theory of evolution stated that **natural selection** can accomplish the same results as selective breeding. If, in nature, *individuals with certain genetically controlled characteristics reproduce more successfully than others do, then future generations will come to resemble those individuals more and more.*

Some people assume, mistakenly, that evolution means "the survival of the fittest," but what really matters for evolution is not survival but *reproduction* (Figure 3.12). Someone who lives to the age of 100 without having a child has

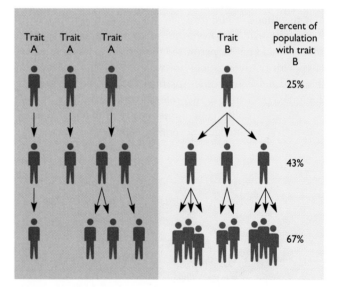

FIGURE 3.12 What's important for evolution is reproduction, not survival. Here, the population starts with three people carrying trait A and one with trait B. The person with B and his or her descendants produce more children, on the average, than people with A do. Consequently, the genes controlling trait B will increase in prevalence from one generation to the next.

---

[1]What about "creation science?" you may ask. Creation scientists argue that certain observations are hard to explain in terms of natural selection; however, no one has yet found evidence supporting the alternative view, that life began suddenly in more or less its present form. It is fair to admit that biologists do not know everything about how evolution operates, but the points that biologists dispute are the details, not the fundamental concept of natural selection.

failed to spread his or her genes. In contrast, a person who has five healthy children before dying at age 30 is a big success, in evolutionary terms.

A gene that increases a person's chance of surviving long enough to reproduce will be favored over a gene that causes death in infancy. But genes that have no influence on the individual's survival can also be favored. For example, a gene that makes an individual more successful at attracting mates would certainly be favored, as would a gene that makes someone more successful at protecting his or her offspring or other close relatives.

CONCEPT CHECK

5. Infertile worker bees are sisters of the queen bee, which lays all the eggs. In comparison with species in which all individuals are fertile, would you expect worker bees to be more likely or less likely to risk their lives to defend their sister? Would you expect a queen bee to be more or less likely than a worker bee to risk her life? (Check your answers on page 74.)

Occasionally, people say something like "every generation our little toes get smaller and smaller because we don't use them," or "through evolution, we will gradually get rid of the human appendix because we don't need it." Such statements reflect a misunderstanding of evolution. We do not add, change, or lose genes because of the way we use some part of the body. Our lack of need for an appendix has no effect on the genes controlling the appendix. The only way that people could evolve, say, a reduction in the size of the little toe would be if people with genes for "smaller than average little toe" reproduced more than other people.

One other common misunderstanding: Evolution does not necessarily mean long-term improvement. Genes will spread within a population if they provide some benefit at the moment. The result could be a population that is beautifully adapted to its current environment but ill-adapted when the environment changes in some way.

The Evolution of Behavior

Psychologists learn about the evolution of behavior largely through studies of animals. The study of animal behavior grew out of two separate pursuits: ethology and comparative psychology. **Ethology** is *the branch of biology that studies animal behavior under natural or nearly natural conditions.* Ethologists emphasize **species-typical behaviors—** *behaviors that are widespread in one animal species but not in others.* Species-specific behaviors are sometimes described as *instinctive,* although many investigators shun that term. (Many people use the term *instinct* as though it constituted an explanation. For example, they might say that a mother squirrel takes care of her young because of her "maternal instinct." But that statement is like saying "she

does it because she does it." Calling something an instinct tells us nothing about how the behavior develops or what processes control it.)

Comparative psychology is *the branch of psychology that compares the behaviors of various animal species.* A comparative psychologist might study which species are best at localizing sounds, how species differ in their means of finding food, or why some species solve a particular problem faster than other species do. Both ethologists and comparative psychologists study how behavioral capacities evolve and how they develop within an individual.

Evolution adapts the behavior of an animal, as well as its anatomy, to its way of life. Consider the mating behavior of the kittiwake, a member of the gull family (Tinbergen, 1958). Kittiwakes, unlike other gulls, nest on narrow ledges of steep cliffs (Figure 3.13). Because there are only so many suitable ledges, kittiwakes fight ferociously to claim territories. By contrast, herring gulls, which nest on the ground, rarely fight over territory, because for them one nesting site is about as good as any other. Kittiwakes use mud to build a hard nest with a barrier to prevent their eggs from rolling off the ledge. Herring gulls make no such effort. When kittiwake chicks hatch, they remain virtually motionless until they are old enough to fly. The advantage of this behavioral tendency is clear: A chick that takes even a step or two may fall off the ledge. Herring gull chicks, in contrast, begin to wander out of their nest long before they can fly.

Each of these kittiwake behaviors—fighting over territory, building secure nests, and remaining motionless—is well adapted to life on a narrow ledge. But have these behaviors been built into the animal by evolution, or are they learned anew by each individual? In the rare cases when kittiwakes nest on the ground, the chicks remain motionless

FIGURE 3.13 The nesting behavior of kittiwakes is superbly adapted for their survival. For example, the parents build a mud barrier on the edge of the nest, and the young remain motionless until they are able to fly.

anyway, even though they are in no danger of falling. If the egg of a herring gull is placed in a kittiwake's nest, the kittiwakes accept the foreign egg and care for the chick after it hatches. But the chick invariably takes a few steps and falls to its death. Evidently, some behavioral differences are products of the evolution of each species, rather than learned behavior.

Sociobiology

Sociobiology is *a field that tries to relate the social behaviors of a species to its biology, particularly to its evolutionary history.* According to sociobiologists, an animal interacts with others of its species in a particular way because similar behaviors in past generations have increased the probability of survival and mating. That is, individuals with a genetic tendency to engage in these social behaviors passed on their genes; individuals that behaved another way were less successful at passing on their genes.

Animal Examples of Sociobiological Explanations

Sociobiologists try to understand how various social behaviors may have helped animals to survive and reproduce. Here are two examples:

• Lions generally live in prides made up of one adult male, several adult females, and their young. If a new male succeeds in driving off the old male, he is likely to kill all the young. Why? Female lions are not sexually receptive while they are nursing their young. By killing the young, the new male brings the females into sexual receptivity and increases the likelihood of spreading his genes (Wilson, 1975).

• In a species of bird called reed buntings, a male-female pair will stick together fairly closely, although some females will also occasionally mate with neighboring males. Males help with incubating the eggs and taking care of the young; however, some males help more than others do. Researchers have found that females that engage in a large number of "extramarital affairs" with neighboring males elicit the least help from their male partners (Dixon, Ross, O'Malley, & Burke, 1994). That is, apparently a male will work hard to help raise the young if the probability is high that he is their father. (We do not assume that he understands all this; evolution has simply prepared him to be more helpful to a faithful mate. Males who behaved this way in the past were more likely to pass on their genes.)

Speculations About Human Sociobiology

Human social behavior is also partly the product of our evolutionary history. In principle, that result is a logical necessity, yet citing precise examples is difficult because we are less certain about which human behaviors are strongly influenced by our genes and which ones are learned from our culture. Consider a couple of speculative, controversial examples:

• People will work very hard to help one another, sometimes even risking their own lives to help other people. *Doing something to help others with no direct benefit to oneself* is called **altruistic behavior.** Similarly, other species engage in some behaviors that appear to be altruistic; for example, a goose that sees a hawk overhead utters an alarm call that warns other geese. A sociobiological explanation for this behavior is that selection has favored genes that promote altruistic behavior toward one's relatives (Trivers, 1972). That is, individuals that help their offspring and other relatives tend to spread their genes, simply because those relatives have many of the same genes as the altruistic individual. And a mechanism that causes one to help relatives may accidentally cause one to help nonrelatives, too.

• Men are more likely than women are to seek multiple sexual partners. A sociobiological interpretation is that a man who impregnates several women is spreading his genes. A woman gains no such advantage in taking multiple sexual partners. Moreover, if she were to do so, she might have trouble getting any one of them to help her rear the children. Therefore, the sociobiologists say, we may have evolved some sex-limited genes that increase males' interest or decrease females' interest in multiple partners (Buss, 1994).

Human sociobiology is controversial, largely because its adherents sometimes seem to be saying, "This is the way people behave; therefore, they must have evolved a tendency to behave this way, and because we have evolved this way, it is natural and almost necessary that we continue to behave this way." That political message does not logically follow from the science. Even if we understand the biological or historical factors that influence us to act in a certain way, we will not necessarily want to continue acting in that way.

Furthermore, sociobiological theories are, in many cases, difficult to test. Sociobiologists know little about the genes that affect human social behaviors, and they can make only uncertain inferences about life in early human societies. Their best approach is to compare cultures. If they find, say, that a male-female difference is consistent across cultures and from one historical era to another, then the difference is probably a real part of human nature. Sociobiological explanations are as appropriate here as they are for lions or reed buntings. However, if a behavior differs greatly across cultures, then we should be skeptical of a sociobiological explanation. Unfortunately for theory-testers, cross-cultural comparisons often show a combination of consistencies and contrasts among cultures. For example, men in every known culture are more interested than women are in multiple sex partners (a consistency across cultures), but the difference between men and women varies from large in some cultures to slight in others (a difference across cultures). In short, human social behavior depends on a combination of evolutionary and cultural influences, and psychologists must try to give both influences due recognition. We shall return to this issue in the section on attraction in Chapter 14.

THE MESSAGE

Genes, Evolution, and Behavior

Many people justifiably criticize the concept of *genetic determinism,* the idea that people may be fated to become criminals, alcoholics, or mental patients because of their genes. Certain claims in sociobiology attract similar criticisms. As you have seen in this module, only a few behavioral differences are rigidly determined by genetics. Genes do fully determine whether you can curl your tongue lengthwise. They also largely determine whether you will get Huntington's disease, Alzheimer's disease, and several other diseases, although future research may find ways to prevent these conditions.

For most behaviors of great interest to psychologists, however, genes alter some aspect of the body (not necessarily the nervous system) so that one behavior or another becomes more likely. It is simply wrong to say that genetic or evolutionary influences on behavior imply that behavior is unmodifiable or that the environment is irrelevant. In fact, understanding how the genes exert their effects may give researchers their best clue about which environmental interventions would be most effective for modifying the behavior.

SUMMARY

✳ *Genes.* Genes, which are segments of chromosomes, control heredity. Because chromosomes come in pairs, every person has two of each gene, one received from the father and one from the mother. The sex chromosomes are an exception; each male has one Y chromosome and one unpaired X chromosome. (page 63)

✳ *Dominant and recessive genes.* A dominant gene exerts its effects even in people who have only one dominant gene, but people must have two of a recessive gene, one on each chromosome, in order to show its effects. (page 64)

✳ *Sex-linked and sex-limited genes.* Genes on the X chromosome are sex linked. A sex-linked recessive gene will show its effects more frequently in males than in females. A sex-limited gene is present in both sexes, but it exerts its effects more strongly in one than in the other. (page 65)

✳ *Identifying and localizing genes.* Researchers have located the gene responsible for Huntington's disease, and they are trying to identify and localize as many other human genes as possible. Identifying people's behavioral tendencies and risks by examining their genes offers the potential for significant benefits and also for possible misuse. (page 66)

✳ *Evidence for genetic influences.* Researchers determine the contribution of genes to human behavior by studying whether monozygotic twins resemble each other more than dizygotic twins do, by comparing monozygotic twins reared in separate environments, and by examining how adopted children resemble their biological parents and their adoptive parents. (page 66)

✳ *How genes affect behavior.* Genes apparently affect an amazing variety of behaviors; however, each gene ordinarily affects a great variety of behaviors, not just one, and a gene can affect behavior indirectly, not necessarily by influencing brain development. (page 68)

✳ *Influence of the environment on gene expression.* It is possible for a behavior that reflects a genetic influence to be highly modified by a change in the environment. (page 70)

✳ *Evolution.* Evolution by natural selection is a logical necessity, given the principles of heredity and the fact that individuals with certain genes leave more offspring than do individuals with other genes. (page 70)

✳ *Study of animal behavior.* Ethologists and comparative psychologists study animal behavior and try to understand how it evolved. (page 71)

✳ *Sociobiology.* Sociobiologists try to explain social behaviors in terms of the survival and reproductive advantages of those behaviors. To interpret human behavior in such terms, one must carefully distinguish behaviors that are part of human nature from those that are highly dependent on culture and individual experience. In many cases, we simply do not know enough yet to make that distinction. (page 72)

Suggestions for Further Reading

Tinbergen, N. (1958). *Curious naturalists.* New York: Basic Books. One of the best books for stimulating interest in animal behavior.

Weiner, J. (1994). *The beak of the finch.* New York: Knopf. Not really about behavior but an excellent book for its explanations of how evolution works.

Terms

chromosome   a strand of hereditary material found in the nucleus of a cell (page 63)

gene   a segment of a chromosome that controls chemical reactions that ultimately direct the development of the organism (page 63)

homozygous   having the same gene on both members of a pair of chromosomes (page 64)

heterozygous   having different genes on a pair of chromosomes (page 64)

dominant gene   a gene that will exert evident effects on development even in a person who is heterozygous for that gene (page 64)

recessive gene   a gene that will affect development only in a person who is homozygous for that gene (page 64)

sex chromosomes   the pair of chromosomes that determine whether an individual will develop as a female or as a male (page 65)

X chromosome   a sex chromosome; females have two per cell and males have only one (page 65)

Y chromosome   a sex chromosome; males have one per cell and females have none (page 65)

sex-linked gene   a gene located on the X chromosome (page 65)

sex-limited gene   a gene that affects one sex more strongly than the other, even though both sexes have the gene (page 65)

heritability   an estimate of the variance within a population that is due to heredity (page 66)

monozygotic twins   (literally, "one-egg" twins) identical twins who develop from the same fertilized egg (page 66)

dizygotic twins   (literally, "two-egg" twins) fraternal twins who develop from two eggs fertilized by two different sperm. Dizygotic twins are no more closely related than are any other children born to the same parents. (page 66)

phenylketonuria (PKU)   an inherited disorder in which a person lacks the chemical reactions that convert a nutrient called phenylalanine into other chemicals; unless the diet is carefully controlled, the affected person will become mentally retarded (page 70)

mutation   a random change in the structure of a gene (page 70)

evolution   changes in the gene frequencies of a species (page 70)

artificial selection   the purposeful breeding, by humans, of animals with certain traits, also known as selective breeding (page 70)

natural selection   the tendency, in nature, of individuals with certain genetically controlled characteristics to reproduce more successfully than others do; future generations will come to resemble those individuals more and more (page 70)

ethology   the branch of biology that studies animal behavior under natural or nearly natural conditions (page 71)

species-typical behavior   a particular behavior that is widespread in one animal species but not in others (page 71)

comparative psychology   the branch of psychology that compares the behaviors of various animal species (page 71)

sociobiology   a field that tries to relate the social behaviors of a species to its biology, particularly to its evolutionary history (page 72)

altruistic behavior   behavior that benefits others without directly benefiting the individual exhibiting that behavior (page 72)

Answers to Concept Checks

1. It is impossible to say whether you are homozygous or heterozygous for the tongue-curling gene. Because it is a dominant gene, it produces the same effects in both the homozygous and heterozygous conditions. Your sister, however, must be homozygous for the noncurling gene. (page 65)

2. Because both of the parents must be homozygous for the inability to curl their tongues, they can transmit only "noncurler" genes, and their children will be noncurlers also. (page 65)

3. The woman will pass a dominant gene for normal color vision to all her children, so they will all have normal color vision. The man will pass a gene for deficient color vision on his X chromosome; the daughters will therefore be carriers for color blindness. (page 65)

4. If all children had equally supportive environments, the heritability of behaviors would *increase*. Remember, heritability refers to how much of the difference among people is due to hereditary variation. If the environment is practically the same for all, then environmental variation cannot account for much of the variation in behavior. Whatever behavioral variation still occurs would be due mostly to hereditary variation. (Note one implication: Any estimate of heritability applies only to a given population. In another population, the heritability could be much different.) (page 67)

5. Because the infertile worker bees cannot reproduce, the only way they can pass on their genes is by helping the queen bee. Consequently, they will sacrifice their own lives to defend the queen. They will also risk their lives to defend other workers in the hive, because these workers also try to defend the queen. The queen, however, will do little to defend a worker, because doing so would not increase her probability of reproducing. (page 71)

Web Resources

Human Genome Project

www.ornl.gov/TechResources/Human_Genome/home.html

This is the definitive site for understanding the Human Genome Project, from the basic science to ethical, legal, and social considerations, to the latest discoveries.

Explanations of Behavior at the Level of the Neuron

Can we explain our experiences and our behavior in terms of the actions of single cells in the nervous system?

Your brain, which controls everything you do, is composed of cells. Does this mean that every one of your experiences—every sight, every sound, every thought—represents the activity of cells in your brain?

One highly productive strategy in science is *reductionism*—the attempt to explain complex phenomena by reducing them to combinations of simpler components. Biologists explain breathing, blood circulation, and metabolism in terms of chemical reactions and physical forces. Chemists explain chemical reactions in terms of the properties of the 92 naturally occurring elements. Physicists explain the structure of the atom and the interactions among atoms in terms of a few fundamental forces.

Does reductionism apply to psychology? Can we explain human behavior and experience in terms of chemical and electrical events in the brain? Here we attempt to answer these questions.

The Cells of the Nervous System

You experience your "self" as a single entity that senses, thinks, and remembers. And yet neuroscientists have found that the nervous system responsible for your experiences consists of an enormous number of separate cells. The brain processes information in **neurons** (NOO-rons), or *nerve cells*. Many of the neurons in the human nervous system are extremely small; the best current estimate is that the nervous system contains nearly 100 billion neurons (Williams & Herrup, 1988), as shown in Figure 3.14. The nervous system also contains another kind of cells called **glia** (GLEE-uh), *which support the neurons in many ways such as by insulating them and by removing waste products.* The glia are about one tenth of the size of neurons but about 10 times more numerous. Until the early 1900s,

many researchers thought it likely that all the neurons physically merged, that the tip of each neuron actually joined the next neuron. We now know that it does not; each neuron remains separate. How do so many separate neurons and glia combine forces to produce the single stream of experiences that is you?

The secret is communication. Each neuron receives information and transmits it to other cells by conducting electrochemical impulses. Sensory neurons carry information from the sense organs to the central nervous system; neurons of the central nervous system process that sensory information and compare it to past information; motor neurons convey commands to the muscles and glands. Within the central nervous system, each neuron sends information to many others, and these in turn send information to still others; eventually, some of those neurons may send information back to the first one. Out of all this rapid exchange of information, about 100 billion neurons produce a single functioning system.

To understand our nervous system, we must first understand the properties of both the individual neurons and the connections among them. Neurons have a variety of shapes, depending on whether they receive information from a few sources or from many and whether they send impulses over a short distance or over a long distance (Figure 3.15).

A neuron consists of three parts—a cell body, dendrites, and an axon (Figure 3.16). The **cell body** *contains the nucleus* of the cell. The **dendrites** (from a Greek word meaning "tree") are *widely branching structures that receive transmissions from other neurons.* The **axon** is a *single, long, thin, straight fiber with branches near its tip.* Some vertebrate axons are covered with *myelin,* an insulating sheath that speeds up the transmission of impulses

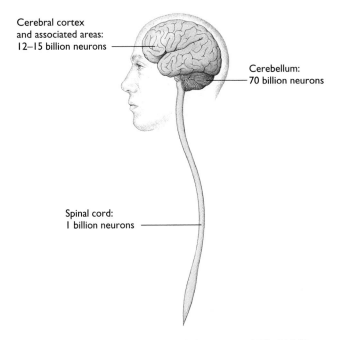

Cerebral cortex and associated areas: 12–15 billion neurons

Cerebellum: 70 billion neurons

Spinal cord: 1 billion neurons

FIGURE 3.14 Distribution of the estimated 83–86 billion neurons in the adult human central nervous system (Based on data of Williams & Herrup, 1988).

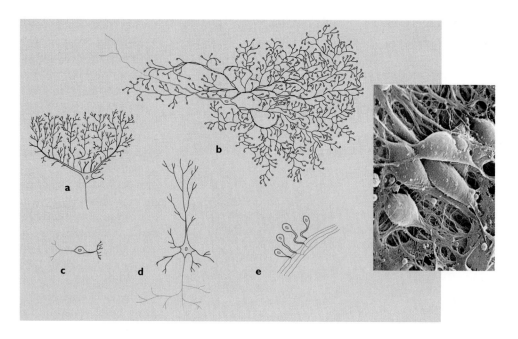

FIGURE 3.15 Neurons vary enormously in shape. In each case, the neuron consists of its cell body and all the branched attachments, called axons and dendrites. The neurons in (a) and (b) receive input from many sources, the neuron in (c) from only a few sources, and the neuron in (d) from an intermediate number of sources. The neurons in (e) are sensory neurons, which carry messages from sensory receptors to the brain or spinal cord. The axons are coded blue for easy identification. [Part (b) courtesy of Richard Coss.]

along an axon. As a rule, an axon transmits information to other cells, and the dendrites or cell body of each cell receives that information. That information can be either excitatory or inhibitory; that is, it can increase or decrease the probability that the next cell will send a message of its own. Inhibitory messages are important for many purposes. For example, during a period of painful stimulation, your brain has mechanisms to inhibit further sensation of pain.

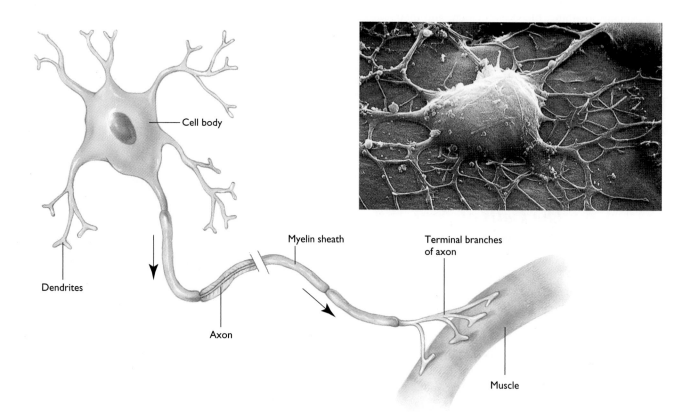

FIGURE 3.16 The generalized structure of a motor neuron shows the dendrites, the branching structures that receive transmissions from other neurons, and the axon, a single, long, thin, straight fiber with branches near its tip. Axons range in length from 1 millimeter to more than 1 meter and carry information to other cells. (inset) A photomicrograph of a neuron.

The Action Potential

Imagine what would happen if axons conveyed information by electrical conduction: Because axons are made of biological materials and not copper wire, the electrical impulse would greatly decrease in intensity as it traveled along the axon. A pinch on your nose would reach the brain at nearly its full intensity; a pinch on your stomach would feel much weaker and a pinch on your toe would feel weaker yet. Short people would be able to feel a pinch on the toe more intensely than tall people would.

So, axons, instead of transmitting electrical impulses, convey information by a special combination of electrical and chemical processes called an **action potential,** *an excitation that travels along an axon at a constant strength, no matter how far it must travel.* An action potential is a yes/no or on/off message. That is, an axon either produces an action potential or it doesn't; it cannot produce larger or smaller or faster or slower action potentials at different times. This principle is known as the *all-or-none law.*

The advantage of an action potential over simple electrical conduction is that action potentials from distant places like your toes reach the brain at full strength, instead of getting weaker as they travel. The disadvantage is that impulses reach your brain more slowly than they would by electrical conduction. Your brain's knowledge is constantly almost one tenth of a second behind what is happening to your toes. Fortunately, that delay does not inconvenience you very often.

To explain how the action potential works, let's start with the resting condition of the axon: Ordinarily, there is *an electrical polarization across the membrane (or covering) of an axon, with a negative charge on the inside of the axon.* This electrical polarization, called the **resting potential** of the membrane, amounts to about 70 millivolts in a typical cell. It is maintained by the different distributions of sodium and potassium ions across the membrane. A mechanism called the sodium-potassium pump keeps sodium more concentrated outside the cell and potassium more concentrated inside. As you probably learned in high-school chemistry, both sodium ions and potassium ions have a $+1$ charge, so you might imagine that the sodium and potassium effects would cancel each other out; however, the body has a great deal more sodium than it has potassium, so the distribution of sodium makes more difference than the distribution of potassium. The net result is that the outside of the axon (where most sodium is located) is relatively positive; the inside is relatively negative (see Figure 3.17). (Naturally, sodium and potassium are not the only ions present; there are also positively charged calcium ions, negatively charged chloride, and other types as well.)

Certain kinds of stimulation can disrupt this stable resting potential. The action potential occurs when the membrane briefly opens little gates (called sodium gates) along its surface to allow sodium ions to enter the axon (Figure 3.18). As those sodium ions cross the membrane, they

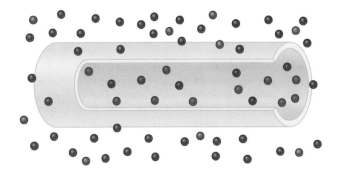

FIGURE 3.17 The axon membrane has a resting potential, when it is not conveying an action potential: the outside is relatively positive and the inside is relatively negative. This difference in electrical potential depends on the distribution of positive ions. The more numerous sodium ions (Na^+) are located mostly outside the axon, whereas the less numerous potassium ions (K^+) are located mostly inside. Here, red spheres represent sodium; blue spheres represent potassium.

eliminate the negative potential that is usually present inside the cell. Then the sodium gates close and potassium gates open to allow potassium ions to leave the axon, returning the axon to its original resting potential (Figure 3.19b). Eventually, the cell pumps the invading sodium ions back out and the lost potassium ions back in.

You will recall that the axon does not conduct like an electrical wire. The action potential travels down the axon like a wave of energy, and the stimulation at each point excites the next point along the axon to create its own action potential. You could imagine the process something like a fire burning along a string: The fire at each point along the string ignites the next point, which in turn ignites the next point. That is, after sodium ions cross at one point along an axon, the electrical

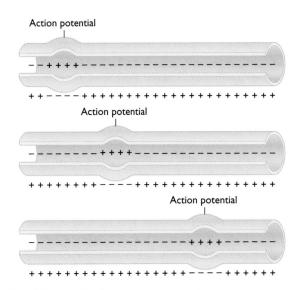

FIGURE 3.18 Ion movements conduct an action potential along an axon. At each point along the membrane, sodium ions enter the axon and alter the distribution of positive and negative charges. As each point along the membrane returns to its original state, the action potential flows to the next point.

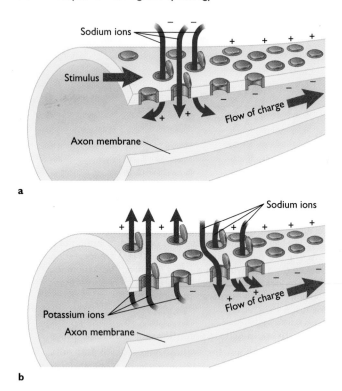

a

b

FIGURE 3.19 (a) During an action potential, sodium gates in the neuron membrane open, and sodium ions enter the axon, bringing a positive charge with them. (b) After an action potential occurs at one point along the axon, the sodium gates close at that point and open at the next point along the axon. When the sodium gates close, potassium gates open, and potassium ions flow out of the axon, carrying a positive charge with them. (Modified from Starr & Taggart, 1992.)

excitation opens channels at the next point along the axon, thus enabling sodium ions to cross there, and so forth, as shown in Figure 3.19. In this manner, the action potential remains equally strong all the way to the end of the axon.

Now, all of this information is clearly important to investigators of the nervous system, but why is it important to you as a general psychology student? First, it explains why sensations on points on your fingers and toes do not fade away by the time they reach your brain. Second, an understanding of action potentials is one step toward understanding the communication between one neuron and the next. Third, certain drugs operate by blocking action potentials. For example, anesthetic drugs (such as Novocaine) silence neurons by clogging the sodium gates (van Dyke & Byck, 1982). When your dentist drills a tooth, the receptors in your tooth send out the message "Pain! Pain! Pain!" But that message does not get through to the brain, because a shot of Novocaine has blocked the sodium gates and thereby halted the sensory messages.

CONCEPT CHECK

6. If you stub your toe, do you feel it immediately or is there a delay before you feel it? Why? (Check your answer on page 84.)

Synapses: The Junctions Between Neurons

Ultimately, each neuron must communicate with other neurons. Communication between one neuron and the next follows a different process from the transmission along an axon. At a **synapse** (SIN-aps), *the specialized junction between one neuron and another* (Figure 3.20), *one neuron releases a chemical that either excites or inhibits the next neuron.* That is, the chemical can make the next neuron either more or less likely to produce an action potential. The events at synapses are central to everything that your brain does, because the synapses are the source of information for the receiving cell.

A typical axon has several branches; each branch ends with a little bulge called a *presynaptic ending,* or **terminal bouton** (or **button**), as shown in Figure 3.21. When an action potential reaches the terminal bouton, it causes the release of molecules of a **neurotransmitter,** *a chemical that has been stored in the neuron and that can activate receptors of other neurons* (Figure 3.21). Different neurons use different chemicals as their neurotransmitters, but each neuron uses the same chemical or same combination of chemicals at all times and at all branches of its axon (Eccles, 1986). The neurotransmitter molecules then diffuse across a narrow gap to *the neuron on the receiving end of the synapse,* the **postsynaptic neuron.** There, the neurotransmitter molecules attach to receptors, which can be located either on the neuron's dendrites or cell body or (for special purposes) on the tip of its axon. The neural communication process is summarized in Figure 3.22.

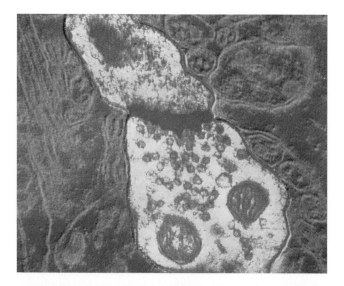

FIGURE 3.20 A synapse, magnified thousands of times in an electron micrograph, includes small round structures in the middle cell called synaptic vesicles, which store neurotransmitter molecules. The thick, dark area at the bottom of the cell is the synapse.

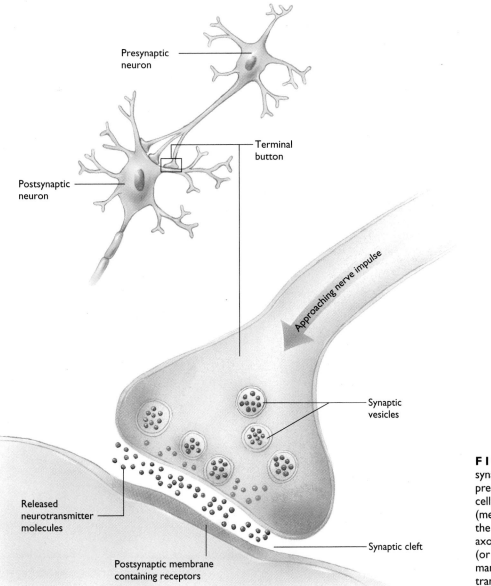

FIGURE 3.21 The synapse is the junction of the presynaptic (message-sending) cell and the postsynaptic (message-receiving) cell. At the end of the presynaptic axon is the terminal bouton (or button), which contains many molecules of the neurotransmitter, ready for release.

Depending on the chemical used as a neurotransmitter and on the type of receptor, the result can be either excitation or inhibition of the neuron. The postsynaptic neuron can receive nearly simultaneous excitation and inhibition from a great many other neurons. This neuron produces an action potential of its own if the total amount of excitation outweighs the total amount of inhibition. That is, positively charged ions can be flowing into the cell at some locations and out at others, while negatively charged ions are also flowing in one direction or the other. The net effect of all these flows can either increase or decrease the frequency of action potentials. The process resembles making a decision: When you are trying to decide whether to do something, you weigh all the pros and cons and then you act if the pros outweigh the cons.

Note that inhibition is not merely the absence of exci-

tation; it is an active braking process. For example, when a pinch on your foot causes you to raise it, thus contracting one set of muscles, inhibitory synapses in your spinal cord block activity in the opposing set of muscles, those that would move your leg the opposite direction. Those inhibitory synapses prevent your spinal cord from sending messages to raise your leg and extend it at the same time.

After a neurotransmitter excites or inhibits a receptor, it displaces from the receptor, terminating the message. From that point on, the fate of the receptor molecule varies. It could become reabsorbed by the axon that released it (through a process called *reuptake*); it could diffuse away, get metabolized, and eventually show up in the blood or urine; or it could bounce around for a moment, return to the postsynaptic receptor and reexcite it. Many drugs, ranging from antidepressants to drugs of abuse, act by blocking

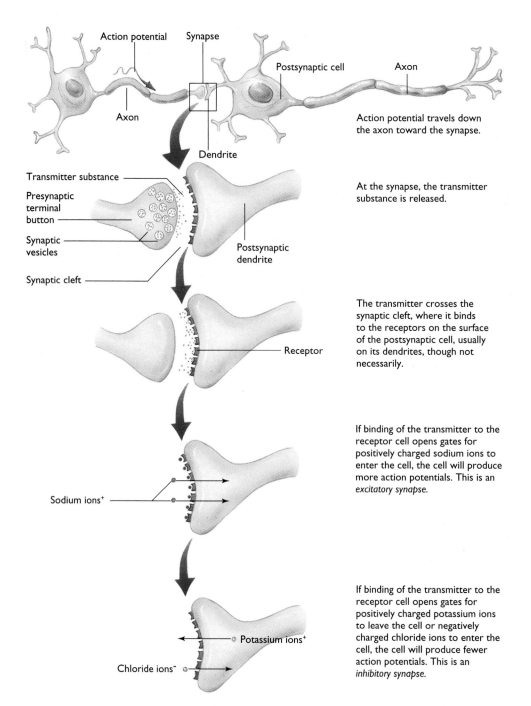

Action potential travels down the axon toward the synapse.

At the synapse, the transmitter substance is released.

The transmitter crosses the synaptic cleft, where it binds to the receptors on the surface of the postsynaptic cell, usually on its dendrites, though not necessarily.

If binding of the transmitter to the receptor cell opens gates for positively charged sodium ions to enter the cell, the cell will produce more action potentials. This is an *excitatory synapse.*

If binding of the transmitter to the receptor cell opens gates for positively charged potassium ions to leave the cell or negatively charged chloride ions to enter the cell, the cell will produce fewer action potentials. This is an *inhibitory synapse.*

FIGURE 3.22 The complex process of neural communication actually takes only 1–2 milliseconds.

reuptake and therefore prolonging the effects of one transmitter or another.

CONCEPT CHECKS

7. Under some conditions, the axons and dendrites of a neuron increase their branching. How will that affect the number of synapses present?

8. Norepinephrine is a neurotransmitter that inhibits postsynaptic neurons. If a drug were injected to prevent norepinephrine from attaching to its receptors, what would happen to the postsynaptic neuron? (Check your answers on page 84.)

WHAT'S THE EVIDENCE?
Neurons Communicate by Releasing Chemicals

You have just learned that neurons communicate by releasing chemicals at synapses. Perhaps you are perfectly content to take my word for it and go on with something else. Still, it is advisable to pause and contemplate the evidence responsible for an important conclusion.

Today, neuroscientists have a wealth of evidence that neurons release chemicals at synapses. They can work with radioactively labeled chemicals that enable investigators to trace where chemicals go and what happens when they get there; they also can inject purified chemicals at a synapse and use extremely fine electrodes to measure the response of the postsynaptic neuron. But scientists have known since the 1920s that neurons communicate by releasing chemicals, although back then they had none of the fancy equipment that they have today. Otto Loewi found evidence of chemical transmission using a very simple, clever experiment, as he later described in his autobiography (Loewi, 1960).

Hypothesis If a neuron releases chemicals, an investigator should be able to collect some of those chemicals and transfer them from one animal to another, and thereby get the second animal to do what the first animal had been doing. Loewi had no method of collecting chemicals released within the brain itself, so he worked with axons communicating with the heart muscle. (Much later research confirmed, as Loewi suspected, that the communication between a neuron and a muscle is similar to that between two neurons.)

Method Loewi began by electrically stimulating some axons connected to a frog's heart. These particular axons slowed down the heart rate. As he continued to stimulate those axons, he collected some of the fluid on and around that heart and transferred it to the heart of a second frog.

Results When Loewi transferred the fluid from the first frog's heart, the second frog's heart rate also slowed down (Figure 3.23).

Interpretation Evidently, the stimulated axons had released a chemical that slows heart rate. At least in this case, neurons send messages by releasing chemicals.

This experiment was remarkably clever; indeed, Loewi eventually won a Nobel Prize in physiology for this and related experiments. Even outstanding experiments have limitations, however. In this case, the main limitation was the uncertainty about whether the conclusion applied only to frog hearts or whether it applied to all communication by neurons. Answering *that* question required enormous efforts and much more elaborate equipment. (The answer is that *almost* all communication by neurons depends on the release of chemicals; a few exceptional neurons communicate electrically.)

✳ ✳ ✳

Neurotransmitters and Behavior: The Example of Parkinson's Disease

Dozens of chemicals serve as neurotransmitters at one brain location or another. It has become increasingly difficult to summarize the behavioral effects of different trans-

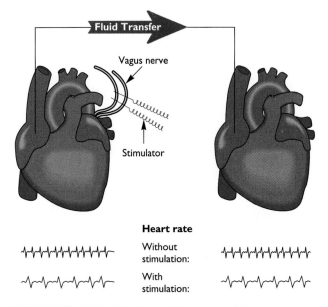

FIGURE 3.23 Otto Loewi demonstrated that axons release chemicals that can affect other cells. Using a frog, he electrically stimulated a set of axons known to decrease the heart rate. Then he collected some fluid from around the heart and transferred it to the surface of another frog's heart. When that heart slowed its beat, Loewi concluded that the axons in the first heart must have released a chemical that slows the heart rate.

mitters, because researchers have discovered that the effects of any neurotransmitter vary among its different kinds of receptors—for example, there are at least 16 receptors for the neurotransmitter glutamate (Westbrook, 1994) and nearly as many for serotonin (Humphrey, Hartig, & Hoyer, 1993). Depending on the receptor, serotonin can affect mood, arousal, motor activity, aggressive behavior, appetite, nausea, and learning. Other transmitters have similarly wide-ranging and miscellaneous effects.

It is difficult to summarize the effects of an overall increase or decrease in a neurotransmitter throughout the brain, although some disorders can be traced to the loss of a particular kind of receptor or the dysfunction of a transmitter in a particular pathway or brain area. One example is Parkinson's disease, a condition that affects about 1% of people over the age of 50. The main symptoms are difficulty in initiating voluntary movement, slowness of movement, tremors, rigidity, and depressed mood, due to a gradual loss of one pathway of neurons that all use the same neurotransmitter, **dopamine** (DOPE-uh-meen), *a chemical that promotes activity levels and facilitates movement* (Figure 3.24). One common treatment is to increase the brain's supply of dopamine. However, dopamine, like many other chemicals, cannot cross directly from the blood into the brain. Instead, physicians often prescribe pills containing L-dopa, which can cross into the brain, which converts L-dopa into dopamine. L-dopa does not prevent the continuing loss of neurons, but it reduces the symptoms of the disease. For people with a mild case of Parkinson's disease, L-dopa can provide added years of nearly normal life; however, it

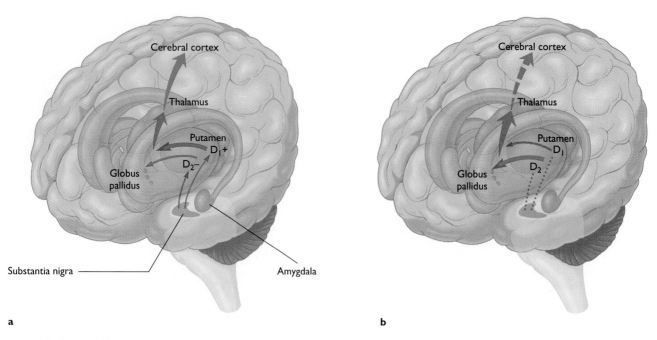

FIGURE 3.24 With Parkinson's disease, axons from the substantia nigra gradually die. (a) Normal brain. (b) Brain of person with Parkinson's disease. Green = excitatory path; red = inhibitory

also produces side effects, including nausea, and the benefits of L-dopa become smaller as the underlying condition deteriorates.

Some additional treatments currently in the experimental stage may become useful in the future. One ap-

Former boxing champion Muhammad Ali developed symptoms of Parkinson's disease, presumably because of blows to his head.

proach is to implant dopamine-containing neurons from the brain of a human fetus, but this approach faces not only the ethical difficulties of dealing with aborted fetuses, but also serious practical and scientific problems (Kupsch, Oertel, Earl, & Sautter, 1995). Another experimental approach is to inject certain chemicals that promote the survival and growth of the remaining neurons in the damaged brain area (Gash et al., 1996; Kolb, Cote, Ribeiro-da-Silva, & Cuello, 1997). That approach appears promising but needs much additional research.

CONCEPT CHECK

9. People suffering from certain disorders are given haloperidol, a drug that blocks activity at dopamine synapses. How would haloperidol affect a person suffering from Parkinson's disease? (Check your answer on page 84.)

THE MESSAGE
From Neurons to Behavior

Here is an imperfect analogy for the nervous system: At U.S. high-school or college football games, one section of the stands is sometimes set aside for fans holding large cards. When their leader calls out a signal, such as "16," each of them holds up the appropriate card. If you were one of the fans, your card #16 might be all red, providing no clue about what the overall message might be. But the pat-

Just as each card-holder has only a small part of the message, which means nothing out of context, each neuron's message has a meaning that depends on what the other neurons are doing at the same time.

tern provided by a few hundred fans might spell out "Go, State." The message of neurons is a little like that. The analogy falters because the message in the cards means something only if someone else on the other side of the field sees the pattern and reads it, whereas there is nothing to "read" the message of the neurons, except for the neurons themselves. But the analogy works in some regards: Each neuron conveys a message that means nothing by itself but becomes part of an important message in context. Also, a mistake by one card holder (or one neuron) is not too costly; the overall message still gets through. But systematic mistakes by a whole group of individuals (neurons) could destroy or garble the message.

S U M M A R Y

✳ *Neuron structure.* A neuron, or nerve cell, consists of a cell body, dendrites, and an axon. The axon conveys information to other neurons. (page 75)

✳ *The action potential.* Information is conveyed along an axon by an action potential, which is regenerated without loss of strength at each point along the axon. (page 77)

✳ *Mechanism of the action potential.* An action potential depends on the entry of sodium into the axon. Anything that blocks this flow will block the action potential. (page 77)

✳ *How neurons communicate.* A neuron communicates with another neuron by releasing a chemical called a neurotransmitter at a specialized junction called a synapse. A neurotransmitter can either excite or inhibit the next neuron. (page 78)

✳ *Neurotransmitters and behavioral disorders.* An excess or a deficit of a particular neurotransmitter can lead to abnormal behavior, such as that exhibited by people suffering from Parkinson's disease. (page 81)

Suggestion for Further Reading

Kalat, J. W. (1998). *Biological psychology* (6th ed.). Belmont, CA: Wadsworth. Chapters 1 through 4 deal with the material discussed in this chapter in more detail.

Terms

neuron   a cell of the nervous system that receives information and transmits it to other cells by conducting electrochemical impulses (page 75)

glia   a cell of the nervous system that insulates neurons, removes waste materials (such as dead cells), and performs other supportive functions (page 75)

cell body   the part of the neuron that contains the nucleus of the cell (page 75)

dendrite   one of the widely branching structures of a neuron that receive transmissions from other neurons (page 75)

axon   a single, long, thin, straight fiber that transmits information from a neuron to other neurons or to muscle cells (page 75)

action potential   an excitation that travels along an axon at a constant strength, no matter how far it must travel (page 77)

resting potential   electrical polarization that ordinarily occurs across the membrane of an axon that is not undergoing an action potential (page 77)

synapse the specialized junction between one neuron and another; at this point, one neuron releases a neurotransmitter, which either excites or inhibits the next neuron (page 78)

terminal bouton (or **button**) a bulge at the end of an axon from which the axon releases a chemical called a neurotransmitter (page 78)

neurotransmitter a chemical that is stored in the terminal of an axon and that, when released, activates receptors of other neurons (page 78)

postsynaptic neuron a neuron on the receiving end of a synapse (page 78)

dopamine a neurotransmitter that promotes activity levels and facilitates movement (page 81)

Answers to Concept Checks

6. You will not feel the pain immediately because the action potential must travel from your foot to your brain. (If the action potentials travel at, say, 30 meters per second and your toe is about 1.5 meters from your brain, you will feel the pain about 0.05 of a second after you stub your toe.) (page 78)

7. Increased branching of the axons and dendrites will increase the number of synapses. (page 80)

8. Under the influence of a drug that prevents norepinephrine from attaching to its receptors, the postsynaptic neuron will receive less inhibition than usual. If we presume that the neuron continues to receive a certain amount of excitation, it will then produce action potentials more frequently than usual. (page 80)

9. Haloperidol would increase the severity of Parkinson's disease. In fact, large doses of haloperidol can induce symptoms of Parkinson's disease in anyone. (page 82)

Web Resources

M.M.M. Brain Tour: Building Blocks

suhep.phy.syr.edu/courses/modules/MM/Biology/biology2.html

Good illustrations and very readable text lead you through this tour of neurons, neurotransmitters, and neural organization, produced by the Mind and Machine MODULE team at Syracuse University.

Explanations of Behavior at the Level of the Nervous system

Does a person who loses part of the brain also lose part of the mind?

Why should psychologists care about the organization of the brain and the effects of brain damage? They have both practical and theoretical reasons.

The practical reason is that they need to distinguish between people who act strangely because they have had bad experiences and people who act strangely because they have a brain disorder. To do so, psychologists need to know how brain damage affects behavior.

The theoretical reason for studying the brain is simply that the study of brain damage helps to explain the organization of behavior. In some manner or another, behavior must be made up of component parts, but what are those parts? Is behavior composed of ideas? sensations? movements? personality characteristics? And how do the various components combine to produce the overall behavior and experience? One way to answer such questions is to examine the effects of brain damage.

A Survey of the Nervous System

Psychologists and biologists distinguish between the central nervous system and the peripheral nervous system. The **central nervous system** consists of *the brain and the spinal cord.* The central nervous system communicates with the rest of the body by the **peripheral nervous system,** which is composed of *bundles of axons between the spinal cord and the rest of the body.* The *peripheral nerves that communicate with the skin and muscles* are collectively called the **somatic nervous system.** Those that control the heart, stomach, and other organs are called the *autonomic nervous system.* Figure 3.25 summarizes these major divisions of the nervous system.

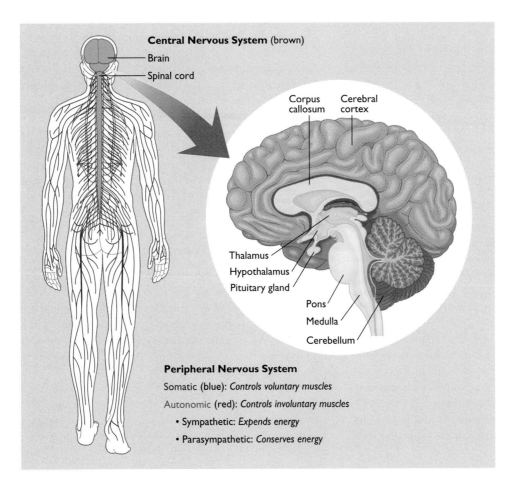

Central Nervous System (brown)
— Brain
— Spinal cord

Corpus callosum
Cerebral cortex

Thalamus
Hypothalamus
Pituitary gland

Pons
Medulla
Cerebellum

Peripheral Nervous System
Somatic (blue): *Controls voluntary muscles*
Autonomic (red): *Controls involuntary muscles*
• Sympathetic: *Expends energy*
• Parasympathetic: *Conserves energy*

FIGURE 3.25 The nervous system has two major divisions; the central nervous system and the peripheral nervous system. Each of these has major subdivisions, as shown.

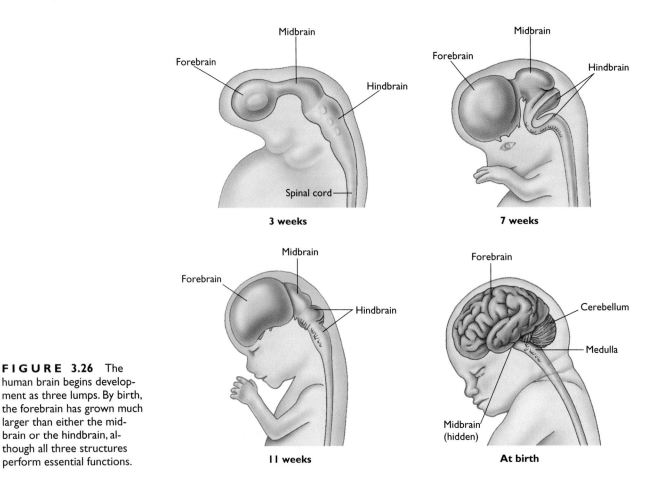

FIGURE 3.26 The human brain begins development as three lumps. By birth, the forebrain has grown much larger than either the midbrain or the hindbrain, although all three structures perform essential functions.

Early in its embryological development, the central nervous system of vertebrates, including humans, is a tube with three lumps, as shown in Figure 3.26. Those lumps develop into the *forebrain*, the *midbrain*, and the *hindbrain*; the rest of the tube develops into the spinal cord. The forebrain, which contains the cerebral cortex and other structures, is by far the dominant portion of the brain in mammals, especially in humans.

The Spinal Cord

The **spinal cord** *communicates with the body below the level of the head by means of sensory neurons and motor neurons* (Figure 3.27). The **sensory neurons** *carry information about touch, pain, and other senses from the periphery of the body to the spinal cord.* The **motor neurons** *transmit impulses from the central nervous system to the muscles and glands.*

The spinal cord serves both reflexive and voluntary behavior. A **reflex** is a *rapid, automatic response to a stimulus.* For example, suppose you put your hand on a hot stove. Stimulation of pain receptors in your finger sends messages along sensory neurons; within the spinal cord, these neurons send messages via interneurons to motor neurons, which then send impulses to the muscles that jerk your hand away from the hot stove.

The spinal cord is also necessary for voluntary behaviors. Every command to walk, talk, or make any other movement requires a message from the brain to the spinal cord and from the spinal cord to the muscles. People who have suffered damage to the spinal cord will lose some part of their muscle control. For example, after damage to the lower part of the spinal cord, a person cannot receive messages from the brain to the bottom of the spinal cord, which controls leg movements as well as bowel and bladder functions. After damage to the upper part of the spinal cord, a person would also lose control of the arm muscles.

The Autonomic Nervous System

The **autonomic nervous system,** closely associated with the spinal cord, *controls the internal organs such as the heart.* The term *autonomic* means involuntary or automatic. The autonomic nervous system is partly, though not entirely, automatic. We are generally unaware of its activity, although it does receive information from, and send information to, the brain and the spinal cord.

The autonomic nervous system consists of two parts: (1) *The sympathetic nervous system,* controlled by a chain of neurons lying just outside the spinal cord, increases heart rate and breathing rate and readies the body for vigorous fight-or-flight activities; and (2) *the parasympathetic nervous system,* con-

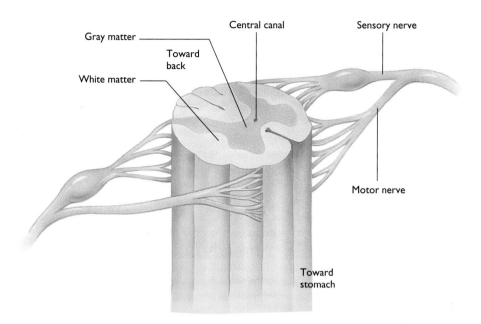

Gray matter

Toward back

White matter

Central canal

Sensory nerve

Motor nerve

Toward stomach

FIGURE 3.27 The spinal cord receives sensory information from all parts of the body except the head. Motor nerves in the spinal cord send messages to control the muscles and glands.

trolled by neurons at the very top and very bottom levels of the spinal cord, decreases heart rate, increases digestive activities, and in general promotes activities of the body that take place during rest (Figure 3.28). We shall return to this topic in more detail in the chapter about emotions (Chapter 12).

The Endocrine System

Although the endocrine system is not part of the nervous system, it is closely related to it—especially to the autonomic nervous system. Messages from the nervous system control the release of hormones from the endocrine system, and several hormones have major effects on certain kinds of brain activity.

The **endocrine system** is *a set of glands that produce hormones and release them into the blood.* Figure 3.29 shows some of the major endocrine glands. **Hormones** are *chemicals released by glands and conveyed via the blood to other parts of the body, where they alter activity.* Hormones are similar to neurotransmitters in that both affect the nervous system. The same chemical can be used both as

a hormone and as a neurotransmitter. The difference is that, when a chemical is used as a neurotransmitter, it is released immediately adjacent to the cell that it is to excite or inhibit. When it is used as a hormone, it is released into the blood, which diffuses it throughout the body.

Hormones can control effects that last from minutes (such as changes in blood pressure) to months (such as preparation for migration in birds). Some hormonal effects are nearly permanent. For example, the amount of the sex hormone testosterone present during prenatal development determines whether one develops a penis and scrotum or a clitoris and labia.

CONCEPT CHECK

10. Just after a meal, the pancreas produces increased amounts of the hormone insulin, which increases the conversion of the digested food into fats in many cells throughout the body. How is a hormone more effective for this purpose than a neurotransmitter would be? (Check your answer on page 101.)

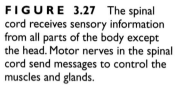

Sympathetic system
uses much energy

- Pupils open
- Saliva decreases
- Pulse quickens
- Sweat increases
- Stomach less active
- Epinephrine (adrenaline) secreted

Parasympathetic system
conserves energy

- Pupils constrict
- Saliva flows
- Pulse slows
- Sweat decreases
- Stomach churns

FIGURE 3.28 The sympathetic nervous system prepares the body for brief bouts of vigorous activity; the parasympathetic nervous system promotes digestion and other nonemergency functions. Although both systems are active at all times, the balance can shift from a predominance of one to a predominance of the other.

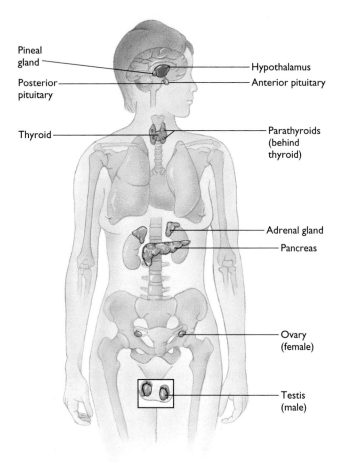

Pineal gland

Posterior pituitary

Thyroid

Hypothalamus

Anterior pituitary

Parathyroids (behind thyroid)

Adrenal gland

Pancreas

Ovary (female)

Testis (male)

FIGURE 3.29 Glands in the endocrine system produce hormones and release them into the bloodstream.

Between the Spinal Cord and the Cerebral Cortex

Above the spinal cord, we find the hindbrain, the midbrain, the subcortical areas of the forebrain, and finally the cerebral cortex. (See Figure 3.30.) Information passing between the spinal cord and the cerebral cortex (in either direction) travels through other structures on the way. In some cases, that route is simple. For example, the primary motor area of the cerebral cortex sends axons that simply pass through other structures until they reach the spinal cord, where they make synapses onto cells that control the muscles. In other cases, the route is complex. For example, when you feel something with your fingers, the axons from your touch receptors send information to the spinal cord, which relays it to cells in the medulla (part of the hindbrain), which relay it to cells in the midbrain, which in turn relay it to cells in the thalamus (part of the forebrain), which in turn relay it to an area in the cerebral cortex. When I mention "relaying" information, I do not mean that the cells literally take the information and pass it along. At each stage, the cells combine and contrast this information with other information, processing it and changing it in various ways.

Furthermore, structures along the way have functions of their own. The **medulla** and **pons,** *structures in the hindbrain* (Figure 3.30), receive sensory input from the head (taste, hearing, touch sensations on the scalp) and send impulses for motor control of the head (for example, chewing, swallowing, and breathing). They also have axons that control breathing, heart rate, and other life-preserving functions.

The medulla, pons, and midbrain also contain the *reticular formation* and several other systems that regulate overall arousal in the brain (Robbins & Everitt, 1995; Szymusiak, 1995). These systems send messages diffusely to most of the forebrain. A malfunction in one of these systems, depending on its nature and location, will render a person either persistently sleepy or persistently aroused.

The **cerebellum** (Latin for "little brain"), *another part of the hindbrain,* is active in the control of rapid sequences of actions, such as playing the piano or dribbling a basketball. A person who suffers damage to the cerebellum can still make muscular movements but must plan each series of movements slowly, one at a time, instead of executing them in a smooth sequence. The cerebellum is also important for any behavior that requires timing, such as tapping out a rhythm, judging which of two visual stimuli is moving faster, and judging whether the delay between one pair of sounds is shorter or longer than the delay between another pair (Ivry & Diener, 1991; Keele & Ivry, 1990).

In later chapters, we shall return to examine some of the other brain structures that you see in Figure 3.30. The hippocampus is important for storing memories; people with damage to the hippocampus can remember most of what happened before the damage but little of what happened afterward (Chapter 7). The hypothalamus makes critical contributions to eating, drinking, sexual behavior, and other emotional or motivated behaviors (Chapter 11).

CONCEPT CHECK

11. People who have become intoxicated on alcohol have slow, slurred speech and cannot walk a straight line. From these observations, which part of the brain would you guess that the alcohol has most greatly impaired? (Check your answer on page 101.)

The Organization and Functioning of the Brain

Somehow, the brain is responsible for all our experiences and all our actions. When we try to explain how this process happens, we immediately encounter a problem: We each experience ourselves as a unity. That is, there seems to be just one "I" who sees, hears, touches, thinks, decides, and acts. Nevertheless, the brain is composed of many separate

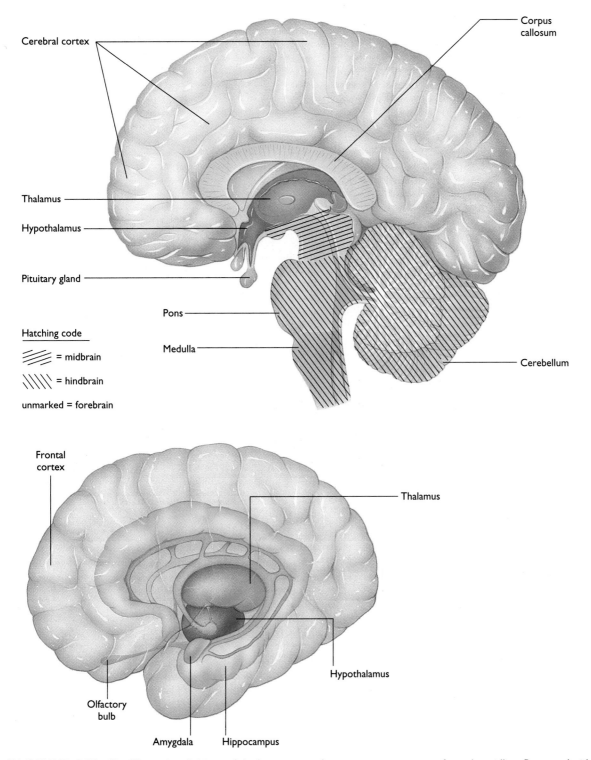

Cerebral cortex

Corpus callosum

Thalamus

Hypothalamus

Pituitary gland

Pons

Medulla

Cerebellum

Hatching code

= midbrain

= hindbrain

unmarked = forebrain

Frontal cortex

Thalamus

Hypothalamus

Olfactory bulb

Amygdala   Hippocampus

F I G U R E 3.30   Top: The major divisions of the human central nervous system, as seen from the midline. Bottom: A side view of the brain, showing internal structures as though the cerebral cortex were transparent.

structures, each composed of substructures; overall, the brain includes tens of billions of neurons. How does one "I" emerge from all these separate voices?

A naive answer would be that all the various parts of the brain funnel their information to a "little person in the head" who puts it all together. Although no one takes that concept seriously, the underlying idea is hard to abandon, and brain researchers have sometimes imagined a "master area" of the brain that would serve the same purpose as the little person—integrating all the information and making decisions.

That master area, if there is such a thing, would presumably be part of the cerebral cortex. The **cerebral cortex** is *the outer surface of the forebrain*—in humans, the largest and most prominent brain area. The cerebral cortex consists of two **hemispheres,** *the left and the right halves* (Figure 3.31). Each hemisphere is responsible for sensation and motor control on the opposite side of the body. (Why the reversal? Why does each hemisphere control the opposite side instead of its own side? Frankly, no one knows.) You have probably heard people talk about "having a lot of gray matter." The cerebral cortex in the forebrain is *gray matter;* it contains a great many cell bodies, which are grayer than the axons. The interior of the forebrain beneath the cerebral cortex contains large numbers of axons, many of them covered with *myelin,* a white insulation. You can see areas of gray matter and white matter in Figure 3.32.

Research on the cerebral cortex, however, has found no "master area" or "central processor." Researchers find few neurons that receive a combination of visual and auditory information or visual and touch information. Apparently, the sensory information does *not* all funnel into one central processor.

Then how does the cortex work? Each part of the brain has some specialized functions but also contributes to a variety of others. By analogy, a medical doctor has a specialized job but also performs many other general functions. If the doctor suddenly left town, we would mainly notice the loss at the hospital but also the losses in the doctor's contributions to home maintenance, feeding

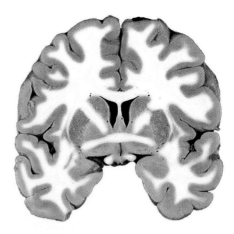

FIGURE 3.32 This cross section of a human brain shows the distinction between gray matter (composed mostly of cell bodies and dendrites) and white matter (composed almost entirely of axons). Myelin, a fatty sheath that surrounds many axons, makes the white matter white.

the family, chauffeuring the children, paying bills, community volunteer activities, and so forth. If the doctor was gone for long, other people would have to take over some of the uncompleted tasks, and as a result these people would become less efficient at their own specialized jobs—and so forth. Similarly, when a brain area becomes damaged or impaired, we primarily notice the loss of its specialized functions, but a variety of other functions will suffer a bit, too, and as other brain areas compensate for the loss, they may become inefficient at their own specialized tasks.

Still, the effects of brain damage sometimes include remarkably limited behavioral deficits. Let us examine some examples of brain damage and the specialized deficits that result.

Effects of Localized Brain Damage: The Visual System

The visual, auditory, and other systems of the brain largely operate independently of one another. The mystery deepens: Even within a given system, such as vision, the brain processes different aspects of the stimulus separately and in parallel. Figure 3.33 illustrates three major pathways in the visual areas of the human cerebral cortex. The main purpose of this figure is to illustrate the idea of separate pathways, not their exact locations. All three pathways begin in the *primary visual cortex,* designated here as V1 (meaning visual area 1), although they each begin with different neurons within that area. These pathways send their information to different neurons in the *secondary visual area,* V2, and from there the information branches out to additional areas. One pathway is mostly responsible for analysis of shape details; another, for color and brightness; another, for motion.

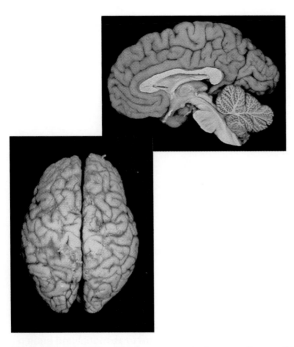

FIGURE 3.31 The human cerebral cortex: (bottom) left and right hemispheres; (top) inside view of a complete hemisphere. The folds greatly extend the brain's surface area.

A person who suffers damage to the entire primary visual cortex (V1) will become completely blind. In contrast, consider what happens to someone with damage to only part of a single pathway. After damage to parts of the inferior temporal cortex, which is part of the shape pathway, some people suffer a specific **faceblindness,** *a specific inability to recognize people by their faces.* Such a person may still be able to read and can see faces well enough to say, "That person is almost bald, has a somewhat thin face, and dark eyes," but lacks the ability to say, "Aha, that's my cousin Ross." The affected person may also fail to identify specific plants, animals, cars, and so forth (Farah, 1990; 1992).

In contrast, people with damage to parts of the color pathway lose an ability called **color constancy,** which is *the ability to continue recognizing colors even after a change in lighting.* For example, suppose you put on blue-tinted glasses. You would not suddenly see everything as blue; you could still identify which objects are red, yellow, and so forth. People with certain kinds of brain damage have trouble with color constancy; for these people, everything in the room would indeed look blue, viewed through the glasses (Zeki, 1980; 1983).

Damage in the motion pathway produces a very surprising deficit: **motionblindness.** People with such damage have *trouble identifying the movement of objects* (Zihl, von Cramon, & Mai, 1983). One such patient found that she could not safely cross a road, because she could not see which cars were moving or how fast. She had trouble pouring coffee into a cup, because she could not see the liquid level gradually rising in the cup. (Eventually, she would stop when she saw coffee all over the table.) For most of us, it is difficult to imagine what the world must look like to a motionblind person. It might be a little bit like living in a world with only strobe lights shining once every few seconds, except that these people experience no blackouts in their perception.

In short, different parts of the visual system of your cerebral cortex process different aspects of each visual stimulus—one part attends to shape, another to color, another to motion. How does your brain put it all together? Again, we have reached the limitations of current knowledge; although the brain must somehow combine different kinds of information, researchers do not currently understand how it does this.

Effects of Localized Brain Damage: Unilateral Neglect

Let's now consider a kind of brain damage that affects attention rather than sensation. Damage in the parietal lobe (see Figure 3.34), especially in the right parietal lobe, leads to **neglect** *(disregard)* of the opposite side of the body and, indeed, the opposite side of their world. Such people may

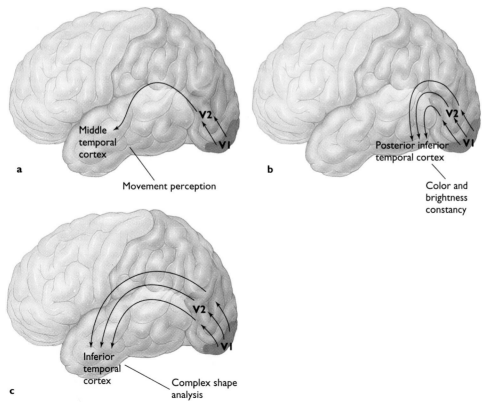

FIGURE 3.33 Three major visual pathways in the cerebral cortex: (a) One path is responsible for movement perception; (b) a second path deals with color and brightness; (c) the third path provides analysis of complex shapes. Because the three paths are largely independent of one another, brain damage can impair one aspect of visual perception without blocking the others.

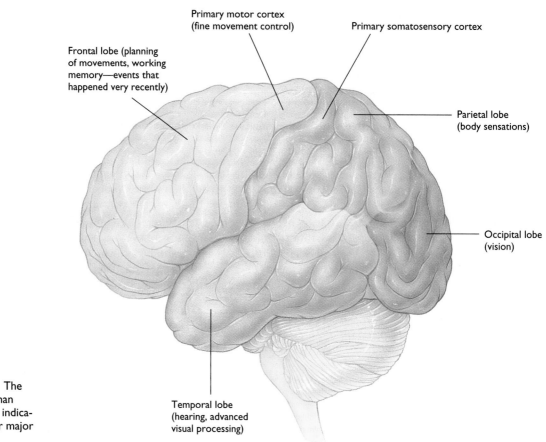

Primary motor cortex
(fine movement control)

Primary somatosensory cortex

Frontal lobe (planning
of movements, working
memory—events that
happened very recently)

Parietal lobe
(body sensations)

Occipital lobe
(vision)

Temporal lobe
(hearing, advanced
visual processing)

FIGURE 3.34 The four lobes of the human cerebral cortex, with indications of some of their major functions.

put clothing on only the right side of the body, insisting that the left half belongs to someone else. They read only the right side of a page and draw only the right side of an object, using only the right side of the paper (Heilman, 1979; see Figure 3.35).

If you were to tickle such a person simultaneously on the left and right sides of the wrist (of either hand, left or right), he or she would report the sensation on the right side of that wrist, ignoring the sensation on the left side. Now, suppose you turn the person's hand upside down and repeat the experiment. He or she now reports the sensation on what has *now* become the right side of the hand, as illustrated in Figure 3.36 (Moscovitch & Behrmann, 1994). That is, the person does not simply neglect a certain area of skin, but detects what part of the arm is on the left, and then neglects it. The impairment is not a loss of sensation; it is a loss of attention.

Effects of Localized Brain Damage: Specific Memory Loss

Brain-damaged people sometimes show remarkably specialized kinds of memory loss, which we shall discuss in Chapter 7. Here, I wish to describe an even more specific kind of memory loss, which has so far been demonstrated only in monkeys.

This brain damage occurs in a tiny portion of the frontal cortex, and the behavior to be measured is a kind of delayed response. **Delayed response** is *any task in which an individual gets a signal and then must wait before it can make the necessary response.* In one set of studies, monkeys were trained to stare at a dot on a screen, as shown in Figure 3.37. A signal light flashed briefly at some spot away from the fixation point. The monkey had to continue looking at the fixation point, until the light went off several seconds later, and then move its eyes to the location where the signal light had been. Monkeys with extensive damage to one area in the frontal lobes of the cerebral cortex showed severe deficits on the task, apparently forgetting where the signal was. With very tiny damage within this brain area, monkeys lose their spatial memory *for just one spot.* For example, a monkey might be unable to remember

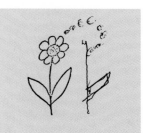

FIGURE 3.35 A person with damage to the right parietal lobe will draw only the right side of an object, as this attempt to copy a picture of a flower shows. (From Heilman, 1979.)

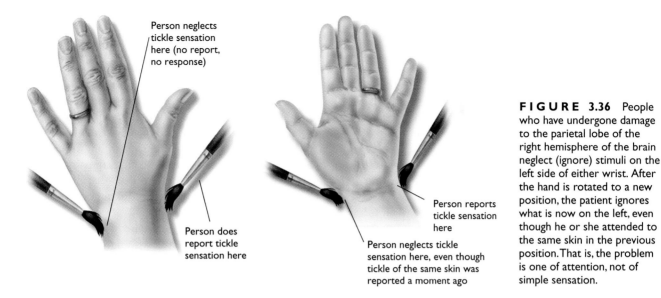

FIGURE 3.36 People who have undergone damage to the parietal lobe of the right hemisphere of the brain neglect (ignore) stimuli on the left side of either wrist. After the hand is rotated to a new position, the patient ignores what is now on the left, even though he or she attended to the same skin in the previous position. That is, the problem is one of attention, not of simple sensation.

a spot directly at the top of the circle or a spot at the left (Goldman-Rakic, 1994). We know the monkey can still see these spots, because the monkey can respond to them on a task requiring no delay. But as soon as we introduce a short delay, the monkey's performance deteriorates. Evidently, the memory for just one location has been lost.

Conclusions About Brain Organization

We have considered examples of damage to the visual system, neglect of half of the body, and loss of a tiny area of spatial memory. I hope that you will find these examples interesting for their own sake, but beyond that, the main point is that the brain is full of separate systems with separate tasks. A small area of brain damage can lead to a signif-

icant loss of a narrowly defined behavioral function, with little loss of other functions.

Here's another way of stating this conclusion, with greater emphasis on the philosophical implications: *If part of the brain is lost, part of behavior and experience is lost as well.* As far as we can tell, *brain activity and "mind" are inseparable; we cannot have one without the other.*

Division of Labor: The Four Lobes of the Cerebral Cortex

In the process of telling you about certain kinds of brain damage, I have already presented the functions of certain parts of the cerebral cortex. Let's now survey the major areas of the cortex more systematically.

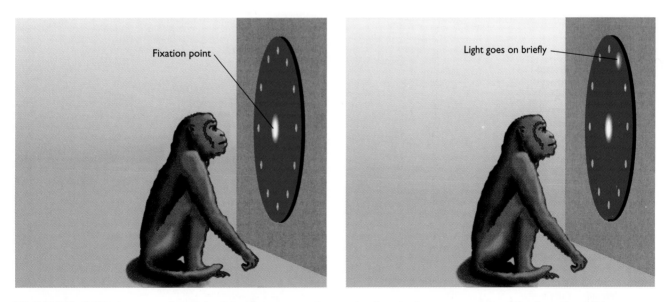

FIGURE 3.37 In one version of the delayed-response task, a monkey is trained to stare at a central fixation point. A light appears briefly at some point along the circle surrounding the fixation point. The monkey keeps its eyes focused on the fixation point during a delay and then must look at the point where the light appeared. The monkey must remember the location of the light during the delay.

For the sake of convenience, we describe the cerebral cortex in terms of four *lobes*—occipital, parietal, temporal, and frontal, as shown in Figure 3.34. The **occipital lobe,** *at the rear of the head, is specialized for vision.* As already discussed, different areas within (and outside) the occipital lobe contribute to different aspects of vision, such as shape, color, and motion. However, all of the occipital lobe apparently contributes to vision in one way or another.

The **parietal lobe,** *just anterior (forward) from the occipital lobe, is specialized for the body senses, including touch, pain, temperature, and awareness of the location of body parts.* The **primary somatosensory** (body-sensory) **cortex,** *a strip in the anterior portion of the parietal lobe, has neurons sensitive to touch in different body areas,* as shown in Figure 3.38. Note that in Figure 3.38a larger areas are devoted to touch in the more sensitive parts of the body,

such as the lips and hands, than to less sensitive areas, such as the abdomen and the back. Damage to any part of the somatosensory cortex will impair sensation from the corresponding part of the body.

The **temporal lobe** of each hemisphere, *located toward the left and right sides of the head, is the main processing area for hearing and also contributes to some of the more complex aspects of vision.* One area in the temporal lobe of the left hemisphere is important for language comprehension. Damage centered here impairs people's ability to understand what other people are saying; they also have trouble remembering the names of objects when they are speaking.

Other parts of the temporal lobe are critical for certain aspects of emotion. People with damage to one part of the temporal lobe, known as the *amygdala,* have almost

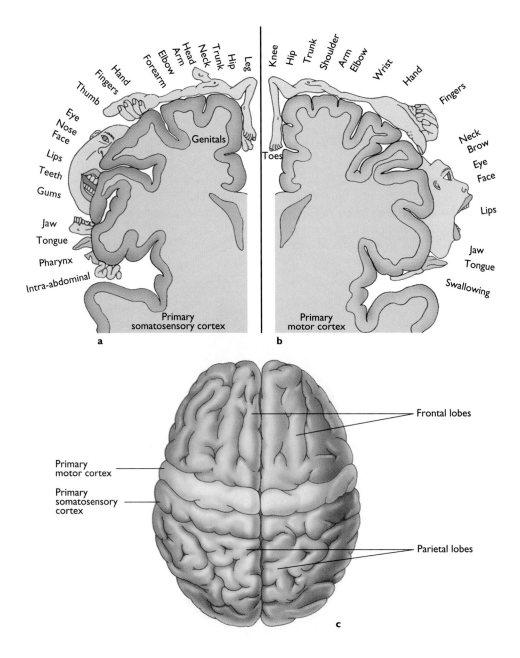

FIGURE 3.38 (a) The primary somatosensory cortex and (b) the primary motor cortex, illustrating which part of the body each brain area controls. Larger areas of the cortex are devoted to body parts that need to be controlled with great precision, such as the face and hands. The figure shows the left primary somatosensory cortex, which receives information from the right side of the body, and the right primary motor cortex, which controls the muscles on the left side of the body. (c) Locations of the primary somatosensory cortex and the primary motor cortex. [(a) and (b) from Geschwind, 1979.]

no fear or anxiety (LaBar, LeDoux, Spencer, & Phelps, 1995). Most people remember emotionally distressing events better than neutral events, but those with damage to the amygdala do not, presumably because they do not feel the emotional distress (Cahill, Babinsky, Markowitsch, & McGaugh, 1995). These people can neither recognize facial expressions of fear in others nor imagine what a frightened face would look like (Adolphs, Tranel, Damasio, & Damasio, 1994).

The **frontal lobe,** *at the anterior (forward) pole of the brain,* includes the **primary motor cortex** (Figure 3.38), *a structure that is important for the control of fine movements,* such as moving one finger at a time. As with the primary somatosensory cortex, each area of the primary motor cortex controls a different part of the body, and larger areas are devoted to precise movements of the tongue and fingers than to, say, the shoulder and elbow muscles. The *anterior sections of the frontal lobe,* called the **prefrontal cortex,** contribute to the organization and planning of movements and to certain aspects of memory. Indeed, planning a movement depends on memory. Recall, for example, the delayed response task (page 92): The individual must remember a signal during a delay and then make the appropriate movement.

Certain areas in the left frontal lobe are essential for human language production. People with extensive damage to the left frontal lobe have trouble speaking, writing, or gesturing in sign language (Bellugi, Poizner, & Klima, 1983; Geschwind, 1970). What they say still makes sense, although they generally omit prepositions, conjunctions, and word endings.

How do we know that these brain areas have the functions that I have described? For many years, nearly all the evidence came from observations of brain damage. Researchers can now supplement such evidence with modern techniques that measure activity in an unanesthetized brain (see Figure 3.39). For example, **functional magnetic resonance imaging (fMRI)** *uses magnetic detectors outside the head to measure the amounts of hemoglobin, with and without oxygen, in different parts of the brain* (Cohen, Noll, & Schneider, 1993). Brain areas that are highly active use much oxygen and therefore decrease the amount of oxygen bound to hemoglobin in the blood. The fMRI technique therefore provides a way of inferring which brain areas are currently more active than others. Figure 3.40 gives an example of an fMRI scan.

CONCEPT CHECK

12. The following five people are known to have suffered damage to the cerebral cortex. From their behavioral symptoms, determine the probable location of the damage for each person: (a) impaired perception of the left half of the body and a tendency to ignore the left half of the body and the left half of the world; (b) impaired hearing and some changes in emotional experience; (c) inability to make fine movements with the right hand; (d) loss of vision in the left visual field; and (e) poor performance on a delayed response task, indicating difficulty remembering what has just happened. (Check your answers on page 101.)

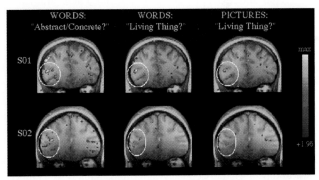

FIGURE 3.40 This brain scan was made with functional magnetic resonance imaging (fMRI). Participants looked at words or pictures and judged whether each item was abstract or concrete, living or nonliving. Yellow shows the areas most activated by this judgment; red shows areas less strongly activated. (From Wagner, Desmond, Demb, Glover, & Gabrieli, 1997. Photo courtesy of Anthony D. Wagner.)

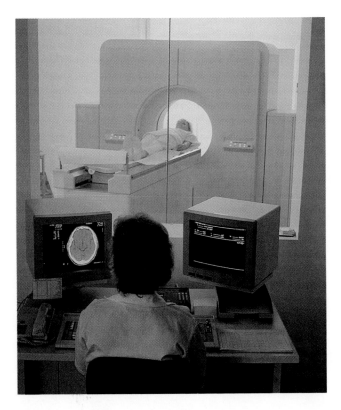

FIGURE 3.39 Devices such as this computerized axial tomography (CAT) scanner produce detailed views of a living human brain.

Effects of Experience on Brain Structure

The drawing in Figure 3.25 shows "the human nervous system." We do not need to specify whose nervous system, because the gross structure is about the same from one person to another. The detailed anatomy does vary, however, and some of these variations depend on people's experiences.

Let's begin with the effects of musical training. Figure 3.38(a) shows how the somatosensory cortex represents different parts of the body. One area, for example, represents the fingers, and researchers have measured the average amount of cortex devoted to the fingers. The results are different, however, for people who have played a stringed instrument (ordinarily, violin) since childhood. Right-handed stringed-instrument players hold the bow with the right hand and finger the strings with the left hand. The result of all those years of practice is that the amount of sensory cortex devoted to the left hand becomes about twice as large as usual (Elbert, Pantev, Wienbruch, Rockstroh, & Taub, 1995).

Many children have *absolute pitch* or "perfect pitch," the ability to hear a note and identify it as B-flat, C-sharp, or whatever. Fewer than one person in 10,000 retains that ability into adulthood, and those few are people who began piano, voice, or other musical lessons in early childhood and continued practicing from then on (Takeuchi & Hulse, 1993). For those who maintain absolute pitch, one area of the temporal lobe of the cerebral cortex is significantly larger than normal (Schlaug, Jäncke, Huang, & Steinmetz, 1995).

What about people who are born blind and who learn to attend to touch stimuli more than other people do? One difference is that part of their occipital cortex, which for other people responds only to visual stimuli, becomes responsive to tactile stimuli, such as Braille characters (Cohen et al., 1997). The section of the somatosensory cortex that represents the index finger (the one ordinarily used for reading Braille) also becomes larger than usual. In fact, small changes in that area occur even from one day to the next; the representation of the index finger will be greater after a day of reading Braille than at the same time on a vacation day (Pascual-Leone, Wasserman, Sadato, & Hallett, 1995).

The biggest effects on brain anatomy appear in those who have had unusual and intensive experiences since early childhood, such as those who started musical training at age four or those who have been blind since birth. The immature brain is probably subject to greater modification than is the adult brain. However, to be fair, we should admit that the evidence does not fully separate the effects of the age of starting practice from the effects of total practice time. For example, a 24-year-old who started violin training at age four has had 20 years of practice, perhaps several hours per day. It would be hard to find, for comparison, a 44-year-old who had started to learn the violin at age 24 and then worked at it for hours each day.

The general point is that our brain anatomy is not fixed at birth. Unusual or prolonged experiences can modify the structure of the brain to improve its efficiency at performing tasks that a given person commonly encounters.

The Corpus Callosum and the Split-Brain Phenomenon

What would happen if the sensory input from one half of your body, represented in one hemisphere, could not travel to the motor cortex in the opposite hemisphere? Such a situation does arise after damage to the **corpus callosum,** *a set of axons connecting the two hemispheres* (Figure 3.41). Corpus callosum damage also prevents someone from comparing sights seen on one side of their world against sights seen on the other side of the world and from comparing something felt with one hand to something felt with the other hand. Information that reaches one hemisphere stays in that hemisphere, because the person no longer has a single cerebral cortex, but rather has two half-cortexes operating side by side. Research on some unusual surgical patients suggests that the result of this operation is two separate spheres of consciousness.

Several teams of brain surgeons have cut the corpus callosum in an effort to relieve *a condition* called **epilepsy,** *in which neurons somewhere in the brain begin to emit abnormal rhythmic, spontaneous impulses.* Such impulses originate in different locations for different people and quickly spread to other areas of the brain, including neurons in the opposite hemisphere. The effects on behavior can vary widely, depending on where the epilepsy originates in the brain and where it spreads. Most people with epilepsy respond well to antiepileptic drugs and can live normal lives. A few people, however, do not respond to any of the known antiepileptic drugs and continue to have major seizures so frequently that they cannot work, go to school, or travel far from medical help. Such people are willing to try almost anything to get relief. In certain cases, surgeons recommended cutting the corpus callosum. The reasoning was that epileptic seizures would be prevented from spreading across the corpus callosum to the other hemisphere and would thus be less severe.

The operation was even more successful than expected. Not only were the seizures limited to one side of the body, but they also became far less frequent. A possible explanation is that the operation interrupted the feedback loop between the two hemispheres that allows an epileptic seizure to echo back and forth. These split-brain patients were able to return to work and to resume other normal activities. There were, however, some interesting behavioral side effects. But before I can discuss these, we need to consider some anatomy.

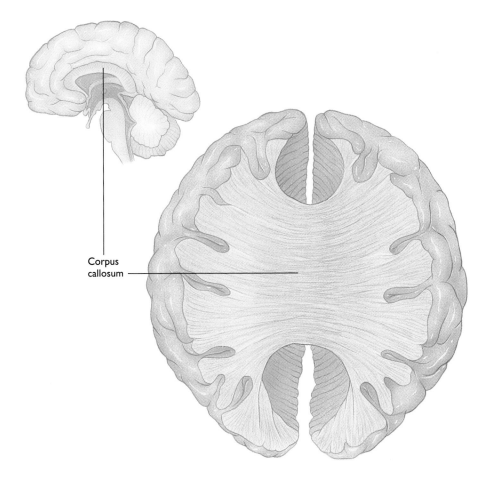

Corpus
callosum

FIGURE 3.41 The corpus callosum is a large set of axons that convey information between the two hemispheres of the cerebral cortex. (left) A midline view showing the location of the corpus callosum. (right) A horizontal section showing how each axon of the corpus callosum links one spot in the left hemisphere to a corresponding spot in the right hemisphere.

Connections Between the Eyes and the Brain

Note: This section presents a simple concept that is contrary to most people's expectations. Even when students are warned that this material will appear on a test and are practically told what the question will be, many of them still answer incorrectly. So please pay attention!

Because each hemisphere of the brain controls the muscles on the opposite side of the body, each half of the brain needs to see the opposite side of the world. This does not mean that your left hemisphere sees with the right eye or that your right hemisphere sees with the left eye. Convince yourself: Close one eye, then open it and close the other. Note that you see almost the same view with both eyes. You see the left half of the world with part of your left eye and part of your right eye.

Figure 3.42, which shows the human visual system, warrants careful study. Light from each half of the world strikes receptors on the opposite side of *each* retina. Information from the left half of each retina travels via the *optic nerves* to the left hemisphere of the cerebral cortex; information from the right half of each retina travels via the optic nerves to the right hemisphere.

Here is one way to remember this material: *Light from each side of the world strikes the opposite side of the retina.*

The brain is connected to the eyes so that each hemisphere sees the opposite side of the world. If you remember those two statements, you should be able to deduce the connections shown in Figure 3.42.

What about the very center of the retina? The cells in a thin strip down the center of each retina send axons to both sides of the brain.

Behavioral Effects of Severing the Corpus Callosum

For almost all right-handed people and for about 60% of left-handed people, the brain area that controls speech is located in the left hemisphere of the brain. For most other left-handers, both hemispheres share control of speech to varying degrees. Complete right-hemisphere control of speech is possible, but rare. The right hemisphere does contribute to the emotional aspects of speech, however. People with right-hemisphere damage speak with little expression and have trouble interpreting the emotions that other people express through tone of voice (Shapiro & Danly, 1985; Tucker, 1981).

If you have the same brain organization as most other people, you can describe only the information that reaches your left hemisphere. However, any information that first enters your right hemisphere passes quickly across the

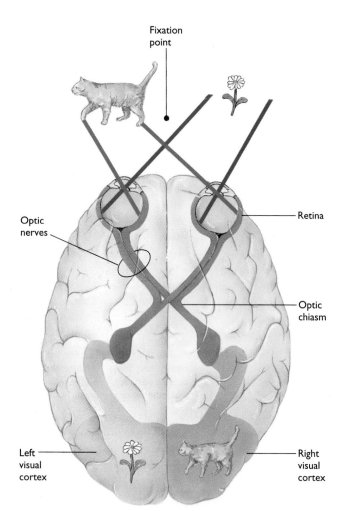

Fixation
point

Optic
nerves

Retina

Optic
chiasm

Left
visual
cortex

Right
visual
cortex

FIGURE 3.42 In the human visual system (viewed here from above), light from either half of the world crosses through the pupils to strike the opposite side of each retina. Axons from the left half of each retina travel to the left hemisphere of the brain; axons from the right half of each retina travel to the right hemisphere of the brain.

corpus callosum to your left hemisphere, so you can talk about anything that reaches any receptor in your body.

But what happens when the corpus callosum is severed? When a woman with a severed corpus callosum touches something with her right hand without looking at it, she can say what it is, because the touch information reaches her left hemisphere (Nebes, 1974; Sperry, 1967). However, if she feels something with her left hand, then she cannot say what it is, because the information reaches only her right hemisphere. If she is given several choices and is asked to point to what her left hand has just felt, she can point to it correctly—but only with her left hand. In fact, she will sometimes point to the correct object with her left hand while saying, "I have no idea what it was. I didn't feel anything." Evidently, the right hemisphere can understand the instructions and answer with the hand it controls, but it cannot talk. Roger Sperry won a Nobel Prize in physiology and medicine in 1981 for these pioneering discoveries.

Now consider what happens when this split-brain woman looks at something (Figure 3.43). Under ordinary conditions, when her eyes are free to move about, she sees almost the same thing in both hemispheres. In the laboratory, however, it is possible to restrict information to one side of the brain or the other by presenting the information faster than the eyes can move. The woman in Figure 3.43 focuses her eyes on a point in the middle of the screen. The investigator flashes a word such as *hatband* on the screen for only a split second so that the woman does not have enough time to move her eyes. If she is asked what she saw, she replies, "band," which is what the left hemisphere saw. (Information from the right side of the screen, you will recall, goes to the left side of each retina and from there to the left hemisphere of the brain.) If she is asked what *kind* of band it might be, she will be puzzled: "I don't know. jazz band? rubber band?" However, if she is asked to point with the left hand at what she saw, the left hand points to a hat (what the right hemisphere saw).

Split-brain people get along reasonably well in everyday life. Walking, for example, is no problem; it is largely controlled by subcortical areas of the brain that exchange information through connections below the corpus callosum.

In special circumstances, the two hemispheres find clever ways to cooperate. In one experiment, a split-brain person was looking at pictures flashed on a screen, as in Figure 3.43a. He could not name most of the objects flashed in the left visual field, but after some delay, he could name such simple shapes as round, square, or triangular. Here is how he did it: After seeing the object (with the right hemisphere), he let his eyes move around the room. (Both hemispheres have control of the eye muscles.) When the right hemisphere saw something with the same shape as the object it had seen on the screen, it would stop moving the eyes. The left hemisphere just waited for the eyes to stop moving and then called out the shape of the object it saw.

CONCEPT CHECKS

13. Information coming to the left hemisphere of the brain comes from which part of the retinas?

14. After damage to the corpus callosum, a person can describe some of what he or she sees, but not all. Where must the person see something in order to describe it in words? one eye or the other? one half of the retina? one visual field or the other? (Check your answers on page 101.)

Split-brain surgery is extremely rare. We study such patients not because you are likely to encounter one but because they can teach us something about the organization of the brain: Although we cannot fully explain our experience of a unified consciousness, we do see that it depends on communication across brain areas. If communication between the two hemispheres is lost, then each hemisphere begins to act and experience independently of the other.

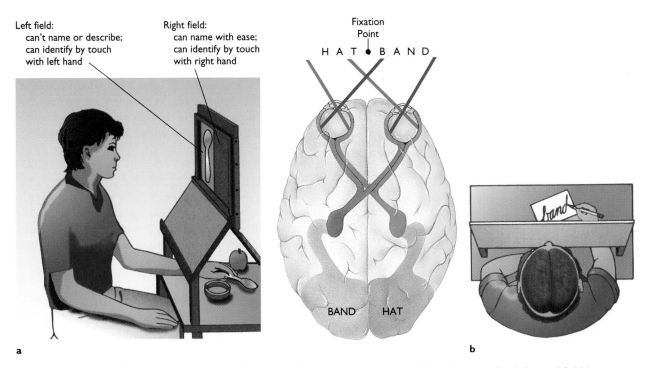

FIGURE 3.43 (a) A woman with a severed corpus callosum cannot name something she sees in her left visual field, but can find the corresponding object with her right hand. (b) When the word *hatband* is flashed on a screen, a woman with a split brain can report only what her left hemisphere saw, *band*. However, with her left hand she can point to a hat, which is what the right hemisphere saw.

Common Misunderstandings About the Brain

Before closing this chapter, I want to caution you about some widespread misperceptions and misunderstandings concerning the brain. One of these concerns the left and right hemispheres. Research on split-brain people and those who have suffered widespread damage to one hemisphere has demonstrated that the two hemispheres have different specializations. The left hemisphere is specialized for language in nearly all right-handers and in most left-handers. The right hemisphere is important for some complex visual-spatial tasks, such as drawing a picture or imagining what something might look like from a different angle. Some writers have gone beyond this generalization, however, to claim that the left hemisphere is logical and the right hemisphere is creative, so some people are logical because they are left-brained people and others are creative because they are right-brained people. Some have even suggested that we could all become more creative if we could find a way to stimulate the right hemisphere or to suppress the competing left hemisphere.

In fact, every task, even the most logical or the most creative, uses both sides of the brain. Certain tasks activate one hemisphere a bit more than the other, but no task relies on just one hemisphere. As for the theory that some people are left brained or that others are right brained, we simply have no evidence to support that claim. The idea that a highly creative person must be relying mostly on their right hemisphere is merely a guess based on that person's behavior, not based on any measurement of brain activity. It is an example of *neuromythology*—making guesses about the brain to account for an observation about behavior.

A second misunderstanding: You have probably heard the expression "They say we use only 10% of our brain." Think about that for a moment: Who are "they"? No brain researcher would say anything of the sort. What does this statement really mean? Does it mean that someone could lose 90% of their brain and still function normally? If so, the statement is false. Does it mean that only 10% of the neurons in the brain are active at any given time? False again. Perhaps it simply means that we could all know more and do more than we know and do now. That is undeniably true, though it has nothing to do with the estimated 10% (or any other number). Suppose that you are not much of an athlete; that doesn't mean that you are using only 10% of your muscles. We all use all of our brain and all of our muscles, even when we do not use them very well. Be wary when anyone says "They say that . . ." if the speaker cannot tell you who "they" are or what evidence they have for the conclusion.

THE MESSAGE
Many Brain Areas, One Brain

Most of us act as a single, unified whole (or at most, two wholes, in the case of some people with a split corpus callosum). This unity emerges despite considerable specialization among brain areas, because each area of the brain communicates with the others. Amazingly, an enormous number of separate areas with separate functions, not guided by a master area, alter their functions, based on what the others are doing, to produce coordinated behavior and a single frame of experience—what you call your "self."

SUMMARY

✳ *Central and peripheral nervous systems.* The central nervous system consists of the brain (forebrain, midbrain, and hindbrain) and the spinal cord. The peripheral nervous system consists of nerves that communicate between the central nervous system and the rest of the body. (page 85)

✳ *Autonomic nervous system and endocrine system.* The autonomic nervous system controls the body's organs, preparing them for emergency activities or for vegetative activities. The endocrine system consists of organs that release hormones into the blood. (page 86)

✳ *Structures of the central nervous system.* Information passing between the cerebral cortex and the spinal cord goes through several intervening structures such as the midbrain and medulla. All the intervening structures have important functions of their own. (page 88)

✳ *Parallel paths and specialized functions of brain areas.* Contemporary research indicates that the various brain areas have specialized functions and that localized brain damage can produce specialized defects. Various brain functions occur in parallel, largely independently. Loss of part of the brain leads to partial loss of behavior and experience. (page 90)

✳ *Lobes of the cerebral cortex.* The four lobes of the cerebral cortex and their primary functions are: occipital lobe, vision; temporal lobe, hearing and some aspects of vision; parietal lobe, body sensations; frontal lobe, movement and preparation for movement. (page 93)

✳ *Imaging brain activity.* Modern technology enables researchers to develop images showing the structure and activity of various brain areas in living, unanesthetized people. (page 95)

✳ *Corpus callosum.* The corpus callosum is a set of axons through which the left and right hemispheres of the cortex communicate. If the corpus callosum is damaged, information that reaches one hemisphere cannot be shared with the other. (page 96)

✳ *Connections from eyes to brain.* In humans, information from the *left* visual field strikes the right half of both retinas, from which it is sent to the *right* hemisphere of the brain. Information from the *right* visual field strikes the left half of both retinas, from which it is sent to the *left* hemisphere. (page 97)

✳ *Split-brain patients.* The left hemisphere is specialized for language in most people, so split-brain people can describe information only if it enters the left hemisphere. Because of the lack of direct communication between the left and right hemispheres in split-brain patients, such people show signs of having separate fields of awareness. (page 97)

✳ *Common misunderstandings.* Many people try to explain either logical thinking or creative thinking by attributing it to extra activity in the left or right hemisphere of the brain. That guess is at best a half-truth, unsupported by direct evidence. Another common misunderstanding is the assertion that we use only a small percentage of our brain. In fact, people are using all of their brain, even when they are not using it very well. (page 99)

Suggestion for Further Reading

Klawans, H. L. (1996). *Why Michael couldn't hit*. New York: W. H. Freeman. Informative and entertaining account of how the rise and fall of various sports heroes relates to what we know about the brain.

Terms

central nervous system   the brain and the spinal cord (page 85)

peripheral nervous system   the bundles of axons that convey messages between the spinal cord and the rest of the body (page 85)

somatic nervous system   peripheral nerves that communicate with the skin and muscles (page 85)

spinal cord   that part of the central nervous system that communicates with sensory neurons and motor neurons below the level of the head (page 86)

sensory neuron   a neuron that carries information about touch, pain, and other senses from the periphery of the body to the spinal cord (page 86)

motor neuron   a neuron that transmits impulses from the central nervous system to the muscles or glands (page 86)

reflex   a rapid, automatic response to a stimulus (page 86)

autonomic nervous system   system of neurons that controls the internal organs such as the heart (page 86)

endocrine system   a set of glands that produce hormones and release them into the bloodstream (page 87)

hormone   a chemical released by glands and conveyed by the blood to other parts of the body, where it alters activity (page 87)

medulla   a structure that is located in the hindbrain and is an elaboration of the spinal cord; controls many muscles in the head and several life-preserving functions, such as breathing (page 88)

pons   a structure adjacent to the medulla that receives sensory input from the head and controls many muscles in the head (page 88)

cerebellum   (Latin for "little brain") a hindbrain structure that is active in the control of movement, especially for complex, rapid motor skills and behaviors that require precise timing (page 88)

cerebral cortex the outer surface of the forebrain (page 90)

hemisphere the left or right half of the brain; each hemisphere is responsible for sensation and motor control on the opposite side of the body (page 90)

faceblindness impairment of the ability to recognize faces, despite otherwise satisfactory vision (page 91)

color constancy the ability to continue recognizing colors even after a change in lighting (page 91)

motionblindness impaired ability to detect motion in visual perception, despite otherwise satisfactory vision (page 91)

neglect the tendency to ignore stimuli on one side of the body or one side of the world (page 91)

delayed response a task in which an individual gets a signal and then must wait before making the necessary response (page 92)

occipital lobe the rear portion of each cerebral hemisphere, critical for vision (page 94)

parietal lobe a portion of each cerebral hemisphere; the main receiving area for the sense of touch and for the awareness of one's own body (page 94)

primary somatosensory cortex a strip in the anterior (forward) part of the parietal lobe that receives most touch sensations and other information about the body (page 94)

temporal lobe a portion of each cerebral hemisphere; the main processing area for hearing, complex aspects of vision, and certain aspects of emotional behavior (page 94)

frontal lobe a portion of each cerebral hemisphere at the anterior pole, with sections that control movement and certain aspects of memory (page 95)

primary motor cortex a strip in the posterior (rear) part of the frontal cortex that controls fine movements, such as hand and finger movements (page 95)

prefrontal cortex an area in the anterior portion of the frontal lobes, critical for planning movements and for certain aspects of memory (page 95)

functional magnetic resonance imaging (fMRI) a technique that uses magnetic detectors outside the head to measure the amounts of hemoglobin, with and without oxygen, in different parts of the brain and thereby provides an indication of current activity levels in various brain areas (page 95)

corpus callosum a large set of axons connecting the left and right hemispheres of the cerebral cortex and thus enabling the two hemispheres to communicate with each other (page 96)

epilepsy a condition characterized by abnormal rhythmic activity of brain neurons (page 96)

Answers to Concept Checks

10. The storage of fats takes place at many sites throughout the body. A hormone diffuses throughout the body; a neurotransmitter exerts its effects only on the neurons immediately adjacent to where it was released. (page 87)

11. Although alcohol impairs activity throughout the brain, one of the first areas to show a substantial effect is the cerebellum. The typical symptoms of alcohol intoxication are also symptoms of impairment to the cerebellum. (page 88)

12. (a) right parietal lobe; (b) temporal lobe; (c) primary motor cortex of the left frontal lobe; (d) right occipital lobe; (e) prefrontal cortex. (page 95)

13. The left hemisphere receives input from the left half of each retina. (page 98)

14. To describe something, a person must see it with the left half of the retina of either eye. The left half of the retina sees the right visual field. (page 98).

Web Resources

A Brief Tour of the Brain

suhep.phy.syr.edu/courses/modules/MM/Biology/biology.html
Scientists at Syracuse University review the structure and functions of the brain and its parts, right down to the neurons; includes illustrations and very readable text.

Human Anatomy On-Line

www.innerbody.com/htm/body.html
Click on the picture of the nervous system or on the images button and select a brain image. Go deeper by clicking on the magnifying glass when your cursor touches a hotspot. Animations show the visual, auditory, and other systems in action.

BrainPoke!

www.wlu.edu/~web/bp/brainpk.html
Tell the surgeon where to poke the brain. See the effect. Does the effect match your expectations?

The L.A. Times Brain Page

www.latimes.com/HOME/NEWS/SCIENCE/REPORTS/THEBRAIN/
The *L.A. Times* Brain Page has one of the more impressive pages you will see on the Web. Note the background of the page itself. You will find several interesting brain facts, articles, and links on this page.

Sensation and Perception

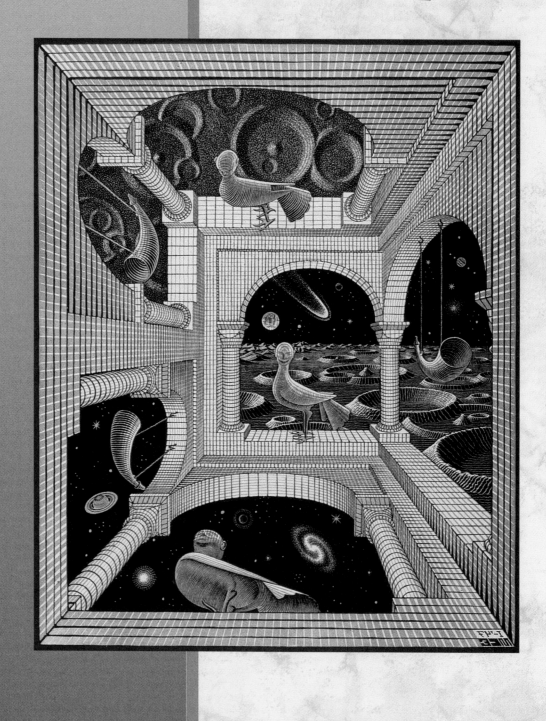

When my son Sam was 8 years old, he asked me, "If we went to some other planet, would we see different colors?" He did not mean just a new shade or a new mixture of familiar colors. He meant colors that were truly new, as different from familiar colors as yellow is from red or blue. I told him that would be impossible, and I tried to explain why.

No matter where we go in outer space, no matter what unfamiliar objects or atmospheres we might encounter, we could never experience a color, or a sound, or any other sensation that would be fundamentally different from what we experience on Earth. Different combinations, perhaps. But fundamentally different sensory experiences, no.

Three years later, Sam told me he was wondering whether people who look at the same thing are all having the same experience: When different people look at something and call it "green," how can we know whether they are all seeing the same "green"? I agreed that there is no way of knowing for sure.

Why am I certain that colors on a different planet would look the same as they do here on Earth and yet uncertain whether colors look the same to different people here? The answer may be obvious to you. If not, I hope it will be after you have read this chapter.

Sensation is the *conversion of energy from the environment into a pattern of response by the nervous system.* It is the registration of information. **Perception** is *the interpretation of that information.* For example, light rays striking your eyes give rise to sensation. When you conclude from that sensation, "I see my roommate," you are expressing your perception. (In practice, the distinction between sensation and perception is often difficult to make.)

Vision

How do our eyes convert light energy into something that we can experience?

How do we perceive colors?

We live in a world full of **stimuli**—*energies that affect what we do.* Our eyes, ears, and other sensory organs are packed with **receptors**—*specialized cells that convert environmental energies into signals for the nervous system.* We see, hear, and so forth because stimuli activate receptors, which in turn send messages to the brain, which eventually uses this information to guide our behavior.

You have probably already been given this account in a biology or health class in high school, perhaps even in elementary school. But did you believe it? Evidently not everyone does. One survey posed the questions, "When we look at someone or something, does anything such as rays, waves, or energy go out of our eyes? into our eyes?" Among first graders (about age 6), 49% answered (incorrectly) that energy went out of the eyes, and 54% answered that energy came into the eyes. (It was possible to say *yes* to both.) Among college students, 33% said that energy went out of the eyes; 88%, that energy came in (Winer & Cottrell, 1996).

The idea that the eyes send out sight rays is hardly the only widespread misconception about vision. We are often led astray because we imagine that what we see is simply a copy of the outside world, and it is not. For example, color is not a property of objects; it is something your brain creates in response to light of different wavelengths. Brightness is not the same thing as the intensity of the light. (Light that is twice as intense does not appear twice as bright.) Our experiences *translate* the stimuli of the outside world into very different representations.

The Detection of Light

What we call *light* is just one part of the electromagnetic spectrum. As Figure 4.1 shows, the **electromagnetic spectrum** is *the continuum of all the frequencies of radiated energy*—from gamma rays and X rays, which have very short wavelengths, through ultraviolet, visible light, and infrared, to radio and TV transmissions, which have very long wavelengths.

What makes "visible light" visible? The answer is our receptors, which are equipped to respond to wavelengths from 400 to 700 nm. With different receptors, we might see a different range of wavelengths. Some species—bees, for example—respond to wavelengths shorter than 350 nm, which are invisible to humans.

The Structure of the Eye

When we see an object, light reflected from that object passes through the **pupil,** an *adjustable opening in the eye through which light enters.* The **iris** is the *colored structure on the surface of the eye, surrounding the pupil.* It is the structure we describe when we say someone has brown, green, or blue eyes. When the light is dim, muscles open the pupil to let in more light. When the light is bright, muscles narrow the pupil.

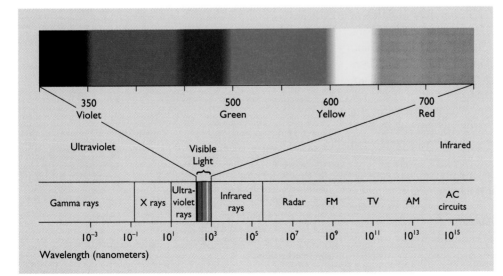

FIGURE 4.1 Visible light, what human eyes can see, is only a small part of the entire electromagnetic spectrum. While experimenting with prisms, Isaac Newton discovered that white light is a mixture of all colors, and color is a property of light. A carrot looks orange because it reflects orange light and absorbs all the other colors.

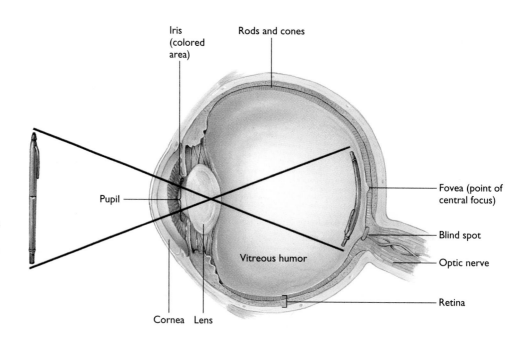

FIGURE 4.2 The lens gets its name from Latin for *lentil,* referring to its shape—an appropriate choice, as this cross section of the eye shows. The names of other parts of the eye also refer to their appearance.

After light passes through the pupil, it travels through the *vitreous humor* (a clear, jellylike substance) and strikes the retina at the back of the eyeball. The **retina** is a *layer of visual receptors covering the back surface of the eyeball* (Figure 4.2). As light passes through the eye, the cornea and the lens focus the light on the retina as shown.

The **cornea,** a *rigid transparent structure on the outer surface of the eyeball,* always focuses light in the same way. The **lens,** however, is a *flexible structure that can vary in thickness,* enabling the eye to **accommodate**—that is, *to adjust its focus for objects at different distances.* When we look at a distant object, for example, our eye muscles relax and let the lens become thinner and flatter, as shown in Figure 4.3a. When we look at a close object, our eye muscles tighten and make the lens thicker and rounder (Figure 4.3b).

Some Common Disorders of Vision

As people grow older, they gradually develop **presbyopia,** *decreased flexibility of the lens and therefore inability to focus on nearby objects.* (The Greek root *presby* means "old." This root also shows up in the word *presbyterian,* which means "governed by the elders.") Many people's eyes are not quite spherical. A person whose eyeballs are elongated, as shown in Figure 4.4a, can focus well on nearby objects but has difficulty focusing on distant objects. Such a person is said to be *nearsighted* or to have **myopia** (mi-O-pee-ah). About half of all 20-year-olds are nearsighted and must wear glasses or contact lenses to see well at a distance. An older person with both myopia and presbyopia needs bifocal glasses to help with both near focus and distant focus. A person whose eyeballs are flattened, as shown in Figure 4.4b, has **hyperopia,** or *farsightedness.* Such a person can focus well on distant objects but has difficulty focusing on close objects.

Two other common visual disorders are glaucoma and cataracts. **Glaucoma** is a *condition characterized by increased pressure within the eyeball;* the result can be damage to the optic nerve and therefore a progressive loss of peripheral vision ("tunnel vision"). A **cataract** is a *disorder in which the lens becomes cloudy.* People with severe cataracts can have the lens surgically removed and replaced with a contact lens. Because the normal lens filters out more blue and ultraviolet light than other light, people with artificial lenses sometimes report seeing blue more clearly and distinctly than they ever had before (Davenport & Foley, 1979). They do, however, suffer increased risk of damage to the retina from ultraviolet light.

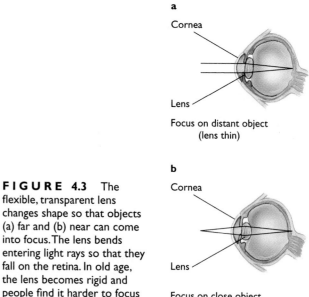

a
Cornea

Lens

Focus on distant object
(lens thin)

b
Cornea

Lens

Focus on close object
(lens thick)

FIGURE 4.3 The flexible, transparent lens changes shape so that objects (a) far and (b) near can come into focus. The lens bends entering light rays so that they fall on the retina. In old age, the lens becomes rigid and people find it harder to focus on nearby objects.

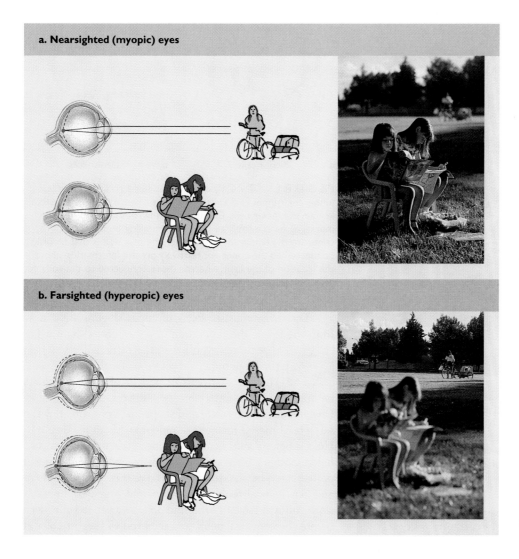

a. Nearsighted (myopic) eyes

b. Farsighted (hyperopic) eyes

FIGURE 4.4 The structure of (a) nearsighted and (b) farsighted eyes distorts vision. Because the nearsighted eye is elongated, light from a distant object focuses in front of the retina. Because the farsighted eye is flattened, light from a nearby object focuses behind the retina. (The dashed line shows the position of the normal retina in each case.)

CONCEPT CHECK

1. Suppose you have normal vision and you try on a pair of glasses made for a person with myopia. How will the glasses affect your vision? (Check your answer on page 117.)

The Visual Receptors

The visual receptors of the eye, specialized neurons in the retina at the back of the eyeball, are so sensitive to light that they are capable of responding to a single photon, the smallest possible quantity of light. There are two types of visual receptors: cones and rods, which differ in appearance, as Figure 4.5 shows, and in function. The **cones** are *receptors adapted for color vision, daytime vision, and detailed vision.* The **rods** are *receptors adapted for vision in dim light.*

About 5–10% of all the visual receptors in the human retina are cones. Most birds have at least as high a proportion of cones as humans and correspondingly have good color vision. Species that are active mostly at night—rats

and mice, for example—have relatively few cones and a great dominance of rods, thus enhancing their perception in faint light.

The proportion of cones is highest toward the center of the retina. The **fovea** (FOE-vee-uh), *the central area of the human retina,* is adapted for highly detailed vision (see Figure 4.2). Of all retinal areas, the fovea has the greatest density of receptors; also, more of the cerebral cortex is devoted to analyzing input from the fovea than input from other areas. If you want to see something in detail, you focus it on the fovea; for example, you can read letters of the alphabet only if you see them in or near the fovea.

Other animal species have eyes that are organized somewhat differently from human eyes. For example, hawks, owls, and other predatory birds have a greater density of receptors on the top of the retina (for looking down) than on the bottom of the retina (for looking up). When these birds are flying, this arrangement enables them to see the ground beneath them in detail. When they are on the ground, however, they have trouble seeing above themselves (Figure 4.6).

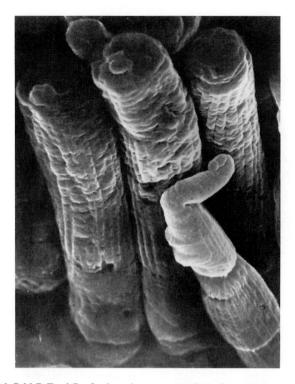

FIGURE 4.5 Rods and cones seen through a scanning electron micrograph. The rods, which number over 120 million in humans, help us see in dim light. The 6 million cones in the retina can distinguish gradations of color in bright light; they enable us to see that roses are red, magenta, ruby, carmine, cherry, vermilion, scarlet, and crimson—not to mention pink, yellow, orange, and white.

FIGURE 4.6 The consequence of having receptors mostly on the top of the retina: Birds of prey, such as these owlets, can see down much more clearly than they can see up. In flight, that arrangement is helpful. On the ground, they have to turn their heads almost upside down in order to see above them.

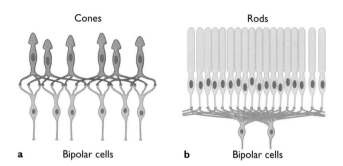

FIGURE 4.7 Only a few cones, but a great many rods, funnel their input into cells of the next layer of the visual system, known as bipolar cells. Because so many rods combine their messages, even a small amount of light falling on the rods can stimulate the bipolar cells. However, the trade-off is that bipolars connected to the cones get relatively precise information about the location of the light, whereas those connected to the rods get only approximate information about the location.

The fovea consists solely of cones (Figure 4.2). Away from the fovea, the proportion of cones drops sharply. For that reason, you have little or no color vision in the far periphery of your eye. Try this experiment: Hold several pens or pencils of different colors behind your back. (Any objects will work as long as they have about the same size and shape and approximately the same brightness.) Pick one at random without looking at it. Hold it behind your head and bring it very slowly into your field of vision. When you just barely begin to see it, you will probably not be able to tell what color it is. (If glaucoma or another medical problem has impaired your peripheral vision, you will have to bring the object closer to your fovea before you can see it at all, and then you will see its color at once.)

The rods are more effective than the cones for detecting dim light, for two reasons: First, a rod is slightly more responsive to faint stimulation than a cone is. Second, the rods pool their resources. In some cases, more than one hundred rods send messages to the next cell in the visual system, whereas only a few cones converge their messages onto a given cell, as shown in Figure 4.7. Table 4.1 summarizes some of the key differences between rods and cones.

CONCEPT CHECK

2. Why is it easier to see a faint star in the sky if you look slightly to the side of the star instead of straight at it? (Check your answer on page 117.)

Dark Adaptation

Suppose you go into a basement at night trying to find your flashlight. The only lightbulb in the basement is burned out. A little moonlight comes through the basement windows, but not much. At first you can hardly see anything. A minute or two later, you are beginning to see well enough to find your way around, and eventually you can see well

TABLE 4.1 Differences Between Rods and Cones

	RODS	CONES
Shape	Nearly cylindrical	Tapered at one end
Prevalence in human retina	90–95%	5–10%
Greatest incidence by species	In species that are active at night	In birds, primates, and other species that are active during the day
Area of the retina	Toward the periphery	Toward the fovea
Contribution to color vision	No direct contribution	Critical for color vision
Response to dim light	Strong	Weak
Contribution to perception in detail	Little	Much

enough to find the flashlight. This *gradual improvement in the ability to see in dim light* is called **dark adaptation.**

The mechanism behind dark adaptation is this: Exposure to light causes a chemical change in certain molecules called *retinaldehydes,* thereby stimulating the visual receptors. (Retinaldehydes are derived from vitamin A.) Under normal (moderate) light, the receptors *regenerate* (rebuild) the retinaldehydes about as fast as the light is altering them, and the person maintains about a constant level of visual sensitivity. In darkness or very dim light, however, the receptors can regenerate their molecules without interruption, so the person gradually becomes better able to detect faint lights.

The cones and rods adapt to the dark at different rates. During the day our vision ordinarily relies overwhelmingly on cones. When we enter a dark place, our cones regenerate their retinaldehydes faster than the rods do, but by the time the rods finish their regeneration, they are far more sensitive to faint light than the cones are. At that point, we are seeing mostly with rods.

Here is how a psychologist demonstrates this process of dark adaptation (Goldstein, 1989): You are taken into a room that is completely dark except for one tiny flashing light. You have a knob that controls the intensity of the light; you are told to make the light so dim that you can barely see it. Over the course of three or four minutes you will gradually decrease the intensity of the light, as shown in Figure 4.8a. Note that a decrease in the intensity of the light indicates an increase in the sensitivity of your eyes. If you stare straight at the point of light, your results will demonstrate the adaptation of your cones to the dim light. (You have been focusing the light on your fovea, which has no rods.)

Now the psychologist repeats the study, with one change in procedure: You are told to stare at a very faint light while another light flashes in the periphery of your vision, where it stimulates both rods and cones. You turn a control knob until the flashing light in the periphery is just barely visible. (Figure 4.8b shows the results.) During the first 7 to 10 minutes, the results are the same as before. But then your rods become more sensitive than your cones, and you begin to see even fainter lights. Your rods continue to adapt to the dark over the next 20 minutes or so.

If you would like to demonstrate dark adaptation for yourself without any apparatus, try this: On a dark night, with only slight amounts of light coming through your

TRY IT YOUR-SELF

windows, turn on a light in your room. Close one eye and cover it tightly with your hand for a few minutes. By the end of that time, your covered eye will be adapted to the dark and your open eye will be adapted to the light. Next, turn off your light and then open both eyes. You will see well with your dark-adapted eye and poorly with the light-adapted eye.

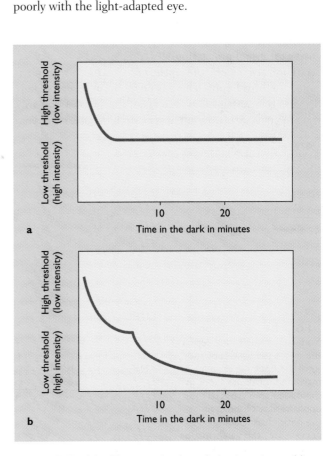

FIGURE 4.8 These graphs show dark adaptation to (a) a light you stare at directly, using only cones, and (b) a light in your peripheral vision, which you see with both cones and rods. (Based on Goldstein, 1989.)

CONCEPT CHECKS

3. You may have heard people say that cats can see in the dark. Is that possible?
4. After you have thoroughly adapted to extremely dim light, will you see more objects in your fovea or in the periphery of your eye? (Check your answers on page 117.)

The Visual Pathway

If you or I were designing an eye, we would probably run the axons of the cones and rods straight to the brain. Nature chose a different method. The visual receptors send their impulses *away from* the brain, toward the center of the eye, where they make synaptic contacts with other neurons called bipolar cells. The *bipolar cells* in turn make contact with still other neurons, the **ganglion cells,** which are *neurons that receive their input from the bipolar cells.* The *axons from the ganglion cells join to form* the **optic nerve,** *which turns around and exits the eye,* as Figures 4.2 and 4.9 show. Half of each optic nerve crosses to the opposite side of the brain at the optic chiasm (KI-az-m). Axons from the optic nerve then separate and go to several locations in the brain. In humans the largest number go to the thalamus, which then sends information to the occipital lobe, the primary area of the cortex for visual processing.

The *area where the optic nerve exits the retina* is called the **blind spot.** There is no room for receptors here because the exiting axons take up all the space. Ordinarily, you are unaware of your blind spot. To illustrate, cover your

 left eye and stare at the center of Figure 4.10, then slowly move the page forward and backward. When your eye is about 25–30 cm (10–12 inches) away from the page, the lion disappears, because it falls into your blind spot. What do you see in its place? Certainly not blackness. Rather, your brain makes an inference about what is in the gap. Do you *see* a continuation of the circle in that gap? Not exactly; you infer it more than you actually perceive it.

Information from the left and right eyes remains separate until it reaches the visual cortex. Each cell in the visual cortex receives input from one part of the left retina and a corresponding part of the right retina—that is, two retinal areas that ordinarily focus on the same point in space. Under normal conditions, the input coming from the left retina is almost the same as that coming from the right retina, and the two effects summate. However, examine Figure 4.11 to see what happens if the retinal images conflict. Move your eyes so close to the page that the two circles seem to merge. You have some neurons in your visual cortex that respond to vertical lines. When you merge the two circles, those cells are getting stimulated by one pattern and inhibited by the other (Logothetis, Leopold, & Sheinberg, 1996). For a short while, the stimulation dominates but then for a while the inhibition dominates. Meanwhile, inhibition and stimulation are also alternating for cells that respond to horizontal lines. The net effect is that you see green lines, then red lines, then green lines again, and so forth. The *alternation between seeing the pattern in the left retina and the pattern in the right retina* is known as **binocular rivalry.**

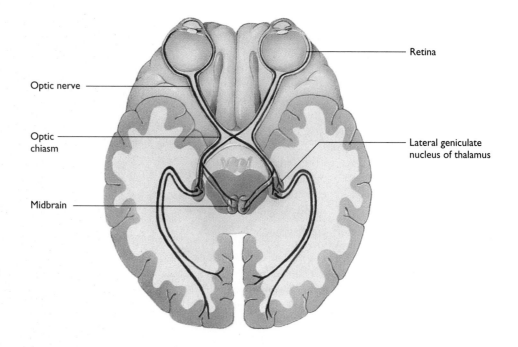

FIGURE 4.9 Axons from cells in the retina depart the eye at the blind spot and form the optic nerve. In humans, about half the axons in the optic nerve cross to the opposite side of the brain at the optic chiasm. Some optic nerve axons carry information to the midbrain; others carry it to the thalamus, which relays information to the cerebral cortex.

Retina

Lateral geniculate nucleus of thalamus

Optic nerve

Optic chiasm

Midbrain

FIGURE 4.10 Close your left eye and focus your right eye on the animal trainer. Move the page toward your eyes and away from them, until you find the point where the lion on the right disappears. At that point, the lion is focused on the blind spot of your retina, where you have no receptors. What you see there is not a blank spot, but a continuation of the circle.

FIGURE 4.11 To produce binocular rivalry, move your eyes toward the page until the two circles seem to merge. You will alternate between seeing red lines and green lines.

Color Vision

As Figure 4.1 shows, different colors of light correspond to different wavelengths of electromagnetic energy. (White light consists of an equal mixture of all the visible wavelengths.) How does the visual system convert these wavelengths into our perception of color? The process begins with three kinds of cones, which respond to different wavelengths of light. Later cells in the visual path code this wavelength information in terms of pairs of opposites—roughly, red versus green, yellow versus blue, and white versus black. Finally, cells in the cerebral cortex compare the input from various parts of the visual field to synthesize a color experience for each object. We shall examine these three stages in turn.

The Trichromatic Theory

Thomas Young was an English physician of the 1700s who, among his many other accomplishments, helped to decode the Rosetta stone (making it possible to understand Egyptian hieroglyphics), introduced the modern concept of energy, revived and popularized the wave theory of light, and offered the first theory about how people perceive color. His theory, elaborated and modified by Hermann von Helmholtz in the 1800s, came to be known as the **trichromatic theory** or the **Young-Helmholtz theory.** It is called *trichromatic* because it claims that our receptors respond to three primary colors. In modern terms, we say that *color vision depends on the*

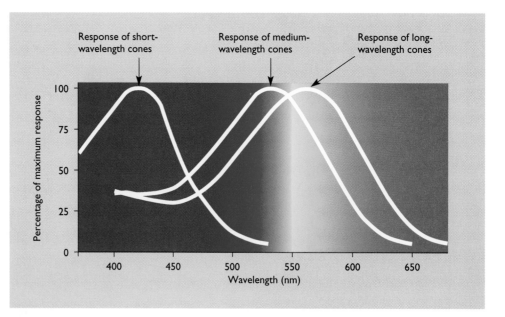

Response of short-wavelength cones

Response of medium-wavelength cones

Response of long-wavelength cones

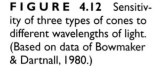

FIGURE 4.12 Sensitivity of three types of cones to different wavelengths of light. (Based on data of Bowmaker & Dartnall, 1980.)

relative rate of response by three types of cones. Each type of cone is most sensitive to a particular range of light wavelengths (Figure 4.12). One type is most sensitive to short wavelengths (which we generally see as blue), another to medium wavelengths (seen as green), and another to long wavelengths (red). Each wavelength prompts varying levels of activity in the three types of cones. So, for example, green light excites mostly the medium-wavelength cones, red light excites mostly the long-wavelength cones, and yellow light excites the medium-wavelength and long-wavelength cones about equally. Every wavelength of light produces its own distinct ratio of responses by the three kinds of cones. White light excites all three kinds of cones equally.

Young and Helmholtz proposed their theory long before experiments confirmed the existence of these three types of cones (Wald, 1968). They relied entirely on a behavioral observation: Observers can take three different colors of light and then, by mixing them in various proportions, match all other colors of light. (Note that mixing light of different colors is not the same as mixing paints of different colors. Mixing yellow and blue *paints* produces green; mixing yellow and blue *lights* produces white.)

The short-wavelength cones, which respond most strongly to blue, are less numerous than the other two types of cones, especially in the fovea. Consequently, a tiny blue

FIGURE 4.13 Blue spots look black unless they cover a sizable area. Count the red dots, then count the blue dots. Try again while standing farther away from the page.

point may look black. For the retina to detect blueness, the blue must extend over a moderately large area. Figure 4.13 illustrates this effect. Count the red spots and then the blue spots. Then stand farther away and count the spots again. You will probably see as many red spots as before but fewer blue spots.

TRY IT YOUR-SELF

CONCEPT CHECK

5. According to the trichromatic theory, how does our nervous system tell the difference between bright yellow-green and dim yellow-green light? (Check your answer on page 117.)

The Opponent-Process Theory

Young and Helmholtz were right about how many cones we have, but our perception of color has some complicated features that the trichromatic theory cannot easily handle. For example, four colors, not three, *seem* to most people to be primary or basic: red, green, yellow, and blue. Yellow simply does not seem like a mixture of reddish and greenish experiences, nor is green a yellowish blue. Furthermore, if you stare at an object of one color, say red, and then look away, you see a colored afterimage—in this case green. Each color appears to have an opposite, and there is no obvious reason why it should, according to the trichromatic theory.

For these reasons, another 19th-century scientist, Ewald Hering, proposed the **opponent-process theory** of color vision, which accounts for much of color information processing after the cones. According to this theory, *we perceive color not in terms of independent colors but in terms of a system of paired opposites: red versus green, yellow versus blue, and white versus black.* Any light stimulus leads to a perception somewhere along each of these three dimensions. Although Hering didn't know it, the dimen-

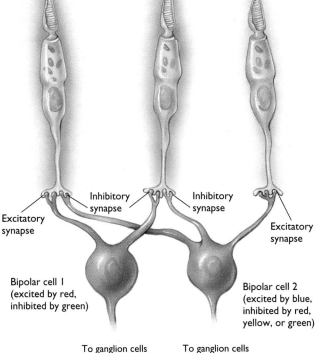

Long-wavelength cone (responds well to red or yellow)

Medium-wavelength cone (responds best to green, less to yellow)

Short-wavelength cone (responds best to blue)

Excitatory synapse

Inhibitory synapse

Inhibitory synapse

Excitatory synapse

Bipolar cell 1 (excited by red, inhibited by green)

Bipolar cell 2 (excited by blue, inhibited by red, yellow, or green)

To ganglion cells   To ganglion cells

FIGURE 4.14 According to the opponent-process theory of color vision, the responses of three kinds of cones excite and inhibit bipolar cells, which relay their responses to other cells in the visual system. For example, red light excites the long-wavelength cone and thereby *excites* bipolar cell 1; green light excites the medium-wavelength cone and thereby *inhibits* bipolar cell 1. Therefore, bipolar cell 1 increases its response in the presence of red light and decreases its response in the presence of green light. After prolonged exposure to red light, the cell will "rebound" to an inhibition of response and therefore report a message of "green."

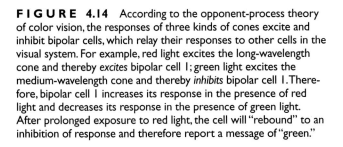

sions correspond to excitation and inhibition of many cells in the visual system (DeValois, 1965; Michael, 1978). For example, some bipolar cells in the eye are excited when green light strikes the cones that connect to them and inhibited when red light strikes.[1] Other bipolar cells are excited by red and inhibited by green. Still other cells are excited by yellow and inhibited by blue or excited by blue and inhibited by yellow. The white/black system is more complicated: If a cell is excited by white light, we cannot meaningfully say that it is inhibited by black. Rather, the cell is inhibited when the light on neighboring areas of the retina is brighter than the light in its own area.

---

[1]Technically, it is wrong to talk about red, green, or blue light. I should say "long-wavelength," "medium-wavelength," or "short-wavelength" light. The light itself is not red, green, or any other color; the color perception is in us. Furthermore, light that is predominantly medium wavelength can, under certain circumstances, be seen as a color other than green. However, to simplify and speed up the conversation, I use terms like *red light* to refer to light that we usually see as red.

For example, in Figure 4.14, bipolar cell 1 receives an excitatory synaptic message from the long-wavelength cone and an inhibitory synaptic message from the medium-wavelength cone. The cell increases its response in the presence of red light and decreases its response in the presence of green light. Bipolar cell 2 receives excitatory synaptic messages from the short-wavelength cone; it is therefore excited by blue light. Cell 2 receives inhibitory messages from both the long-wavelength cone and the medium-wavelength cone; it will be inhibited by either red, yellow, or green light.

Figure 4.15 lends support to the opponent-process theory. Stare at the white dot near the center of the figure and stare at it for a minute or so, preferably under a bright light, without moving your eyes or your head. Then look at a plain white or gray background. *Do this now.*

If you have normal or near-normal vision, you saw the Mona Lisa when you looked away. After bipolar cells and other cells in your visual system have been stimulated long enough they become fatigued, and removal of the stimulus will leave them inhibited. Recall that a cell that is excited by red light is inhibited by green light, and vice versa. Thus, after the removal of a prolonged red light, the cells are responding just as they do in the presence of green light, so

FIGURE 4.15 Use this image to see the negative afterimages of opposite colors, which rebound after sufficient stimulation. Stare at the white dot for a minute or more, then focus on a white background.

FIGURE 4.16 Despite the green and red filters used in producing the center and right-hand photographs, you can still identify the colors of the objects in the photos. The effect would be much more convincing if you were actually on location, looking at this scene through tinted glasses. Here, each photo is surrounded by the white page, which sets an effective standard. Your ability to identify the color of an object, despite changes in the light striking the environment, is called color constancy.

you in fact see green. Similarly, after the removal of a green light you see red, after yellow you see blue, and after blue you see yellow. These *experiences of one color after the removal of another* are called **negative afterimages.**

CONCEPT CHECKS

6. How would bipolar cell 1 in Figure 4.14 respond to yellow light? Why?
7. The negative afterimage that you created by staring at Figure 4.15 may seem to move against the background. Why doesn't it stay in one place? (Check your answers on page 117.)

The Retinex Theory

The opponent-process theory, though it accounts for many phenomena of color vision, overlooks one important one. Suppose you look at a large white screen illuminated entirely with green light, in an otherwise dark room. How would you know whether this is a white screen illuminated with green light or a green screen illuminated with white light? or a blue screen illuminated with yellow light? (Actually, the possibilities go on and on.) The answer is, you would not know. But now someone wearing a brown shirt and blue jeans stands in front of the screen. By comparing what you see of this person to what you see on the screen, you immediately see the shirt as brown, the jeans as blue, and the screen as white, even though all these objects are reflecting more green light than anything else. The point is that we do not ordinarily perceive the color of an object in isolation. We perceive the color of any object by comparing the light it reflects to the light that other objects in that scene reflect. As a result, we can perceive blue jeans as blue and bananas as yellow regardless of whether we are in dim light or bright light, outdoors or indoors, or wearing tinted glasses. This *tendency of an object to appear nearly the same color under a variety of lighting conditions* is called **color constancy.** (See Figure 4.16.)

In response to such observations, Edwin Land (the inventor of the Polaroid Land Camera) proposed the **retinex**

theory. According to this theory, *we perceive color through the cerebral cortex's comparison of various retinal patterns* (Figure 4.17). (*Retinex* is a combination of the words *retina* and *cortex*.) The cerebral cortex compares the patterns of light coming from different areas of the retina and synthesizes a color perception for each area (Land, Hubel, Livingstone, Perry, & Burns, 1983; Land & McCann, 1971).

The strongest evidence for this theory comes from brain-damaged patients. Damage to one region of the occipital cortex destroys color constancy (Wild, Butler, Carden, & Kulikowski, 1985; Zeki, 1993). To a person with such brain damage, an object that looks orange under one light looks red under another; yellow, greenish, or even white under still other lights. As the retinex theory predicts, the phenomenon of color constancy depends on the activity of the cerebral cortex.

In the 1800s, the trichromatic theory and the opponent-process theory were considered rival theories, but vision researchers today consider both of them, as well as the retinex theory, to be correct statements that happen to address different stages of visual processing. The trichromatic theory is certainly correct in stating that human color vision starts with three kinds of cones. The opponent-process theory explains how the bipolar cells and later cells organize color information. The retinex theory adds the final touch, noting that the cerebral cortex compares color information from various parts of the visual field.

SOMETHING TO THINK ABOUT

If you stare for a minute at a small green object on a white background and then look away, you will see a red afterimage. But if you stare at a green wall nearby so that you see nothing but green in all directions, then when you look away you do not see a red afterimage. Why not? ✳

Colorblindness

For a long time, people apparently assumed that anyone with normal vision could see and recognize colors

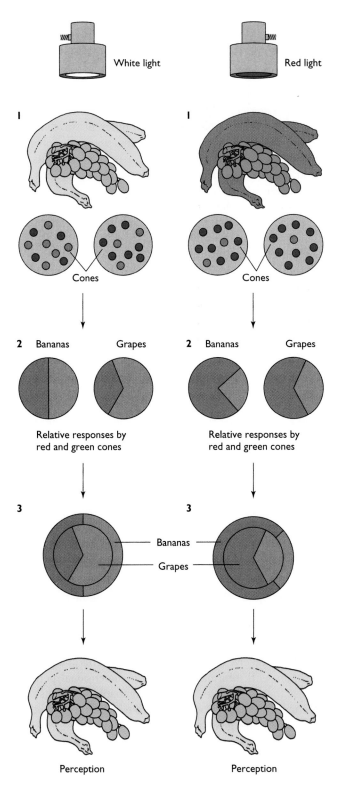

FIGURE 4.17 When bananas and grapes reflect red light, they excite a higher percentage of long-wavelength (red) cones than usual. According to the retinex theory, brain cells determine the red-green percentage for each fruit. Then cells in the visual cortex divide the "red-greenness" of the bananas by the "red-greenness" of the grapes to produce color sensations. In red and white light, the ratios between the fruits are nearly constant.

(Fletcher & Voke, 1985). Then, during the 1600s, the phenomenon of colorblindness (or color deficiency) was un-

ambiguously recognized. Here was the first clue that color vision is a function of our eyes and brains, and not just of the light itself.

The total inability to distinguish one color from another is extremely rare, except as a result of brain damage. However, about 4% of all people are partially colorblind. Investigators believe that most cases of colorblindness result from either the absence of one of the three types of cones or a decreased responsiveness by one of those types (Fletcher & Voke, 1985). People with a deficiency of the medium-wavelength cones are relatively insensitive to medium-wavelength (green) light. I do not mean that such people do not see such light; they perceive a green patch as almost gray, especially if the patch is small (Boynton, 1988).

The most common type of colorblindness is sometimes known as **red-green colorblindness.** People with red-green colorblindness *have difficulty distinguishing red from green and either red or green from yellow.* Actually, red-green colorblindness has two forms, *protanopia* and *deuteranopia.* People with protanopia lack long-wavelength cones; people with deuteranopia lack medium-wavelength cones. People with the rare *yellow-blue colorblindness* (also known as *tritanopia*) have trouble distinguishing yellows and blues. They are believed to lack short-wavelength cones.

 Figure 4.18 gives a crude but usually satisfactory test for red-green colorblindness. What do you see in each part of the figure? (To interpret your answers, refer to answer A on page 118.)

How does the world look to colorblind people? Their descriptions use all the usual color words: Roses are red, violets are blue, bananas are yellow, grass is green. But this does not mean that they perceive colors the same as does a person with normal color vision. Can they tell us what that "red" rose actually looks like to them? In most cases, no. Certain rare individuals, however, are red-green colorblind in one eye but have normal vision in the other eye. Because they know what the color words really mean (from experience with their normal eye), they can tell us what their colorblind eye sees. They say that objects that look red or green to the normal eye look yellow or yellow-gray to the colorblind eye (Marriott, 1976).

If you have normal color vision, Figure 4.19 will show you what it is like to be red-green colorblind. First cover part b, a typical item from a colorblindness test, and stare at part a, a red field, under a bright light for about a minute. (The brighter the light and the longer you stare, the greater the effect will be.) Then look at part b. Staring at the red field has fatigued your red cones, so you will now have only a weak sensation of red. As the red cones recover, you will see part b normally.

Now stare at part c, a green field, for about a minute and look at part b again. Because you have fatigued your green cones, the figure in b will stand out even more strongly than usual. In fact, certain red-green colorblind people may be able to see the number in b only after staring at c. (Refer to answer B on page 118.)

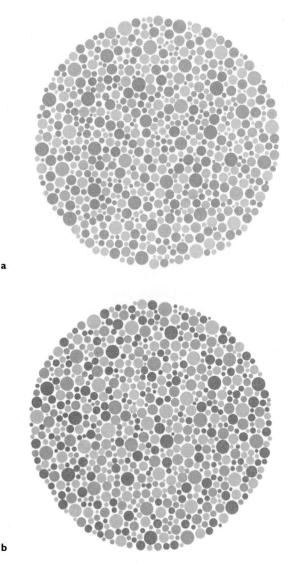

a

b

FIGURE 4.18 These items provide an informal test for red-green colorblindness, an inherited condition that mostly affects men. What do you see? Compare your answers to answer A, page 118.

SOMETHING TO THINK ABOUT

In the introduction to this chapter I suggested that we would see no new colors on another planet and that we cannot be certain that different people on Earth really have the same color experiences. Now try to explain the reasons behind those statements. ✻

Before there were any people or other color-sighted animals, was there any color on Earth? *No.* There was light, to be sure, and different objects reflected different wavelengths of light, but color exists only in brains, not in the objects themselves. Our vision is not just a copy of the outside world; it is a construction that enables us to interact with the world to our benefit.

To many readers, vision and our other senses seem more complicated than some of the later topics in this book, such as emotion. To some extent sensation may really be more complicated than emotion, but the apparent difference in complexity exists partly because researchers have learned so much more about the senses. The more we learn about any topic, the more sophisticated questions we can ask. The complexity of what we now know about vision is a tribute to many generations of researchers.

SUMMARY

✻ *Common misconceptions.* The eyes do not send out "sight rays," nor does the brain build little copies of the stimuli it senses. It converts or translates sensory stimuli into an arbitrary code that represents the information. (page 105)

✻ *Focus.* The cornea and lens focus the light that enters through the pupil of the eye. If the eye is not spherical or if the lens is not flexible, corrective lenses may be needed. (page 106)

✻ *Cones and rods.* The retina contains two kinds of receptors: cones and rods. Cones are specialized for detailed vision and color perception. Rods detect dim light. (page 107)

✻ *Blind spot.* The blind spot is the area of the retina through which the optic nerve exits; this area has no visual receptors and is therefore blind. (page 110)

✻ *Binocular rivalry.* Under normal circumstances, the two retinas receive similar information patterns and provide the brain with information for three-dimensional perception. If the two retinas receive incompatible patterns, we experience a competition in which one pattern or the other dominates at any given moment. (page 110)

FIGURE 4.19 These stimuli induce temporary red-green colorblindness and temporarily enhance color vision. First stare at pattern a under a bright light for about a minute, then look at b. What do you see? Next stare at c for a minute and look at b again. Now what do you see? Compare your answer to answer B, page 118.

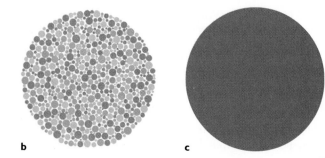

a   b   c

✳ *Color vision.* Color vision depends on three types of cones, each most sensitive to a particular range of light wavelengths. The cones transmit messages so that the bipolar and ganglion cells in the visual system are excited by light of one color and inhibited by light of the opposite color. Then the cerebral cortex compares the responses from different parts of the retina to determine the color of light coming from each area of the visual field. (page 111)

✳ *Colorblindness.* Complete colorblindness is rare. Certain people have difficulty distinguishing reds from greens; in rare cases, some have difficulty distinguishing yellows from blues. (page 114)

Suggestion for Further Reading

Hubel, D. H. (1988). *Eye, brain, and vision.* New York: Scientific American Library. A treatment by an investigator who shared the Nobel Prize in physiology and medicine for his research on the physiology of vision.

Terms

sensation   the conversion of energy from the environment into a pattern of response by the nervous system (page 104)

perception   the interpretation of sensory information (page 104)

stimulus   energy in the environment that affects what we do (page 105)

receptor   a specialized cell that converts environmental energies into signals for the nervous system (page 105)

electromagnetic spectrum   the continuum of all the frequencies of radiated energy (page 105)

pupil   the adjustable opening in the eye through which light enters (page 105)

iris   the colored structure on the surface of the eye, surrounding the pupil (page 105)

retina   a layer of visual receptors covering the back surface of the eyeball (page 106)

cornea   a rigid, transparent structure on the surface of the eyeball (page 106)

lens   a flexible structure that can vary its thickness to enable the eye to focus on objects at different distances (page 106)

accommodation of the lens   adjustment of the thickness of the lens to focus on objects at different distances (page 106)

presbyopia   decreased flexibility of the lens and therefore inability to focus on nearby objects (page 106)

myopia   nearsightedness; the inability to focus on distant objects (page 106)

hyperopia   farsightedness; the inability to focus on nearby objects (page 106)

glaucoma   a condition characterized by increased pressure within the eyeball, resulting in damage to the optic nerve and therefore a loss of vision (page 106)

cataract   a disorder in which the lens of the eye becomes cloudy (page 106)

cone   the type of visual receptor that is adapted for color vision, daytime vision, and detailed vision (page 107)

rod   the type of visual receptor that is adapted for vision in dim light (page 107)

fovea   the central part of the retina that has a greater density of receptors, especially cones, than any other part of the retina (page 107)

dark adaptation   a gradual improvement in the ability to see in dim light (page 109)

ganglion cells   neurons in the eye that receive input from bipolar cells, which in turn receive their input from the visual receptors (page 110)

optic nerve   a set of axons that extend from the ganglion cells of the eye to the thalamus and several other areas of the brain (page 110)

blind spot   the area where the optic nerve exits the retina (page 110)

binocular rivalry   alteration between seeing the pattern in the left retina and the pattern in the right retina (page 110)

trichromatic theory or **Young-Helmholtz theory**   the theory that color vision depends on the relative rate of response of three types of cones (page 111)

opponent-process theory (of color vision)   the theory that we perceive color in terms of a system of paired opposites: red versus green, yellow versus blue, and white versus black (page 112)

negative afterimage   a color that a person sees after staring at its opposite color for a while (page 114)

color constancy   the tendency of an object to appear nearly the same color under a variety of lighting conditions (page 114)

retinex theory   the theory that color perception results from the cerebral cortex's comparison of various retinal patterns (page 114)

red-green colorblindness   impaired ability to distinguish red from green and either red or green from yellow (page 115)

Answers to Concept Checks

1. If your vision is normal, then wearing glasses intended for a myopic person will make your vision blurry. Such glasses alter the light as though they were bringing the object closer to the viewer. Unless the glasses are very strong, you may not notice much difference when you are looking at distant objects, because you can adjust the lens of your eyes to compensate for what the glasses do. However, nearby objects will appear blurry in spite of the best compensations that the lenses of your eyes can make. (page 107)

2. The center of the retina consists entirely of cones. If you look slightly to the side, the light falls on an area of the retina that consists partly of rods, which are more sensitive to faint light. (page 108)

3. As do people, cats can adapt well to dim light. No animal, however, can see in complete darkness. Vision is the detection of light that strikes the eye. (Similarly, the X-ray vision attributed to the comic book character Superman is impossible. Even if he could send out X rays, he would not see anything unless those X rays bounced off an object and back into his eyes. (page 110)

4. You will see more objects in the periphery of your eye. The fovea contains only cones, which cannot become as sensitive as the rods do in the periphery. (page 110)

5. Although bright yellow-green and dim yellow-green light would evoke the same ratio of activity by the three cone

types, the total amount of activity would be greater for the bright yellow-green light. (page 112)

6. Ganglion cell 1 would be almost unaffected by yellow light. Yellow light would stimulate the long-wavelength cone, which excites ganglion cell 1, but it would stimulate the medium-wavelength cone, which inhibits ganglion cell 1, about equally. (page 113)

7. The afterimage is on your eye, not on the background. When you try to focus on a different part of the afterimage, you move your eyes and the afterimage moves with them. (page 114)

Answers to Other Questions in the Text

A. In Figure 4.18a, a person with normal color vision sees the numeral 74; in Figure 4.18b, the numeral 8.

B. In Figure 4.19b, you should see the numeral 29. After you have stared at the red circle in part a, the 29 in b may look less distinct than usual, as though you were red-green color-blind. After staring at the green circle, the 29 may be even *more* distinct than usual. If you do not see either of these effects at once, try again, but this time stare at a or c a little longer, *and* continue staring at b a little longer. The effect does not appear immediately, only after a few seconds.

Web Resources

IllusionWorks

www.illusionworks.com/

Billed as "the most comprehensive collection of optical and sensory illusions on the World Wide Web." There are dozens of illusions, a brief introduction to illusions and perception, comprehensive lists both of books published on illusions and of links to illusion, perception, and cognitive science sites, interactive illusion demonstrations (for which you will need a Java-enabled browser), and interactive antique illusion puzzles (for which you will need the proper Shockwave plug-in, available free at www.macromedia.com/shockwave/download/index.cgi).

MODULE 4.2

The Nonvisual Senses

How do hearing, the vestibular sense, skin senses, pain, taste, and olfaction work?

Consider these common expressions:

I *see* what you mean.
I *feel* sympathy toward your plight.
I am deeply *touched* by everyone's support and concern.
The Senate will *hold* hearings on the budget proposal.
She is a person of great *taste*.
He was *dizzy* with success.
The policies of this company *stink*.
That *sounds* like a good job offer.

Each sentence expresses an idea in terms of sensation, though we know that these terms are not meant to be taken literally. If you compliment people on their "fine taste," you are not referring to their tongues.

The broad, metaphorical use of terms of sensation is not accidental. Our thinking and brain activity deal mostly, if not entirely, with sensory stimuli. Perhaps you doubt that assertion: "What about abstract concepts?" you might object. "Sometimes I think about numbers, time, love, justice, and all sorts of other nonsensory concepts." Yes, but how did you learn those concepts? Didn't you learn numbers by counting objects you could see or touch? Didn't you learn about time by observing changes in sensory stimuli? Didn't you learn about love and justice from specific events that you saw, heard, and felt? Could you explain any abstract concept without referring to something you detect through your senses?

We have already considered how we detect light. Now let's discuss how we detect sounds, head tilt, skin stimulation, and chemicals.

Hearing

Fish detect vibrations in the water by means of a long row of touch receptors along their sides, called the *lateral line system.* The mammalian ear, which probably evolved as a modification of the lateral line system, converts sound waves into mechanical displacements of a membrane that a row of receptor cells can detect.

Sound waves are *vibrations of the air or of another medium.* They vary in both frequency and amplitude (Figure 4.20). The frequency of a sound wave is the number of *cycles (vibrations) that it goes through per second,* designated **hertz (Hz)**. **Pitch** is a *perception closely related to frequency.* We perceive a high-frequency sound wave as high pitched and a low-frequency sound as low pitched. **Loudness** is a *perception that depends on the amplitude of a sound wave*—the vertical range of its cycles. Other things being equal, the greater the *amplitude* of a sound, the louder it sounds to us. Because pitch and loudness are psychological experiences, however, they are influenced by factors other than the physical frequency and amplitude of sound waves. For example, tones of different frequencies may not sound equally loud, even though they have the same physical amplitude.

The ear, a complicated organ, converts relatively weak sound waves into more intense waves of pressure in the *fluid-filled canals of the snail-shaped organ* called the **cochlea** (KOCK-lee-uh), *which contains the receptors for hearing* (Figure 4.21). When sound waves strike the eardrum, they cause it to vibrate. The eardrum is connected to three tiny bones: the hammer, the anvil, and the stirrup (also known by their Latin names: malleus, incus, and stapes). As the weak vibrations of the large eardrum travel

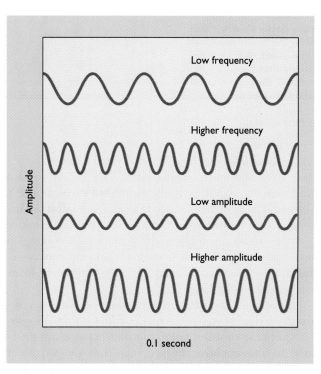

FIGURE 4.20 The period (time) between the peaks of a sound wave determines the frequency of the sound; we experience frequencies as different pitches. The vertical range, or amplitude, of a wave determines the sound's intensity and loudness.

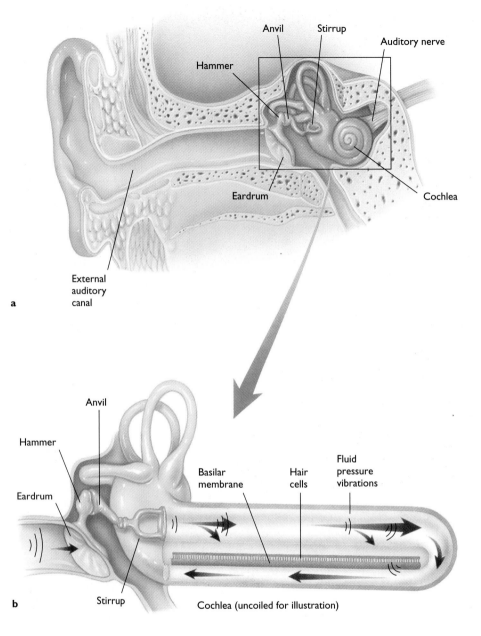

FIGURE 4.21 When sound waves strike the eardrum (a), they cause it to vibrate. The eardrum is connected to three tiny bones—the hammer, anvil, and stirrup—that convert the sound wave into a series of strong vibrations in the fluid-filled cochlea (b). Those vibrations displace the hair cells along the basilar membrane in the cochlea, which is aptly named after the Greek word for *snail*. Here, the dimensions of the cochlea have been changed to make the general principles clear.

through these bones, they are transformed into stronger vibrations of the much smaller stirrup. The stirrup in turn transmits the vibrations to the fluid-filled cochlea, where the vibrations displace hair cells along the **basilar membrane,** *a thin structure within the cochlea.* These hair cells, which act much like touch receptors on the skin, are connected to neurons whose axons form the auditory nerve. Impulses are transmitted along this pathway to the brain areas responsible for hearing.

A person can lose hearing in two ways. One is **conduction deafness,** which *results when the bones connected to the eardrum fail to transmit sound waves properly to the cochlea.* Surgery can sometimes correct conduction deafness by removing whatever is obstructing the movement of those bones. A person with conduction deafness can still hear his or her own voice, because it is conducted through the skull bones to the cochlea, bypassing the eardrum altogether. The other type of hearing loss is

nerve deafness, which *results from damage to the cochlea, the hair cells, or the auditory nerve.* Nerve deafness can result from heredity, from multiple sclerosis and other diseases, or from prolonged exposure to loud noises. Nerve deafness is permanent and cannot be corrected by surgery.

Hearing aids can compensate for hearing loss in most people with either conduction deafness or nerve deafness (Moore, 1989). Hearing aids merely increase the intensity of the sound, however, so they are of little help to people with severe damage to the cochlea or the auditory nerve. Many people have hearing impairments for only certain frequencies, though. For example, people with damage to certain parts of the cochlea have trouble hearing high frequencies or medium-range frequencies. Modern hearing aids can be adjusted to intensify only a certain range of sounds, so that they do not intensify sounds that are already loud enough.

Hearing is the sensing of vibrations. Evelyn Glennie, profoundly deaf since childhood, has become a famous percussionist. Although she cannot hear her music, she detects the vibrations through her stocking feet.

Pitch Perception

Adult humans can hear sound waves from about 15–20 hertz to about 15,000–20,000 Hz (cycles per second). The low frequencies are perceived as deep tones of low pitch; the high frequencies are perceived as tones of high pitch. The upper limit of hearing declines suddenly after exposure to loud noises and declines steadily as a person grows older. Thus, children can hear high-frequency sounds that adults do not.

We hear pitch by different mechanisms at different frequencies. At low frequencies (up to about 100 Hz), the *basilar membrane in the cochlea vibrates in synchrony with the sound waves; that is, it produces action potentials at the same frequency as the sound.* This is the **frequency principle.** A sound with a frequency of 50 Hz excites each hair cell along the membrane 50 times per second, thus sending 50 impulses per second to the brain.

At higher frequencies, the basilar membrane continues to vibrate in synchrony with the sound waves, but the individual hair cells cannot keep pace. (A neuron cannot fire more than about 1,000 action potentials per second, and it cannot maintain that pace for long.) Even so, each vibration of the membrane excites at least a few hair cells, and *groups of them, volleys, respond to each vibration by producing an action potential* (Rose, Brugge, Anderson, & Hind, 1967). This is known as the **volley principle.** Thus, a tone at 1000 Hz might send impulses to the brain 1,000 times per second, even though no single neuron was firing that rapidly. Volleys are adequate for detecting most sounds of speech and music. However, even volleys cannot keep pace with frequencies approaching 5000 Hz (as compared to 4186 Hz, the highest note on a piano).

At high frequencies, sound waves of different frequencies cause vibrations at different locations along the basilar membrane. The membrane is thin and stiff near the stirrup and wide and floppy at the other end. Consequently, *high-frequency sounds cause maximum vibration near the stirrup end, and lower-frequency sounds cause maximum vibration at points farther along the membrane, thereby stimulating hair cells at different locations.* This is the **place principle.** At frequencies less than about 1000 Hz, the difference in location between one tone and another is imprecise, so the place principle does not apply at low frequencies. We do not need it at low frequencies, however, because the frequency and volley principles serve our purposes quite well. The place principle starts to become helpful beyond 1000 Hz and especially beyond 5000 Hz. In short, we detect tones up to about 1000 Hz by the frequency and volley principles, tones above 5,000 Hz by the place principle, and intermediate tones by a combination of volleys and place (Goldstein, 1989; Zwislocki, 1981). Figure 4.22 summarizes the three principles of pitch perception.

CONCEPT CHECKS

8. Suppose a mouse emits a soft, high-frequency squeak in a room full of people. Which kinds of people are least likely to hear the squeak?
9. When hair cells at one point along the basilar membrane produce 50 impulses per second, we hear a

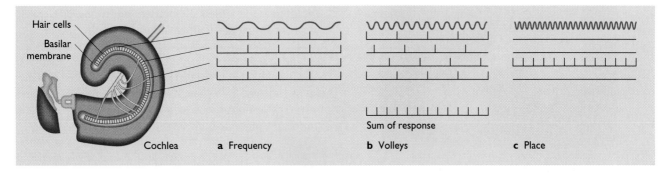

Hair cells
Basilar membrane
Cochlea   **a** Frequency   **b** Volleys   Sum of response   **c** Place

FIGURE 4.22 The auditory system responds differently to low-, medium-, and high-frequency tones. (a) At low frequencies, hair cells at many points along the basilar membrane produce impulses in synchrony with the sound waves. (b) At medium frequencies, different cells produce impulses in synchrony with different sound waves, but the group as a whole still produces one or more impulses for each wave. (c) At high frequencies, only one point along the basilar membrane vibrates; hair cells at other locations remain still.

tone at 5000 Hz. What do we hear when the same hair cells produce 100 impulses per second? (Check your answers on pages 130–131.)

Localization of Sounds

When you hear something, the stimulus is actually on the basilar membrane of your ear, but you do not experience it as such. You experience the sound as "out there," and you can generally estimate its approximate place of origin. How do you do that?

The auditory system determines the direction of a source of sound by comparing the messages coming from the two ears. If a sound is coming from a source directly in front, the messages will arrive at the two ears at the same time and will be equal in loudness. If the sound is coming from a source on the left, however, it will arrive at the left ear slightly before it arrives at the right ear, and it will be louder in the left ear (Figure 4.23). You do not hear two sounds; you have an experience of a single sound coming from the left. A difference between the messages in the two ears indicates how far the sound source is to the left or right of center. (Someone who wears a hearing aid in just one ear may localize sounds inaccurately.)

FIGURE 4.23 The stereophonic hearing of our ears enables us to determine where a sound is coming from. The ear located closest to the sound will receive the sound waves first. A change of less than one ten-thousandth of one second can alter our perception of the location of a sound source.

The auditory system can also detect the approximate distance of a sound source. If a sound grows louder, you interpret it as coming closer. If two sounds differ in pitch, you assume the one with more high-frequency tones is closer. (Low-frequency tones carry better over a long distance than high-frequency tones do.) However, loudness and frequency tell you only the *relative* distances of sound sources; neither one provides information about the *absolute* distance. The only cue for absolute distance is the amount of reverberation (Mershon & King, 1975). In a closed room, you will first hear the sound waves that come directly from the source and then, after a delay, the waves that are reflected off the walls, floor, ceiling, and objects in the room. The more distant the source, the greater the percentage of reflected and delayed sound you will hear. When you hear many reflected sounds (echoes), you judge the source of the sound to be far away. In a noisy room, the echoes are hard to hear, so people have trouble estimating the distances of sounds; because they hear few echoes, they interpret all sounds as coming from a short distance (McMurtry & Mershon, 1985).

CONCEPT CHECKS

10. Why is it difficult to tell whether a sound is coming from directly in front of or directly behind you?
11. Suppose you are listening to a monaural (nonstereo) radio. Can the station play sounds that you will localize as coming from different directions, such as left, center, and right? Can it play sounds that you will localize as coming from different distances? Why or why not? (Check your answers on page 131.)

The Vestibular Sense

In the inner ear on each side of the head, adjacent to the structures responsible for hearing, is a structure called the *vestibule*. The **vestibular sense** that it controls *tells us the direction of tilt and amount of acceleration of the head and the position of the head with respect to gravity*. It plays a key role in posture and balance and is responsible for the sensations we experience when we are riding on a roller coaster or sitting in an airplane during takeoff.

The vestibular sense also enables us to keep our eyes fixated on a target even when our head is moving. When you walk down the street, you can keep your eyes fixated on a distant street sign, even though your head is bobbing up and down. The vestibular sense detects each head movement and controls the movement of your eyes to compensate for it.

To illustrate: Try to read this page while you are jiggling the book up and down and from side to side, keeping your head steady. Then hold the book steady and move your head up and down and from side to side. If you are like most people, you will find it much easier to read when you are moving your head

Twisting, turning, and tilting activate vestibular sensation, which reports the position of the head.

than when you are jiggling the book. That is because your vestibular sense keeps your eyes fixated on the print during head movements. People who have suffered injury to their vestibular sense report that their vision is blurry while they are walking. To read street signs or clocks, they must come to a stop and hold their head steady.

The vestibular system is composed of three semicircular canals, oriented in three separate directions, and two otolith organs (Figure 4.24b). The *semicircular canals* are lined with hair cells and filled with a jellylike substance. When the body accelerates in any direction, the jellylike substance in the corresponding semicircular canal pushes against the hair cells, which send messages to the brain. The two *otolith organs* shown in Figure 4.24b also contain hair cells (Figure 4.24c), which lie next to the *otoliths* (calcium carbonate particles). Depending on which way the head tilts, the particles move about in the direction of gravitational pull and excite different sets of hair cells. The otolith organs report the direction from which gravity is pulling and tell us which way is "up."

What happens if the otoliths fail to provide reliable information? For astronauts in the zero-gravity environment of outer space, the otoliths provide no useful information about up or down; indeed, the up-down dimension is almost meaningless to them. Instead, they learn to rely entirely on visual signals, such as closeness to one object or distance from another (Lackner, 1993).

The Cutaneous Senses

What we commonly think of as the sense of touch actually consists of several partly independent senses: pressure on the skin, warmth, cold, pain, vibration, movement across the skin, and stretch of the skin. These sensations depend on several kinds of receptors in the skin, as Figure 4.25 shows (Iggo & Andres, 1982). A pinch on the skin feels different from a tickle, and both feel different from a cut or a burn, because each of these stimuli excites different recep-

tors. Collectively, these sensations are known as the **cutaneous senses,** meaning the *skin senses.* Although they are most prominent in the skin, we have some of the same receptors in our internal organs as well, enabling us to feel internal pain, pressure, or temperature changes. Therefore, the cutaneous senses are sometimes known by the broader term *somatosensory system,* meaning *body-sensory system.*

On the fingertips, the lips, and other highly sensitive areas of skin, the receptors are densely packed, and each receptor detects stimulation in only a small area of the skin. On the back and other less sensitive areas, the receptors are scattered more widely, and each one is responsible for detecting stimulation over a large surface. Similarly, much

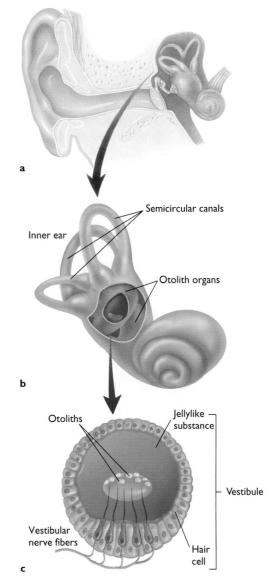

F I G U R E 4.24 (a) Location of and (b) structures of the vestibule. (c) Moving your head or body displaces hair cells that report the tilt of your head and the direction and acceleration of movement.

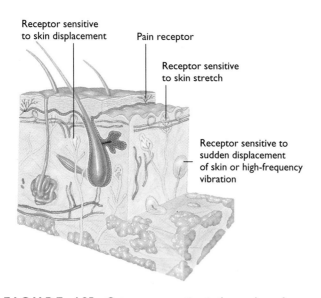

Receptor sensitive
to skin displacement

Pain receptor

Receptor sensitive
to skin stretch

Receptor sensitive to
sudden displacement
of skin or high-frequency
vibration

FIGURE 4.25 Cutaneous sensation is the product of
many kinds of receptors, each sensitive to a particular kind of
information.

more of the parietal lobe is devoted to sensation from the
lips and fingers than from the less sensitive areas.

If you ask someone to place an everyday object in your
hand (such as a pencil or a spoon), without showing it to
you or telling you what it is, you can probably identify the
object just by feeling it. You will probably fail to identify a
more complicated or less familiar object, however, such as a
scale model of the Eiffel Tower, even though you could
identify it easily by sight. With extensive practice, you could
improve your ability to identify objects by touch. Subjects in
one study felt raised-line drawings, like those in Figure
4.26, without seeing them. Some of the subjects were
sighted; some were blind since birth; and some had become
blind later in life. Most sighted people found it very difficult
to identify what the drawings represented, presumably because they had little practice at paying close attention to
touch. People blind since birth also had little success with
this task, but for a different reason: A raised-line drawing of
an umbrella or similar object makes little sense to someone
who has never seen a drawing of the same object. In contrast, people who had lost their vision later in life were able
to identify many of the objects (Heller, 1989). They had the
advantage of previous experience with visual drawings, plus
years of practice in paying close attention to touch.

Pain

Pain receptors are simple, bare nerve endings that send
messages to the spinal cord. The experience of pain, however, is a complicated mixture of sensation (the information
about tissue damage) and emotion (the unpleasant reaction). The sensory and emotional qualities are governed by
different parts of the brain (Craig, Bushnell, Zhang, &
Blomqvist, 1994; Fernandez & Turk, 1992), so the emotional reaction can be either much stronger or weaker than
the sensation itself.

The Gate Theory of Pain   You visit a physician because of severe pain, but as soon as the physician tells you
the problem is minor and nothing to worry about, the pain
starts to subside. Have you ever had such an experience?
Pain can increase or decrease greatly just because of people's expectations. Recall the term *placebo* from Chapter 2:
A placebo is a drug or other procedure that has no pharmacological properties, other than those that result from people's expectations; researchers ordinarily give placebos to
control groups. Placebos can produce such large effects on
pain that they become a research topic on their own. Consider the following: In one experiment, college students
were given a smelly brownish liquid on the index finger of
one hand. It was in fact just a placebo, but they were told
that it was a painkiller. Then the students were given a
painful pinch stimulus to that finger and the index finger of
the other hand. They consistently reported the pain on the
finger with the placebo to be less intense than the pain on
the other finger (Montgomery & Kirsch, 1996). How placebos work is far from clear, but these results eliminate mere
relaxation, which would presumably reduce pain on both
hands equally.

Think about the various times you have had cuts or
other minor injuries. Under most conditions, you have
probably found that you can relieve the pain by gently mas-
saging the skin near the cut, or by applying either cold packs

FIGURE 4.26 Sighted and blind subjects felt these raised-
line drawings and tried to identify what they represented. Most
sighted subjects and subjects blind since birth found the task very
difficult and seldom answered correctly. Subjects who had become blind later in life performed much better (Heller, 1989).

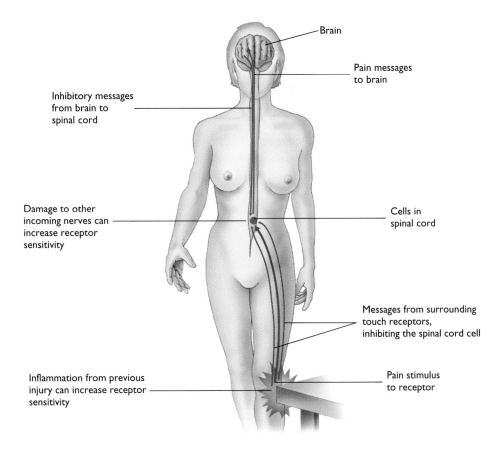

Brain

Pain messages
to brain

Inhibitory messages
from brain to
spinal cord

Damage to other
incoming nerves can
increase receptor
sensitivity

Cells in
spinal cord

Messages from surrounding
touch receptors,
inhibiting the spinal cord cell

Inflammation from previous
injury can increase receptor
sensitivity

Pain stimulus
to receptor

FIGURE 4.27 Pain messages from the skin are relayed from spinal cord cells to the brain. According to the gate theory of pain, those spinal cord cells serve as a gate that can block or enhance the signal. The proposed neural circuitry is simplified in this diagram. Green lines indicate axons with excitatory inputs; red lines indicate axons with inhibitory inputs.

or hot packs (Rollman, 1991). However, when you have had a sunburn, you probably found that even a light touch anywhere on the sunburned area, or stepping into a hot shower, became excruciatingly painful (Devor, 1996). A variety of processes can either increase or decrease the pain caused by a particular injury.

Because of observations such as these, Ronald Melzack and P. D. Wall (1965) proposed the **gate theory** of pain, the idea that *pain messages must pass through a gate, presumably in the spinal cord, that can block these messages.* For example, rubbing the surrounding skin sends inhibitory messages to the spinal cord, closing the pain gates. Various pleasant or distracting brain activities can also send inhibitory messages. Later researchers found that the gate can also enhance the pain messages; for example, damage to some of the incoming axons can induce increased sensitivity of the spinal cord neurons, so that weak stimulation can seem very painful. In short, the activities of the rest of the nervous system can facilitate or inhibit the transmission of pain messages (Figure 4.27).

Mechanisms of Decreasing Pain   Pain alerts us to an injury. A small percentage of people are completely insensitive to pain. They can burn themselves by picking up hot objects; they can scald their tongues on hot coffee; they can cut themselves without realizing it; they can bite their tongues hard, possibly even biting off the tip; they can sit in

a single position for hours without growing uncomfortable, thereby damaging their bones and tendons (Comings & Amromin, 1974).

Although pain messages serve an essential function by alerting us to danger and damage, a prolonged, intense pain message is unnecessary and sometimes disruptive. One way to reduce the sensation of pain is to provide some distraction. In terms of the gate theory, a distraction closes the pain gate. For example, surgery patients in a room with a pleasant view complain less about pain, take less painkilling medicine, and recover faster than do patients in a windowless room or a room with a poor view (Ulrich, 1984).

Pain messages in the nervous system release a neurotransmitter called **substance P,** as well as several others. The neurons that have receptors for substance P are essential for pain; after injections of chemicals that destroy those neurons, laboratory animals have become almost unresponsive to many kinds of painful stimuli (Mantyh et al., 1997). Another set of synapses release **endorphins,** *neurotransmitters that inhibit the release of substance P and thereby decrease pain sensations* (Reichling, Kwiat, & Basbaum, 1988; Terman, Shavitt, Lewis, Cannon, & Liebeskind, 1984). (See Figure 4.28.) The term *endorphin* is a combination of the terms *endogenous* (self-produced) and *morphine.* The drug morphine has long been known for its exceptional ability to inhibit pain; it does so by stim-

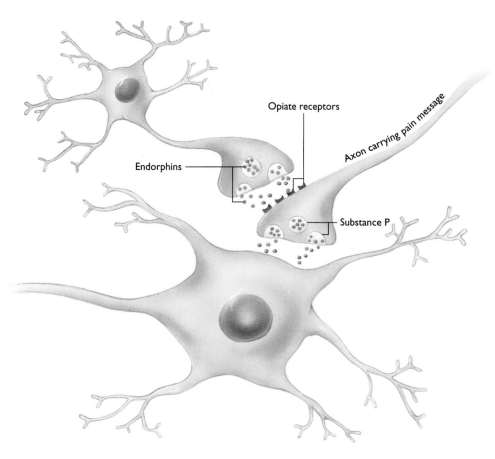

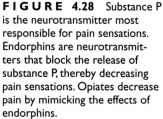

FIGURE 4.28 Substance P is the neurotransmitter most responsible for pain sensations. Endorphins are neurotransmitters that block the release of substance P, thereby decreasing pain sensations. Opiates decrease pain by mimicking the effects of endorphins.

ulating the endorphin synapses in the brain. A variety of nondrug stimuli can also release endorphins. Under some circumstances, a painful stimulus itself releases endorphins so that exposure to one painful stimulus decreases sensitivity to the next painful stimulus (Terman & Liebeskind, 1986). Pleasant stimuli can also release endorphins. (That effect may help to explain why a pleasant view helps to ease postsurgical pain.) In short, endorphins are a powerful method, perhaps the main method, of closing pain "gates."

Paradoxically, another method of decreasing pain begins by inducing it. The *chemical* **capsaicin** stimulates receptors that respond to painful heat (Caterina et al., 1997), and thereby *causes the release of substance P.* Injecting capsaicin or rubbing it on the skin produces a temporary burning or stinging sensation (Karrer & Bartoshuk, 1991; Yarsh, Farb, Leeman, & Jessell, 1979). However, because capsaicin releases substance P faster than the neurons can resynthesize it, after the burning sensation subsides, the result is a fairly long-lasting decrease in pain sensitivity. Several skin creams intended for the relief of aching muscles contain capsaicin. (Don't rub them on right before you go to bed. They produce a burning sensation before they relieve the muscle pain.)

Jalapeños and other hot peppers contain capsaicin. The reason that they taste hot is that their capsaicin releases enough substance P from the tongue to cause a stinging, hot sensation.

CONCEPT CHECKS

12. Naloxone, a drug used as an antidote for an overdose of morphine, is known to block the endorphin synapses. How could we use naloxone to determine whether a pleasant stimulus releases endorphins?

13. Psychologist Linda Bartoshuk recommends candies containing moderate amounts of jalapeño peppers as a treatment for people with pain in the mouth. Why? (Check your answers on page 131.)

The Chemical Senses: Taste and Smell

Most textbooks on sensation concentrate on vision and hearing; some ignore taste and smell or include them in a chapter titled "The Other Senses" or even "The Minor Senses." For most of the animal kingdom, however, these senses are not so minor. If rats or raccoons wrote sensation textbooks, they would probably devote as much coverage to taste and smell as they would to hearing, and they would list vision as one of the "minor senses." Many invertebrates have no vision or hearing at all; they survive with only chemical senses and touch.

Taste

Vision and hearing enable us to find food and water, to avoid danger, to keep our balance, and to find suitable mates. The sense of **taste,** which *detects chemicals on the tongue,* serves just one function: It tells us what to eat and drink.

The *taste receptors are* in the **taste buds,** *located in the folds on the surface of the tongue,* almost exclusively along the outside edge of the tongue in adults (Figure 4.29). (Children's taste buds are more widely scattered.) Try this demonstration (based on Bartoshuk, 1991): Soak something small (the tip of a paper napkin will do) in sugar water, salt water, or vinegar. Then dab it onto the center of your tongue. You will taste nothing. Then slowly move the soaked substance toward the side of the tongue. Suddenly, you taste it.

If you go in the other direction (first touching the side of the tongue and then moving toward the center), you will continue to taste the substance even when it reaches the center of your tongue. The explanation is not that you suddenly grew new taste buds. Rather, your taste buds provide no information about location. Once you have stimulated the taste buds near the edge of the tongue, you will continue tasting the substance, but the taste receptors do not tell you *where* you are tasting the substance. If you now stimulate *touch* receptors elsewhere on your tongue, your brain interprets the taste perception as coming from the spot you are touching, even though the taste sensation is in fact coming from a different location (the side of your tongue).

Different Types of Taste Receptors   Researchers now have a reasonably clear understanding of the structures of the taste receptors and how they work (Margolskee, 1993). Actually, long before neuroscientists began characterizing taste receptors, behavioral researchers had solid evidence that different tastes depend on different kinds of receptors—probably four kinds, representing sweet, sour, salty, and bitter. That conclusion rested partly on demonstrations that people can match most tastes by mixing sweet, sour, salty, and bitter substances (Schiffman & Erickson, 1971). The conclusion was also supported by evidence that certain procedures can affect one taste without affecting others, presumably by acting on only one type of receptor. For example, did you ever drink a glass of orange juice just after brushing your teeth? How can something that ordinarily tastes so good suddenly taste so bad? The reason is that most toothpastes contain sodium lauryl sulfate, a chemical that weakens sweet tastes and intensifies sour and bitter tastes (Schiffman, 1983).

People from different parts of the world have different taste preferences. Contrast, for example, Greek cuisine, Mexican cuisine, and Chinese cuisine. Do the different cultural food preferences relate in any way to differences in people's sense of taste? Evidently not. People are about the same throughout the world in their ability to taste various substances (e.g., Laing et al., 1993). Their food preferences depend mainly on what is familiar to them.

Olfaction

Olfaction is the *sense of smell.* The olfactory receptors, located on the mucous membrane in the rear air passages of the nose (Figure 4.30b), detect the presence of certain air-

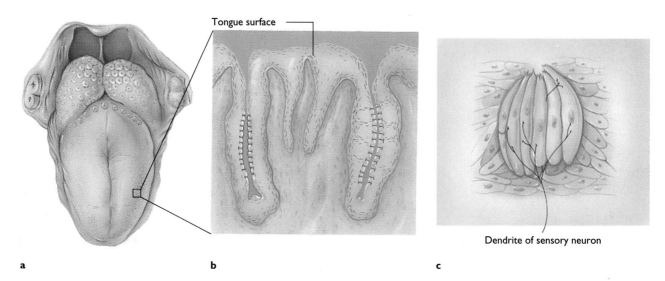

a   **b**   **c**

FIGURE 4.29 (a) The tongue, a powerful muscle used for speaking and eating: Taste buds, which react to chemicals dissolved in saliva, are located along the edge of the tongue in adult humans but are more widely distributed in children. (b) A cross section through part of the surface of the tongue, showing taste buds. (c) A cross section of one taste bud. Each taste bud has about 50 receptor cells within it.

borne molecules. Chemically, these receptors are much like synaptic receptors, except that they are stimulated by chemicals from the environment instead of chemicals released by other neurons. The axons of the olfactory receptors form the olfactory tract, which extends to the olfactory bulbs at the base of the brain.

How many kinds of olfactory receptors do we have? Investigators have long known that color vision depends on three kinds of receptors; they have also long known approximately how many receptor types we have for hearing, touch, and taste. However, until 1991 researchers had virtually no idea how many types of receptors existed for olfaction.

In principle, researchers can determine the number of receptor types through behavioral data, without chemically isolating the receptors. With color vision, for example, the researchers of the 1800s established that people can mix three colors of light in various amounts to match any other color. Therefore, even before the technology existed to examine the cones in the retina, researchers had reason to believe that the retina has three kinds of cones. In taste, the fact that we can mix sweet, sour, salty, and bitter substances to match almost any other taste implies that the tongue has perhaps only four kinds of taste receptors. Regarding olfaction, however, no one knew how many kinds of receptors to expect. Can people match all possible odors by mixing appropriate amounts of three, four, seven, or ten "primary" odors? or do they need 50, 100, or what? No researcher had ever demonstrated that it was possible to match all the possible odors by mixing any number of primaries.

Perhaps it is just as well that no one spent a lifetime investigating this issue. In 1991, Linda Buck and Richard Axel used the latest biochemical technology to demonstrate that the nose has at least a hundred types of olfactory receptors, and probably several hundred (Buck & Axel, 1991). In most cases, a given receptor responds well to only a limited family of odorant molecules (Ressler, Sullivan, & Buck, 1994). We do not yet know exactly how the brain makes sense of hundreds of channels of olfactory information (Figure 4.31). What we do know is that our olfactory system is able to detect and discriminate among an enormous number of possible molecules. When perfume chemists synthesize a brand-new molecule, people do not need to evolve a new receptor to detect it; we can detect any chemical with some combination of the receptors we already have.

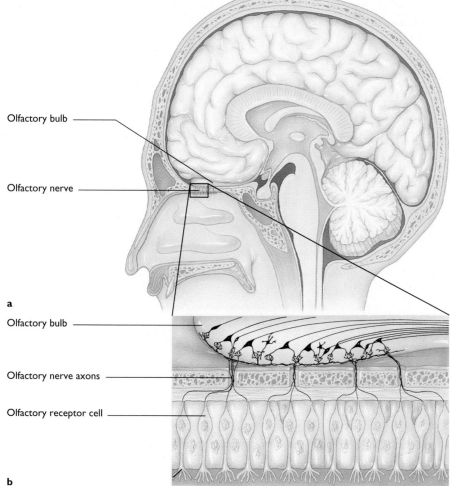

Olfactory bulb

Olfactory nerve

a

Olfactory bulb

Olfactory nerve axons

Olfactory receptor cell

b

FIGURE 4.30 The olfactory receptor cells lining the nasal cavity send information to the olfactory bulb in the brain. There are at least 100 types of receptors with specialized responses to airborne chemicals.

Still, humans' olfactory abilities are unimpressive compared to most other mammals. A single olfactory receptor is probably about as sensitive in humans as it is in any other species, but most other mammals have a greater number of receptors. For example, trained dogs can track a person's olfactory trail across fields and through woods. It is difficult (though humorous) to imagine a human even attempting such a task. People can improve their olfactory discrimination by practice, however. For example, professional wine tasters become highly skilled at discriminating one wine odor from another (Bende & Nordin, 1997).

Olfaction is particularly important for food selection. Neurons in the prefrontal cortex receive both taste and olfactory information, producing the combined sensation that we call *flavor*. These cells also receive input that indicates hunger, and they respond vigorously to the flavor of a food only when the individual is hungry (Rolls, 1997).

Olfaction also serves social functions, especially in nonhuman mammals that identify one another by means of **pheromones,** *odorous chemicals they release into the environment.* Pheromones act primarily on the vomeronasal organ, a set of receptors near, but separate from, the standard olfactory receptors (Monti-Bloch, Jennings-White, Dolberg, & Berliner, 1994). In nearly all nonhuman mammals, the males rely on pheromones to distinguish sexually receptive females from unreceptive females.

Humans prefer *not* to recognize one another by smell. The deodorant and perfume industries exist for the sole purpose of removing and covering up human odors. But perhaps we respond to pheromones anyway, at least under certain conditions. For example, young women who are in frequent contact, such as roommates in a college dormitory, tend to synchronize their menstrual cycles, probably as a result of pheromones they secrete (McClintock, 1971). One study examined women in Bedouin Arab families. The advantages of studying that culture are that the mother and

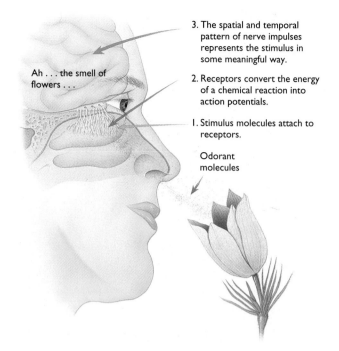

3. The spatial and temporal pattern of nerve impulses represents the stimulus in some meaningful way.

2. Receptors convert the energy of a chemical reaction into action potentials.

1. Stimulus molecules attach to receptors.

Ah . . . the smell of flowers . . .

Odorant molecules

F I G U R E   4.31   Olfaction, like any other sensory system, converts physical energy into a complex pattern of brain activity.

sisters within a family have extensive daily contact, unmarried women have almost no contact with men, and virtually none of the unmarried women and few of the married women use oral contraceptives. Thus pheromones have a maximum opportunity to show their effects in Bedouin culture. The results showed that the women in most families were at least partly synchronized; they might not begin to menstruate on exactly the same day, but they were close (Weller & Weller, 1997).

THE MESSAGE
Sensory Systems

The world as experienced by a bat (which can hear frequencies of 100,000 Hz) or a dog (which can discriminate among odors that you and I would never notice) or a mouse (which depends on its whiskers when exploring the world) is in many ways a different world from the one that people experience. The function of our senses is not to tell us about everything in the world, but to alert us to the information we are most likely to use, given our way of life.

SUMMARY

✱   *Pitch.* At low frequencies of sound, we identify pitch by the frequency of vibrations on the basilar membrane. At intermediate frequencies, we identify pitch by volleys of responses from a variety of neurons. At high frequencies, we identify pitch by the area of the basilar membrane that vibrates most strongly. (page 121)

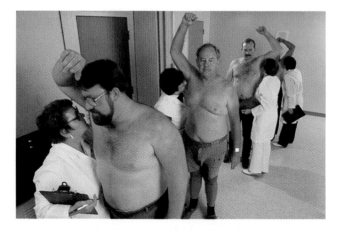

Professional deodorant tester: That's a career option you probably never even considered. Secret, Ban, Arrid—as their names suggest, U.S. industries spend millions of dollars developing and promoting deodorants and antiperspirants so that we can secretly banish sweat and have arid armpits.

✳ *Localizing sounds.* We localize the source of a sound by detecting differences in the time and loudness of the sounds our two ears receive. We localize the distance of a sound source mostly by the amount of reverberation, or echoes, following the main sound. (page 122)

✳ *Vestibular system.* The vestibular system tells us about the movement of the head and its position with respect to gravity. The vestibular system enables us to keep our eyes fixated on an object while the rest of our body is in motion. (page 122)

✳ *Cutaneous receptors.* We experience many types of sensation on the skin, each dependent on different receptors. The fingertips, lips, and face have especially rich supplies of such receptors. (page 123)

✳ *Pain.* The experience of pain can be greatly inhibited or enhanced by other simultaneous experiences, including touch to surrounding skin or the person's expectations. Pain depends largely on stimulation of neurons that are sensitive to the neurotransmitter substance P, which can be inhibited by endorphins. (page 124)

✳ *Taste receptors.* Even before researchers identified the taste receptors, they knew that there must be at least four kinds, because certain procedures affect one taste quality (such as sweetness) without affecting the others. An adult human has taste receptors only along the edges of the tongue. (page 127)

✳ *Olfactory receptors.* The olfactory system—the sense of smell—depends on at least a hundred types of receptors, each with its own special sensitivity. Olfaction is important for many behaviors, including food selection and (especially in mammals) identification of potential mates. (page 128)

Suggestions for Further Reading

Heller, M. A., & Schiff, W. (1991). *The psychology of touch.* Hillsdale, NJ: Erlbaum. Describes research on touch and how people learn to use it for Braille reading and other functions.

McLaughlin, S., & Margolskee, R. F. (1994). The sense of taste. *American Scientist, 82,* 538–545. Highly informative discussion of the physiology and psychology of taste.

Zwislocki, J. J. (1981). Sound analysis in the ear: A history of discoveries. *American Scientist, 69,* 184–192. Review of research on the mechanisms of hearing.

Terms

sound waves   vibrations of the air or of another medium (page 119)

hertz (Hz)   a unit of frequency representing one cycle (vibration) per second (page 119)

pitch   a perception closely related to the frequency of sound waves (page 119)

loudness   a perception that depends on the amplitude of a sound wave (page 119)

cochlea   the snail-shaped, fluid-filled structure that contains the receptors for hearing (page 119)

basilar membrane   a thin structure in the cochlea that vibrates after sound waves strike the eardrum (page 120)

conduction deafness   hearing loss that results when the bones connected to the eardrum fail to transmit sound waves properly to the cochlea (page 120)

nerve deafness   hearing loss that results from damage to the cochlea, the hair cells, or the auditory nerve (page 120)

frequency principle   identification of pitch by the frequency of action potentials in neurons along the basilar membrane of the cochlea, synchronized with the frequency of sound waves (page 121)

volley principle   identification of pitch by groups of hair cells responding to each vibration by producing an action potential (page 121)

place principle   identification of pitch by determining which auditory neurons, coming from which part of the basilar membrane, are most active (page 121)

vestibular sense   a specialized sense that detects the direction of tilt and amount of acceleration of the head and the position of the head with respect to gravity (page 122)

cutaneous senses   the skin senses, including pressure on the skin, warmth, cold, pain, vibration, movement across the skin, and stretch of the skin (page 123)

gate theory   the proposal that pain messages must pass through a gate, probably in the spinal cord, that can block these messages (page 125)

substance P   a neurotransmitter responsible for much of the transmission of pain information in the nervous system (page 125)

endorphin   any of the neurotransmitters that decrease the perception of pain (page 125)

capsaicin   a chemical that stimulates the release of substance P (page 126)

taste   the sensory system that responds to chemicals on the tongue (page 127)

taste bud   the site of the taste receptors, located in one of the folds on the surface of the tongue (page 127)

olfaction   the sense of smell; the detection of chemicals in contact with the membranes inside the nose (page 127)

pheromone   an odorous chemical, released by an animal, that changes how other members of the species respond to that animal socially (page 129)

Answers to Concept Checks

8. Obviously, the people farthest from the mouse are least likely to hear it. In addition, older people would be less likely than young people are to hear the squeak, because the ability to hear high frequencies declines in old age. Another group unlikely to hear the squeak are those who have had repeated exposure to loud noises. For this reason, you should avoid attending loud rock concerts, and listening to recorded music played at a loud volume, especially when you listen on a Walkman or similar device. You could damage your hearing in the long run, even if you do not realize it now. (page 121)

9. We still hear a tone at 5000 Hz, but it is louder than before. For high-frequency tones, the pitch we hear depends on which hair cells are most active, not how many impulses per second they fire. (page 121)

10. We localize sounds by comparing the input into the left ear with the input into the right ear. If a sound comes from straight ahead or from straight behind us (or from straight above or below), the input into the left ear will be identical with the input into the right ear. (page 122)

11. Various sounds from the radio cannot seem to come from different directions, because your localization of the direction of a sound depends on a comparison between the responses of the two ears. However, the radio can play sounds that seem to come from different distances, because distance localization does not depend on a difference between the ears. It depends on the amount of reverberation, loudness, and high-frequency tones, all of which can be varied with a single speaker. Consequently, the radio can easily give an impression of people walking toward you or away from you, but not of people walking left to right or right to left. (page 122)

12. First determine how much the pleasant stimulus decreases the experience of pain for several people. Then give half of them naloxone and half of them a placebo. Again measure how much the pleasant stimulus decreases the pain. If the pleasant stimulus decreases pain by releasing endorphins, then naloxone should impair its painkilling effects. (page 126)

13. The capsaicin in the jalapeño peppers will release substance P faster than it can be resynthesized, thus decreasing the later sensitivity to pain in the mouth. (page 126)

Web Resources

HyperText Psychology—SENSES/Taste
www.science.wayne.edu/~wpoff/cor/sen/taste.html
Learn how we smell odors, what things cause smells, the types of smells, and how the sense of smell can be damaged.

The Interpretation of Sensory Information

What is the relationship between the real world and the way we perceive it?

Why are we sometimes wrong about what we think we see?

which sees one dot of the visual field. What you perceive is not dots, however, but lines, curves, and complex objects. In a variety of ways, your nervous system starts with an enormous array of details and extracts the meaningful information.

Perception of Minimal Stimuli

Some of the very earliest researchers in psychology addressed the question, "What is the weakest sound, the weakest light, the weakest touch, and so forth, that a person can detect?" The early psychologists assumed that this question would be easy to answer and therefore a good starting point for further research. As is often the case, however, this apparently simple question had a complicated answer: What you can detect varies from one occasion to another, and even stimuli that you say you did not see or hear can slightly influence your behavior.

No doubt you have heard people say that "a picture is worth a thousand words." If so, what is one one-thousandth of a picture worth? one word? Ordinarily, one one-thousandth of a picture is worth nothing. (Of course, I grant, "nothing" is *one word!*)

Printed photographs, such as the one on page 129, are composed of a great many dots. Ordinarily, you will be aware of only the overall patterns and objects, but if you magnify a photo, as in Figure 4.32, you can see the individual dots. Although one dot by itself tells us almost nothing, the pattern of dots as a whole constitutes a meaningful picture.

Actually, our vision is like this all the time. Your retina is composed of about 126 million rods and cones, each of

Sensory Thresholds and Signal Detection

In a typical experiment to determine the threshold of hearing—that is, the minimum intensity at which humans can detect sound—subjects are presented with tones of varying intensity in random order, including some trials with no tone at all. During each trial the subjects are asked to say whether or not they heard a tone. Figure 4.33 presents typical results. Notice that people are more likely to report stronger tones than weaker tones, but they occasionally report hearing a tone even when there was no tone at all. No sharp dividing line separates sounds that people can hear from sounds they cannot.

FIGURE 4.32 Although this photograph is composed entirely of dots, we see objects and patterns. The principles at work in our perception of this photograph are at work in all our perceptions.

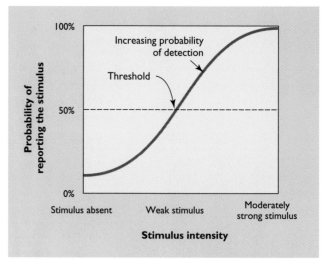

FIGURE 4.33 Typical results of an experiment to measure a sensory threshold. There is no sharp boundary between stimuli that you can perceive and stimuli that you cannot perceive.

Because perception researchers find no sharp dividing line between detectable and nondetectable stimuli, they define a **sensory threshold** as the *intensity at which a given individual can detect a stimulus 50% of the time.* Note, however, that an individual will sometimes detect stimuli below the threshold or fail to detect stimuli above the threshold.

An individual's sensory threshold can change as a result of dark adaptation. For example, if you have been outdoors on a bright, sunny day and you now walk into a movie theater, you will have trouble seeing the seats at first. After a few minutes, your threshold drops (that is, your sensitivity increases) and you can see the seats well. If you stayed in the dark theater after the movie ended, your ability to detect dim light would increase still further. The *sensory threshold at the time of maximum dark adaptation* is called the **absolute threshold.**

When people try to detect weak stimuli, they can be correct in two ways: reporting a stimulus when it is present (a "hit") and reporting no stimulus when it is absent (a "correct rejection"). They can also be wrong in two ways: They can fail to detect a stimulus (a "miss"), or they can say they detected a stimulus when none was present (a "false alarm"). Figure 4.34 outlines these possibilities.

Signal-detection theory is the *study of people's tendencies to make hits, correct rejections, misses, and false alarms* (Green & Swets, 1966). (Psychologists borrowed signal-detection theory from engineering, where this system is applied to such matters as detecting radio signals in the presence of interfering noise.) In signal-detection studies, we compare responses for stimulus-present and stimulus-absent trials. For example, suppose that someone reports a stimulus present on 80% of the trials when we present it. That statistic tells us very little by itself, unless we know how often the person said it was present on trials when it was not. If he or she also said "present" on 80% of trials with no stimulus, then the person was not actually detecting anything at all—just guessing "yes" most of the time. We would be more impressed if the person seldom reported the stimulus present when it was absent.

In a signal-detection experiment, people's responses depend on their willingness to risk a miss or a false alarm. (When in doubt, they have to risk one or the other.) Suppose you are the subject and I tell you that you will receive a 10-cent reward every time you correctly report that a light is present, but you will be fined one cent for saying "yes" if a light was not present. The lights are extremely faint, and sometimes you are not sure whether you saw one or not. When you are not sure, you will probably guess "yes," and the results will resemble those in Figure 4.35a. Then, I change the rules: You will receive a 1-cent reward for correctly reporting the presence of a light, but you will suffer a 10-cent penalty and an electric shock if you report a light when none was present. Now, you will say yes only if you are certain you saw a light, and the results will look like those in Figure 4.35b. In short, people's answers depend on the instructions they receive and the strategies they use, not just what their senses tell them.

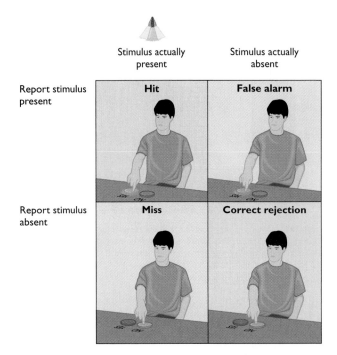

FIGURE 4.34 People can make two kinds of correct judgments (green) and two kinds of errors (red). Someone who too readily reports the stimulus present would get many hits, but also many false alarms.

People can become cautious about false alarms for other reasons, too. In one experiment, participants were asked to try to read words that were flashed on a screen for just a split second. They performed well when ordinary words like *river* or *peach* were shown. For emotionally loaded words like *penis* or *bitch,* however, they generally said they were not sure what they saw. Psychologists have suggested several possible explanations for such results (e.g., Blum & Barbour, 1979); one likely possibility is that subjects hesitate to blurt out an emotionally charged word unless they are certain they are right.

The signal-detection approach is useful in many settings that are remote from a vision or hearing laboratory. For example, if someone uses a personality test to identify people suffering from depression, it is important to evaluate both the number and kinds of errors that the test makes. A "miss" would be a failure to identify a depressed person. A "false alarm" would be calling someone depressed who in fact is not. Depending on the consequences of failing to treat someone who needs help or of providing treatment to someone who doesn't need it, we might be more willing to make one kind of mistake than the other. The legal system is also a signal-detection situation. When we evaluate the suitability of any kind of evidence—DNA matching, lie detector tests, eyewitness testimony, and so forth—the key questions are how often this kind of evidence would label a guilty person as innocent (a miss) and how often it might lead to the conviction of an innocent person (a false alarm). In the legal system, most people are much more willing to accept misses than false alarms. (That is, we reject any evidence that is likely to convict an innocent person.)

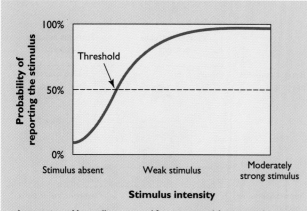

Instructions: You will receive a 10-cent reward for correctly reporting that a light is present. You will be penalized 1 cent for reporting that a light is present when it is not.

a

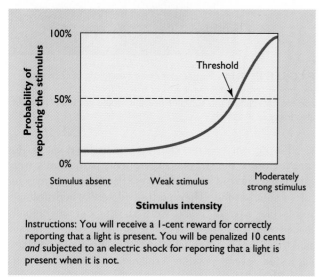

Instructions: You will receive a 1-cent reward for correctly reporting that a light is present. You will be penalized 10 cents *and* subjected to an electric shock for reporting that a light is present when it is not.

b

FIGURE 4.35 Results of experiments to measure a sensory threshold using two different sets of instructions.

CONCEPT CHECK

14. Suppose we find that nearly all alcoholics and drug abusers have a particular pattern of brain waves. Can we now look for that pattern of brain waves and use it to identify people with an alcohol or drug problem? (Check your answer on page 152.)

Subliminal Perception

You have probably heard of **subliminal perception,** the idea that *a stimulus can influence our behavior even when it is presented so faintly or briefly or along with such strong distractors that we do not perceive it consciously.* (*Limen* is Latin for "threshold"; thus, subliminal means "below the threshold.") Some people claim that subliminal perception can powerfully manipulate human behavior.

Are such claims plausible or outright nonsense? The first problem is to define *subliminal.* You already learned that *subliminal* means "below the *threshold.*" Fine, but you also learned that there is no sharp division between perceptible stimuli and imperceptible stimuli. If we define *subliminal* stimuli as those that people detect on fewer than 50% of occasions, then subliminal perception is hardly surprising. In practical terms, when psychologists refer to a "subliminal stimulus," they generally mean "a stimulus that a person *did not* consciously detect on a given occasion," regardless of whether the person could have detected it under other circumstances.

That definition does not solve the problem, however. How do we know whether someone *did* detect a given stimulus? We ask, of course. But a reply that "I did not see" the stimulus could mean "I saw nothing," "I'm unsure what I saw," or "I forget what I saw." You can understand why this kind of research is often difficult to interpret.

What Subliminal Perception Cannot Do

Many of the claims regarding subliminal effects have been so outrageous and so lacking in evidence that many scientists came to doubt that subliminal perceptions had any effect at all. Many years ago, claims were made that subliminal messages could control people's buying habits. For example, an unscrupulous theater owner might insert a single frame reading "EAT POPCORN" in the middle of a film. Customers who were not consciously aware of the message could not resist it, so they would flock to the concession stand to buy popcorn. Despite many tests of this claim, no one found any evidence to support it (Bornstein, 1989).

Another claim is that certain rock recordings contain "satanic" messages that have been recorded backward and superimposed on the songs. Some people allege that the listeners unconsciously perceive these messages and then turn to drugs or devil worship. As far as psychology is concerned, the issue is whether people who heard a backward message could understand it and whether it would influence their behavior. Psychologists have recorded various fairly tame messages (nothing satanic) and asked people to listen to them played backward. So far, no one listening to the backward messages has been able to discern what they would sound like played forward. And listening to those messages has not influenced anyone's behavior in any detectable way (Vokey & Read, 1985). In other words, even if certain music does contain messages recorded backward, we have no reason to believe that these messages will influence the listeners.

A third unsupported claim: Many bookstores and music stores sell "subliminal audiotapes" that claim they can help you to improve your memory, quit smoking, lose weight, raise your self-esteem, and so forth. In one study, psychologists asked more than 200 volunteers to listen to a popular brand of audiotape. But they intentionally mislabeled some of the tapes. That is, some tapes with "self-

The rock group Judas Priest was sued by the families of two teenage boys who committed suicide. The families claimed that subliminal messages on the rock group's album *Stained Class* prompted the boys to commit suicide. A witness for the families demonstrated that, if one song was filtered, slowed down, and played backward, people could hear the phrase "do it." The defense replied that the band had not intentionally inserted this backward message and that, even if they had, the message would not drive a person to suicide. The court found the band not guilty.

If people see a word subliminally, it influences their later perception of an easily visible stimulus (Dixon, 1981). For example, people watch a screen where the word PENCIL is flashed briefly in the midst of a cluttered background. Then they see a set of letters such as TERIW or WRITE and they are supposed to say, as quickly as possible, whether it is a word. People who have just seen the subliminal stimulus PENCIL respond a little quicker than usual that WRITE is a word.

A number of researchers have claimed that brief, subliminal exposure to an emotional message produces an emotional response. In one study, undergraduate students showed mild signs of nervousness or discomfort after viewing a very brief presentation of the message NO ONE LOVES ME but not after viewing the unemotional message NO ONE LIFTS IT (Masling, Bornstein, Poynton, Reid, & Katkin, 1991). This study was not set up to measure how long the effect might last. Other studies have reported fairly long-lasting emotional effects of subliminal stimuli (Hardaway, 1990), but such conclusions remain highly controversial.

The fact that subliminal perception can affect behavior at all is theoretically interesting. It shows that we are not consciously aware of all the information we process or all the events that influence us (Greenwald & Draine, 1997). However, the effects of subliminal perception are much smaller than some people hope and other people fear.

Perception and the Recognition of Patterns

Now let's consider how we perceive complex patterns. People are much better at recognizing complex patterns, especially faces, than at explaining how we do it. When people try to copy a photo of a face, most do a poor job, even though they could trace it reasonably accurately. The problem is not that they cannot control the pencil well enough; it is that they do not pay attention to all the details they need to copy the photo (Cohen & Bennett, 1997), even though they do register those details well enough to recognize the face.

When you attend your 25th high-school reunion, you will probably recognize many people, despite major changes in their appearance. Can you match the high-school photos in Figure 4.36 with the photos of the same people as they looked 25 years later? Probably not, but other people who had attended that high school succeeded with a respectable 49% accuracy (Bruck, Cavanaugh, & Ceci, 1991). They were able to focus on the invariant features that defined each person's face in spite of the changes that had occurred over the years.

But how do we recognize faces? To some extent we do so by unusual characteristics—a peculiar shape of nose, a characteristic mouth, or especially thick eyebrows. However, recognizing a whole face is apparently different in

esteem" messages were labeled "memory tapes" and some tapes with "memory" messages were labeled "self-esteem tapes." After one month of listening, most who *thought* they were listening to self-esteem tapes said they had greatly improved their self-esteem; those who *thought* they were listening to memory tapes said their memory had greatly improved. What they were *actually* hearing made no difference. In other words, if people improved their memory—and some of them did improve, although not nearly as much as they thought they did—the improvement depended on their expectations, not on the tapes themselves (Greenwald, Spangenberg, Pratkanis, & Eskanazi, 1991).

What Subliminal Perception Can Do

We have just considered what subliminal messages *cannot* do. Now let's consider what they apparently *can* do:

If people are subliminally exposed to a simple picture and then asked to choose between that picture and another one (both now plainly visible), about 60–65% will choose the picture they had seen subliminally. Although this is not a very strong effect, it does last for a week or longer (Bornstein, 1989).

TRY IT
YOUR-
SELF

FIGURE 4.36 High-school photos and the same people 25 years later. Can you match the photos in the two sets? (Check answer C on page 152.) (From Bruck, Cavanaugh, & Ceci, 1991.)

some important ways from recognizing other kinds of objects, including pieces of a face. People with certain kinds of brain damage are unable to recognize faces, in spite of being able to read and recognize many kinds of objects (Farah, 1992). People with other kinds of brain damage can recognize faces normally but cannot recognize simple objects such as coffee cups or read even short words (Moscovitch, Winocur, & Behrmann, 1997). Particular parts of the cerebral cortex are more active when people look at faces than when they look at other complex patterns, such as flowers (McCarthy, Puce, Gore, & Allison, 1997), and many psychologists believe that the brain has a special "module" devoted specifically to face recognition.

Regardless of this module hypothesis, we do recognize faces as a whole, not just by specific features such as the eyes and nose. To illustrate, consider Figure 4.37. Presumably, you will identify the two faces immediately as those of U. S. President Bill Clinton and Vice President Al Gore. But now look more closely: The faces were digitally manipulated via computer so that they are exactly alike—about halfway between Clinton's real face and Gore's (Sinha & Poggio, 1996). You recognize the two faces partly by hair, head shape, relative height, and so forth. In short, visual recognition depends on both the isolated features and the overall context.

FIGURE 4.37 Can you easily recognize these faces as Bill Clinton and Al Gore? Note that the faces themselves have been altered to be identical. We recognize the individuals partly by facial features, but also partly by hair, head size, shape, and even the overall context of the picture.

The Feature-Detector Approach

Even explaining how we recognize a simple letter of the alphabet is difficult enough. According to one explanation, we begin recognition by breaking a complex stimulus into its component parts. For example, when we look at a letter of the alphabet, *specialized neurons* in the visual cortex, called **feature detectors,** *respond to the presence of certain simple features, such as lines and angles.* That is, one neuron in your visual cortex might become active only when you are looking at a horizontal line in a particular location. That feature detector would be detecting the feature "horizontal line." Other neurons might detect horizontal lines in other locations, vertical lines, and so forth.

Feature detectors certainly cannot provide the whole explanation for how we perceive letters, much less faces. For example, we perceive the words in Figure 4.38a as CAT and HAT, even though the A in CAT is identical to the H in HAT, and therefore both of them stimulate the same feature detectors. Likewise, the character in the center of 4.38b can be read as either the letter *B* or the number *13.* Feature detectors are essential in the early stages of visual

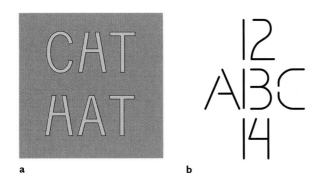

a   **b**

FIGURE 4.38 We perceive elements differently depending on their context. In (a), the A in CAT is the same as the H in HAT, but we perceive them differently. In (b), the central character can appear to be a B or the number 13, depending on whether we read horizontally or vertically. (Part b from Kim, 1989.)

perception, but the perception of a complex pattern requires more than just feature detectors.

WHAT'S THE EVIDENCE?
Feature Detectors in the Human Visual System

We can easily imagine feature detectors in the human brain, and we can imagine all kinds of properties for them. But what evidence do we have for their existence? We have two kinds of evidence, one from laboratory animals and one from humans.

EXPERIMENT 1

Hypothesis Neurons in the visual cortex of cats and monkeys will respond specifically when light strikes the retina in a particular pattern.

Method Two pioneers in the study of the visual cortex, David Hubel and Torsten Wiesel (1981 Nobel Prize winners in physiology and medicine), inserted thin electrodes into cells of the occipital cortex of cats and monkeys and then recorded the activity of those cells when various light patterns struck the animals' retinas. At first they used mere points of light; later they tried lines (Figure 4.39).

Results They found that each cell responds best in the presence of a particular stimulus (Hubel & Wiesel, 1968). Some cells become active only when a vertical bar of light strikes a given portion of the retina. Others become active only when a horizontal bar strikes the retina. In other words, such cells appear to act as feature detectors.

In later experiments, Hubel and Wiesel and other investigators found cells that respond to other kinds of features, such as movement in a particular direction.

Interpretation Hubel and Wiesel reported feature-detector neurons in both cats and monkeys. If the organization of

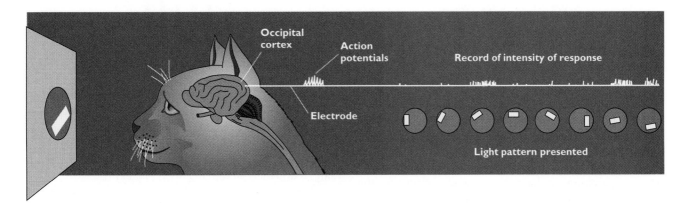

FIGURE 4.39 Hubel and Wiesel implanted electrodes to record the activity of neurons in the occipital cortex of a cat. Then they compared the responses evoked by various patterns of light and darkness on the retina. In most cases, a neuron responded vigorously when a portion of the retina saw a bar of light oriented at a particular angle. When the angle of the bar changed, that cell became silent but another cell responded.

the occipital cortex is similar in species as distantly related as cats and monkeys, it is likely (though not certain) to be similar in humans as well.

A second line of evidence is based on the following reasoning: If the human cortex does contain feature-detector cells, one type of cell should become fatigued after we stare for a time at the features that excite it. When we look away, we should see an aftereffect created by the inactivity of that type of cell. (Recall the negative afterimage in color vision, as shown by Figure 4.15.)

One example of this phenomenon is the **waterfall illusion:** *If you stare at a waterfall for a minute or more and then turn your eyes to some nearby cliffs, the cliffs will appear to flow upward.* By staring at the waterfall, you fatigue the neurons that respond to downward motion. When you look away, those neurons become inactive, but others that respond to upward motion continue their normal activity. Even though the motionless cliffs stimulate those neurons only weakly, the stimulation is enough to produce an illusion of upward motion.

 For another example, here is a demonstration that you can perform yourself.

EXPERIMENT 2

Hypothesis   After you stare at one set of vertical lines, you will fatigue the feature detectors that respond to lines of a particular width. If you then look at lines slightly wider or narrower than the original ones, they will appear to be even wider or narrower than they really are.

Method   Cover the right half of Figure 4.40 and stare at the little rectangle in the middle of the left half for at least 1 minute. (Staring for a longer time will increase the effect.) Do not stare at just one point; move your focus around within the rectangle. Then look at the square in the center of the right part of the figure, and compare the spacing between the lines of the top and bottom gratings (Blakemore & Sutton, 1969).

Results   What did you perceive in the right half of the figure? People generally report that the top lines look narrower than they really are and that the bottom lines look wider.

Interpretation   Staring at the left part of the figure fatigues one set of cells sensitive to wide lines in the top part of the figure and another set sensitive to narrow lines in the bottom part. Then, when you look at lines of medium width, the fatigued cells become inactive. Therefore, your perception is dominated by cells sensitive to narrower lines in the top part and to wider lines in the bottom part.

To summarize, we have two types of evidence for the existence of visual feature detectors: (1) The brains of other species contain cells with the properties of feature detectors, and (2) after staring at certain patterns, we see aftereffects that can be explained as fatigue of feature-detector cells in the brain.

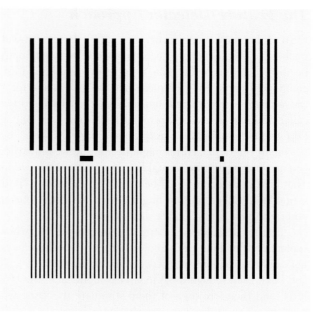

FIGURE 4.40   Use this display to fatigue your feature detectors and create an afterimage. Follow the directions in Experiment 2. (From Blakemore & Sutton, 1969.)

The research just described was only the start of an enormous amount of activity by laboratories throughout the world; later results have led to revised views of what the earlier results mean. For example, even though certain neurons respond better to a single vertical line

than to points or lines of other orientations, the vertical line may not be the best stimulus for exciting those neurons. Most respond even more strongly to a sine-wave grating of lines:

Thus the feature that such cells detect is probably more complex than just a line. Furthermore, because each cell responds to stimuli as different as a line and a group of lines, obviously no one cell provides an unambiguous message about what someone is seeing at any moment. The perception emerges from the pattern of activity of a large population of neurons (Hughes, Nozawa, & Kitterle, 1996).

One important point about scientific advances: A single line of evidence—even excellent, Nobel Prize–winning evidence—seldom provides the final answer to any question. We should always look for multiple ways to test a hypothesis; even if several kinds of evidence support a conclusion, a great many unanswered questions can still remain.

✳   ✳   ✳

Do Feature Detectors Explain Perception?

The neurons I have been describing are active during the early stages of visual processing. Do we simply add up the responses of a great many feature detectors, so that the sum of enough feature detectors constitutes your perception of, say, your psychology professor's face? No, brain researchers doubt that the responses of simple horizontal- or vertical-line feature detectors equal our conscious visual experience (He, Cavanagh, & Intiligator, 1996). Rather, they are just a preliminary step in a complex set of visual processes occupying most of the brain.

To illustrate why simple feature detectors alone cannot explain perception, consider Figure 4.41 (based on Kanizsa, 1979). Parts a and b are composed of small geometric forms. Although we might guess that part a is made up of segments of a three-dimensional cube, we do not *see* the cube. Part b hardly even suggests a cube. In parts c and d, the added lines provide a context that enables us to see the cube. In part e, the deletion of short lines from a enables us to *see* imaginary lines that provide the same context. In c, d, and e, we have perceptually organized a meaningful pattern that goes well beyond the sum of the individual lines, taken one at a time.

Similarly, in Figure 4.42a we see a series of meaningless patches. In Figure 4.42b, the addition of some black glop immediately enables us to perceive these same patches as the word *psychology* (Bregman, 1981). We can perceive the letters in part b only by imposing an active interpretation on the pattern.

The Gestalt Psychology Approach

Figure 4.43, which we see as the overall shape of an airplane, is a photo of several hundred people. Out of context, one person is no more a piece of an airplane than a piece of anything else; the plane is the overall pattern, not the sum of the parts. Recall also Figure 4.32 from earlier in this chapter: The photograph is composed entirely of dots, but we perceive a pattern of objects, not just a collection of dots.

Such observations derive from **Gestalt psychology,** a field that focuses on our ability to perceive overall patterns.

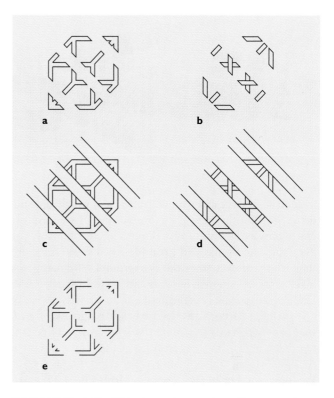

FIGURE 4.41 This picture is a puzzle until a context is introduced. Then a cube "emerges" from meaningless lines. (From Kanizsa, 1979.)

Gestalt (geh-SHTALT) is a German word; there is no exact English equivalent, although *configuration* and *pattern* come close. The founders of Gestalt psychology rejected the idea that a perception can be broken down into its component parts. If a melody is broken up into individual notes, the melody is lost. Their slogan was, "The whole is different from the sum of its parts."

According to Gestalt psychologists, visual perception is an active creation, not just the adding up of lines, dots, or other pieces. We considered examples of this principle in Figures 4.40 and 4.41. Here are some further examples:

 Figure 4.44 shows a photo and a drawing of two animals. As you look at these pictures, you may see the animals almost at once, or you may see

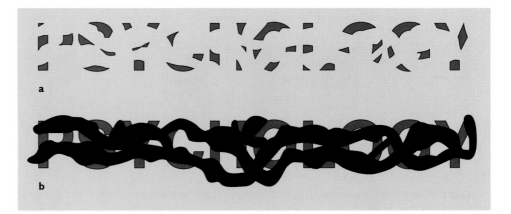

FIGURE 4.42 Someone familiar with only the Hebrew or Arabic alphabet would not see meaningful patterns emerge in part (b). (After Bregman, 1981.)

FIGURE 4.43 According to Gestalt psychology, the whole is different from the sum of its parts. Here, we perceive an assembly of several hundred people as an airplane.

meaningless black and white patches from which you suddenly organize the perception of animals. (If you give up, check answer D, page 152.) To perceive the animals, you must separate **figure and ground**—that is, you must distinguish the *object from the background*. Ordinarily, you make that distinction almost instantly; only in special cases like this one do you become aware of the process.

Figure 4.45 contains five **reversible figures,** *stimuli that can be perceived in more than one way*. In effect, we test hypotheses: "Is this the front of the object or is that the front? Is the object facing left or right? Is this section the foreground or the background?" In Figure 4.45, part a is called the *Necker cube,* after the psychologist who first called attention to it. Which is the front face of the cube? If you look long enough, you will see it two ways. You can see part b either as a vase or as two profiles. In part c, with a little imagination, you might see a woman's face or a man blowing a horn. (If you need help, check answer E on page 152.) Part d (from Boring, 1930) shows both an old woman and a young woman. Almost everyone sees one or the other immediately, but many people lock into one perception so tightly that they cannot see the other one. Part e was drawn by an 8-year-old girl who intended it as the picture of a face. Can you find another possibility? (If you have trouble with parts d or e, check answers F and G, page 152.) Overall, the point of the reversible figures is that we perceive by imposing order on an array, not just by adding up lines and points.

The Gestalt psychologists described some principles of how we organize perceptions into meaningful wholes, as illustrated in Figure 4.46. **Proximity** is the *tendency to perceive objects that are close together as belonging to a group*. The objects in part a form two groups because of

a

b

FIGURE 4.44 Do you see an animal in each picture? If not, check answer D, page 152. (Part b from Dallenbach, 1951.)

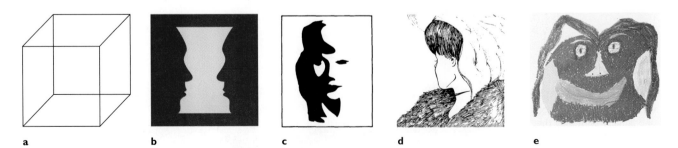

a   b   c   d   e

FIGURE 4.45 Reversible figures: (a) The Necker cube. Which is the front face? (b) Faces or a vase. (c) Sax player and woman's face ("Sara Nader"). (d) An old woman and a young woman. (e) A face or what? (Part d from Boring, 1930.)

FIGURE 4.46 Gestalt principles of (a) proximity, (b) similarity, (c) continuation, (d) closure, and (e) good figure.

their proximity. The *tendency to perceive objects that resemble each other as forming a group* is called **similarity.** The objects in b group into Xs and Os because of similarity. When lines are interrupted, as in c, we may perceive **continuation,** *a filling in of the gaps.* You probably perceive this illustration as a rectangle covering the center of one very elongated hot dog.

When a familiar figure is interrupted, we perceive a **closure** of the figure—that is, *we imagine the rest of the figure.* The figure we imagine completes what we already see in a way that is simple, symmetrical, or consistent with our past experience (Shimaya, 1997). For example, you

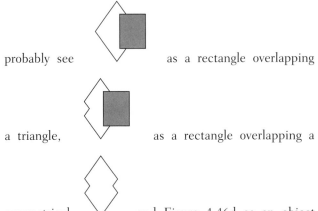

probably see ____ as a rectangle overlapping a triangle, ____ as a rectangle overlapping a symmetrical ____ , and Figure 4.46d as an object overlapping a complete, familiar face.

Of course, the principle of closure is similar to that of continuation. With a complicated pattern, however, closure

takes into account more than just a continuation of the lines. For example, in Figure 4.46c, you fill in the gaps to perceive one long hot dog. With some additional context, you would probably perceive the same pattern as two shorter hot dogs:

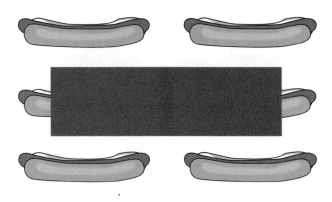

Finally, we tend to perceive a **good figure**—*a simple, symmetrical figure.* As a rule, simple and symmetrical figures are more likely to occur in nature than irregular figures.

If you see ⬭⬭ , it is more likely to be composed of one ellipse overlapping another than to be composed of ⌒ and ⌒ meeting at exactly the right point. In Figure 4.46e, even after we see that the right-hand drawing is a green backward L overlapping part of an irregular object, we continue to perceive it as a red square overlapping a green square. In Figure 4.47, we perceive two striped surfaces, either adjoining side by side or one overlapping the other. That perception is so convincing that you may have to look carefully to persuade yourself that there is no vertical line down the center of the drawing.

Figure 4.48 demonstrates that the principle of good figure does not always lead us to perceive the most likely stimulus (Grossberg, 1997). Most people see part a as a large white cross overlapping a thinner white square, although it is also possible (and equally logical) to see a thin square overlapping a large cross. In parts b and c, we see the thin square clearly superimposed on the left and right arms of the cross; nevertheless, at the top and bottom we tend to see the large cross overlapping the thin square. That is, most people see the square as looping over and

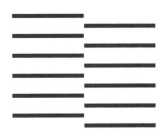

FIGURE 4.47 Two sets of stripes generate an illusion of a vertical line down the center, separating one set of stripes from the other.

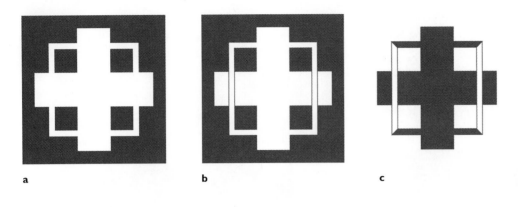

a   b   c

FIGURE 4.48 Do you see a thick cross on top of a thin square, or a square on top of a cross? In part a, both are equally possible, but most people perceive the cross as being on top. In parts b and c, we are shown that the square is on top of the left and right arms of the cross, but most people still see the top and bottom arms of the cross as lying above the square. (Modified from Petter, 1956; and Kanizsa, 1985.)

under the cross, instead of the more likely event that it lies above the cross in all locations.

Perceiving one pattern as lying "on top of" another can have important consequences. Consider Figure 4.49. The dark bars on the right appear to lie on top of a pink rectangle, and therefore the pink rectangle is on a white surface. The contrast between the pink and the white makes the pink appear darker. Meanwhile, the pink on the left appears to lie above the dark bars, making it appear very light by contrast. Overall, the pink bars on the right look much darker than those on the left, even though they are actually the same shade of pink.

CONCEPT CHECK

15. Which of the Gestalt principles were operating in your perception of Figures 4.41 and 4.42? (Check your answers on page 152.)

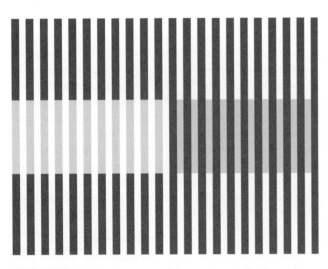

FIGURE 4.49 Because pink bars appear to lie above the dark bars on the left and below them on the right, we see a contrast between pink and dark red on the left, pink and white on the right. Therefore, we see the pink bars on the right as darker, even though they are actually the same shade as the others.

Gestalt Principles in Hearing

The perceptual organization principles of Gestalt psychology apply to hearing as well as to vision. There are reversible figures in sound, just as there are in vision. For instance, you can hear the sound of a clock as "tick, tock, tick, tock" or as "tock, tick, tock, tick." You can hear your windshield wipers going "dunga, dunga" or "gadung, gadung."

As with visual reversible figures, people occasionally get so locked into one interpretation of something they hear that they have trouble hearing it any other way. For example, read this sentence to a friend: "The matadors fish on Friday." Pause long enough to make sure your friend has understood the sentence. Then say: "The cat on the mat adores fish on Friday." If you read the second sentence normally, without pausing between mat and adores, your friend is likely to be puzzled: "Huh? The cat on the matadors . . .?" Had you not just read the first sentence, your friend would have easily understood the second sentence.

Feature Detectors and Gestalt Psychology

The Gestalt approach to perception does not conflict with the feature-detector approach as much as it might seem. The feature-detector approach describes the first stages of perception—how the brain takes individual points of light and connects them into lines and then into more complex features. According to the feature-detector approach, the brain says, "I see these points here, here, and here, so there must be a line. I see a line here and another line connecting with it here, so there must be a letter L."

The Gestalt approach describes how we combine visual input with our knowledge and expectations. According to the Gestalt interpretation, the brain says, "I see what looks like a circle, so the missing piece must be part of a circle too."

Which view is correct? Both, of course. Our perception must assemble the individual points of light or bits of sound, but once it forms a tentative interpretation of the pattern, it uses that interpretation to organize or reorganize the information.

Perception of Movement and Depth

As an automobile drives away from us, its image on the retina grows smaller, yet we perceive it as moving, not as shrinking. That perception illustrates **visual constancy**—our *tendency to perceive objects as keeping their shape, size, and color, even though what actually strikes our retina may be changing from time to time.* Figure 4.50 shows examples of two visual constancies: shape constancy and size constancy. Constancies depend on our familiarity with objects and on our ability to estimate distances and angles of view. For example, we know that a door is still rectangular even when we view it from an odd angle. But to recognize that an object keeps its shape and size, we have to perceive movement or changes in distance or angle. How do we do so?

a

b

FIGURE 4.50 (a) Shape constancy: We perceive all three doors as rectangles. (b) Size constancy: We perceive all three hands as equal in size.

Perception of Movement

It is common sense to assume that anyone who can see a rabbit should be able to see its size, shape, and color, and its direction and speed of movement. In this case, our common sense is wrong. You already know that some people are color-blind and therefore cannot see the rabbit's color. Also, as mentioned briefly in Chapter 3, some people are motion-blind and therefore their ability to see the rabbit's movement is impaired. Motionblindness results from damage to a small area in the temporal lobe of the cortex (Zihl, von Cramon, & Mai, 1983). This rare condition illustrates a major point: The visual system of the brain has separate pathways to analyze different aspects of what we see. One pathway analyzes shape, another analyzes color, and yet another analyzes movement (Zeki, 1993).

The detection of motion in the visual world raises some interesting issues, including how we distinguish between our own movement and the movement of objects. Try this simple demonstration: Hold an object in front of your eyes and then move it to the right. Now hold the object in front of your eyes and move your eyes to the left. The image of the object moves across your retina in the same way, regardless of whether you move the object or move your eyes. Yet, you perceive the object as moving in one case but not in the other. Why?

The object does not appear to move when you move your eyes for two reasons. One reason is that the vestibular system constantly keeps the visual areas of the brain informed of movements of your head. When your brain knows that your eyes have moved to the left, it interprets a change in what you see as being a result of that movement. One man with a rare kind of brain damage was unable to connect his eye movements with his perceptions. Whenever he moved his eyes, he perceived the world as moving. Whenever he watched moving objects or watched anything while he himself moved, he became dizzy and nauseated (Haarmeier, Thier, Repnow, & Petersen, 1997).

The second reason that the object does not appear to move is that we perceive motion when an object moves *relative to the background* (Gibson, 1968). For example, when you walk forward, stationary objects in your environment move across your retina. If something fails to move across your retina, you perceive it as moving in the same direction as you are.

What do we perceive when an object is stationary and the background is moving? That seldom happens, but when it does, we may *incorrectly perceive the object as moving against a stationary background,* a phenomenon called **induced movement.** For example, when you watch clouds moving slowly across the moon from left to right, you generally perceive the clouds as a stationary background and the moon as an object moving from right to left. Induced movement is a form of *apparent movement,* as opposed to *real movement.*

I have already mentioned the waterfall illusion (page 138) as an example of apparent movement. Another example is **stroboscopic movement,** an *illusion of movement created by a rapid succession of stationary images.* When a scene is flashed on a screen and is followed a split second later by a second scene slightly different from the first, you perceive the objects as having moved smoothly from their location in the first scene to their location in the second scene (Figure 4.51). Motion pictures are actually a series of still photos flashed on the screen.

We also experience an *illusion of movement created when two or more stationary lights separated by a short distance blink on and off at regular intervals.* Your brain creates the sense of motion in what is called the **phi effect.** You may have noticed signs in front of restaurants or motels that make use of this effect. As the lights blink on and off, the arrow seems to be moving and inviting you to come inside.

Our ability to detect visual movement played an interesting role in the history of astronomy. In 1930, Clyde Tombaugh was searching the skies for a possible undiscovered planet beyond Neptune. He photographed each region of the sky twice, several days apart. A planet, unlike a star, would move from one photo to the next. However, how would he find one tiny dot that moved, among all the countless unmoving dots in the sky? He put each pair of photos on a machine that would flip back and forth between one photo and the other. When he came to the correct pair of photos, the machine flipped back and forth between them, and he immediately noticed the one moving dot (Tombaugh, 1980). We now know that little dot as the planet Pluto (Figure 4.52).

Depth Perception

Although we live in a world of three dimensions, our retinas are in effect two-dimensional surfaces. **Depth perception,** our *perception of distance,* enables us to experience the world in three dimensions. This perception depends on several factors.

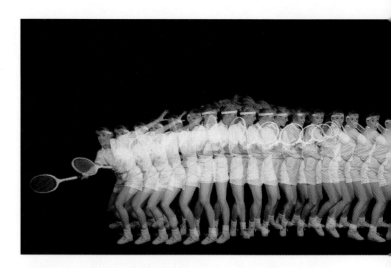

One factor is **retinal disparity**—*the difference in the apparent position of an object as seen by the left and right retinas.* Try this: Hold one finger at arm's length. Focus on it with one eye and then with the other. Note that the apparent position of your finger shifts with respect to the background. Now hold your finger closer to your face and repeat the experiment. Notice that the apparent position of your finger shifts even more. The discrepancy between the slightly different views the two eyes see becomes greater as the object comes closer. We use the amount of discrepancy to gauge distance.

A second cue for depth perception is the **convergence** of our eyes—that is, the *degree to which they turn in to focus on a close object* (Figure 4.53). When you focus on a distant object, your eyes are looking in almost parallel directions. When you focus on something close, your eyes turn in; you can sense the tension of your eye muscles. The more the muscles pull, the closer the object must be.

Retinal disparity and convergence are called **binocular cues,** because they *depend on the action of both eyes.* **Monocular cues** enable a person to *judge depth and distance effectively with just one eye,* or when both eyes see

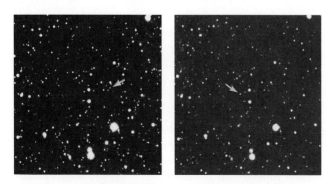

FIGURE 4.52 Clyde Tombaugh used movement perception to discover the planet Pluto. He photographed each area of the sky twice, several days apart. Then he used a machine to flip back and forth between the two photos of each pair. When he came to one part of the sky, he immediately noticed one dot that moved between the two photos. That dot was the planet Pluto.

FIGURE 4.53 Convergence of the eyes as a cue to distance. The more this viewer must converge her eyes toward each other in order to focus on an object, the closer the object must be.

FIGURE 4.51 When you watch a movie, you are unaware of the thousands of still photographs flickering by at a rate of 86,400 per hour. The sequence of photographs printed here conveys a sense of motion in another way.

the same image, as they do when you look at a picture. Several monocular cues help us judge the approximate distance of objects, such as those in Figure 4.54.

Object size: Other things being equal, an object close to us produces a larger image than does one that is farther away. This cue is useful only if we already know the approximate actual size of the objects. For example, the roller skater in the photo produces a larger image than does the parked van, which we know is actually larger. So we see the skater as closer. The rocks in the sea, however, are not of equal size in reality, so the relative sizes of their images do not tell us anything about their distance.

Linear perspective: As parallel lines stretch out toward the horizon, they come closer and closer together. Examine the road in Figure 4.54. At the bottom of the photo (close to the viewer), the edges of the road are far apart; at greater distances,

the edges of the road come closer together. The closer the lines come, the more distant we perceive them to be.

Detail: We see nearby objects, such as the roller skater, in much detail. More distant objects are increasingly hazy and less detailed.

Interposition: A nearby object interrupts our view of a more distant object. Interposition is our surest way of seeing which rocks are closer than others.

Texture gradient: Notice the posts on the safety rail on the right side of the road. At greater distances, the posts come closer and closer together. The "packed together" appearance of objects gives us another cue to their approximate distance.

Shadows: Shadows are hardly prominent in Figure 4.54, but when present they can provide another cue to help us interpret the sizes and positions of objects in a picture.

FIGURE 4.54 We can judge depth and distance in a photograph, using certain useful cues, even if we use only one eye. (1) Closer objects occupy more space on the retina (or in the photograph) than do distant objects of the same type. (2) Nearer objects show more detail. (3) Closer objects overlap certain distant objects. (4) Objects in the foreground look sharper than objects do on the horizon. These are known as monocular cues.

Accommodation: The lens of the eye *accommodates*—that is, it changes shape—to focus on nearby objects, and your brain detects that change and thereby infers the distance to an object. Accommodation could help tell you how far away the photograph itself is, although it provides no information about the relative distances of objects in the photograph.

The ability to use these monocular cues to interpret an illustration depends partly on our experience with photographs and drawings. For example, in the two drawings of Figure 4.55, does it appear to you that the hunter is aiming his spear at the deer? When these drawings were shown to people of certain African cultures that create much sculpture but little drawing, many people said the hunter was aiming at a baby elephant (Hudson, 1960). This comparison illustrates that people have to learn how to use monocular cues to judge depth in drawings.

Another monocular cue helps us to perceive depth when we are looking at a three-dimensional scene, though it does not help us when we are looking at a photograph. When we are moving—riding along in a car, for example—close objects seem to pass by swiftly, although distant objects seem to pass by very slowly. *The faster an object passes by, the closer it must be.* That principle is **motion parallax.**

If you were a passenger on this train, the ground beside the tracks would appear to pass by more quickly than the more distant elements in the landscape. In this photo's version of motion parallax, the ground is blurred and more distant objects are crisp.

CONCEPT CHECKS

16. Which monocular cues to depth are available in Figure 4.55?
17. With three-dimensional photography, cameras take two views of the same scene from different locations through lenses with different color filters or with different polarized-light filters. The two views are then superimposed. The viewer looks at the composite view through special glasses so that one eye sees the view taken with one camera and the other eye sees the view taken with the other camera. Which depth cue is at work here? (Check your answers on page 152.)

Optical Illusions

Many people claim to have seen ghosts, flying saucers, the Loch Ness monster, Bigfoot, Santa's elves, or people floating in the air. Maybe they are lying, maybe they did see something extraordinary, or maybe they saw something ordinary but misinterpreted it. An **optical illusion** is a *mis-*

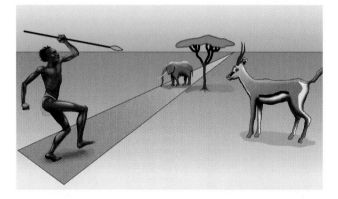

FIGURE 4.55 Which animal is the hunter attacking? Most readers of this text, using monocular cues to distance, will reply that the hunter is attacking the deer. However, many African subjects thought he was attacking "a baby elephant." Evidently, the tendency to use monocular cues to distance depends on experience with photographs and drawings; the African subjects were from cultures with little such experience. (From Hudson, 1960.)

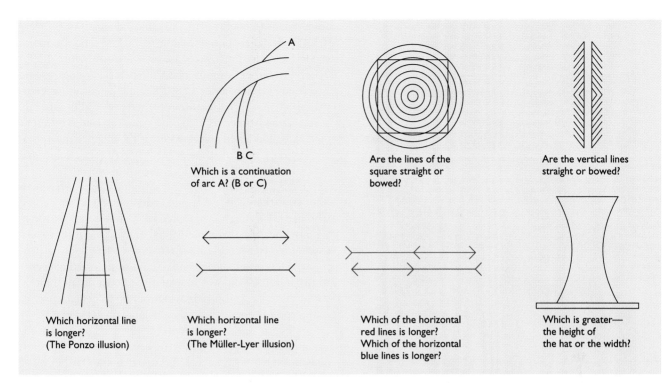

Which is a continuation of arc A? (B or C)

Are the lines of the square straight or bowed?

Are the vertical lines straight or bowed?

Which horizontal line is longer? (The Ponzo illusion)

Which horizontal line is longer? (The Müller-Lyer illusion)

Which of the horizontal red lines is longer? Which of the horizontal blue lines is longer?

Which is greater— the height of the hat or the width?

FIGURE 4.56 Many paintings rely on an optical illusion, but we are more aware of the illusion in geometric figures. (Check your answers with a ruler and a compass.)

interpretation of a visual stimulus. Figure 4.56 shows a few examples. Psychologists would like to develop a single explanation for all optical illusions. (Remember the principle of parsimony from Chapter 2.) Although psychologists have not fully succeeded, today we can explain a fair number of optical illusions based on the relationship between size perception and depth perception.

The Relationship Between Depth Perception and Size Perception

If you can estimate the size of an object, you can deduce its distance. If you can estimate its distance, you can deduce its size. Figure 4.57 shows that a given image on the retina may represent either a small, close object or a large, distant object. Watch what happens when you take a single image and change its apparent distance: Stare at Figure 4.15 again to form a negative af-

terimage. First examine the afterimage while you are looking at the wall across the room. Your afterimage will look fairly large. Then look at the afterimage against the palm of your hand. Suddenly, the image becomes very small. Move your hand backward and forward; you can make the apparent size grow and then shrink.

In the real world, we seldom have trouble estimating the size and distance of objects. When you walk along the street, for instance, you never wonder whether the people you see are giants one kilometer away or miniature people a few centimeters away. However, when you have fewer cues about the size or distance of an object, you can become confused (Figure 4.58). I once saw an airplane overhead and was unsure whether it was a small, remote-controlled toy airplane or a distant, full-size airplane. Airplanes come in many sizes, and the sky has few cues to distance.

A similar issue arises in reported sightings of UFOs. When people see an unfamiliar object in the sky, they can

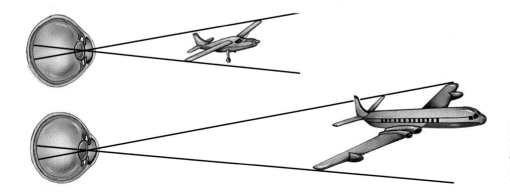

FIGURE 4.57 The trade-off between size and distance: A given image on the retina can indicate either a small, close object or a large, distant object.

FIGURE 4.58 Because fish come in many sizes, we can estimate the size of a fish only if we know how far away it is or if we can compare its size to other nearby objects. See what happens when you cover the man and then cover the hand.

easily misjudge its distance. If they overestimate its distance, they also will overestimate its size and speed.

What does all this have to do with optical illusions? Whenever we misjudge distance, we are likely to misjudge size as well. For example, Figure 4.59a shows people in the

Ames room (named for its designer, Adelbert Ames). The room is designed to look like a normal rectangular room, though its true dimensions are as shown in Figure 4.59b. The right corner is much closer than the left corner. The two young women are actually the same height. If we eliminated all the background cues, then we would correctly perceive the women as being the same size but at different distances. However, the apparently rectangular room provides such powerful (though misleading) cues to distance that the women appear to differ greatly in height.

Even a two-dimensional drawing on a flat surface can offer cues that lead to erroneous depth perception. People who have had much experience with photos and drawings tend to interpret two-dimensional drawings as if they were three-dimensional. Figure 4.60 shows a bewildering two-prong/three-prong device and a round staircase that seems to run uphill all the way clockwise or downhill all the way counterclockwise. Both drawings puzzle us because we try to interpret them as three-dimensional objects.

In Figure 4.61a, we interpret the railroad track as heading into the distance. Similarly, because the background cues in part b suggest that the upper line is farther away than the lower line, we perceive the upper line as being larger. The same is true of the right-hand cylinder in part c. Recall from Figure 4.57 that when two objects produce the same-size image on the retina, we perceive the more distant one as being larger. In short, by perceiving two-dimensional representations as if they were three-dimensional, we misjudge distance and consequently misjudge size. When we are somehow misled by the cues that ordinarily ensure constancy in size and shape, we end up experiencing an optical illusion (Day, 1972).

We can experience an *auditory illusion* by a similar principle: If we misestimate the distance to a sound source, we will misestimate the intensity of the sound. In one study, experimenters misled students about the distance of a sound

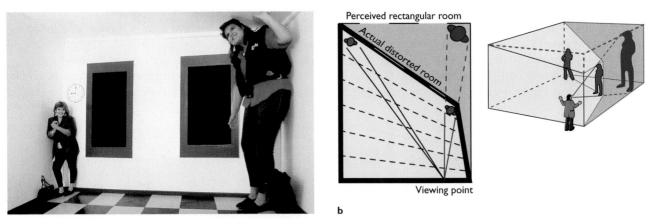

FIGURE 4.59 The Ames room is a study in deceptive perception, designed to be viewed through a peephole with one eye. (a) Both of these people are actually the same height. We are so accustomed to rooms with right angles that we can't imagine how this apparently ordinary room creates this optical illusion. (b) This diagram shows the positions of the people in the Ames room and demonstrates how the illusion of distance is created. [Part (b) from Wilson et al., 1964.]

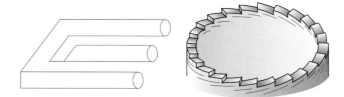

FIGURE 4.60 Expectations shape perceptions. These two-dimensional drawings puzzle us because we try to interpret them as three-dimensional objects.

by using the **visual capture effect,** the *tendency to hear a sound as coming from a visually prominent source.* (You experience this effect when you "hear" a voice coming from a ventriloquist's dummy or from a movie or television screen.) The experimenters had an unchanging sound source that the students never saw, plus a silent "dummy loudspeaker" that moved. The students always thought they heard the sound coming from the dummy loudspeaker, regardless of where the experimenters placed it. When the loudspeaker was far away, most students said the sound was louder than when the speaker was close (Mershon, Desaulniers, Kiefer, Amerson, & Mills, 1981). Remember, the actual sound was the same in all cases. When people thought they heard such a sound from a greater distance, they interpreted it as being more intense.

Cross-Cultural Differences in Seeing Optical Illusions

For most of us, the Müller-Lyer illusion is one of the most convincing. (See Figure 4.62.) According to one attempt at explaining this illusion, the lines with outward-facing arrowheads (on the left in Figure 4.62) appear larger because they resemble the edges of the back of a building; the lines with inward-facing arrowheads resemble the front of a building. (See Figure 4.63.) If we perceive one line (a) as being closer than the other line (b), we are likely to interpret the closer one as shorter.

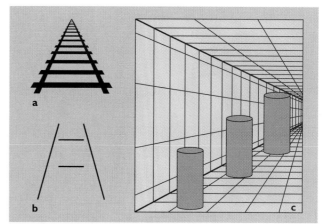

FIGURE 4.61 Some optical illusions depend on misjudgment of distances. In part (b), the top line looks longer because the perspective, resembling the railroad tracks in part (a), suggests a difference in distance. In part (c), the jar on the right seems larger because the context makes it appear farther away.

For several reasons, this explanation is not altogether convincing, but it did lead to the interesting prediction that the Müller-Lyer illusion might be stronger in cultures that have experience with rooms and buildings and weaker in cultures that build circular huts or that live in rain forests or other rural environments. The illusion might also depend on people's experience with drawings of objects.

To test this hypothesis, researchers showed subjects stimuli similar to those in Figure 4.62 and determined which of the horizontal lines with outward arrows appeared the same length as the line with inward arrows. They found that the illusion was stronger for people who lived in cities and weaker for African bushmen (Segall, Campbell, & Herskovits, 1966) and Zambian farm-dwellers (Stewart, 1973). Even the bushmen and farm-dwellers did see the illusion, however; the difference was merely how large an illusion they saw. Furthermore, children generally experienced a larger illusion than adults did, indicating that the ability to see the illusion does not require extensive visual experience.

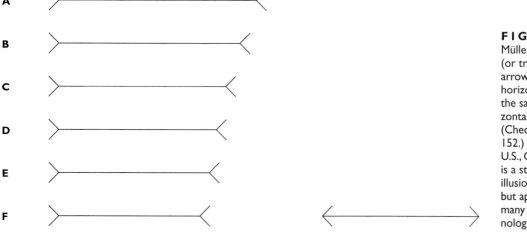

FIGURE 4.62 The Müller-Lyer illusion: Ignoring (or trying to ignore) the arrowheads, which of the horizontal lines on the left is the same length as the horizontal line at the right? (Check answer H on page 152.) For most people in the U.S., Canada, and Europe, this is a strong and convincing illusion. The illusion is present but apparently weaker for many people from less technological societies.

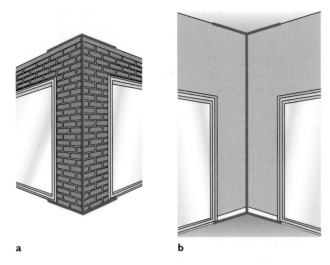

a **b**

F I G U R E 4.63 According to one interpretation of the Müller-Lyer illusion, inward-facing arrowheads make a line appear shorter because they make the line resemble the front of a building (as in a), but outward-facing arrowheads make the line resemble the back of a building (as in b). If we interpret the line with inward-facing arrowheads as closer, we will also interpret the line as shorter.

Clearly the results indicate a cultural influence, but they do not necessarily indicate a cultural difference in depth perception. All the testing was done with drawings on paper, and the differences among cultures probably reflect differences in experience with interpreting two-dimensional drawings (Montello, 1995).

The Moon Illusion

To most people, the *moon close to the horizon appears about 30% larger than it appears when it is higher in the sky*. This **moon illusion** is so convincing that some people have tried to explain it by referring to the bending of light rays by the atmosphere or another physical phenomenon. The explanation, however, must depend on the observer, not the light rays. If you actually measure the moon image with navigational or photographic equipment, you will find that it is the same size at the horizon as it is higher in the sky. For example, Figure 4.64 shows the moon at two positions in the sky; you can measure the two images to demonstrate that they are really the same size. (The atmosphere's bending of light rays makes the moon look orange near the horizon, but it does not increase the size of the image.) However, photographs cannot capture the full strength of the moon illusion as we see it in real life. In Figure 4.64 (or any similar pair of photos), the moon looks almost the same at each position; in the actual night sky, though, the moon looks enormous at the horizon.

One possible explanation is that the vast terrain between the viewer and the horizon provides a basis for size comparison. When you see the moon at the horizon, you can compare it to the other objects you see at the horizon, all of which look tiny. By contrast, the moon looks large. When you see the moon high in the sky, however, it is surrounded only by the vast, featureless sky, so in contrast the moon appears relatively small (Baird, 1982; Restle, 1970).

A second possible explanation is that the terrain between the viewer and the horizon gives an impression of great distance. When the moon is high in the sky, we have no basis to judge distance, and perhaps we thus unconsciously see the overhead moon as closer than the moon is at the horizon. If we see the "horizon moon" as more distant, we will perceive it as larger (Kaufman & Rock, 1989; Rock & Kaufman, 1962). This explanation is appealing, because it relates the moon illusion to our misperceptions of distance, a factor already accepted as important for many other illusions.

Many psychologists are not satisfied with this explanation, however, mostly because they are not convinced that the horizon moon looks farther away than the overhead moon. If we ask people which looks farther away, many say they are not sure. If we prevail upon them to answer, most say the horizon moon looks *closer,* in contradic-

F I G U R E 4.64 Ordinarily, the moon looks much larger at the horizon than it does overhead. In photographs, this illusion disappears completely or almost completely, but the photographs do serve to demonstrate that the physical image of the moon is the same in both cases. The moon illusion requires a psychological explanation, not a physical one.

tion to the theory. Some psychologists reply that the situation is complicated: We unconsciously perceive the horizon as farther away; consequently, we perceive the horizon moon as very large; then, because of the perceived large size of the horizon moon, we secondarily and consciously perceive it as closer (as people report), although we continue to unconsciously perceive it as farther away (Rock & Kaufman, 1962).

One major message arises from work on optical illusions, and indeed from all the research on visual perception: What we perceive is not the same as what is "out there." Our visual system does an amazing job of providing us with useful information about the world around us, but under unusual circumstances we can be very wrong about what we think we see.

THE MESSAGE
Making Sense out of Sensory Information

You have probably heard the expression, "Seeing is believing." The saying is true in many ways, including that what you believe influences what you see. Perception is not just a matter of adding up all the events striking the retina; we look for what we expect to see, we impose order on haphazard patterns, we see three dimensions in two-dimensional drawings, and we see optical illusions. Everything we have experienced in the past, everything that we know (or think that we know) influences what we perceive today.

SUMMARY

✳ *Perception of minimal stimuli.* There is no sharp dividing line between sensory stimuli that can be perceived and sensory stimuli that cannot be perceived. (page 132)

✳ *Signal detection.* To determine how accurately someone can detect a signal or how accurately a test diagnoses a condition, we need to consider not only the ratio of hits to misses when the stimulus is present, but also the ratio of false alarms to correct rejections when the stimulus is absent. (page 133)

✳ *Subliminal perception.* Under some circumstances, a weak stimulus that we do not consciously identify can influence our behavior, at least weakly or briefly. However, the evidence does not support claims of powerful, irresistible effects. (page 134)

✳ *Face recognition.* People are amazingly good at recognizing faces, partly by individual features such as eyes or nose, but also partly by the overall pattern, head size and shape, and the context. (page 135)

✳ *Detection of simple visual features.* In the first stages of the process of perception, feature-detector cells identify lines, points, and simple movement. Feature detectors can-

not account for many of the active, interpretive aspects of perception, however. (page 137)

✳ *Perception of organized wholes.* According to Gestalt psychologists, we perceive an organized whole by identifying similarities and continuous patterns across a large area of the visual field. (page 139)

✳ *Visual constancies.* We ordinarily perceive the shape, size, and color of objects as constant, even though the pattern of light striking the retina varies from time to time. (page 143)

✳ *Motion perception.* We perceive an object as moving if it moves relative to its background. We can generally distinguish between an object that is actually moving and a similar pattern of retinal stimulation that results from our own movement. (page 143)

✳ *Depth perception.* To perceive depth, we use the retinal discrepancy between the views that our two eyes see. We also use other cues that are just as effective with one eye as with two. People need some experience with photos or drawings before they can use depth cues to interpret sizes and distances in the drawings. (page 144)

✳ *Optical illusions.* Many, but not all, optical illusions result from interpreting a two-dimensional display as three-dimensional or from other faulty estimates of depth. (page 146)

✳ *The size-distance relationship.* Our estimate of an object's size depends on our estimate of its distance from us. If we overestimate its distance, we will also overestimate its size. (page 147)

Suggestion for Further Reading

Rock, I. (1984). *Perception.* New York: Scientific American Books. Includes discussions of visual constancies, illusions, motion perception, and the relationship between perception and art.

Terms

sensory threshold   the intensity at which a given individual can detect a sensory stimulus 50% of the time; a low threshold indicates the ability to detect faint stimuli (page 133)

absolute threshold   the sensory threshold at a time of maximum dark adaptation (page 133)

signal-detection theory   the study of people's tendencies to make hits, correct rejections, misses, and false alarms (page 133)

subliminal perception   the ability of a stimulus to influence our behavior even when it is presented so faintly or briefly or along with such strong distractors that we do not perceive it consciously (page 134)

feature detector   a neuron in the visual system of the brain that responds to the presence of a certain simple feature, such as a horizontal line (page 137)

waterfall illusion   a phenomenon in which prolonged staring at a waterfall and then looking at nearby cliffs causes those cliffs to appear to flow upward (page 138)

Gestalt psychology   an approach to psychology that seeks to explain how we perceive overall patterns (page 139)

figure and ground   an object and its background (page 140)

reversible figure   a stimulus that you can perceive in more than one way (page 140)

proximity   in Gestalt psychology, the tendency to perceive objects that are close together as belonging to a group (page 140)

similarity   in Gestalt psychology, the tendency to perceive objects that resemble each other as belonging to a group (page 141)

continuation   in Gestalt psychology, the tendency to fill in the gaps in an interrupted line (page 141)

closure   in Gestalt psychology, the tendency to imagine the rest of an incomplete, familiar figure (page 141)

good figure   in Gestalt psychology, the tendency to perceive simple, symmetrical figures (page 141)

visual constancy   the tendency to perceive objects as unchanging in shape, size, and color, despite variations in what actually reaches the retina (page 143)

induced movement   a perception that an object is moving and the background is stationary when in fact the object is stationary and the background is moving (page 143)

stroboscopic movement   an illusion of movement created by a rapid succession of stationary images (page 144)

phi effect   the illusion of movement created when two or more stationary lights separated by a short distance flash on and off at regular intervals (page 144)

depth perception   the perception of distance, which enables us to experience the world in three dimensions (page 144)

retinal disparity   the difference in the apparent position of an object as seen by the left and right retinas (page 144)

convergence   the degree to which the eyes turn in to focus on a close object (page 144)

binocular cues   visual cues that depend on the action of both eyes (page 144)

monocular cues   visual cues that are just as effective with one eye as with both (page 144)

motion parallax   the apparently swift motion of objects close to a moving observer and the apparently slow motion of objects farther away (page 146)

optical illusion   a misinterpretation of a visual stimulus as being larger or smaller, or straighter or more curved, than it really is (page 146)

visual capture effect   the tendency to localize a sound as coming from a prominent visual feature (such as a loudspeaker or a ventriloquist's dummy) (page 149)

moon illusion   the apparent difference between the size of the moon at the horizon and its size when viewed higher in the sky (page 150)

Answers to Concept Checks

14. We have been told the "hit" rate, but we cannot evaluate it unless we also know the "false alarm" rate. That is, how many people without any alcohol or drug problem have this same pattern of brain waves? If that percentage is large, the test is useless. The smaller that percentage is, the better. (page 134)

15. In Figure 4.41, continuation, closure, and perhaps good figure; in Figure 4.42, closure. (page 142)

16. Object size is a cue that the elephant (usually larger than a deer) must be far away. Interposition is a cue in part a; the deer overlaps a hill that overlaps the hill with the elephant. Linear perspective is a cue in part b. (page 146)

17. Retinal disparity. (page 146)

Answers to Other Questions in the Text

C.   a (7). b (1). c (5). d (9). e (4).

D.

E.

F.

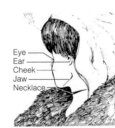

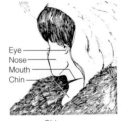

Young woman   Old woman

G.

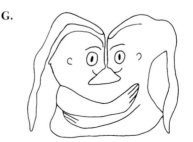

H.   Line d is the same length as the one on the right. (Check it with a ruler.)

Web Resources

Perception & Action Projects

george.arc.nasa.gov/PBA_Group/html/open.html

NASA has posted demonstrations of perceptual illusions and
examples of behavioral adaptation by Malcolm M. Cohen.

Reverse Speech Home Page

www.reversespeech.com/

You've heard that particular recordings contain hidden messages
that can be heard only if the material is played backwards.
One person had the time and patience to research such
claims. You will need the RealAudio plug-in, available for
free at www.realaudio.com/products/player/index.html. Can
you provide a better explanation for the reversed messages?

Altered States

5

During surgery, anesthetized patients are silent, move very little, and show no sign of pain. And if you were to ask them afterward whether they remember anything that happened or anything they heard during the surgery, they would insist that they do not. Nevertheless, if you were to provide a list of words and require them to guess which ones were read aloud during the operation, most of their guesses would be correct—if you ask them within 36 hours (Merikle, 1996).

So, were they conscious during the operation, even though they gave every indication of being unconscious? Or did they remember (weakly) certain events that occurred when they were unconscious? Evidently, the distinction between consciousness and unconsciousness is not a yes-or-no issue: There are various degrees of consciousness.

Consciousness is a fascinating topic, but it is also one of the most difficult phenomena to investigate (Cohen & Schooler, 1997). Does consciousness depend on certain brain areas or processes more than others? Is it really unitary, or do many brain areas each have their own "pieces" of consciousness? Which nonhuman animals (if any) are conscious? What about preverbal children? newborns? fetuses in the middle of pregnancy? brain-damaged people? computers?

Some psychologists regard these questions as answerable; others do not. The main problem is that consciousness, being an internal experience, can be observed by oneself but not by others. The best we can do scientifically is to examine procedures that seem to alter consciousness, such as sleep and dreams, hypnosis, and drugs.

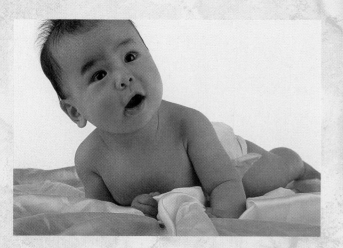

From infancy to adulthood, you repeatedly add and replace material, as did this woman. Only a minuscule fraction of the molecules in your body today are the same as the molecules that were present in infancy. What makes you the same person from one year to the next is your continuous stream of conscious experience.

Sleep and Dreams

Why do we sleep?

What accounts for the content of our dreams?

Ground squirrels hibernate during the winter, a time when they would have trouble finding food. The females awaken in spring as soon as food becomes available. The males also need to awaken in time to eat, but they have another concern as well: The females are ready to mate as soon as they come out of their winter burrows, and each female mates only once a year. Any male who awakens later than the females pays for his extra rest by missing his only mating opportunity for the *entire year*. So males don't take any chances; they all awaken from hibernation a full week before the females do. And then they sit around waiting . . . with no females, nothing to eat, and little to do except to fight with one another (French, 1988).

The point is that animals have evolved internal timing mechanisms to prepare their behavior for predictable needs. Male ground squirrels have a mechanism that awakens them from hibernation while the air is still cold and well before food is available. They awaken not in response to their current situation but in preparation for what will happen a few days later. Similarly, most migrating birds start south in the fall well before their northern homes become inhospitable.

Humans also have built-in timing mechanisms. We do not have an annual mechanism for migration or hibernation, but we do have mechanisms to prepare us for activity during the day and for sleep during the night.

Our Circadian Rhythms

Humans and other highly visual animals are active during the day and inactive at night (Figure 5.1). Rats, mice, and other less visual animals are active at night and inactive during the day. Each species generates a **circadian rhythm,** a *rhythm of activity and inactivity lasting about one day.* (The term *circadian* comes from the Latin roots

circa and *dies*, meaning "about a day.") The rising and setting of the sun provide cues to reset our rhythm each day; in an environment with no cues for time, most people will generate a waking-sleeping rhythm lasting a little longer than 24 hours (Moore-Ede, Czeisler, & Richardson, 1983).

One of the earliest demonstrations of humans' circadian rhythms was a study of two people who spent a few weeks in a remote part of Mammoth Caves in Kentucky (Kleitman, 1963). For 24 hours per day, the temperature was a constant 12° Celsius, and the relative humidity was a steady 100%. They saw no light except the light from lamps that they controlled themselves, and they heard no noises except their own. Any decisions about when to sleep and when to awaken had to come from within, not from the environment. Yet, they went to sleep and awoke at about the same time every day.

Sleepiness and alertness depend strongly on one's position within the circadian rhythm. If you have ever gone all night without sleep—as most college students do at one time or another—you probably grew very sleepy by about 4:00 or 5:00 A.M. But if you were still awake at 7:00 or 8:00 A.M., you began feeling less sleepy, not more so. You became more alert because of your circadian rhythm, even though your sleep deprivation had continued.

In one study, volunteers went without sleep for three nights; an experimenter periodically took their temperature and measured their performance on logical reasoning tasks. Both temperature and logical reasoning declined during the first night and then increased the next morning. During the

FIGURE 5.1 The rising and setting of the sun does not directly produce our daily rhythm of wakefulness and sleepiness, but it synchronizes that rhythm. We adjust our internally generated cycles so that we feel alert during the day and sleepy at night.

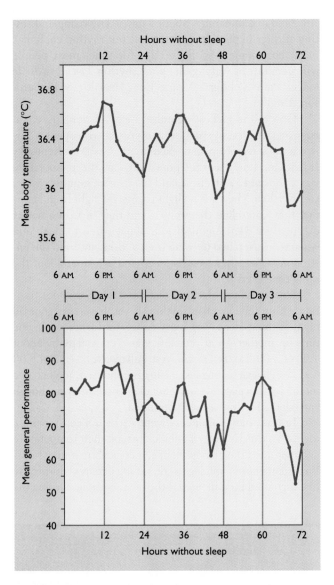

FIGURE 5.2 Cumulative effects of 3 nights without sleep: Both body temperature and logical reasoning decrease each night and increase the next morning. They also deteriorate from one day to the next. (From Babkoff, Caspy, Mikulincer, & Sing, 1991.)

second and third nights, temperature and reasoning decreased more than they had the first night, but they again improved the following morning (Figure 5.2). Thus, sleep deprivation produces a pattern of progressive deterioration that is superimposed on the normal circadian cycle of rising and falling body temperature and alertness (Babkoff, Caspy, Mikulincer, & Sing, 1991). In short, sleepiness apparently depends partly on how long one has gone without sleep and partly on the time of day (that is, where one is within the circadian rhythm).

Morning People and Evening People

Our circadian rhythms do not affect us all in exactly the same way. "Morning people" awaken early and full of energy, doing their best work before noon; "evening people" take longer to become active in the morning and feel best and do their best work in the late afternoon or evening. Most people can diagnose themselves correctly as either morning or evening types. One study found that self-described "morning people" reach their peak body temperature as well as their intellectual and physical peak in the mornings. People who call themselves "evening people" are quite literally slow to warm up in the mornings; their body temperatures are low in the mornings and rise gradually during the day. They also reach their intellectual and physical peak between 5:00 and 10:00 P.M. (Horne, Brass, & Pettitt, 1980).

The morning person/evening person distinction is particularly relevant for research on aging. Most young people are either neutral (about equally alert at all times) or "evening people," whereas nearly all people over age 65 are "morning people." For many years, researchers reported substantial declines in memory with older people. But who did most of this research? Graduate students. How old are graduate students? Most are in their 20s. What time do graduate students choose to conduct their research? Late afternoon or evening, a fine time for 25-year-olds but a miserable time for 65-year-olds. Researchers in one study compared the memories of young adults (18–22 years old) and older adults (66–78 years old) at different times of day. Early in the morning, the older adults did just as well as the younger ones. However, as the day went on, the younger adults either remained steady or improved; the older adults deteriorated steadily (May, Hasher, & Stoltzfus, 1993). Figure 5.3 shows the results of this study.

SOMETHING TO THINK ABOUT

Are most college classes offered in the early morning or late afternoon? Is that because *you* want to take them at that time, or because your aging professors want to schedule them then? ✳

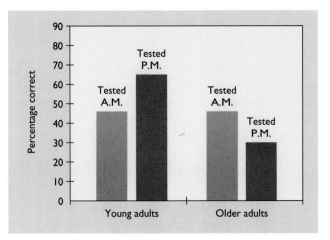

FIGURE 5.3 If tested early in the morning, older people perform as well as younger people on memory tasks. As the day progresses, young people improve and older people deteriorate.

Shifting Sleep Schedules

In ordinary life, the light of early morning serves to reset the body's clock each day to prevent it from gradually slipping out of synchrony with the outside world. If you travel across time zones, the light in your new location will eventually reset your clock to the new time, but until it does so, your internal rhythms will be out of phase with the light and dark cycles of your new environment. For example, if you travel from California to France, it will be 7:00 A.M. (time to get up) when your body says it is 10:00 P.M. (not quite time to go to bed). You will experience **jet lag,** *a period of discomfort and inefficiency, because your internal clock is out of phase with your new surroundings.* You will gradually adjust to the new schedule, although some people adjust much faster than others.

Most people find it easier to adjust when flying west, where they go to bed later, than flying east, where they go to bed earlier (Désir et al., 1981). Thus, east-coast people adjust to west-coast time more easily than west-coast people adjust to east-coast time (Figure 5.4). International pilots, who must constantly adjust to one schedule and then another, develop a variety of techniques to combat fatigue—such as napping, conserving energy, and drinking coffee (Petrie & Dawson, 1997).

It is possible to have an experience akin to jet lag without leaving town. Suppose you stay up late on Friday night and wake up late on Saturday morning. (Many readers will not find this difficult to imagine.) Then, you stay up late again on Saturday and wake up late on Sunday. By Monday morning, when it is time to awaken for school or work, your circadian rhythm has readjusted, so even though the clock on your table says 7:00 A.M., your internal clock thinks you are somewhere far to the west where the time is only 5:00 A.M.

Companies that want to keep their factories going nonstop run three work shifts, such as midnight–8:00 A.M., 8:00 A.M.–4:00 P.M., and 4:00 P.M.–midnight. Because few

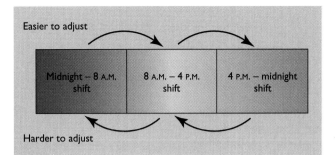

FIGURE 5.5 The graveyard shift is aptly named—serious industrial accidents usually occur at night, when workers are least alert. Night-shift jobs providing emergency services are essential. But few people want to work permanently at night, so workers rotate among three shifts. As in jet lag, the direction of change is critical. Moving forward—clockwise—is easier than going backward.

people want to work regularly on the "graveyard shift" (midnight–8:00 A.M.), many companies rotate their workers among the three shifts. Suppose that you worked the 8:00 A.M.–4:00 P.M. shift today but tomorrow you are scheduled to work the midnight–8:00 A.M. shift. You can't get to sleep at 4:00 in the afternoon, so you show up for work without having slept. You are likely to make many mistakes during the night, and by the time you are ready to drive home the next morning, your coordination and judgment will be as badly impaired as if you were legally drunk (Dawson & Reid, 1997). Even people who work the night shift month after month may continue feeling groggy on the job and sleeping fitfully during the day.

There are two ways for employers to ease the burden on their workers: First, when they transfer workers from one shift to another, they should transfer workers to a *later* shift, not an earlier shift (Czeisler, Moore-Ede, & Coleman, 1982) (Figure 5.5). That is, someone working the 8:00 A.M.–4:00 P.M. shift should switch to the 4:00 P.M.–midnight shift (equivalent to traveling west), instead of the midnight–8:00 A.M. shift (equivalent to traveling east).

Second, employers can help workers adjust to the night shift by providing bright lights to mimic sunlight. In one study, young men exposed to very bright lights at night adjusted well to working at night and sleeping during the day. Within six days, their circadian rhythms had shifted to the new schedule. Another group of men who worked on the same schedule but under dimmer lights showed no indications of altering their circadian rhythms (Czeisler et al., 1990).

CONCEPT CHECK

1. Suppose you are the president of Consolidated Generic Products in the United States. You are negotiating a difficult business deal with someone from

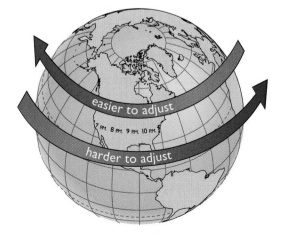

FIGURE 5.4 People traveling east suffer more serious jet lag than people traveling west.

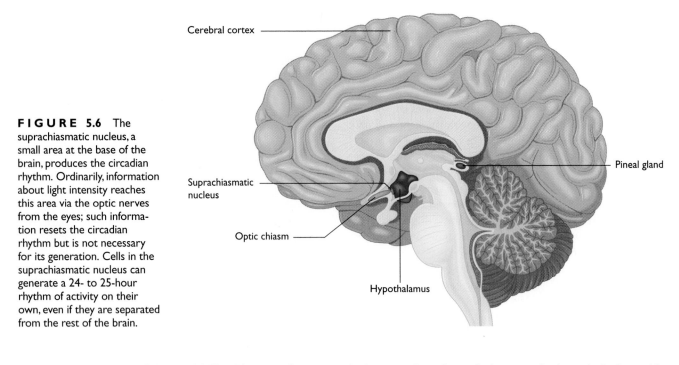

FIGURE 5.6 The suprachiasmatic nucleus, a small area at the base of the brain, produces the circadian rhythm. Ordinarily, information about light intensity reaches this area via the optic nerves from the eyes; such information resets the circadian rhythm but is not necessary for its generation. Cells in the suprachiasmatic nucleus can generate a 24- to 25-hour rhythm of activity on their own, even if they are separated from the rest of the brain.

Cerebral cortex

Pineal gland

Suprachiasmatic nucleus

Optic chiasm

Hypothalamus

the opposite side of the world. Should you prefer a meeting place in Europe or on an island in the Pacific Ocean? (Check your answer on page 172.)

SOMETHING TO THINK ABOUT

Imagine someone who cannot get to sleep until 3:00 A.M.; for months she has been trying to get to bed earlier, but failing. What advice would you offer? (Hint: Remember that our internal clocks can shift more easily to a later time than to an earlier time.) ✳

Brain Mechanisms of Circadian Rhythms

The circadian rhythm of sleep and wakefulness is generated by a tiny structure at the base of the brain, known as the *suprachiasmatic nucleus*. If that area of the brain is damaged, the body's activity cycles become erratic (Rusak, 1977); if cells from that area are kept alive outside the body, they generate a circadian rhythm on their own (Green & Gillette, 1982; Inouye & Kawamura, 1979). In short, this area of the brain serves as the body's built-in clock. (See Figure 5.6.)

The suprachiasmatic nucleus exerts its control partly by regulating secretions of the hormone *melatonin* by the pineal gland. Ordinarily, the human pineal gland starts releasing increased amounts of melatonin at about 8:00 to 10:00 P.M., so people find it easy to fall asleep about two or three hours later. If you take a melatonin pill in the evening, you will notice little if any effect, because you were already producing increased melatonin at that time. However, if you have just flown a few time zones east and want to get to

bed two or three hours before your biological clock would ordinarily allow, then a melatonin pill can be very helpful indeed (Deacon & Arendt, 1996).

CONCEPT CHECK

2. Suppose you are required to work the midnight–8:00 A.M. shift, and you would like to go to sleep at 4:00 P.M. in order to be well-rested before starting work. Would a melatonin pill help? If so, when should you take it? (Check your answer on page 172.)

Why We Sleep

We would not have been born with a mechanism that forces us to sleep for 8 hours or so out of every 24 unless sleep did us some good. But what good does sleep do? Scientists have proposed two theories.

The Repair and Restoration Theory of Why We Sleep

According to the **repair and restoration theory,** *the purpose of sleep is to enable the body to recover from the exertions of the day.* We undeniably need sleep, and we suffer if we do not get it. Sleep deprivation leads to impaired concentration and irritability; prolonged deprivation can impair the function of the immune system and thus increase the risk of becoming ill (Dement, 1972; Everson, 1995; Rechtschaffen & Bergmann, 1995). However, most of the restorative functions that occur during sleep—such as digestion and protein synthesis—also occur during quiet waking periods. Furthermore, in many ways sleeping is different from resting to catch your breath after extensive exercise.

• People need only a little more sleep after a day of extreme physical or mental activity than after a day of inactivity (Horne & Minard, 1985).

• Some people get by with much less than the "normal" 7½ to 8 hours of sleep per day. One extreme case was a healthy 70-year-old woman who slept only about 1 hour each night (Meddis, Pearson, & Langford, 1973).

• Some people fare better than we would have expected after a week or more of sleep deprivation (Figure 5.7). In 1965, a San Diego high-school student, Randy Gardner, stayed awake for 264 hours and 12 minutes—11 days—in a project for a high-school science fair. Gardner suffered no serious psychological consequences (Dement, 1972). On the last night of his ordeal, he played about 100 arcade games against sleep researcher William Dement and won every game. Just before the end of the 264 hours, he held a television press conference and handled himself well. After sleeping for 14 hours and 40 minutes, he awoke refreshed.

If a torturer prevented you from sleeping for the next 11 days, would you do as well as Randy Gardner? Probably not, for two reasons: First, Gardner knew he was in control of the situation and that he could quit if necessary. A torturer would not give you that option. Second, people vary in their ability to tolerate sleep deprivation. We heard about Gardner only because he tolerated it so well. We have no idea how many other people tried to deprive themselves of sleep for several days but gave up.

The summary evaluation of the repair and restoration theory is that the body does do some restoration during sleep, and sleep deprivation *is* harmful, although more so to some people than to others. However, each of us has an urge to sleep, even a need to sleep, at a certain time of day, regardless of how active or inactive we have been during the day. Also, most of the restorative functions of sleep could occur during occasional quiet times, without setting aside an 8-hour period for sleep. Therefore, it is possible that sleep serves other functions as well.

The Evolutionary or Energy-Conservation Theory

Sleep is a way of conserving energy. If we built a solar-powered robot to explore another planet, we would probably program it to shut down most of its activities at night. According to the **evolutionary,** or **energy-conservation, theory of sleep,** *evolution equipped us with a regular pattern of sleeping and waking for the same reason—to conserve fuel and to prevent us from walking into dangers* (Kleitman, 1963; Webb, 1979). Every species has an inefficient time of day; night is that time for humans and other highly visual species. Throughout our evolutionary

FIGURE 5.7 Even near the end of Randy Gardner's 264 consecutive hours without sleep, he was able to perform tasks requiring strength and skill. Here, observers dutifully record his every move.

history, until the invention of electric lights, any activity conducted at night was likely to be wasteful and possibly dangerous. By sleeping, we decrease our energy use by 10 to 25%. At times when food is especially scarce, we either sleep more or we lower our body temperature more than usual, thus conserving even more energy (Berger & Phillips, 1995).

However, sleep protects us only from the sort of trouble we might walk into; it does not protect us from trouble that comes looking for us! So, we sleep well when we are in a familiar, safe place; but we sleep lightly, if at all, when we fear that burglars will break into the house or that bears will nose into our tent.

The evolutionary theory accounts well for differences in sleep among species (Campbell & Tobler, 1984). For example, why do cats sleep so much and horses so little? First, cats can afford to have long periods of inactivity because they eat one or two large, energy-rich meals per day; horses need to spend many hours grazing every day. Second, cats are unlikely to be attacked while they sleep, whereas horses must always be ready to run away from a predator (Figure 5.8). (Woody Allen once said, "The lion and the calf shall lie down together, but the calf won't get much sleep.")

Which of these two theories regarding sleep is correct? Both are, to a large degree. Supporters of the repair and restoration theory concede that the timing and even the amount of sleep depend on when the animal is least efficient at finding food and defending itself. Supporters of the evolutionary theory concede that, during the time

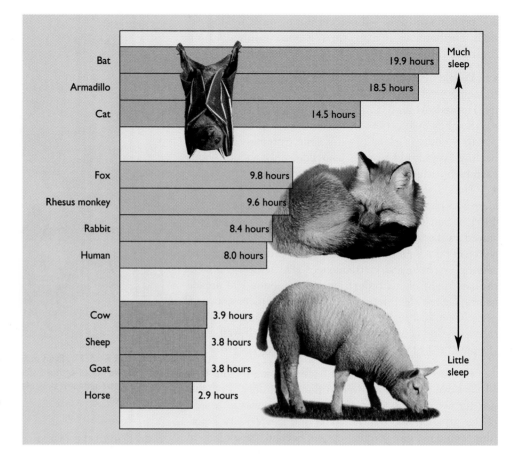

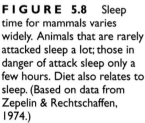

FIGURE 5.8 Sleep time for mammals varies widely. Animals that are rarely attacked sleep a lot; those in danger of attack sleep only a few hours. Diet also relates to sleep. (Based on data from Zepelin & Rechtschaffen, 1974.)

that evolution has set aside for an animal to conserve energy, that animal takes that opportunity to perform repair and restoration functions.

Stages of Sleep

In the mid-1950s, the French scientist Michel Jouvet (Jouvet, Michel, & Courjon, 1959) and the American researchers William Dement and Nathaniel Kleitman (1957a, 1957b) independently discovered a stage of sleep called either *paradoxical sleep* or **rapid-eye movement (REM) sleep.** *During this stage of sleep, the sleeper's eyes move rapidly back and forth under the closed lids.* (All other stages of sleep are known as non-REM, or NREM, sleep.) A paradox is an apparent contradiction; REM sleep is sometimes called paradoxical because it is light in some ways and deep in others. It is light because the brain is active and the body's heart rate, breathing rate, and temperature fluctuate substantially (Parmeggiani, 1982). It is deep because the large muscles of the body, those that control posture and locomotion, are very relaxed. It also has some features that are hard to classify as either deep or light; for example, males typically have an erection of the penis and females have lubrication of the vagina during REM sleep.

People are more likely to report dreams, especially vivid and highly visual dreams, if they are awakened during REM sleep than if awakened during NREM sleep, although some sort of dream report is common in both states. The discovery of REM sleep inspired much research interest in dreaming.

Sleep Cycles During the Night

Sleep researchers distinguish among stages of sleep by recording brain waves with electrodes attached to the scalp (Figure 5.9). *A device* called an **electroencephalograph,** abbreviated **EEG,** *measures and amplifies slight electrical changes on the scalp that reflect patterns of activity in the brain.* Sleep researchers *combine an EEG measure with a simultaneous measure of eye movements* to produce a **polysomnograph** (literally, "many-sleep measure") as shown in Figure 5.10. Upon falling asleep, one enters sleep non-REM stage 1, when the eyes are nearly motionless and the EEG shows many short, choppy waves, as shown in Figure 5.10a. These small waves indicate a fair amount of brain activity, with brain cells firing out of synchrony with one another. Because they are out of synchrony, their activities nearly cancel each other out, like a crowd of people talking at the same time.

As sleep continues, a person progresses into non-REM stages 2, 3, and 4, as shown in Figure 5.10b–e. These stages

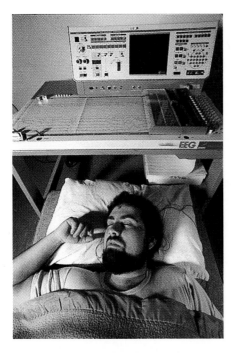

FIGURE 5.9 Electrodes monitor the activity in a sleeper's brain, and an EEG then records and displays brain-wave patterns.

are most easily distinguished by the number of long, slow waves; stage 1 has the fewest, and stage 4 has the most. These large waves indicate *decreased* brain activity. They grow larger from one stage to the next, because a larger proportion of the active neurons are active at the same time. (Note that the eyes remain mostly inactive in each of these stages.)

After stage 4, a sleeper gradually moves back through stages 3 and 2. After that, however, the sleeper enters REM sleep, not stage 1. That is, REM sleep replaces most of stage 1 except for the first episode of the night. In Figure 5.10f, the EEG in REM sleep resembles that of stage 1, but the eyes are moving more extensively and more regularly than they do during any other stage. At the end of REM sleep, the sleeper cycles through stages 2, 3, 4, and then back to 3, 2, and REM again. In a healthy young adult, each cycle lasts 90 to 100 minutes. As shown in Figure 5.11, the cycles continue throughout the night, but as the night progresses, the duration of stages 3 and 4 gets shorter and the duration of REM and stage 2 increases. Figure 5.11 represents sleep under quiet, undisturbed conditions; if the room is noisy, too hot, too cold, or uncomfortable in any other way, the person will have many awakenings and whatever sleep the person does manage will be mostly stage 2 (Velluti, 1997).

Sleep Stages and Dreaming

William Dement's early research indicated that people who were awakened during REM sleep usually reported they had been dreaming but that people who were awakened

during any other period seldom reported dreaming. So, for a while, REM sleep was thought to be almost synonymous with dreaming. However, later studies found that much dreaming also occurs during non-REM sleep, although non-REM dreams are less vivid, less visual, less bizarre, and less likely to be experienced as something that's really happening.

The link between REM sleep and the more vivid dreams prompted sleep investigators to awaken people during REM sleep to ask for dream reports. Scientific progress frequently depends on an improved way of measuring something; in this case, a method for measuring dreaming enabled researchers to answer some basic questions.

For example, does everyone dream? People who claim they do not dream have been taken into the laboratory and attached to a polysomnograph, which revealed normal periods of REM sleep. When these people were awakened during a REM period, they reported dreams (to their own surprise). Apparently, they dream as much as anyone else but forget their dreams faster.

Another question: How long do dreams last? William Dement and Edward Wolpert (1958) awakened people after REM periods of various durations and asked them to describe their dreams. A person awakened after 1 minute of REM sleep would usually tell a brief story; a person awakened after 5 minutes of REM sleep would usually tell a story about 5 times as long, and so on. Evidently, dreams take place in "real time." That is, a dream is not over in a split second; if a dream seemed to last several minutes, it probably did.

Many other questions about dreaming remain unanswerable, however. For example, how accurately do we remember our dreams? Memory distortions occur even for waking events; they are probably much more extreme for dreams, but we do not know how to measure this distortion. Or consider this apparently simple question: Do we dream in color? The fact that people ask this question reveals why it is difficult to answer: They ask because they do not remember whether their dreams were in color. But how could an investigator determine the answer except by asking people? The best evidence we have is that, when people are awakened during REM sleep, when their recall should be as sharp as possible, they report color at least half of the time (Herman, Roffwarg, & Tauber, 1968; Padgham, 1975). This result does not necessarily mean that their other dreams are in black and white; it may mean only that the colors in those dreams were not memorable.

CONCEPT CHECK

3. Is dreaming more common toward the end of the night's sleep or toward the beginning? (Check your answer on page 172.)

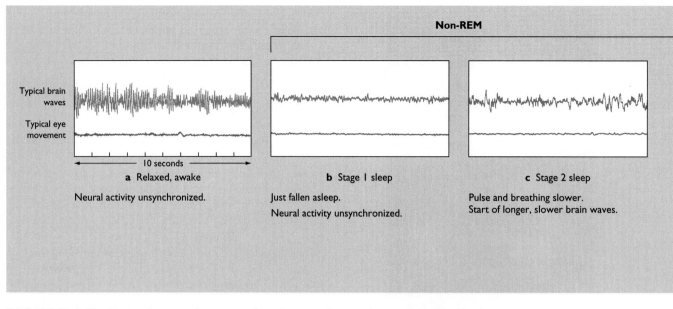

FIGURE 5.10 During sleep, people progress through stages of varying brain activity. The blue line indicates brain waves, as shown by an EEG. The red line shows eye movements. Note that REM sleep resembles stage 1 sleep except for the addition of rapid eye movements. (Courtesy of T. E. LeVere.)

FIGURE 5.11 This fairly typical sleeper had five cycles of REM and non-REM sleep and awakened (A) briefly three times during the night. Note that stage 4 occupies much time early in the night but less later; REM sleep becomes more and more prevalent as the night progresses. (From Dement, 1972.)

The Functions of REM Sleep

Given that people spend 20–25% of an average night in REM sleep, it presumably serves an important function, but what? The most direct way to approach this question is to deprive people of REM sleep to study how this deprivation affects their health or behavior.

In one study, William Dement (1960) monitored the sleep of eight young men for seven consecutive nights and awakened them for a few minutes whenever their EEG and eye movements indicated the onset of REM sleep. He awakened the members of a control group equally often but at random times, so that he did not necessarily interrupt their REM sleep. Over the course of one week, Dement found it harder and harder to prevent REM sleep in the experimental group. On the first night, the average subject had to be awakened 12 times; by the seventh night, 26 times. During the day, REM-deprived subjects experienced anxiety, irritability, and impaired concentration. On the eighth night, all the subjects were permitted to sleep without interruption. Most of them showed a "REM rebound," spending 29% of the night in REM sleep as compared with 19% before the experiment began. The subjects in the

control group, who had not been deprived of REM sleep, showed no such REM rebound.

So, evidently, REM sleep does satisfy a need, and the body will work to catch up on at least some of the REM sleep that it has been forced to miss. However, in this and related studies, the effects of REM deprivation have not been catastrophic, so the question of why we need REM sleep remained.

A second approach to the question is to determine which people get more REM sleep than others. One clear pattern is that infants get more REM sleep than children, and children more than adults. From that observation, many researchers have inferred that REM sleep serves a function that is more acute in younger people. Maybe so, but we should be cautious when interpreting this evidence. Infants not only get more REM sleep but also get more total sleep (Figure 5.12). If we compare species, we find that the species that get the most sleep (such as cats) also generally have the greatest percentage of REM sleep. Among adult humans, those who sleep 9 or more hours per night, spend a large percentage of that time in REM sleep; those who sleep 6 hours or less spend a smaller percentage in REM sleep. In short, the individuals with the greatest

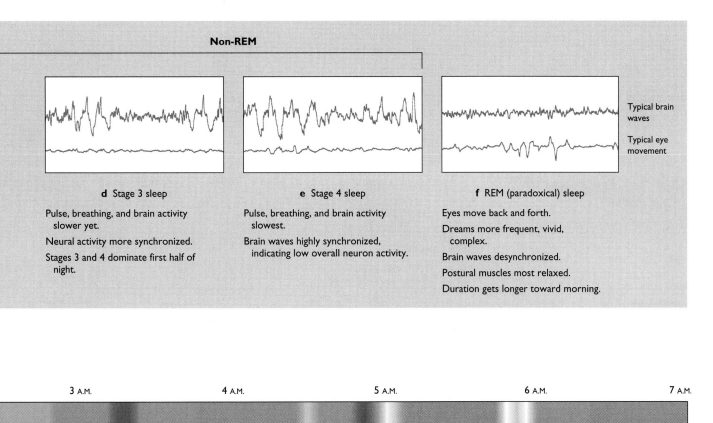

Non-REM

d Stage 3 sleep

Pulse, breathing, and brain activity slower yet.

Neural activity more synchronized.

Stages 3 and 4 dominate first half of night.

e Stage 4 sleep

Pulse, breathing, and brain activity slowest.

Brain waves highly synchronized, indicating low overall neuron activity.

f REM (paradoxical) sleep

Eyes move back and forth.

Dreams more frequent, vivid, complex.

Brain waves desynchronized.

Postural muscles most relaxed.

Duration gets longer toward morning.

Typical brain waves

Typical eye movement

3 A.M.   4 A.M.   5 A.M.   6 A.M.   7 A.M.

2   3   2   REM   1   2   3 2 **A**   REM   **A   A**   2   REM

amount of total sleep time spend the greatest percentage of that time in REM. It is as though a certain amount of *non-REM* sleep is necessary each night; additional amounts of REM sleep can be added if the period of sleep continues long enough (Horne, 1988).

A growing body of research suggests that one function of REM sleep, though not necessarily the main one, is to improve memory storage. When animals are given new learning experiences, they generally get more than the usual amount of REM sleep the following night, and ani-

mals prevented from getting REM sleep learn slowly (Hobson, 1992). As a rule, the animals that learn fastest are also the ones that show the greatest increase in REM sleep (Smith & Wong, 1991). In humans, research indicates that REM sleep is more important for storing some kinds of memories than others. Young adults in one experiment memorized some words and learned a motor skill—tracing some pictures as seen in a mirror—just before a period of sleep either early in the night (mostly non-REM sleep) or late in the night (mostly REM sleep). Other students

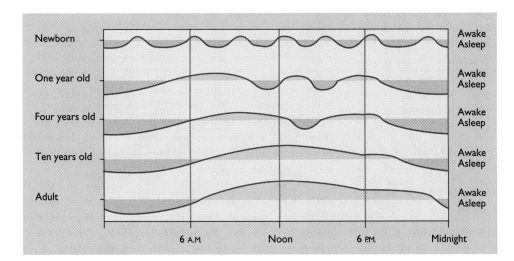

F I G U R E 5.12 Newborns' sleep alternates between wakefulness and naps throughout the day. Within a few months, infants consolidate most of their sleep into one longer period at night, although they continue having one or two naps during the day. As people grow older, the amount of sleep per day decreases. (Based on Kleitman, 1963.)

FIGURE 5.13 Students who learned materials before a period of mostly non-REM sleep thus improved their memory of verbal materials but not motor skills. Those who learned just before a period of mostly REM sleep improved their memory of motor skills but not verbal materials. (Based on results of Plihal & Born, 1997.)

learned the same materials but were then required to stay awake. After three hours of sleep or wakefulness, all were tested for their memory of the two tasks. Those who had experienced three hours of mostly non-REM sleep showed enhanced memory of the word lists. Those who had mostly REM sleep showed enhanced memory of the motor skills (Plihal & Born, 1997). Figure 5.13 summarizes this experiment. The apparent conclusion is that REM sleep is specifically important for strengthening the memories of motor skills but not memories of factual or verbal materials.

The Content of Our Dreams

Even a saint is not responsible for what happens in his dreams.

—ST. THOMAS AQUINAS

What do we dream about and why? People once believed that dreams foretold the future. Occasionally, of course, they do—either by coincidence or because the dreamer

had a reason to expect a certain outcome. Sigmund Freud maintained that dreams reveal a person's unconscious thoughts and motivations. Although Freud's interpretations often revealed more about Freud's imagination than about the dreamer, people's dreams usually do relate somehow to recent thoughts and concerns, though not necessarily unconscious ones (Arkin & Antrobus, 1978). For example, people deprived of fluids frequently dream about drinking; people who have been kept in isolation dream about talking in groups. The dreams of old people differ from those of the young; dreams of women differ from those of men. Curiously, women dream about men more than men dream about women (Domhoff, 1996; Hall & Van de Castle, 1966).

For adult dreamers in the United States—and apparently in other countries, too, according to more limited data—one common dream theme is "things that could go wrong." People often dream of falling, being chased, being naked or almost naked in public, or being unable to do something they need to do. The most common emotion in dreams is apprehension or fear; more dreams include misfortune than good fortune; and the dreamer is more often the victim of aggression than the cause of it (Domhoff, 1996; Hall & Van de Castle, 1966). People occasionally awaken with disappointment that it was only a dream, but more often they awaken with relief. A frequently recurring dream is often a sign of a persistent worry or concern. People who have the same dream over and over tend to report more anxiety, depression, and stress in their waking lives than do other people (Brown & Donderi, 1986).

Dreams are a product of brain activity, and even a sleeping brain experiences a fair amount of sensory information. While you sleep, you can hear any noises in the room, and your vestibular system detects the position of your head (Velluti, 1997). Sometimes these stimuli affect dreams; for example, a noise that is not loud enough to awaken someone might become an explosion or an alarm in a dream. Usually, however, the content of a dream is only remotely related to stimuli in the room, if at all.

A more important correlate of dreams is the spontaneous activity that arises in the brain during REM sleep, particularly in the visual areas. According to the **activation-synthesis theory of dreams,** *the brain experiences this spontaneous activity as sensations, links the sensations together, and tries to synthesize them into a coherent pattern* (Hobson, 1988). A dream is your brain's best effort to make sense of the limited information it is receiving.

For example, the visual areas of the brain become active during REM sleep, especially during the first minutes of a REM period, so nearly all dreams include visual content (Amzica & Steriade, 1996). In one study, a man repeatedly slept in a laboratory; the investigators awakened him during REM periods. They found that the more eye movements he had during his REM periods, the more visual imagery he reported in his dreams, especially imagery of watching other people move (Hong et al., 1997). However, this was just a single study with one participant. Recall from Chapter 2 that we cannot draw cause-and-effect conclusions from correlational studies; that is, we cannot say whether the eye movements controlled the dreams, the dreams affected the eye movements, or another factor controlled both of them.

You might wonder whether blind people have visual dreams. The answer depends on when and how a person became blind. People who had visual experience before eye damage continue to see during their dreams. (The visual cortex is still intact and becomes spontaneously active during REM sleep.) But a person who never had vision or who lost it because of damage to the visual cortex has no visual imagery during dreams, only auditory and touch imagery. People with any degree of visual impairment are more likely than sighted people to dream about touching something (Sabo & Kirtley, 1982).

Many other kinds of dreams also appear to relate to the spontaneous activity of the brain during REM sleep. Many people occasionally dream of flying or falling, probably because the vestibular system detects the body's horizontal position and the brain interprets this sensation as floating or flying (Hobson & McCarley, 1977). Many dreams include strong emotions, especially fear; the *amygdala,* a brain area known to be linked to fear, is highly active during REM sleep (Maquet et al., 1996). Have you ever dreamed that you are trying to walk or run away but you cannot move? One possible reason for this is that the major postural muscles are really paralyzed during REM sleep. Thus, your brain could send messages telling your muscles to move but then receive sensory feedback indicating that they have not moved at all. Finally, consider that many dreams jump incoherently among unrelated scenes and events. One possible explanation is that the prefrontal cortex, which is important for storing recent memories, is substantially *less* active than usual during REM sleep (Maquet et al., 1996).

The problem with the activation-synthesis theory, however, is that it does not make clear, testable predictions. For example, people almost always sleep horizontally but only occasionally dream of flying or falling: Why not always? Our muscles are always paralyzed during REM sleep: Why do we sometimes dream that we're moving but other times dream that we can't? *After* a dream, the activation-synthesis theory can provide explanations, but it offers only vague predictions of who will dream about what and when. This theory can therefore be criticized for not being falsifiable (see Chapter 2).

Finally, however, the activation-synthesis theory does not necessarily imply that our dreams are meaningless. Even if they begin with more-or-less random activity in various brain areas, the dreamer's interpretations of this activity depend on his or her personality, motivations, and previous experiences.

Abnormalities of Sleep

Comedian Steven Wright says that someone asked him, "Did you sleep well last night?" He replied, "No, I made a few mistakes."

We laugh because sleep isn't the kind of activity on which a person makes mistakes; sleep just happens. Sometimes, however, sleep doesn't happen, or it happens at the wrong time, or it does not seem restful, or we have bad dreams. We would not call these unpleasant experiences "mistakes," but in one way or another, our sleep is not what we wanted it to be.

Insomnia

The term *insomnia* literally means "lack of sleep." However, we cannot usefully define insomnia in terms of the number of hours of sleep. Some people feel well rested after less than 6 hours of sleep per night; others feel poorly rested after 9 hours. A complaint of **insomnia** indicates that *the person feels poorly rested the next day.* By this definition,

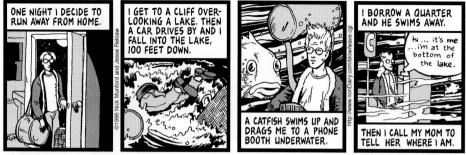

These comic strips represent actual dreams as described to the artist. Dreams often mix possible with impossible events and frequently explore the theme of "things that could go wrong."

about one third of all adults have occasional insomnia and about one tenth have serious or chronic insomnia (Lilie & Rosenberg, 1990). Most of those with serious insomnia have other medical or psychological disorders as well, such as anxiety disorders or depression (Ohayon, 1997).

People sometimes have trouble sleeping because of noise, worries, indigestion, uncomfortable temperatures, use of alcohol or caffeine, and other miscellaneous problems. Overuse of tranquilizers can also cause insomnia. That statement may be surprising, because people often take tranquilizers as a way of *relieving* insomnia. The problem is that no pill will exert its effects for exactly the period of time that someone wants to sleep. Some tranquilizers produce brief effects that wear off before morning, so the person awakens early (Kales, Soldatos, Bixler, & Kales, 1983). Others have effects that last too long, so the person remains sleepy for part of the next day. Moreover, people who use tranquilizers as sleeping pills may come to depend on them, so that they cannot get to sleep without them (Kales, Scharf, & Kales, 1978).

WHAT'S THE EVIDENCE?
Disorders Related to Insomnia

Most people with insomnia suffer from a variety of other complaints and disorders, including tension, depression, personality disturbances, loss of energy, and increases in body temperature and metabolism. Does the lack of sleep *cause* these other problems? Maybe, maybe not; the fact that people with insomnia also tend to have other problems is merely a correlation, and a correlation does not demonstrate causation.

Insomnia is identified not by how many hours one sleeps at night but by how sleepy the person is the following day.

How might we determine whether insomnia leads to these other problems? Here is a clever experiment that addresses this issue (Bonnet & Arand, 1996).

Hypothesis   A previously normal person who is forced to sleep only as long as someone with insomnia, at the same times, will develop a similar pattern of medical and psychological abnormalities.

Method   Experimenters identified 10 adults with insomnia, who were defined as people who, for at least the last year, on more nights than not, took at least 45 minutes to get to sleep and awoke for at least an hour during the night. The experimenters then advertised for volunteers who had no sleeping problems. For each person with insomnia, they matched one volunteer of the same gender and approximately the same age and weight. For seven nights, the experimenters monitored the sleep of the people with insomnia. Whenever one of them went to sleep, the volunteer partner was allowed to go to sleep. When the person with insomnia woke up, the matched volunteer was awakened also. Thus, each volunteer awoke and went to sleep at the same times as one person with insomnia. This kind of design is known as a *yoked control experiment,* because each participant in one group is "yoked" to one person in the other group. At various times during the week, each person was given a variety of medical and psychological tests.

Results   Table 5.1 summarizes the results.

Interpretation   After one week of enforced insomnia, the normal people had less vigor, so we may conclude that lack of sleep decreases pep and energy. In other regards, however, the week of enforced insomnia produced either no effect or effects opposite to those found in people suffering from chronic insomnia. We conclude, therefore, that sleep deprivation by itself does not cause tension, depression, personality disturbances, or increases in body temperature or metabolic rate. Instead, many people develop insomnia because of nervous system disorders that also lead to tension, depression, high body temperature, and so forth.

✶   ✶   ✶

Sleep Apnea

Among the many possible causes of insomnia, one is known as *sleep apnea* (AP-nee-uh). *Apnea* means "no breathing." Many people have either irregular breathing or occasional periods of 10 seconds or so without breathing during their sleep. People with **sleep apnea,** however, may *fail to breathe for a minute or longer and then wake up gasping for breath.* When these people do manage to breathe during their sleep, they generally snore. They may lie in bed for 8 to 10 hours per night but actually sleep less than half that time. During the following day, they are likely to feel sleepy and they may have headaches.

Many people with sleep apnea are obese—especially obese middle-aged or older men, who are unable to find a sleeping position that lets them breathe easily (Mezzanotte, Tangel, & White, 1992). Others have brain abnormalities, especially in the medulla, that interfere with their breathing during sleep.

Narcolepsy   People who experience *sudden attacks of extreme, even irresistible, sleepiness in the middle of the day* are said to have **narcolepsy** (Aldrich, 1993). Such people may also experience sudden attacks of muscle weakness or paralysis. Sometimes they have vivid dreamlike experiences while they are awake. Each of these symptoms could be interpreted as a sudden intrusion of sleep, especially REM sleep, into the waking period of the day.

Narcolepsy is a rare condition, affecting about one person per thousand. Its causes are unknown, although it often runs in families. Physicians prescribe stimulants and antidepressant drugs, both of which are helpful in many cases. Some physicians are hesitant to prescribe these drugs, however, because of side effects and the potential for abuse of stimulant drugs (Kryger, 1993).

Sleep Talking, Sleepwalking, Nightmares, and Night Terrors

Many people, whether or not they suffer from insomnia, nevertheless have unsettling experiences during their sleep. Sleep talking is the most common and least troublesome.

TABLE 5.1 **Test Results in Insomnia Experiment**		
	PEOPLE WITH INSOMNIA	NORMAL PEOPLE AFTER 1 WEEK OF ENFORCED INSOMNIA
Tension	More tense than most people	Decreased tension
Mood	Depressed	Not depressed
Vigor	Low	Low
Personality	Disturbed in several ways	Normal
Estimate of own sleep	Underestimate amount of sleep	Correctly estimate amount of sleep
Body temperature	Higher than normal	Lower than normal
Metabolic rate	Higher than normal	Lower than normal

Most people talk in their sleep more often than they realize, because they do not remember sleep talking themselves and usually no one else is awake to hear them. Sleep talking occurs with about equal probability in REM sleep and non-REM sleep. It can range from a single, indistinct word or grunt to a clearly articulated paragraph. Sleep talkers sometimes pause between utterances, as if they were carrying on a conversation with someone else. In fact, it is possible to engage some sleep talkers in a dialogue. Sleep talking is nothing to worry about. It is not related to any mental or emotional disorder, and sleep talkers rarely say anything that they would be embarrassed to say when awake.

Sleepwalking tends to run (walk?) in families. True sleepwalking occurs mostly in children during stage 4 sleep and lasts less than 15 minutes. Few children hurt themselves when sleepwalking, and most children outgrow it (Dement, 1972). A person who appears to be sleepwalking may really be awake but confused. You have no doubt heard people say that you should never awaken a sleepwalker. This is another of those misconceptions, like "we use only 10 percent of our brain," in which people are quoting each other, each person confident that the others know what they are talking about. In fact, sleep researchers report that waking a sleepwalker is neither dangerous nor harmful, although the person may indeed be disoriented and confused (Moorcroft, 1993).

Other concerns include nightmares and night terrors. A nightmare is an unpleasant dream, but a dream nevertheless. A night terror, however, is a state of extreme panic, including a heart rate three times the normal rate. Night terrors occur during stage 3 or stage 4 sleep but never during REM sleep. They are fairly common in young children and less common in adults (Salzarulo & Chevalier, 1983).

Leg Movements While Trying to Sleep

Have you ever lain in bed, trying to fall asleep, when suddenly one of your legs kicked? An occasional leg jerk while trying to fall asleep is a common experience and no cause for concern. In contrast, some people have *prolonged "creepy-crawly" sensations in their legs, accompanied by repetitive leg movements strong enough to awaken the person, especially during the first half of the night* (Moorcroft, 1993). This condition, known as **periodic limb movement disorder** (or, more informally, as restless leg syndrome), is a common cause of poor sleep in people over the age of 50. Sufferers can stop the leg kicks by standing and walking, but by doing so they of course interrupt their sleep. The causes of this disorder are unknown, and the best advice is to avoid factors that can make the condition worse—such as caffeine, stress, or fatigue. Tranquilizers suppress these leg movements in some people (Schenck & Mahowald, 1996).

4. Why would it be unlikely, if not impossible, for sleepwalking to occur during REM sleep? (Check your answer on page 172.)

Hypersomnia

Finally, consider a disorder that is the opposite of insomnia: A small number of people suffer from **hypersomnia,** *excessive but unrefreshing sleep.* In a typical case, the person sleeps 8 or 9 hours per day during the week, plus an afternoon nap, and then "catches up" by sleeping 18, 20, even 22 hours per day on weekends. Even after this much sleep, the person has trouble awakening and feels confused and poorly rested. In some cases, the disorder can be traced to a history of head trauma, viral infection, or mood disorder, but in many cases the cause is unknown (Bassetti & Aldrich, 1997).

If You Have Trouble Sleeping . . .

Insomnia can be a brief, minor annoyance or a sign of a potentially serious disorder. If you experience persistent difficulties, consult a physician, but for occasional or minor insomnia you can try a few things yourself (Hauri, 1982; Lilie & Rosenberg, 1990):

• Try to associate your bed with sleeping, not with lying awake. If you find that you just can't get to sleep, get up, do something else, and return to bed when you start to feel sleepy.
• Try to wake up at the same time each day. (It is hard to get to sleep at a regular time if you don't also wake up at a regular time.)
• Avoid caffeine and nicotine, especially in the evenings.
• Avoid habitual use of alcohol or sleeping pills. (Either may help you get to sleep occasionally, but they become counterproductive after repeated use.)
• Keep your bedroom cool and quiet.
• Get a consistent amount of exercise daily.

THE MESSAGE
The Mysteries of Sleep and Dreams

Sleep and dreams are unlike wakefulness in some ways, but they do not represent a state of complete unconsciousness. Sounds and other stimuli present in the room can become parts of a dream, and if the stimuli are sufficiently meaningful, such as the sound of a child crying, the dreamer will awaken. The brain is never completely off duty, never completely relaxed.

Although our understanding of sleep and dreams continues to grow, several major questions remain. Even such basic issues as the function of REM sleep remain in doubt. People have long found their dreams a source of wonder, and researchers continue to find much of interest and mystery.

SUMMARY

＊ *Circadian rhythms.* Sleepiness depends on the time of day. Even in an unchanging environment, people become sleepy in cycles of approximately 24 hours. (page 157)

＊ *Theories about our need for sleep.* Several repair and restoration functions take place during sleep. Sleep also serves to conserve energy at times of relative inefficiency. (page 160)

＊ *Sleep stages.* During sleep, people cycle through sleep stages 1 through 4 and back through stages 3 and 2 to 1 again. The cycle beginning and ending with stage 1 lasts about 90 to 100 minutes. (page 162)

＊ *REM sleep and dreams.* A special stage known as REM sleep replaces many of the stage-1 periods. REM sleep is characterized by rapid eye movements, a high level of brain activity, and relaxed muscles. People usually dream during this stage but can dream in other stages also. (page 163)

＊ *Insomnia.* Insomnia—subjectively unsatisfactory sleep—can result from many influences, including a biological rhythm that is out of phase with the outside world, sleep apnea, narcolepsy, overuse of sleeping pills, and periodic limb movement disorder. (page 168)

One recommended strategy if you have trouble sleeping: Don't just lie in bed worrying about your lack of sleep. Get up, do something else, and try going back to sleep later.

Suggestions for Further Reading

Dement, W. C. (1992). *The sleepwatchers.* Stanford, CA: Stanford Alumni Association. An account by one of the founders of sleep research.

Moorcroft, W. (1993). *Sleep, dreaming, and sleep disorders: An introduction.* (2nd ed.). Lanham, MD: University Press of America. An excellent review of research on many aspects of sleep and dreams.

Terms

circadian rhythm　a rhythm of activity and inactivity lasting approximately one day (page 157)

jet lag　the discomfort and inefficiency that travelers experience in a new time zone because their internal clocks are out of phase with the light-dark cycle of their new environment (page 159)

repair and restoration theory　the theory that the purpose of sleep is to enable the body to recover from the exertions of the day (page 160)

evolutionary theory (or **energy-conservation theory**) **of sleep**　the theory that sleep evolved primarily as a means of forcing animals to conserve their energy when they are relatively inefficient (page 161)

rapid eye movement (REM) sleep　a stage of sleep characterized by rapid eye movements, a high level of brain activity, and deep relaxation of the postural muscles; also known as paradoxical sleep (page 162)

electroencephalograph (EEG)　a device that measures and amplifies slight electrical changes on the scalp that reflect brain activity (page 162)

polysomnograph　a device that measures sleep stages using a combination of EEG and eye-movement records (page 162)

activation-synthesis theory of dreams　the theory that parts of the brain are spontaneously activated during REM sleep and that a dream is the brain's attempt to synthesize these sensations into a coherent pattern (page 167)

insomnia　failure to get enough sleep at night in order to feel well rested the next day (page 168)

sleep apnea　a condition causing a person to have trouble breathing while asleep (page 169)

narcolepsy　a condition characterized by suddenly falling asleep, or at least feeling very sleepy, during the day (page 169)

periodic limb movement disorder　a condition occurring during sleep, marked by unpleasant sensations in the legs and many repetitive leg movements strong enough to interrupt sleep (page 170)

hypersomnia　excessive but unrefreshing sleep (page 170)

Answers to Concept Checks

1. You should prefer to schedule the meeting on a Pacific island so that you will travel west and the other person will travel east. (page 159)
2. Try a melatonin pill two or three hours before your desired bedtime—in this case, about 1:00 to 2:00 P.M. (page 159)
3. REM sleep and dreaming are more common toward the end of the night's sleep. (page 163)
4. During REM sleep, the major postural muscles of the body are completely relaxed. (page 170)

Web Resources

SleepNet

shell5.ba.best.com/~ssm/

Learn more about sleep disorders and treatment, with links to many research reports and dream research and analysis sites; forums for discussing sleep and dreams; and The SnoozePaper, a monthly publication devoted to sleep in the news.

MODULE 5.2

Hypnosis

What can hypnosis do?

What are its limitations?

Truth is nothing but a path traced between errors.*

—FRANZ ANTON MESMER

If a hypnotist told you that you were 4 years old and you suddenly starting acting like a 4-year-old, we would say that you are a good hypnotic subject. If the hypnotist said that you see your cousin sitting in the empty chair in front of you, and you said, "yes, I see her"; then again we would remark that you are deeply hypnotized.

But what if you had *not* been hypnotized and you suddenly started acting like a 4-year-old? or insisted that you saw someone in that empty chair? In this case, psychologists would suspect that you were suffering from a serious psychological disorder. Hypnosis induces a temporary state that is sometimes bizarre; no wonder we find it so fascinating.

Psychologists define **hypnosis** as *a condition of increased suggestibility that occurs in the context of a special hypnotist-subject relationship.* The term *hypnosis* comes from Hypnos, the Greek god of sleep. Although it has long been assumed that hypnosis is somehow related to sleep, the connection is only superficial: In both states the eyes are usually closed and the person is without initiative, and a hypnotized person, like a dreamer, accepts contradictory information without protest. A hypnotized person, however, can walk around and respond to objects and events in the real world. Also, the EEG of a hypnotized person is like that of a waking person with closed eyes, not like that of a sleeping person.

Hypnosis was first practiced by an Austrian philosopher and physician, Franz Anton Mesmer (1734–1815). When treating certain medical problems, Mesmer would pass a magnet back and forth across the patient's body to redirect the flow of blood, nerve activity, and certain undefined "fluids." Some of his patients reported dramatic benefits.

---

*Does this sound profound? Or is it nonsense? Mesmer said many things that sound profound at first, but the more we think about them, the less sense they make.

Later, Mesmer discovered that he could dispense with the magnet; a piece of wood, or even his own hand, would work just as well. From this observation, you or I would conclude that magnetism had nothing to do with the phenomenon. Mesmer, however, drew the quirky conclusion that he did not need a magnet because *he himself* was a magnet. With that claim, he gave us the term "animal magnetism."

In his later years, Mesmer grew stranger yet. After his death, his followers carried out serious studies of "animal magnetism" or "Mesmerism," eventually calling it "hypnotism." But by that time, many physicians and scientists associated hypnosis with eccentrics, charlatans, and other practitioners of hocus-pocus. Even today, hypnosis is part of various stage acts. We must therefore carefully distinguish stage hypnotists from psychologists and psychiatrists who are licensed to practice hypnosis.

Ways of Inducing Hypnosis

Mesmer thought that hypnosis was a power that emanated from his own body, like the power that a magnet exerts on metals. If so, only certain people would have the power to hypnotize others. Today, we believe that becoming a successful hypnotist requires a fair amount of practice but no unusual powers or personality traits.

Although Mesmer is often depicted as irresistibly controlling people, psychologists now recognize that hypnosis reflects a willingness by the hypnotized person, not a special power of the hypnotist.

FIGURE 5.14 A hypnotist induces hypnosis by repeating suggestions, relying on the hypnotized person's cooperation and willingness to accept suggestions. No one can force hypnosis on an unwilling person.

There are several ways of inducing hypnosis. The first step toward being hypnotized is simply agreeing to give it a try. Contrary to what you may have seen in the movies or on television, no one can hypnotize an uncooperative person.

A hypnotist might then ask the subject to concentrate, while the hypnotist monotonously repeats such suggestions as, "You are starting to fall asleep. Your eyelids are getting heavy. Your eyelids are getting very heavy. They are starting to close. You are falling into a deep, deep sleep" (Figure 5.14).

In another popular technique, described by R. Udolf (1981), the hypnotist suggests, "After you go under hypnosis, your arm will begin to rise automatically." (Some people, eager for the hypnosis to succeed, shoot their arm up immediately and have to be told, "No, not yet. Just relax; that will happen later.") Then, the hypnotist encourages the subject to relax and suggests that the arm is starting to feel lighter, as if it were tied to a helium balloon. Later, the hypnotist suggests that the arm is beginning to feel a little strange and is beginning to twitch. The timing of this suggestion is important, because when people stand or sit in one position long enough, their limbs really do begin to feel strange and twitch a bit. If the hypnotist's suggestion comes at just the right moment, the subject thinks, "Wow, that's right, my arm does feel a little strange. This is really starting to work!" Wanting to be hypnotized and believing that you are being hypnotized is a big step toward actually being hypnotized.

The Uses and Limitations of Hypnosis

Hypnosis can produce relaxation, concentration, temporary changes in behavior and, sometimes, changes that persist beyond the end of the hypnotic state. A "deeply" hypnotized person will follow many of the hypnotist's suggestions. There is no evidence, however, that hypnosis gives people any new physical or mental abilities.

What Hypnosis Can Do

One well-established effect of hypnosis is to inhibit pain. For some people, a hypnotic suggestion is so effective that they can undergo medical or dental surgery without anesthesia (Figure 5.15). Blocking pain with hypnosis is particularly helpful when people have developed a tolerance for painkilling opiates or if they react unfavorably to anesthetic drugs.

Recall from Chapter 4 that pain has both sensory and emotional components. Hypnosis affects mostly the emotional components. Even when a hypnotized person says that he or she feels no pain, the heart rate and blood pressure still shoot up as much as they do in nonhypnotized people (Hilgard, 1973). Under hypnotic suggestion to feel no unpleasantness, a person subjected to painful stimuli will have high arousal in the parietal cortex areas responsive to body sensations but not in the frontal cortex areas responsive to unpleasant emotions (Rainville, Duncan, Price, Carrier, & Bushnell, 1997). (See Figure 5.16.)

Another constructive use of hypnosis is the **posthypnotic suggestion,** *a suggestion that the person will do or experience something particular after coming out of hypnosis.* The posthypnotic suggestion could be to do something trivial, such as to scratch one's left ear at exactly 9:00. It could also be something more practical, such as a suggestion to give up tobacco, lose weight, stop nail-biting, break other bad habits, become more sexually responsive, or stop having night terrors (Kihlstrom, 1979; Udolf, 1981). The suggestions do not force any change in behavior; the people who agree to be hypnotized have already decided to try to

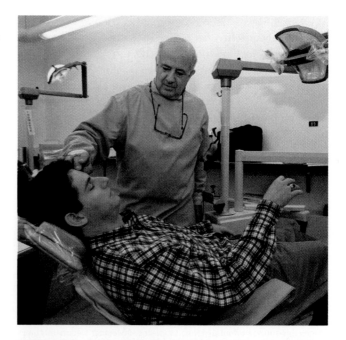

FIGURE 5.15 Some dentists have used hypnosis as their means of relieving pain, even for tooth extractions, root canal surgery, and other seriously painful procedures.

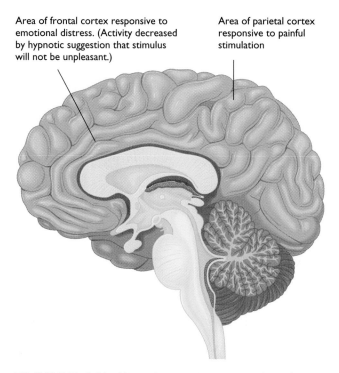

Area of frontal cortex responsive to emotional distress. (Activity decreased by hypnotic suggestion that stimulus will not be unpleasant.)

Area of parietal cortex responsive to painful stimulation

FIGURE 5.16 Hypnotic suggestions to experience less pain can decrease the emotional intensity but generally have less effect on the sensation itself. The hypnotic suggestion that a stimulus will not be unpleasant decreases activity in the frontal cortex areas associated with emotional distress but has little effect on the primary somatosensory cortex.

quit smoking or to change another habit. The hypnosis underscores that resolve.

Posthypnotic suggestions can be effective for helping people to change bad habits, although the effect of a single session wears off in a few days or weeks. In one study, people were taught to use repeated self-hypnosis to quit cigarette smoking. Almost one fourth of those who learned this technique managed to quit smoking for at least the next 2 years (Spiegel, Frischholz, Fleiss, & Spiegel, 1993).

What Hypnosis Cannot Do

Some spectacular claims have been made for the power of hypnotic suggestion, but most of them turn out to be less impressive on closer scrutiny. For instance, people under hypnosis can become as stiff as a board, so stiff that they can balance their head and neck on one chair and their feet on another chair and allow someone to stand on their body (Figure 5.17)! Amazing? Not really. You can probably make yourself stiff enough to balance this way without being hypnotized. It's easier than it looks. (But I do not recommend that you invite someone to stand on you. A person who does not balance just right could injure you.)

Many people have attempted to use hypnosis to enhance memory. For example, a distressed person tells a psychotherapist, "I don't know why I have such troubles. Maybe I had some really bad experience when I was much younger,

but I just can't remember." Or a witness to a crime says, "I saw the culprit for a second or two, but now my memory is vague and I can't give you a good description." Faced with such situations, therapists and police officers have sometimes turned to hypnotism in the hope of uncovering hidden memories. However, hypnotized people are highly suggestible. Even when they are given an innocent suggestion such as "you will remember more than you told us before," many hypnotized people respond with new but incorrect information. One hypnotized witness confidently reported eating a pizza at a restaurant that does not serve pizza. Another person reported seeing tattoos on a person who had none. A third reported being stabbed repeatedly with a knife but had none of the scars that would result from such an injury (Orne, Whitehouse, Dinges, & Orne, 1988).

In several laboratory studies, experimenters have shown participants either photos or videotapes and then asked questions both without hypnosis and with hypnosis. Overall, hypnosis impaired recall at least as often as it improved it (Steblay & Bothwell, 1994). Furthermore, even long after the end of a hypnotic session, many people expressed great confidence in the inaccurate memories that they "gained" during hypnosis.

In response to such findings, a panel appointed by the

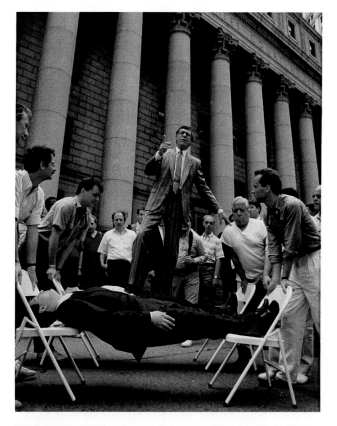

FIGURE 5.17 The U.S. Supreme Court ruled in 1987 that criminal defendants may testify about details they recalled under hypnosis. Its decision sparked this protest by the magician known as "the Amazing Kreskin," who borrowed a stunt usually used to demonstrate the power of hypnosis—standing on a person suspended between two chairs.

American Medical Association (1986) concluded that testimony elicited under hypnosis should not be used in courts of law. The panel voiced no objection to using hypnosis as an investigative tool. For example, if a hypnotized witness reports a license plate number, and the police track down the car and find blood on it, the blood is certainly admissible evidence. However, success stories of that type are rare. Police investigators should therefore disregard a hypnotized witness's report if it does not lead to independent confirmation.

An even more doubtful claim is that hypnosis can help people to recall their early childhood. A hypnotist might say, "You are getting younger. It is now the year _____ ; now it is _____ ; now you are only 6 years old." The hypnotized person may give a convincing performance of being a young child, playing with teddy bears and blankets (Nash, Johnson, & Tipton, 1979). But is this person reliving early childhood experiences? Evidently not. *First,* the childhood "memories" that the hypnotized subject so confidently recalls, such as the names of friends and teachers and the details of birthday parties, are generally inaccurate (Nash, 1987). *Second,* a person who has presumably regressed under hypnosis to early childhood retains spelling and other skills learned later in life. When asked to draw a picture, the subject does not draw as children draw but as adults imagine that children draw (Orne, 1951). (See Figure 5.18.) *Third,* hypnotized subjects will respond just as well to suggestions that they are growing older as to suggestions that they are growing younger. They give just as convincing a performance of being an older person and "remembering" events in the future as of being a younger person (Rubenstein & Newman, 1954). Because these people must be acting out an imagined future, we should assume that they are doing the same with the past.

You may even encounter the astounding claim that hypnosis can help someone to recall memories from a previous life. Hypnotized young people who claim to be recollecting a previous life generally describe the life of a person similar to themselves, married to someone who bears an uncanny resemblance to their current boyfriend or girlfriend. If subjects are asked whether their country (in their past life) is at war or what kind of money is in use, their guesses are seldom correct (Spanos, 1987–88).

CONCEPT CHECK

5. List two practical uses of hypnosis that the evidence supports and one that it does not. (Check your answer on page 180.)

WHAT'S THE EVIDENCE?
The Limits of Hypnosis

Most hypnotists seem to agree about one of the limits of hypnosis: "You don't have to worry," a hypnotist will reassure you. "People never do anything under hypnosis that they

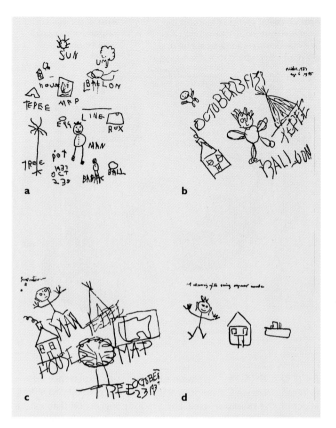

FIGURE 5.18 Regression or role playing? One person made drawing (a) at age 6 and the other three drawings (b, c, & d) as a college student under hypnosis. While under hypnosis, the person was asked to regress to age 6. The drawings created while under hypnosis are not like drawings done in childhood. Orne (1951) concluded that the hypnotized students played the role of a 6-year-old and drew as they thought a child would.

would ordinarily refuse to do." That reassurance is an important strategy in getting you to agree to be hypnotized. But is it true? And how does anyone know whether it is true? Do you suppose that hypnotists have frequently asked clients to perform criminal or immoral acts, so they know that clients consistently refuse? No, of course not. Furthermore, a few investigators have tried to test this statement, but their results are difficult to interpret. The following is one example.

Hypothesis Hypnotized people will sometimes perform acts that nonhypnotized people would refuse to do.

Method Eighteen college students were randomly assigned to three groups. The investigator hypnotized those in one group, instructed those in the second group to pretend they had been hypnotized, and merely asked those in the third group to participate in the study (making no mention of hypnosis). All students were then asked to perform three acts: First, they were told to go to a box in a corner of the room and pick up a poisonous snake. The snake really was poisonous. If a subject got too close to the snake, he or she was restrained at the last moment.

Will hypnotized people do anything that they would otherwise refuse to do? The problem with answering that question is that nonhypnotized people will sometimes perform some strange and dangerous acts, either because an experimenter asked them to or on their own.

Second, the hypnotist poured some highly concentrated, fuming nitric acid into a large container and distinctly stated that it was nitric acid. To dispel any doubts, he threw a coin into the acid and let the subjects watch as it started to dissolve. The hypnotist then told the subjects to reach into the acid with bare hands and remove the coin. Here there was no last-second restraint. Anyone who followed the instructions was told to wash his or her hands in warm soapy water immediately afterward. (Today's ethical procedures would prevent such a study.) Third, the hypnotist instructed the subject to throw the nitric acid into the face of the hypnotist's assistant. Unnoticed, the hypnotist had swapped the container of nitric acid for a container of water, but the hypnotized person had no way of knowing that.

Results Five of the six hypnotized students followed all three directions (Orne & Evans, 1965). Moreover, the six control-group students who were pretending to be hypnotized also followed all three commands! So did two of the six students who were just told to take these actions as part of an experiment, with no mention of hypnosis. (Nonhypnotized subjects did, however, hesitate much longer than the hypnotized subjects.)

Why would people do such extraordinary things? They explained that they simply trusted the experimenter: "If he tells me to do something, it can't really be dangerous."

Interpretation Hypnotized people *will* do some strange things that we assume they would not ordinarily do. However, nonhypnotized people will do the same strange things, at least when they know they are participating in an experiment conducted by someone they regard as reputable.

In short, we simply do not have adequate evidence to decide whether people under hypnosis will do anything that they would utterly refuse to do otherwise, because nonhypnotized people do things we would have expected them to refuse!

There is a message here about psychological research: If the control groups do not behave as the experimenter expects them to behave, it then becomes very difficult to interpret the behavior of the experimental group.

✳ ✳ ✳

Distortions of Perception Under Hypnosis

A few people report visual or auditory **hallucinations** (*sensory experiences not corresponding to reality*) under hypnosis; a larger percentage report touch hallucinations (Udolf, 1981). A hypnotist can bring about a touch hallucination by such suggestions as "your nose itches" or "your left hand feels numb."

When hypnotized people say that they see or hear something or that they fail to see or hear something, are they telling the truth or are they just saying what the hypnotist wants them to say? Or do they perhaps believe that they see or hear something, when in fact they do not?

In one experiment to test this question, people who were highly susceptible to hypnosis looked at the Ponzo illusion, shown in Figure 5.19a. Like other people, they reported that the top horizontal line looked longer than the bottom horizontal line. Then they were hypnotized and told not to see the radiating lines but to see only the two horizontal ones. Those who said that they no longer saw the radiating lines still perceived the top line as longer than the

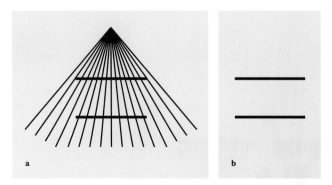

FIGURE 5.19 Horizontal lines of equal length in (a) the Ponzo illusion and (b) without the optical illusion. Researchers employ such visual stimuli to determine how hypnosis may alter sensory perception.

bottom one (Miller, Hennessy, & Leibowitz, 1973). If the radiating lines had truly disappeared, then the subjects would have seen something like Figure 5.19b, where the horizontal lines look equal.

So, does hypnosis alter perception? It does not alter the information that the sensory receptors send to the nervous system. It merely alters how people react to that information and what they do about it.

Is Hypnosis an Altered State of Consciousness?

Hypnosis produces some paradoxical effects. If a hypnotist tells you, "your hand is rising; you can do nothing to stop it," your hand might indeed rise. If you were later asked why, you might reply (as many do) that you lost control over your own behavior. Still, the behavior is neither reflexive nor involuntary; you raised your hand yourself. Psychologists have wrestled with the issue of how a behavior can be voluntary even though one lacks the usual sense of making a decision (Lynn, Rhue, & Weekes, 1990).

At one extreme, some psychologists regard hypnosis as a special state of consciousness, characterized by greatly increased suggestibility. At the other extreme, other psychologists emphasize the similarities between hypnosis and normal wakeful consciousness, especially that hypnotized people are aware of their surroundings and aware of their own behaviors. Most psychologists take intermediate positions, noting that hypnotized people are neither "faking it" nor under the control of the hypnotist. That is, hypnosis is a special state in some ways and not in others (Kirsch & Lynn, 1998).

One way to determine whether hypnosis is a special state of consciousness is to find out whether unhypnotized people can do everything that hypnotized people do. That is, if you agreed to pretend that you were hypnotized, could you do everything that a truly hypnotized person does?

How Well Can an Unhypnotized Person Pretend to Be Hypnotized?

In several experiments, one group of college students was hypnotized while another group was told to pretend they were hypnotized. An experienced hypnotist then examined all the students and tried to determine which ones were really hypnotized.

Fooling the hypnotist turned out to be easier than expected. The pretenders were able to tolerate sharp pain without flinching and could recall or pretend to recall old memories. They could make their bodies as stiff as a board and lie rigid between two chairs. When standing people were told to sit down, they did so immediately (as hypnotized people do) without first checking to make sure there was a chair behind them (Orne, 1959, 1979). When told to experience anger or another emotion, they exhibited physiological changes such as increased heart rate and sweating, just like hypnotized people do (Damaser, Shor, & Orne, 1963). Not even highly experienced hypnotists could accurately identify the pretenders.

However, a few differences between the hypnotized people and pretenders did emerge (Orne, 1979). The pretenders did certain things differently from the way the hypnotized subjects did them—not because they were unable to do them the same way but because they did not know how a hypnotized subject would act. For instance, when the hypnotist suggested, "you see Professor Schmaltz sitting in that chair," people in both groups reported seeing the professor. Some of the hypnotized subjects, however, said they were puzzled. "How is it that I see the professor there, but I can also see the entire chair?" Pretenders never reported seeing this "double reality."

At that point in the experiment, Professor Schmaltz actually walked into the room. "Who is that entering the room?" asked the hypnotist. The pretenders would either say they saw no one, or else they would identify Schmaltz as someone else. The hypnotized subjects would say, "That's Professor Schmaltz." Some of them said that they were confused by seeing the same person in two places at the same time. For some of them, the hallucinated professor faded at that moment, whereas others continued to accept the double image.

So . . . what is our conclusion? Is hypnosis an altered state, or are hypnotized people just playing a role? This is not an easy question to answer. Apparently, unhypnotized people playing the role of "hypnotized subjects" can mimic most of the effects of hypnosis, and they probably could have mimicked the other effects if they had known what those effects were. However, the fact that unhypnotized role-players resemble hypnotized people does not necessarily mean that hypnosis is "nothing but" role-playing (Hilgard, 1971). The induction of hypnosis produces a variety of effects that other people must learn to imitate; those effects happen spontaneously for the hypnotized subjects.

Faked Hypnosis by a Criminal Defendant

In 1979 Kenneth Bianchi was arrested for raping and strangling two women. He was suspected of raping and strangling many others in similar fashion; he was suspected of being the "Hillside Strangler" who had been terrifying the Los Angeles area. While he was awaiting trial, a psychiatrist hypnotized him and claimed to uncover a second personality, "Steve Walker," who had first appeared when Bianchi was 9 years old and who had, Bianchi said, actually committed the crimes. Bianchi pleaded not guilty by reason of insanity.

But was Bianchi really insane, or was he faking the second personality and, indeed, only pretending to be hypnotized (Figure 5.20)? Six psychiatrists were asked to examine Bianchi to try to answer these questions. One of them was Martin Orne, the psychiatrist who had conducted the research on whether college students could effectively pretend to be hypnotized. He knew how difficult it was to detect pretenders, but he had also picked up a few tricks in the course of his earlier research. More importantly, he had cultivated a healthy skepticism. At first, the six psychiatrists were divided about whether Bianchi was really insane or merely faking. Eventually, Orne convinced them that Bianchi was faking, for a variety of reasons including the following (Orne, Dinges, & Orne, 1984):

•   Bianchi behaved in ways that were not typical of hypnotized people. For example, when Orne suggested that someone was sitting in an empty chair, Bianchi not only claimed to see that person but even reached out to shake hands! Orne concluded that Bianchi was trying too hard to prove that he was hypnotized.

FIGURE 5.20 Kenneth Bianchi, accused of being the Hillside strangler, pleaded not guilty on the grounds that he had a "multiple personality" and that his evil second personality was responsible for the crimes. Psychiatrist Martin Orne, however, persuaded the court that Bianchi was faking his second personality and, indeed, that he was only pretending to be hypnotized.

•   In one hypnosis session, Bianchi's "Steve" personality tore the filter tip off a cigarette. After the hypnosis was over, the "Ken" personality expressed amazement and said he couldn't imagine who might have torn the filter tip off. This episode might suggest that Bianchi had completely forgotten his experience under hypnosis. However, Orne observed that Bianchi did exactly the same thing with three other hypnotists. Again, Bianchi was apparently trying to convince everyone that he had been deeply hypnotized.

•   At one point, Orne told Bianchi that he doubted Bianchi was a true case of multiple personality because "real" multiple personalities have three personalities, not just two. (This statement is not true; Orne just wanted to see what would happen.) Later that day, Bianchi developed a third personality.

By uncovering these facts, Orne exposed Bianchi's pretense. Bianchi agreed to plead guilty in return for the state's dropping its request for the death penalty. He also stopped claiming to have multiple personalities.

In short, it is sometimes possible to distinguish between hypnotized people and those who are only pretending, but it is not easy.

Meditation: In Some Ways Like Hypnosis

Hypnosis is not the only method of inducing a relaxed and possibly altered state of consciousness. **Meditation,** *a method of inducing a calm, relaxed state through the use of special techniques,* follows a tradition that has been practiced in various parts of the world for thousands of years. For example, one may sit quietly while repeating a simple sound or chant (such as "om") for 15 to 20 minutes twice a day. The point is "to empty one's mind"—that is, to expel all the worries, troubles, and doubts that otherwise intrude into our thoughts. In that respect, it has some similarities to the relaxed, passive state of hypnosis. However, meditation is different because it includes no hypnotist or suggestions.

Many studies document moderate benefits from meditation in terms of decreased heart rate, blood pressure, and so forth. These benefits are similar to those produced by other means of achieving prolonged relaxation (Holmes, 1984). As with hypnosis, some practitioners of meditation have made exaggerated claims; however, it is possible to dismiss the exaggerations and still respect the real phenomenon.

THE MESSAGE
The Nature of Hypnosis

Researchers have still not reached a consensus on exactly what hypnosis is. They do agree on a few general points, however: Hypnosis is not just faking or pretending to be

Meditation excludes the worries and concerns of the day and thereby induces a calm, relaxed state.

hypnotized, and it does not give people mental or physical powers that they otherwise lack. Hypnosis merely enables people to relax, concentrate, and follow suggestions better than they usually do. Be skeptical of anyone who claims much more than that for hypnosis.

SUMMARY

* *Nature of hypnosis.* Hypnosis is a condition of increased suggestibility that occurs in the context of a special hypnotist-subject relationship. Psychologists try to distinguish the genuine phenomenon, which deserves serious study, from exaggerated claims. (page 173)

* *Hypnosis induction.* To induce hypnosis, a hypnotist asks a person to concentrate and then makes repetitive suggestions. The first steps toward being hypnotized are to be willing to be hypnotized and to believe that one is becoming hypnotized. (page 173)

* *Uses.* Hypnosis can alleviate pain, and through posthypnotic suggestion, it can help someone overcome bad habits, at least temporarily. (page 174)

* *Nonuses.* Hypnosis does not give people special strength or unusual powers. Most of the new "memories" evoked under hypnosis are false. (page 175)

* *Uncertain limits.* Although many hypnotists insist that hypnotized people will not do anything that they would refuse to do when not hypnotized, there is little solid evidence to back up this claim. (page 176)

* *Sensory distortions.* People under hypnosis can be induced to ignore certain stimuli as if they were blind or deaf. However, the ignored information still influences behavior in subtle or indirect ways. (page 177)

* *Hypnosis as an altered state.* Controversy continues about whether hypnosis is a special state of consciousness and, indeed, what we mean by an altered state. (page 178)

* *Meditation.* Meditation can induce a relaxed condition that one might regard as an altered state of consciousness. (page 179)

Suggestion for Further Reading

Rhue, J. W., Lynn, S. J., & Kirsch, I. (Eds.). (1993). *Handbook of clinical hypnosis.* Washington, DC: American Psychological Association. A collection of articles, mostly about the uses of hypnosis for treating psychological disorders.

Terms

hypnosis   a condition of increased suggestibility that occurs in the context of a special hypnotist-subject relationship (page 173)

posthypnotic suggestion   a suggestion made to hypnotized subjects that they will do or experience something particular after coming out of hypnosis (page 174)

hallucination   a sensory experience not corresponding to reality, such as seeing or hearing something that is not present or failing to see or hear something that *is* present (page 177)

meditation   a method of inducing a calm, relaxed state through the use of special techniques (page 179)

Answer to Concept Check

5.   Supported by the evidence: Hypnosis can decrease pain, and posthypnotic suggestions can help people break bad habits. Not supported: Hypnosis does not improve people's memories. (Neither does it give them added strength.) (page 176)

Web Resources

Hypnosis
www.psych-web.com/asc/hyp.html
A collection of FAQs includes Todd Stark on the nature of the hypnotic trance, accuracy of memory, hypnotizability, enhanced mental and physical functioning, and other topics; also articles on "Social Reconstruction of Memories," "Hypnosis in Pain Management," and "Past-Life Hypnotic Regression."

MODULE 5.3

Drugs and Their Effects

What experiences do abused drugs produce?

Why do people experiment with such drugs?

The abuse of alcohol and other drugs is a widespread problem, which we shall consider in Chapter 16. Here, our focus is on the experiences associated with common drugs of abuse. I have tried to present only information that is backed by solid evidence, but in the study of drug effects, it is more difficult than usual to separate fact from fiction. Many people who are trying to discourage drug use have made strong claims about the harms that result from using various drugs. For example, although some drugs—such as MDMA ("ecstasy") and PCP ("angel dust")—can apparently produce brain damage, there is little evidence to support claims of permanent damage from using other drugs (McCann, Lowe, & Ricaurte, 1997). The risk of presenting exaggerated claims is that people stop believing the warnings. At the opposite extreme, many people who defend their own use of drugs have minimized the dangers; again, many of their claims go beyond the facts. As with other topics, we should be skeptical of claims that go beyond the evidence.

Many people assume (incorrectly) that any drug they receive from a physician or from a pharmacy must be safe. In fact, almost any drug is dangerous in large doses, and many legal drugs can become habit-forming after repeated use. Furthermore, many abused drugs—including amphetamines, morphine, and even cocaine—have legitimate medical uses. The dividing line between "good drugs" and "bad drugs" is a blurry one; it depends more on the quantities used and the reasons for their use than it does on the chemistry of the drugs themselves.

A Survey of Abused Drugs and Their Effects

Some abused drugs, such as alcohol and opiates, have predominantly calming effects. Others, such as amphetamines and cocaine, are known for their stimulating effects. Still others, such as LSD, produce hallucinations. Table 5.2 lists some of the commonly abused drugs and their

TABLE 5.2 Commonly Abused Drugs and Their Effects

DRUG CATEGORY	EFFECTS ON BEHAVIOR	EFFECTS ON CENTRAL NERVOUS SYSTEM AND ORGANS
Depressants Alcohol	Relaxant; relieve inhibitions; impair memory and judgment	Widespread effects on membranes of neurons; facilitate activity at GABA synapses
Tranquilizers Barbiturates; benzodiazepines (Valium, Xanax)	Relieve anxiety; relax muscles; induce sleep	Facilitate activity at GABA synapses
Opiates Morphine, heroin	Decrease pain; decrease attention to real world; unpleasant withdrawal effects as drug leaves synapses	Stimulate endorphin synapses
Stimulants Caffeine	Increase energy, alertness	Increase heart rate; indirectly increase activity at glutamate synapses
Amphetamines Cocaine	Increase energy, alertness	Increase or prolong activity at dopamine synapses
Mixed Stimulant-Depressants Nicotine	Stimulate brain activity, but most smokers say cigarettes relax them	Stimulate activity at some (not all) acetylcholine synapses; increase heart rate
Distortion of Experience Marijuana (THC)	Intensifies sensory experiences; distorts perception of time; can relieve glaucoma, nausea; sometimes impairs learning, memory	Attaches to receptors found in hippocampus and other areas; normal role of these receptors is unknown
Hallucinogens LSD; mescaline	Cause hallucinations, sensory distortions, and occasionally panic	Alter pattern of release and binding of serotonin

most prominent effects. Do they have anything in common that would account for their tendency to be abused? Apparently, yes. Nearly all abused drugs increase the activity at dopamine synapses in the brain, especially those with dopamine receptor types D_2, D_3, and D_4 at the postsynaptic membrane (Maldonado et al., 1997). Some drugs (such as amphetamines) increase dopamine release directly; others do so indirectly by stimulating certain synapses which in turn stimulate dopamine release. Of the few abused drugs that are known not to increase dopamine activity, such as phencyclidine (PCP, or "angel dust"), the general pattern is that they inhibit activity at glutamate receptors (Carlezon & Wise, 1996). In a small brain area known as the *nucleus accumbens,* which is apparently critical for either the motivating or the attention-getting effects of experience, glutamate is an excitatory transmitter and dopamine is inhibitory. Thus, drugs that inhibit glutamate (such as PCP) and drugs that stimulate dopamine (most other abused drugs) have the same net effect on the nucleus accumbens. Figure 5.21 shows the location of the nucleus accumbens.

Alcohol

When archeologists unearthed a Neolithic village in Iran's Zagros Mountains, they found a jar that had been constructed about 5400–5500 B.C., which was one of the oldest human-made crafts ever found (Figure 5.22). Inside the

FIGURE 5.22 This jar, dated about 5400–5500 B.C., is one of the oldest human crafts ever found. It was used for storing wine.

jar, especially near the bottom, the archeologists found a yellowish residue. They were curious to know what the jar had held, so they sent some of the residue for chemical analysis. The unambiguous answer came back: The jar had served as a vessel for wine (McGovern, Glusker, Exner, & Voigt, 1996).

Clearly, human use of alcohol is a tradition that has stood the test of time. **Alcohol** is a *class of molecules that includes methanol, ethanol, propyl alcohol (rubbing alcohol), and others. Ethanol is the type that people drink;* the others are highly dangerous if consumed. Alcohol acts primarily as a relaxant. It can lead to heightened aggressive, sexual, and risk-taking behaviors, mainly by depressing the brain areas that ordinarily inhibit such behaviors. Moderate use of alcohol serves as a tension reducer and a social lubricant. It helps people to forget their problems, at least for the moment.

Excessive use can damage the liver and other organs, aggravate or prolong many medical conditions, and impair memory and motor control. A woman who drinks alcohol during pregnancy risks impairment to her baby's brain development (see Chapter 10).

Alcohol abuse occurs throughout the world, although it is more common in some populations than others. Within the United States, alcohol abuse is more common among Native Americans than among other ethnic groups, more widespread among people of African ancestry than those of European ancestry, and more common among people of European ancestry than those of Asian ancestry. The explanation for these ethnic differences is unknown, but it is not true (as many have supposed) that Native Americans get drunk more easily than others. If anything, they are *less* affected than others by a moderate amount of alcohol and therefore continue drinking (Garcia-Andrade, Wall, & Ehlers, 1997). Whatever the explanation, these ethnic differences are worth taking seriously; many observers believe that differences in alcohol use constitute a major reason for

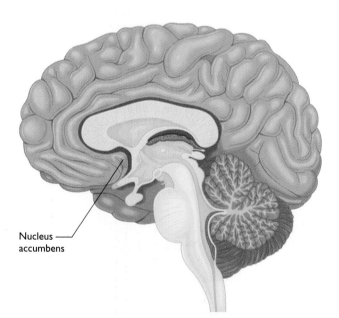

Nucleus
accumbens

FIGURE 5.21 The nucleus accumbens is a small brain area that is critical for the motivating effects of many experiences, including drugs, food, and sex. Most abused drugs increase the activity of dopamine, an inhibitory transmitter in this area. Other abused drugs, such as PCP, inhibit the activity of glutamate, an excitatory transmitter here. That is, a *decrease* in output by the nucleus accumbens is important for the effects of abused drugs and other motivating experiences.

the shorter average life spans of Native Americans and African-Americans, as compared with other groups (Rivers, 1994).

Tranquilizers

Tranquilizers *help people to relax and to fall asleep; they can also decrease muscle tension and suppress epileptic seizures.* Barbiturates, once a common type of tranquilizer, proved to be highly habit-forming and easily fatal in large doses. Today, the most commonly used tranquilizers are a class of chemicals called *benzodiazepines,* which include the drugs diazepam (Valium) and alprazolam (Xanax). Benzodiazepines can also be habit-forming, although less so than barbiturates. Thousands of tons of these drugs are taken in pill form every year in the United States.

Benzodiazepines exert their calming effects by facilitating transmission at synapses that use the neurotransmitter GABA. Alcohol facilitates transmission at the same synapses, though by a different mechanism (Sudzak et al., 1986). Taking alcohol and tranquilizers together can be dangerous, because together they increase GABA transmission more effectively than either alcohol or tranquilizers could alone and thereby suppress activity in the areas of the medulla that control breathing and the heartbeat.

One benzodiazepine drug, flunitrazepam, has attracted attention as the "date rape drug." Flunitrazepam dissolves quickly in water; it has no color, odor, or taste; and it can therefore be easily slipped into a woman's drink without her realizing it. The effects of this drug are similar to those of other tranquilizers; these effects include drowsiness, poor muscle coordination, and memory impairment, which can impair a woman's later ability to describe the attack (Anglin, Spears, & Hutson, 1997; Woods & Winger, 1997). Although flunitrazepam apparently has been used to facilitate date rape, there is no evidence that this drug is fundamentally different from, or more dangerous than, other benzodiazepine tranquilizers, however. When a hospital suspects that a woman has been given flunitrazepam, the hospital can run a simple urine test to determine the presence of this drug.

Opiates

Opiates are either *natural drugs derived from the opium poppy or synthetic drugs with a chemical structure similar to that of natural opiates.* An opiate drug makes people feel happy, warm, and content, with little anxiety or pain. However, the person will experience nausea and will tend to ignore the real world. Once the drug has left the brain, the affected synapses become understimulated, and the user then enters withdrawal. Elation gives way to anxiety, pain, and hyperresponsiveness to sounds and other stimuli.

Morphine (named after Morpheus, the Greek god of dreams) has important medical use as a painkiller. When used for that purpose, morphine is almost never habit-forming.

Here is an important point: No drug is automatically habit-forming. The probability of abuse or habit formation depends partly on the drug but largely on the person taking it and their reasons for doing so.

Opiate drugs such as morphine, heroin, methadone, and codeine bind to a specific set of neurotransmitter receptors in the brain (Pert & Snyder, 1973). The discovery of neurotransmitter receptors prompted neuroscientists to look for naturally occurring brain chemicals that bind to those receptors, because it hardly seemed likely that evolution would equip us with receptors to respond just to extracts of the opium poppy. Researchers found that the brain produces several chemicals, called **endorphins,** that *bind to the opiate receptors* (Hughes et al., 1975). Endorphins serve to inhibit chronic pain.

Marijuana

Marijuana produces a variety of effects, which can include drowsiness, an intensification of sensory experiences, and the illusion that time is passing very slowly (Weil, Zinberg, & Nelson, 1968). It can have certain medical uses, although its medical applications are still controversial. For example, it is sometimes used to reduce pressure in the eyes in an attempt to relieve glaucoma, a common cause of blindness. It also reduces nausea, acts as a weak painkiller, and suppresses tremors, although it is uncertain whether marijuana is ever a better treatment than other medications that have less potential for abuse.

Although people are aware of marijuana's effects for no more than 2 or 3 hours after using it, more subtle effects can

After California legalized marijuana for medical uses, many clubs and stores opened for the sale and distribution of the drug.

persist much longer. Marijuana dissolves in the fats of the body, so traces of it can be found for weeks after the drug has been used (Dackis, Pottash, Annitto, & Gold, 1982).

The literature on marijuana seems to be dominated by people exaggerating the harm of the drug, to discourage people from using it, and people claiming that the drug has almost no dangers, to argue for the reduction or elimination of criminal penalties for using it. Sometimes it is difficult to discern the truth.

One of the arguments emphasizing the dangers of marijuana is that many users are criminals, mentally ill, or otherwise disreputable people. However, correlation does not demonstrate causation. We have no more reason to say that marijuana leads to criminal behavior or mental illness than to say that people with a predisposition toward criminality or mental illness are likely to use marijuana. Many have also attacked marijuana as a "gateway drug," on the grounds that many people who eventually use heroin or cocaine used marijuana first. True, but again we cannot infer cause and effect. Before using heroin, cocaine, or marijuana, most had also used alcohol and tobacco; many had experimented with risky sexual behaviors; and so on. Some of the those who try marijuana, alcohol, or tobacco go on to try heroin or cocaine, but others do not.

On the other hand, marijuana use certainly does pose some risks. Frequent smoking of marijuana increases the risk of lung cancer, just as tobacco smoking does. Many users experience impairment of learning and memory (Miller & Branconnier, 1983). Animal research indicates that marijuana smoke can temporarily shrink the dendrites of brain neurons (Westlake et al., 1991). In short, marijuana use is not enormously risky, but it is hardly risk-free, either.

The active ingredient in marijuana (cannabis) is THC, or tetrahydrocannabinol, which attaches to receptors that are abundant throughout the brain (Herkenham, Lynn, deCosta, & Richfield, 1991), especially in the hippocampus (an important brain area for memory) and brain areas important for the control of movement (Herkenham et al., 1990). The presence of those receptors implies that the brain produces some THC-like chemical of its own. Researchers first discovered a brain chemical that they named *anandamide* (from *ananda*, the Sanskrit word for "bliss") that attaches to the same receptors as THC (Devane et al., 1992). However, the brain has very low levels of anandamide, compared to the abundant THC receptors. A more prevalent compound, discovered later, that attaches to the same receptors, has the not-very-catchy name *sn-*2 arachidonylglycerol, abbreviated 2-AG (Stella, Schweitzer, & Piomelli, 1997). At this point, no one knows the functions of anandamide or 2-AG. In short, we do not yet know why your brain manufactures its own marijuana-like chemicals. Curiously, chocolate also contains three chemicals that probably also attach to the THC receptors (diTomaso, Beltramo, & Piomelli, 1996). So, people who say that they are "addicted to chocolate" may be more literally correct than they had supposed.

The research on THC receptors helps to explain why people frequently die of an overdose of opiates, but rarely of marijuana: Opiate receptors are densely located in the medulla and other brain areas that control heart rate and breathing, whereas these same areas have very few THC receptors (Herkenham et al., 1990). So even rather large doses of marijuana are unlikely to stop the heart or to interfere with breathing.

Stimulant Drugs

Stimulants are *drugs that boost energy, heighten alertness, increase activity, and produce a pleasant feeling.* Coffee, tea, and many soft drinks contain caffeine, which is a stimulant. People who drink a lot of coffee become dependent on caffeine; if someone replaces their regular coffee with decaffeinated coffee, they will experience headaches and drowsiness (Hughes et al., 1991). Surgical patients sometimes report various kinds of distress that can be mistaken for the effects of their operation, when in fact these patients are suffering from caffeine withdrawal.

Amphetamines and cocaine are powerful stimulants with wide-ranging effects. Both drugs prevent neurons from reabsorbing the dopamine they have released; they thereby prolong the effects of the dopamine (Ritz, Lamb, Goldberg, & Kuhar, 1987). Because both of these drugs also increase the activity at norepinephrine and serotonin synapses, their effects on behavior are complex. Both drugs increase the heart rate, blood pressure, and body temperature. Cocaine has additional anesthetic (sensation-blocking) effects, similar to the effects of novocaine and lidocaine.

We regard cocaine as a stimulant because it increases heart rate, makes people excited and alert, and interferes with their sleep. However, cocaine actually *decreases* the overall activity within the brain (London et al., 1990). That effect may seem to contradict the statement that cocaine prolongs the activity of a couple of neurotransmitters; however, those transmitters are predominantly inhibitory transmitters. Thus, by increasing dopamine and norepinephrine activity, cocaine decreases the activity of many brain neurons (Figure 5.23).

If cocaine decreases the activity of neurons, you might ask, how does it act as a stimulant for behavior? The brain is a complicated organ that often operates on the principle of double negatives: Cocaine decreases the activity of neurons, which were in turn acting to inhibit still other neurons. By inhibiting an inhibitor, cocaine has the net effect of stimulating the final behavioral outcome.

Cocaine has long been available in the powdery form of cocaine hydrochloride, a chemical that can be sniffed. It produces mostly enjoyable effects that increase gradually over a few minutes and then decline gradually over about half an hour. It also anesthetizes the nostrils and can in some cases damage the lungs. Sniffed cocaine hydrochloride is only occasionally habit-forming.

Before 1985, the only way to get a more intense effect

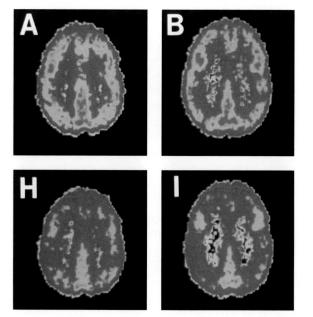

FIGURE 5.23 "Your brain on drugs." Parts A and B show the activity of a normal brain in horizontal section, as measured by PET scans. Parts H and I show activity of the same brain under the influence of cocaine. Red indicates the highest amount of activity, followed by yellow, green, and blue. Note that cocaine has decreased the amount of activity in the brain.

FIGURE 5.24 Because crack is smoked, it reaches the brain in 8 seconds, much faster than other forms of cocaine. All else being equal, the faster that a drug reaches the brain, the more intense the experience will be and the greater the probability of addiction.

from cocaine hydrochloride was to treat it with ether to convert it into *free-base cocaine*—cocaine with the hydrochloride removed. Smoking free-base cocaine enables a high percentage of it to enter the body rapidly and thereby enter the brain rapidly. The faster a drug enters the brain, the more intense the resulting experience will be.

The drug known as *crack cocaine* first became available in 1985. Crack is cocaine that has already been converted into free-base rocks, ready to be smoked (Brower & Anglin, 1987; Kozel & Adams, 1986). (See Figure 5.24.) It is called "crack" because it makes popping noises when smoked. Crack produces a rush of potent effects within just a few seconds, much faster than other forms of cocaine. The effects are generally described as pleasant, although some people report intense anxiety instead, and other people suffer heart attacks or other severe medical complications. Long-term use can lead to a sore throat, mental confusion, lung diseases, and other serious problems.

Because crack cocaine enters the brain so rapidly, it can become powerfully habit-forming, although the habit forms gradually over two to four years, so frequent users may lull themselves into a false sense of security: "I can take it or leave it" (Gawin, 1991). During periods of using the drug, the drug experience itself becomes the focus of so much attention that the person neglects usual activities such as eating, sleeping, going to work, or taking care of family members.

Because selling crack is so lucrative, rival gangs in large cities compete with each other to control the sales. The resulting violence has created a problem for society that goes far beyond the direct harm done by the drug itself.

Tobacco cigarettes deliver nicotine, a chemical that is generally classed as a stimulant although it has complex effects on the body (Stolerman, 1991). Although nicotine increases the heart rate and blood pressure, with many people it also decreases breathing rate (Jones, 1987). Perhaps because of this decreased breathing rate, many smokers say that they find cigarettes relaxing. Nicotine attaches to receptors that increase the release of dopamine in the nucleus accumbens; thus, its effects overlap those of amphetamines, cocaine, and other addictive drugs (Levin & Rose, 1995; Pontieri, Tanda, Orzi, & DiChiara, 1996). Nicotine also stimulates acetylcholine receptors. Nicotine addiction develops relatively slowly, compared to cocaine or opiate addiction, but once it develops, it is very persistent and very hard to break. We shall consider cigarette addiction in more detail in Chapter 16.

Hallucinogens

Drugs that induce sensory distortions are called **hallucinogens** (Jacobs, 1987). Most of these drugs are derived from certain mushrooms or other plants (Figure 5.25); some are manufactured in chemistry laboratories. The hallucinogenic drugs LSD, PCP, and mescaline intensify sensations and can sometimes produce a dreamlike state or an

FIGURE 5.25 Tablas, or yarn paintings, created by members of the Huichol tribe (Mexico), evoke the beautiful lights, vivid colors, and "peculiar creatures" experienced after the people eat the hallucinogenic peyote cactus in highly ritualized ceremonies.

intense mystical experience. Peyote, a hallucinogen derived from a cactus plant, has a long history of use in Native American religious ceremonies.

LSD attaches mainly to one kind of brain receptor sensitive to the neurotransmitter serotonin (Jacobs, 1987). It stimulates those receptors at irregular times and prevents the brain's neurotransmitters from stimulating the receptors at the normal times. We have an interesting gap in our knowledge at this point: We know that LSD's disruption of certain kinds of serotonin receptors leads to hallucinogenic experiences, but we do not understand the relationship between those receptors and the resulting experiences. That is, we know where the hallucinogenic event happens, but not *how* it happens.

Chronic Drug Effects

The intended effects of any drug are temporary. Initially, they produce an effect, such as excitement, relaxation, or a distortion of experience. As the drug leaves the brain and the effects wear off, the person experiences **withdrawal effects,** which are generally *about the opposite of the initial effects.* After someone has taken a drug repeatedly, its effects grow weaker and weaker, unless the person increases the dosage. This *decrease in effect* is called **tolerance.** Drug users often seek the drug partly to combat the withdrawal effects; they increase their dosage to compensate for their tolerance. That is, withdrawal effects and tolerance tend to promote increased use of a drug.

Drug Withdrawal

When habitual users suddenly stop using alcohol or opiate drugs (such as morphine or heroin), they gradually enter a state of withdrawal (Gawin & Kleber, 1986). With alcohol, the typical withdrawal symptoms are sweating, nausea, sleeplessness, and, in severe cases, hallucinations and seizures (Mello & Mendelson, 1978). With opiate drugs, the typical withdrawal symptoms are anxiety, restlessness, loss of appetite, vomiting, diarrhea, sweating, and gagging (Mansky, 1978). People who quit using tranquilizers can experience sleeplessness and nervousness. Users who quit cocaine or other stimulant drugs experience a state of depression. Someone who *feels compelled to use a drug to reduce unpleasant withdrawal symptoms* is said to have a **physical dependence** on the drug.

We distinguish between physical dependence and **psychological dependence,** which is a *strong repetitive desire for something without any accompanying physical symptoms of withdrawal.* For example, habitual gamblers have a psychological dependence on placing bets, even though they can abstain from gambling without undergoing anything like the effects of "cold turkey" heroin withdrawal. A psychological dependence can be extremely insistent, and in many cases, it is pointless to try to decide whether someone's dependence is physical or psychological. (For example, the withdrawal effects for someone who quits using cocaine include mostly "psychological" effects such as a lack of pleasure, with only fairly brief physiological effects. So is the dependence physiological or psychological?)

Drug Tolerance

People who take a drug repeatedly develop a tolerance to its effects. To achieve the desired high, drug users must steadily increase the dose. Some longtime users inject three or four times more heroin or morphine into their veins than it would take to kill a nonuser.

What brings about drug tolerance? It may result in part from automatic chemical changes that occur in cells throughout the body, to counteract the drug's effects (Baker & Tiffany, 1985). It may also result in part from psychological causes. For example, alcohol impairs the coordination of rats as well as that of humans. If rats are simply injected with alcohol every day for 24 days, the rats show no apparent tolerance for alcohol, as indicated by a coordination test given on the last day. However, if their coordination is tested after each of the 24 injections, each test session offers the rats an opportunity to practice their coordination, so their performance steadily improves (Wenger, Tiffany, Bombardier, Nicholls, & Woods, 1981). In other words, by practicing coordination while under the influence of alcohol, the rats develop a tolerance to alcohol. Similarly, people who use stimulant drugs as appetite suppressants start to develop a tolerance to the effects after a few meals. We shall discuss drug tolerance in more detail in the next chapter.

CONCEPT CHECK

6. People who use stimulant drugs as appetite suppressants ordinarily develop a tolerance. How could they prevent the development of this tolerance? (Check your answer later on this page.)

THE MESSAGE
Drugs and Awareness

If you were to change a few of a computer's connections at random, you could produce an "altered state," which would almost certainly not be an improvement. Giving drugs to a human brain is a little like changing the connections of a computer, and almost any drug at least temporarily impairs brain functioning somehow, even if the drug is used under medical supervision and accomplishes some good along with the bad. By examining both the desirable and undesirable effects of drugs on the brain, we can gain greater insight into the brain's normal processes and functions.

SUMMARY

✳ *Alcohol.* Alcohol, the most widely abused drug in our society, relaxes people and relieves their inhibitions. It can also impair judgment and reasoning. (page 182)

✳ *Tranquilizers.* Benzodiazepine tranquilizers are widely used to relieve anxiety; they are sometimes also used to relax muscles or to promote sleep. (page 183)

✳ *Opiates.* Opiate drugs bind to endorphin receptors in the nervous system. The immediate effect of opiates is pleasure and relief from pain. (page 183)

✳ *Marijuana.* Marijuana's active compound, THC, acts on abundant receptors, found mostly in the hippocampus and certain brain areas important for the control of movement. Because the medulla has few THC receptors, a large dose of marijuana is seldom fatal. (page 183)

✳ *Stimulants.* Stimulant drugs such as amphetamines and cocaine increase activity levels and pleasure. Compared to other forms of cocaine, crack produces more rapid effects on behavior, greater risk of addiction, and greater risk of damage to the heart and other organs. (page 184)

✳ *Hallucinogens.* Hallucinogens induce sensory distortions. LSD acts at one type of serotonin synapse; we do not yet know why activity at that type of synapse should produce these effects. (page 185)

✳ *Withdrawal.* After using a drug, the user enters a rebound state known as withdrawal. Drug users often crave drugs as a way of decreasing their withdrawal symptoms. (page 186)

✳ *Tolerance.* People who use certain drugs repeatedly become less and less sensitive to them over time. (page 186)

Suggestion for Further Reading

Rivers, P. C. (1994). *Alcohol and human behavior.* Englewood Cliffs, NJ: Prentice-Hall. Covers all aspects of alcohol use from its effects on physiology to its role in society and culture.

Terms

alcohol   a class of molecules that includes methanol, ethanol, propyl alcohol (rubbing alcohol), and others (page 182)

tranquilizers   drugs that help people to relax (page 183)

opiates   either drugs derived from the opium poppy or synthetic drugs that produce effects similar to those of opium derivatives (page 183)

endorphins   chemicals produced by the brain that have effects resembling those of opiates (page 183)

stimulants   drugs that boost energy, heighten alertness, increase activity, and produce a pleasant feeling (page 184)

hallucinogens   drugs that induce sensory distortions (page 185)

withdrawal effects   experiences that occur as a result of the removal of a drug from the brain (page 186)

tolerance   the weakened effect of a drug after repeated use (page 186)

physical dependence   a condition whereby a habitual drug user is driven to seek the drug to escape or avoid the unpleasant withdrawal effects that occur during abstention from the drug (page 186)

psychological dependence   a strong repetitive desire for something without any physical symptoms of withdrawal (page 186)

Answer to Concept Check

6. Instead of taking a pill just before a meal, people should take it between meals, when they are not planning to eat right away or when they plan to skip a meal altogether. If they eat right after taking a pill, they soon develop a tolerance to its appetite-suppressing effects. However, even if they follow the advice to take the pills between meals, most people are not likely to lose weight in the long run. After their appetite is suppressed for a while, they are likely to experience increased appetite later. (page 187).

Web Resources

Web of Addictions
www.well.com/user/woa/
Andrew L. Homer and Dick Dillon provide factual information about alcohol and other abused drugs. Fact sheets and other material are arranged by drug, with links to net resources related to addictions, in-depth information on special topics, and a list of places to get help with addictions.

National Clearinghouse for Alcohol and Drug Information
www.health.org/survey.htm
Dozens of research and statistical reports about alcohol and drug use. Backtrack to Prevention Online's front page to access even more information, searchable databases, forums, and links.

Learning

Suppose we set up a simple experiment on animal learning. We put a monkey midway between a green wall and a red wall. If it approaches the green wall, we give it a few raisins; if it approaches the red wall, it gets nothing. After a few trials, the monkey always approaches the green wall. After it has made the correct choice, say, 12 times in a row, we are satisfied that the monkey has learned something.

Now let's suppose that we conduct the same experiment with an alligator. We use the same procedure as we did with the monkey, but we get different results. The alligator strains our patience, sitting for hours at a time without approaching either wall. When it finally moves, it is as likely to approach one wall as the other. After hundreds of trials, *we* have learned something: not to go into the trained-alligator business. But we see little evidence that the alligator has learned anything.

Does this mean that alligators are slow learners? Not necessarily. Maybe they are just not motivated to seek food. Maybe they can't see the difference between red and green. Maybe they learn but also forget quickly, so they cannot put

together a long streak of consecutive correct approaches. To decide for sure whether alligators can learn, we would need to test them under a wide variety of circumstances. (I don't know whether you care, but yes, alligators can learn. They're not much good at learning to find food, but according to Davidson [1966], they *can* learn how to get away from unpleasant stimuli.)

Some similar problems arise when evaluating human learning. Suppose that little Joey is having serious academic troubles. Should we consider him a "slow learner"? Not necessarily. Like the alligator, Joey may not be sufficiently motivated, or he may have trouble seeing or hearing, or he may learn and then forget. Maybe he is distracted by his emotional troubles at home. (That's a possibility we probably wouldn't consider with the alligator.) We can imagine all sorts of other reasons why Joey might be having trouble in school.

Psychologists have spent an enormous amount of time studying learning. One of their main discoveries is how important it is to consider all the influences that might interfere with learned performance. Psychologists have developed and polished many of their skills by conducting experiments on learning.

This chapter is about the procedures that produce changes in behavior—why you lick your lips at the sight of tasty food, why you turn away from a food that once made you sick, why you get nervous if a police car starts to follow you, and why you shudder at the sight of a ferocious person with a chain saw. This chapter is also about why you work harder at some tasks than at others and why you sometimes persevere for so long before you give up. Chapter 7 deals with memories. Obviously, one cannot learn a change in behavior without establishing some sort of memory, and one cannot establish a memory without learning something. Still, the study of learning is based on a very different research tradition from that of memory.

MODULE 6.1

Behaviorism

How and why did the behaviorist viewpoint arise?

What is its enduring message?

Different kinds of psychologists disagree about the primary goals of psychology. For example, in later chapters we shall encounter *humanistic psychologists,* who are mainly interested in people's personal experiences and values. Here, we discuss **behaviorists,** *psychologists who insist that psychologists should study only observable, measurable behaviors, not mental processes*. The discussion of behaviorism will lead us into a discussion of learning, a field of research that behaviorists have traditionally dominated.

Because the term *behaviorist* applies to theorists and researchers with quite a range of views, psychologists distinguish between *methodological behaviorists* and *radical behaviorists*. **Methodological behaviorists** *study only the events that they can measure and observe*—in other words, the environment and the individual's actions—*but they sometimes use those observations to make inferences about internal events* (Day & Moore, 1995). For example, depriving an animal of food, or increasing its exercise, or presenting very appealing food will increase the probability that the animal will eat food, work for food, and so forth. From such observations, a psychologist can infer an **intervening variable,** *something that we cannot directly observe but that links a variety of procedures to a variety of possible responses*. In this case, the intervening variable is *hunger:*

Similarly, one could use other kinds of observations to infer other intervening variables, such as thirst, sex drive, anger, fear, and so forth. The important point is that a methodological behaviorist will use such terms only after anchoring them firmly to observable procedures and responses—that is, after giving them a clear operational definition (as discussed in Chapter 2). Most psychological researchers are methodological behaviorists, even if they do not use that term.

Radical behaviorists do not deny that private events such as hunger, anger, or fear exist, and they also agree that it is possible to study the circumstances that cause people to say "I am hungry," "I am angry," and so forth. The distinguishing feature of radical behaviorists is that they *deny that hunger, anger, or any other internal, private event causes behavior* (Moore, 1995). For example, they would say, if food deprivation leads to hunger and hunger leads to eating, what have we gained by introducing the word *hunger*? Why not just say that food deprivation leads to increased eating? According to radical behaviorists, all internal states are caused by an event in the environment (or by the individual's genetics), and therefore the ultimate cause of any behavior lies in the observable events that led up to that behavior, not the internal states.

According to this point of view, most discussions of mental events are just sloppy language. For example, as B. F. Skinner (1990) argued, when you say, "I *intend* to . . . ," what you really mean is "I am about to . . . ," or "In situations like this, I usually . . . ," or "This is in the preliminary stages of happening. . . ." That is, any statement about intentions or mental experiences can be converted into a description of behavior.

The Rise of Behaviorism

Behaviorism can be clearly understood only within the historical context in which it arose. During the early 1900s, one highly influential group within psychology was the *structuralists* (see Chapter 1) who studied thoughts and ideas by asking people to describe their own

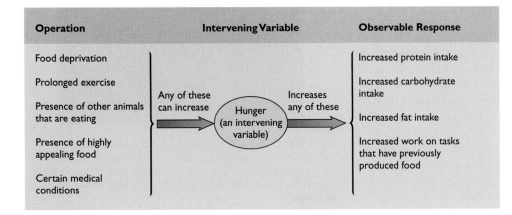

Operation	Intervening Variable	Observable Response
Food deprivation		Increased protein intake
Prolonged exercise		Increased carbohydrate intake
Presence of other animals that are eating	Any of these can increase → Hunger (an intervening variable) → Increases any of these	Increased fat intake
Presence of highly appealing food		Increased work on tasks that have previously produced food
Certain medical conditions		

Behaviorists agree that all psychological investigations should be based on behavioral observations. A methodological behaviorist might use observations of, say, facial expressions to make inferences about such processes as "sadness." A radical behaviorist, however, would study the facial expressions themselves, but not as a means of inferring something else.

every action. Behavior is a product of the individual's past history of stimuli and responses, not simply a product of current stimuli.

If the behaviorist approach is to deal successfully with complex behaviors, it must be able to explain changes in behavior that depend on learning. The behaviorist movement, which was developing during the early 1900s, became the heir to a tradition of animal learning research that had begun for quite different reasons. Charles Darwin's theory of evolution by natural selection inspired many early psychologists to study animal learning and intelligence (Kalat, 1983). At first, those psychologists were interested in comparing the intelligence of various species. By about 1930, however, most psychologists had lost interest in that topic, because the differences in learning performance among species proved to be small and inconsistent. Nevertheless, the early researchers had begun a tradition of studying animal learning in an objective manner; behaviorists carried forth this tradition, although they asked different questions. If nonhumans learn in more or less the same way as humans do, behaviorists reasoned, then it should be possible to discover the basic laws of learning by studying the behavior of a convenient laboratory animal, such as a pigeon or a rat. Most of the rest of this chapter will deal with behaviorists' attempts to outline the basic laws of learning.

experiences. The early behaviorists were, to a large extent, protesting against structuralism. Behaviorists insisted that it is useless to ask people to report on their own private experiences. For example, if someone says, "My idea of roundness is stronger than my idea of color," we have no way to check the accuracy of the report. We are not even certain what it means. If psychology is to be a scientific enterprise, behaviorists insisted, it must deal with only observable, measurable events—that is, behaviors and the environment.

To avoid any mention of the mind, thoughts, or knowledge, some behaviorists went to the opposite extreme. One of the forerunners of behaviorism, Jacques Loeb (1918/1973), argued that much of animal behavior, and perhaps human behavior as well, could be described in terms of simple responses to simple stimuli—for example, approaching light, turning away from strong smells, clinging to hard surfaces, walking toward or away from moisture, and so forth. (See Figure 6.1.) Complex behavior, he surmised, is just the result of adding together many changes of speed and direction elicited by various stimuli. Loeb's view of behavior was an example of **stimulus-response psychology,** *the attempt to explain behavior in terms of how each stimulus triggers a response.*

Although the term *stimulus-response psychology* was an appropriate term for Loeb, it is an inaccurate and misleading description of the behaviorists of today. Behaviorists do not believe that we can point to a simple stimulus to explain

FIGURE 6.1 Jacques Loeb, an early student of animal behavior, argued that much or all of invertebrate behavior could be described as responses to simple stimuli, such as approaching light, turning away from light, or moving opposite to the direction of gravity.

The Assumptions of Behaviorism

Behaviorists make several assumptions, including the validity of the determinist position, the ineffectiveness of mental explanations, and the power of the environment to select behaviors (Moore, 1995). Let's consider each of these points:

Determinism

Behaviorists assume that every behavior has causes that can be understood through scientific methods. In other words, behavior is lawful. One example of a behavioral law is that an individual will increase the rate of a behavior that leads to food and decrease a behavior that leads to a shock. Behaviorists seek to increase their understanding of the laws of behavior, and they test their understanding by trying to predict or control behavior. However, as you will remember from the discussion of free will and determinism in Chapter 1, in complex situations no one can expect completely accurate predictions.

The Ineffectiveness of Mental Explanations

In everyday life, we commonly "explain" our behaviors in terms of their motivations, or emotions, or our mental state. However, behaviorists insist that such statements explain nothing:

Q. Why did she yell at that man?
A. She yelled because she was angry.
Q. How do you know she was angry?
A. We can tell she was angry because she was yelling.

Clearly, references to mental states risk luring us into circular reasoning instead of a more fruitful explanation. To understand the causes of behavior, we should look to the environment and the individual's history. To avoid mental explanations, behaviorists either avoid mental terms altogether or use them very cautiously. B. F. Skinner, the most famous and influential behaviorist, resisted using even apparently harmless words such as *hide* because they imply an intention (L. Smith, 1995). Skinner preferred simply to describe what the individuals *did,* instead of guessing what they were *trying* to do.

The same insistence on description is central to both the British and American legal systems: A witness is asked "What did you see and hear?" An acceptable answer would be, "The defendant was sweating and trembling, and his voice was wavering." It would be unacceptable to say, "The defendant was nervous and worried," because such a statement requires an inference that the witness is not entitled to make. (Of course, after the witness describes the defendant's behavior, the judge or jury might draw a conclusion from it, but at least they know by then what evidence exists to support it.)

The Power of the Environment to Mold Behavior

Behaviors produce outcomes. Eating your carrots has one kind of outcome; insulting your roommate has another. Depending on the kind of outcome, a behavior will occur either more or less often in the future. In effect, our environment selects successful behaviors, much as evolution selects successful animals.

Behaviorists have sometimes been accused of believing that the environment controls practically all aspects of behavior. The most extreme statement of environmental determinism came from John B. Watson, one of the founders of behaviorism, who said, "Give me a dozen healthy infants, well-formed, and my own specified world to bring them up in and I'll guarantee to take any one at random and train him to become any type of specialist I might select—doctor, lawyer, artist, merchant-chief, and yes, even beggar-man thief, regardless of his talents, penchants, tendencies, abilities, vocations, and race of his ancestors" (Watson, 1925, p. 82).

Watson admitted that his statement was an exaggeration. He defended himself by saying that many other people had similarly exaggerated the role of heredity in molding behavior. Today, few psychologists would claim that variations in behavior depend entirely on the environment (or that they depend entirely on heredity, for that matter). Although behaviorists today do not deny the importance of heredity, however, they do not generally emphasize it. Their research focuses on how the environment selects one behavior over another, and their explanations of individual differences concentrate on how different people's behaviors emerge from different learning histories.

Behaviorists emphasize the role of experience in determining our actions—both our current experience and our past experiences in similar situations.

THE MESSAGE
Behaviorism as a Method and Viewpoint

Some behaviorists take more extreme positions than others do. The same could be said for liberals, conservatives, environmentalists, vegetarians, or advocates of any other theoretical position. Just as politicians often attack their opponents by exaggerating their most extreme positions, some psychologists dismiss behaviorism by attacking some of the extreme statements of John Watson, Jacques Loeb, or other early behaviorists. Others abandon behaviorism because they want to investigate knowledge, imagination, or other internal processes, and they find behaviorist procedures and terminology too limiting.

Many students quickly dismiss behaviorism also, because, at least at first glance, it seems so ridiculous: "What do you *mean,* my thoughts and beliefs and emotions don't cause my behavior?!" The behaviorists' reply is, "Exactly right. Your thoughts and other internal states do not cause your behavior, because events in your present and past environment caused those thoughts. The events that caused those thoughts are therefore the real causes of your behavior, and psychologists should spend their time trying to understand the effects of those events, not trying to analyze your thoughts."

Don't be too quick to agree or disagree. Just contemplate this: If you believe that your thoughts or other internal states cause behaviors and that these behaviors were *not* caused by previous events in the environment, what evidence could you provide to support your claim?

SUMMARY

* *Range of positions among behaviorists.* Behaviorists insist that psychologists should study behaviors and their relation to observable features of the environment. Methodological behaviorists use these observables to draw inferences about internal states. Radical behaviorists insist that internal states are of little scientific use and that they do not control behavior. The causes of the internal states themselves, as well as of the behaviors, lie in the environment. (page 191)

* *The origins of behaviorism.* Behaviorism began in part as a protest against structuralists, who were asking people to describe their own mental processes. Behaviorists insisted

that the structuralist approach was futile and that psychologists should study observable behaviors. (page 191)

* *Behaviorists' interest in learning.* Before the rise of the behaviorist movement, other psychologists had studied animal intelligence. Behaviorists adapted some of the methods used in previous studies but changed the questions, concentrating on the basic mechanisms of learning. (page 192)

* *Behaviorists' assumptions.* Behaviorists assume that all behaviors have causes (determinism), that mental explanations are unhelpful, and that the environment acts to select effective behaviors and to suppress ineffective ones. (page 193)

Suggestions for Further Reading

Skinner, B. F. (1974). *About behaviorism.* New York: Knopf. Skinner's elaboration of the behaviorist point of view.

Todd, J. T., & Morris, E. K. (Eds.) (1995). *Modern perspectives on B. F. Skinner and contemporary behaviorism.* Westport, CT: Greenwood Press. A collection of articles in which leading behaviorists assess the past and future of the behaviorist movement.

Terms

behaviorist a psychologist who insists that psychologists should study only observable, measurable behaviors, not mental processes (page 191)

methodological behaviorist a psychologist who studies only measurable, observable events but sometimes uses those observations to make inferences about internal events (page 191)

intervening variable something that we infer without directly observing it and that links a variety of procedures to a variety of possible responses (page 191)

radical behaviorist a behaviorist who denies that internal, private events are causes of behavior (page 191)

stimulus-response psychology a field that attempts to explain behavior in terms of how each stimulus triggers a response (page 192)

Web Resources

Operant Conditioning and Behaviorism

www.biozentrum.uni-wuerzburg.de/genetics/behavior/learning/behaviorism.html

This site provides a historical outline that begins with Thorndike's trial-and-error learning and includes Pavlov's classical conditioning and Skinner's operant conditioning.

Classical Conditioning

When we learn a relationship between two stimuli, what happens?

Do we start responding to one stimulus as if it were the other?

Or do we learn how to use information from one stimulus to predict something about the other?

You are sitting in your room when your roommate flicks a switch on the stereo. You flinch because you know the volume is set to a deafening level. In a case like this, you are not just responding to the flick of the switch; you are responding to what it predicts.

Certain aspects of our behavior consist of learned responses to signals. However, even apparently simple responses to simple stimuli no longer seem as simple as they once did. To explain even the simplest learned responses, we must give an individual credit for having processed a great deal of information.

Psychologists' efforts to discover what takes place during learning have led them to conduct thousands of experiments, many of them on nonhuman animals. For certain kinds of learning, such as birdsong learning, the results depend heavily on which species is being studied, but for many other kinds of learning, the similarities among species are more impressive than the differences. In some ways, it is easier to study rats or pigeons than humans, because a researcher can better control what and when they eat and many other variables likely to influence performance. Besides, to the extent that species do differ, the behavior of a rat or a pigeon will probably be easier to understand than that of a human. Of course, if researchers discover great complexities in the behavior of a rat, they can safely assume that human behavior is at least equally complex.

Pavlov and Classical Conditioning

Suppose you always feed your cat at 4:00 P.M. with food you keep in the refrigerator. As 4:00 P.M. approaches, your cat goes to the kitchen, claws at the refrigerator, meows, and salivates. You might explain the cat's behavior by saying that it "expects" food, that it "knows" there is food in the refrigerator, or that it is "trying to get someone to feed it." Behaviorists reject such mental explanations and instead seek descriptions that do not rely on intentions, thoughts, or knowledge.

When Ivan P. Pavlov proposed a simple, highly mechanical theory of learning, the mood of the time was ready for his message. Pavlov, a Russian physiologist, won a Nobel Prize in physiology in 1904 for his research on digestion. As he continued his research, one day he noticed that a dog would salivate or secrete stomach juices as soon as it saw the lab worker who ordinarily brought the dogs their food. Because this secretion presumably depended on the dog's previous experiences, Pavlov called it a "psychological" secretion. Puzzled, Pavlov enlisted the help of other specialists, who then discovered that "teasing" a dog with the sight

Ivan P. Pavlov (with the white beard) with students and an experimental dog. Pavlov focused on limited aspects of the dog's behavior—mostly salivation—and devised some apparently simple principles to describe that behavior.

of food produced the same quantity and quality of saliva as food in the mouth did and that the secretion was as predictable and automatic as any reflex. Pavlov adopted the term *conditional reflex,* thus implying that he only *conditionally* (or tentatively) accepted it as a real reflex (Todes, 1997). However, this term has usually been translated into English as *conditioned reflex,* a term with different connotations.

Pavlov's Procedures

Pavlov guessed that animals are born with certain *automatic connections*—we call them **unconditioned** (or *unconditional*) **reflexes**—*between a stimulus such as food and a response such as secreting digestive juices.* He conjectured that animals acquire new reflexes by transferring a response from one stimulus to another. For example, if a neutral stimulus—say, a buzzer—always preceded food, an animal might begin to respond to the buzzer just as it responds to food. Thus, the buzzer would also elicit digestive secretions. The *process by which an organism learns a new association between two paired stimuli—a neutral stimulus and one that already evokes a reflexive response*—has come to be known as **classical conditioning** or **Pavlovian conditioning.** (It is called classical because it has been known and studied for a long time.)

Pavlov used an experimental setup like the one in Figure 6.2 (Goodwin, 1991). First, he selected dogs with a moderate degree of arousal. (Highly excitable dogs would not hold still long enough, and highly inhibited dogs would fall asleep.) Then, he attached a tube to one of the salivary ducts in the dog's mouth, to measure salivation. He could have measured stomach secretions, but it was easier to measure salivation.

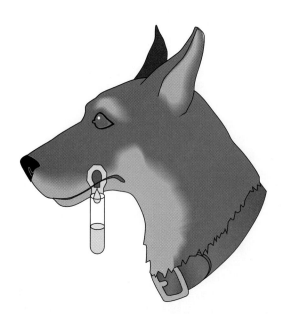

FIGURE 6.2 Pavlov used dogs for his experiments on classical conditioning and salivation. The experimenter can ring a buzzer (CS), present food (UCS), and measure the responses (CR and UCR). Pavlov himself collected saliva with a simple measuring pouch attached to the dog's cheek; his later colleagues used a more complex device.

Pavlov found that, whenever he gave a dog food, saliva flowed in the dog's mouth. The food → salivation connection was automatic, requiring no training. Pavlov called the food the unconditioned stimulus and called the salivation the unconditioned response. The **unconditioned stimulus (UCS)** is *an event that consistently, automatically elicits an unconditioned response,* and the **unconditioned response (UCR)** is *an action that the unconditioned stimulus automatically elicits.*

Next, Pavlov introduced a new stimulus, such as a buzzer. Upon hearing the buzzer, the dog lifted its ears and looked around but did not salivate, so the buzzer was a neutral stimulus with regard to salivation. Pavlov sounded the buzzer a couple of seconds before giving food to the dog. After a few pairings of the buzzer with food, the dog began to salivate as soon as it heard the buzzer (Pavlov, 1927/1960).

We call the buzzer the **conditioned stimulus (CS),** because the dog's *response to it depended on the preceding conditions*—that is, the pairing of the CS with the UCS. The salivation that followed the sounding of the buzzer was the **conditioned response (CR).** The conditioned response is simply *whatever response the conditioned stimulus begins to elicit as a result of the conditioning (training) procedure.* In Pavlov's experiment and in many others, the conditioned response closely resembles the unconditioned response, but in some cases it is quite different. At the start of the conditioning procedure, the conditioned stimulus does *not* elicit a conditioned response. After conditioning, it does.

To summarize: The *unconditioned stimulus* (UCS), such as food or shock, automatically elicits the *unconditioned response* (UCR) at all times. A neutral stimulus, such as a tone or buzzer, that is paired with the UCS becomes a *conditioned stimulus* (CS). At first, this neutral stimulus elicits either no response or some irrelevant response, such as just looking around. After some number of pairings of the CS with the UCS, the conditioned stimulus elicits the *conditioned response* (CR). Figure 6.3 diagrams these relationships.

Here are some other examples of classical conditioning:

- Your alarm clock makes a faint clicking sound a couple of seconds before the alarm goes off. At first, the click by itself does not awaken you, but the alarm does. After a week or so, however, you awaken as soon as you hear the click.

| Unconditioned stimulus, UCS (alarm) | → Unconditioned response, UCR (awakening) |
| Conditioned stimulus, CS (clicking) | → Conditioned response, CR (awakening) |

- You hear the sound of a dentist's drill shortly before the unpleasant experience of the drill on your teeth. From then on, the sound of a dentist's drill arouses anxiety.

| Unconditioned stimulus, UCS (drill on your teeth) | → Unconditioned response, UCR (tensing the muscles) |
| Conditioned stimulus, CS (drill sound) | → Conditioned response, CR (tensing the muscles) |

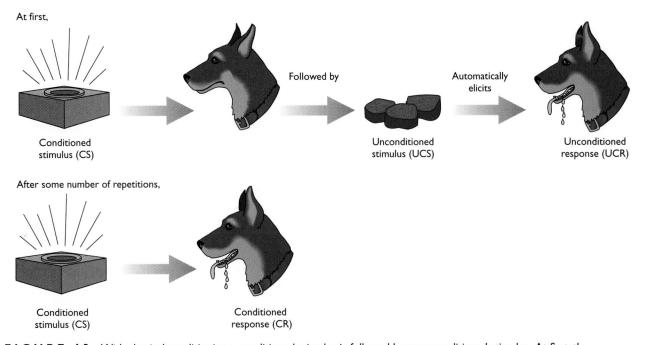

At first,

Conditioned
stimulus (CS)

Followed by

Unconditioned
stimulus (UCS)

Automatically
elicits

Unconditioned
response (UCR)

After some number of repetitions,

Conditioned
stimulus (CS)

Conditioned
response (CR)

FIGURE 6.3 With classical conditioning, a conditioned stimulus is followed by an unconditioned stimulus. At first, the conditioned stimulus elicits no response, and the unconditioned stimulus elicits the unconditioned response. After sufficient pairings, the conditioned stimulus begins to elicit the conditioned response, which can resemble the unconditioned response.

- When your partner is in a romantic mood, he or she puts on some special cologne or perfume and turns on soft music. When in a grouchy mood, he or she scowls, indicating readiness for a quarrel. (Hollis, 1997, describes similar results with fish and birds. The basics of behavior apply across species.)

Unconditioned stimulus, UCS (receptive partner)	→ Unconditioned response, UCR (romantic activities)
Conditioned stimulus, CS (nice smell, soft music)	→ Conditioned response, CR (ready for romance)
Unconditioned stimulus, UCS (grouchy partner)	→ Unconditioned response, UCR (arguments)
Conditioned stimulus, CS (scowling expression)	→ Conditioned response, CR (ready for a fight)

Note the usefulness of classical conditioning in each case: It prepares an individual for likely events.

The unconditioned stimulus can be almost any stimulus that evokes an automatic response. The conditioned stimulus can be almost any detectable stimulus—a light, a sound, the cessation of a light or sound, a smell. . . . Even a mental image can be a conditioned stimulus. Psychologists in general, and behaviorists in particular, are not sure what a mental image really is, but if I tell you to "think about lemon juice," you will salivate, and if I tell you to "think about a painful shock," you will have some changes in breathing and heart rate. For cancer patients who have had repeated chemotherapy treatments, thinking about chemotherapy or even imagining the building where they received it can provoke nausea and vomiting (Dadds, Bovbjerg, Redd, & Cutmore, 1997).

All else being equal, conditioning occurs more rapidly with unfamiliar than with familiar conditioned stimuli. For example, if you heard a tone a thousand times (followed by nothing) and then started hearing the tone followed by a puff of air to your left eye, you would be slow to show signs of conditioning. Similarly, imagine two people who are bitten by a snake. The one who has never been close to a snake before may develop an intense fear of snakes; the one who has spent the past 5 years tending snakes at the zoo will not develop nearly as much fear.

We shall start by discussing mostly laboratory studies but eventually come to an application of classical conditioning to the human phenomenon of drug tolerance. In Chapter 16, we shall consider the role of classical conditioning in the development of phobias.

CONCEPT CHECK

1. A nursing mother consistently responds to her baby's crying by putting the baby to her breast. The baby's sucking causes the release of milk. Within a few days, as soon as the mother hears the baby crying, the milk starts to flow, even before she puts the baby to her breast. What is the conditioned stimulus? the conditioned response? the unconditioned stimulus? the unconditioned response? (Check your answers on page 204.)

The Phenomena of Classical Conditioning

The *process that establishes or strengthens a conditioned response* is known as **acquisition.** Figure 6.4 shows how the strength of a conditioned response increases after pairings of the conditioned and unconditioned stimuli. Acquisition is not the end of the story, however, because any response that can be learned can also be unlearned.

Once Pavlov had demonstrated how classical conditioning occurs, inquisitive psychologists wondered what would happen after various changes were made in the procedures. Their investigations, prompted by practical concerns, theoretical concerns, or simple curiosity, have extended our knowledge of classical conditioning. Here are a few of the main phenomena:

Extinction   Suppose I sound a buzzer and then blow a puff of air into your eyes. After a few repetitions, you will start to close your eyes as soon as you hear the buzzer (Figure 6.5). Now, I sound the buzzer repeatedly without the puff of air. What do you do?

If you are like most people, you will blink your eyes the first time and perhaps the second and third times, but before long you will stop blinking. This decrease of the conditioned response is called **extinction** (see Figure 6.4). *To extinguish a classically conditioned response, repeatedly present the conditioned stimulus (CS) without the unconditioned stimulus (UCS).* That is, acquisition of a response (CR) occurs if the CS predicts the UCS; extinction occurs if the CS no longer predicts the UCS.

Be careful to distinguish between extinction and forgetting. Both serve to weaken a learned response, but they arise in different ways. Forgetting occurs when we have no opportunity to practice a certain behavior over a period of time. Extinction occurs as the result of a specific experience—the presentation of the conditioned stimulus without the unconditioned stimulus.

Extinction does not erase the original connection between the CS and the UCS, though. You might think of acquisition as learning to do something and extinction as learning to inhibit the response. For example, suppose you have gone through original learning in which a tone regularly preceded a puff of air to your eyes. You learned to blink your eyes at the tone. Then you went through an extinction process in which you heard the tone many times but received no puffs of air. You extinguished, so that the tone no longer elicited a blink. Now, without warning, you get another puff of air to your eyes. As a result, the next time you hear the tone, you will blink your eyes! Extinction inhibited your response to the CS (here, the tone), but a sudden puff of air weakens that inhibition (Bouton, 1994).

Spontaneous Recovery   Suppose that we classically condition a response and then extinguish it. Several hours or days later, we present the conditioned stimulus again. In many cases, the conditioned response will reappear. But this return is temporary, lasting only one or a few trials, unless CS-UCS pairings are resumed. **Spontaneous recovery** refers to this *temporary return of an extinguished response after a delay* (see Figure 6.4). For example, the sound of a buzzer (CS) is repeatedly followed by a puff of air blown into the eyes (UCS) until the person learns to blink at the sound of the buzzer. Then the buzzer is presented repeatedly by itself until the person learns to stop blinking. Neither the buzzer nor the puff of air is presented for the next few hours. Then the buzzer is sounded again and the person blinks—not strongly, perhaps, but more noticeably than at the end of the extinction training.

Why does spontaneous recovery take place? Think of it this way: At first, the buzzer predicted a puff of air to the eyes. Then it predicted nothing. The two sets of experiences conflict with each other, but the more recent one predominates, so the person stops blinking. Hours later, neither experience is much more recent than the other, and the effects of the original acquisition are almost as strong as those of extinction.

CONCEPT CHECK

2. In Pavlov's experiment on conditioned salivation in response to a buzzer, what procedure could you use to produce extinction? What procedure could you use to produce spontaneous recovery? (Check your answers on page 204.)

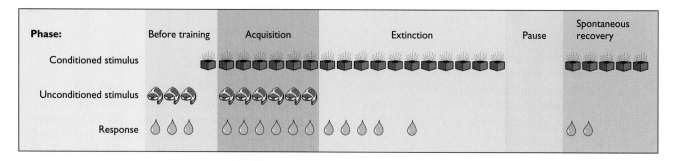

Phase:	Before training	Acquisition	Extinction	Pause	Spontaneous recovery
Conditioned stimulus					
Unconditioned stimulus					
Response					

FIGURE 6.4 Phases of classical conditioning: Classical conditioning proceeds through several phases, depending on the time of presentation of the two stimuli. If the conditioned stimulus regularly precedes the unconditioned stimulus, acquisition occurs. If the conditioned stimulus is presented by itself, extinction occurs. A pause after extinction yields a brief spontaneous recovery.

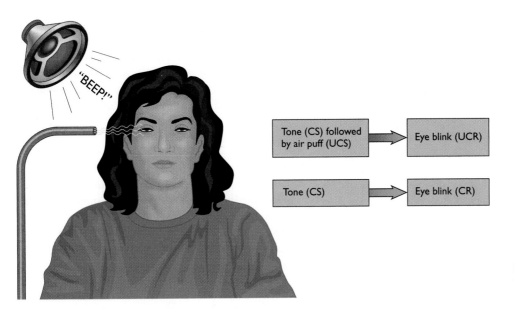

FIGURE 6.5 The procedure for classical conditioning of the eye-blink response

Stimulus Generalization

Suppose your alarm clock makes a faint clicking sound (CS) a few seconds before the alarm (UCS), and you have learned to awaken as soon as you hear the clicking sound. What happens if we now substitute a different alarm clock? It too makes a clicking sound before the alarm goes off, but it is a recognizably different click. Will it awaken you?

It probably will. The closer the sound of the new click is to the original one, the more likely you are to respond by awakening (Figure 6.6). **Stimulus generalization** is the *extension of a conditioned response from the training stimulus to similar stimuli.*

This definition may sound pretty straightforward, but in fact psychologists find it difficult to specify exactly what "similar" means. For example, if you hear a clicking sound somewhere other than in your bedroom or at a time other than your usual time to awaken, it may not be effective at all. So, your response at any moment depends on how similar the total configuration of stimuli is to the set on which you were trained, and that similarity is hard to measure (Pearce, 1994).

Discrimination   Now suppose the experimenter always follows middle C with a puff of air but never follows F-sharp with a puff of air. Eventually, you will learn to **discriminate** between these two tones: You will *respond differently to the two stimuli because different outcomes followed them.* You will blink your eyes when you hear middle C but not when you hear F-sharp. Discrimination is essential in everyday life: You learn that one bell signals that it is time for class to start, and a different bell signals a fire.

SOMETHING TO THINK ABOUT

We can easily determine how well human subjects discriminate between two stimuli. We can simply ask, "Which note has the higher pitch?" or "Which light is brighter?" How could we determine how well a nonhuman can discriminate between two stimuli? ✳

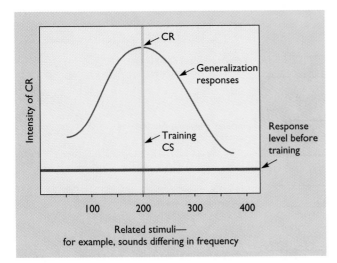

FIGURE 6.6 Stimulus generalization is the process of extending a learned response to new stimuli that resemble the one used in training. As a rule, a stimulus similar to the training stimulus elicits a strong response; a less similar stimulus elicits a weaker response.

Drug Tolerance as an Example of Classical Conditioning

Classical conditioning occurs in many laboratory settings; it also occurs in the outside world, sometimes in unexpected settings. One such setting is **drug tolerance:** *Users of certain drugs experience progressively weaker effects after taking those drugs repeatedly.* One consequence of drug tolerance is that the users crave ever larger amounts of the drug.

Drug tolerance occurs for a variety of reasons, which vary from one case to another (Poulos & Cappell, 1991). In many cases, however, drug tolerance is learned. When drug users inject themselves with morphine or heroin, the procedure is a stimulus that reliably predicts a second stimulus, the drug's entry into the brain. The drug alters experience, but it also triggers a variety of body defenses against its effects—for example, changes in hormone secretions, heart rate, and breathing rate.

Whenever one stimulus predicts a second stimulus that produces a response, the conditions necessary for classical conditioning are present. Shepard Siegel (1977, 1983) has demonstrated that classical conditioning does indeed take place during drug-injecting episodes. Initially, the injection ritual is a neutral stimulus that gives rise to no relevant response. After many pairings of that stimulus with the entry of the drug into the brain, however, the injection procedure by itself can evoke the body's antidrug defenses (Figure 6.7). From then on, the injection procedure, acting as a conditioned stimulus, triggers the defense reactions even before the drug has entered the brain and therefore weakens the effect of the drug.

If we assume that the injection procedure serves as a conditioned stimulus, then the body's defense reactions should be strongest when the drug is administered in the usual way, in the usual location, with as many familiar stimuli as possible. (The whole experience constitutes the conditioned stimulus.) The evidence strongly supports this prediction (Eikelboom & Stewart, 1982; Poulos, Wilkinson, & Cappell, 1981; Siegel, 1983; Tiffany & Baker, 1981). To show strong tolerance in a particular environment, the individual must have previously received the drug in that environment.

Why do some people die of a drug overdose that is no larger than the dose that they normally tolerated? According to the classical-conditioning interpretation, these people probably took the fatal overdose in an unfamiliar setting. For example, someone who is accustomed to taking a drug at home in the evening could suffer a fatal reaction from taking it at a friend's house in the morning. Because the new setting did not serve as a CS, it failed to trigger the usual drug tolerance.

CONCEPT CHECKS

3. When an individual develops tolerance to the effects of a drug injection, what are the conditioned stimulus, the unconditioned stimulus, the conditioned response, and the unconditioned response?
4. Within the classical-conditioning interpretation of drug tolerance, what procedure should extinguish tolerance? (Check your answers on page 204.)

Explanations of Classical Conditioning

What is classical conditioning, really? As is often the case, the process appeared at first to be fairly simple, but later investigation found it to be a more complex, and perhaps more interesting, phenomenon.

Pavlov's Theory of the Causes of Classical Conditioning

Pavlov believed that, for classical conditioning to occur, the conditioned stimulus and the unconditioned stimulus must be close together in time, with the conditioned stimulus occurring first. In the following sketches, read time left to right:

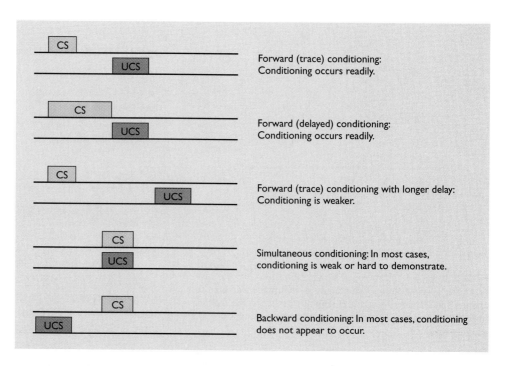

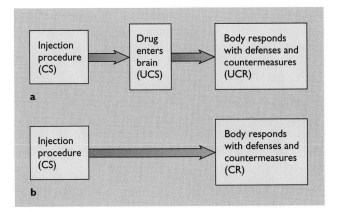

FIGURE 6.7 If a particular injection procedure consistently predicts the entry of a drug into the brain, an individual can develop a conditioned response in defense against the drug. This conditioned response is an important part of drug tolerance.

Conditioning occurs most readily with forward conditioning, with the CS and UCS close in time. *Nearness in time* is called **temporal contiguity.** With rare exceptions, the conditioned stimulus must be presented first, followed quickly by the unconditioned stimulus. In some cases, the conditioned stimulus (such as a buzzer) continues until the presentation of the unconditioned stimulus; in other cases, the conditioned stimulus stops before the unconditioned stimulus does. In either case, however, the delay is short between the start of one stimulus and the start of the other. All else being equal, the longer the delay between the CS and the UCS, the weaker the conditioning will be.

Pavlov proposed a neurological theory, assuming that every stimulus excites a specific area of the brain. A buzzer excites a "buzzer center," and meat excites a "meat center." Exciting both centers at the same time establishes and strengthens a connection between them. From then on, any excitation of the buzzer center (CS) also excites the meat center (UCS) and evokes salivation (Figure 6.8).

Pavlov's theory was appealing because it offered a simple, mechanical explanation of learning, even though he had no evidence for the existence of CS centers or UCS centers, much less connections between them. Later evidence has demonstrated the need for a more complex explanation, however.

A Signal, Not Just a Transfer of Responses

According to Pavlov's view of classical conditioning, an animal comes to respond to the conditioned stimulus as if it were the unconditioned stimulus. With his results, that interpretation was reasonable; the conditioned response and the unconditioned response were both salivation. However, in some situations the conditioned and unconditioned responses can be quite different. For example, a shock (UCS) causes rats to jump and shriek, but a conditioned stimulus predicting the shock makes rats freeze in position. They do

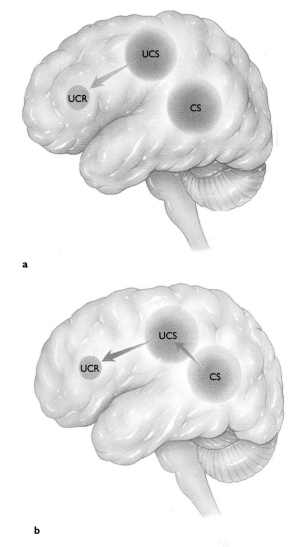

FIGURE 6.8 Pavlov believed that conditioning depended on temporal contiguity: (a) At the start of conditioning, activity in the UCS center automatically causes activation of the UCR center. At this time, activity of the CS center does not affect the UCS center. (b) After sufficient pairings of the CS and UCS, their simultaneous activity causes the growth of a connection between the CS and UCS centers. Afterward, activity in the CS center will flow to the UCS center and therefore excite the UCR center.

not react to the conditioned stimulus as if it were a shock but as they do to signals of possible danger. In short, the conditioned response serves to prepare the individual for the unconditioned stimulus.

WHAT'S THE EVIDENCE?
Contiguity Alone or Contingency

Contrary to what Pavlov believed, temporal contiguity is not always sufficient to establish classical conditioning. We shall consider two highly influential experiments.

EXPERIMENT 1

Hypothesis For this study, we compare two hypotheses: One is that pairing a new stimulus repeatedly with a shock will produce a conditioned response to that stimulus. The other hypothesis is that conditioning to this stimulus will fail if another stimulus already predicted the shock.

Method With one group of rats, a light (CS) was repeatedly followed by a shock (UCS) until the rats showed a clear, consistent response to the light. With a second group, a tone (CS) was followed by the shock until the rats consistently responded to the tone. Then, both groups experienced the light and the tone simultaneously, followed by the same shock. Later, the experimenter tested the rats' reactions to the light and the tone, presented separately (Kamin, 1969). (See Figure 6.9.)

Results After pairing of the combined light-plus-tone with shock, rats continued to respond as before to whichever stimulus they had originally associated with shock (light for one group, tone for the other). However, they responded very weakly to the new, added stimulus. That is, even though the new stimulus was always followed by the shock, animals developed little response to it. These results demonstrate the **blocking effect**: *The previously established association to one stimulus blocks the formation of an association to the added stimulus.*

Interpretation If temporal contiguity were the only factor responsible for learning, the rats should have learned a strong response to both the light and the tone, because both were presented just before the shock. The failure of the rats to learn a response to the new stimulus indicates that conditioning depends on more than just presenting two stimuli together in time; the first stimulus must be informative or predictive of the second stimulus.

EXPERIMENT 2

Hypothesis Again, we compare two hypotheses. The first is that conditioning will occur whenever a CS is consistently followed by a UCS. The second is that conditioning will occur only if the UCS is likely after the CS *and unlikely without the CS.*

Method For rats in Group 1, conditioned stimulus and unconditioned stimulus were presented in the sequence shown at the top of Figure 6.10. The horizontal line represents time; the vertical arrows represent times of stimuli presentation. For rats in Group 2, the two stimuli were presented in the sequence shown at the bottom of Figure 6.10. In both cases, every presentation of the conditioned stimulus immediately preceded a presentation of the unconditioned stimulus. But in the second case, the unconditioned stimulus occurred frequently both in the presence and in the absence of the conditioned stimulus; therefore, the CS was a poor predictor of the UCS (Rescorla, 1968, 1988).

Results Rats receiving the first sequence of stimuli developed a strong response to the conditioned stimulus. Those receiving the second sequence of stimuli developed little or no response (Rescorla, 1968, 1988).

Interpretation Although both groups of rats received the same number of CS-UCS pairings, one group learned a response to the CS and the other group did not. Evidently, *animals (including humans) associate a conditioned stimulus*

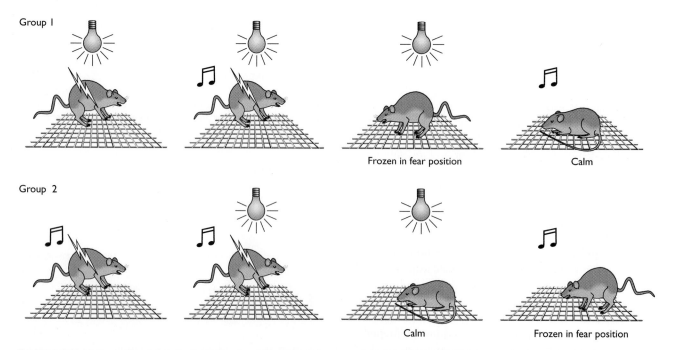

Group 1

Frozen in fear position

Calm

Group 2

Calm

Frozen in fear position

FIGURE 6.9 In Kamin's experiment, each rat first learned to associate either light or sound with shock. Then, it received a compound of both light and sound followed by shock. Even after many pairings, each rat continued to show fear of its old stimulus (the one that already predicted shock). The rats showed little response to the new stimulus.

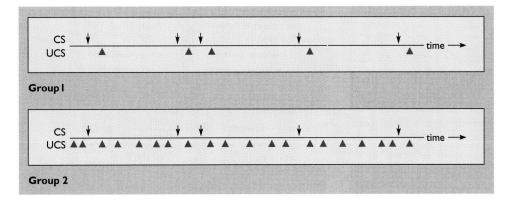

with an unconditioned stimulus only when the CS predicts the occurrence of the UCS. If the conditioned stimulus immediately precedes the unconditioned stimulus but provides no new information, it is ineffective for conditioning.

✳   ✳   ✳

CONCEPT CHECKS

5. If temporal contiguity were the only factor responsible for classical conditioning, what result should the experimenters have obtained in Experiment 2?

6. Suppose you have already learned to flinch when you hear the sound of a dentist's drill, because of the association between that sound and forthcoming pain. Now your dentist turns on some soothing background music at the same time as the drill. That is, the background music is paired with the pain just as much as the drill sound is. Will you learn to flinch at the sound of that background music, if it is presented by itself? (Check your answers on page 204.)

Conditioning, Contiguity, and Contingency

A conditioned response develops only if there is a **contingency** (*predictability*)—that is, only if the UCS is more likely after the CS than it would be otherwise. Classical conditioning has therefore been compared to scientific reasoning (Denniston, Miller, & Matute, 1996): The learner discovers which event predicts which outcome.

However, we should not imagine that a rat literally calculates the probability of a shock after a tone versus the probability of a shock during a period without a tone (Papini & Bitterman, 1990). Indeed, there is no reason to assume that the animal is "thinking" about these events at all. Even in humans, it is possible to produce conditioning when people are not consciously aware of the stimuli. In one study, people looked at photos of faces presented "subliminally" (briefly, followed by an interfering stimulus). One photo was always followed by shock. Even after people developed a conditioned stimulus to that photo, though, they could not describe it. And when they finally got a good, long look at the photo, they described it as unfamiliar (Parra, Esteves, Flykt, & Öhman, 1997).

Therefore, when we say that the results of classical conditioning are *like* scientific reasoning, we mean that both produce an outcome that depends on contingencies, or predictabilities. The underlying mechanisms do not require deep thinking; they might only be combinations of relatively simple processes.

THE MESSAGE
Classical Conditioning Is More than Drooling Dogs

People sometimes use the term "Pavlovian" to mean simple, mechanical, robot-like behavior. But Pavlovian or classical conditioning is not a mark of stupidity: It is a way of responding to relationships among events, a way of preparing us for what is likely to happen. Classical conditioning requires the processing of a fair amount of information.

Classical conditioning is important for some aspects of our behavior but less important for others. It alters our motivational or emotional reactions to stimuli, our "gut feelings"—including responses related to fear, preparations for eating, preparations for a drug injection, and so forth. But it does not control walking toward or away from various stimuli. That is, classical conditioning might tell us to be afraid, but it does not tell us how to avoid the frightening item. It might tell us to salivate in preparation for eating, but it does not tell us how to find food. Other types of learning can answer these other questions, as we shall see later in this chapter.

SUMMARY

✳ *Classical conditioning.* Ivan Pavlov discovered classical conditioning, the process by which an organism learns a new association between two stimuli that have been paired with each other—a neutral stimulus (the conditioned stimulus) and one that initially evokes a reflexive response (the unconditioned stimulus). The organism displays this association by responding in a new way (the conditioned response) to the conditioned stimulus. (page 195)

✳ *Extinction.* After classical conditioning has established a conditioned response to a stimulus, the response can be extinguished by repeatedly presenting that stimulus by itself. (page 198)

✳ *Spontaneous recovery.* If the conditioned stimulus is not presented at all for some time after extinction and is then presented again, the conditioned response may return to some degree. That return is called spontaneous recovery. (page 198)

✳ *Stimulus generalization.* An individual who learns to respond to one stimulus will respond similarly to similar stimuli. However, it is difficult to specify how we should measure similarity. (page 199)

✳ *Discrimination.* If one stimulus is followed by an unconditioned stimulus and another similar stimulus is not, the individual will come to discriminate between these two stimuli. (page 199)

✳ *Drug tolerance.* Drug tolerance is partly a form of classical conditioning in which the drug administration procedure becomes associated with the effects of the drug. (page 199)

✳ *Temporal contiguity versus contingency.* Pavlov believed that temporal contiguity between two stimuli caused classical conditioning. Later studies indicate that conditioning depends also on contingency, or the extent to which the occurrence of the first stimulus predicts the occurrence of the second. (page 200)

Suggestion for Further Reading

Rescorla, R. A. (1988). Pavlovian conditioning: It's not what you think it is. *American Psychologist, 43,* 151–160. A theoretical review by an investigator who has contributed significantly to changing views of classical conditioning.

Terms

unconditioned reflex   an automatic connection between a stimulus and a response (page 196)

classical conditioning or **Pavlovian conditioning**   the process by which an organism learns a new association between two paired stimuli—a neutral stimulus and one that already evokes a reflexive response (page 196)

unconditioned stimulus (UCS)   a stimulus that automatically elicits an unconditioned response (page 196)

unconditioned response (UCR)   an automatic response to an unconditioned stimulus (page 196)

conditioned stimulus (CS)   a stimulus that comes to evoke a particular response after being paired with the unconditioned stimulus (page 196)

conditioned response (CR)   Whatever response the conditioned stimulus begins to elicit as a result of the conditioning procedure (page 196)

acquisition   the process by which a conditioned response is established or strengthened (page 198)

extinction   in classical conditioning, the dying out of the conditioned response after repeated presentations of the conditioned stimulus without the unconditioned stimulus (page 198)

spontaneous recovery   the temporary return of an extinguished response after a delay (page 198)

stimulus generalization   the extension of a conditioned response from the training stimulus to similar stimuli (page 199)

discrimination   making different responses to different stimuli that have been followed by different outcomes (page 199)

drug tolerance   the progressively weaker effects of a drug after repeated use (page 199)

temporal contiguity   nearness in time (page 201)

blocking effect   the tendency of a previously established association to one stimulus to block the formation of an association to an added stimulus (page 202)

contingency   the prediction of one stimulus from the presence of another (page 203)

Answers to Concept Checks

1. The conditioned stimulus is the baby's crying. The unconditioned stimulus is the baby's sucking at the breast. Both the conditioned response and the unconditioned response are the release of milk. Many nursing mothers experience this classically conditioned reflex. (page 197)

2. To bring about extinction, present the buzzer repeatedly without presenting any food. To bring about spontaneous recovery, first bring about extinction; then wait hours or days and present the buzzer again. (page 198)

3. The conditioned stimulus is the injection procedure. The unconditioned stimulus is the entry of the drug into the brain. Both the conditioned response and the unconditioned response are the body's defenses against the drug. (page 200)

4. To extinguish tolerance, present the injection procedure (conditioned stimulus) without injecting the drug (unconditioned stimulus). Instead, inject just water or salt water. Shepard Siegel (1977) demonstrated that repeated injections of salt water do reduce tolerance to morphine in rats. (page 200)

5. If temporal contiguity were the only factor responsible for classical conditioning, the rats exposed to the first sequence of stimuli should have responded just as those exposed to the second sequence of stimuli. In both cases, the CS was always followed by the UCS. (page 203)

6. No, you will not learn to flinch at the sound of the background music. Because the drill sound already predicted the pain, the new stimulus is uninformative and will not be strongly associated with the pain. Your results will be an example of the blocking effect. (page 203)

Web Resources

Factors Determining the Effectiveness of Classical Conditioning

www.biozentrum.uni-wuerzburg.de/~brembs/classical/classical.html

This fairly technical discussion also covers the intricacies of learned associations.

MODULE 6.3

Operant Conditioning

How do the consequences of our behaviors affect future behaviors?

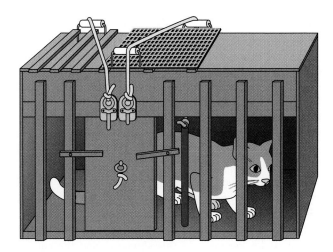

FIGURE 6.11 Each of Thorndike's puzzle boxes had a device that could open it. Here, tilting the pole will open the door. (Based on Thorndike, 1911/1970.)

Sometimes a very simple idea can be amazingly powerful. Consider democracy, for example: What could be simpler than the idea that every person gets one vote? Or consider the idea of natural selection, an extremely simple concept that brings order to an enormous array of biological facts that would otherwise seem unrelated. In this module we shall consider the idea that behaviors become more likely or less likely because of their consequences. In other words, we either repeat a behavior or cease doing it, depending on the outcome. This simple, even obvious, idea is quite powerful.

Thorndike and Operant Conditioning

Shortly before Pavlov performed his innovative experiments, Edward L. Thorndike (1911/1970), a Harvard graduate student, had begun to train and test some cats in a basement. Saying that earlier experiments had dealt only with animal intelligence, never with animal stupidity, he devised a simple, behavioristic explanation of learning.

Thorndike put cats into puzzle boxes (Figure 6.11) from which they could escape by either pressing a lever, pulling a string, or tilting a pole. Sometimes he placed food outside the box. (Usually, though, just escaping from the small box was reinforcement enough.) The cats learned to make whatever response opened the box. Thorndike discovered that they learned faster if the response opened the box immediately; any delay would impair learning.

When a cat had to tilt a pole to escape from the box, it would first paw or gnaw at the door, scratch the walls, or pace back and forth. Eventually, it would bump against the pole by accident and the door would open. The next time, the cat would go through the same repertoire of behaviors but might bump against the pole a little sooner. Over many trials, the time it took the cat to escape grew shorter, in a

gradual and irregular fashion. Figure 6.12 shows a learning curve to represent this behavior. A *learning curve* is a graph of the changes in behavior that occur over successive trials in a learning experiment.

Had the cat "figured out" how to escape? Had it come to "understand" the connection between bumping against the pole and opening the door? No, said Thorndike. If the cat had gained some new insight at some point along the way, he explained, its speed of escaping would have suddenly increased at that point. Actually, the cat's performance improved slowly, gradually, and inconsistently. One could not designate at which point the cat understood.

Thorndike concluded that learning occurs only when certain behaviors are strengthened at the expense of others. An animal enters a given situation with a certain repertoire of responses—pawing the door, scratching the walls, pacing,

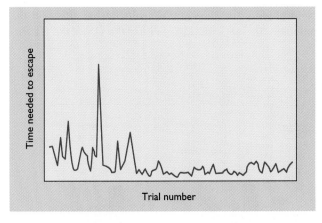

FIGURE 6.12 Trial and error or insight? As the data from one of Thorndike's experiments show, the time that a cat needs to escape from a puzzle box gradually grows shorter, but in an irregular manner. Thorndike concluded that the cat did not at any point "suddenly get the idea." Instead, reinforcement gradually increased the probability of the successful behavior.

and so forth (labeled R_1, R_2, R_3, . . . in Figure 6.13). First, the animal engages in its most probable response for this situation (response R_1 in the figure). If nothing special happens, it proceeds to other responses. Eventually, it attempts a lower-probability response—for example, bumping against the pole—that opens the door (response R_7 in the figure). The opening of the door serves as a reinforcement.

A **reinforcement** is *an event that increases the future probability of the most recent response.* Thorndike said that it "stamps in," or strengthens, the response. The next time Thorndike's cat is in the puzzle box, it may have a slightly higher probability of bumping the lever; after another reinforcement, the probability will go up another notch. Eventually, the pole-bumping response becomes the most probable response in this situation, and the cat escapes quickly (Figure 6.13c).

Thorndike summarized his views in the **law of effect** (Thorndike, 1911/1970, p. 244): *"Of several responses made to the same situation, those which are accompanied or closely followed by satisfaction to the animal will, other things being equal, be more firmly connected with the situation, so that, when it recurs, they will be more likely to recur."* In other words, the animal becomes more likely to repeat the responses that led to favorable consequences. This process does not require that the animal "think" or "understand," however. A fairly simple machine could produce responses at random and then repeat the ones that led to reinforcement.

The process of changing behavior by following a response with reinforcement is known as **operant conditioning** (because the subject operates on the environment to produce an outcome) or **instrumental conditioning** (because the subject's behavior is *instrumental* in producing the outcome). The defining difference between operant conditioning and classical conditioning is one of procedure: *In operant conditioning, the subject's behavior determines an outcome and is affected by that outcome. In classical conditioning, the subject's behavior has no effect on the outcome (the presentation of either the CS or the UCS).*

In general, the two kinds of conditioning also differ in the behaviors that they affect. That is, classical conditioning applies primarily to **visceral responses** (*responses of the internal organs*), such as salivation and digestion, whereas operant conditioning applies primarily to **skeletal responses**—that is, *movements of leg muscles, arm muscles, and so forth.* However, this distinction sometimes breaks down. For example, if a tone is consistently followed by an electric shock (a classical-conditioning procedure), the tone will make the animal freeze in position (a skeletal response) as well as increase its heart rate (a visceral response).

CONCEPT CHECK

7. When I ring a bell, an animal sits up on its hind legs and drools; then I give it some food. Is the animal's behavior an example of classical conditioning or of operant conditioning?

    So far, you do not have enough information to answer the question. What else would you need to know before you could answer? (Check your answer on page 218.)

Extinction, Generalization, Discrimination, and Discriminative Stimuli

No doubt you are familiar with the saying, "If at first you don't succeed, try, try again." Better advice is to try again, but differently. If a particular action fails or used to succeed but is now failing, perhaps you should quit that action and try something else instead.

In operant conditioning, **extinction** *occurs if responses stop producing reinforcements.* For example, you were once in the habit of asking your roommate to join you for supper. The last five times you asked, your roommate said no, so you stop asking. In classical conditioning, extinction is achieved by presenting the CS without the UCS. Table 6.1 compares operant conditioning and classical conditioning.

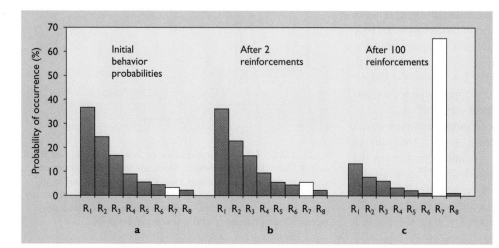

FIGURE 6.13 According to Thorndike, a cat starts with a large set of potential behaviors in a given situation. When one of these, such as pushing at a door, leads to reinforcement, the future probability of that behavior increases. We do not need to assume that the cat understands what it is doing or why.

T A B L E 6.1	**Comparison of Classical Conditioning and Operant Conditioning**	
	CLASSICAL CONDITIONING	OPERANT CONDITIONING
Terminology	CS, UCS, CR, UCR	Response, reinforcement
Subject's behavior . . .	Does not control UCS	Controls reinforcement
Paired during acquisition	Two stimuli (CS and UCS)	Response and reinforcement (in the presence of certain stimuli)
Responses studied	Mostly visceral (internal organs)	Mostly skeletal (movements)
Extinction procedure	CS without UCS	Response without reinforcement

You will recall the phenomena of stimulus generalization and discrimination in classical conditioning. Similar phenomena occur in operant conditioning. An individual who receives reinforcement for a particular response to a certain stimulus will probably make the same response to a similar stimulus. *The more similar a new stimulus is to the original reinforced stimulus, the more strongly the subject is likely to respond.* This phenomenon is known as **stimulus generalization.** For example, you might reach for the turn signal in a rented car in the same place where you would find it in your own car.

An individual who is *reinforced for responding to one stimulus and not for responding to another stimulus* will come to **discriminate** between them and *will respond more vigorously to one than to the other.* For example, you walk toward a parked car that you think is yours but then you realize it is not. After several such experiences, you learn to identify your own car from a distance.

A *stimulus that indicates which response is appropriate or inappropriate* is called a **discriminative stimulus.** A great deal of our behavior is governed by discriminative stimuli. For example, your professor standing at the front of the class is a discriminative stimulus to stop talking and get ready to take notes. When class is about over, the hands on the clock provide a discriminative stimulus to get ready to leave the room. A scowl on your roommate's face is a discriminative stimulus for you to keep quiet. Road signs provide discriminative stimuli to tell you when to speed up, slow down, or change lanes. Throughout your day, one stimulus after another signals which behaviors are likely to be reinforced and which ones are not.

Why Are Certain Responses Learned More Easily Than Others?

Thorndike's cats quickly learned to push and pull various devices in their efforts to escape from his puzzle boxes. But when Thorndike tried to teach them to scratch or lick themselves to receive the same reinforcement, they learned slowly and performed inconsistently. Why?

One possible reason is **belongingness,** the *concept that certain stimuli "belong" together or that a given response is more readily associated with certain outcomes*

than with others. Belongingness is an idea that Thorndike himself suggested, although psychologists neglected it for decades, preferring to believe that animals could just as easily associate almost any stimulus with any response. Eventually, psychologists revived the concept of belongingness, also sometimes known as "preparedness" (Seligman, 1970). For example, dogs can readily learn that a sound coming from one location means "raise your left leg," and a sound coming from another location means "raise your right leg." But it takes them virtually forever to learn that a ticking metronome means raise the left leg and a buzzer means raise the right leg (Dobrzecka, Szwejkowska, & Konorski, 1966). (See Figure 6.14.)

Presumably, Thorndike's cats were slow to associate scratching themselves with escaping from a box because the two activities do not "belong" together. (Cats evolved the ability to learn "what leads to what" in the real world, and scratching oneself is very unlikely to open doors in the real world.) But there is another possible explanation for why cats have trouble learning to scratch themselves for reinforcement: Perhaps a cat will scratch itself only when it itches (Charlton, 1983). Consider what would happen if you knew that you could win a large prize if you finished first in a rapid swallowing contest. (Why not? People compete at everything else.) You quickly swallow once, twice, maybe three times, but each successive swallow gets harder and harder. (Go ahead and try it.) Some behaviors are just not easy to produce in large quantities.

TRY IT YOUR- SELF

B. F. Skinner and the Shaping of Responses

The most influential radical behaviorist, B. F. Skinner (1904–1990), demonstrated many uses of operant conditioning. Skinner was an ardent practitioner of parsimony, always seeking simple explanations in terms of reinforcement histories rather than more complex explanations in terms of mental states.

One problem confronting any student of behavior is how to define a response. For example, imagine watching a group of children and trying to count "aggressive behaviors."

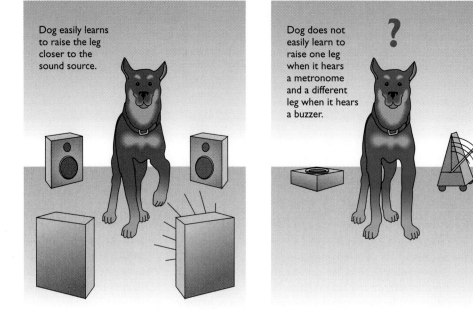

FIGURE 6.14 According to Thorndike's principle of belongingness, some items are easy to associate with each other because they "belong" together; others do not. For example, dogs easily learn to use the direction of a sound as a signal for which leg to raise, but they have trouble using the *type* of sound as a signal for which leg to raise.

What is an aggressive act and what isn't? Psychologists studying intelligence, emotion, or personality spend much of their time trying to find the best method of measurement. Even simple food-getting or shock-escaping responses are hard to define and measure. Skinner dispensed with the arguments (Zuriff, 1995): He set up a box, called an *operant chamber* (or *Skinner box,* a term that Skinner himself never used), in which a rat presses a lever or a pigeon pecks an illuminated disk, or "key," to receive food (Figure 6.15). He then operationally defined the response as anything that the animal did to depress the lever or key. So, if the rat pressed the lever with its snout instead of its paw, the response still counted; if the pigeon batted the key with its wing instead of pecking it with its beak, it still counted. The behavior was defined by its outcome, not the muscle movements.

Does that definition make sense? Skinner's reply was that it did, because it led to consistent results in his experiments. Many other researchers agreed, and Skinner's procedures became standard in many laboratories. When deciding how to define a term (such as *response*), the best definition is the most useful one. If our purposes change, we can change the definition later.

Shaping Behavior

Suppose that you want to train a rat to press a lever. If you simply put the rat in a box and wait, the rat might never press the lever. To avoid interminable waits, Skinner introduced a powerful technique, called **shaping,** for *establishing a new response by reinforcing successive approximations to it.*

To *shape* a rat to press a lever, you might begin by reinforcing the rat for standing up, a common behavior in rats. Before long, the rat has received several reinforcements and is beginning to stand up more frequently. Now you change

FIGURE 6.15 B. F. Skinner examines one of his laboratory animals in an operant-conditioning chamber, or "Skinner box." When the light above the bar is on, pressing the bar is reinforced. A food pellet rolls out of the storage device (left) and down the tube into the cage.

the rules, giving food only when the rat stands up while facing in the general direction of the lever. Soon, the rat spends much of its time standing up and facing the lever. (It extinguishes its behavior of standing and facing in any other direction, because those responses are not reinforced.) Next, you provide reinforcement only when the rat stands facing in the right direction and in the half of the cage nearest the lever. You gradually move the boundary, and the rat moves closer to the lever. Then the rat must touch the lever and, finally, apply weight to it. Through a series of short, easy steps, you might thus shape the rat to press levers in a matter of minutes. Similarly, education is a kind of shaping procedure: First, your parents or teachers praise you for counting your fingers; later, you must add and subtract to earn their congratulations; step by step, your tasks get more complex, until you are doing calculus.

Chaining Behavior

To produce complex sequences of behavior, psychologists use a procedure called **chaining.** Assume that you want to train an animal, perhaps a guide dog or a show horse, to go through a sequence of actions in a particular order. You could *chain* the behaviors, *reinforcing each one with the opportunity to engage in the next behavior.* That is, first the animal learns the final behavior for a reinforcement; then it learns the next-to-last behavior, which is reinforced by the opportunity to perform the final behavior. And so on.

For example, a rat might first be placed on the top platform in Figure 6.16, where it eats food. Then it is placed on the intermediate platform with a ladder in place leading to the top platform. The rat learns to climb the ladder. After it has done so repeatedly, it is placed again on the intermediate platform but this time the ladder is not present. It must learn to pull a string to raise the ladder so that it can climb to the top platform. Finally, the rat is placed on the bottom platform. It now has to learn to climb the ladder to the intermediate platform, pull a string to raise the ladder, and then climb the ladder again. For each response in the chain, the reinforcement is the opportunity to engage in the next behavior; the final response in the chain leads to food.

Humans learn to make chains of responses, too. As an infant you learned to eat with a fork and spoon. Later, you learned to put your own food on the plate before eating. Eventually, you learned to plan a menu, go to the store, buy the ingredients, cook the meal, put it on the plate, and then eat it. Each behavior is reinforced by the opportunity to engage in the next behavior.

To show how effective shaping and chaining can be, Skinner sometimes performed this demonstration: First, he

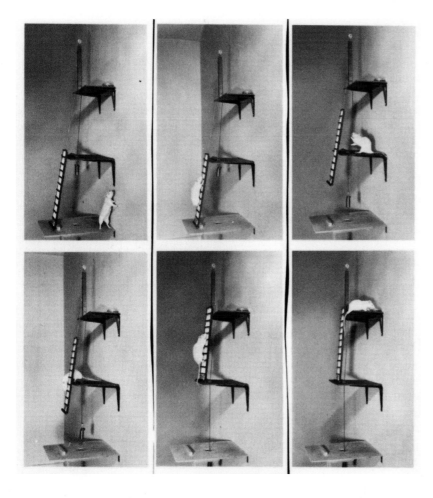

FIGURE 6.16 Chaining is a procedure in which the reinforcement for one behavior is the opportunity to engage in the next behavior. To reach food on the top platform, this rat must climb a ladder and pull a string to raise the ladder so that it can climb up again. Behavior chains longer than this can be sustained by reinforcement at the end of the chain.

TABLE 6.2   Four Categories of Operant Conditioning

	ITEM SUCH AS FOOD OR PRAISE	ITEM SUCH AS PAIN OR DISCOMFORT
Behavior produces the item.	**Positive reinforcement** (behavior increases in frequency) Example: You write a short story and *receive a prize* for it. (You learn to write more short stories and submit them in contests.)	**Punishment,** also called *passive avoidance* (behavior decreases in frequency) Example: You insult someone who then *slaps* your face. (You learn not to insult people.)
Behavior prevents or removes the item.	**Omission training,** also called *punishment* or *negative punishment* (behavior decreases in frequency) Example: You eat too much in winter and then in spring you can't fit into your swimsuit. (You learn not to overeat.)	**Escape or active avoidance,** also called *negative reinforcement* (behavior increases in frequency) Example: You carry an umbrella with you all day and as a result you *avoid getting wet* when the rains come. (You learn to carry your umbrella when you hear a forecast of rain.)

trained a rat to go to the center of a cage. Then he trained it to do so only when he was playing a certain record. Then he trained it to wait for the record to start, go to the center of the cage, and sit up on its hind legs. Step by step, Skinner eventually trained the rat to wait for the record to start (which happened to be the "Star-Spangled Banner"), move to the center of the cage, sit up on its hind legs, put its claws on a string next to a pole, pull the string to hoist a flag, and then salute the flag until the record had finished. Only then did the rat get its reinforcement. Needless to say, a show of patriotism is not part of a rat's natural repertoire of behavior; it learns to go through the motions only by successive approximations.

Increasing and Decreasing the Frequency of Responses

Nearly all of our behavior is governed by its consequences. Investigators of operant conditioning try to determine in detail how those consequences exert their effects.

Reinforcement and Punishment

Recall that *reinforcement* is an event that increases the probability that a response will be repeated. A **punishment** is *an event that decreases the probability of a response.* A reinforcement can be either the presentation of an item such as food or the removal or avoidance of an item such as pain. A punishment can be either the presentation of an item such as pain or the removal of an item such as

food. One is tempted to say that reinforcement is a pleasant event and punishment an unpleasant event, but we do not really know what rats, pigeons, and other species experience. Moreover, addicts work extremely hard for alcohol, drugs, and gambling activity, even when they seem to receive virtually no pleasure from these things (Berridge & Robinson, 1995). So, we should not equate reinforcement with pleasure.

Table 6.2 outlines the four possibilities for reinforcement and punishment and introduces some terms, including a couple that are potentially confusing. Let's go through these terms and procedures carefully. **Positive reinforcement** (on the upper left of the table) is the *presentation of an event that strengthens or increases the likelihood of a behavior.* Examples are food, water, or access to a sexual partner.

Punishment (upper right) occurs when a response is followed by an event such as pain. For example, you put your hand on a hot stove and burn yourself; you insult someone and that person slaps you. Punishment is also called **passive avoidance learning** because *the individual learns to avoid a particular outcome by being passive* (for example, by *not* putting your hand on the stove or by *not* insulting people).

Omission training (lower left) occurs *when the omission of the response produces reinforcement.* Therefore, producing the response also leads to a lack of reinforcement. For example, "If you make one more snotty remark, you will get no dessert!" Omitting the snotty remark is reinforced with dessert; producing the response leads to a lack of dessert. (This procedure is occasionally called *negative punishment* to indicate that the response is punished by the absence of an event that would have otherwise occurred.)

Finally, **escape learning** or **active avoidance learning** (lower right) occurs if the *responses lead to escape from or avoidance of something painful*. One therefore learns to make the response, even though it is followed by nothing happening. Examples are learning to come indoors when a storm is brewing (to avoid getting wet) and learning to get out of the way when you hear a driver blowing a horn (to avoid getting hit). Because the *response is reinforced by the absence of a painful event*, escape or avoidance learning is also sometimes known as *negative reinforcement*. Note that a negative reinforcement is not a punishment; reinforcement increases a behavior. The difference between positive and negative reinforcement is whether the reinforcement is the presentation of something (like food) or the avoidance of something (like pain). The terms "escape learning" and "avoidance learning" are more widely used and less confusing than the term "negative reinforcement" (see Kimble, 1993), but you should understand all of these terms.

In summary, responses are increased by gaining something like food (positive reinforcement) or avoiding something like pain (escape or avoidance training or negative reinforcement). Responses are decreased by receiving pain (punishment) or by losing a chance for food or the like (omission training).

CONCEPT CHECK

8. Identify each of the following examples, using the terms shown in Table 6.2:
    a. Your employer gives you bonus pay for working overtime.
    b. You learn to stop playing your accordion at 5:00 A.M., because your roommate threatens to kill you if you do it again.
    c. You turn off a dripping faucet, ending the "drip drip drip" sound.
    d. You drink less beer than you once did, because you feel sick after drinking more than one glass.
    e. Your swimming coach says you cannot go to the next swim meet (which you were looking forward to), because you broke a training rule.
    f. Because you drive recklessly, you temporarily lose the privilege of driving the family car.
    g. You stay away from some fellow students who are coughing and sneezing, because you do not want to catch whatever illness they have. (Check your answers on page 218.)

How effective is punishment? That depends. If an individual has only one way to satisfy a strong motivation, punishing that act is generally ineffective. In one experiment, B. F. Skinner (1938) first trained food-deprived rats to press a bar to get food and then stopped delivering food for bar presses—an extinction procedure. For the first 10 minutes of extinction, some rats not only failed to get food

but the bar slapped their paws every time they tried to press it. They temporarily suppressed their bar-pressing, but in the long run they made as many presses as did the rats that never received any punishment.

Skinner concluded that punishment was ineffective, except for a temporary suppression of behavior. That conclusion, however, is an overstatement from the results of a single experiment (Staddon, 1993). Punishment can be quite effective, if it occurs quickly and consistently after the punished response and if alternative responses are available (Walters & Grusec, 1977). For example, if you want to teach your 3-year-old daughter not to put her hand on the stove, a gentle slap on the hand, or even a stern, sharp "NO!" is more effective than reinforcing her for another, competing behavior. Note that the quickness and consistency of the rebuke are important; making the punishment more intense will not make it more effective. Children respond more readily to mild punishment accompanied by a parent's explanation of why they were punished than they do to more intense punishment without an explanation.

Punishment is least effective when it is applied in response to a strongly motivated behavior for which the individual has no alternative. For example, if you were punished for eating or drinking, you would continue to do so anyway. In the experiment in which Skinner reported punishment to be ineffective, he was punishing food-deprived rats for pressing the lever that had in the past produced food. Bar-pressing was the only food-getting behavior the rats could perform. Punishment can also be ineffective with attention-starved children who find that they can get more attention for "bad" behavior than for "good" behavior.

Being ejected from a game for using foul language is an example of effective punishment: It is quick and consistent, and the player has other available behaviors that can achieve good results without incurring punishment.

And punishment can backfire in other ways. For example, a parent who spanks a child for nervous fidgeting may find that the spanking makes the child even more nervous and fidgety. In short, punishment can be either effective or ineffective, depending on a variety of circumstances.

CONCEPT CHECK

9. The U.S. government imposes strict punishments for selling illegal drugs. Based on what you have just read, why are those punishments ineffective for many people? (Check your answer on page 218.)

SOMETHING TO THINK ABOUT

Your local school board proposes to improve class attendance by lowering the grades of any student who misses a certain number of classes. Might the board achieve the same goal more effectively by using positive reinforcement? ✳

Different items can serve as reinforcements for different people. This man has devoted an enormous amount of time, effort, and money to collecting old comic books. Some people pay thousands of dollars for old stamps, coins, or baseball cards.

What Constitutes Reinforcement?

With operant conditioning, a response becomes more common because it is followed by a reinforcer. But what is a reinforcer? It is "something that increases the probability of the preceding response." So far, we are just going around in circles. It would be helpful to specify the basis of reinforcement, so we would know better how to reinforce a child for studying or how to reinforce a worker for doing a job well.

Thorndike suggested a trial-and-error approach to finding reinforcers: We could simply try a number of likely reinforcers to see what works. If some event serves as a reinforcer for one behavior, it will also serve as a reinforcer for other behaviors. That approach is, however, theoretically unsatisfactory. *Why* is food reinforcing, for example?

Many reinforcers satisfy biological needs (hunger, thirst, sex, temperature regulation, and so forth). However, for many people, alcohol and tobacco, which can be biologically harmful, act as stronger reinforcers than exercise and a healthy diet. Saccharin, a sweet but biologically useless chemical, can also be a reinforcer.

David Premack (1965) proposed a simple rule: *The opportunity to engage in frequent behavior* (such as eating) *will be a reinforcer for any less-frequent behavior* (such as lever-pressing). This relationship is known as the **Premack principle.** Thus, for example, if you spend more time reading than watching television, someone could increase your television watching by reinforcing you with books. For someone else, it might be possible to reinforce reading with opportunities to watch television. In short, a given opportunity may or may not be a reinforcer, depending on the individual and the response to be reinforced.

The limitation of the Premack principle is that we are sometimes reinforced by an opportunity to do an uncommon behavior. For example, you probably spend little time clipping your toenails, but if you are badly overdue for clipping them, the opportunity to do so can be a reinforcer. According to the **disequilibrium principle** of reinforcement, *each of us has a normal, or "equilibrium," state in which we divide our time among various activities in some preferred way, and if we are removed from that state, a return to it will be reinforcing.* If you have recently spent less time than usual clipping toenails, playing video games, or talking with friends, then the opportunity to do so will be a reinforcer. However, if you have already completed your usual amount of an activity, then the opportunity to do it again will be an ineffective reinforcer (Timberlake & Farmer-Dougan, 1991).

CONCEPT CHECK

10. Anorexia nervosa is a condition in which someone is obsessed with weight loss and refuses to eat enough to survive. Suppose you are trying to encourage such a person to eat and you wish to use positive reinforcement. According to the disequilibrium principle, how should you begin? (Check your answer on page 218.)

Unconditioned and Conditioned Reinforcement   Food and drink are reinforcers for virtually everyone, even infants. By contrast, money is a reinforcer only for those who have learned what they can do with it. Psychologists therefore distinguish between **unconditioned reinforcers,** *which are reinforcing because of their own properties,* and **conditioned reinforcers,** *which became reinforcing because of their previous association with an unconditioned reinforcer.* Food and water are unconditioned reinforcers. Coins and bills (conditioned reinforcers) have no value in themselves, but become reinforcing because they can be exchanged for food or other unconditioned reinforcers. A student learns that good grades will win the approval of parents and teachers; an employee learns that increased sales will win the approval of an employer. We spend most of our time working for conditioned reinforcers.

Reinforcement as Learning What Leads to What

Thorndike, you will recall, believed that reinforcement strengthens the response that preceded it. According to that view, reinforcement is a mechanical process; the animal or person who experiences reinforcement simply engages in the response more frequently, without necessarily understanding *why*.

According to another view, individuals learn what leads to what (Tolman, 1932). A rat may learn that running down an alley leads to food. Having learned that, the rat does not automatically go running down the alley all the time. It runs down the alley only when it needs food.

For example, suppose an animal has managed to find its way through a maze. We present it with something it does not need at the moment, such as food just after it has eaten a meal. If we test the rat again after its next meal, it shows no increased speed at getting through the maze. However, if tested several hours after its most recent meal, the rat scurries through the maze, indicating that it had learned more than it had previously shown (Tolman & Honzik, 1930). This procedure is known as *latent learning*, because what is learned is at first *latent* (not apparent to the observer). Latent learning is generally taken as evidence that operant conditioning establishes cognitions or knowledge and does more than just strengthen response tendencies.

Many conditioned reinforcers are surprisingly powerful. Consider, for example, how hard some first-graders will work for a little gold star that the teacher pastes on an assignment.

Another example: A rat is reinforced with sugar water for making response A and is reinforced with food pellets for making response B. After both responses have become well established, the rat is made ill after consuming, say, the sugar water. Now, when given the opportunity to make either response, the rat makes mostly response B. Evidently, the original training did not just increase two responses; the rat learned which response produced which outcome (Colwill, 1993).

In other words, we must distinguish between learning and performance. A subject's behavior depends on which outcome is associated with that behavior and how strongly motivated the subject is to achieve the outcome.

Schedules of Reinforcement

The simplest procedure in operant conditioning is to provide reinforcement every time the correct response occurs. **Continuous reinforcement** refers to *reinforcement for every correct response.* As you know, not every response in the real world leads to reinforcement.

Reinforcement for some responses and not for others is known as **intermittent reinforcement.** We behave differently when we know that only some of our responses will be reinforced. Psychologists have investigated the effects of many **schedules of reinforcement,** which are *rules or procedures for the delivery of reinforcement.* Four schedules for delivery of intermittent reinforcement are fixed ratio, fixed interval, variable ratio, and variable interval. (See Table 6.3.) A ratio schedule provides reinforcements depending on the number of responses. An interval schedule provides reinforcements depending on the timing of responses.

Fixed-Ratio Schedule　A **fixed-ratio schedule** *provides a reinforcement only after a certain (fixed) number of correct responses have been made*—after every fifth response, for example. Some animals continue responding even with a fixed-ratio schedule that reinforces every one-hundredth or every two-hundredth response. We see similar behavior among pieceworkers in a factory, whose pay depends on how many pieces they turn out or among fruit pickers who get paid by the bushel.

The response rate for a fixed-ratio schedule tends to be rapid and steady. However, if the schedule requires a large number of responses for reinforcement, there may be a temporary interruption after each reinforced response. For example, if you have just completed 10 calculus problems, you may pause briefly before starting your French assignment; after completing 100 problems, you would pause even longer.

Variable-Ratio Schedule　A **variable-ratio schedule** is similar to a fixed-ratio schedule except that *reinforcement is provided after a variable number of correct responses.* For example, reinforcement may come after an average of 10 responses, but sometimes comes after as

T A B L E 6.3 Some Schedules of Reinforcement

TYPE	DESCRIPTION
Continuous	Reinforcement for every response of the correct type
Fixed ratio	Reinforcement following completion of a specific number of responses
Variable ratio	Reinforcement for an unpredictable number of responses that varies around a mean value
Fixed interval	Reinforcement for the first response that follows a given delay since the previous reinforcement
Variable interval	Reinforcement for the first response that follows an unpredictable delay (varying around a mean value) since the previous reinforcement

few as 1 or 2 and sometimes after 20 or more responses. Variable-ratio schedules generate steady response rates. Gambling is reinforced on a variable-ratio schedule, because the gambler receives payment on an irregular basis for some responses and not for others.

In everyday life, we sometimes perform a behavior in which every response has an equal, fairly low probability of yielding a reinforcement. When that is true, we are reinforced on a variable-ratio schedule. For example, every time you apply for a job, you might or might not get it. The more times you apply, the better your chances, but you cannot predict how many applications you need to send in before you get a job offer.

Fixed-Interval Schedule A **fixed-interval schedule** *provides reinforcement for the first response made after a specific time interval.* For instance, an animal might get food for only the first response it makes after each 2-minute interval. Then it would have to wait another 2 minutes before another response would be effective. Animals (including humans) on such a schedule usually learn to pause after each reinforcement and begin to respond again only as the end of the time interval approaches.

Checking your mailbox is an example of behavior on a fixed-interval schedule. If your mail is delivered at about 3:00 P.M., you will get no reinforcement for checking your mailbox at 2:00 P.M. If you are eagerly awaiting an important letter, you might begin to check around 2:30 and continue checking every few minutes until it arrives.

Variable-Interval Schedule In a **variable-interval schedule**, *reinforcement is available after a variable amount of time has elapsed.* For example, reinforcement may come for the first response after 2 minutes, then for the first response after 7 seconds, then for the first response after 3 minutes 20 seconds, and so forth. There is no way to know how much time will pass before the next response is reinforced. Consequently, responses on a variable-interval schedule occur at a slow but steady rate. For example, you call your best friend and you get a busy signal. You don't

know how soon your friend will hang up, so you try again every few minutes.

Stargazing is another example of a response that is reinforced on a variable-interval schedule. The reinforcement for stargazing—seeing a new comet, for example—appears at irregular, unpredictable intervals. Consequently, both professional and amateur astronomers scan the skies regularly.

Extinction of Responses Maintained by Ratio or Interval Reinforcement After a schedule of intermittent reinforcement (either a ratio schedule or an interval schedule), the extinction of responses tends to be slower than it is after a schedule of continuous reinforcement (reinforcement for every response). For example, suppose that every time you have put money into a vending machine you received a can of soda (continuous reinforcement), but now you put in your money and the machine gives you nothing. You will not try many times before you quit. However, suppose you have frequently put money into a slot machine (a gambling device that reinforces on a variable-ratio schedule), sometimes winning some money but usually not. When the machine no longer produces reinforcements (ever), you might continue putting money into it for quite a while before your responses extinguish.

CONCEPT CHECKS

11. Identify which schedule of reinforcement applies to each of the following examples:
    a. You attend every new movie that appears at your local theater; you find most of them dull (not reinforcing) but really enjoy about one-fourth of them.
    b. You occasionally check your e-mail to find out whether you have any new messages.
    c. You tune your television set to an all-news cable channel, and you look up from your studies to check the sports scores every 30 minutes.
12. Stargazing in the hope of finding a comet was cited as an example of a variable-interval schedule. Why is it *not* an example of a variable ratio?

13. A novice gambler and a longtime gambler both lose 20 bets in a row. Which one is more likely to continue betting? Why? (Check your answers on page 218.)

Practical Applications of Operant Conditioning

Although operant conditioning arose from purely theoretical concerns, it has a long history of practical applications. Here are four examples.

Animal Training

Most animal acts today are based on training methods similar to Skinner's. To induce an animal to perform a trick, the trainer first trains it to perform a simple act that is similar to its natural behavior. Then the trainer shapes the animal, step by step, to perform progressively more complex behaviors. Most animal trainers rely on positive reinforcement rather than on punishment.

During World War II, Skinner proposed a military application of his training methods (Skinner, 1960). The military was having trouble designing a guidance system for its air-to-ground missiles. It needed apparatus that could recognize a target and guide a missile toward it but that was compact enough to leave room for explosives. Skinner said that he could teach pigeons to recognize a target and peck in its direction. If pigeons were placed in the nose cone of a missile, the direction of their pecking would guide the missile to the target. Skinner demonstrated that pigeons would do the job more cheaply and more accurately and would take up less space than the apparatus then in use, but the military laughed off the whole idea.

Persuasion

How could you persuade someone to do something that he or she did not want to do? To use an extreme example, how could you convince a prisoner of war to cooperate with the enemy?

The best way is to start by reinforcing a very small degree of cooperation and then working up to the goal, little by little. This principle has been applied by people who had probably never heard of B. F. Skinner, positive reinforcement, or shaping. During the Korean War, the Chinese Communists forwarded some of the letters written home by prisoners of war but intercepted others. (The prisoners could tell from the replies which letters had been forwarded.) The prisoners began to suspect that they would have better luck getting their letters through if they said something mildly favorable about their captors. So, from time to time, they would include a brief remark that the Communists were not really so bad, or that certain aspects of the Chinese system seemed to work pretty well, or that they hoped the war would end soon.

After a while, the Chinese captors devised essay contests; the soldier who wrote the best essay (in the captors' opinion) would win a little extra food or some other privilege. Most of the winning essays contained a statement or two that complimented the Communists on a minor matter or admitted that "the United States is not perfect."

Gradually, more and more soldiers started to include such statements in their essays. Occasionally, the Chinese might ask one of them, "You said the United States is not

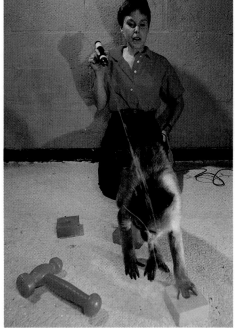

The high-tech hope of robots handling housekeeping chores has yet to materialize, but in the meantime, simian aides—trained monkeys—are helping the disabled. Monkeys are proving useful for indoor tasks for people with limited mobility. The monkey at left is being trained to retrieve objects identified with a laser beam. Such training relies on shaping behavior Skinner-style—building a new response by reinforcing sequential approximations to it.

perfect. We wonder whether you could tell us some of the ways in which it is not perfect, so that we can better understand your system." Then they would ask the soldiers who had cooperated to read aloud their lists of what was wrong with the United States. And so on. Gradually, without torture or coercion and with only modest reinforcements, the Chinese induced many prisoners to make public statements denouncing the United States, to make false confessions, to inform on fellow prisoners, and even to reveal military secrets (Cialdini, 1993).

The point is clear: Whether we want to get rats to salute the flag or soldiers to denounce it, the most effective training technique is to start with easy behaviors, to reinforce those behaviors, and then to shape gradually more complex behaviors.

Applied Behavior Analysis / Behavior Modification

In one way or another, people are almost constantly trying to influence other people's behavior. Psychologists have developed procedures based on operant conditioning for strengthening their influence for various purposes.

In **applied behavior analysis,** also known as **behavior modification,** *a psychologist first determines the reinforcers that are sustaining an unwanted behavior and then tries to alter that behavior by reducing the reinforcements for the unwanted behavior and providing suitable reinforcers for more acceptable behaviors.* For example, consider the use of safety belts in cars. Many adults still do not habitually wear safety belts, even though the use of such belts would prevent an estimated 50% of the fatalities and serious injuries in automobile accidents. Many states impose fines for failing to wear seat belts, but such laws are only moderately effective.

One alternative is to reinforce people for wearing safety belts. Virginia Polytechnic Institute invited people parking on campus to sign cards pledging to wear safety belts. All those signing the pledge became eligible for drawings for prizes. Drivers were also invited to affix a display in their car windows, indicating that they wear seat belts. Campus police randomly distributed prize coupons to cars containing that display. This procedure increased the percentage of drivers wearing safety belts from its previous level of 53 to 72% (Thyer & Geller, 1990).

Similarly, applied behavior analysis is used in therapy for psychologically disturbed people, to teach techniques of effective parenting, to encourage medical patients to follow the doctor's instructions, and in business and industry. In each case, the purpose is to provide clear and immediate reinforcements for the desired behaviors.

CONCEPT CHECK

14. Of the procedures characterized in Table 6.2, which one applies to laws that penalize people for not wearing seat belts? Which one applies to giving prizes to people who do wear seat belts? (Check your answers on page 218.)

Breaking Bad Habits

Some people learn to conquer their own bad habits by means of reinforcements. Nathan Azrin and Robert Nunn (1973) recommend this three-step method:

1. Become more aware of your bad habit. Interrupt the behavior and isolate it from the chain of normal activities. Then, you might imagine an association between the behavior and something repulsive (Yates, 1985). For example, to break a nail-biting habit, imagine your fingernails covered with sewage.

2. If no one else will reinforce you for making progress, provide your own reinforcements. For example, buy yourself a special treat after you have abandoned your bad habit for a certain period of time.

3. Do something incompatible with the offending habit. For example, if you have a nervous habit of hunching up your shoulders, practice depressing your shoulders.

Figure 6.17 shows an example of a college student setting up a list of reinforcements and punishments to support his goal of decreasing his smoking. If he successfully limited his smoking, he would treat himself to a movie. If he

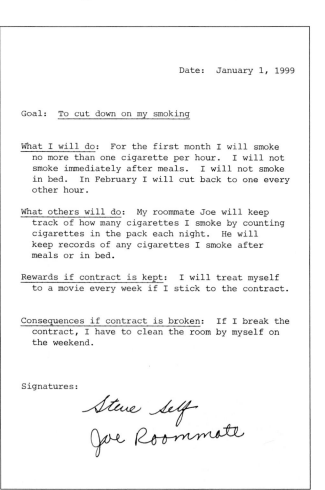

FIGURE 6.17 Sometimes, people try to change their own behavior by setting up a system of reinforcements and punishments.

exceeded the limit he had set for himself, he would have to clean the room by himself on the weekend, and he would not go to a movie. Many people set up similar patterns of reinforcement and punishment for themselves, generally without a written contract. If you decide to try this approach, set clear goals, choose realistic reinforcers, and keep track of your successes and failures.

THE MESSAGE
Operant Conditioning and Human Behavior

Suppose one of your instructors announced that everyone in the class would receive the same grade at the end of the course, regardless of performance on tests and papers. Would you study hard in that course? Probably not. Or suppose your employer said that all raises and promotions would be made at random, with no regard to how well you do your job. Would you continue working as hard as possible? Not likely. Do not take it as an insult that some aspects of your behavior resembles that of a pigeon or a rat in a Skinner box. For any organism to survive, its behavior must increase or decrease depending on its consequences. That is the main point of operant conditioning.

SUMMARY

* *Reinforcement.* Edward Thorndike introduced the concept of reinforcement. A reinforcement increases the probability that the preceding response will be repeated. (page 205)

* *Operant conditioning.* Operant conditioning is the process of controlling the rate of a behavior through its consequences. (page 206)

* *Extinction.* In operant conditioning, a response becomes extinguished if it is no longer followed by reinforcement. (page 206)

* *Shaping.* Shaping is a technique for training subjects to perform difficult acts by reinforcing them for successive approximations to the desired behavior. (page 207)

* *Reinforcement and punishment.* Behaviors can be reinforced (strengthened) by presenting favorable events or by omitting unfavorable events. Behaviors can be punished (suppressed) by presenting unfavorable events or by omitting favorable events. (page 210)

* *The nature of reinforcement.* The opportunity to engage in a more probable behavior will reinforce a less probable behavior. Something that an individual can exchange for a reinforcer becomes a reinforcer itself. (page 212)

* *Learning what leads to what.* Animals (and people) learn which reinforcement is associated with which behavior. The frequency with which they repeat a given behavior depends on their motivation to receive the reinforcement at the moment. (page 213)

* *Schedules of reinforcement.* The frequency and timing of a response depends on the schedule of reinforcement. In a ratio schedule of reinforcement, an individual is given reinforcement after a fixed or variable number of responses. In an interval schedule of reinforcement, an individual is given reinforcement after a fixed or variable period of time. (page 213)

* *Applications.* People have applied operant conditioning to animal training, persuasion, applied behavior analysis, and the breaking of bad habits. (page 215)

Suggestions for Further Reading

Skinner, B. F. (1953). *Science and human behavior.* New York: Macmillan. A systematic statement of Skinner's positions, written for students.

Staddon, J. (1993). *Behaviorism.* London: Duckworth. A critique of both the strengths and weaknesses of Skinner's views.

Terms

reinforcement   an event that increases the future probability of the most recent response (page 206)

law of effect   Thorndike's theory that a response followed by favorable consequences becomes more probable and a response followed by unfavorable consequences becomes less probable (page 206)

operant conditioning or **instrumental conditioning**   the process of changing behavior by following a response with reinforcement (page 206)

visceral responses   activities of the internal organs (page 206)

skeletal responses   movements of the muscles that move the limbs, trunk, and head (page 206)

extinction   in operant conditioning, the weakening of a response after a period without reinforcement (page 206)

stimulus generalization   in operant conditioning, the tendency to make a similar response to a stimulus that resembles one that has already been associated with reinforcement (page 207)

discrimination   in operant conditioning, learning to respond in one way to one stimulus and in a different way to another stimulus (page 207)

discriminative stimulus   stimulus that indicates on which occasion a response will produce a certain consequence (page 207)

belongingness   the concept that certain stimuli are readily associated with each other and that certain responses are readily associated with certain outcomes (page 207)

shaping   a technique for establishing a new response by reinforcing successive approximations (page 208)

chaining   a procedure for developing a sequence of behaviors in which the reinforcement for one response is the opportunity to engage in the next response (page 209)

punishment   an event that decreases the probability that a response will be repeated (page 210)

positive reinforcement   strengthening a behavior through the presentation of an event such as food (page 210)

passive avoidance learning   learning to avoid an outcome such as shock by being passive—that is, by inhibiting a response that would lead to the outcome (page 210)

omission training   learning to suppress a behavior that would lead to the omission of an event such as food (page 210)

escape learning   learning to escape from an event such as shock (page 211)

active avoidance learning   learning to make a response to avoid an event such as shock (page 211)

Premack principle   the principle that the opportunity to engage in a frequent behavior will reinforce a less frequent behavior (page 212)

disequilibrium principle   the principle that an opportunity to engage in any deprived activity will be a reinforcer because it restores equilibrium (page 212)

unconditioned reinforcer   an event that is reinforcing because of its own properties (page 212)

conditioned reinforcer   an event that becomes reinforcing because it has previously been associated with an unconditioned reinforcer (page 212)

continuous reinforcement   reinforcement for every correct response (page 213)

intermittent reinforcement   reinforcement for some responses and not for others (page 213)

schedule of reinforcement   a rule or procedure linking the pattern of responses to the reinforcements (page 213)

fixed-ratio schedule   a rule for delivering reinforcement only after the subject has made a specific number of correct responses (page 213)

variable-ratio schedule   a rule for delivering reinforcement after varying numbers of correct responses (page 213)

fixed-interval schedule   a rule for delivering reinforcement for the first response that the subject makes after a specified period of time has passed (page 214)

variable-interval schedule   a rule for delivering reinforcement after varying amounts of time (page 214)

applied behavior analysis or **behavior modification**   a procedure for determining the reinforcers that sustain an unwanted behavior and then reducing the reinforcements for the unwanted behavior and providing suitable reinforcers for more acceptable behaviors (page 216)

Answers to Concept Checks

7. You would need to know whether the bell was always followed by food (classical conditioning) or whether food was presented only if the animal sat up on its hind legs (operant conditioning). (page 206)

8. **a.** positive reinforcement; **b.** punishment or passive avoidance; **c.** escape learning or negative reinforcement; **d.** punishment or passive avoidance; **e.** omission training or negative punishment; **f.** omission training or negative punishment; **g.** avoidance learning or negative reinforcement. (page 211)

9. To be effective, punishments must be quick and consistent. Punishments for drug dealing are neither quick nor consistent. Furthermore, punishment most effectively suppresses a response when the individual has alternative responses that can gain reinforcements. Many people who gain enormous profits by selling drugs would have no alternative legal way to gain similar profits. (page 212)

10. Begin by determining how this person spends his or her time—for example, exercising, reading, watching television, visiting with friends. Then determine something that he or she has recently not had much opportunity to do. Activities for which one has only limited opportunities become good reinforcers. (page 212)

11. **a.** variable ratio. (You will be reinforced for about one-fourth of your entries to the theater but on an irregular basis.) **b.** variable interval. (The messages appear at unpredictable times, so your responses are reinforced at unpredictable intervals.) **c.** fixed interval. (page 214)

12. In a variable-ratio schedule, the number of responses matters but the timing does not. If you have already checked the stars tonight and found no comets, checking three more times tonight will probably be fruitless. Checking at a later date gives you a better chance. (page 214)

13. The habitual gambler will continue longer, because he or she has a history of being reinforced for gambling on a variable-ratio schedule, which retards extinction. (For the same reason, an alcoholic who has had both good experiences and bad experiences while drunk is likely to keep on drinking even after several consecutive bad experiences.) (page 215)

14. If you think of "not wearing seat belts" as a behavior, then penalizing people for that behavior is a punishment. If (more reasonably) you think of wearing seat belts as the behavior to be changed, wearing seat belts is a way of avoiding punishment, and the example is therefore one of avoidance behavior or negative reinforcement. Giving prizes to people who agree to wear seat belts is an example of positive reinforcement. (page 216)

Web Resources

Positive Reinforcement

server.bmod.athabascau.ca/html/prtut/reinpair.htm

Lyle K. Grant of Athabasca University helps students understand what does and what does not constitute positive reinforcement. Be sure you understand the examples before you begin the practice exercise.

Dr. P's Dog Training

www.uwsp.edu/acad/psych/dog/dog.htm

Mark Plonsky of the University of Wisconsin discusses obedience competition, K9 training, assistance dogs, and working dogs, and offers lots of general information.

Animal Training at Sea World

www.seaworld.org/animal_training/atcontents.html

Sea World trainers use operant conditioning principles with performing animals. The discussion covers primary and conditioned reinforcers, shaping, observational learning, and other principles.

Operant Conditioning

snycorva.cortland.edu/~ANDERSMD/OPER/operant.HTML

This site offers a basic introduction to the key concepts involved in operant conditioning.

Other Kinds of Learning

What kinds of learning do not fit neatly into the categories of classical or operant conditioning? What are the special features of these kinds of learning?

How do we learn from the successes and failures of others without trying every response ourselves?

Operant and classical conditioning both depend on an association between a first event (response or CS) and a second event (reinforcement or UCS). The main difference is that, in operant conditioning, the first event is something the individual does, whereas in classical conditioning, the first event is a stimulus presented from the outside. It might seem that all possible examples of learning would fall into either of these two categories; several, however, are difficult to classify or else require another category altogether.

Conditioned Taste Aversions

First, suppose an experimenter repeatedly presents a light followed by a shock. After a few pairings, the animal in the experiment shows an increased heart rate whenever it sees that light. Which kind of learning is this?

Second, suppose the experimenter turns on the light and then waits to see what the animal does. If (and only if) it looks toward the light, it gets a shock. Before long, the animal consistently turns away from the light. Which kind of learning is this?

The first is classical conditioning; the second is operant. But now consider a third experiment: The experimenter turns on a light. The animal looks toward it. Then it gets a shock. Now suppose *on the very next trial* and from then on, the animal avoids the light. What kind of learning took place? It's hard to say. Did the light itself predict the shock (as in classical conditioning) or did the animal's response to the light produce the shock (as in operant conditioning)? When learning occurs reliably after just one pairing, it is difficult to distinguish between classical and operant conditioning.

One kind of learning that does occur reliably after a single trial is an *association between eating something and getting sick,* which we call **conditioned taste aversion,** first documented by John Garcia and his colleagues. This kind of learning shows some special features, including strong learning despite delays of minutes or hours. For example, imagine an experiment conducted using a rat. The same process occurs in other species, including humans, but most of the research is with rats. The experiment begins with a rat drinking a saccharin solution. The effect is strongest with an unfamiliar taste, so let's suppose the rat has never tasted saccharin before. Saccharin tastes sweet, and in small amounts it is neither healthful nor harmful. After the rat has drunk the solution for a few minutes, the experimenter removes the bottle, waits minutes or even hours, and then injects a small amount of poison, thus making the rat moderately ill. The experimenter then waits a day or longer to let the rat recover and then offers it a choice between the saccharin solution and unflavored water. The rat will strongly prefer the unflavored water (Garcia, Ervin, & Koelling, 1966). In contrast, rats that had not been poisoned, or rats poisoned after drinking something else, strongly prefer the saccharin solution to plain water. Evidently, the first group of rats had learned a connection between taste and illness, in spite of the long delay and their having experienced the pairing only once. In many other cases of either classical or operant conditioning, learning is greatest with a 1- or 2-second delay between the events to be associated and hard to demonstrate at all with delays over 20 seconds (Kimble, 1961).

An animal that learns a conditioned taste aversion to a particular food treats that food as if it were foul-tasting (Garcia, 1990). Some ranchers in the western United States have used this type of learning to deter coyotes from eating sheep. They offer the coyotes sheep meat containing low levels of lithium salts or similar poisons. Afterward, as shown in Figure 6.18, the coyotes no longer attack sheep and act as if sheep meat tasted bad. This technique has the advantage of protecting the ranchers' sheep without killing the coyotes, which are a threatened species.

Conditioned taste aversions are special in another regard as well: Recall that an animal can associate something it ate with getting ill hours later. No doubt the animal had many other experiences between its meal and the illness, so why didn't it associate the illness with something else instead? The answer is that animals are predisposed to associate illness mostly with what they eat. In one classic experiment (Garcia & Koelling, 1966), rats were allowed to drink saccharin-flavored water from tubes that were set up so that, whenever the rats licked the water, a bright light flashed and a loud noise sounded. Some of the rats were exposed to X rays (which can induce nausea) while they drank. Others were given electric shocks to their feet 2 seconds after they had begun to drink. After the training was complete, each rat was tested separately with a tube of saccharin-flavored water and a tube of unflavored water that produced lights and noises. (Figure 6.19 illustrates this experiment.)

FIGURE 6.18   This coyote previously fell ill after eating sheep meat containing a mild dose of lithium salts. Now it reacts toward both live and dead sheep as it would toward bad-tasting food.

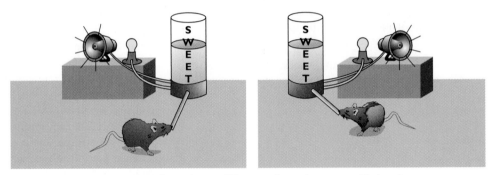

Rats drink saccharin-flavored water. Whenever they make contact with the tube, they turn on a bright light and a noisy buzzer.

Then

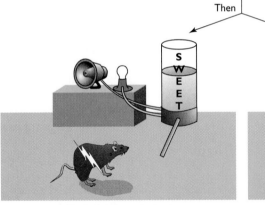

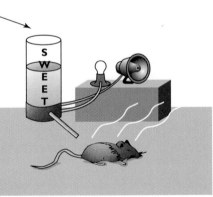

Some rats get electric shock.

Some rats are nauseated by X rays.

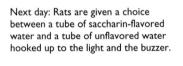

Next day: Rats are given a choice between a tube of saccharin-flavored water and a tube of unflavored water hooked up to the light and the buzzer.

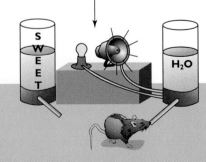

FIGURE 6.19   An experiment by Garcia and Koelling (1966): Rats "blame" tastes for their illness; lights and sounds, for their pain.

Rats that had been shocked avoided the tube with the lights and noises but drank the saccharin-flavored water.

Rats that had been nauseated by X rays avoided the saccharin-flavored water but drank the water hooked up to the lights and the buzzer.

A male white-crowned sparrow learns his song in the first months of life, but does not begin to sing it until the next year.

The rats that had been exposed to X rays avoided only the flavored water. The rats that had received shocks while drinking avoided only the tube that produced lights and noises. Evidently, rats (and other species) have a built-in predisposition to associate illness mostly with what they have eaten or drunk and to associate skin pain mostly with what they have seen or heard. (The predisposition to associate illness with food is an example of preparedness, mentioned earlier in this chapter.) Such predispositions are presumably beneficial because foods are more likely to cause internal events, and lights and sounds are more likely to signal external events.

CONCEPT CHECK

15. Name the unusual features of conditioned taste aversions. (Check your answer on page 225.)

Birdsong Learning

Birdsongs brighten the day for people who hear them, but for birds it is earnest business. For most species, the song is limited to males, mostly during spring, the mating season. As a rule, a song indicates, "Here I am. I am a male of _____ species. If you're a female of my species, please come closer. If you're a male of my species and you can hear me, you're too close. If I find you, I'll attack." (Among the delights of birdsongs are the exceptions to the rule. Mockingbirds copy all the songs they hear and defend their territory against intruders of any species—sometimes even squirrels, cats, people, automobiles. . . . And Carolina

wrens sing male-and-female duets throughout the year. But on to more relevant matters.)

If you were to rear an infant songbird in isolation from others of its species, would it develop a normal song on its own? Maybe or maybe not, depending on its species. Some species have to learn their song. For example, in several sparrow species, a male will develop a normal song only if he hears the song of his own species. He *learns most readily* during a **sensitive period** *early in life*. The duration of that period varies among species, but generally ends by fall, when the adult males stop singing. The sensitive period lasts longer if the infant hears a live male, such as his father, under natural conditions and ends sooner if he is hearing just a tape recording of the song in a laboratory experiment (Baptista & Petrinovich, 1984; Marler & Peters, 1987, 1988). But if the infant hears the song of another species, he will not imitate it. Evidently, a fledgling sparrow is equipped with mechanisms to produce approximately the right song and ways of identifying which songs to imitate and which to disregard (Marler, 1997).

Song learning differs from the other kinds of learning we have examined. During the sensitive period, the infant bird just listens. We cannot call the song he hears an unconditioned stimulus, because it elicits no apparent response. At no time in this sensitive period does the bird receive any apparent reinforcement. Nevertheless, he forms a representation of how his song should sound, and he begins to practice singing when he reaches sexual maturity the following spring. At that point, we can recognize a trial-and-error process with a strange form of operant conditioning. At first, his song is a disorganized mixture of sounds, somewhat like a babbling human infant. As time passes, he eliminates some sounds and rearranges others until he matches the songs he heard the previous summer (Marler & Peters, 1981, 1982). Once he establishes a song, he can continue singing it even if he becomes deaf.

The point is that the principles of learning vary from one situation to another. If a situation poses special problems—such as food selection, song learning in birds, probably language learning in humans—we can expect to find that species have evolved their own special ways of learning (Rozin & Kalat, 1971).

CONCEPT CHECK

16. What aspects of birdsong learning set it apart from classical and operant conditioning? (Check your answers on page 225.)

Social Learning

According to the **social-learning approach** (Bandura, 1977, 1986), *we learn about many behaviors before we try them the first time. Much learning, especially in humans,*

According to the social-learning approach, we learn many behaviors by observing what others do, imitating behaviors that are reinforced, and avoiding behaviors that are punished. This girl is being blessed by the temple elephant. Others who are watching may later imitate her example.

results from observing the behaviors of others and from imagining the consequences of our own behavior. For example, if you want to learn how to swim, paint pictures, play bridge, or drive a car, you *could* try to learn strictly by trial and error, but you would probably start by watching someone who already knows how to do the activity. When you eventually try it yourself, your attempt will be subject to reinforcement and punishment and therefore falls into the general realm of operant conditioning, but your attempt will be facilitated by your observations of others. It is therefore useful to examine social learning as a special case.

Although psychologists frequently speak of "social-learning theory," it is not a theory in the sense described in Chapter 2. The social-learning approach is closer to a point of view or a field of emphasis. It focuses on the effects of observation, imitation, setting goals, and self-reinforcement. In this sense, much of human behavior depends on social learning; after all, most school learning is an attempt to learn from the experiences of other people.

Modeling and Imitation

If you visit another country, especially one with customs very different from your own, you may find yourself bewildered about things you used to take for granted. Ordering food in a restaurant is not done the way you did it back home; paying the bill is done differently, too. A hand gesture such as ✋ is considered friendly in some countries but rude or vulgar in others. Americans visiting Japan often have trouble understanding how to use the baths and toilets. With effort, you can learn foreign customs. Someone may explain them to you, or you may simply watch and copy. You either *model* your behavior after that of others or you

A child will mimic an adult's behavior even when neither one is reinforced for the behavior. This girl attacks a doll after seeing a film of a woman hitting it. People who witness violent behavior, including violence at home, may be more prone than others to turn to violent behavior themselves.

imitate others. On a smaller scale, you follow the same processes to learn the customs of a religious organization, a fraternity or sorority, or a new place of employment.

Albert Bandura, Dorothea Ross, and Sheila Ross (1963) studied the role of imitation for learning aggressive behavior. They asked two groups of children to watch films in which an adult or a cartoon character violently attacked an inflated "Bobo" doll. They had another group watch a film in which the characters did not attack the doll. They then left the children in a room with a Bobo doll. The children who had watched films showing attacks on the doll (and only those children) attacked the doll vigorously, using many of the same movements they had just seen. The clear implication is that children copy the aggressive behavior they have seen in others.

Is the same true for adolescents and adults? This issue warrants our concern, because many popular movies include so much violence. As you read in Chapter 2, the available evidence does not demonstrate that watching violence on television or in movies necessarily causes violent behavior. However, some individuals are more highly influenced than others; some viewers (especially adolescents with a history of violent behavior) identify strongly with a highly violent character in a film. Others may be highly influenced by a film because it resembles an event they have witnessed in their own lives. Many cases have been reported in which people have reenacted scenes they had just seen in a film (Snyder, 1991).

CONCEPT CHECK

17. Many people complain that they cannot find much difference between the two major political parties in the United States, because so many American politicians campaign using similar styles and take similar stands on the issues. Explain this observation in terms of social learning. (Check your answer on page 225.)

Vicarious Reinforcement and Punishment

Six months ago, your best friend quit a job with Consolidated Generic Products in order to open a restaurant. Now you are considering quitting your own job with Consolidated Generic and opening your own restaurant. How do you decide whether to take this step?

Perhaps the first thing you do is find out how successful your friend has been. You do not automatically imitate the behavior of someone else, even someone you admire. Rather, you imitate behavior that has proven reinforcing for that person. In other words, you learn by **vicarious reinforcement** or **punishment**—that is, by *substituting someone else's experience for your own.*

When a new business venture succeeds, other companies try to figure out the reasons for that success and then try to follow the same course. When a venture fails, other companies try to learn the reasons for that failure and try to avoid making the same mistakes. When a football team wins consistently, other teams copy its style of play. And when a television program wins high ratings, other producers are sure to present look-alikes the following year.

SOMETHING TO THINK ABOUT

Might vicarious learning lead to a certain monotony of behavior and contribute to the lack of variety in the television programs and movies that are offered to the public? How can we learn vicariously without becoming just like everyone else? ✸

In many cases, vicarious punishment seems to affect behavior less than vicarious reinforcement does. We are bombarded by reminders that failure to wear seat belts will lead to injury or death, and yet many of us fail to buckle up. Despite widespread publicity about the consequences of driving while intoxicated, using addictive drugs, or engaging in unsafe sex, many people ignore the dangers. Even the death penalty, an extreme example of vicarious punishment, has little demonstrable effect on the murder rate.

Why does vicarious punishment so frequently produce such weak effects? One explanation is that, to be influenced, we must identify with the person who is receiving a vicarious reinforcement or punishment. Most of us think of ourselves as successful people; we see someone who is getting punished as a "loser" and "not like us." We can therefore continue to ignore the dangers.

The Role of Self-Efficacy in Social Learning

People are selective when choosing who to imitate. We imitate people we regard as successful, people we would like to resemble. Advertisers, keenly aware of this tendency, try to feature endorsements from people consumers are likely to admire and imitate. Cereal and candy advertisements feature happy, healthy children; soft-drink ads feature attractive young adults; ads for luxury cars feature people who look wealthy.

So, when you watch an Olympic diver win a gold medal for a superb display of physical control, do you then go out and try to make some spectacular dives into a pool? The person is successful, you would like to identify with that person, and if you do, you have just experienced vicarious reinforcement for the diver's success. And yet you probably do not try to imitate the dives. Why not?

If you are like most people, the reason is that you doubt you are capable of duplicating the diver's performance. People imitate someone else's behavior only if they have a sense of **self-efficacy**—*the perception that they themselves could perform the task successfully.* You observe your past successes and failures, compare yourself to the successful person, and estimate your chance of success.

People's sense of self-efficacy generally correlates well with their persistence at a task. For example, people who believe they can succeed at losing weight or quitting smoking or giving up alcohol have a much better chance of prolonged success than do people who doubt their own ability to succeed (Curry, Marlatt, & Gordon, 1987). Of course, as with other correlations, we cannot draw conclusions about cause and effect. Perhaps their sense of self-efficacy helps people to break bad habits; just as likely, people may develop that sense of self-efficacy because they know they can break their bad habits.

Self-Reinforcement and Self-Punishment in Social Learning

We learn by observing others who are doing what we would like to do. If our sense of self-efficacy is strong enough, we try to imitate their behavior. But actually succeeding often requires prolonged efforts. People typically set a goal for themselves and monitor their progress toward that goal. They even provide reinforcement or punishment for themselves, just as if they were training someone else. They say to themselves, "If I finish this math assignment on time, I'll treat myself to a movie and a new magazine. If I don't finish on time, I'll make myself clean the stove and the sink."

We tend to imitate the actions of successful people, but only if we feel self-efficacy, a belief that we could perform the task well.

We acquire a sense of self-efficacy mostly through our own successes but also partly by watching and identifying with role models.

(Self-punishments are usually pretty mild and seldom actually imposed.)

People who have never learned to use self-reinforcement can be taught to do so. Donald Meichenbaum and Joseph Goodman (1971) worked with a group of elementary-school children who acted impulsively, blurted out answers, and failed to consider the consequences of their actions. To encourage them to set appropriate goals for themselves and to practice self-reinforcement in achieving them, Meichenbaum and Goodman taught the children to talk to themselves while working on a task. For example, a child might say, "Okay, what do I have to do? You want me to copy the picture. . . . Okay, draw the line down, down, good; then to the right, that's it; now down some more and to the left. Good, I'm doing fine so far. Remember, go slowly. Now back up again. No, I was supposed to go down. That's okay. Just erase the line carefully. . . ." After only four training sessions, the children had learned to pause before answering questions, and they were answering more questions correctly.

Unfortunately, self-reinforcement and self-punishment do not always succeed. One psychologist, Ron Ash (1986), tried to teach himself to stop smoking by means of punishment. He decided to smoke only while he was reading *Psychological Bulletin* and other highly respected but tedious publications. By associating smoking with boredom, he hoped to eliminate his desire to smoke. Two months later he was smoking as much as ever, but he was starting to *enjoy* reading *Psychological Bulletin*!

THE MESSAGE
Why We Do What We Do

Almost everything you have done today was a learned behavior—from getting dressed and combing your hair this morning to reading this chapter right now. In fact, you probably would have trouble listing many things you have done today that were not learned. Even your bad habits are examples of learning.

One point that I hope has emerged in this chapter is that learning takes many forms. Classically conditioned salivation, operantly conditioned movements, conditioned taste aversions, and socially learned behaviors occur under diverse circumstances. The underlying mechanisms in the brain may or may not be the same, but at a descriptive level these types of learning differ in some important ways. In short, your behavior is subject to a wide variety of learned influences.

SUMMARY

✳ *Conditioned taste aversions.* Animals, including people, learn to avoid foods, especially unfamiliar ones, if they become ill afterward. This type of learning occurs reliably after a single pairing, even with a delay of hours between the food and the illness. Animals are predisposed to associate illness with what they eat or drink, not with other events. (page 219)

✳ *Birdsong learning.* Infant birds of some species must hear their song during a sensitive period in the first few months of life, if they are to develop a fully normal song the following spring. During the early learning, the bird makes no apparent response and receives no apparent reinforcement. (page 221)

✳ *Learning by observation.* We learn much by observing what other people do and what consequences they experience. (page 221)

✳ *What we imitate.* We tend to imitate behaviors that have led to reinforcement for other people. We are less consistent in avoiding behaviors that have led to punishment. (page 222)

✳ *Whom we imitate.* We are more likely to imitate the actions of people we admire and people with whom we identify. (page 223)

✳ *Self-efficacy.* Whether we decide to imitate a behavior that has led to reinforcement for others depends on whether we believe we are capable of duplicating that behavior. (page 223)

✳ *Self-reinforcement and self-punishment.* Once people have decided to try to imitate a certain behavior, they set goals for themselves and may even provide their own reinforcements and punishments. (page 223)

Suggestion for Further Reading

Bandura, A. (1986). *Social foundations of thought and action.* Englewood Cliffs, NJ: Prentice-Hall. A review of social learning by its most influential investigator.

Terms

conditioned taste aversion   the tendency to avoid eating a substance that has been followed by illness when it was eaten in the past (page 219)

sensitive period   a time early in life during which some kind of learning occurs most readily (page 221)

social-learning approach   the view that people learn by observing and imitating the behavior of others and by imagining the consequences of their own behavior (page 221)

vicarious reinforcement or **vicarious punishment**   observed reinforcement or punishment experienced by someone else (page 223)

self-efficacy   the perception of one's own ability to perform a task successfully (page 223)

Answers to Concept Checks

15. Conditioned taste aversions develop after a single trial, despite delays of minutes or hours between food and illness—a longer delay than any that could produce rapid learning in any other situation that psychologists have studied. Also, animals are predisposed to associate foods and not other events with illnesses. (page 221)

16. The most distinctive feature is that birdsong learning occurs during a time when the learner makes no apparent response and receives no apparent reinforcement. Also, at least in certain sparrow species, birdsong learning occurs most readily during an early sensitive period, and the bird is capable of learning its own species' song but not the song of another species. (page 221)

17. One reason that most American politicians run similar campaigns and take similar stands is that they all tend to copy the same models—candidates who have won elections in the past. Another reason is that they all pay attention to the same public-opinion polls. (page 221)

Web Resources

Albert Bandura

www.ship.edu/~cgboeree/bandura.html

C. George Boeree of Shippensburg University provides a short biography of Albert Bandura, describes early research in social learning, and defines many key terms and concepts.

Memory

7

Suppose I offer you—for a price—an opportunity to do absolutely anything you want to do for one day. You will not be limited by any of the usual constraints on what is possible. You can travel in a flash from one place to another, visiting as many places as you care to crowd into that single day. You can even travel into outer space, searching for life on other planets. You can travel forward and backward through time, finding out what the future holds in store and witnessing the great events of history, or even prehistoric times. (But you will not be able to alter history.) Anything you want to do—just name it and it is yours. Furthermore, I guarantee your safety: No matter where you choose to go or what you choose to do, you will not get hurt.

Now, how much would you be willing to pay for this once-in-a-lifetime opportunity? Oh, yes, I should mention . . . there is one catch. When the day is over, you will forget everything that happened. You will never be able to recover any memory of that day. Any notes or photos will vanish. And anyone else who takes part in your special day will forget it, too.

Now, how much would you be willing to pay? Much less than before, I am sure; perhaps nothing. Living without remembering is hardly living at all: Our memories are almost the same as our "selves."

Kutbidin Atamkulov travels from one Central Asian village to another singing from memory the tale of the Kirghiz hero, Manas. The song, which lasts 3 hours, has been passed from master to student for centuries. Human memory can hold an amazing amount of information.

Types of Memory

Do we have different types of memory?

Why do we remember some types of material better than others?

John Horton Conway, a Princeton University mathematics professor, is an accomplished mathematician, magician, game theorist, and computer programmer who is also known for his impressive memory. For example, he has memorized the names of all the stars visible in the northern hemisphere. As he told one interviewer (Seife, 1994, p. 13): "I like knowing things. When a constellation is covered up by a cloud, I predict where the stars will be when the cloud moves away. I really get a feeling of power—knowing what will happen is almost like making it happen." He can also recite poetry that he learned as a child but has not thought about since then. He memorized π to 1,000 decimal places and persuaded his wife to learn it too. They take long, romantic walks during which he recites a few places of π, then she says a few, then he says a few. . . .

So, Conway has an outstanding memory, right? Yes, except that during the 20 years he spent at Cambridge University, he never did learn the names of all his colleagues in the math department (Seife, 1994). Examples such as this illustrate a point that psychologists took decades to learn: It is possible to have an excellent memory for some kinds of material but only an average or even a poor memory for other kinds of material, depending on your interest in the material, how and under what circumstances you learned it, and so forth.

Why No One Experiment Characterizes All of Memory

If you have an important test on Wednesday morning, how much do you study on Tuesday night? Some professors advise their students against last-minute cramming, and students occasionally misinterpret that advice to mean that last-minute *reviewing* is useless. (I met one student who proudly told me that he didn't study at all the day before a test. He seemed puzzled by his mediocre grades.) What professors mean is that you should study as you go, not wait until the last night to start. But even if you take this advice, a last-minute refresher does help.

A few years ago someone wrote a proposal for a book called "How to Study in College"; the author offered the opposite advice: Students should postpone their studying until the last possible moment, because if they studied earlier, they would forget it all. If you have ever waited until the night before a test to start your study, you *know* this manuscript was offering bad advice. So how could its author, a college professor who had read at least some research on memory, have come to such a faulty conclusion? And what evidence do we have to refute it?

Ebbinghaus's Pioneering Studies of Memory

The German psychologist Hermann Ebbinghaus (1850–1909) founded the experimental study of memory. Previous researchers had asked people to describe their memories, but they could not measure the accuracy of these reports. Ebbinghaus conducted his research by teaching new material and then measuring memory for that material after various delays. To make sure that the material to be memorized would be unfamiliar, Ebbinghaus invented *nonsense syllables,* meaningless three-letter combinations such as GAK or VUB. He wrote out 2,300 such syllables, arranged them in random lists (Figure 7.1), and then set out to determine how well people could memorize and retain such lists. He had no cooperative introductory psychology students to draw from

Professor Conway is a brilliant mathematician with an excellent memory for most matters, but he has trouble remembering his colleagues' names.

FIGURE 7.1 Hermann Ebbinghaus pioneered the scientific study of memory by observing his own capacity for memorizing lists of nonsense syllables.

for his study, nor friends who would volunteer to memorize lists of nonsense syllables, so he ran all the tests on himself. Over a period of about 6 years, he memorized thousands of lists of nonsense syllables. (He was either very dedicated to his science or uncommonly tolerant of boredom.)

In one experiment, Ebbinghaus memorized several lists of 13 nonsense syllables each and then tested his memory after various delays. (The results appear in Figure 7.2.) He forgot a mean of more than half of each list after one hour and still more after 24 hours. If you take these results seriously, you will decide to do your studying as close as possible to the time of the test. After all, any earlier study is likely to be forgotten.

Of course, then you should also conclude that education itself is pointless. If you will forget most of what you learn within 24 hours, how much will you still remember by the time you graduate, much less a few years after graduation? So, unless the whole idea of education is fundamentally flawed, Ebbinghaus's results must not apply to all memory.

Differences Among Individuals Because of Interference

Suppose we repeat Ebbinghaus's experiment, but instead of doing all the studies on one person, we persuade a large number of college students to learn a list of nonsense syllables, testing some of them after short delays and some after long delays. The top line of Figure 7.2 shows the results of one such study: Even after 24 hours, most students still remember most of the nonsense syllables on the list (Koppenaal, 1963).

Why do you suppose most college students can remember a list so much better than Ebbinghaus did? You may be tempted to say that college students did so well because they are so intelligent. True, no doubt, but Ebbinghaus was no dummy either. Or you might suggest that college students have had "so much practice at memorizing nonsense." (Sorry if you think that's true.) But Ebbinghaus had memorized a lot of nonsense himself. In fact, the problem was that poor Hermann Ebbinghaus had memorized *too much* nonsense—literally thousands of lists of syllables (Figure 7.3). When anyone memorizes large amounts of similar material, the memory becomes a bit like a cluttered room: Something seems to be lost just because it is buried among other items and hard to find. Learning vast amounts of information does not block new learning (any more than a cluttered room prevents you from bringing in another piece of clutter), but it increases the risk of confusing old items with new ones and therefore forgetting.

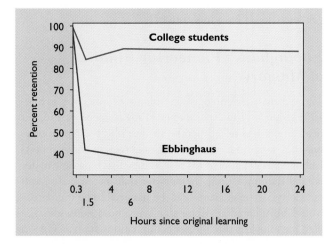

FIGURE 7.2 Blue line: Recall of lists of syllables by Ebbinghaus (1913) after delays of various lengths. Red line: Recall of lists of words by college students after delays of various lengths (based on Koppenaal, 1963). Ebbinghaus learned as fast as other people but forgot faster.

FIGURE 7.3 Ebbinghaus could learn new lists of nonsense syllables, but he forgot them quickly because of interference from all the previous lists he had learned. People who memorize many similar lists start to confuse them with one another.

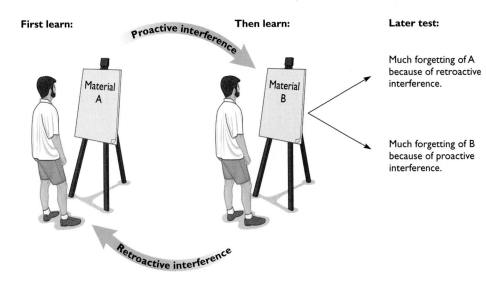

FIGURE 7.4 When someone learns two similar sets of materials, each interferes with the other. The old interferes with the new by proactive interference; the new interferes with the old by retroactive interference.

If you learn several sets of related materials, the old interferes with the new and the new interferes with the old. The *old materials increase forgetting of the new materials* through **proactive interference** (acting forward in time); the *new materials increase forgetting of the old materials* through **retroactive interference** (acting backward in time).

Figure 7.4 shows the difference between these two kinds of interference. Interference is responsible for a great deal of our everyday forgetting. You may forget where you parked your car at the local shopping mall, because of proactive interference from all the previous times you parked in the same lot. You may forget the French vocabulary list that you studied three weeks ago, because of retroactive interference from other lists you have studied since then.

The application of this idea to Ebbinghaus is simple: Because he had memorized so many lists of syllables, he had massive proactive interference and he forgot new lists much faster than other people would. Therefore, the results he collected on himself are very misleading if they are applied to anyone else. The moral of the story: When you want to memorize something, beware of studying anything else very similar to it. (Studying unrelated material poses no problem.)

CONCEPT CHECKS

1. Professor Tryhard learns the names of his students every semester. After several years, he learns them as quickly as ever but forgets them faster. Does he forget because of retroactive interference or proactive interference?
2. Remember the concept of spontaneous recovery from Chapter 6, page 198? Can you explain it in terms of proactive interference? (What is learned first? What is learned second? What would happen if the first interfered with the second?) (Check your answers on page 240.)

The Importance of Meaningfulness

Ebbinghaus, you will recall, was memorizing nonsense syllables. As you might guess, people tend to remember meaningful material better than they remember nonsense.

For example, in one experiment, two groups of people examined either picture (a) or picture (b) in Figure 7.5 and listened to the paragraph in part (c) (Bransford & Johnson, 1972, p. 131). Note that the paragraph makes sense if you have seen picture A but not if you have seen only picture B. As you might expect, the people who had seen picture A remembered about twice as much of the paragraph as those who had seen only picture (b).

How well do you suppose you remember the meaningful, important events of your life? Marigold Linton (1982) wrote notes about at least two important personal events each day for 6 years and recorded the date on the back of each note. At various times, she drew notes at random from the pile and tested her ability to recall the approximate date of each event. She found that she remembered the dates of about 95% of events 1 year old and a slightly lower percentage of older events. Similarly, Willem Wagenaar (1986) wrote index cards recording 2,400 personal events over 6 years. At the end of the 6 years, he tested himself by reading part of each card (for example, "what happened") and trying to recall the rest (for example, who, where, and when). He was able to recall at least a little information about almost every event. In short, we generally remember meaningful events well, even years later.

The Importance of Distinctiveness

 We also tend to remember distinctive or unusual material. Read the following list and then recall immediately, in any order, as many items as you can:

potato, asparagus, cauliflower, turnip, broccoli, Egypt, beans, corn, peas, rutabaga, squash, cabbage

If the balloons popped, the sound would not be able to carry since everything would be too far away from the correct floor. A closed window would also prevent the sound from carrying since most buildings tend to be well insulated. Since the whole operation depends on a steady flow of electricity, a break in the middle of the wire would also cause problems. Of course, the fellow could shout, but the human voice is not loud enough to carry that far. An additional problem is that a string could break on the instrument. Then there could be no accompaniment to the message. It is clear that the best situation would involve less distance. Then there would be fewer potential problems. With face to face contact, the least number of things could go wrong.

a   b   c

FIGURE 7.5   In an experiment by Bransford and Johnson (1972), one group of people looked at picture (a) and another group looked at picture (b). Then both groups heard the paragraph in part (c). The paragraph is meaningful only if you have seen picture (a).

One of the items you are most likely to recall is *Egypt,* because it is different from the others: It is the only word beginning with a capital letter and the only word that refers to anything other than a vegetable.

Similarly, we tend to remember unusual people or people with unusual names. If you meet several men of rather ordinary appearance and similar names, like John Stevens, Steve Johnson, and Joe Stevenson, it may take you a long time to get their names straight. You will be quicker to remember a 7-foot-tall, redheaded man named Stinky Rockefeller. *The tendency to remember unusual items better than more common items* is known as the **von Restorff effect,** after the psychologist who first demonstrated it (von Restorff, 1933).

Dependence of Memory on the Method of Testing

Ebbinghaus tested his memory by requiring himself to repeat the correct syllables in the correct order. Might his method have underestimated his memory? For example, most of us occasionally find ourselves unable to remember someone's name, or the formula for the volume of a sphere, or another fact that we once knew. Still, we know we haven't forgotten it altogether; later, a reminder may bring back the memory.

How well someone appears to remember something depends on how a psychologist tests the memory. The simplest way is to ask for **recall.** To recall something is *to produce it,* as you do on essay tests or short-answer tests. For instance, if I ask you, "Please name all the children in your fourth-grade class," you will probably have trouble doing so, partly because you confuse the names of the children in your fourth-grade class with those you knew in other grades. (Remember the influence of proactive and retroactive interference.)

You will remember more with **cued recall,** a method in which you *receive significant hints about the material.*

For example, I might show you a photograph of all the children in your fourth-grade class, or else I might give you a list of their initials (Figure 7.6). Try this: Cover the right side of Table 7.1 with a piece of paper and try to identify the authors of each book on the left. (This is the recall method.) Then uncover the right side, revealing each author's initials, and try again. (This is cued recall.)

TRY IT YOURSELF

With **recognition,** a third method of testing memory, a person is asked to *identify the correct item from several choices.* People can usually recognize more items than they can recall. For example, I might give you a list of 60 names and ask you to check off the correct names of children in your fourth-grade class. Multiple-choice tests use the recognition method to test memory.

FIGURE 7.6   Can you recall the names of the students in your fourth-grade class? Trying to remember without any hints is *recall.* Using a photo or a list of initials is *cued recall.* If you tried to choose the correct names from a list, you would be engaged in *recognition.* If you compared how fast you relearned the correct names and how fast you learned another list, you would be using the *savings* (or *relearning*) method.

TABLE 7.1 The Difference Between Recall and Cued Recall

Instructions: First try to identify the author of each book listed in the left column while covering the right column (recall method). Then expose the right column, which gives each author's initials, and try again (cued recall).

BOOK	AUTHOR
Moby Dick	H. M.
Emma and *Pride and Prejudice*	J.A.
Hercule Poirot stories	A.C.
Sherlock Holmes stories	A.C.D.
I Know Why the Caged Bird Sings	M.A.
War and Peace	L.T.
This book	J.K.
Canterbury Tales	G.C.
The Origin of Species	C.D.
Gone with the Wind	M.M.
The Color Purple	A.W.
Les Misérables	V.H.

(For answers, see page 240, Answer A.)

A fourth method, the **savings,** or **relearning, method,** can detect weaker memories than the other methods will. Suppose you cannot name some of the children in your fourth-grade class (recall method) and cannot pick out their names from a list of choices (recognition method). If I presented you with the correct list of names, you might learn it faster than you would learn an unfamiliar list of names. You *relearn something more quickly than you learn something new.* In other words, you save time when you relearn material that you learned in the past. The amount of time saved (time needed for original learning minus the time for relearning) is a measure of memory.

An overall conclusion: We revere Ebbinghaus as the pioneer who started scientific memory research. However, many memories are remembered far longer and better than Ebbinghaus's results implied. His memory was impaired by proactive interference and by dealing with meaningless and nondistinctive information.

CONCEPT CHECK

3. Each of the following is an example of one method of testing memory. Identify each method.

   a. Although you thought you had completely forgotten your high-school French, you do much better in your college French course than your roommate, who never had French in high school.

   b. You don't have a telephone directory and are trying to remember the phone number of the local pizza parlor.

   c. After witnessing a robbery, you have trouble describing the thief. The police show you several photographs and ask whether any of them was the robber.

   d. Your friend asks, "What's the name of our chemistry lab instructor? I think it's Julie or Judy something." (Check your answers on page 240.)

The Information-Processing View of Memory

One important theme of memory research since about 1950 has been the search for distinctions among types of memory. According to one view, the **information-processing model** of memory, human memory is analogous to the memory system of a computer: *Information enters the system, is processed and coded in various ways, and is then stored* (Figure 7.7). According to a version of this model that was long considered the standard, information first enters temporary storage (as when information is typed into a computer) and later enters permanent storage (as when information is entered onto a disk). Still later, in response to a cue from the environment, a person can recover the information from permanent storage (Atkinson & Shiffrin, 1968). According to this model, we distinguish three types of memory: a very brief sensory store, short-term memory, and long-term memory. We shall examine this model and its strengths and weaknesses and then consider alternative views.

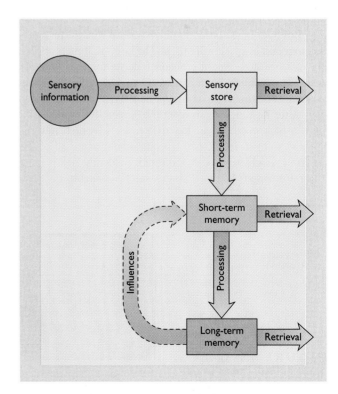

FIGURE 7.7 The information-processing model of memory resembles a computer's memory system, including temporary and permanent memory.

A bolt of lightning flashes through the sky for just a split second, but you can visualize it in detail for a short time afterward. That image is held momentarily in your sensory store.

The Sensory Store

Every memory begins as an exposure to a sensory stimulus. After you see or hear something for even a split second, you can temporarily recall minor details about it, because it has entered the **sensory store**, *a very brief storage of sensory information.* However, unless you immediately and actively attend to this information, it will fade rapidly as new information replaces it in the sensory store.

George Sperling (1960) tested how much information people can retain in the sensory store. He flashed an array like the one shown in Figure 7.8 onto a screen for 50 milliseconds. When he asked viewers to report as much of the whole array as they could, he found that they could recall a mean of only about four items. If he had stopped his experiment at that point, he might have concluded that viewers stored only a small fraction of an array.

But Sperling knew that it takes several seconds for a person to report even a few items, and he knew that memories in the sensory store would probably fade during that time. To test that possibility, he told viewers he would ask them to report only one row of the array, but he did not tell them which row. After flashing the array on the screen, he immediately used a high, medium, or low tone to signal which row the viewers were to recall. Most people could name all of the items in whichever row he indicated. Evidently, nearly all of the information in the array was briefly available to them.

When he waited for even one second before signaling which row to recall, though, viewers were less likely to recall that row. That is, for information in the sensory store, the rule is "use it or lose it," and you had better use it fast.

Is this phenomenon really memory, or is it perception? It is a borderline case. Not everything falls neatly into our human-made categories.

SOMETHING TO THINK ABOUT

Sperling demonstrated the capacity of the sensory store for visual information. How could you demonstrate the capacity of the sensory store for *auditory* information? ✳

Short-Term Memory Versus Long-Term Memory

Of all the vast information that passes through our sensory store, a small amount catches our attention enough to get stored and processed a little longer. But even for information that catches our attention, some gets stored permanently and some does not. According to the traditional version of information-processing theory, we should distinguish between **short-term memory,** *temporary storage of the information that someone has just experienced,* and **long-term memory,** *a relatively permanent store of mostly meaningful information.* Figure 7.9 compares the sensory store and short- and long-term memory. Short-term and long-term memory differ in their dependence on retrieval cues, their capacity, and their tendency to decay.

Dependence on Retrieval Cues If you try to recall a telephone number that you read just seconds ago, presumably stored in your short-term memory, either you can recall it easily or it is already gone. You don't need reminders or hints, and chances are that no reminder or hint would do you much good anyway. In contrast, to get information from long-term memory, you need a *retrieval cue*, an association that elicits the memory. Some retrieval cues work better than others. For example, the retrieval cue "the city you were born in" should enable you to retrieve the name of one

Stimulus arrary flashed on screen for 0.05 seconds

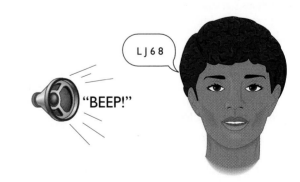

"BEEP!"

LJ68

Within the next 0.1 to 0.3 seconds, high, medium, or low tone signals indicate which row to say

Participant says the correct row

FIGURE 7.8 George Sperling (1960) flashed arrays like this on a screen for 50 milliseconds. After the display went off, a signal told the viewer which row to recite.

city from your long-term memory. The retrieval cue "U.S. city whose name is also the name of an animal" probably does not enable you to retrieve anything quickly. You laboriously go through all the cities (or animals) you can think of until eventually you come up with an answer—most likely, Buffalo, New York. (Conceivably, you might also think of Caribou, Maine; White Pigeon, Michigan; Anaconda, Montana; or Deadhorse, Alaska.) Retrieving long-term memories is sometimes a difficult, effortful task.

Differences in Capacity   The capacity of long-term memory is so vast that we cannot easily measure it. Unlike computers, people never fill their memories so full that they have no room to store something new. (Of course, also unlike computers, people are constantly dumping some of their memories.) Short-term memory, in contrast, has a relatively small, easily measured capacity. Read each of the following sequences of letters; then look away and try to repeat them from memory. Or read each aloud and ask a friend to repeat it.

EHGPH
JROZNQ
SRBWRCN
MPDIWFBS
ZYBPIAFMO
BOJFKFLTRC
XUGJDPFSVCL

Most normal adults can repeat a list of approximately seven items—letters, in this case. Some people can remember eight or nine; others, only five or six. George Miller (1956) referred to the short-term memory capacity as "the magical number seven, plus or minus two." When people try to repeat a longer list, however, they may fail to remember even the first seven items. It is somewhat like trying to hold several objects in one hand: You can hold a certain number, depending on their size, but if you try to hold too many you will drop them all (Figure 7.10). However, when we refer to a limit of about seven "items," the size of an item can vary. You can store more information if you can organize it into familiar **chunks,** or *meaningful units*. (See Figure 7.11.) As an illustration, examine each of these sequences of numbers and then try to repeat them:

106614921776

31416–271828–1414–1732

Could you do it? The first list was either easy or impossibly long, depending on whether you recognized the sequence as three historical dates (the Norman invasion of England in 1066, Columbus's arrival in America in 1492, and the Declaration of Independence in 1776). The second number is already separated into four chunks, but the separation will help you only if you recognize the chunks as the approximate values of π, 3.1416 . . . ; e, 2.71828 . . . ; the square root of two, 1.414 . . . ; and the square root of three, 1.732.

With practice, people can learn to recognize larger and larger chunks of numbers. One student from Carnegie-Mellon University (Ericsson, Chase, & Falcon, 1980) volunteered for an experiment on memorizing digits. At the beginning, he could repeat only about seven digits at one time. But over the course of a year and a half, working 3 to 5 hours per week, he gradually improved until he could repeat

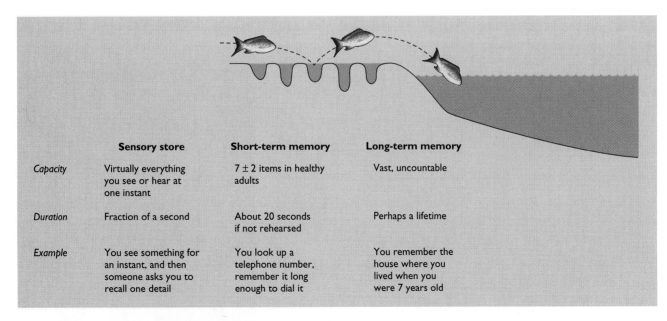

	Sensory store	Short-term memory	Long-term memory
Capacity	Virtually everything you see or hear at one instant	7 ± 2 items in healthy adults	Vast, uncountable
Duration	Fraction of a second	About 20 seconds if not rehearsed	Perhaps a lifetime
Example	You see something for an instant, and then someone asks you to recall one detail	You look up a telephone number, remember it long enough to dial it	You remember the house where you lived when you were 7 years old

FIGURE 7.9 After about 1 second, you can no longer recall information from the sensory store. Short-term memories can be recalled up to about 20 seconds without rehearsal—much longer if you continually rehearse them. Long-term memories decline somewhat, especially at first, but you may be able to retrieve them for a lifetime. Your address from years ago is probably in your long-term memory and will continue to be for the rest of your life.

FIGURE 7.10 Short-term memory is like a hand full of eggs; it can hold only a limited number of items at a time.

as many as 80 digits, as shown in Figure 7.12, by using extraordinary strategies for chunking. He was a competitive runner, so he might store the sequence "3492 . . ." as "3 minutes, 49.2 seconds, a near world-record time for running a mile." He might store the next set of numbers as a good time for running a kilometer, a mediocre marathon time, or a date in history. However, when he was tested on his ability to remember a list of letters, his performance was only average, because he had not developed any special chunking strategies for letters.

As a rule, a psychologist who reads a list of numbers and asks someone to repeat them assumes that the results measure short-term memory. The possibility of chunking, however, shows that the test is not a pure measure of short-term memory. Someone who recognizes 1492 and 1776 as meaningful units is clearly bringing long-term memories into this short-term memory test. In the case of the Carnegie-Mellon student, it is not clear whether he was using short-term memory at all or whether he had actually developed ways to rapidly organize large amounts of information into long-term memory.

Decay of Short-Term Memories over Time People can forget long-term memories, largely through proactive and retroactive interference, but the mere passage of time (decay) does not weaken long-term memories by very

much. In contrast, short-term memories can disappear quickly, apparently through simple decay, unless people continually rehearse them.

Lloyd Peterson and Margaret Peterson (1959) demonstrated the decay of short-term memory with an experiment that you can easily repeat if you coax a friend to volunteer. First, read aloud a meaningless sequence of letters, such as HOZDF. Then wait for a bit and ask your friend to repeat it—an easy task, because your friend spent the delay rehearsing, "H-O-Z-D-F, H-O-Z-D-F, . . ."

Forgetting will occur, however, if you prevent rehearsal during the delay. Say "I am going to read you a list of letters, such as HOZDF. Then I'm going to tell you a number, such as 231. When you hear the number, begin counting backward by threes: 231, 228, 225, 222, 219, and so on. When I tell you to stop, I'll ask you to repeat the sequence of letters." Record your data as in Table 7.2.

Try this experiment with several friends, and compute the percentage of those who recalled the letters correctly after various delays. Figure 7.13 gives the results that Peterson and Peterson obtained. Note that only about 10% of their subjects could recall the letters correctly after a delay of 18 seconds. In other words, if we fail to rehearse something that has entered short-term memory, it will generally fade away within 20 seconds or less.

This demonstration breaks down, however, if you use highly meaningful material. If you ask your friend to memorize "there is a poisonous snake under the chair," he or she is likely to remember it well even after counting backward by threes from 231. Highly meaningful material enters long-term memory quickly.

Furthermore, Peterson and Peterson's experiment does not demonstrate such a distinct difference between short-term and long-term memory as we once thought existed. Let's reconsider the demonstration: You read off, say,

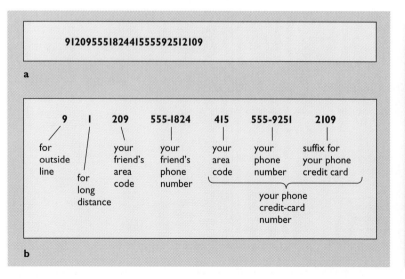

FIGURE 7.11 We overcome the limits of short-term memory through chunking. You probably could not remember the 26-digit number in (a), but by breaking it up into a series of chunks, you can remember it and dial the number correctly.

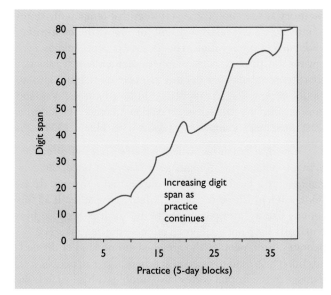

FIGURE 7.12 Most people can repeat a list of about seven numbers. One college student gradually increased his ability to repeat a list of numbers, over 18 months of practice. With practice, he greatly expanded his short-term memory for digits but not for letters or words. (From Ericsson, Chase, & Falcon, 1980.)

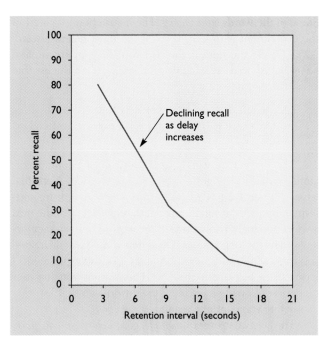

FIGURE 7.13 In a study by Peterson and Peterson (1959), people remembered a set of letters well after a short delay, but their memory faded greatly over 20 seconds if they were prevented from rehearsing during that time.

"BKLRE," asked someone to count backward by threes for 5 seconds, and then probably found that the person could recall the letters. After two more trials you came to "DSJGT" and a 20-second delay, and the person probably could not recall it. But DSJGT was the fourth trial, potentially subject to a fair amount of proactive interference. Suppose you try this with another volunteer, but now you *start* with DSJGT and a 20-second delay. Your new volunteer will probably remember DSJGT (Keppel & Underwood, 1962; Wickens, 1970). Evidently, the forgetting of items stored in short-term memory depends partly on interference, as it does with long-term memory.

CONCEPT CHECK

4. Name one way in which short-term memory and long-term memory are evidently different and one way in which they are similar. (Check your answers on page 240.)

TABLE 7.2			
LETTER SEQUENCE	STARTING NUMBER	DELAY IN SECONDS	CORRECT RECALL?
BKLRE	712	5	
ZIWOJ	380	10	
CNVIU	416	15	
DSJGT	289	20	
NFMXS	601	25	

The Transfer from Short-Term Memory to Long-Term Memory

For many years, psychologists thought of short-term memory and long-term memory as separate stages: Information first enters short-term memory and stays there for a while. If rehearsal kept it there long enough, it would **consolidate** to *form a long-term memory* (Figure 7.14).

Now we suspect that consolidation depends on much more than just time and that holding something for a long time in short-term memory does not automatically shift it into long-term memory. As an illustration, try the following experiment (based on Craik & Watkins, 1973): Read the list of words below to yourself, or read them to your roommate.

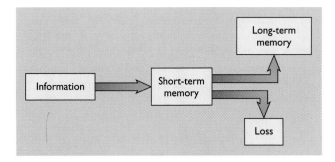

FIGURE 7.14 According to the original conception of the relationship between short-term and long-term memory, if a short-term memory is rehearsed long enough, it becomes a long-term memory; without consolidation, it is lost. This view is now considered oversimplified.

Some of the words start with *g*. The instruction for part 1 of the experiment is to keep track of the most recent *g*-word.

 At the end of the list, you (or your roommate) should say what was the last word on the list that began with *g*:

table, giraffe, frog, goose, key, window, banana, pencil, spoon, grass, road, garden, house, tree, lake, paper, chicken, glove, paint, garlic, stone.

The correct answer is *garlic*, and most people easily come up with the right answer. So far, so good. Note that what you needed to do was to store each *g*-word in short-term memory until you dumped it to replace it with the next *g*-word. You had to hold some of the words briefly in memory and others for longer times. Okay, now that I have distracted you for a while, let's move on to part 2 of the experiment: I didn't warn you about this, but I now want you (or your roommate) to write a list of *all* the *g*-words on that list. (Try this before you continue reading.)

The correct answers are *giraffe, goose, grass, garden, glove,* and *garlic*. Considering the delay between when you first read the words and when you recalled them, we must assume you recalled them from long-term memory. The question is, which terms made it into your long-term memory? In general, researchers find that people are about equally likely to remember *giraffe, grass,* and *glove* (which stayed in short-term memory only briefly) as to remember *goose* or *garden* (which stayed longer in short-term memory before being replaced). Evidently, how long a word stays in short-term memory has little to do with whether it moves into long-term memory.

Another problem with the traditional concept: If short-term memory is just a holding station on the way to long-term memory, then any defect in short-term memory should block the formation of long-term memories. However, a few brain-damaged patients can form and retrieve new long-term memories normally, despite serious defects in short-term memory. One such patient had a short-term memory capacity of only *two* items. For example, he might be able to repeat "7, 4" but would fail at repeating "7, 4, 8" (Shallice & Warrington, 1970). However, with extensive repetitions, he could memorize lengthier materials (just as a normal person could memorize something longer than seven items), and after memorizing it, he could retain it over the long term.

It appears to be possible to have a poor short-term memory and still store a great deal into long-term memory. That conclusion implies that short-term memory is not just a holding stage on the way to long-term memory.

A Modified Theory: Working Memory

The concept of short-term memory has a status similar to that of many other psychological concepts: The original concept is partly right, but not quite. Most memory researchers today have substituted a different term, working memory. **Working memory** is seen not just as a system that temporarily stores information, but also as *a system for processing or working with current information.* That is, the concept is almost synonymous with one's current sphere of attention. It includes short-term memory (events that just occurred), but it also includes information already stored in long-term memory and now recalled for current use. Working memory includes at least three major components (Baddeley & Hitch, 1994):

• *A central executive,* which governs shifts of attention. When someone tries to manage two tasks at once, the central executive has to allocate resources to the two and determine when to attend to one and when to the other. If all this sounds like a "little person in the head," it is because psychologists have not yet figured out how the central executive operates. Still, people who are good at one kind of divided-attention task tend to be good at others also, and people with damage to the frontal cortex have trouble with all such tasks (Cummings, 1995). So the central executive is a meaningful process, even if we do not yet understand it very well.

• *A phonological loop,* which stores and rehearses speech information. The phonological loop enables us to repeat seven or so numbers or letters immediately after hearing them; it more or less corresponds to the traditional view of short-term memory.

• *A visuospatial sketchpad,* which stores and manipulates visual and spatial information, providing for vision what the phonological loop provides for speech. Research indicates that its limit is about four visual items (Luck & Vogel, 1997).

The reason for distinguishing between the phonological and visuospatial stores is that two word tasks or two visuospatial tasks performed at the same time interfere with each other, but people can perform one of each at the same time without interference (Baddeley & Hitch, 1974; Hale, Myerson, Rhee, Weiss, & Abrams, 1996). People may have working memory stores for touch, smell, and taste also, but so far researchers have concentrated mostly on the auditory and visual stores.

Consistent with the idea of a phonological loop, it is easier to remember a list of short words that are easy to pronounce than a list of longer words that are harder to pronounce (Cowan, Wood, Nugent, & Treisman, 1997), and it is easier to remember words that sound different than

 words that sound similar to one another (Awh et al., 1996). For example, try to memorize the following lists. Most will find List 1 the easiest.

List 1 (short words)	List 2 (longer words)	List 3 (similar-sounding words)
fit	prayer	Swiss
blue	yield	stress
tell	crowd	sauce
pin	blouse	sells
trip	strolls	swells
high	thrill	sews
deck	flour	space

The concept of a phonological loop helps to explain differences in reading comprehension. Imagine various people reading either of the following sentences:

Because Ken really liked the boxer, he took a bus to the nearest pet store to buy the animal.

Because Ken really liked the boxer, he took a bus to the nearest sports arena to see the match.

Then, the readers are asked true-false questions such as

T   F   Ken liked a dog.
T   F   Ken liked a fighter.

Many English words have several unrelated meanings—for example, *boxer, bass, tire, leaves.* To understand such words, we must wait until the context of the sentence identifies the correct meaning. In the "Ken" sentences, the context remained ambiguous about the meaning of "boxer" until eight words later—a serious strain for any reader with a short phonological loop (Miyake, Just, & Carpenter, 1994).

CONCEPT CHECK

5. Would readers who have a shorter phonological loop show greater reading comprehension in English, which has many words with two or more meanings, or in Italian, which has few such words? (Check your answer on page 241.)

Other Memory Distinctions

Later in this chapter we shall encounter the distinction between declarative memories and procedural memories. A *declarative memory* is the ability to state a fact; a *procedural memory* is a skill, a memory of how to do something. Certain kinds of brain damage impair declarative memory without damaging procedural memories. That is, a man who forgets his address and telephone number may nevertheless remember how to tie his shoes and how to ride a bicycle.

Psychologists also find it useful to distinguish between two kinds of long-term declarative memory—**semantic memory,** *memory of general principles,* and **episodic memory,** *memory for specific events in a person's life, generally including details of when and where they happened* (Tulving, 1989). For example, your memory of the rules of tennis is a semantic memory; your memory of the most recent time you played tennis is an episodic memory. Your memory of the periodic table of chemistry is a semantic memory; your recollection of breaking a test tube in a chemistry lab is an episodic memory.

Episodic memories are in many cases more fragile than semantic memories. For example, people sometimes remember a statement they have heard (a semantic memory) but forget when, where, and from whom they heard it (an episodic memory). That phenomenon is known as **source**

amnesia, *remembering the content but not the context of learning it.* Because of source amnesia, people sometimes confuse reliable information with the unreliable: "Did I hear this idea from my professor or was it on *South Park?* Did I read about brain transplants in *Scientific American* or in the *National Enquirer?*" As a result, you might dismiss an idea at first ("Oh, that's just a rumor!" or "Oh, that's just my nutty roommate's idea!") but later remember the idea, forget where you heard it, and start to take it seriously (Johnson, Hashtroudi, & Lindsay, 1993; Riccio, 1994).

CONCEPT CHECK

6. Is your memory of your current mailing address a semantic memory or an episodic memory? What about your memories of the day you moved to your current address? (Check your answers on page 241.)

THE MESSAGE
Varieties of Memory

Although researchers still disagree with one another on many points about memory, they do agree about what memory is *not:* Memory is not a single store into which we simply dump things and later take them out. When Ebbinghaus conducted his studies of memory in the late 1800s, he thought he was measuring the properties of memory, period. We now know that the properties of memory depend on the type of material being memorized, the individual's experience with similar materials, the method of testing, and the recency of the event. Memory is not one process, but many.

SUMMARY

✱ *Ebbinghaus's approach.* Hermann Ebbinghaus pioneered the experimental study of memory by testing his own ability to memorize and retain lists of nonsense syllables. Although the general principles he reported were valid, his measurements of the speed of learning and forgetting do not apply to all memory. (page 229)

✱ *Variations in memory strength.* People remember material best if they have minimal interference from similar materials, if the material is meaningful and distinctive, and if the method of testing is capable of detecting a weak memory. (page 230)

✱ *The information-processing model.* Psychologists distinguish among various types of memory. According to the information-processing model of memory, information is stored first as short-term memories and later processed to become long-term memories. (page 233)

✱ *Memory capacity.* Short-term memory has a capacity of only about seven items in normal adults, although chunking can enable us to store much information in each item. Long-term memory has a very large, not easily measured capacity. (page 234)

✳ *Weaknesses of the traditional information-processing model.* Contrary to what psychologists once believed, how long an item remains in short-term memory is a poor predictor of whether it will enter long-term memory. Furthermore, some people with a defective short-term memory have a normal long-term memory. Evidently, short-term memory is not simply a holding station on the way to long-term memory. (page 237)

✳ *Working memory.* As an alternative to the traditional description of short-term memory, most current researchers identify working memory as a system for storing and processing several kinds of current information. (page 238)

✳ *Semantic and episodic memories.* An additional distinction can be drawn between semantic memories (memories of general principles) and episodic memories (memories of personal experiences). In most cases episodic memories are more fragile and more easily lost or distorted. (page 239)

Suggestion for Further Reading

Schacter, D. L. (1996). *Searching for memory.* New York: Basic Books. Discusses current theories and research in an accessible manner.

Terms

proactive interference   the hindrance that an older memory produces on a newer one (page 231)

retroactive interference   the impairment that a newer memory produces on an older one (page 231)

von Restorff effect   the tendency to remember distinctive or unusual items on a list better than other items (page 232)

recall   a method of testing memory by asking someone to produce a certain item (such as a word) (page 232)

cued recall   a method of testing memory by asking someone to remember a certain item after being given a hint (page 232)

recognition   a method of testing memory by asking someone to choose the correct item from a set of alternatives (page 232)

savings method or **relearning method**   a method of testing memory by measuring how much faster someone can relearn something than learn something for the first time (page 233)

information-processing model   the view that information is processed, coded, and stored in various ways in human memory as it is in a computer (page 233)

sensory store   a very brief storage of sensory information (page 234)

short-term memory   a temporary storage of a limited amount of information (page 234)

long-term memory   a relatively permanent store of information (page 234)

chunking   the process of grouping digits or letters into meaningful sequences (page 235)

consolidation   the formation and strengthening of long-term memories (page 237)

working memory   a system that processes and works with current information, including three components—a central executive, a phonological loop, and a visuospatial sketchpad (page 238)

semantic memory   memory of general principles (page 239)

episodic memory   memory for specific events in a person's life (page 239)

source amnesia   remembering content but not the context of learning it (page 239)

Answers to Concept Checks

1. It is due to proactive interference—interference from memories learned earlier. Much of the difficulty of retrieving long-term memories is due to proactive interference. (page 231)

2. First, the subject learns the response; second, the subject learns the extinction of the response. If the first learning proactively interferes with the later learning, spontaneous recovery will result. (page 231)

3. **a.** savings; **b.** recall; **c.** recognition; **d.** cued recall. (page 233)

4. Short-term memory has a limited capacity of about seven items in normal adults, whereas long-term memory has an extremely large capacity (difficult to estimate). Both short-term memory and long-term memories are more rapidly forgotten in the presence of interference. (page 237)

5. Readers with a shorter phonological loop should show greater comprehension of Italian, which will seldom require them to remember a word for very long before deciding on its meaning. (page 239)

6. Your memory of your current address is a semantic memory. Your memory of the events of moving day is an episodic memory. (page 239)

Answer to Other Questions in the Text

A. Hermann Melville, Jane Austen, Agatha Christie, Arthur Conan Doyle, Maya Angelou, Leo Tolstoy, James Kalat, Geoffrey Chaucer, Charles Darwin, Margaret Mitchell, Alice Walker, Victor Hugo. (page 233)

Web Resources

The Magic Seven, Plus or Minus Two
www.well.com/user/smalin/miller.html
This is George Miller's classic article about the limits of short-term memory, complete with graphs and references, as it originally appeared in the *Psychological Review* in 1956.

MODULE 7.2

Memory Improvement

How can we improve our memory?

There you are, sitting in class taking a geography test, unable to remember the major rivers of Africa. You remember reviewing that section in your book last night; you even remember that it was on the upper left side of the page, and there was a diagram to the right of it. You even remember the cappuccino you were sipping as you were studying. And that it was about 9:30 P.M. at the time. You just don't remember the names of the rivers.

How is it that we sometimes remember so much useless information while forgetting what we really wanted to remember? And how can we improve our memory?

The short answer is that, to improve your memory, you must improve the way you store the material in the first place. The rest of this module elaborates on that point.

The Influence of Emotional Arousal

People usually remember emotionally arousing events. Chances are you can vividly remember your first day of college, your first kiss, the time your team won the big game, and various times when you were extremely frightened or extremely excited.

The effects of arousal on memory have been known for centuries. In England in the early 1600s, when people sold land, they did not yet have the custom of recording the sale on paper. (Paper was expensive and most people were illiterate anyway.) Instead, residents of the city or village would gather together in a ceremony; someone announced the sale and instructed everyone to remember it. The children's memory was especially important, because they would live the longest. To increase the chances that the children would remember, the adults would kick the children while telling them about the business deal. (Avoiding such abuse is just another of the many benefits of literacy.)

Unfortunately, emotional intensity does increase the vividness and intensity of a memory, but it does not guarantee the memory's accuracy. Many people report "flashbulb" memories of where they were, what they were doing, or even the weather at the time they heard shocking news—the assassination of John Kennedy, the explosion of the *Challenger,* the death of Princess Diana, and so on. One investigator asked English people to remember the moment they first heard about the Hillsborough football disaster, when a stampede of fans trying to enter the stadium crushed 95 people to death. Large numbers of people claimed to have clear recollections of the moment when they first heard the news. However, when the same people were interviewed on different occasions, the "clear, vivid" memories they once reported were not always the same as what they reported another time (Wright, 1993). So, emotionally charged memories are subject to distortion, just as other memories are.

Why are emotionally arousing events so memorable (even if the memories are not always accurate)? First, emotionally exciting events stimulate certain kinds of norepinephrine synapses in the brain, known as β-adrenergic synapses, which enhance memory storage. Drugs that block those synapses decrease the storage of emotionally exciting events (Cahill, Prins, Weber, & McGaugh, 1994). Second, exciting experiences arouse your sympathetic nervous system, increasing the conversion of stored glycogen into glucose (a sugar) and therefore raising the level of blood glucose (McGaugh, 1990). Recall from Chapter 3 that glucose is the brain's primary fuel; elevating the glucose level facilitates brain functioning.

Could you enhance your memory by taking drugs that stimulate β-adrenergic synapses? In principle, maybe;

Do you remember the first time you saw a comet? Most people recall emotionally arousing events, sometimes in great detail, although not always accurately.

however, such drugs produce unwanted side effects, including headaches, nausea, and heart problems. Could you enhance your memory by increasing your blood glucose levels? Yes, but don't try to do that by eating chocolate. Excess carbohydrates raise your blood glucose only briefly before you store them, so your waistline will increase more than your test scores. The best solution is to try to increase your interest in the material and, therefore, your emotional response to it.

Meaningful Storage and Levels of Processing

If you want to memorize something, such as a definition, you might try repeating it many times. Other things being equal, repetition does aid memory, but other things are seldom equal. To illustrate: Examine Figure 7.15, which shows a real U.S. penny and 14 fakes. If you live in the United States, you have seen pennies countless times, but can you now identify the real one? Most U.S. citizens cannot (Nickerson & Adams, 1979). (If you do not have a penny in your pocket, check answer B on page 248. If you are not from the United States, try drawing the front and back of a common coin in your own country.) In short, mere repetition, such as looking at a coin many times, does not guarantee a strong memory.

According to the **levels-of-processing principle** (Craik & Lockhart, 1972), *how easily we can retrieve a memory depends on the number and types of associations we form.* When you read something—this chapter, for example—you might simply read over the words, giving them no more thought than necessary to complete your reading assignment. In that case, you have engaged in shallow processing, and whatever memories you store will

T A B L E 7.3	**Levels-of-Processing Model of Memory**
Superficial processing	*Simply repeat the material to be remembered: "Hawk, Oriole, Tiger, Timberwolf, Blue Jay, Bull."*
Deeper processing	*Think about each item. Note that two start with T and two with B.*
Still deeper processing	*Note that three are birds and three are mammals. Also, three are major league baseball teams and three are NBA basketball teams. Use whichever associations mean the most to you.*

be hard to retrieve at test time. Alternatively, you might stop and think about various points that you read, relate them to your own experiences, and think of your own examples of the principles discussed. The more ways you think about the material, the deeper your processing is and the more easily you will remember it later. Table 7.3 summarizes this model.

As an example, imagine several groups of students who study a list of words in several ways. One group simply reads the list over and over, and a second counts the letters in each word. Both procedures produce *superficial processing* and poor recall later. A third group tries to think of a synonym for each word or tries to use each word in a sentence. As the students think about the words, they store them at a *deeper level of processing,* so they will recall them better than the first two groups. Students in the fourth group try to relate each word to themselves: "How does this apply to me? What experiences have I had that relate to this word?" This group does even better than the third group. For a while, psychologists thought that relating words to yourself produces a special kind of strengthening, but later research found equally strong memories in students who tried to relate each word to their mothers (Symons & Johnson,

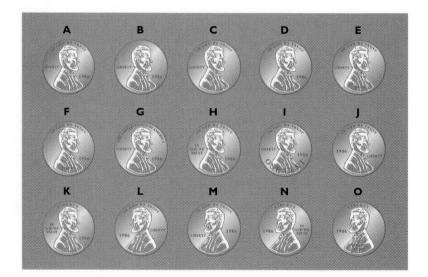

FIGURE 7.15 Can you spot the genuine penny among 14 fakes? (Based on Nickerson & Adams, 1979.) If you're not sure (and you don't have a penny with you), check answer B on page 248.

Most actors prepare for a play by spending much time thinking about the meaning of what they say (a deep level of processing) and spending only a little time simply repeating the words (a shallow level of processing).

1997). The conclusion is that memory grows stronger when people elaborate and organize the material and relate it to other things that they know and care about.

You can improve your level of processing in one of two ways (Einstein & Hunt, 1980; McDaniel, Einstein, & Lollis, 1988): First, you can think about each individual item on the list you are trying to remember. Second, you can look for relationships among the items. You might notice, for example, that the list consists of five animals, six foods, four methods of transportation, and five objects made of wood. One of the skills we gain through education is learning to organize material in this way. According to one study of Kpelle children in West Africa, teenage children who had gone to school organized a list of words into categories, such as foods, types of clothing, and hunting materials. Unschooled children did not sort the list into categories and generally did not remember the words very well (Scribner, 1974).

CONCEPT CHECKS

7. Many of the best students in a course (those who get the best grades) read the assigned text chapters more slowly than average. Why?
8. Most actors and public speakers who have to memorize lengthy passages spend little time simply repeating the words and more time thinking about them. Why? (Check your answers on page 248.)

Self-Monitoring of Understanding

Whenever you are studying a text, you must periodically decide, "Should I keep on studying this section, or do I already understand it well enough?" Even when you are reading a single sentence, you have to decide whether you understand the sentence or whether you should stop and reread it. This sentence was once published in the student newspaper at North Carolina State University:

> He said Harris told him she and Brothers told French that grades had been changed.

Ordinarily, when good readers encounter such a confusing sentence, they notice their own confusion and reread the sentence or, if necessary, the whole paragraph. Poor readers tend to read at the same speed for both easy and difficult materials, instead of slowing down when they come to difficult sentences.

Monitoring one's own understanding is difficult and often inaccurate, yet it is not impossible. After you have read a chapter, you can probably make a somewhat accurate (better than chance) estimate of how well you will perform when you are tested on the material later (Maki & Serra, 1992). If you wait a while (at least a few minutes) after studying something and then try to predict how well you will remember it later, your prediction will improve (Weaver & Kelemen, 1997). Evidently, you monitor how much you have already forgotten and use that to estimate your later memory losses.

When Mozart was a boy he visited the Vatican, where he heard a performance of a piece of music. The next day, he had a handwritten score of the piece. The Pope was furious, because he had decreed that no one could copy the score of that music, but Mozart had written down the entire piece from memory—eight voice parts—after one hearing. The Pope was so impressed, he awarded Mozart a medal.

People need to monitor their understanding of a text to decide whether to continue studying or whether they already understand it well enough. Most readers have trouble making that judgment correctly.

One systematic way to monitor your own understanding of a text is by using the **SPAR method:**

Survey. Get an overview of what the passage is about. Scan through it; look at the boldface headings; try to understand the organization or goals of the passage.

Process meaningfully. Read the material carefully. Think about how you could use the ideas, or how they relate to other things you have read. Evaluate the strengths and weaknesses of the argument. The more actively you think about what you read, the better you will remember the material.

Ask questions. If the text provides questions, like the concept checks in this text, try to answer them. Then pretend you are the instructor; write the questions you would ask on a test, and then answer them yourself. In the process, you will discover which sections of the passage you need to reread.

Review. Wait a day or so, and then retest your knowledge. Spacing out your study over time increases your ability to remember it over the long term.

The Effects of Spacing Out Study Sessions

Suppose someone reads you a list of 20 words and asks you to recall as many of them as possible. You cannot store that many words in your phonological loop, but you will probably remember a few words, *especially the items at the beginning and end of the list.*

That tendency, known as the **serial-order effect,** includes two aspects: The *primacy effect* is the tendency to remember the first items, and the *recency effect* is the tendency to remember the last items. One explanation for the primacy effect is that the listener has a chance to rehearse the first few items for a few moments by themselves with no interference from the others. One explanation for the recency effect is that the last items are still in the listener's phonological loop at the time of the test.

The phonological loop cannot provide the whole explanation for the recency effect, however. In one study, British rugby players were asked to name the teams they had played against in the current season. Players were most likely to remember the last couple of teams they had played against, thus showing a clear recency effect, even though they were recalling events that occurred weeks apart (Baddeley & Hitch, 1977). (The phonological loop holds information for only seconds.)

So, studying material—or, rather, *reviewing* material—shortly before a test is likely to improve recall, via the recency effect. Now consider something you once studied and have not reviewed since then, such as a foreign language you studied several years ago. If you resumed your study, would much of it come back to you?

Harry Bahrick (1984) tested people who had studied Spanish in school anywhere from 1 to 50 years previously. People who had studied it 1 or 2 years ago remembered more than those who had studied it 3 to 6 years ago, but beyond 6 years the retention appeared to be stable (Figure 7.16). In other words, we do not completely forget old memories even if we seldom use them.

In a later study, Bahrick and members of his family studied foreign-language vocabulary either on a moderately frequent basis (practicing once every 2 weeks) or on a less-frequent basis (as seldom as once every 8 weeks); both schedules eventually reached the same total study time.

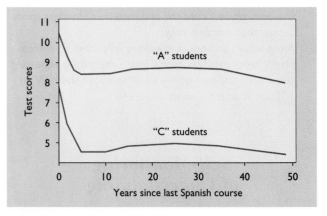

FIGURE 7.16 (Left) Spanish vocabulary as measured by a recognition test shows a rapid decline in the first few years but then long-term stability. (From Bahrick, 1984.)

The result: More frequent study led to faster learning; however, less frequent study led to better long-term retention, as measured years later (Bahrick, Bahrick, Bahrick, & Bahrick, 1993).

The principle here is a general one: *If you want to remember something for as long as possible*—and presumably that is why you are getting an education in the first place—you should study and review under varying conditions with substantial intervals between study sessions. Spreading out your study will slow down your original learning but will improve your ability to recall the information long afterward (Schmidt & Bjork, 1992).

CONCEPT CHECKS

9. The results shown in Figure 7.16 demonstrate how well people recognize the Spanish they studied years ago. Might they actually remember more than this figure indicates? If so, how could you determine how much more they remember?

10. If you want to do well on the final exam in this course, what should you do now—review this chapter or review the first three chapters in the book? (Check your answers on page 248.)

The Use of Special Coding Strategies

A librarian who places a new book on the shelf also enters some information into the retrieval system, so that anyone who knows either the title, author, or topic can find the book. Similarly, when you store a memory, you store it in terms of **retrieval cues,** *associated information that might help you regain the memory later.* We shall examine two illustrations of retrieval cues, the encoding specificity effect and the use of mnemonic devices.

Encoding Specificity

When you learn something, the associations you form with the learned material become retrieval cues that can remind you of the material later. According to the **encoding specificity principle** (Tulving & Thomson, 1973), *the associations you form at the time of learning will be the most effective retrieval cues* (Figure 7.17).

 TRY IT YOUR- SELF Here is an example (modified from Thieman, 1984). First, read the pairs of words (in psychological jargon, *paired associates*) in Table 7.4a. Then, turn to Table 7.4b on page 247. For each of the words on that list, try to recall a related word on the list you just read. *Do this now.* (The answers are on page 248, answer C.)

Most people find this task difficult. Because they initially coded the word *cardinal* as a type of clergyman, for ex-

FIGURE 7.17 According to the principle of encoding specificity, the way we code a word during original learning determines which cues will remind us of that word later. For example, when you hear the word *queen,* you may think of that word in any of several ways. If you think of *queen bee,* then the cue *playing card* will not remind you of it later. If you think of the *Queen of England,* then *chess piece* will not be a good reminder.

ample, they do not think of it when they see the retrieval cue *bird.* Consequently, you can improve your memory by storing information in terms of the same retrieval cues you will most likely use when you try to recall it. (Or store it with as many different retrieval cues as possible.)

The principle of encoding specificity extends to practically any aspect of experience at the time of storage. If you experience something while you are in a particular mood, you are somewhat more likely to think of it again when you are in the same mood (Bower, 1994). If you learn something while under the influence of a drug, such as a tranquilizer, you will probably remember it more easily when you take that drug again than at other times. **State-dependent memory** is *the tendency to remember something better if your body is in the same condition during recall as it was*

TABLE 7.4a

Clergyman — Cardinal
Trinket — Charm
Social event — Ball
Shrubbery — Bush
Inches — Feet
Take a test — Pass
Weather—Fair
Geometry — Plane
Tennis — Racket
Stone — Rock
Magic — Spell
Envelope — Seal
Cashiers — Checkers

Nobel Peace Prize Winners

1901	H. Dunant and F. Passy
1902	E. Ducommun and A. Gobat
1903	Sir W. R. Cremer
1904	Institute of International Law
1905	Baroness von Suttner
1906	T. Roosevelt
1907	E. T. Moneta and L. Renault
1908	K. P. Arnoldson and F. Bajer
1909	A. M. F. Beernaert and Baron d'Estournelles de Constant
1910	International Peace Bureau
1911	T. M. C. Asser and A. H. Fried

1957	L. B. Pearson
1958	G. Pire
1959	P. J. Noel-Baker
1960	A. Luthuli
1961	D. Hammarskjöld (posthumously)
1962	L. Pauling (awarded 1963)

1990	M. Gorbachev
1991	A. S. Suu Kyi
1992	Rigoberta Menchú
1993	Nelson Mandela and Frederik W. de Klerk
1994	Yasir Arafat, Yitzhak Rabin, and Shimon Peres
1995	Joseph Rotblat and Pugwash Conferences on Science and World Affairs
1996	Carlos Felipe Ximenes Belo and José Ramos-Horta
1997	Jody Williams and International Committee to Ban Landmines

FIGURE 7.18 A list of Nobel Peace Prize winners: Mnemonic devices can be useful when people try to memorize long lists like this one.

during the original learning. The point is that, if you want to remember something easily and under a wide variety of conditions, study it under a wide variety of conditions, not just one.

Mnemonic Devices

If you needed to memorize something lengthy and not terribly exciting—for example, a list of all the bones in the body—how would you do it? One effective strategy is to attach systematic retrieval cues to each term, so that you can remind yourself of the terms when you need them.

A **mnemonic device** is *any memory aid that is based on encoding each item in a special way.* The word *mnemonic* (nee-MAHN-ik) comes from a Greek root meaning "memory." (The same root appears in the word *amnesia,* "lack of memory.")

Mnemonic devices come in many varieties. Some are simple: thinking up a little story that reminds you of each item to be remembered (such as "Every Good Boy Does Fine" to remember the notes EGBDF on the musical staff). Suppose you had to memorize the list of Nobel Peace Prize winners (Figure 7.18). You might try making up a little story: "Dun (Dunant) passed (Passy) the Duke (Ducommun) of Gob (Gobat) some cream (Cremer). That made him internally ILL (Institute of International Law). He suited (von

Suttner) up with some roses (Roosevelt) and spent some money (Moneta) on a Renault (Renault) . . . ." You'd still have to study the names, but your story might help.

Another effective mnemonic device is the **method of loci** (method of places). *First, you memorize a series of places, and then you use a vivid image to associate each of these locations with something you want to remember.* For example, you might start by memorizing every location along the route from your dormitory room to, say, your psychology classroom. Then you link the locations, in order, to the names.

Suppose the first three locations you pass are the desk in your room, the door to your room, and the corridor. You should first form a mental image linking the first pair of Nobel Peace Prize winners, Dunant and Passy, to the first location, your desk. You might imagine a Monopoly game board on your desk, with a big sign "DO NOT (Dunant) PASS (Passy) GO." Then you link the second pair of names to the second location, your door: A DUKE student (as in Ducommun) is standing at the door, giving confusing signals. He says "DO COME IN (Ducommun)" and "GO BACK (Gobat)." Then you link the corridor to Cremer, perhaps by imagining someone has spilled CREAM (Cremer) all over the floor (Figure 7.19). You continue in this manner until you have linked every name to a location. Now, if you can remember all those locations in order and if you have good visual images for each one, you will be able to recite the list of Nobel Peace Prize winners.

A similar mnemonic device is called the **peg method.** *You start by memorizing a list of objects, such as "One is a bun, two is a shoe, three is a tree, . . ." Then you form mental images to link the names with these peg words,* just as you would with the method of loci. For example, for number one, "I ate a BUN at the DUNE PASS (Dunant, Passy)," imagining *dune pass* as a passageway between sand

FIGURE 7.19 The method of loci is one of the oldest mnemonic devices. First learn a list of places, such as "my desk, the door of my room, the corridor, . . ." Then link each of these places to the items on a list of words or names, such as a list of the names of Nobel Peace Prize winners.

TABLE 7.4b

Instructions: For each of these words, write a related word that you remember from the *second column* of the list in Table 7.3.

Exhibition —

Animal —

Part of body —

Transportation —

Football —

Crime —

Former U.S. president —

Music —

Personality —

Write —

Bird —

Board game —

Sports —

dunes. Later, you use all your peg words to help you remember the list of names. To use mnemonic devices well, you need to be clever and resourceful in producing images. (What image can you devise for Nobel Peace Prize winner Mikhail Gorbachev?)

How useful are elaborate mnemonic devices? Learning to use mnemonics takes some time and effort, but the rewards are substantial for someone who wants to memorize long lists of names or words. Some people find mnemonics useful for remembering people's names. (For example, you might remember someone named Harry Moore by picturing him as "more hairy" than everyone else.) Few people find mnemonics useful for everyday tasks such as remembering where you parked your car, but mnemonics can be helpful in their proper place.

THE MESSAGE
Improving One's Memory

We often speak of "storing" and "retrieving" memories, as if we were putting items on a shelf and then taking them off. For some purposes, this analogy is satisfactory, but only if we don't take it too seriously. The more you know about something and the more interested you get, the easier it is to establish new memories and find them when you need them. It is as though putting a certain kind of item on your "shelf" makes it easier to add more items of the same kind.

SUMMARY

✳ *Emotional arousal.* Emotionally exciting events tend to be remembered vividly, if not always accurately. Such events stimulate β-adrenergic synapses in the brain and act to increase blood glucose levels. (page 241)

✳ *Levels-of-processing principle.* According to the levels-of-processing principle, a memory becomes stronger (and easier to recall) if we think about the meaning of the material and relate it to other material. (page 242)

✳ *Self-monitoring of understanding.* Good readers check their own understanding of a text and slow down or reread when they do not understand. Self-monitoring is difficult, but people can learn techniques to improve their self-monitoring. (page 243)

✳ *Timing of study.* Studying under consistent conditions as close as possible to the time of the test will increase your memory during the test. However, reviewing under varied conditions at long, irregular intervals is better for establishing memories that will be available at varied times and places. (page 244)

✳ *Encoding specificity.* When we form a memory, we store it with links to the way we thought about it at that time. When we try to recall the memory, a cue is most effective if it is similar to the links we formed at the time of storage. (page 245)

✳ *Mnemonics.* Specialized techniques for establishing systematic retrieval cues can help people to remember ordered lists of names or terms. (page 246)

Suggestion for Further Reading

Cermak, L. S. (1975). *Improving your memory.* New York: McGraw-Hill. A lively book about mnemonic devices and other ways to improve memory.

Terms

levels-of-processing principle   the concept that the number and types of associations established during learning determines the ease of later retrieval of a memory (page 242)

SPAR method   a systematic way to monitor and improve understanding of a text by surveying, processing meaningfully, asking questions, and reviewing (page 244)

serial-order effect   the tendency to remember the items near the beginning and end of a list better than those in the middle (page 244)

retrieval cue   information associated with remembered material, which can be useful for helping to recall that material (page 245)

encoding specificity principle   the tendency for the associations formed at the time of learning to be more effective retrieval cues than other associations (page 245)

state-dependent memory   the tendency to remember something better if your body is in the same condition during recall as it was during the original learning (page 245)

mnemonic device   any memory aid that is based on encoding each item in a special way (page 246)

method of loci   a mnemonic device that calls for linking the items on a list with a memorized list of places (page 246)

peg method   a mnemonic device in which a person first memorizes a list of objects and then forms mental images linking those objects ("peg words") to a list of names to be memorized (page 246)

Answers to Concept Checks

7. Students who read slowly and frequently pause to think about the meaning of the material are engaging in deep processing and are likely to remember the material well, probably better than those who read through the material quickly. (page 243)

8. Simply repeating the words would produce a shallow level of processing and poor retention. A more efficient means of memorizing is to spend most of one's time thinking about the meaning of the speech and only a little time actually memorizing the words. (page 243)

9. People would probably show even greater retention if they were tested by the savings method. (page 245)

10. To prepare well for the final exam, you should review all the material at irregular intervals. Thus, you might profit by skimming over Chapters 2 and 3 right now. Of course, if you have a test on Chapter 7 in a day or two, your goal is different and your strategy should be different. (page 245)

Answers to Other Questions in the Text

B. The correct coin is A. (page 242)
C. (page 247)

Exhibition—Fair
Animal—Seal
Part of body—Feet
Transportation—Plane
Football—Pass
Crime—Racket
Former U.S. president—Bush
Music—Rock
Personality—Charm
Write—Spell
Bird—Cardinal
Board game—Checkers
Sports—Ball

Web Resources

Memory Techniques and Mnemonics
www.demon.co.uk/mindtool/memory.html
MindTools offers commercial software designed to improve memory, and more than 25 free articles about memory and how to improve it, stress management, time management, and other topics.

MODULE 7.3

Memory Loss

What are some of the causes of memory loss?

What do various types of memory loss teach us about memory?

Computer operators are advised to protect their computers from strong magnetic fields. Suppose you defied that advice and passed your computer through the strongest magnetic field you could find. Chances are, you would erase all your computer's memory, but suppose it erased all of the text files but none of the graphics files. Or perhaps it left all the old memories intact but made it impossible to store new ones. From the damage, you would receive hints about how your computer's memory works.

The same is true of human memory. Passing your head by a magnet would not erase your memories. (At least not with ordinary magnets; I don't know what would happen at extreme levels.) However, the kinds of damage that do impair memory affect different kinds of memory in different ways. The study of severe memory loss helps us to understand systems of memory.

"Normal" Forgetting

Pick your favorite meal. I'm going to imagine that you said pizza, but substitute something else if you wish. List all the pizza meals you can remember. You will probably start with your most recent pizza meals and then add some especially interesting or unusual meals from long ago. You will recall more recent than remote examples, but you will recall a few from many years ago, and if you still recall a memory that is a few years old now, you will probably continue to remember it indefinitely. In short, most memories fade rapidly, but the longer you have held onto a memory, the less it tends to fade. The overall trend of memory and forgetting looks approximately as shown in the following diagram (Rubin & Wenzel, 1996). The family of curves shows that the rate of forgetting varies among individuals and even

among situations for a given individual. Nevertheless, the shape of the curve is consistent.

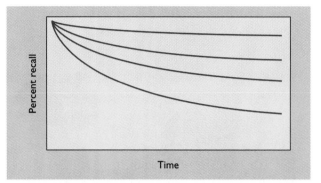

Why do we forget? Let us review the possibilities already discussed in this chapter. One explanation is interference. For example, sports fans will forget most of the details of a game they saw a year ago, largely because of interference from their memories of all the games they saw before it (proactive interference) and after it (retroactive interference).

A second explanation is that memory traces gradually decay, like old photographs that fade in the sunlight. The effects of decay and interference are difficult to disentangle experimentally. That is, during any delay, a memory is subject to the effects of both time and interference from other experiences. Nevertheless, researchers have considered decay a likely explanation of forgetting from working memory, because some information in the phonological loop disappears within seconds if it is not rehearsed. Decay is a less likely explanation of forgetting from long-term memory, because some long-term memories remain available after years even without use.

A third possible explanation is that memories seem to be forgotten because we no longer have the appropriate retrieval cues. For example, if you learned certain facts in an eighth-grade geography class, the retrieval cues included the context—when and where you learned it (the classroom, the city, the other students around you). If you try to remember these facts years later, you no longer have the contextual cues to help remind you. Sometimes, if people return to the place where they learned something (at least in their imagination), they remember information that they thought they had forgotten.

You are, of course, most likely to forget material when you were paying little attention at the time you learned it. In particular, people often remember an idea and forget where they heard it. Have you ever told someone something—a joke, a bit of gossip perhaps—only to have that person say, "Yes, I was the one who told *you* that"? In one experiment, students sat in a group trying to think of solutions to a problem. A week later, each student was asked separately to think of other possible solutions. Many of them offered, as their own "original" idea, something that they had heard another student suggest the previous week (Marsh, Landau, & Hicks, 1997). They had simply forgotten where they got the

Bob Williams was one of 40 aging former paratroopers who reenacted his parachute jump on the 50th anniversary of D day. Ordinarily we forget most events from 50 years ago. However, this was a very distinctive, emotionally arousing event, followed by very few other experiences that were similar enough to produce interference. Returning to the scene of the original jump provides contextual cues that would help to retrieve the memory.

idea. The result is unintentional plagiarism: More often than we realize, we claim an idea to be new, not remembering that we first heard it from someone else.

Amnesia After Brain Damage

In contrast to normal forgetting, **amnesia** is a *severe loss or deterioration of memory.* Even in the most severe cases of amnesia, people do not forget everything they have ever learned. The specific deficits of amnesic patients tell us

much about the distinctions among the various types of memory. We shall consider amnesia based on several types of brain damage, plus amnesia of infancy and old age.

The Case of H. M., a Man with Hippocampal Damage

In 1953, a man with the initials H. M. was subjected to unusual brain surgery in an attempt to control his severe epilepsy. Even while taking antiepileptic drugs, H. M. had suffered such frequent and severe seizures that he was unable to keep a job or live a normal life. In desperation, surgeons removed his **hippocampus,** *a large forebrain structure in the interior of the temporal lobe* (Figure 7.20),

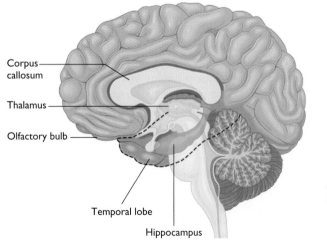

a

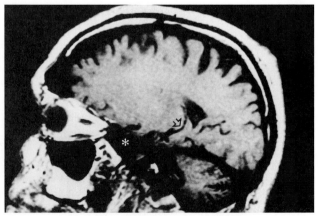

FIGURE 7.20   The hippocampus is a large subcortical structure of the brain. After damage to the hippocampus and related structures, patient H. M. had great difficulty storing new long-term memories. The photo shows a scan of the brain of H. M. formed by magnetic resonance imaging. The asterisk indicates the area from which the hippocampus is missing. The arrow indicates a portion of the hippocampus that is preserved. (Photo courtesy of Suzanne Corkin and David Amaral.)

where they believed his epileptic seizures were originating. They also removed some surrounding brain areas. At the time, researchers knew little about the functions of the hippocampus or the kinds of memory deficits likely to result from its removal.

The results of the surgery were favorable in some regards. H. M.'s epileptic seizures decreased in frequency and severity. His personality and intellect remained the same; in fact, his IQ score increased slightly after the operation, presumably because of the decreased epileptic interference.

However, he suffered severe memory problems (Corkin, 1984; Milner, 1959), particularly a massive **antero-grade** (ANT-eh-ro-grade) **amnesia,** *inability to store new long-term memories.* For years after the operation, he cited the year as 1953 and his own age as 27. Later, he took wild guesses (Corkin, 1984). He would read the same issue of a magazine repeatedly without realizing that he had read it before. He could not even remember where he had lived for the last few years. He also suffered a moderate **retrograde amnesia,** *loss of memory for events that occurred shortly before the brain damage;* see Figure 7.21). That is, he had some trouble recalling events that had happened within the last 1 to 3 years before the operation, although he could recall older events. People who suffer a head injury with loss of consciousness generally have retrograde amnesia for the events leading up to the injury.

H. M. could form normal short-term memories, such as repeating a brief list of items, and if he was permitted to rehearse them without distraction, he could even retain the list of items for several minutes. He could also learn new skills, as we shall see in a moment.

Like Rip van Winkle (the story character who slept for 20 years and awakened to a vastly changed world), H. M. became more and more out of date with each passing year (Gabrieli, Cohen, & Corkin, 1988; Smith, 1988). He did not

recognize the names or faces of people who became famous after the mid-1950s. He could not name the president of the United States even when Ronald Reagan was president, though he remembered Reagan as an actor from before 1953. He did not understand the meaning of words that had entered the English language after the time of his surgery. For example, he guessed that *biodegradable* means "two grades," that *soul food* means "forgiveness," and that a *closet queen* is a "moth." For H. M., watching the evening news was like visiting another planet.

In spite of H. M.'s massive memory difficulties, he can still acquire new skills and retain them later. We refer to *skill retention* as **procedural memory,** in contrast to **declarative memory,** *the ability to recall factual information.* For example, H. M. has learned to read material written in mirror fashion (Cohen & Squire, 1980):

with the words reversed like this

Although H. M. has learned to read mirror writing, he does not remember having learned it. He has also learned a simple finger maze, and he has learned the correct solution to the Tower of Hanoi puzzle shown in Figure 7.22 (Cohen, Eichenbaum, Deacedo, & Corkin, 1985). He does not *remember* learning these skills, however. He claims that he has never seen any of these tasks before, and he is always a bit surprised by his success.

Because H. M.'s memory deficits are so severe, surgeons today would not attempt the same surgery. Occasionally, people suffer accidental damage to the hippocampus from stroke or other means; those people also show extensive memory impairment, especially when describing events in their lives (Reed & Squire, 1997; Vargha-Khadem et al., 1997). Both human and animal studies confirm that memories are not stored *in* the hippocampus, but the hippocampus must function in order to store certain kinds of memories. Once these memories are stored, however, they can persist after removal of the hippocampus. (After all, H. M. remembers most of what happened before his operation.)

Frontal-Lobe Amnesia

Amnesia can also arise after damage to the frontal lobes, especially the prefrontal cortex (see Figure 7.20). Because the frontal lobes receive a great deal of input from the hippocampus, the symptoms of frontal-lobe damage overlap those of hippocampal damage. However, frontal-lobe damage produces some special memory impairments of its own.

Frontal-lobe damage can be either the result of a stroke or of trauma to the head. Frontal-lobe deterioration is also commonly associated with **Korsakoff's syndrome,** *a condition caused by a prolonged deficiency of vitamin B_1, usually as a result of chronic alcoholism.* This vitamin deficiency leads to a loss or shrinkage of neurons in many parts of the brain, especially the prefrontal cortex and parts

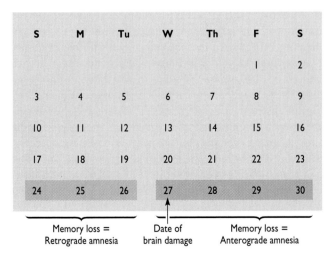

FIGURE 7.21 Retrograde amnesia is loss of memory for events in a certain period *before* brain damage or another trauma. Anterograde amnesia is difficulty forming new memories *after* some trauma.

FIGURE 7.22 In the Tower of Hanoi puzzle, the task is to transfer all the disks to another peg, while moving only one at a time and never placing a larger disk onto a smaller disk. Patient H. M. learned the correct strategy and retained it from one test period to another, although he did not remember ever seeing the task before. That is, he showed procedural memory but not declarative memory.

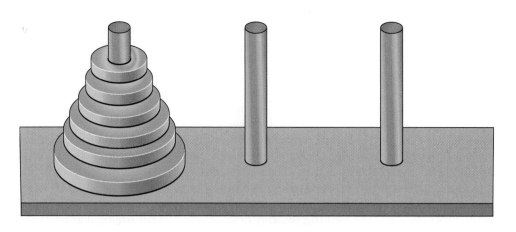

of the thalamus. Patients suffer multiple impairments of memory, apathy, and confusion (Oscar-Berman, 1980; Squire, Amaral, & Press, 1990). Patients with Korsakoff's syndrome suffer severe retrograde amnesia, generally covering most events beginning about 15 years before the onset of their illness (Squire, Haist, & Shimamura, 1989). They also suffer from anterograde amnesia. If given a long list of words to remember, they temporarily remember the words at the end of the list, but they forget those at the beginning of the list (Stuss et al., 1994). A few minutes later, they forget even the words at the end.

Such patients have particular difficulty remembering when and where various events took place (Shimamura, Janowsky, & Squire, 1990). For example, if asked what they ate this morning or what they did last night, they give a confident but wrong answer—although it may have been true at some time in the past. In spite of their severe loss of declarative memories, they acquire new procedural memories reasonably well.

Patients with frontal-lobe damage, whatever the cause, have a characteristic pattern of answering questions with a bewildering mixture of correct information, out-of-date information, and wild guesses. Their guesses, or **confabulations,** are apparent *attempts to fill in the gaps in their memory.* Other people confabulate, too, when they cannot quite remember something that they believe they should (Moscovitch, 1995), but people with frontal-lobe damage confabulate in self-contradictory or preposterous ways, as the following example illustrates (Moscovitch, 1989, pp. 135–136):

Psychologist: How old are you?
Patient: I'm 40, 42, pardon me, 62.
Psychologist: Are you married or single?
Patient: Married.
Psychologist: How long have you been married?
Patient: About 4 months.
Psychologist: What's your wife's name?
Patient: Martha.
Psychologist: How many children do you have?
Patient: Four. (He laughs.) Not bad for 4 months.
Psychologist: How old are your children?

Patient: The eldest is 32; his name is Bob. And the youngest is 22; his name is Joe.
Psychologist: How did you get these children in 4 months?
Patient: They're adopted.
Psychologist: Who adopted them?
Patient: Martha and I.
Psychologist: Immediately after you got married you wanted to adopt these older children?
Patient: Before we were married we adopted one of them, two of them. The eldest girl Brenda and Bob, and Joe and Dina since we were married.
Psychologist: Does it all sound a little strange to you, what you are saying?
Patient: I think it is a little strange.
Psychologist: I think when I looked at your record it said that you've been married for over 30 years. Does that sound more reasonable to you if I told you that?
Patient: No.
Psychologist: Do you really believe that you have been married for 4 months?
Patient: Yes.

Why do these patients confabulate? According to Morris Moscovitch (1992), the frontal lobes are necessary for *working with memory,* the strategies we use to reconstruct memories that we cannot immediately recall. For example, if someone asks you who Romeo's girlfriend was; whether helium is a gas, liquid, or solid; or whether you have ever been to Puerto Rico, you can probably answer at once without much effort or concern. But if you are asked what you did Tuesday evening last week, or what is the farthest north that you have ever traveled, or what was the most recent time you saw any modern art, your answer will require effort and reasoning. People with frontal-lobe damage have difficulty inferring what must have happened in their past, so they make unlikely guesses.

Implicit Memory in Amnesic Patients

Brain damage can cause defects in some kinds of memory while leaving others almost intact. For example, people with amnesia have poor factual memories but can acquire new procedural memories. Moreover, these people show evidence of memories if they are tested in a special way for *implicit* memory (Reber, 1997). The kinds of memory tests we have considered so far—recall, recognition, and so forth—have been tests of **explicit memory**—*a person who states the correct answer recognizes that it is the correct answer and that it tapped his or her memory.* For example, to the question "who is your psychology instructor?" you would have to state the name or choose it from a list of choices. In contrast to such explicit or direct tests of memory, a test of **implicit** or *indirect* **memory** *does not require any recognition that one is using memory.* In fact, the subjects may not even realize that they are taking part in a memory test.

TRY IT YOUR-SELF Before we proceed, try the demonstration below: Here, you see some three-letter combinations. Add letters to form each of these into an English word:

BEL	_____
HEL	_____
CON	_____
TRA	_____
MOD	_____
DEF	_____

You could have thought of any number of words—the dictionary lists well over a hundred familiar CON—words alone. Did you happen to write any of the following: *below, helium, concern* or *consider* or *contrast, travel, modern, defect*? Each of these words had appeared in the two paragraphs before this demonstration. Reading or hearing a word temporarily *primes* that word and increases the chance that you will use it yourself (Graf & Mandler, 1984; Schacter, 1987). If you wrote any of these words, you probably did not realize you were using your memory, and if I had asked you to use your memory explicitly ("Please write everything you can remember from the last two paragraphs"), you still might not have included any of these words.

Brain-damaged amnesic patients show relatively normal priming, despite deficits in explicit memory. For example, one brain-damaged patient can listen to a list of words and then fill in the stems to complete them (CON-cern, TRA-vel, MOD-ern, and so forth). However, if he is asked explicitly to guess which of a pair of words was on the list (concern or contest, travel or tractor, modern or modify), he guesses with only chance accuracy. In fact, even after 40 sessions of such tests, he says he does not recognize the psychologist testing him and does not remember being tested before (Hamann & Squire, 1997).

Table 7.5 contrasts priming with several other ways of testing memory.

TABLE 7.5 Several Ways to Test Memory

	DESCRIPTION	EXAMPLE
Recall	You are asked to say what you remember.	Name the Seven Dwarfs.
Cued recall	You are given significant hints to help you remember.	Name the Seven Dwarfs. Hint: One was always smiling, one was smart, one never talked, one always seemed to have a cold. . . .
Recognition	You are asked to choose the correct item from among several items.	Which of the following were among the Seven Dwarfs: Sneezy, Sleazy, Dopey, Dippy, Hippy, Happy?
Savings (relearning)	You are asked to relearn something: If it takes you less time than when you first learned that material, some memory has persisted.	Try memorizing this list: Sleepy, Sneezy, Doc, Dopey, Grumpy, Happy, Bashful. Can you memorize it faster than this list: Sleazy, Snoopy, Duke, Dippy, Gripey, Hippy, Blushy?
Priming	You are asked to generate words, without necessarily recognizing them as memories.	You hear the story "Snow White and the Seven Dwarfs." A while later you are asked to fill in these blanks to make words:

```
_____L_____        _____P_____
_____N_____        _____Z_____
_____ _____C
_____O_____E_____
_____R_____        _____P_____
_____ _____PP_____
_____A_____H_____U_____
```

CONCEPT CHECKS

11. a. Is remembering how to tie your shoes a procedural memory or a declarative memory?

   b. You remember an event that happened to you the first day of high school. Is that a procedural or a declarative memory?

12. Which of the following is an example of implicit memory?

   a. You read a chapter about Central America and then try to answer some practice questions about it. Although you cannot answer questions in the format "name the capital of Honduras," you do answer most of the multiple-choice items correctly.

   b. Two people near you are talking about Tibet, and you are not paying attention. After they leave, someone asks you what they had been talking about and you reply that you have no idea. A few minutes later you spontaneously comment, "I wonder what's going on in Tibet these days."

13. Which kinds of memory are most impaired in H. M. and frontal-lobe patients? Which kinds are least impaired? (Check your answers on page 256.)

The Implications of Brain-Damage Amnesia

Studies of amnesic patients highlight the differences between declarative and procedural memories, between explicit and implicit memories, and between the ability to recall old memories and the ability to store new memories. The phenomenon of implicit memory demonstrates that a memory can be active and capable of influencing behavior, at least temporarily, even though a person may not be consciously aware of it.

These memory distinctions require further research, however. Many researchers are not at all convinced that psychologists can usefully distinguish between explicit and implicit memories on the basis of whether they require "conscious awareness" (Rudy & Sutherland, 1992). (Imagine trying to draw that distinction with rats' or monkeys' memories, for example.) In the future, psychologists may clarify the current distinctions or else introduce different ones. The growing consensus, however, is that some sort of distinction is necessary; we have different kinds of memory, not just one.

Infant Amnesia

Most adults remember only a few events, if any, from before age 5, although they have some memories from ages 5, 6, and beyond. Some people remember events from as far back as age 2, but those memories are isolated and fragmentary.

The *relative lack of early declarative memories*, known as **infant amnesia** or **childhood amnesia**, is difficult to explain (Howe & Courage, 1997). Young children do form some reasonably long-lasting memories. Even children younger than 2 years old show clear signs of remembering events from months ago, and 4-year-olds can accurately describe experiences from ages 3, 2, and even earlier—such as their birthday parties, Christmas celebrations, and visits to grandparents (Bauer, 1996). So, it is not that young children fail to form long-term memories but that almost all of those early memories fade away.

Psychologists have proposed several theories to explain infant amnesia, none of them convincing. Sigmund Freud's theory was that infant memories are hidden or repressed because of the emotional traumas of infancy. However, he offered no evidence for this role of early trauma nor for his claim that a therapist could reaccess those memories accurately.

Another possibility is that early memories are nonverbal and later memories are verbal. One fault with that hypothesis is that 4- and 5-year-olds (who clearly rely on language) do remember events from ages 2 and 3 but older children do not.

Another possibility is that infant amnesia is related to the immaturity of the hippocampus (Moscovitch, 1985). The hippocampus is indeed slow to mature, and young children perform poorly on tests of the kinds of memory that are most dependent on the hippocampus (Overman, Pate, Moore, & Peuster, 1996). However, its development is gradual, and it evidently matures fast enough for a 4-year-old to remember events from age 2. So why can't a 10- or 20-year-old remember those same events?

Still another proposal is that a permanent memory of an experience requires the "sense of self" that develops between ages 3 and 4 (Howe & Courage, 1993). This theory, though certainly worth considering, is vague and difficult to test. Also, rats and pigeons develop long-term memories, but do we really want to say that they have a "sense of self"? In summary, the phenomenon of infant amnesia remains unexplained.

People retain many procedural memories from early childhood, such as how to eat with chopsticks or a fork and spoon, but they forget nearly all the specific events from that time of their life.

SOMETHING TO THINK ABOUT

Does the encoding specificity principle (page 245) suggest another possible explanation for infant amnesia? (Hint: Your physiological condition always differs somewhat at the time of attempted recall from what it was when originally learned.) ✳

Amnesia of Old Age

Some older people suffer from Alzheimer's disease or other degenerative conditions that gradually destroy brain cells and thereby impair attention and memory. But what about the memory of healthy older people? Years ago, psychologists tended to overstate the memory loss of old age, because they compared the average young people of their era with the average older people. The younger generation had advantages of much better nutrition, health care, and education than the older generation had ever had. Later, better research, which followed a given set of individuals over the years, found that most healthy people show little decline of memory in old age (Schaie, 1994).

On the average, older adults show only mild deficits on the simplest memory tasks, such as short-term retention of a list of words; they show greater deficits on more complex tasks (Babcock & Salthouse, 1990; Salthouse, Mitchell, Skovronek, & Babcock, 1989). If given a short narrative to remember, older adults remember the central points of the narrative almost as well as younger adults, although they are likely to forget the odd and irrelevant details (Hess, Donley, & Vandermaas, 1989).

Some old people deteriorate more than others, and we would all like to know how to increase our chances of remaining alert and productive in old age. One study found that professors at the University of California, Berkeley, deteriorated less in old age than did other people in the same region (Shimamura, Berry, Mangels, Rusting, & Jurica, 1995). The suggestion is that intellectual activity helps to protect the brain against deterioration, but we cannot draw that conclusion with confidence; it is also possible that the kinds of people least likely to deteriorate in old age are the ones most likely to pursue intellectual activities from youth on.

THE MESSAGE
The Impermanence of Memories

The various ways in which memory fails after brain damage shows us how complicated memory really is. The hippocampus and frontal cortex are clearly important for memory, but in one way or another, just about all other brain areas are, too: Memory requires sensory processing, storing information, retrieving it when necessary, reasoning about available information to fill in the gaps, and finally using the information in action. Considering all the ways that memory *could* fail, it is quite impressive that our memory is usually as accurate as it is.

SUMMARY

✳ *Normal forgetting.* Forgetting depends partly on interference from related memories. At least for memories in the phonological loop, passive decay also contributes to forgetting. We also have trouble remembering when we do not have adequate retrieval cues. (page 249)

✳ *Amnesia after damage to the hippocampus.* H. M. and other patients with damage to the hippocampus have great difficulty storing new declarative memories, although they form normal procedural and implicit memories. (page 250)

✳ *Korsakoff's syndrome and other damage to the frontal lobes.* After suffering damage to the frontal lobes, people make illogical inferences about their past and therefore make odd confabulations. (page 251)

✳ *Lessons from amnesia.* Studies of brain-damaged people demonstrate the value of distinguishing among different types of memory, such as declarative and procedural, or explicit and implicit. (page 254)

✳ *Infant amnesia.* Most people remember little from early childhood, even though preschoolers have clear recollections of experiences that happened months or even years ago. So far, psychologists have no convincing theory to explain the loss of early memories. (page 254)

✳ *Loss of memory in old age.* Most older people suffer some loss of memory, especially for details and for the contexts of events. (page 255)

Suggestion for Further Reading

Squire, L. R., & Butters, N. (Eds.) (1992). *Neuropsychology of Memory* (2nd ed.). New York: Guilford Press. Collection of chapters by several leading investigators of memory and amnesia.

Terms

amnesia   severe loss or deterioration of memory (page 250)

hippocampus   a forebrain structure in the interior of the temporal lobe that is important for storing certain kinds of memory (page 250)

anterograde amnesia   the inability to store new long-term memories (page 250)

retrograde amnesia   loss of memory for events that occurred before the brain damage (page 251)

procedural memory   retention of learned skills (page 251)

declarative memory   recall of factual information (page 251)

Korsakoff's syndrome   a condition caused by a prolonged deficiency of vitamin B_1, which results in both retrograde amnesia and anterograde amnesia (page 251)

confabulations   guesses made by amnesic patients to fill in the gaps in their memory (page 252)

explicit memory   a memory that a person can state, generally recognizing that it is the correct answer (page 253)

implicit memory   a memory that influences behavior without requiring conscious recognition that one is using a memory (page 253)

infant amnesia or **childhood amnesia**   a relative lack of declarative memories from early in life (page 254)

Answers to Concept Checks

11. Remembering how to tie your shoes is a procedural memory. Remembering the first day of school is a declarative memory. (page 254)

12. Item b is an example of implicit memory. Both recall and recognition are examples of explicit memory. (page 254)

13. With H. M. and other amnesic patients, declarative memories are the most impaired and procedural memories are the least impaired. (page 254)

Web Resources

Amnesia Lab HomePage

hermes.cns.uiuc.edu/

The Amnesia Research Laboratory at the University of Illinois at Urbana-Champaign conducts neuropsychological studies of patients with memory disorders, eye movement monitoring, and functional neuroimaging. You can ask questions about amnesia that might be included in a FAQ that is being developed, although you will not receive an individual response.

MODULE 7.4

The Reconstruction of Memory

Why do we sometimes report memories that turn out to be incorrect?

How do later events sometimes change people's recollections?

Forgetting has often been compared to a fading photograph, but in one important way it is very different: As we start to forget, we don't just lose the facts; we sometimes exaggerate or distort them. For example, many people who have visited India report seeing an amazing feat in which

FIGURE 7.23 Some visitors to India report seeing a boy climb a rope (or maybe a bamboo pole). Some claim they also saw him disappear and later reappear. Generally, the more spectacular the account, the less recent the event.

a magician throws one end of a rope into the air, where it becomes stiff long enough for a boy to climb it (Figure 7.23). Climbing an unsupported rope would be magical enough, but some people claim to have seen even more amazing feats. Researchers located 21 people who had seen the Indian rope trick and others with second-hand reports. They compared the reports to how recently the witnesses claimed to have seen the trick (Wiseman & Lamont, 1996). Here are the results:

Reported event	When seen (mean)
Saw a boy climb a rope and then climb down, but admittedly it might have been a bamboo pole instead of a rope.	4 years ago
Saw a boy start to climb a rope, then seem to vanish, then reappear at the top of the rope.	12.67 years ago
Saw a boy climb a rope, reach the top, then vanish and reappear behind the crowd.	32.5 years ago
Saw a boy climb a rope, reach the top, then vanish and reappear in a basket that had been in plain view of the audience.	41.75 years ago
Still more amazing reports...	Didn't actually see it, but heard about it from someone else.

One possible interpretation of these results is that, over the years, Indian boys have become less magical. The more parsimonious interpretation is that, over the years, the witnesses' memories have become distorted.

Another example: You have probably heard claims that a UFO crashed near Roswell, New Mexico, in 1947, and that the U.S. government hid the spacecraft and the aliens' bodies. However, according to Kal Korff (1997), one of the most serious UFO investigators, the facts are these:

In 1947, a Roswell man reported that he might have found the remains of a flying saucer. The local Air Force commander sent Major Jesse Marcel to retrieve the wreckage. The next day, the commander announced, with Marcel present, that it was nothing but a weather balloon. (Much later, the government admitted it had actually been the remains of an experimental spying device.) No one said anything more about it until 1978—more than 30 years later—when Marcel met a UFO enthusiast and told him a version of the "wrecked saucer" story. Marcel, whose military file indicates that he had a long history of exaggerating to impress people, apparently continued that habit. For example, he bragged to the *National Enquirer* that he had shot down five enemy aircraft during the war, although his military file indicates that he was never even a pilot.

UFO enthusiasts nevertheless believed Marcel's report and boast that they then interviewed "more than ninety witnesses." However, of those, only seven claim to have actually seen anything; the other "witnesses" had just heard about it from someone else. Since then, some of those seven have changed their stories several times, contradicting themselves and one another. Some of them are apparently confusing events that they remember from the 1950s or later with the original 1947 event. In short, the parsimonious interpretation is that the memories are as distorted as those of the Indian rope trick.

Distortions of memory over time, even fairly short times, are common. They tell us much about how memory normally works and how skeptical we should be of eyewitness reports of long-ago events.

Reconstruction of the Past

If you try to recall what you did three nights ago, you will start with the details that you remember clearly and **reconstruct** the rest to fill in the gaps: *During an original experience, we construct a memory. When we try to retrieve that memory, we reconstruct an account based partly on surviving memories and partly on our expectations of what must have happened.* For example, suppose you recall that you studied in the library three nights ago. With a little effort, you may remember where you sat, what you were reading, who sat next to you, and where you went for a snack afterward. As time passes, you will probably forget that evening altogether, unless you happen to fall in love with the person who sat down next to you. If so, you will long remember that chance meeting and perhaps even where you went for a snack, but probably not which book you were reading. If you wanted to recall the book, you might reconstruct the event: "Let's see, that semester I was taking a chemistry course that took a

lot of study, so maybe I was reading a chemistry book. No, wait, I remember that when we went out to eat, we talked about politics. So, I was probably reading my political science text."

We also depend on inferences to reconstruct the times of various memories. In one study, investigators located 82 adults who consistently kept up with the news and routinely watched the television program *60 Minutes*. They asked each participant to estimate the approximate dates of various news events and of various *60 Minutes* episodes. The results: People could recall the approximate dates of most news events, but their guesses about the dates of *60 Minutes* episodes were virtually worthless, except for episodes aired during the last two months (Friedman & Huttenlocher, 1997). (See Figure 7.24.) The reason for this difference is that news stories have a logical order and connections to other events in one's life. ("Oh, yeah, I remember what I did when I heard about . . .") With *60 Minutes* episodes, however, we have few links to any other experience. The important conclusion of this study is that, except for very recent events, we cannot attach a date to a memory based on its freshness or sharpness. Our attempts to date a memory involve mostly reconstructions and logical inferences.

Reconstruction and Inference in List Memory

TRY IT YOURSELF Try this demonstration: Read the words in list A, then turn away from the list and pause for a few seconds, and then write as many of the words as you can remember. Then repeat the same procedure for lists B and C. (*Please do this now, before reading the following paragraph.*)

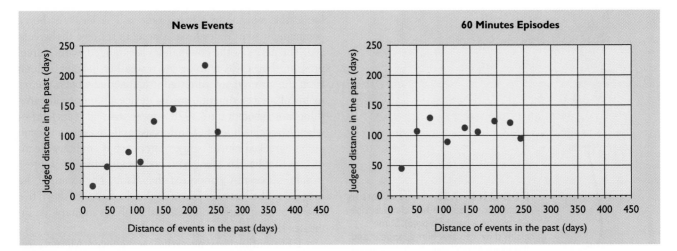

F I G U R E 7.24 People who followed the news and regularly watched the television program *60 Minutes* could estimate the time of various news events but guessed almost randomly about when they saw various *60 Minutes* episodes, except those from the most recent two months. (From Friedman & Huttenlocher, 1997.)

List A	List B	List C
bed	candy	fade
rest	sour	fame
awake	sugar	face
tired	dessert	fake
dream	salty	date
wake	taste	hate
snooze	flavor	late
blanket	bitter	mate
doze	cookies	rate
slumber	fruits	
snore	chocolate	
nap	yummy	

After you have written out your lists, check how many you got right. If you missed several of them, you are normal. The point of this demonstration is not how many you got right, but whether you included *sleep* on the first list, *sweet* on the second, or *fate* on the third. Many people include one or more of these words (which were not on the lists), and some do so with great confidence (Deese, 1959). Apparently, while learning the individual words, people also learn the "gist" of what they are all about, and from that they reconstruct a memory of another word that the list implied. This effect is powerful; even adding a few unrelated words on each list does not weaken it (Robinson & Roediger, 1997). Evidently, even when we are just trying to remember a list of words, we reconstruct or infer what "must have" been on the list.

If you did include *sleep, sweet,* or *fate,* don't worry. Your error is not a sign of a bad memory; in fact, people with really bad memories *don't* make this kind of error (Schacter, Verfaellie, & Anes, 1997). They don't remember the words that *were* on the list and therefore don't use them to infer related words. If you did not include *sleep, sweet,* or *fate,* well . . . actually, this demonstration works better when people hear the list than when they read it. Try reading the lists to your roommate or another friend, and see whether they "remember" the implied words.

Reconstructions of Stories

Suppose people listen to a story about a teenager's day, including a mixture of normal events (watching television) and oddities (clutching a teddy bear and parking a bicycle in the kitchen). Which would people remember better—the normal events or the oddities? You might predict that they would remember the unusual and distinctive events, and you would be right—*if* people are tested quickly enough to show a good memory. However, if we wait long enough for people to start to forget the story, they reconstruct a more typical day for the teenager, recalling the normal events, omitting the unlikely ones, and adding some that "should have happened," even though the story did not mention them—such as "the teenager went to school in the morning." In short, the less certain people's memories are, the more they rely on their expectations (Heit, 1993; Maki, 1990).

A witness at a trial is asked to recall an event that happened months or years ago. It is neither likely nor necessary that this witness will recall every detail or every word of a conversation. Rather, the report will be a mixture of clear memories and reconstructions.

In a study that highlights the role of expectations, U.S. and Mexican adults tried to recall three stories. Some were given U.S. versions of the stories; others were given Mexican versions. (For example, in the "going out on a date" story, the Mexican version had the man's sister go along as a chaperone.) On the average, U.S. participants remembered the U.S. versions better, whereas the Mexicans remembered the Mexican versions better (Harris, Schoen, & Hensley, 1992).

Hindsight Bias

TRY IT YOUR-SELF Let's try another demonstration. First read the following paragraph, and then answer the question that follows:

For some years after the arrival of Hastings as governor-general of India, the consolidation of British power involved serious war. The first of these wars took place on the northern frontier of Bengal where the British were faced by the plundering raids of the Gurkas of Nepal. Attempts had been made to stop the raids by an exchange of lands, but the Gurkas would not give up their claims to country under British control, and Hastings decided to deal with them once and for all. The campaign began in November, 1814. It was not glorious. The Gurkas were only some 12,000 strong; but they were brave fighters, fighting in territory well-suited to their raiding tactics. The older British commanders were used to war in the plains where the enemy ran away from a resolute attack. In the mountains of Nepal it was not easy even to find the enemy. The troops and transport animals suffered from the extremes of heat and cold, and the officers learned caution only after sharp reverses. Major-General Sir D. Octerlony was the one commander to escape from these minor defeats. (Woodward, 1938, pp. 383–384)

Question In light of the information appearing in this passage, what was the probability of occurrence of each of the four possible outcomes listed below? (The probabilities should total 100%.)

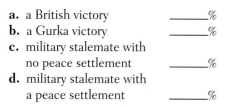

a. a British victory _____%
b. a Gurka victory _____%
c. military stalemate with
no peace settlement _____%
d. military stalemate with
a peace settlement _____%

Note that each of these possible outcomes had some likelihood, given the facts as stated. Now that you have made your estimates of the probabilities, I can tell you what really happened: The two sides reached a military stalemate without any settlement. The British had the advantages of superior numbers and superior equipment, but the Gurkas knew the territory and refused to give up. Battles continued sporadically and indecisively for years.

Now that you know the outcome, would you like to revise your estimates of the probabilities? Perhaps if you reread the paragraph, you will decide that you had overestimated the probabilities of some outcomes and underestimated others.

Subjects in one experiment read the preceding passage about the British and the Gurkas. Some were told the correct outcome, and others were told one of the other outcomes; all were then asked to estimate the probabilities of the four possible outcomes. Each group listed a high estimated probability for the "actual" outcome they had been given (Fischhoff, 1975). That is, once they knew what "really" happened (or incorrectly *thought* they knew), they reinterpreted the previous interpretation to make that outcome seem likely, or perhaps even unavoidable (Figure 7.25). The subjects' behavior illustrates **hindsight bias,** *the tendency to mold our recollection of the past to fit how events later turned out.* Something happens and we then say, "I *knew* that was going to happen!" (Oh, incidentally, I lied about the outcome of the British-Gurkas war. Actually, the British won, although the war dragged on for 2 years. Would you like to reevaluate your estimates *again*?)

Examples of hindsight bias are abundant. As columnist Meg Greenfield (1997, p. 104) once wrote, if we believe what people say today, they always thought that "Harry Truman was a wonderful, gutsy, honest president; that the Vietnam War was a loser and we should get out; that Watergate represented a really big, serious, clearcut offense, . . . and that civil-rights legislation that upheld and enforced the principle of colorblind treatment of citizens by government was a good thing. And needless to say, everyone also always knew that the Soviet Union . . . was going to collapse and disappear." At the times of those events, however, many people who now remember thinking these things were in fact saying something quite different.

We can explain hindsight bias in several ways (Hawkins & Hastie, 1990), including that memory fades—especially

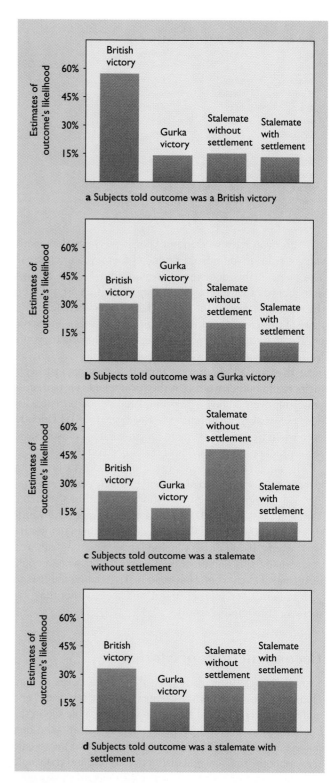

FIGURE 7.25 Mean estimates of the likelihood of four outcomes varied, depending on what each group was told about the "actual" outcome. Those who thought the British had won said that, under the circumstances, the British had a very high probability of victory. Those who thought the Gurkas had won said that was the most likely outcome under the circumstances—and so forth. (Based on data of Fischhoff, 1975.)

for intangible, private events such as expectations and emotions (Levine, 1997). After people find out how an event turns out, they remember best the previous facts that fit with the final outcome. From the facts that stand out in their memory, they reconstruct what they "must have" previously thought.

SOMETHING TO THINK ABOUT

Can you interpret people's beliefs that they had a "psychic hunch" in terms of hindsight bias? ✳

Eyewitness Identifications

Suppose you witness a crime: several hours, days, or weeks later, the police ask you to identify the culprit. You still remember the face somewhat, but your memory has faded. To help you, the police offer you a lineup of five or so possible suspects and ask whether you recognize any of them as the guilty party. Might you make a mistake?

Psychologists have conducted studies with staged crimes and various kinds of lineups. They find that witnesses are not always accurate. Witnesses who express higher confidence tend to be more accurate, although they make mistakes too (Sporer, Penrod, Read, & Cutler, 1995). When the police try to develop an unbiased lineup, they often start with someone they suspect and then add others who look similar. (If the witness described a young man with a mustache, it would obviously be unfair to set up a lineup with one young, mustached man and four older, clean-shaven men.) Unfortunately, a lineup with the main suspect and others chosen because they resemble the suspect is also biased, for a subtler reason (Wogalter, Marwitz, & Leonard, 1992): If all the others are selected because they resemble the suspect, the suspect stands out as the one who is *most similar* to all the others in the group! For instance, examine the lineup in Figure 7.26.

 TRY IT YOUR-SELF Without even having witnessed the crime, would you be more likely to pick out one of these people than the others? (Check answer D, page 265.) It is difficult to make a lineup fair (Wells, 1993; Wogalter, Marwitz, &

Leonard, 1992). The point is that, because memory is so suggestible, it is difficult to ask a totally unbiased, nonsuggestive question.

The "False Memory" Controversy

Occasionally, someone tells a therapist about vague unpleasant feelings, and the therapist replies, "Symptoms like yours are usually found among people who were abused, especially sexually abused, in childhood. Do you think you were?" In some cases, the client says yes; in other cases, the client says no, and the therapist accepts the denial and moves on to other topics. A major controversy has arisen, however, about cases in which a therapist does not accept "no" for an answer: "The fact that you can't remember doesn't mean that it didn't happen. It may have been so painful that you repressed it." The therapist may then recommend hypnosis, repeated attempts to remember, or other techniques. Several sessions later, the client may say, "It's starting to come back to me . . . I think I do remember . . . ." *Reports of long-lost memories, prompted by clinical techniques,* are known as **recovered memories.**

Sexual abuse in childhood does occur, and no one knows how often. Some abused children do develop long-lasting psychological scars. But when people claim to recover long-forgotten memories, should we assume their reports to be accurate? Some reports are bizarre. In one case, two sisters accused their father of raping them many times, both vaginally and anally, bringing his friends over on Friday nights to rape them, forcing them to participate in satanic rituals that included cannibalism, the slaughter of babies, and so forth (Wright, 1994). The sisters had not remembered any of these events until they spoke with a therapist. In another case, a group of 3- and 4-year-old children, after urgings from a therapist, accused their Sunday school teacher of sexually abusing them with a curling iron, forcing them to drink blood and urine, hanging them upside down from a chandelier, dunking them in toilets, and killing an

| Suspect # 1 | Suspect # 2 | Suspect # 3 | Suspect # 4 | Suspect # 5 |

FIGURE 7.26   Here, a lineup is composed of one "suspect" and others chosen to resemble the suspect. Does one of these stand out as the probable suspect? (Check answer D, page 265.)

elephant and a giraffe during Sunday school class (Gardner, 1994). In neither of these cases, nor in several similar cases, was there any physical evidence to support the claims—scarred tissues or giraffe bones, for example.

Recovered-memory claims are not always so bizarre, but their accuracy is almost always uncertain. Suppose a 30-year-old woman claims that her father sexually abused her when she was 10. She had not remembered it until now, when her therapist repeatedly asked her to imagine "what it would have been like if she had been abused." In almost all cases, it is impossible to check the accuracy of such recovered memories. One might consult school records of long ago to see whether they described a happy, healthy child or one showing physical and emotional scars, but even the best of such records are incomplete and possibly misleading. Psychological researchers can, however, address these questions: When people have miserable, abusive experiences, are they likely to forget them for a long time? And is it possible to persuade someone to "remember" an event that never actually happened, just by suggesting it?

Repression

Sigmund Freud, whom we shall consider more fully in Chapter 13, introduced the term **repression** as *the process of moving a memory, motivation, or emotion from the conscious mind to the unconscious mind.* Although many therapists continue to use the concept of repression, the research on memory and forgetting has not supported it (Holmes, 1990). Controlled experiments designed to produce repression have produced small, inconsistent, ambiguous effects.

Other studies have examined people known to have had dreadful experiences. One study examined 16 children who had witnessed the murder of one of their parents. All had recurring nightmares, haunting thoughts, and painful flashbacks of the experience; none showed any indication of forgetting or repressing the memories (Malmquist, 1986). Another study examined 20 children who, at ages less than 5 years old, had survived a plane crash, or had been kidnapped, or had been forced to participate in the filming of pornographic movies. Of those who were at least 3 years old at the time of the trauma, 6 out of 9 had good recall of the events even years later, and the other 3 had partial memories—in contrast to the poor recall of most early childhood experiences (Terr, 1988). From such results, we cannot conclude that repression never occurs. (It is almost impossible to prove that something *doesn't* exist. Could you prove that unicorns don't exist?) However, the harder it is to demonstrate a phenomenon, the rarer it must be in real life—if it exists at all.

People do *forget* some painful memories, especially from early childhood, if given enough time. But because we are as likely to forget happy memories as unhappy ones—maybe even more likely—we should not attribute our memory loss to repression.

WHAT'S THE EVIDENCE?
Suggestions and False Memories

Critics of the concept of recovered memories have suggested that a therapist, by repeatedly suggesting that a client recall certain kinds of memories, can unintentionally "implant" a **false memory,** *a report that someone believes to be a memory but that does not actually correspond to real events* (Lindsay & Read, 1994; Loftus, 1993). Researchers cannot determine whether a particular report of recovered memory was true or false, but they can test how easy it is to implant a false memory. We shall examine three representative experiments.

EXPERIMENT I

Hypothesis If people are asked questions that suggest or presuppose a certain fact, many people will later report remembering that "fact," even if it never happened.

Method Elizabeth Loftus (1975) asked two groups of students to watch a videotape of an automobile accident. Then she asked one group but not the other, "Did you see the children getting on the school bus?" In fact, the videotape did not show a school bus. A week later, she asked both groups 20 new questions about the accident, including this one: "Did you see a school bus in the film?"

Results Of the first group (those who were asked about seeing children get on a school bus), 26% reported that they had seen a school bus; of the second group, only 6% said they had seen a school bus.

Interpretation The question "Did you see the children getting on the school bus?" presupposes that there *was* a school bus in the film. Some of the students who heard that question reconstructed what happened by combining what they actually saw with what they believed might reasonably have happened and what someone (the researcher) had suggested to them afterward.

EXPERIMENT 2

The first experiment demonstrated that a suggestion can distort memories of something that people watched. But could a suggestion also distort a personal memory, or even implant a memory of an experience that never really occurred?

Hypothesis If people are told about a childhood event by people they trust, they will come to remember it as something they actually experienced, even if in fact they did not.

Method The participants, aged 18 to 53, were told that the study concerned their memories of childhood. Each was given four paragraphs; each paragraph described a different event. Three of the events had actually happened.

(The experimenters had contacted parents to get descriptions of childhood events.) A fourth event was a plausible story about getting lost, which had not actually happened, described in terms of family members. An example for one Vietnamese woman: "You, your Mom, Tien and Tuan, all went to the Bremerton K-Mart. You must have been five years old at the time. Your Mom gave each of you some money to get a blueberry ICEE. You ran ahead to get into the line first, and somehow lost your way in the store. Tien found you crying to an elderly Chinese woman. You three then went together to get an ICEE."

After reading the four paragraphs, each participant was asked to write whatever additional details they could remember of the event. They were asked to try again one week later, and then again after another week.

Results Of 24 participants, 6 reported remembering the suggested (false) event. Participants generally described the false memories in fewer words than the correct memories, but some did provide a fair amount of "additional detail." The woman in the example above said, "I vaguely remember walking around K-Mart crying and looking for Tien and Tuan. I thought I was lost forever. I went to the shoe department, because we always spent a lot of time there. I went to the handkerchief place because we were there last. I circled all over the store it seemed 10 times. I just remember walking around crying. I do not remember the Chinese woman, or the ICEE (but it would be raspberry ICEE if I was getting an ICEE) part. I don't even remember being found" (Loftus, Feldman, & Dashiell, 1995).

Interpretation A simple suggestion can provoke some people to recall a personal experience in moderate detail, even though the event never happened. Granted, the suggestion affected fewer than half of the people tested, and most of them reported only vague memories. Still, the researchers used only a brief suggestion, without hypnosis or other techniques that probably would have increased the effect.

EXPERIMENT 3

Defenders of the concept of recovered memories are not impressed with false memories such as being lost at a Kmart. Even if this woman was not lost at Kmart at age 5, she was probably lost somewhere else at some other time. Implanting a false memory of such a likely event does not demonstrate that one could implant a false memory of, say, childhood sexual abuse.

To this criticism, researchers reply that it would be unethical to try to implant memories of something so traumatic. However, it is possible to compare the difficulty of implanting a memory of a reasonably likely event with an implanted memory of an implausible one.

Hypothesis When adults hear a suggestion about a childhood religious experience, they will be more likely to accept it and claim to remember it if it pertains to the kind of ceremony they practice in their own religion. They will probably not accept a suggestion about a ceremony from another religion.

Method The experimenters began by contacting the mothers of 29 Roman Catholic and 22 Jewish teenage girls. All had been active in their religious practices through childhood and into the present. The mothers provided descriptions of events (not necessarily religious) that actually happened to their daughters at about age 8.

The experimenters told each girl five brief episodes and asked them to provide any additional details they could remember. Three of these were real events, as described by the mothers. Another one was a false event that would be plausible to the Catholic girls but not to the Jewish girls: taking Communion and returning to the wrong seat. The other was a false event that should be plausible to the Jews but not to the Catholics: conducting Friday night prayers before sunset and dropping the bread.

Results Most girls remembered all three of the correct events and provided additional information. Here are the results for the false events (Pezdek, Finger, & Hodge, 1997):

	Recalled neither	Recalled the Catholic event	Recalled the Jewish event	Recalled both
Catholic girls (total of 29)	19	7	1	2
Jewish girls (total of 22)	19	0	3	0

Interpretation As predicted, it was easier to implant plausible than implausible memories, but three of the Catholic girls did report false memories corresponding to a Jewish ceremony. Evidently, the more likely a suggested event and the more similar it is to one's actual experience, the easier it is to implant a false memory. But there is probably no sharp line between implantable and nonimplantable memories.

So, what conclusion should we draw about the possibility of implanting false memories of sexual abuse and the like? The experiments described here are just examples of a large body of research, but they all follow about the same pattern: Researchers use either a single suggestion or a few repetitions. The more repetitions, the bigger the effect (Zaragoza & Mitchell, 1996). The suggestions pertain to nontraumatic events, and the participants are normal people with no known psychological problems. In contrast, therapists who are seeking recovered memories use repeated suggestions, sometimes accompanied by hypnosis or other techniques. They suggest highly traumatic experiences, and they deal with troubled people. Obviously, we cannot directly extrapolate from one to the other. In particular, the research evidence does not demonstrate that all recovered memories must be false (Pope, 1996).

On the other hand, it is clearly unfair to dismiss the research simply because it has not demonstrated false memories of sexual abuse or satanic rituals. Ethically, researchers cannot attempt such, and they should not need to do so. If you can build a small fire with a few twigs, you shouldn't have to demonstrate that, with more fuel, you could build a bigger fire.

The main conclusion is that a therapist, police investigator, or anyone else who repeatedly suggests that something "might have" or "must have" occurred runs a major risk of implanting or distorting a memory. People who are seeking the truth need to become more aware of this risk and more cautious about the questions they ask. Furthermore, if someone claims to have recovered a long-forgotten memory, other people should treat it as no more than a hypothesis, one that might be true but could be false. Such testimony, by itself, in the absence of supporting evidence, should not be a basis for making an arrest, breaking up a family, or taking any other drastic action.

✳ ✳ ✳

Children as Eyewitnesses

Finally, what about children who are witnesses or victims of a crime? Young children forget more rapidly than adults do, and they sometimes confuse fantasy with reality. Are they therefore unreliable as witnesses?

They do tend to be more vulnerable than adults are to suggestion, and they can quickly become unreliable witnesses if the interviewers ask the wrong kind of questions. In one study, preschool children were repeatedly asked to "think about" getting their hand caught in a mousetrap. Eventually, most of them provided elaborate details about the injury and the ensuing trip to the hospital. They provided as much detail about this false memory as about a real injury, and they gave every indication of believing their reports (Ceci, 1995).

However, in two other studies, children were asked about the events of their medical examinations at delays ranging from 3 days to 6 weeks after the event. Children of ages 3 to 7 reported the events accurately and in detail. Researchers then asked suggestive or leading questions such as "Did the nurse cut your hair?" and "Did the person hit you?" Even at younger ages, only a few children reported events that had not happened (Baker-Ward, Gordon, Ornstein, Larus, & Clubb, 1993; Goodman, Aman, & Hirschman, 1987). These results, of course, do not deny that one could induce children to give false testimony by more prolonged and insistent suggestions, but they do indicate that children can give accurate reports under favorable circumstances.

The general recommendations for children's eyewitness testimony are as follows: If a child is simply asked to describe the events, in a nonthreatening atmosphere, without suggestions or pressure, reasonably soon after the event, even children as young as 3 can be believable (Ceci & Bruck, 1993). Asking a child the same questions repeatedly within a single interview, though, can confuse the child. (Some will change their answers on the assumption that their first answer must have been wrong.) However, asking the child to repeat the story every few days may help the child to remember; this may be necessary if the child is to testify in a trial many months later (Poole & White, 1995).

SOMETHING TO THINK ABOUT

Some people claim to have been abducted by aliens from another planet. Presuming that they are not deliberately lying to get attention, that they are not mentally ill, and that they were not in fact abducted by aliens, how might we explain their reports? ✳

THE MESSAGE
Memories, True, False, and Uncertain

A historian who writes about times long ago reconstructs events based on the remaining records and the historian's inferences about what must have happened. We do the same with our own memories. If someone suggests that "surely you remember the time when you got lost at Kmart . . . ," you might reconstruct a memory of something that did not actually happen. Have you ever reminisced with someone about an event from years ago, only to discover that the two of you remembered that event very differently? If you want to record an event accurately forever, take notes or photographs. Your notes or photos will fade, too, but at least they won't be transformed into something entirely different.

He: *We met at nine.*
She: *We met at eight.*
He: *I was on time.*
She: *No, you were late.*
He: *Ah, yes! I remember it well.*
　　We dined with friends.
She: *We dined alone.*
He: *A tenor sang.*
She: *A baritone.*
He: *Ah, yes! I remember it well.*
　　That dazzling April moon!
She: *There was none that night.*
　　And the month was June.
He: *That's right! That's right!*
She: *It warms my heart to know that you*
　　Remember still the way you do.
He: *Ah, yes! I remember it well.*

—"I REMEMBER IT WELL" FROM THE MUSICAL *GIGI*
BY ALAN JAY LERNER AND FREDERICK LOEWE

S U M M A R Y

✳ *Reconstruction.* When remembering stories or events from their own lives, people recall some of the facts and fill in the gaps, based on logical inferences of what must have happened. They rely particularly heavily on inferences when they are uncertain about their memory of the events. (page 258)

✳ *Reconstructions from a word list.* If people read or hear a list of related words and try to recall them, they are likely to include closely related words that were not on the list. (page 258)

✳ *Hindsight bias.* People often revise their memories of what they previously expected, saying that how events turned out was what they had expected all along. (page 259)

✳ *Eyewitness testimony.* Eyewitness testimony is sometimes accurate, sometimes not. Lineups can bias a witness toward identifying a particular suspect. (page 261)

✳ *False memory debate.* Some therapists have used hypnosis or very suggestive lines of questioning to try to help people remember painful experiences. Some of the reported memories include extreme or bizarre events that people claim they experienced long ago but did not remember until much later. It is important to try to distinguish actual cases of abuse from false memories that depend on suggestion. (page 261)

Suggestion for Further Reading

Schacter, D. (Ed.) (1995). *Memory distortion.* Cambridge, MA: Harvard University Press. Collection of chapters about false memories and other kinds of distorted memories.

Terms

reconstruction   putting together an account of past events, based partly on memories and partly on expectations of what must have happened (page 258)

hindsight bias   the tendency to mold our recollection of the past to fit how events later turned out (page 260)

recovered memory   a report of a long-lost memory, prompted by clinical techniques (page 261)

repression   according to Freudian theory, the process of moving a memory, motivation, or emotion from the conscious mind to the unconscious mind (page 262)

false memory   a report that someone believes to be a memory but that does not actually correspond to real events (page 262)

Answer to Question in the Text

D. Face #5 is the suspect. All the others have been chosen to resemble him, but each has a different unusual feature. (page 261)

Web Resources

False Memory Syndrome Foundation home page
advicom.net/~fitz/fmsf/
The scientific community in general does not support the notion that recovered memories are reliable. *The Skeptic* magazine addresses the issue; the APA delivers a policy statement and a Q&A about memories of childhood abuse.

Cognition and Language

Consider the statement, "This sentence is false." Is the statement itself true or false? Declaring the statement to be true agrees with its own assessment that it is false. But declaring it to be false would make its assessment correct.

A sentence about itself, called a *self-referential* sentence, can be utterly confusing, like the one above. It can also be true (e.g., "This sentence consists of six words"), false ("Anyone who reads this sentence will be suddenly transported to the planet Neptune"), untestable ("Whenever no one is reading this sentence, it changes into the passive voice"), or amusing ("This sentence no verb" or "This sentence sofa includes an unnecessary word").

In this chapter, you will be asked to think about thinking, talk about talking, and read about reading. Doing so is self-referential, and if you try to "think about what you are thinking now," you can easily go into a confusing loop similar to the one in "This sentence is false." For that reason, among many others, psychological researchers focus as much as possible on results obtained from carefully controlled experiments, not just on what people say they think about their own thought processes.

Cognition includes both old knowledge (such as knowing how to read a blueprint) and the use of that knowledge in a new situation.

How do we think about categories of objects?

How accurate are our mental images and maps?

To what extent can we control our attention, and do certain stimuli capture it automatically?

Cognition is psychologists' word for *thinking, gaining knowledge, and dealing with knowledge.* Cognitive psychologists study how people think, how they acquire knowledge, what they know, how they imagine, and how they solve problems. They also deal with how people organize their thoughts into language and communicate with others.

Perhaps it seems to you that cognitive psychology should be trivially simple. "If you want to find out what people think or what they know, why not just ask them?" Sometimes psychologists can and do ask them; however, in many cases, people are not fully aware of their own thought processes (Kihlstrom, Barnhardt, & Tataryn, 1992). Recall, for example, implicit memory, as discussed in Chapter 7: Sometimes you see or hear something that influences your behavior in the next minute or so, without your realizing it. Similarly, we often solve a problem so fast that we do not know how we did it.

Cognitive psychology increased in popularity during the 1950s through the 1970s, the era of vastly increased use of computers. Although brains and computers do not work the same way, computers provide a valuable way of modeling theories of cognitive processes. A researcher may say, "Imagine that cognitive processes work as follows. . . . Now let's program a computer to go through those same steps in the same order. If we then give the computer the same information that a human has, will it draw the same conclusions a human does and make the same errors?" In short, computer modeling provides a good method to test theories of cognition. Today, cognitive psychology uses a variety of methods to measure mental processes and to test theories about what we know and how we know it.

SOMETHING TO THINK ABOUT

The Turing Test, suggested by computer pioneer Alan Turing, proposes the following operational definition of artificial intelligence: A person poses questions to a human source and to a computer, both in another room. The human and the computer send back typewritten replies, which are identified only as coming from "source A" or "source B." If the questioner cannot determine which replies are coming from the computer, then the computer has passed a significant test of understanding.

Suppose a computer did pass the Turing Test. Would we then say that the computer "understands," just as a human does? Or would we say that it is merely mimicking human understanding? ✻

Categorization

An ancient Greek philosopher once wrote that we can never step into the same river twice. In a sense, of course, he was right; everything is constantly changing. However, we generally find it useful to think of the Nile as "the same" river from one minute to the next, even from one century to the next. It also suits our purposes to use "river" as a general concept, lumping together the Nile, the Amazon, the Mississippi, and thousands of others, despite their differences.

Forming useful categories enables us to make educated guesses about features we have never seen for ourselves (Anderson, 1991). For example, your concept of a river enables you to infer that a river that you have never seen probably has many of the features of familiar rivers, such as a flow of water, navigability by boats, a certain degree of curviness, and the presence of fish.

We often take our categories for granted, as if our own way of categorizing objects were the only possible way (Figure 8.1). But people in other cultures sometimes use categories that seem strange to us (Lakoff, 1987). The Japanese word *hon* refers to sticks, pencils, trees, hair, hits in baseball, shots in basketball, telephone calls, television programs, a mental contest between a Zen master and a student, and medical injections. Clearly, people from different cultures categorize objects in different ways.

How do people decide how to categorize objects? To understand thinking, we need to understand how we categorize.

Categorization by Prototypes

If you look up a word such as *river* in a dictionary, you will find a definition. Do we also look up our concepts in a mental dictionary to determine their meaning? In some cases, probably yes. For example, we think of the term *bachelor* as an unmarried male. Because we would not ordinarily apply the term bachelor to a 3-year-old boy or to a Catholic priest, we might want to modify the definition to "a male who has never married but who could decide to get married." Such a definition pretty well explains the concept of a bachelor.

Few concepts can be so clearly defined, however. More frequently, we deal with loosely defined categories such as

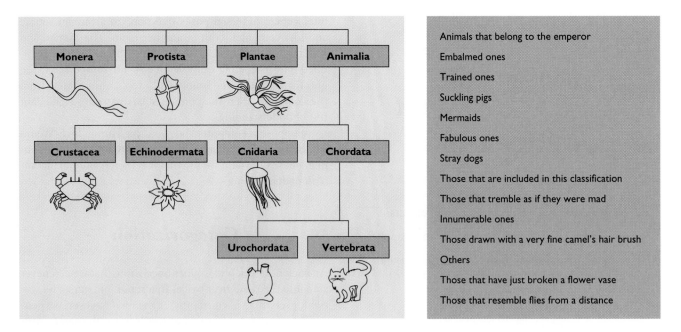

Animals that belong to the emperor

Embalmed ones

Trained ones

Suckling pigs

Mermaids

Fabulous ones

Stray dogs

Those that are included in this classification

Those that tremble as if they were mad

Innumerable ones

Those drawn with a very fine camel's hair brush

Others

Those that have just broken a flower vase

Those that resemble flies from a distance

FIGURE 8.1 Left: A much-abridged chart of the current scientific classification of the animal kingdom. Right: An alleged listing from an ancient Chinese encyclopedia—actually the product of someone's imagination (Rosch, 1978). The point is that there are many ways to categorize animals or anything else, and some methods of categorizing are better than others.

interesting novels or embarrassing experiences, in which we could not list the defining features. Even for such a simple, everyday concept as a table, we have trouble describing the necessary and sufficient features: Most tables are made of wood, but they need not be. Most have four legs, but they can have more or fewer. The top surface must be reasonably flat, but not everything with a flat surface is a table.

According to Eleanor Rosch (1978; Rosch & Mervis, 1975), many categories are defined by *familiar or typical examples* called **prototypes.** According to the categorization by prototypes approach, we decide whether an object belongs to a category by determining how well it resembles the protypical members of that category.

For example, we define the category *vehicle* by giving examples: *car, bus, train, airplane, boat.* To decide whether another object is a vehicle, we compare it to these examples. If we ask people whether a truck is a vehicle, they quickly respond "yes." They have longer reaction times to the atypical example *blimp* and still longer reaction times to *elevator* or *water skis.* The main point of Rosch's prototype approach is that category membership can be a matter of degree.

Conceptual Networks

TRY IT YOUR-SELF Choose any word and try to think about just that one word, nothing else, for 30 seconds. Why is this task so difficult? Because any word reminds you of something else. You do not store words in your brain in isolation, but in networks of related ideas.

First, you might link your word to subcategories and supercategories. For example, you link the word *bird* to more general and more specific terms as follows:

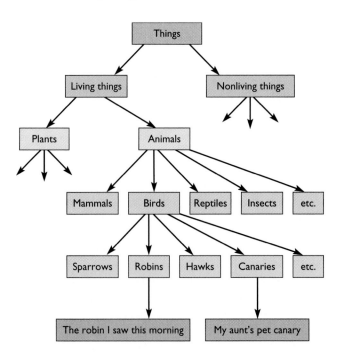

Researchers can demonstrate the reality of this kind of hierarchy (Collins & Quillian, 1969, 1970). Suppose you are asked several true-false questions about canaries:

Canaries are yellow.
Canaries sing.
Canaries lay eggs.
Canaries have feathers.
Canaries have skin.

Almost everyone will correctly answer "true" to all five items. As in many cognitive psychology experiments, the dependent variable is the reaction time (speed of answering). If you are like most people, your response is fastest on the *yellow* and *sing* items, a bit slower (in milliseconds) on the *eggs* and *feathers* items, and still slower on the *skin* item. Why? It is because yellowness and singing are distinctive, well-known characteristics of canaries. You probably do not think of eggs or feathers as specific features of canaries; instead you reason (quickly), "Canaries are birds, and birds lay eggs. So canaries lay eggs." Skin is not a particularly distinctive feature of canaries or even of birds, so you have to reason, "Canaries are birds and birds are animals. Animals have skin, so canaries must have skin."

Even though this way of categorizing things causes you slight delays in answering certain questions, such as whether canaries have skin, it actually saves you time and effort in the long run. When you learn that all birds have body temperatures above 40° C., you don't have to learn this fact again separately for every species of bird. When you learn that all animals have mitochondria in their cells, you don't have to relearn that fact for every animal species. Thus, reasoning in terms of categories and subcategories makes our lives easier.

CONCEPT CHECK

1. Which would take longer to answer: whether fashion models wear dresses, or whether fashion models sometimes get sick? Why? (Check your answer on page 278.)

We also link a word or concept to other concepts that relate to it in a variety of ways. Figure 8.2 shows a possible network of conceptual links for one person (Collins & Loftus, 1975). The links will, of course, vary from one person to another and from one moment to another. Suppose this network describes your own concepts. *When you hear about or think about one of the concepts shown in this figure, exciting that concept will activate, or prime, the concepts linked to it* (Collins & Loftus, 1975). The process of doing so is called **spreading activation.** As a result of spreading activation, thinking of one concept makes it easier to think of its related concepts also. For example, if you hear the word *flowers,* you are temporarily more likely than usual to think of the word *roses.* If you hear *flowers* and then see the word *roses* flashed briefly on a screen or hear it spoken very softly, your probability of identifying *roses* correctly will be higher than usual. Spreading activation can also combine from two sources. For

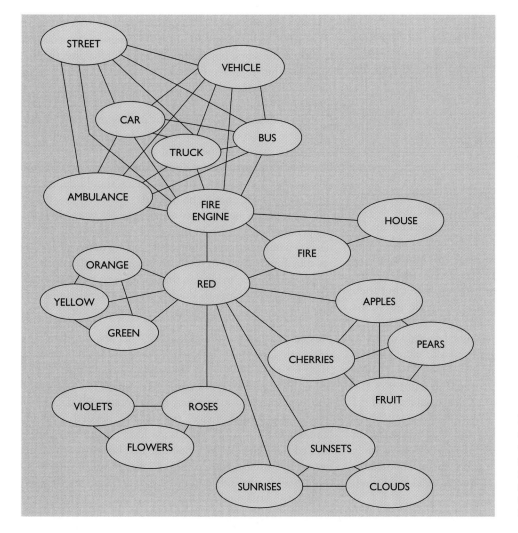

FIGURE 8.2 We link each concept to a variety of other related concepts. Any stimulus that activates one of these concepts will also partly activate (or "prime") the ones that are linked to it. (From Collins & Loftus, 1975.)

example, if you hear the words *flowers* and *red,* you have an even higher probability of thinking of the word *roses.*

As this theory would predict, a concept that is linked to many other concepts will activate each of them only slightly, whereas a concept that is linked to only a few will activate them more strongly. For example, *fruit* is linked with a relatively small number of items—more than shown in Figure 8.2, but still not an enormous number. The concept *red* is linked to a much larger number of other items. Suppose we ask various people the following questions and then measure their speed of response:

What is something red that is a fruit?
What is something that is a fruit and is red?

On average, people respond slightly faster to the second question, and the spreading-activation theory explains why (Collins & Loftus, 1975). With the first question, *red* produces only a small spreading activation for *apple* (the most likely correct answer). So the person answering the question does not get much of a start on this question until hearing the word *fruit*. With the second question, the word *fruit* provides a good start and has significantly activated *apple* before the person hears *red*.

CONCEPT CHECK

2. Would people respond faster to naming "something that makes sounds and tells time" or "something that tells time and makes sounds"? (Check your answer on page 278.)

Mental Imagery

When people think about three-dimensional objects or about places where they have been, do their mental images actually resemble vision? You might think this is a trivial question that does not need to be researched: "Of course mental images are like real vision," you might reply. "I see mental images all the time." Your self-reports are not solid evidence, however. After all, people sometimes insist that they have a clear mental image of an object but then find that they cannot correctly answer simple questions about it.

To illustrate: Imagine a simple cube balanced with one point (corner) on the table and the opposite point straight up. Imagine that you are holding the highest point with one finger. Now, with a finger of the opposite hand, point to all the remaining corners of the cube. How many corners do you touch?

You probably will say that you answered this question by "picturing" a cube in your mind as if you were actually seeing it. However, most people answer the question incorrectly, and only a few get the right answer quickly (Hinton, 1979). (Check answer A, page 278.)

So our mental images are sometimes wrong. Further, it is not obvious that we need mental images to answer visual or spatial questions. Computers can answer such questions quite accurately without drawing little pictures inside themselves. Can we demonstrate that mental images are at least sometimes useful, though, and that they have some of the properties we ordinarily associate with vision? Answering this question was one of the early triumphs of experimental research in cognitive psychology.

WHAT'S THE EVIDENCE?
Mental Imagery

Roger Shepard and Jacqueline Metzler (1971) conducted a classic study of how humans solve visual problems. They reasoned that, if people actually visualize mental images, then the time it takes them to rotate a mental image should be similar to the time it takes to rotate a real object.

Hypothesis When people have to rotate a mental image to answer a question, the farther they have to rotate it, the longer it will take them to answer the question.

Method The experimenters showed subjects pairs of two-dimensional drawings of three-dimensional objects, as in Figure 8.3 and asked whether the drawings in each pair represented the same object rotated in different directions or whether they represented different objects. (Try to answer this question yourself before reading further. Then, check answer B, page 278.)

The subjects could answer by pulling one lever to indicate *same* and another lever to indicate *different.* When the correct answer was *same,* a subject might determine that answer by rotating a mental image of the first picture until it matched the second. If so, the delay should depend on how far the image had to be rotated.

The delays before answering *different* were generally longer and less consistent than those for answering *same*— as is generally the case. Subjects could answer *same* as soon as they found a way to rotate the first object to match the second. However, to be sure that the objects were different, subjects might have to double-check several times and imagine more than one way of rotating the object.

Results Subjects were almost 97% accurate in determining both *same* and *different.* As predicted, their reaction time for responding *same* depended on the angular difference in orientation between the two views. For example, if the first image of a pair had to be rotated 30 degrees to match the second image, the subject needed a certain amount of time to pull the *same* lever. If the two images looked the same after the first one had been rotated 60 degrees, the subject took twice as long to pull the lever. In other words, the subjects reacted as if they were actually watching a little model of the object rotate in their head; the

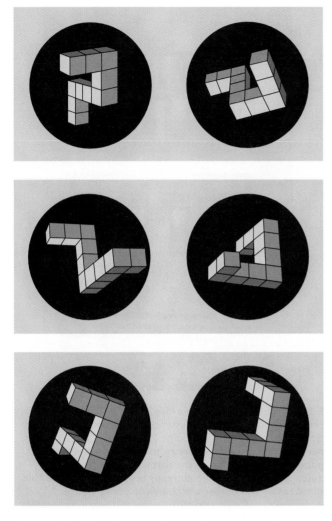

FIGURE 8.3 Examples of pairs of drawings used in an experiment by Shepard and Metzler (1971). Do the drawings for each pair represent the same object being rotated, or are they different objects? (See answer B on page 278.)

more the object needed to be rotated, the longer they took to determine the answer.

Interpretation Viewing a mental image is at least partly like real vision.

Whenever possible, researchers try to test a hypothesis in different ways. Even what appears to be an excellent experiment may have some hidden flaw or be subject to an alternative explanation. An alternative way of studying visual imagery is to ask people to imagine various objects while researchers record their eye movements. One study found that, while people were imagining objects, their eyes moved almost the same way as when they were actually looking at the same objects (Brandt & Stark, 1997). Even this study, of course, does not fully establish the relationship between imagined vision and real vision, but it helps to confirm a similarity.

✳   ✳   ✳

SOMETHING TO THINK ABOUT

Some people report that they have auditory images as well as visual images. They "hear" words or songs "in their head." What kind of evidence would we need to test this claim? ✳

Using Mental Images: Cognitive Maps

You are staying at a hotel in an unfamiliar city. You walk a few blocks to get to a museum; then you turn and walk in another direction to get to a restaurant; after dinner, you turn again and walk to a theater. After the performance, how do you get back to the hotel? Do you retrace all of your steps? Can you find a shorter route? Or do you give up and hail a cab?

If you can find your way back, you do so by using a **cognitive map,** *a mental image of a spatial arrangement.* One way to measure the accuracy of people's cognitive maps is to test how well they can find the route from one place to another. Another way is to ask them to draw a map. As you might expect, people draw a more complete map of the areas they are most familiar with. When students try to draw a map of their college campus, they generally include the central buildings on campus and the buildings they enter most frequently (Saarinen, 1973). The longer students have been on campus, the more detail they include (Cohen & Cohen, 1985).

The errors people make in their cognitive maps follow some interesting patterns. First, they tend to remember street angles as being close to 90 degrees, even when they are not (Moar & Bower, 1983). We can easily understand that error. For practical purposes, all we need to remember is "go three blocks and turn left" or "go two blocks and turn right"; we do not burden our memory by recalling "turn 72 degrees to the right."

Second, people generally imagine geographic areas as being aligned neatly along a north-to-south axis and an east-to-west axis (Stevens & Coupe, 1978; B. Tversky, 1981). Try to answer these questions, for example: Which city is farther west—Reno, Nevada, or Los Angeles, California? And which is farther north—Philadelphia, Pennsylvania, or Rome, Italy? Most people reason that, because California is west of Nevada, Los Angeles is "obviously" west of Reno. (Figure 8.4 shows the true position of the cities.) Rome is in southern Europe, and Philadelphia is in the northern part of the United States; therefore, Philadelphia should be north of Rome, right? In fact, Rome is north of Philadelphia.

You now see the differences between a cognitive map and a real map: Cognitive maps, like other mental images, highlight some details, distort some, and omit others. Nevertheless, they are accurate enough for most practical purposes.

Attention

Much of intelligent behavior depends on successfully managing your attention. For example, while driving a car, you might devote most of your attention to the conversation, but

FIGURE 8.4 Logical versus actual: location of Reno and Los Angeles. Most people imagine that Los Angeles is farther west because California is west of Nevada.

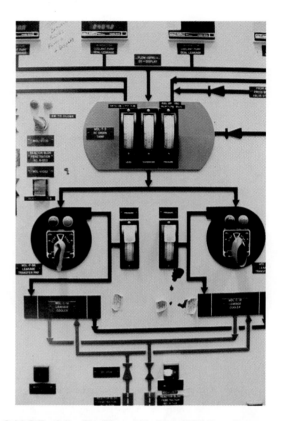

FIGURE 8.5 The Three Mile Island TMI-2 nuclear power plant had a complex and confusing control system, a small portion of which is shown here. Some of the important gauges were not easily visible to the operators, some of the gauges were poorly labeled, and many of the alarm signals had ambiguous meanings. The nuclear plant currently in operation at Three Mile Island has a much simpler and clearer operating system.

if the traffic gets bad or if you have to look for a particular street, you might shift your attention more to your driving. You might even tell your friend to be quiet until you find your turn. People who either cannot shift their attention or shift it too easily, have trouble in school, on the job, and in everyday life.

Very complex tasks overload almost anyone's attention span. For example, Figure 8.5 shows a small part of the control room of the Three Mile Island nuclear power plant as it looked before the nearly disastrous accident in 1979. You notice immediately the enormous number of knobs and gauges; a nuclear power plant is, after all, a complicated system. What you cannot see in the picture is that, in certain cases, the knob that controlled a variable was in one place and the gauge measuring that variable was in another place. After the 1979 accident, ergonomists (human factors psychologists) helped redesign the plant so that mere humans could master the task of running it.

Preattentive and Attentive Processes

Sometimes you recognize familiar patterns automatically, without requiring any attention or working memory (Schneider & Shiffrin, 1977; Shiffrin & Schneider, 1977). For example, you might drive home along a familiar route, recognizing the landmarks and turning at the correct time even while thinking about something else. When you reach your driveway, you might realize that you do not even remember driving there. In other situations, you have to pay careful attention to what you are doing, one step at a time, as when you write an essay for your English class and have to tell your friends not to interrupt you until you finish. To illustrate the difference between these two types of processing, first examine Figure 8.6. In each part of the figure, find the circle that is intersected by a vertical line.

You probably spotted the vertical line in *b* about as quickly as the vertical line in *a,* even though *b* has far more distracters (circles without lines) (Treisman & Souther,

1985). Apparently, people examine all the circles *in parallel.* That is, we can look at all the circles at once; finding the vertical line does not require attending to one circle at a time. Finding the line relies on a **preattentive process**— *a procedure for extracting information automatically and simultaneously across a large portion of the visual field* (Enns & Rensink, 1990).

Now look at Figure 8.7. Each part contains several pentagons, most of them pointing upward. Find the one pentagon in each part that points downward.

Most people take longer to find the pentagon pointing down in part *b* than in part *a,* because part *b* contains more distracters. The greater the number of distracters, the longer it takes to find the pentagon that is different; people must turn their attention to one pentagon at a time until they come to the correct one. In contrast to the preceding example, this task requires an **attentive process**—*a procedure that considers only one part of the visual field at a time.* An attentive process is ordinarily a *serial* process, because a person must attend to each part one after another in a series.

 Here is another example of a preattentive or automatic process: Read the following instructions and then examine Figure 8.8 on page 276:

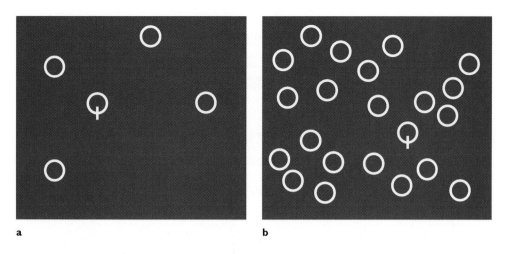

FIGURE 8.6 Demonstration of preattentive processes: Find the vertical line in each part. Most people find it about equally fast in both parts.

Notice the blocks of color at the top of the figure. Scanning from left to right, give the name of each color as fast as you can. Then notice the nonsense syllables printed in different colors in the center of the figure. Don't try to pronounce them; just say the color of each one as fast as possible. Then turn to the real words at the bottom. Don't read them; quickly state the color in which each one is printed.

Most people find it very difficult not to read the words at the bottom of the figure. After all the practice you have had reading English, you can hardly bring yourself to look at the word RED, written in green letters, and say "green." *The tendency to read the word, instead of saying the color of ink as instructed,* is known as the **Stroop effect,** after the psychologist who discovered it. The effect is particularly strong when the discrepancy is small between the word and the color of the ink. That is, it is difficult enough to look at the word YELLOW in blue ink and say "blue"; it is even more difficult to look at YELLOW in orange ink and say "orange" (Klopfer, 1996).

With the Stroop effect, preattentive or automatic processing acts as interference, but in many situations we can harness it to our advantage. For example, if you were an ergonomist designing a piece of machinery, you could design warning signs that stand out by use of preattentive processes: The gauges in both the top and bottom rows of Figure 8.9 represent the current measurements of several

items. If the machine is running properly, the first gauge should read about 70, the second should read about 40, the third should read about 30, and the fourth should read about 10. Note that, in the bottom row, all the safe readings point in the same direction, so an operator can detect a dangerous reading quickly, preattentively. In the top row, a person must attend to one gauge at a time, however.

The Attentional Blink

Sometimes you can do two things at once, especially if one of them is a simple, routine task such as driving your car down a familiar road. However, when any stimulus catches your attention, it briefly blocks your attention to anything else. Psychologists speak of a "perceptual bottleneck," implying that only one stimulus at a time can get through to your attentional processor (Pashler, 1994).

The clearest demonstration of this principle is a phenomenon called the **attentional blink,** which was named by analogy to a blink of the eyes; during the moment it takes you to blink, you cannot see anything. Similarly, *during the moment after perceiving one stimulus, it is difficult to attend to something else.*

For example, consider the display shown in Figure 8.10. Participants watched a screen that briefly displayed two letters, one in green and one in red. A nonsense pat-

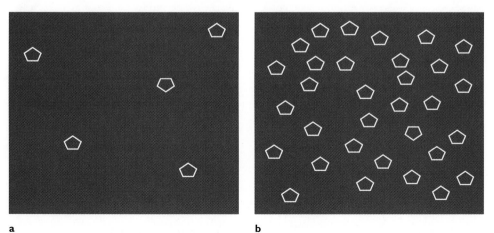

FIGURE 8.7 Demonstration of attentive processes: Find the pentagon pointing down in each part. Most people take longer to find it in part b.

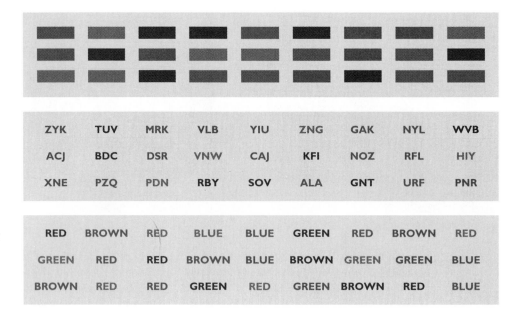

ZYK	TUV	MRK	VLB	YIU	ZNG	GAK	NYL	WVB
ACJ	BDC	DSR	VNW	CAJ	KFI	NOZ	RFL	HIY
XNE	PZQ	PDN	RBY	SOV	ALA	GNT	URF	PNR

RED	BROWN	RED	BLUE	BLUE	GREEN	RED	BROWN	RED
GREEN	RED	RED	BROWN	BLUE	BROWN	GREEN	GREEN	BLUE
BROWN	RED	RED	GREEN	RED	GREEN	BROWN	RED	BLUE

FIGURE 8.8 Read (left to right) the color of the ink in each part. Try to ignore the words themselves. Your difficulties on the lowest part illustrate the Stroop effect.

tern followed to make the identification more difficult. If the two letters appeared on the screen simultaneously, participants could identify both of them with reasonable accuracy. However, if one letter preceded the other, participants named the first one correctly but had more trouble with the second one. The interference was especially severe with a delay of 200 milliseconds(ms) but still noticeable at a delay of 600ms (Duncan, Ward, & Shapiro, 1994). Similar results occur with many kinds of stimuli: Someone sees a letter or a word or hears a sound and then another one of the same kind; the result is decreased identification of the second one (Duncan, Martens, & Ward, 1997).

This period of several tenths of a second after presentation of the first stimulus is the attentional blink, the time when it is hard to register a second stimulus. What happens to information that is presented during the attentional

blink? The brain does not shut it out completely. Evoked potentials recorded from the scalp indicate that the information reaches the cerebral cortex (Luck, Vogel, & Shapiro, 1996). Also, although you would ordinarily ignore a word or name you read during the attentional blink, you do notice it if it is your own name (Shapiro, Caldwell, & Sorensen, 1997).

CONCEPT CHECK

3. Suppose you are in a field full of brownish bushes and one brown rabbit that is not moving. If you want to find the rabbit, will you rely on attentive or nonattentive processes? What if the field has many stationary rabbits and one that is hopping? Will you then find it by attentive or nonattentive processes? (Check your answer on page 278.)

FIGURE 8.9 Each gauge represents a measurement of a different variable in a machine, such as an airplane. The top row shows one way of presenting the information. The operator must check each gauge one at a time to find out whether the reading is within the safe range for that variable. The bottom row shows the information represented in a way that is easier to read. The safe range for each variable is rotated to the same visual position. At a glance, the operator can detect any reading outside the safe zone.

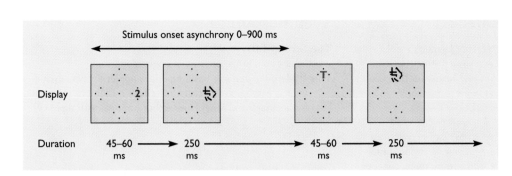

FIGURE 8.10 Participants watched a screen that showed a green number (2 or 5) and a red letter (L or T). Sometimes they appeared simultaneously, sometimes with a delay of up to 900 milliseconds between them. Immediately after each stimulus disappeared, an interfering pattern took its place. The results demonstrated interference from the first stimulus upon the second stimulus. (Modified from Duncan, Ward, & Shapiro, 1994).

THE MESSAGE
Thinking as a Laboratory Phenomenon

Throughout this module, we have considered experiments from which psychologists drew inferences about people's categorization, conceptual networks, cognitive maps, and attention. Drawing inferences is a time-honored way of doing science: Physicists describe the properties of electrons and quarks; astronomers estimate the age of the universe; biologists reconstruct the probable structure of dinosaurs and other species long since extinct. When dealing with unobservables—whether it be attention processes or quarks—we should remember that any one line of evidence is tentative. The conclusions never become certain, but they become stronger if we find many kinds of studies, using different methods, whose results all point in the same direction.

SUMMARY

✴ *Categorization.* People use many categories for which we have no clear or simple definition; we determine whether something fits the category by how closely it resembles a few familiar examples. (page 269)

✴ *Conceptual networks.* We store representations of words or concepts with links to related concepts. Hearing or thinking about one concept will temporarily prime the linked concepts. (page 270)

✴ *Mental imagery.* Mental images resemble vision in certain respects. For example, the time required to answer questions about a rotating object depends on how far the object would actually rotate and, therefore, the necessary time. (page 272)

✴ *Cognitive maps.* People learn to find their way by using cognitive maps, but they make certain consistent errors in these maps, such as remembering all turns as being close to 90-degree angles. (page 273)

✴ *Attentive and preattentive processes.* We notice some items—such as a straight line among circles or a moving object among stationary ones—almost at once, in spite of

many potential distracters. Noticing other, less distinct items requires more careful attention to one possible target after another. However, this difference is one of degree; all tasks require attention, although some require more than others. (page 274)

✴ *Automatic attention.* Sometimes it is difficult to avoid attending to certain stimuli; for example, it is difficult to state the color of the ink in which words are written while ignoring the words themselves (especially if they are color names). (page 275)

✴ *Attentional blink.* Immediately after perceiving a stimulus, there is a brief moment when it is difficult to perceive other stimuli, although they may exert subtle effects on later perceptions. (page 275)

Suggestion for Further Reading

Johnson-Laird, P. N. (1988). *The computer and the mind.* Cambridge, MA: Harvard University Press. Description of cognitive psychology and its relationship to computer science, written in nontechnical language.

Terms

cognition   the processes of thinking, gaining knowledge, and dealing with knowledge (page 269)

prototype   a familiar or typical example of a category (page 270)

spreading activation   the process by which the activation of one concept also activates or primes other concepts that are linked to it (page 271)

cognitive map   a mental representation of a spatial arrangement (page 273)

preattentive process   a procedure for extracting information automatically and simultaneously across a large portion of the visual field (page 274)

attentive process   a procedure that extracts information from one part of the visual field at a time (page 274)

Stroop effect   the tendency to read a word, especially if it is a color name, in spite of instructions to disregard the word and state the color of the ink in which it is printed (page 275)

attentional blink   a brief period after perceiving a stimulus, during which it is difficult to attend to another stimulus (page 275)

Answers to Concept Checks

1. It would take longer to answer whether fashion models sometimes get sick. Wearing dresses is a distinctive feature of fashion models; becoming ill is not. To answer the second question, you have to reason that models are people, and people sometimes get sick. (page 271)

2. People should answer *alarm clock* or *cuckoo clock* faster to the second question. The cue "tells time" strongly activates only a few concepts and therefore provides a strong start, whereas the cue "makes sounds" activates so many concepts that it only very weakly primes the correct answer. (page 272)

3. Finding a motionless brown rabbit in a field full of brown objects will require attentive processes, but you could use preattentive processes to find a hopping rabbit in a field where nothing else is moving. (For this reason, small animals that are in danger of predation stay motionless when they can.) (page 276)

Answers to Other Questions in the Text

A. The cube has six (*not* four) remaining corners. (page 272)

B. The objects in pair (a) are the same; in (b), they are the same; and in (c), they are different. (page 273)

Web Resources

The Stroop Effect

www.conex.com.br/user/hermann/eng/stroop.htm
This student-created site has a nice Java applet for demonstrating the Stroop effect. Test yourself, or a friend or classmate, for accuracy and time: Does either improve with practice?

MODULE 8.2

Problem Solving, Expertise, and Error

What do experts know or do that sets them apart from other people?

How can we improve our ability to solve problems?

Why do people sometimes reason illogically?

On a college physics exam, a student was once asked how to use a barometer to determine the height of a building. He answered that he would tie a long string to the barometer, go to the top of the building, and carefully lower the barometer until it reached the ground. Then, he would cut the string and measure its length.

How would you carry 98 water bottles—all at one time, with no wheelbarrow or truck? When faced with a new problem, sometimes people find a novel and effective solution, and sometimes they do not.

When the professor marked this answer incorrect, the student asked why. "Well," said the professor, "your method would work, but it's not the method I wanted you to use." When the student objected, the professor offered, as a compromise, to let the student try again.

"All right," the student said. "Take the barometer to the top of the building, drop it, and measure the time it takes to hit the ground. Then, from the formula for the speed of a falling object, using the gravitational constant, calculate the height of the building."

"Hmmm," replied the professor. "That too would work. And it does make use of physical principles. But it still isn't the answer I had in mind. Can you think of another way?"

"Another way? Sure," replied the student. "Place the barometer next to the building on a sunny day. Measure the height of the barometer and the length of its shadow. Also measure the length of the building's shadow. Then, use the formula

$$\frac{\text{height of barometer}}{\text{length of barometer's shadow}} = \frac{\text{height of building}}{\text{length of building's shadow}}$$

The professor was becoming more and more impressed, but he was still reluctant to give credit for the answer. He asked for yet another method.

The student suggested, "Measure the barometer's height. Then walk up the stairs of the building, marking it off in units of the barometer's height. At the top, take the number of barometer units and multiply by the height of the barometer to get the height of the building."

The professor sighed: "Just give me one more way— any other way—and I'll give you credit, even if it's not the answer I wanted."

"Really?" asked the student with a smile. "Any other way?"

"Yes, any other way."

"All right," said the student. "Go to the man who owns the building and say, 'Hey, buddy, if you tell me how tall this building is, I'll give you this neat barometer!'"

We sometimes face a logical or practical problem that we have never tried to solve before. We must devise a new solution; we cannot rely on a memorized or practiced solution. Sometimes people develop creative, imaginative solutions, like the ones that the physics student proposed. Sometimes they offer less imaginative, but still reasonable, solutions. Other times they suggest something quite illogical or offer no solution at all. Psychologists study problem-solving behavior partly to understand the thought processes behind it and partly to look for ways to help people reason more effectively.

Expertise

People vary in their performance on problem-solving and decision-making tasks. In the barometer story just described, we would probably talk about the student's creativity; in other cases, we might talk of someone's expertise. In either case, some people seem more able than others to understand a problem and to find feasible solutions.

Expert performance in music, art, athletics, and other fields can be extremely impressive. An expert crossword puzzle solver not only completes the *New York Times* Sunday crossword—an amazing feat in itself—but finds it too easy and has to have a race with another expert puzzle solver to make the task interesting. An expert birdwatcher can look at a small photo that is slightly out of focus and identify not only the species of bird, but also the subspecies, the sex, the age, and whether the bird is in summer or winter plumage. An expert at the game of bridge will say something like, "It was obvious from the bidding that East had to have the king of diamonds, so obviously it was better to try for an endplay than a finesse." (And a casual bridge player like me wonders "Huh? How was any of that obvious?")

Practice Makes Perfect (or Nearly Perfect)

Confronted by such amazing skills, it is tempting to assume that these experts were born with a special talent. Not so, say psychologists who have studied expertise (Ericsson & Charness, 1994; Ericsson, Krampe, & Tesch-Römer, 1993). In virtually every kind of endeavor, people need years of concentrated practice before they emerge as experts. For most kinds of performance, ranging from chess to sports to violin playing, the general rule is that one needs about ten years of concentrated practice. For decades, the Russians have dominated world chess competitions. Is that because Russians have a special talent for chess? Probably not; the more parsimonious explanation is that more Russians play chess, beginning in childhood, than people in other countries. In general, researchers find, if you know how many people in a given country play chess, you can predict fairly accurately how good the best player is in that country (Charness & Gerchak, 1996).

Hungarian author Laszlo Polgar set out to demonstrate his conviction that almost anyone can become an expert at something, with sufficient effort. He allowed his three young daughters to explore several fields; when they showed an interest in chess, he devoted enormous efforts to nurturing their chess skills. Today, all three daughters are outstanding chess players. One of them, Judit Polgar, reached grand master status about ten years after she started studying the game. (See Figure 8.11.)

Similarly, most of the world's best violinists began learning the violin in early childhood and continue practicing 3–4 hours a day throughout their lives. The top tennis and golf players also spend many hours practicing. Those hours of practice do not include performances; while performing, one does not have the opportunity to correct one's mistakes. Thus, an expert violinist practices the especially difficult passages; a tennis player spends hours working on the backhand shot; a golfer spends hours practicing chip shots. Practice is even more effective if a coach is present to provide extra feedback.

FIGURE 8.11 Judit Polgar confirmed her father's confidence that prolonged effort could make her an expert in her chosen field, chess. By reaching the status of grand master at age 15 years and 5 months, she beat Bobby Fisher's previous record for being the youngest.

Some researchers have argued that becoming an expert depends *entirely* on practice and is independent of any inborn talents or predispositions. That claim is almost certainly an overstatement (Gardner, 1995). If ten people began developing a skill at exactly the same age and practiced for exactly the same amount of time for the same number of years, would they all reach exactly the same level of expertise? Probably not. At a minimum, we must admit the obvious: A person with genes for being short and slow will not become an expert basketball player, a person born blind will not become an expert photographer, and so forth. Furthermore, in any field, those who show early success are most likely to devote the necessary practice time to become experts. The main point, however, is that, in any field, most of the difference between the experts and the merely average-to-good performers depends on effort and practice.

So, does all this mean that *you* could become an expert at something? Well, if you have waited until you are college age to start on a skill as competitive as chess, violin, or basketball, you are very late; nearly all experts in those fields were early starters. Still, if you choose an appropriate field and devote enough effort, you can become an expert at something. However, do not underestimate the effort and sacrifice that will be necessary. For Judit Polgar to become a grand master at chess, she devoted about 8 hours a day to chess, from age 5 to 15. She did not go to public school, so

FIGURE 8.12 Pieces arranged on a chessboard as they might actually occur in a game (a) and in a random manner (b). Master chess players can memorize the realistic pattern much better than average players can, but they are no better than average at memorizing the random pattern.

she missed most of the usual childhood activities. Whatever your chosen field, if you want to excel in it, you will have to commit yourself to an enormous amount of work.

Expert Pattern Recognition

Once someone has become an expert, what exactly does that person do that other people do not? In other words, what makes someone an expert? One important characteristic of experts is that they can look at a pattern and recognize its important features quickly. Much of the research in this area deals with chess, because it is easier to identify the experts in chess than in most other fields. In a typical experiment (de Groot, 1966), people were shown pieces on a chessboard, as in Figure 8.12, for 5 seconds. Then, they were asked to recall the position of all the pieces. When the pieces were arranged as they might occur in an actual game, expert players could recall 91% of the positions, whereas novices could recall only 41%. When the pieces were arranged randomly, however, the expert players did no better than the nonexperts. That is, on the average, expert chess players are not superior in overall memory or intelligence; they have simply learned to recognize and remember a great many of the most common chessboard patterns.

Further evidence for this conclusion includes the fact that the top-level grand master chess players can play simultaneous games against six or so other highly ranked opponents and play almost as well as if they were facing only one opponent (Gobet & Simon, 1996). Simultaneous play offers little opportunity for planning five or six moves ahead and for considering all the possible countermoves by one's opponent; in simultaneous play, one is forced to rely on quickly recognizing a pattern and knowing what is a good move for that situation.

Problem Solving

Can people learn general skills of problem solving, which they could apply to new and unfamiliar questions? To some extent, yes, they can (Bransford & Stein, 1984).

Generally, we go through four phases when we set about solving a problem (Polya, 1957): (1) understanding the problem, (2) generating one or more hypotheses, (3) testing the hypotheses, and (4) checking the result (Figure 8.13). A scientist goes through those four phases when approaching a new, complex phenomenon, and you would probably go through these phases when trying to assemble a bicycle that came with garbled instructions. We shall discuss these four phases of problem solving in detail.

Understanding and Simplifying a Difficult Problem

You are facing a question or a problem, and you have no idea how to begin. You may even think the problem is unsolvable. Then someone shows you how to solve it, and you realize, "I could have done that, if I had only thought of trying it that way."

When you do not know how to solve a problem, try starting with a simpler version of it. For example, here is what may appear to be a difficult, even impossible, problem:

> A professor hands back students' test papers at random. On the average, how many students will accidentally receive their own paper?

Note that the problem does not specify how many students are in the class. At first, you may not know how to approach the problem, but see what happens if you start with some simpler cases: How many students will get their own paper back if there is only one student in the class? One, of course. What if there are two students? There is a 50% chance that both will get their own paper back and a 50% chance that neither will. On the average, one student will get the correct paper. What if there are three students? Each student then has one chance in three of getting his or her own paper. A one-third chance times three students means that, on the average, one student will get the correct paper. Already you can see the pattern: If there are 100 students,

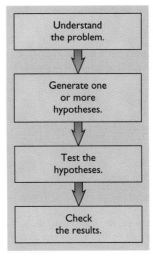

FIGURE 8.13 The four steps to solving a problem.

Understand the problem.

Generate one or more hypotheses.

Test the hypotheses.

Check the results.

each student has one chance in a hundred of getting his or her own paper back. No matter how many students are in the class, on average, one student will get his or her own paper back.

Generating Hypotheses

After you have simplified a problem as much as possible, you need to generate *hypotheses*—preliminary interpretations that you can evaluate or test. In some cases, you can generate a complete list of possibilities and then test them all. For example, suppose you want to connect your television set to a pair of stereo amplifiers and a VCR or DVD player, but you have lost the instruction manuals (or you refuse to read them). You have several cables to attach, and each device has some input and output channels. You could simply connect the cables by trial and error, testing every possibility until you find one that works. *A mechanical, repetitive mathematical procedure for solving a problem* is called an **algorithm.** Testing every possible hypothesis is one example of an algorithm. The rules for alphabetizing a list are another example. You can also learn an algorithm for how to win, or at least tie, every time you play tic-tac-toe.

In many situations, however, you could not list all the hypotheses, much less test them. For example, consider the question, "What should I do with my life?" Confronted with a vast and confusing array of possibilities, you must simplify the task. **Heuristics** are *strategies for simplifying a problem or for guiding an investigation.* In this career-choice example, you might limit yourself to a few possible careers

that tap your interests and skills and then try to learn as much as you can about those few careers.

To illustrate the contrast between algorithms and heuristics, consider chess. At a typical point in a game of chess, a player has about 25 legal moves, for each of which the opponent has 25 legal replies. If you wanted to choose the best possible move by an algorithm, you would consider each of your 25 possible moves, each of your opponent's possible replies, each of your possible next moves, and so forth—say, five or six moves ahead. Finally, you would select the move that gives you the best result, assuming that your opponent made the best possible reply at each point. This algorithm, however, will overburden your memory, so you simplify it with some heuristics: On each move, you select just a few possible moves for serious consideration, aided by your recognition of similar positions you have faced in past games. You consider just a few of your opponent's likely responses, a few of your possible next moves, and so forth. If you decide that one of your possible moves would be disastrous, you do not waste time reconsidering it after your opponent's move.

In contrast, the best chess-playing computers do rely on algorithms to test every possible move. The Deep Blue computer program that beat Garry Kasparov, the best human player, did so by considering every possible move and every possible reply, 14 or 15 moves ahead, and as many as 45 moves ahead when necessary (Mechner, 1998). The computer succeeded because it can consider 200 million positions per second (and remember the outcomes). With such a powerful algorithm, no heuristics are necessary.

However, in the game of Go (Figure 8.14), which has a 19 × 19 grid and very complex strategies, each player has an average of about 250 possible moves, for each of which the opponent would have 250 possible replies. Whereas

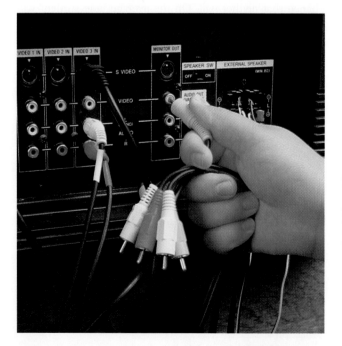

To find the right way to connect the lines, you could use the simple algorithm of trying every possible combination, one after the other.

FIGURE 8.14 In the Chinese game Go, opponents alternate placing their markers on a 19 × 19 grid, attempting to arrange their own pieces in a safe arrangement or to surround opposing pieces that are not in safe arrangements. For this game, an algorithm of imagining every possible move and then every possible reply would be extemely inefficient; effective strategies require heuristics to restrict the moves under consideration.

Deep Blue can run its algorithm to find the best possible chess move in 3 minutes, a computer would need an estimated 70 years to complete a comparable algorithm for Go! At the time that Deep Blue beat Kasparov, the best available computer program for playing Go was at the level of a beginner (Mechner, 1998). Even if we assume that computers will continue to get faster and more powerful, programming a computer to play Go successfully will probably require developing some heuristics—in effect, programming the computer to think more like a human.

CONCEPT CHECK

4. Suppose you are a traveling salesperson. You must start from your home city, visit each of several other cities, and then return home. Your task is to find the shortest route. What would be the appropriate algorithm? What would be a possible heuristic for simplifying the problem? (Check your answer on page 295.)

Testing Hypotheses and Checking the Results

If you think you have solved a problem, test your idea to see whether it will work. Many people who think they have a great idea never bother to try it out, even on a small scale. One inventor applied for a patent on the "perpetual motion machine" shown in Figure 8.15. Rubber balls, being lighter than water, rise in a column of water and flow over the top. The balls are heavier than air, so they then fall, thus moving a belt and thereby generating energy. At the bottom, they reenter the water column. Do you see why this system could never work? You would if you tried to build it. (Check your answer on page 296, answer C.)

The final step for solving a problem is to check and recheck the results, or at least to find out whether the result is plausible. For example, one article in the journal *Science* reported that fields in California's Imperial Valley produce 750,000 melons per acre. One reader wrote to the journal to point out that 750,000 melons per acre meant about 17 melons per square foot. With tongue in cheek, he asked whether the weight of all those melons might be causing California's earthquakes (Hoffman, 1992).

Generalizing Solutions to Similar Problems

After laboriously solving one problem, can people then solve a related problem more easily? Can they at least recognize that the new problem is related to the old problem, so that they know where to start?

Sometimes, but all too frequently they do not. Many people who understand the laws of probability fail to see how those laws might apply to real-life situations (Nisbett, Fong, Lehman, & Cheng, 1987). For example, most people who flipped a coin 10 times and got 10 consecutive heads

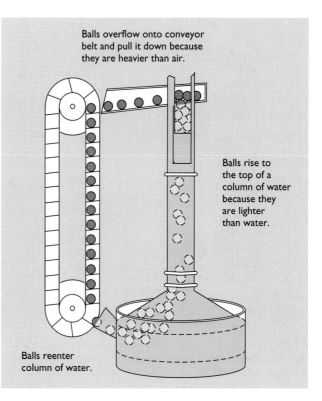

Balls overflow onto conveyor belt and pull it down because they are heavier than air.

Balls rise to the top of a column of water because they are lighter than water.

Balls reenter column of water.

F I G U R E 8.15 What is wrong with this perpetual motion machine?

would not expect more than 5 heads out of the next 10 flips. But the same people might expect a basketball team that won 10 consecutive games to win the next 10 games as well. The basketball situation is not exactly the same as coin flipping, but it does have some similarities: A long winning streak depends partly on chance.

In other situations as well, people who have solved one problem correctly fail to solve a second problem that is basically similar, unless someone explains that the two problems are similar (Gick & Holyoak, 1980). For example, Figure 8.16a shows a coiled garden hose. When the water spurts out, what path will it take? (Draw it.) Figure 8.16b shows a curved gun barrel. When the bullet comes out, what path will it take? (Draw it.)

Almost everyone draws the water coming out of the garden hose in a straight path. Even after doing so, however, many people draw a bullet coming out of a gun in a curved path, as if the bullet remembered the curved path it had just taken (Kaiser, Jonides, & Alexander, 1986). The physics is the same in both situations: Except for the effects of gravity, both the water and the bullet will follow a straight path.

Sometimes we recognize similar problems and use our solution to an old problem as a guide to solving a new one (Figure 8.17), but sometimes we do not. What accounts for the difference? It is easier to generalize a solution after we have seen several examples of it; if we have seen only a single example, we may think of the solution in only that one context (Gick & Holyoak, 1983).

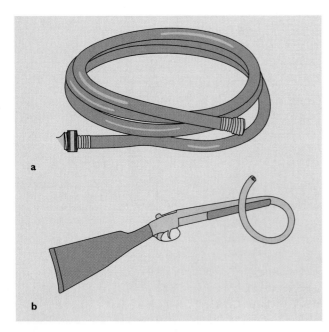

FIGURE 8.16 (a) Draw the trajectory of water as it flows out of a coiled garden hose. (b) Draw the trajectory of a bullet as it leaves a coiled gun barrel.

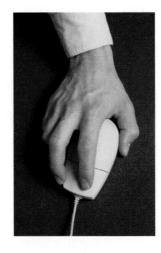

FIGURE 8.17 The computer mouse was invented by a computer scientist who was familiar with an engineering device called a planimeter that he believed could be modified for use with computers. Such insights are unusual; most people do not generalize a solution from one task to another.

Special Features of Insight Problems

Some of the problems we have been discussing are "insight" problems or "aha!" problems—the kind in which the correct answer occurs to you suddenly or not at all. Here is a clear example of an insight problem (Gardner, 1978): Figure 8.18 shows an object that was made by just cutting and bending an ordinary piece of cardboard. How was it made? If you think you know, take a piece of paper and try to make it yourself. (The correct answer is on page 296, answer D.)

 TRY IT YOUR-SELF

FIGURE 8.18 This object was made by cutting and folding an ordinary piece of cardboard, with nothing left over. How was it done?

Insightful Problem Solving: Sudden or Gradual?

Solving insight problems differs from solving, say, algebra problems. Most people can look at an algebra problem and rather accurately predict whether they will be able to solve it, and if so how quickly. As they work on the problem, they can estimate how close they are to reaching a solution. On insight problems, however, people give inaccurate estimates about whether they are about to solve the problem or not (Metcalfe & Wiebe, 1987). Frequently, someone will say, "I have no idea whether I will ever solve this problem," and then suddenly announce the correct answer a minute or so later.

So, it appears that the answer comes suddenly, or not at all. But does it, really? If you were groping your way around in a dark room, you would have no idea how soon you were going to find the door, but that does not mean that you had made no progress. You would have learned much about the room, including many places where the door was *not*.

So, maybe people are making progress without realizing it, when they struggle with insight problems. To test this possibility, psychologists gave students problems having the following form:

The following three words are all associated with one other word. What is that word?

color   numbers   oil

In this case, the correct answer is *paint*. As with other insight questions, subjects reported that the answer came to them suddenly or not at all and that they could not tell whether they were about to think of the answer or not. Then, the experimenters gave the subjects paired sets of three words each, like those shown here in Sets 1 and 2, to examine for 12 seconds. In each pair, one set had a correct answer (like *paint* in the example just given). For the other set, no one word was associated with all three items. Subjects were asked to generate a

 TRY IT YOUR-SELF

correct answer if they could; if not, they were to guess *which* set had a correct answer and to say how confident they were of their guess. Examples:

Set 1

playing   credit   report   *or*   still   pages   music

Set 2

town   root   car   *or*   ticket   shop   broker

(You can check your answers on page 296, answer E.)

The main result was that, when subjects could not find the correct answer, they still guessed with greater than 50% accuracy which set had a correct answer (Bowers, Regehr, Balthazard, & Parker, 1990). Even when subjects said they had "no confidence" at all in their guesses, they were still right more often than not. In short, insight solutions are not as sudden as they seem; people may be approaching a solution without even realizing it.

The Characteristics of Creative Problem Solving

Solving a problem or developing a new product is always a creative activity, but some solutions and products seem more creative than others. Psychologists frequently define **creativity** as *the development of novel, socially valued products* (Mumford & Gustafson, 1988). In principle this is a reasonable definition, although in practice it can be hard to apply; many unusual works of art, music, and literature were very lightly regarded in their own time but later hailed as classics. By the usual definition of *creativity*, these works became creative many decades after they were produced!

Could you or I develop a great scientific theory, if we addressed the right question and had all the necessary in-formation? If you want to try this challenge, examine the data in the table below. Five pairs of numbers, arbitrarily labeled s and q, are measurements of two physical variables. I won't tell you what the variables are, because you might be familiar with the theory in question. Examine each of the pairs of variables to see whether you can find a single mathematical equation relating s to q.

In one study, 4 of 14 university students managed to find the correct equation within one hour, thus reproducing a great scientific discovery (Qin & Simon, 1990). You may use a calculator. Recommendation: Either copy these data onto another sheet of paper or cover the text that follows so that you do not accidentally read the correct formula.

s	q
36	88
67.25	224.7
93	365.3
141	687
483.8	4332.1

The data represent measurements regarding the first five planets of our solar system. Column s gives the distance

Creative problem solving, evident in this temporary bridge made of old railroad cars, has two elements: novelty and social value.

from the sun in millions of miles; column q gives the time (in Earth days) required for rotation around the sun. The German astronomer Johannes Kepler (1571–1630) is regarded as a genius and as the founder of modern astronomy for discerning the relationship between these two sets of data.

The correct formula can be expressed in any of the following ways:

$$s^3/q^2 = 6.025$$
$$s^3/6.025 = q^2$$
$$q^{2/3} = 0.55\,s$$
$$s^{1.5} = 2.45\,q$$

That is, the cube of the distance from the sun is related to the square of the period of rotation. The fact that 4 university students solved this problem, in far less time than Kepler needed, indicates that the actual problem solving requires only good mathematical skill and persistence, not a special talent available to only one person in a million. Kepler was a true genius because he guessed that there *was* a relationship between the two sets of numbers: He guessed that it was a solvable problem.

SOMETHING TO THINK ABOUT

Are people of normal talents also capable of great creative achievements in art and literature? How could we test that ability? ✳

The Characteristics of Creativity

Are some people naturally more creative than other people are? The Torrance Tests of Creative Thinking measure creativity using items similar to the one shown in Figure 8.19 (Torrance, 1980, 1981, 1982). We know that such tests measure something consistent; if you took tests of this type on several occasions, you would probably get approximately the same score each time. Several other tests have also been devised for measuring creativity of various sorts. The best summary is that there are many kinds of creativity: You might be creative in art but not in writing, or creative in writing but not in scientific problem solving (Sternberg & Lubart, 1996).

FIGURE 8.19 A "what-is-it?" picture, similar to those in one part of the Torrance Tests of Creative Thinking.

So, it doesn't make sense to talk about "creative people"; it is better to talk about people who are "creative in a particular situation." As a rule, people are creative only within the domains that they know well (Gardner, 1993). The key to creative success is primarily to generate many new ideas or products, more or less at random, and then judge which ones to develop and which to abandon (Simonton, 1997). Making that judgment requires extensive knowledge of the field. Therefore, you want a creative solution to a problem in automobile repair, try a good auto mechanic, not a painter or poet.

Howard Gardner (1993) studied creativity by examining in detail the lives of seven 20th-century people who are widely regarded as creative in very different fields: Sigmund Freud (psychology), Albert Einstein (physics), Pablo Picasso (painting), Igor Stravinsky (musical composition), T. S. Eliot (poetry), Martha Graham (dance), and Mahatma Gandhi (political resistance, religion, and spirituality). Gardner inquired what, if anything, these highly creative people had in common. He found a few patterns, which

may perhaps be accidents based on his particular choice of "creative people," but these patterns deserve at least serious consideration. Among them were the following:

- Creativity thrives in an atmosphere of moderate tension; the person senses that the old ways of doing things are not quite right.
- The highly creative person must have enough of a background in the topic to feel self-confident but not so much experience that he or she has become trapped into the traditional habits of procedure. Just as people need about ten years to become an expert in a field, people generally need about ten years in a field before they are ready to make their first major creative contribution.
- During a period early in life, when a creative genius is working on some new ideas, he or she is likely to rely heavily on one or a small number of close, trusted friends for advice and encouragement. This advice is necessary for polishing the ideas, and the encouragement is necessary to enable the creative person to persist in the face of criticism.
- A creative genius throws him- or herself wholeheartedly into the work, sacrificing any possibility of a "well-rounded" life. Each of the creative people that Gardner studied had a very limited family life and very strained relationships with other people. Even Gandhi, who was famous as an advocate for love and justice, loved people in the abstract but had trouble developing close relationships with real, live people.

Creative careers, however, are extremely variable (Simonton, 1997). As a rule, poets are recognized for their greatness early in life, generally in their 20s, whereas the greatest, most creative historians seldom do their best work before their 40s or 50s. Within any field, some people start early and quit early and others bloom late; some—such as Bach, Picasso, and Thomas Edison—produce enormous quantities of good work, whereas others produce only one or two works worthy of recognition.

Howard Gardner studied the lives of seven highly creative people, including political and spiritual leader Mahatma Gandhi and dance pioneer Martha Graham, to find the features that promote creativity.

CONCEPT CHECK

5. It has been long reported that great creative poets die younger, on the average, than equally recognized historians. Why? (Hint: The average depends on the whole distribution, from youngest at death to oldest. Imagine the distribution of ages at death for both groups.) (Check your answer on page 295.)

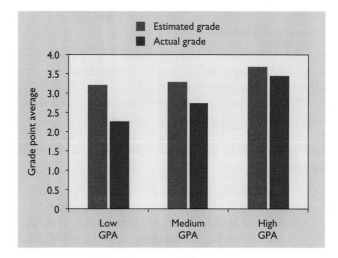

FIGURE 8.20 At the beginning of a semester, undergraduates in an advanced psychology course estimated their probable semester grade. Students with low, medium, or high grade-point averages generally predicted that they would get an A or a B. The best students were slightly overpredicting their success; the worst students were greatly overpredicting. (Based on data of Prohaska, 1994).

Common Errors in Human Cognition

Although we humans pride ourselves on our intelligence and our ability to solve problems, we sometimes err with fairly simple problems. After someone points out the correct answer, we may be surprised by our own mistake. Sometimes we err because we relied on inappropriate heuristics. (Recall that heuristics are methods for simplifying a problem and facilitating an investigation.) Ordinarily, relying on heuristics enables us to find a reasonable, if not perfect, answer. Occasionally, however, certain heuristics can lead us astray. Let's now consider several reasons why people sometimes arrive at illogical conclusions.

Overconfidence

TRY IT YOUR-SELF Let's start with a demonstration. Answer each of the following questions and then estimate the probability that your answer is correct. For example, you might feel 99%, 50%, or 10% sure that you are correct.

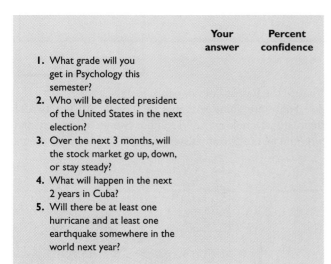

	Your answer	Percent confidence
1. What grade will you get in Psychology this semester?		
2. Who will be elected president of the United States in the next election?		
3. Over the next 3 months, will the stock market go up, down, or stay steady?		
4. What will happen in the next 2 years in Cuba?		
5. Will there be at least one hurricane and at least one earthquake somewhere in the world next year?		

Most people are overconfident of their answers to questions 1–4 and underconfident of their "yes" answer to question 5. (You did say "yes," didn't you?) For statistical reasons, the average person is almost sure to be underconfident of his or her answer to question 5: Because the actual probability is virtually 100%, no one will overstate the probability, and if even a few people guess less than 100%,

the average will be an understatement (Erev, Wallsten, & Budescu, 1994).

When people try to predict events that are actually quite uncertain, however, most people tend to be overconfident of their predictions (Juslin & Olsson, 1997). People are especially likely to be overconfident about their own accomplishments. For example, at the beginning of each semester, most students (even poor students) estimate that they will get mostly A's and B's (Prohaska, 1994). (See Figure 8.20.) Most students also slightly overestimate the grades they *already* received; that is, they remember slightly higher grades than they actually got (Bahrick, Hall, & Berger, 1996). Similarly, most athletes and coaches predict that they will have better seasons this year than they had last year, and most people entering a contest think they have a better-than-average chance of winning. A certain amount of optimism and self-confidence is probably good for our mental health, but objectively speaking, people overestimate their probable success. (For example, it is impossible for *every* team in the league to win more games this year than last year.)

Philip Tetlock (1994) conducted a study of government officials and consultants, foreign policy professors, newspaper columnists, and others who make their living by analyzing and predicting world events. He asked them to predict some events in U.S. and world politics over the next several years—such as what will happen in Korea, the Middle East, Eastern Europe, and Cuba—and to state their confidence in these predictions (such as 70%); 5 years later, he checked their accuracy. He found that most of the experts' predictions were no more accurate than the guesses you or I might have made, although they had stated great confidence in their predictions. Curiously, the few experts whose predictions showed more than random accuracy shared a few common characteristics:

• They showed no strong political leaning. (Experts who consistently favored one political party or viewpoint were wrong as often as they were right.)
• They relied on complex information, instead of arguing from analogy to a single historical pattern.
• They were not overly sure of themselves. That is, the ones most likely to be right were the ones who admitted they might be wrong.

Of all the people who make their living by predicting the future, weather forecasters are among the most accurate. Although we tend to remember only their errors, of all the times when meteorologists foretell a "70% chance of rain," it actually rains close to 70% of the time. One advantage of weather forecasting over, say, predicting political events, is that meteorologists get day-by-day feedback on their predictions; when they are wrong, they cannot avoid admitting they were wrong.

Premature Commitment to a Hypothesis

Sometimes we make mistakes because we commit ourselves prematurely to a particular hypothesis and fail to consider other possibilities. For example, examine the extremely out-of-focus photo in Figure 8.21a and guess what it depicts. Then see Figures 8.21b and 8.21c. Most people find that seeing the extremely out-of-focus photo makes it harder to identify the items in the slightly out-of-focus photo. When they saw the first photo, they formed a hypothesis, almost certainly a wrong one, which interfered with correct perception of the later photo (Bruner & Potter, 1964). This interference continues even after people are told that their first hypothesis was wrong (Snodgrass & Hirshman, 1991).

Peter Wason (1960) asked students to discover a certain rule he had in mind for generating sequences of numbers. One example of the numbers the rule might generate, he explained, was "2, 4, 6." He told the students that they could ask about other sequences, and he would tell them whether or not those sequences fit the rule. As soon as they thought they had enough evidence, they could guess what the rule was.

Most students started by asking, "8, 10, 12?" When told "yes," they proceeded with, "14, 16, 18?" Each time, they were told, "Yes, that sequence fits the rule." Soon most of them guessed, "The rule is three consecutive even numbers."

"No," came the reply. "That is not the rule." Many students persisted, trying "20, 22, 24?" "26, 28, 30?" "250, 252, 254?" And so forth. Eventually, they would say, "Three even numbers in which the second is two more than the first and the third is two more than the second." Again, they were told that the guess was wrong. "But how can it be wrong?" they complained. "It always works!"

The rule Wason had in mind was, "Any three positive numbers of increasing magnitude." For instance, 1, 2, 3,

would be acceptable; so would 5, 21, 24601. Where many students went wrong was in testing only the cases that their hypothesis said would fit the rule. One must also examine the cases that the hypothesis says will not fit the rule (Klayman & Ha, 1987).

One special case of premature commitment to a hypothesis is the phenomenon of **functional fixedness,** *the tendency to adhere to a single approach to a problem or a single way of using an item.* Here are three examples:

TRY IT YOURSELF

1. You are provided with a candle, a box of matches, some thumbtacks, and a tiny piece of string that is shorter than the width of the candle, as shown in Figure 8.22. Using no other equipment, find a way to mount the candle to the wall so that it could be lit.
2. Consider an array of nine dots:

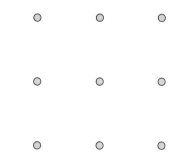

Connect all nine dots with a series of connected straight lines, such that the end of one line is the start of the next.

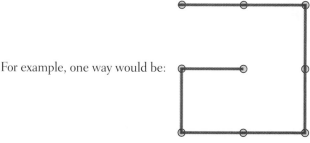

For example, one way would be:

But use the fewest lines possible.
3. There are some students in a room. All but two of them are psychology majors, all but two are chemistry majors, and all but two are history majors. How many students

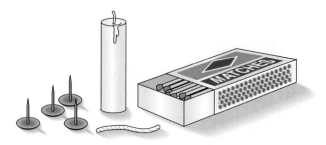

FIGURE 8.22 You are provided with a candle, a box of matches, some thumbtacks, and a very tiny piece of string. What is the best way, using no other equipment, to attach the candle to a wall?

are in the room, and what are their majors? (Note: If your first impulse is to say "two of each," try it out: It doesn't work.) Now here's the interesting part: There are two possible solutions. After you have found one solution, discard it and find another.

After you have either found solutions to these questions or given up, check answer F on page 296. Question 1 was difficult because most people think of the matchbox as simply a container for the matches, not as a potential tool on its own. The box is "functionally fixed" for one way of using it. Question 2 was difficult because most people assume that the lines must remain within the area defined by the nine dots. Question 3 has a double difficulty: It is difficult to think of even one solution, and after thinking of it, it is hard to abandon it to think of an entirely different approach.

The Representativeness Heuristic and Base-Rate Information

Perhaps you have heard the saying: "If something looks like a duck, waddles like a duck, and quacks like a duck, chances are it's a duck." This saying is an example of the **representativeness heuristic,** *the tendency to assume that, if an item is similar to members of a particular category, it is probably a member of that category itself.*

This assumption is usually correct. It can lead us astray, however, if we are dealing with something rare. For example, suppose you see a bird that looks like an Eskimo curlew, walks like an Eskimo curlew, and whistles like an Eskimo curlew. Does that mean you have found an Eskimo curlew? Not likely. Eskimo curlews are extremely rare, almost extinct; chances are, you have sighted another bird that resembles an Eskimo curlew.

When we must decide whether something belongs in category A or category B—for example, an Eskimo curlew versus another bird—we should consider three questions: (1) How closely does it resemble the items in the first category? (2) How closely does it resemble the items in the second category? (3) Which is more common, category A or category B? The answer to the third question is known as **base-rate information**—that is, *data about the frequency or probability of a given item,* how rare or how common it is.

People frequently overlook the base-rate information and follow only the representativeness heuristic. As a result, they identify something as a member of an uncommon category, disregarding the more likely category. For example, consider the following question (modified from Kahneman & Tversky, 1973):

TRY IT YOUR-SELF

Psychologists have interviewed 30 engineers and 70 lawyers. One of them is Jack, a 45-year-old married man with four children. He is generally conservative, cautious, and ambitious. He shows no interest in political and social issues and spends most of his free time on home carpentry, sailing, and

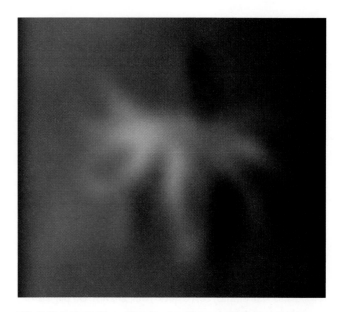

FIGURE 8.21a People who form a hypothesis based on the first photo look at succeeding photos to find evidence that they are right. Because their first guess is generally wrong, they don't do as well as people who look at the later photos before making any preliminary guesses. Try to guess what this shows. Then examine parts (b) and (c) on pages 291 and 293.

solving mathematical puzzles. What is the probability that Jack is one of the 30 engineers in the sample of 100?

Most people think that this description is more representative of engineers than it is of lawyers. Based on representativeness, they estimate that Jack is probably an engineer, neglecting to take into account that the sample includes more than twice as many lawyers as engineers. That base-rate information should influence their estimates. In fact, however, most people virtually ignore the base-rate information, making the same estimates regardless of whether the sample includes 30% or 70% engineers (Kahneman & Tversky, 1973).

Here is another example of overreliance on the representativeness heuristic. Read the following description, and then answer the questions following it:

Linda was a philosophy major. She is 31, bright, outspoken, and concerned about issues of discrimination and social justice.

Now, what would you estimate is the probability that Linda is a bank teller? What is the probability that she is a *feminist* bank teller? (Answer before you read on.)

The true probabilities, which are hard to estimate, are not the point. The interesting result is that most people estimate a higher probability that Linda is a *feminist* bank teller than the probability that she is a bank teller (Tversky & Kahneman, 1983). However, she could clearly not be a feminist bank teller without being a bank teller. Apparently, people regard this description as fairly typical for a feminist and therefore also for a feminist bank teller (or feminist anything else) but do not regard the description as typical for bank tellers in general (Shafir, Smith, & Osherson, 1990). Because of the representativeness heuristic, people overestimate the probability that Linda is a feminist bank teller.

CONCEPT CHECK

6. Suppose an improved lie-detector test can determine with 90% accuracy whether people are telling the truth. An employer proposes to administer the test to all employees, asking them whether they have ever stolen anything valuable from the company and summarily firing everyone who fails the test. Is this policy reasonable? Assume that the company has 1,000 employees; of these, only 20 have ever stolen anything. Hint: Think about the base-rate probability of finding a dishonest employee. (Check your answer on page 295.)

The Availability Heuristic

When we are asked how common something is, we generally start by trying to think of examples. Try this question: In the English language, are there more words that start with *k* or more words that have *k* as the third letter? If you are like most people, you guessed that there are more words that start with *k*. How did you decide that? You tried to think of words that start with *k*: "king, kitchen, kangaroo, key, knowledge, . . ." Then you tried to think of words that have *k* as the third letter: "ask, ink, . . . uh . . ." You were relying on the **availability heuristic**, *the strategy of assuming that the number of memories of an event that are available indicates how common the event actually is* (Table 8.1). Because it was easier to think of words that start with *k* than words with *k* as the third letter, you assumed that there really are more words that start with *k*. In fact, however, words with *k* as the third letter are considerably more numerous.

The availability heuristic leads to illusory correlations, as we saw in Chapter 2. Someone asks, "Do people act strange on nights with a full moon?" If you have always expected people to act strange on such nights, you may be able to remember more times when they did act strange than times when they did not.

Here is another example of the availability heuristic: Suppose I ask you to fill out a survey of your beliefs on a variety of controversial political, social, and religious issues. Then, for each of those questions, I ask you to estimate what percentage of other people agree with your position. You will probably overestimate that percentage, for two reasons: One reason is that, as mentioned before, most people are overconfident of their own opinions. The other reason is that you probably associate with friends who share most of your opinions. Because you can think of many people who share your opinions, you overestimate how many others do also.

Another example: Do you consider yourself a better-than-average driver, an average driver, or a worse-than-average driver? Almost all people call themselves better than average or average in this regard. Where are all the below-average drivers? Evidently, some people overestimate their driving skills. One reason is this: When you think about other drivers, the ones you remember most vividly are the unusually bad drivers. Because the worst drivers are the easiest to remember, we overestimate their numbers.

You can guard against overuse of the availability heuristic. When you try to estimate whether one type of event is more common than another, look for systematic data. Don't just trust your memory of how often various events occur.

Framing Questions

If we were truly logical beings, we would give the same answer to a question no matter how it was worded. In fact, most people give one answer to a question that is phrased in terms of gain but give a different answer to the same question when it is phrased in terms of loss.

For example, you have recently been appointed head of the Public Health Service. A new contagious disease has been detected, and you must choose between two plans of action. If you do nothing, 600 people will die. If you adopt plan A, you will save the lives of 200 people. If you adopt plan B, there is a 33% chance that you will save all 600 and 67% chance that you will save no one. (Choose plan A or B before reading further.)

Now another contagious disease breaks out; again you must choose between two plans. If you adopt plan C, 400

TABLE 8.1	The Representativeness Heuristic and the Availability Heuristic		
	A TENDENCY TO ASSUME THAT . . .	*LEADS US ASTRAY WHEN . . .*	*EXAMPLE OF ERRONEOUS ASSUMPTION*
Representativeness heuristic	any item that resembles members of a particular category is probably itself a member of that category.	an item resembles members of a rare category.	You see something that looks the way you imagine a UFO would look, so you decide it is a UFO.
Availability heuristic	how easily we can think of examples of a category indicates how many examples really exist.	one kind of example is easier to think of than another is.	You remember more newspaper reports of airline crashes than of car crashes, so you assume that air crashes are more common than car crashes.

people will die. If you adopt plan D, there is a 33% chance that no one will die and a 67% chance that 600 will die. Choose one plan now, and then compare your choices with the results in Figure 8.23. *The tendency to answer a question differently when it is framed (phrased) differently* is called the **framing effect.**

Consider another example; this one deals with money instead of lives. Which would you rather have?

      W. a gain of $240

or   X. a 25% chance to win $1,000

Now you need to make another decision. You have just received an outright gift of $1,000, but you must choose between two unpleasant alternatives:

      Y. a loss of $750

or   Z. a 75% chance of losing the whole $1,000
         (a 25% chance of losing nothing)

Tversky and Kahneman (1981) found that 84% of all people chose W over X (avoiding risk), whereas 87% chose Z over Y (taking a risk). Note that W is actually $10 less than choice Y and that X is the same as Z. Again, people generally avoid taking a risk when considering gains but accept a risk when considering losses. Put another way, people try to avoid losses.

The framing effect has consequences for persuasion. Suppose you want to encourage people to wear seat belts, exercise, take vitamins, quit smoking cigarettes, practice "safe sex," or whatever. Should you say, "If you do this you

FIGURE 8.21b

will probably live longer"? Or should you say, "If you don't do this, you will probably die sooner"? We need research to establish the results in each case, but the point is that we cannot assume that the "live longer" and "die sooner" messages will yield the same results (Rothman & Salovey, 1997). How we frame a question changes the way people respond to it.

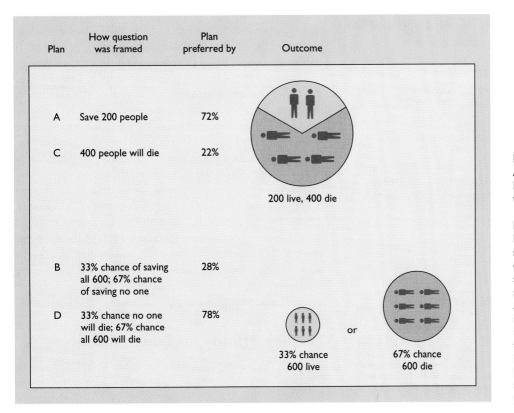

FIGURE 8.23 When Amos Tversky and Daniel Kahneman (1981) offered these choices to more than 150 people, 72% chose A over B, and 78% chose D over C. However, plan A is exactly the same as plan C (200 live, 400 die), and plan B is exactly the same as plan D. Why then did so many people choose both A and D? The reason, according to Tversky and Kahneman, is that most people avoid taking a risk when a question is phrased in terms of gain, but they are willing to accept a risk when the question is phrased in terms of loss.

CONCEPT CHECK

7. a. Someone says, "More than 90% of all college students like to watch late-late night television, whereas only 20% of older adults do. Therefore, more watchers of late-late night television are college students." What error in thinking has this person made?

b. Someone tells me that, if I say "abracadabra" every morning, I will stay healthy. I say it daily and, sure enough, I stay healthy. I conclude that saying this magic word really does ensure health. What error of thinking have I made? (Check your answers on page 296.)

Learning, Memory, Cognition, and the Psychology of Gambling

Suppose your professor asks everyone in class to hand in $10. The professor collects all the money, keeps half of it, and hands the other half to one of the students, chosen at random. Presuming you were not the winner of the money, would you encourage your professor to repeat this exercise every week from now on?

Casino gambling and state lotteries operate much like this example. Table 8.2 illustrates the odds for one state lottery game. Actually, casinos offer much better odds than a state lottery; a casino keeps less than 5% of the gambled money, whereas a state government keeps about 50%. In either case, the great majority of the bettors are going to lose money, although they continue gambling anyway.

Gambling has been a common human behavior throughout history and throughout the world. Here we shall focus on why people make apparently illogical bets, where they are likely to lose more than they win. This issue illustrates several of the principles of learning, memory, and thinking we have discussed in the last three chapters.

TABLE 8.2	**Expected Winnings on a $1 Decco Ticket (a California Lottery Game)**			
PROBABILITY	×	PAYOFF	=	EXPECTED VALUE
.9573084	×	$0	=	$0.000
.040404	×	$5	=	$0.202
.0022409	×	$50	=	$0.112
.0000467	×	$5,000	=	$0.233
Total	1.0			$0.547

NOTE: Someone who purchases a $1 ticket has more than a 95% chance of winning nothing, slightly more than a 4% chance of winning $5, and so forth. Overall, the person should expect to receive about 55 cents back for the $1. No one actually receives the 55 cents for a single ticket, but that should be the average payoff after someone has bought many Decco tickets.

FIGURE 8.24 Most chronic gamblers believe that some people can win consistently at games of chance. Even with slot machines, many gamblers believe their skill in pulling the handle can influence their results.

Overestimation of Control

Rationally, you should not spend even $1 when your chance of winning $5,000 in a lottery is 1 in 21 thousand. But what if you thought that *your* chances were significantly better than everyone else's? Most gamblers believe that some people can win consistently at games of chance. Even most people who play the slot machines (Figure 8.24) believe that their skill in pulling the arm can influence their winnings (Griffiths, 1990).

In one study, people were given a chance to buy $1 lottery tickets for a $50 prize (Langer, 1975). Some of them were simply handed a ticket; others were permitted to choose their own ticket. Those who chose their own ticket thought they had a better chance of winning. Days later, all the ticket-holders were asked whether they were willing to sell their ticket to someone else. Those who had chosen their own tickets were much less willing to sell, and some refused to sell for less than the full $50 they expected to win!

As a general rule, whenever we have an intention to achieve an outcome, we are inclined to assume that our actions will achieve that outcome, or at least make it more likely (Matute, 1996; Thompson, Armstrong, & Thomas, 1998). We are especially likely to believe that our actions matter in any competititive situation. Most of the time, our choices do influence the outcome, and healthy, successful people keep trying and believing that they are succeeding. That tendency backfires, however, in gambling situations where the outcomes are actually random.

People's Affinity for Long-Shot Bets

 Which would you rather have, $100,000 for sure, or a 10% chance of winning a million dollars? What about a choice between $10,000 for sure and a 1% chance at a million dollars? Would you prefer

$1,000 for sure or a 0.1% chance at a million? A sure profit of $100 or a 0.01% chance at a million? A $10 profit or a 0.001% chance at a million? A $1 profit or a 0.0001% chance at a million?

If you are like most people, you chose the $100,000 over a 10% chance at a million, and you also chose $10,000 over a 1% chance. But at some point, you switched from the sure profit to the gamble. Especially if the sure profit is $10 or less, most people prefer a chance at winning a million. In fact, almost half of college students who were asked would forego $10 to have even one chance in a million of winning a million—a gamble of very bad odds (Rachlin, Siegel, & Cross, 1994).

Why? First, for most students, $10 does not sound like very much. Oh, sure, you would rather have $10 than not have it, but another $10 is not going to raise most people's standard of living enough to notice. A million dollars would. Furthermore, although it is easy to understand the difference between a 10% chance and a 1% chance, most of us are not very concerned about the difference between a 0.001% chance and a 0.0001% or even a 0.000001% chance. Beyond a certain point, they all blur together as just "unlikely," and as long as the chance is even slightly above 0, we think, "Someone is going to win, and it might be me." Finally, it may be that the extreme unlikeliness of winning makes the bet even more appealing: People report more pleasure from a surprising gain than from an expected gain (Mellers, Schwartz, Ho, & Ritov, 1997). That is, a long-shot gambling win, which is a big surprise, provides more fun than your paycheck at work, or the money you knew your aunt would send you on your birthday, or any other routine gain.

Schedules of Reinforcement

Anyone who makes many bets will win some and lose some. The effect is similar to a variable-ratio schedule, as discussed in Chapter 6, but not exactly the same. (In a variable-ratio schedule, an unpredictable number of responses will eventually lead to reinforcement. In gambling, it is possible to keep on betting forever without winning.) Intermittent schedules of reinforcement lead to continued responding, even during a long period without reinforcement.

Howard Rachlin (1990) suggests that gamblers evaluate their success at the end of a string of bets that ends in a win. For example, suppose you lose bets on six horse races and then bet on a winner. If your bet on the winner pays more than the amount you lost on the first six bets, then you don't count your progress as "six losses, one win," but as "a net gain on the day, one overall win."

Now, imagine a man who buys tickets in a state lottery. Every year he spends hundreds of dollars, maybe thousands, without winning anything. Does he give up? If so, he must admit that all he had invested was a loss. If he continues to buy tickets, he maintains the hope of eventually hitting the jackpot, winning more than enough to make up

FIGURE 8.21c

for all the money he lost. One single payoff could make the whole string of bets a net win.

Vicarious Reinforcement and Punishment

Recall from the discussion of social-learning theory that people learn what to do and what to avoid by observing what happens to others. Recall also that vicarious reinforcement tends to be more effective than vicarious punishment.

State governments want to encourage people to buy lottery tickets (because they provide revenue for the government), so they encourage massive publicity for everyone who wins a big jackpot (Figure 8.25). You often see news reports

FIGURE 8.25 States that sponsor lotteries provide publicity and an exciting atmosphere for each big payoff. They hope that this publicity will provide vicarious reinforcement to encourage other people to buy lottery tickets. They do not publicize all the people who lost money on the lottery.

Gambling occurs in almost every culture that has possessions and money. Here, Egyptian men place bets at a racetrack.

showing some instant millionaire, delirious with excitement. (The state hopes that this vicarious reinforcement will induce you to buy lottery tickets.) You seldom see reports about the millions of people who bought tickets and won nothing.

The Influence of Heuristics

Using the availability heuristic, people assume that, if they can recall many examples of an event, that event must be common. You can see how this combines forces with vicarious reinforcement. Someone who sees a big lottery winner on television almost every week remembers many such examples and therefore overestimates the likelihood of winning the lottery.

The representativeness heuristic also plays a role in gambling. Suppose you are flipping a coin, recording the order of heads (H) and tails (T). Which of the following sequences do you think is more likely?

1. H H H H H H H H
2. H H H H H H H T

Although both sequences are equally likely, most people who have no training in probability theory think sequence 2 is more likely (Kahneman & Tversky, 1973). A sequence of all heads seems *unrepresentative* of usual experiences. However, representativeness does not alter the odds: Even after seven heads, another head is just as likely as a tail on the next flip.

The **gambler's fallacy,** an example of the representativeness heuristic, is *the belief that, if a particular outcome has not occurred for a while, its "turn" has come.* With regard to human behavior, this assumption usually succeeds: If your friends have gone out for pizza four nights in a row, they are indeed due to switch to something else. But truly random events do not "take turns." If the last seven spins on the roulette wheel landed on black numbers, red does not become more likely for the next spin. Losing your last 20 bets does not make you more likely to win your next bet.

Self-Esteem

Many gamblers have an additional reason for gambling that we cannot explain in terms of learning, memory, or errors in reasoning: They want to beat their opponent. For many habitual gamblers, their self-esteem is strongly tied to proving themselves to be "winners," and they like to make that point by winning someone else's money (Peck, 1986). Their self-esteem becomes more of an issue when gambling among friends and acquaintances than it does when gambling in a casino. Consequently, a habitual gambler who has been losing at a game of, say, craps or poker will sometimes bet wildly and foolishly in an effort to catch up.

In summary, we have the following explanations for why some people continue to gamble despite consistent losses:

- They believe that by skillfully choosing the right numbers they can increase their probability of winning a game of chance.
- If the potential prize is large, people act as if they do not understand the difference between a small chance of winning and an *extremely* small chance of winning.
- They can continue through a long losing streak if the (imagined) eventual payoff would be large enough to repay all their losses.
- They remember seeing or hearing about many people who have won big jackpots. They thus receive vicarious reinforcement for gambling, and they overestimate the probability of winning.
- They may believe that, after a long series of losses, the probability of winning increases.
- They are so eager to beat an opponent that they will take risks they know to be foolish.

Similar explanations apply to the gambles that people take in everyday life. If you drink and drive, or date someone who mistreated you in the past, you are taking a gamble—perhaps a foolish gamble. People take such risks for some of the same reasons just described.

One general point is that people usually have multiple reasons for their behavior. People do not gamble for just one reason any more than you went to college for just one reason. A second general point is that the principles of learning, memory, and cognition do not apply to separate domains; we can apply all of those principles to a single behavior, such as gambling.

SOMETHING TO THINK ABOUT

Recall the discussion on page 290 about how the phrasing of a question can influence someone's answer. For example, most people will take more risks to avoid a loss than they will to increase a gain. Can you use this principle to explain why many gamblers on a losing streak will continue betting, sometimes increasing their bets? Is there a different way for a gambler to think about the situation, to decrease the temptation to continue gambling? ✳

THE MESSAGE
Successful and Unsuccessful Problem Solving

After reading about all the common reasoning errors people make and the foolish gambles that people take, it is easy to despair of human intelligence and assume that we are all a bunch of fools. In a way we are, but in a way we are all geniuses too. Each of us has areas of expertise and near-expertise where we make excellent decisions, and areas of incompetence where we make embarrassing blunders. Learning about common errors may help us to avoid these blunders . . . at least sometimes.

SUMMARY

✳ *Becoming an expert.* Experts are made, not born. Becoming an expert requires years of practice and effort. (page 279)

✳ *Expert pattern recognition.* Experts recognize and memorize familiar and meaningful patterns more rapidly than less experienced people do. (page 281)

✳ *Steps for solving a problem.* People take four steps to solve a problem: understanding the problem, generating hypotheses, testing the hypotheses, and checking the result. (page 281)

✳ *Algorithms and heuristics.* People can solve problems by using algorithms (repetitive means of checking every possibility) or heuristics (ways of simplifying the problem to get a reasonable solution). (page 282)

✳ *Generalizing.* People who have learned how to solve a problem will not necessarily apply that solution to a similar problem. (page 283)

✳ *Insight.* With insight problems, people have trouble estimating how close they are to a solution. However, they may be making progress even if they do not realize that they are. (page 284)

✳ *Creativity.* Creative people do their creative work in a field in which they have knowledge and self-confidence; creativity does not generalize well from one field of endeavor to another. Many highly creative people go through a period in which they rely on a small group of friends, perhaps just one, for support and encouragement. They dedicate their lives to their work, often to the exclusion of all else. (page 285)

✳ *Reasons for errors.* People tend to be overconfident about their own judgments. Other common mistakes in human reasoning include premature commitment to a hypothesis, overreliance on the representativeness heuristic and the availability heuristic, and altering one's answer when the same question is framed in different terms. (page 287)

✳ *Reasons for gambling.* Gambling illustrates the combined influences of learning, memory, and cognition. Many people gamble despite consistent losses, because they overestimate their control, because they are insensitive to the difference between a small chance and an extremely small chance

of winning, because they experience vicarious reinforcement, and because they believe a series of losses makes an eventual win more likely. Some people gamble as a way of competing with others and of establishing their own self-esteem. (page 292)

Suggestion for Further Reading

Bransford, J. B., & Stein, B. S. (1984). *The ideal problem solver.* New York: Freeman. Advice about how to approach and solve both "mind-bender" problems and practical problems.

Terms

algorithm a mechanical, repetitive mathematical procedure for solving a problem (page 282)

heuristics strategies for simplifying a problem or for guiding an investigation (page 282)

creativity the development of novel, socially valued products (page 285)

functional fixedness the tendency to adhere to a single approach to a problem or a single way of using an item (page 288)

representativeness heuristic the tendency to assume that, if an item is similar to members of a particular category, it is probably a member of that category itself (page 289)

base-rate information data about the frequency or probability of a given item (page 289)

availability heuristic the strategy of assuming that the number of available memories of an event indicates how common the event actually is (page 290)

framing effect the tendency to answer a question differently when it is framed (phrased) differently (page 291)

gambler's fallacy the belief that, if a particular outcome has not occurred for a while, it becomes more likely than before (page 294)

Answers to Concept Checks

4. An algorithm would check each of the possible routes: If you had your home city (H) and three other cities (1, 2, and 3), the possible routes would be H-1-2-3-H, H-1-3-2-H, and H-2-1-3-H. (Three other routes that you could generate would be the mirror images of these three and therefore not necessary to consider.) As the number of cities increases, the number of possible routes rises rapidly. If you had to visit 10 cities, your algorithm would have to consider almost 2 million routes. One possible heuristic would be to consider only those routes from each city to one of the closest two other cities. (page 283)

5. Because many poets are recognized for their greatness while they are still young, it is possible to be a great poet and die young. As a rule, historians are in their 40s or later when they do their first outstanding work; therefore, it is almost impossible to be recognized as a great historian and to die young. (page 287)

6. The employer would fire 18 dishonest employees (90% of the 20 who had stolen). The employer would also fire 98 honest employees (10% of the 980 who had not stolen). That is, a clear majority of those identified as dishonest are

actually honest. (An employer might be willing to fire that many honest people in order to get rid of some dishonest people, but most employees would consider this action most unfair.) (page 290)

7. **a.** Failure to consider the base rate: 20% of all older adults is a larger number than 90% of all college students;
b. Premature commitment to one hypothesis without considering other hypotheses (such as that one could stay healthy without any magic words). (page 292)

Answers to Other Questions in the Text

C. The water in the tube would leak out of the hole in the bottom. Any membrane heavy enough to keep the water in would also keep the rubber balls out. (page 283)

D. This illustration shows how to cut and fold an ordinary piece of paper or cardboard to match the figure, with nothing left over. (page 284)

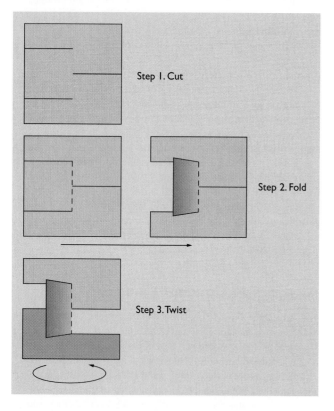

E. Set 1: The words *playing, credit,* and *report* are all associated with *card.* Set 2: The words *ticket, shop,* and *broker* are all associated with *pawn.* (page 285)

F. (1) The best way to attach the candle to the wall is to dump the matches from the box and thumbtack the bottom of the box to the wall, as shown in this picture. The tiny piece of string is useless.

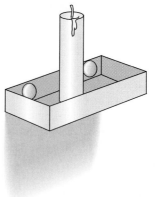

(2) The dots can be connected with four lines:

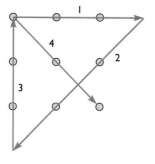

(3) One possible answer is that there are three students: one psychology major, one chemistry major, and one history major. The other possibility is that there are two students who are majoring in something else—music, for example. (If there are two music majors, all but two of them are indeed majoring in psychology, etc.) (page 288)

Web Resources

Creativity and Star Trek

www2.shore.net/~sek/STCreativity.html

Robert Sekuler and Randolph Blake, authors of *Star Trek on the Brain: Alien Minds, Human Minds,* offer an interesting exploration of creativity and some of the limitations on human creativity. Before you visit the creativity page, take a few minutes to draw a picture of a member of an alien race that no human has ever seen. Make it as different from human as you can. Click the link to the "Star Trek on the Brain" page for several interesting links.

MODULE 8.3

Language

How do we learn to understand language, to speak, and to read?

Does language have special properties that set it apart from other intelligent behaviors?

Language is an extremely versatile system. Other species have various ways of sending signals to one another, but only human languages have the property of **productivity,** *the ability to express new ideas.* Every day we say and hear a few stock sentences, such as "Nice weather we're having," or "I can't find my shoes," but we also say and hear sentences that no one has ever said before.

You might ask, "How can you know that no one has ever said that particular sentence before?!" Well, of course, we cannot know for sure that a particular sentence is new, but we can be confident that many sentences are new (without specifying which ones). Imagine trying this exercise (don't really try it unless you have an enormous amount of time to spare): Pick a sentence of 10 to 20 words from any book you choose. How long would you need to keep reading, in that book or any other, until you found exactly the same sentence again?

In short, we do not memorize all the sentences we will ever use; instead, we learn rules for making sentences and for interpreting other people's sentences. The famous linguist Noam Chomsky (1980) has described those rules as a **transformational grammar,** which is *a system for converting a deep structure into a surface structure.* The deep structure is the underlying logic of the language. The surface structure is the sequence of words as they are actually spoken or written (Figure 8.26). According to this theory, whenever we speak we transform the deep structure of the language into a surface structure. Two surface structures can resemble each other without representing the same deep structure, or conversely, they can represent the same deep structure without resembling each other.

For example, "John is easy to please" has the same deep structure as "pleasing John is easy" and "it is easy to please John." These sentences all represent the same underlying idea.

In contrast, consider the sentence, "Never threaten someone with a chain saw." The surface structure of that sentence maps into two quite different deep structures:

It is not nice to swing a chain saw around and threaten someone with it.

If you meet someone carrying a chain saw, don't make any threatening gestures.

The productivity of language enables humans to communicate and elaborate on ideas to a far greater extent than any other species can. Language researcher Terrence Deacon describes a brief talk about language and the brain that he presented to his 8-year-old son's elementary school class. One child in the class asked whether other animals have their own languages. Deacon explained that other species have various methods of communication, but none of them has a flexible system similar to human language. The child persisted, asking whether other animals had at least a *simple* language, perhaps one with only a limited vocabulary and a very simple grammar. No, he replied, they do not have even a simple language.

Then another child asked, "Why not?" (Deacon, 1997, p. 12). Deacon paused. And then paused some more. Why not, indeed. He realized that this 8-year-old child had asked a most profound question. If language is so extremely useful to humans, why haven't other species evolved at least a little of it?

Language comes easily to humans. Almost all children, even many mentally retarded children, learn their native language, even though their parents may know nothing about how to teach it. Meanwhile, nonhumans can learn only a little language at best, despite psychologists' concentrated efforts to teach it. Evidently, we humans are highly specialized for acquiring language.

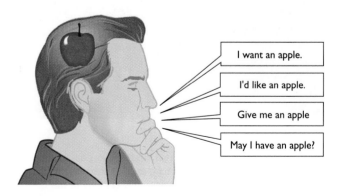

FIGURE 8.26 According to transformational grammar, we can transform a sentence with a given surface structure into any of several other sentences with different surface structures. All of them represent the same deep structure, which is the underlying logic of the sentence.

Precursors to Language in Chimpanzees and Bonobos

One way to examine humans' specialization for language is to determine how far other species could progress toward language, given sufficient training. Beginning in the 1920s, several psychologists reared chimpanzees in their homes and tried to teach them to talk. The chimpanzees learned many human habits (Figure 8.27) but showed only very limited understanding of language. Later, Allen Gardner and Beatrice Gardner (1969) taught a chimpanzee named Washoe to use the sign language that American deaf people use (Ameslan). Sign language is closer to the hand gestures that chimpanzees use naturally, and it does not require them to imitate human voice sounds, for which their vocal tracts are poorly adapted. Washoe eventually learned the symbols for about 100 words, which she occasionally linked into meaningful combinations, such as "cry hurt food" for a radish.

Other chimpanzees also learned to use such symbols, but a controversy arose about whether their use of symbols and gestures really resembles human language. In many

a

b

c

d

e

FIGURE 8.27 Speaking is physically impossible for chimpanzees, but some psychologists have tried to teach them to communicate by using gestures or symbols. (a) One of the Premacks' chimps arranges plastic chips to make a "sentence" request for food. (b) Viki in her human home, helping with the housework. After years with the Hayeses, she could make only a few sounds similar to English words. (c) Kanzi, a bonobo, presses symbols to indicate words. Among the primates, bonobos have shown the most promising ability to acquire language. (d) A chimp signing *toothbrush.* (e) Roger Fouts with Alley the chimp, who is signing *lizard.*

cases, chimpanzees' gestures were an imitation of symbols their human trainers had recently used (Terrace, Petitto, Sanders, & Bever, 1979). Moreover, they used their symbols almost exclusively to make requests, only rarely to describe things, and they seldom linked gestures together in anything like a sentence (Pate & Rumbaugh, 1983; Terrace et al., 1979; Thompson & Church, 1980). By contrast, a human child with a vocabulary of 100 words or so starts to link them together to make many original combinations and short sentences.

That, at any rate, was the conclusion derived from studies of the common chimpanzee, *Pan troglodytes*. Closely related to the common chimp is a rare and endangered species, *Pan paniscus*, sometimes known as the pygmy chimpanzee (a misleading term because these animals are almost as large as common chimpanzees) and sometimes known as the bonobo. Their social behavior resembles that of humans in several regards: Males and females form strong, long-lasting attachments; females are sexually responsive throughout the month, not just during their fertile period; males contribute much more to infant care than do other nonhuman primate males; and adults often share food with one another.

Several bonobos have used symbols in impressive ways. First, they occasionally use the symbols to name and describe objects that they are not requesting. Second, they sometimes use the symbols to describe past events. (One explained a cut on his hand by using gestures to indicate that his mother had bit him.) Third, they frequently make original, creative requests, such as asking one person to chase another person while the bonobo watched. Their comprehension is better than their production; a couple of bonobos seem to comprehend symbols about as well as a 2- to 2½-year-old child understands language (Savage-Rumbaugh et al., 1993).

A couple of bonobos have also shown considerable understanding of spoken English (Figure 8.28), responding correctly to unfamiliar spoken commands such as "throw your ball into the river" and "go to the refrigerator and get out a tomato" (Savage-Rumbaugh, 1990; Savage-Rumbaugh, Sevcik, Brakke, & Rumbaugh, 1992). They even passed the test of responding to commands issued over earphones, used to eliminate the possibility of unintentional "Clever Hans"-type signals, as discussed in Chapter 2.

The explanation for this impressive success probably pertains partly to species differences: Perhaps bonobos have greater language capacities than common chimpanzees. Another part of the explanation may pertain to the method of training: Learning by observation and imitation probably promotes better understanding than the formal training methods that were used in previous studies. (Savage-Rumbaugh, Sevcik, Brakke, & Rumbaugh, 1992). Finally, the bonobos began their language experience early in life. Songbirds learn their song more easily during an early sensitive period; humans apparently have a sensitive period for easy language acquisition early in life; perhaps the same is true for bonobos.

FIGURE 8.28 Kanzi, a bonobo, points to answers on a board in response to questions he hears through earphones. Experimenter Rose Sevcik sits with him but does not hear the questions, so she cannot intentionally or accidentally signal the correct answer.

CONCEPT CHECK

8. Based on the studies with bonobos, can you offer some good advice about how to teach language to children born with a disability that impairs language learning? (Check your answer on page 311.)

Human Specializations for Learning Language

Is the glass half full or half empty? Should we be impressed that bonobos understand language almost as well as a 2½-year-old child, or wonder why they do not progress further? Yes, bonobos sometimes construct two- or three-symbol combinations, but they do not produce full sentences. Humans are clearly specialized to learn language in a way that no other species can.

Susan Carey (1978) has estimated that children between the ages of 1½ and 6 learn an average of nine new words per day—almost one new word per hour! Deciphering the meanings of words would seem to be an overwhelmingly difficult task (Markman, 1990). Suppose someone points to a pillow and says "makura." If you were a Japanese child, you would accept *makura* as the word for *pillow*. You would also accept it as an adult trying to learn Japanese as a second language. But how did you know that the word *makura* meant *pillow?* Logically, it could have referred to all soft things, all cloth-covered things, all throwable things, or all things important at bedtime (including pajamas, darkened rooms, storybooks, and goodnight kisses). Sometimes children do guess wrong. For example, if you point to a dog and say "dog," most young children assume that the word also applies to other small animals. Similarly, many young children first use the word *daddy* to refer to all adult men. But it is remarkable that, when children learn new words, they more or less understand the meanings.

Noam Chomsky has argued that language is so complex, and so easily learned, that its development must not depend on ordinary types of learning. For example, consider this sentence: *The boy who is unhappy is watching Mickey Mouse.* How would you convert that sentence to a question, to ask whether it was true? I assume you find this easy: "Is the boy who is unhappy watching Mickey Mouse?" (You might also have asked, "Is the boy who is watching Mickey Mouse unhappy?") Even most preschool children phrase the question correctly; virtually none of them say, "Is the boy who unhappy is watching Mickey Mouse?" How did those preschoolers know the right way to phrase the question? Chomsky argues that children have so seldom heard such questions that they have not had adequate opportunity to learn the rather complicated grammatical rule. He and his followers therefore suggest that people are born with a **language acquisition device** or "language instinct," *a built-in mechanism for acquiring language* (Pinker, 1994). The basis for this theory is known as the **poverty of the stimulus argument:** *What children hear does not provide enough information for them to learn or infer grammar, so they must be born with that knowledge.*

Most psychologists concede that people must be born with some sort of language predisposition; after all, children who are taught under the worst conditions acquire far more language than chimpanzees taught under the best conditions. However, many researchers still question the poverty of the stimulus argument, because grammar differs enormously from one language to another. If you grew up in an English-speaking family, you quickly learned to phrase questions like, "Is the boy who is unhappy watching Mickey Mouse?" But if you had been adopted in infancy by a family living somewhere else in the world, you could have learned to speak Finnish, Mandarin, Hindi, Navajo, Zulu, or any other language, which might have a grammar radically different from English. It is easy to agree that infants must be born with something that facilitates language learning, but it is implausible to suppose that this something would "tell" the infant how to phrase an English question about an unhappy boy who might be watching Mickey Mouse (Deacon, 1997; Seidenberg, 1997).

We are forced, then, to reexamine the idea that infants can actually learn all the complexities of word meanings and grammar from apparently meager information. Perhaps this task is not as nearly impossible as it sounds. In one study, researchers fed the text of an electronic encyclopedia into a computer that was programmed to detect which words were used in similar contexts. At the end, the computer was able to pass simple language tests, such as identifying synonyms for a word (Landauer & Dumais, 1997). Furthermore, parents throughout the world simplify language by speaking "parentese." I am not talking about idiotic "goo-goo" baby talk, but a pattern of speech that emphasizes and prolongs the vowels, making more clear than usual the difference between words such as *cat* and *cot* (Kuhl et al., 1997). Infants listen more intently to *parentese* than to normal speech and learn more from it.

Some psychologists have even proposed that language learning is easy for children specifically *because* their memory is imperfect (Newport, 1990). They cannot remember everything they hear, so they remember the patterns that occur regularly; in effect, they ignore the trees and perceive the forest.

Language and the Human Brain

What aspect of the human brain enables us to learn language so easily? One hypothesis is that language is simply an accidental by-product of humans' large brains and superior intelligence. One major problem with that hypothesis is that dolphins and whales have larger brains than humans have but do not develop language. (Yes, they communicate, but not in a flexible system resembling human language.) Furthermore, some people with massive brain damage have less total brain mass than a chimpanzee, but depending on the location of the damage, they can continue to speak and understand language. Also, people with certain genetic abnormalities develop normal intelligence except for impaired language (Gopnik & Crago, 1991), or impressive language skills despite mental retardation in all other regards (Bellugi, Wang, & Jernigan, 1994). So language is not just a by-product of overall intelligence or brain size; it must reflect a special organization of our brain.

Studies of brain-damaged people have long pointed to two brain areas as particularly important for language. People with damage in the frontal cortex, including *Broca's area* (Figure 8.29), develop **Broca's aphasia,** *a condition characterized by inarticulate speech and by difficulties with both using and understanding grammatical devices— prepositions, conjunctions, word endings, complex sentence structures, and so forth.* These people do not really lose all grammatical understanding; they merely find it much more difficult to use and understand language, much as undamaged people do when they are extremely distracted (Blackwell & Bates, 1995). People with damage in the temporal cortex, including *Wernicke's area* (Figure 8.29), develop **Wernicke's aphasia,** *a condition marked by difficulty recalling the names of objects and impaired comprehension of language.* Because these people do not remember names, their speech is nonsensical, even when it is grammatical. For example, one patient responded to a question about his health, "I felt worse because I can no longer keep in mind from the mind of the minds to keep me from mind and up to the ear which can be to find among ourselves" (Brown, 1977).

However, language did not evolve by simply adding a language circuit to an otherwise nonlinguistic brain. The

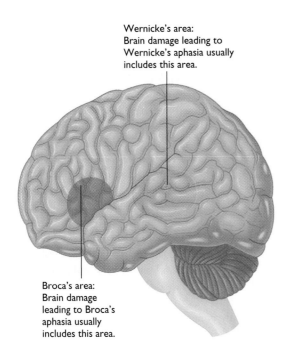

Wernicke's area:
Brain damage leading to
Wernicke's aphasia usually
includes this area.

Broca's area:
Brain damage
leading to Broca's
aphasia usually
includes this area.

F I G U R E   8.29 Brain damage that produces major deficits in language usually includes the left-hemisphere areas shown here. However, the deficits are severe only if the damage is more extensive, including these areas but extending to others as well. Many areas of the human brain contribute to language comprehension and production.

human brain is not just an ape brain with language ability tacked on; it displays enormous expansion of the prefrontal cortex, increased connections among cortical areas, and numerous other specializations to facilitate language (Deacon, 1997). Broca's area and Wernicke's area are important for language, but they are hardly the only important areas. Brain damage that seriously impairs language generally includes either Broca's or Wernicke's area but also includes other areas. Furthermore, PET scans or other recordings of the brain show widespread activation during speech or

language listening. It is hardly an exaggeration to say that the whole human brain is specialized to use and manipulate symbols to make language possible.

Stages of Language Development

Table 8.3 lists the average ages at which children reach various stages of language ability (Lenneberg, 1969; Moskowitz, 1978). Progression through these stages depends largely on maturation, not just extra experience (Lenneberg, 1967, 1969). Parents who expose their children to as much language as possible find that they can increase the children's vocabulary a bit, but they hardly affect the ages at which children reach various stages of language development (Figure 8.30). At the other extreme, in terms of exposure to language, hearing children of deaf parents are exposed to very little spoken language, but if they have periodic contact with speaking people, they progress through the various stages of language development almost on schedule.

For the first 6 months or so, deaf infants babble as much as hearing infants do. After that, deaf infants babble less. At first, babbling produces only haphazard sounds, but soon the infant starts repeating the sounds that are common in the language that the baby has been hearing, while discarding other sounds that the baby has not been hearing. Thus, by the age of 1 year, French babies babble French sounds, Chinese babies babble Chinese sounds, and so forth (Locke, 1994).

By the age of 1 year, infants begin to understand language, and most can say at least a word or two. Throughout the world, one of the first sounds to be uttered is *muh.* Parents in most parts of the world have defined *muh-muh* (or something similar to it) as meaning "mother." Infants also typically make the sounds *duh, puh,* and *buh;* they almost never make the sound *s.* In many languages, the word for father is similar to *daddy* or *papa. Baba* is the word for grandmother in several languages. In effect, infants tell

AGE	TYPICAL LANGUAGE ABILITIES (MUCH INDIVIDUAL VARIATION)
TABLE 8.3 Stages of Language Development	
3 months	Random vocalizations.
6 months	More distinct babbling.
1 year	Babbling that resembles the typical sounds of the family's language; probably one or more words including "mama"; language comprehension much better than production.
1½ years	Can say some words (mean about 50), mostly nouns; no phrases.
2 years	Speaks in two-word phrases.
2½ years	Longer phrases and short sentences, with some errors and unusual constructions. Can understand much more.
3 years	Vocabulary of about 1,000 words; longer sentences with fewer errors.
4 years	Close to adult speech competence.

FIGURE 8.30 Some overeager parents try to teach their children language at a very early age. The child may enjoy the attention, but the activity is unlikely to accelerate the child's progress in language development.

their parents what words to use for certain concepts. Indeed, Deacon (1997) makes the point that languages in general evolve to become easy for infants to learn.

By age 1½, most toddlers can say a few words. (The mean is about 50.) However, they seldom link words together. Thus, a toddler who can say "Daddy" and "bye-bye" may still be unable to say "Bye-bye, Daddy." In context, parents can usually discern considerable meaning in these single-word utterances. *Mama* might mean, "That's a picture of Mama," "Take me to Mama," "Mama went away and left me here," or "Mama, I'm hungry."

Some toddlers follow a pattern of language development that is different from the usual one (Nelson, 1981). Instead of speaking one word at a time and learning the names of objects, these children speak poorly articulated, compressed phrases, such as "Do-it-again" or "I-like-read-Goodnight-Moon." At first, these expressions are so poorly pronounced that adults may not realize the child is doing anything but babbling. Children who start off by generating these complex requests and phrases tend to continue doing so (Nelson, Baker, Denninger, Bonvillian, & Kaplan, 1985).

By age 2, children start producing "telegraphic" phrases of two or more words, including combinations such as "more page," "allgone sticky," and "allgone outside," to indicate "read some more," "my hands are now clean," and "someone has closed the door," respectively. Note the originality of such phrases; it is unlikely that children learned them by imitating their parents!

By age 2½ to 3 years, most children are generating full sentences, though each child maintains a few peculiarities. For example, many young children have their own rules for forming negative sentences. A common one is to add *no* or *not* to the beginning or end of a sentence, such as, "No I want to go to bed!" One little girl formed her negatives just by saying something louder and at a higher pitch; for instance, if she shrieked, "I want to share my toys!" she really meant, "I do *not* want to share my toys." Presumably, she had learned this "rule" by remembering that people screamed at her when they told her not to do something. My son Sam made negatives for a while by adding the word *either* to the end of a sentence: "I want to eat lima beans

either." Apparently, he had heard people say, "I don't want to do that either" and had decided that the word *either* at the end of the sentence made it an emphatic negative.

At this same age, children act as if they were applying grammatical rules. (I say "as if" because they cannot state the rules. By the same token, baseball players who anticipate exactly where a fly ball will come down act "as if" they understood complex laws of physics and calculus.) For example, a child may learn the word *feet* at an early age and then, after learning other plurals, abandon it in favor of *foots*. Later, the child begins to compromise by saying "feets," "footses," or "feetses," before eventually returning to "feet." Children at this stage say many things they have never heard anyone else say, such as "the mans comed" or "the womans goed and doed something." Clearly, they are applying rules for how to form plurals and past tenses, although they *overregularize* or *overgeneralize* those rules. My son David invented the word *shis* to mean "belonging to a female." He had apparently generalized the rule "He—his, she—shis." Note that all these inventions imply that children are learning rules, not just repeating word combinations.

CONCEPT CHECK

9. At what age do children begin to string words into novel combinations that they have never heard anyone say before? Why do psychologists believe that even very young children learn some of the rules of grammar? (Check your answers on page 311.)

Children Exposed to No Language or to Two Languages

If children weren't exposed to any language at all, would they make up one of their own? In rare cases, an infant who was somehow separated from all humans has grown up in a forest until discovered a few years later. Those children not only failed to show a language of their own but also failed to learn much of human language after they were given the opportunity (Pinker, 1994). However, we have no way of knowing for sure whether those children tried to develop a language when they were younger, or whether they would have tried, if they had had companions capable of responding to them.

The closest we can come to duplicating such an experience is the unfortunate condition of some deaf children. A child who cannot hear well enough to learn speech and who never sees anyone using sign language is effectively isolated from all language. The results are consistent: Those children make up their own sign language. As they grow older, they make the system more complex, linking signs together into sentences with fairly consistent word order and grammatical rules—for example, "Mother, twist open the jar, blow a bubble, so I can clap it" (Goldin-Meadow, McNeill, & Singleton, 1996; Goldin-Meadow & Mylander, 1998). Most deaf children manage to teach their system, or at least part of it, to one or both parents, although the parents do not become as fluent as the children. Deaf children who spend much time together adopt each other's signs and eventually develop a unified system.

Although each deaf child invents a different system, most systems share some interesting similarities. For example, most include some sort of marker to indicate the difference between a subject that is doing something to an object ("the mouse eats the cheese") and a subject that is doing something without an object ("the mouse is moving"). The sign languages invented by children in Taiwan resemble those of children in the United States, even though the hearing adults in those countries are using languages with very different grammars—Chinese and English (Goldin-Meadow & Mylander, 1998).

Some children grow up in a **bilingual** environment, *learning two languages about equally well.* Bilingualism is especially common among immigrant children, who are generally bicultural as well, learning both their parents' customs and those of their new country. The representation of language in the brain is almost the same in bilingual people as it is in those who speak only one language. The research results clearly indicate that bilingual language capacity is neither more nor less lateralized to the left hemisphere than is a single language (Paradis, 1990; Solin, 1989). In the frontal cortex, in and around Broca's area, bilingual people use slightly different areas when speaking in one language or the other, but the difference is even smaller among people who have been bilingual since infancy (Kim, Relkin, Lee, & Hirsch, 1997).

If the brain representations are so similar, how do bilingual people keep their two languages separate? The answer is that they do not, at least not completely (Bijeljac-Babic, Biardeau, & Grainger, 1997). For example, one study asked people to say the ink color of various English and Spanish words, saying them all in English. You can try this task yourself with the following display:

TRY IT YOUR-SELF

literature than someone who speaks only one language. The benefits are particularly obvious for someone who learns two widely used languages, such as English and Chinese.

A second advantage of bilingualism is more subtle: A bilingual person gains extra cognitive flexibility by learning that there are different ways of expressing the same idea. For example, children younger than 6 years old who speak only one language show a strong belief that every object has one and only one name. For example, if an adult gestures toward a cup and a gyroscope and says, "please bring me the gyroscope," a child who knows the word *cup* will immediately bring the gyroscope, assuming that if one object is the cup, the other one must be the gyroscope. But the child would also fetch the gyroscope if asked to bring the *vessel,* the *chalice,* or any other synonym for *cup.* A bilingual child, however, is more likely to hesitate or to ask for clarification, showing an understanding that the unfamiliar word could refer to the cup just as easily as it could refer to the unknown object (Davidson, Jergovic, Imami, & Theodos, 1997).

CONCEPT CHECK

10. Suppose you know that someone understands both English and another language, and you want to determine what that language is without even asking. How could you do this, using one of the tasks described in this section? (Check your answer on page 311.)

Understanding Language

Making sense of what we see and hear is a complex process that requires knowledge about the world. For example, consider the following sentences (from Just & Carpenter, 1987):

YELLOW GREEN **RED BLUE VERDE AZUL AMARILLO** ROJO

If you speak only English, you probably had more trouble with the first four than with the second four. However, if you knew that *verde, azul, amarillo,* and *rojo* are the Spanish words for *green, blue, yellow,* and *red,* respectively, then you probably had some difficulty with the second four as well, demonstrating the *bilingual Stroop effect.* The better your knowledge of Spanish, the more difficult those last four items will be, even though you know you are supposed to suppress your Spanish and answer in English (Altarriba & Mathis, 1997).

Bilingualism has two disadvantages: Children take longer to master two languages than to master one (naturally), and even adult bilinguals occasionally confuse or intermix words from the two languages. The primary advantage is obvious: Someone who understands two languages well can speak with more people and read a greater variety of

That store sells horse shoes.

That store sells alligator shoes.

We would not interpret the second sentence as referring to "shoes for alligators to wear," because alligators do not wear shoes. But that is a fact you had to know; the sentences themselves do not tell you that horses wear horseshoes but people wear alligator shoes. Here is another example:

I'm going to buy a pet hamster at the store, if it's open.

I'm going to buy a pet hamster at the store, if it's healthy.

Nothing about the sentence structure told you that *it* in the first sentence refers to the store and in the second sentence to the hamster. You understood because you know that stores (but not hamsters) can be open, whereas hamsters (but not stores) can be healthy. In short, language comprehension depends on assumptions that the speaker and the listener—or the writer and the reader—share.

The context can change the meaning of whole sentences as well as individual words (Just & Carpenter, 1987). (See Figure 8.31.) For example, we generally interpret the proverb "time flies like an arrow" to mean that time passes quickly. But consider the same sentence in two other (far-fetched) contexts:

Q: You taught me one method to time the motion of cars, and a different way to time the flight of arrows. But how should I time the flight of houseflies?
A: Time flies like an arrow.

This science-fiction world has some weird insects—space flies, gravity flies, and time flies. They all eat wood, but each fly likes a different kind. Space flies like to eat a desk. Most gravity flies like chairs. Time flies like an arrow.

Language comprehension is immensely complicated, as people discover when they try to program a computer to understand language (Just & Carpenter, 1987). And yet, most of the time, we understand what we hear and read without any noticeable effort. Although many questions remain to

be answered, researchers have also made some discoveries about how comprehension takes place.

Hearing a Word as a Whole

We customarily describe the word *cat* as being composed of three sounds, *kuh, ah,* and *tuh.* In a sense this is misleading: The first sound in cat is not quite the same as the consonant sound in *kuh;* the *a* and *t* sounds are changed also. Each letter changes its sound depending on the other sounds that precede it and follow it. We cannot hear the separate letters of a word; we must hear the word as a whole.

One of the clearest demonstrations of this principle was an experiment in which students listened to a tape recording of a sentence with one sound missing (Warren, 1970). The sentence was, "The state governors met with their respective legislatures convening in the capital city." However, the sound of the first *s* in the word *legislatures,* along with part of the adjacent *i* and *l,* had been replaced by a cough or a tone. The students were asked to listen to the recording and try to identify the location of the cough or tone. None of the 20 students identified the location correctly, and half thought the cough or tone interrupted one of the other words on the tape. They all claimed to have heard the *s* plainly. In fact, even those who had been told that the *s* sound was missing still insisted that they had heard the sound. Apparently, the brain uses the context to fill in the missing sound.

Understanding Words in Context

Many words have different meanings in different contexts. *Rose* can refer to a flower, or it can be the past tense of the verb *to rise.* Consider the word *mean* in this sentence: "What did that mean old statistician mean by asking us to find the mean and mode of this distribution?"

Just as we hear the word *legislatures* as a whole, not as a string of separate letters, we interpret a sequence of words as a whole, not one at a time. For example, suppose you hear a tape-recorded sound that is carefully engineered to sound halfway between *dent* and *tent.* If you simply hear it and are asked to say what you heard, you might reply "dent," "tent," or "something sort of intermediate between dent and tent." But now, suppose you hear that same sound in context:

1. When the *ent in the fender was well camouflaged, we sold the car.
2. When the *ent in the forest was well camouflaged, we began our hike.

Most people who hear sentence 1 report the word *dent.* Most who hear sentence 2 report *tent.* Now consider two more sentences:

3. When the *ent was noticed in the fender, we sold the car.
4. When the *ent was noticed in the forest, we stopped to rest.

Great wall of china.

Our new china patterns underscore Gorham's commitment to dinnerware that can proudly stand next to our highly popular crystal stemware and our inveterately successful sterling flatware. To see it all, talk to your Gorham representative or write Gorham. P.O. Box 6150, Providence. RI 02940.

GORHAM. THE PERFECT SETTING.

GORHAM

FIGURE 8.31 Many clever ads take advantage of the fact that a given word can have several meanings and that the readers will figure out the intended meaning based on the context.

For sentences 3 and 4, the context does not help. People are as likely to report hearing *dent* in one sentence as they are in the other (Connine, Blasko, & Hall, 1991). Think for a moment what this means: In the first two sentences, the fender or forest showed up three syllables after *ent. In the second pair, the fender or forest showed up six syllables later. Evidently, when you hear an ambiguous sound, you can hold it in a temporary "undecided" state for about three syllables for the context to help you understand it. Beyond that point, it is too late for the context to help; you hear it one way or the other and stick with your decision, even if the later context contradicts it.

Although a delayed context cannot help you hear an ambiguous word correctly, it can help you understand what it means. Consider the following sentence from Karl Lashley (1951):

> Rapid righting with his uninjured hand saved from loss the contents of the capsized canoe.

If you hear this sentence spoken aloud, so that spelling is not a clue, you are likely at first to hear the second word as *writing*. That is a perfectly reasonable interpretation, until you reach the final two words of the sentence. Suddenly the phrase *capsized canoe* changes the whole scenario; now we understand that *righting* meant "pushing with a paddle." In summary, only the immediate context can influence what you hear, but even a much delayed context can influence what you think the sentence means.

Understanding Negatives

Suppose you are trying to decide whether to buy a product at the supermarket. You notice on the package, "Contains no cyanide or rat pieces." Do you become more likely or less likely to buy it? Less likely, if you are like most people. It is as though you did not fully believe the "no." (After all, why would the manufacturer even mention the absence of poisons and disgusting contaminants unless there were some reason to believe these might be present?) Similarly, people who read that "Bob Talbert is not linked with the Mafia" tend to remember the hint that he might have been linked with the Mafia (Wegner, Wenzlaff, Kerker, & Beattie, 1981).

Even if you had every reason to believe the denial, you still might act as though you did not believe it. Students in one study watched as an experimenter poured sugar into two jars. The students were then told to place whichever label they wanted on each jar. One label said "sucrose, table sugar." The other said "not sodium cyanide, not poison." Then, the experimenter made two cups of Kool-Aid, one with sugar from one jar and one from sugar in the other jar, and asked the students to choose one cup of Kool-Aid (Figure 8.32). Almost half the students said they had no preference, but of those who did have a preference, 35 of 44 wanted the Kool-Aid made from the jar marked "sucrose," not from the one that denied having cyanide and poison (Rozin, Markwith, & Ross, 1990). The students acted as though the label "not cyanide" meant something was wrong with the sugar in that jar.

People have particular trouble understanding double negatives, such as "she is not unfriendly." The state of Illinois gives the following instructions to the jurors in a murder case; note the four (!) negatives in this one sentence (emphasis added):

> If you do *not* unanimously find from your consideration of all the evidence that there are *no* mitigating factors sufficient to *preclude* the imposition of a death sentence, then you should sign the verdict requiring the court to impose a sentence *other than* death.

Does that sound clear to you? Do you think the author of these instructions was trying to make the point clear to a jury?

SOMETHING TO THINK ABOUT

Sometimes, a newspaper prints an accusation ("Joe Shmo accused of selling drugs to children") and later admits that the information was wrong. The accused person sometimes complains that the original charge was made in the form of a prominent headline but the retraction is buried in

FIGURE 8.32 Most students preferred Kool-Aid made with sugar labeled "sugar" instead of sugar labeled "not cyanide," even though they had placed the labels themselves. Evidently, people do not fully believe the word "not." (Based on results of Rozin, Markwith, & Ross, 1990.)

the back pages where most readers overlook it. Should the accused person *want* the retraction ("Joe Shmo did not sell drugs to children") to be a prominent headline? ✳

Reading

As you will recall from earlier in this chapter, expertise in a chosen field, achieved after years of practice, enables one to recognize complex patterns at a glance. You may not think of yourself as an "expert" reader, but only because we usually reserve the term *expert* for someone who is far more skilled than everyone else. Nevertheless, your years of practice at reading enable you to recognize words almost instantaneously.

Consider the following experiment: The investigator flashes a single letter on a screen for less than a quarter of a second and then flashes an interfering pattern on the screen and asks, "What was the letter, C or J?" Then the experimenter flashes an entire word on the screen for the same length of time and asks, "What was the first letter of the word, C or J?" (Figure 8.33). Which question do you think would be easier to answer? Most people can *identify the letter more accurately when it is part of a whole word than when it is presented by itself* (Reicher, 1969; Wheeler, 1970). This is known as the **word-superiority effect.**

In a follow-up experiment, James Johnston and James McClelland (1974) briefly flashed words on the screen and asked students to identify one letter (whose position was marked) in each word (Figure 8.34). On some trials, they told the students to focus on the center of the area where the word would appear and to try to see the whole word. On other trials, they showed the students exactly where the critical letter would appear on the screen and told them to focus on that spot and ignore the rest of the screen. Most students more successfully identified the critical letter when they were told to look at the whole word than when they focused on just the letter itself.

The context of other letters aids recognition only if the combination is a word or something similar. For example, it is easier to recognize the difference between COIN and JOIN than the difference between C and J. But it is easier to recognize the difference between C and J than the difference between XQCF and XQJF (Rumelhart & McClelland, 1982).

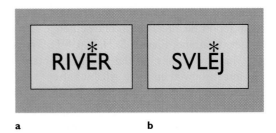

a   b

FIGURE 8.34 Students performed better at identifying an indicated letter when they focused on an entire word (a) than when they were asked to remember a single letter in a designated spot among random letters (b).

You may have experienced the word-superiority effect yourself. A common game on long car trips is to try to find every letter of the alphabet on the billboards along the way. Many people find it easier to spot a particular letter by reading whole words than by checking letter by letter.

What accounts for the word-superiority effect? According to one model (McClelland, 1988; Rumelhart, McClelland, & the PDP Research Group, 1986), our perceptions and memories are represented by vast numbers of connections among "units," presumably corresponding to neurons or sets of neurons. Each unit is connected to other units (Figure 8.35).

Each unit, when activated, excites some of its neighbors and inhibits others to varying degrees. Suppose that, at a given moment, units corresponding to the letters C, O, I, and N are moderately active—not quite active enough for a firm identification of each letter. These units excite a higher-order unit corresponding to the word COIN. Although none of the four letter units sends a strong message by itself, the collective impact is strong (McClelland & Rumelhart, 1981). This higher-level perception COIN then feeds excitation back to the letter-identifying units and confirms their tentative decisions, because they make sense in context.

Figure 8.36 is an example of the kind of phenomenon this model attempts to explain. Why do you see the top word in that figure as *RED* instead of *PFB*? After all, in the three other words of that figure, you do see those letters as *P, F,* and *B.* But in the top word, one ambiguous figure activates some *P* units and some *R* units; the next figure activates *E* and *F* units, and the third figure activates *D* and *B* units. All of those units in turn activate other, more complex

FIGURE 8.33 Do you *C a J?* (a, b) A student watches either a word or a single letter flashed on a screen. (c, d) An interfering pattern is then flashed on the screen and the student is asked, "Which was presented: *C* or *J*?" More students were able to identify the letter correctly when it was part of a word.

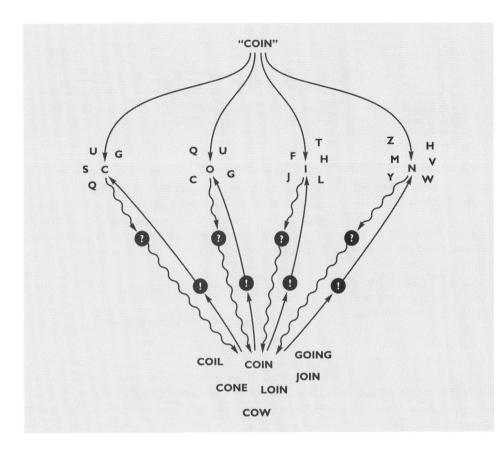

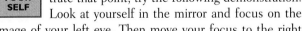

FIGURE 8.35 According to one version of the connectionist model, a visual stimulus activates certain letter units, some more strongly than others. Those letter units then activate a word unit, which in turn strengthens the letter units that compose it. For this reason, we recognize a whole word more easily than we recognize a single letter.

units corresponding to *RFB, PFB, PFD,* and *RED.* Because *RED* is the only English word in the group, the units that correspond to *RED* are easier to activate than those for *PFB* and the others. Consequently, you perceive the word as *RED.* As the *RED* unit becomes active, it in turn provides feedback to strengthen the activity of the *R, E,* and *D* units.

Reading and Eye Movements

In an alphabetic language such as English, the printed page consists of letters, which often form familiar clusters, which in turn form words and, finally, sentences. One kind of cluster is a **phoneme,** *a unit of sound.* A phoneme can be a single letter (such as *f*) or a combination of letters (such as *sh*). Another kind of cluster is a **morpheme,** *a unit of meaning.* For example, the word *thrills* has two morphemes (*thrill* and *s*). The final *s* is a unit of meaning because it indicates that the word is plural. (See Figure 8.37.)

CONCEPT CHECK

11. How many phonemes are in the word *thoughtfully?* How many morphemes? (Check your answers on page 311.)

When we read, do we ordinarily read one letter, one phoneme, one morpheme, or one word at a time, or do we read several words at once? And do we move our eyes steadily or in a jerky fashion? The movements are so fast that we cannot answer these questions by self-inspection.

Psychologists have arranged devices to monitor people's eye movements during reading. Their first discovery was that a reader's eyes move in a jerky fashion, not steadily. You can move your eyes steadily when they are following a moving object, but when you are scanning a stationary object such as a page of print, you alternate between *periods called* **fixations,** *when your eyes are stationary,* and *quick eye movements called* **saccades** *that take your eyes from one fixation point to another.* You read during your fixations; you are virtually blind during the saccades. To illustrate that point, try the following demonstration: Look at yourself in the mirror and focus on the image of your left eye. Then move your focus to the right

TRY IT YOUR-SELF

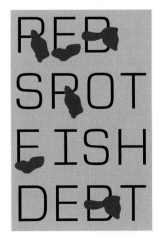

FIGURE 8.36 A pattern across letters enables us to identify a word; word recognition in turn helps to confirm the letter identifications. Although each of the letters in the top word is ambiguous, a whole word—RED—is perceived. (From Rumelhart, McClelland, & the PDP Research Group, 1986.)

FIGURE 8.37 The word *shamelessness* has nine phonemes (units of sound) and three morphemes (units of meaning).

eye. Can you see your eyes moving in the mirror? (Go ahead; try it.) People generally agree that they cannot see their eyes move; that is, they are virtually blind during the eye movement.

"Oh, but wait," you say. "That slight movement of my eyes in the mirror was simply too quick and too small a movement to be seen." Wrong. Try again, but this time get someone else to look at your left eye and then shift his or her gaze to your right eye. Now you do see the other person's eye movement, so the movement itself is not too fast or too small to be seen. Go back and try your own eyes in the mirror again and observe the difference. You can see someone else's eyes moving, but you cannot see your own eyes moving in the mirror.

There are two reasons for this: First, certain areas in the parietal cortex monitor impending eye movements and send a message to the primary visual cortex, in effect telling the visual cortex, "The eyes are about to move, so shut down activity for a moment." Even if you are in total darkness, the visual cortex decreases its activity during saccadic eye movements (Burr, Morrone, & Ross, 1994; Paus, Marrett, Worsley, & Evans, 1995). Second, what you see at the end of a saccade interferes with what you saw during the saccade (Matin, Clymer, & Matin, 1972). That is, when you see a brief blur followed by a distinct stimulus, your brain concentrates on the distinct stimulus and ignores the blur.

An average adult reading a newspaper or magazine article fixates on each point for an average of about 200 milliseconds (ms). Good readers generally have shorter fixations than poor readers do (Just & Carpenter, 1987), and everyone has shorter fixations on familiar words like *girl* than on difficult words like *ghoul*. After each fixation, the saccade lasts about 25–50 ms. Thus, a typical reader has about four fixations per second.

(In the attentional blink experiments discussed earlier, a letter that is flashed on the screen interferes with another letter that is flashed 200 ms later. So why doesn't one fixation interfere with another one when you are reading? The main explanation is that the flashes are very brief in the attentional blink experiments. The other explanation relates to the word-superiority effect: It is easier to read whole words, especially in the context of a meaningful sentence, than to identify isolated letters.)

How much can a person read during one fixation? Many people have the impression that they see quite a bit of the page at each instant. Like many informal impressions, this one is wrong. Research indicates that we generally read only about 11 characters—one or two words—at a time. Recall

from Chapter 4 that human vision has its greatest acuity in the fovea, an area in the center of the retina. You can read letters when you fixate them in the fovea, but your ability to read drops sharply in the surrounding area. To demonstrate this phenomenon, focus on the point marked by an arrow (↓) in the sentences below.

↓
1. This is a sentence with no misspelled words.
↓
2. Xboc tx zjg rxunce with no mijvgab zucn.
↓
3. Xboc tx zjg rxuhnj with zw cjvvgab zucn.

If you permit your eyes to wander back and forth, you quickly notice that sentences 2 and 3 are mostly gibberish. But as long as you dutifully keep your eyes on the fixation point in sentence 2, it may look all right. You can read the letter on which you fixated plus about three or four characters (including spaces) to the left and about seven to the right. This is enough for you to see—*ce with no m*—, or possibly—*nce with no mi*—. You cannot see the more distant letters well enough to be sure whether or not they spell out real words. In sentence 3, however, you do notice something wrong. Even while keeping your eyes carefully fixated on the *i* in *with,* you can see that the next word is the nonsense combination *zw* and that the previous word ends with *j,* unlike any English word you can think of.

In a study documenting this phenomenon, college students read text on a computer screen while a machine monitored their eye positions and fed that information to the computer. The computer correctly displayed whatever word a student was fixating on, plus a certain number of letters on each side of it. Beyond those letters, the computer displayed only gibberish. Students very rarely noticed that anything was unusual, unless the computer started displaying gibberish letters closer than three characters to the left or seven characters to the right of the fixation point (Underwood & McConkie, 1985). Apparently, we read in a "window" of about 11 letters—the fixated letter, about three characters to its left, and about seven to its right.

In many cases, that window includes one word plus a fragment of the next word. For example, suppose you have fixated on the point shown by an arrow in the sentence below:

↓
The government made serious mistakes.

Because of the research just described, we know that readers can see the word *serious* plus about the first three letters of *mistakes.* Three letters do not identify the word *mistakes;* from what the reader knows, that next word could be *misspellings, misbehavior, missiles, mishmash,* or any of a number of other *mis*-things that a government might make. Does the "preview" of the next word facilitate reading? Yes. In one study, college students again read passages on a computer screen while a machine monitored their eye movements. The computer correctly displayed the word the student fixated on plus the next zero, three, or four letters. So the display might look like this:

↓
The government made xxxxxxx xxxxxxxx.
↓
The government made serious xxxxxxxx.
↓
The government made serious mistakes.

or like this:

↓
The government made serxxxx xxxxxxxx.
↓
The government made serious misxxxxx.
↓
The government made serious mistakes.

Students who could preview the first three or four letters of the next word read significantly faster than those who could not (Inhoff, 1989). Evidently, we do not read just one word at a time. While we are reading one word, we are previewing the next.

Would it be possible to learn to read more letters in each fixation? Perhaps, but doing so might not be helpful. Some people do read more letters per fixation, especially to the right of the fixation point. Far from gaining an advantage, such people suffer from *dyslexia,* a specific impairment of reading (Geiger, Lettvin, & Zegarra-Moran, 1992). They see too many words at once, thus confuse them, and consequently have trouble identifying any of them.

Some people read much faster than others; for example, you might wonder what "speed readers" do differently from normal readers. An average adult reader has about four or five fixations per second with occasional backtracks, for an overall rate of about 200 words per minute. Speed readers have more and briefer fixations and fewer backtracks and can double or triple their reading speed while maintaining normal comprehension. However, those who claim that they can increase their reading speed to five or ten thousand words per minute must be skipping over many of the words altogether. Saccadic eye movements last 25 to 50 ms by themselves, and the results clearly indicate that reading does not occur during saccades. Thus, it would be impossible to exceed 20–40 fixations per second, even if each fixation lasted no time at all! Given that each fixation identifies one or two words, depending on the length of the word, the theoretical maximum would be 20–80 words per second, or 1,200–4,800 words per minute. And, remember, this calculation unrealistically assumes a fixation time of

Reading is a complex skill that includes many stages, from eye movements through understanding and using the material. Investigators find that they cannot separate these stages, though how well a reader understands the material influences the speed of the eye movements. By studying reading, psychologists hope to improve methods of teaching reading.

zero. People who read faster than about 600 words per minute are actually reading some of the content and skipping over and guessing about the remainder. That strategy works well enough for fairly predictable content (like a James Bond novel), but don't try it with your chemistry textbook (Just & Carpenter, 1987).

CONCEPT CHECKS

12. Why can we sometimes read two or three short words at a time, whereas we need a saccade or two to read the same number of longer words?
13. If a word is longer than 11 letters, will a reader need more than one fixation to read it? (Check your answers on page 311.)

Reading and Understanding in Context

Good reading requires understanding word meanings. Some English words, such as *bachelor* and *uranium,* have only one meaning, so understanding them poses no special problems. Other English words, however, have multiple meanings, and we have to discern the correct one in context. For example, consider this sentence: *A pelican dove into the water and scared away the dove.* The word *dove* is potentially ambiguous, but the context enables you to infer, so fast that you were unaware of what you were doing, that the first *dove* rhymes with *stove* and means "plunged"; the second *dove* rhymes with *love* and means a "pigeonlike bird." Now, consider another sentence: *A flying fish jumped out of the water and scared the pigeon and dove away.* In this case, the word *dove* is hopelessly ambiguous. The sentence might mean that the flying fish scared two birds (a pigeon and a dove), or that the fish scared the pigeon and then dove (plunged) away.

Good writers try to avoid severe ambiguities of this type; however, the context of a sentence is usually sufficient to clarify the meaning of each word. In some cases, a word appears early in a sentence and the context that explains it occurs later. Consider the italicized words in each of the following sentences:

The *table* that was full of errors was an embarrassment to the owners of the furniture store.

The *table* that was full of errors was an embarrassment to the publishers of the mathematics text.

When they chose the *lead,* they were very careful, because they wanted the new play to be a success.

When they chose the *lead,* they were very careful, because they wanted to produce high-quality pencils.

In cases such as these, most readers have a fairly long fixation time when they read an ambiguous word such as *table* or *lead.* If the previous context has made it clear which meaning is correct, a good reader almost immediately selects the correct meaning and discards the other possibilities. If the previous context provided no help, good readers keep in mind several possible meanings of the ambiguous word until later in the sentence. They show long fixation times on later words (such as *furniture* or *mathematics, play* or *pencils*) that clarify the meaning of the ambiguous word (MacDonald, Pearlmutter, & Seidenberg, 1994; Sereno, Pacht, & Rayner, 1992).

Poor readers are less efficient at selecting the correct meaning. Even after the context has established the correct meaning of a word, poor readers continue to keep in mind both of the possible meanings (Gernsbacher, 1993; Gernsbacher & Faust, 1991). For example, if people read the sentence "he dug with the spade," and then an experimenter asks whether the sentence included anything related to the word "ace," good readers promptly say no, but poor readers hesitate and sometimes say yes. Evidently, good readers suppressed the irrelevant meaning of *spade* as a playing card, but the poor readers suppressed it more slowly or less completely.

THE MESSAGE
Language as a Defining Feature of Humans

At the start of this module, we considered the question, "If language is so extremely useful to humans, why haven't other species evolved at least a little of it?" None of the research directly answers this question, but we can speculate. Certain adaptations are much more useful on a large scale than on a small scale. For example, skunks survive because they are very stinky; it wouldn't do another species much good to be just a little bit stinky. Porcupines survive because they have long, sharp quills; having a few short quills might be slightly helpful, but not very. Similarly, a little language

might be slightly helpful (like a little stink or a few short quills), but better developed language is so enormously useful that a little bit of language development is probably an unstable condition, evolutionarily speaking. Once a species, such as humans, had evolved a little language, those individuals with still better language abilities would be at a selective advantage compared to the others. (However, of course, we are still faced with the ultimate question: Why has no other species ever evolved that first little bit of language?)

SUMMARY

✳ *Language productivity.* Human languages enable us to create new words and phrases to express new ideas. (page 297)

✳ *Language training in nonhumans.* Bonobos, and to a lesser extent other chimpanzees, have shown an ability to learn certain aspects of language. Human evolution evidently elaborated on potentials found in our ape-like ancestors but developed that potential well beyond the level it reached in other species. (page 298)

✳ *Rapid language learning in children.* Children learn language at such an amazing rate, considering the unsystematic training they receive, that many psychologists believe humans are born with a predisposition to learn language. However, exactly *what* we are born with is controversial; it is hard to believe that we are born with a predisposition to learn the grammar of a particular language. (page 299)

✳ *Brain organization and aphasia.* Brain damage, especially in the left hemisphere, can impair people's ability to understand or use language. However, the brain areas that contribute to language are diffuse, and the exact brain organization varies from one person to another. (page 300)

✳ *Stages of language development.* Children advance through several stages of language development, probably reflecting maturation of brain structures necessary for language and not just the total amount of experience. From the start, children's language is creative and shows an effort to understand and use rules of grammar. (page 301)

✳ *Children exposed to no language or to two.* If deaf children of hearing parents are not exposed to language, they invent a sign language of their own. Children in a bilingual environment sometimes have trouble keeping the two languages separate but gain the ability to converse with many people and, in certain ways, show greater than usual cognitive flexibility. (page 302)

✳ *Understanding language.* Much of speech is ambiguous; we understand words and sentences in context by applying the knowledge we have about the world in general. (page 303)

✳ *Reading.* When we read, we have fixation periods separated by eye movements called saccades. We read during the fixations, not the saccades. Even good readers can read only about 11 letters per fixation; people increase their speed of reading by increasing the number of fixations per second. (page 306)

Suggestions for Further Reading

Deacon, T. W. (1997). *The symbolic species.* New York: W. W. Norton and Co. A brilliant, profound analysis of human language and how it relates to the evolution of the human brain.

Pinker, S. (1994). *The language instinct.* New York: William Morrow and Company. Clear, often entertaining discussion of the psychology of language.

Terms

productivity   the ability to express new ideas (page 297)

transformational grammar   a system for converting a deep structure into a surface structure (page 297)

language acquisition device   a built-in mechanism for acquiring language (page 300)

poverty of the stimulus argument   the belief that children do not receive enough information from what they hear for them to learn or infer grammar, so they must be born with that knowledge (page 300)

Broca's aphasia   a condition characterized by inarticulate speech and by difficulties with both using and understanding grammatical devices—prepositions, conjunctions, word endings, complex sentence structures, and so forth (page 300)

Wernicke's aphasia   a condition marked by difficulty recalling the names of objects and impaired comprehension of language (page 300)

bilingual   learning to use two languages about equally well (page 303)

word-superiority effect   identifying a letter with greater ease when it is part of a whole word than when it is presented by itself (page 306)

phoneme   a unit of sound (page 307)

morpheme   a unit of meaning (page 307)

fixations   periods when the eyes are stationary (page 307)

saccade   a quick jump in the focus of the eyes from one point to another (page 307)

Answers to Concept Checks

8. Start language learning when a child is young. Rely on imitation as much as possible, instead of providing direct reinforcements for correct responses. (page 299)

9. Children begin to string words into novel combinations as soon as they begin to speak two words at a time. We believe that they learn rules of grammar because they overgeneralize those rules, creating such words as *womans* and *goed.* (page 302)

10. Set up a Stroop task, asking the person to read off the color of the ink of all the words. Let the words be color names from many languages. The person should show some delay at naming the colors of ink for English words (*red, green,* and so forth) and for whatever other language he or she knows well. (page 303)

11. The word *thoughtfully* has seven phonemes: th-ough-t-f-u-ll-y. (A phoneme is a unit of sound, not necessarily a letter of the alphabet.) It has three morphemes: thought-ful-ly. (Each morpheme has a distinct meaning.) (page 307)

12. Two or three short words can fall within the "window" of about 11 letters that we can fixate on the fovea at one time. If the words are longer, it may be impossible to get them all onto the fovea at once. (page 309)

13. Probably, but not always. Suppose your eyes fixate on the fourth letter of *memorization.* You should be able to see the three letters to its left and the seven to its right—in other words, all except the final letter. Because there is only one English word of the form *memorizatio-,* you have enough information to recognize the word. (page 309)

Web Resources

Chimpanzee and Human Communication Institute

www.cwu.edu/~cwuchci/main.html

Visit Central Washington University's Chimpanzee and Human Communication Institute (CHCI), and learn more about Washoe, her "adopted son" Loulis, and three other chimps who have learned to use American Sign Language to communicate with humans. You might even want to apply for the 10-week Summer Apprenticeship Program.

The Gorilla Foundation

www.gorilla.org/GF/index.html

The Gorilla Language Project, or Project Koko, is the longest continuous interspecies communication project of its kind in the world. Koko, Michael, and Ndume are the western lowland gorillas involved in this study of language acquisition.

Intelligence and Its Measurement

The famous mathematician Alan Turing bicycled to and from work each day. Occasionally, the chain fell off his bicycle and he had to replace it. Eventually, Turing began to keep records and noticed that the chain fell off at mathematically regular intervals. In fact, it fell off after exactly a certain number of turns of the front wheel. Turing then calculated that this number was an even multiple of the number of spokes in the front wheel, the number of links in the chain, and the number of cogs in the pedal. From these data, he deduced that the chain came loose whenever a particular link in the chain came in contact with a particular bent spoke on the wheel. He identified that spoke, repaired it, and never again had trouble with the bicycle chain (Stewart, 1987).

Turing's solution to his problem qualifies as highly intelligent, according to what we usually mean by *intelligent*. But hold your applause. Your local bicycle mechanic could have solved the problem in just a few minutes, without using any mathematics at all.

So, you might ask, what's my point? Was Turing unintelligent? Not at all. He was highly intelligent. If you have a new, complicated, unfamiliar problem to solve, you should probably take it to someone like Turing, not to your favorite bicycle mechanic.

My point is that intelligence is a combination of general abilities and practiced skills. The term *intelligence* can refer to the highly practiced skills shown by a good bicycle mechanic, a Micronesian sailor, a hunter-gatherer of the Serengeti Plain, or any other person with extensive experience and special expertise in a particular area. *Intelligence* can also refer to the generalized problem-solving ability that Turing displayed—the kind of ability that one can apply in an unfamiliar situation. But even that sort of ability develops gradually, reflecting the contributions of many kinds of experience.

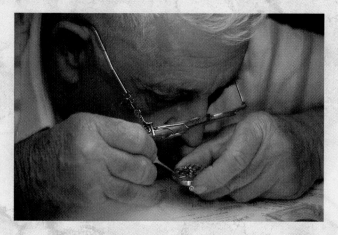

The term *intelligence* refers to both generalized problem solving and to highly practiced skills.

MODULE 9.1

Intelligence and Intelligence Tests

What is intelligence?

What is the purpose of IQ tests?

What do the scores on IQ tests mean?

Intelligence testing has a long history of controversy, partly because of misconceptions about its purpose. Consider this analogy: You have just been put in charge of choosing the members of your country's next Olympic team. However, the Olympic rules have been changed: Each country can send only 30 men and 30 women, and each athlete must compete in every event. Furthermore, the competitive events will be new ones, not exactly like any of the familiar events, and the Olympic Committee will not publish the rules for any of the new events until all of the athletes have arrived at the Olympic site. Clearly, you cannot hold the usual kind of tryouts, but neither will you choose people at random. How will you proceed?

Your best bet would be to devise a test of "general athletic ability." You might measure the abilities of all the applicants to run, jump, change direction, maintain balance, throw and catch, kick, lift weights, respond rapidly to signals, and perform other athletic feats. Then, you would choose the applicants who had the best scores, confident that they will do reasonably well at whatever events the Olympic Committee selects.

No doubt, your test would be imperfect. But if you must choose 60 athletes, and if you want to maximize their chances of winning, you must certainly use some sort of test. So, you go ahead with your test of general athletic ability.

As time passes, other people begin to use your test, and it becomes well accepted and widely used. Does its acceptance imply that athletic ability is a single quantity, like speed or weight? Not at all. For certain purposes, you found it useful to act as if athletic ability were a single quantity, even though you know that great basketball players are not necessarily great swimmers or gymnasts.

What Is Intelligence?

Intelligence tests resemble our imaginary test of athletic ability. If you were in charge of choosing which applicants to admit to a school or college, you would want to select those who would profit most from the experience. Because students may be studying subjects that they have never studied before, it makes sense to measure their general ability to profit from education rather than any specific knowledge or specialized ability.

Intelligence tests were developed for the practical function of selecting students for admission or placement in schools. These tests were not based on any theory of intelligence, and those who administer them have often been content to define *intelligence* as the ability to do well in school. Given that definition, IQ tests do measure intelligence.

For theoretical purposes, however, that definition is hardly satisfactory. What would be a better definition? Here are some of the ways that psychologists have defined *intelligence* (Sternberg, 1997; Wolman, 1989):

- The mental abilities that enable one to adapt to, shape, or select one's environment.
- The ability to judge, comprehend, and reason.
- The ability to understand and deal with people, objects, and symbols.
- The ability to act purposefully, think rationally, and deal effectively with the environment.

Note that these definitions use such terms as *judge, comprehend, understand,* and *think rationally*—terms that are themselves only vaguely defined. Psychologists would like to better organize this list of intelligent abilities, so that it has some structure or organization. Just as all the objects in the world are composed of compounds of only 92 elements, most psychologists expect to find that all the various kinds of intelligence are compounds of a few basic abilities. They have proposed several models of how intelligence is organized.

Spearman's Psychometric Approach and the g Factor

The **psychometric approach** to intelligence, pioneered by Charles Spearman (1904), features *the measurement (metric) of individual differences in behaviors and abilities.* Spearman began by measuring how well a variety of people performed a variety of tasks, such as following complex directions, judging musical pitch, matching colors, and performing arithmetic calculations. He then found that performance on any single task correlated positively with performance on all the other tasks. He therefore deduced that all these tasks must have something in common. To perform well on any test of mental ability, Spearman argued, people need a certain *"general" ability*, which he called **g.** (The g is always italicized and always lowercase.) Later researchers have confirmed that scores on virtually all kinds of cognitive tests correlate fairly strongly with one another, including tests that do not require any particular knowledge or schooling. Consider, for example, the following task: Either ⊓ or ⊓ is flashed on a screen for a fraction of a second.

Then, ⊓ is flashed on the screen in the same location, to serve as a "masking stimulus" (to make the task a bit more difficult). The observer's task is to say whether the left or right arm was longer on the first stimulus. The investigator varies the duration of the first stimulus to determine the briefest flash that still enables the observer to answer correctly. Performance on this perceptual task has a correlation of at least .4 to .5 with scores on a standard intelligence test (Deary & Stough, 1996). So, intelligence tests are measuring something that shows up in a wide variety of situations.

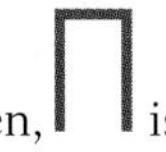

To account for the fact that performance on various tasks does not correlate perfectly, Spearman suggested that each task requires the use of a *"specific" ability,* **s,** in addition to the general ability, g, that all tasks require (Figure 9.1). Thus, intelligence consists of a general ability plus an unknown number of specific abilities, such as mechanical, musical, arithmetical, logical, and spatial ability. Later research has found that many of these specific abilities develop somewhat independently and may rely on partly separate genetic influences (Loehlin, Horn, & Willerman, 1994; Pedersen, Plomin, & McClearn, 1994). Spearman

called his theory a "monarchic" theory of intelligence because it included a dominant ability, or monarch (g), which ruled over the lesser abilities.

Psychologists do not entirely agree on what g represents. That is, the ability to do well on one task does correlate with the ability to do well on another task, but that correlation could indicate either a single, unitary process—such as the ability to perceive and manipulate relationships—or else the correlation could represent the fact that many separate processes depend on the same growth factors (Petrill, Luo, Thompson, & Detterman, 1996). Consider the following analogy:

First, consider the high correlation among the tasks shown in Figure 9.2: People who excel at running a 100-meter race also generally do well at the high jump and the long jump. A particular athlete might be a little better at one of these events than the others, but we can hardly imagine an outstanding high jumper who could not manage a decent long jump. The reason for this high correlation is that all

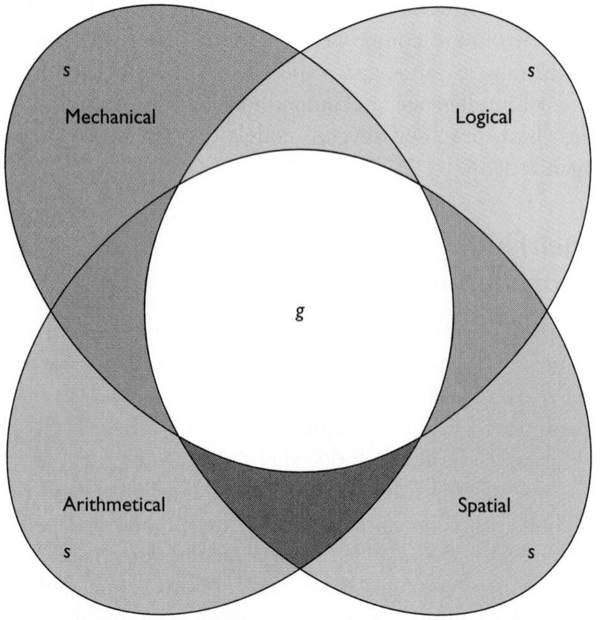

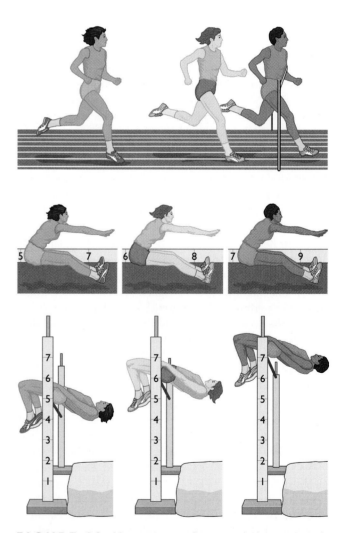

FIGURE 9.1 According to Spearman (1904), all intelligent abilities have an area of overlap, which he called g (for "general"). Each ability also depends partly on an s (for "specific") factor.

FIGURE 9.2 Measurements of sprinting, high jumping, and long jumping correlate with one another because they all depend on the same leg muscles. Similarly, the g factor that emerges in IQ testing could reflect a single ability that all tests tap.

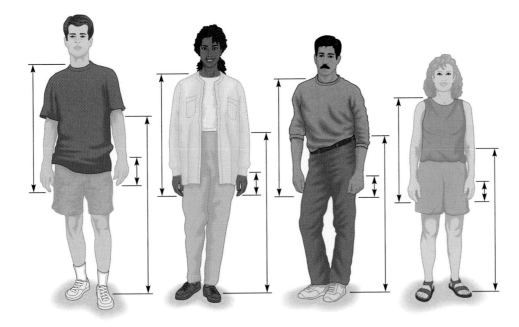

FIGURE 9.3 Measurements of leg, arm, and finger length correlate with one another only because the genes, nutrition, and health factors that promote the growth of any one of these also promote the growth of the others. Similarly, the *g* factor that emerges in IQ testing could reflect that different intellectual abilities depend on the same nutritional, health, and educational influences.

three events depend on the same leg muscles. An injury that impaired performance on one event would impair performance on all three.

Second, consider the lengths of three body parts—the left leg, the right arm, and the left index finger—as illustrated in Figure 9.3: Within a normal population of people, these three measurements will correlate strongly with one another. That is, people with a long left leg also tend to have a long right arm and a long left index finger. Why? These measurements definitely do not measure the same thing. (Amputation of one of them would not affect the others at all.) Lengths of leg, arm, and finger correlate because the *causes* of growth are the same for all three—nutrition, health, age, and certain genes.

Now, which of these cases is most like intelligence? Do we find a positive correlation among the performances of various intellectual skills because they all measure a single underlying ability or because they all grow together, dependent on the same factors of health, nutrition, education, genetics, and so forth?

The evidence suggests that both of these hypotheses are partly correct. For example, certain kinds of brain damage impair performance on a wide variety of intellectual tasks, because the damage impairs a function such as attention that is necessary for almost any task. Thus, various intellectual abilities will correlate with one another partly because they depend on some of the same underlying processes. However, as we have seen in previous chapters, some people can lose a specific kind of memory or perceptual ability without much loss of other abilities. That is, different intellectual abilities do not share *all* of their underlying processes. To a considerable degree, various intellectual skills correlate with one another because health, nutrition, education, and the other factors that promote the development of any one skill also promote the development of others.

Fluid Intelligence and Crystallized Intelligence

Raymond Cattell accepted Spearman's psychometric approach but proposed one important modification. According to Cattell (1987), the *g* factor has two components: fluid intelligence and crystallized intelligence. Thus, intelligence can be compared to water: Fluid water can take any shape, whereas ice crystals are rigid. **Fluid intelligence** is *the power of reasoning and using information.* It includes the ability to perceive relationships, solve unfamiliar problems, and gain new types of knowledge. Fluid intelligence mostly relates to the ability to store large amounts of information in working memory and then to process that information quickly (Fry & Hale, 1996). (If you cannot process the information quickly enough, it will start to fade from your working memory.) **Crystallized intelligence** consists of *acquired skills and knowledge and the application of that knowledge to the specific content of a person's experience.* For example, fluid intelligence is the ability to learn new skills in a new job. Crystallized intelligence includes the skills already learned and practiced by someone who has had the job for years. Eventually those skills become almost automatic.

Fluid intelligence, according to Cattell and his colleagues, reaches its peak before age 20; beyond that age, it remains fairly constant, although it can decline sharply as a result of Alzheimer's disease or any other deteriorative condition or source of brain damage (Horn, 1968). Crystallized intelligence, on the other hand, continues to increase as long as a person remains healthy and active (Cattell, 1987; Horn & Donaldson, 1976). A 20-year-old may be more successful than a 65-year-old at solving a problem that is unfamiliar to both of them, but the 65-year-old will excel at solving problems in his or her area of specialization.

Although the distinction between crystallized and fluid intelligence is useful, it is not an absolute. Some tasks require mainly crystallized or mainly fluid intelligence, but any task taps at least a little of both.

CONCEPT CHECK

1. Was Alan Turing's solution to the slipping bicycle chain (at the start of this chapter) an example of fluid or crystallized intelligence? Would the solution provided by a bicycle mechanic be an example of fluid or crystallized intelligence? (Check your answers on page 326.)

Gardner's Theory of Multiple Intelligences

The traditional defense of theories proposing a single kind of intelligence has rested on the concept of *g*: Tests of all kinds of intellectual abilities—mathematical, verbal, and others—correlate with one another and therefore support the idea of a single underlying ability called *g*. However, critics reply, the statistical emergence of *g* merely indicates that mathematics, language, and the other tested skills happen to be related. If we expand the concept of *intelligence* to include other skills that society values, the concept of *g* may fade away or even disappear.

In particular, Howard Gardner (1985) has claimed that people have **multiple intelligences**—*numerous unrelated forms of intelligence.* Gardner distinguishes language abilities, musical abilities, logical and mathematical reasoning, spatial reasoning, body movement skills, self-control and self-understanding, and sensitivity to other people's social signals. He points out that people can be outstanding in one type of intelligence but not in others. For example, a *savant* (literally, "learned one") is a person whose performance in one area is outstanding but whose performance in other areas is just ordinary, or perhaps well below average. One pair of twins were intellectually impaired in most regards and could not even do simple arithmetic, but they could perform amazing feats of calendar calculation. You could call out any date, past or future (such as August 28, 1591), and they would quickly state the day of the week—in this case, Wednesday (Horwitz, Kestenbaum, Person, & Jarvik, 1965).

More generally, an athlete can excel at body movement skills but lack musical abilities; an outstanding musician can be insensitive to other people; a politician can be outstanding at understanding other people's needs but quite inept at controlling his or her own body movements. Because of the differences among multiple kinds of intelligence, someone who seems very intelligent in certain regards may surprise us by doing something utterly foolish in a different setting.

Gardner certainly makes an important point: People do have a variety of socially valued abilities, and almost no one is strong in all abilities or weak in all abilities. Gardner encourages us to seek better ways of teaching and encouraging a full range of abilities, including self-control, social responsiveness, and other intelligent skills that educators have not traditionally emphasized.

Do we want to use one word, *intelligence,* to refer to every valued skill from writing a novel to dribbling a basketball? If we do, then Gardner is correct that people have many unrelated kinds of intelligence. However, in this case, we shall need a new term (perhaps *cognitive ability*) to refer more narrowly to mathematical, logical, and verbal skills.

Sternberg's Triarchic Theory of Intelligence

Spearman concluded that intelligence depends on one overall ability; Cattell suggested two kinds of ability, and Gardner suggested many. Still, the concept of ability tells us nothing about *how* a person processes information or engages in "intelligent" behavior (Das, 1992).

Robert Sternberg (1985) has offered one of the most influential attempts to specify in detail the processes of intelligent behavior. Sternberg's description is called a **triarchic theory** (in contrast to Spearman's monarchic theory), because Sternberg deals with *three aspects of intelligence: (1) the cognitive processes that occur within the individual, (2) the situations that require intelligence, and (3) how intelligence relates to the external world.*

According to Sternberg, the first part of the triarchy—the cognitive processes within the individual—includes three components: learning the necessary information,

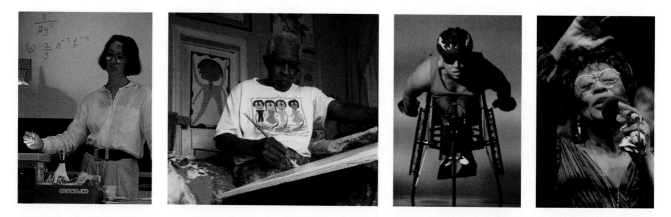

According to Howard Gardner, we have many intelligences, including mathematical ability, artistic skill, muscle skills, and musical abilities.

In Garrison Keillor's fictional *Lake Wobegon,* "all the children are above average." Although that description sounds impossible, in one sense it is true: Everyone is above average at something. A given individual may excel at mathematics, dancing, piano playing, juggling, poetry, cooking, or whatever. A single measurement of "intelligence" necessarily overlooks people's specialized skills.

planning an approach to a problem, and combining the knowledge with the plan to actually solve a problem.

Standard IQ tests do not try to measure the learning or planning components; these concentrate on the third component—how well someone actually solves a problem. For example, a test might ask you to complete an analogy, such as

Washington is to 1 as Lincoln is to:
(a) 5,   (b) 10,   (c) 20,   (d) 50.

To solve this problem, you must have already learned a fair amount of relevant information, and you must develop a strategy for applying it to this question. Ultimately, if you are successful, you decide that the question must be referring to George Washington and the $1 bill and that the answer is a, because Abraham Lincoln's picture is on the $5 bill. This question is reasonable, as far as it goes, although we need to recognize that it measures only the final outcome, not the steps that led up to it. An improved measure of intelligence might separate the learning and planning components from the performance component.

The second part of Sternberg's triarchy is the identification of situations that require intelligence. It is important to distinguish novel situations from repeated situations, because they require different responses. In a novel situation, we must examine a problem in various ways until we find a successful approach. (Recall, for example, the insight problems of Chapter 8.) In a repeated situation, we profit by developing automatic habits, so that we can quickly make a successful response.

The third part of the triarchy is the relationship between intelligence and the outside world. An intelligent person either adapts to the environment or tries to improve the environment, or if all else fails, escapes to a better environment. Sternberg (1985) and others (Weinberg, 1989) have tried to develop special tests of people's practical intelligence—for example, the ability of a young person to identify the steps most likely to lead to career advancement. (See Figure 9.4.) Sternberg explicity recognizes that, because intelligent behavior must be practical, the term *intelligence* is meaningful only in a sociocultural context. For example, we cannot meaningfully compare the intelligence of a European city-dweller with that of someone living in the Amazon rain forests or the Serengeti Plain. What is important and practical for a member of one group may not be for the others.

Table 9.1 summarizes four theories of intelligence.

CONCEPT CHECK

2. In Sternberg's theory, novel situations call for creative problem solving, whereas repeated situations call for automatic habits. Using Cattell's terminology, which kind of situation calls for fluid intelligence and which calls for crystallized intelligence? (Check your answer on page 326.)

Theories of Intelligence and Tests of Intelligence

The standard IQ tests, which we shall consider momentarily, were devised decades ago, before most of the discoveries about memory and cognition that we discussed in the last two chapters. Today, there are several theories

FIGURE 9.4 In these two photos, which person is the supervisor and which is the worker? Robert Sternberg has used these photos to evaluate people's "practical intelligence"—their ability to understand nonverbal cues.

TABLE 9.1 Four Theories of Intelligence

THEORY	PRINCIPAL THEORIST	KEY IDEAS AND TERMS	EXAMPLES
Psychometric approach	Charles Spearman	g factor: general abstract reasoning ability common to various tasks	Perceiving and manipulating relationships
		s factor: specific ability required for a given task	Mechanical, verbal, spatial abilities
Fluid and crystallized intelligence	Raymond Cattell	Fluid intelligence: reasoning and using information; peaks in young adulthood	Finding a solution to an unfamiliar problem.
		Crystallized intelligence: acquired skills and knowledge; continues growing throughout life	Knowing how to play the piano, build a cabinet, write a novel, calculate a sales tax
Multiple intelligences	Howard Gardner	Intelligence includes all the abilities that one's society values	Music, social attentiveness, dancing, language skills, mathematics, etc.
Triarchic theory	Robert Sternberg	Cognitive mechanisms	Gaining knowledge, planning a strategy, actually solving a problem
		Situations that require intelligence	Novel situations; repeated situations
		Relationship to the environment	Adapting to one's environment, improving it, or escaping from it

about intelligence and a variety of intelligence tests, but these theories have little relationship to the tests.

Can we measure something—in this case, intelligence—without fundamentally understanding what it is? Possibly so; physicists measured gravity and magnetism long before they understood them theoretically. Maybe psychologists can do the same with intelligence.

But then again, maybe not. Physicists of the past measured not only gravity and magnetism, but also "phlogiston," a substance that, they later discovered, does not exist. Measurements of a poorly understood phenomenon are risky. Many psychologists are dissatisfied with the currently available intelligence tests, and some are working toward eventually producing a fundamentally better test. The available tests have both strengths and weaknesses, however. Let's examine some of these tests.

IQ Tests

You have no doubt spent a significant portion of your life taking tests. Some need for testing is clear, even if our society does overdo it. More students want to attend medical school than our medical schools could possibly accommodate; more people would like to be airplane pilots than the airlines can hire; more people would like to play on their college basketball teams than those teams can include. We must somehow determine which applicants are most likely to perform the task well.

Schools and colleges base their admissions decisions partly on students' grades and teachers' recommendations, but they know that the value of such information is limited. (Some schools are better than others; some teachers grade more strictly than others.) To compare students from different schools, admissions officials also look at students' scores on standardized tests.

Intelligence quotient (IQ) tests attempt to *measure an individual's probable performance in school and similar settings.* (The term *quotient* dates from the time when IQ was determined by dividing *mental age* by *chronological age.* That method is now obsolete, but the term remains.) The first IQ tests were devised for a practical purpose by two French psychologists, Alfred Binet and Theophile Simon (1905). The French Ministry of Public Instruction wanted a fair way to identify children who had such serious intellectual deficiencies that they could not succeed in the public school system and who therefore should not be placed in the same classes with other students. The task of identifying such children had formerly been left to medical doctors; however, doctors had different standards, and the school system was looking for a fair, impartial test. Binet and Simon produced a test to measure the skills that children need for success in school, such as understanding and using language, computational skills, memory, and the ability to follow instructions.

Their test, and others like it, do make reasonably accurate predictions. But suppose that a test correctly predicts that one student will perform better than another in school. Can we then say that the first student did better in school *because of* a higher IQ score?

No. Consider this analogy: Suppose we ask why a certain basketball player misses so many of his shots. Someone answers, "Because he has a low shooting average." Clearly, that explains nothing. (The reason for his low shooting average is that he misses so many shots.) Similarly, saying that a student does poorly in school because of a low IQ score isn't much of an explanation; after all, the IQ test was designed to measure the very skills that schoolwork requires. An IQ score measures performance; it does not explain it.

The Stanford-Binet Test

The test that Binet and Simon designed was later modified for English speakers by Lewis Terman and other Stanford psychologists and published as the **Stanford-Binet IQ test.** This test is administered to individual students by someone who has been carefully trained how to present the items and how to score the answers. It contains items that range in difficulty, designated by age (see Table 9.2). An item designated as "age 8," for example, will be answered correctly by 60–90% of all 8-year-olds. (A higher percentage of older children will answer it correctly, as will a lower percentage of younger children.) Those who take this test are asked only those items that are pegged at about their level of functioning. For example, the psychologist testing an 8-year-old might start with the items designated for 7-year-olds. Unless that child missed many of the items for 7-year-olds, the psychologist would simply give credit for all the 6-year-old items without bothering to test them. Presuming that the child answered nearly all of the 7-year-old items correctly, the psychologist would proceed to the items for 8-year-olds, 9-year-olds, and so forth, until the child began to miss item after item. At that point, the psychologist would end the test without proceeding to the still more difficult items.

T A B L E 9.2	**Examples of the Types of Items on the Stanford-Binet Test**
AGE	**SAMPLE TEST ITEM**
2	Test administrator points at pictures of everyday objects and asks, "What is this?" "Here are some pegs of different sizes and shapes. See whether you can put each one into the correct hole."
4	"Why do people live in houses?" "Birds fly in the air; fish swim in the _____."
6	"Here is a picture of a horse. Do you see what part of the horse is missing?" "Here are some candies. Can you count how many there are?"
8	"What should you do if you find a lost puppy?" "Stephanie can't write today because she twisted her ankle. What is wrong with that?"
10	"Why should people be quiet in a library?" "Repeat after me: 4 8 3 7 1 4."
12	"What does *regret* mean?" "Here is a picture. Can you tell me what is wrong with it?"
14	"What is the similarity between high and low?" "Watch me fold this paper and cut it. Now, when I unfold it, how many holes will there be?"
Adult	"Make up a sentence using the words *celebrate, reverse,* and *appointment.*" "What do people mean when they say, 'People who live in glass houses should not throw stones' "?

SOURCE: Modified from Nietzel and Bernstein, 1987.

Ordinarily, the entire test lasts anywhere from 1 hour to 1½ hours. However, unlike most other IQ tests, the current edition of the Stanford-Binet imposes no time limit; people are allowed to think about each item for as long as they wish (McCall, Yates, Hendricks, Turner, & McNabb, 1989).

Stanford-Binet IQ scores are computed from tables set up to ensure that a given IQ score will mean the same at different ages. The mean IQ at each age is 100. A 6-year-old, with an IQ score of, say, 116, has performed better on the test than 84% of other 6-year-olds; similarly, an adult with an IQ score of 116 has performed better than 84% of other adults. The Stanford-Binet also provides subscores reflecting crystallized intelligence, abstract visual reasoning, and short-term memory (Daniel, 1997; McCall et al., 1989).

In Table 9.2, note that the Stanford-Binet test includes questions designated for children who are only 2 years old. However, scores below age 4 or 5 fluctuate markedly (Honzik, 1974; Morrow & Morrow, 1974), because younger children are sometimes attentive to a task and sometimes not. The test scores of very young children are useful for certain research purposes, but they should not be weighed heavily when making placement decisions about individual children.

The Wechsler Tests

Two IQ tests devised by David Wechsler, known as the **Wechsler Adult Intelligence Scale–Third Edition (WAIS–III)** and the **Wechsler Intelligence Scale for Children–Third Edition (WISC–III),** produce the same average, 100, and almost the same distribution of scores as the Stanford-Binet. The WISC is given to children up to age 16; beyond that age, everyone takes the WAIS. As with the Stanford-Binet, the Wechsler tests are administered to one individual at a time. A Wechsler test provides an overall score and scores in two major categories (verbal and performance); each of these is further divided into component abilities. (Table 9.3 shows examples of test items, and Figure 9.5 shows one individual's test profile.) Thus, a Wechsler test provides a profile of the individual's strengths and weaknesses. People who learned English as a second language, for example, ordinarily receive higher scores on the performance section than on the verbal section.

Each of the 12 parts of the WISC–III or the WAIS–III begins with the simplest questions and progresses to increasingly difficult items. Six of the parts constitute the Performance Scale; these call for nonverbal answers (Figure 9.6), although the test-taker must know enough English to understand the instructions. The other parts, constituting the Verbal Scale, require spoken or written answers.

The inclusion of questions that ask for factual information (such as "From what animal do we get milk?") has caused much controversy. Critics complain that such items measure knowledge, not ability. Defenders reply as follows:

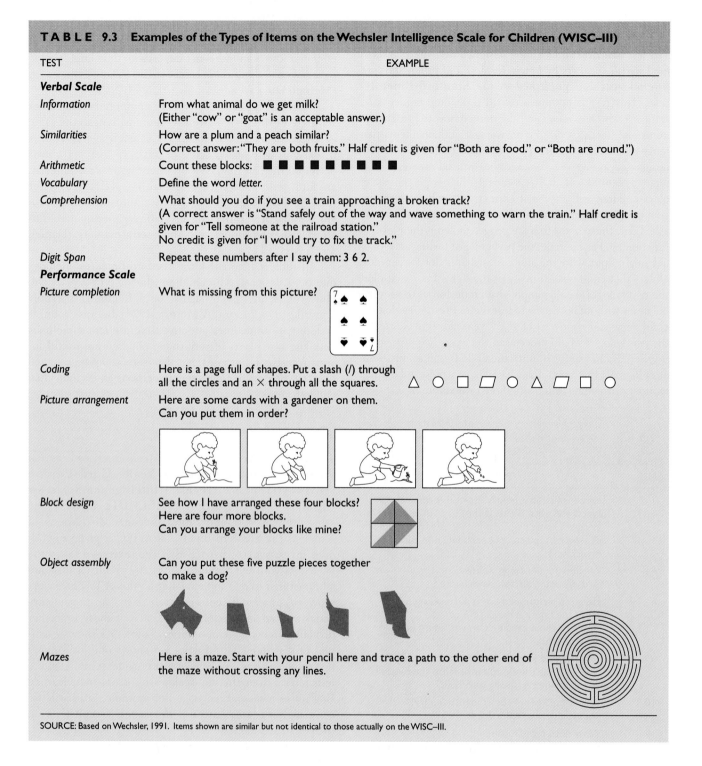

TABLE 9.3 Examples of the Types of Items on the Wechsler Intelligence Scale for Children (WISC–III)

TEST	EXAMPLE
Verbal Scale	
Information	From what animal do we get milk? (Either "cow" or "goat" is an acceptable answer.)
Similarities	How are a plum and a peach similar? (Correct answer: "They are both fruits." Half credit is given for "Both are food." or "Both are round.")
Arithmetic	Count these blocks: ■ ■ ■ ■ ■ ■ ■ ■ ■
Vocabulary	Define the word *letter*.
Comprehension	What should you do if you see a train approaching a broken track? (A correct answer is "Stand safely out of the way and wave something to warn the train." Half credit is given for "Tell someone at the railroad station." No credit is given for "I would try to fix the track."
Digit Span	Repeat these numbers after I say them: 3 6 2.
Performance Scale	
Picture completion	What is missing from this picture?
Coding	Here is a page full of shapes. Put a slash (/) through all the circles and an ✕ through all the squares.
Picture arrangement	Here are some cards with a gardener on them. Can you put them in order?
Block design	See how I have arranged these four blocks? Here are four more blocks. Can you arrange your blocks like mine?
Object assembly	Can you put these five puzzle pieces together to make a dog?
Mazes	Here is a maze. Start with your pencil here and trace a path to the other end of the maze without crossing any lines.

SOURCE: Based on Wechsler, 1991. Items shown are similar but not identical to those actually on the WISC–III.

- "Intelligent" people tend to learn more facts than others do, even if they have had no more exposure to the information.
- As researchers in artificial intelligence have discovered, most of what we call intelligence requires a vast store of factual knowledge (Schank & Birnbaum, 1994). That is, factual knowledge is not *sufficient* to demonstrate intelligence, but it is *necessary*.
- The purpose of an IQ test is to predict performance in school, and in that respect it works. Students who already know a great many facts tend to do well in school.

We shall consider further criticism of intelligence tests in the second module of this chapter.

Raven's Progressive Matrices

The Stanford-Binet and Wechsler tests, though useful for many purposes, have certain limitations. First, they call for specific information that may be much more familiar to some people than to others. Second, because they require use and comprehension of the English language, they are

Subtest Scores

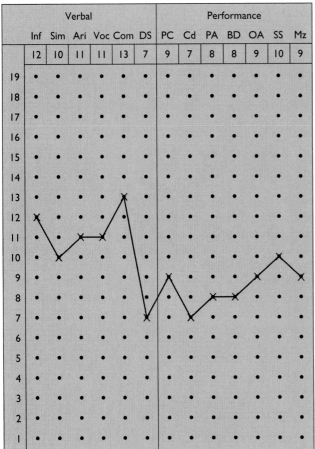

	Verbal						Performance						
	Inf	Sim	Ari	Voc	Com	DS	PC	Cd	PA	BD	OA	SS	Mz
	12	10	11	11	13	7	9	7	8	8	9	10	9

FIGURE 9.5 A score profile for one child on the WISC–III IQ test. Each subtest score represents this child's performance on one type of task compared with other children of the same age. Besides providing an overall IQ score, a profile such as this highlights an individual's strengths and weaknesses. Note that this child performed better on verbal tasks than on performance tasks. (Data courtesy of Patricia Collins.)

unfair to people who do not speak English well, including immigrants and hearing-impaired people. "Why not simply translate the tests into other languages?" you might ask. Psychologists sometimes do, but it is difficult to equate the translation with the original. For example, one part of the Stanford-Binet presents certain words and asks for words that rhyme with them. Generating rhymes is moderately easy in English, extremely easy in Italian, but, I am told, virtually impossible in Zulu (Smith, 1974).

To overcome such problems, psychologists have tried to devise a "culture-fair" or culture-reduced test that would make minimal use of language and would not ask for any specific facts. *One example of a culture-reduced test* is the **Progressive Matrices** test devised by John C. Raven. Figure 9.7 presents matrices of the type that this test uses.

These matrices, which progress gradually from easy items to difficult items, attempt to measure abstract reasoning; to answer the questions, a person must generate hypotheses, test them, and infer rules (Carpenter, Just, & Shell, 1990).

FIGURE 9.6 Much of the WAIS–III involves nonverbal tests where a person is asked to perform certain tasks. Here, to evaluate visual-spatial organization, a woman arranges colored blocks according to a specified pattern while a psychologist times her.

The Progressive Matrices test does not call for any verbal responses or specific information, and the instructions are easy to explain to almost anyone. It therefore gives a non-English-speaking immigrant or a deaf person a much better opportunity than most other IQ tests do (Powers, Barkan, & Jones, 1986; Vernon, 1967). The main disadvantage of this test is that it provides only a single overall score, instead of also identifying an individual's strengths and weaknesses, as other IQ tests do (Sternberg, 1991).

How culture-fair, then, is the Progressive Matrices test? It is fairer than the Wechsler or Stanford-Binet tests, but it does assume familiarity with pencil-and-paper, multiple-choice tests, and several other Western customs. For example, children from some cultures have been taught that it is disrespectful to express their own opinions without first checking with their parents, or not to speak to unfamiliar adults, such as the person administering the test (Greenfield, 1997). In Western culture, if a child is asked to sort items into categories, the response considered "most intelligent," for example, is to put all the metal tools in one category, all the foods in another, and so forth. But among the Kpelle people of Africa, the "intelligent" response would be to link objects that might be used together—such as placing a knife with a potato, because one would use the knife to cut the potato (Greenfield, 1997). In short, any test is based on the assumptions of a particular culture.

The Scholastic Assessment Test

The test once known as the Scholastic Aptitude Test, *designed to measure a student's likelihood of doing well in college,* is now titled the **Scholastic Assessment Test (SAT).** Because the term *assessment* means *test,* the title really means *school-based test test.* Many people call it the "SAT test," adding yet another layer of redundancy.

The Scholastic Assessment Test serves the same function as an IQ test: It predicts college performance. (Figure 9.8 shows the relationship between SAT scores and grade-point average during the freshman year in college at one university.) The basic SAT is administered to large groups of students at a time; it consists of multiple-choice items divided into two sets, verbal and quantitative. The SAT also offers subject tests in individual fields, such as history. Each test is scored on a scale from 200 to 800. The mean was originally set at 500. Over the years, the mean gradually drifted downward, partly because a wider range of students were taking the test, instead of just the best. In 1995, the scoring system was readjusted to return the mean to 500. (Thus, scores reported before the readjustment do not mean the same thing as scores reported after the readjustment.)

Figure 9.9 presents examples of the types of items found on the SAT. If you are a college student in the United States, you are probably familiar with either the SAT or the similar American College Test (ACT). Recent changes to the SAT have included the addition of a writing test and the option of taking the test on a computer.

The SAT was designed to help colleges to select among applicants for admission. Although the best predictor of col-

lege success is success in high school, high-school grades by themselves are not entirely satisfactory. Grading standards differ among various high schools, and some students take more challenging courses than others do. The SAT offers a method for comparing students from different high-school backgrounds. As a predictor of college success, the SAT by itself is less satisfactory than high-school grades alone. However, a combination of high-school grades and SAT scores significantly improves the prediction of college success (Weitzman, 1982).

Because many students worry about doing well on the SAT, a coaching industry has developed. Students can pay to attend these sessions after school or on weekends. If you attended such sessions, did you get your money's worth? If you did not attend them, did you miss a chance for a much higher SAT score? Several studies have compared the SAT scores of students who attended coaching sessions to the scores of students of similar ability who did not. The results have been consistent: On the average, participation in SAT-coaching sessions raises a student's score by about 10 to 20 points (on a scale from 200 to 800). Students who attend longer, more intensive coaching sessions score only slightly higher than those who attend briefer sessions. To improve scores by more than

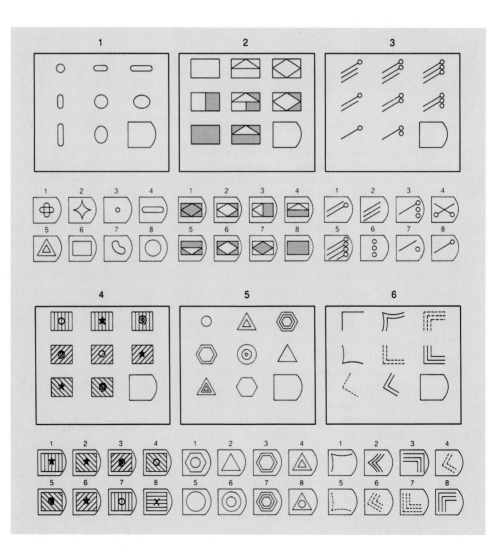

FIGURE 9.7 Items similar to those in Raven's Progressive Matrices test. The instructions are: "Each pattern has a piece missing. From the eight choices provided, select the one that completes the pattern, both going across and going down." (You can check your answers against answer A, page 326.)

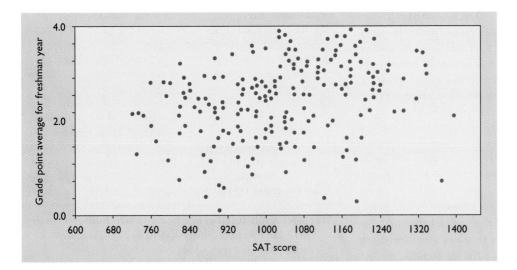

FIGURE 9.8 In this scatter plot, each point represents one freshman student at a particular university. That student's SAT score is given on the *x*-axis; the grade-point average, on the *y*-axis. Note that SAT scores predict college grades moderately well, with a correlation of .3 for this sample. Also note the exceptions—students with high SAT scores but poor grades and students with low SAT scores but good grades.

30 points, though, a student must spend almost as much time in the coaching sessions as attending school (Kulik, Bangert-Drowns, & Kulik, 1984; Messick & Jungeblut, 1981).

THE MESSAGE
Measuring Something We Don't Fully Understand

The standard IQ tests and related tests have survived for decades, despite persistent criticism. These tests have their pluses as well as their minuses. An IQ score is useful for certain practical purposes, such as selecting students for special programs. It also relates roughly to some biological variables. For example, studies using modern methods such as MRI scans have found a moderate, positive correlation between students' IQ scores and their brain volumes (Willerman, Schultz, Rutledge, & Bigler, 1991).

In a way, the overall intelligence of an individual is like the gross national product of a country; both figures provide a summary that may be useful for certain purposes. However, if we want to understand the processes in any detail, we need to go beyond those summaries and explore the detailed components that underlie them.

Psychologists hope to develop new tests that tap a wider range of abilities, including interpersonal (social) intelligence, creativity, practical intelligence, and learning style (Daniel, 1997). However, producing a significantly improved IQ test will not be as easy as it may sound. The current tests, even with their shortcomings, are the products of decades of research and effort; devising a valid measure of more complex and varied abilities will require at least as much research.

In the next module of this chapter, we shall consider how psychologists evaluate tests, including the currently available IQ tests and any new tests that might someday be proposed to take their place. Psychologists have devised some clear criteria for evaluating tests and deciding which tests are better than others.

At this point, let's simply stress that the value of an IQ test, like that of any tool, depends on how it is used. Just as a hammer can be used to build a door or to break one down, a test score can be used to open the doors of opportunity or to close them. A test score, if cautiously interpreted, can aid schools in making placement decisions. If the score is treated as an infallible guide, however, it can be seriously misleading.

SUMMARY

✳ *Defining intelligence.* The designers of the standard IQ tests defined intelligence simply as the ability to do well in school. Psychologists with a more theoretical interest have defined intelligence by listing the abilities that it includes. (page 315)

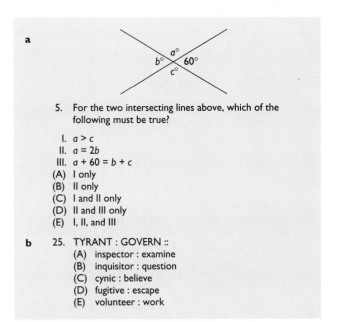

FIGURE 9.9 These two sample items from the Scholastic Assessment Test (SAT) reflect its two parts, which measure mathematical and verbal skills. (From the College Entrance Examination Board and the Educational Testing Service.)

✳ *g factor.* Various "intelligent" abilities apparently share a common element, known as the *g* factor, which is closely related to abstract reasoning. The *g* factor may arise either because various tests tap the same ability or because the health and educational factors that promote the growth of one intellectual ability also promote the development of other intellectual abilities. (page 315)

✳ *Fluid and crystallized intelligence.* Psychologists distinguish between fluid intelligence (a basic reasoning ability that can be applied to any problem, including unfamiliar ones) and crystallized intelligence (acquired abilities to solve familiar types of problems). (page 317)

✳ *Abilities that make up intelligence.* Psychologists have drawn up different lists of the abilities that make up intelligence. Some define intelligence fairly narrowly; others include such abilities as social attentiveness, musical abilities, and motor skills. According to the theory of multiple intelligences, people possess many independent types of intelligence. (page 318)

✳ *Triarchic theory.* According to Sternberg's triarchic theory of intelligence, intelligence consists of three aspects: the cognitive mechanisms within the individual, the situations that require intelligence, and the ways that intelligent behavior relates to the environment. (page 318)

✳ *IQ tests.* The Stanford-Binet and other IQ tests were devised to predict the level of performance in school. (page 320)

✳ *Wechsler IQ tests.* The Wechsler IQ tests measure separate abilities, grouped into a Verbal Scale and a Performance Scale of six parts each. (page 321)

✳ *Culture-reduced tests.* Culture-reduced tests such as Raven's Progressive Matrices can be used to test people who are unfamiliar with English. (page 322)

✳ *SAT.* The Scholastic Assessment Test is similar to IQ tests because it predicts performance in school, specifically in college. (page 323)

Suggestion for Further Reading

Ceci, S. J. (1990). *On intelligence . . . more or less.* Englewood Cliffs, NJ: Prentice-Hall. Perceptive critique of traditional assumptions about intelligence.

Terms

psychometric approach   the measurement of individual differences in abilities and behaviors (page 315)

g   Spearman's "general" factor that all IQ tests and all parts of an IQ test are believed to have in common (page 316)

s   a "specific" factor that is more important for performance on some portions of an intelligence test than it is for others (page 316)

fluid intelligence   the basic power of reasoning and using information, including the ability to perceive relationships, solve unfamiliar problems, and gain new types of knowledge (page 317)

crystallized intelligence   acquired skills and knowledge and the application of that knowledge to the specific content of a person's experience (page 317)

multiple intelligences   Gardner's theory that intelligence is composed of numerous unrelated forms of intelligent behavior (page 318)

triarchic theory   Sternberg's theory that intelligence has three aspects: the cognitive processes that occur within the individual, the situations that require intelligence, and how intelligence relates to the external world (page 318)

intelligence quotient (IQ)   a measure of an individual's probable performance in school and in similar settings (page 320)

Stanford-Binet IQ test   a test of intelligence, the first important IQ test in the English language (page 321)

Wechsler Adult Intelligence Scale–Third Edition (WAIS–III)   an IQ test originally devised by David Wechsler, commonly used with adults (page 321)

Wechsler Intelligence Scale for Children–Third Edition (WISC–III)   an IQ test originally devised by David Wechsler, commonly used with children (page 321)

Progressive Matrices   an IQ test that attempts to measure abstract reasoning without the use of language or recall of facts (page 323)

Scholastic Assessment Test (SAT)   a test designed to measure a student's likelihood of performing well in college (page 323)

Answers to Concept Checks

1. Turing's solution reflected fluid intelligence, a generalized ability that could apply to any topic. The solution provided by a bicycle mechanic would reflect crystallized intelligence, ability developed in a particular area of experience. (page 318)

2. Using Cattell's terminology, a novel situation calls for fluid intelligence, whereas a repeated situation calls for crystallized intelligence. (page 319)

Answers to Other Questions in the Text

A.   **1.** (8); **2.** (6); **3.** (3); **4.** (4); **5.** (6); **6.** (2) (page 324)

Web Resources

Barbarian's Online Test Page
www.iglobal.net/psman/intelligence.html
Take a deep breath before you try any of the dozen or so tests of intelligence on this page, because your brain is going to get a real workout!* You can also link to the EQ test on Barbarian's "Other Online Tests" page.

---

*Note: Any psychological test that is readily available to the public, while entertaining and possibly informative, should not be used to make important decisions about yourself or others. The most powerful, valid, and reliable psychological assessment devices are usually kept under the tight control of their creators or copyright holders.

MODULE 9.2
Evaluation of Intelligence Tests

What do scores on IQ tests mean?

What accounts for the variations in intelligence among different groups of people?

Edward Thorndike, a pioneer in the study of both animal and human learning, is often quoted as saying, "If something exists, it exists in some amount. If it exists in some amount, it can be measured." Douglas Detterman (1979) countered, "Anything which exists can be measured incorrectly."

Both of these quotes apply well to intelligence: If intelligence exists at all, it must be measurable, but it can also be measured incorrectly. One of the major tasks now facing researchers is to determine whether IQ tests measure what their designers claim they measure and whether they apply fairly to all groups. Because much is at stake here, the conclusions are often controversial.

The Standardization of IQ Tests

To specify what various scores mean, those who devise a test must *standardize* it. **Standardization** is *the process of establishing rules for administering a test and for interpreting the scores.* One of the main steps in standardization is to find the **norms,** which are *descriptions of the frequencies of occurrence of particular scores.*

Psychologists try to standardize a test on a large, representative population. For example, if a test is to be used with children throughout the United States and Canada, psychologists need to measure the norms with a large random or representative sample of U.S. and Canadian children, not just with children of one ethnic group or one geographic region.

The Distribution of IQ Scores

Binet, Wechsler, and the other pioneers who devised the first IQ tests chose items and arranged the scoring method to establish the mean score at 100, with a standard devia-

tion of 15 for the Wechsler test, as Figure 9.10 shows, and 16 for the Stanford-Binet. (Recall from Chapter 2 that the standard deviation is a measure of the degree of variability of performance. If most scores are close to the mean, the standard deviation is small; if scores vary widely, the standard deviation is larger.) The scores of almost any population approximate a *normal distribution* or bell-shaped curve, as shown in Figure 9.10; the distribution is symmetrical, and most scores are close to the mean.

In any normal distribution, 68% of all people fall within one standard deviation above or below the mean; about 95% are within two standard deviations. Someone with a score of 115 on the Wechsler test exceeds the scores of people within one standard deviation from the mean, plus all of those more than one standard deviation below the mean—a total of 84% of all people, as shown in Figure 9.10. We say that such a person is "in the 84th percentile." Someone with an IQ score of 130 is in the 98th percentile, which means that his or her score is higher than the scores of 98% of others in the same age group.

Psychologists sometimes refer to people more than two standard deviations above the mean as "gifted." That designation is arbitrary. It makes little sense to say that a child with an IQ of 130 is gifted but a child with an IQ of 129 is not.

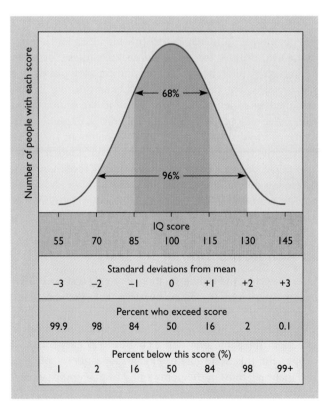

FIGURE 9.10 The scores on an IQ test form an approximately bell-shaped curve. The curve shown here represents scores on the Wechsler IQ test, with a standard deviation of 15 (15 points above and below the mean, which is 100). The results on the Stanford-Binet test are very similar, except that the standard deviation is 16, so the spread is slightly wider.

People with IQ scores at least two standard deviations below the mean are classified as "retarded." Many can be "mainstreamed" in regular classes; severely retarded children are taught in special classes.

Psychologists also classify people more than two standard deviations below the mean as "retarded." Many retarded children, especially those who are severely retarded, suffer from biological disorders, including chromosomal abnormalities and fetal alcohol syndrome (Zigler & Hodapp, 1991). In the United States, the *Individuals with Disabilities Act* requires public schools to provide "free and appropriate" education for all children, regardless of their limitations. Children with severe handicaps are placed in a special class, but those with milder handicaps are "mainstreamed" as much as possible, placed in the same classes with other children but given special consideration. For example, a child with a mild hearing impairment might sit close to the front of the room or a child with a motor handicap might be given extra time when taking tests. Unfortunately, we do not know as much as we wish we did about how to educate people with special needs (Detterman & Thompson, 1997).

Restandardization of IQ Tests

Over the years, the standardization of any IQ test eventually becomes obsolete. In 1920, a question that asked people to identify "Mars" was fairly difficult, because most people knew little about the planets. Today, in an era of space exploration, the same question would be very easy for most people. But this trend goes beyond just questions about factual material; most of the items on IQ tests seem to get easier from one decade to the next.

Consequently, the publishers of IQ tests periodically update them, replace easy questions with slightly harder ones, and make the scoring standards a bit stricter, to keep the mean score at 100. In other words, *decade by decade, generation by generation, people have been getting better and better at whatever it is that IQ tests are measuring.* If

your generation were to take the same IQ test as your parents' generation, graded the same way, yours would score about 5–10 points higher, on the average. This tendency is known as the **Flynn effect,** after the psychologist who first called attention to it (Flynn, 1984, 1987). What accounts for the Flynn effect? Psychologists are not certain. Evolution is not a plausible explanation for such a rapid change. Improved health and nutrition are probably contributors, at least for improving scores at the lower end. Greater availability of education may be a factor, although the Flynn effect applies even to children 5–10 years old, and it seems doubtful that elementary schools have been getting steadily better from one decade to the next. One appealing hypothesis is that children have been receiving more and more benefits—yes, benefits—from television, movies, and computer programs (Neisser, 1997). Scores have been rising especially on highly visual tests, such as Raven's Progressive Matrices, which relate to the less verbal, more visual processing that television and other technologies promote. Regardless of the explanation, the Flynn effect demonstrates that changes in the environment can alter IQ scores.

Evaluation of Tests

At some point in your academic career, you probably complained that a test was unfair. Similarly, many people complain about intelligence tests. Much is at stake in this dispute; intelligence tests substantially influence the future of millions of people. Psychologists try to avoid simply arguing about whether or not a test appears to be reasonable; they examine specific kinds of evidence to determine whether the test achieves what it is intended to achieve. The main ways of evaluating any test are to check its reliability and validity.

Reliability

The **reliability** of a test is defined as *the repeatability of its scores* (Rogers, 1995). A reliable test measures something consistently. To determine the reliability of a test, psychologists calculate a correlation coefficient. They may test the same people twice, either with the same test or with equivalent versions of it, and compare the two sets of scores. Or they may compare the scores on the first and second halves of the test or the scores on the test's odd-numbered and even-numbered items. If all items measure approximately the same abilities, the scores on one set of items should be highly correlated with the scores on the other set of items. As with any other correlation coefficient, the reliability of a test can (theoretically) range from +1 to −1. In the real world, however, reliability is always positive. (A negative reliability would mean that most of the people who score high on one set of items score low on the other set. That pattern simply never happens.) Figure 9.11 illustrates **test-retest reliability,** *the correlation between scores on a first test and on a retest.*

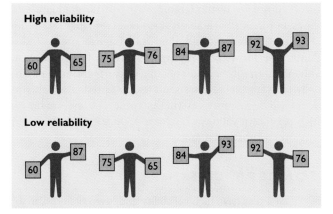

High reliability

60 65   75 76   84 87   92 93

Low reliability

60 87   75 65   84 93   92 76

FIGURE 9.11 On a test with high reliability, people who score high the first time will score high when they take the test again. On a test with low reliability, scores fluctuate randomly.

If a test's reliability is perfect (+1), the person who scores the highest on the first test will also score highest on the retest, the person who scores second highest on the first test will also score second highest on the retest, and so forth. If the reliability is 0, scores will vary randomly from one test to another. The reliability of the WISC–III has been measured at .96 (Wechsler, 1991), and the reliabilities of the Stanford-Binet, Progressive Matrices, and SAT are similar. These figures indicate that these IQ tests are measuring *something*, but they do not tell us what that something is or how useful it is.

CONCEPT CHECKS

3. I have just devised a new "intelligence test." I measure your intelligence by dividing the length of your head by its width and then multiplying by 100. Would that be a reliable test?

4. Most students find that their SAT scores increase the second time they take the test. Does that improvement indicate that the test is unreliable? (Check your answers on page 340.)

Validity

A test's **validity** is *a determination of how well it measures what it claims to measure.* One type of validity is **content validity.** We say that a test has high content validity if *its items accurately represent the information that the test is meant to measure.* For example, a test for a driver's license has content validity if it includes important laws and regulations that pertain to driving. A licensing examination for psychologists would have high content validity if it tested information that a practicing psychologist is expected to know.

A second type of validity is **construct validity.** A test has construct validity if *what it measures corresponds to a theoretical construct.* For example, intelligence is a theoretical construct that should have certain properties, such

as increasing as a child grows older. For an IQ test to have construct validity, older children should, as a rule, answer more questions correctly than younger children do. It should also have the property of being independent of eyesight; a test would lack construct validity if blind people could not do well on it. In short, a test has good construct validity if the scores depend on factors we believe to be important and do not depend on factors we believe to be unimportant (Messick, 1995).

Predictive validity, a third type of validity, is *the ability of a test's scores to predict some real-world performance.* For example, an interest test that correctly predicts what courses a student will enjoy has predictive validity, as does an IQ test that correctly predicts how well a student will perform in school.

As with reliability, psychologists measure predictive validity by a correlation coefficient. To determine the predictive validity of an IQ test or the SAT, psychologists determine how well those scores predict students' grades. A validity of +1 would mean that the scores perfectly predicted performance; a validity of 0 would mean that the scores were worthless as predictors. A common problem in psychology is that the criterion that tests try to predict, such as grades in school, is itself an inaccurate measure of performance. The less accurately we measure the criterion, the harder it is for test scores to correlate highly with it.

The predictive validity of standard IQ tests and the SAT generally ranges from about .3 to .6, varying from one school to another (Anastasi, 1988; Siegler & Richards, 1982). As these figures suggest, success in school depends not only on academic skills, but also on motivation, persistence, and other personality attributes that are hard to measure—as well as what courses one takes, what teachers one has, and other factors that are impossible to predict.

In some countries, test scores determine a student's future almost irrevocably. Students who perform well are almost assured of future success; those who perform poorly will have very limited opportunities.

Validity of Test Scores for Selecting among Job Applicants Besides predicting school performance, IQ tests also have some validity (about .2 to .3) for predicting success in a variety of jobs (Wagner, 1997). To select people for advanced jobs, the best predictor is workers' current job performance or job knowledge. For entry-level jobs, however, tests of cognitive abilities help to identify workers who will learn a job quickly and well. According to Frank Schmidt and John Hunter (1981, p. 1128), "Professionally developed cognitive ability tests are valid predictors of performance on the job . . . for all jobs . . . in all settings." That is probably an overstatement. (It could hardly be an understatement!) Also, the controversy continues about whether job performance is more accurately predicted by more-or-less standard cognitive test scores or by measures of "practical knowledge" or common sense (Sternberg, Wagner, Williams, & Horvath, 1995). Personality factors such as persistence and willingness to listen and learn would probably be excellent predictors also, if we had better ways to measure them (Wagner, 1997). Still, for many jobs, using some type of cognitive test score to select employees increases the chances that those who are hired will succeed at their jobs.

In some cases, job applicants have challenged the right of an employer to deny them a job based on a test score or even based on their education. Their claim is that those criteria create unnecessary barriers for people who have little formal education but who can nevertheless perform the job well. U.S. courts have ruled that an employer can use test scores to select employees only if the employer can demonstrate that the scores are valid predictors of performance on that particular job. In fact, employers may use almost any criterion that they can demonstrate to be valid. If a police department wants to hire only tall police officers or an airline wants to hire only thin flight attendants, the courts ask a simple question (Hogan & Quigley, 1986): Can you demonstrate that people who meet this criterion do the job better than people who don't?

Special Problems in Measuring Validity Measuring the validity of a test can be tricky, especially at a school that relies heavily on the test scores for its admissions decisions. Consider data for the Graduate Record Examination (GRE), a test that is similar to the SAT. For predicting grades in the first year of graduate school, the verbal and quantitative parts of the GRE have the following predictive validities (Educational Testing Service, 1994):

	GRE verbal score	GRE quantitative score
Graduate students in Physics	.19	.13
Graduate students in English	.23	.29

Note that, for physics students, the verbal score is the better predictor of grades, whereas for English students, the quantitative score is a better predictor! How can we explain

these surprising results? Simply. Almost all graduate students in physics have about the same (very high) score on the quantitative test, and almost all English graduate students have the same (very high) score on the verbal test. When almost all the students in a department have practically the same score, that score cannot predict which students will be more successful than others. A test can have a high predictive validity only for a population whose scores vary over a substantial range.

CONCEPT CHECKS

5. Can a test have high reliability and low validity? Can a test have low reliability and high validity?
6. If physics graduate departments tried admitting some students with low quantitative scores on the GRE and English departments tried admitting some students with low verbal scores, what would happen to the predictive validity of those tests?
7. Would you expect the SAT scores to show higher predictive validity at a university with extremely competitive admissions standards, such as MIT, or at a university that admits almost anyone who applies? (Check your answers on page 341.)

Utility

In addition to reliability and validity, a good test should have utility. **Utility** is defined as *usefulness for a practical purpose.* Not every test that is reliable and valid is also useful.

For example, one study found that first-year grades at the University of Pennsylvania correlated positively with both SAT aptitude test scores and SAT achievement test scores. That is, both aptitude scores and achievement scores were valid. However, the investigators found that they could predict first-year grades just as well from achievement scores alone as they could from a combination of aptitude and achievement scores (Baron & Norman, 1992). That is, if the university already had students' SAT achievement scores, the SAT aptitude test had little or no utility. Those results may not apply to other colleges, and they are of course irrelevant for colleges that do not require the achievement tests. The point is that any institution should determine whether a given test has utility for its purposes.

Table 9.4 summarizes the criteria for evaluating intelligence tests.

Interpreting Fluctuations in Scores

Suppose that your score on the first test in your Psychology course is 94% correct. On the second test (which was equally difficult), you achieve a score of only 88%. Does that score indicate that you studied harder for the first test than for the second test? Not necessarily. Whenever you take tests that are not perfectly reliable, your scores are likely to fluctuate. The lower the reliability, the greater the fluctuation.

T A B L E 9.4 Evaluating Intelligence Tests

RELIABILITY	VALIDITY	UTILITY	BIAS
How consistent are the same person's scores?	How well does the test measure what it claims to measure? Content: Do the test items represent the pertinent information? Construct: Do the results match theoretical expectations? Prediction: Do the test scores predict real-world performance?	How useful is the test for a particular purpose?	Do test scores make equally accurate predictions from all groups?

When people lose sight of this fact, they sometimes offer complex explanations for random fluctuations in results. In one well-known study, Harold M. Skeels (1966) tested infants in an orphanage and identified those who had the lowest IQ scores. He then placed those infants in an institution that provided more personal attention. Several years later, most of those infants showed major increases in their IQ scores. Should we conclude, as many psychologists did, that the extra attention improved the children's IQ performances? Not necessarily (Longstreth, 1981). IQ tests for infants have low reliability—in other words, the scores tend to fluctuate widely. If someone selects a group of infants with low IQ scores and retests them later, the mean IQ score is almost certain to improve, simply because the scores had nowhere to go but up. Many of the infants were, no doubt, brighter than their original test scores indicated and received bad test scores because they were not feeling well, were not paying attention, or had other temporary problems.

SOMETHING TO THINK ABOUT

What would be the proper control group for the study by Skeels? ✳

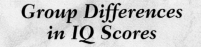

Group Differences in IQ Scores

Binet and the other pioneers in IQ testing discovered that girls tend to do better than boys on certain kinds of language tasks, especially verbal fluency. Boys, however, tend to do better than girls on visual-spatial rotations and certain kinds of mathematical reasoning. By loading the test with one type of item, they could have "demonstrated" that girls are smarter than boys or that boys are smarter than girls. Instead, they carefully balanced these two types of items to ensure that the mean score of both girls and boys would be 100.

Over the years, studies have continued to demonstrate the same kinds of male-female differences in many countries and cultures (Halpern, 1997). Note that these are differences between the *averages*; the distribution of male scores completely overlaps the distribution of female scores, and the differences within either group are large compared to the differences between the two groups:

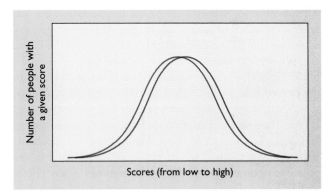

Males tend to show greater individual variability. Thus, the data on a variety of intellectual measures show a higher percentage of males than females at the very top of the range and also at the very bottom of the range (Lubinski & Benbow, 1992). For example, one finds more males than females among the top achievers in many fields but also among those with mental retardation, attention deficit disorder, and reading and speaking impairments (Halpern, 1997). (*Why* this is true, we do not know.)

Ethnic groups in the United States also differ in their mean performances on IQ tests (Herrnstein & Murray, 1994). One problem when dealing with these data is that any group—such as "Black" or "African-American"—refers to a diverse population who vary among themselves both genetically and environmentally. Ordinarily, researchers classify people by simply asking them how they classify themselves; therefore, these categories are only partly satisfactory (at best) from either a biological or sociological standpoint. Nevertheless, these are the data, for whatever they are worth (Neisser et al., 1996; Suzuki & Valencia, 1997): The mean score of European-Americans as a whole is about 100, with the Jewish subpopulation averaging a few

Many immigrants to the United States settle in ethnic neighborhoods where they can use their original language. Most first-generation immigrants do not score highly on English-language intelligence tests; as a rule, their children and grandchildren get higher scores.

points above other European-Americans. The mean for African-Americans used to be 85 but has risen over the last several decades to about 88 or 90; African-Americans' scores on the SAT and other tests have risen also (Williams & Ceci, 1997). The mean score for Latinos is in the 90s, but many of those people are first-generation immigrants to the United States who are hampered by language problems; most Latinos score lower on the Verbal part of the Wechsler IQ test than on the Performance part, which relies less on language. The means for East Asians (those of Japanese, Chinese, or Korean descent) vary from one sample to another, sometimes about 100 and sometimes a few points higher. East Asians' school performance is even higher than one would predict from their test scores and is presumably the result of a culture that encourages diligent study.

Please bear in mind that these data reflect the means for entire populations. Each ethnic group includes many individuals with extremely high scores and many others with very low scores. These data do not justify prejudices or assumptions about any given individual.

What accounts for the observed differences among ethnic groups? In a famous but controversial book, *The Bell Curve*, Richard Herrnstein and Charles Murray (1994) argued that these IQ differences may be partly due to genetic differences. In response to this book and the ensuing controversy, a panel of distinguished investigators reviewed the evidence and issued a report (Neisser et al., 1996). The panel largely agreed with Herrnstein and Murray, with slightly different wording and emphases, about the following points:

- IQ tests, imperfect as they are, reliably measure something, regardless of whether we choose to call it intelligence.
- Whatever IQ tests measure correlates with school performance, the likelihood of getting certain jobs, and many other behavioral measures. It is not an all-important characteristic of a person, but it is not trivial either.

- Measured differences among groups are not illusions that we can attribute to faulty tests.
- IQ differences within the European-American population reflect a combination of environmental and genetic differences. Not much is known about the genes that affect intelligence. Important environmental factors include the fairly obvious ones such as education (Brody, 1997; Ceci & Williams, 1997; Perkins & Grotzer, 1997), but also such factors as early nutrition, exposure to lead and other toxins, and whether the mother drank alcohol during pregnancy.
- IQ differences among ethnic groups may also reflect a combination of environmental and genetic differences.

The first and second of those points say, in effect, that IQ tests are reliable and valid for certain purposes. As already mentioned earlier in this chapter, the data clearly support those two points. According to a consensus of 52 leading researchers in this area (Arvey et al., 1994), Herrnstein and Murray's third and fourth points also fit the data: The apparent group differences are not due to faulty testing, and differences among European-Americans are probably due to both genetic and environmental influences. On the fifth point, however, the evidence is too weak to justify any conclusion beyond saying that it *may* be true. The available evidence does not demonstrate a genetic basis for ethnic differences, but it also fails to eliminate that possibility. Quite simply, we do not have much strong evidence. With that preview in mind, let us proceed.

Should We Care?

On such a politically charged question, it is risky to say anything at all. Even discussing the differences between blacks and whites calls extra attention to such matters and runs the risk of supporting prejudices against minority groups. No doubt most of us look forward to the day when race and ethnicity are no longer a divisive issue and no one asks or much cares about IQ differences among groups; however, that day has not yet come. Many people do care about why blacks and whites differ, and many people form opinions about the issue, some of them very strong, frequently without knowing any of the evidence. If people are going to have opinions, they may as well know the evidence.

Are IQ Tests Biased?

One often-proposed explanation for group differences in IQ scores is that the tests are biased against certain groups. That is, ethnic groups do not actually differ in mean IQ; they merely appear to differ because of unfair or inappropriate tests. Presumably, according to this viewpoint, a better test would indicate no group differences.

The first point to emphasize here is that the existence of measurable group differences does not, by itself, demonstrate bias in the tests. If, on the average, one group gets

Students who return to school in their 30s or later usually get better grades than their test scores would predict. That is, the tests are "biased" against them in the technical sense of the term *bias*. Saying this does not mean the tests were designed to be unfair to them, just that the test scores underpredict their performance.

higher scores than the second group, it could be that the test is biased against the second group, but it is also possible that the groups really do differ in their performances. For example, on the average, 20-year-olds answer more questions correctly on almost any information test than do 6-year-olds. This fact does not indicate that information tests are biased against 6-year-olds; the difference in scores accurately reflects that 20-year-olds are better informed than 6-year-olds. If two groups differ in their performances, we need to collect evidence to find out whether the test is biased or not.

To determine whether or not a test is **biased** against a group, psychologists determine *whether the test systematically underestimates group members' performance*. To understand what it means for a test to be biased, consider two examples: First, the Stanford-Binet and Wechsler IQ tests are biased against non-English speaking immigrants to the United States. In the long run (after immigrants have learned the language), such people usually succeed beyond what their initial test scores would indicate. That is, the test scores underestimate the immigrants' eventual performance. Psychologists of an earlier era, either unaware of this bias or insensitive to it, drew some conclusions that now seem ludicrous about the "feeblemindedness" of immigrants (Gelb, 1986).

A second example: Women who enter or return to college in their 30s or later, generally receive better grades than their scores on the SAT, ACT, or any other test would predict. They also do better than their high-school grades would predict. When we say, therefore, that these tests are biased against such women, we are not suggesting that the test authors rigged the tests against them. We are merely saying that a given test score means something different for a 40-year-old woman than it does for a 19-year-old. Why do the women who return to school get better grades than their

test scores predict? There are a couple of hypotheses: (1) Because they have been away from school for a while, their test-taking skills are rusty but will recover with a little practice. (2) To return to school at all at that point, they must have strong motivation.

To determine whether a test is biased—against middle-aged women, ethnic minorities, or whatever—psychologists must find out whether such individuals do better in school or college than the test scores predict. Psychologists try to identify bias both in individual test items and in the test as a whole.

Evaluating Possible Bias in Single Test Items

To determine whether a particular item on a test is biased, psychologists must go beyond an "armchair analysis" that says "this item seems unfair." They look for evidence that an item that is relatively easy for one group might be relatively difficult for another group (Schmitt & Dorans, 1990).

Figure 9.12, an item that once appeared on the SAT, shows a diagram of an American football field and asks for the ratio of the distance between the goal lines to the distance between the sidelines. For men, this was one of the easiest items on the test. The few men who missed it generally did poorly on the rest of the test as well. However, a higher percentage of women missed this item, including some women who did very well on the rest of the test. The reason was that some very bright women did not know which were the goal lines and which were the sidelines. This pattern of evidence indicated that the item was biased against women, and the publishers of the SAT therefore

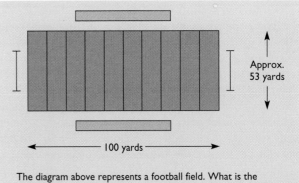

The diagram above represents a football field. What is the ratio of the distance between the goal lines to the distance between the sidelines?

a. 1.89
b. 1.53
c. 0.53
d. 5.3
e. 53

F I G U R E   9.12 This item was once included on the SAT, until psychologists determined that it was biased against women. Some women who did very well on the rest of the test did not know which were the goal lines and which were the sidelines.

"Students will rise to your level of expectation," says Jaime Escalante (left), the high-school teacher portrayed by Edward James Olmos (right), in *Stand and Deliver*. The movie chronicles Escalante's talent for inspiring average students to excel in calculus. School counselors warned that he asked too much of his students; parents said their kids didn't need calculus. And when his students first passed the advanced placement test, they were accused of cheating, a charge that seemed to reflect prejudice against the students, who were not European-American, middle-class, college-prep types.

removed the item from the test. As a rule, standardized tests such as the SAT are routinely purged of any items with demonstrable bias against a particular group.

Evaluating Possible Bias in a Test as a Whole

By definition, a biased test is one that systematically underestimates (underpredicts) the performance of a group. If an IQ test is indeed biased against African-Americans, for example, then African-Americans who score, say, 100 really have greater abilities than European-Americans with the same score and should outperform them in school.

The evidence, however, indicates that minority-group students with a given IQ score generally do about as well in school and at school-related tasks as do European-Americans with the same IQ score (Barrett & Depinet, 1991; Cole, 1981; Lambert, 1981; Svanum & Bringle, 1982). Likewise, minority-group students with a given SAT score generally do about as well in college as do European-Americans with the same scores (McCornack, 1983). The unpleasant fact is that, on the average, European-American students get better grades in school in the United States than African-Americans do. The IQ tests simply report that fact. In short, the tests show no evidence of ethnic-group bias, so continued claims of test bias could be described as "blaming the messenger" (the IQ tests) for the bad news.

Some critics have argued that African-American students perform more poorly than they might be expected to on various tests because they are either intimidated by a European-American tester or because they are confused by the language of the test. However, research studies have found no consistent increase in black children's test scores when the test is administered by an African-American measiner, using an African-American dialect (Sattler & Gwynne, 1982).

Saying that IQ tests show no demonstrable bias against minority groups does *not* mean, though, that the differences in scores are due to differences in innate ability. It merely means that whatever causes children to differ in school performance also causes them to differ in test performance. Whether this difference reflects hereditary or environmental influences is an entirely separate question.

Also note that even defenders of IQ tests do not claim that the tests are perfect. At best, they measure one kind of intelligence, the kind of intelligence that helps people to do well in school. They do not measure the multiple kinds of intelligence that Gardner discusses and certainly not all the kinds of skills that any human culture might value.

CONCEPT CHECKS

8. A test of driving skills includes items requiring people to describe what they see. People with visual impairments score lower than people with good vision. Is the test therefore biased against people with visual impairments?

9. Suppose someone devises a new IQ test, and we discover that tall people generally get higher scores on this test than short people do. How could we determine whether this test is biased against short people? (Check your answers on page 341.)

How Do Heredity and Environment Affect IQ Scores?

The British scholar Francis Galton (1869/1978) was the first to offer evidence that the tendency toward high intelligence is hereditary. As evidence, he simply pointed out that eminent and distinguished men—politicians, judges, and the like—generally had several distinguished relatives. We no longer consider that evidence convincing, because distinguished people share environment as well as genes with their relatives. Besides, becoming a distinguished person is only partly a result of intelligence.

The question of how heredity affects intelligence has persisted to this day and continues to be difficult to answer. The issue is complicated because intellectual development undoubtedly depends on many genes (Chorney et al., 1998) and many environmental influences, each of which makes a small contribution. Here are descriptions of the available kinds of evidence, with their strengths and limitations:

Family Resemblances

Figure 9.13, based on a review of the available literature by Thomas Bouchard and Matthew McGue (1981), shows the correlations of IQ scores for people with various degrees of genetic relationship. These data are based almost entirely on European-American families; we do not know how well the results apply to other ethnic groups.

Because no IQ test has perfect reliability, a single individual taking the test on two occasions will get slightly different scores, and the correlation between the two test scores will be close to .9. The scores of monozygotic (identical) twins correlate with each other almost that well (Plomin & DeFries, 1980). Monozygotic twins resemble each other not only in overall IQ, but also in individual tests of verbal ability, spatial ability, processing speed, and memory; they continue to resemble each other throughout life—even beyond age 80 in one study (McClearn et al., 1997). Fraternal twins and nontwin siblings differ more than monozygotic twins do, but their scores are still fairly close. More remote relatives, such as cousins, have IQ scores that correlate positively but not strongly. A resemblance among relatives is consistent with the possibility of a genetic influence, but it is also consistent with the possibility of an environmental influence. (Closer relatives have more similar environment as well as more similar heredity.)

Note also in Figure 9.13 the positive correlation between unrelated children adopted into the same family. That correlation indicates a significant contribution from the environment. However, because this correlation is lower than the correlation between siblings (brothers or sisters) suggests that family environment does not account for all variations in IQ. (Alternatives include genetics, prenatal environment, and "nonshared" factors in the environment that differ from one family member to another.)

The comparison between monozygotic (identical) and dizygotic (fraternal) twins also shows a greater correlation between monozygotic twins than between dizygotic twins. This presumably reflects a genetic contribution, unless we can attribute these results to a tendency for monozygotic twins to spend more time together and to be treated more alike. However, researchers have found that identical twins who always *thought* they were fraternal twins resemble each other as much as other identical twins do; fraternal twins who always *thought* they were identical twins resemble each other no more than other fraternal twins do (Scarr, 1968; Scarr & Carter-Saltzman, 1979). That is, the main determinant of similarity in IQ is whether twins are actually identical, not whether they think they are identical.

Identical Twins Reared Apart

In Figure 9.13, note the high correlation between monozygotic twins reared apart. That is, identical twins who have been adopted by different parents and reared in separate environments nevertheless strongly resemble each other in IQ scores (Bouchard & McGue, 1981; Farber, 1981). That resemblance implies a genetic contribution to IQ. Skeptics point out that the "separate" environments have often been very similar (Farber, 1981; Kamin, 1974). In some cases, the biological parents raised one twin, and close relatives or

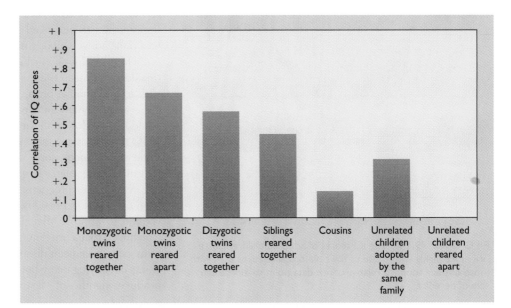

FIGURE 9.13 Mean correlations for the IQs of children with various degrees of genetic and environmental similarity. (Siblings are non-twin children in the same family.) (Adapted from Bouchard & McGue, 1981.)

next-door neighbors raised the other twin. Yet, it is difficult to escape the suggestion of at least a small genetic contribution, because it is unlikely that monozygotic twins reared apart would have *more* similar environments than dizygotic twins who grow up in the same household.

Twins and Single Births

One final point about Figure 9.13: Dizygotic twins resemble each other more closely than single-birth siblings do. That finding, consistent across several studies, indicates an influence from being born at the same time, since the genetic similarity between dizygotic twins is the same as that between siblings. These results may reflect the importance of prenatal and early postnatal environment. Twins share a prenatal environment, and therefore get the same nutrition, body temperature, alcohol or tobacco, and all other influences, while the brain is going through some critical stages of development (Devlin, Daniels, & Roeder, 1997). In fact, it is often difficult to distinguish between the role of genetics and that of prenatal environment.

Adopted Children

Another line of evidence comes from studies of adopted children. Children who are reared by their biological parents generally have IQ scores similar to those of their parents (Figure 9.14). For adopted children, IQ scores in early childhood are generally intermediate between those of their biological parents and those of their adoptive parents; as they become older children and then adolescents, their IQ scores gradually become closer to those of their biological parents, and it thus becomes harder to demonstrate the influence of their adoptive parents (Loehlin, Horn, & Willerman, 1989; Plomin, Fulker, Corley, & DeFries,

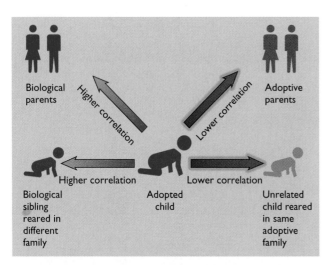

FIGURE 9.14 The IQ scores of adopted children correlate more highly with those of their biological relatives than with those of their adoptive relatives. Such data point to a probable role of heredity.

1997). Furthermore, the IQ scores of unrelated children adopted by the same family resemble each other less than do the IQs of related children who are adopted by separate families (Teasdale & Owen, 1984).

The interpretation of these results is confounded to some extent by the policies of adoption agencies. Many adoption agencies place children of parents with high IQs with the brightest available adoptive parents, thereby providing an environment that should help the children to resemble their biological parents. Still, because adopted children resemble their biological parents *more* than they resemble their adoptive parents, heredity seems to play a significant role in IQ scores.

Gene Identification

The most direct kind of evidence is the identification of specific genes linked to intelligence. One set of investigators compared the chromosomes of children with very high IQ scores (mean 136) and those with average scores (mean 103). They found one gene, of the 37 they examined, that was significantly more common in the high-IQ group (Chorney et al., 1998). Because they had examined so many genes, they knew that a discrepancy in one gene could arise by accident, so they repeated their study with other samples of people with high and average IQs, and again they found that the gene in question was more common in the high-IQ groups. Overall, 46% of the high-IQ people and 23% of the low-IQ people had this gene. Obviously, this gene is neither necessary nor sufficient for high intelligence; it can be only one contributor among dozens of other genes and a great many environmental influences.

Most researchers agree that hereditary and environmental factors both contribute to the observed variations in IQ scores, at least within the European-American population, the subjects of most studies (Thompson, Detterman, & Plomin, 1991; Turkheimer, 1991). The important question is no longer *do* heredity and environment contribute to IQ, but *how* do they contribute? (The one identified gene that appears to be linked to IQ controls a receptor whose functions are very poorly understood.)

Heredity does contribute to variations in IQ scores, but this does not mean that people are somehow limited by the abilities they had at birth. Obviously, if we gave every child either an extremely good or extremely bad environment, we could raise or lower all their IQ scores. Positive heritability of IQ scores merely means that, if children grow up in the same environment, some do better than others, and part of that difference relates to genetics.

A variety of programs have attempted to take children from extremely deprived homes and give them special intervention to improve their intellectual development. People who hoped that a brief intervention might lead to huge, long-term gains have been disappointed. However, intensive programs occupying many hours per week for several years can produce significant, lasting benefits (Ramey & Ramey,

1998). Again, the point is that conceding that heredity plays a role does not minimize the importance of the environment.

Heredity, Environment, and Ethnic Differences

Is it likely that hereditary differences contribute to part of the observed differences in IQ scores among ethnic groups? Some psychologists believe so but others do not. Many, on each side of this argument, state their case with more confidence than their data would seem to support.

Those who believe that heredity is a likely contributor to ethnic differences offer the following simple proposition: Hereditary differences do appear to contribute to IQ differences within at least one ethnic group (Europeans and European-Americans), so therefore they probably also contribute to the differences among ethnic groups. However, this conclusion is unfounded. To illustrate: Imagine that someone finds that the children in a certain city differ in their IQ scores and that part of this difference is due to genetics. Now, we take a random sample of the families and move them to a second city, with worse health, nutrition, education, and overall opportunities. We would probably find that the children now perform worse on the tests. If we compared children within one city or the other, *those* differences might be partly genetic, but the difference between cities could still be entirely due to environment. (See Figure 9.15.)

People who argue that heredity could not contribute to ethnic differences in IQ argue as follows: The various human ethnic groups have diverged for only a brief period of evolutionary history. The great majority of human genes either show no variation at all among individuals or differ widely *within*

each ethnic group. Only a few genes (such as the genes controlling hair and skin color) have a greater difference among ethnic groups than they have within each group. (Actually, there are probably *no* genes that are present in all members of one group but none of another. At most, a gene might be present in a higher percentage of one group than the other.)

Granting all of that, the implications for the genetics of intelligence are still unclear, however. Different ethnic groups do share most of their genes in common, but within a given country such as the United States, different ethnic groups also share a good deal of their environment in common (Rowe, Vazsonyi, & Flannery, 1994). Furthermore, researchers do not know which genes, or even how many genes, make significant contributions to intelligence or how such genes exert their effects. Do such genes differ more within each human population than they differ among populations? Or are these genes some of the few that differ significantly between one population and another? In short, we do not yet know enough about either the environmental or the genetic influences on IQ to say what is possible. Arguing about probabilities and likelihoods is no substitute for collecting evidence.

WHAT'S THE EVIDENCE?

Environmental Contributors to Ethnic Differences

Many studies attempting to evaluate the role of environmental factors have followed the design of providing improved early education, improved nutrition, or a change in

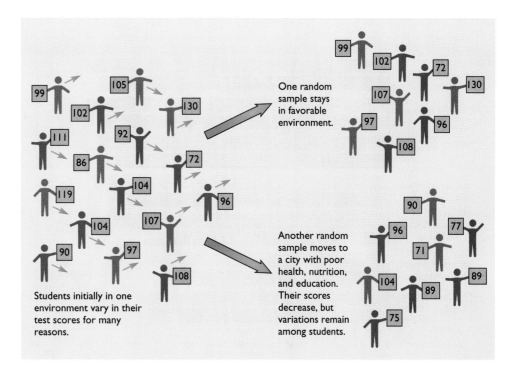

FIGURE 9.15 If two sets of children grow up in very different circumstances, it is possible that the difference between the two groups is entirely due to environmental differences, even if the differences within each group are partly due to genetic factors.

Students initially in one environment vary in their test scores for many reasons.

One random sample stays in favorable environment.

Another random sample moves to a city with poor health, nutrition, and education. Their scores decrease, but variations remain among students.

If ethnic differences in IQ are largely the result of environmental differences, African-American children adopted by upper-middle-class European-American families should score higher, on average, than similar children reared in African-American homes. The results of research have been unimpressive and also hard to interpret, because many of the children studied were adopted relatively late.

another environmental factor for an experimental group of extremely low-income children and then examining the effects on the children's eventual IQ scores and school performances. Most such studies have found genuine but fairly small benefits (e.g., Darlington, Royce, Snipper, Murray, & Lazar, 1980).

A more drastic approach is to examine African-American children who have been adopted by upper-middle-class European-American families. The idea behind this approach is that such families are likely to provide a variety of environmental supports helpful for performance on IQ tests, including good nutrition, better education, and general familiarity with "the culture of the test."

Hypothesis If the IQ differences among the races is partly due to early experiences, then African-American children reared by European-American families should perform better on IQ tests than most other African-American children will.

Method Sandra Scarr and Richard Weinberg (1976) studied European-American families in Minnesota that had adopted African-American children (with two African-American parents) or ethnically mixed children (one African-American and one European-American parent). Many of these parents also had biological children of their own; many had also adopted European-American or Asian or Native American children. The investigators tested the IQs of the children and the adopting parents and tested them again 10 years later (Scarr & Weinberg, 1976; Weinberg, Scarr, & Waldman, 1992).

Results Figure 9.16 shows the mean scores for only those individuals who were tested both times. All the means were lower at the second test because of changes in the IQ test itself. (As mentioned earlier, psychologists restandardize the test every few years, generally making it more difficult.)

Interpretation The data of interest are the mean scores for the adopted children. The adopted European-American children scored higher than adopted children with one African-American parent ("ethnically mixed"), who in turn scored higher than adopted children with two African-American parents. However, the ethnically mixed adopted children scored near 100 (above 100 on the first test but

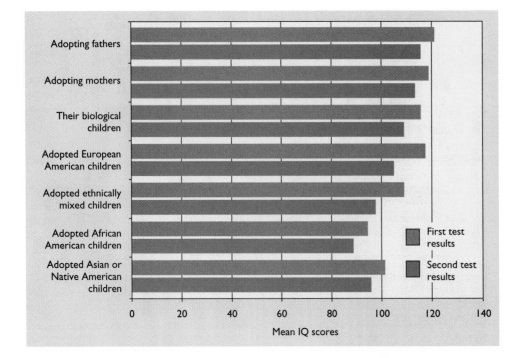

First test results

Second test results

FIGURE 9.16 During childhood, African-American children adopted by upper-middle-class European-American families showed IQ scores well above the national average for African-Americans, but 10 years later they showed only small benefits.

slightly below that on the second). Adopted children with two African-American parents scored a mean of 95 on the first test; 89, ten years later.

Psychologists are frankly divided about how to interpret these results (e.g., Levin, 1994; Waldman, Weinberg, & Scarr, 1994). African-American children adopted by upper-middle-class European-American families did perform better on IQ tests than the national average for African-Americans (85), but not much better. Furthermore, the mean for African-Americans in Minnesota is not 85, but 88.

If these data suggest a disappointingly small environmental influence, one possible reason is that the presumed benefits of an "advantaged" family began well after birth. For whatever reason, the African-American mothers of the adopted children in this study gave their babies up for adoption significantly later than did the European-American mothers. Many of the adopted African-American and ethnically mixed children lived in several foster homes of unknown quality before being adopted. Perhaps these children demonstrated the effects of their very early environment, as well as their prenatal environment. (Many African-American mothers who give their babies up for adoption are teenagers who received poor health care and nutrition during pregnancy.) In short, this study, which was designed to demonstrate environmental influences, instead produced small and equivocal effects.

✳   ✳   ✳

Hereditary Contributors to Ethnic Differences

In comparison, let us now examine a study with the potential to show a strong hereditary contribution.

Hypothesis   If heredity is responsible for even part of the difference between the races in IQ performance, then African-Americans with a high percentage of European ancestry should obtain higher IQ scores than African-Americans with a lower percentage. (Few U.S. African-Americans have 100% African ancestry.)

Method   Determining the ethnic ancestry of an African-American child is difficult. Most family trees do not go back enough generations, and skin color is an inaccurate indicator. (Even in Africa, skin darkness varies greatly from one subpopulation to another.) Blood-typing, however, provides a somewhat better estimator.

The investigators (Scarr, Pakstis, Katz, & Barker, 1977) examined 362 African-American children in Philadelphia, testing 14 different blood factors—the familiar ABO blood types, the Rh factor, the Duffy factor, and 11 others. Certain blood factors are more common in Europe than in Africa and vice versa. For example, type B blood is present in only 9% of Europeans but in 21% of Africans. Few if any

Variations in skin darkness are an inaccurate indicator of degree of African ancestry. Blood-typing provides a somewhat better indicator, although it is also far from certain.

Europeans have Duffy type A− B− blood, whereas 94% of Africans do. By comparing each child's blood factors to the frequency of those blood factors in both Europe and Africa, the investigators estimated the degree of European ancestry for each child. Then, the investigators correlated their estimates of European ancestry with performance on Raven's Progressive Matrices and four other tests of intellectual performance.

Results   The investigators tried several methods of weighting the importance of various blood factors to estimate European and African ancestry. Regardless of which method they used, however, they found virtually zero correlation between the estimates of European ancestry and measures of performance.

Interpretation   If hereditary factors were a major contributor to ethnic differences in IQ scores, we would expect to find a positive correlation between the amount of European ancestry and IQ scores. The absence of such a correlation indicates either that heredity contributes nothing to the ethnic differences or that it contributes so little that this research method could not detect it. Another possibility is that the investigators estimated African and European ancestry too inaccurately (Reed, 1997). Perhaps the main point here is simply that it is difficult to determine the roles of heredity and the environment for differences among human groups.

✳   ✳   ✳

Heredity and Environment

Where does this leave us? The best designed studies, attempting to demonstrate an environmental contributor to ethnic differences, found only weak and uncertain effects. The best study capable of demonstrating a hereditary contributor found no evidence of any influence at all. Sometimes, even good research fails to answer the question being posed; here, we have such a case. Future research may help to resolve the issues; in the meantime, the best recommendation is to draw no conclusion at all and to be suspicious of anyone who seems too sure of the answer.

What kind of research should psychologists do in the future? Actually, I would not encourage a young psychologist to begin research on the roles that heredity and environment play in IQ differences. Never mind the political explosiveness of the issue; the topic is scientifically difficult, and it is not clear what use (if any) the results would have. There is, however, one related topic that definitely does deserve more and improved research: Given that environmental factors do contribute to differences in intelligence (as everyone agrees, even if we don't all agree how much they contribute), what are the important environmental factors? Simply growing up in an upper-middle-class home is apparently insufficient to boost IQ or school performance by much. But what is sufficient? prenatal health and nutrition, perhaps? other factors in an infant's environment? If we could identify those factors, we might be able to accomplish something that would benefit everyone.

SUMMARY

* *Standardization.* To determine the meaning of a test's scores, the authors of a test determine the mean and the distribution of scores for a random or representative sample of the population. IQ tests are revised periodically. To keep the same mean, test authors make the tests more difficult from time to time. (page 327)

* *Distribution of IQ scores.* IQ tests have a mean of 100 and a standard deviation of about 15 or 16, depending on the test. Items are carefully selected so that performance on each item correlates positively with performance on the test as a whole. (page 327)

* *Reliability and validity.* Tests are evaluated in terms of reliability and validity. Reliability is a measure of a test's consistency, or the repeatability of its scores. Validity is a determination of how well a test measures what it claims to measure. (page 328)

* *Test bias.* Psychologists try to remove from a test any item that tends to be easy for one group of people to answer but difficult for another. They also try to evaluate the possible bias of a test as a whole. Bias is defined as a systematically incorrect estimation of how well a group will perform. By that definition, IQ tests are biased against immigrants but apparently not against racial minorities; they predict the school performance of African-Americans about as accurately as that of European-Americans. (page 332)

* *Hereditary and environmental influences.* To determine the contribution of heredity to the variations in scores on IQ tests, investigators compare identical twins and fraternal twins, study identical twins reared apart, and compare adopted children with their biological and adoptive parents. For European-American families (about whom we have the most information), both hereditary and environ-

mental factors appear to contribute to observed differences in performance. (page 334)

* *The controversy concerning ethnic differences in IQ.* Ethnic groups differ, on the average, in IQ performance, although the group mean scores cannot tell us what to expect from each individual. Research designed to show environmental contributors to these ethnic differences have generally produced disappointingly small effects that are difficult to interpret. The best-designed study capable of demonstrating a hereditary contribution failed to show even marginal effects. At present, the existing research evidence does not justify a confident conclusion about the origin of ethnic differences. (page 337)

Suggestion for Further Reading

Neisser, U., et al. (1996). Intelligence: knowns and unknowns. *American Psychologist, 51,* 77–101. Although much dispute surrounds the meaning of IQ scores and the reasons why individuals differ, psychologists have also found areas of agreement. This article describes the consensus of most psychologists today, the evidence behind their conclusions, and the questions that still remain unanswered.

Terms

standardization   the process of establishing rules for administering a test and for interpreting the scores (page 327)

norms   descriptions of the frequencies of occurrence of particular scores (page 327)

Flynn effect   the tendency for people's performance on IQ tests to improve from one decade or generation to the next (page 328)

reliability   the repeatability of a test's scores (page 328)

test-retest reliability   the correlation between scores on a first test and on a retest (page 328)

validity   the determination of how well a test measures what it claims to measure (page 329)

content validity   the similarity between the items in a test and the information that the test is meant to measure (page 329)

construct validity   the correspondence of a test's measurements to a theoretical construct (page 329)

predictive validity   the ability of a test's scores to predict some real-world performance (page 329)

utility   the usefulness of a test for a practical purpose (page 330)

bias   the tendency for test scores to exaggerate a difference between groups or to report a nonexistent difference (page 333)

Answers to Concept Checks

3. Yes! To say that a test is "reliable" is simply to say that its scores are repeatable—that and only that. My test would give perfectly reliable (repeatable) measurements. True, they would be utterly useless, but that is beside the point. Reliability is not a measure of usefulness. (page 329)

4. No. An individual's score may be higher on the retest, either because of the practice at taking the test or because of the

additional months of education. But the rank order of scores does not change much. That is, if some people retake the test, all of them are likely to improve their scores, but those who had the highest scores the first time will probably also have the highest scores the second time. (page 329)

5. Yes, a test can have high reliability and low validity. A measure of intelligence determined by dividing head length by head width has high reliability (repeatability) but presumably no validity. A test with low reliability cannot have high validity, however. Low reliability means that the scores fluctuate randomly. If the test scores cannot even predict a later score on the same test, then they can hardly predict anything else. (page 330)

6. The predictive validity of the tests would increase. The predictive validity tends to be low when almost all students have practically the same score; it is higher when students' scores are highly variable. (page 330)

7. The predictive validity of SAT scores will be higher at the university that admits almost anyone. At the university with extremely competitive admissions standards, almost all students have nearly the same SAT scores, and the slight variation in scores cannot predict which students will get the best grades. (page 330)

8. No, this test is not biased against people with visual impairments. It correctly determines that they are likely to be poor drivers. (page 334)

9. We would need to determine whether the test accurately predicts the school performances of both short and tall people. If short people with, say, an IQ score of 100 perform better in school than tall people with an IQ score of 100, then the test is underpredicting the performances of short people, and we can thus conclude that this test is biased against them. (Merely that the test reports a difference between short people and tall people is not in itself evidence of test bias.) (page 334)

Web Resources

The Bell Curve and Its Critics

www.cycad.com/cgi-bin/Upstream/People/Murray/bc-crit.html
Charles Murray, co-author of *The Bell Curve,* responds to criticism of the ideas advanced in the book.

Development

10

Suppose you buy a robot. When you get home, you discover that it does nothing useful. It cannot even maintain its balance. It makes irritating, high-pitched noises, moves its limbs about haphazardly, and leaks. The store you bought it from refuses to take it back. And you discover that, for some reason, it is illegal to turn it off. So you are stuck with this useless machine.

A few years later, your robot can walk and talk, read and write, draw pictures, and do arithmetic. It will follow your directions (most of the time), and sometimes it will even find useful things to do without being told. It beats you consistently at checkers and destroys you at memory games.

How did all this happen? After all, you knew nothing about how to program a robot. Did your robot have some sort of built-in programming that simply took a long time to phase in? Or was it programmed to learn all these skills by imitating what it saw?

Children are a great deal like that robot. Nearly every parent wonders, "How did my children get to be the way they are?" The goal of developmental psychology is to understand everything that influences human behavior "from womb to tomb."

As we grow older, we change in many ways—we gain in some ways and lose in others. Developmental psychologists seek to understand the changes in our behavior and the reasons behind these changes.

The Study of Early Development

What are the capacities of the newborn and the young infant?

How can psychologists determine those capacities?

The artwork of young children can be amazingly inventive and can reveal a great deal about what the children are thinking. One toddler, 1½ years old, showed off a drawing that consisted only of dots on a sheet of paper. Puzzled adults did not understand the drawing. It is a rabbit, the child explained, while making more dots: "Look: hop, hop, hop. . . ." (Winner, 1986).

When my daughter, Robin, was 6 years old, she drew a picture of a boy and a girl drawing pictures (Figure 10.1). The overall drawing has features that may not be clear; for example, both children are wearing Halloween costumes.

For the little girl's drawing, Robin pasted on some wildlife photos. This array, she maintained, was what the little girl had drawn. Now look at the little boy's drawing: It's just a scribble. When I asked why the little girl's drawing was so much better than the little boy's, Robin replied, "Don't make fun of him, Daddy. He's doing the best he can."

Sometimes, as in this case, a child's drawing can tell us a great deal about the child's worldview. As children grow older, their art changes. Robin Kalat, now a high-school student, draws pictures with a skill that I envy. Still, I sometimes miss the highly expressive drawings of her early childhood.

The point is this: As we grow older, we develop; we gain many new abilities and skills. But we lose something too.

Studying the abilities of children, especially infants and very young children, is extremely challenging. The very young are often capable of far more than we realize, simply because they misunderstand our questions or we misunderstand their answers, or because we assume that, if they cannot do very much, they probably don't think very much either. It is also easy to underestimate the abilities of the very old. Developmental psychologists have made much progress by devising increasingly careful and sensitive ways to measure behavioral abilities.

The Fetus and the Newborn

Even at the time of birth, a human infant can see, hear, and show indications of a certain amount of learning and memory. Within the next few weeks or months, the infant is ready to acquire new skills at an impressive rate.

FIGURE 10.1 A drawing of two children drawing pictures, courtesy of 6-year-old Robin Kalat.

Prenatal Development

During **prenatal development**—*development before birth*—everyone starts life as a *fertilized egg cell,* or **zygote.** That fertilized egg develops through several stages, known as *blastula, gastrula, embryo* (from about 2 to 8 weeks after conception in humans), and **fetus** (from about 8 weeks after conception until birth, in humans). A human embryo does not look much different from a hog embryo or that of any other vertebrate (Figure 10.2).

Even a human fetus still has a long way to go. All of its organs, including the brain, must mature a great deal before birth. Different structures and substructures mature at different times; consequently, traumas and *teratogens* (poisons) produce various kinds of impairments at different ages.

The growing body receives its nutrition from the mother. If she eats little, the baby receives little nourishment. If she takes drugs, the baby gets them too. Undernourished mothers generally give birth to small babies (Figure 10.3), and investigators have long known that newborns

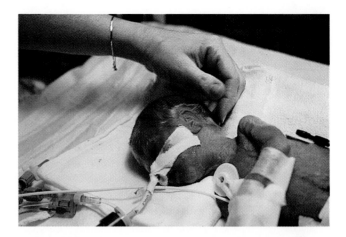

FIGURE 10.3 Advances in modern medicine enable us to keep babies alive even when they are born premature or very small. Low-birth-weight babies are prone to a variety of physical and behavioral difficulties later in life; however, we cannot be sure that low birth weight causes these problems. Many of these babies are born to mothers who are very young or impoverished, who take illegal drugs, or who fail to provide good nutrition and care.

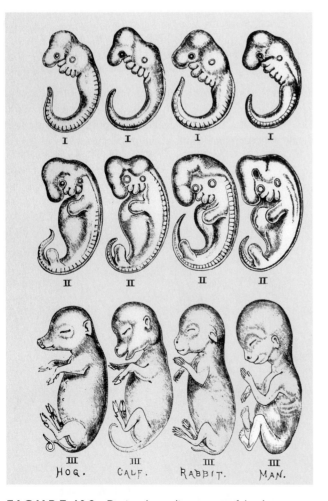

FIGURE 10.2 During the earliest stages of development, a human embryo looks much the same as the embryo of any other vertebrate species. The differences emerge later.

weighing less than about 1,750–2,000 grams (4 pounds) are at high risk of dying in infancy (Kopp, 1990). If such babies survive, they have an increased risk of eventual mental retardation, low academic achievement, and various behavior problems (Morgan & Winick, 1989). Those facts are beyond dispute, but let's consider how difficult it is to interpret them.

The apparently obvious interpretation is that low birth weight leads to impaired brain development and thus to later academic and behavior problems. However, many low-birth-weight babies are born to mothers who are poor, uneducated, unhealthy, teenaged, unmarried or unhappily married, victims of family violence, having a low-vitamin or low-mineral diet, possibly smoking or drinking during pregnancy, not visiting a doctor for care and advice during pregnancy, and unable to provide a good home after delivering the baby (Garcia Coll, 1990; McCormick, 1985). In short, many low-birth-weight babies have other, probably more serious problems as well, which combine to increase the risk to the child (Brooks-Gunn & Furstenberg, 1989; Zeanah, Boris, & Larrieu, 1997).

One way to study the effect of low birth weight separately from other problems is to examine pairs of twins where one twin was born much heavier than the other. The twins differ in birth weight but have the same parents and the same environment both before and after birth. In most cases, the low-birth-weight infant develops about as well as the heavier twin (Wilson, 1987). In short, low birth weight *by itself* is not necessarily a serious problem; it correlates with developmental difficulties partly because many low-birth-weight babies have other disadvantages.

A more severe risk arises if the fetus is exposed to alcohol or other substances. *If the mother drinks alcohol during pregnancy,* the infant may develop signs of **fetal alcohol** syndrome, *a condition marked by stunted growth of the head and body; malformations of the face, heart, and ears; and nervous system damage, including seizures, hyperactivity, learning disabilities, and mental retardation* (Streissguth, Sampson, & Barr, 1989). In milder cases, the child's appearance may be normal, but the child is still likely to have impaired academic skills and deficits in language, memory, and fine motor speed (Mattson, Riley, Grambling, Delis, & Jones, 1998). The more alcohol the mother drinks and the longer she drinks during pregnancy, the greater the risk to the fetus (see Figure 10.4). Similarly, women who smoke during pregnancy have an increased probability that their babies will be born very small and that the babies will have a variety of serious health problems early in life. These mothers also run an increased risk that their children, especially sons, will develop *conduct disorder*, a condition marked by discipline problems both at school and at home, and potentially even criminal behavior in adulthood. Conduct disorder has been found to correlate more strongly with the mother's smoking during pregnancy than with the father's antisocial behavior, the family's economic status, lack of supervision of the child, or excessive punishment (Wakschlag et al., 1997). To be safe, pregnant women should avoid alcohol and tobacco and should get a physician's advice before taking even routine, over-the-counter drugs.

Still, it is remarkable that an occasional "high risk" child—small at birth, perhaps exposed to alcohol or other drugs before birth, perhaps from an impoverished or turbulent family—overcomes all odds and becomes a healthy, productive, outstanding person (Werner, 1989). Resilience (the ability to overcome obstacles) is hardly well understood, but the general pattern is that the more positive influences one has in life, the easier it is to overcome a negative one. That is, people who overcome a great disadvantage tend to have some special source of strength—a close relationship with one or more supporting people, an effective school, a strong faith, some special skill, or just a naturally easygoing disposition (Masten & Coatsworth, 1998).

Behavioral Capacities of the Newborn

A human newborn is a little like a computer that is not attached to a monitor: It may be processing a great deal of information, but it cannot tell us about it. The challenge of studying the newborn is to figure out how to attach some sort of "monitor" to find out what is going on inside the newborn's head.

Newborns have very little control of their muscles. At first, they cannot keep their head from flopping over, and their arms and legs flail about aimlessly. They gradually gain more muscle control, partly through growth and maturation of the muscles and nerves and partly from practice. For example, babies are much more persistent at waving their arms if they can see their arms than if they have to wave without watching (van der Meer, van der Weel, & Lee, 1995). Also, babies who are too young to support their own weight flail their arms and legs in varied and haphazard ways; as soon as they are capable of supporting their weight, they quickly abandon most of their varied movement patterns and settle on the standard patterns and rhythms of human crawling (Freedland & Bertenthal, 1994).

About the only useful movements that newborns can make are mouth and eye movements. As the months pass, and as their control spreads from the head muscles downward, they are able to make progressively finer movements, eventually culminating in the ability to move a single finger at a time.

If we want to test an infant's sensory and learning abilities, we must test them by means of responses that the infant can control. For example, if we want to test what an infant can see, we should examine eye movements or head movements; if we try to train an infant to reach out and grab something, we will almost certainly underestimate the infant's capacities.

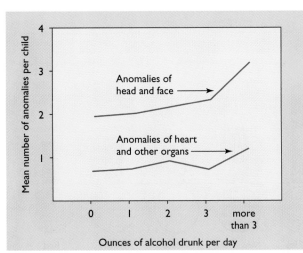

FIGURE 10.4   (a) The more alcohol a woman drinks during pregnancy, the more likely her baby is to have anomalies of the head, face, and organs. (Based on data of Ernhart et al., 1987.) (b) A child with fetal alcohol syndrome: Note especially the wide separation between the eyes, a common feature of this syndrome.

a   b

Newborns' Vision

William James, a pioneer in American psychology, once said that as far as an infant can tell, the world is a "buzzing confusion," full of meaningless sights and sounds. Since James's time, psychologists have substantially increased their estimate of what an infant can see.

One research method is to record the infant's eye movements. In general, infants direct their eyes toward the same kinds of objects that attract adults' attention. For example, even 2-day-old infants spend more time looking at drawings of human faces than at other patterns with similar areas of light and dark (Fantz, 1963). (See Figure 10.5.)

By the age of 5 months or so, infants have had extensive visual experience but almost no experience at crawling or reaching for objects. As they start to gain control of their arm and leg movements, they suddenly have to reach out to pick up toys, crawl around objects, avoid crawling off ledges, and in other ways coordinate what they see with what they do.

Apparently, infants must have some experience of controlling their own movements before they show a fear of heights. Infants begin to show a fear of heights shortly after they begin to crawl—presumably also the age when they have their first experience of slipping and falling. Infants who crawl early develop a fear of heights early; infants who are late to crawl are also late to develop a fear of heights (Campos, Bertenthal, & Kermoian, 1992).

Although visual-motor coordination develops quickly, infants need practice to maintain and improve that coordination. Kittens are ideal for studies of visual-motor development because they can move about quite well by the time they first open their eyes. In one experiment, kittens were permitted to walk around in a dark room for 21 hours a day (Held & Hein, 1963). For the other 3 hours, half of the kittens (the "active" group) were permitted to walk around in a well-lit cylindrical room, as Figure 10.6 shows. The other kittens (the "passive" group) were confined to boxes that were propelled around the room by the active kittens.

The active kittens gradually developed good paw-eye coordination, but the passive kittens lagged far behind. In

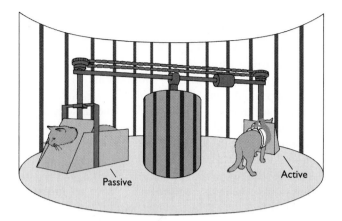

FIGURE 10.6 As the kitten carousel experiment demonstrates, experience influences development. These two kittens see the same thing, but only one can correlate what it sees with its own movements. Only the active kitten develops normal paw-eye coordination. (Modified from Held & Hein, 1963.)

fact, the passive kittens' coordination actually grew worse instead of better as the experiment continued. Evidently, kittens need to see and move at the same time in order to maintain and improve their visually guided behavior. The same is almost certainly true for humans as well.

Newborns' Hearing

At first it might seem difficult to measure newborns' responses to sounds; after all, we cannot observe anything similar to eye movements. However, we can record the effects of sounds on an infant's sucking. Infants suck more vigorously when they are aroused, and certain sounds arouse them more than others do.

In one study, the experimenters played a brief sound and noted how it affected the infant's sucking rate (Figure 10.7). On the first few occasions, the sound increased the sucking rate. After the sound had been played repeatedly, it produced less and less effect. We say that the infant became *habituated* to the sound. **Habituation** is *decreased response*

FIGURE 10.5 Infants pay more attention to faces than to other patterns. (Based on Fantz, 1963.) These results suggest that infants are born with certain visual preferences that do not depend on learned associations. Their preference for faces facilitates the development of social attachments.

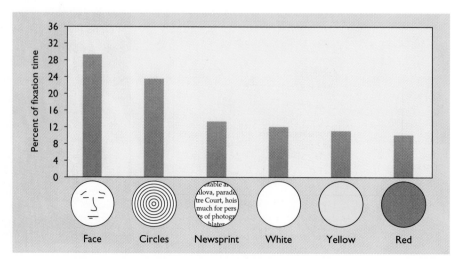

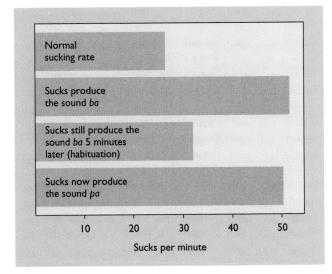

FIGURE 10.8 Inspired by research showing that a fetus learns to recognize its mother's voice, some women have made special efforts to talk to their fetuses—and some enterprising capitalists have sold them "pregaphones," manuals, tapes, and lessons. (Don't assume that the fetus is the one getting the greatest benefit from all of this.)

FIGURE 10.7 After 5 minutes of hearing the same sound, the infant's sucking habituates. When a new sound, *pa*, follows, the sucking rate increases, an indication that infants do hear a difference between the two sounds *ba* and *pa*. (Based on results of Eimas, Siqueland, Juscyk, & Vigorito, 1971.)

to a repeated stimulus. When the experimenters substituted a new sound, it produced a sharp increase in the sucking rate. Evidently, the infant was aroused because he or she heard a new, unfamiliar sound. *When a change in a stimulus produces an increase in a previously habituated response,* we say that the stimulus has produced **dishabituation.**

Psychologists use this technique to determine whether infants hear a difference between two sounds (Jusczyk, 1985). For example, an infant who has become habituated to the sound *ba* will increase the sucking rate in response to the sound *pa* (Eimas, Siqueland, Jusczyk, & Vigorito, 1971). Apparently, even month-old infants can tell the difference between *ba* and *pa*. Evidently, infants have some preliminary skills of attending to language sounds long before they develop other language skills.

The Learning and Memory of Newborns

Infants certainly cannot describe their memories to us. But if they respond differently to a stimulus because of previous experience with it, we can infer that they remember it.

Several studies have begun with the observation that infants learn to suck harder on a nipple if their sucking turns on a sound. Investigators then tried to determine whether infants will work harder to turn on certain sounds than they will for others. In one study, 26 babies less than 3 days old could turn on a tape recording of their mother's voice by sucking on a nipple at certain times and at certain rates. By sucking at different times or at different rates, they could turn on a tape recording of another woman's voice. When their manner of sucking produced their own mother's voice, their rate of sucking increased significantly (De-Casper & Fifer, 1980); it increased less when it produced a different voice. Apparently, even very young infants recog-

nized their own mother's voice and preferred it to an unfamiliar voice. Because they showed this preference so early—in some cases, on the day of their birth—developmental psychologists believe that the infants are displaying a memory of what they heard *before* birth (Figure 10.8).

CONCEPT CHECK

1. Suppose that a newborn sucks to turn on a tape recording of its father's voice. Eventually, the baby habituates and the sucking rate decreases. Now, the experimenters substitute the recording of a different man's voice for the father's. What would you conclude if the sucking rate increased? What if it remained the same? What if it decreased? (Check your answers on page 353.)

Using somewhat older infants, Carolyn Rovee-Collier (1984) demonstrated an ability to learn a response and remember it for days afterward. She attached a ribbon to one ankle so that an infant could activate a mobile by kicking with one leg (Figure 10.9); 2-month-old infants quickly learned this response and generally kept the mobile going nonstop for a full 45-minute session. (I know I said infants cannot control their leg muscles, but they don't need much control to keep the mobile going.) Once they have learned, they quickly remember what to do when the ribbon is reattached several days later—to the infants' evident delight.

WHAT'S THE EVIDENCE?
The Infant's Thought Processes About Object Permanence

Measuring an infant's vision, hearing, and memory can be difficult enough. Inferring the infant's thoughts and knowledge is trickier yet, although researchers have found some clever

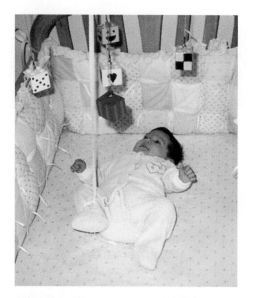

FIGURE 10.9 By the age of 8 weeks, infants can rapidly learn to kick one of their legs to activate a mobile attached to their ankle with a ribbon. After just a little practice, they can keep the mobile going for a full 45-minute session. These infants also remember how to activate the mobile from one session to the next. (From Rovee-Collier, 1984.)

ways to do just that. As you can imagine, however, these inferences must be made cautiously and tentatively.

Jean Piaget (peah-ZHAY), whose theories we shall consider in more detail in the next module, inferred that infants in the first few months of life lack the concept of **object per-**

toy in front of a 6-month-old infant, who reaches out and grabs it. Later, place a toy in the same place, but before the infant has a chance to grab it, cover it with a clear glass. No problem; the infant removes the glass and takes the toy. Now, you repeat that procedure, but this time you cover the toy with an opaque (nonclear) glass. The infant, who watched you place the glass over the toy, makes no effort to remove the glass and obtain the toy. Or you put the toy down and then place a thin barrier between the infant and the toy. The infant will reach for a toy that is partly visible but not for one that is completely hidden (Piaget, 1937/1954). (See Figure 10.10.)

Why not? According to Piaget, the infant *does not know* that the hidden toy is there; not until about the age of 9 months does he or she fully understand object permanence. However, one can imagine other possible explanations for Piaget's results. One later study suggests that infants do show signs of understanding object permanence when they are tested differently.

Hypothesis An infant who sees an event that should be impossible (if objects are permanent) will stare longer than will an infant that sees a similar but possible event.

Method Infants aged 6 or 8 months watched a series of events staged by the researcher. First, the child watched the experimenter raise a screen to show nothing behind it and then watched a toy car go down a slope and emerge on the other side, as shown in the drawing below. The researchers measured how long the child stared after the car went down the slope; they repeated the procedure until the child decreased the staring time for three trials in a row (showing habituation).

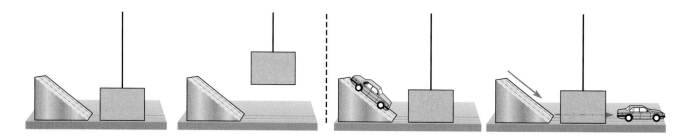

manence, *the idea that objects continue to exist even when we do not see or hear them.* How could he know? He drew the inference from observations of the following type: Place a

Then, the experimenters presented two kinds of events, three times each, as shown on page 351. In a Possible event, the raised screen showed a box that was behind the screen but not

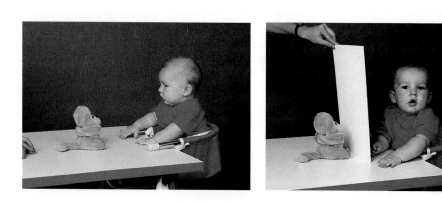

FIGURE 10.10 During the sensorimotor period, a child will reach for a visible toy (left) but not one that is hidden behind a barrier (right)—even if the child sees someone hide the toy. According to Piaget, this observation indicates that the child lacks the concept of object permanence.

on the track. In an Impossible event, the raised screen showed a box that was on the track, right where the car would pass. After the screen lowered, the car went down the slope and (for both Possible and Impossible events) emerged on the other side. (For Impossible events, the experimenters had pulled the box off the track after lowering the screen.) The experimenters measured each child's staring times after both kinds of events.

Interpretation Why did the infants stare longer at the "Impossible" event? The inference—and admittedly it is only an inference, not a certainty—is that the infants found the Impossible event surprising. To be surprised, the infants had to expect that the box would continue to exist where it was hidden and that a car could not go through it. If this inference is correct, even 6-month-old infants understand a

Possible event

Impossible event

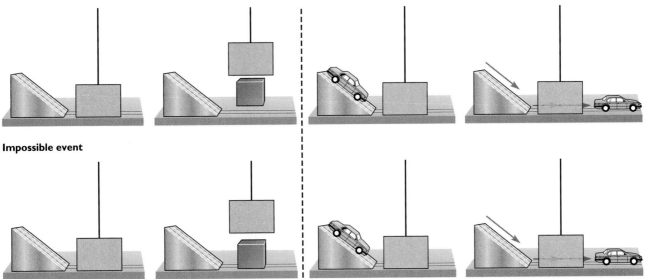

Results Figure 10.11 shows the mean looking times. Infants stared longer after seeing an Impossible event than after seeing a Possible event. They also stared longer during the first pair of events than after the second pair and longer after the second than the third (Baillargeon, 1986).

fair amount about the permanence of objects. One later study with a slightly different method again measured how long infants stared at Possible and Impossible events and demonstrated object permanence in infants as young as 3½ months (Baillargeon, 1987).

Still, remember that infants as old as 9 months failed Piaget's object permanence task of reaching out to pick up a hidden object. Do infants have the concept of object permanence or do they lack it? Perhaps there is something wrong with that question. It is possible to "have" a concept but use it in some situations and not in others (Munakata, McClelland, Johnson, & Siegler, 1997). Even college students can pass a physics test and then fail to apply the laws of motion in a new situation or understand the rules of grammar and yet make grammatical errors.

The important point about research is this: Especially when we are dealing with infants or anyone else whose thought processes are likely to be different from our own, we should be cautious about inferring what they can or cannot do. The results may vary depending on exactly what procedures and tests we use.

＊　＊　＊

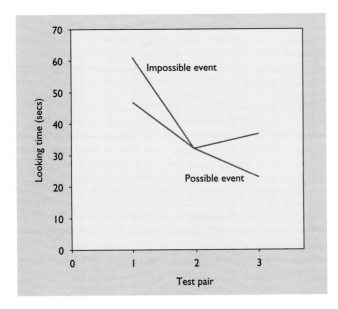

FIGURE 10.11 Mean looking times of 6- and 8-month-old infants after they had watched either Possible or Impossible events. (From Baillargeon, 1986.)

Further Capacities of the Infant

Using the technique of measuring infants' staring time, researchers have also made a surprising inference about infants' concept of number: Karen Wynn (1992) showed an

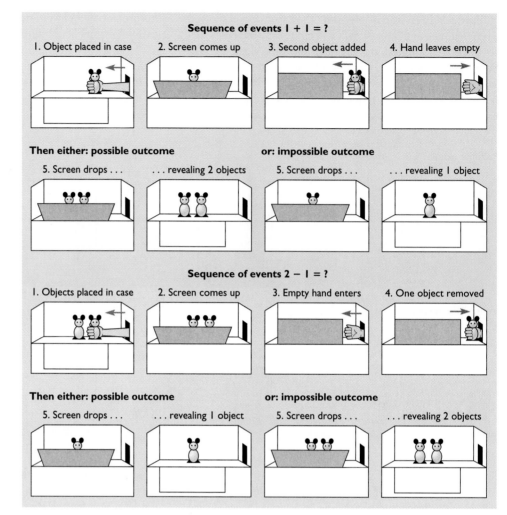

Sequence of events 1 + 1 = ?

1. Object placed in case   2. Screen comes up   3. Second object added   4. Hand leaves empty

Then either: possible outcome   **or: impossible outcome**

5. Screen drops . . .   . . . revealing 2 objects   5. Screen drops . . .   . . . revealing 1 object

Sequence of events 2 − 1 = ?

1. Objects placed in case   2. Screen comes up   3. Empty hand enters   4. One object removed

Then either: possible outcome   **or: impossible outcome**

5. Screen drops . . .   . . . revealing 1 object   5. Screen drops . . .   . . . revealing 2 objects

FIGURE 10.12 Five-month-old infants stare longer at an "impossible" display than at the possible display. Evidently, even at this age, children understand that adding or subtracting an object should change the number present.

infant an object, then raised a screen, and then placed another object behind the screen. Or else she showed the infant two objects, raised a screen, and then removed one of the objects from behind the screen. Finally, the screen dropped, revealing either the correct, expected number of objects (1 + 1 = 2 or 2 − 1 = 1) or an "impossible" total (1 + 1 = 1 or 2 − 1 = 2). Figure 10.12 shows these procedures. On the average, 5-month-old infants stared longer at an impossible total than at an expected total. Evidently, even at the age of 5 months, infants have a primitive concept that adding something should make the total more and subtracting should make it less.

THE MESSAGE
Infants—Capable of So Little and So Much

Notice that the experiments just described enable psychologists to explore infant thought and perception long before the infants can talk. The trend has been a steady increase in our estimation of infants' capacities. Because of infants'

poor control of their muscles, they are indeed like a computer with a faulty monitor: They have a lot more going on inside than they can show us.

SUMMARY

✳ *Prenatal development.* Behavioral development begins before birth. During prenatal development, an individual is especially vulnerable to the damaging effects of alcohol and other drugs. Babies who are very small at birth have a high risk of later problems, mainly because they generally do not get good care or stimulation later in life. (page 346)

✳ *Inferring infant capacities.* It is easy to underestimate the capacities of newborn human infants, because they have so little control over their muscles. With careful testing procedures, we can demonstrate that newborns can see, hear, and remember more than we might have supposed. (page 347)

✳ *Inferring infant thought processes.* Infants behave differently from older children in many ways. For example, infants fail to reach for a toy after watching someone hide it within their reach. We can try to draw inferences about infants' thinking, but we must be cautious about these inferences. An infant who fails to reach for a toy may not know the toy still exists, may be distracted by other sights, may have forgotten the hiding place, or may be following a motor habit that is inconsistent with reaching in the correct direction. (page 349)

Suggestion for Further Reading

Mandler, J. M. (1990). A new perspective on cognitive development in infancy. *American Scientist, 78,* 236–243. An interesting article describing the often surprising capabilities of infants less than 6 months old.

Terms

prenatal development   development before birth (page 346)

zygote   a fertilized egg cell (page 346)

fetus   an organism more developed than an embryo but not yet born (from about 8 weeks after conception until birth, in humans) (page 346)

fetal alcohol syndrome   a condition marked by stunted growth of the head and body; malformations of the face, heart, and ears; and nervous system damage, including seizures, hyperactivity, learning disabilities, and mental retardation (page 346)

habituation   a decrease in a person's response to a stimulus after it has been presented repeatedly (page 348)

dishabituation   an increase in a previously habituated response as a result of a change in the stimulus (page 349)

object permanence   the concept that objects continue to exist even when one does not see, hear, or otherwise sense them (page 350)

Answer to Concept Check

1. If the rate increased, we would conclude that the infant recognizes the difference between the father's voice and the other voice. If the rate remained the same, we would conclude that the infant did not notice a difference. If it decreased, we would assume that the infant preferred the sound of the father's voice for some reason. (page 349)

Web Resources

Classic Theories of Child Development
idealist.com/children/cdw.html
In a hypertext tutorial about the theories of Freud, Mahler, and Erikson, Linda Chapman also takes a month-by-month look at the normal developmental sequence from birth to three years.

The Development of Thinking and Reasoning

What goes on in the mind of a small child?

How do the thoughts of children differ from those of adults?

How does moral reasoning develop?

Preschool children ask some profound questions: "Why is the sky blue? What makes ice cubes cold? If it's dangerous to look at the sun, why is it safe to look at a picture of the sun? Where does the sun go at night?" They are relentlessly curious about how things work and why. (Moreover, when you answer their questions, they never interrupt to ask, "Is this going to be on the test?")

These same budding little scientists also believe in Santa Claus and the tooth fairy. Adults find it difficult to recapture what it is like to be a child. It is clear that children think differently from adults in a variety of ways, although it is not easy to specify those ways. Nevertheless, we try.

The Development of Thought and Knowledge: Piaget's Contributions

Attending a rousing political rally can have a profound effect on a young adult, less effect on a preteen, and no effect at all on an infant. However, playing with a pile of blocks will be a more stimulating experience for a young child than for someone older. The effect of a certain experience on a person's thinking processes and knowledge depends on the level of that person's maturity and his or her previous experiences. The theorist who made this point most strongly and most influentially was Jean Piaget (1896–1980). (See Figure 10.13.)

Early in Piaget's career, he administered IQ tests to French-speaking children in Switzerland. He grew bored with the IQ tests because he felt he was not learning anything about intelligence, but he was fascinated by the incorrect answers that children consistently gave in response to certain questions. For example, when asked, "If you mix

some water at a temperature of 50 degrees with an equal amount of water at 70 degrees, what temperature will the mixture be?" most 9-year-olds answer, "120 degrees" (Jensen, 1980).

Unless someone was going around mischievously misinforming all the children in Switzerland, the children must be reaching incorrect conclusions on their own. In other words—and this is one of Piaget's central insights—*children's thought processes are different from those of adults.* Children are not merely inexperienced adults, and they are not just less skillfully going through the same thought processes that adults use. The difference between children's thought processes and those of adults is *qualitative* as well as *quantitative*—that is, it is both a difference in kind and a difference in amount. Piaget supported this conclusion with extensive studies of children, especially his own.

Intellectual Growth: Some Piagetian Terminology

According to Piaget, a child's intellectual development is not merely an accumulation of experience or a maturational unfolding. Rather, the child constructs new mental processes as he or she interacts with the environment.

In Piaget's terminology, behavior is based on schemata (the plural of *schema*). A **schema** is *an organized way of interacting with objects in the world.* For instance, infants

FIGURE 10.13 Jean Piaget (1896–1980), the most influential theorist on intellectual development in children, demonstrated that the influence of an experience on a person's way of thinking depends on that person's age and previous experience.

FIGURE 10.14 According to Piaget, assimilation and accommodation occur whenever we interact with an object. Here, an infant assimilates new objects to the grasp schema, applying an established behavior to them. However, the infant also accommodates the grasp schema, adjusting it to fit objects of different shapes and sizes.

have a grasping schema and a sucking schema. Older infants gradually add new schemata to their repertoire and adapt their old ones. This adaptation takes place through the processes of assimilation and accommodation.

With **assimilation,** a person *applies an old schema to new objects*—for example, an infant may suck an unfamiliar object or use the grasp response when trying to manipulate it. With **accommodation,** a person *modifies an old schema to fit a new object*—for example, an infant may suck a breast, a bottle, and a pacifier in different ways or modify the grasp response to accommodate the size or shape of a new toy (Figure 10.14).

Infants shift back and forth from assimilation to accommodation. For example, an infant who tries to suck on a rubber ball (assimilating it to her sucking schema) may find that she cannot fit it into her mouth. First, she may try to accommodate her sucking schema to fit the ball; if that fails, she may try to shake the ball. She is assimilating the new object to her grasping schema, but she is also accommodating that schema—changing it—to fit the ball.

Adults do much the same thing. You are given a new mathematical problem to solve. You try several of the methods you have already learned until you hit upon the one schema that works. In other words, you assimilate the new problem to your old schema. However, if the new problem is quite different from any problem you have ever solved before, you modify (accommodate) your schema until you work out a solution. Through processes like these, said Piaget, intellectual growth occurs.

Piaget's Stages of Intellectual Development

Piaget contended that children progress through four major stages of intellectual development:

1. *The sensorimotor stage* (from birth to about 1½ years)
2. *The preoperational stage* (from about 1½ to 7 years)
3. *The concrete-operations stage* (from about 7 to 11 years)
4. *The formal-operations stage* (from about 11 years onward)

The ages given here are only approximate, and Piaget was rightly more interested in the sequence of stages than the exact age at which someone reaches a particular stage

(Lourenço & Machado, 1996). Let us consider the capacities of children at each of these stages.

The Sensorimotor Stage: Infancy

Piaget called the first stage of intellectual development the **sensorimotor stage,** because *at this early age (birth to 1½ years) behavior consists mostly of simple motor responses to sensory stimuli*—for example, the grasp reflex and the sucking reflex. The fact that infants do not look for objects that they cannot see indicated to Piaget that infants respond only to what they see and hear, rather than to what they might remember or imagine.

Infants do, nevertheless, notice relationships among their experiences (Mandler, 1990). For example, even infants as young as 4 months old pay more attention to a film when the sound track matches the action than one in which the sound track is unrelated to the action. Also, an infant who has been sucking on a pacifier will stare longer at a pacifier of the same shape than a pacifier of a different shape.

As children progress through the sensorimotor stage of development, they appear to gain some concept of self. The data are as follows: A mother puts a spot of unscented rouge on an infant's nose and then places the infant in front of a mirror. Infants less than 1½ years old either ignore the red spot they see on the baby in the mirror or else reach out to touch the red spot. At some point after age 1½ years, infants in the same situation will touch themselves on the nose, indicating that they recognize themselves in the mirror (Figure 10.15). Infants show this sign of self-recognition at varying ages; the age when they start to show self-recognition is also the age when they sometimes begin to act embarrassed (Lewis, Sullivan, Stanger, & Weiss, 1991). That is, they show a sense of self either in both situations or in neither.

The Preoperational Stage: Early Childhood

By about age 1½, most children are learning to speak; within a few years, they will have nearly mastered their language. Nevertheless, they do not understand everything in the same way that adults do. For example, they have difficulty

FIGURE 10.15 If someone places a bit of unscented rouge on a child's nose, a child about 2 years old or older shows self-recognition by touching his or her own nose. A younger child ignores the red spot or points at the mirror.

understanding that a mother can be someone else's daughter. A boy with one brother will assert that his brother has no brother. Piaget refers to this period as the **preoperational stage,** because *the child lacks* **operations,** *which are reversible mental processes.* For example, for a boy to understand that his brother has a brother, he must be able to reverse the concept of "having a brother."

Distinguishing Appearance from Reality in the Preoperational Stage

Children in the early preoperational stage do not distinguish clearly between appearance and reality. A child who sees you put a white ball behind a blue filter will say that the ball is blue. When you ask, "Yes, I know the ball *looks* blue, but what color is it *really*?" the child grows confused. As far as the child is concerned, any ball that *looks* blue *is* blue (Flavell, 1986).

However, as we found in the case of object permanence, a child can appear to have an ability or to lack it, depending on how one tests that ability. Consider first the following experiment: A psychologist shows a child a playhouse room that is a scale model of a full-size room. Then, the psychologist hides a tiny toy in the small room (while the child watches) and explains that a bigger toy just like it is "in the same place" in the bigger room. (For example, if the little toy was behind the sofa in the little room, the big toy would be behind the sofa in the big room.) Then, the psychologist asks the child to go into the big room and find the big toy. Most 3-year-olds look in the correct place and find the toy immediately. Most 2½-year-olds, however, search haphazardly, instead of using the little room as a "map" for the big room. If the experimenter shows the child

the big toy in the big room and asks the child to find the little toy "in the same place" in the little room, the results are the same: 3-year-olds can find it but 2½-year-olds cannot. It appears that 3-year-olds have an ability that 2½-year-olds still lack, and this is in fact a striking example of a rapid intellectual change (DeLoache, 1989).

Before we speak too confidently about what a 2½-year-old cannot do, however, consider this clever follow-up study: The psychologist hides a toy in the small room while the child watches. Then, they step out of the room, and the psychologist shows the child a "machine that can expand things." The psychologist aims a beam from the machine at the room and takes the child out of the way. For the next couple of minutes they hear chunkata-chunkata-clunkata-clunkata sounds, and then the psychologist shows the child the full-sized room and asks the child to find the toy hidden in the blown-up room. Even 2½-year-olds have no trouble with this task; they go immediately to the correct location (DeLoache, Miller, & Rosengren, 1997). (See Figure 10.16.) Evidently, these children can use one room as a "map" of the other *if* they think of them both as "the same room," even though they don't seem to understand the idea that one room is a model of the other. (Incidentally, hardly any of the children showed any doubt that the machine had actually expanded the room, and many continued to believe it even after the psychologist tried to explain what had really happened!)

Egocentric Thinking in the Preoperational Period

Piaget concluded that children's thought processes are **egocentric.** In using this term, Piaget did *not* mean that children are selfish; instead, he meant that *a child sees the world as centered around himself or herself and cannot take the perspective of another person.* If you and a

Young children's thinking is egocentric: They have trouble understanding someone else's point of view. If asked to describe how a complicated pile of blocks appears to someone else, they instead describe how it appears from their own position.

a 2½-year-old shown in small room where stuffed animal is hidden

2½-year-old is unable to find the stuffed animal in the larger room

b 3-year-old shown in small room where stuffed animal is hidden

3-year-old is able to find the stuffed animal in the larger room

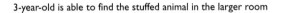

F I G U R E   10.16   If an experimenter hides a small toy in a small room and asks a child to find the larger toy "in the same place" in the larger room, a 2½-year-old will search haphazardly. However, the same child knows exactly where to look, if the experimenter says this is the same room as before, except that a machine has expanded it.

preschool child sit on opposite sides of a complicated pile of blocks and you ask the child to draw what the blocks would look like from your side, the child will draw them as they look from his or her own side. When speaking, children often omit the necessary background information, as if assuming that the listener understands everything the speaker understands. (The same can be said for adults, unfortunately. Someone may start discussing the details of a topic before the listener has any idea what the speaker is talking about.)

CONCEPT CHECK

2.   Which of the following is the clearest example of egocentric thinking?

   a. A writer who uses someone else's words without giving credit.

   b. A politician who blames others for everything that goes wrong.

   c. A professor who gives the same complicated lecture to a freshman class that she gives to a convention of professionals. (Check your answer on page 367.)

To say that a child is egocentric is to say that he or she has trouble understanding other people's point of view— what they know and what they do not know. Some psycho-

logical researchers have explored the very difficult topic of what children understand about other people's thoughts and knowledge.

> **WHAT'S THE EVIDENCE?**
> *Children's Understanding*
> *of Other People's Cognitions*

How and when do children first understand that other people have minds and knowledge? Researchers have developed some very cleverly designed experiments to try to answer this difficult question.

Hypothesis   A child who understands that other people have minds will distinguish between someone who is in a position to know certain information and someone who could not know it.

Method   A 3- or 4-year-old child sat in front of four cups. (Figure 10.17.) The child watched as one adult hid a candy or toy under one of the cups, although a screen prevented the child from seeing which cup. Then, another adult entered the room. The "informed" adult pointed to the cup under which he or she had just hidden the surprise; the "uninformed" adult pointed to one of the other cups. The child was then given an opportunity to look under one cup to try to find the surprise.

FIGURE 10.17 A child sat in front of a screen covering four cups and watched as one adult hid a surprise under one of the cups. Then, that adult and another (who had not been present initially) each pointed to one of the cups to signal where the surprise was hidden. Many 4-year-olds consistently followed the advice of the informed adult; 3-year-olds did not.

This procedure was repeated 10 times for each child. The two adults alternated roles, but on each trial one or the other hid the surprise when the other was absent. That is, one was in a position to know where the surprise was hidden, and the other was not.

Results Of the 4-year-olds, 10 out of 20 chose the correct cup (the one indicated by the informed adult) at least 8 times out of 10 tries. That is, many of the 4-year-olds showed that they understood who had the relevant knowledge and who did not. However, none of 14 3-year-olds chose the correct cup as many as 8 times out of 10; they were just as likely to follow the lead of the uninformed adult as that of the informed adult (Povinelli & deBlois, 1992).

Interpretation Evidently, 4-year-olds have a greater understanding of other people's knowledge (or lack of it) than 3-year-olds have.

✳ ✳ ✳

Other experiments, using a somewhat different procedure, have yielded similar results. For example, children in one study watched a dramatization where a girl who had a marble in her basket left the room temporarily. During her absence, a second girl moved the marble from the first girl's basket to her own basket. When the first girl returned to the room, the children were asked "Where is the marble?" and "Where will the girl look for it?" Most 4-year-olds answered that she would look in her own basket; younger children thought she would look in the other basket (Wimmer & Perner, 1983). As in the previous study, 4-year-olds are better able than younger children to make inferences about what various people might or might not know.

Although these are important results, we should avoid drawing too broad a conclusion. Using other methods, we can produce evidence that even younger children understand something about the experiences or knowledge of other people. For example, children less than 1 year old act sad and sometimes cry when they see another child get hurt (Hobson, 1993). That is, a child may show an understanding of other people's thoughts and feelings in some ways but not in others.

Lack of the Concept of Conservation in the Preoperational Period

According to Piaget, preoperational children lack the concept of **conservation.** Just as they fail to understand that something can still be white even though it looks blue, they fail *to understand that objects conserve such properties as number, length, volume, area, and mass after the shape or arrangement of the objects has changed.* They cannot perform the mental operations necessary to understand such transformations. (Table 10.1 shows some typical conservation tasks.)

For example, if we set up two glasses of the same size

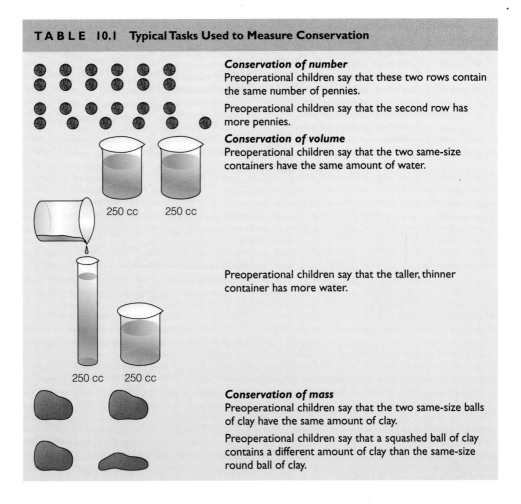

T A B L E 10.1   Typical Tasks Used to Measure Conservation

Conservation of number
Preoperational children say that these two rows contain the same number of pennies.

Preoperational children say that the second row has more pennies.

Conservation of volume
Preoperational children say that the two same-size containers have the same amount of water.

250 cc   250 cc

Preoperational children say that the taller, thinner container has more water.

250 cc   250 cc

Conservation of mass
Preoperational children say that the two same-size balls of clay have the same amount of clay.

Preoperational children say that a squashed ball of clay contains a different amount of clay than the same-size round ball of clay.

containing the same amount of water and then pour the contents of one glass into a taller, thinner glass, preoperational children will say that the second glass contains more water (Figure 10.18).

I once doubted whether children really believed what they were saying in such a situation. I thought perhaps the phrasing of the questions somehow tricks them into saying something they do not believe. If you have these same doubts, borrow someone's 6-year-old child and try it yourself, with your own wording. Here's my own experience: One year when I was discussing Piaget in my introductory psychology

TRY IT YOUR-SELF

F I G U R E 10.18   Looks can be deceptive: The conservation concept shows one way that children think less logically than adults do. Preoperational children, up to about the age of 7 years, don't understand that a property of a substance—such as the volume of water—remains constant despite changes in its appearance. During the transition from preoperational thinking to concrete operations at around age 7, conservation tasks seem difficult and confusing to the child.

class, I invited my son Sam, then 5½ years old, to take part in a class demonstration. I started with two glasses of water, which he agreed contained equal amounts of water. Then I poured the water from one glass into a wider glass, lowering the water level. When I asked Sam which glass contained more water, he confidently pointed to the tall, thin one.

After class he complained, "Daddy, why did you ask me such an easy question? Everyone could see that there was more water in that glass! You should have asked me something harder to show how smart I am!"

The following year, I brought Sam to class again for the same demonstration. He was now 6½ years old, about the age when children make the transition from preoperational thinking to the next stage. I again poured the water from one of the tall glasses into a wider one and asked him which glass contained more water. He looked and paused. His face got red. Finally, he whispered, "Daddy, I don't know!" After class he complained, "Why did you ask me such a hard question? I'm never coming back to any of your classes again!" The question that was embarrassingly easy one year ago had, in the interim, become embarrassingly difficult.

The next year, when he was 7½, I tried again (at home). This time, he answered confidently, "Both glasses have the same amount of water, of course. Why? Is this some sort of trick question?"

The Concrete Operations Stage: Later Childhood

At about the age of 7, children enter the stage of concrete operations and begin to understand the conservation of physical properties. This transition is not sudden, however. The ability to understand the conservation of various properties emerges sequentially, at different ages. For instance, a 6-year-old child may understand that squashing a ball of clay will not change its weight but may not realize until years later that squashing the ball will not change the volume of water it displaces when it is dropped into a glass.

The **stage of concrete operations** is Piaget's term for the stage *when children can perform mental operations on concrete objects but still have trouble with abstract or hypothetical ideas.* For example, ask this question: "How could you move a 4-mile-high mountain of whipped cream from one side of the city to the other?" Older children find the question amusing and try to think of an imaginative answer. But children in the concrete operations stage (or younger) are likely to complain that the question is silly.

Or ask, "If you could have a third eye anywhere on your body, where would you put it?" Children in this stage generally respond immediately that they would put it right between the other two, on their forehead. They seem to regard the question as uninteresting. Older children come up with more imaginative possibilities—on the back of their head or on the tip of a finger (so they could peek around corners).

The Formal Operations Stage: Adolescence and Adulthood

Formal operations is Piaget's term for *the mental processes used to deal with abstract, hypothetical situations. Those processes demand logical, deductive reasoning and systematic planning.* According to Piaget, children reach the stage of formal operations at about age 11. He attributed some fairly sophisticated abilities to children in this stage, although later research indicates that many children take much longer to reach this stage, if they ever do.

Suppose we ask three children, ages 6, 10, and 14, to arrange a set of 12 sticks in order from the longest to the shortest. The 6-year-old (preoperational) child fails to order the sticks correctly. The 10-year-old (concrete operations) eventually gets them in the right order, but only after a great deal of trial and error. The 14-year-old (formal operations) holds the sticks upright with their bottom ends on the table and then removes the longest one, the second-longest one, and so on.

A second example: We set up five bottles of clear liquid and explain that it is possible, by mixing the liquids together in a certain combination, to produce a yellow liquid. The task is to find the right combination. Children in the concrete operations stage plunge right in with an unsystematic trial-and-error search. They try combining bottles A and B, then C and D, then perhaps A, C, and E, and so on. By the time they work through five or six combinations, they have forgotten which ones they've already tried. They may try one combination several times and others not at all; if and when they do stumble onto the correct combination, it is mostly by luck.

Children in the formal operations stage approach the problem more systematically. They may first try all the two-bottle combinations: AB, AC, AD, AE, BC, and so forth. If all those fail, they then try three-bottle combinations: ABC, ABD, ABE, ACD, and so on. By adopting a strategy for trying every possible combination only once, they are bound to succeed.

Children do not reach the stage of formal operations any more suddenly than they reach the concrete operations stage. Before they can reason logically about a particular problem, they must first have a fair amount of experience in dealing with that problem. A 9-year-old who has spent a great deal of time playing chess reasons logically about chess problems and plans several moves ahead. The same child reverts to concrete reasoning, however, when faced with an unfamiliar problem.

Table 10.2 summarizes Piaget's four stages.

CONCEPT CHECK

3. You are given the following information about four children. Assign each of them to one of Piaget's stages of intellectual development. (Check your answers on page 367.)

   a. Child has mastered the concept of conservation; still has trouble with abstract and hypothetical questions.

TABLE 10.2 Summary of Piaget's Stages of Cognitive Development

STAGE AND APPROXIMATE AGE	ACHIEVEMENTS AND ACTIVITIES	LIMITATIONS
Sensorimotor (birth to 1½ years)	Reacts to sensory stimuli through reflexes and other responses	Little use of language; seems not to understand object permanence; does not distinguish appearance from reality
Preoperational (1½ to 7 years)	Develops language; can represent objects mentally by words and other symbols; can respond to objects that are remembered but not present	Lacks operations (reversible mental processes); lacks concept of conservation; focuses on one property at a time (such as length or width), not on both at once; still has trouble distinguishing appearance from reality
Concrete operations (7 to 11 years)	Understands conservation of mass, number, and volume; can reason logically with regard to concrete objects that can be seen or touched	Has trouble reasoning about abstract concepts and hypothetical situations
Formal operations (11 years onward)	Can reason logically about abstract and hypothetical concepts; develops strategies; plans actions in advance	None beyond the occasional irrationalities of all human thought

b. Child performs well on tests of object permanence; still has trouble with conservation.
c. Child has schemata; does not speak in complete sentences; fails tests of object permanence.
d. Child performs well on tests of object permanence, conservation, and hypothetical questions.

Are Piaget's Stages Distinct?

According to Piaget, the four stages of intellectual development are distinct, and each transition from one stage to the next requires a major reorganization of the child's way of thinking. He contended that children in the sensorimotor stage fail certain tasks because they lack the concept of object permanence and that children in the preoperational stage fail conservation tasks because they lack the necessary mental processes. In other words, intellectual growth is marked by periods of revolutionary reorganization, as a child advances from one stage of thinking to another.

Later research has thrown much doubt upon this conclusion. If it were true, then a child in a given stage of development—say, the preoperational stage—should perform consistently at that level. In fact, a given child's performance will fluctuate, and one can increase that fluctuation by altering the difficulty of a task. For example, preschool children ordinarily fail conservation-of-number tasks, where an investigator presents two rows of coins or candies with seven or more objects in each row, then spreads out one row and asks which row "has more." Preoperational children reply that the spread-out row has more. However, when Rochel Gelman (1982) presented two rows of only three objects each (Figure 10.19) and then spread out one of the rows, even 3- and

4-year-old children answered that the rows had the same number of items. (Most of the 3-year-olds counted first, to make sure.) After much practice with these short rows, most of the 3- and 4-year-olds also answered correctly that a spread-out row of eight items had the same number of items as the tightly packed row of eight.

In general, the progression from one stage of thinking to another appears to be gradual and not sudden (Siegler, 1994). That is, the difference between older children and younger children is not so much a matter of *having* an ability or of *lacking* it; the difference is between readily using the ability or using it only for simple tasks. As the children develop, they use the ability for increasingly more complex tasks.

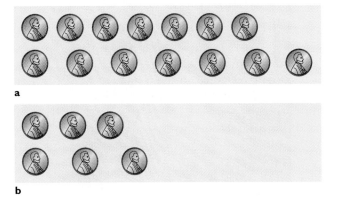

FIGURE 10.19 (a) With the standard conservation-of-number task, preoperational children answer that the lower row has more items. (b) With a simplified task, the same children say that both rows have the same number of items.

Implications for Education: Piaget and Lev Vygotsky

One implication of Piaget's findings is that children must discover certain concepts, such as the concept of conservation, mainly on their own. Teaching any such concept means directing children's attention to the key aspects and then letting them discover the concept for themselves.

Another implication frequently drawn from Piaget's work is that teachers should determine a child's level of functioning and then teach material appropriate to that level. For example, teachers should not try introducing abstract concepts to children who are at the concrete operations stage of development.

In contrast to this view, the Russian psychologist Lev Vygotsky (1978) argued that education cannot simply wait for children to reach the next stage of development on their own; children have to learn in order to develop. Indeed, Vygotsky argued, the one distinguishing characteristic of human thought is that it is based on language and symbols. We use language both to influence others and to control our own behavior (as when we tell ourselves what to do and what not to do). Therefore, it is inefficient to expect children to explore and discover what we want them to know; adults should indeed teach them (Karpov & Haywood, 1998).

However, when Vygotsky said that adults should teach children, he did not necessarily mean to teach by lecturing them, and he certainly did not mean that adults should ignore the child's developmental level. What he meant was this: Every child has a **zone of proximal development,** which is *the distance between what a child can do on his or her own and what the child can do with the help of adults or other children.* Instruction should always remain within that zone. For example, one should not try to teach a 4-year-old the concept of conservation of volume, and it would be a waste of time to try to teach it to an 8-year-old, who probably understands the concept already. But a child

around 6 years old who does not yet understand the concept might be able to learn it with help and guidance from an adult or older child. Similarly, children improve their recall of a story when adults provide appropriate hints and reminders, and they can solve more complicated math problems with help than they can solve alone. Vygotsky compared this help to *scaffolding,* the temporary supports that builders use when constructing a new building: After the building is complete, the scaffolding can be removed.

Good advice for an educator, therefore, is to be sensitive to a child's zone of proximal development, to try to detect how much further he or she can successfully push the child's development. In some cases, the child may provide clues. For example, several preoperational children who are asked which beaker has more water may all point to the tall, thin one; however, the children who could most easily learn conservation of volume describe the various beakers by using hand gestures that indicate both height and width (Goldin-Meadow, Alibali, & Church, 1993). An educator sensitive to those gestures could infer which children have the largest zone of proximal development and, therefore, which children are ready for certain kinds of instruction.

The Development of Moral Reasoning

As children develop their reasoning powers, they apply their new reasoning abilities to moral issues. Just as 11-year-olds reason differently from 5-year-olds about what happens when water is poured from one beaker to another, they also reason differently about issues of right and wrong.

Kohlberg's Method of Evaluating Levels of Moral Reasoning

Psychologists once regarded morality as a set of arbitrary, learned rules with no logical basis. Lawrence Kohlberg (1969; Kohlberg & Hersh, 1977) rejected that view, arguing instead that moral reasoning is the result of a reasoning process that resembles Piaget's stages of intellectual development. Young children mostly equate "wrong" with "punished." Adults understand that certain acts are wrong even though they may never lead to punishment and that other acts are right even if they do lead to punishment. Children younger than about 6 years old think that accidentally breaking something valuable is worse than intentionally breaking something of less value; older children and adults give more regard to people's intentions.

Kohlberg proposed that people pass through distinct stages as they develop moral reasoning. Although those stages are analogous to Piaget's stages, they do not follow the same time sequence. For example, an individual may progress rapidly through Piaget's stages but move more slowly through Kohlberg's stages.

Lev Vygotsky called attention to a child's zone of proximal development: The gap between what a child can do alone and what the child can do with help. Education within the zone of proximal development can advance a child's reasoning abilities.

Kohlberg suggested that moral reasoning should not be evaluated according to the decisions a person makes but according to the reasoning behind them. For example, do you think that designing nuclear bombs is a moral way to make a living? According to Kohlberg, whether it shows good moral reasoning depends on one's reasons for taking the job. Hugh Gusterson (1992) interviewed nuclear bomb designers at the Lawrence Livermore National Laboratory. When he asked them about the morality of their actions, nearly everyone said something like, "You're lucky you chose me to interview, because I, unlike all the others, think deeply about these matters." (Clearly, all of them were thinking about the morality of their profession, but they were not discussing it with one another.) The vast majority said they were confident that the weapons they designed would never be used and that the only function of the bombs was to threaten and, thereby, to prevent a war. If you disagree with these bomb designers' assumptions, you might disagree with the morality of their *actions,* but according to Kohlberg's system, you should concede that they are operating at a high level of moral *reasoning,* because they explained their actions in terms of the expected benefits to humanity.

Kohlberg believed that we all start with a low level of moral reasoning and mature through higher stages. To measure the maturity of a person's moral judgments, Kohlberg devised a series of **moral dilemmas**—*problems that pit one moral value against another.* Each dilemma is accompanied by a question, such as "What should this person do?" or "Did this person do the right thing?" Kohlberg was not concerned about the choice a person makes, because the dilemmas pit one value against another and well-meaning people do disagree on the right answer. More revealing than the answer itself is the explanation behind it. The respondent's explanations are then matched to one of Kohlberg's six stages, which are grouped into three levels (see Table 10.3). Because very few people operate consistently at stage 6, many authorities combine stages 5 and 6. To emphasize: In Kohlberg's scheme, there are no moral or immoral decisions, just moral and immoral *reasons* for making a decision. (See Figure 10.20.)

SOMETHING TO THINK ABOUT

Suppose a military junta overthrows a democratic government and sets up a dictatorship. In which of Kohlberg's stages of moral reasoning would you classify the members of the junta? Would your answer depend on the reasons they gave for setting up their dictatorship? ✶

People's responses to Kohlberg's moral dilemmas suggest the level of moral reasoning at which they *usually* operate. Few people are absolutely consistent in their moral reasoning, any more than they are consistent in any other kind of reasoning.

Kohlberg and others have found that people begin at

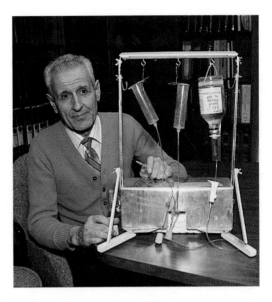

F I G U R E   10.20   Here is a real-life moral dilemma: Michigan physician Jack Kevorkian developed a device to help terminally ill patients kill themselves painlessly. Is it morally right or wrong to aid in someone else's suicide? According to Kohlberg's viewpoint, the morality of an act does not depend on the act itself, but on the reasoning behind the act.

the first stage and progress through the others in order, although they do not all reach the highest stages. (The order of progression is an important point: If people were just as likely to progress in the order 3-5-4 as in the order 3-4-5, then we would have no justification for regarding stage 5 as more advanced than stage 4.) People seldom skip a stage or revert to an earlier stage after reaching a higher one.

Figure 10.21 shows that most 10-year-olds' judgments are at Kohlberg's first or second stage, but that the mode of 16-year-olds' judgments is at stage 5. What accounts for this rather swift development of moral reasoning? Kohlberg suggests that it results from cognitive growth: 16-year-olds are capable of more mature reasoning than 10-year-olds. Rachael Henry (1983) proposed a different possibility: Adolescents reject parental authority. In stages 1 and 2, parents are the source of moral judgments, and what they say determines what is right and what is wrong. In stage 3, other people become the source of moral judgments. In stage 4, the source is the law; in stages 5 and 6, society as a whole or some abstract truth is the source of moral judgments. As adolescents continue to mature, they move farther and farther away from regarding their parents as the ultimate authority on questions of morality.

CONCEPT CHECK

4. For the moral dilemma described at the top of Table 10.3, suppose someone says that Heinz was wrong to steal the drug to save his wife's life. Which level of moral reasoning is characteristic of this judgment? (Check your answer on page 367.)

TABLE 10.3   **Responses to One of Kohlberg's Moral Dilemmas by People at Six Levels of Moral Reasoning**

The dilemma: Heinz's wife was near death from cancer. A druggist had recently discovered a drug that might be able to save her. The druggist was charging $2,000 for the drug, which cost him $200 to make. Heinz could not afford to pay for it, and he could borrow only $1,000 from friends. He offered to pay the rest later. The druggist refused to sell the drug for less than the full price paid in advance: "I discovered the drug, and I'm going to make money from it." Late that night, Heinz broke into the store to steal the drug for his wife. Did Heinz do the right thing?

LEVEL/STAGE	TYPICAL ANSWER	BASIS FOR JUDGING RIGHT FROM WRONG	DESCRIPTION OF STAGE
The Level of Preconventional Morality			
1. Punishment and obedience orientation	"No. If he steals the drug he might go to jail." "Yes. If he can't afford the drug, he can't afford a funeral, either."	Wrong is equated with punishment. What is good is whatever is in the man's immediate self-interest.	Decisions are based on their immediate consequences. Whatever is rewarded is "good" and whatever is punished is "bad." If you break something and are punished, then what you did was bad.
2. Instrumental relativist orientation	"He can steal the drug and save his wife, and he'll be with her when he gets out of jail."	Again, what is good is whatever is in the man's own best interests, but his interests include delayed benefits.	It is good to help other people, but only because they may one day return the favor: "You scratch my back and I'll scratch yours."
The Level of Conventional Morality			
3. Interpersonal concordance, or "good boy/nice girl" orientation	"People will understand if you steal the drug to save your wife, but they'll think you're cruel and a coward if you don't."	Public opinion is the main basis for judging what is good.	The "right" thing to do is whatever pleases others, especially those in authority. Be a good person so others will think you are good. Conformity to the dictates of public opinion is important.
4. "Law and order" orientation	"No, because stealing is illegal." "Yes. It is the husband's duty to save his wife even if he feels guilty afterward for stealing the drug."	Right and wrong can be determined by duty or by one's role in society.	You should respect the law — simply because it *is* the law — and work to strengthen the social order than enforces it.
The Level of Postconventional or Principled Morality			
5. Social-contract legalistic orientation	"The husband has a right to the drug even if he can't pay now. If the druggist won't charge it, the government should look after it."	Laws are made for people's benefit. They should be flexible. If necessary, we may have to change certain laws or allow for exceptions to them.	The "right" thing to do is whatever people have agreed is the best thing for society. As in stage 4, you respect the law, but in addition recognize that a majority of the people can agree to change the rules. Anyone who makes a promise is obligated to keep the promise.
6. Universal ethical principle orientation	"Although it is legally wrong to steal, the husband would be morally wrong not to steal to save his wife. A life is more precious than financial gain."	Right and wrong are based on absolute values such as human life. Sometimes these values take precedence over human laws.	In special cases, it may be right to violate a law that conflicts with higher ethical principles, such as justice and respect for human life. Among those who have obeyed a "higher law" are Jesus, Mahatma Gandhi, and Martin Luther King, Jr.

SOURCE: Kohlberg, 1981

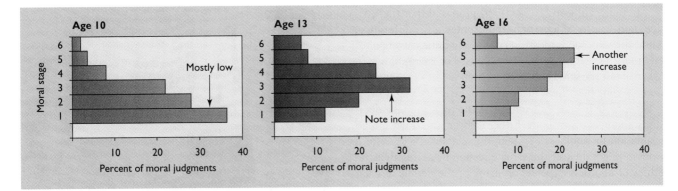

FIGURE 10.21 Distinguishing right from wrong: The development of moral reasoning. Most younger adolescents give answers corresponding to Kohlberg's earlier moral stages. By age 16, most are at Kohlberg's fourth and fifth stages. (Based on Kohlberg, 1969.)

The Limitations of Kohlberg's Views of Moral Development

Kohlberg's theories have had an enormous impact on psychology, although they do have certain limitations. Some critics point out that moral reasoning is just one part of moral behavior. James Rest (1983) divides moral behavior into four components:

1. Interpreting the situation
2. Deciding on the morally correct thing to do
3. Deciding what you will actually do, which may not be the same as the morally correct thing to do
4. Actually doing what you have decided to do

Kohlberg's stages relate only to the first and second of these components. Many juvenile delinquents and adult criminals make mature responses to Kohlberg's moral dilemmas but then engage in destructive behavior (Jurkovic, 1980; Link, Sherer, & Byrne, 1977). Apparently, a person can distinguish between right and wrong in the abstract and then behave in a way that ignores that reasoning (Figure 10.22).

Another criticism is that Kohlberg may have misinterpreted the lower stages of moral reasoning because they are characteristic of children or others who have trouble articulating their views. For example, many children say that stealing is wrong "because you might get caught." However, if children are asked whether they would steal something if they were sure they would not be caught, many say no. Apparently, they have a feeling of moral obligation, a sense of right and wrong, even if they are unable to state this idea clearly. In many cultures, such as the Hindu culture of India, almost all moral reasoning is stated in terms of natural obligations, not in terms of the laws and social conventions that figure so heavily in Western thought. For example, in Hindu custom, people should never eat beef, widows should not eat fish, and menstruating women should seclude themselves and not touch the family's meals. The Hindus defend these customs, which seem arbitrary to outsiders, as part of a natural moral order. In short, contrary to

Kohlberg's views, the idea of moral obligation may be a natural concept of human thought, even in childhood—and not something that we develop later in life after passing through the stage of conventional reasoning (Shweder, Mahapatra, & Miller, 1987).

Yet another criticism is that Kohlberg concentrated entirely on one type of moral reasoning, which we might call the "justice" orientation, based on people's rights. Carol Gilligan (1977, 1979) pointed out a different way of approaching moral decisions, the "caring" orientation: what would help or hurt other people. For example, consider a situation during the Vietnam War, when a group of soldiers were ordered to kill a group of unarmed civilians. One soldier, who regarded the order as immoral, refused to shoot. So, in terms of "justice," this soldier acted at a high moral level, following a "higher law" that required him not to kill. However, his actions made no difference, as the other soldiers killed all the civilians. In terms of "caring," he would have been more moral if he had found a way to hide a few of the Vietnamese civilians (Linn & Gilligan, 1990).

FIGURE 10.22 Critics of Kohlberg's approach to moral reasoning point out that moral reasoning is not the same thing as moral action. This cadet at a Russian military academy could probably explain why cheating is immoral, but he cheats nevertheless.

Initially, Gilligan (1977, 1979) proposed that the "justice" and "caring" orientations represented a sex difference. Men, she said, focus mostly on rights and duties; women focus more on caring and relationships. For example, when asked about the ethics of abortion, men might say that abortion is wrong because it takes a life, or else they might say it is acceptable because a woman has the right to make decisions about her own body. Either answer would get a high evaluation in Kohlberg's system, if explained clearly. But a woman might answer the same question by saying that the ethics of abortion depends on many of the details of each situation. An "it depends" answer does not get high marks in Kohlberg's system, because his system does not rely on abstract principles of right and wrong. Nevertheless, this type of answer may reflect a sympathetic, caring approach to solving people's problems.

Gilligan therefore proposed alternative stages of moral development, outlined in Table 10.4. The postconventional stage is the most mature; the preconventional stage is the least mature. Like Kohlberg, Gilligan concentrates on the reasons behind someone's moral decisions, not on the decisions themselves. But unlike Kohlberg, Gilligan emphasizes the "caring" aspect of the reasons: Will this action help or hurt the people it affects?

Later researchers have agreed with Gilligan that people have two ways of reasoning about moral issues, one based on justice and the other based on caring, although they have failed to confirm any consistent difference between men's and women's moral reasoning (Shweder & Haidt, 1993). Nearly everyone, male or female, shows concern with both justice and caring.

Gilligan has therefore modified her position: Each of us has within ourselves two "voices" of morality—a voice of justice and rights and a voice of caring and relationships. One voice may speak a little louder in some people, but both voices are valid (Gilligan & Attanucci, 1988). Sometimes, the two voices are in conflict; that is, one may feel an obligation to help a person and yet find that the only way to help requires breaking a general principle of justice (Linn & Gilligan, 1990). In short, moral decisions can be complicated. (See Figure 10.23.)

FIGURE 10.23 Sometimes the two "voices" of moral reasoning—justice and caring—are in conflict with each other. From a caring standpoint, you want to help a person in distress. From a justice standpoint, though, you may think it wrong to encourage begging. In many controversial situations, ranging from abortion to the death penalty to animal protection, well-meaning people disagree about what actions are moral.

THE MESSAGE
Developing Cognitive Abilities

The universe is a complicated place, and even well-educated adults continue working throughout their lives to understand it. For a young child, this work is an enormous challenge, and we adults find it difficult to reconstruct what the world looks like through a child's eyes. In childhood, as throughout life, a person is constantly constructing one hypothesis after another, discarding old conceptions of the world to make way for new ones.

SUMMARY

✳ *Piaget's view of children's thinking.* According to Jean Piaget, children's thought processes are more intuitive, less logical, and more egocentric than adults' thought processes are. (page 354)

✳ *Piaget's stages of development.* Piaget described four stages of development of thought processes and knowledge. Children progress through those stages in order. (page 355)

✳ *Egocentric thinking.* Young children sometimes have trouble understanding other people's point of view. Before about age 4, children have trouble inferring what someone else is likely or unlikely to know. (page 356)

✳ *Restricted uses of abilities.* Young children do not always use all the abilities they have. Although children in the preoperational stage ordinarily fail to demonstrate their understanding of conservation of number, it is clear from other tasks that they do understand the concept of number. (page 361)

TABLE 10.4	Carol Gilligan's Stages of Moral Development
STAGE	**BASIS FOR DECIDING RIGHT FROM WRONG**
Preconventional	What is helpful or harmful to myself?
Conventional	What is helpful or harmful to other people?
Postconventional	What is helpful or harmful to myself and others?

✳ *Implications for education.* Teaching must be at a level appropriate to the developmental stage of the child. However, as Lev Vygotsky argued, children can advance with an adult's help and thus do more than they could on their own. Therefore, educators should try to push children somewhat beyond their current level of performance. (page 362)

✳ *Kohlberg's view of moral reasoning.* Lawrence Kohlberg contended that moral reasoning can also be described in terms of stages. According to Kohlberg, a person's moral reasoning should be evaluated on the basis of the reasons the person gives for a decision, rather than on the basis of the decision itself. (page 362)

✳ *Gilligan's view of moral reasoning.* Carol Gilligan demonstrated that not all people decide moral dilemmas primarily on the basis of principles of justice. Some decide primarily on the basis of a caring orientation. (page 365)

Suggestion for Further Reading

Hobson, R. P. (1993). *Autism and the development of mind.* Hove, East Sussex, UK: Lawrence Erlbaum Associates. Despite the title, this book is only partly about autism; it is about how children come to understand other people and to communicate with them.

Terms

schema (plural: **schemata**)   an organized way of interacting with objects in the world (page 354)

assimilation   Piaget's term for the application of an established schema to new objects (page 355)

accommodation   Piaget's term for the modification of an established schema to fit a new object (page 355)

sensorimotor stage   according to Piaget, the first stage of intellectual development; an infant's behavior is limited to making simple motor responses to sensory stimuli (page 355)

preoperational stage   according to Piaget, the second stage of intellectual development, in which children lack operations (page 356)

operation   according to Piaget, a mental process that can be reversed (page 356)

egocentric   the inability to take the perspective of another person, a tendency to view the world as centered around oneself (page 356)

conservation   the concept that objects retain their weight, volume, and certain other properties in spite of changes in their shape or arrangement (page 358)

stage of concrete operations   according to Piaget, the third stage of intellectual development; children can deal with the properties of concrete objects but cannot readily comprehend hypothetical or abstract questions (page 360)

stage of formal operations   according to Piaget, the fourth and final stage of intellectual development; in this stage, people deal with abstract, hypothetical situations, which demand logical, deductive reasoning and systematic planning (page 360)

zone of proximal development   the distance between what a child can do on his or her own and what the child can do with the help of adults or older children (page 362)

moral dilemma   a problem that pits one moral value against another (page 363)

Answers to Concept Checks

2.   (c) is the clearest case of egocentric thought, a failure to recognize another person's point of view. It is not the same as selfishness. (page 357)

3.   **a.** Stage of concrete operations; **b.** preoperational stage; **c.** sensorimotor stage; **d.** stage of formal operations. (page 360)

4.   Not enough information is provided to answer this question. In Kohlberg's system, any judgment can represent either a high or a low level of moral reasoning; we evaluate a person's moral reasoning entirely by the explanation for the judgment, not by the judgment itself. (page 363)

Web Resources

Jean Piaget's Theory of Development

snycorva.cortland.edu/~ANDERSMD/PIAGET/OPEN.HTML

A student-created, concise tutorial on the basic concepts advanced by Piaget covers the stages of intellectual development, conservation experiments, and a biological theory of intelligence.

Social and
Emotional Development

What special social and emotional problems do people face at different stages of their life?

What determines how we develop socially and emotionally?

You are a contestant on a new TV game show called "What's My Worry?" Behind the curtain is someone with an overriding concern. You are to identify that concern by questioning a psychologist who knows what it is. (You can neither see nor hear the person.) You must ask questions that can be answered with a single word or a short phrase. If you identify the worry correctly, you can win as much as $50,000.

But there is one catch: The more questions you ask, the smaller your prize will be. If you guess correctly after only one question, you win $50,000. After two questions, you win $25,000. And so on. It would therefore be poor strategy to keep asking questions until you were sure of the

As people grow older, they mature in their social and emotional behaviors. However, many revert quickly to childlike behaviors in situations where such behavior is acceptable.

answer; instead, you should ask one or two questions and then guess.

What would your first question be? Mine would be: "How old is this person?" The principal worries of teenagers are different from those of most 20-year-olds, which in turn differ from those of most 40-year-olds and 70-year-olds. Each age has its own characteristic concerns, opportunities, and pleasures.

Research Designs for Studying Development

Comparing the psychology of people of different ages sounds easy: We study a group of, say, 10-year-olds and a group of 20-year-olds to see how they differ. But how do we know whether those differences are due to age or to another difference between the groups? We may get different results depending on exactly how we conduct the study. Depending on the circumstances, psychologists can use either cross-sectional studies or longitudinal studies. A **cross-sectional study** *compares groups of individuals of different ages all at the same time.* For example, we could compare the drawing abilities of 6-year-olds, 8-year-olds, and 10-year-olds. The main weakness of cross-sectional studies is the difficulty of obtaining equivalent samples at different ages. For example, suppose you want to do a cross-sectional study comparing 20-year-olds and 60-year-olds. You study a sample of 20-year-olds from the local college, but how will you find a comparable group of 60-year-olds? The 60-year-olds you eventually select may have been less educated from the start, perhaps less wealthy, perhaps different in many other regards.

A **longitudinal study** *follows a single group of individuals as they develop.* For example, we could study a group of 6-year-olds and then study the same children again when they reach ages 9 and 12. Table 10.5 contrasts the two kinds of studies.

Longitudinal studies also face certain practical difficulties. A longitudinal study of children from the ages of 6 to 12 necessarily requires 6 years to complete; a longitudinal study from 6 to 60 would take much too long for any one investigator to complete. To make matters worse, many of the children who begin in a study at, say, age 6 may move out of town by age 9 or 12. A longitudinal study of the elderly faces the likelihood that many people will die or become seriously ill before the end of the study. Furthermore, those who leave a study may be different in important ways from those who continue. For example, suppose a creature from outer space observes humans for the first time and discovers that about 50% of young adults are males but that only 10–20% of 90-year-olds are males. The creature then concludes that, as human males grow older, most of them transform into females.

You can see why that conclusion is wrong. Males—with a few exceptions—do not change into females, but on the av-

TABLE 10.5 Cross-Sectional and Longitudinal Studies

	DESCRIPTION	ADVANTAGES	DISADVANTAGES	EXAMPLE
Cross-sectional	Several groups of subjects of various ages studied at one time	1. Quick 2. No risk of confusing age effects with effects of changes in society	1. Risk of sampling error by getting different kinds of people at different ages 2. Risk of cohort effects	Compare memory abilities of 3-, 5-, and 7-year-olds
Longitudinal	One group of subjects studied repeatedly as they grow older	1. No risk of sampling differences 2. Can study effects of one experience on later development 3. Can study consistency within individuals over time	1. Takes a long time 2. Some subjects quit 3. Sometimes hard to separate effects of age from changes in society	Study social and emotional behavior of children at time of parents' divorce and at various times afterward

erage they die earlier, leaving a greater percentage of older females. Similarly, in any longitudinal study, it is possible that those who left a study (for whatever reason) are brighter or less bright, more motivated or less motivated, or different in a variety of other ways from those who continued in the study. If so, the differences between the average person at the beginning of the study and the average person at the end of the study are not really due to the process of aging. **Selective attrition,** also known as *differential survival,* is *the tendency for some kinds of people to be more likely than others to drop out of a study.* Psychologists can partly reduce this problem by reporting the data only for the people who completed the study and disregarding the data for those who left.

A longitudinal study also faces the difficulty of separating the effects of age from the effects of changes in society. For example, suppose we found that a group of people who were 20 years old in 1970 became politically more conservative by age 40. We would not know whether these people became more conservative because of their age or because of changes in the political situation between 1970 and 1990.

Why, then, would investigators ever conduct a longitudinal study? One reason is that certain questions logically require a longitudinal study. For example, to study the effects of divorce on children, we can learn much by comparing how each child reacts at first with how that same child reacts several years later. To study whether happy children are likely to become happy adults, we would have to follow a single group of people for a substantial period of time.

What happens if a cross-sectional study gets one result and a longitudinal study gets another? Psychologists look

for the reasons behind the different results. For example, suppose someone conducting a study in 1955 finds that the mean IQ score of the 20-year-olds is much higher than that of the 60-year-olds. However, on a retest in 1995, the former 20-year-olds (now 60 years old) score as high as they did in 1955. Thus, the longitudinal part of the study indicates that IQ scores are fairly stable from age 20 to age 60. Why, then, did the 20-year-olds score so much higher than the 60-year-olds in 1955? There are two possible reasons: First, perhaps in 1955 the investigators selected a particularly bright group of 20-year-olds or a dull group of 60-year-olds. Secondly, maybe the generation of people who were 20 years old in 1955 were healthier and better educated than the older generation had ever been. That is, the 20-year-olds of 1955 may have performed better than the 20-year-olds of 1915 would have. Psychologists call this a *cohort effect* (Figure 10.24). A **cohort** is *a group of people born at a particular time or a group of people who entered an organization at a particular time.* Psychologists try to distinguish whether a difference among people of different ages is really due to age or whether it is a difference among cohorts.

CONCEPT CHECKS

5. Suppose you want to study the effect of age on artistic abilities, and you want to be sure that any apparent differences are due to age and not to a cohort effect. Which should you use, a longitudinal study or a cross-sectional study?

FIGURE 10.24   Children of the 1920s, 1960s, and 1990s differed in their behavior because they grew up in different historical eras, with different options regarding education, nutrition, and health care. Differences among age groups based on such influences are called cohort effects.

6. Suppose you want to study the effect of age on choice of clothing, but you are concerned that clothing fashions change from one year to the next. (It would not be fair to compare the people of today with people of previous years.) Which should you use, a longitudinal study or a cross-sectional study?

7. At Santa Enigma College, the average first-year student has a C-minus average, and the average senior has a B-plus average. An observer concludes that, as students progress through college, they improve their study habits. Based on the idea of selective attrition, propose another possible explanation. (Check your answers on page 381.)

Using a combination of cross-sectional and longitudinal studies, psychologists study changes in people's abilities and also changes in their life situations. The decisions and social environment that young adults face are very different from those experienced by children on the one hand or elderly people on the other hand.

Erikson's Ages of Human Development

How people spend their time is largely determined by their current role in life—preschool child, student, worker, or retired person. Moreover, a person's role in life is determined largely, though not entirely, by his or her age. To understand why people behave as they do, we need to know the decisions they are facing at the current stage of their life.

Erik Erikson (Figure 10.25) divided the human life span into eight ages, each with its own social and emotional conflicts. First is *the age of the newborn infant,* whose main conflict is **basic trust versus mistrust.** The infant asks, in effect, *"Is my social world predictable and supportive?"* An infant whose early environment is supportive, nurturing, and loving will form a strong attachment to the parents that will also positively influence future relationships with other people (Erikson, 1963).

Erikson's second age is *the age of the toddler,* 1–3

years old, whose main conflict is **autonomy versus shame and doubt.** The toddler faces the issue, *"Can I do things by myself or must I always rely on others?"* Experiencing independence for the first time, the toddler begins to walk and talk, to become toilet trained, to obey some instructions and defy others. Depending on how the parents react, children either develop a healthy feeling of autonomy (independence) or a self-critical sense of shame and the doubt that they can accomplish things on their own.

Erikson's third age is the age of *the preschool child,* whose main conflict is **initiative versus guilt.** At ages 3–6, as children begin to broaden their horizons, their boundless energy comes into conflict with parental restrictions. Sooner or later, the child breaks something or makes a big mess. The child then faces the question, *"Am I good or bad?"* In contrast to the previous stage, where the child was concerned about what he or she is *capable* of doing, at this stage the child is concerned about the morality or acceptability of his or her actions.

In the fourth age, *preadolescence* (about ages 6–12), **industry versus inferiority** is the main conflict. The

FIGURE 10.25   Erik Erikson argued that each age group has its own special social and emotional conflicts.

question is: *"Am I successful or worthless?"* Children widen their focus from the immediate family to society at large and begin to prepare for adult roles. They fantasize about the great successes ahead, and they begin to compete with their peers in an effort to excel in the activities popular with their age group. Children begin to develop a sense of either competence or inadequacy.

Erikson's fifth age is *adolescence (the early teens),* where the main conflict is **identity versus role confusion.** Adolescents begin to seek independence from their parents and try to answer the question *"Who am I?"* or *"Who will I be?"* They may eventually settle on a satisfactory answer—form an identity—or they may continue to experiment with goals and lifestyles—a state of role confusion.

Erikson's sixth age is *young adulthood,* in which **intimacy versus isolation** is the main conflict: *"Shall I share my life with another person or live alone?"* Young adults who marry or live with a friend find that they must adjust their habits to make the relationship succeed. Those who choose to live alone may experience loneliness and pressure from their parents and friends to find a suitable partner.

Erikson's seventh age is *middle adulthood.* Here, the major conflict is **generativity versus stagnation:** *"Will I produce something of real value? Will I succeed in my life, both as a parent and as a worker? Will I in some way give something back to society?"*

Finally comes *old age* (the years after retirement), where the main conflict is **ego integrity versus despair.** *"Have I lived a full life or have I failed?"* Integrity is a state of contentment about one's life, past, present, and future. Despair is a state of great disappointment about the past and the present, coupled with fear of the future. Table 10.6 summarizes Erikson's ages.

Is Erikson's view of development accurate? This question is unanswerable. Some psychologists find Erikson's description of development a useful way to organize our thinking about human life; others find it less useful, and it is not the kind of theory that one can test scientifically. Erikson described development; he did not explain it. For example, he hardly addressed the question of how or why a person progresses from one stage to the next.

Now let's take a closer look at some of the major issues that confront people in their social and emotional development at different ages. Beyond the primary conflicts that Erikson highlighted, development is marked by a succession of other significant problems.

SOMETHING TO THINK ABOUT

Suppose you disagreed with Erikson's analysis; for example, suppose you believe that the main concern of young adults is not "intimacy versus isolation" but "earning money versus not earning money" or "finding meaning in life versus meaninglessness." How might you determine whether your theory or Erikson's is more accurate? ✳

Infancy: Forming the First Attachments

Before the late 1950s, if someone had asked, "What causes an infant to develop an attachment to its mother?" almost all psychologists would have replied, "Mother's milk." They were wrong.

Studies of Attachment Among Monkeys

Attachment—*a long-term feeling of closeness between people, such as a child and a caregiver*—depends on more than just being fed. Attachment is part of trust, in Erikson's

---

TABLE 10.6 **Erikson's Ages of Human Development**

AGE	MAIN CONFLICT	TYPICAL QUESTION
Infant	Basic trust versus mistrust	Is my social world predictable and supportive?
Toddler (ages 1–3)	Autonomy versus shame and doubt	Can I do things by myself or must I always rely on others?
Preschool child (ages 3–6)	Initiative versus guilt	Am I good or bad?
Preadolescent (ages 6–12)	Industry versus inferiority	Am I successful or worthless?
Adolescent (early teens)	Identity versus role confusion	Who am I?
Young adult (late teens and early 20s)	Intimacy versus isolation	Shall I share my life with another person or live alone?
Middle adult (late 20s to retirement)	Generativity versus stagnation	Will I succeed in my life, both as a parent and as a worker?
Older adult (after retirement)	Ego integrity versus despair	Have I lived a full life or have I failed?

FIGURE 10.26 In Harlow's studies, monkeys who got milk from the wire mother still clung to the cloth mother as much as they could.

sense of "trust versus mistrust." That attachment or trust comes only partly from the satisfaction of biological needs. It also depends on the emotional responses provoked by such acts as hugging.

Some highly influential evidence comes from an experiment that Harry Harlow conducted with monkeys. Harlow (1958) separated eight newborn rhesus monkeys from their mothers and isolated each of them in a room containing two artificial mothers. Four of the infant monkeys had a mother made out of wire and equipped with a milk bottle in the breast position and a mother made out of cloth with no bottle (Figure 10.26); the other four monkeys had a cloth mother with a bottle and a wire mother with no bottle. Harlow wanted to find out how much time the baby monkeys would spend with the artificial mother that fed them.

Figure 10.27 shows the mean number of hours per day that the monkeys spent with the two kinds of mothers. Regardless of whether they got their milk from the cloth mother or from the wire mother, they all spent more than half of their time clinging to the cloth mother and very little time with the wire mother. Evidently, their attachment depended more on *contact comfort*—comfortable skin sensations—than on the satisfaction of their hunger or sucking needs.

At first, Harlow thought that the cloth mothers were adequately serving the infants' emotional needs. He discovered, however, that the monkeys failed to develop normal social and sexual behavior (Harlow, Harlow, & Suomi, 1971). (See Figure 10.28.) When some of the females finally became pregnant, they proved to be woefully inadequate mothers, rejecting every attempt their babies made to cling to them or to be nursed. Clearly, the monkeys that had been reared by artificial mothers did not know how to react to other monkeys. With monkeys, as with humans, a good parent interacts with the infant, giving out social signals as well as responding to the infant's signals. Being warm and cuddly is a good start, but it is hardly enough.

What are the messages of this study? The data do *not* mean that an infant needs a mother's constant attention. They do mean that an infant needs social attention from *someone*. In later studies, Harry Harlow and Margaret Harlow (1965) found that infant monkeys reared by artificial mothers could develop fairly normally if they had frequent opportunities to play with other infant monkeys.

Early Attachment in Humans

In the first year of life, an infant forms attachments to the parents and to many others. Suppose we want to answer some questions about early attachment: Why do some infants form stronger attachments to their parents than others do? In the long run, does a strong attachment to one person, such as the mother, produce a better psychological outcome

FIGURE 10.27 All the baby monkeys preferred the cloth mothers, regardless of which artificial mother fed them; the two bottom lines show hours per day spent with the wire mothers.

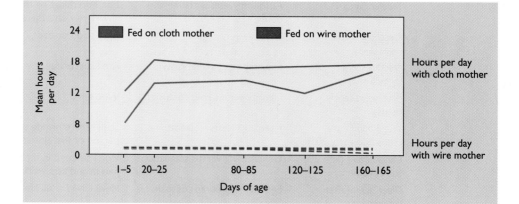

FIGURE 10.28 Much of what we need and learn depends on interaction with others. This mother monkey reared in isolation ignores her baby.

than moderate attachments to several people? Does a good relationship with the mother (or mother substitute) early in life make it easier for the infant to develop close bonds with other people later in life?

Before we can begin to answer questions like these, we first need a good way to measure attachment. One method that has proven to be both versatile and reliable is the **Strange Situation** (usually capitalized), pioneered by Mary Ainsworth (1979). In this procedure, *a mother and the infant* (typically 12 or 18 months old) *come into a room with many toys. Then, a stranger enters the room. The mother leaves and then returns.* A few minutes later both the stranger and the mother leave; then the stranger returns, and finally the mother returns. Through a one-way mirror, a psychologist observes the infant's reactions to each of these events.

Infants' responses fall into four major categories:

- *Securely attached.* The infant uses the mother as a base of exploration, often showing her a toy, cooing at her, or making eye contact with her. The infant shows some distress when the mother leaves, but cries only a little, if at all. When she returns, the infant goes to her with apparent delight, cuddles for a while, and then returns to the toys.
- *Anxiously attached.* Responses toward the mother fluctuate between happy and angry. The infant clings to the mother and cries profusely when she leaves, as if worried that the mother might not return. When she does return, the infant clings to her again.
- *Anxious and avoidant.* While the mother is present, the infant does not interact with her much and does not stay near her. The infant cries when she leaves but does not go to her when she returns.
- *Disorganized.* The infant pays little attention to the mother and seems not to notice when she leaves or returns.

Most of the existing research concerns mothers, although it has not been limited to them. As you might expect, many infants show a secure attachment not only to the mother, but also to the father (Belsky, 1996), the grandparents and other caregivers. As a rule, the quality of one relationship correlates with the quality of another; for example, if the parents have a stable marriage, usually they also develop a good relationship with their children, but if the parents have a troubled marriage, they are likely to have trouble with their children as well (Erel & Burman, 1995).

Behavior in the Strange Situation correlates strongly with behavior at home, and one can predict the pattern of attachment from how the parents treat the infant at an earlier age. The more time that parents spend affectionately interacting with an infant at the age of 3 months, the more likely that infant is to show a secure attachment at 12 months (Cox, Owen, Henderson, & Margand, 1992), and when parents learn techniques to increase their sensitivity to their infant's needs, the infant often develops a more secure relationship (van IJzendoorn, Juffer, & Duyvesteyn, 1995). Quality of attachment also depends on temperament; some infants seem to be calmer and easier to please from the start. Through a combination of parenting styles and infant temperaments, infants in Japan are more likely than U.S. infants to develop a secure attachment, and infants in northern Germany are less likely (Grossman, Grossman, Spangler, Suess, & Unzner, 1985; Miyake, Chen, & Campos, 1985):

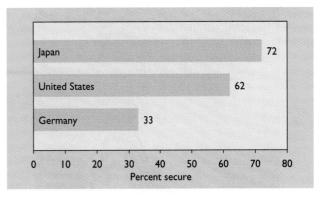

Furthermore, an infant who shows a secure attachment to the mother is also likely to relate well to playmates (Elicker, Englund, & Sroufe, 1992). It is tempting to suggest that a secure attachment to the mother forms a model that facilitates other social relationships, but the results do not justify cause-and-effect conclusions. (For example, perhaps some infants are born with an easygoing disposition, and they therefore bring out the best in both their mothers and their playmates.) Still, we do see a consistency across relationships: Children with one good relationship are likely to have others.

An infant with an anxious or avoidant attachment is not necessarily doomed to a lifetime of difficulties, but one with a disorganized attachment may indeed be at risk. One study found a strong relationship between a disorganized attachment in infancy and deviant or highly aggressive behavior at the age of 5 years (Lyons-Ruth, Alpern, & Repacholi, 1993).

The Effects of Different Parenting Styles

If and when you become a parent, you will rely partly on advice from other parents, books about child care, and your own memories of how your parents treated you. Your children are excellent teachers themselves. When you do your parenting job right, they will let you know; when you make a mistake, they will definitely let you know. Parenting is difficult, but be reassured: You don't need to be perfect. Parental behavior can vary within a fairly wide range without having drastic effects on children's personality development (Harris, 1995).

Diana Baumrind (1971) conducted extensive studies of the behaviors of parents and children, identifying the various styles of parenting. The following are the most common or most basic:

Authoritative parents: These parents *set high standards and impose controls, but they are also warm and responsive to the child's communications.* They encourage their children to set their own goals and to strive toward them. Therefore, although these parents set limits, they adjust those limits appropriately as the child grows older. Their children show self-reliance and self-control, cooperating with others and generally doing well in school.

Authoritarian parents: Like the *authoritative* parents, *authoritarian* parents set firm controls. However, they tend to be *less warm* and emotionally more distant from the child; *they set rules without explaining why they are good rules.* Their children tend to be socially responsible, law-abiding citizens, but they tend also to be discontent, distrustful, and not very independent.

Permissive parents: Permissive parents are *warm and loving but undemanding.* Their children generally lack self-control and lack a sense of social responsibility.

Indifferent or uninvolved parents: Some parents *spend little time with their children and do little more than provide them with food and shelter.* Their children, as you might imagine, tend to be impulsive and undisciplined.

We should not assume that parents' behavior causes their children's behavior. These are correlational studies, and as with nearly all correlational studies, we can imagine other possible explanations for the results. For example, children's behavior can affect their parents as much as the parents affect the children. (Perhaps children who act in self-reliant, self-controlled ways elicit authoritative parenting styles.) Another possibility is that parents and children show certain patterns of behavior because they share certain genes. (Perhaps the genes that promote permissive behavior in parents increase the probability of irresponsible behavior in children.)

Baumrind's research focused mainly on European-American children; later research found that the effects of different parenting styles vary somewhat among different ethnic groups (Darling & Steinberg, 1993). For example, the *authoritative* parenting style is associated with strong academic success and social cooperativeness for European-American children; the effects are less consistent for Asian-American and African-American families. Also, *authoritarian* European-American parents tend to have somewhat withdrawn children; authoritarian African-American parents have rather assertive children. At present, the reasons for these apparent differences are uncertain. These results remind us not to assume that the results found in one group will apply to all groups; they also emphasize the need for further research in this area.

Social Development in Childhood

The social and emotional development of children depends in part on how successful they are in forming friendships with other children (Figure 10.29). Some

Physical contact and cuddling are essential for the attachment that develops between parent and child. The early parent-child relationship serves as a prototype for later social attachments.

FIGURE 10.29 Children learn social skills by interacting with brothers, sisters, and friends close to their own age.

children are "popular," having many friends and admirers. Others are "rejected," with most other children avoiding their company. Still others are "controversial," liked by some and rejected by others. Controversial children are generally those with some social skills but an aggressive streak. A child's status as popular, rejected, or controversial tends to be fairly consistent from year to year (Coie & Dodge, 1983). Children with few friends tend to suffer from low self-esteem and do poorly in both schoolwork and athletics. (But does the lack of friends lead to poor performance, or does poor performance lead to a lack of friends?)

Many studies have been made of the effects of being a firstborn child or being born later. A number of those birth-order studies report that firstborn children do better in school, are more ambitious, are more honest, and have a greater need to affiliate with others. Children born later tend to be more popular, more independent, less conforming, better adjusted emotionally, and possibly more creative. These tendencies are small and inconsistent, however, and some of the evidence is based on poorly conducted studies (Ernst & Angst, 1983; Schooler, 1972). Be skeptical of recommendations that parents should space their children many years apart to give each of them the alleged benefits of the firstborn.

SOMETHING TO THINK ABOUT

Psychologists have offered two explanations for the effects of birth order on behavior: (1) Depending on whether there are older, younger, or no other children in the family, each child is subjected to different social influences. (2) Because the mother undergoes physical changes, such as changes in her hormones after giving birth, younger children experience different prenatal influences from those experienced by the firstborn child. What kind of evidence would you need to decide whether one of these explanations was more satisfactory than the other? ✳

Adolescence

Adolescence begins when the body reaches *puberty*, the onset of sexual maturation. In North America, the mean ages are around 12 to 13 in girls and about a year or two later in boys. The end of adolescence is harder to identify. Adolescence merges into adulthood, and adulthood is more a state of mind than a condition of the body. Some 12-year-olds act like adults, and some 30-year-olds act like adolescents.

Adolescence is a time of transition from childhood to adulthood. Children think of themselves as part of their parents' family; young adults are ready to become parents. Adolescents are somewhere in between, still closely tied to their parents but spending more and more time with their peer group. They do not have as much freedom and independence as adults, but they have far more than they did a few years before. Adolescence has sometimes been portrayed as a period of "storm and stress," and for some it is indeed. Some teenagers find themselves in serious conflict with their parents (Paikoff & Brooks-Gunn, 1991); some are deeply depressed or violent; and still others make choices that will haunt them for years. Most teenagers, however, like and respect their parents and are, in turn, liked and respected by their parents. Not everyone will look back on the high-school years as "the best time of my life," but most have a reasonably good experience of adolescence.

Identity Development

Adolescence is a time of "finding yourself," of determining "Who am I?" or "Who will I be?" In some societies, children are expected eventually to enter the same occupation as their parents and to live in the same town. The parents may even choose marriage partners for their children. In such societies, adolescents have few major choices to make.

Western society offers young people a great many choices. They decide how much education to get, what job to seek, and where to live, whether to marry and whom and when, what political and religious affiliation to adopt, and what standards to follow regarding sex, alcohol, and drugs. Remember from Chapter 8 that, even when people are given all the information they need to answer a question, they sometimes still rely on inappropriate heuristics and make illogical decisions. With regard to one's most important choices, such as a career and a life partner, we must often make decisions based on very limited information. No one needs to make a perfect decision, but even making a satisfactory decision is difficult.

An adolescent's *concerns with decisions about the future and the quest for self-understanding* has been called an **identity crisis.** The term *crisis* implies emotional turbulence, but in fact most adolescents go through this experience quite calmly. There are two major elements of identity development—whether one is actively exploring the issue and whether one has made any decisions (Marcia, 1980). We can diagram the possibilities, using the following grid:

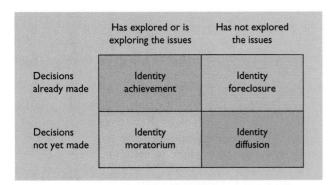

	Has explored or is exploring the issues	Has not explored the issues
Decisions already made	Identity achievement	Identity foreclosure
Decisions not yet made	Identity moratorium	Identity diffusion

Those who have not yet given any serious thought to making any decisions and who, in fact, have no clear sense of identity are said to have **identity diffusion.** People in this stage are not actively concerned with their identity and are waiting until later to clarify the issues.

People in **identity moratorium** are *seriously considering the issues but have not yet made any decisions.* They experiment with various possibilities and imagine themselves in different roles before deciding which one is best.

Identity foreclosure is a state of *having firm decisions without having given them much thought.* Ordinarily, those decisions originate from one's parents or from society. For example, a young man might be told that he is expected to go into the family business with his father, or a young woman might be told that she is expected to marry and raise children. Decrees of that sort were once common in North America and Europe, and they are still common in many other societies today. Someone who accepts such decisions has little reason to explore the possibility of alternative identities.

Finally, **identity achievement** is *the outcome of having explored various possible identities and then making one's own decisions.* Identity achievement does not come all at once. For example, someone might be fully decided about a career but not about marriage, or about marriage but not a career and might be just starting to struggle with questions of religion and politics. It is also possible, even common, to reach identity achievement and then, years later, rethink some of those decisions.

The "Personal Fable" of Teenagers

TRY IT YOURSELF

Are the following statements true or false?

- Other people may fail to realize their life ambitions, but I will realize mine.
- I understand love and sex in a way that my parents never did.

- Tragedy may strike other people, but it will probably never strike me.
- Almost everyone notices how I look and how I dress.

According to David Elkind (1984), teenagers are particularly likely to harbor such beliefs. Taken together, he calls them the "personal fable," the conviction that "I am special—what is true for everyone else is not true for me." Up to a point, this fable can help us to maintain a cheerful, optimistic outlook on life, but it becomes dangerous when it leads people to take foolish chances (See Figure 10.30.)

For example, one study found that high-school girls who were having sexual intercourse without contraception estimated that they had only a small chance of becoming pregnant through unprotected sex. Girls who were either having no sex or having sex using contraception estimated a much higher probability that unprotected sex would lead to pregnancy (Arnett, 1990). Because this was a correlational study, we do not know which came first—the girls' underestimation of the risk of pregnancy, or their willingness to have unprotected sex. Nevertheless, in either case, these results illustrate the "it can't happen to me" attitude.

That attitude is hardly unique to teenagers, however. Middle-aged adults also overestimate their own chances of winning a lottery, regard themselves as more likely than other people to succeed on the job and as less likely than average to have an injury or a serious illness (Quadrel, Fischhoff, & Davis, 1993). That is, few people fully outgrow the "personal fable."

FIGURE 10.30 Some teenagers seriously risk their health and safety. According to David Elkind, one reason for such risky behavior is the "personal fable," the secret belief that "nothing bad can happen to me."

Adulthood and Aging

Adults hope that life begins at 40—but the great anxiety is that it ends there.

—DANIEL LEVINSON (1978)

From their 20s until retirement, the main concern of most adults is: "What will I achieve and contribute to society and my family? Will I be successful at the activities I have chosen?"

The adult years begin with a flurry of major decisions about marriage, career, having children, where to live, and how to live. After one settles those decisions, adulthood becomes a time of relative security and stability. A typical middle-aged adult spends little time worrying about "what will I be doing next year?" or "who will go with me to the show on Friday night?" Whether middle age is a time of satisfaction and contentment or feeling stuck in a rut depends on the quality of the decisions made in adolescence and early adulthood.

Job Satisfaction

Adults who are satisfied with their job are generally satisfied with their life, and people who like their life generally like their job (Keon & McDonald, 1982). Some adults manage to be happy even though they work at an unrewarding job, but the daily work routine is bound to influence their satisfaction with life.

How satisfied *are* most workers? The answer depends on how the question is phrased. When pollsters simply ask, "Are you satisfied with your job?" about 85–90% say yes (Weaver, 1980). But when pollsters ask, "If you could start over, would you seek the same job you have now?" less than half of white-collar workers and only one fourth of blue-collar workers say yes. Although most workers say they are "satisfied" with their job, they could easily imagine being *more* satisfied.

The level of satisfaction is lower, on the average, among young workers than among older workers (Bass & Ryterband, 1979). (See Figure 10.31.) One possible explanation is that older workers have better, higher-paying jobs. Another is that today's young people are harder to satisfy. Another possibility is that many young workers start out in the wrong job and find a more suitable one later on. Still another is that many young people are still considering the possibility of changing jobs; by age 40, most people have reconciled themselves to whatever job they have.

Your choice of career has a profound effect on the quality of your life. A student once told me that he found the courses in his major boring, but at least they were preparing him for a job. I cautioned him that he would probably find the job just as boring. Between the ages of 20 and 70, you will probably spend about half of your waking hours on the job—a long time to live with work you find unsatisfying.

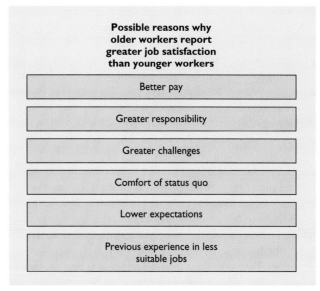

Possible reasons why older workers report greater job satisfaction than younger workers

Better pay
Greater responsibility
Greater challenges
Comfort of status quo
Lower expectations
Previous experience in less suitable jobs

F I G U R E 10.31 Most older workers report higher job satisfaction than younger workers do. Psychologists propose several reasons for this tendency.

The Midlife Transition

People enter adulthood with a great many hopes and goals. Then, as they settle into the daily round of activities, they tend to postpone their ambitions. Around the age of 40, some adults experience a **midlife transition,** *a reassessment of personal goals.* Up to this point, they had clung to the personal fable that their life would be a success in every way. There was always plenty of time to get that better job, start that family, write that great novel, take that trip up the Amazon, or get an advanced degree. But at some point, they begin to realize that the opportunity to make major life changes is rapidly fading.

The Russian novelist Leo Tolstoy wrote, at age 47:

> I have lived through the period of childhood, adolescence and youth when I climbed higher and higher up the mysterious hill of life, hoping to find at its summit a result worthy of the effort put in; I have also lived through the period of maturity during which, having reached the summit, I went on calmly and contentedly . . . searching all round me for the fruits of life which I had attained . . . and I have lived through the conviction that nothing of what I expected on this summit was there and that now, only one thing remained to me—to descend to the other side to the place where I came from. And I have begun that descent. . . . I call such a condition old age, and at the present moment I have reached that condition. [Tolstoy, 1875/1978, pp. 288–289.]

Daniel Levinson (1977, 1978) reports that about 80% of all adults experience such a midlife transition. Other psychologists deny that the prevalence of the experience is anywhere near that figure. But it may only be a matter of degree: Most middle-aged adults do not experience the distress that Tolstoy described, but many go through a minor, nontraumatic readjustment in which they review the direction that their life has been taking. When you are young, you have many goals and dreams of all the great things you will experience and accomplish. You know you are not achieving all of them, but you can tell yourself, "I'll do that later." As you get to middle age, you discover that you are running out of "later." Some of your earlier dreams are becoming unrealistic, but others are still achievable. But even if they are still achievable, you realize that time is passing: "What am I waiting for?"

The resolution of this midlife transition can take any of several directions. Some people accept their lives more or less as it is, abandon their unrealistic goals, and reset new goals that are consistent with the direction their lives have taken. Others decide that they had some earlier dreams that have not been achieved but that they are not willing to abandon. They quit their unsatisfactory jobs and go back to school, set up a business of their own, or do something else they had always wanted to try. The least satisfactory outcome is to decide, "I can't abandon my dreams, but I can't do anything about them either. I need to keep this job that I hate and press on with a life that has no joy."

The moral is clear: To increase your chances of feeling good in middle age and old age, make the right decisions now. If there is something you really care about, something you will feel bad about if you don't at least try it, get started on it now. Take chances on yourself. If you fail, well, at least you tried, and you won't always wonder what would have happened if you had only tried. Besides, in the process of trying to do what you want, you might discover a related opportunity that you would not have found otherwise. And you never know: You just might succeed.

Old Age

The percentage of people who live into their 70s and 80s has risen steadily throughout the 20th century. Their health has also improved, and so has their activity level and intellectual performance (Schaie, 1994). People age in different ways. Some people, especially those with Alzheimer's disease or other serious ailments, deteriorate both intellectually and physically—in some cases, quite rapidly. Other older people remain almost as active and alert as ever, well into their 80s or even 90s.

One common concern of old age is to maintain a sense of dignity and self-esteem. How well older people maintain their dignity depends largely on how they are treated by their family, their community, and their society (Figure 10.32). Some cultures, including the people of Korea, observe a special ceremony to celebrate a person's retirement or 70th birthday (Damron-Rodriguez, 1991). African-American and Native American families traditionally honor their elders, giving them a position of status in the family and calling upon them for advice. Japanese families follow a

FIGURE 10.32 In Tibet and many other cultures, children are taught to treat old people with respect and honor. Most older people say that maintaining a sense of dignity is very important to them.

similar tradition, at least publicly (Koyano, 1991). Dignity and self-esteem also depend upon a feeling of having lived life well. To feel dignity in old age, spend your time well in your youth.

As people age, they have to deal with changes in social status as well as changes in their bodies. Figure 10.33 shows the percentage of people in the United States who

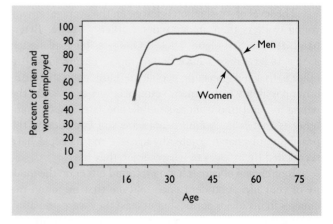

FIGURE 10.33 The percentage of people employed rises and falls as a function of age. These figures include students, patients in hospitals, and others who are not looking for a job. (Based on data from U.S. Department of Labor, 1989.)

are employed at various ages (U.S. Department of Labor, 1989). For about 40 to 50 years of life, people spend much of their time at work, taking pride and gaining prestige from their accomplishments. Then sometime between the ages of 60 and 70, they face voluntary or mandatory retirement. Many continue to be active, doing volunteer work, taking a part-time job . . . or serving as a U.S. senator. . . .

People adjust to retirement in different ways (Atchley, 1980). Those who were active and had a variety of interests before retirement usually find the adjustment easiest. Most retirees go through a "honeymoon" period at first, doing all the things they never had time to do before. However, their reborn hopes for great achievement soon fade. Just as many 20-year-olds start out with lofty goals that they can never achieve, many 65-year-olds enter retirement with unrealistic expectations. Before long, they review their prospects and revise their goals.

It is important for old people to maintain some sense of control over their lives, even if their health fails. Consider someone who has spent half a century managing a household or running a business, who is now living in a nursing home where staff members make all the decisions, from scheduling meals to choosing television programs. This loss of control can be both frustrating and degrading. When the nursing home staff leaves some of the choices up to the residents and lets them perform some tasks by themselves, their health, alertness, and memory tend to improve (Rodin, 1986; Rowe & Kahn, 1987).

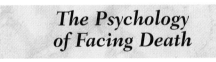

The Psychology of Facing Death

A man who has not found something he is willing to die for is not fit to live.

—MARTIN LUTHER KING, JR. (1964)

This is perhaps the greatest lesson we learned from our patients: LIVE, so you do not have to look back and say, "God, how I have wasted my life!"

—ELISABETH KÜBLER-ROSS (1975)

The worst thing about death is the fact that when a man is dead it's impossible any longer to undo the harm you have done him, or to do the good you haven't done him. They say: live in such a way as to be always ready to die. I would say: live in such a way that anyone can die without you having anything to regret.

—LEO TOLSTOY (1865/1978, p. 192)

We commonly associate death with older people, although a person can certainly die at any age. Not only do we have trouble dealing with the prospect of our own death, but we also find it difficult to deal with the death of others. Each society provides standards and guidance for how people should deal with the death of a loved one, and Western society has changed its standards over the last century. In the 1800s, the death of a spouse was expected to lead to a

Linda McCartney battled cancer for several years before her death in 1998. In the "acceptance" stage of facing death, people take a realistic approach to their impending death.

long-lasting, almost permanent grief. Today, society encourages people to try to return to normal functioning (Stroebe, Gergen, Gergen, & Stroebe, 1992). Most people need about a year to work through their grief, but the course of bereavement varies greatly from one person to another.

Most people deal with anxiety about their own death by telling themselves that death is far in the future. When they learn that they have a fatal disease, they react in many ways. Elisabeth Kübler-Ross (1969), in her book *On Death and Dying,* suggests that dying people go through five stages of adjustment, as listed below. Dying people can move from stage to stage in any order and sometimes skip some stages altogether.

- *Denial:* the refusal to accept the information about having an incurable condition. The person visits doctors, faith healers, and anyone else who promises a chance for recovery.
- *Anger:* rage at doctors, nurses, and relatives. One characteristic utterance is, "Why me?"
- *Bargaining:* promising good behavior in the future in return for recovery. Religious people often make promises to God; some people also try offering the doctor a special inducement.
- *Depression:* sadness about losing life. Some people become very depressed, but not all do.
- *Acceptance:* a readiness to die. People who reach this stage lose interest in most of what is happening around them.

SOMETHING TO THINK ABOUT

Do Kübler-Ross's stages apply only to people who are dying? Or do people react in similar fashion to lesser losses, such as a poor grade or being fired from a job? Have you ever had a personal experience when you went through some of the same stages? ✳

> ### THE MESSAGE
> ## Social and Emotional Issues Through the Life Span

People confront crises and issues at different ages, but whatever one does at one age strongly affects life at a subsequent age. A young child who fails to develop a sense of trust or autonomy, or an adolescent who fails to achieve a sense of identity, enters the next age with some catching up to do. A young adult who makes poor decisions about marriage and career—sometimes no decision at all is the worst decision—causes problems that may linger into middle age and beyond. People do recover from earlier problems: The point is simply that issues that we face at one age may persist to later stages of life. No stage of development is ever completely over.

SUMMARY

* *Cross-sectional and longitudinal studies.* Psychologists study development by means of cross-sectional studies, which examine people of different ages at the same time, and by means of longitudinal studies, which look at a single group of people at various times as they grow older. Each method has its advantages and disadvantages. (page 368.)

* *Cohort effects.* In some cases, a difference between young people and old people is not due to age itself but to a cohort effect: People born in one era differ from those born in a different era. (page 369)

* *Erikson's ages of development.* Erik Erikson described the human life span as a series of eight ages, each with its own social and emotional conflicts. (page 370)

* *Infant attachment.* The initial attachment of an infant to his or her mother depends on the comfort of physical contact rather than on being fed. Later, other kinds of parent-child contact become increasingly important for developing the infant's social behaviors. (page 371)

* *Parenting styles.* Different parenting styles are associated with varying behavior patterns in children; the nature of that association appears to vary across ethnic groups. (page 374)

* *Social development of children.* The social development of a child depends on the influences of other children, including brothers and sisters. (page 374)

* *Adolescent identity crisis.* Adolescents have to deal with an identity crisis, the question "Who am I?" Many experiment with several identities before deciding which one seems right. (page 375)

* *Adults' concerns.* One of the main concerns of adults is balancing the competing demands of family and career. For most adults, satisfaction with life is closely linked with their satisfaction on the job. Some adults experience a midlife transition and reevaluate their goals. (page 377)

* *Old age.* In old age, people make new adjustments, including the adjustment to retirement. Maintaining dignity and independence is a key concern. (page 378)

* *Facing death.* People at all ages must face the anxieties associated with the inevitability of death. People go through some characteristic reactions when they know that they are likely to die soon. (page 379)

Suggestions for Further Reading

Elkind, D. (1984). *All grown up and no place to go.* Reading, MA: Addison-Wesley. An account of the problems that teenagers and young adults face.

Kail, R. V., & Cavanaugh, J. C. (1996). *Human development.* Pacific Grove, CA: Brooks/Cole. A good textbook on all aspects of developmental psychology.

Terms

cross-sectional study   a study of groups of individuals of different ages all at the same time (page 368)

longitudinal study   a study of a single group of individuals over time (page 368)

selective attrition   the tendency of some kinds of people to be more likely than others to drop out of a study (page 369)

cohort   a group of people born at a particular time (as compared to people born at different times) (page 369)

basic trust versus mistrust   the conflict between trusting and mistrusting that parents and other key figures will meet one's basic needs; the first conflict in Erikson's eight ages of human development (page 370)

autonomy versus shame and doubt   the conflict between independence and doubt about one's abilities (page 370)

initiative versus guilt   the conflict between independent behavior and behavior inhibited by guilt (page 370)

industry versus inferiority   the conflict between feelings of accomplishment and feelings of worthlessness (page 370)

identity versus role confusion   the conflict of discovering who one is or will be (page 371)

intimacy versus isolation   the conflict between spending one's life with a partner and living alone (page 371)

generativity versus stagnation   the conflict between a productive life and an unproductive one (page 371)

ego integrity versus despair   the conflict between satisfaction and dissatisfaction with one's life; the final conflict in Erikson's eight ages of human development (page 371)

attachment   a long-term feeling of closeness between people, such as a child and a caregiver (page 371)

Strange Situation   procedure in which a psychologist observes an infant's behavior in an unfamiliar room when the mother leaves and returns (page 373)

authoritative parents   those who are demanding and impose firm controls, but who are also warm and responsive to the child's communications (page 374)

authoritarian parents   those who exert firm controls on their children, generally without explaining the reasons for the rules and without providing much warmth (page 374)

permissive parents   those who are warm and loving but undemanding (page 374)

indifferent or uninvolved parents   those who pay little attention to their children beyond doing what is necessary to feed and shelter them (page 374)

identity crisis   concerns with decisions about the future and the quest for self-understanding (page 375)

identity diffusion   the condition of having not yet given any serious thought to identity decisions and having no clear sense of identity (page 376)

identity moratorium   the state of seriously considering one's identity without yet having made any decisions (page 376)

identity foreclosure   the state of having made firm identity decisions without having thought much about them (page 376)

identity achievement   the outcome of having explored various possible identities and then making one's own decisions (page 376)

midlife transition   a time of goal reassessment (page 377)

Answers to Concept Checks

5. Use a longitudinal study. A longitudinal study studies the same people repeatedly instead of comparing one cohort with another. (page 369)

6. Use a cross-sectional study, comparing people of different ages all in the same year. (page 370)

7. Another possible explanation is that the first-year students who have the lowest grades (and therefore pull down the grade average for first-year students) do not stay in school long enough to become seniors. (page 370)

Web Resources

The Child Psychologist

www.childpsychology.com/

Rene Thomas Folse's site focuses on "Specific Disorders and Other Reasons for Concern" about the behavior of children, and on "Treatment, Resources and Remediation." There are links to information about several specific diagnostic tests used with children.

MODULE 10.4

Growing Up the Same and Different: Temperament, Family, Gender, and Cultural Influences

Do people's temperamental differences remain consistent as they grow older?

How does family life guide children's social and emotional development?

How do boys and girls differ, and why?

How does ethnic identity influence development?

If you had to describe yourself in 200 words or less, what would you say? You would probably mention your age, whether you are male or female, where you live, your main interests and activities, and something about your family. You might mention your political or religious affiliation, if these are important to you. Would you also mention your ethnic identity? Some would; some would not.

The point is this: You are a unique individual, and you are also a member of various identifiable groups. Your group memberships mold what you think of yourself and how other people treat you. You are a complex product of both what you bring to a situation (your personality and temperament) and how a situation affects you. Let's begin with temperament.

Temperament and Lifelong Development

People differ markedly in their **temperament**—their *tendency to be either active or inactive, outgoing or reserved.* Would you rather go to a party where you will meet new

people, or would you prefer to spend a quiet evening with a few old friends? Do you like to try a new, somewhat risky adventure, or would you prefer to watch while someone else tries it first? In general, are you more impulsive or more reserved than most of the people you know?

Now, consider how you just described yourself: Is that the way you have always been, more or less? Or have you changed considerably? Were you at one time a great deal more outgoing and adventurous, or more shy and reserved, than you are now?

According to the research, most people are fairly consistent in their temperament over long periods of time. We can begin to measure temperament even before birth. During the last two months before birth, infants differ substantially in the amount of kicking and other movements, and the ones that are most active before birth tend to remain the most active after birth (Eaton & Saudino, 1992).

Jerome Kagan and Nancy Snidman (1991) measured how often 4-month-old infants kicked, how often they cried, and how tense their hands were. A few months later, they examined the same infants' responses to mildly frightening situations. (For example, the experimenter might uncover a rotating toy, frown, and scream a nonsense phrase.) Infants who showed the most kicking, crying, and tension at the age of 4 months also tended to show the most fears at the ages of 9 and 14 months. That is, their temperaments were consistent from one test to the next.

CONCEPT CHECK

8. Was Kagan and Snidman's study longitudinal or cross-sectional? (Check your answer on page 388.)

Infants who seldom kick, cry, or display fear are called "easy" or "uninhibited" (Thomas & Chess, 1980; Thomas, Chess, & Birch, 1968). Easy infants develop regular sleeping and eating habits, show interest in new people and new objects, and are easily comforted. The kicking, crying, highly fearful infants are, as you might guess, termed "difficult" or "inhibited." Their eating and sleeping habits are irregular, they show frequent signs of tension, and they are hard to comfort (Kagan, 1989). These infants are also more likely to contract various contagious diseases (Lewis, Thomas, & Worobey, 1990). Evidently, temperament is connected to all aspects of how the body functions. Not all infants fit into either the "inhibited" or "uninhibited" categories; many are

Most people's temperaments remain fairly consistent over time. An outgoing, uninhibited child will probably continue to be outgoing and uninhibited for years, perhaps even into adulthood.

intermediate. Some fit a special category called "slow to warm up": They withdraw at first from unfamiliar people and new experiences, but after repeated exposures they begin to react positively.

How long do infant temperaments last? The answer varies. Infants identified as highly inhibited at the age of 21 months are more likely than others to end up as shy, quiet, nervous, and fearful 7½-year-olds (Kagan, Reznick, & Snidman, 1988). Similarly, many uninhibited infants develop into socially interactive, highly talkative 7½-year-olds. However, major changes occur, too; about 10% of *uninhibited* infants develop into shy 7½-year-olds (Kagan, 1989).

What causes differences in temperament? Genetic differences make some contributions. Monozygotic (identical) twins resemble each other in temperament more than dizygotic (fraternal) twins do (Matheny, 1989). Monozygotic twins reared in separate and apparently rather different environments still generally end up with similar temperaments (Bouchard, Lykken, McGue, Segal, & Tellegen, 1990). Environmental factors obviously play a major role also; otherwise, monozygotic twins would always exactly match each other in temperament.

Heredity and environment can interact in some complex ways to influence temperament. Furthermore, a child's developing temperament can alter the environment, which in turn influences the further development of temperament (Bouchard et al., 1990; Collins & Gunnar, 1990). For example, a child with an uninhibited temperament will meet more people and try more new experiences than an inhibited child will; while doing so, the child learns new skills and develops new behaviors that can alter later reactions to new situations.

The Family

One of the most powerful influences in the human environment is the family. Children in a loving family gain a sense of security and learn, "I am a lovable person." By playing with brothers, sisters, or other children, they begin to learn social skills. They also learn social skills by observation, especially by watching how their parents relate to each other. How do variations in early family environments affect a child's social and emotional development?

Parental Employment and Child Care

Many people assume that the "normal" way of rearing infants is for the mother to stay with them full-time, because that custom was prevalent in much of North America and Europe for many years. However, child-rearing customs vary greatly from one culture to another, one era to another, even from one social class to another (see Figure 10.34). In many cultures, especially subsistence cultures, a mother returns to her usual tasks of gathering food and so forth shortly after giving birth, leaving her infant most of the day

F I G U R E 10.34 In many cultures, it has long been the custom for a mother to leave her infant for much of the day with friends, relatives, and other children. An infant with multiple caregivers can develop just as healthy emotional and social behaviors as one having a single caregiver.

with other women, relatives, and any older children in the family (McGurk, Caplan, Hennessy, & Moss, 1993). For example, in the Efe culture of Africa, a mother stays with her infant only about half of the day, but the infant is seldom alone. Within the first few months, the infant will establish strong attachments to several adults and children (Tronick, Morelli, & Ivey, 1992). In wealthy families in Europe, it has long been the custom for "nannies" (paid caregivers) to take care of the children for most of the day.

Still, many psychologists in Europe and North America developed a theoretical belief that healthy emotional development required an infant to establish a strong attachment to a single caregiver—ordinarily, the mother. When more and more families began placing infants in day care so that both parents could return to work shortly after their infant's birth, a question arose about whether those children would be psychologically harmed.

The research on day care indicates that children from good homes generally develop satisfactorily, both intellectually and socially, if they receive at least adequate day care (Scarr, 1998). The quality of the day care makes a greater difference for children from disadvantaged homes. (Evidently, development is satisfactory when either home life or day care is good; problems arise when both are bad.) When children from disadvantaged homes get good day care (with a consistent, affectionate staff and adequate facilities), they develop better than if they had stayed at home (McGurk et al., 1993; Scarr, Phillips, & McCartney,

1990). Children from deprived homes who also get poor day care—which is often all the parents can afford—are at a definite disadvantage.

The most enduring controversy has concerned the effects of starting day care before a child is 1 year old. Several studies have reported that children who attend day care for 20 hours or more per week during the first year of their life fail to develop a secure relationship with their mothers, as measured in the Strange Situation (discussed earlier). However, the problem may be in the measurement (McGurk et al., 1993). Remember, in the Strange Situation, the mother leaves the infant in a room with a stranger and later returns; an infant who does not greet her return eagerly is considered to have an avoidant relationship. But think about this situation from the standpoint of an infant who is left in day care 5 days per week: Your mother has frequently left you in a room with a stranger before. Now she has done it again. Every time she left you in the past, you have been safe and well cared for; so, it's no big deal. When she returns three minutes later . . . perhaps the main surprise is that she came back so soon.

In other words, failing to greet the mother on her return might have different implications for an infant accustomed to day care than it does for an infant accustomed to spending all day with the mother. The research to date does not document that day care harms the infant's social development, provided that the day care is of good quality. (Unfortunately, of course, affordable good-quality day care is often hard to find.)

Nontraditional Families

The "traditional" family consists of a mother, a father, and their children. Many people who grew up in a reasonably happy traditional family think of such an arrangement as so "right" that anything else must be wrong.

Nevertheless, most children grow up in families that are significantly different from the traditional model. For example, psychologists have studied the children of unmarried mothers (Weissman, Leaf, & Bruce, 1987), children reared by a gay or lesbian couple (Patterson, 1994), and children of families where the mother works full-time and the father stays home with the children (Parke, 1995). Parenting styles do differ a bit; for example, fathers generally play with their children more and talk to them less. However, the usual finding is that children in nontraditional families turn out about the same as those from more traditional families. Many of the differences that do emerge are due to economics: Most unmarried mothers have very limited finances and cannot provide their children with the same opportunities that middle-class children have.

Parental Conflict and Divorce

At an earlier time in the United States, divorce was unusual and frowned upon. When Adlai Stevenson was defeated in the presidential campaign of 1952, one explanation given was that American voters would never elect a divorced candidate as president. By 1980, when Ronald Reagan was elected president, hardly anyone considered his divorce and remarriage to be an issue at all. By then, divorce was simply a fact of life.

An estimated 75% of African-American children and 38% of European-American children will experience the divorce of their parents before the children reach the age of 16. Most of those children show a variety of academic, social, and emotional problems, compared to children in two-parent households. One reason is that the children of divorced families receive less attention and suffer greater economic hardship. The main reason, however, is that children in divorced families often endure the prolonged conflict and hostility between their parents (Amato & Keith, 1991). If the divorce takes place while the children are still too young to realize what is happening, the effects on the children will be milder (Tschann, Johnston, Kline, & Wallerstein, 1990).

Mavis Hetherington and her associates have conducted longitudinal studies of middle-class, elementary-school children and their families following a divorce (Hetherington, 1989; Hetherington, Cox, & Cox, 1982). In each case, the mother had custody of the children. Hetherington found that most of the children and many of the parents suffered considerable upheaval after the divorce, especially during the first year.

During this first year, the children resorted to pouting and other forms of seeking attention. They were generally angry about their parents' divorce, and they let the parents know about it. Many of the divorced mothers had very difficult relationships with their sons; one exasperated divorced mother described their relationship as "like getting bitten to death by ducks." Boys in particular became very aggressive toward other children, and much of their aggressive behavior was unprovoked and ineffective (Figure 10.35). After 2 years following the divorce, these boys became better adjusted, but by then they had been rejected by their peers.

FIGURE 10.35 Sons of divorced parents often go through a period when they act out their frustrations by starting fights.

Boys who changed schools after the first year managed to escape their reputation and make a fresh start.

The degree of distress varied from one child to another. Generally, a child's distress was greater if the mother had not worked before the divorce and had taken a job immediately afterward—often an economic necessity. The children in such families felt that they had lost both parents. In the studies by Hetherington and her associates, boys showed more distress and more negative behavior than girls did, partly because the mothers retained custody of the children. When the father had custody, the boys reacted better than the girls did (Santrock, Warshak, & Elliott, 1982). (Because many other factors are at work, we cannot conclude, however, that a father should always be granted custody of sons or that a mother should always be granted custody of daughters.)

In families where the mother remarried, the children—especially the girls—were often indifferent or hostile to the stepfather and showed poorer adjustment than children of mothers who did not remarry (Hetherington, Bridges, & Insabella, 1998). Many of the girls rejected every attempt their stepfathers made to establish a positive relationship, until eventually the stepfather simply gave up (Hetherington, 1989). When stepfathers were asked to name "all the members of your family," most did not even mention their stepdaughters.

Hetherington's studies concentrated on European-American, middle-class children, and the results are somewhat different for other cultures. Divorce is more common in African-American families, but in most cases it is more accepted and less stressful (Fine & Schwebel, 1987). Many African-American families ease the burden of single parenthood by having a grandmother or other relative share in the child care. As in European-American families, the more upset the mother is by the divorce, the more upset the children are likely to be (Phillips & Alcebo, 1986).

Exceptions can be found to almost any generalization about the effects of divorce on children, however (Hetherington, Stanley-Hagan, & Anderson, 1989). Some children show emotional distress for a year or two and then gradually feel better. Others continue to act depressed 5 or 10 years after the divorce. A few seem to do well for a while and then show signs of distress years later, especially during adolescence. Other children are amazingly resilient throughout their parents' divorce and afterward. They keep their friends; they do all right in school; they maintain good relationships with both parents. Generally, these children were well-adjusted before the divorce, and their parents displayed a minimum of conflict toward each other (Hetherington, 1989; Kline, Tschann, Johnston, & Wallerstein, 1989).

Given the emotional trauma commonly associated with divorce, should parents stay together "for the children's sake"? The answer depends on how serious the parents' conflicts are. Children who grow up in households where the parents are constantly angry or distressed develop emotional problems similar to those of the children of divorced families

(Emery, 1982). Indeed, most children (especially boys) in divorced families begin to show signs of distress years *before* the divorce itself, perhaps in response to the parental conflict they already experience (Cherlin et al., 1991).

The Influence of Gender

How would you be different if you had been born female instead of male, or male instead of female? We all have certain impressions of how boys act differently from girls, and men from women. But how many of those impressions are correct, how many are exaggerations, and how many are simply false? Remember the phenomenon of *illusory correlations* from Chapter 2: We tend to remember most clearly the examples that fit a pattern we expect to find; therefore, we convince ourselves that our expectations were correct. Sex differences do occur, but we must base our conclusions on systematic data and not on casual impressions.

Sex Differences in Behavior

In 1974, Eleanor Maccoby and Carol Jacklin published an extensive review of the literature on sex differences in behavior. They concluded that the evidence supported a few generalizations. For example, females tend to perform better on certain aspects of language use, whereas males tend to perform better on certain mathematical and visual-spatial tasks. These differences are marked in adolescents and adults but questionable in children. Also, males tend to fight more. Sex differences in other aspects of behavior were possible but not clear from the evidence (Maccoby & Jacklin, 1974).

Maccoby and Jacklin's review drew two kinds of criticisms. First, some argued that they had either ignored or understated many behavioral differences between the sexes: On the average, men swear more than women. Women tend to know more than men do about flowers. Men and women generally carry books and packages in different ways (Figure 10.36). The list of miscellaneous differences could go on and on.

Secondly, others argued that Maccoby and Jacklin had overstated the differences and that in fact the behavior of males and females hardly differs at all. According to this point of view, boys and girls—and men and women—act differently only because our society tells them to. (Actually, even if this idea is true, it is not a fair criticism of Maccoby and Jacklin, who were trying to describe the differences, not explain them.)

Much time has passed since Maccoby and Jacklin's 1974 review. Most of the same conclusions still hold, although we must modify them somewhat (Maccoby, 1990). For example, the female advantage on verbal tasks seems to have faded (for unknown reasons). Also, it now appears that women are, on the average, more easily influenced by other people's opinions. (Depending on your point of view, you

FIGURE 10.36 One of many poorly understood differences between the sexes: Beyond the age of puberty, most males carry packages at their side, whereas females carry them in an elevated position.

Sex Differences in Social Situations It is now clear that certain important differences between males and females emerge only in a social context (Maccoby, 1990). Psychologists ordinarily test people in isolation. When tested one at a time, boys and girls tend to behave about the same in most regards. However, in a group setting, boys usually get together with other boys and girls get together with other girls; suddenly, the two groups act very differently (Figure 10.37).

Girls sometimes play competitive games, but they are more likely than boys to spend long times at quiet, cooperative play. They take turns; they present their desires as "suggestions" instead of demands; they exchange compliments; and they generally try to avoid hurting each other's feelings.

Meanwhile, boys are almost always competing with each other. They compete even when they are just talking: They shout orders, they interrupt, they make threats and boasts, and they exchange insults. Their play is often rough and aggressive and almost always competitive. When a group of elementary-school boys play a game, sooner or later they will have a dispute about the rules; invariably, they work out a compromise and continue playing, but they may continue screaming "you cheater!" or "you liar!" while they play. Still, when the game is over, they almost always part as friends.

When boys grow up, do they change their ways of interacting with one another? Not entirely. Deborah Tannen (1990) reports one episode at a college basketball game: At the University of Michigan, student tickets have seat numbers on them, but students generally ignore those assignments and take seats on a first-come, first-served basis. One night, several men from the visiting team, Michigan State, tried to go to the seats listed on their tickets, only to find some University of Michigan students, both men and women, already seated there. The Michigan State students

could say that women are more conformist or more flexible and that men are more independent or more stubborn.) Males and females also differ in helping behavior. It is not a simple case of one sex being more helpful than the other; men and women tend to help in different ways. For example, men are generally more likely to help a stranger change a flat tire; women are more likely to help people who need long-term nurturing support (Eagly & Crowley, 1986).

FIGURE 10.37 One girl tested alone behaves about the same as one boy tested alone. But when boys play together, they "show off" to one another and to other observers; girls play more cooperatively.

asked the others to get out of their seats; the men in those seats then replied rudely, and the dispute quickly grew loud, heated, and insulting. The women were mortified with embarrassment.

Within a few minutes, however, the Michigan State men settled into seats next to the University of Michigan students, and before long the two groups of men were happily discussing basketball strategies. The women didn't understand why the men had screamed insults in the first place or why they had made friends so quickly afterward.

Male-Female Relationships in Childhood and Adulthood   What do you suppose happens when boys and girls play together? If they are working on a task that requires cooperation, few sex differences are evident (Powlishta & Maccoby, 1990). However, in an unsupervised situation with no need to cooperate, the boys often dominate and intimidate the girls. In some cases, the boys take control and the girls simply watch (Maccoby, 1990).

When boys and girls become young men and women, romantic interests may draw them together, but both are ill prepared to deal with the other sex. Men are used to demanding what they want; women are used to a cooperative give-and-take. Men worry about their status in relation to other men; women often fail to understand these status contests. When women discuss their problems, they expect their listeners to express sympathy; men often fail to understand this need. Here are some examples of the resultant misunderstanding (Tannen, 1990):

• A man invites an out-of-town friend to spend the night in the guest bedroom. The man's wife is upset that her husband did not check with her before inviting his friend. He replies that he would feel embarrassed to say, "I have to ask my wife first."

• A woman asks her husband to get their VCR to record a TV movie. The husband says this particular kind of VCR plays tapes but cannot record. The woman then asks their next-door neighbor to check the VCR. He too tells her the VCR cannot record. The husband feels resentful about this episode for years, because his wife implied that he was too incompetent to understand their VCR.

• A woman who has had breast surgery tells her husband she is unhappy about the scar left by the surgery. Instead of expressing sympathy, he replies, "You can have plastic surgery. . . ." She is upset by the implication that he doesn't like the way she looks. He replies that he doesn't care about the scar; he was trying to help because *she* said she was unhappy.

Are male-female relationships always like this? Of course not. There are many differences *on the average* between men and women, just as there are between 25-year-olds and 20-year-olds or between Northerners and Southerners, or between almost any other identifiable groups. The distributions may overlap completely; therefore, the discussion of averages may not tell us what to expect from a given individual.

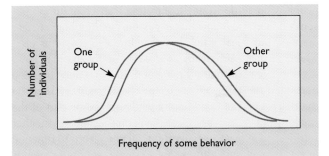

Frequency of some behavior

Ethnic and Cultural Influences

Membership in a minority group molds a child's development in two major ways: First, the customs of the minority group may in fact differ from those of other groups. For example, many Japanese parents put great emphasis on educational achievement and bringing honor to one's family (Yamamoto & Kubota, 1983). Secondly, members of a minority group are affected by the attitudes of other people, who may treat them differently or expect certain behaviors from them simply because they are members of that minority group.

Immigrants to the United States or any other country undergo a period of **acculturation**, *a transition from feeling part of the culture of their original country to the culture of the country they enter.* Acculturation is gradual; people sometimes require a generation or more before they or their descendants feel fully comfortable in a new culture.

In many cases, a person may have to function as a member of two or more cultures or subcultures. For example,

Many immigrants are bicultural, having reasonable familiarity with two sets of customs. These Asian immigrants to Australia adopt some Australian customs while maintaining some of their own.

people who settle in an Italian-American community may speak Italian and follow Italian customs in their home neighborhood but speak English and follow U.S. customs elsewhere. African-Americans and Asian-Americans may identify strongly with their ethnic group, live in a neighborhood populated mostly by others of the same group, and rely on the help of an extended family, while also being part of the "melting pot" U.S. culture at school, on the job, and in other settings. To at least a small extent, all of us learn to function in a variety of subcultures. For example, you enter slightly different subcultures at home, at college, on the job, at a religious ceremony, and so forth. You learn to adjust what you say and do depending on the setting and the people present. Although everyone has this experience to some extent, the transitions are more noticeable and more intense for ethnic minority members.

People react to these transitions in different ways. Some minority group members become more or less completely assimilated into the majority or melting-pot culture. However, they may pay a price for doing so. For example, some high-achieving, African-American students worry that their school and occupational success may alienate them from other African-Americans—that "if you succeed, you're betraying your color" (Fordham, 1988).

One alternative to full assimilation is **biculturalism,** *the ability to alternate between membership in one culture and membership in another.* Although doing so is difficult, many people succeed. The advantages of biculturalism are similar to those of bilingualism: A bilingual person (one who speaks two languages) can communicate with more people and read a greater variety of literature than can a monolingual person. Also, bilingual people come to understand their primary language from a new perspective and often become more sensitive to the multiple meanings of a word. Similarly, a bicultural person can speak with and interact with a great variety of other people and can become more aware of both the strengths and the weaknesses of each culture (Harrison, Wilson, Pine, Chan, & Buriel, 1990; LaFromboise, Coleman, & Gerton, 1993).

THE MESSAGE
Understanding and Accepting Many Ways of Life

Each of us can easily fall into the trap of thinking that our own way of growing up and relating to other people is the "right" or "normal" way. In fact, people differ substantially in their social development; we have examined some of the major reasons for this difference—temperament, family influences, gender, and ethnic and cultural identity. As a society, we are beginning to recognize and appreciate the resulting diversity of behavior that these influences create.

SUMMARY

* *Temperament.* Even infants who are only a few months old show clear differences in temperament, their own characteristic way of reacting to new experiences and new people. Temperament remains fairly consistent as a person grows older. (page 382)

* *Changes in the U.S. family.* As U.S. society has changed over the decades, the role of women has changed, and therefore family life has also changed. The research suggests that children who spend much of their early life in a day-care arrangement can develop without difficulties, provided that the day care is of good quality. Most children in nontraditional families develop normally, except for the effects of the poverty that is common among unmarried mothers. (page 383)

* *Effects of divorce.* Children of divorcing families often show signs of distress, sometimes even before the divorce. The distress is generally more marked in European-American families than in African-American families. (page 384)

* *Male-female differences.* Behavioral differences between males and females are small, on the average, when people are tested one at a time. However, in social settings males tend to associate with other males while females associate with females. Males tend to be more competitive, sometimes aggressively so. (page 385)

* *Ethnic and cultural differences.* People also differ because of ethnic and cultural influences. Acculturation is the process of transition from one culture to another. Many people can function successfully as members of two or more cultures simultaneously. (page 387)

Suggestions for Further Reading

Hetherington, E. M. (1989). Coping with family transitions: Winners, losers, and survivors. *Child Development, 60,* 1–14. Review of the effects of divorce on children.

Maccoby, E. E. (1990). Gender and relationships. *American Psychologist, 45,* 513–520. Review of findings concerning sex differences in social behavior.

Tannen, D. (1990). *You just don't understand.* New York: William Morrow. A popular book that discusses the various reasons that men and women often fail to understand one another.

Terms

temperament   people's tendency to be either active or inactive, outgoing or reserved (page 382)

acculturation   a transition from feeling part of the culture of one's original country to the culture of the country that one enters (page 387)

biculturalism   the ability to alternate between membership in one culture and membership in another (page 388)

Answer to Concept Check

8. Kagan and Snidman's study was longitudinal; they studied the same children at different ages. (page 382)

Web Resources

American Demographics

www.demographics.com/

American Demographics Magazine uses U.S. Census Bureau
   statistics to describe consumer trends for business leaders.
   Search the archives, using such search terms as *divorce,
   diversity, personality, gender,* or whatever else is of interest to
   you to find articles about trends in these topics.

Motivation

During the summer of 1996, the proprietors of London's Kew Gardens announced that they had a most unusual plant, native to Sumatra and rarely cultivated elsewhere, which was about to bloom for the first time since 1963. So, if you had been in London then, with enough time available, would you have made a point of visiting Kew Gardens to witness this rare, once-or-twice-in-a-lifetime event? No? What if I told you that it was a truly beautiful flower? with a lovely, sweet smell? Still no?

Then, what if I told you the truth—that it has the nastiest, most obnoxious smell of any flower on Earth—that the name of the flower is the *stinking lily,* because it smells like a huge, week-old carcass of rotting meat or fish . . . and that one whiff of it can make a strong person retch. Now would you want to go visit the flower? If so, you would have to wait in line. When Kew Gardens announced that the stinking lily was about to bloom, an enormous crowd gathered, forming a line that stretched to the length of a soccer field (MacQuitty, 1996). (The first day that the flower bloomed, it had hardly begun to stink. Disappointed visitors vowed to return later.)

Human motivations are surprising, puzzling, and often seemingly illogical. Psychologists have made progress in understanding complex motivated behaviors, but much still remains to be learned. We begin this chapter with an overview of some general principles of motivation. Then, we shall explore three examples of motivated behaviors: hunger, sexual activity, and striving for achievement.

These examples of motivation deserve emphasis largely because they are each an important part of human life, but also because they illustrate how our biology interacts with our social setting. Hunger is based on a biological need, but what, when, and how much we eat also depends on what we learn from other people. Sexual motivation also serves a biological need, but the search for a suitable partner is a complex social behavior. Striving for achievement is learned as a method of pleasing and impressing others. Although it is primarily a social motivation, it is also an outgrowth of the competition for dominance that we can observe throughout the animal kingdom.

There are good reasons why this flower is seldom cultivated outside its native Sumatra. Would you stand in line to visit it?

MODULE 11.1

General Principles of Motivation

What is motivation?

How could a psychologist determine whether an act is motivated?

$\mathbf{Y}$ou are sitting quietly, reading a book, when suddenly you hear a loud noise. You jump a little and gasp. Was that

was an accident." Your friend, who promised to drive you somewhere and then left without you, says, "I didn't do it on purpose. I just forgot." Maybe so and maybe not. How can we determine whether a behavior is motivated or accidental, intentional or unintentional? We need a clear understanding of how motivated behaviors differ from unmotivated behaviors.

General Properties of Motivated Behavior

What, if anything, do the various types of motivated behavior have in common? The foremost characteristic of motivated behaviors is that they are goal directed. Highly motivated individuals persist with a behavior or alter their behavior until they reach their goal; they frequently set up subgoals that they will need to achieve on the way to their final goal (Austin & Vancouver, 1996). For example, if you were motivated to improve your house, you might make a list of the items that need repair and then determine the tools needed for each repair:

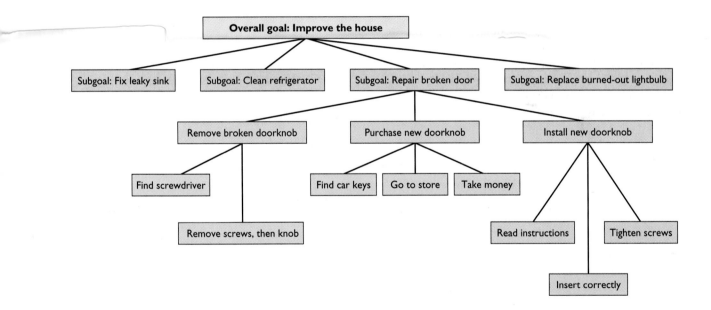

action motivated? "No," you say. "I jumped involuntarily." Now I tell you that I want to do a little experiment. I shall tap my pencil; as soon as you hear it, you should try to jump and gasp just as you did the first time. I tap my pencil and, sure enough, you jump and gasp. Was that action motivated? "Yes," you reply.

So, what appears to be approximately the same behavior can be motivated at one time and unmotivated at another time. Can we trust people to tell us whether their behavior was motivated or unmotivated? Not always. Someone accused of murder says, "I didn't mean to kill him. It

To determine whether a particular behavior is motivated, as opposed to automatic or reflexive, an observer needs to watch an individual over a period of time in a variety of circumstances. If the individual varies the behavior at different times and persists until reaching a goal, then the behavior is motivated, or intentional.

SOMETHING TO THINK ABOUT

A frog flicks its tongue at a passing insect, captures it, and swallows it. The behavior serves to satisfy the frog's need for

393

food, so we might guess that it is motivated. However, the behavior appears to be as constant as a reflex. How might you determine whether this behavior is motivated? ✷

A second characteristic of motivated behaviors is that they vary from time to time and from one individual to another, under the influence of both internal (biological) and external (social) controls. For example, you wear different clothes from one day to the next, and you wear different clothes from your roommate on any given day.

Views of Motivation

What is motivation? Let's try some definitions: "Motivation is what activates and directs behavior." That description fits many examples well enough, but it also fits other, nonmotivational phenomena. For example, light activates and directs the growth of plants, but we would hardly say that light motivates plants.

"Motivation is what makes our behavior more vigorous and energetic." The problem with that definition is that some people are strongly motivated to lie motionless for hours on end.

How about this: "Motivation is what changes one's preferences or choices"? That might do, except that we would first have to define preference and choice.

Frankly, it is hard to state precisely what we mean by motivation. Psychologists have repeatedly altered their views of motivation. By considering one theory after another, they have seen the shortcomings of each and have in the process developed some idea of what motivation is and is not.

Motivation as an Energy

Motivation, which comes from the same root as *motion,* is literally something that "moves" a person. So, we might think of it as a type of energy. According to Konrad Lorenz (1950), a pioneer in the study of animal behavior, animals engage in instinctive acts when specific energies reach a critical level. For example, a male stickleback fish has no specific energy for mating outside the breeding season, so it will not respond sexually. At the start of the breeding season, it has a small amount of mating energy, and it will then court female stickleback fish and attack male stickleback fish. At the height of the breeding season, it has a great amount of mating energy, so it will court females vigorously; it may even respond sexually to a piece of wood painted to resemble a female of its species.

Figure 11.1 illustrates Lorenz's model. A specific kind of energy builds up in the reservoir and flows into the tray below. The outlets in that tray represent ways of releasing this energy. If conditions are right, the energy is released through the lowest outlet—for example, mating with a

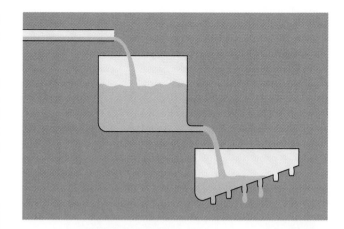

FIGURE 11.1   According to Konrad Lorenz, energy (represented as a fluid) builds up in a "reservoir" in the brain and needs to be discharged. Ordinarily, an instinct is released through natural or preferred outlets. If those outlets are blocked, however, energy spills over into another outlet, and the animal engages in an unrelated behavior. (After Lorenz, 1950.)

normal partner. If that outlet is blocked and energy continues to build up, the energy will spill through one of the higher, less preferred outlets. However, Lorenz's theories reflect an obsolete conception of how the nervous system works. He believed that every impulse to action had to be carried out, so that if one response was blocked, the energy would activate something else. We now know that an individual can simply inhibit the impulses toward disadvantageous behavior.

Drive Theories

Related to the instinctive energy theories are theories that describe motivation as a **drive,** *a state of unrest or irritation that energizes one behavior after another until one of them removes the irritation* (Hull, 1943). For example, when you get a splinter in your finger, the discomfort motivates you to engage in various actions until you get rid of the splinter.

According to the *drive-reduction theory* that was popular among psychologists of an earlier era, animals including humans strive to reduce their needs and drives as much as possible. That is, they eat to reduce their hunger, drink to reduce their thirst, have sexual activity to reduce their sex drive, and so forth. This view implies that we all strive for a state where all our needs have been met, at which time we would become inactive. The primary shortcoming of this view is that, in fact, most people seek variety and activity in life; the ideal state is one with a moderate amount of stimulation, not one with as little as possible.

Another flaw in this drive theory is that it ignores the role of external stimulation. For example, a person's interest in food depends not only on hunger (an internal drive) but also on what foods are available. Similarly, interest in sex depends partly on an internal drive and partly on the presence or absence of a suitable partner.

Homeostasis

One important advance upon the idea of drive reduction is the concept of **homeostasis,** *the maintenance of an optimum level of biological conditions within an organism* (Cannon, 1929). The idea of homeostasis recognizes that we are motivated to seek a state of equilibrium, not to reduce all stimuli to zero. For example, people maintain a nearly constant body temperature through a combination of physiological and behavioral means. We fight against both increases and decreases in body temperature. Each of us also works to maintain a fairly steady body weight, a nearly constant amount of water in the body, a reasonably stable level of sensory stimulation, and so on.

Unlike a rock, which remains static only because nothing is acting upon it, the homeostasis of the body is more like a spinning top; someone must apply additional energy from time to time to keep it spinning. For example, we maintain constant body temperature partly by shivering, sweating, and other involuntary physiological responses and partly by putting on extra clothing, taking off excess clothing, or finding a more comfortable location.

Human motivated behaviors differ from the actions of a thermostat in one important regard: Our behavior often anticipates future needs. For example, you might eat a large breakfast one morning, even though you are not terribly hungry, just because you know you are going to be too busy to stop for lunch. If you are angry or frightened, you begin to sweat even before you begin the vigorous actions that might heat up your body. (We call this phenomenon a "cold sweat.") Thus, one fruitful way of describing motivation is that it maintains current homeostasis and anticipates future needs to maintain future homeostasis (Appley, 1991).

Still, even that conception of motivation overlooks the power of new stimuli to arouse motivated behaviors. For example, nonhungry people may eat or drink just to be sociable or because someone has offered them something especially tasty.

Incentive Theories

Why do people ride roller coasters? It is doubtful that they have any special need to go thundering down a steep decline. Or suppose you have just finished a big meal and someone offers you a slice of a very special cake. If you are like most people, you eat it but not because you need it. Evidently, motivation includes more than the internal forces that push us toward certain behaviors; it also includes **incentives**—*external stimuli that pull us toward certain actions.*

The distinction between a drive and an incentive is not clear-cut. Jumping into a swimming pool on a hot summer day may satisfy your biological drive to maintain normal body temperature, but the prospect of splashing around in the water may serve as a strong incentive as well.

Most motivated behaviors are controlled by a combination of drives and incentives. You eat because you are hungry (a drive) and because you see appealing food in front of you (an incentive). How much you eat depends on both the strength of the drive and the appeal of the incentive.

Intrinsic and Extrinsic Motivations

Similar to the distinction between drives and incentives, psychologists also distinguish between intrinsic and extrinsic motivations. An **intrinsic motivation** is *a motivation to engage in an act for its own sake;* an **extrinsic motivation** is *based on the reinforcements and punishments that the act may bring.* For example, if you eat because you are hungry, you are following an intrinsic motivation; if you eat something you don't like just to please the cook, you are following an extrinsic motivation. Most behaviors follow a combination of both kinds of motivation. For instance, an artist paints partly for the joy of creation (intrinsic) and partly for the eventual profit (extrinsic). You read this book partly because you enjoy reading it (I hope), partly because you want to get a good grade in the course, partly because you know you will feel guilty if you spend a lot of money on a college education and then fail your courses, and partly because you saw your roommate studying a textbook and decided to follow the example.

Does a combination of intrinsic and extrinsic motivations lead to more persistent and effective performance than, say, an intrinsic motivation alone? Not always. In a classic study, researchers let four monkeys play with a device like the one in Figure 11.2. To open it, a monkey had to remove the pin, lift the hook, and then lift the hasp, in that order. The monkeys played with the device from time to time over a period of 10 days. They received no reinforcements; they played with it apparently just for the fun of it (an intrinsic motivation). By the end of the 10 days, each

We eat because of both intrinsic and extrinsic motivations. Even when the hunger (an intrinsic motivation) is satisfied, we eat because of the taste and the desire to socialize (extrinsic motivations).

FIGURE 11.2 Monkeys learned to open this device by removing the pin, the hook, and the hasp, in that order. At first, they received no reward but continued to open the device just for the fun of it. Then, when they could open it to obtain a raisin, their performance deteriorated. Evidently, in some cases an individual performs better with just intrinsic motivation (here, the joy of the task itself) than with a combination of intrinsic and extrinsic motivations.

monkey was able to open the device quickly, almost always taking the steps in the right order. Then, the device was placed over a food well in a place where the monkeys were accustomed to finding a raisin (an extrinsic motivation). If they opened the device they could get the raisin. Suddenly, their ability to open the device deteriorated. Instead of patiently removing the pin, the hook, and the hasp as they had done before, they attacked the hasp forcefully. They took longer to open the device for food than they had for play. Later, when they were offered the device by itself with no food available, they opened it less frequently than before and made more errors in their attempts (Harlow, Harlow, & Meyer, 1950). Evidently, opening the device for food had become work, so the monkeys no longer saw it as play.

Might the same principle apply to human behavior? In a typical experiment to test this idea, college students were asked to try to arrange seven plastic pieces with complex shapes to match figures in a drawing. At one point halfway through the experiment, students in the experimental group were paid $1 for each correct match. (Students in the control group did not know that the experimental group was being paid.) Then, the experiment continued without pay for anyone. After pay was suspended, the experimental group did less work than the control group did (Deci, 1971). Results such as these illustrate the **overjustification effect:** *When people are given more extrinsic motivation than necessary to perform a task, their intrinsic motivation declines.* According to one interpretation, people ask themselves, "Why am I doing this?" They then answer, "It's not because I enjoy the task. It's because I'm being paid." If they stop getting paid, they lose interest in the task.

The overjustification effect, like various other psychological principles, applies under some conditions but not others (Eisenberger & Cameron, 1996). It is wrong to conclude, as some have, that we should never reward people or even praise them for a job well done. Verbal praise, especially if it is well earned, strengthens people's enjoyment of a task. The overjustification effect applies only when people are given physical rewards for doing a task, and even then it is sometimes a weak effect.

Table 11.1 summarizes four views of motivation.

CONCEPT CHECK

1. Suppose you want to encourage your younger cousin to continue taking piano lessons. Based on the overjustification effect, would it be wise to pay him for practicing? (Check your answer on page 399.)

TABLE 11.1 Four Views of Motivation

VIEW	BASIC POSITION	MAJOR WEAKNESSES
Instinct theories *According to instinct theories, motivation is a kind of energy that builds up until it finds a release.*	Motivations are energies that accumulate; each energy specifies a preferred action, although it might spill over into a less preferred outlet.	Based on obsolete view of the nervous system.
Drive theories *According to drive theories, motivation is an irritation that continues until we find a way to reduce it.*	Motivations are based on needs or irritations that we try to reduce; they do not specify particular actions.	Implies that we always try to reduce stimulation, never to increase it. Also overlooks importance of external stimuli.
Homeostasis (plus anticipation) *Homeostasis is the process of maintaining a variable, such as body temperature, within a set range.*	Motivations tend to maintain body states near some optimum, intermediate level. They may react to current needs and anticipate future needs.	Overlooks importance of external stimuli.
Incentive theories *Incentives are external stimuli that attract us, even if we have no biological need for them.*	Motivations are responses to attractive stimuli.	Incomplete theory unless combined with drive or homeostasis.

Types of Motivation

How many motivations do people have? They are motivated to obtain food, water, shelter, and clothing; to have social contact with others; to smell the stinking lily in Kew Gardens. . . . The list could go on and on. Can we group these motivations into a few coherent categories?

Primary and Secondary Motivation

One way to categorize motivations is to distinguish primary motivations from secondary motivations. **Primary motivations**—such as the search for food and water—are *automatic, built-in processes.* **Secondary motivations** *develop as a result of specific learning experiences,* presumably because the secondary motivation has, in the past, led to the satisfaction of a primary motivation. Primary motivations and secondary motivations are analogous to the unconditioned reinforcers and conditioned reinforcers that we considered in Chapter 6.

Presumably, we learn secondary motivations because they help us to satisfy primary motivations. For example, we learn to have a desire for money (a secondary motivation) because it helps us to obtain food, water, and shelter (primary motivations). Often, however, a secondary motivation seems to develop a momentum of its own, thus becoming apparently independent of the original primary motivations associated with it. For example, many people start a coin or stamp collection because they think it might be worth something and eventually start spending money to add to the collection for its own sake. Some people try to do something spectacular to get into the *Guinness Book of World Records.* Why? to achieve fame? In any case, they sometimes lose

This man is trying to set the world record for being covered by bees. The desire for fame is an amazingly strong motivator.

sight of the fact that they are devoting more effort than the fame or any other reward is likely to be worth. One man holds the record for the longest fingernails, at 41.6 inches and still growing; another man has been growing his fingernails for 30 years in hopes of eventually catching up and surpassing the current champion. Other people have performed such feats as smoking 114 cigarettes in 3 minutes, pushing a pea with their nose for 3 miles, French-kissing snakes, and allowing their body to be covered with a record number of scorpions—all in failed attempts to get into the *Guinness* book (Spaeth, 1995). (The Guinness people refuse to publicize such records because they don't want to encourage self-destructive behaviors.)

CONCEPT CHECK

2. Is your interest in graduating from college a primary motivation or a secondary motivation? (Check your answer on page 399.)

Maslow's Hierarchy of Needs

Abraham Maslow (1970) attempted to bring some organization to the listing of human motivations, including both primary and secondary motivations. According to Maslow, our behavior is governed by a **hierarchy of needs,** *an organization from the most necessary and insistent to the ones that receive attention only when all others are under control.* The most basic are the physiological needs for food, drink, oxygen, and warmth, as shown at the bottom level of Figure 11.3. According to Maslow, these basic needs ordinarily take priority over all others (Figure 11.4). For example, people who are gasping for breath will not take time out to do something else until they have satisfied their need for oxygen. Once people have satisfied all of their physiological needs, they seek to satisfy their safety needs, such as security from attack and avoidance of pain. When those needs are satisfied, they proceed to the needs for love and belonging—making friends and socializing with them. Next come the needs for esteem, such as gaining prestige and a feeling of accomplishment. At the apex of Maslow's hierarchy is the need for **self-actualization,** *the need to achieve one's full potential.*

Maslow's theory is appealing because it recognizes that the various motivations are not equal. When they conflict, people will generally give priority to the tasks most necessary for survival. However, there is no evidence to support the idea that motivations fall into five distinct categories (Wahba & Bridwell, 1976). That is, the differences between the need for oxygen and the need for food (both basic physiological needs) are as great as the differences between the need for love and the need for self-esteem. Furthermore, people sometimes work to satisfy higher-level needs before they satisfy lower-level needs. Even when you are ravenously hungry, you might skip a meal to be with someone you love, or to study for a test, or to accept an award. Martyrs have willingly

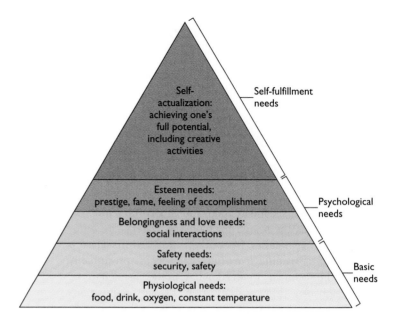

FIGURE 11.3 Maslow's hierarchy of needs suggests a hierarchical order to human motivations. If you are thirsty, you will want to drink something to fill that basic need. If your primary physical needs are met, you can then focus on meeting your psychological needs for companionship and achievement. Your final efforts will be devoted to reaching your full potential. But do all people follow this principle? Some people, including Olympic performers, sacrifice eating, entertainment, and companionship to strive toward athletic accomplishment and prestige. Artists might also give up physical comforts and social pleasures to focus on their inner vision and to realize their creative potential.

sacrificed their lives to advance a political or religious cause. Depending on the circumstances, almost any motivation may take priority over the others, at least temporarily.

THE MESSAGE
Many Types of Motivation

People frequently puzzle over why someone did something. For example, why would someone stand in line for hours to smell a stinking lily? We almost exclusively puzzle over behaviors that contribute little or nothing to survival. That

FIGURE 11.4 According to Maslow's hierarchy of needs, we concentrate first on the lowest level of needs—such as the need for food, oxygen, and constant temperature—until we meet them. Then we move on to higher and higher needs. Thus, an impoverished and homeless person would be unlikely to devote much effort to creative endeavors. (Some exceptions to this rule do occur, however.)

is, we do not bother to ask why when someone gasps for breath, eats, drinks, or runs away from a tiger. For the unusual behaviors such as trying to smell a stinking lily, people seldom have just one simple motivation. More often, it is a combination: curiosity, the desire to have something unusual to talk about with friends, perhaps even a desire for fame of a very local variety.

SUMMARY

✳ *Characteristics of motivated behaviors.* Motivated behaviors persist until the individual reaches the goal. They are controlled by internal and external forces and by biological and social forces. Motivated behaviors vary from time to time, from situation to situation, and from person to person. (page 393)

✳ *Motivation as energy or drive reduction.* Psychologists have sometimes viewed motivation as an energy that must be used up in one way or another, or as a process that persists until all drives are reduced. Each of these views has serious limitations. (page 394)

✳ *Motivation as a way of maintaining homeostasis.* To a large degree, motivated behaviors tend to maintain body conditions and stimulation at a near-constant, or homeostatic, level. This view of motivation can account for much behavior, if we also assume that behaviors anticipate future needs instead of just responding to current needs. However, the homeostatic view of motivation overlooks the role of external stimuli for arousing behavior. (page 395)

✳ *Motivation as incentive.* Motivations are partly under the control of incentives—external stimuli that pull us toward certain actions. Both drives and incentives control most motivated behaviors. (page 395)

✳ *Intrinsic and extrinsic motivations.* People and animals engage in some actions because the actions themselves are interesting or pleasing (intrinsic motivation). Providing a physical reinforcement (extrinsic motivation) for the actions sometimes backfires by reducing the interest or pleasure they provide. (page 395)

✱ *Types of motivations.* Psychologists have made several attempts to list or categorize various motivations. One prominent attempt, offered by Abraham Maslow, arranged needs in a hierarchy ranging from basic physiological needs at the bottom to the need for self-actualization at the top. His claim that people satisfy their lower needs before their higher needs does not apply in all cases, however. (page 397)

Terms

drive   an internal state of unrest or irritation that energizes one behavior after another until one of them removes the irritation (page 394)

homeostasis   the maintenance of biological conditions at an optimum level within an organism (page 395)

incentive   an external stimulus that prompts an action to obtain the stimulus (page 395)

intrinsic motivation   motivation to engage in an act for its own sake (page 395)

extrinsic motivation   motivation based on the rewards and punishments that an act may bring (page 395)

overjustification effect   the tendency of people who are given more extrinsic motivation than necessary to perform a task to experience a decline in their intrinsic motivation (page 396)

primary motivation   motivation that serves biological needs (page 397)

secondary motivation   motivation that serves no direct biological need but develops as a result of specific learning experiences (page 397)

hierarchy of needs   Maslow's categorization of human motivations, ranging from basic physiological needs at the bottom to the need for self-actualization at the top (page 397)

self-actualization   the need to achieve one's full potential (page 397)

Answers to Concept Checks

1. According to the overjustification effect, you should not pay him enough that he starts practicing just for the reward. However, verbal praise would be good. (page 396)

2. Your interest in graduating from college is a secondary motivation, because it is something you had to learn to value. Such secondary motivations can become very strong. (page 397)

Web Resources

Autobiography of Konrad Lorenz

www.nobel.se/laureates/medicine-1973-2-autobio.html

Konrad Lorenz is one of psychology's few Nobel Laureates. The 1973 Nobel Prize in Physiology or Medicine was jointly awarded to Konrad Lorenz and two other ethologists "for their discoveries concerning organization and elicitation of individual and social behaviour patterns." The press release (www.nobel.se/laureates/medicine-1973-press.html) explains the significance of their contributions.

Maslow's Hierarchy of Needs Theory

snycorva.cortland.edu/~andersmd/maslow/homepage.html

A brief tutorial about Maslow's theory of motivation, the hierarchy of needs, and the application of the theory to education. Can you spot the fairly major error in the description of the hierarchy?

MODULE 11.2

Motivation and Biological States: The Case of Hunger

How do we choose which foods to eat?

Why do some people gain so much more weight than others do?

Small birds eat only as much as they need to meet their immediate needs, storing almost no fat at all. The advantage is that they remain light and therefore fast, just as they need to be to escape predators. The disadvantage is that they have no reserves; if they have trouble finding food for even a short time, they can starve to death. Bears follow a different strategy. Sometimes they can find food in abundance and sometimes they find almost nothing for days or even weeks at a time. So, they feast on all the food they can eat, when they can find it, and store enough fat to meet their energy needs during times of famine.

Which strategy is better for humans? It depends. Something midway between these two extremes is probably best, although the ideal varies depending on circumstances:

FIGURE 11.5 Mealtime is more than just an opportunity to satisfy hunger: It is an occasion to bring the family and sometimes friends together, to share a pleasant experience, to discuss the events of the day, and even to pass on a culture from one generation to the next. We expect family members to participate in these meals, even if they are not hungry.

Can you always find good food, or might there be a famine? Does your survival depend on being as quick as a small bird, or could you afford to slow down like a fat bear and still survive?

How much we eat, and what and when we eat, also depends on factors that have nothing to do with our energy needs (Figure 11.5). When you visit friends or relatives, they may offer you food as a gesture of affection, and they may act hurt if you refuse their hospitality. Say that you visit the family of your boyfriend or girlfriend, and you want to make a good impression. "Dinner's ready!" someone calls. You go into the dining room and find a huge meal spread out before you, which your hosts clearly expect you to enjoy. Do you explain that you are not hungry because you already made a pig of yourself at lunch? Probably not.

Motives in Food Selection

Have you ever wondered how people first figured out which foods were edible? It was easy for you and me; our parents and other people told us what to eat, and we did not have to try all the weeds in the field to decide which ones were good. Our parents learned from their parents and they in turn from their parents, but way back when, somebody had to discover what was edible by trial and error. Furthermore, they had to discover many principles of how to prepare foods (Rozin, 1996). For example, cassava, a root native to South America, is poisonous unless someone washes it and pounds it for about 3 days. Cashews are covered with a thin membrane that must be carefully removed; anyone who touches it will react as if they had touched poison ivy. American corn (maize) has an abundance of certain nutrients and a deficit of others, and beans have nearly the opposite set of abundances and deficits, so it is best to combine corn with beans—as the Native Americans discovered long ago.

We learn our food choices largely by learning what *not* to eat. Toddlers around the age of 1½ will try to eat almost anything they can fit into their mouths (Figure 11.6). Up to the age of 7 or 8, about the only reason children give for refusing to eat something is that they think it would taste bad (Rozin, Fallon, & Augustoni-Ziskind, 1986). As children grow older, they give a wider variety of reasons for accepting certain foods and rejecting others. As with other motivations, food selection depends on a combination of physiological, social, and cognitive factors. Let's consider some of the most important factors.

Acceptance or Rejection of Foods Based on Taste

Some taste preferences are present at birth. Infants readily consume sweet liquids; when they taste something bitter or sour, they turn their head and spit it out.

FIGURE 11.6 Infants and young children will try eating almost anything and refuse food only if it tastes bad. As they grow older, they learn to avoid foods for other reasons. People avoid eating some substances to avoid getting sick; they avoid other substances because the very idea of eating them is disgusting.

At least one taste preference can be triggered by an abnormal condition within the body. One boy showed a strong craving for salt. As an infant, he licked the salt off crackers and bacon but refused to eat the food itself. One of the first words he learned was *salt*. He put a thick layer of salt on everything he ate, and sometimes he ate salt by itself. When deprived of salt, he ate almost nothing and began to waste away. At the age of 3½, he was taken to the hospital and fed the usual hospital fare. He soon died of salt deficiency (Wilkins & Richter, 1940).

It turned out that the boy's adrenal glands were defective. These glands secrete hormones that enable the body to retain salt. The boy craved great amounts of salt because salt was being excreted so rapidly from his body. (We are often told to limit our salt intake for health reasons, but too little salt can also be dangerous.)

Research on animals confirms that a deficiency of salt in the body triggers an immediate craving for salty foods. As soon as animals, including humans, become salt deficient, they show a heightened preference for salty tastes (Rozin & Kalat, 1971). People who have lost large quantities of salt as a result of bleeding or heavy sweating often express a craving for salt. Apparently, salty foods actually taste better to salt-deficient people and animals than they do to others (Jacobs, Mark, & Scott, 1988). In short, changes in body chemistry can alter a person's motivation to choose a particular food.

Preference for Familiar Foods

Although most people eat a wide variety of foods, they are cautious about eating anything unfamiliar. Think about the first time you tried jalapeño peppers or coffee, for example. Even foods that taste reasonably good at first—artichokes, for example—taste even better after they become familiar.

Members of every culture and every ethnic group become familiar with its preferred ways of preparing and seasoning foods (Rozin, 1996). Children who grow up in Italian families come to prefer foods flavored with tomato, garlic, and olive oil. Mexican infants dislike hot peppers at first, but by the time they are a few years old, many insist on having them with almost every meal. Cuisine is one of the most stable and defining features of any culture. In one study, researchers interviewed Japanese high-school and college students who had spent a year in another country as part of an exchange program. The researchers asked the students how much they enjoyed their experience and how much distress they felt at various times. The amount of pleasure or displeasure had little relationship to the religion, family life, recreation, or dating customs of the host country. The main determinant was the food: Students who could at least occasionally get something similar to Japanese food had a good time; those who could not became unhappy and homesick (Furukawa, 1997).

Learned Associations with Food

As I mentioned in Chapter 6, animals associate foods with the gastrointestinal consequences of eating them. The same is true of humans. When you eat something and later feel sick, you may form a strong aversion to that food, especially if it was an unfamiliar one. Ordinarily, the aversion forms because something in the food made you ill, but the same learning takes place regardless of what caused the illness. If you eat something at an amusement park and then go on a wild ride and get sick, you may never again like that food (Figure 11.7). Even though you know the ride was at fault, an area deep in your brain still associates the food with the sickness.

People can also develop preferences by associating a food with another food that they already enjoy (Capaldi, 1996). For example, parents who want their child to learn to like broccoli might mix a little broccoli with some cheese or other food that the child already likes. Later, they could gradually reduce the amount of cheese.

People also reject safe, nutritious foods because of the very idea of where those foods came from (Rozin & Fallon, 1987; Rozin, Millman, & Nemeroff, 1986). In the United States, most people refuse to eat dog meat, cat meat, or horse meat. Many vegetarians consider any kind of meat disgusting and are distressed even to watch other people eat it. The longer people have been vegetarians, the more firmly they tend to reject meat-eating as not only undesirable but even immoral (Rozin, Markwith, & Stoess, 1997).

How would you like to try the tasty morsels described in Figure 11.8? Most people find the idea of eating insects

FIGURE 11.7 People associate the foods they eat, especially unfamiliar foods, with the way they feel afterward. If you ate corn dogs and cotton candy just before getting on a wild roller coaster ride and then got sick from the ride, something in your brain would "blame" the food for your feeling ill, even though you consciously believe that the food had nothing to do with your illness. Ordinarily, however, this kind of learning teaches us to avoid harmful substances.

repulsive, even if the insects were sterilized to kill all the germs (Rozin & Fallon, 1987). People also say they would refuse to drink a glass of apple juice after a dead, sterilized cockroach had been dipped into it. After seeing a cockroach dipped into a glass of apple juice, some people even refuse to drink other apple juice that was poured into a different glass (Rozin, Millman, & Nemeroff, 1986).

Crispy Cajun Crickets

Adapted from a recipe in the *Food Insects Newsletter,* March 1990

Tired of the same old snack food? Perk up your next party with Crispy Cajun Crickets ("pampered" house crickets, *Acheta domesticus,* available from Flucker's Cricket Farm, P.O. Box 378, Baton Rouge, LA 70821, 800-735-8537).

  1 cup crickets
  1 pinch oatmeal
  4 ounces butter, melted
    Salt
    Garlic
    Cayenne

1. Put crickets in a clean, airy container with oatmeal for food. After one day, discard sick crickets and freeze the rest.
2. Wash frozen crickets in warm water and spread on a cookie sheet. Roast in a 250-degree oven until crunchy.
3. Meanwhile heat butter with remaining ingredients and sprinkle this sauce on crickets before serving.

Yield: 1 serving

FIGURE 11.8 People avoid eating some potential foods because they are disgusted by the very idea of eating them. For example, most people would refuse to eat insects, regardless of any assurances that the insects were nutritious and harmless.

Different cultures have different taboos. Here is an assortment of insect and reptile dishes. (Yum, yum?)

The Physiological Mechanisms of Hunger

Hunger is a (partly) homeostatic drive that serves to keep fuel available for the body to use. Specialized mechanisms in the brain monitor how much fuel is available; when supplies begin to drop, the brain triggers behaviors that lead to eating. But how does the brain know how much fuel is available and, therefore, how much a person should eat and how often?

The problem is far more complex than keeping enough fuel in the gas tank of a car. When the fuel gauge shows that the tank is running low, you fill it with gas. By contrast, keeping track of how much fuel is in your stomach does not tell you how much more you need. Right now, in addition to the fuel in your stomach and intestines, a fair amount of fuel is present in every cell of your body, ready to be used. Additional fuel is circulating in your blood, ready to enter cells that need it. Still more fuel is stored in the fat cells, available to be converted into a form that can enter the bloodstream. If necessary, your body can break down muscle tissues to provide additional fuel. Your car will stop within seconds after it uses up all the fuel in the gas tank, whereas your body can keep going for days, even weeks, after your stomach is empty.

How do you know how much to eat, especially considering that each meal has a different density of nutrients from any other? Fortunately, you don't have to get it exactly right. You have one set of mechanisms that control short-term changes in hunger and a separate set of long-term mechanisms that act as a correction if your short-term mechanisms cause you to eat too much or too little.

Short-Term Regulation of Hunger

The factors responsible for ending a meal are several, but they are easy to describe. Under most circumstances, the main factor is distension of the stomach and intestines; we feel "full" because the digestive system is literally full (Seeley, Kaplan, & Grill, 1995). We also monitor how much we have eaten (Spiegel, 1973); with familiar foods we calibrate approximately how much nutrition we are getting per amount swallowed (Deutsch & Gonzalez, 1980); and we have receptors in the intestines that detect the sugars in the food (Lavin et al., 1996). The fact that these receptors detect sugars and not fats may be one reason that people tend to overeat on a high-fat diet.

The main factor responsible for the onset of hunger and the start of a meal is a drop in how much glucose enters the cells, but the control of glucose is a more complicated story (Figure 11.9). **Glucose,** *the most abundant sugar in your blood, is an important source of energy for all parts of the body and almost the only source for the brain.* Most foods can be converted at least partly into glucose. Excess

blood glucose can be converted into fats and other stored fuels, and stored fuels can be converted back into blood glucose when necessary. The flow of glucose to or from the blood depends on two hormones released by the pancreas, insulin and glucagon.

Insulin is *a hormone that increases the flow of glucose and several other nutrients into body cells.* At the beginning of a meal, before the nutrients have even started entering the blood, the brain sends messages to the pancreas to increase its secretion of insulin. Insulin promotes the movement of glucose and other nutrients out of the blood and into both the cells that need fuel (such as muscles and neurons) and the cells that store the nutrients as fats and other supplies. As the meal continues, the digested food enters the blood, but almost as fast as it enters, insulin helps to move excess nutrients out of the blood and into the liver

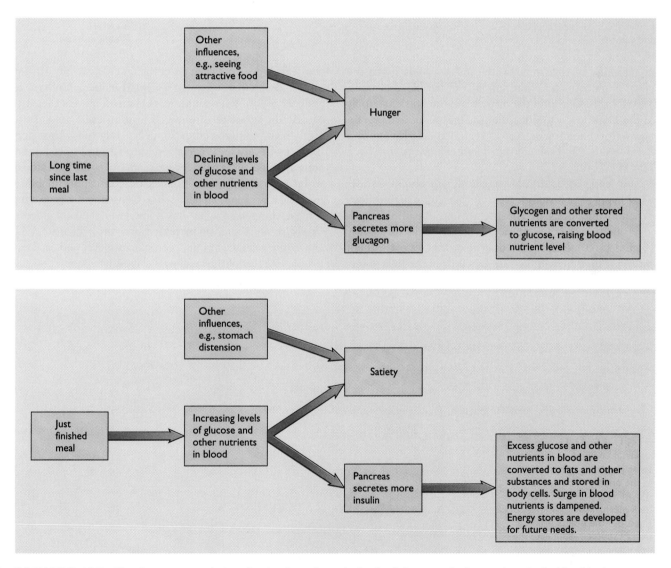

FIGURE 11.9 The short-term regulation of eating depends on the levels of glucose and other nutrients in the blood; it also depends on the appearance and flavor of the food, social influences, and so forth. Varying secretions of the hormones insulin and glucagon help to keep the blood nutrient levels reasonably constant. During and shortly after a meal, insulin moves blood nutrients into storage in the liver and fat cells; during a period without food, glucagon converts stored nutrients into blood glucose.

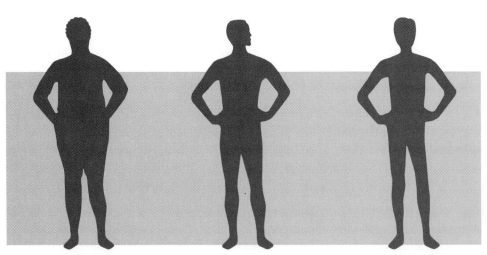

High insulin
Food is stored as fat.
Little glucose in blood.
Appetite increases.
Weight increases.

Lower insulin
Fat supplies are
converted to glucose.
Appetite is lower.

Very low insulin
Glucose cannot enter
cells. Appetite is high,
but much of nutrition
is excreted.
Weight decreases.

FIGURE 11.10 How insulin affects glucose, appetite, and weight.

or fat cells. In that manner, the insulin holds down the surge of glucose and other nutrients in the blood (Woods, 1991). Later, long after the meal, when the nutrient supply in the blood starts to drop, the pancreas reduces its secretion of insulin and increases its secretions of **glucagon,** *a hormone that helps to convert stored energy supplies back into blood glucose.*

At least that is the story for healthy people. Consider what happens if insulin levels stay constantly high or low: When insulin levels are consistently low, as with the medical condition diabetes, nutrients enter the cells very slowly (Figure 11.10). People with untreated diabetes eat without satisfying their hunger because very little of the food enters

the cells. It does not even enter the fat cells, so they can eat a great deal without gaining weight (Lindberg, Coburn, & Stricker, 1984). They simply excrete much of what they eat.

At the opposite extreme, if insulin levels are consistently high, nutrients enter the cells easily, but a large percentage of every meal is converted to fats and stored in fat cells. Because the insulin level remains high, the food stored in fat cells simply stays there; glucagon cannot mobilize much of it back into blood glucose. Consequently, soon after a meal, the person again has a low level of blood glucose *(hypoglycemia)* and an increased appetite. (Figure 11.11 shows the relationship between glucose level and food intake.) Note that, if the insulin level is either consistently low

FIGURE 11.11 To maintain equilibrium, homeostatic regulating systems such as the one for food intake shown here provide a feedback mechanism. Low levels of glucose—the brain's primary energy source—stimulate the hypothalamus, which prompts the pancreas to release insulin and raise the levels of glucose. Once the glucose reaches a certain level, control mechanisms act to lower it.

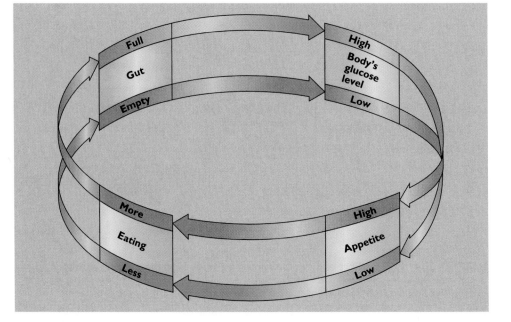

or consistently high, the result will be an increased appetite; however, very low insulin levels lead to weight loss and very high insulin levels lead to weight gain.

CONCEPT CHECK

3. Insulin levels fluctuate cyclically over the course of a day. Would you guess that they are higher in the middle of the day, when people tend to be hungry, or late at night, when they are generally less hungry? (Check your answer on page 412.)

The Long-Term Regulation of Hunger

Stomach distension, intestinal distension, and the other mechanisms for ending a meal are far from perfect. Depending on the caloric density of your next meal, you may eat a bit more or a bit less than you need to replenish your resources. If you misjudged in the same direction with every meal, you would eventually have a problem. If you consistently ate 5% more than you needed, it is estimated that you would gain 15 pounds (7 kilograms [kg]) per year (Jéquier, 1987). If you consistently ate 5% less than you needed, you would eventually starve to death.

However, you have long-term mechanisms to correct short-term errors. If you overeat for several meals, you will begin to feel less hungry and you will start eating smaller meals until you get back to about your normal weight. Conversely, if you undereat for a few meals, you will start feeling hungrier than usual, and you will increase your intake until you get back to normal. Most people's weight fluctuates from one day to the next but remains remarkably stable from one month to the next, even if they seldom check the scales. That mean weight is referred to as a **set point**—*a level that the body works to maintain* (Figure 11.12).

The mechanism for this correction is now partly understood. *The body's fat cells produce a hormone* called **leptin** *in amounts proportional to the total amount of fat* (Halaas et al., 1995). When the body gains fat, the extra leptin alters activity in parts of the hypothalamus (an area of the brain), causing meals to satisfy hunger faster (Campfield, Smith, Guisez, Devos, & Burn, 1995). Among the many other effects of leptin, it triggers the start of puberty: When the body reaches a certain size and weight, the increased leptin levels combine with other forces to induce all the hormonal changes of puberty (Chehab, Mounzih, Lu, & Lim, 1997).

FIGURE 11.12 For most people, weight fluctuates around a set point, somewhat like a diving board that bounces up and down from a central position.

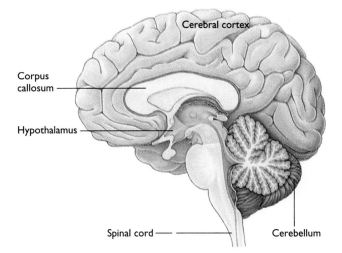

FIGURE 11.13 The hypothalamus, a small area on the underside of the brain, contains several subareas that contribute in various ways to eating, drinking, sexual behavior, and other motivated activities. Damage to the lateral hypothalamus inhibits eating; damage to other hypothalamic areas can provoke overeating.

The Brain Mechanisms of Hunger and Satiety

The brain must somehow monitor information from the blood, cells, and digestive system to determine when to eat and when to stop eating. Several brain areas, especially those in the hypothalamus (Figure 11.13), are especially important in this process.

The **lateral hypothalamus** appears to be *a critical area for starting meals.* Animals, including humans, with damage to the lateral hypothalamus have trouble salivating, swallowing, and digesting foods (Hernandez, Murzi, Schwartz, & Hoebel, 1992). Also, such individuals secrete higher levels of glucagon than of insulin; consequently, the fat supplies are constantly converted into blood glucose, so the individual has little immediate need for further nutrition.

Two areas of the hypothalamus are important for ending meals. One is the **ventromedial hypothalamus.** *After damage that includes the ventromedial hypothalamus and the axons that pass nearby, an individual digests food more rapidly than usual and secretes more insulin.* The high insulin level causes a disproportionate amount of each meal to be stored as fat. Because the food passes quickly through the digestive system and into the fat cells, where it stays, the individual becomes hungry again shortly after each meal (Hoebel & Hernandez, 1993). Figure 11.14 shows a very obese rat with this kind of brain damage. One woman with a tumor in this area gained an average of more than 10 kg (15 pounds) per month (Reeves & Plum, 1969).

Another area of the hypothalamus contributes to ending meals in a different way. *After damage to or chemical inhibition of the* **paraventricular hypothalamus,** *meals are of normal frequency but each individual meal is*

FIGURE 11.14 An obese rat with a damaged ventromedial hypothalamus (left) can eat less than an ordinary rat (right) and still gain weight. This rat's excess fat prevents it from grooming its fur.

enormous (Leibowitz & Alexander, 1991; Leibowitz, Hammer, & Chang, 1981). An individual with such brain damage can continue eating until the stomach and intestines are about to burst.

CONCEPT CHECKS

4. Many young ballet dancers and other female athletes who exercise heavily and keep their weight low are slower to start puberty than most other girls. Why?
5. After damage to the ventromedial hypothalamus, an animal's weight eventually reaches a higher than usual level and then fluctuates around that amount. What has happened to the set point? (Check your answers on page 412.)

Eating Disorders

The mechanisms I have discussed so far enable most people to select a reasonable, well-balanced diet and to maintain their weight within normal limits. In some individuals, though, the motivational mechanisms go awry. They feel hungry all the time and eat too much, or they alternate between stuffing themselves and starving themselves, or they feel hungry but refuse to eat. Some of these disorders result from physiological abnormalities; others result from social and cognitive influences that are competing with the normal physiological mechanisms.

Obesity

Obesity is *the excessive accumulation of body fat.* A body weight 20–40% above the standard for a person's height is considered mild obesity. Weight 41–100% above the standard is considered moderate obesity, and still greater obe-

sity is considered severe (Berkow, 1987). Why do some people become seriously overweight? Obviously, because they take in more calories than they use up. But *why* do they do that?

The Limited Role of Emotional Disturbances

Are overweight people more likely than others are to have psychological problems? One prevalent idea has been that anxiety, depression, or other emotional problems can lead to overeating and weight gain. Another theory is that extreme weight gain leads to anxiety or depression. The research, however, fails to support either hypothesis. Anxiety, depression, and other psychological concerns are not unusually common among obese people (Wadden & Stunkard, 1987). Nevertheless, there may be a subpopulation of obese people who react strongly to the unfavorable way in which they are treated. Because prejudices against the obese are so common, many obese people have a restricted social life and have trouble getting a good job. Dealing with such prejudices and barriers leads some obese people to psychological distress and low self-esteem (Friedman & Brownell, 1996).

Although emotional distress is not the cause of obesity, it can produce temporary fluctuations in eating and body

Although obesity is not significantly linked with either anxiety or depression, some obese people feel distressed and suffer from low self-esteem because of how other people react to them.

weight for almost anyone. In one survey of 100 adults (Edelman, 1981), 40 said that they overeat three or more times per month when they feel nervous, tired, lonely, or sorry for themselves. The eating binge enables them to focus their attention on eating and away from their other concerns (Heatherton & Baumeister, 1991). Such eating binges are most frequent and most extreme with people who have been dieting to lose weight (Greeno & Wing, 1994). Evidently, dieters actively inhibit their desire to eat, until a stressful experience breaks these inhibitions and releases the pent-up desire to eat.

Genetics

Obesity tends to run in families, and the weight of adopted children correlates more closely with that of their birth parents than with that of their adoptive parents (Stunkard et al., 1986). What this evidence means is that, other things being equal, certain genes increase the chances that someone will become overweight. This evidence does not mean that genetics fully explains obesity, however. In particular, consider the fact that obesity is far more common in the United States today than it was in the early 1900s or earlier. The spread of obesity is certainly not due to genetic changes, but rather to changes in lifestyle. Not that long ago, most of our ancestors were active most of the day in farming or manual labor. Today, many people drive to work, take an elevator instead of the stairs, and then sit all day in an office. Eating habits have also changed. Fast-food hamburger outlets provide inexpensive high-fat meals, restaurants with all-you-can-eat buffets encourage gluttony, and even grocery stores and supermarkets offer great varieties of very tempting high-calorie convenience foods. Most obese people show a strong preference for foods that are rich in both fats and carbohydrates, such as cake frosting, and such foods are more readily available today than ever before (Drewnowski, 1996).

Probably the best illustration of the relationship between genetics and lifestyle for the onset of obesity comes from the Pima Indians of Arizona. At least 75 percent of Pima adults have a genetic predisposition to obesity (Thompson, Ravussin, Bennett, & Bogardus, 1997), and most also have high blood pressure and diabetes. However, before the 1940s, when they were mainly eating the vegetables that grow in the Sonoran desert, such as those shown in Figure 11.15, they were not generally obese. Evidently, their digestive systems were well adapted to that diet but not to hamburgers, French-fried potatoes, and various other convenience foods. The fact that the Pimas became obese on a "standard" U.S. diet, whereas most other people do not, points to a genetic difference. However, the impact of the change in diet indicates the importance of nongenetic factors as well. That is, a gene can either lead to obesity or not, depending on the diet. Today, many of the Pimas are trying to return to their traditional foods (Zastaury, 1996).

Decreased Energy Output

Many overweight people who claim that they eat only normal amounts of food actually eat more than they admit, maybe even more than they admit to themselves. However, some really do eat only normal-sized meals (DeLuise, Blackburn, & Flier, 1980). The overweight condition of these people is not due to high energy intake but to low energy output. Not only do they fail to exercise, but they also have a low overall metabolic rate. Presumably, one effect that the genes for obesity have is to decrease the use of energy.

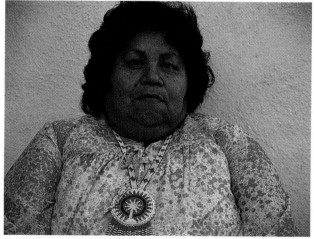

FIGURE 11.15   Native Americans ate desert plants such as the beans and seeds at left. Most Pima Indians have a gene that leads to obesity if they eat a standard U.S. diet. However, few were obese when they ate their traditional diet.

One group of investigators compared the infants of 12 overweight mothers and six normal-weight mothers over their first year of life. All the babies weighed about the same at birth, but six of the babies of the overweight mothers had become overweight by the end of that first year. Those babies had also been relatively inactive since birth. During the first 3 months, they had expended about 20% less energy per day than the babies who maintained normal weight (Roberts, Savage, Coward, Chew, & Lucas, 1988).

Low energy expenditure is a good predictor of weight gain in adults as well. Eric Ravussin and his associates (1988) found that the adults with the lowest energy expenditure over a 24-hour period were the most likely to gain weight over the next 2 to 4 years.

Other Physiological Factors

People can be predisposed to obesity for many physiological reasons. For example, people who have a steadily high level of insulin store most of each meal as fat and thus become hungry soon after eating.

Certain genetic strains of mice become obese because their fat cells fail to produce leptin. Leptin, as you will recall, is the messenger that tells the brain how much fat the body has. If the fat cells do not produce leptin, the brain reacts as if the body had no fat—that is, as if the body were starving. Injections of leptin cause these mice to eat less, exercise more, and lose weight (Pellymounter et al., 1995). Naturally, this discovery led many people to hope that leptin injections would work similar wonders for overweight people. Indeed, a few obese people are deficient in leptin, and leptin injections would probably be a very safe and effective treatment for them (Montague et al., 1997). However, the great majority of obese people produce leptin in proportion to their fat stores, resulting in leptin levels several times larger than average (Considine et al., 1996). These people are evidently insensitive to leptin; perhaps their leptin receptors in the brain are unresponsive. Although leptin itself would be no remedy for such people, researchers may someday find another way to accomplish what leptin ordinarily accomplishes.

Losing Weight

If you talk to enough people about weight loss, some will tell you that it is almost impossible to lose weight and keep it off, but others will recount stories of people who succeeded. The reason for the discrepancy is simple: Some people do manage to lose weight and keep it off (Schachter, 1982), and then neither you nor any weight-loss clinic will hear much more about them. Those who show up at a weight-loss clinic are people who have failed repeated attempts to diet on their own, and many of them have difficult problems.

For those who seek professional help in losing weight, a variety of approaches are available. Most therapists recommend starting with the simplest methods; if those methods fail, then consider trying more intensive methods (Friedman & Brownell, 1996):

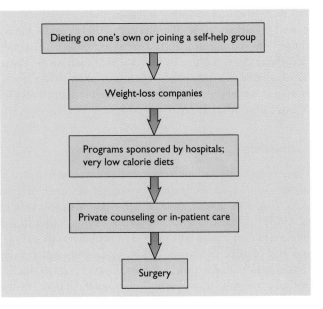

A survey of weight-loss experts found that they disagreed about much but did agree on a few recommendations (Schwartz & Brownell, 1995):

• Except for people with unusual medical problems, almost everyone who needs to lose weight should include increased exercise as part of the strategy. The best advice is to set realistic exercise goals and then stick to them: Someone who has hardly lifted a muscle in years should not plan to run great distances every day. It is better to start with a more modest goal, such as walking three times around the block every other day, and then gradually increase the activity.

• The severity of the problem should dictate the approach. For example, only people with severe, life-threatening obesity should even consider surgical removal of fat.

• Programs such as Overeaters Anonymous (OA) are often helpful to people who feel comfortable with the strong spiritual focus and the emphasis on overeating as an addiction or disease. However, such programs should not be recommended to people who feel uncomfortable with this approach.

• Private counseling is an option mainly useful for people who have other psychological problems in addition to their weight problem.

The Effect of Intentional Weight Loss on Appetite

Are you satisfied with your own weight? In the United States, almost everyone says "no." Even among women who have a normal weight for their height (according to life insurance tables) and who *know* that they are of normal weight, nearly all want to be thinner. Among men of normal weight, some wish they were heavier and some wish they were thinner, but again very few are content (Raudenbush & Zellner, 1997).

The motivation for women is cultural standards that depict thin women as especially attractive or fashionable. April Fallon and Paul Rozin (1985) asked women to indicate on a diagram which body figure they thought men considered most attractive. The investigators also asked men which female figure *they* considered most attractive. As Figure 11.16 shows, women thought that men preferred thinner women than most men actually do. (The same study also found that men thought women preferred heavier men than most women actually do.)

Given the social pressure to be thin, many normal-weight people deprive themselves of food they would like to eat, keeping themselves thinner than they would have been by eating naturally (Polivy & Herman, 1987). They continue to have a strong drive to eat, however, and many factors can weaken their resolve. In one experiment, participants were told that they were taking part in market research on ice cream flavors. Some of these people were first asked to drink a milkshake; others were not. Then, they were all asked to taste three flavors of ice cream. (The dependent variable was how much ice cream they ate.) When this experiment was conducted with people who were not dieting, participants tasted about the same amount of ice cream regardless of whether or not they had already drunk a milkshake (Figure 11.17). But when the experiment was conducted with people who were dieting, those who had first drunk a milkshake ate *more* ice cream than those who had not (Ruderman, 1986; Ruderman & Christensen, 1983). Apparently, the dieters said to themselves, "What the heck. As long as I've already broken my diet, I may as well eat all I want." Not all dieters react this way when they have consumed a calorie-rich snack; as is generally the case in psychology, we can find many individual differences (Lowe, 1993). However, the point is that many dieters can be easily shaken off their diet.

Some become "yo-yo dieters," alternating periods of weight loss with periods of weight gain. The resulting fluctuations in body weight may be harmful to health, although little research has been done to measure the degree of that risk. Consequently, authorities are not certain what advice to give to people of near-normal weight who are considering trying to lose weight. Certainly, if someone is extremely obese, then losing weight is medically important. When less obese people

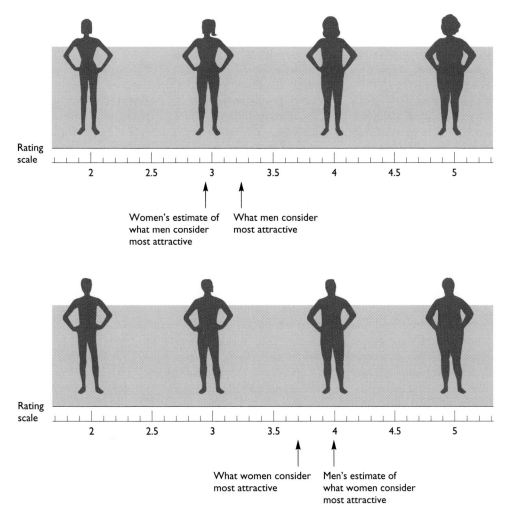

FIGURE 11.16 In a study by Fallon and Rozin (1985), women and men were asked which figure of the opposite sex they considered most attractive and which figure they believed the opposite sex considered most attractive. Each sex had systematic misestimates of the other's preferences.

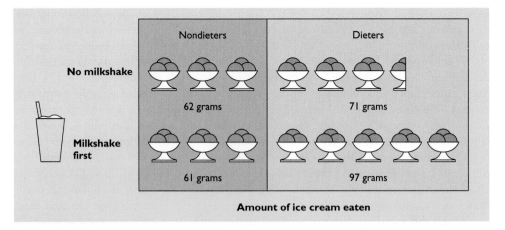

FIGURE 11.17 Dieters who drank a milkshake before tasting ice cream ate more ice cream than did dieters who had not drunk a milkshake. Apparently, those who drank the milkshake thought, "I've broken my diet anyway, so I may as well eat all I want." (Data from Ruderman & Christensen, 1983.)

succeed at keeping their weight down, again dieting is clearly beneficial. However, when people who are already close to normal weight find themselves repeatedly losing and regaining weight by "yo-yo dieting," no one can be sure whether the benefits outweigh the risks (Brownell & Rodin, 1994).

Anorexia Nervosa

Some people go beyond reasonable limits in their passion to lose weight. The Duchess of Windsor once said, "You can't be too rich or too thin." She may have been right about being too rich, but she was definitely wrong about being too thin. Some people are so strongly motivated to be thin (for social and cognitive reasons) that they manage to overrule their physiological drives almost completely.

Here is a case history: A somewhat chubby 11-year-old girl who weighed 118 pounds (53 kg) was told to watch her weight (Bachrach, Erwin, & Mohr, 1965). She did so all through her teens. Along the way, she suffered certain hormonal difficulties, including menstrual irregularity, heavy menstrual bleeding, and deficient activity of her thyroid gland. At age 18, she still weighed 118 pounds (53 kg), but with her taller frame that weight was normal for her.

After she was married, she moved from her home in Virginia to her husband's place of employment in California. She immediately became homesick. Because the couple could afford only a small apartment with no cooking facilities, they ate most of their meals at a very inexpensive restaurant. Soon she began to lose weight and stopped menstruating. She found sexual relations painful and unpleasant. Her physician warned her that, if she did not start regaining some weight, he would be forced to send her home to her parents. He intended this as a threat, but she took it as a promise. By the time she visited the physician again, she had lost even more weight and soon went back to Virginia.

Even after returning to familiar surroundings and home cooking, however, she continued to lose weight. The weight loss seemed to have developed a momentum of its own, and she continued to get thinner, eventually reaching a weight of only 47 pounds (21 kg).

This is a case of **anorexia nervosa,** *a condition in which a person refuses to eat adequate food and steadily loses weight.* (*Anorexia* means "loss of appetite." *Nervosa* means "for nervous reasons," to distinguish it from disorders of the digestive system.) At the outset, the person may have decided to lose weight for health reasons, or to become a dancer, or for some other reason. But the person continues losing weight well beyond the original goal. Surprisingly, though, even when anorexic women are on the verge of starvation, they have unusually high energy levels (Falk, Halmi, & Tryon, 1985). They run long distances, engage in sports, work diligently on their school assignments, and sleep very little. As with other psychological conditions, anorexia nervosa comes in all degrees, but in its most severe form it can lead to atrophy of the heart muscle and death.

Anorexia nervosa usually begins during the teenage years. Earlier onset is almost unheard of. Later onset is uncommon, although anorexia that begins during the teenage years can continue on into the 20s or beyond. Reports from before the 1980s described anorexia as almost limited to women of European ancestry. Since then, researchers have found that anorexia is indeed far more common in women than in men, although men can become anorexic too. Asian or African ancestry is no protection against anorexia; apparently, vulnerability to the disorder has far more to do with socioeconomic status and cultural pressure to be thin than with ethnic background (Le Grange, Telch, & Agras, 1997). One of the major contributors to anorexia is societal pressure, especially on women, to be very thin. Anorexia is less likely to occur in cultures that either tolerate or cherish a somewhat plumper look, such as Jamaica (Smith & Cogswell, 1994) or Europe in an earlier era (Figure 11.18).

Some psychologists have tried to explain anorexia nervosa in terms of a malfunction of the lateral hypothalamus, the brain area that seems to be so central for hunger. That explanation is unlikely, however. Many people with anorexia enjoy preparing food, seem quite interested in food, and enjoy the taste, but they avoid food in far more extreme ways than people who are merely not hungry. For example, some people with anorexia even refuse to lick

FIGURE 11.18 Beauty is in the eye of the beholder. Many cultures, including Europe in earlier centuries, have had a standard of female beauty that is noticeably plumper than that of Western society today. Presumably, a society with no pressure for extreme thinness is also a culture with little likelihood of anorexia nervosa.

postage stamps, for fear that the glue might contain some tiny fraction of a calorie. A mere lack of hunger could hardly explain such behavior.

A better description of anorexia nervosa is that it reflects a "pathological fear of fatness." Even when anorexic women become painfully thin, they often describe themselves as "looking fat" and "needing to lose weight" (Figure 11.19).

What motivates someone to become anorexic? The motivations are complex and vary from one individual to another. First, many women who become anorexic have always prized self-control. Their massive weight loss demonstrates extreme self-control and thereby raises their self-esteem. Also, maintaining a dangerously low weight can be a way of rebelling quietly and attracting attention. Before the onset of the disorder, most anorexic girls are described as having been obedient, high-achieving perfectionists (Bruch, 1980; Goldstein, 1981). Their severe weight loss attracts attention and gives them prestige.

Bulimia

Other people, again mostly young women, starve themselves at times but occasionally throw themselves into an eating binge. They may consume as many as 20,000 calories at a time (Schlesier-Stropp, 1984)—the equivalent of about 30 Big Macs, 10 helpings of French fries, and 10 chocolate milkshakes. Some, but not all, force themselves to vomit or use laxatives after gorging on these enormous meals. People who *alternate between self-starvation and excessive eating* are said to suffer from **bulimia** (literally,

"ox hunger"). We might imagine that people who go on eating binges might starve themselves for a while to make up for it. According to Janet Polivy and Peter Herman (1985), however, the causation goes in the other direction: It is the dieting that causes the binges. Bulimic people starve themselves for a while, fight their persistent feelings of hunger for a while, and then go on an eating binge.

Most people with bulimia have low self-esteem, a tendency toward depression, and a history of growing up in a somewhat troubled family (Fairburn, Welch, Doll, Davies, & O'Connor, 1997). Of course, so do many other people who do not develop bulimia. Some people with bulimia are thin (as with anorexia), but others fluctuate around a normal or high body weight. One study of women who sought psychological help for bulimia found that, 6 years after the end of treatment, 60% no longer had an eating disorder, 30% still had a moderate problem, and 10% either had serious disorders or had died (Fichter & Quadflieg, 1997).

Eating disorders including anorexia and bulimia increased in prevalence in the United States during the 1980s and 1990s, especially among women. Meanwhile, most surveys also found an increasing percentage of young women who report feeling dissatisfied with their appearance, especially those who think they are too heavy (Feingold & Mazzella, 1998). The pressure on women to try to look thin is probably a major contributor to both anorexia and bulimia.

FIGURE 11.19 A fun house mirror causes a temporary distortion of anyone's body appearance. People with anorexia nervosa experience a similar distortion of body image at all times, seeing themselves as much fatter than they really are.

THE MESSAGE
The Complexities of Hunger

The research on anorexia and bulimia underscores the idea that our motivations are controlled by a complex mixture of physiological, social, and cognitive forces. People become overweight (or falsely perceive themselves as overweight) for a variety of reasons, relating to everything from genetics to culture, and they then try to lose weight mostly for social reasons, such as trying to look attractive. Sometimes, the physiological factors and the social factors collide, as when normal-weight people try to make themselves thinner and thinner.

The overall point is this: All our motivations interact and combine. How much we eat and what and when we eat depend not only on our need for food, but also on social needs and the need for self-esteem.

SUMMARY

✳ *Food selection.* Food preferences can be altered by changes in body chemistry, such as a deficiency of salt. Other things being equal, we tend to prefer familiar foods. We avoid foods that have been associated with something nauseating or repulsive and prefer foods previously associated with other good-tasting foods. (page 400)

✳ *Short-term regulation of hunger.* Meals are ended by several mechanisms, principally distension of the stomach and intestines. Hunger resumes when the cells begin to receive less glucose and other nutrients. The hormones insulin and glucagon regulate the flow of nutrients from the blood to storage and from there back into the blood. (page 402)

✳ *Long-term regulation of hunger.* An individual meal can be larger or smaller than necessary to provide the energy that the body needs. The body's fat cells secrete the hormone leptin in proportion to their mass; an increase of leptin decreases hunger, and a decrease of leptin increases hunger. (page 405)

✳ *Causes of being overweight.* People become overweight for many reasons, but emotional difficulties are rarely a major factor. Some people are predisposed to obesity for genetic reasons; whether they become obese or how obese they become depends on what kinds of food their culture provides. Among the mechanisms leading to obesity are low energy output and insensitivity to leptin. (page 406)

✳ *Weight-loss techniques.* People in our society resort to a variety of strategies to lose weight, ranging from dieting to surgery. Increased exercise is a good idea for almost anyone who needs to lose weight. (page 408)

✳ *Anorexia nervosa and bulimia.* People suffering from anorexia nervosa deprive themselves of food, sometimes to the point of starvation. They suppress their physiological drives to satisfy other motivations, including self-esteem. People suffering from bulimia alternate between periods of strict dieting and brief but spectacular eating binges. (page 410)

Suggestions for Further Reading

Capaldi, E. D. (Ed.) (1996). *Why we eat what we eat.* Washington, DC: American Psychological Association. A collection of articles about food selection and the regulation of hunger.

Logue, A. W. (1991). *The psychology of eating and drinking* (2nd ed.). New York: Freeman. Discusses normal and abnormal eating, including anorexia and bulimia.

Terms

glucose   the most abundant sugar in the blood (page 403)

insulin   a hormone that the pancreas releases to increase the entry of glucose and other nutrients into the cells (page 403)

glucagon   a hormone that the pancreas releases to convert stored energy supplies back into blood glucose (page 404)

set point   a level of some variable (such as weight) that the body works to maintain (page 405)

leptin   a hormone released by fat cells; among other effects, it signals the brain to decrease meal size (page 405)

lateral hypothalamus   an area of the brain that contributes to the control of hunger (page 405)

ventromedial hypothalamus   an area of the brain in which damage leads to weight gain via an increase in the frequency of meals (page 405)

paraventricular hypothalamus   an area of the brain in which damage leads to weight gain via an increase in the size of meals (page 405)

obesity   the excessive accumulation of body fat (page 406)

anorexia nervosa   a psychological condition in which a person refuses to eat adequate food and steadily loses weight (page 410)

bulimia   a condition in which a person alternates between self-starvation and excessive eating (page 411)

Answers to Concept Checks

3.   Insulin levels are higher in the middle of the day (LeMagnen, 1981). As a result, much of the food you eat is stored as fats and you become hungry again soon. Late at night, when insulin levels are lower, some of your fat supplies are converted to glucose, which enters the blood. (page 405)

4.   By keeping their fat levels very low, they also keep their leptin levels low, and leptin is one of the triggers for puberty. (page 406)

5.   The set point has increased. (page 406)

Web Resources

Hunger and Eating

www.csun.edu/~vcpsy00h/students/hunger.htm

This student essay is about the biological, learning, and cognitive factors that affect hunger, obesity, and eating disorders.

Eating Disorders

www.psych.org/public_info/eating.html

In the *Let's Talk Facts* series, the American Psychiatric Association describes eating disorders, their major symptoms, what we know about causes, and treatment.

Sexual Motivation

What causes sexual arousal?

What sexual customs are prevalent in our society?

What accounts for some of the variations in sexual practices?

For most of us, sexual activity does not occupy a major fraction of the average day, but thinking about sex does. If you have any doubts about people's interest in sex, consult

Sexual customs vary sharply from one society to another. These people play "kiss-a-girl" in traditional Ukrainian costumes while riding galloping horses. The point of the game is ostensibly to develop horseback-riding skills, but clearly that is not the only motivation.

the television listings, popular books and magazines, and films. (In fact, one way that people can tell they are getting old is that they only think about sex most of the time . . . instead of all the time.)

Humans, unlike most other mammalian species, are interested in sex even at times of the month when a woman is unlikely to get pregnant; in fact, we often take measures to prevent pregnancy. Worldwide, most couples stay together not only long enough to rear children but also long after the children are grown up. Sexual motivation can bind people together in powerful and intimate relationships and also sometimes drive them apart.

Sexual motivation, like hunger, depends on both a physiological drive and available incentives. Also like hunger, the sex drive increases during times of deprivation, at least up to a point, and it can be inhibited for social and symbolic reasons, including religious ones.

However, the sex drive differs from hunger in important ways. We do not need to be around food to feel hungry; many people do need the presence of an attractive partner to feel sexual arousal. Eating in public is normal; sexual intercourse in public is not. We need to eat regularly to stay alive; sexual deprivation is not life-threatening.

What Do People Do, and How Often Do They Do It?

Researchers have many reasons for inquiring about the frequency of various sexual behaviors. For example, if we want to predict how fast and how far the AIDS virus is likely to spread in the population, it is important to know how many people are having unsafe sex with a variety of partners.

In addition to the important scientific and medical reasons for investigating sexual behavior, let's admit it: Most of us are curious about what other people do. We would like to know, "Am I normal? Am I doing something wrong or shameful? Am I missing out on something?"

The answer to the first question depends on what we mean by "normal." If that term means "reasonably common in the population," then it is hard to think of anything you might be doing—or not doing—that would make you abnormal. People vary enormously in their sexual behavior and interests.

The Kinsey Survey

The first important survey of human sexual behavior was conducted by Alfred C. Kinsey (Figure 11.20), a shy and studious insect biologist who once agreed to teach the biological portion of Indiana University's course on marriage. When he found that the library included very little information about human sexuality, he decided to conduct a survey. What he intended as a small-scale project eventually grew into a survey of 18,000 people.

FIGURE 11.20 Alfred C. Kinsey pioneered survey studies of sexual behavior. As an interviewer he was peerless—he always put people at ease so that they could speak freely, but he was also alert to probable lies. His results should be interpreted cautiously, however, because he did not obtain a random or representative sample of the population.

Although Kinsey had a large sample, it was neither random nor representative. He obtained most of his interviews by going to organizations, ranging from fraternities to nunneries, and trying to get everyone in the organization to talk to him. As a result, he interviewed mostly midwestern European-Americans who belonged to organizations that agreed to cooperate. Furthermore, with any sample, not everyone gives honest and accurate replies about their sexual activities. Consequently, Kinsey's data do not provide a trustworthy estimate of the frequencies of various behaviors in the U.S. population. Nevertheless, he did document that human sexual behavior is extremely variable (Kinsey, Pomeroy, & Martin, 1948; Kinsey, Pomeroy, Martin, & Gebhard, 1953). For example, he found some men and women who had rarely or never experienced orgasm. At the other extreme, he found one man who reported an average of four or five orgasms per day over the preceding 30 years (with a diary) and several women who sometimes had 50 or more orgasms within 20 minutes.

Kinsey found that most people were unaware of the great variation in sexual behavior in the population at large. For example, when he asked people whether they believed that "excessive masturbation" causes physical and mental illness, most said they did. (We now know it does not.) He then asked what would constitute "excessive." For each person, "excessive" meant a little more than what he or she did. One young man who masturbated about once per month said he thought three times per month would be excessive and would cause mental illness. Another man, who masturbated three times per day, said he thought five times per day would be excessive. (In reaction to these findings, Kinsey once defined a *nymphomaniac* as "someone who wants sex more than you do.")

Contemporary Surveys

Kinsey did not even try to interview a random sample of the population, because he assumed that most people would refuse to cooperate and perhaps even take offense at being asked. He may have been right about people in the 1940s; however, his assumptions clearly do not hold true today. In the 1980s and 1990s, researchers identified random samples of the U.S. population and managed to get cooperation from most of the people they approached (Fay, Turner, Klassen, & Gagnon, 1989; Laumann, Gagnon, Michael, & Michaels, 1994).

(Some advice if anyone ever asks you to participate in a sex survey: Do not cooperate until you know who the questioner is. Legitimate researchers are careful to present their credentials to show their affiliation with a research institute. They also take elaborate precautions to guarantee the confidentiality of people's responses. If "researchers" who want to ask you questions about your sex life fail to present their credentials or seem unconcerned about your confidentiality, do not trust them. Be especially wary of sex surveys conducted by telephone. Although a few sex researchers do conduct research by telephone, most use a face-to-face interview. When in doubt, assume that the alleged survey is an obscene phone call in disguise.)

A survey of a random sample of almost 3,500 U.S. adults (Laumann, Gagnon, Michael, & Michaels, 1994) has added greatly to our knowledge of U.S. sexual practices and customs. First, what would people *like* to be doing? Figure 11.21 shows the percentage of men and women who describe various sexual activities as "very appealing." Clearly, the most popular sexual activity is vaginal intercourse. Watching one's partner undress is "very appealing" to many people; so is oral sex. Other possible options lag well behind. Note one ambiguity in people's responses: A response of "very appealing" might mean, "I have frequently enjoyed doing that activity," "I would like to try that activity," or even "I enjoy fantasizing about that activity, although I might decline to do it in real life." (One wonders, for example, about the 13% of men who say they find group sex very appealing.)

Note also that a higher percentage of men than women report an interest in every activity on the list. Other studies have reported similar results. Besides the differences shown in Figure 11.21, men are much more likely than women to masturbate frequently and to look forward to opportunities for casual sex (Oliver & Hyde, 1993). However, in spite of men's desire for more frequent and varied sexual activities, men and women are equally likely to express satisfaction with their current sex lives.

Figure 11.22 shows the number of sex partners during the past year for people of various ages. At all ages, most people report either no partner or just one. The percentage of people having multiple partners is greatest in young adulthood and declines steadily with age.

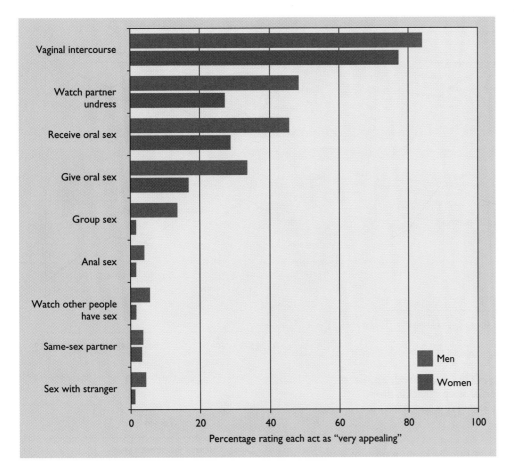

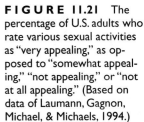

FIGURE 11.21 The percentage of U.S. adults who rate various sexual activities as "very appealing," as opposed to "somewhat appealing," "not appealing," or "not at all appealing." (Based on data of Laumann, Gagnon, Michael, & Michaels, 1994.)

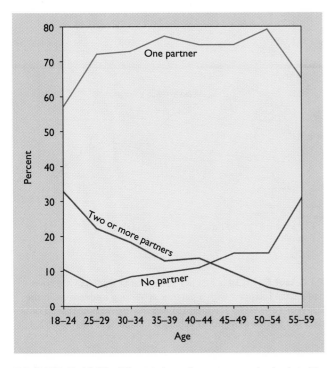

FIGURE 11.22 The number of sex partners in the last 12 months, by U.S. adults of various ages, both sexes combined. (Based on data of Laumann, Gagnon, Michael, & Michaels, 1994.)

The results in Figure 11.22 are cross-sectional, not longitudinal. That is, the 20-year-olds and 50-year-olds grew up in different eras. Figure 11.23 emphasizes these differences among cohorts. People were asked how many sex partners they had had in their lifetime. As Figure 11.23 shows, people in their 40s were more likely to report a large number of partners than were people in their 50s. The reason is that people who were in their 40s at the time of the survey were young and unmarried during the 1970s, an era of a relatively high degree of sexual freedom. People in their 50s were young during a more restrictive era.

In Figure 11.24, you can see differences in current sexual activity reported by people of different ages. The older respondents are less likely than the young ones to report having sex more than twice per week. That trend is probably a real effect of age, not a cohort effect. That is, most 50- to 60-year-olds agree that they are having sexual relations less often than they did when they were younger.

Finally, how many people have a homosexual orientation? You may have heard people announce the figure "ten percent," as if it were an established fact. That number is derived from Kinsey's survey from the 1940s and 1950s. Kinsey reported that about 13% of the men and 7% of the women he interviewed reported a predominantly homosexual orientation. The often-quoted figure of 10% is simply the mean of Kinsey's results for men and women.

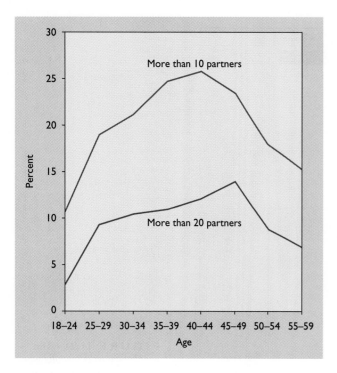

FIGURE 11.23 The percentage of U.S. adults (both sexes combined) reporting more than 10 or 20 sex partners in their lifetime. (Based on data of Laumann, Gagnon, Michael, & Michaels, 1994.)

However, Kinsey's data were based on a very nonrandom sample of the population.

According to a survey of a random sample of 3,500 U.S. adults, 2.8% of men and 1.4% of women describe themselves as having a homosexual (gay or lesbian) orientation (Laumann et al., 1994). As Figure 11.25 illustrates, heterosexuality versus homosexuality is a continuum. Just as many left-handed people perform some tasks with their right hand, and most right-handed people have at least tried various tasks with their left hand, a number of people have at least experimented with both homosexual and heterosexual activities: More than 4% of both men and women report at least one adult homosexual experience. If we expand the scope to "lifetime," including early puberty, 9% of men report at least one homosexual experience.

If you have frequently heard the prevalence of homosexual orientations estimated at 10%, you may be skeptical of the report that only 1–3% of people identify themselves as gay or lesbian. However, three other large surveys of U.S. men reported that 1–2%, 3%, or 6% of U.S. men were either gay or bisexual (Billy, Tanfer, Grady, & Klepinger, 1993; Cameron, Proctor, Coburn, & Forde, 1985; Fay, Turner, Klassen, & Gagnon, 1989). The study reporting the 6% figure had the least satisfactory sampling technique. Surveys in Great Britain and in France have reported a slightly lower prevalence of homosexual orientations, as shown in Figure 11.26 (Spira, et al. 1993; Wellings, Field, Johnson, & Wadsworth, 1994).

The frequencies of various sexual practices vary, of course, among cultures and historical eras. Certainly a sex

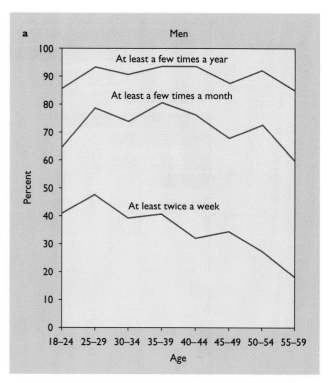

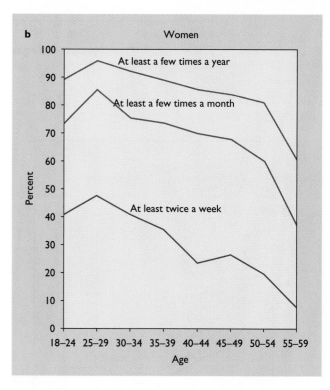

FIGURE 11.24 The percentage of U.S. adults who have had sexual relations with a partner at varying frequencies in the last year. (a) Results for men. (b) Results for women. (Based on data of Laumann, Gagnon, Michael, & Michaels, 1994.)

survey of the United States in 1992 does not apply to other locations or other times. Several studies have reported on the exotic sexual customs of people in certain non-Western

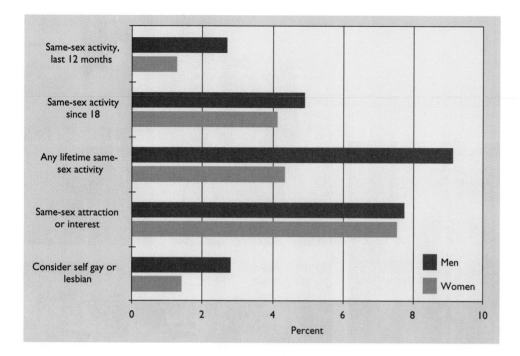

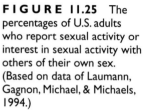

FIGURE 11.25 The percentages of U.S. adults who report sexual activity or interest in sexual activity with others of their own sex. (Based on data of Laumann, Gagnon, Michael, & Michaels, 1994.)

cultures (Davenport, 1977). When we consider how difficult it has been to get reasonably accurate data about U.S. sexual practices, we should be skeptical about studies where anthropologists have interviewed a few people about the sexual customs of their culture. Nevertheless, observable practices (such as dating, marriage, and public display of the human body) vary so strikingly that we can clearly say that much of sexual behavior is the product of learned customs, not just of biological necessity.

Sexual Behavior in the Era of AIDS

During the 1980s, a new factor entered into people's sexual motivations: the fear of **acquired immune deficiency syndrome (AIDS),** *a new and deadly sexually transmitted disease that gradually destroys the body's immune system.*

For the AIDS virus to spread from one person to another, it must enter the second person's blood. (The virus does not survive long outside body fluids.) There are three common routes of transmission: transfusions of contaminated blood, sharing needles used for intravenous injections of illegal drugs, and sexual contact. Other contacts between people, even kissing, cannot spread the AIDS virus (unless perhaps both people had a cut on the mouth that was actively bleeding at the time).

An infected male has an estimated 3% chance of transmitting the virus to a female during vaginal intercourse; an infected woman has no more than a 2% chance, probably much less, of transmitting it to a male (Kaplan, 1988). The likelihood of transmission increases if either partner has an open wound on the genitals or if the woman is menstruating. The probability of transmission during anal intercourse

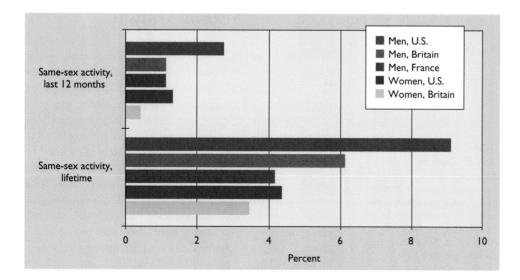

FIGURE 11.26 Comparisons of the results of surveys conducted in three countries, asking people whether they have experienced homosexual activity. (Based on data of Laumann, Gagnon, Michael, & Michaels, 1994; Spira et al., 1993; Wellings, Field, Johnson, & Wadsworth, 1994.)

Human cultures have very different standards regarding public display of the human body, dating, marriage, and premarital sex.

is higher, about 7–10%, because the lining of the rectum is likely to be torn (Kaplan, 1988). These estimates are just approximations, of course.

For generations, people have known how to avoid contracting syphilis, gonorrhea, and other sexually transmitted diseases: Don't have sex with someone who might be infected, or when in doubt, use a condom. If people had consistently followed this advice, we could have eliminated those diseases long ago. The same advice is now offered to combat AIDS, and many people have followed it, though certainly not all. One study of men leaving a homosexual bathhouse found that only 10% were engaging in anal sex without a condom—a far lower percentage than was common before the AIDS crisis (Richwald et al., 1988).

Some heterosexual couples have also become more

Right to life

AIDS is a preventable disease. By using condoms during sex and by not sharing injection needles with other people, one can greatly decrease the probability of transmitting or receiving the AIDS virus. Advertisements such as this one have prompted many people to change their behavior.

cautious, although that increase is not impressive overall. According to one national survey in 1990, only 17% of heterosexuals with multiple sexual partners and 12.6% of heterosexuals with "risky" sexual partners used condoms consistently (Catania et al., 1992). Choosing whether or not to have sex, or how or with whom, is a special kind of decision-making. The continuing spread of the AIDS virus and the continuing number of unwanted pregnancies indicates that many people are still making some unwise sexual decisions (Wyatt, 1994).

Sexual Arousal

Sexual motivation depends on both physiological and cognitive influences. William Masters and Virginia Johnson (1966), who pioneered the study of human sexual response, discovered that physiological arousal during the sex act is about the same in men and women. They observed hundreds of people engaging in masturbation and sexual intercourse in a laboratory and monitored their physiological responses, including heart rate, breathing, muscle tension, blood engorgement of the genitals and breasts, and nipple erection. Masters and Johnson identified four physiological stages in sexual arousal (Figure 11.27). During the first stage, *excitement,* a man's penis becomes erect and a woman's vagina becomes lubricated. Breathing grows rapid and deep. Heart rate and blood pressure increase. Many people experience a flush of the skin, which sometimes re-

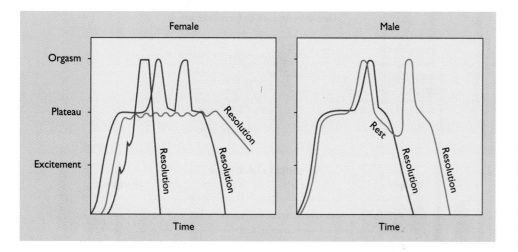

FIGURE 11.27 Sexual arousal usually proceeds through four stages—excitement, plateau, orgasm, and resolution. Each line represents the response of a different individual. (After Masters & Johnson, 1966.)

sembles a measles rash. Women's nipples become erect, and if women have never nursed a baby, their breasts swell slightly. Although this stage is referred to as excitement, it actually requires some degree of relaxation. Nervousness interferes with sexual excitement; so do stimulant drugs (even coffee).

During the second stage, called the *plateau,* excitement remains fairly constant. This stage lasts for varying lengths of time, depending on the person's age and the intensity of the stimulation. During the third stage, excitement becomes intense and is followed by a sudden relief of tension known as *climax* or *orgasm,* which is felt throughout the entire body. During the fourth and final stage, *resolution,* the person returns to an unaroused state.

As Figure 11.27 shows, the pattern of excitation varies from one person to another. During a given episode, a woman may experience either no orgasm at all, a single orgasm, or many. Men do not experience multiple consecutive orgasms, although they can achieve orgasm again following a rest (or refractory) period. In both sexes, the intensity of the orgasm ranges among individuals from something like a sigh to an extremely intense experience.

At any rate, that is the usual pattern. Some people are unable to complete the four stages of arousal. Some men cannot produce or maintain an erection. Others have premature ejaculations, advancing from excitement to orgasm sooner than they or their partners wish. A substantial number of women, perhaps as many as 10%, and a few men stay at the plateau stage without experiencing orgasm. The reasons for such sexual dysfunctions are largely unknown. Some people have physiological disorders; others may have trouble enjoying sexual relations because they feel ashamed.

Sexual Identity and Orientation

Just as hunger includes two major aspects—how much food to eat and which foods to choose—sexual motivation includes two aspects: how frequently to have sex and with

whom. People vary in their sexual preferences, just as they do in their food preferences or any other aspect of life. Why do some people prefer partners of the opposite sex and others prefer partners of their own sex?

Psychologists distinguish between gender identity and sexual orientation. **Gender identity** (or sexual identity) is *the sex that a person regards him- or herself as being.* Ordinarily, people with male genitals have a male identity and people with female genitals have a female identity, although exceptions do occur. **Sexual orientation** is *a person's preference for male or female sex partners (or both or neither).* People who prefer partners of their own sex have a homosexual (gay or lesbian) orientation. Psychologists do not yet fully understand the causes of sexual orientation.

Influences on Sexual Anatomy

In the earliest stages of development, the human fetus has a "unisex" appearance (Figure 11.28). One structure subsequently develops into either a penis or a clitoris; another structure develops into either a scrotum or labia. The direction this development takes depends on hormonal influences during prenatal development. Beginning in the seventh or eighth week after conception, genetic *male fetuses generally secrete higher levels of the hormone* **testosterone** *than do females* (although both sexes produce some), and over the next couple of months the testosterone causes the tiny fetal structures to grow into a penis and a scrotum. In genetic female fetuses, with lower levels of testosterone, the structures develop into a clitoris and labia. Levels of *the hormone* **estrogen** *increase more in females than in males* at this time; estrogen is important for female development but has little effect on whether one develops a penis or clitoris, scrotum or labia.

Remember: In humans and other mammals, high testosterone levels produce a male anatomy; low testosterone levels produce a female anatomy. Within normal limits, the amount of circulating estrogen does not determine whether one develops a male or female appearance.

At least one child in two thousand is born with genitals that are hard to classify as male or female. For example, some genetic female fetuses have overactive adrenal glands

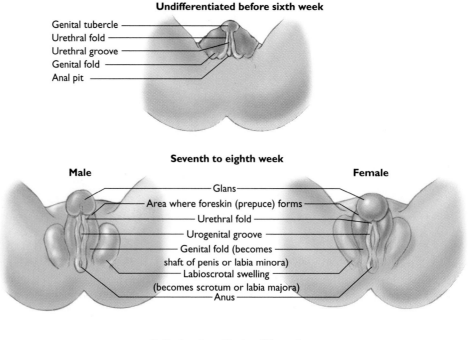

Undifferentiated before sixth week

Genital tubercle
Urethral fold
Urethral groove
Genital fold
Anal pit

Seventh to eighth week

Male   Female

Glans
Area where foreskin (prepuce) forms
Urethral fold
Urogenital groove
Genital fold (becomes
shaft of penis or labia minora)
Labioscrotal swelling
(becomes scrotum or labia majora)
Anus

Fully developed by twelfth week

Urethral   Male   Female
opening
(meatus)   Prepuce
(Penis) Glans (Clitoris)
(Penis) Shaft (Clitoris)
Labia minora   Urethral opening
(meatus)
Scrotum   Labia majora   Vaginal
opening
Anus

FIGURE 11.28 The human genitals look the same with both male and female fetuses for about the first 6 or 7 weeks after conception (a). Differences begin to emerge over the next couple of months (b) and are well developed at birth (c).

that secrete enough testosterone to partially masculinize development. The genetic female may then develop a sexual anatomy that looks intermediate between male and female (Money & Ehrhardt, 1972). In rarer cases, a genetic male develops an intermediate condition because of a gene that alters hormone receptors (Misrahi et al., 1997). *People with an anatomy that appears intermediate between male and female* are known as **intersexes** or **hermaphrodites** (Figure 11.29).

How should parents and others treat intersexes? The main question is how these people can be most successful and satisfied socially. For decades, the standard medical recommendation has been, when in doubt, call the child female, and perform surgery to make her anatomy look female. This surgery includes creating or lengthening a vagina and reducing the ambiguous penis/clitoris to the size of an average clitoris. In many cases, the additional surgery is unsatisfactory and additional operations are performed later. That is a lot of surgery, but most physicians think it is easier and produces a more normal appearance than any attempts to expand an ambiguous penis/clitoris to the size of a penis.

That recommendation has been based on the assumption that, if a child looks like a girl and is treated like a girl,

she will develop psychologically as a girl. Physicians never had much evidence for that assumption, and some adult intersexes, in spite of their appearance and rearing, develop a male identity. Furthermore, a great many complain that genital surgery—reducing or removing the penis/clitoris—

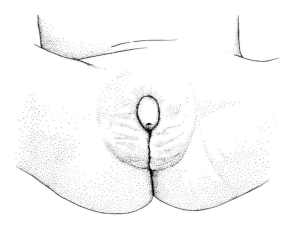

FIGURE 11.29 External genitals of a 3-month-old genetic female: This infant was masculinized before birth by excess androgens from the adrenal gland.

left them with greatly reduced sexual excitation and a feeling of mutilation. Finally, they object that, in many cases, physicians lied to them about what surgery they had done and why. The standard, traditional approach in medicine is now being opposed by those who recommend complete honesty with intersexes and avoiding surgery until or unless such people request it themselves as adults (Diamond & Sigmundson, 1997).

CONCEPT CHECK

6. If a human fetus were exposed to very low levels of both testosterone and estrogen throughout prenatal development, how would the sexual anatomy appear? (Check your answer on page 424.)

Influences on Sexual Orientation

Society's attitudes toward homosexuality have changed repeatedly over time. As far as we know, the ancient Greeks and Romans considered it fairly typical for men to engage in occasional sexual activities with each other as well as with women (Boswell, 1990). (The Greek and Roman writers had little to say about women's sexual interests.) During a later era, Europeans regarded male homosexuality as sinful or criminal. By the early 20th century, the "enlightened" view was that homosexuality was not sinful but "merely" a sign of disease or mental illness. The evidence, however, was based on a badly distorted sample: Psychiatrists and psychologists were acquainted with homosexual men who had sought help for psychological troubles. But homosexual men without psychological problems never consulted therapists, and therefore the therapists did not know about them. Studies of homosexual men who have never visited a therapist revealed that many homosexual men are content and well adjusted (Siegelman, 1974). Consequently, psychologists and psychiatrists today consider a homosexual orientation to be a natural variation in sexual motivation.

The origins and determinants of sexual orientation are not yet well understood. Adult homosexuals often report that their sexual preference was apparent to them from as early an age as they can remember. They did not choose it voluntarily, and they could not change it, even if they wanted to, any more easily than a left-hander could decide to be right-handed. What causes some people to develop a heterosexual preference and others to develop a homosexual preference?

Most of the available research deals with gay men. Lesbians (women with a homosexual orientation) are less numerous, and many are sufficiently private about their orientation that they become invisible to researchers. The research we do have suggests that genetic factors contribute toward sexual orientation for both men and women. Figure 11.30 shows the results of studies concerning homosexuality in twins and other relatives of adult gays and lesbians (Bailey & Pillard, 1991; Bailey, Pillard, Neale, & Agyei, 1993). Note that homosexuality is more prevalent in the monozygotic (identical) twins than in the dizygotic (fraternal) twins. That trend suggests a genetic influence toward homosexuality, although a gene could hardly be the only factor. (If it were, then 100% of the monozygotic twins would have a homosexual orientation.) Note also that homosexuality is more common among the dizygotic twins than among adopted brothers or sisters. That trend also suggests a genetic factor, although it could also indicate the influence of a factor in the prenatal environment that is shared by twins but not by boys who simply grow up in the same family. If genetic influences contribute to homosexuality, the genes influencing males are different from those influencing females. That is, gay men have a high percentage of gay relatives but not of lesbian relatives; lesbian women have a high percentage of lesbian relatives but not of gay relatives.

If genes affect sexual orientation, they must do so by altering the development of some part of the body, possibly the brain. Other possible influences on sexual orientation, such as prenatal hormones, may also alter brain anatomy. Regardless of the roles of genetics, hormones, and other factors, the evidence suggests a measurable difference in brain anatomy between homosexual and heterosexual men. Let's examine that evidence.

Attitudes toward homosexual relationships have varied among cultures and among historical eras.

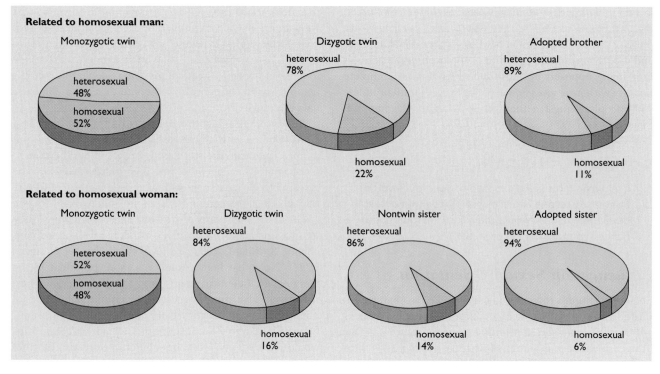

FIGURE 11.30 The probability of a homosexual orientation is higher among monozygotic twins of adult homosexuals than among their dizygotic twins. The probability is higher among dizygotic twins than among adopted brothers or sisters who grew up in the same family. These data suggest a possible genetic role in the development of sexual orientation. (Based on results of Bailey & Pillard, 1991; Bailey, Pillard, Neale, & Agyei, 1993.)

WHAT'S THE EVIDENCE?
The Relationship Between Sexual Orientation and Brain Anatomy

Animal studies have demonstrated that one section of the anterior hypothalamus, known to neuroanatomists as INAH3, is generally larger in males than it is in females and that this portion of the brain is necessary for the display of male-typical sexual activity. Its growth is known to depend on prenatal hormones. This, then, is an interesting area to compare in the brains of homosexual and heterosexual men.

Hypothesis   INAH3, a particular cluster of neurons in the anterior hypothalamus, will be larger, on average, in the brains of heterosexual men than it is in the brains of homosexual men or heterosexual women.

Method   Simon LeVay (1991) examined the brains of 41 young or middle-aged adults (ages 26–59), who had died of AIDS or other causes. AIDS was the cause of death for all 19 of the homosexual men in the study, 6 of the 16 heterosexual men, and 1 of the 6 heterosexual women. No brains of homosexual women were available for study. LeVay measured the sizes of four clusters of neurons in the anterior hypothalamus, including two clusters for which sex differences are common and two that do not differ between the sexes.

Results   LeVay found that three of the four neuron clusters did not consistently vary in size among the groups he studied. However, area INAH3 was, on the average, about twice as large in heterosexual men as it was in homosexual men and about the same size in homosexual men as it was in heterosexual women. Figure 11.31 shows results for two representative individuals. The results probably do not simply reflect the cause of death; among heterosexual men, the size of this brain area was about the same for men who died of AIDS and men who died of other causes.

Interpretation   These results suggest that the size of the INAH3 area of the anterior hypothalamus may be related to heterosexual versus homosexual orientation, at least for some individuals. These results are consistent with the idea that genes or prenatal hormones guide brain development, thus altering the probabilities of developing various sexual orientations. However, the results are not entirely conclusive. Conceivably, a homosexual or heterosexual lifestyle might alter brain anatomy instead of the other way around. Also, we do not know whether the people that LeVay studied were representative of other people; certainly, we must await replications on other samples. Finally, the variations in brain structure from one person to another indicate that brain anatomy does not completely control sexual orientation. (The INAH3

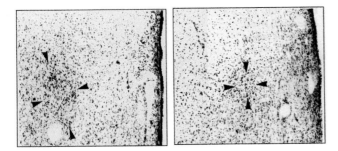

FIGURE 11.31 One section of the anterior hypothalamus (marked by arrows) is larger, on the average, in the brains of heterosexual men (left) than in the brains of homosexual men (right) or heterosexual women (LeVay, 1991). Review Figure 11.13 for the location of the hypothalamus.

nucleus was fairly large in some homosexual men and fairly small in some heterosexual men.)

So, where do all these studies leave us? At this point, the evidence links certain biological factors, including genes and brain anatomy, to male homosexuality, at least for some individuals. We know little, however, about how those biological predispositions combine with experience to produce sexual orientation. Indeed, researchers do not know which kinds of experiences are most crucial. We need to await additional studies before we can draw any confident conclusions.

Uncertainty and tentative conclusions are not unusual in psychology. If you decide to become a psychologist, you will need to get used to the words *maybe* and *probably*. As I pointed out in Chapter 2, psychologists rarely talk about "proving" a conclusion; they merely increase or decrease their confidence in a conclusion.

* * *

CONCEPT CHECK

7. Most studies find that adult homosexual men have approximately the same levels of testosterone in their blood as heterosexual men of the same age. Do such results conflict with the suggestion that prenatal hormonal conditions can predispose certain men to homosexuality? (Check your answer on page 424.)

THE MESSAGE
The Biology and Sociology of Sex

Sexual motivation at any moment reflects an interplay of biological readiness and the availability of a suitable partner. Similarly, the development of sexual interest and sexual orientation reflects a complex combination of biological predisposition and experiences. Researchers are making progress, but much remains to be learned.

SUMMARY

* *Variability in human sexual behavior.* Alfred Kinsey, who conducted the first extensive survey of human sexual behavior, found that sexual activity varies more widely than most people realize. (page 413)

* *Prevalence of sexual behaviors.* Modern surveys indicate that most U.S. adults have either one sex partner or none during a given year. Men express a greater interest than women do in varied sexual practices with varied partners. Nevertheless, sexual satisfaction is reported to be about equal for men and women. (page 414)

* *Prevalence of homosexuality.* According to several surveys, about 1–3% of U.S. and Western European adults regard themselves as either gay or lesbian. A larger percentage of people, especially men, who regard themselves as heterosexual have experimented with homosexual activities, especially during adolescence. (page 415)

* *Sexual arousal.* Sexual arousal proceeds through four stages: excitement, plateau, orgasm, and resolution. For a combination of physiological and motivational reasons, some people fail to pass through all four stages or pass through them more quickly than they wish. (page 418)

* *Development of genitals.* In the early stages of development, the human fetus possesses anatomical structures that may develop into either male genitalia (if testosterone levels are high enough) or female genitalia (if testosterone levels are lower). (page 419)

* *Homosexuality.* For reasons that are unclear, some people develop a heterosexual orientation and others develop a homosexual orientation. Genetic influences can apparently alter the probability of a homosexual orientation, although these influences alone cannot account for all variations in sexual orientation. On the average, heterosexual and homosexual men differ in the size of one structure in the hypothalamus that contributes to certain aspects of sexual behavior. (page 421)

Suggestion for Further Reading

Laumann, E. O., Gagnon, J. H., Michael, R. T., & Michaels, S. (1994). *The social organization of sexuality in the United States.* Chicago, IL: University of Chicago Press. Provides survey data and also a discussion of the role of sexuality in human life.

Terms

acquired immune deficiency syndrome (AIDS)   a disease often transmitted sexually that gradually destroys the body's immune system (page 417)

gender identity   the sex that a person regards him- or herself as being (page 419)

sexual orientation   a person's preference for either male or female sex partners (page 419)

testosterone   a hormone present in higher quantities in males than in females (page 419)

estrogen a hormone present in higher quantities in females than in males (page 419)

Answers to Concept Checks

6. A fetus exposed to very low levels of both testosterone and estrogen throughout prenatal development would develop a normal female appearance. High levels of testosterone lead to male anatomy; low levels lead to female anatomy. The level of estrogen does not play a decisive role. (page 421)

7. Not necessarily. The suggestion is that prenatal hormones can alter early brain development. In adulthood, hormone levels are normal, but certain aspects of brain development have already been determined. (page 423)

Web Resources

Sexual Motivation
www.csun.edu/~vcpsy00h/students/sexmotiv.htm
Follow the complex relationships among hormones, cognitions, learning, and culture as they influence sexual motivation.

MODULE 11.4

Achievement Motivation

What motivates some people to work harder than others?

Your 2-year-old nephew is building a stack of blocks. You say, "Here, let me help you," and you finish stacking the blocks. Will he smile and thank you? Hardly. He is more likely to cry, "I wanted to do it myself!" His goal was not to *have* a tall stack, but to *build* a tall stack.

Say that you are doing something creative yourself—painting a picture, writing a story, playing chess perhaps—something you do moderately well. Someone who is more expert than you says, "Here, let me help you. I see you're having a little trouble, and I think I can fix it." How do you react? You might not burst into tears, but you probably resent the help. It was your task, and you wanted to do it yourself.

Most of us strive for the joy of accomplishment, some of us more than others. What occupation do you hope to enter after graduation? Have you chosen it because it is the surest way for you to earn a lot of money? Or have you chosen it because it will enable you to take pride in your achievements? Many people have forgone better-paying jobs to take one that will give them a greater feeling of achievement.

Measuring the Need for Achievement

The **need for achievement** is *a striving for accomplishment and excellence.* That sounds like a rather straightforward definition, but it confuses two quite distinct types of motivation (McClelland, Koestner, & Weinberger, 1989). As a rule, when people describe themselves as having a strong achievement motivation, they are referring to an extrinsic motivation. That is, they are drawn by the rewards they have been receiving or expect to receive for various accomplishments. But, as we saw in the first module of this chapter, there is a second kind of need for achievement, a more intrinsic motivation. People with this intrinsic need for achievement may not describe themselves as striving for achievement, but they do take pleasure in accomplishing goals for their own sake. They are likely to persist at a task for a long time and probably develop great skills in the long run. For example, people who spend every spare moment studying and playing chess may be driven by an intrinsic motivation to excel at chess, even if they do not think of themselves as "highly motivated" toward achievement. (They may even think that they are wasting their time.) We shall concentrate here on the intrinsic need for achievement.

The intrinsic need for achievement was first inferred from the performance of schoolchildren. Some children are much more successful in school than others who, as far as we can tell, have equal ability and are equally interested in the rewards that good grades might eventually bring. The same is true in athletics, business, and other aspects of life. Apparently, some people simply try harder than others. If this is true, then we should be able to measure and study this tendency as a personality variable. But how?

If you wanted to determine which workers or schoolchildren were most highly motivated to achieve, what would you measure and how? You could not simply measure how *much* people achieve, because you are trying to explain *why*

The need for achievement includes both extrinsic and intrinsic motivation. The artist who created this wooden cow probably hoped for recognition and money (an extrinsic motivation) but also must have enjoyed the creative process itself (an intrinsic motivation). The inside of the back of the cow folds out to form a desk.

some people achieve more than others. You would need to measure the need for achievement separately from the achievements themselves.

Another way *not* to measure the need for achievement is to ask people whether they are strongly motivated for success. Many people say yes because they believe it is socially desirable to do so. Psychologists measure achievement motivation indirectly, without even telling people what they are measuring.

One of the most popular methods of measuring the need for achievement makes use of the *Thematic Apperception Test (TAT),* which we shall examine again in Chapter 13 (McClelland, Atkinson, Clark, & Lowell, 1953). Investigators show people some pictures and ask them to tell a story about each. Before reading further, try it yourself: Examine the picture in Figure 11.32 and tell a story about it that includes what led up to this scene, what is happening now, and what will happen next.

If you ever take the TAT, after you finish your stories about all the pictures, psychologists will count the number of times you mentioned various themes, including striving for goals and achievements. For example, this story would get a high score on need for achievement:

> This girl is taking an important test. First, she went through the test and answered all the items she knew well. Now, she is trying to remember the answer to one of the more difficult questions. She gazes off into the distance, trying to remember everything she has read about this topic. She finally remembers, writes down the correct answer, and gets a perfect score. Later, she goes on to college, becomes a Rhodes scholar, and eventually becomes a famous inventor.

Contrast that story with this one:

> This girl is sitting through a very boring class. She is gazing off into the distance, thinking about the party she went to last weekend. As soon as class is over, she goes out and has a good time with her friends.

Such a story would rate a zero on the need for achievement. (It might rate high on other motives, of course.) Your answer on any one picture is not critical; for example, you might tell stories on a few pictures that have nothing to do with achievement and stories rich in achievement themes on the other pictures. What matters is the total over the series.

How well does the Thematic Apperception Test measure need for achievement? The data suggest that it provides a moderately useful measure. Children who score high on the need for achievement generally work harder and get higher grades in school than do children of equal IQs who score low on need for achievement (Khalid, 1991). Need for achievement also correlates reasonably well with various measures of career success (Spangler, 1992). It does not correlate highly with people's self-reports of their "strength of motivation." In other words, the test does seem to tap something related to intrinsic motivation.

FIGURE 11.32 In the Thematic Apperception Test, each person looks at a series of pictures similar to this one and tells a story about each one. Psychologists count the number of achievement themes mentioned by each person, to measure that person's need for achievement. They can also measure other motivations by counting other kinds of themes.

The Need for Achievement and Setting Goals

Suppose you have a choice of three video games to play. One game is easy; you know you can get a high score on it, but so could anyone else. The second game is more difficult; you are not sure how well you would do. The third is so difficult that you are sure you would lose quickly, as most people do. Which do you choose? Most people prefer the difficult but not impossible game, especially people with a strong need for achievement (Atkinson & Birch, 1978).

People sometimes prefer especially easy or especially difficult tasks if they are dominated by a **fear of failure,** *a concern with avoiding defeat as opposed to gaining victory.* When they try very easy tasks, they avoid failure, although they never achieve any remarkable success. When they try very difficult tasks, they provide themselves with an excuse for failure. Apparently, they would rather fail at an impossible task than run the risk of failing at a realistic task.

People with a strong fear of failure will make a normal effort, or even an extraordinary effort, when given an easy task or when in a relaxed, low-pressure situation. But if they are told, "This is an important test; you are going to be evaluated, so do your best," they expend less effort. In contrast, people with a strong need for achievement make little effort on an easy task or when the situation puts little pressure on them. When they are told that they are going to be evaluated, they try harder (Nygard, 1982).

When people receive feedback on their performance, such as "you got 82% correct on the first test," those with a strong need for achievement usually increase their efforts, no matter what the results were. Apparently, they interpret almost any feedback as meaning that they have room for improvement and need to try harder. People with a low need for achievement or a high fear of failure react to feedback by decreasing their efforts. The feedback either tells them that they are achieving their modest goals, or that they are failing and may as well quit (Matsui, Okada, & Kakuyama, 1982).

SOMETHING TO THINK ABOUT

Some people have suggested that our society has become less ambitious and less motivated by achievement than it once was. How could we test that hypothesis? ✻

CONCEPT CHECK

8. The new basketball coach at Generic Tech has set up a game schedule for next year. The team will play only opponents that had about average records last year, winning as many as they lost. Does this coach have a high need for achievement or a high fear of failure? (Check your answer on page 431.)

Effective and Ineffective Goals

High goals are especially effective in motivating people with a strong need for achievement, and they also tend to be somewhat effective with most people. (See Figure 11.33.) At the start of the college semester, four young women are asked to state their goals. One is aiming for a straight-A average. Another hopes to get at least a C average. A third plans to "do as well as I can." A fourth has no set goals. Which student will work hardest and get the best grades?

The student aiming for a straight-A average will do the best, under certain circumstances (Locke & Latham, 1991):

•   She must have enough ability for the goal to be realistic. If she has previously struggled just to get passing grades, she will quickly become discouraged.
•   She must take her goal seriously. If she casually says she is aiming for straight A's and then never thinks about it again, it will make no difference to her. She can increase her commitment to the goal by stating it publicly. The more people who know about her goal, the harder it will be for her to ignore it.
•   She must get some feedback from periodic test scores and grades on assignments to tell her what topics she needs to study harder (Figure 11.34).
•   She will be most likely to pursue her goal diligently if she is *not* being paid to achieve it or at least if the payment

FIGURE 11.33 People with a high need for achievement prefer high goals. Research findings indicate that people work hardest when they set high goals for themselves, provided they think they have a realistic chance of succeeding.

does not require an extremely outstanding performance. If she must get all As in order to earn a financial reward, she is likely to become discouraged if it appears that she might get even one B. At that point, she may quit trying. An offer of money helps people to achieve lower goals, but they need intrinsic motivations to pursue high goals.

The same conditions hold for workers (Locke, Shaw, Saari, & Latham, 1981). A very high goal leads to the best performance, provided that the goal seems realistic. A vague "do your best" goal is no better than no goal at all. For a goal to be effective, workers must be committed to achieving it and must receive periodic feedback on their progress. Once they reach their goal, they must be rewarded; otherwise, they will be indifferent toward setting goals later on.

Setting goals leads to vigorous activity if:

The goal is realistic.

A serious commitment is made, especially if it is made publicly.

Feedback is received.

FIGURE 11.34 Conditions for high activity toward achieving goals.

CONCEPT CHECK

9. Under what conditions would people be most likely to keep their New Year's resolutions? (Check your answer on page 431.)

Age and Sex Differences in Need for Achievement

Some people have such a strong need for achievement that they will devote every available moment to an ambitious task they have set for themselves. How does the need for achievement develop, and why does it become stronger in some people than in others?

The Development of Need for Achievement in Childhood

Achievement and success mean different things to different people (Phalet & Claeys, 1993). In some cultures, and for some people within a given culture, the emphasis is on individual accomplishments, such as gaining wealth, fame, and influence. For others, the emphasis is on identification with the group, such as serving one's country or helping one's family. The Japanese culture in particular stresses bringing honor to one's family. In nontechnological societies, success is not defined in terms of jobs and money.

Achievement also has different meanings for people of varying ages. For older people, jobs and earnings become less important goals (Maehr & Kleiber, 1981); hobbies become more important, and even mere competence in taking care of one's own needs can be a source of feelings of accomplishment. Still, even within a sometimes restricted range, people strive for some kind of achievement.

In early childhood, achievement also means something more like competence than prestige. Even children who are only 18 months old clearly show pride in their accomplishments, such as building a tall stack of blocks. By age 2½, they understand the idea of competition; they show pleasure at outdoing someone else, disappointment at losing (Heckhausen, 1984).

Although preschool children show great pleasure when they have completed a task, they seldom appear distressed by their inability to complete it. Heinz Heckhausen (1984) tried to find out how children less than 4 years old would react to failure. He rigged up various contraptions so that a child's stack of blocks would topple or fall through a trap door. He often managed to arouse the children's curiosity, but never their discouragement. He could not find a way to make young children feel that they had failed.

Preschool children are highly optimistic about their own abilities. Even when they have failed a task repeatedly, they confidently announce that they will succeed the next

Preschool children show delight in their successes, but show no clear sign of discouragement after their failures. Perhaps they are ever-confident of their eventual success, or perhaps they simply do not yet understand the concept of failure.

time. An adult asks, "Who is going to win this game the next time we play?" Most preschool children shout "me!" even if they have lost time after time in the past (Stipek, 1984).

Perhaps optimism comes naturally to humans. We quickly learn how it feels to succeed; we learn more slowly what it means to fail. When children enter school, their teachers force them to compare themselves to one another. Within a few years, some children begin to approach tasks with a fear of failure instead of a joyful striving for success (Stipek, 1984).

Psychologists have not yet determined when and why children change their attitudes toward success and failure, but they suspect that teachers unintentionally convey the message, "You probably aren't going to like this or do it very well, but you have to do it anyway." Jere Brophy (1987, p. 190) reports the following quotes from junior-high teachers:

- "If you get done by ten o'clock, you can go outside."
- "This penmanship assignment means that sometimes in life you just can't do what you want to do. The next time you have to do something you don't want to do, just think: 'Well, that's part of life.'"
- "You'll have to work real quietly, otherwise you'll have to do more assignments."
- "This test is to see who the really smart ones are."

Sex Differences in Need for Achievement

Times change. In the United States, before the 1960s, relatively few women sought long-term careers; most expected to quit work when they got married or when they had their first child. However, by the mid-1980s, most women, even mothers of preschoolers, had jobs outside the home (Matthews & Rodin, 1989). Even many older women, who had grown up in an earlier era with much less support for women's careers, reentered the job market (Clausen &

Gilens, 1990). For women as well as for men, work provides an opportunity to gain a sense of accomplishment as well as a source of income.

Nevertheless, industrial-organizational psychologists find that most women still do not advance as rapidly as men do in business. Companies hire women about as frequently as men for their lower-level management positions, but they tend to give men faster promotions and salary increases. When women do reach high levels of leadership, they are generally rated as about equally effective as men at the same level, except in a few settings such as in the military (Eagly, Karau, & Makhijani, 1995).

Why? One possibility is that women place themselves at a disadvantage by interrupting their careers for child care or by refusing promotions that would require moving to another city. However, even women who accept transfers to other cities and who never interrupt their careers still fail to advance as rapidly as men, on the average (Stroh, Brett, & Reilly, 1992).

The seemingly obvious conclusion is that companies continue to discriminate against women, in spite of their claims that they try hard not to do so. Still, there is one more possibility: According to some reports, women, on the average, score lower than men do on need for achievement, as measured by the Thematic Apperception Test. That is, perhaps many women are simply content with a lower rate of advancement, or maybe more men are willing to sacrifice everything else to get ahead.

If men and women really do differ in need for achievement, the explanation must include the fact that society discourages girls and women from setting high goals. Many girls set high goals for themselves while they are in high school but lower their goals within the next few years (Farmer, 1983). In one study, a group of adult women filled out a job-interest questionnaire. The interests they checked most frequently included secretary, elementary school teacher, home economics teacher, and dietitian. Two weeks later, they filled out the same questionnaire again, but this time they were given these instructions:

> I want you to pretend with me that men have come of age and that: (1) Men like intelligent women; (2) Men and women are promoted equally in business and the professions; and (3) Raising a family well is very possible for a career woman. (Farmer & Bohn, 1970, p. 229).

After hearing these instructions, the women expressed a significantly increased interest in becoming an author, psychologist, lawyer, insurance salesperson, or physician. They largely lost interest in becoming a secretary, teacher, or dietitian (Farmer & Bohn, 1970). Evidently, women lower their career aspirations because they fear that high ambitions will scare men away, or because they believe businesses will not promote them fairly, or because they fear that a full-time career will interfere with raising a family (Farmer, 1987).

Jobs That Encourage or Discourage Achievement Motivation

Imagine that you are either starting up or reorganizing a company, and you must decide how to divide up the workload. Should you make the jobs challenging and interesting, at the risk that they might be difficult? Or should you make them simple and foolproof, at the risk of being boring?

Your answer will depend on what you assume about the workers and their motivations. *According to the* **scientific-management approach** *to job design, also known as Theory X, most employees are lazy, indifferent, and uncreative.* Therefore, employers should make the work as foolproof as possible and supervise the workers to make sure they are doing each task the right way, not only to save time but also to avoid injury (Figure 11.35). The employer leaves nothing to chance or to the worker's own initiative (McGregor, 1960).

According to an alternative view, the **human-relations approach** *to job design, also known as Theory Y, employees like to take responsibility for their work, to enjoy some variety in their job, and to feel a sense of accomplishment* (McGregor, 1960). In short, they have a need for achievement. According to this approach, employers should enrich the jobs, giving each employee responsibility for meaningful tasks. For example, a financial services corporation that followed the scientific-management approach would have one employee keep one kind of records, another keep another kind of records, and so on. The same company, reorganized according to the human-relations approach, would put each employee in charge of the services for particular clients, therefore keeping a variety of records, doing different things at various times, and seeing how all the pieces come together. Employees with enriched jobs generally report greater satisfaction (Campion & McClelland, 1991). From the employer's standpoint, the enriched jobs

FIGURE 11.35 Psychologists have conducted research to determine the best, safest, most efficient ways to perform even simple tasks. For example, the drawing on the left shows the right way to lift a brick, and the drawing on the right shows the wrong way, according to Gilbreth (1911).

are beneficial in most ways, although they pose two possible disadvantages: It takes longer to train the workers than it would with simpler jobs, and the workers performing enriched jobs expect to be paid more than before!

So, which approach is better? Before you answer, consider an analogy to education: Professor X tells students exactly what to read on which day, what facts to study for each test, and precisely what to do to get a good grade. (This course is analogous to the scientific-management approach; it leaves nothing to the students' initiative.) Professor Y outlines some general issues to be discussed in the course, provides a long list of suggested readings, lets the students control class discussion, and invites students to create their own ideas for projects instead of taking tests. (This course is analogous to the human-relations approach, though perhaps a little more extreme.) Which class would you like better?

My answer would be, "It depends." If I am extremely interested in the topic of the course and I would like to pursue some ideas of my own, then I would prefer Professor Y's course, and I would consider Professor X's course tedious and insulting. But if I am just taking the course to satisfy a requirement and I have no enthusiasm for the topic, I might appreciate the precise structure of Professor X's class.

The same is true of jobs. Some workers, especially the younger and brighter ones, thrive on the challenge of an enriched job. Others, especially those who have been doing a simple job for many years, dislike the insecurity of learning new skills and solving problems on their own (Arnold & House, 1980; Campion & Thayer, 1985; Hackman & Lawler, 1971).

CONCEPT CHECK

10. "I want my employees to enjoy their work and to feel pride in their achievements." Does that statement reflect a belief in the human-relations approach or the scientific-management approach? (Check your answer on page 431.)

THE MESSAGE
What the Need for Achievement Says About Motivation

Although we sometimes regard hunger as a "typical" motivation, it differs in some striking ways from the need for achievement. For example, people can satisfy their hunger but seldom satisfy their need for achievement. At the end of a big meal, you are quite uninterested in food. In contrast, no matter how marvelous people's achievements are, they seldom lose interest in further achievements. Almost no one reaches his or her life goal and then stops; after reaching a previous life goal, people simply set new goals (Cantor &

People who have already achieved much, such as author Stephen King, seldom rest on their successes. They set new goals and try to achieve even more.

Fleeson, 1994). We would be distressed if we had no further goals. We constantly strive to build a perfect world, but we might not enjoy living in one.

In the words of the Russian novelist Fyodor Dostoevsky (1864/1960, pp. 29, 30): "Man likes to create and build roads; that is beyond dispute. But why does he also have such a passionate love for destruction and chaos? . . . May it not be that he loves chaos and destruction . . . because he is instinctively afraid of attaining his goal and completing the edifice he is constructing? . . . [P]erhaps the only goal on earth to which mankind is striving lies in this incessant process of attaining, or in other words, in life itself, and not particularly in the goal. . . . He feels that as soon as he has found it there will be nothing for him to look for. . . . He likes the process of attaining, but does not quite like to have attained."

SUMMARY

❉ *Measurement of need for achievement.* Some people work harder than others because of their strong need for achievement. Need for achievement can be measured by the stories a person tells when looking at pictures in the Thematic Apperception Test. (page 425)

❉ *Goal setting.* People with a strong need for achievement prefer to set goals that are high but realistic. Given such a goal, they will work as hard as possible. In contrast, people with a low need for achievement or a strong fear of failure prefer goals that are either easy to achieve or so difficult that they provide a ready excuse for failure. (page 426)

❉ *Effectiveness of goal setting.* Almost all of us are motivated to achieve a goal if the goal is realistic, if we make a serious commitment to achieving it, and if we get feedback on our efforts to reach the goal. (page 427)

❉ *Achievement motivation in children.* Children begin showing delight in their accomplishments by the age of 1½. Preschool children are highly optimistic about their own abilities. After they enter school, they learn the meaning of failure and start to show discouragement. (page 428)

✻ *Sex differences in need for achievement.* According to some reports, men have a stronger need for achievement than women have, on the average, although some of the results are difficult to replicate. To some extent, women lower their aspirations because they fear that their success may displease men or because they believe that employers will not promote them fairly. (page 428)

✻ *Jobs that encourage or discourage need for achievement.* According to the scientific-management approach, jobs should be made simple and foolproof. According to the human-management approach, jobs should be made interesting enough to give workers a sense of achievement. (page 429)

Suggestion for Further Reading

McClelland, D. C. (1987). *Human motivation.* New York, NY: Cambridge University Press. A text by one of the pioneers in the study of achievement motivation.

Terms

need for achievement   a striving for accomplishment and excellence (page 425)

fear of failure   a preoccupation with avoiding failure, rather than taking risks in order to succeed (page 426)

Answers to Concept Checks

8. The answer depends on how good a team Generic Tech has. If they won most of their games last year and return most of their top players, then the coach has set a very low goal for them, and we can therefore assume that the coach has more fear of failure than need for achievement. If, however, Generic Tech has a mediocre team, then the coach may have set a realistic challenge. We would then assume that the coach has a high need for achievement. (page 427)

9. A New Year's resolution is like any other goal: People are more likely to keep it if it is realistic, if they state the resolution publicly, and if they receive feedback on how well they are doing. (page 428)

10. It reflects the human-relations approach. (page 430)

Web Resources

McGregor—Theory X and Y

sol.brunel.ac.uk/~jarvis/bola/motivation/mcgregor.html

Consider the assumptions and consequences of McGregor's theory of management and motivation: Which management style do you prefer?

David McClelland, Psychologist

fox.nstn.ca/~dmcclel2/psych.html

A brief biography of the famous psychologist, by the not-yet-famous actor.

Motivation

spider.rowan.edu/edlead/marcus/page29.htm

Laurence R. Marcus of Rowan University outlines 10 theories of motivation, including McGregor's, McClelland's, and Maslow's.

Emotions, Health Psychology, and Stress

The *Star Trek* character Mr. Spock is reputed to have emotions but to suppress them almost always. Suppose you are the first astronaut to land on a planet where the inhabitants experience no emotions at all (but who conveniently speak English). They gather around and ask you, their first visitor from Earth, what *emotion* is. What do you tell them?

"Well," you might say, "emotion is how you feel when something surprisingly good or surprisingly bad happens to you." "Wait a minute," they reply. "We don't understand these words *feel* and *surprisingly*."

"All right, how about this: Emotions are experiences like anger, fear, happiness, sadness. . . . "

"*Anger, fear* . . . what do those terms mean?" they ask.

Defining such terms would be more difficult than trying to explain *color* to a blind person. Even though blind people cannot experience color, they can determine whether someone else has color vision by showing the appropriate stimuli. Could you set up a similar test that would allow emotionless people to determine whether someone else was experiencing an emotion? If so, what sort of test could you use? The problem is that *color vision* has a well-established meaning, whereas *emotion* has an imprecise meaning that is defined mostly by example.

In this chapter, we shall consider what psychologists have learned so far about emotions, while leaving some major questions unanswered. We begin with general theories and principles. Later, we turn to the role of emotions in health and how people cope with the emotions associated with stress.

When we experience emotions, we are in some way moved. (*Movement* is the root of emotion.) Our feeling of disturbance is a positive or negative excitement; sometimes we cry for joy, sometimes in grief.

Emotional Behaviors

What causes us to feel one emotion or another?

How many kinds of emotion do people have?

The philosopher Paul Griffiths (1997, p. 14) wrote, "My central conclusion is that the general concept of emotion is unlikely to be a useful concept in psychological theory." He compares the concept of emotion to ancient astronomy's concept of "superlunary objects," which referred to all objects beyond the orbit of the moon: The items that fit the concept are too diverse to form a useful category.

If you would like to defend the category *emotion,* first try to define it. When you find it difficult to define (as you will), you may object, "Even if I can't define it in so many words, I can recognize it when I see it." Can you? When you swat at a housefly and it flies away, is it frightened? If you poke at a beehive and the bees attack you, are they angry? If fear and anger refer only to the behaviors, then, yes, the fly is frightened and the bees are angry. But if emotions are experiences, like what you and I feel when we experience fear and anger, then it is difficult—maybe even impossible—for us to know whether insects have emotions.

Never mind insects; what about humans: Is boredom an emotion? interest? pain? courage? confidence? sexual desire? How do we decide what is an emotion and what is not?

Emotion is often a slippery concept, difficult to define and difficult to measure. It is, nevertheless, so important that psychologists can hardly ignore it. The cautious approach is to anchor our discussion as carefully as possible in observable, measurable behaviors.

Emotion, Decision-Making, and Emotional Intelligence

When drawing conclusions, you are generally advised to look at the evidence "calmly, rationally, unemotionally." The *Star Trek* character Mr. Spock, the personification of this advice, is extremely logical and rarely emotional. If emo-

tions only get in the way of intelligent decision-making, why do we have them at all?

The answer is that, except for extremely intense emotions, they don't get in the way. In fact, the capacity to feel emotion may even be necessary for good decision-making. Antonio Damasio (1994) described some patients who suffered severely impoverished emotions following damage to parts of the prefrontal cortex. One was the famous patient Phineas Gage, who survived a freak accident in 1848 when an iron bar shot through his head, damaging his prefrontal cortex. Nearly one-and-a-half centuries later, researchers examined his skull (which is still on display in a Boston museum) and reconstructed the route that the bar must have taken through Gage's brain (Damasio, Grabowski, Frank, Galaburda, & Damasio, 1994). As you can see in Figure 12.1, the accident damaged a portion of his prefrontal cortex. The result, according to medical reports of the time, was that Gage showed little emotion and also seemed to lose his former values. He had formerly been a conscientious worker, but he became unreliable in both his work and his personal habits. He ignored the usual polite restraints when making sexual advances and in his use of profane language. He followed each whim of the moment, unable to carry out any long-term plans.

A parallel case in more recent times is a person known to us as "Elliot" (Damasio, 1994). Elliot, too, suffered damage to his prefrontal cortex, as a result of surgery to remove

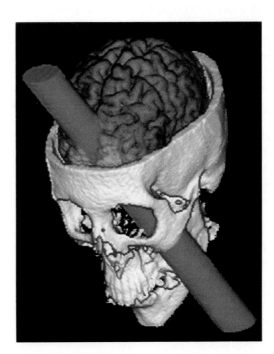

FIGURE 12.1 In the 1990s, researchers used modern technology to reconstruct the path that an iron bar must have taken through the brain of Phineas Gage, who survived this injury in 1848. The damage impaired Gage's judgment and decision-making. (From Damasio, Grabowski, Frank, Galaburda, & Damasio, 1994.)

a brain tumor. Therefore, he reports almost no emotional experiences. He shows no impatience, no frustration; he experiences no joy from music or art; he rarely expresses anger; he describes his brain surgery and the resulting deterioration of his life with calm detachment, as if he were describing events that happened to a stranger. Besides his loss of emotions, he has great difficulty making or following any reasonable plans. If given an array of information, he can discuss the probable outcome of each decision he might make, but after describing those outcomes, he seems to have no idea which decision to make. Or if he does announce a decision, he abandons it soon after. As a result, Elliot cannot keep a job, cannot invest his money intelligently, and cannot maintain normal relationships with his friends or acquaintances.

According to Damasio (1994), Elliot's difficulty with decision-making is closely related to his lack of emotions. Ordinarily, when you or I consider possible decisions, we contemplate the possible outcomes and feel a brief "as if" emotion with each. For example, you consider a job offer from a company that pollutes the environment, and you get a feeling of revulsion, so you decide to reject the offer. When you consider another offer from a company that recently fired your best friend, you imagine the unpleasant scene when you next face that friend, and again you decide to reject the offer. You continue until you come to a job offer that will make you feel good if you accept it. Now, imagine eliminating all those emotions, and you can see that the capacity for emotion is helpful, even necessary, for making many decisions.

Many psychologists therefore speak of **emotional intelligence,** *the ability to perceive, imagine, and understand emotions and to use that information in decision-making* (Mayer & Salovey, 1995, 1997). For example, imagine that you are standing in line for lunch but you have left a bit of a gap between you and the person in front. Someone else steps into the line in front of you. You have to judge whether this person was being rude, or merely making an honest mistake by not realizing you were in this line. Should you scream threats and insults? Or should you calmly inform this person of the mistake? Or ignore it altogether?

Or imagine a man who is trying to decide whether to tell a certain joke to a couple of women. He needs to gauge how they will probably respond: Will they enjoy it, or will they regard it as sexist, offensive, or worse? Suppose he tells it. Now, the women have to judge his intentions: Did he mean no harm, or was this joke potentially the start of some sort of sexual harassment?

In short, we frequently need to make complicated judgments, and people who often make the wrong judgments can get themselves into trouble. Undoubtedly, some people are better than others at judging the emotional content of a social situation, although psychologists know little about how to measure this sort of skill. Ultimately, it would be useful to find ways to teach emotional

intelligence, although no one is yet sure how. As with any other kind of teaching, it is possible to teach with good intentions and still produce more confusion than clarity (Mayer & Salovey, 1997).

Excitement and Physiological Arousal

Originally, the word *emotion* was a general term for any sort of turbulent movement. People used to talk about thunder as an "emotion of the atmosphere." Eventually, the word came to refer only to feelings associated with vigorous motion of the body, such as fear, anger, and joy.

We experience emotional arousal, or excitement, when we have a strong tendency either to approach or to avoid something, generally in an energetic way. For example, love includes a strong drive to be close to another person. Anger includes a tendency to charge toward someone and to attack either verbally or physically. Fear and disgust are associated with a tendency to escape. All emotions share certain features related to physiological arousal. So, although anger, fear, and happiness are very different emotional states, we can express any one of these by screaming or by engaging in frenzied activity.

"But wait," you say. "Sometimes when I feel highly emotional, I can hardly do anything at all. Like the time I borrowed a friend's car and then wrecked it. When I had to explain what had happened to the car, I could hardly speak." True, but even then your emotion was associated with a tendency to take vigorous action. While you were reporting the wreck to your friend, you undoubtedly felt a strong urge to run away. Although you suppressed that urge, it made itself apparent in your trembling voice and shaking hands.

Ordinarily, an emotional state elicits a tendency toward vigorous action, even if we suppress that tendency. Here, a soldier disarms a mine during the war in the former Yugoslavia. No doubt he feels an intense desire to run away, and no doubt his heart is racing, but he manages to restrain himself from acting upon these impulses.

The Role of the Autonomic Nervous System

Any stimulus that arouses an emotion—such as a hug, a fire alarm, or a slap on the face—alters the activity of the **autonomic nervous system,** *the section of the nervous system that controls the functioning of the internal organs.* The word *autonomic* means independent; biologists once believed that the autonomic nervous system operated independently of the brain and the spinal cord. We now know that the brain and the spinal cord send messages to alter the activity of the autonomic nervous system, but we continue to use the term *autonomic.*

The autonomic nervous system consists of the sympathetic and the parasympathetic nervous systems (Figure 12.2). *Two chains of neuron clusters just to the left and right of the spinal cord* make up the **sympathetic nervous system,** *which arouses the body for "fight or flight."* (See Figure 12.3.) For example, if someone charges at you, you may have to choose between fighting and running away,

but in either case, your sympathetic nervous system prepares you for a burst of vigorous activity. It does so by increasing your heart rate, breathing rate, production of sweat, and flow of epinephrine (EP-i-NEF-rin; also known as adrenaline).

The **parasympathetic nervous system** consists of *neurons whose axons extend from the medulla* (Figure 12.2) *and the lower part of the spinal cord to neuron clusters near the internal organs. The parasympathetic nervous system decreases the heart rate, promotes digestion, and in general supports nonemergency functions.* Both the sympathetic and parasympathetic systems send axons to various organs of the body, such as the heart and digestive organs. A few organs, such as the adrenal gland, receive input from only the sympathetic nervous system.

Both systems are constantly active. The alternation or shifting balance between the two systems helps to keep the body in homeostasis (see Chapter 10), but one system can be temporarily dominant over the other. An emergency that demands a vigorous response will predominantly activate

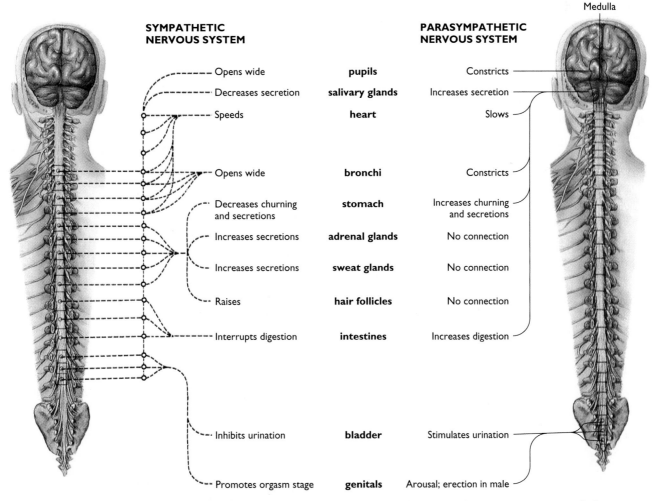

FIGURE 12.2 The autonomic nervous system consists of the sympathetic and parasympathetic nervous systems, which sometimes act in opposing ways and sometimes in cooperative ways. The sympathetic nervous system readies the body for emergency action; the parasympathetic nervous system supports digestive and other nonemergency actions.

FIGURE 12.3 The sympathetic nervous system prepares the body for a vigorous burst of activity.

the sympathetic system; a restful situation predominantly activates the parasympathetic system. Some situations activate parts of both systems at once (Berntson, Cacioppo, & Quigley, 1993). For example, a frightening situation may increase your heart rate and sweating (sympathetic responses) and also promote bowel and bladder evacuation (parasympathetic responses). Remember the last time you were seriously frightened. Chances are, your heart was beating wildly, you found yourself gasping for breath, and you were afraid you were going to lose your bladder control. Both your sympathetic and parasympathetic nervous systems were responsible for those responses.

The Opponent-Process Principle of Emotions

After the cessation of a stimulus that has excited sympathetic activity, the system "rebounds" with increased parasympathetic activity (Gellhorn, 1970). (See Figure 12.4.) For example, while you are running away from an attacker, your sympathetic nervous system increases your heart rate and your breathing rate. If the police suddenly in-

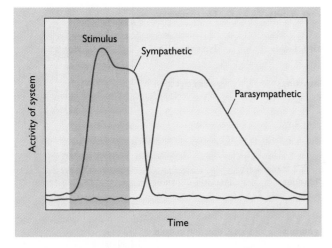

FIGURE 12.4 After removal of the stimulus eliciting the sympathetic response, that response is reduced, while the opposing parasympathetic response is enhanced. This is why people feel faint at the end of an exciting experience.

tercept your attacker, your sympathetic arousal ceases, and your parasympathetic system becomes highly activated on the rebound. If the rebound is large enough, a person who has just escaped from danger may faint because of the sudden decrease in heart rate.

This tendency is related to a larger, general principle, the **opponent-process principle of emotions** (Solomon, 1980; Solomon & Corbit, 1974). According to this principle, *the removal of a stimulus that excites one emotion causes a swing to an opposite emotion* (Figure 12.5). This principle is similar to the opponent-process principle of color vision (discussed in Chapter 4). Recall that, when you stare for a long time at one color and then look away, you see its opposite. (After staring at yellow, you see blue.) Solomon and Corbit suggest that the same principle holds true with emotional states.

For example, suppose you are making a parachute jump for the first time. As you start your fall, you probably experience a state akin to terror. As you continue to fall and your parachute opens, your terror begins to subside. When you land safely, your emotional state does not simply return to normal; it rebounds to relief. As time passes, your relief gradually fades until, at last, you return to a normal state. Figure 12.6 shows these changes in emotional response over time. Solomon and Corbit refer to the initial emotion as the A state and the opposite, rebound emotion as the B state.

Here is another example: You hear on the radio that you have just won $1 million in the lottery; you become elated. Later, you discover that the winner was not you, but someone else with a similar name. Now, you feel sad, even though you "lost" something you never really had.

Solomon and Corbit further propose that repetition of an experience strengthens the B state but not the A state. For example, after you have made several parachute jumps, your rebound pleasure becomes greater and starts to occur earlier and earlier. Eventually, you may not be aware of any initial terror at all; the entire experience becomes pleasant.

Figure 12.6 illustrates the changes in emotional response that occur when the experience-and-rebound cycle is repeated many times. Note that the A state has become weaker and the B state has become stronger and more prolonged.

FIGURE 12.5 According to *the opponent-process principle of the emotions*, removing the stimulus for one emotion elicits a rebound to the opposite emotion. A hiker who sees a snake may feel terrified; when the threat passes, the terror gives way to relief and elation.

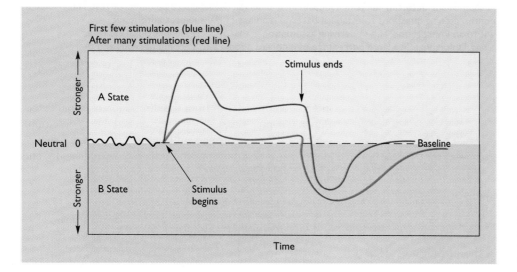

FIGURE 12.6 According to *the opponent-process theory of emotions*, removal of the stimulus for one emotion (A state) induces the opposite emotion (B state). The blue line shows emotional responses to a stimulus that is introduced and then withdrawn. The red line shows emotional responses to a stimulus that has been introduced and withdrawn repeatedly. Note how the intensity of the response changes over time. (Based on Solomon & Corbit, 1974.)

CONCEPT CHECKS

1. When you ride a roller coaster, does your heart rate increase or decrease? What happens after you get off the ride?

2. If we apply the opponent-process principle to the experiences that drugs produce, we can describe the initial "high" as the A state and the subsequent unpleasant withdrawal experience as the B state. If someone takes a drug repeatedly, how will the A state and the B state change? (Check your answers on page 452.)

The Sympathetic Nervous System and Lie Detection

Frequently, the police interview a suspect who denies any participation in a crime, or an employer interviews a prospective employee who claims to be skillful, honest, and trustworthy. In such cases, the interviewer would like to know whether the person is telling the truth. Unfortunately, most of us are not very good at detecting lies. In one study, a well-known British political commentator gave two consecutive interviews about his favorite films. In one, he told the truth; the other time, he lied on every question. Both interviews were broadcast on radio and television and printed in a newspaper. Members of the public were invited to guess which of the interviews was the honest one and which one was full of lies. Of the more than 41,000 people who responded, only 53% got the right answer (Wiseman, 1995). Curiously, the television viewers were less accurate than the radio listeners or newspaper readers.

For centuries, people have tried to find a simple test to determine who is lying. One of the best-known attempts is the **polygraph,** *an instrument that simultaneously records several indications of sympathetic nervous system arousal, generally including blood pressure, heart rate, breathing rate, and electrical conduction of the skin* (Figure 12.7). (Slight sweating, a sympathetic nervous system response, increases electrical conduction of the skin.) The assumption is that people feel nervous when they lie, and consequently their sympathetic nervous system will show more arousal when they lie than when they tell the truth.

The polygraph sometimes accomplishes its goal simply because an accused person hooked up to a polygraph believes that it can detect lies and confesses, "Oh, what's the use. You're going to figure it out now anyway, so I may as well tell you . . . ." But with people who do not break down and confess, how effectively does a polygraph detect lying? Let's examine the evidence.

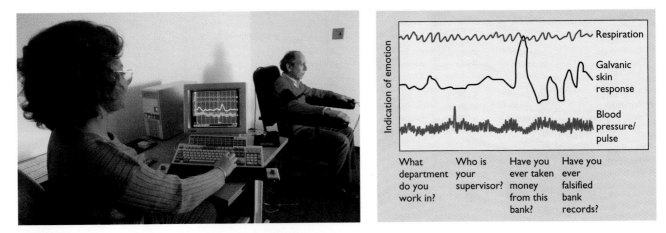

FIGURE 12.7 The polygraph, a method for detecting nervous arousal, is the basis for the so-called lie detector test. The polygraph operator asks a series of nonthreatening questions to establish baseline readings of the subject's autonomic responses, then asks questions relevant to an investigation. The underlying assumption is that an increase in arousal indicates nervousness, which in turn indicates lying. Unfortunately, a large percentage of innocent people also become nervous and therefore appear to be lying.

WHAT'S THE EVIDENCE?
The Effectiveness of a Polygraph in Detecting Lies

Hypothesis Polygraph administrators will identify guilty suspects as liars more often than they identify innocent suspects as liars.

Method To test this hypothesis, the investigators need a sample of people who are known to be guilty and another sample who are known to be innocent but who are otherwise similar to the guilty people. In one study, the investigators selected 50 criminal cases where two suspects had taken a polygraph test, and one suspect had later confessed to the crime (Kleinmuntz & Szucko, 1984). Thus, the investigators knew which 50 suspects were guilty, and they knew that the 50 innocent people were similar enough to have been plausible suspects. It is important to note that all suspects had denied their guilt at the time of the polygraph test.

During the administration of the polygraph, suspects were asked two kinds of questions: *Relevant* questions pertained to the crime itself; for example, "Did you steal $125 from the convenience store last Tuesday?" *Control* questions took the following form: "Have you ever taken anything of value that was not yours?" Theoretically, someone who robbed the convenience store should be more nervous about the first question; anyone else should be, if anything, more nervous about the second.

Six professional polygraph administrators examined all the polygraph results and judged which suspects were lying and which were telling the truth.

Results Figure 12.8 shows the results. The polygraph administrators did manage to identify 76% of the guilty suspects as liars; however, they also classified 37% of the innocent suspects as liars.

Interpretation Recall from the discussion of signal detection in Chapter 4 that, when a person is trying to determine whether something is present or absent, there are two possible correct decisions (green in the following diagram) and two possible errors (red).

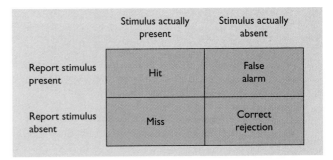

Polygraph administrators can also make two kinds of correct decisions and two kinds of errors:

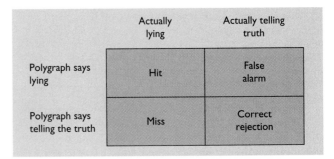

A polygraph user obtains more "hits" than most people do on their own. However, most of the errors made by polygraph users are "false alarms" (also known as "false positives")—falsely identifying innocent people as lying. Given the usual belief that we would prefer to let guilty people go

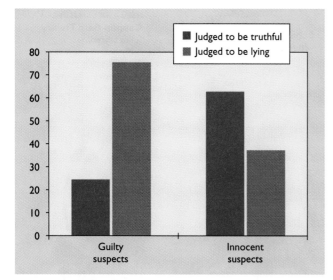

FIGURE 12.8 Polygraph examiners correctly identified 76% of guilty suspects as lying. However, they also identified 37% of innocent suspects as lying. (Based on data of Kleinmuntz & Szucko, 1984.)

free than to convict innocent people, these polygraph results are disturbing.

✳ ✳ ✳

The results of this study are typical of similar research; in fact, this study may have even underestimated the tendency of polygraph administrators to call innocent people liars. In some studies, polygraph administrators have called half or more of the innocent people liars (Forman & McCauley, 1986; Horvath, 1977; Patrick & Iacono, 1989).

Imagine the consequences: Suppose we give polygraph tests to ten suspects, one of whom is guilty. The test would have about a 76% chance of identifying the guilty person as lying, but it would also identify several of the innocent people as liars. Or imagine giving a polygraph to all the people who work for a company, asking whether they have ever stolen from the company. Even if every employee is loyal and innocent, the test may identify almost half of them as liars. Because of the low accuracy of polygraph tests, the U.S. Congress passed a law in 1988 prohibiting private employers from giving polygraph tests to employees or job applicants, except under special circumstances (Camara, 1988). Polygraph results are only rarely admissible as evidence in a court of law.

An Alternative: The Guilty-Knowledge Test

The **guilty-knowledge test,** *a modified version of the polygraph test,* produces more accurate results by *asking questions that should be threatening only to someone who knows the facts of a crime that have not been publicized* (Lykken, 1979). Instead of asking, "Did you rob the gas station?" the interrogator asks, "Was the gas station robbed at

8:00 P.M.? at 10:30? at midnight? at 1:30 in the morning? Did the robber carry a gun? a knife? a club?" Someone who shows heightened arousal only in response to the correct details of the crime is presumed to have "guilty knowledge"—knowledge that only someone who had committed the crime or had talked to the guilty person would possess. The guilty-knowledge test, when properly administered, identifies a large percentage of guilty people and only rarely makes the mistake of classifying an innocent person as guilty (Balloun & Holmes, 1979; Bashore & Rapp, 1993; Elaad, 1990).

SOMETHING TO THINK ABOUT

How might the results of the guilty-knowledge test be biased by a questioner who knows the correct details of the crime? How should the test be administered to minimize that bias? ✳

Pencil-and-Paper Integrity Tests

Suppose you are an employer who wants to know whether someone applying for a job at your company is likely to be an honest worker. Giving a polygraph test is illegal and would not be very accurate anyway, and you can't give a guilty-knowledge test, because no one can have guilty knowledge about a crime that has not yet occurred. So what do you do?

One approach is to administer pencil-and-paper "integrity tests" that ask such questions as these:

- Have you ever stolen money or property from a previous employer?
- Do you think that most employees occasionally steal from their employers?
- On previous jobs, have you ever left work early while claiming to work a full day?
- Have you sometimes come to work while under the influence of illegal drugs?
- If you were sure you wouldn't get caught, would you ever make personal long-distance phone calls and charge them to your employer?

You might imagine that anyone who has a history of dishonest dealings with previous employers would lie about it. Amazingly, many people fill out the questionnaire honestly, admitting a long history of past dishonesty. (Perhaps they assume the new employer will find out about this history anyway by checking with previous employers.) Research on such tests is limited, but it suggests that these tests manage to identify a good percentage of dishonest people (Camara & Schneider, 1994).

However, the integrity tests have two major problems: First, they misidentify some extremely ethical and scrupulous people who "confess" to being imperfect (Lilienfeld, Alliger, & Mitchell, 1995). For example, someone may read the question, "Have you ever stolen property from a previous employer?" and think, "Well, there was that one time when I used a business envelope to mail a personal letter, and technically that was stealing."

Second, if the tests become widely used, job applicants will surely learn how to pretend to be honest: Say you have never stolen from an employer, you have never cheated your employer, you don't think most other people do either, and you think anyone who does should be punished. Test designers can then reword the questions to make their point less obvious, asking questions about conscientiousness, impulse control, and other characteristics that correlate with honesty. They can also include *social desirability* items: People who say no to items like *Occasionally I overeat* or who say yes to *I donate money to every worthy charity that I know* can be suspected of answering dishonestly to the more relevant items. In short, it may be possible to design valid integrity tests, but at present we have no guarantees (Alliger, Lilienfeld, & Mitchell, 1996).

Three General Theories of Emotion

Psychologists generally agree that emotions are related to the activity of the autonomic nervous system and the activity of the body in general. The nature of that relationship is less clear. Let us consider three theories that have offered different descriptions of that relationship.

The James-Lange Theory of Emotions

In 1884, William James and Carl Lange independently proposed a theory that immediately became highly influential and still remains highly influential, although psychologists have often misunderstood it. Indeed, even today people often confuse what James and Lange actually said, what they meant to say, and what casual readers thought they said (Ellsworth, 1994).

Common sense suggests that you feel sad and therefore you cry; you become afraid and therefore you tremble; you feel angry and therefore your heart beats faster and your face turns red. James and Lange turned this concept around. According to the **James-Lange theory** (Figure 12.9), *a person's interpretation of a stimulus evokes the autonomic changes directly; the emotion is the perception of those changes.* You decide that you are sad *because* you cry, you feel afraid *because* you tremble, and you feel angry *because* your heart is racing and your face is turning red. Similarly, the act of smiling brings happiness and frowning brings sadness. The body responses alone, James and Lange would agree, are not sufficient for emotions, but they are necessary. For example, trembling itself would not make you afraid. (You might be trembling because you are cold.) Nevertheless, if you did not tremble, you could not have the full experience of fear.

According to this theory, how would you know which emotion you are feeling? Actually, William James was skeptical of separating emotion into different categories such as

FIGURE 12.9 Three traditional theories of emotion differ concerning the relationship between physiological arousal and the cognitive experience of emotion. According to the James-Lange theory, the physiological arousal determines the nature of the emotion. According to the Cannon-Bard theory, the physiological arousal is independent of the cognitive experience. According to Schachter and Singer's theory, the physiological arousal determines the intensity of the emotion, but it does not determine which emotion one experiences.

fear, anger, and disgust. He regarded emotions as endlessly varying, with no firm border between one and the next. Still, as far as it makes sense to label emotions, the James-Lange theory suggests that we distinguish our emotions by observing our bodily responses, especially our autonomic responses. We sense one pattern of autonomic responses when we are angry, another pattern when happy, still another when we are frightened or sad. (Remember, according to this theory, an emotion is the *perception* of what is happening in the body, not the *cause* of that change.) But is the autonomic state associated with anger noticeably different from the state associated with anxiety or any other emotion?

Heart rate and respiration increase during the experience of almost any emotion. Beyond that basic similarity, each emotional state has certain distinguishing physiological features (Levenson, 1992). With its "butterflies in the stomach" sensation, anxiety is probably the most distinctive emotional experience (Neiss, 1988). Your heart rate increases a little more when you are angry or frightened than when you are happy; the temperature of your hands increases more when you are angry than when you feel any other emotion. Your facial muscles respond in different ways when you experience various emotions, even though you may not actually be smiling or frowning (Tassinary & Cacioppo, 1992).

Granted that emotional states produce different physiological states, can those differences account for the differences in emotions, as James and Lange suggested? If you begin to breathe rapidly and your heart begins to race, do you decide whether you are angry or frightened by checking the temperature of your hands—or any other physiological indicator? Probably not. The physiological differences among emotions are small, probably too small to identify an emotional state accurately (Lang, 1994). In fact, most people cannot accurately report even the intensity of their autonomic arousal.

A somewhat more promising possibility is that we judge our emotions by monitoring our facial expressions, or that having a certain facial expression at least increases the probability of feeling the associated emotion. James Laird (1974) molded people's faces into a smile or a frown by telling them to contract first this muscle, then that one, without ever using the words *smile* or *frown*. He found that an induced smile made people more likely to feel happy and that an induced frown made them more likely to feel sad or angry. You might try this yourself: Smile for a while; then frown for a while. Do you feel happier when you are smiling, even though it was a purely voluntary smile?

If you do, remember the problem of *demand characteristics*: Maybe you say you felt happier when you smiled, just because you knew you were supposed to. Similarly, participants in an experiment often report what they think the experimenter expects them to report. Even though Laird never used the words *smile* or *frown,* the subjects may have identified their expressions and guessed that they were supposed to be related to their mood.

In another study, the experimenters found a clever way to conceal their purpose. They told subjects that the experiment had to do with how people with disabilities learn to write after losing control of their arms. The subjects were told to hold a pen either with their teeth or with their protruded lips, as Figure 12.10 shows. Then they were to use the pen in various ways, such as drawing lines between dots and making checkmarks to rate the funniness of cartoons. When they held the pen with their teeth, their face was forced into a near-smile and they rated the cartoons as very funny. When they held the pen with protruded lips, they rated the cartoons as significantly less funny (Strack, Martin, & Stepper, 1988). (Try holding a pen one way and then the other, while reading newspaper cartoons. Do you notice any difference?)

The Cannon-Bard Theory of Emotions

Walter Cannon (1927), a prominent American physiologist, argued against the idea that autonomic responses were essential to emotion. Instead, he said, emotions produce autonomic changes and the cognitive experience of emotion independently. This view, as modified by Philip Bard (1934), is known as the **Cannon-Bard theory of emotions** (Figure 12.9). According to this theory, *certain areas of the brain evaluate sensory information and, when appropriate, send one set of impulses to the autonomic nervous system and another set to the forebrain, which is responsible for the subjective and cognitive aspects of emotion.*

The key assumption here is that the cognitive aspect of emotions is independent of the autonomic aspect. This assumption is only partly true. After spinal cord damage, people experience little sensation from their heart beating, stomach fluttering, and other autonomic responses; yet, they continue to experience fear, anger, and other emotions. They may report, however, that their emotions feel less intense than they did before. For example, one man with spinal cord damage reported that he occasionally *acted* angry without actually feeling angry, just because he knew that, if he did not respond to the situation with anger, other people would take advantage of him (Hohmann, 1966).

Similarly, after people with an intact nervous system take tranquilizing drugs, they generally report that their emotions, especially anxiety, seem less intense than before.

a   b

FIGURE 12.10 Facial expression can influence mood. When people hold a pen with their teeth (a), they rate cartoons as funnier than when they hold a pen with their protruded lips (b).

That is, the cognitive aspect of emotions may be partly independent of the autonomic changes, but it is not as independent as Cannon and Bard originally suggested.

Schachter and Singer's Theory of Emotions

Suppose we wire you to another person so that you share the other person's heart rate, breathing rate, skin temperature, and muscle tension. When the other person feels a particular emotion, will you feel it, too?

We cannot perform that experiment, but we can do the next best thing: We can use a drug to induce nearly the same physiological state in two people, and then see whether they both report the same emotion. To make things a little more interesting, we can put them in different situations. If emotion depends only on a person's physiological state, then both people will report the same emotion, even if they happen to be in different situations. Stanley Schachter and Jerome Singer (1962) put these ideas to the test in a now-famous experiment.

Schachter and Singer gave injections of the hormone epinephrine (adrenaline) to a group of college students who agreed to participate in the experiment. (Epinephrine mimics the effects of arousal of the sympathetic nervous system for about 20 to 30 minutes.) The experimenters told some of the subjects that the injections were vitamins; they did not warn them about the likely autonomic effects. Others were told to expect increased heart rate, butterflies in the stomach, and so forth. (Therefore, when these people did have such experiences, they would attribute the effects to the injection, not to the situation.)

Subjects were then placed in different situations. Some were placed, one at a time, in a situation designed to arouse euphoria (excited happiness). The others were placed in a situation designed to arouse anger.

Each student in the euphoria situation was asked to wait in a room with a very playful confederate, or accomplice, of the experimenter. The confederate flipped wads of paper into a trash can, sailed paper airplanes, built a tower with manila folders, shot paper wads at the tower with a rubber band, and played with a hula hoop. He encouraged the subject to join him in play.

Each subject in the anger situation was put in a waiting room with an angry confederate and asked to fill out an insulting questionnaire that included such items as these:

Which member of your immediate family does not bathe or wash regularly?

With how many men (other than your father) has your mother had extramarital relationships?

4 or fewer   5–9   10 or more

Most students in the euphoria situation showed strong emotional responses. Some joined the confederate in his play (Figure 12.11), and some of them initiated play of their own. (One jumped up and down on the desk, and another opened a window and threw paper wads at passersby.) The students in the anger situation responded in various ways; some muttered angry comments, and a few refused to complete the questionnaire.

But another factor was important in this experiment. Some of the subjects had been informed beforehand that the injections would produce certain autonomic effects, including hand tremors and increased heart rate. No matter which situation those subjects were in, they showed only slight emotional responses. When they felt themselves sweating and their hands trembling, they said to themselves, "Aha! I'm getting the side effects, just as they said I would."

What can we conclude from this experiment? According to **Schachter and Singer's theory of emotions,** a physiological state is not the same thing as an emotion (see Figure 12.9). *The intensity of the physiological state—that is, the degree of sympathetic nervous system arousal—determines the intensity of the emotion, but not the type of emotion.* Depending on all the information people have about themselves and the situation, they can interpret a particular type of arousal as either anger, euphoria, or just an interesting side effect from taking a pill. That is, arousal intensifies an emotion, but cognitive appraisal of the situation tells us *which* emotion we are feeling. Table 12.1 contrasts Schachter and Singer's theory with the James-Lange and Cannon-Bard theories.

Unfortunately, Schachter and Singer's conclusions neglect another group of subjects—subjects whose results raise problems for their theory. These subjects, who were given placebo injections instead of epinephrine, showed about as much euphoria in the euphoria situation and as much anger in the anger situation as did the subjects injected with epinephrine. Therefore, critics argue, the epinephrine injections may have had nothing to do with the results. If we accept that possibility, we are left with this summary of the results from Schachter and Singer's experiment: People in a situation designed to induce euphoria act happy; people in an anger situation act angry. This result is not very interesting (Plutchik & Ax, 1967).

Schachter and Singer were right to call attention to the importance of cognition, but they may have ventured too far. By emphasizing how cognition determines our emotions, they downplayed the contributions of physiological states. To some extent, fear, anger, and happiness really do feel different physiologically, and those physiological differences contribute to the experience of our emotions.

The overall questions related to the James-Lange, Cannon-Bard, and Schachter-Singer theories are complex and difficult to investigate. Most investigators today believe that a more fruitful strategy is to explore the nature of specific emotions and their causes and expressions. Perhaps some day, after we know enough about specific emotions, we can return to study the issue of emotions in general.

CONCEPT CHECK

3. You are in a small boat far from shore, and you see a storm approaching. You feel frightened and start to

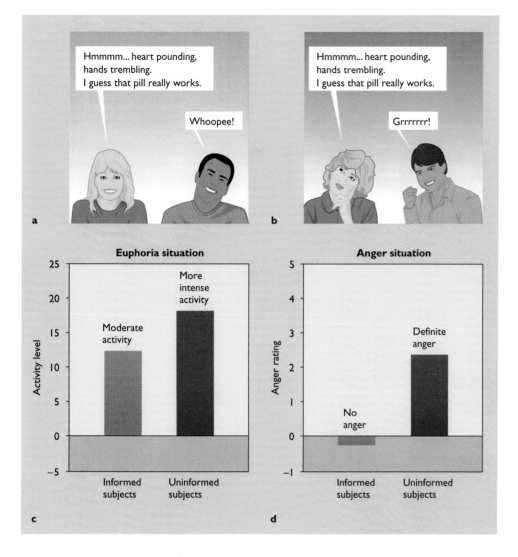

FIGURE 12.11 In Schachter and Singer's experiment, people who were uninformed about the effects of epinephrine reported strong emotions appropriate to their situation. According to Schachter and Singer, the autonomic arousal controls the strength of the emotion, but cognitive factors tell us which emotion we are experiencing.

tremble. According to the James-Lange theory, which came first—the fright or the trembling? According to Schachter and Singer's theory, which came first? (Check your answers on page 452.)

The Range of Emotions

How many different emotions do humans experience? Do we perhaps have a few "basic" emotions that combine to form other emotional experiences, just as three primary colors combine to produce all the other colors we see?

Psychologists have not yet agreed on a single list of basic emotions. Some psychologists have proposed a very short list, such as "pain and pleasure" or "happiness, sadness, and anger." Most theorists who have tried to list the basic emotions have included happiness, sadness, anger, fear, disgust, surprise, contempt, and shame. However, most also include one or more other emotions, such as guilt, interest, hope, pride, relief, frustration, love, awe, boredom, jealousy, regret, or embarrassment (Keltner & Buswell, 1997). Still other theorists have questioned the whole con-

cept of basic emotions (e.g., Ortony & Turner, 1990). For example, anger, which is ordinarily considered a basic emotion, may be a combination of more primitive elements—widening the eyelids, lowering the eyebrows, pursing the lips, and making a fist.

How can we decide what is a basic emotion? The English language draws a distinction among shame, guilt, and embarrassment, but using different words does not guarantee that each is a distinct and basic emotion. English also distinguishes among red, orange, and pink (as well as scarlet, crimson, and other variants), but we do not accept each of these as a basic color. Psychologists have generally accepted the following criteria for establishing a basic emotion:

•   Basic emotions should emerge early in life, without requiring much experience. For example, *fear* and *anger* are reasonable candidates to be considered basic emotions, because we see them even in infants. *Nostalgia* and *pride,* which emerge later in life, are weaker candidates to be considered basic emotions (Lewis, 1995).

•   The basic emotions should be similar for people in different cultures. For example, if happiness and sadness are basic emotions, then people from one culture should easily

TABLE 12.1   Three Theories of Emotion

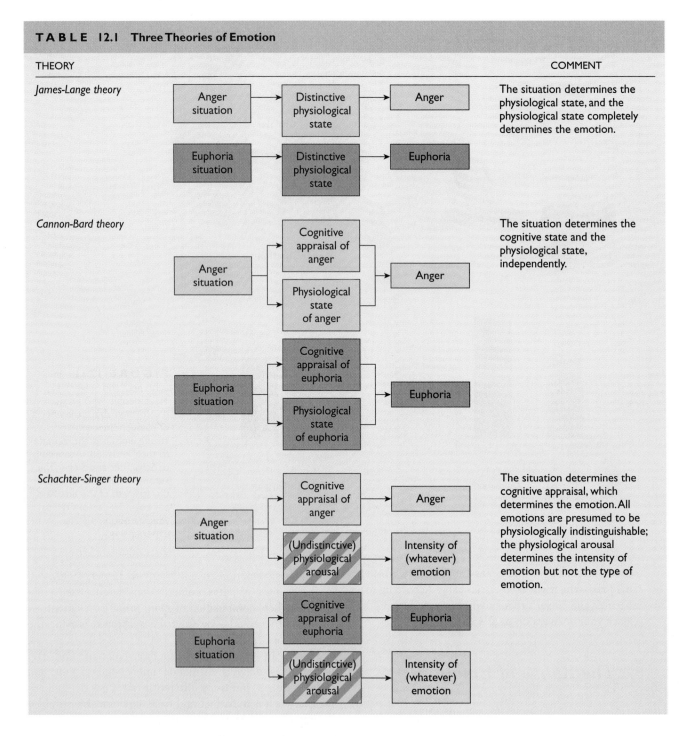

THEORY		COMMENT
James-Lange theory		The situation determines the physiological state, and the physiological state completely determines the emotion.
Cannon-Bard theory		The situation determines the cognitive state and the physiological state, independently.
Schachter-Singer theory		The situation determines the cognitive appraisal, which determines the emotion. All emotions are presumed to be physiologically indistinguishable; the physiological arousal determines the intensity of emotion but not the type of emotion.

recognize expressions of happiness and sadness by people of another culture. Cultures could differ, however, in their rules for such matters as when people should laugh and cry, what events should provoke jealousy, how much fear is normal, and how often people should get angry at others instead of taking the blame upon themselves (Mesquita & Frijda, 1992; Roseman, Dhawan, Rettek, Naidu, & Thapa, 1995).

• Basic emotions should have distinct biological bases. That is, a basic emotion probably depends on its own system of brain activity and triggers its own pattern of body activity, including perhaps a facial expression.

Producing Facial Expressions

Does each emotion have its own special expression? And why do we have facial expressions of emotions, anyway?

Quite simply, the function of facial expressions is communication. All primates (humans, apes, and monkeys) communicate their emotional states through gestures and facial expressions (Redican, 1982). (See Figure 12.12.) We humans can use spoken language as well, but we ordinarily prefer to use nonverbal expressions. You wink, nod, or smile to show a possible romantic interest; you withhold

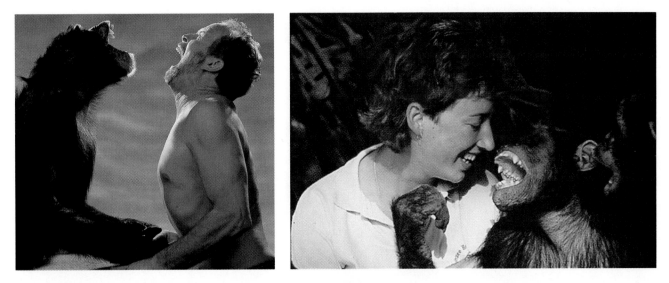

F I G U R E 12.12   The facial expressions of chimpanzees are similar to those of humans.

such expressions to indicate a lack of interest. (You *could* actually tell a stranger "I find you sexually attractive" or "please don't approach me." If you try this direct verbal approach, you will probably discover why most people prefer to rely on facial expressions.)

Facial expressions provide a kind of "truth in advertising." That is, your expression reflects your internal state— such as being happy, sad, or angry—and therefore tells other people whether you are likely to interact with them in a friendly or an uncooperative manner (Buck, 1994). Emotional expressions occur mostly in the presence of other people. For example, one study found that people bowling with friends often smiled after making a strike or a spare; people bowling alone seldom smiled (Kraut & Johnston, 1979). In another study, Olympic medal winners smiled often while waiting for the awards ceremony with others but seldom when they were waiting alone (Fernández-Dols & Ruiz-Belda, 1997). Even 10-month-old infants smile more when their mothers are watching than when their mothers are sitting nearby but reading a magazine (Jones, Collins, & Hong, 1991). Laughter occurs vastly more often in social settings than when people are alone, and it is highly contagious (Provine, 1996, 1997). That is, we laugh mostly when others are laughing. Many televised comedies include a laugh track to help the viewers at home start laughing.

Voluntary smiles, frowns, and other facial expressions do not exactly match the full, spontaneous expressions (except in the case of skilled actors). For example, the smile of a truly happy person includes movements of the mouth muscles and the muscles surrounding the eyes (Figure 12.13a). Voluntary smiles (Figure 12.13b) include the mouth movements but generally do not include the muscles around the eyes (Ekman & Davidson, 1993). *The full expression including the muscles around the eyes* is called the **Duchenne smile,** named after Duchenne de Boulogne, the first person to describe it.

Understanding Facial Expressions

Do we learn how to make appropriate facial expressions, or are they part of our biological heritage? One way to approach this question is through naturalistic observations. Charles Darwin (1872/1965) asked missionaries and other people stationed in remote parts of the world to describe the facial expressions of the people who lived there. He found that people everywhere had similar facial expressions, including expressions of grief, determination, anger, surprise, terror, and disgust.

One century later, Irenäus Eibl-Eibesfeldt (1973, 1974) photographed people in different cultures, documenting the similarities in their facial expressions. He found smiling, frowning, laughing, and crying present

a   b

F I G U R E 12.13   A spontaneous, happy smile (a) includes movements of both the mouth muscles and the muscles surrounding the eyes. This expression is sometimes called the "Duchenne smile." A voluntary smile (b) ordinarily includes only the mouth muscles. Most people cannot voluntarily control the eye muscles associated with the Duchenne smile.

FIGURE 12.14 This laughing girl was born deaf and blind. (From Eibl-Eibesfeldt, 1973.)

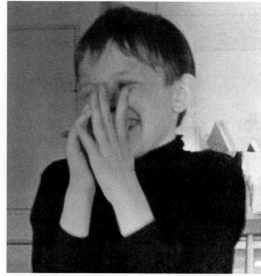

FIGURE 12.15 A boy, blind since birth, covers his face in embarrassment. (From Eibl-Eibesfeldt, 1973.) He prevents others from seeing his face, even though he has never experienced sight himself.

throughout the world, even in children who are born deaf and blind (Figures 12.14 and 12.15). Evidently, at least some of our facial expressions develop spontaneously, without any need for imitation. Eibl-Eibesfeldt also found that people everywhere expressed a friendly greeting by briefly raising their eyebrows (Figure 12.16). The mean duration of

FIGURE 12.16 People throughout the world, such as this man from New Guinea, raise their eyebrows as a greeting. Traveling around the world, you could communicate anywhere by using such universal facial expressions of emotion as smiling and frowning. But you might give the wrong message if you didn't know that nodding your head in some cultures means "no" or which hand and foot gestures are insulting. (From Eibl-Eibesfeldt, 1973.)

that expression is the same in all cultures: one third of a second from start to finish, including one sixth of a second in the fully elevated position.

To move beyond naturalistic observations, researchers typically use photos of people showing the presumed "basic" facial expressions, as shown in Figure 12.17. Try identifying these expressions yourself. First, look at each face and try to name its expression. (Please try now.)

Then look at each and match the expressions to the following labels (one face per label): anger, disgust, fear, happiness, sadness, and surprise.

Most people can match all six of the labels accurately. After researchers translate the labels into other languages, people in other cultures can also match them quite accurately, though not perfectly (Ekman, 1992). In other experiments, this procedure is reversed, and Europeans or Americans are asked to identify the facial expressions of people from other parts of the world. Here, again, the accuracy is fairly good.

What can we conclude from such data? We can conclude that people's facial expressions have approximately the same meaning throughout the world (Ekman, 1994). However, the results do not necessarily indicate that people have precisely six basic emotions (Russell, 1994). One problem is that most expressions are somewhat ambiguous. For example, if you had looked only at face f, would you have been sure that it expressed fear? Using a matching procedure, you can label it as fear because it looks more like fear than any of the others do, and you can find other expressions to fit the other labels. But if you looked at f by itself, you might have called the expression sadness, anger, or even surprise. If you looked at d by itself, you might have called the expression fear or hope instead of surprise. In real

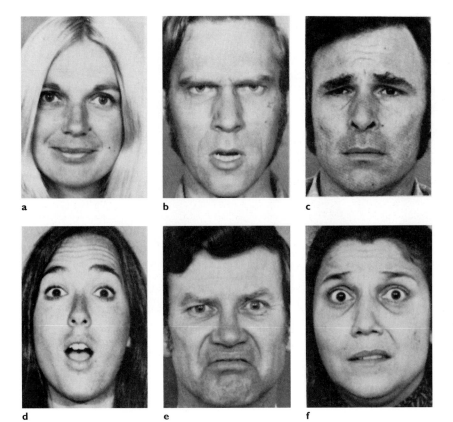

FIGURE 12.17 Paul Ekman has used these faces in experiments testing people's ability to recognize expressions of emotions. Can you identify which face conveys anger, disgust, fear, happiness, sadness, and surprise? Check the answer on page 452. (From Ekman & Friesen, 1984.)

life, we identify people's emotions only partly by their facial expression and also partly by the situation (Russell, 1997).

Furthermore, the fact that people of all cultures can recognize facial expressions for six emotions does not necessarily mean that these are basic emotions, much less that they are the *only* basic emotions. Consider an analogy to color: No doubt people throughout the world could match an array of colors to the names red, green, yellow, blue, pink, orange, brown, and purple, and probably even light green, dark green, yellowish green, and so forth. We do not conclude from this evidence that all those colors are "basic." Similarly, agreement on the label of a facial expression is weak evidence for calling the underlying emotion basic.

A Biological Approach to Identifying Basic Emotions

If people do have basic emotions, one way to identify them would be to find a brain area that is active during only one kind of emotion. For example, if researchers found some kind of brain damage that eliminated one kind of emotion without having much effect on the others, we could conclude that the eliminated emotion was a basic one, independent of the others.

Researchers have found evidence linking fear or anxiety to part of the amygdala, as shown in Figure 12.18. This figure shows a human brain, although much of the research has been conducted with rodents. A sudden loud noise will evoke a startle response (tensing the muscles, etc.) in practically any mammal—human, rat, whatever—unless the individual

is deaf or unless damage has occurred to certain areas of the pons and medulla. Ordinarily, this startle response is even greater in anxiety-provoking situations. For example, people show a greater startle response in a dark room than in one that is well-lit. Just attaching shock electrodes to the skin enhances the startle response, even before any shocks are delivered (Grillon & Ameli, 1998). However, after damage to the amygdala in either humans or rats, many frightening stimuli no longer produce much of a fear response on their own and no longer enhance the startle response to a sudden noise (LaBar, LeDoux, Spencer, & Phelps, 1995; Phillips & LeDoux, 1992).

People who have suffered damage to the amygdala report feeling few fears or anxieties. They also cannot recognize other people's facial expressions of fear (Broks et al., 1998) and have trouble inferring other people's emotions from their tone of voice (Scott et al., 1997). However, their problems are not limited to depictions of fear or anxiety; they also have some trouble recognizing expressions of anger, disgust, and surprise.

Research has also identified a brain area apparently associated with disgust. In one study, people looked at photos of other people's facial expressions. Whenever they looked at photos showing disgust, activity increased in a brain area known as the anterior insular cortex (Phillips et al., 1997). That finding is particularly interesting because the anterior insular cortex is also known to respond strongly when people taste something offensive. Taste is also known as *gustation*, so *dis-gust* is literally *bad taste.* Our brains actually respond to disgusting things as if they tasted bad.

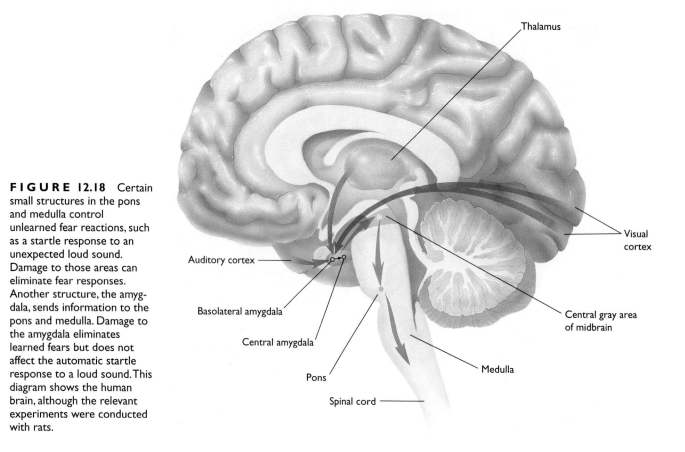

FIGURE 12.18 Certain small structures in the pons and medulla control unlearned fear reactions, such as a startle response to an unexpected loud sound. Damage to those areas can eliminate fear responses. Another structure, the amygdala, sends information to the pons and medulla. Damage to the amygdala eliminates learned fears but does not affect the automatic startle response to a loud sound. This diagram shows the human brain, although the relevant experiments were conducted with rats.

Happiness

What makes you happy? What makes you unhappy? The answers are more elusive than you might expect. The following quote is from Leo Tolstoy, the author of *War and Peace, Anna Karenina,* and other famous novels. At the time of this writing, Tolstoy was rich and famous but desperately unhappy:

> I wandered about in the forest of human knowledge. . . . From one branch of human knowledge I received an endless number of precise answers to questions I had not asked, answers concerning the chemical composition of the stars, the movement of the sun toward the constellation Hercules, the origin of the species and of man, the forms of infinitely small atoms. . . . But the answer given by this branch of knowledge to my question about the meaning of my life was only this: You . . . are a temporary, random conglomeration of particles. The thing that you have been led to refer to as your life is simply the mutual interaction and alteration of these particles. This conglomeration will continue for a certain period of time; then the interaction of these particles will come to a halt, and the thing you call your life will come to an end and with it all your questions. You are a little lump of something randomly stuck together. The lump decomposes. . . . There is no more to be said.
>
> My life came to a stop. . . . There was no life in me because I had no desires whose satisfaction I would have found reasonable. . . . If a fairy had come and offered to fulfill my every wish, I would not have known what to wish for. . . . I

did not even want to discover truth anymore because I had guessed what it was. The truth was that life is meaningless. (Tolstoy, 1882/1983, pp. 40–41, 27–28)

What would it take to make Tolstoy happy? Fame, wealth, family, and friends had failed to bring him happiness. If he were alive today, no doubt someone would recommend giving him antidepressant drugs. But I wouldn't count on drugs to do him much good either. What Tolstoy needed was a belief that the universe made sense and that life had meaning. Eventually, he found contentment, if not exactly happiness, by seeking spiritual (though not church-oriented) values.

 How happy would you rate yourself on a scale from 0 to 10, where 10 is extremely happy, 0 is extremely unhappy, and 5 is average? Then answer two more questions: What do you think would make you happier than you are now? And what *does* make you happy, on a typical day? (Please try answering these questions before you read on.)

In almost all countries except those that are war-torn or overrun with famine and disease, most people rate themselves somewhat above average in happiness (Diener & Diener, 1996). If you are like many people, your answer to "what would make you happier" probably included something like money, possessions, a good job, a boyfriend or girlfriend (or a "better" boyfriend or girlfriend), or more leisure time. However, the things that people think would make them happy generally do not keep them happy for long. Lottery winners report great happiness shortly after winning but return to their usual happiness level (or even less!) within weeks or months. To the question "what does make you happy?" almost no one mentions money or possessions. Most people include spending time with family or friends, enjoying nature, doing something well enough to get a sense of accomplishment, or a system of beliefs.

In one study, more than 2,000 twins in Minnesota rated their own happiness. Their ratings correlated only slightly with their wealth, education, job prestige, marital status, or religious commitment, but in most cases, either both twins were happy, both were neutral, or both were unhappy (Lykken & Tellegen, 1996). We should nurture a little skepticism here: Maybe how happy people *say* they are isn't how happy they *actually* are; after all, how could we check the accuracy of someone's happiness report? Nevertheless, whatever it is that these happiness reports measure is apparently part of someone's personality, more rooted in genetics or the prenatal environment than it is in people's recent experiences. Some people tend to be gloomy and others tend to be cheerful, and most events shift the level of happiness only temporarily.

THE MESSAGE
Determining the Range of Emotions

When psychologists debate about how many basic emotions people have (if any), it may seem to you that the answer to this question is not terribly important. In a practical sense, it may not be, but it is part of a much larger issue. Similarly, in a practical sense, it may not matter whether there are 92 naturally occurring chemical elements or some other number, but when chemists established the number with confidence, they knew that they then understood something important about elements and that they were on the way to still greater understanding. Any field must start out by understanding its elements as clearly as possible. The psychology of emotions continues to be a difficult and sometimes frustrating field, simply because researchers are still searching for the answers to some basic questions.

SUMMARY

* **The usefulness of emotions.** We make many decisions by imagining the emotional consequences of the possible outcomes. Brain-damaged people who suffer a loss of emotions also have trouble making and executing long-term plans. (page 435)

* **Emotional intelligence.** In social situations, people need special skills to judge other people's emotions and intentions and the probable emotional outcomes of their own possible behaviors. People who misjudge others' emotions can easily cause themselves trouble. (page 436)

* *Emotions and autonomic arousal.* Emotions are generally associated with arousal of either the sympathetic or parasympathetic branch of the autonomic nervous system. The sympathetic nervous system readies the body for emergency action. The parasympathetic nervous system promotes digestion and other less vigorous activities. (page 437)

* *Opponent-process principle.* Removing the impetus for a given emotion instigates a sudden swing to the opposite emotion. For example, removing something that had made you happy would make you unhappy. (page 438)

* *Polygraph.* The polygraph measures the activity of the sympathetic nervous system through such variables as heart rate, breathing rate, blood pressure, and electrical conductance of the skin. The polygraph is sometimes used as a "lie detector," although it is not very accurate for that purpose. (page 439)

* *James-Lange theory.* According to the James-Lange theory of emotions, an emotion is the perception of a change in the body's physiological state. (page 442)

* *Cannon-Bard theory.* According to the Cannon-Bard theory, the cognitive experience of an emotion occurs at the same time as physiological arousal, but the two are independent of each other. (page 443)

* *Schachter and Singer's theory.* According to Schachter and Singer's theory, autonomic arousal determines the intensity of an emotion but does not determine what that emotion will be. We identify an emotion on the basis of how we perceive the situation. (page 444)

* *Range of emotions.* Psychologists do not fully agree about which emotions, if any, are basic. (page 445)

* *Facial expressions.* Many human facial expressions have similar meanings in cultures throughout the world. (page 446)

* *Measuring happiness.* Happiness is difficult to measure, and most of what we know about it is based on correlational data. Material possessions alone cannot guarantee happiness. Happiness level is a fairly stable aspect of personality despite changes in people's lives. (page 450)

Suggestions for Further Reading

Damasio, A.R. (1994). *Descartes' error.* New York: G.P. Putnam's Sons. Argues that emotion is a necessary contributor to intelligent decision-making.

LeDoux, J.E. (1996). *The emotional brain.* New York: Simon & Schuster. Discussion of the biological bases of emotion, by a pioneering researcher.

Russell, J.A., & Fernández-Dols (Eds.) (1997). *The psychology of facial expression* (pp. 295–320). Cambridge, England: Cambridge University Press. Good review of research on how we express emotions.

Terms

emotional intelligence   the ability to perceive, imagine, and understand emotions and to use that information in decision-making (page 436)

autonomic nervous system   a section of the nervous system that controls the functioning of the internal organs (page 437)

sympathetic nervous system   a system composed of two chains of neuron clusters lying just to the left and right of the spinal cord; these neurons send messages to the internal organs to prepare them for a burst of vigorous activity (page 437)

parasympathetic nervous system   a system of neurons located in the medulla and the bottom of the spinal cord; these neurons send messages to the internal organs to prepare the body for digestion and related processes (page 437)

opponent-process principle of emotions   the principle that the removal of a stimulus that excites one emotion causes a swing to an opposite emotion (page 438)

polygraph   a machine that simultaneously measures heart rate, breathing rate, blood pressure, and electrical conduction of the skin (page 439)

guilty-knowledge test   a test that uses the polygraph to measure whether a person has information that should be known only by someone guilty of a certain crime or someone who talked with the guilty person (page 441)

James-Lange theory   the theory that emotion is merely our perception of autonomic changes and movements evoked directly by various stimuli (page 442)

Cannon-Bard theory of emotions   the theory that certain areas of the brain evaluate sensory information and, when appropriate, send one set of impulses to the autonomic nervous system and another set to the forebrain, which is responsible for the subjective and cognitive aspects of emotion (page 443)

Schachter and Singer's theory of emotions   the theory that the intensity of sympathetic arousal determines the intensity of an emotion but that cognitive factors determine the type of emotion. (page 444)

Duchenne smile   a spontaneous expression that includes movement of both the mouth muscles and certain muscles near the eyes (page 447)

Answers to Concept Checks

1.   When you ride a roller coaster, your heart rate increases (sympathetic activity). After you get off the ride, your heart rate falls to lower than usual (rebound increase in parasympathetic activity). (page 439)

2.   After someone takes a drug repeatedly, the A state becomes weaker. (That is known as tolerance, as discussed in Chapter 7.) The B state (withdrawal) becomes stronger. (page 439)

3.   According to the James-Lange theory, the trembling and shaking came first. Schachter and Singer's theory agrees. However, according to the James-Lange theory, your perception of the trembling and shaking leads immediately and automatically to the experience of fear. According to Schachter and Singer's theory, you first interpret your trembling on the basis of the circumstances before you experience fear: "Am I shaking because of that pill I took? Because someone made me angry? Because I'm excited? Because I'm frightened?" (page 444)

Answers to Other Question in the Text

Figure 12.17, page 449: From left to right, top to bottom, the faces express happiness, anger, sadness, surprise, disgust, and fear.

Web Resources

What's Your EQ?

www.utne.com/cgi-bin/eq/

How well do you know or recognize your feelings and use them to make effective life decisions?*

Drugs, Brains & Behavior

daniel.drew.edu/~ctimmons/drugs/chap04.htm#James-Lange Theory of Emotion

C. Robin Timmons of Drew University and Leonard W. Hamilton of Rutgers University briefly describe the James-Lange, Cannon-Bard, and Schachter and Singer theories of emotions.

---

*Note: Any psychological test that is readily available to the public, while entertaining and possibly informative, should not be used to make important decisions about yourself or others. The most powerful, valid, and reliable psychological assessment devices are usually kept under the tight control of their creators or copyright holders.

MODULE 12.2

Anger and Violent Behaviors

What are the circumstances that lead to violence?

Why are some people more violent than others?

During World War II—while nearly all the industrialized nations were at war, while the Nazis were exterminating the Jews, and while the United States was preparing a nuclear bomb that it later dropped on Japan—Mohandas K. Gandhi, the world's foremost advocate of nonviolence, was in jail for leading a protest march against British rule in India. The charge against Gandhi was, ironically, "disturbing the peace." Someone asked Gandhi what he thought of Western civilization. He replied that he thought it might be a good idea.

Human beings are capable of ghastly acts of cruelty against one another. They are also capable of acts of nobility, heroism, and courageous opposition to violence, as in Gandhi's case. The struggle to understand violence is among the most important goals facing humanity in general, and psychology in particular.

Provocations of Anger and Violence

Most people become angry far more often than they actually attack anyone. Participants in one study kept an "anger diary" for a week (Averill, 1983). Most of their experiences with anger were provoked by people they knew well, such as, "My roommate locked me out of the room when I went to the shower. That's the third time. If he does it one more time, I'm gonna kill him." The diaries also included descriptions of what people did in response to each event. Nearly all the replies were either, "I talked to the person who made me angry," "I talked to someone else about it," or "I did nothing about it." Very few admitted to issuing even threats of violence, and certainly no one said, "The next day he locked me out again, so I killed him."

If you try keeping track of your own anger experiences, you will probably find that you are often provoked when someone prevents you from doing something you wanted to do, such as if someone borrows something you needed without asking you. You will also probably find that few or none of your angry episodes lead to violence. Psychologists have long spoken of the **frustration-aggression hypothesis,** *the idea that frustration—a failure to obtain something that one expected—leads to aggressive behavior* (Dollard, Miller, Doob, Mowrer, & Sears, 1939). However, this hypothesis has several limitations. First, frustration produces anger and the potential for aggression mainly when one attributes an intention to the person who caused the frustration. For example, if someone runs down the hall, bumps into you, and knocks you down, you might feel angry. But if someone slipped on a wet spot on the floor and knocked you down, you would probably not feel angry, because you do not assess blame. Secondly, even when frustration leads to anger, the anger will not necessarily lead to aggression. Finally, frustration is important only for emotional aggression, not for calm aggressive behaviors that people learn as strategies for getting what they want.

Leonard Berkowitz (1983, 1989) therefore proposed a more comprehensive theory: Any unpleasant event—frustration, pain, foul odors, a hot environment, frightening information, whatever—excites both the impulse to fight and the impulse to flee. Which impulse dominates depends on the circumstances, and one of the main circumstances is the expected result of an attack. If you have frequently struck people before, have won most of your fights, and have seldom been punished, and you think the person who just spilled coffee on you looks easy to beat, you may threaten this person or even strike. But if you have had mostly bad experiences when you got into fights, or if the offending person looks large and ferocious, you will suppress your anger. And if the one who spilled the coffee is your boss, or the loan and scholarship officer at your college, you will most likely smile and apologize for being in the way.

Although any kind of frustration or disappointment can lead to anger, and potentially to violence, the likelihood is particularly strong in a sexual context. Throughout the animal kingdom, who are more likely to fight with one another—males or females? Males. When do they fight the most? During the reproductive season. And what are they fighting about? Access to females. In some cases, they are fighting for a position of dominance, but the main value of dominance is increased access to sexual partners. In humans as well, one of the leading causes of murder is sexual jealousy (Daly, Wilson, & Weghorst, 1982).

Characteristics of Relatively Violent People

Can we identify the people who are most likely to commit violent acts? In at least one regard, many psychologists were on the wrong track for a long time, assuming that people committed violence because of low self-esteem. According

Throughout the animal kingdom, aggressive behavior is common among males when they are competing for the attention and affection of females.

to that idea, people who thought little of themselves tried to build themselves up by tearing someone else down. Perhaps (but only perhaps) that hypothesis works in certain cases of group violence. A fair number of outbreaks of ethnic violence have occurred when a group has suffered defeats and humiliations and then embraced an ideology that blamed another group for their problems and promised them a glorious future after the destruction of the offending group (Staub, 1996).

For individual violence, however, the research supports little or no link between low self-esteem and violent behavior. The *victims* certainly report low self-esteem, sometimes extremely low, but the aggressors tend to be arrogant, egotistical, and quite self-confident. At most, it may be that violence results when something threatens someone's high self-esteem, and that person then strikes out against another person to reaffirm a sense of superiority (Baumeister, Smart, & Boden, 1996).

One extensive study of Norwegian and Swedish bullies, ages 7 through 16, found that hardly any of them suffered from feelings of anxiety or insecurity. They were as a rule large, strong, impulsive, and indifferent to their victims. Why did they do it? They said it was fun. They enjoyed taking another child's money, forcing him to eat weeds, leading him around as a pet with a string around his neck . . . and, most importantly, they got away with it. Psychologists found they could reduce the bullying by increasing adult supervision, enforcing rules, and having serious talks with the offending children and their parents (Olweus, 1995).

If low self-esteem is not a good predictor of violence, what is? Sometimes psychologists or other mental-health professionals are asked to predict how violent someone will be. For example, a judge may be trying to decide between a prison sentence and a period of probation for someone recently convicted of a crime. Or perhaps someone has been in prison and is now eligible for parole, or has been in a hospital for mentally disordered criminal offenders and is now being considered for release.

Under such circumstances, how accurate would you guess that a psychologist's predictions are? Predictions based on interviews are a bit more accurate than they would be by flipping a coin, but they are not impressive (Monahan, 1984). One reason for these mediocre results is that violent behavior is sporadic and situation-dependent. Even the most violence-prone people can be pleasant and charming, especially when they are talking to a psychologist who has the power to decide whether they belong in prison. The best basis for predicting violence is past behavior; people with a long history of violent acts are likely to commit some more, whereas those having committed only a single violent act are much less dangerous. From an examination of someone's past, it is possible to make moderately useful predictions, although it is still best to admit uncertainty, just as weather forecasters usually qualify their predictions, such as, "the chance of rain is 80% for Tuesday and 60% for Wednesday." Many psychologists prefer to say something like, "This defendant has a less than 25% risk of violence if he gets a job and a higher than 50% chance if he does not" (Borum, 1996; Grisso & Tomkins, 1996; Monahan & Steadman, 1996).

Specifically, people who were physically abused as children and who witnessed violence between their parents are more likely than others to commit repeated acts of violence, including murder (Malinosky-Rummell & Hansen, 1993). The physical pain of being beaten may provoke future violence, and a violent parent provides a model for the child to imitate. (Recall the principles of social learning from Chapter 6.) Even this predictor is far from foolproof, however; only about one third of abused children become abusive parents (Widom, 1989).

Several other factors are associated with a tendency toward violent behavior (Lewis et al., 1985; Lynam, 1996; Osofsky, 1995; Raine, Venables, & Williams, 1990):

- A history of violent or impulsive acts and of frequent associations with antisocial individuals
- Growing up in a violent neighborhood

- Not feeling guilty after hurting someone
- Weaker-than-normal physiological responses to arousal
- A history of suicide attempts
- Watching a great deal of violence on television

The probability of attack also depends on biological factors. In all cultures, violent and criminal activities are more common in men than in women, and the probability of such activities increases sharply during puberty, when testosterone levels are increasing. Figure 12.19 shows the probability of arrest for robbery, burglary, and aggravated assault as a function of age in the United States. For each crime, the age of the maximum number of arrests was set at 100%, so the graph does not show that burglary is more than three times more common than either of the other two crimes. Note that, for each crime, the rate of occurrence rises sharply during the teen years, reaches a peak at 17 to 21 years, and then declines steadily.

Figure 12.20 shows the percentage of male juvenile delinquents born in 1945 or 1958 who had their first arrest at various ages. Note that the probability of a first arrest increases sharply between the ages 12 and 16 and then drops (Tracy, Wolfgang, & Figlio, 1990). The probability of an arrest does not drop at age 17, but the probability of a *first* arrest does; that is, a boy who did not get himself into trouble before age 17 will probably not start later.

With humans as well as with other species, testosterone increases the probability of violence (Bernhardt, 1997; Brooks & Reddon, 1996; Dabbs, Carr, Frady, & Riad, 1995). (Recall the link between violence and sexual jealousy.) A variety of drugs, notably alcohol and tranquilizers, increase the probability of violent behavior (Bushman, 1993; Bushman & Cooper, 1990). Tranquilizers presumably increase violent behavior by decreasing people's fear of the possible retaliation by the person being attacked. Also, the probability of violent behavior is highest

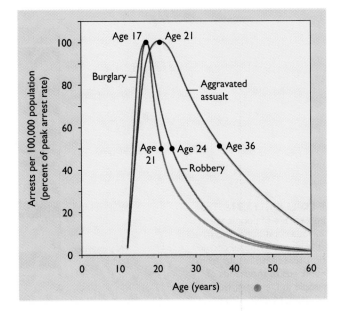

FIGURE 12.19 Relative frequencies of arrest at different ages in the United States. For each crime, the age of the maximum number of arrests was set at 100%. Note that the arrest rate rises for each crime until ages 17–21 and thereafter declines. (From data of the Federal Bureau of Investigation, 1984.)

among adults with low activity of the neurotransmitter serotonin. Exactly how a deficit of serotonin activity could lead to violence is unknown, but measurements of serotonin metabolites in the blood or urine have provided moderately accurate predictors of which paroled prisoners will be arrested again (Virkkunen, Eggert, Rawlings, & Linnoila, 1996) and which survivors of violent suicide attempts will attempt it again (Roy, DeJong, & Linnoila, 1989). Drugs that increase serotonin activity help to decrease aggressive acts among people with a history of such (Coccaro & Kavoussi, 1997).

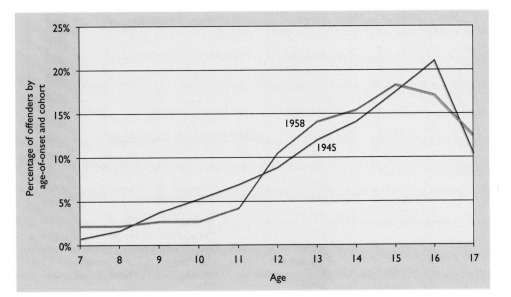

FIGURE 12.20 The percentage of juvenile delinquents in Philadelphia, Pennsylvania, who had their first arrest at each age. The number of total arrests does not decline at age 17, but the number of first-time arrests does. (From Tracy, Wolfgang, & Figlio, 1990.)

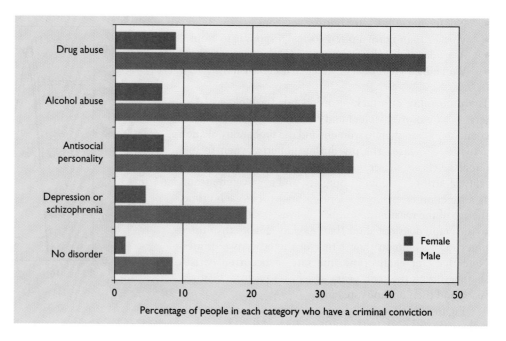

FIGURE 12.21 The percentage of people with various conditions who have at least one criminal conviction. (Based on results from hundreds of thousands of people in Denmark, from Hodgins, Mednick, Brennan, Schulsinger, & Engberg, 1996.)

Violence by Mental Patients

Decades ago, psychologists believed that mental patients or former mental patients were no more dangerous than anyone else and no more likely to commit crimes. However, that conclusion was based on distorted evidence. At the time, most mental patients who were admitted to mental hospitals stayed there indefinitely, so only the best recovered and least dangerous ones were released. Today, nearly all mental patients are released after brief stays, so our data are more representative.

The results vary from one study to another, but in general it appears that patients with most kinds of mental disorders are somewhat more likely than other people to be arrested for serious crimes (Eronen, Hakola, & Tiihonen, 1996; Hodgins, Mednick, Brennan, Schulsinger, & Engberg, 1996; Teplin, Abram, & McClelland, 1996). (See Figure 12.21.) A few (very few) deeply disturbed mental patients commit extreme, senseless acts of violence, such as pushing a stranger in front of a subway train in a large city, and thereby receive a disproportionate amount of publicity (Martell & Dietz, 1992).

One type of mental disorder that is associated with a high probability of crime is *antisocial personality disorder* (Hodgins et al., 1996). However, the criteria for diagnosing that condition include lack of remorse and repeatedly performing acts that are grounds for arrest (American Psychiatric Association, 1994), so its association with crime is hardly a mystery. The other mental disorder associated with a high crime rate is drug and alcohol abuse (Hodgins et al., 1996; Monahan, 1992; Teplin et al., 1996). One interesting, unresolved question is to what extent the violence is due to the drugs and to what extent it is a product of the kind of person who abuses drugs. Curiously, one study found that giving methylphenidate (Ritalin), a stimulant

drug, to adolescents with conduct problems actually decreased their troublesome behaviors (Klein et al., 1997).

Still, even though certain disorders are associated with an increased risk of violence, the task remains to predict which individuals with a given disorder are dangerous. As with anyone else, interviews and personality measures provide only weak predictors of violence (Bonta, Law, & Hanson, 1998). The best predictor is the person's past history of violent or criminal behavior. As shown in Figure 12.22,

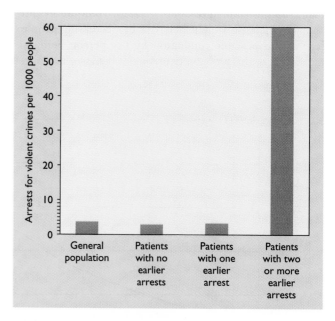

FIGURE 12.22 The arrest rates for mental patients and for the general public. Patients with a history of criminal offenses are likely to continue to be dangerous, but those without such a history are not. (After data of Cocozza, Melick, & Steadman, 1978.)

mental patients with a past history of criminal arrests are likely to be arrested again; those with no previous arrests are likely to continue keeping a clean record (Cocozza, Melick, & Steadman, 1978).

Sexual Violence

Rape is *sexual contact obtained through violence or threats.* Although that definition sounds simple enough, in practice, offenses range on a continuum from forcible rape through ambiguous resistance. For example, 9% of the women surveyed at 32 colleges reported that they had been forced into unwanted sexual intercourse, and 25% said they had participated in unwanted intercourse in response to verbal coaxing or while under the influence of alcohol (Koss, Gidycz, & Wisniewski, 1987; see Figure 12.23). At the same colleges, only 4.4% of the men said they had forced a woman to have sex (Koss & Dinero, 1988). Although it is possible that a small percentage of the men forced themselves sexually on a larger percentage of women, a more likely interpretation is that men and women interpreted the same events differently. In many cases, a couple had kissed and petted voluntarily; when the man wished to progress to intercourse, evidently the woman said no but the man either disbelieved or disregarded her refusal. Preventing date rape is partly a matter of persuading men to respect a woman's refusal and partly a matter of advising women to express their refusal clearly and firmly.

What kind of men commit rape? Unfortunately, most of our data are based on convicted rapists, who are generally those who committed violent attacks and who may therefore not be representative of other rapists. Still, the best available evidence indicates that most men who sexually attack women have a history of hostility and violence against both men and women (Malamuth, Sockloskie, Koss, & Tanaka, 1991). Many rapists were abused children; many feel anger toward women and a need to dominate or control them. Although much less is known about date rapists, one survey of admitted date rapists found that they also reported anger toward women and a drive to dominate them (Lisak & Roth, 1988). The probability of rape is also elevated when a man becomes so intoxicated from alcohol or other drugs that he sheds the inhibitions that would ordinarily prevent such an attack (Lisak & Roth, 1988).

Just as psychologists do with other kinds of criminals, they sometimes try to predict whether convicted sex offenders (such as rapists and child molesters) are still dangerous—for example, when a sex offender is under consideration for parole. It would be pointless to ask sex offenders whether they are still attracted by the idea of rape or sexual contact with children; someone hoping for parole is not likely to answer honestly. The preferred approach is to present photos or audiotapes of various kinds and measure erections of the penis. Many rapists become sexually aroused by portrayals of rape, and many child molesters become aroused by photos of naked children, whereas most other men are not sexually aroused by either of these kinds of stimuli (Earls, 1988; Harris & Rice, 1996). However, although most psychologists feel comfortable in assuming that this procedure indicates whether someone is likely to commit rape or child abuse, we have little direct evidence to test this assumption.

What should a woman do if a man is trying to rape her? Some psychologists recommend fighting back; others recommend trying to appeal to the would-be rapist's better nature; others recommend doing something to upset or offend the rapist, such as vomiting. However, for each of these recommendations, one can find other psychologists who say it is a bad idea that is likely to backfire (Fischhoff, 1992). The problem is that no one approach is sure to succeed; the results depend on the woman, the man, and the setting.

SOMETHING TO THINK ABOUT

Rapists and child molesters sometimes pore over sexually explicit magazines and watch videotapes just before committing an offense (Malamuth & Donnerstein, 1982; Marshall, 1988). Can we conclude that such materials lead to the offenses? (Remember, correlation does not mean causation.) What kind of evidence would we need to determine whether sexually explicit materials lead to sexual offenses? ✷

THE MESSAGE
Controlling Violence

Most of us would like to believe that people are fundamentally good and that acts of violence and cruelty are an abnormality: If only we could get rid of poverty, injustice, ignorance, low self-esteem, and so forth, then people would stop being cruel to one another. The problem with this noble belief is that some perpetrators of unspeakable cruelty have had all the advantages of wealth and opportunity. Improvements in society can decrease violent crime—after all, the crime

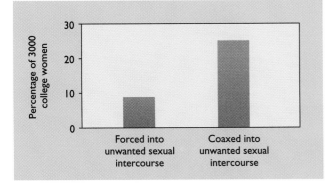

FIGURE 12.23 How common is date rape on college campuses? The answer depends on how we define rape.

rate usually does go down when the economy improves—but we are unlikely to eliminate violence completely.

Is punishment therefore the answer? Only in part. Children are less likely to be bullies if they have enough adult supervision, and adults are also less likely to abuse others if they believe someone will retaliate against them. However, making punishments quicker and more certain is more effective than making them harsher. In fact, excessively painful punishment actually triggers aggressive behavior.

Finally, it is possible to help people control their aggressive tendencies, if they wish to receive help. People can be taught to accept frustration and to react to disappointments in less disruptive ways. Those who are accustomed to gaining attention or other reinforcements from violent outbursts can learn other ways to get what they want (Fehrenbach & Thelen, 1982). People are less likely to turn to violence, even as a "last resort," if they can see other options.

SUMMARY

✳ *Anger.* People experience anger frequently, although it seldom leads to violent acts. Aggressive behavior often occurs in defense of territory or in competition for a mate. Frustration or other unpleasant experiences often prompt aggressive behavior. (page ●●●)

✳ *Predicting violence.* Psychologists and psychiatrists find it difficult to predict whether a particular prisoner would be dangerous, if released. The best way to make such predictions is to review someone's past behavior, especially the history of violent behavior. (page ●●●)

✳ *Violence by mental patients.* People with certain kinds of psychological disorders, especially substance abusers, are more likely than other people to commit violent acts. Still, the best predictor of violence among mental patients, as among other people, is their past behavior. (page ●●●)

✳ *Sexual violence.* Most of the men who are convicted of violent rape have a history of other kinds of violent acts also. (page ●●●)

Suggestion for Further Reading

Staub, E. (1989). *The roots of evil.* New York: Cambridge University Press. An inquiry into why people engage in extremely violent behavior.

Terms

frustration-aggression hypothesis   the theory that frustration leads to aggressive behavior (page ●●●)

rape   sexual contact obtained through violence or threats (page ●●●)

Web Resources

MINCAVA: Global Links on Violence

www.mincava.umn.edu/global.asp

The Minnesota Center Against Violence & Abuse (MINCAVA) maintains hundreds of links to sites that provide information about all forms of violence.

Health Psychology

How do our emotions affect our health?

I magine you meet a man who is suffering from, say, multiple sclerosis. Would you say, "It's his own fault he's sick; he's being punished for his sins"? I presume you would neither say nor believe anything so cruel. However, in the Middle Ages and in ancient times, many people believed just that. We congratulate ourselves today on having advanced beyond that way of thinking; we know it is wrong to blame the victim.

Or do we? We may think that cigarette smokers are at least partly at fault if they develop lung cancer. We note that AIDS is usually contracted by people with a history of intravenous drug use or unsafe sex. If women drink alcohol during pregnancy, we hold them partly responsible for the deformities or mental retardation of their infants. As we learn more and more about the causes of various illnesses,

we expect people to accept more responsibility for their own health, even if we do not exactly use the word *blame* when people become ill.

People's behavior does, in fact, influence their health. Unfortunately, we can easily overstate the extent of that influence. Some people are always as careful as possible about their diet, exercise regularly, and have healthy habits but develop serious illnesses anyway. Psychological factors influence our health, but these are not the only influences.

Health psychology *is concerned with how people's behavior can enhance health and prevent illness and how behavior contributes to recovery from illness* (Brannon & Feist, 1992). It deals with such issues as why people smoke, why they sometimes ignore their physician's advice, and how to reduce pain. In this section, we shall focus mainly on how stress and other emotional conditions affect health.

Stress

Have you ever gone without sleep several nights in a row trying to finish an assignment before a deadline? Or waited what seemed like forever for someone who was supposed to pick you up? Or had a close friend suddenly not want to see you anymore? Or tried to explain why you no longer want to date someone? Each of these experiences provokes an emotional response and causes stress.

Selye's Concept of Stress

According to Hans Selye (1979), an Austrian-born physician who worked at McGill University in Montreal, **stress** is *the nonspecific response of the body to any demand made upon it.* Every demand on the body evokes certain specific responses as well. The body responds in one way to the loss of blood, in another way to the lack of sleep. But all demands on the body evoke generalized responses such as increased response of the sympathetic nervous system, increased release of the hormone epinephrine, and impaired concentration.

When people say, "I've been under a lot of stress lately," they are generally referring to a string of unpleasant experiences. Selye's concept of stress is broader: He includes any experience that brings about change in a person's life. For example, getting married and being promoted are presumably pleasant experiences, but they also demand that you make changes in the way you live, so in Selye's sense, these events produce stress. It is unclear, however, whether a favorable stressor makes the same demands on the body as does an unfavorable stressor. According to Selye, dealing with the effects of poverty, racism, sexism, or a lifelong disability would *not* count as stress, however; only *changes* in your life count as stress.

Selye believed that the body goes through three stages in its response to a stressor: The first is **alarm,** *a brief period of high arousal of the sympathetic nervous system, readying*

Health psychology deals with all the various ways that people's behavior affects their health, ranging from why some people neglect to take their prescribed medication to why some people persist in smoking, heavy drinking, and other risky behaviors.

the body for vigorous activity. Some stressors last longer than the body can maintain this high state of arousal, however. Perhaps you have a high-stress job or you live near the runway of a busy airport. If so, you cannot overcome your problem with a brief burst of intense activity. You enter **resistance,** *a stage of prolonged but moderate arousal.* Your epinephrine levels remain at a high level day after day, week after week (Figure 12.24). Your adrenal cortex secretes cortisol and several other hormones that elevate blood sugar and enhance metabolism. The increased fuel supply to the cells enables them to sustain a high, steady level of activity to endure prolonged stress. However, you no longer feel ready for vigorous activity; you feel withdrawn and inactive much of the time, your performance deteriorates, and you complain of a decreased quality of life (Evans, Bullinger, & Hygge, 1998).

If the stress is even more intense and long-lasting, the body enters the third stage, **exhaustion.** *As cortisol and other hormones shift energy toward increasing blood sugar and metabolism, they shift it away from synthesis of proteins, including the proteins necessary for activity of the immune system.* In the short term, that shift may not be a problem; however, severe stress over many months can weaken the immune system and leave an individual vulnerable to a variety of illnesses (Cohen, 1996). The end result is characterized by weakness, fatigue, loss of appetite, and a general lack of interest.

Posttraumatic Stress Disorder

Perhaps the most powerful demonstration of the effects of severe stress is **posttraumatic stress disorder (PTSD).** *People who have endured extreme stress feel prolonged anxiety and depression* (Pitman, Orr, Forgue, DeJong, & Claiborn, 1987). This condition has been recognized in postwar periods throughout history and given such names as "battle fatigue" or "shell shock." One nationwide survey reported posttraumatic stress disorder in 20% of the American veterans who were wounded in Vietnam (Helzer, Robins, & McEnvoy, 1987). It also occurs in rape or assault victims, torture victims, survivors of an air-

This group of Vietnam vets met regularly for a year to work on problems related to posttraumatic stress. Since the group disbanded, one member has had an exhibition of his hand-colored photographs. (This group portrait is a sample of his work.) Another member has started his own company. Some members have created new careers; some have been in and out of substance-abuse programs. Most continue to experience vivid dreams full of war images.

plane crash or a severe automobile crash, and witnesses to a murder.

Anyone who suffers through a traumatic event experiences severe stress at the time and shortly afterward. People differ greatly, however, in their long-term reactions. For example, in 1980, a man kidnapped three college cheerleaders and raped and murdered one of them. The other two escaped and eventually testified against their assailant. One of the two quickly put the events behind her; she completed her education, married, got a job, had children, and only occasionally thought about her gruesome ordeal. The other woman suffered a clear case of PTSD, including long bouts of depression and intense flashbacks. She found herself unable to focus on her studies and became very uneasy in her relationships with men. At one point, she rented a room with a view of the prison, so that she could keep an eye on it, to make sure that her assailant didn't escape (Krueger & Neff, 1995). Why do some people develop PTSD, whereas others who had similar experiences do not? Psychologists do not yet know.

People with posttraumatic stress disorder can suffer from frequent nightmares, outbursts of anger, constant unhappiness, and guilt. The guilt is a special kind of experience, often called *survivor's guilt,* common to people who survive a catastrophe in which many other people died. People with PTSD may also have difficulty concentrating or relating emotionally to other people (Keane, Wolfe, & Taylor, 1987). A brief reminder of the tragic experience can trigger a flashback that borders on panic. Many mundane events become stressful, even years after the original event (Solomon, Mikulincer, & Flum, 1988). In one study, eight Vietnam veterans with PTSD watched a 15-minute videotape of dramatized combat. Watching the film elevated their endorphin levels just as people generally react to an actual injury (Pitman, van der Kolk, Orr, & Greenberg, 1990).

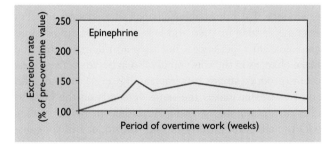

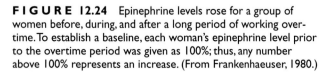

FIGURE 12.24 Epinephrine levels rose for a group of women before, during, and after a long period of working overtime. To establish a baseline, each woman's epinephrine level prior to the overtime period was given as 100%; thus, any number above 100% represents an increase. (From Frankenhaeuser, 1980.)

Measuring Stress and Its Effects on Health

Most investigators agree that severe stress can endanger a person's health. For example, prolonged job stress is significantly correlated with anxiety and depression (deWolff, 1985). People who experience severe stress on the job report frequent illnesses as well. (At least, they often call in sick and stay home from work!)

How much stress is injurious to one's health? Is it true that the more stress a person experiences, the more that person's health suffers?

To answer such questions, we need to measure both stress and health. Measuring health is tough enough; measuring stress is even more difficult. One approach is to give people a checklist of stressful experiences. For example, Thomas Holmes and Richard Rahe (1967) devised a Social Readjustment Rating Scale (Table 12.2) that assigns points for both desirable and undesirable events, in accordance with Selye's idea that any change in a person's life is stressful. Note, for example, that you could get 35 points for "change in number of arguments with spouse"—the same number of stress points for an increase *or* a decrease in arguments! To measure the amount of your stress, you are supposed to check off all the experiences you have had within a given period of time, such as the last 6 months, and total up the points assigned to each.

Although this scale has been widely used, it is subject to many criticisms: First, the assumption that we can simply add stress points from various events is probably incorrect (Birnbaum & Sotoodeh, 1991). For example, suppose you graduate from college (26 points), treat yourself to a vacation (13), and then start a new job (36). That adds up to 75 points—more than you would get for a divorce (73) or the death of a close family member (63).

Second problem: The scale includes 53 points for suffering the stress associated with "personal injury or illness." It also ascribes points for sexual difficulties, change in sleeping habits, and change in eating habits—all symptoms of illness. So, it is hardly surprising that people with high scores on this rating scale have an increased probability of being ill.

Third, the scale fails to measure some important stressors. Selye defined stress as a response to changes in one's life, and accordingly, this scale ignores the stress of coping with ongoing problems, such as racism or poverty. It also ignores the stress we experience from events that *almost* happened. For example, all year long you expect to

---

T A B L E   12.2   Social Readjustment Rating Scale

RANK	LIFE EVENT	POINT VALUE	RANK	LIFE EVENT	POINT VALUE
1	Death of spouse	100	22	Change in responsibilities at work	29
2	Divorce	73	23	Son or daughter leaving home	29
3	Marital separation	65	24	Trouble with in-laws	29
4	Jail term	63	25	Outstanding personal achievement	28
5	Death of close family member	63	26	Wife begin or stop work	26
6	Personal injury or illness	53	27	Begin or end school	26
7	Marriage	50	28	Change in living conditions	25
8	Fired at work	47	29	Revision of personal habits	24
9	Marital reconciliation	45	30	Trouble with boss	23
10	Retirement	45	31	Change in work hours or conditions	20
11	Change in health of family member	44	32	Change in residence	20
12	Pregnancy	40	33	Change in schools	20
13	Sex difficulties	39	34	Change in recreation	19
14	Gain of new family member	39	35	Change in church activities	19
15	Business readjustment	39	36	Change in social activities	18
16	Change in financial state	38	37	Mortgage or loan less than $10,000	17
17	Death of a close friend	37	38	Change in sleeping habits	16
18	Change to different line of work	36	39	Change in number of family get-togethers	15
19	Change in number of arguments with spouse	35	40	Change in eating habits	15
20	Mortgage over $10,000	31	41	Vacation	13
21	Foreclosure of mortgage or loan	30	42	Christmas	12
			43	Minor violations of the law	11

SOURCE: Homes & Rahe, 1967.

be laid off from your job. You keep waiting, but the rumored plant closing never happens. Or you have been counting on a promotion at work, and you have told all your friends that you are expecting it, but then you do not get promoted. You will get no points on the rating scale for "not getting fired" or "not being promoted." And yet anyone who has lived through such an experience can tell you that it was very stressful.

SOMETHING TO THINK ABOUT

Can you think of a better way to measure stress? Some psychologists have given people a list of events and have asked them to check off events they have experienced and also to assign a value to each event, on the basis of how stressful they found it to be. Is that an improvement, or does it introduce problems of its own? ✳

Lazarus's Approach to Stress

Aside from the problems with the Social Readjustment Rating Scale, however, many psychologists challenge the basic assumption that a particular life change necessarily produces a specific amount of stress and that a given event will be equally stressful for all people. As Richard Lazarus (1977) pointed out, the amount of stress evoked by an event depends on how people interpret the event and what they can do about it. Pregnancy can be much more stressful for a 16-year-old unmarried woman than it is for a 27-year-old married woman. Being fired may be a disaster for a 50-year-old who expects to have trouble finding another job; it may be only a minor annoyance to a 19-year-old.

According to Lazarus, *a stressful situation is one that someone regards as threatening and as possibly exceeding his or her resources* (Lazarus, 1977). (See Figure 12.25.) Note that this view of stress assumes a major role for people's knowledge, experience, and cognitions: If you are bitten by a snake, you might remain calm if you recognize the snake as a harmless variety. If your boss criticizes your work, you might shrug off the insult if you know your boss had reason to be in a bad mood.

To the extent that stress depends on our interpretation of an event, not simply on the event itself, people can learn to cope with potentially stressful events, as we shall see later in this chapter. People can learn to deal with events actively instead of feeling threatened by them. Given this view, the proper measure of stress would include not only the unpleasant events ("hassles") that we have to deal with but also the pleasant events ("uplifts") that brighten our day and help to cancel out the unpleasant events (Kanner, Coyne, Schaefer, & Lazarus, 1981). Table 12.3 presents one example of this approach.

In short, stress is difficult to measure accurately. Nevertheless, we can identify particular kinds of stressful experiences that endanger many people's health. Study-

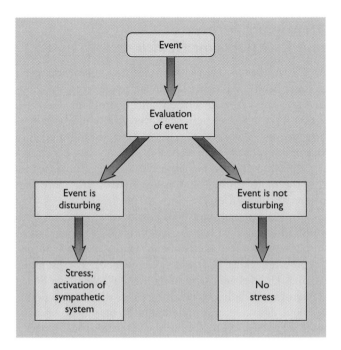

FIGURE 12.25 Lazarus stated that evaluation of some kind, conscious or unconscious, always precedes emotion. Thus, a given event can be highly stressful for one person yet only slightly stressful or not at all for a second person.

ing the effects of experience on health and illness can offer us insights into the relationships among stressful experiences, interpretation of those experiences, and body functioning.

TABLE 12.3 Ten Most Frequent Hassles and Uplifts

HASSLES	UPLIFTS
1. Concerns about weight	1. Relating well with your spouse or lover
2. Health of a family member	2. Relating well with friends
3. Rising prices of common goods	3. Completing a task
4. Home maintenance	4. Feeling healthy
5. Too many things to do	5. Getting enough sleep
6. Misplacing or losing things	6. Eating out
7. Yard work or outside home maintenance	7. Meeting your responsibilities
8. Property, investment, or taxes	8. Visiting, phoning, or writing someone
9. Crime	9. Spending time with family
10. Physical appearance	10. Home (inside) pleasing to you

SOURCE: Kanner, Coyne, Schaefer, & Lazarus, 1981.

Stress and Psychosomatic Illness

A **psychosomatic illness** is not an imagined or a feigned illness. Rather, it is *an illness that is influenced by a person's experiences—particularly stressful experiences—or by his or her reactions to those experiences.* That is, something about the person's behavior or way of life influenced the onset and progression of the disease. Most illnesses are partly psychosomatic in this sense.

For many years, physicians looking for the sources of illness concentrated on physical agents such as germs or injuries, giving no thought to the possibility of a psychosomatic influence. Then, in the early 1800s, they found soldiers who were suffering from what we would now call posttraumatic stress disorder. Some of them showed serious (though temporary) physical ailments, including blindness or paralysis, even though they had never been injured. A few even died on the battlefield when a cannonball landed nearby without striking them. Physicians of the time suggested that the soldiers were injured by the wind of the cannonball passing by, or by atmospheric electricity stirred up by the wind, or by the heat or the temporary vacuum it left in its wake. Today, those hypotheses sound extremely farfetched; at the time, they seemed more reasonable than the "ridiculous" idea that mere fear or other psychological states could influence someone's health (McMahon, 1975).

Physicians and psychologists still have difficulty explaining how emotional states affect the body. They do not assume that emotions lead directly to illness. They know, however, that people who have certain emotional experiences are more likely than others to overeat, to smoke, or to engage in other habits that increase the risk of illness. Certain behaviors and experiences can damage the immune system and increase a person's vulnerability to a variety of disorders, ranging from minor infections to cancer (Shavit et al., 1985).

One young woman died of fear in a most peculiar way: When she was born, on Friday the 13th, the midwife who delivered her and two other babies that day announced that all three were hexed and would die before their 23rd birthday. The other two did die young. As the third woman approached her 23rd birthday, she checked into a hospital and informed the staff of her fears. The staff noted that she dealt with her anxiety by extreme hyperventilation (deep breathing). Shortly before her birthday, she hyperventilated to death.

How did this happen? Ordinarily, when people do not breathe voluntarily they breathe reflexively; the reflex is triggered by carbon dioxide in the blood. By extreme hyperventilation, this woman had exhaled so much carbon dioxide that she did not have enough left to trigger reflexive breathing. When she stopped breathing voluntarily, she stopped breathing altogether ("Clinicopathologic conference," 1967). This

is a clear example of a self-fulfilling prophecy: The fact that the woman believed in the hex caused it to be fulfilled. This is also a clear example of the indirect influence of emotions on health.

We shall examine heart disease and cancer as examples of diseases that may be linked to particular emotional experiences or personality types. In both cases, the evidence has both strengths and weaknesses.

Heart Disease

An upholsterer repairing the chairs in a physician's waiting room once noticed that the fronts of the seats wore out before the backs. To figure out why, the physician began watching patients in the waiting room. He noticed that his heart patients habitually sat on the front edges of their seats, waiting impatiently to be called in for their appointments. This observation led the physician to hypothesize a link between heart disease and an impatient, success-driven personality, now known as the Type A personality (Friedman & Rosenman, 1974).

People with **Type A personality** are *highly competitive; they believe that they must always win. They are impatient, always in a hurry, and often angry and hostile.* By contrast, people with a **Type B personality** are *relatively easygoing, less hurried, and less hostile.* For example, Gary Schwartz (1987) described his observations of two men fishing: One (a Type B) slowly baited his hook, dropped his line into the water, and sat back watching the gulls and waiting for a bite. Another man (a Type A), fishing with two poles, spent much of his time rushing back and forth between the two poles, cursing when the two lines got tangled with each other. When another fisher caught a large fish, this man pulled up his anchor in frustration and raced his boat off to another part of the bay. (Are you a Type A or a Type B? Test yourself by answering the questions in Figure 12.26.)

TRY IT YOUR-SELF

Statistically, a link does exist between Type A personality and susceptibility to heart disease. People with a Type A personality tend to have a higher heart rate and higher blood pressure than most other people. The difference is larger in competitive situations, where people with a Type A personality show great increases in heart rate and blood pressure (Lyness, 1993).

Additional evidence for this linkage comes from studies comparing heart disease in various cultures (Levine, 1990). Some cultures have a hurried pace of life; people walk fast; they talk fast; almost everyone wears a watch; storekeepers pay prompt attention to their customers. Other cultures have a more relaxed pace of life; people are seldom in a rush; few people wear watches; the buses and trains seldom arrive on schedule but no one seems to care (Figure 12.27). As you might guess, the rate of heart disease is higher in countries with a hurried pace of life than it is in countries with a more relaxed pace. In the United States, the risk of

Measuring the Type A Personality
_____ 1. Do you find it difficult to restrain yourself from hurrying others' speech (finishing their sentences for them)?
_____ 2. Do you often try to do more than one thing at a time (such as eat and read simultaneously)?
_____ 3. Do you often feel guilty if you use extra time to relax?
_____ 4. Do you tend to get involved in a great number of projects at once?
_____ 5. Do you find yourself racing through yellow lights when you drive?
_____ 6. Do you need to win in order to derive enjoyment from games and sports?
_____ 7. Do you generally move, walk, and eat rapidly?
_____ 8. Do you agree to take on too many responsibilities?
_____ 9. Do you detest waiting in lines?
_____ 10. Do you have an intense desire to better your position in life and impress others?

FIGURE 12.26 If you answer yes to a majority of these items, Friedman and Rosenman (1974) would say that you probably have a Type A personality. But they would also consider your explanation of your answers, so this questionnaire gives only a rough estimate of your personality. Friedman and Rosenman classified everyone as either Type A or Type B, but most psychologists believe that people can exhibit various degrees of Type A traits.

heart attacks and the pace of life are generally highest in large northeastern cities; they are lowest in the small towns in the west and the south. Of course, these are correlational data; they do not demonstrate conclusively that a frantic pace of life causes heart problems. (For example, something about cultural differences in diet or climate might simultaneously influence people's activity levels and their heart muscles.)

At first, researchers focused on the role of impatience and competitiveness as the main links between Type A behavior and heart disease. However, later evidence has indicated that heart disease correlates more strongly with unpleasant emotions, especially hostility. A hostile attitude is only a small contributor to heart disease, however, in comparison to genetics, diet, exercise, and other factors (Miller, Smith, Turner, Guijarro, & Hallet, 1996). Still, even a small contributor to heart disease is worth taking seriously.

CONCEPT CHECK

4. People with a Type A personality are likely to develop stress-related heart disease. Yet, when they fill out the Social Readjustment Rating Scale, mentioned earlier, their scores are often low. Why might that scale understate the stress levels of Type A people? (Check your answer on page 466.)

Cancer

There are many kinds of cancer and many causes that are not yet well understood. Behavior can also influence the onset and spread of cancer, at least indirectly. For example, women who examine their breasts regularly can detect breast cancer at an early stage, when treatment is more likely to be successful. However, most women do not conduct regular, competent self-examinations, either because they do not know how, or because they are fearful, or because they feel helpless to do any good (Miller, Shoda & Hurley, 1996). Latina women in the United States have a higher rate of cervical cancer than other women, partly because they are less likely than other women to see doctors regularly for Pap smear tests (Meyerowitz, Richardson, Hudson, & Leedham, 1998). In many ways, preventing or treating cancer requires behavioral as well as medical interventions.

FIGURE 12.27 People in some cultures have a frantic pace of life: Everyone seems to be in a rush; people walk fast, talk fast, and push one another around. In other cultures, no one is sure what time it is and no one cares. The risk of heart disease is greatest in cultures or subcultures with a frantic pace of life.

Do our emotions contribute directly to cancer? Because the brain influences the immune system, which fights cancer, an emotional experience might lead to an impairment of the immune system and therefore to a greater risk of certain kinds of cancer.

The two emotional states most likely to lead to cancer are depression and stress. Many cancer patients are depressed (Weinstock, 1984), and many of them report that they were depressed, often following the death of a loved one, long before they knew they had cancer. Severe depression suppresses the activity of the immune system and leaves a person more vulnerable than usual to all sorts of infections and diseases, including the spread of certain types of tumors (Anisman & Zacharko, 1983; Baker, 1987).

While conducting research on the effects of stress in animals, investigators have found that stress increases the spread of cancer and shortens the animal's lifespan. But it is difficult to extrapolate from those results to humans. First, the results vary from one study to another, depending on the duration and type of stress and the genetic makeup of the animals. Second, nearly all animal studies deal with cancers caused by viruses, and viruses cause fewer than 5% of human cancers (Fox, 1983).

Depression, stress, and severe emotional problems probably do increase the risk of cancer in humans. Still, their influence is minor; emotional factors are far less important in causing cancer than are genes and toxic substances (Anisman & Zacharko, 1983; Derogatis, 1986; Fox, 1983). Keeping a positive outlook on life may help to prevent cancer; still, many people suffering from serious, long-lasting depression manage to survive into old age (Stein, Miller, & Trestman, 1991).

Psychological factors exert a stronger influence on what happens after the onset of cancer. For many people, the stress of dealing with cancer decreases the pleasures of life, impairs eating and sleeping, and directly or indirectly weakens the ability of the immune system to attack the cancer cells (Andersen, Kiecolt-Glaser, & Glaser, 1994). People who receive steady support from their family and friends, or from a psychotherapist or a self-help group, have a better chance of recovery and a better quality of life while they are fighting the disease (Fawzy, Fawzy, Arndt, & Pasnau, 1995).

THE MESSAGE
Health is Both Psycho and Somatic

The important point to remember about health psychology is that personality, emotions, and behavior are just one aspect of health. Good diet, good exercise, and quitting tobacco improve one's chances for good health; regular breast self-exams help to detect possible problems early; controlling hostility and other negative emotions will decrease the

risk of heart disease. Still, we should not set unrealistic expectations for behavioral strategies. No matter how much someone follows the best psychological advice, health is also subject to the influence of genetics, toxic substances in the environment, and other factors that are hard to control. So, yes, do what you can to improve your behavior and attitude, but if problems arise, don't expect attitude readjustment to take the place of medical help. And if you become ill, don't feel guilty that you just didn't have the right attitude. What happens to your health is partly under your control, but not entirely.

SUMMARY

❋ *Selye's concept of stress.* According to Hans Selye, stress is "the nonspecific response of the body to any demand made upon it." Any event, pleasant or unpleasant, that brings about change in a person's life produces some measure of stress. This theory, though influential, has some problems and limitations. (page 459)

❋ *Stages of response to stress.* The body goes through three stages in response to a stressful experience: alarm, resistance, and exhaustion. In the resistance and exhaustion stages, prolonged channeling of energy toward resisting stress can weaken the immune system. (page 459)

❋ *Influence of past experiences.* The degree of stress that an event evokes depends not only on the event itself but also on the person's interpretation of that event. People with posttraumatic stress disorder react strongly to daily events because of their previous experiences with war, rape, or other deeply upsetting occurrences. (page 460)

❋ *Difficulties of measuring stress.* The stress that an individual experiences is difficult to measure. Two people who have gone through similar experiences may show different levels of stress. (page 460)

❋ *Psychosomatic illness.* Stress, hostility, and other emotional experiences may increase the probability of certain illnesses. A psychosomatic illness is somehow related to a person's experiences or to his or her reactions to those experiences. (page 463)

❋ *Heart disease.* People with a Type A personality are competitive, impatient, and hostile. They are more likely than others to suffer heart disease, although the strength of that relationship and the reasons behind it are still in dispute. The emotional states of depression and hostility pose a greater risk than competitiveness and impatience. (page 463)

❋ *Cancer.* Depression and stress can increase the risk of cancer, at least slightly. Social support improves people's chances of recovery from cancer and also improves their quality of life while fighting the disease. (page 464)

Suggestion for Further Reading

Brannon, L., & Feist, J. (1997). *Health psychology* (3rd ed.). Belmont, CA: Wadsworth. A textbook that surveys the relationship between behavior and health.

Terms

health psychology   a field of psychology concerned with how people's behavior can enhance health and prevent illness and how behavior contributes to recovery from illness (page 459)

stress   according to Hans Selye, the nonspecific response of the body to any demands made upon it; according to Lazarus, a situation that someone regards as threatening and as possibly exceeding his or her resources (pages 459)

alarm   the first stage of response to stress, a brief period of high arousal of the sympathetic nervous system, readying the body for vigorous activity (page 459)

resistance   the second stage of response to stress, a stage of prolonged but moderate arousal (page 460)

exhaustion   the third stage of response to stress, when the body's prolonged response to stress decreases the synthesis of proteins, including the proteins necessary for activity of the immune system (page 460)

posttraumatic stress disorder (PTSD)   a condition in which people who have endured extreme stress feel prolonged anxiety and depression (page 460)

psychosomatic illness   an illness that is influenced by a person's experiences—particularly stressful experiences—or by his or her reactions to those experiences (page 463)

Type A personality   a personality characterized by constant competitiveness, impatience, anger, and hostility (page 463)

Type B personality   a personality characterized by an easygoing attitude, with little hurry or hostility (page 463)

Answer to Concept Check

4.   The Social Readjustment Rating Scale measures events that change a person's life; it does not measure constant sources of stress such as the pressures of work. The scale also fails to measure people's reactions, such as impatience, competitiveness, and hostility. (page 464)

Web Resources

Lifescan Health Risk Appraisal

wellness.uwsp.edu/Health_Service/services/lifeScan.shtml

Do you know what your *appraised health age* is? Answer a few health questions and find out. If possible, first check your blood pressure, total cholesterol, and HDL cholesterol levels.

MODULE 12.4

Coping with Stress

How can we reduce the harmful effects of stress on the body?

How can we learn to cope with stress?

An eccentric millionaire whom you have never met before hands you a $10 bill for no apparent reason, no strings attached. How do you feel? Pleased, I assume.

Now let's change the circumstances a bit: The millionaire had been handing out $100 bills until it was your turn, but then: "Sorry, I just ran out of $100 bills. So I'll have to give you a $10 bill instead." Now how do you feel? disappointed, sad, angry? You may even feel *cheated,* even though you have just received something for nothing.

Just as your reaction to a gift of $10 depends on the circumstances, so does your reaction to bad news. How would you feel if you had studied hard for a test and then got a C−? Unhappy, I presume. But if you then discovered that everyone around you had failed the test, you would begin to feel much better about your C−.

How you feel about an event depends not just on the event itself but also on how you interpret it (Frijda, 1988; Lazarus, Averill, & Opton, 1970). Was it better or worse than you had expected? Better or worse than what happened to other people? Was it a one-time event, or did it carry a hint of what might happen in the future? How you feel about an event also depends on your personality. Some people manage to keep their spirits high even in the face of tragedy; others are devastated by minor setbacks.

Coping with stress is the process of developing ways to decrease its effects and to get through difficult tasks despite the stress. How do people cope with disappointments, anxieties, and stress? And can we learn to cope more successfully?

Coping Styles and Strategies

People cope with stress in a great many ways, but we can group most of them into two major categories. In the style known as **monitoring,** *one attends carefully to the stressful event and one's reaction to it and tries to take effective action.* In **blunting,** *one tries to avoid the stressful event or at least avoid thinking about it.* Some people tend to rely more on one style than on the other, but it is best to alternate between the two depending on circumstances, as most people do (Heszen-Niejodek, 1997). In particular, when the stressful event is controllable, the best policy is to take action, using the monitoring approach. For example, if you have test-taking anxieties, you could try to relax and not think about the test, but if you instead spend time studying for the test, you will probably improve your grade and reduce your anxiety. Similarly, if you have troubles in your marriage or with your job, the best way to reduce the stress is to search for a solution to the problem.

The stressfulness of an event depends on how we interpret it, not just on the event itself. For example, most people would be delighted to finish second or third in an Olympic event, but someone who was expecting to finish first may consider any lesser result to be a defeat and a disappointment.

"Cabin fever"—the distress people feel when they are cooped up and cannot leave—is largely due to one's feeling unable to predict or control events.

However, suppose your stress comes from having to lie in a hospital bed awaiting an operation or recovering from one. Or having to sit in a dentist's chair for some unpleasant procedure. Now, you have few active responses that will make much difference. You can't run away or attack, for example; you just have to sit there and endure the situation. In such cases, one must turn to a blunting strategy.

Monitoring Strategies

Whenever a stressful situation is at all controllable, people feel better if they take action. In fact, they feel better even if the action they take is ineffective, as long as they *think* it might be effective. Here, we will consider the importance of a sense of control and then discuss a few additional monitoring strategies.

The Importance of Predictability and Control

Let's start by contrasting two hypothetical situations. First, imagine that some torturer is keeping you awake 24 hours per day. You have no way of escaping and no way of knowing how long the torture will last, but in fact it lasts 3 days until someone finally liberates you. Contrast that experience with an experiment in which you agree to go without sleep for 3 days. You could quit if you wanted to, but in fact you don't.

Another comparison: An enormous snowstorm has trapped you in a small cabin. You have an ample supply of food and fuel, but you have no idea how long you will be stuck in the cabin. In fact, the snow melts 5 days later, thus allowing you to leave. Contrast that with a case where you decide to isolate yourself in a cabin for 5 days so you can finish a painting or a musical composition.

In both cases, the physical circumstances are the same—3 days without sleep or 5 days without leaving a cabin. But if you are doing something voluntarily, if you know what to expect, and if you know that you could quit if you wanted to, the events are far less stressful. When hospital patients or nursing-home residents are told what to expect and are given the opportunity to make even a few choices, they feel better and on the average live longer (Shapiro, Schwartz, & Astin, 1996). Many people find that religious faith helps them to cope with stress by giving them some sense of control over matters that are otherwise uncontrollable.

In several experiments, people were asked to perform difficult tasks while listening to loud bursts of noise that might impair their performance. Some participants had no power to control the noise; others were shown a switch that could cut off the noise, although the experimenters preferred that the subjects not use that switch unless it became necessary. Even though none of the subjects flipped the switch, simply knowing that they *could* turn off the noise made it less disturbing to them. They performed better on a proofreading task than did the subjects with no sense of control (Glass, Singer, & Pennebaker, 1977; Sherrod, Hage, Halpern, & Moore, 1977).

Why do you suppose people who consistently blame other people for their misfortunes tend to have a poor psychological adjustment (Tennen & Affleck, 1990)? One explanation is that, if you think other people are maliciously thwarting your plans, you no longer feel in control of the situation.

CONCEPT CHECK

5. Which would disrupt your studying more, your own radio or your roommate's radio? Why? (Check your answer on page 473.)

Practice at self-defense serves as a kind of inoculation against fear. The thought of being attacked is less frightening to one who has some idea of how to handle the situation.

Why does a predictable or controllable event produce less stress than an unpredictable or uncontrollable event does? One explanation is that we fear an unpredictable, uncontrollable event may grow so intense that it will eventually become unbearable (Thompson, 1981). As long as we know what will probably happen next, we assume that things won't get any worse. And as long as we have some measure of control over an event, we tell ourselves that we can take action if the situation becomes unbearable.

A second explanation is that, when an event is predictable, we can prepare for it at the appropriate time and relax at other times. If you dread being called upon to answer questions in class and your professor calls on students at random, you have to remain tense and ready at all times. But if your professor calls upon students in alphabetical order, you can relax until shortly before your turn comes, and then get ready.

Inoculation

A stressful experience is less disturbing if you know what to expect, but it is hard to know what to expect if you have not been through the experience before. Sometimes, a good solution is to provide people with a small-scale preview of a stressful experience that they may need to face later. In other words, we can "inoculate" or immunize someone against certain kinds of stressful experiences.

One way to **inoculate** people against stressful events is *to expose them to smaller amounts of such events beforehand* (Janis, 1983; Meichenbaum, 1985; Meichenbaum & Cameron, 1983). For example, many armies have

soldiers practice combat skills under realistic conditions, sometimes under actual gunfire. Another way is through role-playing. A police trainee might pretend to intervene while two people act like a husband and wife engaged in a violent quarrel. If you are nervous about going to your landlord with a complaint, you might get a friend to play the part of the landlord and then practice what you plan to say.

Inoculation has proved successful with young people suffering from "dating anxiety." Some young people are so nervous about saying or doing the wrong thing that they avoid all opportunities to go out on a date. By means of role-playing, they can practice dating behaviors with assigned partners and thus feel less apprehensive about dating (Jaremko, 1983).

CONCEPT CHECK

6. Suppose you are nervous about giving a speech before a group of 200 strangers. How could you inoculate yourself to reduce the stress? (Check your answer on page 473.)

Social Support

Have you ever had a secret too shameful to tell? Have you stopped yourself from disclosing a personal experience because you thought others would think less of you? . . . Have you ever lied to yourself by claiming that a major upheaval in your life didn't affect you or, perhaps, didn't occur? If so you may be hurting yourself. Not because you have had a troubling experience but because you can't express it.

—JAMES W. PENNEBAKER (1990)

Simply writing about one's deepest feelings or painful experiences helps relieve the tension. It demonstrates that the events were not too painful even to think about.

A great many people have undergone a severely painful experience at one time or another. Perhaps you were beaten or sexually molested; perhaps you were responsible for someone else's injury; perhaps you attempted suicide; perhaps someone humiliated you in public. Whatever your experience, you may decide that it was too painful even to think about, much less talk about. Therefore, the pain builds up inside.

People who have had painful experiences report that they feel much better after they have a chance to talk about them to someone, or even just write about them. In one series of experiments, college students were randomly assigned to two groups. For about half an hour per day on 3–5 consecutive days, the experimental group was asked to write about their deepest thoughts and feelings about an emotional issue that had affected them. For example, many wrote about the death of a loved one, a personal failure, or sexual or physical abuse. The psychologists conducting the study said nothing to them about what they had written, and in fact kept no record of which student had written which essay. The control group spent the same amount of time writing about unemotional topics, such as how they budgeted their time in a typical day. The experimental group described the experience as extremely valuable, in spite of the fact that many of them had become very upset, even tearful, during the experiment. A follow-up measurement found that the experimental group members had better health over the next few months, got better grades, and drank less alcohol (Pennebaker, 1997). Evidently, just expressing their feelings reduced their stress and enabled them to relax and deal more effectively with life.

In many cases, people gain the greatest support by talking with people who have lived through similar crises. Alcoholics Anonymous, for example, is composed of recovering alcoholics who try to help one another. To give another example, the nurses who work in the intensive care units of hospitals undergo constant, often severe stress (Hay & Oken, 1977). The unspoken (but rigidly obeyed) rule is never to refuse help to either a patient or a fellow nurse. These nurses are surrounded by the sights, sounds, and smells of patients who are suffering and dying. When a patient dies, it is often the nurse, not the doctor, who must inform the relatives. At the end of the day, these nurses cannot simply go home and resume life as usual. They need to unwind, and they often do so by sharing their experiences with other nurses. Receiving social support, especially from sympathetic people who have endured similar problems, improves overall health and actually increases life expectancy (Uchino, Cacioppo, & Kiecolt-Glaser, 1996).

Beliefs as Coping Strategies

- In the long run, I shall be more successful than most.
- Sure, I have my strengths and weaknesses, but my strengths are in areas that are important; my weaknesses are in areas that don't really matter.
- When I fail, it is because I didn't try hard enough or because I got some bad breaks—not because of any lack of ability.
- No matter how bad (or good) things are, they are going to get better.
- Right now I'm sad that my wife (husband) left me, but in the long run I'll be better off without her (him).
- I lost my job, but in many ways it was a crummy job. The more I think about it, the happier I am about it. I can get a better one.

Any of these statements may be correct or incorrect for a given person at a given time. Remember the "personal fable" of adolescence from Chapter 10? Most normal, happy people nurture various versions of that fable throughout life. They emphasize their strengths, downplay their weaknesses, and distort bad news to make it seem not so bad, maybe even good (Taylor & Brown, 1988). To some extent, these beliefs can help people to deal with the difficult and stressful times of life.

When a situation is undeniably bad, people can still find ways to deny the problem. Medics serving in the Vietnam War knew they were risking their lives every time they boarded a helicopter to go to the aid of wounded soldiers. Because they had no way to predict or control the enemy's actions, we might expect them to have experienced extreme stress. In general, however, measurements of the activity of their autonomic nervous system showed low levels of arousal on both flight days and nonflight days (Bourne, 1971). Why? They had managed to convince themselves of their own invulnerability. They even told exaggerated stories about their close brushes with death as evidence that they led a charmed life.

People also look for an optimistic outlook to help them cope with severe illness. One study of 78 women who had surgery for the removal of breast cancer found that they coped with their stress and anxiety in three ways (Taylor, 1983):

First, they searched for meaning in the experience. Many of them said that they had become better people and had developed a new attitude toward life.

Second, they tried to regain a feeling of mastery over their lives. They wanted to believe that they knew why they had developed cancer and that they knew how to avoid a recurrence.

Third, they all sought to boost their self-esteem by comparing themselves with someone else who was worse off: "I'm glad I had only one breast removed instead of both, like some other women." "Sure, I had both breasts removed, but at least I was 70 years old at the time. It would have been worse if it had happened when I was young." "It was terrible to have both breasts removed at age 35, but I was already married, and my husband has been sympathetic and supportive."

Relaxation and exercise are strategies that people can use to manage their reactions to problems. People who devote a short time each day to relaxation report less stress, and exercise can be a way of working off excess energy, allowing greater relaxation.

In short, people tell themselves: "I'm in control; my life is getting better; at least, things are better than they might have been." Is it good for our mental health for us to remain unrealistically optimistic? On that question, psychologists disagree (Colvin & Block, 1994; Taylor & Brown, 1994). Certainly, some people manage to maintain excellent mental health without maintaining any apparent illusions about themselves. Although researchers have not yet measured the limits of optimistic thinking, it seems likely that the best general attitude might be *slightly* unrealistic optimism.

Blunting Strategies

Blunting strategies do not attempt to solve the underlying problems, but they help us to manage our reactions to them. Three common examples are relaxation, exercise, and distraction.

Relaxation

Sometimes people have a real problem, such as an impending medical operation, but they cannot do much about it. At other times, people get nervous even when they have no real problem (Manuck, Cohen, Rabin, Muldoon, & Bachen, 1991). In such situations, it is helpful to try to relax. Here are some suggestions that may help (Benson, 1985):

• Find a quiet place. Do not insist on absolute silence; just find a spot where the noise is least disturbing.
• Adopt a comfortable position, relaxing your muscles. If you are not sure how to do so, start with the opposite: *Tense* all your muscles so you become fully aware of how they feel. Then relax them one by one, starting from your toes and working systematically toward your head.
• Reduce sources of stimulation, including your own thoughts. Focus your eyes on a simple, unexciting object. Or repeat something over and over—a sentence, a phrase, a prayer, or even a meaningless sound like *om*—whatever feels comfortable to you.
• Don't worry about anything, not even about relaxing. If worrisome thoughts keep popping into your head, dismiss them with an "oh, well."

Some people call this practice meditation. People who practice this technique daily report that they feel less stress. Many of them improve their overall health (Benson, 1977, 1985). One study found that people who went through a 12-week meditation program had a long-lasting decrease in anxiety and depression, as compared with a control group who spent the same amount of time listening to lectures about how to reduce stress (Sheppard, Staggers, & John, 1997).

Another step toward relaxation is to learn to interpret situations realistically. Some people fret forever about disasters that *might* happen or about something someone said that *might* be taken as an insult. Psychologists encourage people to reinterpret situations and events in less threatening ways.

Exercise

Exercise also can help to reduce stress. It may seem contradictory to say that both relaxation and exercise reduce stress, but exercise does help people to relax (Mobily, 1982). Suppose you are tense about something that you have to do tomorrow. Your sympathetic nervous system becomes highly aroused in preparation for that event, and there is nothing you can do about it. Under those conditions, the best approach may be to work off some of your excess energy through exercise and then relax afterward.

Regular exercise also prepares people for the unexpected. People in good physical condition react less strongly than other people do to stressful events (Crews & Landers, 1987). An event that would elevate the heart rate enormously in other people elevates it only moderately in a person who has been exercising regularly.

Distraction

Another powerful blunting strategy is distraction (Cioffi, 1991). For example, many people find that they can reduce dental or postsurgical pain by playing video games or by watching comedies on television. The Lamaze method teaches pregnant women to suppress the pain of childbirth by concentrating on breathing exercises.

How effective a distraction is depends partly on whether a person believes that it will help. In one experiment, college students were asked to hold their fingers in ice water until the sensation became too painful to endure (Melzack, Weisz, & Sprague, 1963). Some of them listened to music of their own choice and were told that listening to music would lessen the pain. Others also listened to music but were given no suggestion that it would ease the pain. Still others heard nothing but were told that a special "ultrasonic sound" was being transmitted that would lessen the pain. The group that heard music and expected it to lessen the pain tolerated the pain better than either of the other two groups. Evidently, neither the music nor the suggestion of reduced pain is as effective as both are together.

Distraction also helps us to cope with stress that is not painful. People who are concentrating on a difficult task find it helpful to take a break once in a while. They may go to a movie, read something entertaining, play a round of golf, or just daydream. Furthermore, trying to find the humor in a stressful situation often provides an effective distraction.

SOMETHING TO THINK ABOUT

Many experiments report that a placebo alone serves as an effective painkiller for certain patients. Why might that be? ✳

We discuss various aspects of psychology in different chapters—cognition, motivation, emotion, and so forth. This seems a reasonable way to organize a psychology textbook, but our experiences do not divide up so neatly into separate parts. As you have seen in this chapter, our emotions are closely linked to our biology, our motivations, and our memory and cognitions. Any factor that changes one aspect of our experience—say, cognition—will have rippling effects on emotions and motivations as well.

SUMMARY

✳ *Coping styles.* People's strategies for dealing with stress fall into two major categories. Monitoring is an attempt to focus on the source of the problems; blunting is an attempt to distract oneself and to reduce the distress without addressing the problem. (page 467)

✳ *Prediction and control.* Events are generally less stressful when people think they can predict or control them. (page 468)

✳ *Inoculation.* Someone who has experienced a mildly stressful experience is less stressed than other people are by a later, more intense version of the same experience. (page 469)

✳ *Social support.* Support and encouragement from friends and family help to alleviate stress. Many people cope with problems by talking with other people who have dealt with similar problems, such as members of self-help groups. (page 469)

✳ *Beliefs.* A belief in one's capacity to succeed may help to reduce stress, even if this belief is not entirely accurate. (page 470)

✳ *Relaxation and exercise.* One way of coping with stress is to find a quiet place, relax the muscles, and eliminate distracting stimuli. Exercise can be a helpful way of channeling nervous energy and enabling oneself to relax. (page 471)

✳ *Distraction.* Distracting a person's attention from the source of the stress helps to reduce the stress. (page 472)

Suggestion for Further Reading

Pennebaker, J. W. (1990). *Opening up.* New York: William Morrow and Company. A description of the stress-relieving values of discussing your most painful experiences, either with other people or to yourself in writing.

Terms

monitoring   attending carefully to the stressful event and one's reaction to it and trying to take effective action (page 467)

blunting   trying to avoid the stressful event or at least avoid thinking about it (page 467)

inoculation   protection against the harmful effects of stress by earlier exposure to smaller amounts of it (page 469)

Answers to Concept Checks

5. Your roommate's radio would be more disruptive. You can turn your own radio on or off, switch stations, or reduce the volume. You have no such control over your roommate's radio (unless your roommate happens to be very cooperative). (page 468)

6. Practice giving your speech to a small group of friends. If possible, practice giving the speech in the room where you will ultimately deliver it. (page 469)

Web Resources

Stress Assess

wellness.uwsp.edu/Health_Service/services/stress.shtml
Evaluate your current stress sources, distress symptoms, and lifestyle behaviors. A personalized assessment includes strategies to counteract stress.

How To Fight & Conquer Stress

www.coolware.com/health/medical_reporter/stress.html
Material from the Rose Men's Health Resource defines stress, examines its positive and negative aspects, identifies some major life stressors, and provides tips on how to combat the negative effects of stress.

Personality

Geronimo with His Spirit by Frederick Brown (1984)

13

Several thousand people have the task of assembling the world's largest jigsaw puzzle, which contains more than one trillion pieces. Connie Conclusionjumper examines 20 pieces very closely, stares off into space, and announces, "When the puzzle is fully assembled, it will be a picture of the Houston Astrodome!" Prudence Plodder says, "Well, I don't know what the whole puzzle will look like, but I think I've found two little pieces that fit together."

Which of the two is making the greater contribution to completing the puzzle? We could argue either way. Clearly the task would require an enormous number of little, unglamorous accomplishments like Prudence's. But if Connie is right, her flash of insight will be extremely valuable for assembling all the little pieces. Of course, if the puzzle turns out to be a picture of two sailboats on Lake Erie, then Connie will have made us waste time looking for nonexistent connections.

Some psychologists have offered grand theories about the nature of personality. Others have investigated why people with a certain type of personality act the way they do in a specific situation. In this chapter, we shall explore several methods of approaching personality, ranging from large-scale to small-scale, from theoretical to descriptive.

Characters in ancient plays wore masks to indicate their personalities, and we still look to people's faces as one marker of their personalities—although it is often a misleading cue. Caricature, a popular art style, exaggerates facial expression.

Major Approaches to Personality

What is personality and how does it develop?

What are some effective ways to study personality?

Every individual is virtually an enemy of civilization.... Thus civilization has to be defended against the individual.... For the masses are lazy and unintelligent... and the individuals composing them support one another in giving free rein to their indiscipline.

—SIGMUND FREUD (1927/1953)

It has been my experience that persons have a basically positive direction. In my deepest contacts with individuals in therapy, even those whose troubles are most disturbing, whose behavior has been most anti-social, whose feelings seem most abnormal, I find this to be true.

—CARL ROGERS (1961)

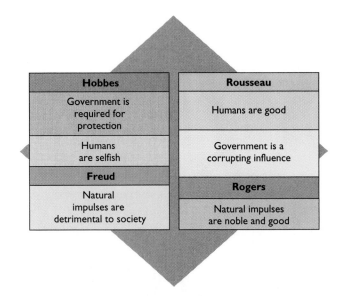

Hobbes	Rousseau
Government is required for protection	Humans are good
Humans are selfish	Government is a corrupting influence

Freud	Rogers
Natural impulses are detrimental to society	Natural impulses are noble and good

FIGURE 13.1 Philosophers Thomas Hobbes and Jean-Jacques Rousseau expressed opposing views of human nature. Psychologists Sigmund Freud and Carl Rogers also expressed opposite views. Freud, like Hobbes, stressed the more negative aspects of human nature; Rogers, the more positive or optimistic aspects.

Which point of view is correct? Or does the truth lie somewhere in between? The study of human personality is complicated, and we can easily be tempted to emphasize one aspect of personality to the exclusion of the others.

Conceptions of Personality

The term *personality* comes from the Latin word *persona,* meaning "mask." In the plays of ancient Greece and Rome, actors wore masks to indicate whether they were comic or tragic characters. Unlike a mask that one can either put on or take off, however, the term *personality* implies something stable. **Personality** consists of *all the consistent ways in which the behavior of one person differs from that of others, especially in social situations.* (Differences among people in their learning, memory, or sensory functions are not generally considered part of personality.)

The ancient Greeks believed that personality depended on which of four different "humors" predominated in a person's body (Figure 13.2). A predominance of yellow bile made people hot tempered. A predominance of black bile made people depressed. An excess of phlegm made people sluggish and apathetic. An excess of blood made people courageous, hopeful, and amorous. The ancient Greek theory persists in the English language in such terms as *phlegmatic* and *melancholic* (literally, "black-bile-ic").

Today, although we no longer believe in the four humors, we do believe that personality is influenced by other chemicals, such as hormones and neurotransmitters. It is further influenced by our experiences, including our observation and imitation of other people's behavior.

What makes us tick? What makes us the way we are? Way down deep, are humans mostly good or mostly bad?

The 17th-century philosopher Thomas Hobbes argued that humans are by nature selfish. Life in a state of nature, he said, is "nasty, brutish, and short." If we are to protect ourselves from one another, we must be restrained by a watchful government.

The 18th-century political philosopher Jean-Jacques Rousseau disagreed. He maintained that humans are basically good and that "civilized" governments are the problem, not the solution. Although he conceded that society could never return to "noble savagery," he believed that education and government should promote the freedom of the individual. Rational people acting freely, he maintained, would advance the welfare of all.

The debate between those two viewpoints survives in modern theories of personality (Figure 13.1). Some theorists, including Sigmund Freud, have held that people are born with sexual and destructive impulses that must be held in check if civilization is to survive. Others, including Carl Rogers, believed that people will achieve good and noble goals once they have been freed from unnecessary restraints.

FIGURE 13.3 Sigmund Freud offered interpretations of dreams, slips of the tongue, psychological disorders, and other behaviors that people had previously considered "random" or "unexplainable." According to Freud, even apparently purposeless behaviors reveal the influence of unconscious thoughts and motivations. Freud's theories have had an immense influence on many people, not just on psychologists. For example, many literary commentators have offered psychoanalytic interpretations of novels and plays. Most psychological researchers, however, are skeptical of Freud's approach.

FIGURE 13.2 According to the second-century Greek physician Galen, people's personalities depended on four humors. These were, clockwise from top left: sanguine, melancholic, phlegmatic, and choleric. Galen's theory was popular in medieval Europe.

In this brief first module, we shall quickly survey the major approaches to the study of personality: the *psychodynamic* approach (see the second module), the *trait* approach (see the third module), the *learning* approach (already discussed in the social learning module of Chapter 6), and the *humanistic* or *phenomenological* approach. The humanistic approach will receive a little more attention here because it does not have a module of its own.

The Psychodynamic Approach

Sigmund Freud's theory was the first of several psychodynamic theories. A **psychodynamic theory** *relates personality to the interplay of conflicting forces within the individual, including some that the individual may not consciously recognize.* That is, we are being pushed and pulled by internal forces that we do not fully understand.

The nature of these forces varies from one theory to another. For example, Freud (Figure 13.3) emphasized sexual motivation. Suppose you go to visit someone but you forget your umbrella and leave it behind. You didn't "just forget," Freud would say; perhaps you secretly love the person you were visiting, and by leaving your umbrella you create an excuse to go back and visit again—"to pick up the umbrella." Your secret love might be so secret that you are not even aware of it yourself; it is an unconscious feeling but nevertheless it influences your behavior.

Carl Jung proposed that your behavior is guided by a different kind of unconscious influence: If you dream about a beetle, for example, it might be because beetles have played an important part in human mythology at least dating back to the ancient Egyptians. If you draw a circle inside a square inside a circle, you are also recreating symbolism that has appeared in various cultures throughout the world. Somehow, Jung said, the experiences of your ancestors have caused you to be born with a predisposition to develop certain thoughts and images. (Jung accepted the theory of inheritance of acquired characteristics, a theory that biologists have thoroughly discredited.)

Alfred Adler suggested that people are guided by their ambitions—that, above all else, we are striving for success or superiority, or at least a belief in our potential for success. However, we are sometimes unaware of our strategies for maintaining this belief. If you marry someone who is likely to thwart your ambitions, perhaps your underlying motivation is to be able to maintain an illusion: "I could have been a great success if my husband/wife hadn't prevented me." Failure to study can have a similar motivation: "I could have done well on this test, but my friends talked me into going out to a party the night before."

Although Freud, Jung, Adler, and other theorists differ strongly about the nature of people's underlying motivations, they agree that people become more effective in their lives by becoming more aware of their thoughts and feelings. In short, the psychodynamic approaches claim that many of the influences behind anyone's personality are hidden and that much of our behavior is the result of competing motivations.

The Trait Approach

Whereas psychodynamic theorists try to explain the underlying basis for personality, many contemporary researchers concentrate on simply describing the differences among personalities. The point of the **trait approach to personality** is that *people have consistent personality characteristics that can be measured and studied.* If you try to describe someone you know, you will almost certainly list some personality traits, such as "she's friendly, honest, has a good sense of humor, but sometimes gets too upset by criticism." Psychologists try to make these descriptions more accurate and systematic. It would be helpful, for example, to specify *how* friendly or honest this person is, compared to others, or to specify in which situations he or she is friendly or honest.

Let's start with this example: Some people match their gender stereotypes rather closely, being either very "masculine" men or very "feminine" women. According to the usual or stereotypical meanings of the terms, *masculinity* includes ambitiousness, self-assertiveness, and an interest in sports. *Femininity* includes an enjoyment of children, an enjoyment of beautifying the house and garden, and a tendency to be sympathetic to and understanding of other people.

We could therefore identify masculinity and femininity as personality traits. One of the tasks for researchers, then, is to determine whether these are really just two ends of a single continuum (just as outgoingness is the opposite of isolation), or whether they are separate dimensions. Sandra Bem (1974) proposed that it is possible to be *high in both masculinity and femininity, or flexible enough to switch between masculinity and femininity depending on the situation.* She defined this trait as **androgyny** (from the Greek roots *andr-* meaning "man" and *gyne-* meaning "woman"). According to Bem, androgynous people are not limited by one stereotype or the other and can combine masculine strengths such as ambition with feminine strengths such as sympathy for the needs of others.

Table 13.1 presents part of a checklist of masculine

TRY IT YOUR- SELF

and feminine traits. In the original scoring system, you would be considered androgynous if you checked about the same number of masculine items as feminine items. However, one way to be *equal* in both categories is to be very low in both. It is hard to see any advantage in being unassertive, unambitious, indifferent to children, unsympathetic to other people, and low in all the other masculine and feminine characteristics. Consequently, most investigators now define androgyny as a personality that is high in both masculinity and femininity.

Consider a second example of personality traits: Do you think that your successes and failures depend mostly on your own efforts or mostly on circumstances beyond your control? Presumably, we all agree that both are important, but people differ in how much they emphasize one or the other. People who *believe they are largely in control of their lives* are said to have an **internal locus of control.** Those who *believe they are controlled mostly by external forces* are said to have an **external locus of control** (Rotter, 1966). Table 13.2 lists some items from a questionnaire designed to measure locus of control. After you complete these items, check answer A, page 484.

Generally, people with an internal locus of control like to choose tasks where they believe they can control the outcome, and then they persist at these tasks. At the end, they take the credit for their successes and the blame for their failures. People with an external locus of control are more likely to feel helpless (Lefcourt, 1976).

TABLE 13.1 Sample Items from the Bem Sex-Role Inventory

MASCULINE ITEMS	FEMININE ITEMS
Ambitious	Affectionate
Assertive	Cheerful
Competitive	Compassionate
Makes decisions easily	Loves children
Self-reliant	Loyal
Willing to take risks	Sympathetic

SOURCE: Bem, 1974, p. 156.

TABLE 13.2 Sample Items from the Internal-External Scale

For each item, choose the statement you agree with more.

1. a. Without the right breaks, one cannot be an effective leader.
   b. Capable people who fail to become leaders have not taken advantage of their opportunities.
2. a. Becoming a success is a matter of hard work; luck has little or nothing to do with it.
   b. Getting a good job depends mainly on being in the right place at the right time.
3. a. As far as world affairs are concerned, most of us are the victims of forces we can neither understand nor control.
   b. By taking an active part in political and social affairs, people can control world events.
4. a. Many times I feel that I have little influence over the things that happen to me.
   b. It is impossible for me to believe that chance or luck plays an important role in my life.

SOURCE: Rotter, 1966, pp. 11–12.

CONCEPT CHECK

1. Who would be more likely to buy lottery tickets—someone with an internal or external locus of control? (Check your answer on page 484.)

Androgyny and locus of control are just two personality traits; obviously, we could define and measure a great many more. We describe the sizes of objects in terms of three dimensions of space (length, width, and height) and one dimension of time. How many dimensions would we need to describe people's personalities? We shall explore that question later in this chapter.

The Learning Approach

How does someone develop a personality trait, such as androgyny or locus of control? Genetics and other biological factors no doubt exert some influence, but specific behaviors must be learned. Indeed, some psychologists have argued that the whole concept of general personality traits is vastly overrated, and that most of our personality is learned on a situation-by-situation basis (Mischel, 1973, 1981). For example, you might consider yourself honest because you would always return a lost wallet to its owner and because

you would never cheat on your income taxes; nevertheless, you may find yourself telling each of your dating partners, "You are the only one I have ever loved." So how useful is it to say that you are an honest person, or even that you are "more honest than 80% of other people"? It might be more useful to describe specific behaviors, such as honesty about returning a lost wallet or dishonesty toward romantic partners, or conscientiousness in particular situations, or friendliness in particular situations (Mischel & Shoda, 1995). And, presumably, these specific behaviors are learned.

The Social Learning module of Chapter 6 described some ways in which we learn our personality. We learn much by imitation or by vicarious reinforcement and punishment. That is, we copy behaviors that we know led to success for other people but avoid behaviors that led to failure for others.

Let's illustrate this idea by applying this approach to masculinity, femininity, and androgyny. One major part of those traits is **gender role,** *the pattern of behavior that each person is expected to follow because of being male or female.* A gender role is the psychological aspect of being male or female, as opposed to sex, which is the biological aspect. We know that gender role is at least partly learned, because certain aspects of it vary strikingly among cultures (Figure 13.4). For example, some cultures define cooking as "women's work" and others define it as "men's work." Men wear their hair short in some cultures and long in others.

FIGURE 13.4 Gender roles vary greatly from one culture to another, and even from one time period to another within a single culture. Here, a male Palestinian farmer near Jerusalem (upper left) and a woman in Vietnam (upper right) plow the fields. Men in Dacca, East Pakistan (lower left), and a Hmong woman in Thailand (lower right) do the wash.

When we say that children learn their gender role, we do not necessarily mean that anyone teaches it to them deliberately or intentionally. For example, most adults do *not* teach boys that they are supposed to fight with one another, and adults usually do what they can to stop the fighting. Nevertheless, little boys tend to be bossy and aggressive, especially when they think no adults are watching (Powlishta & Maccoby, 1990). Some of that aggressiveness probably arises from biological tendencies, but boys may have also learned some of it by following adults' examples. Boys tend to imitate men, and girls tend to imitate women. In one experiment, children watched adults choose between an apple and a banana. If all the men chose, say, the apple and all the women chose the banana, the boys who were watching wanted an apple and the girls wanted a banana (Perry & Bussey, 1979). The choice of fruit is, in itself, trivial, but the study shows the potential for influence on more important behaviors.

Perhaps even more importantly, children learn gender roles from other children. Children have a "playground culture" of their own; each cohort teaches the slightly younger set what is expected of them, and in many ways the peer group has a stronger influence than parents do (Harris, 1995). Even parents who try to raise their sons and daughters to be nonsexist find that their children come back from the playground with strong prejudices about what boys do and what girls do (Figure 13.5).

FIGURE 13.5 Children learn their gender roles partly by imitating adults, but they probably learn more from other children.

In short, the learning approach focuses on more specific behaviors than does the trait approach and attempts to relate specific behaviors to specific experiences. Some of these are the person's own experiences and some are those of others whom the person has imitated.

Humanistic Psychology

Another general perspective on personality, **humanistic psychology,** *deals with consciousness, values, and abstract beliefs, including spiritual experiences and the beliefs that people live by and die for.* According to humanistic psychologists, personality depends on what people believe and how they perceive the world. If you *believe* that a particular experience was highly meaningful, then it *was* highly meaningful. A psychologist can understand your behavior only by asking you for your own evaluations and interpretations of the events in your life. (In theology, a *humanist* glorifies humans, generally denying or at least giving little attention to a Supreme Being. The term *humanistic psychologist* implies nothing about a person's religious beliefs.)

Humanistic psychology emerged in the 1950s and 1960s as a protest against both behaviorism and psychoanalysis, which were the dominant viewpoints in psychology at that time (Berlyne, 1981). Behaviorists and psychoanalysts often emphasize the less noble, or at least morally neutral, aspects of people's thoughts and actions, whereas humanistic psychologists see people as essentially good and striving toward perfection. Also, behaviorism and psychoanalysis, despite their many differences, are both rooted in *determinism* (the belief that every behavior has a cause) and in *reductionism* (the attempt to explain behavior in terms of its component elements). Humanistic psychologists reject these attempts to explain behavior in terms of its parts or causes. They claim that people make deliberate, conscious decisions about what to do with their lives. People can decide to devote themselves to a great cause, to sacrifice their own well-being, and to risk their lives. To the humanistic psychologist, it is fruitless to ascribe such behavior to past rewards and punishments or to unconscious thought processes.

Humanistic psychologists generally study the special experiences of a given individual, as opposed to seeking means or medians for large representative groups. For example, humanistic psychologists study growth experiences—the moments that people identify as points of transition, when they may say, "Aha! Now I have become an adult," or "Now I have truly committed my life to this goal" (Frick, 1983). They also study **peak experiences,** *moments in which a person feels truly fulfilled and content.* Some people report that they "feel at one with the universe" when they hear "thrilling" music, or take part in an emotional religious ceremony, or achieve a great accomplishment.

Carl Rogers and the Goal of Self-Actualization

Carl Rogers, an American psychologist, studied theology before turning to psychology, and the influence of those early studies is apparent in his view of human nature. Rogers (Figure 13.6) became probably the most influential humanistic psychologist.

According to Rogers (1980), human nature is basically good. People have a natural drive toward **self-actualization,** which means *the achievement of one's full potential.* According to Rogers, it is as natural for people to strive for excellence as it is for a plant to grow. The drive for self-actualization is the basic drive behind the development of personality. (Rogers's concept of self-actualization is similar to Adler's concept of striving for superiority. Adler was a forerunner of humanistic psychology.)

Children evaluate themselves and their actions, beginning at an early age. They learn that what they do is sometimes good and sometimes bad. They develop a **self-concept,** *an image of what they really are,* and an **ideal self,** *an image of what they would like to be.* Rogers measured a person's self-concept and ideal self by handing the person a stack of cards containing statements such as "I am honest" and "I am suspicious of others." The person would then sort the statements into piles representing *true of me* and *not true of me,* or arranging them in a continuum from *most true of me* to *least true of me.* (This method is known as a *Q-sort.*) Then Rogers would provide an identical stack of cards and ask the person to sort them into two piles: *true of my ideal self* and *not true of my ideal self.* In this manner, he could determine whether someone's self-concept was similar to his or her ideal self; people who perceive a great discrepancy between the two generally experience distress. Humanistic psychologists try to help people overcome this distress, either by improving their self-concept or by changing their ideal self.

To promote human welfare, Rogers maintained that people should relate to one another with **unconditional positive regard,** a relationship that Thomas Harris (1967) described with the phrase "I'm OK—you're OK." Unconditional positive regard is *the complete, unqualified acceptance of another person as he or she is,* much like the love of a parent for a child. If someone expresses anger, or even a desire to kill, the listener should accept that as an understandable feeling, even while discouraging the person from taking certain possible actions. The listener must convey the message that the other person is inherently good, even though certain actions might be bad. This view resembles the Christian admonition to "hate the sin but love the sinner." The alternative is *conditional positive regard,* the attitude that "I shall like you only if . . . " People who are treated this way may feel restrained about opening themselves to new ideas or behaviors, for fear of losing someone else's esteem.

Abraham Maslow and the Self-Actualized Personality

Abraham Maslow (Figure 13.7), another of the founders of humanistic psychology, proposed that people have a hierarchy of needs, an idea we considered in Chapter 11. The highest of those needs is *self-actualization,* the fulfillment of a person's potential. What kind of person achieves self-actualization, and what is the result of achieving it? Maslow (1962, 1971) sought to describe the self-actualized personality. He complained that psychologists concentrate on disordered personalities, thus reflecting the medical view that health is merely the absence of disease. They seem to assume that all personality is either "normal" (that is, bland) or undesirable. Maslow insisted that personality can differ from the normal in positive, desirable ways.

To determine the characteristics of the self-actualized personality, Maslow made a list of people who, in his opinion,

FIGURE 13.6 Carl Rogers maintained that people naturally strive toward positive goals and that they do not need special urging. He recommended that people relate to one another with "unconditional positive regard."

FIGURE 13.7 Abraham Maslow, one of the founders of humanistic psychology, introduced the concept of a "self-actualized personality," a better-than-merely-normal personality associated with high productivity and enjoyment of life.

FIGURE 13.8 Harriet Tubman, left, one of the people Maslow identified as having a self-actualized personality, was one of the leaders of the Underground Railroad, a system for helping black slaves to escape from the southern states during the period before the Civil War. Maslow described the self-actualized personality by identifying highly productive and admirable people, such as Tubman, and then determining which personality features these people had in common.

had achieved their full potential. His list included people he knew personally as well as figures from history (Figure 13.8). He then sought to discover what these people had in common.

According to Maslow (1962, 1971), people with a self-actualized personality show the following characteristics:

• An accurate perception of reality: They perceive the world as it is, not as they would like it to be. They are willing to accept uncertainty and ambiguity when necessary.
• Independence, creativity, and spontaneity: They follow their own impulses.
• Acceptance of themselves and others: They treat people with unconditional positive regard.
• A problem-centered outlook, rather than a self-centered outlook: They think about how best to solve a problem, not how to make themselves look good. They also concentrate on significant problems, such as philosophical or political issues, not just the petty issues of getting through the day.
• Enjoyment of life: They are open to positive experiences, including "peak experiences."
• A good sense of humor.

Critics have attacked Maslow's description on the grounds that, because it is based on his own choice of subjects, it may simply reflect the characteristics that he himself admired. In any case, Maslow paved the way for other attempts to define a healthy personality as something more than personality without disorder.

THE MESSAGE
In Search of Human Nature

You have no doubt heard the parable of the blind people describing an elephant: One feels the tusks and says an elephant is like a smooth rock; another feels the tail and says an elephant is like a rope; and so forth. The full description of an elephant can emerge only from the combination of narratives. Similarly, a full description of personality emerges from a combination of research approaches. Saying that people have personality traits does not necessarily conflict with saying that personality is learned, or that it has unconscious influences (the psychodynamic approach), or that it is largely under conscious control (the humanistic approach).

However, although these approaches are not necessarily in conflict, their advocates are not necessarily in full agreement, either: We began with contrasting quotes about people being either fundamentally bad (Freud) or good (Rogers). Various personality theorists have sharply different views of human nature, and much is at stake. The challenge for personality researchers is to take such global questions about human nature and try to convert them into scientifically testable hypotheses.

SUMMARY

✳ *Personality theories as views of human nature.* Personality consists of all the stable, consistent ways that the behavior of one person differs from that of others. Theories of personality are closely related to conceptions of human nature. Some observers believe that human beings are basically hostile and need to be restrained (Hobbes, Freud). Others believe that human beings are basically good and are hampered by restraints (Rousseau, Rogers). (page 477)

✳ *Psychodynamic theories.* Several historically influential theories have described personality as the outcome of internal forces of which people are not fully conscious. (page 478)

✳ *Trait theories.* Many contemporary researchers try to describe and measure the consistent ways that one person's personality differs from another's. (page 479)

✳ *The learning approach.* The behaviors that constitute personality are learned. They can be learned through individual experience, or as social learning psychologists emphasize, they can be learned by imitation or vicarious reinforcement and punishment. Because people's experiences vary, they can have very specialized characteristics, showing a trait such as honesty in one situation but not in another. Gender roles vary among cultures because of social learning. (page 480)

✳ *Humanistic psychology.* Humanistic psychologists emphasize conscious, deliberate decision-making; they oppose attempts to reduce behavior to its elements or to seek explanations in terms of unconscious influences. (page 481)

Suggestion for Further Reading

Maslow, A. H. (1962). *Toward a psychology of being.* Princeton, NJ: Van Nostrand. A good introduction to humanistic psychology.

Terms

personality   all the consistent ways in which the behavior of one person differs from that of others, especially in social situations (page 477)

psychodynamic theory   a system that relates personality to the interplay of conflicting forces within the individual, including some that the individual may not consciously recognize (page 478)

trait approach to personality   the study and measure of consistent personality characteristics (page 479)

androgyny   a condition of being high in both masculine and feminine traits, or flexible enough to switch between masculinity and femininity depending on the situation (page 479)

internal locus of control   the belief that one is largely in control of the events of one's life (page 479)

external locus of control   the belief that external forces are largely in control of the events of one's life (page 479)

gender role   the pattern of behavior that each person is expected to follow because of being male or female (page 480)

humanistic psychology   a field that is concerned with consciousness, values, and abstract beliefs, including spiritual experiences and the beliefs that people live by and die for (page 481)

peak experiences   moments in a person's life when he or she feels truly fulfilled and content (page 481)

self-actualization   the achievement of one's full potential (page 482)

self-concept   an image of what one really is (page 482)

ideal self   an image of what one would like to be (page 482)

unconditional positive regard   the complete, unqualified acceptance of another person as he or she is (page 482)

Answer to Concept Check

1.   People with an external locus of control would be more likely to buy lottery tickets. Those with an internal locus of control prefer tasks where they can control the outcome. (page 480)

Answer to Other Question in the Text

A.   Choices 1b, 2a, 3b, and 4b indicate internal locus of control; the other choices indicate external locus of control. Your answers to a longer list of such items could more accurately assess your locus of control. (page 479)

Web Resources

Personality and Consciousness
www.wynja.com/personality/theorists.html
This growing site includes papers about Adler, Freud, Jung, Kelly, Lewin, Maslow, Rogers, Skinner, and others. You are invited to submit your own paper(s) for others to read; you will retain the copyright.

Grand Theories of Personality

Is personality rooted in one or two dominant motivations, such as sexuality or the desire for superiority?

What is a "healthy" personality?

The most famous person associated with psychology is surely Sigmund Freud. His influence on society is vast, extending into sociology, literature and the arts, even religion and politics (Figure 13.9). And yet, here we are, about three-fourths of the way through this text on psychology, and until now I have barely mentioned Freud. Why?

The reason is that, although Freud continues to be highly influential outside psychology, his influence within psychology is very much on the decline. According to one psychologist, Frederick Crews (1996), ". . . independent studies have begun to converge toward a verdict that was once considered a sign of extremism or even of neurosis: that there is literally nothing to be said, scientifically or therapeutically, to the advantage of the entire Freudian system or any of its constituent dogmas."

Think about that: *nothing* to be said in favor of *any* of Freud's theories. Needless to say, not everyone agrees with Crews. Some psychologists still loyally adhere to Freud's theories and methods, and even many who do not regard

themselves as Freudians have been influenced by him, perhaps in ways they do not realize. Still, the decline of Freud's influence is striking. In this module, we shall consider how Freud developed his theories and how he used or misused evidence. We shall also consider the ideas of several other theorists who also developed grand and ambitious theories of personality based on different assumptions.

Sigmund Freud and Psychoanalysis

Sigmund Freud (1856–1939; Figure 13.3), an Austrian physician, would have liked to become a professor of cultural history or anthropology; he wrote several books and articles about those topics in his later years. As a Jew in late 19th-century Austria, however, he knew that he had little chance of becoming a university professor. The only professional careers open to Jews in his time and place were in law, business, and medicine. Freud chose medicine, but without any deep commitment to the field.

Psychoanalysis and the Unconscious

Early in his career, Freud worked with the psychiatrist Josef Breuer, who had been treating a young woman with a fluctuating variety of physical complaints. As she talked with Breuer about her past, she recalled various traumatic, or emotionally damaging, experiences. Breuer, and later Freud also, proposed that recalling these experiences produced **catharsis,** *a release of pent-up emotional tension,* and thereby relieved her illness. However, later scholars who reexamined the medical records of the time found that this woman was not at all cured by this treatment. She ended the treatment and entered a hospital, where she was treated with drugs. Eventually, she recovered, although the cause of her problems and the basis for her recovery remain mysterious (Ellenberger, 1972).

Regardless of whether Breuer's "talking cure" had been successful, Freud began applying it to his own emotionally disturbed patients. He referred to *his method of explaining and dealing with personality, based on the interplay of conscious and unconscious forces,* as **psychoanalysis.** To this day, psychoanalysts remain loyal to that method and to Freud's theories.

Psychoanalysis started out as a fairly simple theory: Each of us has an unconscious mind as well as a conscious mind (Figure 13.10). The **unconscious** is *the repository of memories, emotions, and thoughts, many of them illogical, that affect our behavior even though we cannot talk about them.* Traumatic experiences force thoughts and emotions into the unconscious, and the goal of psychoanalysts is to bring those memories to consciousness. Doing so produces catharsis and enables the person to confront irrational and self-defeating impulses.

FIGURE 13.9 The fame of Sigmund Freud far exceeds that of any other psychologist. His picture has even been placed on the Austrian 50-schilling bill.

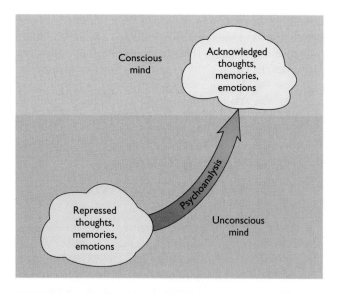

FIGURE 13.10 Freud believed that, through psychoanalysis, parts of the unconscious could be brought into the conscious mind, where a person could deal with them.

As Freud listened to his patients, however, he became convinced that the traumatic events they recalled were not sufficient to account for their abnormal behavior. Some patients reacted strongly to events that others took in stride. Why? At first, in the early 1890s, Freud attributed their overreactions to sexual difficulties (Macmillan, 1997). People with excessive anxiety, he said, were suffering from a lack of sexual gratification, and they could solve their problems by increased sexual activity. (For a while, Freud claimed that this recommendation cured their problems, but he soon abandoned it, and since then no one has found it to be effective.) People suffering from nervous exhaustion, he said, were suffering from the results of masturbation. His "evidence" for this idea was that all of his patients suffering from nervous exhaustion had masturbated (!). You can see the problem: Freud was practicing long before the Kinsey report had been published, and no one knew yet how common masturbation was. Freud boldly asserted that normal, mentally healthy people do not masturbate. Now, suppose you were in his audience. Would you raise your hand and say, "Wait a minute; I think I'm mentally normal, and I masturbate. . . "? Probably not, and neither did anybody else, so Freud concluded that he was right.

A few years later, however, Freud abandoned these hypotheses and suggested instead that the ultimate cause of psychological disorders was traumatic experiences from early childhood, especially early sexual experiences. In some of his writings, he attributed those experiences to seductions by other children; in later reports, he said that the father or other adults had sexually abused the children. He had no evidence for any of his accusations; his patients did not even recall any of these events, but Freud inferred that they must have happened anyway. He put together parts of the patients' dream reports, slips of the tongue, and so forth, and claimed that these all pointed to early sexual abuse. At

this point, Freud's problems with evidence began to become serious. His ideas about inadequate sex or too much masturbation may sound ridiculous, but at least they were testable. But how was anyone to determine whether the events that Freud inferred from dreams and so forth had actually happened?

A few years later, he backed down from saying that psychological disorders resulted from childhood sexual abuse. According to Freud's own description of these events, he realized that his patients had "misled" him into believing they had been sexually abused in early childhood; in fact, Freud said, their claims of sexual contact with their parents were "wishful phantasies" (Freud, 1925). Although he never fully developed his views of girls' early sexual development, he was more explicit about boys: During early childhood, every little boy goes through an **Oedipus complex;** he *develops a sexual interest in his mother and competitive aggression toward his father.* (Oedipus—EHD-ah-puhs—a figure in an ancient Greek play by Sophocles, unknowingly murdered his father and married his mother.) In short, Freud said people become psychologically disturbed not because their parents sexually molested them, but because as children they had wanted to have sex with their parents and couldn't.

Why did Freud switch from his idea about early sexual abuse to a theory about early sexual fantasies? According to one view (Masson, 1984), Freud was right the first time, and he simply lost the courage to defend his views about childhood sexual abuse. According to other scholars, however, Freud never had any justification for either set of views (Esterson, 1998; Powell & Boer, 1994; Schatzman, 1992). In his earliest writings, Freud had inferred his patients' sexual abuse from their symptoms and dreams, despite their own denials of such sexual abuse. It was hardly fair, therefore, to complain that the patients had "misled" him into believing they had been sexually abused. When he switched to saying that the patients had had an Oedipus complex or other childhood sexual fantasies, he was again drawing inferences that his patients denied. (Freud considered his patients' protests to be signs of emotional resistance and therefore confirmation that his interpretations were correct.)

Apparently, Freud's main evidence for his interpretations was simply that he was able to construct a coherent story linking a patient's symptoms, dreams, and so forth to the sexual fantasies that Freud inferred must have occurred (Esterson, 1993). In short, he did not distinguish between his "results" and his "interpretations."

Further Examples of Casual Use of Evidence

Freud preferred complicated explanations to more parsimonious ones. At one point, his friend Wilhelm Fliess performed a surgical operation on a woman's nose to try to relieve her stomach and menstrual pains—no, that's not a misprint—and absentmindedly left half a meter of surgical gauze in her nasal cavity after the operation. Her nose became infected and her face disfigured, and she almost bled to death. In a letter to Fliess, Freud suggested that the reason the woman continued to bleed for so long was that she had "an old wish to be loved in her illness" (Masson, 1985, Letter of May 4, 1896).

Another patient, known as Dora, came to Freud at her father's insistence. Since about age 8, Dora had suffered from headaches, coughing, and shortness of breath, all of which Freud interpreted as psychological in nature. She had also avoided a certain friend of her father, Mr. "K," ever since one episode when K grabbed Dora, then 14 years old, and kissed her on her lips. Freud wrote that Dora surely experienced sexual pleasure at this time, partly because K's presumably erect penis rubbed up against her clitoris and excited it. Freud described Dora's reaction of disgust as ". . . entirely and completely hysterical. I should without question consider a person hysterical in whom an occasion for sexual excitement elicited feelings that were preponderantly or exclusively unpleasurable" (Freud, 1905/1963, p. 44). He then proceeded to try to explain Dora's hysterical behavior, tracing it to her love for both K and her father and her homosexual attraction to Mrs. K. As one reads Freud's elaborate discussion, one wonders what was wrong with Dora's simpler explanation—that she really was repulsed by the sexual advances of this middle-aged man.

Stages of Psychosexual Development in Freud's Theory of Personality

Right or wrong, Freud's theory is so well known that, as a student of psychology, you should know what these terms mean when you hear someone else talking about them. One of his central points was that psychosexual interest and pleasure begin in infancy. He used the term **psychosexual pleasure** in a broad sense to include *all strong, pleasant excitement arising from body stimulation.* He maintained that how we deal with our psychosexual development influences nearly all aspects of our personality.

Freud proposed that young children have sexual tendencies that resemble those of more primitive mammals. Just as nonhuman mammals respond sexually to sounds and smells that do not excite most adult humans, children respond sexually to stimulation of the mouth, the anus, and other body zones. Freud based his views on his own and his patients' reconstructions of their childhood; he did not systematically observe children himself.

According to Freud (1905/1925), people have a *psychosexual energy,* which he called **libido** (lih-BEE-doh), from a Latin word meaning "desire." Normally, libido is focused in an infant's mouth and "flows" to other parts of the body as the child grows older. Children go through five stages of psychosexual development, each with a characteristic sexual focus that leaves its mark on the adult personality. If normal sexual development is blocked or frustrated at any stage, Freud said, part of the libido becomes **fixated** at

The beginning of psychosexual development is the oral stage, when infants enjoy stimulation of their mouth—which for them means sucking, swallowing, and biting. They like putting things in their mouths and gnawing on them. According to Freud, if normal sexual development is blocked at this stage, the child will grow up continuing to get much pleasure from drinking and eating, as well as from kissing and smoking. Perhaps this pipe smoker's mother weaned him too quickly—or let him nurse too long. And perhaps such an explanation is incorrect. Like many of Freud's ideas, this one is difficult to test.

that stage; that is, it *continues to be preoccupied with the pleasure area associated with that stage.* Table 13.3 summarizes these stages.

The Oral Stage   In the **oral stage,** from birth through the first year or so (Freud was vague about the age limits of each stage), *the infant derives intense psychosexual pleasure from stimulation of the mouth, particularly while sucking at the mother's breast.* In the later part of the oral stage, the infant begins to bite as well as suck. A person fixated at this stage continues to receive great pleasure from eating, drinking, and smoking and may also have lasting concerns with dependence and independence.

The Anal Stage   At about 1 to 3 years of age, children enter the **anal stage.** At this time *they get psychosexual pleasure from stimulation of the anal sphincter, the muscle that controls bowel movements.* A person fixated at this stage goes through life "holding things back"—being orderly, stingy, and stubborn—or, less commonly, may go to the opposite extreme and become wasteful, messy, and destructive.

The Phallic Stage   Beginning at about age 3, in the **phallic stage,** children begin to *play with their genitals,* and, according to Freud, become sexually attracted to the opposite-sex parent. Freud claimed that boys with a phallic fixation are afraid of being castrated; girls with such a fixation develop "penis envy." These ideas have long been controversial; developmental psychologists almost never observe castration fear or penis envy in children.

TABLE 13.3 Freud's Stages of Psychosexual Development

STAGE (approximate ages)	SEXUAL INTERESTS AT THIS STAGE	EFFECTS OF FIXATION
Oral Stage (birth to 1 year)	Sucking, swallowing, biting	Lasting concerns with dependence and independence; pleasure from eating, drinking, and other oral activities
Anal stage (1 to 3 years)	Expelling feces, retaining feces	Orderliness, stinginess, stubbornness
Phallic stage (3 to 5 or 6 years)	Touching penis or clitoris; Oedipus complex	Difficulty feeling closeness. Males: fear of castration Females: penis envy
Latency period (5 or 6 to puberty)	Sexual interests suppressed	—
Genital stage (puberty onward)	Sexual contact with other people	—

The Latent Period From about age 5 or 6 until adolescence, Freud said, most children enter a **latent period** in which they *suppress their psychosexual interest*. At this time, they play mostly with peers of their own sex. The latent period is evidently a product of the culture and is not apparent in certain nonindustrialized societies.

The Genital Stage Beginning at puberty, young people *take a strong sexual interest in other people*. This is known as the **genital stage.** According to Freud, anyone who has fixated a great deal of libido in an earlier stage has little libido left for the genital stage. But people who have successfully negotiated the earlier stages can now derive primary satisfaction from sexual intercourse.

Evaluation of Freud's Stages Freud's theory makes such vague predictions that it is difficult to test (Grünbaum, 1986; Popper, 1986). When it has been tested, the results have been mostly unimpressive or inconclusive. For example, the characteristics of being orderly, stingy, and stubborn, which Freud described as due to anal fixation, do tend to correlate with one another, suggesting that they are part of a single personality type. However, we have no evidence that these attributes actually result from any aspect of toilet training (Fisher & Greenberg, 1977).

Freud's Description of the Structure of Personality

Personality, Freud claimed, consists of three aspects: the id, the ego, and the superego (Figure 13.11). (Actually, he used German words that mean *it, I,* and *over-I.* A translator used Latin equivalents instead of English words.) The **id** consists of *all our biological drives,* such as sex and hunger. The id demands immediate gratification. The **ego** is *the rational, decision-making aspect of the personality.* The **superego** contains *the memory of our parents' rules and prohibitions,*

such as, "Nice little boys and girls don't do that." Sometimes the id produces sexual or other motivations that the superego considers repugnant, thus evoking feelings of guilt. The ego may side with either the id or the superego; if it sides with the superego, it tries to avoid even thinking about the id's unacceptable impulses. Most psychologists today find it difficult to imagine the mind in terms of three warring factions and therefore regard Freud's description as only a metaphor.

CONCEPT CHECK

2. What kind of behavior would Freud expect of someone with a strong id and a weak superego? What behavior would you expect of someone with an unusually strong superego? (Check your answers on page 496.)

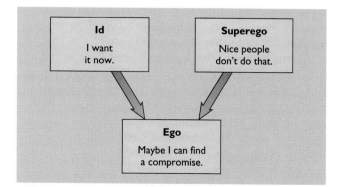

FIGURE 13.11 Freud described personality as a collection of three parts that are often in conflict with one another. The *id* asks for immediate gratification of biological urges, such as the sex drive. The *superego* counters these impulses with lists of rules that we learned from our parents. The *ego,* torn between these two forces, makes the decisions about what to do. According to Freud, we can understand certain people's behavior by assuming that their id is stronger than their superego or that their superego is stronger than their id.

Defense Mechanisms Against Anxiety

According to Freud, *the ego defends itself against conflicts and anxieties by relegating unpleasant thoughts and impulses to the unconscious.* Among the **defense mechanisms** that the ego employs are repression, denial, rationalization, displacement, regression, projection, reaction formation, and sublimation (Figure 13.12). Ordinarily, we are not aware of our own repressions, rationalizations, and so forth. Defense mechanisms are normal ways of suppressing anxiety and are often adaptive, becoming a problem only when they prevent a person from effectively dealing with reality.

Repression   The defense mechanism of **repression** is *motivated forgetting*—the rejection of unacceptable thoughts, desires, and memories and their relegation to the unconscious. Repression is perhaps the most central concept in Freud's theory.

One example of repression would be a woman seeing someone beating another person to death and later not being able to remember what she saw. Another example: A man gives a speech, and several members of the audience raise serious objections to what he says; later, he forgets their objections.

Researchers have struggled to find unambiguous evidence to support the concept of repression. Investigators have exposed subjects to various unpleasant or threatening experiences, in the expectation that repression would interfere with their memories. However, whenever subjects did have trouble remembering the events, a variety of alternative explanations appear to be possible (Holmes, 1990). Outside the laboratory, repression is certainly not common in situations where we might expect it. As discussed in Chapter 7, kidnapping victims, children who watched the death of their own parents, and others who endured similar misery almost always remember the events intensely.

Denial   *The refusal to believe information that provokes anxiety* ("This can't be happening") is called **denial.** Whereas repression is the motivated forgetting of certain information, denial is an assertion that the information is incorrect. For example, someone with a serious alcohol problem may insist, "I'm not an alcoholic. I can take it or leave it."

Rationalization   When people *attempt to prove that their actions are rational and justifiable and thus worthy of approval,* they are using **rationalization.** For example, a

FIGURE 13.12 The ego—the rational I—has numerous ways of defending itself against anxiety, that apprehensive state named for the Latin word meaning "to strangle." These defense mechanisms try to ignore or avoid facing unpleasant realities, and they are part of an internal battle that you fight against yourself.

student who wants to go to the movies instead of studying says, "More studying won't do me any good anyway." Someone who misses a deadline to apply for a job says, "I didn't really want that job anyway."

Displacement *By diverting a behavior or thought away from its natural target toward a less threatening target,* **displacement** lets people engage in the behavior they prefer without experiencing severe anxiety. For example, a man who is angry at his boss might come home and kick his dog. He really wants to kick his boss, but that would cause him too much anxiety. Or a student who is angry at her professor screams at her roommate.

Regression *A return to a more juvenile level of functioning,* **regression** is an effort to avoid the anxiety of facing one's current role in life. By adopting a childish role, a person can escape responsibility and return to an earlier, perhaps more secure way of life. For example, after a new sibling is born, a 5-year-old child may start wetting the bed again. Following a divorce or a business setback, a man may resort to daydreaming, getting drunk, or other immature behaviors.

Projection *The attribution of one's own undesirable characteristics to other people* is known as **projection.** When people project their own faults onto others, they do not necessarily deny that they possess those faults themselves (Holmes, 1978; Sherwood, 1981). However, by suggesting that the faults are widespread, they make them more acceptable and less anxiety provoking. For example, someone who secretly enjoys pornography might accuse other people of enjoying it.

Reaction Formation To reduce anxiety and to keep undesirable characteristics repressed, people may use **reaction formation** to *present themselves as the opposite of what they really are.* In Shakespeare's play *Hamlet,* Gertrude says, "The lady protests too much, methinks." People who insist too vehemently that something is "absolutely" true often harbor secret doubts about whether it is really true. For example, a man troubled by doubts about his religious faith may try to convert others to the faith. Someone with unacceptable aggressive tendencies may join a group dedicated to preventing violence against babies or animals. (Not everyone who proselytizes for a faith has deep doubts about it, of course, and not everyone who tries to prevent violence is secretly a violent person. Different people can have a variety of reasons for the same actions.)

Sublimation *The transformation of sexual or aggressive energies into culturally acceptable, even admirable, behaviors* is **sublimation.** According to Freud, sublimation enables a person to express the impulse without admitting its existence. For example, painting and sculpture may represent a sublimation of sexual impulses. Someone with unacceptable aggressive impulses may sublimate them by be-

coming a surgeon. However, if the true motives of a painter are sexual, as Freud proposed, they are well hidden indeed. Sublimation is the one proposed defense mechanism that is associated with socially constructive behavior.

CONCEPT CHECK

3. Match the Freudian defense mechanisms in the top list with the situations in the list that follows:

1. Repression	**5.** Regression
2. Denial	**6.** Projection
3. Rationalization	**7.** Reaction formation
4. Displacement	**8.** Sublimation

_____ **a.** A man who is angry with his neighbor goes hunting and kills a deer.

_____ **b.** Someone with a smoking habit insists there is no convincing evidence that smoking impairs health.

_____ **c.** A woman with doubts about her religious faith tries to convert others to her religion.

_____ **d.** A man who beats his wife writes a book arguing that people have an instinctive need for aggressive behavior.

_____ **e.** A woman forgets a doctor's appointment for a test for cancer.

_____ **f.** Someone who has difficulty dealing with certain people resorts to pouting, crying, and throwing tantrums.

_____ **g.** A boss takes credit for a good idea suggested by an employee because, "It's better for me to take the credit so that our department will look good and all the employees will benefit."

_____ **h.** Someone with an unacceptable impulse to shout obscenities becomes a writer of novels.

(Check your answers on page 496.)

Manifestations of the Unconscious in Everyday Life

Freud believed that the unconscious made itself felt in nearly all aspects of ordinary life. Even an act that may be explained as "just a meaningless accident" reflects an unconscious motivation. For example, whenever one of Freud's patients "forgot" an appointment, Freud assumed the patient did not want to keep it.

Freud also interpreted *slips of the tongue,* or what have come to be called "Freudian slips," as revelations of unconscious thoughts or motives. If you said "I leave you" instead of "I love you," Freud would assume that your error revealed an unconscious rejection of your professed love.

Today, psychologists believe that most slips of the tongue have multiple causes. Here is an example that is not really a slip of the tongue, but it helps to illustrate the point.

 Ask someone to repeat the word "poke" ten times, about once every two seconds. At the end, quickly ask, "What do you call the white of an egg?" Your friend will almost certainly say "yolk," instead of the correct answer, "albumin" (Baars, Fehling, LaPolla, & McGovern,

1997). Saying "poke" had primed your friend to say a similar-sounding word. Similarly, someone who reads "the Alpha and the Omega" as "the Alfalfa and the Omega" may have some interesting unconscious thoughts but has probably just confused two similar sounding words. Most slips of the tongue produce meaningless gibberish, and the occasional slips that seem meaningful could be just accidents.

Nevertheless, it is also possible that people's motives do sometimes influence slips of the tongue. Let's examine a clever attempt to test this idea.

WHAT'S THE EVIDENCE?
Freudian Slips

How might one test the relation between people's motives and their slips of the tongue? If we followed people around and recorded all their slips of the tongue, we would still have to guess or infer their hidden motives.

A second method would be to induce a motive—hunger, for example—for the purposes of an experiment. Then, we could ask the hungry subjects to read a certain passage, and we could count how many of their slips of the tongue had something to do with eating. We could repeat the experiment, inducing a different motive, to see whether people made corresponding slips.

However, most people make so few slips of the tongue that the experiment might go on for months with few results. We need a procedure that increases the frequency of slips of the tongue. Michael Motley and Bernard Baars (1979) devised just such a procedure.

Hypothesis When people are performing a difficult task on which they are likely to make slips of the tongue, the kinds of slips they make will depend on the motivations they are feeling at the moment.

Method The experimenters divided 90 male college students into three groups: a "sex" group, a "shock" group, and a control group. Those in the sex group were greeted by a very attractive female experimenter dressed in a sexy outfit and behaving seductively. Those in the shock group were met by a male experimenter who attached electrodes to

their arms and told them the electrodes were connected to a "random shock generator" that might give them one or more painful shocks at unpredictable times during the experiment. (No shocks were actually given.) Those in the control group were met by a male experimenter who attached no electrodes to them and made no mention of shocks. Thus, one group should have a heightened sexual motivation, one group should have a strong fear of shock, and one group should be concerned with neither sex nor shock.

The students watched a screen on which the experimenters flashed pairs of words or nonsense syllables, such as "HAT-RAM" and "RUF-GAM." Each pair was flashed for 1 second. A buzzer sounded 0.4 second after each pair appeared, telling the students to speak aloud the *previous* pair. So, for example, after seeing "RUF-GAM," they would have to say "HAT-RAM" (the previous pair), and remember "RUF-GAM" to say after the next pair. Students made slips of the tongue about 30% of the time. For example, they would say "HAT-RAM" as "RAT-HAM" and "RUF-GAM" as "GUF-RAM."

Some of the syllable pairs were designed to promote sex-related slips. For example, "GOXI-FURL" and "LOOD-GEGS" might be repeated as "FOXY-GIRL" and "GOOD-LEGS." Other pairs were designed to promote shock-related slips. For example, "SHAD-BOCK" and "WOT-HIRE" might be pronounced as "BAD-SHOCK" and "HOT-WIRE." Other pairs did not suggest any slips related to either sex or shock.

Results The men in the sex group made more than twice as many sex-related slips as shock-related slips. The opposite was true for the men in the shock group. Those in the control group made both types of errors about equally. Figure 13.13 illustrates the results.

Interpretation The results support Freud's claim that a strong motivation can increase the frequency of slips of the tongue related to that motivation. Slips of the tongue may indeed sometimes reflect a person's thoughts and desires.

But the results do not support Freud's contention that hidden motivations are the main cause of slips of the tongue. Slips were common in this experiment because the task was so difficult. Having to say one pair while preparing

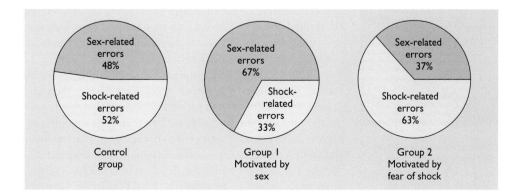

FIGURE 13.13 In the presence of an attractive woman, men made many sex-related slips of the tongue. When they were worried about shocks, they made shock-related slips of the tongue.

to say another produced conflict between the two pairs that a subject was trying to remember.

✴   ✴   ✴

Freud's Legacy

Undeniably, Freud was a great pioneer in identifying new questions. The validity of his answers is quite controversial, however. He based his conclusions on inferences he drew from what his patients said and did, and he had no sure way of testing the validity of those inferences. A growing number of psychologists today contend that Freud imposed theories onto his data instead of drawing conclusions from the data.

It is possible, of course, for a visionary leader to induce correct theories based on weak evidence, and Freud could have been right even if his methods were faulty. How well his theories stand up today depends on who you ask, but the aspects of his theories that attract the fewest arguments are generalities such as the following:

- Our behavior is molded by earlier experiences dating back to childhood.
- Every behavior has multiple causes, and we are unaware of many of them.
- Someone can react strongly to a fairly normal experience because of its symbolic significance to that individual.
- We have a variety of ways of defending ourselves against anxiety.
- Talking about a psychological problem sometimes helps.

Compared to what Freud was trying to accomplish, however, giving him credit for such generalities is "damning by faint praise." Freud thought he had devised a method to discover the contents of people's unconscious minds. Such inferences might sometimes be correct; the problem, however, is to distinguish valid inferences from fanciful ones. On that point, many psychologists are most skeptical.

Freud's own couch is now part of our history. What is the future of psychoanalysts' couches? Psychoanalytic interpretations range from reasonable to doubtful; in any individual case, it is difficult or even impossible to judge the accuracy of an analyst's interpretation.

FIGURE 13.14 Karen Horney, a major neo-Freudian, revised some of Freud's theories and gave greater attention to cultural influences. She was a pioneer in the development of feminine psychology.

Neo-Freudians

Some psychologists, known as **neo-Freudians,** have *remained faithful to parts of Freud's theory while modifying other parts.* One of the most influential neo-Freudians was the German physician Karen Horney (HOR-nigh; 1885–1952; Figure 13.14), who believed that Freud had exaggerated the role of the sex drive in human behavior and had misunderstood the sexual motivations of women. She believed, for example, that the conflict between a child and his or her parents was a reaction to parental hostility and intimidation, not a manifestation of sexual desires. Horney contended that Freud had slighted the importance of cultural influences on personality and that he neglected to help his patients work out practical solutions to their problems. Still, Horney's views were more a revision than a rejection of Freud's theories. Other theorists, including Carl Jung and Alfred Adler, broke more sharply with Freud. Although some psychologists call Jung and Adler neo-Freudians, the followers of Jung and Adler do not. Each offered a very different, distinctly non-Freudian view of personality.

Carl Jung and the Collective Unconscious

Carl G. Jung (YOONG; 1875–1961; Figure 13.15), a Swiss physician, was an early member of Freud's inner circle. Freud regarded Jung as a son, the "heir apparent" or "crown prince" of the psychoanalytic movement, until their father-son relationship began to deteriorate (Alexander, 1982). At one point, Freud and Jung agreed to analyze each other's dreams. Freud described one of his dreams, but then refused to provide the personal associations that would enable Jung to interpret it, insisting that "I cannot risk my authority."

Jung was more forthcoming. He described a dream in which he explored the upper stories of a house, then explored its basement, and finally discovering that the house had a subbasement, began to explore that. Jung thought the dream referred to his explorations of the mind. The top floor was the conscious mind; the basement was the unconscious; and the subbasement was a still deeper level of the unconscious, yet to be explored. Freud, however, insisted

FIGURE 13.15 Carl G. Jung rejected Freud's concept that dreams hide their meaning from the conscious mind: "To me dreams are a part of nature, which harbors no intention to deceive, but expresses something as best it can" (Jung, 1965).

that the dream referred to Jung's personal experiences and frustrations (Hannah, 1976).

Jung's own theory of personality incorporated some of Freud's ideas but put greater emphasis on people's search for a spiritual meaning in life and on the continuity of human experience, past and present. Jung believed that every person has not only a conscious mind and a "personal unconscious" (equivalent to Freud's "unconscious"), but also a collective unconscious. The personal unconscious represents a person's own experience. The **collective unconscious,** which is present at birth, represents *the cumulative experience of preceding generations.* Because all humans share a common ancestry, all have the same collective unconscious. The collective unconscious contains **archetypes,** which are *vague images that we all inherit from the experiences of our ancestors.* As evidence for this view, Jung pointed out that similar images emerge in the art of cultures throughout the world (Figure 13.16) and that similar themes emerge in various religions, myths, and folklore. Those images and themes also appear in dreams and in the hallucinations of people with severe psychological disorders.

Given what biologists now know of genetics, Jung's ideas are hard to defend. Having an experience does not change one's genes, and even if we did somehow develop genes that represented common human experiences, those genes would certainly vary among people, as other genes do. (Jung was quite insistent that the collective unconscious was the same for all people.) Jung's alternative to a genetic explanation was that perhaps archetypes exist on their own, independent of time, space, and brains. That is a difficult idea even to contemplate, much less test. In short, Jung's views of the collective unconscious and archetypes are vague and mystical, although a much modified version could be developed that would be scientifically testable (Neher, 1996).

Alfred Adler and Individual Psychology

Alfred Adler (1870–1937; Figure 13.17), an Austrian physician who, like Jung, had been one of Freud's early associates, broke with Freud because he believed Freud was overemphasizing the sex drive and neglecting other, more important influences on personality. They parted company in 1911, with Freud insisting that women experience "penis envy" and

with Adler contending that women were more likely to envy men's status and power. The two were never reconciled.

Adler founded a rival school of thought, which he called **individual psychology.** To Adler, this term did not mean "psychology of the individual." Rather, it meant *"indivisible psychology,"* a psychology of the person as a whole rather than a psychology of parts, such as id, ego, and superego. Adler emphasized the importance of conscious, goal-directed behavior and deemphasized (though he did not deny) unconscious influences.

Adler's Description of Personality

Several of Adler's early patients were acrobats who had had an arm or a leg damaged by a childhood illness or injury. These people were determined to overcome their disabilities, and they had worked hard to develop the strength and coordination they needed to perform as acrobats. Perhaps, Adler surmised, people in general try to overcome their weaknesses and to transform them into strengths (Adler, 1932/1964).

As infants, Adler pointed out, we are small, dependent creatures who strive to overcome our inferiority. People who do not succeed go through life with an **inferiority complex,** *an exaggerated feeling of weakness, inadequacy, and helplessness.* Even those who do manage to overcome their feelings of inferiority persist in their efforts to achieve.

According to Adler, everyone has a natural **striving for superiority,** *a desire to seek personal excellence and fulfillment.* Each person creates a **style of life,** or *master plan for achieving a sense of superiority.* That style of life may be directed toward success in business, sports, politics, or another competitive activity. Or it may be directed toward "success" of a different sort: For example, someone who withdraws from life may gain a sense of accomplishment or superiority from being uncommonly self-sacrificing. Someone who constantly complains about real or imagined illnesses or disabilities may, by demanding help from friends and family, win a measure of control or superiority over them. Or someone may commit crimes to savor the attention that they bring.

Adler recognized that people are not always aware of their own style of life and the assumptions behind it and may fail to realize that the real motive behind a word or action is to manipulate others. They may engage in self-defeating behavior because they have not admitted to themselves what their goals really are. Adler tried to determine people's real motives. For example, he would ask someone who complained of a backache, "How would your life be different if you could get rid of your backache?" Those who said they would become more active were presumably suffering from real ailments that they were trying to overcome. Those who said they could not imagine how their life would change, or said only that they would get less sympathy from others, were presumably suffering from psychologically caused ailments or, at least, were exaggerating their discomfort.

FIGURE 13.16 Carl Jung was fascinated with the similar images that show up in the artwork of different cultures. One recurring image is the mandala, which Jung believed to be a symbol of the self's striving for unity and wholeness. These mandalas are (upper left) a Hindu painting from Bhutan; (upper right) a mosaic from Beth Alpha Synagogue, Israel; (lower left) a tie-dye tapestry created in the United States; and (lower right) a Navajo sand painting from the southwestern United States.

CONCEPT CHECK

4. In Adler's theory, what is the relationship between striving for superiority and style of life? (Check your answer on page •••.)

Adler's View of Psychological Disorders

Any personality based on a selfish style of life is unhealthy, Adler (1928/1964) said. People's need for one another requires that they develop a **social interest,** *a sense of solidarity and identification with other people.* People with a strong social interest strive for superiority in a way that contributes to the welfare of the whole human race, not just to their own welfare. They want to cooperate with other people, not to compete. In equating mental health with a strong social interest, Adler saw mental health as a positive state, not just the absence of impairments.

In Adler's view, people with psychological disorders are not suffering from an "illness." Rather, they have set immature goals, are following a faulty style of life, and show little social interest. Their response to new opportunity is "Yes, but . . ." (Adler, 1932/1964). They are striving for superiority in ways that are useless to themselves and to others.

FIGURE 13.17 Like Horney, Alfred Adler thought that Freud overemphasized the sex drive. Adler was very interested in feelings of self-esteem. He was the first to talk about the possibility of a "healthy" personality as not just a personality free from disorders. According to Adler, the key to a healthy personality was "social interest," a desire for the welfare of other people.

For example, one of Adler's patients was a man who lived in conflict with his wife because he was constantly trying to impress her and dominate her (Adler, 1927). When discussing his problems, the man revealed that he had been very slow to mature physically and had not reached puberty until he was 17 years old. Other teenagers had ignored him and had treated him like a child. He was now a physically normal adult, but he was overcompensating for those years of feeling inferior by trying to seem bigger and more important than he really was.

Adler tried to get patients to understand their own style of life and to correct the faulty assumptions on which they had based their lives. He urged them to strengthen their social interest and to strive for superiority in ways that would benefit both themselves and others.

Adler's Legacy

Adler's influence on psychology exceeds his fame. His concept of the "inferiority complex" has become part of the common culture. He was the first to talk about mental health as a positive state rather than as merely the absence of impairments. Many later forms of therapy drew upon Adler's innovations, especially his emphasis on the assumptions underlying a patient's behavior. Humanistic psychologists followed Adler by urging people to take responsibility for their own behavior and for modifying their style of life.

THE MESSAGE
Grand Theories, Grand Ambitions

Freud, Jung, and Adler lived and worked in an earlier era that was apparently more conducive to building major theories of how personality fits together. It is easy to fault these theorists for jumping to conclusions and for their other shortcomings. Still, one should admire the scope of what they were trying to accomplish and the influence that they had on later investigators. Previously, personality was entirely in the realm of philosophers and novelists. The grand theory builders made personality a topic for research and progress.

SUMMARY

✳ *Freud.* Sigmund Freud, the founder of psychoanalysis, proposed that human behavior is greatly influenced by unconscious thoughts and motives and that much of what we do and say has hidden meanings. (page 485)

✳ *Freud's psychosexual stages.* Freud believed that many unconscious thoughts and motives are sexual in nature. He proposed that people progress through stages or periods of psychosexual development—oral, anal, phallic, latent, and genital—and that frustration at any one stage can lead to a lasting fixation of the libido at that stage. (page 487)

✳ *Slips of the tongue.* Unconscious thoughts influence many aspects of everyday life, including slips of the tongue, although other influences may be more important. (page 490)

✳ *Jung.* Carl Jung believed that all people share a "collective unconscious" that represents the entire experience of humanity. (page 492)

✳ *Adler.* Alfred Adler proposed that people's primary motivation is a striving for superiority. Each person adopts his or her own "style of life," or method of striving. (page 493)

✳ *Adler's view of a healthy personality.* According to Adler, the healthiest style of life is one that emphasizes "social interest"—that is, concern for the welfare of others. (page 494)

Suggestions for Further Reading

Adler, A. (1954). *Understanding human nature.* Greenwich, CT: Fawcett. (Original work published 1927.) Adler's most general and most popular book.

Freud, S. (1924). *Introductory lectures on psychoanalysis.* New York: Boni & Liveright. Available in various paperback editions. This is Freud's attempt to describe the fundamentals of his theory to a general audience.

Macmillan, M. (1997). *Freud evaluated.* Cambridge, MA: MIT Press. A thorough criticism of Freud's theories and his use of evidence.

Terms

catharsis   the release of pent-up emotional tension (page 485)

psychoanalysis   Freud's approach to personality, based on the interplay of conscious and unconscious forces (page 485)

unconscious   according to Freud, the repository of memories, emotions, and thoughts—often illogical thoughts—that affect our behavior even though we cannot talk about them (page 485)

Oedipus complex   according to Freud, a young boy's sexual interest in his mother accompanied by competitive aggression toward his father (page 486)

psychosexual pleasure   according to Freud, any strong, pleasant enjoyment arising from body stimulation (page 487)

libido   in Freud's theory, psychosexual energy (page 487)

fixation   in Freud's theory, a persisting preoccupation with an immature psychosexual interest as a result of frustration at that stage of psychosexual development (page 487)

oral stage   Freud's first stage of psychosexual development; here, psychosexual pleasure is focused on the mouth (page 487)

anal stage   Freud's second stage of psychosexual development; here, psychosexual pleasure is focused on the anus (page 487)

phallic stage   Freud's third stage of psychosexual development; here, psychosexual interest is focused on the penis or clitoris (page 487)

latent period   according to Freud, a period in which psychosexual interest is suppressed or dormant (page 488)

genital stage   Freud's final stage of psychosexual development, in which sexual pleasure is focused on sexual intimacy with others (page 488)

id   according to Freud, the aspect of personality that consists of all our biological drives and demands for immediate gratification (page 488)

ego   according to Freud, the rational, decision-making aspect of personality (page 488)

superego   according to Freud, the aspect of personality that consists of memories of rules put forth by one's parents (page 488)

defense mechanism   a method employed by the ego to protect itself against anxiety caused by the conflict between the id's demands and the superego's constraints (page 489)

repression   motivated forgetting; the relegation of unacceptable impulses or memories to the unconscious (page 489)

denial   the refusal to believe information that provokes anxiety (page 489)

rationalization   attempting to prove that one's actions are rational and justifiable and thus worthy of approval (page 489)

displacement   the diversion of a thought or behavior away from its natural target toward a less threatening target (page 490)

regression   the return to a more juvenile level of functioning as a means of reducing anxiety or in response to emotionally trying circumstances (page 490)

projection   the attribution of one's own undesirable characteristics to other people (page 490)

reaction formation   presenting oneself as the opposite of what one really is, in an effort to reduce anxiety (page 490)

sublimation   the transformation of sexual or aggressive energies into culturally acceptable, even admirable, behaviors (page 490)

neo-Freudians   personality theorists who have remained faithful to parts of Freud's theory while modifying other parts (page 492)

collective unconscious   according to Jung, an inborn level of the unconscious that symbolizes the collective experience of the human species (page 493)

archetypes   according to Jung, vague images inherited from our ancestors and contained in the collective unconscious (page 493)

individual psychology   the psychology of the person as an indivisible whole, as formulated by Adler (page 493)

inferiority complex   an exaggerated feeling of weakness, inadequacy, and helplessness (page 493)

striving for superiority   according to Adler, a universal desire to seek personal excellence and fulfillment (page 493)

style of life   according to Adler, a person's master plan for achieving a sense of superiority (page 493)

social interest   a sense of solidarity and identification with other people (page 494)

Answers to Concept Checks

2.   Someone with a strong id and a weak superego could be expected to give in to a variety of sexual and other impulses that other people would inhibit. Someone with an unusually strong superego would be unusually inhibited and dominated by feelings of guilt. (page 488)

3.   **a.** 4, displacement; **b.** 2, denial; **c.** 7, reaction formation; **d.** 6, projection; **e.** 1, repression; **f.** 5, regression; **g.** 3, rationalization; **h.** 8, sublimation. (page 490)

4.   In Adler's theory, a person's style of life is a method of striving for superiority. (page 494)

Web Resources

The Freud Web

www.stg.brown.edu/projects/hypertext/landow/HTatBrown/freud/Freud_OV.html

David B. Stevenson offers an in-depth look at Freud the man and at major elements of Freudian theory.

The Jung Index

www.jungindex.net/

One of the best psychology sites on the Web includes a detailed introduction to Jung's theory, a glossary of Jungian terms, a newsletter, and other valuable features.

Alfred Adler Institute of San Francisco

ourworld.compuserve.com/homepages/hstein/

The definitive Adler site includes dozens of articles about classical Adlerian psychology, how to become an Adlerian therapist, biographical sketches of Adler and prominent Adlerian therapists, and more.

Personality Traits

Is personality consistent over time and from one situation to another?

What are personality traits?

In many ways, all rocks are the same. If you want to predict when a dropped rock will hit the ground, you do not need to know what kind of rock it is. If you skip a rock across a lake, throw it against a window, or use it to crack open a coconut, you can predict what will happen if you know the size and shape of the rock. You don't need to know much more.

For other purposes, however, you can't treat all rocks the same way. If you want to predict what will happen if you run an electric current through it, you have to know how much metal is in the rock. If you want to determine a fair sale price for the rock, you need to know whether it is a diamond or a piece of granite.

Similarly, people resemble one another in some ways and differ in others. Psychologists investigate individual differences in two ways, called the nomothetic and the idiographic approaches. The word *nomothetic* (NAHM-uh-THEHT-ick) comes from the Greek *nomothetes,* meaning "legislator"; the **nomothetic approach** *seeks general laws about how an aspect of personality affects behavior,* often based on statistical comparisons of large groups of people. For example, we might make the nomothetic statement that people with a more *Machiavellian* personality tend to be highly manipulative and that people with a less Machiavellian personality tend to cooperate with others. We could apply that statement fairly directly to anyone, simply by measuring that person's degree of Machiavellianism.

In contrast, the word *idiographic* is based on the root *idio-,* meaning "individual." The **idiographic approach** concentrates on *intensive studies of individuals* (Allport, 1961). For example, certain psychologists have studied how people's life goals affect their moods and their reactions to various events. Because people have different goals, the investigators draw carefully qualified conclusions about how people with one kind of goal behave and how people with another kind of goal behave (Emmons, 1991). The idiographic approach can lead to a conclusion that applies to more than just one person, but it is not meant to generalize to the whole population.

Actors, such as this man playing the role of a woman in Japanese Kabuki theater, can present personalities that are very different from their private personalities. All of us occasionally display temporary personality states different from our usual selves.

Personality Traits and States

Meteorologists distinguish between climate (the usual conditions) and weather (the current conditions). For example, the climate in London, England, is moister and cooler than the climate in south Texas, but on a given day the weather could be warm in London and cool in Texas. Similarly, psychologists distinguish between long-lasting personality conditions and temporary fluctuations.

A consistent, long-lasting tendency in behavior, such as shyness, hostility, or talkativeness, is known as a **trait.** In contrast, a **state** is *a temporary activation of a particular behavior.* People's behavior varies from time to time because they are in different states. For example, stage fright is a state; general nervousness is a trait. Being quiet in a library is a state; being quiet most of the time is a trait. A trait is like a climate condition that manifests itself in the long run, though not at every moment.

Note that both traits and states are descriptions of behavior, not explanations. To say that someone is nervous or quiet does not explain the person's behavior; it merely tells us what we are trying to explain.

5. Suppose someone becomes nervous as soon as he sits down in a dentist's chair. Is this experience "trait anxiety" or "state anxiety"? (Check your answer on page 502.)

The Search for Broad Personality Traits

If we choose to describe people's personalities in terms of traits, how many personality traits should we identify? One way to begin is by examining our language. Presumably, if a particular personality trait is really important, any human language should have a word for it. Although this assumption could be wrong, it seems reasonable, considering how much attention people pay to other people's personalities.

Gordon Allport and H. S. Odbert (1936) plodded through an English dictionary and found almost 18,000 words that might be used to describe personality. Using this list, psychologists deleted words that were merely evaluations (such as *pleasant* or *nasty*) and terms referring to temporary states (such as *confused*). In the remaining list, they looked for clusters of synonyms, such as *affectionate, warm,* and *loving,* and kept only one of these terms. When they found opposites, such as *honest* and *dishonest,* they also kept just one of the terms. (*Honesty* and *dishonesty* are different degrees of a single trait, not two separate traits.) After eliminating synonyms and antonyms, Raymond Cattell (1965) narrowed the original list down to 35 traits.

The "Big Five" Personality Traits

Although some of the 35 personality traits that Cattell identified are not exactly synonyms or antonyms of one another, many of them overlapped enough to suggest that they were not independent traits. Furthermore, for practical purposes, psychologists usually prefer to deal with a smaller number. Remember the principle of parsimony from Chapter 2: If we can explain most aspects of personality with, say, 5 or 10 traits, we do not need to measure 35 or more.

To determine which traits correlate with one another, psychologists use a method called *factor analysis.* For example, if measurements of *warmth, gregariousness,* and *assertiveness* correlate strongly with one another, we can group them together into a single trait. But if this combined trait does not correlate highly with *self-discipline,* then we should distinguish *self-discipline* as a separate trait.

Using this approach, many researchers have found that they can describe most of the variance in human personality with what they call the **big five personality traits:** *neuroticism, extraversion, agreeableness, conscientiousness, and openness to new experience* (McCrae & Costa, 1987). These five factors offer a powerful description of personality

The Japanese artist Morimura Yasumasa reconstructs famous paintings, substituting his own face. Some people love his work; others dislike it or object to the whole idea. People high in "openness to experience" delight in new, unusual forms of art, literature, and music.

because each pertains to behavior in a wide variety of situations and because each of them correlates only weakly with any of the others. The big five dimensions are described below (Costa, McCrae, & Dye, 1991). Note that the first two, neuroticism and extraversion, are the "biggest" of the big five. Even psychologists who are skeptical of the big five model agree that neuroticism and extraversion are powerful traits that influence much of human behavior (Block, 1995).

Neuroticism is *a tendency to experience unpleasant emotions relatively easily.* People who test high in neuroticism are relatively likely to experience anxiety, hostility, depression, self-consciousness, and impulsiveness. The opposite of neuroticism is emotional stability or self-control.

Extraversion is *a tendency to seek stimulation and to enjoy the company of other people.* The opposite of extraversion is introversion. Extraversion is associated with warmth, gregariousness, assertiveness, impulsiveness, and a need for excitement. People high in extraversion enjoy meeting new people and tend to be happy under most circumstances (Francis, Brown, Lester, & Philipchalk, 1998). However, they are also more prone than other people to heavy use of alcohol, on the average (Martsh & Miller, 1997), and to risk taking in general.

Agreeableness is *a tendency to be compassionate toward others and not antagonistic.* It implies a concern for the welfare of other people, closely related to Adler's concept of social interest. People high in agreeableness generally trust other people and expect other people to trust them.

Conscientiousness is *a tendency to show self-discipline, to be dutiful, and to strive for achievement and competence.* Research has shown that people high in conscientiousness tend to be good workers on almost any job (Barrick & Mount, 1991). They are likely to complete whatever task they say they will perform.

Openness to experience, an uncommon trait in many populations, is *a tendency to enjoy new intellectual experiences and new ideas.* Someone high in this trait would be likely to enjoy modern art, unusual music, thought-provoking films and plays and would enjoy meeting different kinds of people and exploring new ideas and opinions (McCrae, 1996).

CONCEPT CHECK

6. Some psychologists suggest that we should divide extraversion into two traits—which they call *ambition* and *sociability*—changing the big five into the big six. How should psychologists determine whether to do so? (Check your answer on page 502.)

Pros and Cons of the Big Five Description

To demonstrate that the "big five" traits provide a useful description for human personality, researchers must demonstrate that these five traits are nearly independent of one another and that they account for a major portion of the personality variation in many population samples, including both sexes, a wide range of ages, and a variety of cultures. For the most part, researchers have tested this hypothesis by repeating their original procedure on new samples of people. That is, they administer a questionnaire containing many personality descriptions (e.g., *friendly, competitive, shy,* and so forth) and ask people to rate themselves or other people on each description. Then, the psychologists conduct a factor analysis to determine which descriptions correlate with one another.

Support for the Big Five Description   Many studies using this approach have concluded that the five-factor description is satisfactory for characterizing personality in both men and women, and that (in translation) the description also works in a variety of languages and cultures (McCrae & Costa, 1997). Certain differences do occur among cultures, however. For example, the research sometimes finds that one or another of the personality traits, such as openness, does not show enough individual variation to be

useful in some cultures (John, 1990). Also, some studies have found five personality traits to be useful—but five somewhat *different* traits from the more-established big five (Ormerod, McKenzie, & Woods, 1995). Psychologists need to make a judgment about whether these discrepancies create a serious problem, but most have concluded that the five-factor model works "well enough" across cultures.

How consistent does personality remain with age, as described by the five traits? As a rule, personalities seldom change drastically during adulthood (Costa & McCrae, 1994). We do find a few trends in personality as people grow older. Generally, between ages 20 and 30, most people decline in the "thrill-seeking" aspect of extraversion (McCrae & Costa, 1994). Over the entire course of adulthood, most people show a slight increase in agreeableness and conscientiousness and a moderate decrease in neuroticism, extraversion, and openness. The decrease in openness relates to the common observation that young adults are much more likely than older adults to enjoy new types of music and to try new kinds of foods, new styles of clothing, and so forth (Sapolsky, 1998). (Who listens more to new popular music—you or your parents? Who listens more to the "oldies" radio station?)

In some cases, people make a deliberate effort to change some aspect of their personality—to overcome an addiction or to decrease their neuroticism. Although changes can and do occur, they are almost always slow and difficult (DiClemente, 1994). In short, the personality of a young adult is likely to mature with age, but it is not likely to change drastically.

Criticisms of the Big Five Description   In spite of the apparent success of the big five personality traits, several prominent psychologists caution against its wholehearted acceptance.

First problem: Nearly all of the data so far depend on written responses to questionnaires. Maybe what people say on questionnaires captures all the important dimensions of their personalities, but maybe it doesn't.

Second problem: The five-factor structure is theoretically unsatisfying. We have neither a psychological nor a biological explanation for why humans should have five main personality traits instead of another number, or why, if there *are* five, they should be these particular five (Block, 1995; Eysenck, 1992; Zuckerman, 1992).

Third problem: Choosing precisely five traits is arbitrary. Remember that Raymond Cattell initially identified 35 traits; factor analysis suggests that we can combine those 35 into 5 because various groups of the 35 traits correlate highly with one another. Still, the groups do not correlate perfectly. Some psychologists believe that we could describe personality more adequately with 7 or 8 traits (Block, 1995; Cloninger, 1994), or even with Cattell's original 35. Still other psychologists, noting a positive correlation between extraversion and openness and a negative correlation between neuroticism and conscientiousness, believe we could get by with 3 factors instead of 5 (Eysenck, 1992).

Overall, how should we evaluate the five-factor description? The answer depends on our purposes. If we are interested in a good, practical way to describe a great deal of the variation in human personality while using only a few terms, the five-factor description works well. However, if we are interested in a theoretical understanding of personality, it is an overstatement to call the five-factor description a fact of nature (as some have done).

The Origins of Personality

A description of personality differences is not an explanation. The question is: What makes some people more extraverted, neurotic, agreeable, conscientious, or open than other people are?

The two major categories of influence are heredity and environment. To measure these influences, researchers have relied mostly on two kinds of data. First, they compare the similarities between monozygotic (identical) twins and dizygotic (fraternal) twins. As Figure 13.18 shows, five studies conducted in separate locations indicated much greater similarities in extraversion between monozygotic pairs than between dizygotic pairs (Loehlin, 1992). However, such results are not easy to interpret. Some dizygotic twins make

a special effort to highlight their distinctiveness, and their parents also encourage them to be different from each other. Therefore, twin studies probably overstate the role of heredity in personality (Saudino, 1997).

Second, researchers compare the personalities of parents, their biological children, and their adopted children. As Figure 13.19 shows, parents' levels of extraversion correlate moderately with those of their biological children and hardly at all with those of their adopted children. Similarly, biologically related brothers or sisters growing up together resemble each other moderately; unrelated children adopted into the same family do not develop similar personalities (Loehlin, 1992). The results shown in Figures 13.18 and 13.19 pertain to extraversion; similar studies provide a largely similar pattern for neuroticism and other personality traits (Heath, Neale, Kessler, Eaves, & Kendler, 1992; Loehlin, 1992; Viken, Rose, Kaprio, & Koskenvuo, 1994).

Overall, these results indicate a moderate influence of hereditary factors, although no one knows exactly how they contribute. One possibility is that genetically determined differences in neurotransmitter receptors influence how strongly people respond to new stimuli, thereby predisposing some people to be more sensation-seeking or extraverted than others (Benjamin et al., 1996; Blum, Cull, Braverman, & Comings, 1996; Ebstein et al., 1996). However, we need

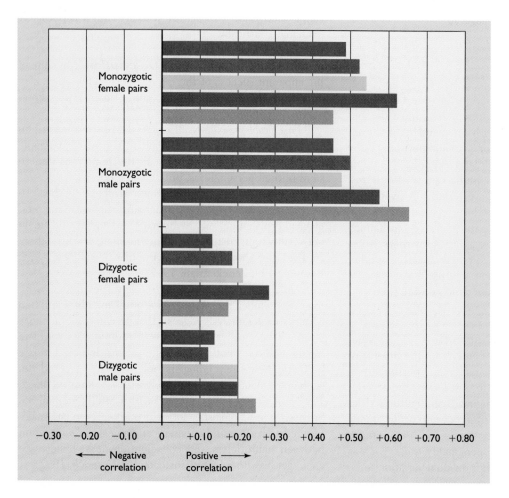

FIGURE 13.18 Five studies—conducted in Great Britain, the United States, Sweden, Australia, and Finland—found larger correlations between the extraversion levels of monozygotic (MZ) twins than those of dizygotic (DZ) twins. (Based on data summarized by Loehlin, 1992.)

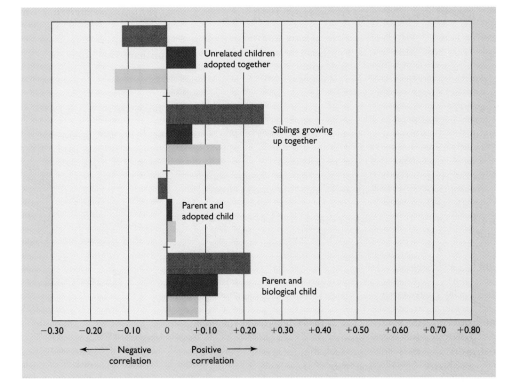

FIGURE 13.19 Three studies—from Britain, Minnesota, and Texas—measured extraversion in members of hundreds of families. Each found moderate positive correlations between parents and their biological children and between pairs of biologically related brothers and sisters. However, all found low or even negative correlations between parents and adopted children or between adopted children living in the same family. (Based on data summarized by Loehlin, 1992.)

far more research to explore this and other possible links between genes and behavior.

The nongenetic contributors are even less understood. Even children who grow up with their biological parents resemble their parents in personality only to a moderate degree (Bratko & Marušić, 1997), and the personality correlations between adopted children and adoptive parents are even lower, sometimes even zero or negative. Evidently, children learn rather little of their personality by imitating their parents. Many researchers believe that much of the variation among people's personalities relates to the **unshared environment,** *the aspects of environment that differ from one individual to another, even within a family.* Unshared environment is, because of its idiosyncratic nature, very difficult to investigate. To some extent, unshared environment actually reflects genetic influences: People with various predispositions choose different activities and thereby create individual environments for themselves (Saudino, 1997).

THE MESSAGE
The Challenges of Classifying Personality

Just as rocks are the same in some ways and different in others, personalities are the same in some regards and different in others. We find it useful to categorize personalities along a few dimensions, just as we find it useful to talk about different types of rocks.

In some ways, however, the analogy between classifying rocks and classifying personalities breaks down. The

problem is not just that every individual personality is different from every other; after all, every piece of granite is a little different from every other piece, too. Rather, the problem is that human personalities change from one situation to another far more than the properties of rocks do. As well as you know your closest friends and relatives, aren't you still sometimes surprised by how one of them acts in a new situation? Aren't you sometimes surprised even at your own behavior? The complexities of human personality make this area of research particularly challenging.

SUMMARY

✸ *Nomothetic and idiographic laws.* Psychologists seek both nomothetic laws, which apply to all people, and idiographic laws, which apply to individual differences. (page 497)

✸ *Traits and states.* Traits are personality characteristics that persist over time; states are temporary changes in behavior in response to particular situations. (page 497)

✸ *Five major traits.* Psychologists seek a short list of traits that describes as much of behavior as possible. Much can be explained by these five traits: neuroticism, extraversion, openness to new experience, agreeableness, and conscientiousness. (page 498)

✸ *Determinants of personality.* Studies of twins and adopted children indicate that heredity contributes to part of the observed differences in personality. Family environment evidently contributes rather little. Much of the variation in personality may be due to unshared environment, the special experiences that vary from one person to another even within a family. (page 500)

Suggestion for Further Reading

Pervin, L. A. (1990). *Handbook of personality.* New York: Guilford Press. Contains summaries of theory and research on a wide variety of topics related to personality.

Terms

nomothetic approach   an approach to the study of individual differences that seeks general laws about how an aspect of personality affects behavior (page 497)

idiographic approach   an approach to the study of personality differences that concentrates on intensive studies of individuals (page 497)

trait   a consistent, long-lasting tendency in behavior (page 497)

state   a temporary activation of a particular behavior (page 497)

big five personality traits   five traits that account for a great deal of human personality differences: neuroticism, extraversion, agreeableness, conscientiousness, and openness to new experience (page 498)

neuroticism   the tendency to experience unpleasant emotions relatively easily (page 498)

extraversion   the tendency to seek stimulation and to enjoy the company of other people (page 498)

agreeableness   the tendency to be compassionate toward others and not antagonistic (page 499)

conscientiousness   the tendency to show self-discipline, to be dutiful, and to strive for achievement and competence (page 499)

openness to experience   the tendency to enjoy new intellectual experiences, the arts, fantasies, and anything that exposes a person to new ideas (page 499)

unshared environment   the aspects of environment that differ from one individual to another, even within a family (page 501)

Answers to Concept Checks

5.   This nervousness is state anxiety, because it is evoked by a particular situation. Trait anxiety is a strong tendency to become nervous in many situations. (page 498)

6.   They should determine whether measures of ambition correlate strongly with measures of sociability. If they do, then ambition and sociability can be considered two aspects of a single trait, extraversion. If they do not correlate strongly, then they are indeed separate personality traits. (page 499)

Web Resources

Personality Traits And Heart Disease Risk
www.pslgroup.com/dg/358ae.htm
This is a news report of a study that found that personality traits can increase or decrease the risk of heart attack. The trait that increases the risk, and who it affects most, may surprise you.

Personality Measures and the Big 5
fas.psych.nwu.edu/perproj/theory/big5.table.html
The different terms used by 16 different personality theorists to describe dimensions of personality are organized into five broad dimensions in this tabular comparison.

Personality Assessment

How can we measure personality?

How can we use measurements of personality?

A new P. T. Barnum Psychology Clinic has just opened at your local shopping mall and is offering a Grand Opening Special on personality tests. You have always wanted to know more about yourself, so you sign up. Here is Barnum's true-false test:

Questionnaire for Universal Assessment of Zealous Youth (QUAZY)

1. I have never met a cannibal I didn't like.   T   F
2. Robbery is the only major felony I have ever committed.   T   F
3. I eat "funny mushrooms" less frequently than I used to.   T   F
4. I don't care what people say about my nose-picking habit.   T   F
5. Sex with vegetables no longer disgusts me.   T   F
6. This time I am quitting glue-sniffing for good.   T   F
7. I generally lie on questions like this one.   T   F
8. I spent much of my childhood sucking on telephone cords.   T   F
9. I find it impossible to sleep if I think my bed might be clean.   T   F
10. Naked bus drivers make me nervous.   T   F
11. Some of my friends don't know what a rotten person I am.   T   F
12. I usually find laxatives unsatisfying.   T   F
13. I spend my spare time playing strip solitaire.   T   F

You turn in your answers. A few minutes later, a computer prints out your individual personality profile:

> You have a need for other people to like and admire you, and yet you tend to be critical of yourself. While you have some

personality weaknesses, you are generally able to compensate for them. You have considerable unused capacity that you have not turned to your advantage. Disciplined and self-controlled on the outside, you tend to be worrisome and insecure on the inside. At times, you have serious doubts as to whether you have made the right decision or done the right thing. You prefer a certain amount of change and variety and become dissatisfied when hemmed in by restrictions and limitations. You also pride yourself as an independent thinker and do not accept others' statements without satisfactory proof. But you have found it unwise to be too frank in revealing yourself to others. At times you are extraverted, affable, and sociable, while at other times you are introverted, wary, and reserved. Some of your aspirations tend to be rather unrealistic. (Forer, 1949, p. 120)

Do you agree with this assessment?

Several experiments have been conducted along these lines with psychology classes (Forer, 1949; Marks & Kammann, 1980; Ulrich, Stachnik, & Stainton, 1963). Students started by filling out a questionnaire—one that looked fairly reasonable, not something as preposterous as the QUAZY. Several days later, each student received a sealed envelope with his or her name on it. Inside was a "personality profile," supposedly based on the student's answers to the questionnaire. The students were asked, "How accurately does this profile describe you?" About 90% rated it as good or excellent. Some expressed amazement at its accuracy: "I didn't realize until now that psychology was an exact science." None of them realized that everyone had received exactly the same personality profile—the same one you just read.

The students accepted this personality profile partly because it vaguely describes almost everyone, much like newspaper horoscopes do, and partly because people tend to accept almost *any* statement that an "expert" makes about them. Richard Kammann repeated this experiment but substituted a strange, unflattering personality profile that included statements like "your boundless energy is a little wearisome to your friends" and "you seem to find it impossible to work out a satisfactory adjustment to your problems."

People tend to accept almost any personality assessment that someone offers them, especially if it is stated in vague, general terms that each person can interpret to fit himself or herself. To determine the accuracy of a personality test, we need objective information, not just self-reports by satisfied customers.

More than 20% of the students rated this unlikely assortment of statements a "good to excellent" description of their own personality (Marks & Kammann, 1980).

The moral of the story is this: Psychological testing is tricky. If we want to know whether a particular test measures a particular person's personality, we cannot simply ask whether that person thinks it does. Even if a test is totally worthless, many people will describe its results as a "highly accurate" description of themselves. To devise a psychological test that not only *appears* to work but also actually *does* work, we need to follow some elaborate procedures to design the test carefully and to determine its reliability and validity.

Standardized Personality Tests

Psychologists have devised a great variety of personality tests; they add new ones every year. A **standardized test** is *one that is administered according to specified rules and whose scores are interpreted in a prescribed fashion.* One important step for standardizing a test is to determine the distribution of scores for a large number of people. We need to know the mean score and the range of scores for people in general and the mean and the range for various special populations, such as severely depressed people. Given such information, we can determine whether a given individual's score on the test is within the normal range or whether it is more typical of people with a particular disorder.

Most of the tests published in popular magazines have never been standardized. A magazine may herald an article: "Test Yourself: How Good Is Your Marriage?" or "Test Yourself: How Well Do You Control the Stress in Your Life?" After you take the test and compare your answers to the scoring key, the article may tell you that "if your score is greater than 80, you are doing very well . . . if it is below 20, you need to work on improving yourself!"—or some such nonsense. Unless the magazine states otherwise, you can safely assume that the author pulled the scoring norms out of thin air and never even bothered to make sure that the test items were clear and unambiguous.

Over the years, psychologists have developed an enormous variety of tests to measure both normal and abnormal personality. A great deal of research focused on trying to standardize their interpretation and measure their reliability and validity. We shall examine a few prominent examples and explore some creative possibilities for future personality measurement.

Objective Tests of Personality

Some of the most widely used personality tests are based on simple pencil-and-paper responses. We shall consider one of them—the MMPI—in some detail because it is the most widely used of all personality tests (Piotrowski & Keller, 1989). We shall then examine the 16-PF more briefly.

The Minnesota Multiphasic Personality Inventory

The **Minnesota Multiphasic Personality Inventory** (mercifully abbreviated **MMPI**) consists of *a series of true-false questions intended to measure certain personality dimensions and clinical conditions such as depression.* The original MMPI, developed in the 1940s and still in use, has 550 items; *the second edition,* **MMPI-2,** published in 1990, has 567. Typical items are "my mother never loved me" and "I think I would like the work of a pharmacist." (The items I mention in this text are rewordings of the actual items.)

The original MMPI was devised *empirically*—that is, by trial and error (Hathaway & McKinley, 1940). The authors developed hundreds of true-false questions that they thought might be useful for identifying personality dimensions. They put these questions to people who were known to be suffering from depression, paranoia, and other psychological disorders and to a group of hospital visitors, who were assumed to be psychologically normal. The researchers selected those items that most of the people in a given clinical group answered differently from most of the normal people. Their assumption was that, if you answer many questions just as depressed people usually answer them, you are probably depressed too. The MMPI had 10 scales—for reporting a depression score, a paranoia score, a schizophrenia score, and others. Later, other researchers found that they could use MMPI items to measure other dimensions of personality as well (Helmes & Reddon, 1993).

The result was a test that worked, and still works, moderately well in practice. For example, most people with scores above a certain level on the depression scale are in fact depressed. Some of the items on the MMPI made sense theoretically; some did not. For example, some items on the depression scale asked about feelings of helplessness or worthlessness, which are an important part of depression. But two other items were "I attend religious services frequently" and "occasionally I tease animals." If you answered *false* to either of those items, you would get one point on the depression scale! These items were included simply because more depressed people than nondepressed people answered *false* to these items. Why they did is not obvious. (Perhaps depressed people do not tease animals just because they do hardly anything just for fun.)

Revisions of the Test

The MMPI was standardized in the 1940s. As time passed, the meaning of certain items, or at least of certain answers, changed. For example, how would you respond to the following item?

I believe I am important.   T   F

In the 1940s, fewer than 10% of all people marked this item *true*. At the time, the word "important" meant about the same thing as "famous," and people who called themselves important were thought to have an inflated view of themselves. Today, we are more likely to say that every person is important.

What about this item?

I like to play drop the handkerchief.   T   F

Drop the handkerchief, a game similar to tag, dropped out of popularity in the 1950s. Most people born since then have never even heard of the game, much less played it.

To bring the MMPI up to date, a group of psychologists rephrased some of the items, eliminated some, and added new ones to deal with drug abuse, suicidal ideas, Type A personality, and other issues that did not concern psychologists in the 1940s (Butcher, Graham, Williams, & Ben-Porath, 1990). Then, they tried out the new MMPI-2 on 2,600 people selected to resemble the current mix of age, sex, race, and education in the United States. In other words, the psychologists restandardized the test. (Any test must be restandardized from time to time. You may recall from the discussion of IQ tests in Chapter 9 that certain items once considered difficult are now considered relatively easy.) These psychologists also developed a new form, the MMPI-A, intended for use with adolescents.

The MMPI-2 has 10 clinical scales, as shown in Table 13.4. The various scales have 32 to 78 items each, scattered throughout the test, rather than clustered. Most people get at least a few points on each scale; a score above a certain level indicates a probable difficulty. Figure 13.20 shows how MMPI-2 scores are plotted.

The Generalizability of the MMPI

Your personality is such an integral part of who you are. Is it really possible for one test to measure personality for all kinds of people? In particular, is the MMPI (or MMPI-2 or MMPI-A) a fair measure of personality for people of different ethnic and cultural backgrounds?

This is a difficult question to answer. In general, the means and ranges on each scale are about the same for many ethnic groups (Negy, Leal-Puente, Trainor, & Carlson, 1997). A few small differences in scores do occur, but they could reflect either real differences in personality or differences in interpreting what certain questions mean. Consequently, psychologists use the same norms for all groups, but they are slightly more cautious about interpreting the scores of racial minorities, especially those people who are most impoverished and least educated (Gynther, 1989).

Detection of Deception on the MMPI and Elsewhere

Suppose you were taking the MMPI or another personality test and you wanted to make yourself look mentally healthier than you really are. Could you lie on the test? Yes. Could anyone catch you in your lies? Probably.

The designers of the MMPI and the MMPI-2 included in their test certain items designed to identify people who consistently lie (Woychyshyn, McElheran, & Romney, 1992). For example, consider the items "I like every person I have ever met" and "occasionally I get angry at someone." If you answer *true* to the first question and *false* to the second, you are either a saint or a liar. The test authors, convinced that there are more liars than saints, would give you one point for each of these answers on a special "lie scale." If you get too many points on the lie scale, a psychologist will distrust your answers to the other items. Strangely enough, some people lie on the test to try to make themselves look bad. The test has some special items to detect that kind of faking also.

A similar method is used to detect deception on other types of tests. For example, many employers ask job applicants to fill out a questionnaire that asks them how much experience they have had with certain job-related skills.

TABLE 13.4 The Ten MMPI-2 Clinical Scales	
SCALE	TYPICAL ITEM
Hypochondria (Hs)	I have chest pains several times a week. (T)
Depression (D)	I am glad that I am alive. (F)
Hysteria (Hy)	My heart frequently pounds so hard I can hear it. (T)
Psychopathic deviation (Pd)	I get a fair deal from most people. (F)
Masculinity-femininity (Mf)	I like to arrange flowers. (T = female)
Paranoia (Pa)	There are evil people trying to influence my mind. (T)
Psychasthenia (obsessive-compulsive) (Pt)	I save nearly everything I buy, even after I have no use for it. (T)
Schizophrenia (Sc)	I see, hear, and smell things that no one else knows about. (T)
Hypomania (Ma)	When things are dull I try to get some excitement started. (T)
Social introversion (Si)	I have the time of my life at parties. (F)

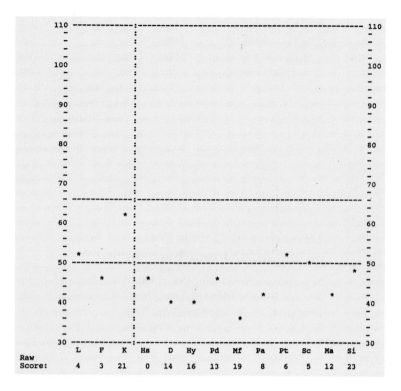

Raw Score:	L	F	K	Hs	D	Hy	Pd	Mf	Pa	Pt	Sc	Ma	Si
	4	3	21	0	14	16	13	19	8	6	5	12	23

F I G U R E 13.20 For the MMPI-2's 10 clinical scales, a score is plotted to profile an individual, as shown here. This is the profile of a middle-aged man with no psychological problems. A person with a disorder such as hypochondria or paranoia would have scores in the range of 65 or higher on the hypochondria or paranoia scales. (Source: Minnesota Multiphasic Personality Inventory-2, © by the Regents of the University of Minnesota. Data courtesy of R. J. Huber.)

What is to prevent eager applicants from exaggerating or even lying about their experience? To find out whether applicants are lying, some employers include among the authentic items a few bogus items referring to nonexistent tasks, as shown in Table 13.5.

According to the results of one study, almost half of all job applicants claimed to have experience with one or more nonexistent tasks (Anderson, Warner, & Spencer, 1984). Moreover, applicants who claimed a great deal of experience with nonexistent tasks also overstated their abilities on real tasks. An employer can use answers on bogus items as a correction factor. The more skill an applicant claims to have on a nonexistent task, the more the employer will discount that applicant's claims of skill on real tasks.

SOMETHING TO THINK ABOUT

Could you use this strategy in other situations? Suppose a political candidate promises to increase aid to college students. You are skeptical. How could you use the candidate's statements on other issues to help you decide whether to believe this promise? ✳

Uses of the MMPI

The MMPI is useful to psychologists who want to measure personality for research purposes. It is also useful to clinical psychologists who want to learn something about a client before beginning therapy or who want an independent measure of how much a client's personality has changed during the course of therapy (McReynolds, 1985).

How informative are the results to the client who actually takes the MMPI test? In some cases, the results point out a problem to which the person had paid little attention. In other cases, however, the results do little more than restate the obvious. For example, suppose you gave the following answers:

I doubt that I will ever be successful.	True
I am glad that I am alive.	False
I have thoughts about suicide.	True
I am helpless to control the important events in my life.	True

A psychologist analyzes your answer sheet and tells you, "Your results show indications of depression." Yes, of course; you already knew that. But even in a case like this, the results can be useful—not just for telling you that you are depressed (which you already knew), but for measuring *how* depressed you are at this moment (a basis for comparison of future results).

The 16-PF Test

The **16-PF Test** is another widely used standardized personality test. The term "PF" stands for personality factors. The test *measures 16 factors, or traits, of personality.* Unlike the MMPI, which was intended primarily to identify abnormal personalities, the 16-PF Test was devised to assess various aspects of normal personality. Raymond Cattell (1965) used factor analysis to identify the traits that contribute most significantly to personality. As we saw earlier in this chapter, other psychologists used factor analysis to identify 5 major traits; Cattell found 35 and then narrowed them

TABLE 13.5 Part of an Employment Application Designed to Determine Whether Applicants Are Lying About Their Skills

How much experience have you had at …	None	A Little	Much
Matrixing solvency files?	☐	☐	☐
Typing from audio-Fortran reports?	☐	☐	☐
Determining myopic weights for periodic tables?	☐	☐	☐
Resolving disputes by isometric analysis?	☐	☐	☐
Stocking solubility product constants?	☐	☐	☐
Planning basic entropy programs?	☐	☐	☐
Operating a matriculation machine?	☐	☐	☐

to 16. He then devised a test to measure each of those traits. Because of the large number of factors, the results of his test apply to a rather wide range of behaviors (Krug, 1978).

When someone takes the 16-PF Test, the results are printed out as a **personality profile,** *a representation of that person's relative status on each dimension,* as Figure 13.21 shows. By examining such a profile, a psychologist can determine the person's dominant personality traits.

Although the 16-PF Test was originally designed to assess normal personality, it does enable clinicians to identify various abnormalities, such as schizophrenia, depression, and alcoholism. Each disorder is associated with a characteristic personality profile (Figure 13.22). As with any test, this test should be used cautiously, especially with people

from different cultural backgrounds. Psychologists have translated this test into other languages, but something is often lost in translation. One study found that Mexican-Americans taking the 16-PF in Spanish had substantially different personality profiles than did Mexican-Americans taking supposedly the same test in English (Whitworth & Perry, 1990).

Projective Techniques

The MMPI, the 16-PF, and similar personality tests are easy to score and easy to handle statistically, but they restrict how a person can respond to a question. To find out

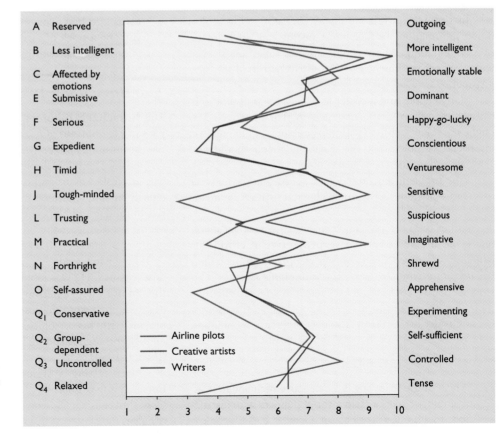

FIGURE 13.21 Personality profiles on the 16-PF Test for airline pilots, creative artists, and writers. A personality profile shows whether people are high or low on a given trait. In this sample, writers were the most imaginative group. (Adapted from *Handbook for the Sixteen Personality Factors,* copyright 1970 by the Institute for Personality and Ability Testing, Inc. Reproduced by permission of the copyright owners.)

A Reserved — Outgoing
B Less intelligent — More intelligent
C Affected by emotions — Emotionally stable
E Submissive — Dominant
F Serious — Happy-go-lucky
G Expedient — Conscientious
H Timid — Venturesome
J Tough-minded — Sensitive
L Trusting — Suspicious
M Practical — Imaginative
N Forthright — Shrewd
O Self-assured — Apprehensive
Q₁ Conservative — Experimenting
Q₂ Group-dependent — Self-sufficient
Q₃ Uncontrolled — Controlled
Q₄ Relaxed — Tense

—— Airline pilots
—— Creative artists
—— Writers

1 2 3 4 5 6 7 8 9 10

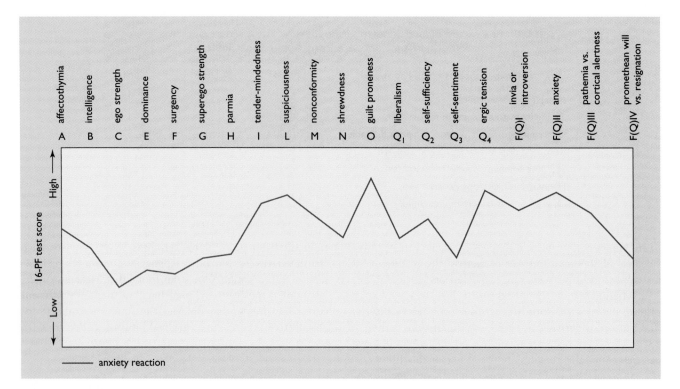

FIGURE 13.22 This personality profile, based on the 16-PF Test, shows that this person is high in guilt and low in "ego strength." Cattell made up his own words for familiar concepts so that he could provide a precise definition that would not be confused with the everyday and vague meaning of a term such as *depression*. For example, *surgency* means something similar to cheerfulness and sociability. *Parmia* describes adventurousness or boldness. (From Cattell, 1965).

more, psychologists must ask open-ended questions that permit an unlimited range of responses.

To simply say "tell me about yourself" rarely evokes much information. In fact, most people find such invitations threatening. Many people are not fully honest even with themselves, much less with a psychologist they have just met.

Many people find it easier to discuss their problems in the abstract than in the first person. For instance, they might say, "I have a friend with this problem. Let me tell you my friend's problem and ask what my friend should do." They then describe their own problem. They are "projecting" their problem onto someone else, in Freud's sense of the word—attributing their own characteristics to someone else.

Rather than discouraging projection, psychologists often make use of it. They use **projective techniques,** which are *designed to encourage people to project their personality characteristics onto ambiguous stimuli.* This strategy helps people to reveal themselves more fully than they normally would to a stranger, or even to themselves. Let's consider two of the best-known projective techniques.

CONCEPT CHECK

7. Which of the following is a projective technique? **a.** A psychologist gives a child a set of puppets with instructions to act out a story about a family. **b.** A psycholo-

gist hands you a stack of cards, each containing one word, such as *tolerant,* with instructions to sort the cards into two piles—a stack of cards that apply to you and a stack of cards that do not apply to you. (Check your answer on page 513.)

The Rorschach Inkblots

The **Rorschach Inkblots,** *a projective test based on people's interpretations of ten ambiguous inkblots,* is probably the most famous projective technique of personality. It was created by Hermann Rorschach, a Swiss psychiatrist, who was interested in art and the occult. He read a book of poems by Justinus Kerner, a mystic writer, who had made a series of random inkblots and had then written a poem about each one. Kerner believed that anything that happens at random reveals the influence of occult, supernatural forces.

Rorschach made his own inkblots but put them to a different use. He was familiar with a word-association test then in use where a person was given a word and was asked to say the first word that came to mind. Combining this approach with his inkblots, Rorschach showed people an inkblot and then asked them to say whatever came to mind (Pichot, 1984).

After testing a series of inkblots on his patients, Rorschach was impressed that their interpretations of the blots differed from his own. In a book published in 1921 (English translation 1942) he presented the 10 inkblots that still constitute the Rorschach Inkblot Technique. (Originally, he had worked with a larger number, but the publisher insisted on cutting the number to 10 to save printing costs.) As other psychiatrists and psychologists began using these blots, they gradually developed the Rorschach into the projective technique we know today.

Administering the Rorschach　The Rorschach Inkblot Technique consists of 10 cards similar to the one in Figure 13.23. Five are black and white; five are in color. A psychologist administering this procedure hands you a card and asks, "What might this be?" The instructions are intentionally vague. The assumption is that everything you do in an ill-defined situation will reveal something significant about your personality to the psychologist—so, the more poorly defined the situation, the better. The psychologist may keep a record of almost everything you do, including what you say you see, where and how you hold the cards, the length of any pauses between your responses, and so forth.

Sometimes people's answers reveal much, either immediately or in response to a psychologist's probes. Here is an example (Aronow, Reznikoff, & Moreland, 1995):

(Card 5). **Client:**　Some kind of insect; it's not pretty enough to be a butterfly.
Psychologist:　Any association to that?
Client:　It's an ugly black butterfly, no colors.
Psychologist:　What does that make you think of in your own life?
Client:　You probably want me to say "myself." Well, that's probably how I thought of myself when I was younger—I never thought of myself as attractive—my sister was the attractive one. I was the ugly duckling— I did get more attractive as I got older.

CONCEPT CHECK

8.　Why would it be impossible to receive a copy of the Rorschach Inkblot Test by mail, fill it out, and mail it back to a psychologist to evaluate your answers? (Check your answer on page 513.)

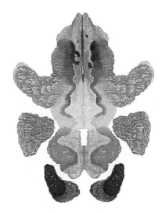

FIGURE 13.23　In the Rorschach Inkblot Test, people look at a pattern similar to this one and say what it looks like to them. The underlying theory is that, in an ambiguous situation, anything that someone does and says will reveal the individual's personality.

Evaluation of the Rorschach　Granted that people's answers on the Rorschach often contain a wealth of personal information, the key issue is whether psychologists can accurately interpret that information. In the 1950s and 1960s, certain psychologists made exaggerated claims, even calling the Rorschach "an X ray of the mind." Those claims provoked equally enthusiastic criticism. The trouble is partly that the Rorschach provides unstructured answers that must be interpreted by a psychologist who, in many cases, has preconceived notions about the client's problems.

For example, one depressed man replied as follows to one blot: "It looks like a bat that has been squashed on the pavement under the heel of a giant's boot" (Dawes, 1994, p. 149). Psychologist Robyn Dawes initially thought that this response illustrated the great power of the Rorschach: The client was expressing a sense of being overwhelmed and crushed by powers beyond his control. However, after further contemplation, Dawes realized that he had already known the client was depressed, so he interpreted the response accordingly. If a client with a history of violence had made the same response, the therapist would have focused on the aggressive nature of the giant's foot stomp. If the client had been prone to hallucinations or to paranoia, the psychologist would have made still other interpretations. That is, Rorschach interpretations depend on the psychologist's expectations at least as much as they do on what the client actually says. (Recall the need for double-blind procedures, as discussed in Chapter 2.)

A person's responses to the Rorschach can be used in either of two ways, as a projective technique or as an objectively scored test. The more traditional method of using it as a projective technique focuses on the content, such as themes of violence or depression. Used in this manner, the Rorschach faces the problem just described: The interpretations depend heavily on the therapist's expectations. Nevertheless, defenders of the technique reply that they use it only as a way of starting a conversation and getting clients to talk more freely about topics they might be reluctant to discuss (Aronow, Reznikoff, & Moreland, 1995). Used in that way, the Rorschach is beyond criticism, but its limitations are clear.

When the Rorschach is used as an objectively scored test, a psychologist counts particular kinds of responses and compares the results to the norms for the population. The use of standards developed by James Exner (1986) has greatly improved psychologists' ability to agree on their interpretation of a person's responses to the Rorschach. Thus, the test is now more reliable than it once was. Recall from Chapter 9, however, the difference between reliability and validity. Although interpretations of Rorschach responses are now reasonably reliable (repeatable), their validity is less certain.

Researchers have reported reasonably good results when using Rorschach responses to predict how well a client will respond in psychotherapy (Meyer & Handler,

1997). The test is also reasonably valid for identifying schizophrenia and for determining that someone has a psychological problem, without necessarily identifying the problem (Vincent & Harman, 1991). However, critics charge that, what the Rorschach does tell us, we could learn more easily or with greater certainty by other means (Wood, Nezworski, & Stejskal, 1996). In short, the Rorschach can be useful as a conversation starter and maybe as a supplement to other means of assessment, but it should not be the sole basis for making a confident judgment about someone. Many psychologists have serious qualms when their colleagues use Rorschach results to recommend that someone be committed to a mental hospital, or to recommend for or against a prisoner's parole (Dawes, 1994).

The Thematic Apperception Test

The **Thematic Apperception Test (TAT)** consists of pictures like the one shown in Figure 13.24. *The subject is asked to make up a story for each picture, describing what is happening, what events led up to the scene, and what will happen in the future.* The test was devised by Christiana Morgan and Henry Murray as a means of measuring people's needs; it was revised and published by Murray (1943) and later revised by others. There are 31 pictures in all; no more than 20 are used with a given individual. Some pictures are used just for men, women, boys, or girls, and some are used for anyone. The pictures are all somewhat ambiguous but, except for one (which is blank!), they provide a better-defined stimulus than does the Rorschach.

People who take the TAT are expected to identify with the people shown in the pictures. For this reason, men are given pictures showing mostly men, and women are given pictures showing mostly women. People usually tell stories that relate to recent events and concerns in their own lives, possibly including concerns that they would be reluctant to talk about openly.

For example, one young man told the following story about a picture of a man clinging to a rope:

> This man is escaping. Several months ago he was beat up and shanghaied and taken aboard ship. Since then, he has been mistreated and unhappy and has been looking for a way to escape. Now the ship is anchored near a tropical island and he is climbing down a rope to the water. He will get away successfully and swim to shore. When he gets there, he will be met by a group of beautiful native women with whom he will live the rest of his life in luxury and never tell anyone what happened. Sometimes he will feel that he should go back to his old life; but he will never do it. (Kimble & Garmezy, 1968, pp. 582–583)

This young man had entered divinity school, mainly to please his parents, but was quite unhappy there. He was wrestling with a secret desire to "escape" to a new life with greater worldly pleasures. In his story, he described someone doing what he really wanted to do but would not openly admit.

The TAT is often used in a clinical setting to induce clients to speak freely about their problems. It is also used for research purposes. As mentioned in Chapter 11, an investigator might measure someone's "need for achievement" by counting all the stories that he or she tells about achievement. The same could be done for aggression, passivity, control of outside events, or dominance. The investigator could then use these findings to study the forces that strengthen or weaken various needs.

When different psychologists examine the same TAT replies, they generally agree, more or less, on their interpretations. Most studies find a correlation of about .85 between different raters' interpretations—known as the *interrater reliability* (Cramer, 1996). When a given individual takes the TAT at two different times, months apart, the test-retest reliability is generally lower, usually less than .5 and sometimes much less than that (Cramer, 1996). That instability may not be a fault of the test, however; the test indicates people's needs and motivations, which do change over time.

Less Successful Projective Techniques

Based on the theory that your personality affects everything you do, some psychologists (and others) have tried analyzing people's handwriting. For example, perhaps people who dot their i's with a dash— *i* —are especially energetic, or perhaps people who draw large loops above the line—as in *allow* —are highly idealistic. Carefully collected data, however, show only random relationships between handwriting and personality (Tett & Palmer, 1997).

Another projective technique is to offer children dolls and invite them to act out a story. The dolls might be chosen, for example, to represent two parents and a child. The idea is that a child who is unable or unwilling to describe physical or sexual abuse might act out a story in which the adults abuse the child. The problem is with the interpretation of the results: Suppose a child acts out sexual contact between two dolls. Should we surmise that an adult has sexually molested the child? Maybe not; the child may have discovered sex play with other children or may have watched late-night cable-television shows. This form of doll

FIGURE 13.24 In the Thematic Apperception Test, people look at a picture such as this one and tell a story about what is going on. Most people include material that relates to current concerns in their lives. Reprinted by permission of the publisher from Henry A. Murray, *Thematic Apperception Test*, Cambridge, Mass.: Harvard University Press, Copyright ©1943 by the President and Fellows of Harvard College, ©1971 by Henry A. Murray.

play tells us nothing for certain about the child's own experiences (Ceci, 1995; Koocher et al., 1995).

Prospects for New Personality Tests

Each of the currently popular personality tests has limitations, but some psychologists are experimenting with creative new techniques. One approach that a few researchers have tried is the *emotional Stroop test.* Recall the Stroop effect from Chapter 8: People are asked to look at a display like this and read the color of the ink instead of reading the words:

Uses and Misuses of Personality Tests

Before any drug company can market a new drug in the United States, the Food and Drug Administration (FDA) requires that it be carefully tested. If the FDA finds the drug safe and effective, it approves the drug for certain purposes, with a warning label that lists precautions, such as an advisory that pregnant women should not take it. After the drug is approved, however, the FDA cannot prevent a physician from prescribing it for an unapproved purpose and cannot keep it out of the hands of people who should not be taking it.

purple brown green blue yellow purple yellow red brown

In the **emotional Stroop test,** *a person examines a list of words, some of which relate to a possible source of worry or concern to the person, and tries to say the color of the ink of each word.* For example, in the display below, say the color of the ink of each word as fast as possible:

Personality tests are a little like drugs: They ought to be used with great caution and only for the purposes for which they have demonstrable usefulness. They are, at a minimum, helpful to psychologists as an interviewing technique, to help "break the ice" and get a good conversation started. Tests can also be useful as an aid in personality assessment by a clini-

cancer venom defeat hospital rattler failure fangs blood loser slither nurses bite jobless cobra inadequate disease

As a rule, people who are known to have an anxiety about snakes have an extra-long delay in reading the color of snake-related words—*venom, rattler, fangs, slither, bite, cobra.* Similarly, people worried about their health have long delays on the disease-related words; people concerned about success and failure have delays on words like *loser* and *jobless.* Therefore, it is possible to measure people's delays in stating the ink color for a variety of words and from these results infer each person's main worries or concerns (Williams, Mathews, & MacLeod, 1996). Researchers are just beginning to explore the potential uses of this method.

CONCEPT CHECK

9. On the preceding sample items of an emotional Stroop test, if you had the greatest delay in naming the ink color for *cancer, hospital, blood, nurses,* and *disease,* what would these results imply about your emotions? (Check your answer on page 513.)

cal psychologist. Note that I said "as an aid," *not* "as a sufficient method of personality assessment." For example, suppose someone has an MMPI personality profile that resembles the profile typical for schizophrenia. Identifying schizophrenia or any other unusual condition is a signal-detection problem, as we discussed in Chapter 4—a problem of reporting a stimulus when it is present without falsely reporting it when it is absent. Suppose (realistically) that people without schizophrenia outnumber people with schizophrenia by 100 to 1. Suppose further that a particular personality profile on the MMPI-2 is characteristic of 95% of people with schizophrenia and only 5% of other people. As Figure 13.25 shows, 5% of the normal population is a *larger* group than 95% of the schizophrenic population. Thus, if we labeled as "schizophrenic" everyone with a high score, we would be wrong more often than right. (Recall the representativeness heuristic and the issue of base-rate information, discussed in Chapter 8: Someone who seems "representative" of people in a rare category does not necessarily belong to that category.) Therefore, a conscientious psychologist will

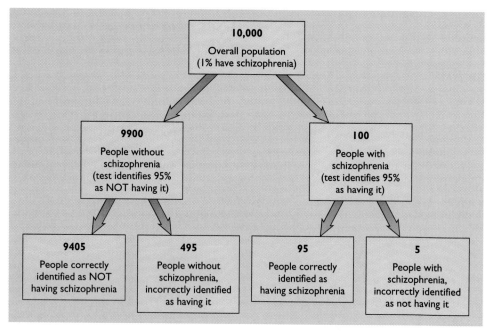

FIGURE 13.25 Even the best personality tests make mistakes. A test to detect an unusual condition will often identify normal people as having the condition. Here, we assume that a certain profile occurs in 95% of people with schizophrenia and 5% of other people. If we relied entirely on this test, we would correctly identify 95 schizophrenic people, but we would also misidentify 495 normal people as schizophrenic.

look for other evidence beyond the test score before drawing a firm conclusion. (The same, of course, should be said of any test, including IQ tests.)

Some employers use personality tests to screen job applicants, selecting only those who have the "right" personality. The underlying idea is correct: What makes a good worker is at least as much a matter of personality as it is intelligence. A good worker is conscientious, cooperative with other workers, calm under pressure, persistent about achieving goals, responsive to the client's needs, and so forth—all personality traits. The difficulty is not that personality is unimportant but that many personality tests do not measure the right factors (Hogan, Hogan, & Roberts, 1996). For example, a personality test that claims to measure an "aggressive" personality may not measure the kind of aggressiveness that is presumably useful in a sales job. For ethical, legal, and practical reasons, employers should use a personality test *only* when they have clear evidence that the results help them to select among job applicants more accurately than they could without the test.

THE MESSAGE
Trying to Measure Personality

As you have been reading about personality tests, you may have objected that no test could adequately describe the factors that make you the unique individual that you are. You are right. Just try to imagine how long it would take to measure everything that is worth knowing about your personality. After all, even family members who have known you all your life are sometimes surprised by what you say and do.

The goals of personality testing are more modest—just to measure a few aspects that are useful for certain pur-

poses. But we need to remember what these purposes are and determine how well (or poorly) various tests can achieve them. Within their proper place tests can be useful; the problems arise when people try to draw strong conclusions from weak data.

SUMMARY

✱ *People's tendency to accept personality test results.* Because most people are inclined to accept almost any interpretation of their personality based on a personality test, tests must be carefully scrutinized to ensure that they are measuring what they claim to measure. (page 503)

✱ *Standardized personality tests.* A standardized test is one that is administered according to explicit rules and whose results are interpreted in a prescribed fashion. Standards are based on the scores of people who have already taken the test. (page 504)

✱ *The MMPI.* The MMPI, a widely used personality test, consists of a series of true-false questions selected in an effort to distinguish among various personality types. The MMPI-2 is a modernization of the version first developed in the 1940s. (page 504)

✱ *Detection of lying.* The MMPI and certain other tests guard against lying by including items on which nearly all honest people will give the same answer. Any other answer is probably a lie. An unusual number of "lying" answers will invalidate the results. (page 505)

✱ *The 16-PF Test.* The 16-PF Test, another standardized personality test, measures 16 personality traits. Although it was designed primarily to measure normal personality, its results do distinguish between normal and abnormal personalities. (page 506)

✱ *Projective techniques.* A projective technique—such as the Rorschach Inkblots or the Thematic Apperception Test—lets people describe their concerns indirectly while talking about "the person in the picture" or about other ambiguous stimuli. The results from projective techniques are difficult to interpret and have unimpressive validity for making decisions about any individual. (page 507)

✷ *Uses and misuses of personality tests.* Personality tests can be used as an aid for assessing personality, but their results should be interpreted cautiously and in conjunction with other evidence. These tests should be used for job selection only when evidence clearly indicates that the results are valid for this purpose. (page 511)

Suggestion for Further Reading

Anastasi, A. (1988). *Psychological testing* (6th ed.). New York: Macmillan. A good textbook on both personality testing and IQ testing.

Terms

standardized test a test that is administered according to specified rules and whose scores are interpreted in a prescribed fashion (page 504)

Minnesota Multiphasic Personality Inventory (MMPI) a standardized test consisting of true-false items and intended to measure various personality dimensions and clinical conditions such as depression (page 504)

MMPI-2 the modernized edition of the MMPI (page 504)

16-PF Test a standardized personality test that measures 16 personality traits (page 506)

personality profile a graph that shows an individual's scores on scales measuring various personality traits (page 507)

projective techniques procedures designed to encourage people to project their personality characteristics onto ambiguous stimuli (page 508)

Rorschach Inkblots a projective personality technique; people are shown 10 inkblots and asked what each might be depicting (page 508)

Thematic Apperception Test (TAT) a projective personality technique; a person is asked to tell a story about each of 20 pictures (page 510)

Answers to Concept Checks

7. **a.** The puppet activity could be a projective technique, because the child is likely to project his or her own family concerns onto the puppets, using them to enact various problems. (page 508)

8. The Rorschach Inkblot Test must be administered in person by a psychologist who observes how you hold the cards, whether you rotate them, and anything else you do. The psychologist may also ask you to explain where you see something or why it looks as you say it does. (page 509)

9. The results would suggest that you are especially worried about health-related matters. (page 511)

Web Resources

Barbarian's Online Test Page

www.iglobal.net/psman/personality.html

The Barbarian provides links to dozens of sites that feature personality tests, including the Kiersey Temperament Sorter, the Enneagram Test, the Type A Personality Test, and the Locus of Control test. Additional tests can be found in the *Other Online Tests* section.*

---

*Note: Any psychological test that is readily available to the public, while entertaining and possibly informative, should not be used to make important decisions about yourself or others. The most powerful, valid, and reliable psychological assessment devices are usually kept under the tight control of their creators or copyright holders.

Social Psychology

14

In the *Communist Manifesto*, Karl Marx and Friedrich Engels wrote, "Mankind are more disposed to suffer, while evils are sufferable, than to right themselves by abolishing the forms to which they are accustomed. But when a long train of abuses and usurpations, pursuing invariably the same object, evinces a design to reduce them under absolute despotism, it is their right, it is their duty, to throw off such government." Fidel Castro wrote, "A little rebellion, now and then, is a good thing."

Do you agree with those statements? Why or why not? Can you think of anything that would change your mind?

Oh, pardon me. . . . That first statement was not from the *Communist Manifesto*—it was from the United States' Declaration of Independence. Sorry. And that second statement was a quotation from Thomas Jefferson, not Castro.

Do you agree more with these statements now that you know they came from democratic revolutionaries instead of communist revolutionaries? What determines who or what will influence you? This question is one example of the issues of interest to **social psychologists**—*the psychologists who study social behavior and how individuals influence other people and are influenced by other people.*

Social psychology is a broad, diverse field that is difficult to define. I know I have just defined it as the study of social behavior and influence, but the term *social behavior* is in turn defined very broadly to include such things as attitudes, persuasion, and certain aspects of self-understanding. One characterization of social psychology, if not exactly a definition, is that it is a field that studies the everyday behaviors of relatively normal people, generally in relationship to other people. In this chapter, we shall consider several of the major fields of research and application in social psychology.

Social psychologists find that influence depends not only on what someone says, but also on who says it, and on what the listeners think of that person.

MODULE 14.1

Social Perception and Cognition

How do we form impressions of other people?

How do we determine why someone behaves in a certain way?

Shortly after a massacre in Lebanon in 1982, several audiences were polled concerning their reactions to the television news coverage. Pro-Israeli audiences were angry about the news programs' anti-Israeli bias, whereas pro-Arab audiences were angry about the *same* programs' anti-Arab bias (Vallone, Ross, & Lepper, 1985).

We inevitably form attitudes about other people and

If you were a new patient of Dr. Balamurali Ambati, the world's youngest doctor (at age 17), what would your first impression probably be? If you formed a first impression based only on his youthful appearance, you could be badly mistaken about his abilities. First impressions do not always linger, but sometimes they do.

groups of people—whether good, bad, or indifferent. Once we have formed such attitudes, they can be very persistent, altering the way we perceive new information about those people. **Social perception and cognition** describe *the process we use to gather and remember information about others and to make inferences based on that information.* Social perception and cognition are similar in many ways to the principles of visual perception and nonsocial cognition that we examined in earlier chapters, particularly because our expectations can strongly influence what we observe, remember, and conclude.

First Impressions

Other things being equal, *the first information we learn about someone influences us more than later information does* (Belmore, 1987; Jones & Goethals, 1972). This tendency is known as the **primacy effect**. For example, if a professor seems energetic and engaging on the first day of class, you will start out with a favorable attitude and thus probably forgive his or her lackluster performance later in the semester. But a professor who seems dull from the first will have a hard time regaining your attention later in the semester. Similarly, your professors' early impressions of their students can have lasting effects. Also, think about the first impressions you formed of various fellow students and coworkers.

Why are first impressions so influential? Partly because, if our first impression of someone is unfavorable, we may not spend enough time with that person to form an alternative view. Also, once we have formed an impression, it alters our interpretation of later experiences. Suppose that your first impression of someone is that he talks about himself too much. Later, when he talks about himself again, even in a modest or appropriate way, you will take his comments as further support for your initial impression. Anything he says about someone else will merely seem like an "exception to the rule." Similarly, if your first impression of someone is unfavorable, when you walk past her and she says nothing, you will interpret her behavior as unfriendly. If your first impression had been favorable, you might interpret the same behavior as an indication that she was busy or distracted.

Thus, our first impressions can become self-fulfilling prophecies. For example, suppose a psychologist hands you a telephone receiver and invites you to have a conversation with an attractive, appealing person of the opposite sex. Later, the psychologist hands you the same receiver and invites you to talk with a person described as much less attractive. You will act very differently toward these two people and probably elicit cheerful, sparkling conversation from the first and rather bland conversation from the second—even though the two people were actually similar. (The psychologist chose at random which person would get which description; neither knew how the psychologist was describing them.) In short, your first impression of someone changes how you act, and thereby influences the other person to try to live up to (or down to) your first impression (Snyder, Tanke, & Berscheid, 1977).

SOMETHING TO THINK ABOUT

In a criminal trial, the prosecution presents its evidence first. Might that give the jury an unfavorable first impression of the defendant and increase the probability of a conviction? ✳

CONCEPT CHECK

1. Why do some professors avoid looking at students' names when they grade essay exams? Why is it more important for them to avoid looking at the names on tests given later in the semester than on the first test? (Check your answer on page 523.)

Stereotypes and Prejudices

A **stereotype** is *a generalized belief or expectation about a group of people.* We generally reserve the term **prejudice** for *an unfavorable stereotype, a negative attitude toward a group of people,* such as a belief that members of a particular group are lazy or hostile. Prejudices are frequently unyielding and harmful. For example, someone who has a prejudice against black people may not give blacks a fair chance to show their abilities. Black children who battle repeated instances of prejudice in school sometimes become so discouraged that they stop trying. For example, Claude Steele (1997) has found that, if black students are given a task but are told that it is not a test of their abilities, they perform well. But if they are told that the test will measure their abilities, many perform poorly. Steele's interpretation is that a test of abilities raises the threat that, if blacks perform poorly, they tend to confirm the hated prejudices about their abilities, and their concerns about that threat are counterproductive to their performance (Steele & Aronson, 1995).

Many stereotypes and prejudices are not only harmful but also false. False beliefs can emerge through a simple feature of human memory: We tend to remember the unusual. If we see an unusual person doing something unusual, the event is doubly memorable. For example, if you have met only a few left-handed redheads in your life, and maybe two of them did something unusual, you might remember those events and form a stereotype about left-handed redheads that might be entirely wrong—an illusory correlation, as discussed in Chapter 2.

Stereotypes can also be based on a grossly exaggerated grain of truth. In particular, people tend to perceive and describe their political opponents as being far more extreme than they really are (Keltner & Robinson, 1996). For example, some English-literature professors in the United States have been arguing for a revision of the curriculum to include more feminist and non-Western writers. When defenders of the standard curriculum (Shakespeare, Homer, Chaucer, and so forth) were asked to guess what the revisionists really wanted, most guessed that the revisionists wanted students to read *nothing but* feminist and multicultural authors. In fact, the revisionists wanted a mixture of such authors along with some traditional choices (Robinson & Keltner, 1996).

Researchers have, however, belatedly discovered that stereotypes are sometimes correct. For example, who do you think are more aggressive, on the average—men or women? Who express their feelings more easily, on the average—men or women? If you answered "men" to the first question and "women" to the second, you expressed stereotypes, but the evidence says you are correct. Similarly, who do you think is more likely to be sensitive to the subtle social connotations of what people say—a liberal-arts major or an engineering major? Again, if you said "liberal-arts major," you are endorsing a stereotype, but you are generally right (Ottati & Lee, 1995).

In some cases, two ethnic groups agree on a stereotype, although they put different values on it. For example, many Americans describe the Chinese as "inhibited," whereas the Chinese would use the term "self-controlled." U. S. businesspeople complain that Mexicans "don't show up on time for meetings and don't keep to schedules," whereas the Mexicans complain that people in the United States "are always in a rush" and "act like robots" (Lee & Duenas, 1995). In short, it may be wrong to try to eliminate all stereotypes. Instead, we should try to gauge the accuracy of various stereotypes, and if groups do differ, accept those differences as part of the valuable, enjoyable diversity of human life. Further, even though we might recognize someone as a member of a group and therefore statistically more likely to behave in a particular way, we need to be able to readjust our expectation if it doesn't fit that individual. For example, it is natural to hold the stereotype that most 70-year-olds are less active and athletic than most 20-year-olds. But if I meet a 70-year-old woman who likes to play tennis, I should treat her as the active woman she is, not as mirroring my image of a typical 70-year-old.

It is easy to measure most attitudes by simply asking people to describe their attitudes or to put a check mark on an answer sheet. Stereotypes and prejudices are different, however. When people are asked how much racism they think occurs in the United States, most say they perceive "some" or "much" racism. But if asked whether they themselves are racist, almost everyone says "no." Similarly, most people deny being sexist or holding stereotypes about any group. We all believe in fair treatment for everyone, or so we say. But if no one is a racist or a sexist and no one holds any stereotypes or has any prejudice, where is all the racism, sexism, and so forth coming from?

Psychologists can measure prejudice in subtle ways. For example, suppose you watch a videotape of several young men who are talking loudly although you cannot hear exactly what they are saying. After a while, one of them pushes another. Now, you are asked whether you think the push was aggressive or playful. Do you think your decision would be influenced by whether the men were black or white? Many people *are* influenced, even if they think they would not be. If the man doing the pushing is either white or a well-dressed black man, most people guess "playful," but if he is black and not neatly dressed, most guess "aggressive" (Banaji & Greenwald, 1994; Kunda & Thagard, 1996).

Imagine yourself in the following study to measure gender stereotypes: On each trial, a word will be flashed on a screen, then the screen will go blank, and then a name will be flashed on the screen. You don't need to do anything about the first word, but when you see the name, you must identify it as either male or female. For example:

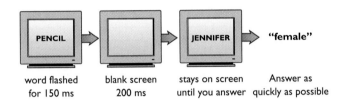

| word flashed for 150 ms | blank screen 200 ms | stays on screen until you answer | Answer as quickly as possible |

Even though you don't have to do anything with the first word, you are sure to read it anyway. (It's flashed on the same part of the screen as the name.) If the first word has definite male or female connotations, it will either increase or decrease your speed of identifying the gender of the name. For example, if the first word is KING, it will facilitate saying "male" after the name STEVE but inhibit saying "female" after the name JANE. The word PRINCESS would have the opposite effects.

 So, what happens if we use words that are generally associated with either male or female stereotypes? On the following list, cover the items at the right. First read a word at the left, and then uncover the name to the right and, as quickly as possible, identify it as either male or female.

Prime Word	Name	Male or Female?
Athletic	Dave	
Birthday	Michael	
Sentimental	Nancy	
Gentle	Jack	
Vulgar	Judy	
Thorn	Sarah	
Ballet	José	
Briefcase	Karen	
Tattoo	Bob	
Sleep	Linda	
Gossip	Barbara	
Hostile	Maria	
Mildew	Brian	
Sewing	Frank	

The effect here is small, so you probably did not notice yourself responding faster to some names than others, but at least you get the idea of the experiment. Taking the mean of a large number of subjects, researchers found that people identify a name as female about 8 ms faster if the priming word was stereotypically female (such as *sentimental* or *ballet*) than if it was stereotypically male (such as *vulgar* or *briefcase*). Similarly, people identified a name as male about 8 ms faster after a male than a female priming word (Blair & Banaji, 1996). Speeds were intermediate after neutral words such as *prairie* or *sleep*.

In a similar study, participants were shown word pairs such as *white—stubborn*, where the words *white* and *black* were understood to refer to white and black people, and subjects were asked to press one button if the connection could be true (as in *white—stubborn*) and another button if the connection was never true (as in *black—metallic*). On the average, people pressed the button slightly faster when the pairings were consistent with common stereotypes (as in *white—ambitious* or *black—musical*) than if they were reversed (as in *white—musical* or *black—ambitious*), even though people still answered "yes" (Dovidio, Evans, & Tyler, 1986).

So. . . what's my point? Is it, "See, way down deep you really are a sexist or racist, you nasty so-and-so"? Not at all. Most of the people in these studies were well-meaning and doing their best to overcome stereotypes and prejudice, and they would be embarrassed to discover that they exhibited signs of them (Monteith, Devine, & Zuwerink, 1993). The point is that racism, sexism, and all the other -isms can operate without our awareness (Greenwald & Banaji, 1995). People sometimes argue that we should eliminate all preferential treatment for blacks, women, and other groups, and instead select among applicants "entirely on the basis of their qualifications." The problem, according to the research just described, is that we may have prejudices and embrace stereotypes that we do not consciously recognize. Even when we think we are looking just at the qualifications, we may actually look at these differently, depending on whether the person we are considering is white or black, male or female.

Overcoming Prejudice

After prejudices and hostility have arisen between two groups, what can anyone do to break down those barriers? Simply getting to know each other better sometimes helps, but not dependably. A more effective technique is to get the two groups to work toward a common goal.

Many years ago, psychologists demonstrated the power of this technique using two arbitrarily chosen groups, not different races (Sherif, 1966). At a summer camp at Robbers' Cave, Oklahoma, 11-to-12-year-old boys were divided into two groups in separate cabins. The groups competed for prizes in sports, treasure hunts, and other activities. With each competition, the antagonism between the two groups grew more intense. The boys made threatening posters, shouted insults, and engaged in food fights. Each group had clearly developed prejudice and hostility toward the other.

Up to a point, the "counselors" (the experimenters) allowed the hostility to take its course, neither encouraging

People who work together for a common goal can overcome prejudices that initially divide them.

nor prohibiting it. Then, they tried to reverse it by stopping the competitions and setting common goals. First, they asked the two groups to work together to find and repair a leak in the water pipe that supplied the camp. Later, they had the two groups pool their treasuries to rent a movie that both groups wanted to see. Still later, they had the boys pull together to get a truck out of a rut. Gradually, hostility turned into friendship—except for a few holdouts who nursed their hatred to the bitter end! The point of this study is that competition leads to hostility; cooperation leads to friendship.

Attribution

We often try to figure out why the people we observe behave as they do. Yesterday, you won 1 million dollars in the state lottery. Today, a classmate who had never seemed to notice you before asks you for a date. You wonder why. When we are not sure what is causing the behavior of someone we are observing, we *attribute* causes that seem appropriate. **Attribution** is *the set of thought processes we use to assign causes to our own behavior and to the behavior of others.*

Internal Causes Versus External Causes

Fritz Heider, the founder of attribution theory, maintained that people often try to decide whether someone's behavior is the result of internal or external causes (Heider, 1958). **Internal attributions** are *explanations based on someone's stable characteristics, such as attitudes, personality traits, or abilities.* **External attributions** are *explanations based on the situation, such as stimuli in the environment, the events of the day, and the rewards and penalties associated with certain acts.* For example, your brother decides to walk to work this morning instead of driving. You could offer an internal attribution ("He likes fresh air and exercise") or an external attribution ("His car is broken"). Internal attributions are also known as *dispositional*; external attributions are also known as *situational.*

We make internal attributions when someone does something unexpected—something that makes us say, "I wouldn't have done that." For example, if I told you I would like to visit Hawaii, you would draw no conclusions about me, because the appeal of Hawaii is obvious. However, if I said I would like to visit Antarctica, you would wonder what about me could explain this unusual interest (Krull & Anderson, 1997).

This tendency sometimes leads to misunderstandings between members of different cultures. Each person views the other's behavior as "something I would not have done" and therefore grounds for making an attribution about the other individual's personality. In fact, such behavior may actually be what the other person's culture dictates. For example, some cultures expect people to cry loudly at funerals or to be emotionally demonstrative in other ways; other cultures expect people to be more restrained under these circumstances. People who are unfamiliar with other cultures may attribute a behavior to someone's personality and thus overlook the influence of the situation and the culturally determined response to that situation.

Harold Kelley (1967) proposed the theory that we rely on three types of information when deciding whether to make an internal or an external attribution for someone's behavior:

- **Consensus information** (*how a person's behavior compares with other people's behavior*). If someone be-

We are sometimes surprised by people's behavior and attribute an internal cause when in fact the people are acting in accord with the customs of their culture.

haves the same way that other people do in a situation, or the same way you imagine other people would, then you would probably make an external attribution. If someone behaves in an unusual way, you look for an internal attribution, pertaining to something about that person instead of something about the situation.

- **Consistency information** (*how the person's behavior varies from one time to the next*). If someone almost always seems friendly, for example, you would make an internal attribution ("this person is friendly"). If someone seems friendly at times and less friendly at other times, you look for external attributions ("something just happened to cause this person's bad mood").
- **Distinctiveness** (*how the person's behavior varies from one object or social partner to another*). For example, if someone is friendly to most people, but unfriendly to one particular person, you make an external attribution for the unfriendly behavior. That is, you assume that person elicits unfriendly behavior from an otherwise friendly person and that, therefore, the behavior does not reveal a personality trait.

CONCEPT CHECKS

2. Classify the following as either internal or external attributions:

   a. She contributed money to charity because she is generous.

   b. She contributed money to charity because she wanted to impress her boss, who was watching.

   c. She contributed money to charity because she owed a favor to the man who was asking for contributions.

3. Your friend Juanita returns from watching *The Return of the Son of Sequel Strikes Back Again Part 2* and says it was excellent. Most other people who commented on this film disliked it. Will you be inclined to make an internal or an external attribution for Juanita's enjoyment of this movie? Why? (Distinctiveness, consensus, or consistency?) (Check your answers on page 523.)

Errors and Biases

In most cases, people judge the evidence intelligently and make appropriate internal or external attributions for people's behavior. However, one error they are especially likely to make is *to make internal attributions for other people's behavior, even when they see evidence for an external influence on behavior.* That tendency is known as the **fundamental attribution error** (Ross, 1977).

For example, students in one study were asked to read an essay that another student had written, praising Fidel Castro, the Communist leader of Cuba, and then estimate the writer's actual attitudes toward Castro. Even students who were told that the writer had been assigned to write a pro-Castro essay assumed that the writer was at least mildly pro-Castro (Jones & Harris, 1967). In a later study, experi-

menters explained that one student in a creative writing class had been assigned to write a pro-Castro essay and an anti-Castro essay, at different times in the course. They then showed the subjects the two essays and asked them to estimate the writer's true beliefs. Most said they thought that the writer had significantly changed his or her attitudes toward Castro between the first essay and the second (Allison, Mackie, Muller, & Worth, 1993). That is, even when people are told of a powerful external reason for someone's behavior, they still sometimes make internal attributions. Apparently, they believe that the situational pressure could not have been sufficient and that the person must have had internal reasons as well (McClure, 1998).

Moreover, *people are more likely to make internal attributions for other people's behavior than they are for their own behavior* (Jones & Nisbett, 1972). This tendency is called the **actor-observer effect**. You are an "actor" when you try to explain the causes of your own behavior and an "observer" when you try to explain someone else's behavior.

The actor-observer effect has been demonstrated in several studies (Watson, 1982). In one of these, Richard Nisbett and his colleagues (1973) asked college students to rate themselves, their fathers, their best friends, and Walter Cronkite (a television news announcer at the time) on several personality traits. For each trait (such as "leniency"), the subjects were given three choices: (1) the person possesses the trait, (2) the person possesses the opposite trait, and (3) the person's behavior "depends on the situation." Subjects checked "depends on the situation"—an external attribution—most frequently when they were rating themselves, less frequently when they were rating their fathers and friends, and least often when they were rating Walter Cronkite. Figure 14.1 shows the results.

Why do we tend to explain our own behavior differently from that of others? There are several possibilities (Jones & Nisbett, 1972; Watson, 1982). *First,* because we observe our own behavior in many different situations, we realize how much it varies from one situation to another. (Recall Kelley's theory: You make external attributions when someone's behavior varies across time and across situations.) We are less aware of the variations in someone else's behavior.

Second, we tend to attribute unexpected, surprising behavior to internal causes. Our own behavior seldom surprises us, so we do not attribute it to internal causes.

The *third* reason is perceptual. We do not see ourselves as objects, because our eyes look outward and focus on our environment. We see other people, however, as objects in our visual field.

The perceptual explanation for the actor-observer effect has an interesting implication: If you could somehow become an object in your own visual field, then you might explain your own behavior in terms of internal traits, just as you tend to explain the behavior of others. In one innovative study, Michael Storms (1973) videotaped several subjects as they carried on a conversation. Before showing them the videotape, he asked them why they had said certain things

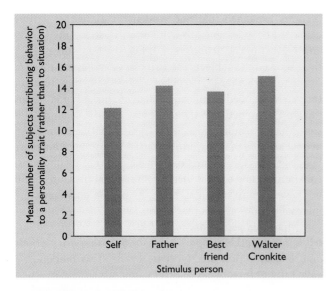

FIGURE 14.1 Subjects were asked whether certain people had certain traits, such as "leniency," or the opposite traits, such as "firmness," or whether "it depended on the situation." They attributed the most personality traits to news announcer Walter Cronkite (the person they knew least) and the fewest to themselves. That is, they were most likely to say that their own behavior depended on the situation. (Based on data of Nisbett, Caputo, Legant, & Marecek, 1973.)

and why they thought the others had said what they had. At first, most of the subjects attributed their own remarks to external causes ("I was responding to what the other person said") and attributed what the other people had said to internal causes "he was showing off" or "she always says things like that"). Then Storms showed them the videotape and asked them the same questions. This time, many of them attributed their own behavior more often to internal causes ("I was being smart-alecky. . . . I was trying to act friendly"). That is, when people watched themselves, they reacted just as they did when watching other people—by making mostly internal attributions for behavior.

SOMETHING TO THINK ABOUT

Try to explain these examples of behavior:

- Why did you choose to go to the college you are attending?
- Why did your roommate choose this college?
- Why are you reading this book right now?
- Why does your roommate study so much (or so little)?

Did you attribute internal causes or external causes for these behaviors? Did you rely more on external causes to explain other people's behavior or to explain your own? ✱

Using Attributions to Control Perceptions of Ourselves

Although we generally attribute our own behavior largely to external causes, we vary our attributions to try to pre-

sent ourselves in a favorable light. For example, you may credit your intelligence for the good grades you get (an internal attribution) and blame unfair tests for your bad grades (an external attribution). Members of groups that are frequent victims of discrimination often blame their defeats on prejudice and discrimination—sometimes rightly, sometimes wrongly (Crocker & Major, 1989). *Attributions that we adopt to maximize our credit for our success and minimize our blame for our failure* are called **self-serving biases** (Miller & Ross, 1975; Van Der Pligt & Eiser, 1983).

People can also protect their image by adopting **self-handicapping strategies**, when they *intentionally put themselves at a disadvantage to provide an excuse for an expected failure.* Suppose you expect to do poorly on a final exam. You go to a party the night before and stay out until three in the morning. Now, you can blame your low score on your lack of sleep and avoid having to admit even to yourself that you might have done poorly anyway.

In an experiment on self-handicapping strategies, Steven Berglas and Edward Jones (1978) asked college students to work on problems; some students were given solvable problems, and others were given a mixture of solvable and unsolvable problems. Then, the experimenters told all the students that they had done well. The students who had been given solvable problems (and had solved them) felt good about their success. Those who had worked on unsolvable problems were unsure in what way they had "done well," because they knew they had not understood many of the problems. They certainly had no confidence that they could continue to do well.

Next, the experimenters told the subjects that the purpose of the experiment was to investigate the effects of drugs on problem solving and that they were now going to hand out another set of problems. The subjects could choose between taking a drug that supposedly impaired problem solving abilities and another drug that supposedly improved them. The subjects who had worked on unsolvable problems the first time were more likely than the others to choose the drug that supposedly impaired performance. Because they did not expect to do well on the second set of problems anyway, they chose to provide themselves with a convenient excuse.

THE MESSAGE
How Social Perceptions Affect Behavior

We are seldom fully aware of the reasons for our own behavior, much less someone else's, but we make our best guesses. If someone you know passes by without saying hello, you might attribute that person's behavior to either absentmindedness, indifference, or outright hostility. If someone acts unusually friendly, you might attribute that response to your own personal charm, the other person's extraverted personality, or that person's devious and manipulative personality. Whatever attributions you make are sure to influence your own social behaviors.

SUMMARY

✳ *First impressions.* Other things being equal, we pay more attention to the first information we learn about someone than to later information. (page 517)

✳ *Stereotypes.* Stereotypes are generalized beliefs about groups of people. They are sometimes illusory correlations that arise from people's tendency to remember unusual actions clearly, especially unusual actions by members of minority groups. However, some stereotypes are also correct or partly correct. (page 518)

✳ *Prejudice.* A prejudice is an unfavorable stereotype. Many people will not admit, even to themselves, that they have prejudices. Through indirect measures, researchers have found ways to demonstrate subtle effects of stereotypes and prejudices even in people who deny having them. (page 518)

✳ *Attribution.* Attribution is the set of thought processes by which we assign causes to behavior. We attribute behavior either to internal causes or to external causes. According to Harold Kelley, we are likely to attribute behavior to an internal cause if it is consistent over time, different from most other people's behavior, and directed toward a variety of other people or objects. (page 520)

✳ *Fundamental attribution error.* People frequently attribute other people's behavior to internal causes, even when they see evidence of external influences. (page 521)

✳ *Actor-observer effect.* We are more likely to attribute internal causes to other people's behavior than to our own. (page 521)

✳ *Self-serving bias and self-handicapping.* People sometimes try to protect their self-esteem by attributing their successes to skill and their failures to outside influences. They can also intentionally place themselves at a disadvantage to provide an excuse for their expected failure. (page 522)

Suggestion for Further Reading

M. P. Zanna & J. M. Olson (Eds.) (1994). *The psychology of prejudice: The Ontario Symposium, Volume 7.* Hillsdale, NJ: Lawrence Erlbaum. Good collection of research on stereotypes and prejudices.

Terms

social psychologists   the psychologists who study social behavior and how individuals influence other people and are influenced by other people (page 516)

social perception and cognition   the process of gathering and remembering information about others and making inferences based on that information (page 517)

primacy effect   the tendency to be more influenced by the first information learned about someone than by later information about the same person (page 517)

stereotypes   overgeneralizations of either positive or negative attitudes toward people (page 518)

prejudice   an unfavorable stereotype; a negative attitude toward a group of people (page 518)

attribution   the set of thought processes we use to assign causes to our own behavior and to the behavior of others (page 520)

internal attribution   an explanation based on someone's stable characteristics, such as attitudes, personality traits, or abilities (page 520)

external attribution   an explanation based on the situation, such as stimuli in the environment, the events of the day, and the rewards and penalties associated with certain acts (page 520)

consensus information   comparisons of one person's behavior with that of others (page 520)

consistency information   observations of how a person's behavior varies from one time to another (page 521)

distinctiveness   observations of how a person's behavior varies from one object or social partner to another (page 521)

fundamental attribution error   the tendency to make internal attributions for other people's behavior, even when an observer sees evidence for an external influence (page 521)

actor-observer effect   the tendency to attribute internal causes more often for other people's behavior than for one's own behavior (page 521)

self-serving biases   attributions that people adopt to maximize their credit for their successes and to minimize their blame for their failures (page 522)

self-handicapping strategies   techniques for intentionally putting oneself at a disadvantage to provide an excuse for an expected failure (page 522)

Answers to Concept Checks

1. They want to avoid being biased by their first impressions of the students. This procedure is less important with the first test, because they have not yet formed strong impressions of the students. (page 518)

2. **a.** internal; **b.** and **c.** external. An internal attribution relates to a stable aspect of personality or attitudes; an external attribution relates to the current situation. (page 521)

3. You will probably make an internal attribution for Juanita's enjoyment, attributing it to her characteristic of being easy to please instead of attributing it to the quality of the movie. The reason is *consensus:* When one person's behavior differs from that of others, we make an internal attribution. (page 521)

Web Resources

Interpersonal Perception

nw3.nai.net/~dakenny/interp.htm

David A. Kenny of the University of Connecticut, author of *Interpersonal Perception: A Social Relations Analysis,* offers an outstanding tutorial on the judgments that one person makes about another.

Attitudes and Persuasion

What are attitudes?

What methods of persuasion are most effective, and under what circumstances?

"If you want to change people's behavior, first you have to change their attitudes." Do you agree?

Suppose you say "yes." Now, answer two more questions: (1) What is your attitude about paying higher taxes? (2) If the government raises taxes, will you pay the higher taxes?

If you're like most people, you will say that (1) your attitude about paying higher taxes is unfavorable, but that (2) if the taxes are raised, you will pay them. In other words, by changing the law, the government can change your behavior without changing your attitude.

So what effects do attitudes have on behavior? And what leads people to change their attitudes?

Attitudes and Their Influence

An **attitude** is *a like or dislike that influences our behavior toward a person or thing* (Allport, 1935; Petty & Cacioppo, 1981). Your attitudes include an evaluative or emotional component (how you feel about something), a cognitive component (what you know or believe), and a behavioral component (what you are likely to do). *Persuasion* is an attempt to alter your attitudes or behavior.

One common way of measuring attitudes (and thus the effectiveness of persuasion) is through the use of attitude scales, such as Likert scales, also known as summated rating scales (Dawes & Smith, 1985). On a Likert scale (named after psychologist Rensis Likert), a person checks a point along a line ranging from 1, meaning "strongly disagree," to 5 or 7, meaning "strongly agree," for each of several statements about a topic, as shown in Figure 14.2.

Check marks on an answer sheet are imperfect measurements of attitudes, partly because people have different styles of responding. For example, Japanese and Chinese people tend to put their check marks at or near the middle of the scale, whereas people in the United States tend to choose more extreme values (Chen, Lee, & Stevenson, 1995). Therefore, a check mark of 1 may not have quite the same meaning on an Asian answer sheet as it does on a North American answer sheet.

Even if we measure attitudes well, they do not always correlate strongly with actual behavior (McGuire, 1985; Wicker, 1969). For example, your favorable attitude toward getting good grades is no guarantee that you will devote yourself to your studies.

The behavior of some people is more consistent with

Indicate your level of agreement with the items below, using the following scale:

	Strongly disagree		Neutral		Strongly agree
1. Labor unions are necessary to protect the rights of workers.	1	2	3	4	5
2. Labor union leaders have too much power.	1	2	3	4	5
3. If I worked for a company with a union, I would join the union.	1	2	3	4	5
4. I would never cross a picket line of striking workers.	1	2	3	4	5
5. Striking workers hurt their company and unfairly raise prices for the consumer.	1	2	3	4	5
6. Labor unions should not be permitted to engage in political activity.	1	2	3	4	5
7. America is a better place for today's workers because of the efforts by labor unions in the past.	1	2	3	4	5

Note: Items 2, 5, and 6 are scored the opposite of 1, 3, 4, and 7.

FIGURE 14.2 Likert scales—such as this one assessing attitudes toward labor unions—are commonly used in attitude research. Subjects rate the degree to which they agree or disagree with items that measure various aspects of a particular attitude.

their attitudes than is the behavior of others. When you enter an unfamiliar situation, do you immediately look around to determine what other people are doing and what is expected of you? Some do. These people are known as **high self-monitors** because they *constantly monitor their own behavior to try to behave in the appropriate manner* (Snyder, 1979). Other people, *low self-monitors,* pay less attention to others' expectations and simply do what they feel like doing.

CONCEPT CHECK

4. Whose behavior matches their attitudes more closely—high self-monitors or low self-monitors? (Check your answer on page 533.)

Two Routes of Attitude Change and Persuasion

Remember from Chapter 2 that many of the people responding to one survey said "no" to *I believe there is intelligent life in outer space* and "yes" to *I believe the government is concealing evidence of intelligent life in outer space.* The most likely explanation is that people answer survey questions impulsively without thinking through their answers. The same is true of attitudes: Sometimes people ponder the evidence carefully and develop a carefully reasoned attitude, and sometimes they form attitudes with only a flimsy, superficial basis.

Richard Petty and John Cacioppo (1981, 1986) proposed the following distinction: *When people take a decision seriously, they invest the necessary time and effort to carefully evaluate the evidence and logic behind each message.* Petty and Cacioppo call this logical approach the **central route to persuasion.** In contrast, *when people listen to a message on a topic of little importance to them, they pay more attention to such factors as the speaker's appearance and reputation or the sheer number of arguments presented, regardless of their quality.* This superficial approach is the **peripheral route to persuasion.**

CONCEPT CHECK

5. You are listening to someone who is trying to persuade you to change your major from astrology to psychology. Your future success may depend on making the right decision. You also listen to someone explain why a trip to the Bahamas is better than a trip to the Fiji Islands. You had no intention of going to either place. In which case will you follow the central route to persuasion? (Check your answer on page 533.)

Most political candidates will try both the central and peripheral routes to persuasion, depending on the situation. In debate and interviews, they try to impress with their knowledge and logic. In brief campaign appearances, they are more concerned with presenting an image, such as that of a "regular person just like you."

Highly Resistant Attitudes

Most people's attitudes fall along a continuum: You know much and care deeply about a few topics; regarding these, you have firm, well-informed attitudes that you would change only by solid evidence and logic—the central route. At the other end of the continuum, many topics hardly interest you at all; you might express an opinion, if asked, but you have little basis for that opinion, so you could change it easily, even by the peripheral route.

On a few topics, however, many people form strong, unshakable attitudes based on hardly any information at all. One such topic is the death penalty. In the United States, about 60–75% say that they support the death penalty, whereas 20–30% oppose it, and the others are undecided. The percentages vary a bit from year to year, but unlike most other topics, the answers hardly change at all after the question has been reworded (Ellsworth & Gross, 1994).

 Before we continue, answer the following questions:

Knowledge items

1. The death penalty has been abolished by a majority of Western European nations.

True	I don't know	False
☐	☐	☐

2. Over the years, states which have had the death penalty have shown lower murder rates than neighboring states which did not have the death penalty.

True	I don't know	False
☐	☐	☐

3. Studies have shown that the rate of murder usually drops in the weeks following a publicized execution.

True	I don't know	False
☐	☐	☐

4. Poor people who commit murder are more likely to be sentenced to death than rich people.

True	I don't know	False
☐	☐	☐

5. After the U.S. Supreme Court struck down the death penalty in 1972, the murder rate in the United States showed a sharp upturn.

True	I don't know	False
☐	☐	☐

6. On the average, the death penalty costs the taxpayers less than life imprisonment.

True	I don't know	False
☐	☐	☐

Reasons for support or opposition

1. We need capital punishment to provide support and protection for the police.

Agree	I don't know	Disagree
☐	☐	☐

2. Even when a murderer gets a life sentence, he usually gets out on parole, so it is better to execute him.

Agree	I don't know	Disagree
☐	☐	☐

3. We need capital punishment to show criminals that we mean business about wiping out crime in this country.

Agree	I don't know	Disagree
☐	☐	☐

4. Society has a right to get revenge when a very serious crime like murder has been committed.

Agree	I don't know	Disagree
☐	☐	☐

5. Sometimes I have felt a sense of personal outrage when a convicted murderer was sentenced to a penalty less than death.

Agree	I don't know	Disagree
☐	☐	☐

6. One problem with the death penalty is that only the poor and unfortunate are likely to be executed.

Agree	I don't know	Disagree
☐	☐	☐

7. There is too much danger of executing an innocent man.

Agree	I don't know	Disagree
☐	☐	☐

8. Executions set a violent example which may even encourage violence and killing in our society.

Agree	I don't know	Disagree
☐	☐	☐

9. It is immoral for society to take a life regardless of the crime the individual has committed.

Agree	I don't know	Disagree
☐	☐	☐

10. Any execution would make me sad, regardless of the crime the individual had committed.

Agree	I don't know	Disagree
☐	☐	☐

For the knowledge items, the correct answers are: (1) true, (2) false, (3) false, (4) true, (5) false, and (6) false. When these questions were asked of 500 Californians, the average person said "uncertain" to 1.5 of these 6 items, and answered 2.4 correctly and 2.0 incorrectly (Ellsworth & Ross, 1983). However, most said that, even if their guesses on these items and others were wrong, they couldn't imagine any facts that would change their attitude. Regarding the reasons for support or opposition, many people agreed with all or almost all of the reasons supporting their attitude and none of those against it.

You can see the difficulties of trying to persuade people, or even to arrange a compromise, on highly divisive issues such as the death penalty or abortion. People adopt a position and then accept any argument that favors it, and they reject or ignore any contrary information or argument.

Much is at stake here. In U.S. states that have instituted the death penalty, anyone who says "I could never vote for the death penalty under any circumstances" is excluded from jury service on a murder trial, because he or she cannot abide by the laws that state that a jury should consider the death penalty under certain circumstances.

Because many opponents of the death penalty say that they are opposed under *all* circumstances, trial juries in murder cases are composed almost entirely of death-penalty supporters—who are more often white than black, male than female, old than young, and more sympathetic to the prosecution than to the defense (Cowan, Thompson, & Ellsworth, 1984; Fitzgerald & Ellsworth, 1984).

Delayed Influence of Messages

In certain cases, a message may have no apparent influence on you at the time you hear it, but an important effect later. There are several reasons for a message to have a delayed effect; we shall consider two examples.

The Sleeper Effect

Suppose you reject a message because of peripheral route influences. For example, you reject a new idea without giving it much thought, because you have a low opinion of the person who suggested it. If the idea is a good one, it may have a delayed effect. Weeks or months later, you may forget where you heard the idea and remember only the idea itself; at that time you can evaluate it on its merits (Hovland & Weiss, 1951; Pratkanis, Greenwald, Leippe, & Baumgardner, 1988). Psychologists use the term **sleeper effect** to describe *delayed persuasion by an initially rejected message*.

Minority Influence

Delayed influence also occurs when a minority group, especially one that is not widely respected, proposes a worthwhile idea: The majority may reject the idea at first but adopt it later in some form. By "minority group," I do not necessarily mean an ethnic minority; the minority may be a political minority or any other outnumbered group.

If a minority group continually repeats a single, simple message and if its members seem to be united, it has a good chance of eventually influencing the majority's decision. The minority's united, uncompromising stance is important; it forces the majority to wonder, "Why won't these people conform? Maybe their idea is better than we thought." The minority's influence often increases gradually, even if the majority hesitates to admit that the minority has swayed them (Wood, Lundgren, Ouellette, Busceme, & Blackstone, 1994). A minority, by expressing its views, can also prompt the majority to generate new ideas of its own (Nemeth, 1986). That is, by demonstrating the possibility of disagreement, the minority opens the way for other people to offer new suggestions that are different from the original views of both the majority and the minority.

One powerful example of minority influence is that of the Socialist Party of the United States, which ran candidates for elective offices from 1900 through the 1950s. The party never received more than 6% of the vote in any presidential election. No Socialist candidate was ever elected senator or governor, and only a few were elected to the

A persistent and determined group can exert major influences on public policy, with or without an election. Here, a woman waves as she climbs a redwood tree to protest logging in a California forest. Tree sitters sometimes stay in the treetops for days to prevent the cutting of trees.

House of Representatives (Shannon, 1955). Beginning in the 1930s, the party's membership and support began to dwindle, until eventually the party stopped nominating candidates.

Was that because the Socialists had failed? No. It was because they had already accomplished most of their original goals! Most of the major points in the party's 1900 platform had been enacted into law (see Table 14.1). Of course, the Democrats and Republicans who voted for these changes always claimed that the ideas were their own. Still, the Socialist Party, though always a minority, had exerted an enormous influence on the country.

CONCEPT CHECK

6. At a meeting of your student government, you suggest a new method of testing and grading students. The other members immediately reject your plan. Should you become discouraged and give up? If not, what should you do? (Check your answer on page 533.)

Ways of Presenting Persuasive Messages

Most persuasive messages fall into one of two categories—do this to make something good happen, and do this to prevent something bad from happening. Either one can be effective, depending on the circumstances. Figure 14.3

TABLE 14.1 The Political Platform of the U.S. Socialist Party, 1900

PROPOSAL	EVENTUAL FATE OF PROPOSAL
Women's right to vote	Established by 19th amendment to U.S. Constitution; ratified in 1920
Old-age pensions	Included in the Social Security Act of 1935
Unemployment insurance	Included in the Social Security Act of 1935; also guaranteed by other state and federal legislation
Health and accident insurance	Included in part in the Social Security Act of 1935 and in the Medicare Act of 1965
Increased wages, including minimum wage	First minimum-wage law passed in 1938; periodically updated since then
Reduction of working hours	Maximum 40-hour work week (with exceptions) established by the Fair Labor Standards Act of 1938
Public ownership of electric, gas, and other utilities and of the means of transportation and communication	Utilities not owned by government but heavily regulated by federal and state governments since the 1930s
Initiative, referendum, and recall (mechanisms for private citizens to push for changes in legislation and for removal of elected officials)	Adopted by most state governments

SOURCES: Foster, 1968; and Leuchtenburg, 1963.

shows a chain letter that has been circulated widely throughout the world over several decades. It has been called a "mind virus" because of its ability to get people to duplicate and spread the letter (Goodenough & Dawkins, 1994). Many people who receive this letter cannot resist its command to make copies and send them to others, even if they regard its message as a silly superstition. The letter claims to be offering "good luck" and "love," but it follows those promises with an implied threat: Allegedly, people who have failed to follow the instructions have been victims of terrible events. (They lost their job, lost a loved one, died,

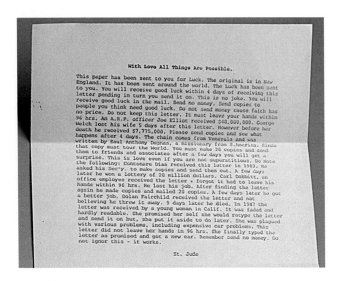

FIGURE 14.3 If you received a copy of this chain letter, would you copy it and send it on to other people, as it requests? Why or why not?

or had car problems!) The threat makes people feel nervous and uneasy if they decline to follow the instructions.

Fear messages are effective in some cases, as in the St. Jude letter, but not always. Appeals for money are often accompanied by implied threats, such as "If you don't send enough money to support our cause, then our political opponents will gain power and do terrible things." According to the research, messages that appeal to fear are effective only if they can convince people that the danger is real (Leventhal, 1970). People tend to disbelieve an organization that exaggerates the threats or sends "emergency" appeals too often.

Moreover, a fear message is most effective if people believe they can do something to reduce the danger, especially if they need to act only on rare occasions. For example, most people will visit a physician to get an immunization against a contagious disease or to get an X ray to test for cancer. Many people will also change their sex habits to avoid herpes or AIDS, but not everyone remains consistent in these practices. Even fewer people consistently change their behavior to conserve natural resources or to avoid damaging the world's climate, because most people doubt that their behavior will exert a major influence.

Audience Variables

Some people are more easily persuaded than others are, and an individual may be more easily influenced at some times than at others. The ease of persuading someone depends on both person variables and situation variables.

Person Variables Who would you guess would be persuaded more easily—highly intelligent or less intelligent people? Actually, the answer depends on the message. Other things being equal, the peripheral route to persuasion is generally more effective with less intelligent people, who are more likely to accept an illogical or poorly supported idea (Eagly & Warren, 1976). The central route to persuasion is generally more effective with highly intelligent people, who are better able to understand complicated evidence and more likely to devote the energy necessary to evaluate it.

However, the effectiveness of the central or peripheral route depends not only on the listener's intelligence but also his or her level of interest. Suppose you listen to a debate about raising the tuition at Santa Enigma Junior College to pay for new buildings and equipment. You have never heard of the college, so you pay little attention. A neatly dressed, smooth-talking speaker can probably persuade you, using the peripheral route, even though you are an intelligent, well-educated person. But now imagine that you listen to a debate about raising tuition at your own college. The speaker could be the same, stating the same evidence and arguments, but you will now evaluate the arguments much more carefully, and the central route to persuasion will be more effective for you.

Situation Variables   Other things being equal, a persuasive message is more effective if the speaker can convey the message, "I am similar to you" or "my message is right for people like you." We like people who resemble ourselves in almost any way. In one striking illustration of this tendency, students were asked to read a very unflattering description of Grigory Rasputin, the "mad monk of Russia," and then rate Rasputin's personality on several scales such as pleasant to unpleasant, effective to ineffective, and strong to weak. All students read the same description except for Rasputin's birthdate: In some cases, Rasputin's actual birthdate had been changed to match the student's own birthdate. Students who thought Rasputin had the same birthdate as their own liked him better than other students did. Nobody thought he was "pleasant," but many did rate him as "strong" and "effective" (Finch & Cialdini, 1989).

You can probably think of examples where a speaker began by stressing his or her resemblance to the audience: "I remember when I was a student like you." "I grew up in a town similar to this one." "I believe in family values, and I'm sure you do too." This technique is part of the peripheral route to persuasion, but it can be used effectively on almost anyone.

People with Heightened Resistance   A persuasive message can become ineffective if people can generate arguments against it. For example, *simply informing subjects a few minutes ahead of time that they are about to hear a persuasive speech on a certain topic weakens the effect of the talk on their attitudes* (Petty & Cacioppo, 1977). This tendency is called the **forewarning effect**.

With the **inoculation effect**, *people first hear a weak argument, then a stronger argument supporting the same conclusion.* After they have rejected the first argument, they

Grigory Rasputin was a contemptible person. However, people who are told he resembled them, even in trivial ways, soften their criticisms.

are likely to reject the second one also. In one experiment, subjects listened to speeches *against* brushing their teeth after every meal. Some of them heard just a strong argument (for example, "Brushing your teeth too frequently wears away tooth enamel, leading to serious disease"). Others first heard a weak argument, then the strong argument 2 days later. Still others first heard an argument *for* toothbrushing, then the strong argument against it. Only the subjects who heard the weak antibrushing argument before the strong one resisted its influence; the other two groups found it highly persuasive (McGuire & Papageorgis, 1961). So, if you want to convince someone, present some good evidence first; don't start with evidence that they may consider faulty.

CONCEPT CHECK

7. If you want your children to preserve the beliefs and attitudes you try to teach them, should you give them only arguments that support those beliefs or should you also expose them to attacks on those beliefs? Why? (Check your answer on page 533.)

Strategies of Persuasion

Many people, ranging from salespeople selling worthless products to people representing noble charities, will sometimes ask you to give more of your time or money than you would rationally choose to spend. You should understand several of their techniques so that you can resist these appeals.

One technique is to make a modest request at first and then to follow it with a larger second request. This procedure is called the **foot-in-the-door technique**. When Jonathan Freedman and Scott Fraser (1966) asked suburban residents in Palo Alto, California, to put a small "Drive Safely" sign in their window, most of them agreed to do so. A couple of weeks later, other researchers asked the same residents to let them set up a large, unsightly "Drive Safely" billboard in their front yard for 10 days. They made the same request to a group of residents that had not been approached by the first group of researchers. Of those who had already agreed to display the small sign, 76% agreed to let them set up the billboard. Only 17% of the others agreed. Even agreeing to make as small a commitment as signing a petition to support a cause significantly increases the probability that people will later donate money to that cause (Schwarzwald, Bizman, & Raz, 1983).

In another approach, called the **door-in-the-face technique** (Cialdini et al., 1975), *someone follows an outrageous initial request with a much more reasonable second one,* implying that, if you refused the first request, you should at least compromise by agreeing to the second one. For example, I once received a telephone call from a college alumni association, asking me to show my loyalty by contributing $1,000. When I apologetically declined, the caller acted sympathetic (as if to say, "It's too bad you don't have a high-paying job like all our other alumni . . .") and then asked whether I could contribute $500. And if not $500, how about $200? And so forth. The implication was that, if I had refused the original request, I should "compromise" by giving a smaller amount.

Robert Cialdini and his colleagues (1975) demonstrated the power of the door-in-the-face technique with a clever experiment. They asked one group of college students, chosen randomly, whether they would be willing to chaperone a group from the juvenile detention center on a trip to the zoo. Only 17% said they would. They asked other students to spend 2 hours per week for 2 years working as counselors with juvenile delinquents. Not surprisingly, all of them refused. But then the researchers asked them, "If you won't do that, would you chaperone a group from the juvenile detention center on one trip to the zoo?" Half of them said they would. Apparently, they felt that the researchers were conceding a great deal and that it was only fair to meet them halfway.

Someone using the **lowball technique** *first offers an extremely favorable deal and then makes additional demands after the other person has committed to the deal* (Cialdini, 1993). For example, a car dealer offers you an exceptionally good price on a new car and a most generous price for the trade-in of your old car. You weren't sure you wanted this make of car, but the deal is too good to resist. After you have committed yourself to buying this car, the dealer checks with the boss, who rejects the deal. Your salesperson comes back saying, "I'm so sorry. I forgot that this car has some special features that raise the value. If we sold it for the price I originally quoted, we'd lose money." So you agree to a higher price. Then the company's used car specialist looks at your old car and "corrects" the trade-in value to a lower amount. Still, you have already committed yourself, so you don't back out. Eventually, you leave with a deal that you would probably not have accepted at the start.

In the **that's-not-all technique,** *someone makes an offer and then improves the offer before anyone has a chance to reply.* The television announcer says, "Here's your chance to buy this amazing combination paper shredder and coffeemaker for only $39.95. But wait, there's more! We'll throw in a can of dog deodorant! And this handy windshield wiper cleaner and a subscription to *Modern Lobotomist!* And if you act now, you can get this amazing offer, which usually costs $39.95, for only $19.95! Call this number!" People who hear the first offer and then the "improved" offer are more likely to comply than are people who first hear the "improved" offer (Burger, 1986).

CONCEPT CHECK

8. Identify each of the following as an example of the foot-in-the-door technique, the door-in-the-face technique, or the that's-not-all technique.

   a. Your boss says, "We need to cut costs drastically around here. I'm afraid I'm going to have to cut your salary in half." You protest vigorously. Your boss replies, "Well, I suppose we could cut expenses some other way. Maybe I can give you just a 5% cut." "Thanks," you reply. "I can live with that."

   b. A store marks its prices "25% off," then scratches that out and marks them "50% off!" Though the prices are now about the same as at competing stores, customers flock into the store.

   c. A friend asks you to help carry some supplies over to the elementary school for an afternoon tutoring program. When you get there, the principal says that one of the tutors is late and asks whether you could take her place until she arrives. You agree and spend the rest of the afternoon tutoring. The principal then talks you into coming back every week as a tutor. (Check your answers on page 533.)

Cognitive Dissonance

On page 561, we considered whether a change in people's attitudes will change their behavior. The theory of cognitive dissonance reverses the direction: It holds that, when people's behavior changes, their attitudes will change (Festinger, 1957).

Cognitive dissonance is *a state of unpleasant tension that people experience when they hold contradictory attitudes or when their behavior is inconsistent with their attitudes, especially if they perceive this inconsistency as a threat to their self-esteem.* For example, if you pride yourself on honesty and find yourself saying something you do not believe, you feel tension. You can reduce that tension in three ways: You can change what you are saying to match your attitudes, change your attitude to match what you are saying, or adopt an explanation that justifies your behavior under the circumstances (Wicklund & Brehm, 1976). (See Figure 14.4.) Although you might adopt any of these options, most of the existing research has focused on how cognitive dissonance changes people's attitudes.

Evidence Favoring the Cognitive Dissonance Theory

Leon Festinger and J. Merrill Carlsmith (1959) carried out the following classic experiment on cognitive dissonance. Imagine yourself as one of the participants. The experimenters explain that they are studying motor behavior. They show you a board full of pegs. Your task is to take each peg out of the board, rotate it one-fourth of a turn, and return it to the board. When you finish all the pegs, you start over from the top, rotating all the pegs again as quickly and accurately as possible. . . for an hour. As you proceed, an experimenter silently takes notes. You find your task tedious and boring.

At the end of the hour, the experimenter thanks you for participating and "explains" to you (falsely) that the study's purpose was to determine whether people's performances are influenced by their attitudes toward the task. You were in the neutral-attitude group, but those in the positive-attitude group are told before they start that this will be an enjoyable, interesting experience. In fact, the experimenter continues, right now the research assistant is supposed to give that instruction to the next participant, a young woman waiting in the next room. The experimenter excuses himself to find the research assistant and then returns distraught. The assistant is nowhere to be found, he says. He turns to you and asks, "Would you be willing to tell the next subject that you thought this was an interesting, enjoyable experiment? If so, I will pay you."

Assume that you consent, as most students in the study did. After you tell that woman in the next room that you enjoyed the study, what would you actually think of the study, assuming the experimenter paid you $1? What if he paid you $20? (This study occurred in the 1950s, before decades of inflation. In today's money, that $20 would be worth more than $100.)

In the actual study, after participants told the woman how much fun this experiment was, they left, believing the study was over. As they walked down the hall, they were met by a representative of the psychology department who explained that the department wanted to find out what kinds

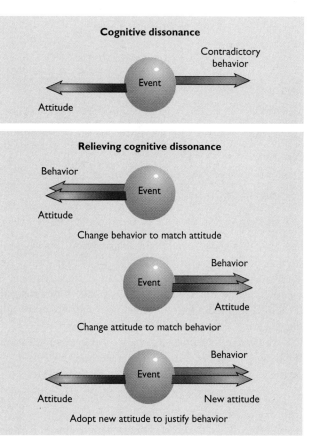

FIGURE 14.4 Cognitive dissonance is a state of tension that arises when people perceive that their attitudes do not match their behavior. Theoretically, they could resolve this discrepancy by changing either their attitudes or their behavior, or by developing a new attitude or excuse to explain the discrepancy. Most of the research, however, has focused on how cognitive dissonance leads to a change of attitude.

of experiments were being conducted and whether they were educationally worthwhile. (The answers to these questions were the real point of the experiment.) Participants were asked how enjoyable they considered the experiment to be and whether they would be willing to participate in a similar experiment later.

The students who received $20 said they thought the experiment was boring and that they wanted nothing to do with another such experiment. However, contrary to what you might guess, those who received just $1 said they enjoyed the experiment and would be willing to participate again (Figure 14.5).

Why? According to the theory of cognitive dissonance, those who accepted $20 to tell a lie experienced little conflict. They knew they were lying, but they also knew why: for the $20. They had no reason to change their original opinion of the experiment—that they had been bored to tears. However, the students who had told a lie for only $1 felt a conflict between their true attitude toward the boring experiment and what they had said about it. The small payment provided little reason for lying, so they experienced

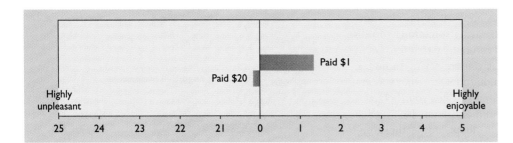

FIGURE 14.5 In a classic experiment demonstrating cognitive dissonance, subjects were paid either $1 or $20 for telling another subject that they enjoyed an experiment (which was actually boring). Later, they were asked for their real opinions. Those subjects who were paid the smaller amount said that they enjoyed the study more than the others. (Based on data from Festinger & Carlsmith, 1959.)

cognitive dissonance—an unpleasant tension. They did not want to feel bad about telling a lie, so the only way they could reduce their tension was to change their attitude, to decide that the experiment really had been interesting after all. ("I learned a lot of interesting things about myself, like . . . uh . . . how good I am at rotating pegs.")

The idea of cognitive dissonance attracted much attention and inspired a great deal of research in the 1960s and 1970s (Aronson, 1997). Two representative examples:

• An experimenter left a child in a room with toys but forbade the child to play with one particular toy. If the experimenter threatened the child with severe punishment for playing with the toy, the child avoided it but still regarded it as desirable. However, if the experimenter merely said that he or she would be unhappy or disappointed if the child played with that toy, the child avoided the toy and said (even weeks later) that it was not a good toy (Aronson & Carlsmith, 1963).

• The experimenter asked college students to write an essay defending a position that the experimenter knew, from previous information, was contrary to the students' actual beliefs. For example, college students who favored freer access to alcohol might be asked to write essays on why the college should increase restrictions on alcohol. Those who were told they must write the essays did not change their views significantly, but those who were asked to "please" write the essay but were also reminded that they did so voluntarily generally came to agree with what they wrote (Croyle & Cooper, 1983).

Some people are more likely than others to alter their attitudes as a result of cognitive dissonance. A few studies have found weaker cognitive dissonance effects in Japanese than in North American people, perhaps because the Japanese are more accustomed to subordinating their own attitudes to do what someone else asks of them (Heine & Lehman, 1997).

The general principle is that, if you ask people to do something they would not otherwise do, by means of a minimum reward or a tiny threat, so that they are acting voluntarily or almost voluntarily, they will change their attitudes to defend what they are doing to reduce cognitive dissonance. This procedure is a particularly powerful way of changing people's attitudes because people are actively participating, not just quietly listening to someone else explain the reasons for an opinion. You have probably heard people say, "If you want to change people's behavior, you have to change their attitudes first." The results of cognitive dissonance experiments tell us quite the opposite: If you start by changing people's behavior, their attitudes will change too.

CONCEPT CHECKS

9. Suppose your parents pay you to get a good grade in a course that you consider boring. According to cognitive dissonance theory, are you more likely to develop a positive attitude toward your studies if your parents pay you $10 or $100?
10. The effort to avoid cognitive dissonance leads to consistency in behavior. Use that principle to explain the foot-in-the-door technique. (Check your answers on pages 533, 534.)

THE MESSAGE
Attitudes, Persuasion, and Manipulation

When you are forming an attitude toward something of little consequence to you, it is understandable that you will follow the peripheral route, paying little attention to the complexities of the evidence. When you are dealing with important matters, however, such as how you will spend your time and money, or who to choose for your partner in life, you will almost certainly follow the central route, examining the facts as carefully as you can. It is important to be alert to some of the influences that might throw you off course, such as the foot-in-the-door technique, lowballing, and cognitive dissonance. Advertisers, politicians, and vast numbers of others are trying to polish their techniques of persuasion, and not everyone has your best interest at heart.

SUMMARY

✳ *Attitudes.* An attitude is a like or dislike of something or somebody that influences our behavior toward that thing or person. (page 524)

✱ *Two routes to persuasion*. When people are considering an appeal regarding a topic of little importance, they are easily persuaded by the speaker's appearance and other superficial factors, regardless of the strength or weakness of the evidence. When people consider an appeal on a matter of importance to them, they pay more attention to logic and to the quality of the evidence. (page 525)

✱ *Resistant attitudes*. On a few topics, such as the death penalty, many people form entrenched attitudes that are based on little real information. (page 525)

✱ *Sleeper effect*. When people reject a message because of their low regard for the person who proposed it, they sometimes forget where they heard the idea and later come to accept it. (page 527)

✱ *Minority influence*. Although a minority may have little influence at first, it can, through persistent repetition of its message, eventually persuade the majority to adopt its position or to consider other alternatives. (page 527)

✱ *Influence of fear-inducing messages*. Whether messages that appeal to fear prove effective depends on whether people perceive the danger as real and whether they think they can do anything about it. (page 527)

✱ *Forewarning and inoculation effects*. People evaluate the reasoning behind the persuasive messages they hear. If they have been warned that someone will try to persuade them of something, or if they have previously heard a weak version of the persuasive argument, they tend to resist the argument more strongly than they otherwise would have. (page 529)

✱ *Strategies of persuasion*. Several procedures can influence people to do something they would not have done, if asked directly. These include starting with a tiny request and then increasing it, starting with an enormous request and offering to compromise, offering a generous deal and then demanding more, and offering a moderate deal and then adding inducements. (page 529)

✱ *Cognitive dissonance*. Cognitive dissonance is a state of unpleasant tension that arises from contradictory attitudes or from behavior that conflicts with a person's attitudes. When people's behavior does not match their attitudes, they try to eliminate the inconsistency by changing either their behavior or their attitudes. (page 530)

Suggestion for Further Reading

Petty, R. E., & Cacioppo, J. T. (1996). *Attitudes and persuasion: Classic and contemporary approaches* (2nd ed). Dubuque, IA: Times Mirror Higher Education. A complete yet readable review of research on attitudes and attitude change.

Terms

attitude   a like or dislike that influences our behavior toward a person or thing (page 524)

high self-monitor   a person who constantly monitors his or her own behavior to try to behave in what others consider an appropriate manner for each situation (page 525)

central route to persuasion   a method of persuasion based on careful evaluation of evidence and logic (page 525)

peripheral route to persuasion   a method of persuasion based on such superficial factors as the speaker's appearance and reputation or the sheer number of arguments presented, regardless of their quality (page 525)

sleeper effect   delayed persuasion by an initially rejected message (page 527)

forewarning effect   the tendency of a brief preview of a message to decrease its persuasiveness (page 529)

inoculation effect   the tendency of a persuasive message to be weakened if people first hear a weak argument supporting the same conclusion (page 529)

foot-in-the-door technique   a method of eliciting compliance by first making a modest request and then following it with a larger request (page 530)

door-in-the-face technique   a method of eliciting compliance by first making an outrageous request and then replying to the refusal with a more reasonable request (page 530)

lowball technique   the procedure of first offering an extremely favorable deal and then making additional demands after the other person has committed to the deal (page 530)

that's-not-all technique   a method of eliciting compliance whereby someone makes an offer and then improves the offer before anyone has a chance to reply (page 530)

cognitive dissonance   a state of unpleasant tension that people experience when they hold contradictory attitudes or when their behavior is inconsistent with their attitudes, especially if they perceive this inconsistency as a threat to their self-esteem (page 531)

Answers to Concept Checks

4. The attitudes of low self-monitors will more often match their behavior. High self-monitors are more likely to do what they think is expected of them, independent of their attitudes. (page 525)

5. You will pay more attention to the evidence and logic, following the central route to persuasion, for the decision about your major. (page 525)

6. The fact that your idea was overwhelmingly rejected does not mean that you should give up. If you and a few allies continue to present this plan in a simple way, showing apparent agreement among yourselves, the majority may eventually endorse a similar plan—but probably without giving you credit for suggesting the idea. (page 527)

7. You should expose them to weak attacks on their beliefs so that they will learn how to resist such attacks. Otherwise, they will be like children who grow up in a germ-free environment: They will develop no "immunity" and will thus be vulnerable when their beliefs are attacked. (page 529)

8. **a.** Door-in-the-face technique; **b.** that's-not-all technique; **c.** foot-in-the-door technique. (page 530)

9. You will come to like your studies more if you are paid $10 than if you are paid $100. If you are paid only $10, you won't be able to tell yourself that you are studying harder only for the money. Instead, you will tell yourself that you must be really interested. The theory of intrinsic and extrinsic motivation leads to the same prediction: If you study hard in the absence of any strong external reason, you will perceive that you have internal reasons for studying. (page 532)

10. Once you have agreed to a small request, you can maintain consistency (decrease dissonance) by agreeing to similar requests in the future. (page 532)

Web Resources

Cognitive Dissonance Theory

ccwf.cc.utexas.edu/~benj/patty/

A student paper describes cognitive dissonance and lists techniques for reducing dissonance, with help from Calvin and Hobbs.

Cognitive Dissonance

thanatos.uoregon.edu/~galahad/cogdiss.html

A student examines "The Role of Cognitive Dissonance in Decision Making."

Interpersonal Attraction

How do people choose their friends?

How do people select their romantic partners?

William Proxmire, a former U.S. senator, used to give "Golden Fleece Awards" to those who, in his opinion, most flagrantly wasted the taxpayers' money. He once bestowed an award on some psychologists who had received a federal grant to study how people fall in love. According to Proxmire, the research was pointless because people do not want to understand love. They prefer, he said, to let such matters remain a mystery.

This module presents the information Senator Proxmire thought you did not want to know.

People's Need for One Another

Think back to your first week at college. Did you feel lonely? Maybe not, if you went to the same college as some close friends, or if you made some good friends rapidly. But many college students do feel lonely at the start. If you did, you may have spent hours on the telephone with friends and family back home, or you may have worked hard at establishing new friendships.

Clearly, people crave close, long-term relationships with other people. We have a "need to belong," to identify with a family or close group of friends and to be able to talk with someone about personal, confidential matters (Collins & Miller, 1994). Why? Some psychologists have proposed that we learn this need from our early experiences with a nurturing parent. I shall not deny the importance of early nurturing experiences, but those experiences do not fully explain our strong social needs. If they did, we would find similar social needs in all other mammalian species. Bears, humans, porcupines, deer, and all the rest start life with a nurturing mother-infant relationship; nevertheless, some species develop a rich social life and some do not (Figure 14.6). Humans' need for social relationships might therefore best be regarded as a basic need, a part of our biological nature (Baumeister & Leary, 1995).

Besides lasting relationships, we sometimes cultivate temporary friends for a limited purpose. For example, you might want to get together with other students in a particular class to study for a test, or you might get together with a group for recreational sports.

Brief, casual affiliations can also be important to us for our own self-understanding. If you have just had an intense and trying emotional experience, you might want to be with other people who have had a similar experience, to compare your reactions to theirs and (you hope) demonstrate that you coped with the experience at least as well as they did (Kruglanski & Mayseless, 1990). People also like to associate with people who can set a good example. For example, cancer patients generally like to associate with other cancer patients, especially patients who are showing signs of recovery and who can thus provide an encouraging role model (Taylor & Lobel, 1989).

When people expect to face a difficult experience in the near future, they generally like to be with other people

FIGURE 14.6 Although all mammalian species start life with a nurturing mother-infant relationship, some species become highly social and some do not. Humans are among the highly social species. Evidently, our tendency to be social is part of our basic nature.

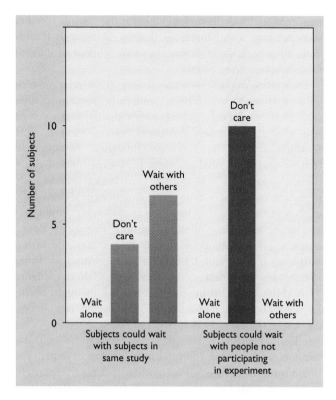

FIGURE 14.7 In Schachter's experiment, people who thought they were waiting for a procedure in which they would receive strong shocks preferred to wait with others who were about to undergo the same procedure. They had no particular desire to wait with people who were not participating in the same study. That is, miserable people like to be with other miserable people. In more general terms, we like to compare our reactions to those of other people who have had, or expect to have, similar experiences.

facing a similar predicament. As the old saying goes, "Misery loves company." To test this hypothesis, Stanley Schachter (1959) told subjects that he intended to measure the effects of electric shock on their heart rate and blood pressure. He told one group to expect substantial shocks; he told the other group to expect mild tickling or tingling sensations. Then, he told the subjects that they would have to wait about 10 minutes while the experimenter made some last-minute adjustments to the equipment. Some subjects were given a choice between waiting alone or waiting with other subjects in the same experiment. Other subjects were given a choice between waiting alone and waiting with students who just happened to be in the building (not subjects in the experiment). Subjects who expected only mild shocks had little preference; they were willing to wait anywhere or with anybody. But the subjects who expected strong shocks strongly preferred to wait with other subjects in the same experiment, as Figure 14.7 shows. In short, people in distress crave the company of people in similar distress. That is, misery loves *miserable* company. Short-term relationships like these can serve a variety of purposes, even if they do not develop into anything deeper or more lasting.

Establishing Lasting Relationships

Out of all the people you meet, how do you choose those few who become your friends? Here, we shall consider factors relevant to both friendships and dating relationships; later, we shall specifically discuss dating and marriage.

Proximity and Familiarity

Proximity means *closeness.* (It comes from the same root as *approximate.*) Not surprisingly, *we are most likely to become friends with people who live or work in close proximity and who become familiar to us.* In one study, residents of a graduate housing project at the Massachusetts Institute of Technology were asked to list their three closest friends (Festinger, Schachter, & Back, 1950). The residents lived in two-story buildings with five apartments on each floor (Figure 14.8). On the average, they reported that about two-thirds of their closest friends lived in the same building, mostly on the same floor. People were most likely to make friends with their next-door neighbors.

At the start of a school year, Robert Hays (1985) asked college students to name two other students with whom they thought they might become friends. After 3 months, he found that more of the potential friends who lived close together had become friends than had those who lived farther apart.

Proximity increases the probability that two people will become friends or lovers, partly by giving them more opportunities to meet and talk and partly by just making them familiar with each other. Other things being equal, *the more often we come in contact with someone—or with an inanimate object such as a food or a painting—the more we tend to like that person or object* (Saegert, Swap, & Zajonc, 1973; Zajonc, 1968). This tendency is known as the **mere exposure effect**.

Similarity

Here's another finding that will hardly surprise you: Most close friends resemble one another in age, physical attractiveness, political and religious beliefs, intelligence, academic interests, religion, and attitudes (Laumann, 1969).

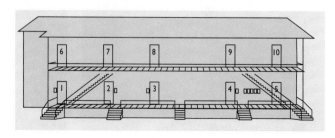

FIGURE 14.8 Students who lived in this graduate housing project generally chose friends who lived nearby. (From Festinger, Schachter, & Back, 1950.)

Even when friends differ in some ways, they generally have much in common, such as interests, attitudes, and level of education.

Most people also date and eventually marry people who closely resemble themselves in many ways. Couples who differ markedly in their education and interests may date for a while, but they are not likely to marry (Plomin, De-Fries, & Roberts, 1977). Couples who marry in spite of major differences in personality are likely to have troubled marriages (Russell & Wells, 1991).

Do you like people better when you find out that their beliefs and attitudes are similar to yours? That question turns out to be a little trickier than it sounds at first. You probably like most of the people you meet, until you have a reason to alter your judgment. If you think at all about a new acquaintance's beliefs and attitudes, you probably assume that he or she shares your own beliefs and attitudes. . . because most people do, don't they? After all, your opinions and actions are normal and correct, so of course most other people share them (Alicke & Largo, 1995). Therefore, finding a disagreement with someone may *lower* your regard for them more than finding agreement with someone *increases* your regard (Rosenbaum, 1986).

Confirmation of Self-Concept

You might well be saying, "Big deal. People make friends with others who live nearby and resemble them. Psychologists needed research to demonstrate *that?*"

Sometimes, it is worthwhile to do research to demonstrate the obvious, just because what appears to be obvious is not always so. For example, suppose you are in a research study. First, you are asked to describe yourself. Then, two other people tell you how they reacted. After you have described yourself, the first person says, "I think you seem a pleasant, honest person. You're intelligent and you have some interesting ideas and a nice sense of humor."

The second says, "I hate to be rude, but frankly I think you seem rather superficial. You're trying to make a good

impression, but for me, you're failing. You drift aimlessly from one topic to another; you can't even organize your thoughts."

Which one would you choose as a partner? The obvious answer is the first one; indeed, just about everyone enjoys hearing some flattering comments. However, many people who have low self-esteem choose the person who gave them a low evaluation (Swann, 1997). Evidently, people believe and seek the company of someone who confirms their self-evaluation. Some who think little of themselves find it cognitively satisfying to be with others who share that low evaluation.

You can see the harmful consequences of this tendency. Someone with a low self-evaluation chooses friends and perhaps even a husband or wife who constantly criticizes. The result of all that criticizing is even lower self-esteem.

The Equity Principle

A friendship or romance works best if each partner believes that he or she is getting just about as good a deal as the other party is. The situation is not unlike a business relationship. According to **exchange** or **equity theories,** *social relationships are transactions in which partners exchange goods and services.* In some cases, the businesslike nature of the exchange is fairly blatant. In the "Singles' Ads" sections of many newspapers, those seeking a relationship describe what they have to offer ("35-year-old divorced male, 6'1", business executive, athletic. . .") and what they want in return ("seeks warm, caring, attractive woman, age 27–33 . . ."). The ads resemble the "asked" and "bid" columns for the stock exchange (Kenrick & Trost, 1989). People run ads for nonromantic friendships less often, but the same principle applies: A good friendship has a balance of giving and taking. Each partner gets enough reinforcement to support continued efforts.

As in business, a friendship or romantic relationship is most stable if both partners believe in the fairness of the deal. It is easiest to establish a stable relationship if the partners are about equally attractive and intelligent and contribute about equally to the finances and the chores, and so forth. With some couples, one partner is wealthier but the other is more attractive, or one is more intelligent but the other is very kind and considerate, or some other kind of compensation exists. Those arrangements can also seem fair, although it is more difficult to be sure.

CONCEPT CHECK

11. A person your own age from another country moves in next door to you. Neither of you speaks the other's language. Are you likely to become friends? What factors will tend to strengthen the likelihood of your becoming friends? What factors will tend to weaken it? (Check your answers on page 542.)

Special Concerns for Selecting a Mate

Choosing a partner for a marriage (or the equivalent of a marriage) is not the same as choosing other kinds of friends, mostly because of the extra dimension of raising children. Yes, I know, not everyone wants to get married, not all married couples plan to have children, and many unmarried people rear children. What I shall describe does not apply to everyone. Still, it applies to those who hope to marry and have children.

Physical Attractiveness

What characteristics do you look for in a person you date and perhaps eventually marry? If you are like most college students, you say that you want "someone who is intelligent, honest, easy to talk to, with a good sense of humor."

Now imagine a friend says, "Hey, you're not doing anything this weekend, right? How about going out on a blind date with my cousin who is visiting here for the weekend?"

"Well, I don't know," you reply. "Tell me about your cousin."

"My cousin is intelligent, honest, easy to talk to, and has a good sense of humor."

Are you eager to date this person? Probably not. Your friend did not even mention the cousin's appearance, so you infer the worst. So, were you being dishonest when you said you wanted someone intelligent, honest, and easy to talk to? Not really. You did not mention appearance, because you assumed that people would take for granted your preference for good looks. (You also didn't say that you hope your date speaks English; you don't need to mention the obvious.)

In one study, social psychologists arranged blind dates for 332 freshman couples for a dance before the start of classes. They asked all the participants to fill out lengthy questionnaires, but the experimenters actually paired students at random. Midway through the dance, the experimenters separated the men and women and asked them to rate how much they liked their date and whether they hoped to date this person again. The only factor that influenced how much each liked the other was appearance (Walster, Aronson, Abrahams, & Rottman, 1966). Similarities of attitudes, personality, and intelligence counted for very little. We should not find this result surprising; after all, during a couple of hours at a dance, how much opportunity does a couple have to explore each other's deepest beliefs and values? About all they knew about each other was related to appearance. Intelligence, honesty, and other character values do become important in a relationship, but not until later.

Physical attractiveness is influential not just for its own sake but also because it biases how we respond to what people say and do. As a rule, people regard their physically attractive acquaintances as highly sociable, dominant, sexually responsive, mentally healthy, intelligent, and socially skilled (Feingold, 1992a). One group of experimenters asked subjects to rate the personality and intelligence of students in a series of yearbook photographs (Dion, Berscheid, & Walster, 1972). Participants rated the attractive students as more sensitive, kind, poised, and sociable than the others.

The Possible Biological Value of Attractiveness

Why is physical appearance so important to us? We take it so much for granted that we don't even understand why there is a question. But think about other species: In many bird species, the male is more brightly colored than the female. Early in the mating season, brightly colored males sing vigorously from perches exposed at the treetops. Females shop around among the unmated males of their species and generally choose the one that is brightest in color and sings most often and most vigorously. In a few species, a female also prefers a male with an especially long tail (Figure 14.9). From an evolutionary standpoint, isn't she making a foolish choice? The male she chooses has devoted a lot of his energies to feather color. (It takes much more energy to produce bright colors than dull ones.) Singing loudly from the treetop is practically an invitation to hawks and other predators. If he has a long tail, it may look pretty, but it interferes with his flying. Why should the female prefer a mate who wastes his energies and endangers his life?

Biologists eventually discovered that wasting energy and risking life was precisely the point (Zahavi & Zahavi, 1997). Only a healthy, vigorous male can afford to spend that much energy on colorful feathers or a long tail, or to risk predation by singing from an exposed perch. A weak or sickly male who spent his energies on "false advertising" would probably die. In effect, a colorful, singing male is screaming, "Look at me! I am so vigorous that I can afford to take crazy risks, and I have so much energy to spare that I can afford to waste it. You will certainly want me to be the father of your children!" The female, we presume, does not understand why she is attracted to colorful, loudly singing males. She just is, because throughout her evolutionary history, females who chose colorful, loudly singing males

FIGURE 14.9 In a few bird species, males with very long tails attract more mates. However, they pay a price: The long tail impairs their flying abilities. As a rule, only very healthy and vigorous males have extra long tails.

generally had energetic partners who provided them with plenty of food while they were sitting on the nest and probably also provided good genes to the babies.

Now, back to humans: Is attractiveness in humans also a valid indicator of health, fertility, and other favorable characteristics? Theoretically, it should be. Certainly, many illnesses decrease people's attractiveness. Also, *good-looking* is in many regards similar to *normal*. A computer can take photographs of a large number of moderately similar people, all sitting in the same position and looking in the same direction, and average their faces. Most people regard the resulting averaged face as more attractive than most of the original faces (Langlois & Roggman, 1990; Langlois, Roggman, & Musselman, 1994). (See Figure 14.10.) In other words, a highly attractive face has an average nose, about an average mouth, about an average distance between the eyes, and so forth. If we note anything "unusual" about an attractive face, it is the absence of irregularities—no crooked teeth, no skin blemishes, no asymmetries or peculiarities.

Why is normal attractive? The hypothesis is that a normal face is probably a healthy face. The genes for an average face have spread in the population, presumably because they are linked to success. Any face that departs much from the average could show signs of disease or genetic mutation. So it would seem, at least. However, in one study, researchers obtained photos of hundreds of teenagers from long ago. Then, they asked people to examine the photos and rate the faces for attractiveness; they also obtained extensive medical records for the people in the photos. The ratings of attractiveness did not correlate reliably with health, either for adolescence or later life. People who were rated attractive were more likely to marry, and especially to marry early, but unattractive people who did marry were just as likely to have children as the more attractive people (Kalick, Zebrowitz, Langlois, & Johnson, 1998). Evidently, at least for this one sample, attractiveness was false advertising; it had nothing to do with health or fertility.

If facial attractiveness is a poor cue to health, what about the rest of the body? According to one theory, men prefer women with a narrow waist and wide hips—a hip-to-waist ratio of about 0.7—because women with that ratio are most likely to be fertile. However, in one study, both men and women examined line drawings of women's figures, as in Figure 14.11, and selected which ones were most attractive and most likely to bear children successfully. Contrary to this theory, neither men nor women showed any consistent preference for a .7 waist-to-hip ratio. Most rated one of the thinner women as most attractive and one of the heavier women as most likely to bear children (Tassinary & Hansen, 1998). In short, the women who people generally regard as most attractive are neither the ones that scientists estimate to be most fertile (.7 ratio) nor the ones that most nonscientists estimate to be most fertile (more than .7 ratio). Attractiveness is generally honest advertising about a bird's health and vigor, but in humans, the evidence so far suggests that attractiveness is frequently false advertising.

SOMETHING TO THINK ABOUT

The studies just described were conducted in the United States. Would you expect attractiveness to be better correlated with health and vigor in any other societies? ✳

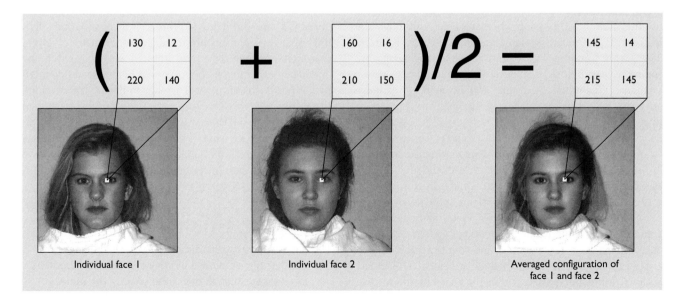

FIGURE 14.10 A computer averaged a set of faces by measuring the gray value of each point on each picture and then producing a new picture with the average of the grays at each point. This set of photos illustrates the procedure for two original faces. The numbers are for illustrative purposes only. Especially when a large number of faces have been averaged, most people rate the resulting "average" face more attractive than most of the originals. (From Langlois, Roggman, & Musselman, 1994).

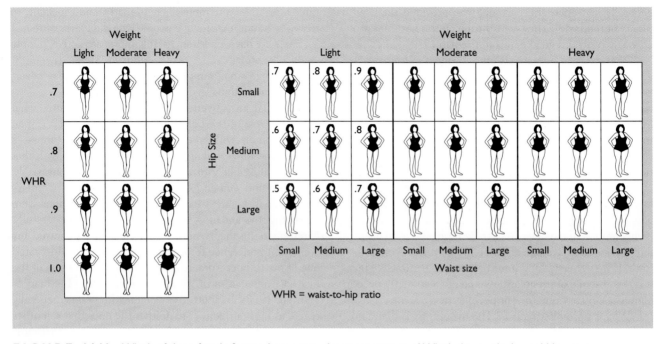

FIGURE 14.11 Which of these female figures do you regard as most attractive? Which do you think would be most likely to have babies successfully? In one study, most men and women picked one of the thinner women as most attractive but one of the heavier women as most likely to be fertile, thereby failing to support the theory that attractive means fertile. (From Tassinary & Hansen, 1998).

Men's Preferences and Women's Preferences

With most couples, who is older, the man or the woman? Who is more concerned about the other partner's appearance, the man or the woman? And who is more concerned about the partner's ability to earn a living and provide resources, the man or the woman?

You probably answered "the man" to the first and second questions and "the woman" to the third. The answers are the same in every known human society, although the degree of preference varies (Feingold, 1992b; Kenrick, 1994). (For example, in societies where a man must work for many years before he achieves economic success, young women prefer much older men. Where men can achieve success more quickly, women prefer men closer to their own age.)

Can we explain why men prefer younger women? Recall from Chapter 3 the *sociobiological approach,* also known as *evolutionary psychology,* which emphasizes the idea that social behavior is a product of evolutionary pressures (Buss, 1994; Kenrick, 1994). According to this approach, men prefer young women because women reach menopause and therefore stop being fertile at about age 40–50. Men have therefore evolved a tendency to find younger (probably fertile) women more attractive than older women. This theory sounds rather persuasive, although it is difficult to test. And, as we just saw, the evidence so far has not supported other speculations about a link between attractiveness and fertility.

Consider another difference between men and women: In every known culture, extramarital affairs by husbands are generally more tolerated than those by wives. The degree of that difference varies; for example, the Swedes tolerate a woman's extramarital affairs more than the Chinese or Arabs do (Buss, 1994). In no culture, however, are affairs by wives considered more acceptable than those by husbands. From a sociobiological standpoint, one explanation is that a man cannot be sure he is the father of his wife's baby unless he knows that she has had sex with him alone. Consequently, a wife's infidelity is a threat; it means that he might unknowingly spend his life rearing another man's children. A woman does not have that problem; she knows that any child she bears must be her own. For her, a greater concern is that her husband might leave her to devote his attention to another woman. Surveys in several cultures find that men are more distressed than women by a partner's sexual affair with someone else; women tend to be more jealous when a partner becomes emotionally close to another woman (Buss, Larsen, Westen, & Semmelroth, 1992; Buunk, Angleitner, Oubaid, & Buss, 1996).

CONCEPT CHECK

12. Suppose astronauts discover humanlike beings on another planet, whose biology and culture resemble ours except that all men have exactly the same wealth, and women remain fertile all their lives instead of losing their fertility at menopause. What would you predict about the mate preferences of men and women on this planet? (Check your answer on page 542.)

Romantic and Passionate Love

A couple that decides to marry announces to each other and to the world that they love each other more than anyone else and that they pledge to stay together as long as they both shall live. And yet a distressing percentage of marriages end in divorce. What went wrong?

Sometimes people change in ways they could not have foreseen, but in many cases the problem is that people simply marry the wrong partners. The Western custom of dating is well adapted for determining whether two people enjoy the same kinds of entertainment but not for determining the factors that are critical for long-term family life. Questionnaire studies have found that, as couples continue to date, their estimates of each other's sexual histories, activity preferences, and so forth become more *confident,* but not more *accurate* (Swann & Gill, 1997). Answer the questions below, first for yourself and second *as you think your dating partner would answer them.* (Several of these questions assume a heterosexual relationship; please disregard any items that do not apply to you.)

1. After you marry or establish another long-term relationship, how often would you want to visit your parents? your in-laws?
2. How many children do you want to have? how soon?

3. How do you want to raise your children? Should one partner stay home with the children full-time while they are young? Or should both partners share the responsibility for child care? Or should the children be placed in a day-care center?
4. Suppose one of you is offered a good job in one city and the other is offered a good job in a city a hundred miles away. Neither of you can find a satisfactory job in the other's city. How would you decide where to live?
5. Suppose a sudden financial crisis strikes. Where would you cut expenses to balance the budget? clothes? food? housing? entertainment?
6. How often do you plan to attend religious services?
7. How and where do you like to spend your vacations?
8. How often would you expect to spend an evening with friends, apart from your partner?

Were you uncertain about how your dating partner would answer any of these questions? If so, you are in the majority. And yet, disagreements about such questions are among the most common reasons for conflict in marriage or other long-term relationships. I am not suggesting that you should ask every person you date to fill out this questionnaire. However, before you get far enough into a relationship that love and marriage become a realistic possibility, you should discuss anything that is important to you. If you care about having children, find out what your partner thinks. If you want your eventual husband or wife to share your religious beliefs (or lack of them), discuss religion and your deepest values.

In a mature, lasting relationship, a couple can count on each other for care and affection through both the good times and the bad times.

Romantic Relationships that Last

When you hear about the high percentage of marriages that end in divorce, it is easy to despair, but many marriages still remain strong for a lifetime. Most characteristics of successful marriages are what you would probably expect (Karney & Bradbury, 1995):

- The husband and wife have similar attitudes and personalities.
- Both find sexual satisfaction in the relationship.
- The couple has a steady and adequate income.
- The husband has a good enough job to maintain self-respect.
- The wife was not pregnant before they married.
- The couple's parents also had successful marriages.

A successful marriage changes over the years, just as individual lives do. At first, the couple has the intense excitement of learning about each other and doing new things together. Years later, the two have worked out a complex system of shared work and understandings. Although they do not arouse each other's emotions as intensely or as frequently as before (Berscheid, 1983), they still love each other, perhaps even more deeply. If one of them becomes ill or dies, the emotion inherent in the mature relationship becomes vividly apparent.

THE MESSAGE
People Need Other People

Few people enjoy living as a hermit, isolated from others. In prisons, one of the harshest forms of punishment is solitary confinement. Almost any social contact is better than none at all. However, many people may choose their friends and their spouse poorly. This module began with the observation that former Senator Proxmire thought people did not want or need to learn about research on the topic of love. Let's end with the observation that people definitely need to know more about love.

SUMMARY

❋ *People's need for one another.* People crave the companionship of other people, especially others to whom they have felt emotionally close for a long time. This need can be regarded as part of human nature. (page 535)

❋ *Short-term affiliation.* People in distress gain strength from associating even briefly with other people, especially others who have undergone or who expect to undergo similar distressing experiences. (page 536)

❋ *More lasting relationships.* People generally choose friends and romantic partners who live near them, resemble them, and confirm their self-esteem. Relationships are most likely to survive and grow if each person believes that he or

she is getting about as good a deal as the other person is. (page 536)

❋ *Marriage and similar attachments.* People have special considerations when choosing a potential marriage partner, because marriage usually implies a commitment to rearing children together. The behavior and interests of men are somewhat different from those of women. (page 538)

❋ *Physical attractiveness.* In many nonhuman species, physical attractiveness is a reliable cue to the individual's health, vigor, and therefore desirability as a mate. In humans, attractiveness is a powerful determinant of mate choice but has not been demonstrably linked to health or other biologically useful functions. (page 538)

❋ *Long-term romantic relationships.* Marriage and similar relationships often break up because the partners had chosen each other for the wrong reasons, without learning about the values and attitudes that are important for daily life and rearing a family. Marriages are successful when the partners have much in common and find ways to satisfy each other's needs. (page 541)

Suggestions for Further Reading

Berscheid, E. (1994). Interpersonal relationships. *Annual Review of Psychology, 45,* 79–129. Review of research about how people establish relationships and how those relationships change over time.

Buss, D. (1994). *The evolution of desire: Strategies of human mating.* New York: Basic Books. Discussion of the evolutionary influences on men's and women's preferences in a mate.

Terms

proximity (literally, "closeness")   the tendency to choose as friends people with whom we come in frequent contact (page 536)

mere exposure effect   the tendency to increase our liking for everything and everyone that has become familiar (page 536)

exchange or **equity theories**   theories maintaining that social relationships are transactions in which partners exchange goods and services (page 537)

Answers to Concept Checks

11. Proximity and familiarity will strengthen the likelihood of your becoming friends. The similarity principle will weaken it. Because of the difference in languages, you will have little chance, at least at first, to discover any similarities in interests or attitudes. In fact, proximity will probably not be a potent force, because it serves largely as a means of enabling people to discover what they have in common. (page 537)

12. If all men are equally wealthy, women should have no reason to prefer older men and would presumably prefer men who are close to their own age. If women's fertility lasts as late in life as men's does, then the men on this

planet should not have a strong preference for younger women. (page 541)

Web Resources

Physical Attraction

miavx1.muohio.edu/~psybersite/attraction/

Four students in an advanced social psychology course developed this tutorial examining physical attraction and how it is affected by attributions and gender, and provide some cross-cultural comparisons and a quiz.

Dating, Love, Marriage, and Sex

www.cmhc.com/psyhelp/chap10/

The nature of attraction and love is one of the topics discussed in this chapter of the on-line book *Psychological Self-Help*.

MODULE 14.4

Interpersonal Influence

Under what circumstances do we conform to the behavior of others?

Why do people act differently in groups than when they are alone?

In the spring of 1983, a strange epidemic swept through a Palestinian village in one of the territories occupied by Israel. The hospitals were flooded with people, mostly adolescents, complaining of headaches, dizzy spells, stomach pains, blurred vision, and labored breathing. The Palestinians accused the Israelis of poisoning the air or the water, perhaps in an effort to sterilize young Palestinian women. The Israelis replied with indignant denials.

Meanwhile, although physicians conducted extensive tests on all the patients, they could find nothing medically wrong with them. They studied the food, the air, the water, and every possible source of poison or contagious disease. They found no signs of anything that could cause illness. Finally, they concluded that all the symptoms were the result of anxiety, coupled with the power of suggestion (Paicheler, 1988). The Palestinians, understandably nervous about the political tensions in the region, *believed* they had been poisoned; this belief and the accompanying symptoms of illness spread from person to person just like a contagious disease.

We live in an ambiguous world. We often fail to understand what is happening or what we should do about it; when in doubt, we take our cues from what other people are doing. And following their lead is fine, if they happen to be better informed or wiser than we are.

Other people influence us in two major ways: First, they provide us with *information* (or misinformation). For example, if almost everyone else is flocking toward or away from something, they probably have a reason, so we should at least pay attention to whatever is driving their actions. Second, people set *norms*, defining what we are expected to do. In much of our social behavior, we follow rules of politeness, such as "do not interrupt," "raise your hand if you want to speak in class," and "wait in line after the people who arrived before you do." People who persistently violate these rules will anger other people and suffer the consequences. Here, we shall encounter many examples of both informational and normative influences.

Conformity

Conformity means *maintaining or changing one's behavior to match the behavior of others.* The pressure to conform sometimes exerts an overwhelming normative influence. Koversada, on the coast of the Adriatic Sea, is a small, totally nudist city (although people do sometimes dress for dinner at a formal restaurant). If a first-time visitor walks around the city wearing clothes, other people stop and stare, sometimes shaking their heads with disapproval. The visitor begins to feel awkward, out of place, and just as self-conscious as a naked person would be in a city of fully clothed people. Most visitors soon undress like everyone else (Newman, 1988).

Conformity can also serve informational functions, especially when we are not quite sure what we are seeing or hearing. One example is an illusion known as the **autokinetic effect:** *If you sit in a darkened room and stare at one small, stationary point of light, the point will eventually seem to move.* If someone says, "I see it moving in a zigzag manner" or "I see it moving slowly in a counterclockwise direction," you are likely to perceive it the same way.

People tend to conform to the behavior of others, especially in ambiguous situations. Sometimes they will even conform when they doubt the wisdom of the other people's behaviors.

You will perceive some movement on your own, but other people's suggestions can greatly alter the apparent speed and direction of the movement.

Early research suggested that people are most likely to conform their opinions in ambiguous situations that make it difficult for people to be sure of their own judgment (Sherif, 1935). For example, there are no absolutely right or wrong styles of clothing; in matters such as politics, religion, or the movement of a single point of light in a darkened room, there may be a right answer, but we do not have enough information to be sure of that answer. Consequently, we rely on other people's opinions to help form our own.

Would we also conform to the opinions or behaviors of others if we were sure that we were right and they were wrong? To answer that question, Solomon Asch (1951, 1956) carried out a now-famous series of experiments.

Asch assembled groups of students and asked them to look at a vertical bar, as shown in Figure 14.12, which was defined as the model. He also showed them three other vertical bars (right half of Figure 14.12), and asked them which bar was the same length as the model. As you can see, the task is simple. Asch asked the students to give their answers aloud. He repeated the procedure with 18 sets of bars.

Only one student in each group was a real subject. All the others were confederates who had been instructed to give incorrect answers on 12 of the 18 trials. Asch arranged for the real subject to be the next-to-the-last person in the group to announce his answer so that he would hear most of the confederates' incorrect responses before giving his own (Figure 14.13). Would he go along with the crowd?

To Asch's surprise, 37 of the 50 subjects conformed to the majority at least once, and 14 of them conformed on more than half of the trials. When faced with a unanimous wrong answer by the other group members, the mean subject conformed on 4 of the 12 trials. Asch was disturbed by these results: "That we have found the tendency to conformity in our society so strong . . . is a matter of concern. It raises questions about our ways of education and about the values that guide our conduct" (Asch, 1955, p. 34).

Why did the subjects conform so readily? When they were interviewed after the experiment, some said they thought the rest of the group was correct or they guessed that an optical illusion was influencing the appearance of the bars. Others said they knew their "conforming" answers

FIGURE 14.13 Three of the eight subjects in one of Asch's experiments on conformity: The one in the middle is the real subject; the others are the experimenter's confederates. (From Asch, 1951.) In this test of the power of group pressure to induce conformity, people were asked to disagree with strangers for only a short time. The correct answers were clear—yet most subjects felt a strong pressure to conform to what the majority said.

were wrong but went along with the group for fear of being ridiculed. Reactions of the nonconforming subjects were interesting, too: Some were very nervous but felt dutybound to say how the bars looked to them. A few seemed socially withdrawn, as if they paid no attention to anyone else. Still others were supremely self-confident, as if to say, "I'm right and everyone else is wrong. It happens all the time."

Asch (1951, 1955) found that the amount of conforming influence depended on the size of the opposing majority. In a series of studies, he varied the number of confederates who gave incorrect answers from 1 to 15. He found that the subjects conformed to a group of 3 or 4 just as readily as they did to a larger group (Figure 14.14). However, the subjects conformed much less if they had an "ally." Being a minority of one is painful, but being in a minority of two is not as bad (Figure 14.15).

Over the years since Asch's experiments were conducted, similar studies have been conducted many times in

FIGURE 14.12 Choosing conformity: In Asch's conformity studies, subjects were asked to match one line with one of three other lines on another card. They were surrounded by people who gave obviously wrong answers.

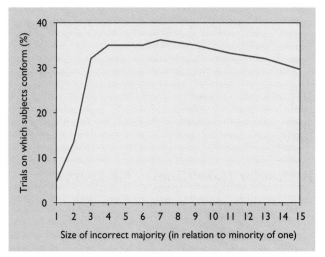

FIGURE 14.14 Asch (1955) found that conformity became more frequent as group size increased to about three, and then it leveled off.

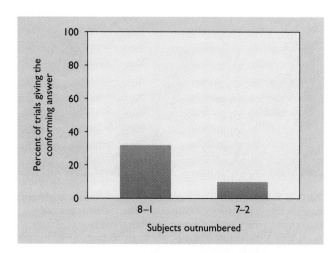

FIGURE 14.15 In Asch's experiments, subjects who were faced with a unanimous majority giving wrong answers conformed to the majority view on 32% of trials. Subjects who had one "ally" giving the correct answer were less likely to conform. Evidently, it is difficult to be in a minority of one, but less difficult to be in a minority of two.

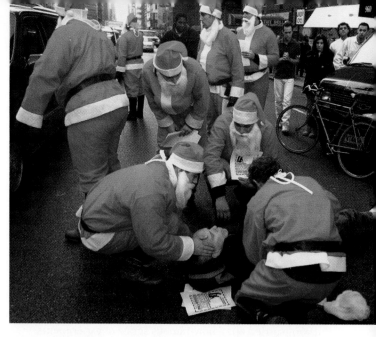

People watch other people's responses to help decide what their own should be. When a group of sidewalk Santas—who had gathered in Manhattan to promote a back-rub business—came to the aid of an injured cyclist, a few Santas made the first move and then the others decided to follow suit.

many countries. In the United States, most studies show a slight decrease in the amount of conformity since the 1950s. In cultures that emphasize collectivist values, such as most Asian cultures, the percentage of conforming answers tends to be higher than in cultures that stress individualism. However, in those collectivist cultures, people seem to be motivated mostly by politeness, not wishing to embarrass the others by correcting their errors (Bond & Smith, 1996). That is, when researchers use what appears to be the "same" task in a different culture, they may not actually be testing the same psychological processes.

Accepting or Denying Responsibility Toward Others

Sometimes other people encourage us to do something we would not have done on our own, as in Asch's studies. Sometimes other people inhibit us from doing something that we would have done on our own. We look around to see what others are doing—or *not* doing—and we say, "Okay, I'll do that too. I'll do my fair share—no more, no less." Why do people sometimes work together to help one another and sometimes ignore the needs of others?

Bystander Helpfulness and Apathy

Suppose, while you are waiting at a bus stop, you see me trip and fall down, just 10 meters away from you. I am not screaming in agony but I don't get up right away either, so you are not sure whether I need help. Do you think you would probably come over and offer your help? Or would you just stand there and ignore me? Before you answer, try imagining the situation two ways: First, you and I are the

only people in sight. Second, there are a lot of other people nearby, none of whom is rushing to my aid. Does the presence of those other people make any difference in your response? (Note that it doesn't change *my* predicament. I am in the same amount of pain, regardless of whether one person or many people ignore me.)

Late one night in March, 1964, Kitty Genovese was stabbed to death near her apartment in Queens, New York. For 30 minutes, 38 of her neighbors listened to her screams. A few stood at their windows watching. None of them came to her aid or called the police. Why?

Bibb Latané and John Darley (1969) proposed that one reason the neighbors failed to help was **diffusion of responsibility:** *We tend to feel less responsibility for helping when other people are around than when we know that no one else can help.* Latané and Darley suggested that no one helped Kitty Genovese because everyone knew that many other people *could* help her.

In an experiment designed to test this hypothesis, a young woman ushered either one or two students into a room and asked them to wait a few minutes for the start of a market research study (Latané & Darley, 1968, 1969). She then went into the next room, closing the door behind her. There, she played a tape recording that made it sound as though she had climbed onto a chair and had fallen off. For about 2 minutes, she could be heard crying and moaning, "Oh . . . my foot . . . I can't move it. Oh . . . my ankle. . . ." Of the subjects who were waiting alone, 70% went next door and offered to help. Of the subjects who were waiting with someone else, only 13% offered to help.

Diffusion of responsibility is one possible explanation. Each person thinks, "It's not my responsibility to help any more than it is the other person's. And if we get blamed for not helping, it's as much that person's fault as it is mine." A second possible explanation is that the presence of other people who are also doing nothing provides information (or misinformation). At first the situation is ambiguous: "Do I need to act, or not?" When you see other people doing nothing, you assume they know something you don't know, and thus that the situation requires no action. In fact, the others are just as uncertain as you are, and they are drawing conclusions from *your* inaction. Social psychologists use the term **pluralistic ignorance** to describe *a situation where people say nothing and each person falsely assumes that everyone else has a different, perhaps better informed opinion.* Notice that the presence of other people exerts both normative and informational influences: Their inactivity implies that doing nothing is acceptable (a norm) and that the situation is not an emergency (information).

Social Loafing

Sometimes your success and rewards depend entirely on your own efforts. For example, when you take a test in one of your college courses, you are required to work alone. In many other cases, however, you work with other people as part of a team. For example, if you work for a company that gives workers a share of the profits, your rewards depend on both your own productivity and that of the other workers. Do you work as hard when the rewards depend on the group's productivity as you do when they depend on your own efforts alone?

In many cases, the answer is "no." In one experiment, students were told to scream and clap and try to make as loud a noise as possible, like cheerleaders at a sports event. Sometimes each student screamed and clapped alone; sometimes students acted in groups of two to six; and sometimes they acted alone but *thought* that other people

In a tug-of-war or other task in which individuals pool their efforts, most people do not work as hard as they would when working alone. This is called "social loafing." However, if participants know that each individual's contribution will be measured separately, social loafing ceases and everyone puts out a full effort.

were screaming and clapping too. (They wore headphones so that they could not hear anyone else.) As a rule, students who screamed and clapped alone made more noise than students who were (or thought they were) part of a group (Latané, Williams, & Harkins, 1979). Social psychologists call this phenomenon **social loafing**—*the tendency to "loaf" (or work less hard) when sharing work with other people.* Social loafing has been demonstrated with several other behaviors as well. For example, suppose you were asked to "name all the uses you can think of for a brick" (such as *crack nuts, anchor a boat,* or *use as a doorstop*) and write each one on a card. You would probably use many cards if you were working by yourself, but you would fill out fewer cards if you were tossing them into a pile along with other people's suggestions, to be evaluated as a group (Harkins & Jackson, 1985).

At this point you may be thinking, "Wait a minute. When I'm playing on a basketball team, I try as hard as I can. I don't think I loaf just because others are working together." And you are right; social loafing seldom occurs in team sports. (When it does, the fans boo.) The reason is that observers, including teammates, can easily see who is contributing and who is not. Even though the team wins or loses as a group, individual players also compete for recognition as individuals. People loaf in group projects only if they expect no reward for extra effort; they put out a serious effort if they expect other people to notice their effort, or if they think they can contribute something that other group members cannot (Shepperd, 1993; Williams & Karau, 1991).

Social loafing is a robust phenomenon, easy to demonstrate in many settings. Generally, the effect is large when people consider the task unimportant and smaller when they believe that much is at stake. (See Figure 14.16.) Other things being equal, men do more social loafing than women. (Perhaps women are more accustomed to working hard without getting credit.) Also, people in Western cultures do more social loafing than do people in Asian cultures, which stress the value of helping one's group instead of just helping oneself (Karau & Williams, 1995). Japanese people will scorn anyone who does not do a fair share of a group effort. If some people continue to loaf, the ones who had been working generally quit. That is, in Japanese society, either everyone works or no one works (Shepperd, 1995).

CONCEPT CHECKS

13. Given what we have learned about social loafing, why are most people unlikely to work hard to clean up the environment?

14. Suppose the head of a large library wants the library staff to pay more attention to getting all the books into their correct locations. Currently, many of the books are misplaced, and the staff seem to be "loafing" at rearranging them. What could be done to encourage greater efforts? (Check your answers on page 550.)

FIGURE 14.16 During a catastrophe, people abandon their usual tendencies toward bystander apathy and social loafing. Just after an earthquake in the San Francisco area, authorities ordered the residents in one area to evacuate their residences within 15 minutes. People who usually ignored one another immediately pitched in to help move their valuables.

Group Decision-Making

An organization that needs to make a decision will frequently set up a committee to look into the issues and make recommendations. We prefer a committee to an individual because the committee has more time, more total information, and fewer peculiarities and biases than any individual has. Nevertheless, a group is subject to the influences of conformity and social loafing, which sometimes interfere with reaching the best possible decisions.

Group Polarization

If nearly all the people who compose a group lean in the same direction on a particular issue, the group as a whole will tend to move even further in that direction after they discuss that issue. This phenomenon is known as **group polarization.** Note that, in this case, *polarization* does not mean that the group breaks up into fragments favoring different positions. Rather, it means that, after discussing the issues, the members of a group move *together* toward one pole (extreme position) or the other. For example, a group of

people who are opposed to abortion or in favor of animal rights or opposed to gun regulations will, after discussing the issue among themselves, generally become more extreme in their views than they had been at the start (Lamm & Myers, 1978).

Group polarization occurs because of both informational and normative influences (Isenberg, 1986). During the group discussion, the members become aware of new arguments and new information. If most of the members were leaning in one direction at the start, the group will hear many new arguments favoring that side of the issue and few or none for the opposition (Burnstein & Vinokur, 1973, 1977). The lack of balance between positive and negative arguments is essential for group polarization (Kuhn & Lao, 1996). Also, as the members of the group become aware of the consensus during the discussion, they feel pressure to conform. The pressure to conform is strongest for people who believe that they are not fully accepted by the rest of the group (Noel, Wann, & Branscombe, 1995). They can increase their acceptance by the group if they emphasize how vigorously they support its views and goals.

CONCEPT CHECK

15. Is a jury more likely to reach a biased or extreme decision than a single individual would be? (Check your answer on page 550.)

Groupthink

One extreme form of group polarization is known as **groupthink,** when *the members of a group suppress their doubts about a group's poorly thought-out decision, for fear of making a bad impression or disrupting the harmony of the group* (Janis, 1972, 1985). In some cases, dominant members of the group actually ask dissenters to be quiet; more often, dissenters silence themselves. One dramatic example of groupthink led to the Bay of Pigs fiasco of 1962. President John F. Kennedy and his advisers were considering a plan to support a small-scale invasion of Cuba at the Bay of Pigs. They assumed that a small group of Cuban exiles could overwhelm the Cuban army and trigger a spontaneous rebellion of the Cuban people against Fidel Castro and his government. Most of the advisers who doubted this assumption felt pressured to keep quiet; one who did express his doubts was told that he should loyally support the president, who had already made up his mind. Within a few hours after the invasion began, all the invaders were either killed or captured. The decision-makers themselves wondered how they could have made such a stupid decision.

Another example of groupthink was NASA's ill-fated decision to launch the space shuttle *Challenger* on a cold morning in 1986. The top decision-makers let it be known that they had strong economic and public-relations reasons for launching the shuttle on schedule. Project engineers who

ASSAI BEN BALLA, À CVI FORTVNA SVONA. 16

Gettisi à basso, ò si solleui in alto
Chi concorde a suoi passi hà la Fortuna,
Che sarà in tempo e la cadenza, e l'salto.

Many organizations try to resist the tendency toward groupthink—the tendency to stifle dissenting views and proceed to a possibly disastrous decision. During the Renaissance, European kings sometimes called on a "fool" (or court jester) to describe some proposal in a fresh and possibly amusing light. In a court composed largely of yes-men, the fool sometimes was the only one who could openly point out the folly of a proposed action without fear of reprisals.

knew the rocket booster was unsafe at low temperatures dutifully kept quiet and hoped for the best. Then, 73 seconds after the launch, the *Challenger* exploded because of an O-ring that was unable to function at low temperatures.

In both the Bay of Pigs incident and the *Challenger* disaster, group members who doubted the wisdom of the decision kept quiet and thus created an illusion of unanimous support. Originally, psychologists believed that groupthink occurs mostly in highly cohesive groups, such as fraternal or religious organizations, where the members think that it would be rude to criticize one another's views. Later research has found that almost all groups, not just cohesive ones, are capable of exerting pressure to conform (Aldag & Fuller, 1993).

Irving Janis (1985) suggests several techniques for reducing the likelihood of groupthink: Leaders should encourage dissent. The group can be divided into subgroups to see whether they arrive at the same conclusions in independent discussions. Leaders should consult their advisers one by one in private. The group should seek the advice of outside experts, including those with dissenting opinions. In any case, group members who entertain doubts about a leader's decision should remember the lessons of the Bay of Pigs and the *Challenger*: When much is at stake, it is better to risk angering one's leader than to go along with a possibly disastrous decision.

THE MESSAGE
To Conform or Not to Conform?

Conforming to what others do is not, in itself, a bad idea. When I drive on the right side of the road, I am rather relieved that other people are being conformists and also driving on the right side. Problems arise when we are surrounded by people who are expressing an extreme and possibly wrong opinion (as in group polarization) or by people who are doing nothing when something needs to be done (as in bystander apathy). We need to be alert: to conform when conformity is helpful or at least harmless but to resist when conformity is dangerous.

SUMMARY

* *Types of social influence.* People influence our behavior by providing information (right or wrong) and by setting norms that they enforce by providing or withholding their approval. (page 544)
* *Conformity.* Many people conform to the majority view even when they are confident that the majority is wrong. An individual is as likely to conform to a group of three as to a larger group, but an individual who has an ally is less likely to conform to the majority. (page 544)
* *Diffusion of responsibility.* People in groups are less likely than an isolated individual to come to the aid of another because they experience a diffusion of responsibility. (page 546)
* *Social loafing.* People working together on a task tend to exert less effort than people who are working independently. However, people will work just as hard on the group task if they are evaluated on the basis of their individual performances or if they believe their contributions will make a big difference to the group's success. (page 547)
* *Group polarization.* Groups of people who lean mostly in the same direction on a given issue often make decisions that are more extreme than the decisions that most individuals would have made on their own. (page 548)
* *Groupthink.* Groupthink occurs when members of a cohesive group fail to express their opposition to a decision, for fear of making a bad impression or harming the cohesive spirit of the group. (page 548)

Suggestion for Further Reading

Cialdini, R. B. (1993). *Influence: Science and practice* (rev. ed.). New York: William Morrow. One of the most enjoyable and entertaining books in psychology. Buy a copy and take it with you on vacation.

Terms

conformity   maintaining or changing one's behavior to match the behavior of others (page 544)

autokinetic effect   the illusory perception that a point of light in a darkened room is in motion (page 544)

diffusion of responsibility   the tendency to feel less responsibility for helping when other people are around than when we know that no one else can help (page 546)

pluralistic ignorance   a situation where people say nothing and each person falsely assumes that everyone else has a different, perhaps better informed opinion. (page 547)

social loafing   the tendency to "loaf" (or work less hard) when sharing work with other people (page 547)

group polarization   the tendency of a group whose members lean in the same direction on a particular issue to become more extreme in its views after discussing the issue as a group (page 548)

groupthink   a process by which the members of a group suppress their doubts about a group's poorly thought-out decision, for fear of making a bad impression or disrupting the harmony of the group (page 548)

Answers to Concept Checks

13. For the task of protecting the environment, each person is part of a group containing billions of other people. Social loafing is likely because many one-person contributions, such as picking up litter, would not earn individual credit or recognition. Also, each person thinks, "What good could one person do with such a gigantic problem?" When people believe that their own contribution would not make a noticeable difference, they tend to engage in social loafing. (page 547)

14. One approach would be to make the contributions of each staff member more apparent (because social loafing is common when people do not see that their own efforts

make much difference). For example, assign each person a different set of shelves and report which shelves have shown the greatest improvement in orderliness. A similar approach can be used for other examples of loafing on the job. (page 547)

15. Group polarization occurs when nearly all the members of a group lean in the same direction before they start discussing the issue. If a jury were almost unanimous, with one or two uncertain members, group polarization would probably move the group toward a unanimous verdict. However, a jury that starts out divided would be more likely to compromise than to move toward an extreme. Most research has found juries and similar groups to be no more extreme or biased than the average individual (Kerr, MacCoun, & Kramer, 1996). (page 548)

Web Resources

Groupthink

www.nwmissouri.edu/nwcourses/martin/socialpsych /groupthink/sld001.htm

Doug Martin of Northwest Missouri State University developed this slide presentation that summarizes Janis's concept of Groupthink.

Groupthink: Theoretical Framework

choo.fis.utoronto.ca/FIS/Courses/LIS2149/Groupthink.html

This three-page series by Chun Wei Choo of The University of Toronto begins with an elaborate diagram showing the antecedent conditions and observable consequences of Groupthink; on pages 2 and 3 are steps to minimize its development.

The Power of the Social Situation

Why do people sometimes engage in self-defeating behavior?

How can we change the situation to minimize such behavior?

Back in the 1960s, several world problems seemed to threaten the very future of civilization. The Vietnam War seemed to go on forever; the nations of the world seemed to be preparing for global nuclear war; racial injustice and discrimination were widespread in the United States; we were beginning to recognize how badly people were damaging the environment. As a high-school and college student at the time, I had grandiose dreams that I was going to save the world. I wasn't sure how, but I thought psychological research was one possibility. I hoped to somehow change human nature so that people would stop being so cruel and selfish.

Now here we are, many years later, and I reflect on the people who really did make the world a better place. Some made their impact through moral leadership or politics—Martin Luther King, Jr., Mother Teresa, Alexander Solzhenitsyn, Nelson Mandela, and others. But there have also been many who improved the world through technology—a route that I never even contemplated during my youthful "save the world" fantasies. For example, the engineers who devised spy satellites made possible the international treaties banning tests of nuclear weapons. (Without the capacity to watch one another, competing countries would never have agreed to such treaties.) The engineers who developed computers, printers, and modems spread freedom of the press to every technologically advanced country. (Any country that allows people to have computers is giving them printing presses.) These technological advances changed human *behavior* without changing human *nature*.

The general point here is that much of our behavior is controlled by the situation—sometimes the technological situation, sometimes the social situation. A situation can pressure us, or virtually compel us, to behave either in constructive ways or else in uncooperative and self-

defeating ways. We need to recognize the power of these situations, so that we can avoid or change the most harmful ones.

Behavior Traps

What would you think of someone who knowingly paid a great deal more for something than it was worth? Or someone who confessed to a crime even though the police admitted they did not have enough evidence for a conviction? Or someone who used up all of his or her resources at once instead of saving some for later? You would probably question that person's intelligence or sanity. And yet, under certain circumstances, you might act the same way yourself. Sometimes, we fall into a **behavior trap**—*a situation that coerces us into self-defeating behaviors.* We call such situations "traps" because people wander into them without realizing the danger; once they see the danger, they cannot find their way out. We shall consider three examples: escalation of conflict, the prisoner's dilemma, and the commons dilemma.

Escalation of Conflict

Sometimes a conflict or competition between two sides progressively escalates: After one side increases its effort and investment, the other side increases and then surpasses the first side's effort, thus prompting the first side to retaliate, and so forth. Eventually, both sides have invested far more than the original dispute was worth, but neither wants to quit and admit defeat.

Social pressures drive people to expose themselves to many kinds of risk. It is easier to avoid these situations than to escape them after the danger is evident.

For example, imagine that you and I and a few other people are at an auction. The auctioneer explains that the next item up for bids is a dollar bill, which she will sell to the highest bidder, even if the highest bid is only a few cents. There is one catch, however; at the end, when someone finally buys the dollar bill, the second-highest bidder must pay his or her bid to the auctioneer also, receiving nothing in return. So, for example, if I bid 5 cents, you bid 10 cents, and the bidding stops there, you would buy the dollar bill for 10 cents and I would simply lose my 5 cents.

Suppose that we both think this sounds like a good deal and we plunge right in. I bid 5 cents, you bid 10, I bid 15, and the bidding continues. Eventually you bid 90 cents and I bid 95. Now, what do you do? If you let me have the dollar bill for 95 cents, you will lose 90 cents. So you bid one dollar, hoping at least to break even. What do I do? If I stop bidding, I lose 95 cents. But if I can buy the dollar for $1.05, I sustain a net loss of only 5 cents. So I bid $1.05. Then you bid $1.10, because you would rather lose 10 cents than lose a whole dollar. And so on. After a while, we start to lose track of the economics and begin to get angry with each other. After all, as soon as one of us quits bidding, the other one will "win."

Psychologists have repeatedly set up such situations to see what would happen. They have usually managed to sell their dollar bills for prices over $1, usually in the range of $3 to $5, and once for $25 (Brockner & Rubin, 1985). As soon as the bidding went over $1, bidders became increasingly distressed—sweating, trembling, sometimes even crying. Many of them offered excuses for themselves, such as "I'm sorry I behaved so irrationally, but I had a couple of beers before I came over here." (At the end of the experiment, the psychologists always returned the money that the bidders paid them, although they had not promised to do so.)

The point of this study is *not*: "Here's a good scam you can use to work your way through college." The point is that, once a person gets into a situation like this, it is hard to get out. And similar situations do arise in real life. The arms race between the United States and the Soviet Union was a classic example: From the end of World War II until 1991 (when the Soviet Union collapsed), the two countries devoted enormous sums of money to building weapons. Periodically, critics would ask, "Does it really make sense to spend this much money on weapons?" And the reply was, "We have already spent an enormous amount. Having spent so much already, we may as well spend a little more to be sure that we have more weapons than the other side."

Similar situations occur in everyday life (Staw & Ross, 1989). Someone who has lost money by gambling may continue gambling to avoid admitting that the original gamble was a mistake. Someone who has invested in a stock that lost money may hold onto the stock (and perhaps continue losing money) rather than sell it and accept the loss. A company that has invested millions on developing a new, unsuccessful product may invest additional millions to finish the product. Labor negotiations may persist fruitlessly

because both sides need a "victory" to justify the strike they have already endured. Perhaps you can think of additional examples.

Cooperation and Competition in the Prisoner's Dilemma

In some situations, you have a choice between two actions—an action that seems best for you and one that seems best for your group. However, if everyone in the group chooses the action that seems best for himself or herself, everyone will suffer. The problem is not simply human selfishness; the problem is inherent in the situation itself.

For example, consider the **prisoner's dilemma,** *a situation where people must choose between a cooperative act and an act that could benefit only themselves while hurting others.* There are many versions of this dilemma, but let's start with the original: You and a partner are arrested and charged with armed robbery. The police take each of you into separate rooms and ask you to confess. If neither of you confesses, the police will not have enough evidence to convict you of armed robbery, but they can convict you of a lesser offense that carries a sentence of 1 year in prison. If either of you confesses and testifies against the other, the confessor will go free and the other will get 20 years in prison. If you both confess, you will each get 5 years in prison. Each of you knows that the other person has the same options. Figure 14.17 illustrates your choices.

If your partner does not confess, it is to your own advantage to confess, because you will go free. (Your partner

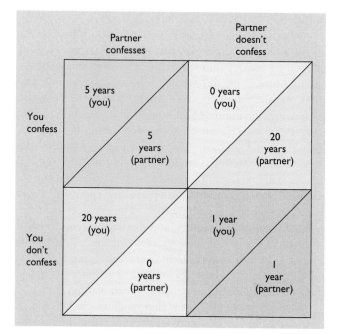

FIGURE 14.17 In the prisoner's dilemma, each person considering the choice alone finds it beneficial to confess. But when both people confess, they suffer worse consequences than if both had refused to confess.

will get 20 years in prison, but let's assume you are mostly interested in yourself.) If your partner does confess, it is still to your advantage to confess—you get only 5 years in prison instead of 20. So, you confess. Your partner, reasoning the same way, also confesses, so you both get 5 years in prison. If you had both kept quiet, you would each have served only 1 year in prison. The situation led you both to uncooperative, self-defeating behavior.

If you and your partner could have discussed your strategy, you would have agreed not to confess. Then, when the police took you to separate rooms, you would each hope that the other would keep the bargain. And if your friend did keep the bargain, what should you do? Confess, of course! We're back where we started.

The two of you are likely to cooperate only if you can stay in constant communication with each other (Nemeth, 1972). If each can listen to everything the other one says, you know that, if one confesses, the other will retaliate immediately. Indeed, as a general principle, self-defeating behaviors often arise because of lack of communication. Marriages fail, labor unions start costly strikes, and countries go to war because the two sides do not communicate enough about what each side is willing to do and willing to accept in return (Thompson & Hrebec, 1996).

The prisoner's dilemma can also be stated in terms of gains instead of losses. Social psychologists have invented games where each player chooses between two moves, one cooperative and the other competitive. The moves the players make determine their costs and rewards (Figure 14.18). To complicate matters (and make them more interesting), the game continues through many rounds. If one player

chooses the competitive response for one trial, the other player can retaliate on the next. Players earn the most rewards if both choose the cooperative move. Frequently, however, one player chooses the competitive response, the other retaliates, and both players lose rewards (Axelrod & Dion, 1988).

In the long run, which is the better strategy in life? The prisoner's dilemma is much like a business deal: One person promises to mail a product and the other person promises to mail a check, and then both have to choose whether to cooperate (send the promised product or check) or compete (send nothing and hope to get something in return). If you dealt with a different person each time, you would gain more by competitive moves than by cooperative moves. But real life isn't like that. People who like to cooperate find other people who cooperate, and they do business among themselves. The uncooperative people who are always trying to cheat their opponents have more and more difficulty getting anyone to do business with them (Wilson, Near, & Miller, 1996).

CONCEPT CHECK

16. Suppose you are playing the prisoner's dilemma game shown in Figure 14.18. Both you and the other player know that you will play for exactly ten times. Also, suppose that you are interested only in the economic outcome, not in the morality of your decision, and that you do not expect to meet the other player ever again. In this situation, many people would make the cooperative choice on the first nine rounds of the game and the competitive move on the final round. Why? (Check your answer on page 557.)

The Commons Dilemma

Here is another case where people hurt themselves and others by considering only their own short-term interests (Hardin, 1968): In the **commons dilemma,** *people who share a common resource tend to overuse it and therefore make it unavailable in the long run.* The commons dilemma takes its name from this parable: You are a shepherd in a small village with a piece of land, called the commons, that everyone is free to share. Most of the time, your sheep graze on your own land, but when a few of them need a little extra grass, you are free to take them to the commons. There are 50 shepherds in the village, and the commons can support about 50 sheep a day. So, if each shepherd takes an average of one sheep per day to the commons, everything works out fine. But suppose a few shepherds decide to take several sheep per day to the commons to save the grass on their own land. Not to be outdone, other shepherds do the same. Soon the commons is barren and useless to all.

Social psychologists have simulated the commons dilemma, like the prisoner's dilemma, in laboratory games. In one study, college students were asked to sit around a

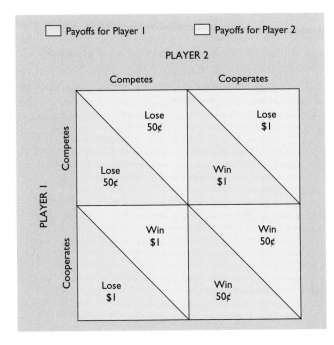

FIGURE 14.18 In this game based on the prisoner's dilemma, each player can choose either the cooperative move or the competitive move. If both cooperate, each wins 50 cents; in other choices, one or both players lose money.

bowl that contained 10 nuts (Edney, 1979). They were told that they could take as many nuts as they wanted any time they chose. Every 10 seconds, the number of nuts remaining in the bowl would be doubled. The object of the game was to collect as many nuts as possible. Clearly, the rational strategy is to let the nuts double every 10 seconds for a while and then to "harvest" some to divide among the participants. But most of the groups never made it past the first 10 seconds. The subjects simply plunged in and grabbed as many nuts as they could, immediately exhausting the resources.

Some people do cooperate, however. Consider this scenario: Imagine you are in the fishing business. The numbers of fish have been declining, and the government has asked you and all the other fishing companies to reduce your annual catch. However, you know the government cannot enforce this regulation, so you can still catch more than your assigned share without penalty. What do you do? About half of college students who were asked this question said they would cooperate and limit their catch (Baron, 1997). If they were actually depending on fishing to make a living, they might decide differently (Figure 14.19). Still, the reasons they gave were interesting. Students said that they wanted to do their part to make the world a better place and that they thought, by cooperating, they would influence others to cooperate too, and thus benefit themselves in the long run.

WHAT'S THE EVIDENCE?
Obedience to Authority

One final example of a self-defeating situation arises when people obey an authority who gives bad orders. Ordinarily, if someone you hardly know orders you to do something unpleasant, saying "you *have* to do this," you would probably refuse quite vehemently. Sometimes, however, you may get into a situation where you feel obligated to obey unreasonable orders. We might have thought that only people with a rigid, authority-worshiping personality would follow objectionable orders, but evidence has shown that some situations build up such powerful pressures that almost anyone obeys.

Research on this topic was inspired by reports of atrocities in the Nazi concentration camps during World War II. Those who had committed the atrocities defended themselves by saying that they were only obeying orders. International courts rejected that defense, and outraged people throughout the world told themselves, "If I had been there, I would have refused to follow such orders" and "It couldn't happen here."

What do you think? Could it happen here? Stanley Milgram (1974) set up an experiment to discover whether a carefully designed situation could trap people into obeying apparently dangerous orders. Milgram's experiment quickly became one of the most famous studies in psychology, with major ethical and scientific implications.

Hypothesis When an authority figure gives normal people instructions to do something that might hurt another person, at least some of them will obey, under carefully designed circumstances.

Method Two adult male subjects arrived at the experimental room—the real subject and a confederate of the experimenter pretending to be a subject. (They were not college students. The experimenters wanted results that would generalize to a broad population. They also wanted to minimize the risk that the subjects would guess the true purpose of the experiment.) The experimenter told the subjects that this was an experiment on learning and that one subject would be the "teacher" and the other the "learner." The teacher would read lists of words through a microphone to the learner, who would sit in a nearby room. The teacher would then test the learner's memory for the words. Every time the learner made a mistake, the teacher was to deliver an electric shock as punishment.

The experiment was rigged so that the real subject was always the teacher and the confederate was always the learner. The teacher watched as the learner was strapped into the shock device, so he or she knew that the learner could not escape (Figure 14.20). The learner never actually received any shocks, but the teacher was led to believe that he did. In fact, before the start of the study, the experimenter also had the teacher feel a "sample shock" from the machine, demonstrating that the machine really worked.

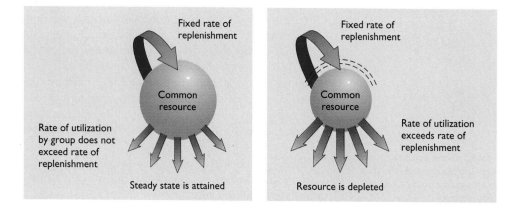

FIGURE 14.19 The commons dilemma: Unless the users agree to moderate their use of a common resource, it will soon be used up. For example, years of overfishing off the coast of Newfoundland so throroughly depleted the fish population that the Canadian government finally had to ban commercial fishing.

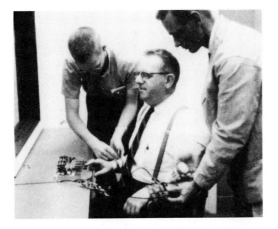

F I G U R E   14.20   In Milgram's experiment, a rigged drawing selected a confederate of the experimenter to be the "learner." Here, the learner is strapped to a device that is supposedly designed to deliver shocks.

The experiment began uneventfully. The teacher read the words and tested the learner's memory for them. The learner made many mistakes. The teacher sat at a shock generator that had levers to deliver shocks ranging from 15 volts up to 450 volts, in 15-volt increments (Figure 14.21). The experimenter instructed the teacher to deliver a shock every time the learner made a mistake, beginning with the 15-volt switch and raising the voltage by 15 volts for each successive mistake. As the voltage went up, the learner in the next room cried out in pain and even kicked the wall.

In one version of the experiment, the learner complained that he had a heart condition. If a teacher asked who would take responsibility for any harm done to the learner, the experimenter replied that he (the experimenter) would take responsibility but insisted that "while the shocks may be painful, they are not dangerous." When the shocks reached 150 volts, the learner called out in pain and begged to be let out of the experiment, complaining that his heart was bothering him. Beginning at 270 volts, he responded to shocks with agonized screams. At 300 volts, he shouted that he would no longer answer any questions. After 330 volts, he

made no response at all. Still, the experimenter ordered the teacher to continue asking questions and delivering shocks. (Remember, the learner was not really being shocked. The screams of pain were being played from a tape recorder.)

Results   Of 40 subjects, 25 continued to deliver shocks all the way up to 450 volts. The people who did so were not sadists. They were normal adults, recruited from the community through newspaper ads. They were paid a few dollars for their services, and those who asked were told that they could keep the money even if they quit. (Not many asked.) People from all walks of life obeyed the experimenter's orders, including blue-collar workers, white-collar workers, and professionals. Most of them grew quite upset and agitated while they were supposedly delivering shocks to the screaming learner, but they kept right on.

Interpretation   The level of obedience Milgram observed depended on certain factors that he injected into the situation. One was that the experimenter agreed to take responsibility. (Remember the diffusion of responsibility principle.) Another factor was that the experimenter started with a small request, asking the subject to press the lever for a 15-volt shock, and then gradually progressed to stronger shocks. (Remember the foot-in-the-door principle; remember also Skinner's shaping principle.)

We can identify many other contributing factors, and we can imagine many ways to change the procedure that would probably also change the results. Figure 14.22 and Figure 14.23 illustrate the results of a few variations in procedure that Milgram tried. For example, subjects were more obedient to an experimenter who remained in the same room than to one who left. They were less obedient if they needed to force the learner's hand back onto the shock plate. If additional "teachers" divided the task—the other "teachers" also being confederates of the experimenter—a participant was very likely to obey if the others obeyed, but unlikely to obey if the others disobeyed.

F I G U R E   14.21   The "teacher" in Milgram's experiment flipped switches on this box, apparently delivering stronger and stronger shocks for each successive error that the "learner" made. The situation was designed to appear realistic, although the device did not actually shock the learner.

F I G U R E   14.22   In one variation of Milgram's standard procedure, he asked the teacher to hold the learner's hand on the shock electrode. This close contact with the learner decreased obedience to less than half of its usual level; still, some teachers continued following orders to deliver shocks. (From Milgram's 1965 film, *Obedience*.)

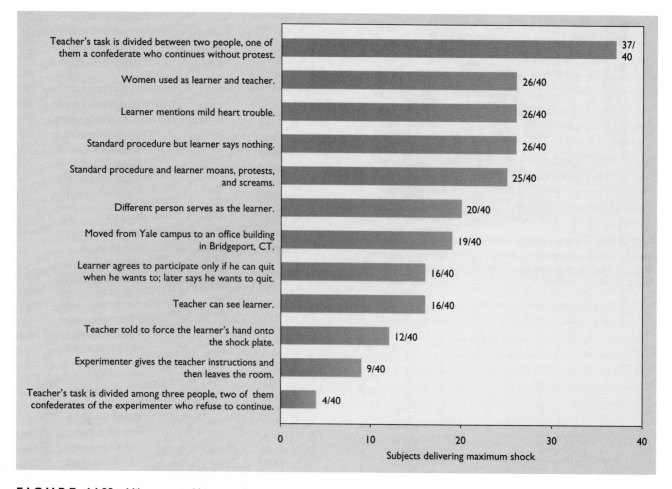

FIGURE 14.23 Milgram varied his procedure in many ways to find out what elements promoted or inhibited obedience. Division of responsibility increased obedience; an implication of personal responsibility decreased obedience. Under all conditions, some people obeyed and others did not.

Still, the remarkable conclusion remains that, under a variety of conditions, many normal people followed orders from an experimenter they had just met, even though they thought they might hurt or even kill someone. Imagine how much stronger the pressure to obey orders from a government or military leader would be.

Ethical Issues Milgram's experiment told us something about ourselves that we did not want to hear. No longer could we say, "Something like what happened in the Nazi concentration camps could never happen here." We found that most of us tend to follow orders, even quite offensive orders. We are indebted to Milgram's study for this important, if unwelcome, information. However, although I am glad to know about Milgram's results, I doubt that I would have enjoyed being a subject in his experiment. Most of his subjects were emotionally drained by the experience, and some were visibly upset to discover how readily they had obeyed orders to deliver dangerous shocks to another person.

Milgram's study prompted psychology researchers to establish much clearer and stricter rules about what an experimenter can ethically ask a subject to do. Today, before the start of any psychological experiment—even the simplest and most innocuous—the experimenter is required to submit a plan to a Human Subjects Committee that must either approve or reject the ethics of the experiment.

If anyone today submitted a proposal to conduct research similar to Milgram's study, the local Human Subjects Committee would almost certainly refuse permission. However, if the same procedures had been in place *at the time of Milgram's study*, would a committee have prohibited his study? The curious fact is that we aren't sure. Before Milgram's research, very few people expected his results to turn out as they did. Milgram had asked various psychologists and psychiatrists to predict the results; nearly all replied that only a rare psychopathic weirdo would press levers to deliver severe shocks. A Human Subjects Committee that shared this expectation might have foreseen little ethical difficulty with Milgram's study. The unforeseen ethical problem underscores just how surprising Milgram's results were.

SOMETHING TO THINK ABOUT

Here is one version of the experiment that Milgram never tried: At the start of the experiment, we announce that the teacher and the learner will trade places halfway through the experiment so that the previous "learner" will start delivering shocks to the teacher. How do you think the teachers would behave then? What other changes in procedure can you imagine that might influence the degree of obedience?

✳   ✳   ✳

THE MESSAGE
Fix the Situation, Not Human Nature

If you are in a crowded theater when a fire breaks out, you know you are supposed to file out quietly, because the risk of being trampled to death in a panic is greater than the danger from the fire itself. But what would you actually do? If a panic does develop, the first few to panic will get out safely; it would do you no good to keep calm if everyone else is about to panic. Because other people reason in the same way, before long someone does try to rush out, and then panic develops.

How could we prevent people from panicking? The best solution is not to tell people about the virtues of cooperation; it is to build more exits. Similarly, it is difficult to teach people to behave productively in any of the behavior traps presented in this chapter; the best advice is to avoid those situations. Also, if you have already been following someone's dangerous orders, as in Milgram's experiment, it is difficult to quit. The best time to quit is before the situation gets started. In short, instead of just finding the right act to take in each situation, it is important to choose one's situations.

S U M M A R Y

✳ *Behavior traps.* Certain situations—such as the dollar auction, the prisoner's dilemma, and the commons dilemma—pressure even intelligent and rational people into self-defeating behavior. (page 551)

✳ *Obedience.* Many people obey the orders of a person in authority even if they believe their actions will injure someone else. They are less likely to obey if they can see the person who would be injured. They are more likely to obey if other people are following orders without protest. (page 554)

Suggestions for Further Reading

Brockner, J., & Rubin, J. Z. (1985). *Entrapment in escalating conflicts*. New York: Springer-Verlag. Describes research on the dollar auction and similar behavior traps.

Milgram, S. (1975). *Obedience to authority*. New York: Harper & Row. Describes Milgram's classic experiments on obedience.

Terms

behavior trap   a situation that almost forces people into self-defeating behaviors. (page 551)

prisoner's dilemma   a situation where people must choose between an act that is beneficial to themselves but harmful to others and an act that is moderately beneficial to all. (page 552)

commons dilemma   a situation where people who share a common resource tend to overuse it and therefore make it unavailable in the long run. (page 553)

Answer to Concept Check

16. In the early rounds, you know that any competitive move that you make is likely to provoke the other player to retaliate on the next move. You will gain more if both players cooperate than if you exchange retaliations. However, in the last round, you know that the other player will have no further opportunities to retaliate. (page 553)

Web Resources

Prisoners' Dilemma

serendip.brynmawr.edu/bb/pd.html

Play the Prisoners' Dilemma Game with Serendip. Win as much as you can!

Abnormalities
and Therapies I:
General Principles

15

Over the past 4 months, George has struck and injured several dozen people, most of whom he hardly knew; 2 of them had to be sent to the hospital. George expresses no guilt, no regrets. He says he would attack every one of them again if he got the chance. What should society do with George?

1. Send him to jail?
2. Commit him to a mental hospital?
3. Give him an award for being the best defensive player in the league?

Before you can answer these questions, you must know the context of George's behavior. Behavior that would seem normal at a party might seem bizarre in a business meeting. Behavior that earns millions for a rock singer might earn a trip to the mental hospital for a college professor. Behavior that is perfectly routine in one culture might be considered criminal in another.

Even when we know the context of someone's behavior, we may wonder whether it is "normal." Suppose your rich Aunt Tillie starts to pass out $5 bills to strangers on the street corner and vows that she will keep on doing so until she has exhausted her entire fortune. Is she mentally ill? Should the court commit her to a mental hospital and turn her fortune over to you as her trustee?

A man claims to be Jesus Christ and asks permission to appear before the United Nations to announce God's message to the world. A psychiatrist is sure that he can relieve this man of his disordered thinking by giving him anti-psychotic drugs, but the man refuses to take the drugs and insists that his thinking is perfectly normal. Should we force him to take the drugs, just ignore him, or place his address on the agenda of the United Nations?

What we consider normal behavior for a New Zealand Maori man might be considered abnormal for a business executive or a college professor.

An Overview of Abnormal Behavior

Why do some people behave abnormally?

What are the most common kinds of abnormal behavior?

Students in medical school often contract what is known as "medical students' disease." Imagine that you are just beginning your training in medicine. One of your textbooks describes "Cryptic Ruminating Umbilicus Disorder":

"The symptoms are very minor, until the condition becomes hopeless. The first symptom is a pale tongue." (You go to the mirror. You can't remember what your tongue is supposed to look like, but it *does* look a little pale.) "Later, a hard spot forms in the neck." (You feel your neck. "Wait! I never felt *this* before! I think it's something hard!") "Just before the arms and legs fall off, there is shortness of breath, increased heart rate, and sweating." (Already distressed, you *do* have shortness of breath, your heart *is* racing, and you *are* sweating profusely.)

Sooner or later, most medical students decide they have a dreaded illness, usually by misunderstanding the description of some disease and confusing it with their own normal condition. When my brother was in medical school, he diagnosed himself as having a rare, fatal illness, checked himself into a hospital, and wrote out his will. (Today, he is a successful physician.)

"Medical students' disease" is even more common among students of psychological disorders. As you read this chapter and the next one, you may decide that you are suffering from one of the disorders you read about. Well, perhaps you are, but recognizing a little of yourself in the description of a psychological disorder does not necessarily mean that you have the disorder. All of us feel sad, nervous, or angry occasionally, and many of us have mood swings, bad habits, or beliefs that strike other people as odd. A diagnosis of a psychological disorder should be reserved for people with problems that seriously interfere with their lives.

Concepts of Normal and Abnormal Behavior

How should we define abnormal behavior? If we try to be completely objective, we might define *abnormal* in a statistical manner as any behavior that differs very much from the average. However, by that definition, unusually happy or successful people are abnormal, and severe depression would become normal if enough people suffered from it. Ordinarily, when we say "abnormal," we mean something other than "different."

The American Psychiatric Association (1994) has defined

What we consider normal or abnormal depends on the context. Here, people dressed as witches ski down a mountain as part of an annual festival in Belalp, Switzerland, in which dressing as witches is supposed to chase away evil spirits. A woman gets painted in stripes in preparation for Mardi Gras celebration in New Orleans. A Malaysian boy kisses a deadly king cobra as part of a competition to win $2000 for performing various feats with three species of snakes.

abnormal behavior as behavior that leads to distress (pain), disability (impaired functioning), or an increased risk of death, pain, or loss of freedom. We can question that definition as well. For example, when Martin Luther King, Jr., fought for the rights of African-Americans, he risked death, pain, and loss of freedom. But we regard his acts as heroic, not abnormal.

Another way to define abnormal would be to let people decide for themselves whether they are troubled. For example, someone who appears to be successful might say, "Everyone thinks I'm doing fine, but inside I feel miserable." According to a definition that focuses on distress, anyone who thinks he has a psychological problem does have a problem.

Fair enough, but what do we do about people who behave very strangely but insist that they do *not* have a problem? Imagine a woman who babbles incoherently, urinates and defecates in the street, insults strangers, begs for $1 bills and then sets fire to them, while claiming to be doing all this in obedience to messages from the planet Chlorox. Suppose also that she reports feeling no distress, does not wish to change, and refuses all offers of help. If we call her abnormal or disordered, then what we mean by "abnormal" does not require a feeling of distress. Perhaps, when we say "abnormal," we inevitably imply that the condition is somehow undesirable.

SOMETHING TO THINK ABOUT

How would *you* define abnormal behavior? ✳

Abnormal Behavior as a Culturally Determined Phenomenon

Each of us learns from our culture the expected or normal behaviors for various situations. We also learn from our culture some of the options for *abnormal* behavior. For example, in one culture in Sudan, women have low status and very limited rights; if a woman's husband mistreats her, she has almost no defense. However, people in this society believe that a woman can sometimes be possessed by a demon, who causes her to lose control and scream all sorts of "crazy" things that she "could not possibly believe," including insults against her own husband (!). Her husband cannot scold or punish her for acting this way, because after all it is not really she, but only the demon who is saying these things. The standard way to remove the demon is to provide the woman with luxurious food, new clothing, an opportunity to spend lots of time with other women instead of with her husband, and almost anything else she demands until the demon departs. You can guess how common demon possession is in this culture (Constantinides, 1977).

More examples: *Brain fag syndrome* is a psychiatric condition with headache, eye fatigue, and inability to concentrate—a common complaint among West African students just before exams. You might try explaining to your own professor that you cannot take a test tomorrow because you

have brain fag syndrome, but unless you live in West Africa, I doubt that your explanation will do you much good. You have probably heard the expression "to run amok." *Running amok* is a type of abnormal behavior recognized in parts of Southeast Asia; someone (usually a young man) runs around engaging in furious, almost indiscriminate, violent behavior (Berry, Poortinga, Segal, & Dasen, 1992). Such behavior is considered an understandable reaction to psychological stress, not a criminal offense.

Does running amok remind you of anything common in North America or Europe? How about the "celebrations" that occur after a sports team wins a major championship? (See Figure 15.1.) Like running amok, we regard such wild displays as temporary, excusable responses to overwhelming emotion.

Although we consider the fans' destructive celebrations to be "normal," their behavior illustrates one important point about conditions that we call "abnormal": Some people who behave "abnormally" are responding to suggestions or examples. For example, one U.S. psychiatrist found that several patients in one mental hospital had cut off one of their ears. Assuming that this behavior must be a common symptom of a psychological disorder, he contacted therapists at other hospitals to ask how often they had observed the same thing. None of them ever had. Apparently, the first patient who cut off his ear gave the idea to the others at the same hospital. (Why they copied that behavior is, of course, an interesting question.)

A related controversy has arisen with regard to **dissociative identity disorder,** previously known as **multiple personality disorder,** in which *a person alternates among two or more distinct personalities, each with its own behavioral patterns, memories, and even name, almost as if each personality were really a different person.* Such conditions were once considered to be extremely rare. Then,

FIGURE 15.1 Following the victory in a major sports event, the home-town fans often celebrate with a destructive rampage. Under other circumstances, such acts would be considered criminal or insane; under these circumstances, we are more tolerant.

FIGURE 15.2 Chris Sizemore, the real "Eve" in *The Three Faces of Eve,* exhibited a total of 22 personalities, including her final, permanent identity. A person who periodically changes personality and identity is said to have *dissociative identity disorder.* Each of those personalities, by itself, seems reasonably normal. Films, television, and other media often mistakenly refer to this condition as "schizophrenia." People with schizophrenia have only one personality; that personality, however, is abnormal in serious ways.

beginning in the 1950s, a few such cases received much publicity, such as the case of Chris Costner White Sizemore, featured in the book and movie *The Three Faces of Eve,* written by her psychiatrists (Thigpen & Cleckley, 1957). Sizemore ("Eve") eventually told her own story, which was very different from her psychiatrists' version (Sizemore & Pittillo, 1977; Sizemore & Huber, 1988). (See Figure 15.2.) Then a few other people with dissociative identity disorder also received extensive publicity; by the early 1990s, some therapists were reporting many such cases. Why has the apparent prevalence increased so much? According to one hypothesis, patients copy the example of other patients with dissociative identity disorder who they have read about, heard about, or met. Researchers have now assembled convincing evidence against that hypothesis; this is not a condition that people are likely to choose voluntarily (Eich, Macaulay, Loewenstein, & Dihle, 1997; Gleaves, 1996). A more likely hypothesis is that the apparent prevalence of the disorder encourages therapists to look for it and even to suggest to clients—sometimes under hypnosis—that they might have another personality. By doing so, therapists may cause, aggravate, or complicate the problem in vulnerable people (Gleaves, 1996; Spanos, 1994). In short, just as we learn from our culture how we are supposed to act, we also learn—from our culture and even from our therapists—some of our options for abnormal behavior.

The Origins of Abnormal Behavior

Each time and place has interpreted abnormal behavior according to its own worldview. People in the Middle Ages, for example, regarded peculiar behavior as a sign that the disturbed person was possessed by a demon. To

exorcise the demon, priests resorted to prescribed religious rituals (Figure 15.3).

In Western cultures today, the predominant view is the **biopsychosocial model,** which emphasizes that *abnormal behavior has three major aspects—biological, psychological, and sociological.* Many researchers and therapists focus more on one aspect than another, but few would deny that all three are important.

The biological roots of abnormal behavior include genetic factors, which can lead to abnormal brain development, excesses or deficiencies in the activity of various neurotransmitters, hormonal abnormalities, and so forth. Behavior can also be affected by brain damage, infectious diseases, brain tumors, poor nutrition, inadequate sleep, and overuse of certain drugs, including over-the-counter medications.

The psychological component of abnormality consists of a person's reactions to events. The reactions depend both on the events themselves and on people's vulnerability. For example, someone with a genetic predisposition or a history of past abuse might be so vulnerable that relatively minor events could trigger a depression. Someone else might become depressed only in the face of a much more serious loss. Regardless of how a problem develops, a psychologist must deal with how a person copes with the current events of life. Depending on the therapist's theoretical orientation, he or she might try to understand thoughts and motivations or might focus strictly on behavior.

FIGURE 15.3 Peculiar behavior was once explained as demon possession. Here St. Zenobius exorcises devils, fleeing from the mouths of the possessed. At the time of this late 15th-century work, attributed to Botticelli, the priest Savonarola was exorcising the city with public burnings of luxury goods.

Finally, the behavior must be understood in a social and cultural context. People are greatly influenced by how other people act toward them and what other people expect of them. When someone acts strangely, in many cases that person is part of a disordered family or social network, where the others are acting just as strangely, or even worse.

I could say that abnormality depends on both biological and social influences, but that slogan wouldn't tell us much about an individual case. For example, suppose you are a therapist and you meet someone who is crying almost constantly. Before you begin treatment for depression, you need to rule out other possibilities: Maybe the person recently lost a loved one and belongs to a culture that expects people to continue grieving for weeks or months. Another possibility is that the person has a brain tumor that causes uncontrollable crying. Before you can decide how to treat the problem, you need to define the problem as clearly as possible.

The Classification and Prevalence of Psychological Disorders

Any scientific study must be based on agreed standards for classifying information. Imagine what would happen if several psychologists conducted research on the causes or treatment of some disorder (depression, for example) but were all defining depression differently. Chaos would result. Various psychologists might conduct solid research and yet arrive at different conclusions.

That kind of chaos *has* often occurred in psychology, and as a result, psychologists have worked hard to establish uniform definitions and standards for diagnosis. The result of that effort is *a reference book* called **The Diagnostic and Statistical Manual of Mental Disorders** (DSM)—now in

its fourth edition and therefore known as **DSM-IV**—which *lists the acceptable labels for all psychological disorders* (alcohol intoxication, exhibitionism, pathological gambling, anorexia nervosa, sleepwalking disorder, stuttering, and hundreds of others), with a description of each disorder.

Uses of DSM-IV

DSM-IV functions partly like a nature field guide, describing the defining characteristics of each psychological disorder and how to distinguish it from similar disorders. However, people with psychological disorders do not always fit neatly into one particular category. For example, many have combinations of depression, anxiety, alcohol abuse, and other disorders and may qualify for several diagnoses. Other people have mild problems, requiring a difficult judgment about whether to give them any diagnosis at all.

Psychologists and psychiatrists do their best to make consistent diagnoses, although borderline cases make statistics somewhat uncertain. In one survey of a random sample of about 20,000 people in three U.S. cities, trained interviewers tried to reach all the "usual residents" of each selected neighborhood, including those who lived at home and those who lived in institutions such as prisons, mental hospitals, and nursing homes. They reported that about one fifth of all adults were suffering from a psychological disorder of some sort (as defined by DSM) and that close to one third had suffered from such a disorder at some point (Myers et al., 1984; Robins et al., 1984). A similar study conducted 10 years later estimated that about one half of all people endure a diagnosable psychological disorder at some point in their lives (Kessler et al., 1994). According to both surveys, the most common psychological disorders are phobia and related anxiety disorders, alcohol or drug abuse, and mood disorders (including depression), as shown in Figure 15.4.

Many people are skeptical of any diagnostic system that

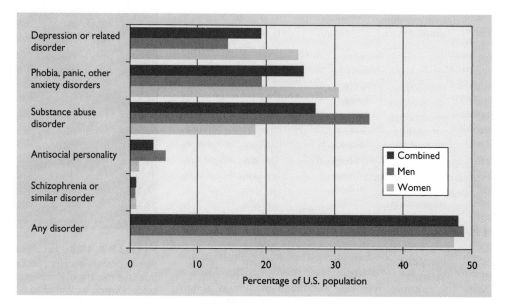

FIGURE 15.4 According to one extensive survey, about half of the population of the United States will suffer at least one psychological disorder at some time in life. (The figures for the individual conditions do not add up to the total percentage for "any disorder" because some people have more than one disorder.) However, the exact percentages depend on where one draws the dividing line between "normal" and "abnormal"; for each condition, we can find many borderline cases. (Based on data of Kessler et al., 1994.)

classifies half of all people as psychologically disordered at some point in life. Remember, however, that the exact numbers depend on difficult judgments about how to classify borderline cases. With stricter criteria, the percentages would be lower; with looser criteria, they could be higher.

CONCEPT CHECK

1. Which are the most common psychological disorders? (Check your answer on page 568.)

Criticisms of DSM-IV

Suppose a child who is frequently bullied or ridiculed starts protesting vehemently against going to school, sometimes even vomiting on school mornings. Or imagine a woman who has been in an abusive relationship for years and is now trying to escape from it and restore her damaged self-esteem. Both of these people might consult a psychologist or psychiatrist for help.

In an earlier era, the therapist probably would have talked with them without making any DSM diagnosis. After all, their problems appear to be understandable reactions to their social situations, and most people prefer to avoid the possible stigma of a psychiatric diagnosis. However, today, many insurance policies will pay for visits to a psychotherapist only if the person has a psychiatric diagnosis. Similarly, school systems get extra money to help children with special needs *if* those children have psychiatric diagnoses. The consequence is that many therapists will try to give almost any client a psychiatric diagnosis. With just a little exaggeration, the child who resists going to school and the woman recovering from an abusive relationship might be said to have one of several anxiety or stress disorders. Similarly, someone who consults a therapist because of diminished sexual pleasure can be diagnosed with *hypoactive sexual desire disorder;* someone who bears a grudge can be diagnosed with *paranoid personality disorder;* and so forth. Of the hundreds of diagnoses described in DSM-IV, many pertain to serious disorders, but some seem to be making normal worries into psychiatric conditions (Kutchins & Kirk, 1997).

DSM-IV's Classifications

The clinicians and researchers who use DSM-IV classify each client along five separate *axes* (lists). A person may have one or more disorders on a given axis—for example, alcohol abuse and depression—or none at all. The axis that gets the most attention is Axis I, *Clinical disorders.* Table 15.1 lists the major categories of disorder on Axis I. Every disorder on Axis I has its onset at some time after infancy and thus represents a deterioration of functioning. That is, the person is doing worse now than at some point in the past. Axis I conditions include the most common psychological disorders—anxiety disorders, substance abuse, and depression. They also include schizophrenia, a condition

that can be extremely disabling. (Chapter 16 will explore anxiety disorders, substance abuse, depression, and schizophrenia in detail.) Axis I also includes eating disorders, sleep disorders, and impulse control disorders—which have all been mentioned in previous chapters—as well as several others.

Axis II, *Personality disorders and mental retardation,* lists disorders that generally persist throughout life (see Table 15.2). These conditions seem to be an integral part of the self, rather than something that a person acquires. A **personality disorder** is *a maladaptive, inflexible way of dealing with the environment and other people,* such as antisocial behavior or avoidance of other people. Many other psychological disorders resemble medical diseases to some extent, whereas personality disorders are more of an integral part of the person, like being tall, or left-handed, or red-headed. People with personality disorders seldom complain about their condition and seldom seek treatment, except at the insistence of family, acquaintances, or an employer. Even when they do seek treatment, substantial improvement is uncommon.

Axis III, *General medical conditions,* lists physical disorders, such as diabetes or alcoholic cirrhosis of the liver, that can affect a person's behavior. Ordinarily, a psychotherapist does not treat a person for an Axis III disorder but should be aware of the Axis III disorders because they might affect interpretation of behavior.

Stress can intensify a psychological disorder and thus affect the course of treatment. Axis IV, *Psychosocial and environmental problems,* indicates how much stress the person has had to endure, on a scale from 0 (almost no stress) to 6 (stress equivalent to being held hostage or to experiencing the death of a child).

Some people with a psychological disorder are able to proceed with their normal work and social activities; others are not. Axis V, *Global assessment of functioning,* evaluates a person's overall level of functioning, on a scale from 1 (serious attempt at suicide or complete inability to take care of oneself) to 90 (happy, productive, with many interests).

The Importance of Differential Diagnosis

In abnormal psychology, as in any field of medicine, any diagnosis (identification) of a disorder requires ruling out other possibilities. For example, suppose someone says, "I feel unenergetic and pessimistic; I have trouble sleeping at nights; I don't have much appetite; and nothing brings me pleasure anymore." That description sounds very much like depression, but some people have those symptoms as a result of a malfunctioning thyroid gland, a stroke, the side effects from taking certain medications, withdrawal effects after quitting cocaine, a grief reaction following the death of a loved one, or fatigue after a period of being overworked. Similarly, many psychological disorders have symptoms that resemble the effects of various kinds of brain damage,

TABLE 15.1 Some Major Categories of Psychological Disorders According to Axis I of DSM-IV

Disorders usually first evident in childhood or adolescence	*Examples:* *Attention-deficit hyperactivity disorder:* impulsivity; hyperactivity; inability to pay attention to school or work *Tourette's disorder:* repetitive movements, such as blinking an eyelid or twitching a hand; chanted sounds—in some cases, obscene words *Elimination disorders:* bed-wetting; urinating or defecating in one's clothes *Stuttering:* frequent repetition or prolongation of sounds, interfering with speech
Substance-related disorders	Alcohol abuse, cocaine abuse, opiate abuse, and abuse of other mind-altering substances
Schizophrenia	Deterioration of everyday functioning, along with either a lack of emotional response, or thought disorders, or hallucinations or delusions
Delusional (paranoid) disorder	Irrational beliefs, such as the belief that "everyone is talking about me behind my back" or that "I have discovered the secret that will solve all the world's problems if I can just get people to listen to me"
Mood disorders	Periods of depression serious enough to interfere with daily life, sometimes alternating with periods of mania, which is the opposite of depression
Anxiety disorders	Lingering anxiety at almost all times, unpredictable attacks of severe anxiety, or periods of anxiety that regularly occur when the person is confronted with a particular object or thought
Somatoform disorders	*Examples:* *Conversion disorder:* One or more physical ailments, such as blindness or paralysis, caused at least in part by psychological factors but not intentionally produced *Hypochondriasis:* Repetitive, exaggerated complaints of illness *Somatization disorder:* Recurrent complaints of pain and other ailments that are not apparently due to any physical disorder
Dissociative disorders	Loss of the memory of a person's own identity or the memory of past events, not caused by brain damage
Sexual disorders	*Examples:* *Pedophilia:* Sexual attraction to children *Exhibitionism:* Sexual pleasure from exposing oneself in public *Voyeurism:* Sexual arousal primarily from watching other people undressing or engaging in sexual intercourse *Fetishism:* Sexual arousal primarily from leather or other inanimate objects
Eating disorders	*Examples:* *Anorexia nervosa:* Refusal to eat, fear of being fat *Bulimia nervosa:* Binge eating alternating with weight loss
Sleep disorders:	*Examples:* *Insomnia:* Frequent feeling of not being rested after a night's sleep *Sleep terror disorder:* Repeated periods of awakening suddenly in an experience of panic *Sleepwalking disorder:* Repeated episodes of leaving the bed, walking about, and not remembering the episode later
Impulse control disorders	A tendency to act on impulses that other people usually inhibit, such as the urge to gamble large amounts of money foolishly, the urge to steal something, or the urge to strike someone

nutritional deficiencies, hormonal disorders, and so forth. Psychiatrists and clinical psychologists must learn to make a **differential diagnosis**—that is, *a determination of what problem a person has, in contrast to all the other possible problems that might produce similar symptoms.* Only after the therapist knows exactly what the problem is can he or she decide on the best treatment.

THE MESSAGE
Is Anybody Normal?

Most people believe there is an unpleasant stigma attached to being diagnosed with a psychological disorder. Almost any synonym for "mental illness" is considered an insult.

And yet, as you read earlier in this module, according to one study, about one-half of all people in the United States will have at least one DSM-IV disorder at some point in life. If that statistic is accurate, or even close, the implication is obvious: Most of the people who qualify for a psychological diagnosis are not very different from normal. At some point in your life, you may have a bout of depression or anxiety or suffer from substance abuse or other psychological distress. If so, remember that you have plenty of company.

SUMMARY

✳ *Normal and abnormal behavior.* Although psychologists and psychiatrists try to be objective and scientific when identifying abnormal behavior, some judgments are necessarily difficult and dependent on value judgments. To

TABLE 15.2   Some Major Categories of Psychological Disorders, According to Axis II of DSM-IV

Mental retardation	Intellectual functioning significantly below average; significant deficits in adaptive behavior
Personality disorders	*Examples:*
	Paranoid personality disorder: Suspiciousness; habitual interpretation of other people's acts as threatening
	Schizotypal personality disorder: Poor relationships with other people; odd thinking; neglect of normal grooming. This disorder is similar to schizophrenia but less extreme
	Antisocial personality disorder: Lack of affection for other people; tendency to manipulate other people without feeling guilty; high probability of getting into trouble with the law; low probability of keeping a job
	Borderline personality disorder: Lack of a stable self-image; trouble establishing lasting relationships with other people or making lasting decisions about values, career choice, even sexual orientation; repeated self-endangering behavior, such as drug abuse, reckless driving, casual sex, binge eating, shoplifting, and running up large debts
	Histrionic personality disorder: Excessive emotionality and attention-seeking; constant demand for praise
	Narcissistic personality disorder: Exaggerated opinion of one's own importance and a lack of regard for others (Narcissus was a figure in Greek mythology who fell in love with himself)
	Avoidant personality disorder: Avoidance of social contact; lack of friends
	Dependent personality disorder: Preference for letting other people make decisions; lack of initiative and self-confidence

avoid tyrannical subjugation of eccentric people, we should be cautious about applying psychiatric labels. (page 561)

✳ *Cultural influences on abnormal behavior.* Any culture provides not only examples of how to behave normally but also how to behave abnormally. (page 562)

✳ *Multiple causes of abnormal behavior.* Abnormal behavior is the result of various combinations of biological factors, early experiences, and learned responses to a stressful or unsupportive environment. (page 563)

✳ *The Diagnostic and Statistical Manual.* Psychological disorders are classified in the *Diagnostic and Statistical Manual of Mental Disorders, Fourth Edition* (DSM-IV). This manual classifies disorders along five axes. Axis I and Axis II deal with psychological disorders; Axis III deals with physi-

cal ailments that can affect behavior; Axes IV and V provide the means of evaluating a person's stress level and overall functioning. (page 564)

✳ *Axis I—disorders that affect part of a person's life.* Axis I of DSM-IV lists disorders that usually begin after infancy and that have at least some likelihood of recovery. Three common disorders of this sort are anxiety disorders, substance abuse, and depression. (page 565)

✳ *Axis II—lifelong disorders.* Axis II of DSM-IV lists conditions that arise early and persist throughout a lifetime, such as mental retardation and personality disorders. (page 565)

✳ *Personality disorders.* Personality disorders are stable characteristics that impair a person's effectiveness or ability to get along with others. Examples of personality disorders are excessive dependence on others and excessive self-centeredness. (page 565)

✳ *Differential diagnosis.* Psychiatrists and clinical psychologists need to learn to consider all the possible diagnoses of a given set of symptoms and to identify the correct one by eliminating all the other possibilities. (page 565)

Suggestions for Further Reading

Barlow, D. H., & Durand, V. M. (1995). *Abnormal psychology.* Pacific Grove, CA: Brooks/Cole. A good general textbook on abnormal behavior.

Holmes, D. S. (1997). *Abnormal psychology.* White Plains, NY: Longman. Another outstanding textbook.

Terms

Almost everyone has an unpleasant mood or shows strange behaviors once in a while. Many people who qualify for a DSM-IV diagnosis are not much different from anyone else.

dissociative identity disorder   a rare condition in which the personality separates into several identities; also known as multiple personality disorder (page 562)

biopsychosocial model the concept that abnormal behavior has three major aspects—biological, psychological, and sociological (page 563)

Diagnostic and Statistical Manual of Mental Disorders, Fourth Edition (DSM-IV) a book that lists the acceptable labels for all psychological disorders, with a description of each and guidelines on how to distinguish it from similar disorders (page 564)

personality disorder a maladaptive, inflexible way of dealing with the environment and other people (page 565)

differential diagnosis a determination of what problem a person has, in contrast to all the other possible problems that might produce similar symptoms (page 566)

Answer to Concept Check

1. The most common diagnoses are anxiety disorders, substance-related disorders, and depression. (page 565)

Web Resources

Mental Illness (Overview)

www.psych.org/public_info/overview.html

The American Psychiatric Association provides an overview of Mental Illness in this pamphlet from the *Let's Talk Facts* series.

Psychotherapy

What methods are used to help people overcome psychological disorders?

How effective are these methods?

Observation
If I don't drive around the park,
I'm pretty sure to make my mark.
If I'm in bed each night by ten,
I may get back my looks again.
If I abstain from fun and such,
I'll probably amount to much.
But I shall stay the way I am,
Because I do not give a damn.

—DOROTHY PARKER (1944)

Psychotherapy is *a treatment of psychological disorders by methods that include a personal relationship between a trained therapist and a client.* But psychotherapy does little good unless the client gives the proverbial damn.

A psychotherapist, like this military psychologist in a Haitian refugee camp, tries to help people overcome problems, or, better yet, to help themselves.

Psychotherapy is used for many well-defined disorders that are listed in DSM-IV and also for adjustment and coping problems. Some psychotherapy clients are virtually incapacitated by their problems, but others are reasonably happy, successful people who would like to function even more successfully.

Before World War II, almost all psychotherapists were psychiatrists, and most of them used Freudian methods. Today, psychotherapy is available from clinical psychologists, social workers, counseling psychologists, and others, using hundreds of methods and approaches that differ markedly. For example, in psychoanalysis and cognitive therapy, the therapist does much of the talking; in person-centered therapy, the therapist says little. Psychoanalysts examine past emotions; cognitive therapists emphasize current emotions; behavior therapists try to change behaviors and practically ignore emotions. Many therapists focus on the problems of the individual; family therapists and community psychologists focus on problems of larger groups. Nevertheless, as you will see, the various forms of therapy have a few fundamental points in common, such as the need for a close relationship between the client and the therapist.

Psychoanalysis

Several types of psychotherapy, known as **psychodynamic therapies,** *attempt to uncover people's underlying drives and motivations.* For example, both Sigmund Freud's procedure (looking for underlying sexual motives) and Alfred Adler's procedure (looking for underlying power and superiority motives) are considered psychodynamic, despite the differences between them. Here, we shall focus on the procedure developed by Freud, although its practitioners have modified and developed it further since Freud's time.

Psychoanalysis, the first of the "talk" therapies, is *a method based on identifying unconscious thoughts and emotions and bringing them to consciousness, to help people understand their thoughts and actions.* Psychoanalysis is therefore described as an "insight-oriented therapy," in contrast to therapies that focus on changing thoughts and behaviors (Figure 15.5).

Freud believed that psychological problems were the result of unconscious thought processes and that the only way to control self-defeating behavior is to make those processes conscious. Bringing them to consciousness, he thought, would produce **catharsis,** *a release of pent-up emotions associated with unconscious thoughts and memories.* Among his methods of bringing unconscious material to consciousness were free association, dream analysis, and transference.

Free Association

Free association is a method that Freud and his patients developed together. (Actually, a more accurate translation of the original German expression would be "free intrusion.")

569

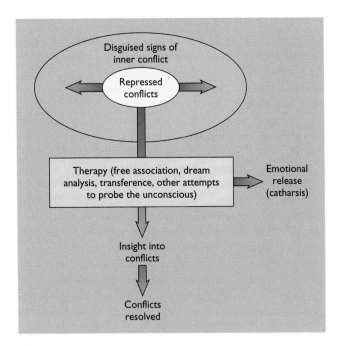

FIGURE 15.5 The goal of psychoanalysis is to resolve psychological problems by bringing to consciousness the unconscious thought processes that are responsible for the difficulty. *Analysis* literally means "to loosen or break up, to look at the parts."

In **free association,** the client *starts thinking about a particular symptom or problem and then reports everything that comes to mind—a word, a phrase, a visual image.* The client is instructed not to omit or censor anything or even try to speak in complete sentences.

The psychoanalyst listens for links and themes that might tie the patient's fragmentary remarks together. The assumption is that all behavior is determined, that nothing happens without a cause. (Recall from Chapter 6 that behaviorists make the same assumption.) Every jump from one thought to another reveals a relationship.

Here is a paraphrased excerpt from a free-association session:

> A man begins by describing a conference he had with his boss the previous day. He did not like the boss's policy, but he was in no position to contradict the boss. He had had a dream. It was something about an ironing board, but that was all he remembered of the dream. He comments that his wife has been complaining about the way their maid irons. He thinks his wife is being unfair; he hopes she does not fire the maid. He complains that his boss did not give him credit for some work he did recently. He recalls a childhood episode: He jumped off a cupboard and bounced off his mother's behind while she was leaning over to do some ironing. She told his father, who gave him a spanking. His father never let him explain; he was always too strict. (Munroe, 1955, p. 39)

To a psychoanalyst, the links in this story suggest that the man is associating his wife with his mother. His wife was unfair to the maid about the ironing, just as his mother had been unfair to him. Moreover, his boss is like his father, never giving him a chance to explain his errors and never giving him credit for what he did well.

Dream Analysis

Each dream has a **manifest content**—*the content that appears on the surface*—and a **latent content**—*the hidden content that is represented only symbolically in the actual experience.* Freud (1900/1955) sought to understand the latent content but rejected the view that each item in the manifest content represents the same latent content for everyone. To understand a dream, he said, one must determine what each detail of the manifest content means to the dreamer.

To illustrate, Freud (1900/1955) interpreted one of his own dreams, in which one of his friends was his uncle. He described the following associations: Two of his friends had been recommended for an appointment as a university professor, but both had been turned down, probably because they were Jews. Freud himself had recently been recommended for the same appointment, but he feared that he, too, would be turned down because he was Jewish. Freud's only uncle had once been convicted of illegal business dealings and had not been very intelligent.

Freud considered one of his friends to be somewhat unintelligent, like the uncle. Another friend had once been taken to court by a woman who accused him of sexual misconduct, although the charges were dropped. By linking these two friends to his uncle, Freud interpreted the dream as meaning, "Maybe they didn't get rejected for the university appointment because they were Jews, but because one was a simpleton (like my uncle) and the other was accused of a crime (like my uncle). If so, I still have a chance for the appointment."

To Freud, every dream represents a form of wish fulfillment. The wish may be disguised, but it is always there. For example, in his dream, Freud was not wishing that his friend were his uncle. Rather, he was wishing that he would get the university appointment, and he was wishing that his friends had been rejected for another reason besides being Jewish.

Contrary to what you may have heard, Freud did not see sexual symbolism in all dreams. Curiously, however, the examples he gives of dreams with nonsexual symbolism are his own dreams, and his examples of dreams containing sexual symbolism are described as other people's dreams.

CONCEPT CHECK

2. A popular paperback purports to tell you what your dreams mean. The author says that every element of a dream has a symbolic meaning—in many cases, a sexual meaning. A ballpoint pen represents a penis, for example, and walking up a flight of stairs represents sexual arousal. Would Freud agree or disagree with the author of this book? (Check your answer on page 583.)

Transference

Some clients show either exaggerated love or hatred for their therapist, which seems inappropriate under the circumstances. Psychoanalysts call this reaction **transference;** they mean that clients are *transferring onto the therapist what they actually feel toward their father or mother or another important figure.* Transference often provides clues to the client's feelings about those people.

Psychoanalysts are fairly active in their **interpretation** of what the client says—that is, they *explain the underlying meaning*—and may even argue with the client about interpretations. They may regard the client's disagreement as **resistance,** *continued repression that interferes with therapy.* Resistance can take many forms; for example, a client who has begun to touch on an extremely anxiety-provoking topic may turn the conversation to something trivial or may simply "forget" to come to the next session.

Psychoanalysts today remain largely loyal to Freud's approach, although they modify it in many ways (Karon & Widener, 1995). The goal is still to bring about a major reorganization of the personality, changing a person from the inside out, by helping people understand the hidden reasons behind their actions.

Behavior Therapy

Behavior therapists assume that human behavior is learned and that it can be unlearned. They identify the behavior that needs to be changed, such as a phobia or an addiction or a nervous twitch, and then set about changing it through reinforcement, punishment, and other principles of learning. They may try to understand the causes of the behavior, as a first step toward changing it, but unlike psychoanalysts, they are more interested in directly changing behaviors than in understanding their hidden meanings.

Behavior therapy *begins with clear, well-defined behavioral goals, such as eliminating test anxiety or getting the client to quit smoking, and then attempts to achieve those goals through learning.* Setting clear goals enables the therapist to judge whether the therapy is succeeding. As in the examples of operant conditioning that we encountered in Chapter 6, the psychologist uses a shaping procedure—that is, starts by reinforcing simple behaviors and then progresses to more complex ones. If the client shows no improvement after a few sessions, the therapist tries a different procedure. We shall consider three examples of behavior therapy here and more in Chapter 16.

Behavior Therapy for Anorexia Nervosa

A behavior therapist treats anorexia nervosa (Chapter 11) by providing reinforcement for eating or gaining weight. For example, one woman with severe anorexia nervosa was isolated from her family and placed in a small, barren hospital room (Bachrach, Erwin, & Mohr, 1965). She was told that she could not leave the room and could see no one except the nurse who came at mealtimes. She could obtain privileges—such as having a television or reading material, the right to leave the room, or the right to have visitors—only as a reward for gaining weight. This method may seem heartless, but life-threatening cases like this one demand drastic measures. The woman gradually gained weight and was released from the hospital when she reached 77 pounds (35 kilograms). After leaving, she lost some of the weight she had gained but not enough to endanger her life.

Behavior therapy can be combined with other therapeutic methods. In cases of anorexia nervosa, this therapy is most effective when it is combined with family counseling designed to alter the family interactions that may have led to the problem (Russell, Szmukler, Dare, & Eisler, 1987).

Behavior Therapy for Bed-Wetting

Some children continue to wet the bed long after the usual age of toilet training. Most of them outgrow the problem, but it occasionally lingers on to age 5, 10, or even into the teens.

We now know that many bed wetters have small bladders and thus have difficulty getting through the night without urinating. We also know that many are unusually deep sleepers who do not wake up when they wet the bed (Stegat, 1975).

Behavior therapists treat anorexia nervosa patients by providing privileges as reinforcements for weight gain. A life-threatening disorder requires drastic interventions.

The most effective procedure uses classical conditioning to train the child to wake up at night and go to the bathroom when the bladder is full (Houts, Berman, & Abramson, 1994). The simplest procedure uses a small battery-powered device that fits into the child's underwear at night. During the night, when the child urinates, the device detects the moisture and produces a pulsing vibration that awakens the child. (Alternative devices work on the same principle but produce loud noises.)

The vibration acts as an unconditioned stimulus (UCS) that evokes the unconditioned response (UCR) of waking up. In this instance, the body itself generates the conditioned stimulus (CS): the sensation produced by a full bladder (Figure 15.6). Whenever that sensation is present, it serves as a signal that the vibration is imminent. After a few pairings (or more), the sensation of a full bladder is enough to wake the child.

Actually, the situation is a little more complicated, because the child is positively reinforced with praise for waking up to use the toilet. Thus, the process includes both classical and operant conditioning. Training by use of an alarm or vibration eliminates bed-wetting in most children, though not all, and is sometimes effective after as little as one night.

Aversion Therapy

Although behavior therapists rely mostly on positive reinforcement, they occasionally use punishment to try to teach clients an aversion (dislike) to a stimulus. For example, they might ask someone who is trying to quit smoking to smoke twice as many cigarettes as usual for a few days, to inhale rapidly (one puff every 6 seconds), or to smoke nonstop in a small, airtight room with overflowing ashtrays, until there is little oxygen left to breathe. The goal is to teach the client

A small device called a "Potty Pager" fits into a child's underwear and produces a vibration when it becomes moist. It thereby awakens the child, who then learns to awaken when the bladder is full. (Photo courtesy of Ideas for Living, Inc., Boulder, CO.)

an aversion to smoking. At the end of this treatment, most people stop smoking at least temporarily, although they are likely to start up again within a year (Poole, Sanson-Fisher, & German, 1981). It is apparently difficult to undo years of enjoyable smoking with a few unpleasant sessions of aversion therapy.

Therapies That Focus on Thoughts and Beliefs

Someone says to you, "Look how messy your room is! Don't you ever clean it?" How do you react? You might say, "Big deal. Maybe I'll clean it tomorrow." Or you might feel worried, angry, or even depressed. If you get upset, it may not be merely because you were criticized but because you want everyone to believe that you are scrupulously clean and tidy. Some therapists focus on the thoughts and beliefs that underlie people's emotional reactions. Unlike psychoanalysts, these therapists are more concerned about what their clients are thinking right now than about the early experiences that led to these thoughts.

FIGURE 15.6 A child can be trained not to wet the bed by the use of classical-conditioning techniques. At first, the sensation of a full bladder (the CS) produces no response, and the child wets the bed. This causes a vibration or other alarm (the UCS), and the child wakes up (the UCR). By associating the sensation of a full bladder with a vibration, the child soon begins waking up to the sensation of a full bladder alone, and will not wet the bed.

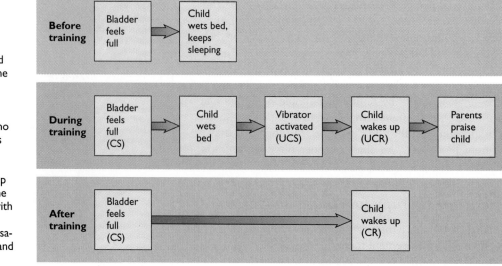

Cognitive and Rational-Emotive Therapies

Cognitive therapy *seeks to improve people's psychological well-being by changing their cognitions*—their thoughts and beliefs (Beck, 1976; Hollon & Beck, 1979). For example, someone who has undergone an extremely stressful experience, such as being raped or witnessing a fatal accident, may harbor irrational and harmful beliefs such as "it was my fault" or "it will happen to me again" (Marks, Lovell, Noshirvani, Livanou, & Thrasher, 1998). A cognitive therapist tries to identify these thoughts and encourage the client to explore the evidence behind them. Generally, the client discovers that these beliefs are unjustified. Eventually, the client learns to identify and challenge his or her own disruptive thoughts. (We shall discuss cognitive therapy for depression in Chapter 16.)

A related approach, **rational-emotive therapy** is *a treatment based on the assumption that people's emotions depend on their "internal sentences," such as "I can't be happy unless I succeed at all times"* (Dryden & DiGiuseppe, 1990). This therapy is called "rational-emotive" because it assumes that thoughts (rationality) lead to emotions. The problem therefore is not the unpleasant emotions themselves, but the irrational thoughts that lead to them.

Rational-emotive therapists (Ellis, 1987) believe that abnormal behavior often results from such irrational beliefs as these:

- I must perform certain tasks successfully.
- I must perform well at all times.
- I must have the approval of certain people at all times.
- Others must treat me fairly and with consideration.
- I must live under easy, gratifying conditions.

The word *must* makes these beliefs irrational. Rational-emotive therapists try to identify irrational beliefs (which people may never have verbalized) and then contradict them. They urge clients to substitute other, more realistic "internal sentences." Rational-emotive therapists intervene directly to instruct and persuade. Here is an excerpt from a rational-emotive therapy session with a 25-year-old physicist:

Client: The whole trouble is that I am really a phony. I am living under false pretenses. And the longer it goes on, the more people praise me and make a fuss over my accomplishments, the worse I feel.

Therapist: What do you mean you are a phony? I thought that you told me, during our last session, that your work has been examined at another laboratory and that some of the people there think your ideas are of revolutionary importance.

Client: But I have wasted so much time. I could be doing very much better. . . . Remember that book I told you I was writing . . . it's been three weeks now since I've

spent any time on it. And this is simple stuff that I should be able to do with my left hand while I am writing a technical paper with my right. I have heard Bob Oppenheimer reel off stuff extemporaneously to a bunch of newspaper reporters that is twice as good as what I am mightily laboring on in this damned book!

Therapist: Perhaps so. And perhaps you're not quite as good—yet—as Oppenheimer or a few other outstanding people in your field. But the real point, it seems to me, is that . . . here you are, at just twenty-five, with a Ph.D. in a most difficult field, with an excellent job, much good work in process, and what well may be a fine professional paper and a good popular book also in progress. And just because you're not another Oppenheimer or Einstein quite yet, you're savagely berating yourself.

Client: Well, shouldn't I be doing much better than I am?

Therapist: No, why the devil should you? As far as I can see, you are not doing badly at all. But your major difficulty—the main cause of your present unhappiness—is your utterly perfectionistic criteria for judging your performance. (Ellis & Harper, 1961, pp. 99–100)

CONCEPT CHECK

3. How does the concept behind rational-emotive therapy compare to the James-Lange theory of emotions, from Chapter 12? (Check your answer on page 583.)

Cognitive-Behavior Therapy

Many therapists combine important features of both behavior therapy and cognitive therapy to form **cognitive-behavior therapy.** Cognitive-behavior therapists *set explicit goals for changing people's behavior, but in contrast to most behavior therapists, they place more emphasis on changing people's interpretation of their situation.* For example, most of us get very upset if we see a video news report showing a fatal automobile accident; we would be much less upset if someone told us that the film was just a special-effects simulation (Meichenbaum, 1995). Similarly, cognitive-behavior therapists try to help clients distinguish between serious, real problems and imagined or distorted problems. They help clients change their interpretations of past events, current concerns, and future possibilities. Cognitive-behavior therapy has become one of the most widespread forms of therapy in the United States.

Humanistic Therapy

As we saw in Chapter 13, humanistic psychologists believe that people can decide consciously and deliberately what kind of person to be and that people naturally strive to

The crash of the *Challenger* (left) was deeply upsetting to a great many people. Tragedies in fictional films, like the one in *Con Air* shown at right, are far less disturbing. The impact of any event depends not just on the event itself, but also on how we interpret it.

achieve their full potential. However, people sometimes learn to dislike themselves because others criticize and reject them. They become distressed by the **incongruence** (*mismatch*) *between their self-concept and their ideal self.* Humanistic therapists hold that, once people are freed from the inhibiting influences of a rejecting society, they can solve their own problems.

The best-known version of humanistic therapy is **person-centered therapy** pioneered by Carl Rogers. It is also known as nondirective or client-centered therapy. *The therapist listens to the client sympathetically, with total acceptance and unconditional positive regard, like the love of a parent for a child.* Most of the time, the therapist restates what the client has said, to clarify it, thus conveying the message, "I'm trying to understand your experience from your point of view." The therapist strives to be genuine, empathic, and caring, rarely offering any interpretation or advice. Here is an example (shortened from Rogers, 1951, pp. 46–47):

Client: I've never said this before to anyone. This is a terrible thing to say, but if I could just find some glorious cause that I could give my life for I would be happy. I guess maybe I haven't the guts—or the strength—to kill myself—and I just don't want to live.

Counselor: At the present time things look so black to you that you can't see much point in living.

Client: Yes. I wish people hated me, because then I could turn away from them and could blame them. But no, it is all in my hands. I either fight whatever it is that holds me in this terrible conflict, or retreat clear back to the security of my dream world where I could do things, have clever friends, be a pretty wonderful sort of person.

Counselor: It's really a tough struggle, digging into this like you are, and at times the shelter of your dream world looks more attractive and comfortable.

Client: My dream world or suicide.

Counselor: Your dream world or something more permanent than dreams.

Client: Yes. (A long pause. Complete change of voice.) So I don't see why I should waste your time. I'm not worth it. What do you think?

Counselor: It's up to you, Gil. It isn't wasting my time. I'd be glad to see you, whenever you come, but it's how you feel about it. If you want to come twice a week, once a week, it's up to you.

Client: You're not going to suggest that I come in oftener? You're not alarmed and think I ought to come in every day until I get out of this?

Counselor: I believe you are able to make your own decision. I'll see you whenever you want to come.

Client: I don't believe you are alarmed about . . . I see. I may be afraid of myself, but you aren't afraid for me.

The therapist provides an atmosphere in which the client can freely explore feelings of guilt, anxiety, and hostility. By accepting the client's feelings, the therapist conveys the message, "You can make your own decisions. Now that you are more aware of certain problems, you can deal with them constructively yourself."

CONCEPT CHECK

4. Answer the following questions with reference to psychoanalysis, cognitive or rational-emotive therapy, humanistic therapy, and behavior therapy.
   a. With which type of therapy is the therapist least likely to offer advice and interpretations of behavior?
   b. Which type focuses more on changing what people do than on exploring what they think?
   c. Which two types of therapy try to change what people think? (Check your answers on page 583.)

Family Systems Therapy

In **family systems therapy,** *the guiding assumption is that a troubled individual is probably part of a troubled family.* In some cases, the person who first seeks treatment is the least disturbed member of the family; in any case, therapists are usually more effective if they can deal with a person's problems in the context of other family members. Marriage counseling is a special kind of family system therapy, in which the therapist deals with a married couple.

Family systems therapy is not exactly an alternative to other forms of therapy; a family therapist can use psychoanalysis, behavior therapy, cognitive therapy, or any other technique. What distinguishes family therapists is that they prefer to talk with two or more members of a family together; even when they do talk with just one member of a family, they focus on how that individual fits into the family. Their assumption is that many problems arise from poor communication or unreasonable expectations within the family. Even when the problem is primarily that of an individual (such as alcoholism), other family members have learned to treat the disordered person in certain ways; solving the problem requires changing the family environment as well as changing the individual's behavior (Clarkin & Carpenter, 1995; Rohrbaugh, Shoham, Spungen, & Steinglass, 1995).

For example, one young man who had been caught stealing a car was taken to a psychologist. The psychologist, a family therapist, asked to talk with the parents as well. As it turned out, the father had been a heavy drinker until his boss pressured him to quit drinking and join Alcoholics Anonymous. Until that time, the mother had made most of the family decisions in close consultation with her son, who had become almost a substitute husband. When the father quit drinking, he began to assume more authority over the

Most people with psychological problems are members of troubled families. A family systems therapist focuses on how each individual's problems fit into the family's problems.

family, and his son came to resent him. The mother felt less needed and grew depressed. Each member of the family had problems that they could not resolve separately. The therapist worked to help the father improve his relationship with both his son and his wife and to help all three find satisfying roles within the family (Foley, 1984).

General Trends in Psychotherapy

Hundreds of other types of therapy are available, including some that are quite different from the five listed here. About half of all U.S. psychotherapists, however, profess no strong allegiance to any single form of therapy. Instead, they practice **eclectic therapy,** meaning that they *use a combination of methods and approaches.* An eclectic therapist might use behavior therapy with one client and rational-emotive therapy with another or else start with one therapy and then shift to another when the first seems ineffective. The therapist might also borrow insights from several approaches. Table 15.3 contrasts five major types of psychotherapy.

The early practitioners of psychotherapy insisted on seeing each client one at a time, frequently, and on a long-term basis. Over the years, new methods have arisen for making psychotherapy less costly, less time-consuming, and therefore available to more people. We shall now consider the alternatives of brief therapy, group therapy, and self-help groups.

Brief Therapy

Psychotherapy can require a major commitment of time and money. An individual psychotherapy session generally lasts about 50 minutes; depending on the therapist and the nature of the client's problems, the sessions are generally scheduled once per week but can be as often as every day. If the therapy begins with an open-ended plan to continue "as long as necessary," it can easily drag on for years. Indeed, many therapists, especially psychoanalysts, have assumed that frequent sessions conducted over a long period of time are essential for a successful outcome, and they regarded any client who quit after a few sessions as a dropout, a failure.

Eventually, therapists realized that some of the apparent failures were really "premature successes" who did not need further treatment. In fact, about half of all people who enter psychotherapy show significant improvement within 8 sessions, and three-fourths show improvement within 26 sessions (Howard, Kopta, Krause, & Orlinsky, 1986).

As a result, many therapists began to plan limits on the duration of therapy. At the start of **brief therapy,** or *time-limited therapy, the therapist and the client reach an agreement about what they can expect from each other and how long the treatment will last*—such as once per week for 2 months (Koss & Butcher, 1986). As the deadline

TABLE 15.3   Comparison of Five Types of Psychotherapy

TYPE OF PSYCHOTHERAPY	THEORY OF WHAT CAUSES PSYCHOLOGICAL DISORDERS	GOAL OF TREATMENT	THERAPEUTIC METHODS	ROLE OF THERAPIST
Psychoanalysis	Unconscious thoughts and motivations	To bring unconscious thoughts to consciousness; to achieve insight	Free association, dream analysis, and other methods of probing the unconscious mind	To interpret associations
Cognitive therapies	Irrational beliefs and unrealistic goals	To establish realistic goals, expectations, and interpretations of a situation	Dialogue with the therapist	To help the client reexamine assumptions
Humanistic (person-centered) therapy	Reactions to a rejecting society; incongruence between self-concept and ideal self	To enable client to make personal decisions; to promote self-acceptance	Client-centered interviews	To focus the client's attention; to provide unconditional positive regard
Behavior therapy	Learned inappropriate, maladaptive behaviors	To change behaviors	Positive reinforcement and other learning techniques	To develop, direct, and evaluate the behavior therapy program
Family systems therapy	Distorted communication and confused roles within a family	To improve the life of each individual by improving functioning of the family	Counseling sessions with whole family or with individual talking about life in the family	To promote better family communication and understanding

approaches, both the therapist and the client are strongly motivated to bring the therapy to a successful conclusion. (How hard would you work on a term paper if you had no deadline to meet? How would a professor conduct the class if a course were scheduled to continue "as long as necessary"? Without deadlines, few of us would apply ourselves as diligently as possible.)

Moreover, with a deadline that's agreed-upon in advance, clients do not feel deserted or rejected when the therapy ends. They may return for an occasional extra session months later, but for a time they must get along without help. Any client who fails to make progress by the deadline should consider going to a different therapist. Many clients, probably most, prefer brief therapy to an indefinitely long commitment, and most clients with mild problems respond well to brief therapy.

Unfortunately, however, recent economic trends have created pressure for therapy to be extremely brief, sometimes too brief. People who receive health care through health maintenance organizations (HMOs) pay a fixed amount per month and then receive whatever medical care they need from the staff of the organization. Most HMOs offer brief therapy or "crisis intervention" as part of their services. In other words, anyone who belongs to such an HMO can get a few psychotherapy sessions (typically 3–20, depending on the HMO), without any extra payment. The advantage of this system is that many people who could not otherwise afford psychotherapy can get help during a time of distress (Hoyt & Austad, 1992). The disadvantage is that the HMO saves money by minimizing ser-

vices and therefore authorizes only brief therapy even for people with more extensive problems. Any client who needs more than the allotted amount of treatment is either given a prescription for drugs instead of psychotherapy or encouraged to see a therapist outside the HMO at the client's own expense (Karon, 1995).

Economically speaking, it is impossible to maximize the quality of care and minimize the cost at the same time. The goal of HMOs, to provide good yet inexpensive therapy, is understandable; however, some HMOs provide simply too little. Working out a cost-effective solution will be a serious challenge.

Group Therapy

The pioneers of psychotherapy dealt with their clients on a one-on-one basis. Individual psychotherapy has advantages—most of all, privacy. But for many purposes, it is helpful to treat clients in groups. **Group therapy** is *therapy that is administered to a group of people all at once.* It first became popular as a method of providing help to people who could not afford to pay for individual sessions. (Spreading the costs of a session among 5–10 group members reduces the cost for each.) Eventually, therapists found that group therapy has other advantages as well. In particular, many clients seek help because of failed relationships or because they have trouble dealing with other people. A group therapy session enables them to examine how they relate to others and to practice better social skills (Ballinger & Yalom, 1995).

Group therapy can be less expensive than individual therapy. Moreover, participants learn from one another and explore their ways of relating to other people.

Self-Help Groups

Self-help groups, such as Alcoholics Anonymous, operate much like group therapy sessions, except that they do not include a therapist. Each participant both gives and receives help. People who have experienced a particular problem themselves can offer special insights to others with the same problem. They are especially well prepared to deal with someone who says, "You just don't understand." They reply, "Oh, yes, we do!" Self-help groups have another advantage: The members are available to help one another whenever someone needs help—often or seldom, without an appointment, without charge.

Some self-help groups are composed of current or former mental patients. The members feel a need to talk to others who have gone through a similar experience, either in addition to or instead of treatment by a therapist. The Mental Patients' Association in Canada was organized by former patients who were frustrated and angry at the treatment they had received (or failed to receive), especially in mental hospitals (Chamberlin, 1978). Similar organizations in the United States and Europe enable former patients to share experiences with one another, provide support, and work together to defend the rights and welfare of mental patients.

Evaluating the Effectiveness of Psychotherapy

For the purpose of healing what ails your psyche, you can talk to someone who will be very curious about your childhood toilet training, someone who will compare your dreams to ancient myths and folktales, someone who will listen sympathetically and wait for you to solve your own problems, or someone who will use learning principles to change your habits. Hundreds of forms of therapy are available, ranging from traditional, mainstream approaches to

some odd and untested procedures. You can, if you wish, crawl naked into a hot tub with your therapist to reenact the moment of birth. However, if you want your insurance company to pay for your treatment, the company will question whether the treatment will be effective enough to be worth the cost.

How can we measure the effectiveness of a treatment? You might imagine that it would be simple to determine how much people improve in their psychological well-being from the start to the end of treatment. However, when would you guess that people usually enter psychotherapy—when they are feeling better than usual or when they are feeling worse? Naturally, they seek therapy when they are feeling worse, perhaps even the worst they have ever felt. From that starting point, they have almost nowhere to go but up. That is, an apparent improvement in someone's condition might be due to natural fluctuations in psychological well-being instead of the results of therapy.

Hans Eysenck (1952) called attention to this issue by pointing out that about 65% of the people who never receive therapy for their psychological problems nevertheless improve in a year or two. *Improvement without therapy* is called **spontaneous remission.** So, to measure the effectiveness of psychotherapy, an investigator must compare the improvement of psychotherapy clients to the spontaneous remission rate.

WHAT'S THE EVIDENCE?

How Effective is Psychotherapy?

In other chapters in this book, the "What's the evidence?" section has highlighted a particular study. Here, I want to describe a general research approach. Hundreds of research studies similar to this have been conducted, although each of them varies in its details (Kazdin, 1995).

Because everyone's moods and effectiveness fluctuate over time, an apparent improvement between the start and the end of therapy is hard to interpret. How much of the improvement depended on the therapy and how much would have occurred even without therapy? Adequate research on this issue requires a control group.

Hypothesis   Psychologically troubled people who receive psychotherapy will show greater improvements in their condition than similar people who do not receive therapy.

Method   For the results to be meaningful, participants must be assigned at random to the therapy and nontherapy groups. (Comparing people who sought therapy to those who did not seek it would be unfair, because the two groups might differ in the severity of their problems or their motivation for overcoming them.) In the best studies, people who contact a clinic about receiving therapy are all given a preliminary examination and are then randomly assigned to receive therapy at once or to be placed on a "waiting list" for therapy at a later time. A few months later, the investigators compare the amount of improvement shown by the therapy group and the waiting-list group.

How should the investigators measure the amount of improvement? Researchers cannot rely on the judgments of the therapists, who, after all, want to demonstrate the effectiveness of their procedures. For similar reasons, they cannot ask the clients for an unbiased opinion about how much they have improved. Therefore, the researchers may ask a "blind" observer (see Chapter 2) to evaluate each client, without knowing who has received therapy and who has been on the waiting list. Or they may ask each person to take a standardized personality test, such as the MMPI. Unfortunately, the personality tests are far from perfect, and a single evaluation by a blind observer uncovers only a limited amount of information. In short, this research method should be able to detect major changes in clients' well-being, but it may overlook smaller changes.

Many experiments on psychotherapy simply compare a group that received therapy to a control group that was on the waiting list. Other experiments, however, have compared groups receiving different kinds of therapy or different frequencies of therapy.

Results   Here, we are not interested in the results of any single study. Most experiments have included only a modest number of people, such as 10 or 20 receiving therapy and a similar number on the waiting list. To draw a conclusion, we need to pool the results from a great many similar experiments. Psychologists use a method called **meta-analysis,** *taking the results of many experiments, weighting each one in proportion to the number of participants, and determining the overall average effect.* According to one meta-analysis that pooled the results of 475 experiments, the average person in therapy shows greater improvement than 80% of similarly troubled people who are not receiving therapy (Smith, Glass, & Miller, 1980). Figure 15.7 illustrates this effect.

Interpretation   One could easily complain that investigators have invested a great deal of effort for rather little payoff. After 475 experiments, we can confidently say that getting therapy is usually better than not getting therapy. This conclusion is like saying that, if you are ill, some medicine is better than no medicine. However, even if this conclusion seems unimpressive, it does pave the way for further, more detailed studies about which kinds of therapy are best, how therapy produces its benefits, and so forth.

* * *

CONCEPT CHECK

5. Although well-designed experiments on psychotherapy use a blind observer to rate clients' mental health, double-blind studies are virtually impossible. Why? (Check your answer on page 583.)

Comparisons of Different Therapies and Therapists

Next, of course, we want to know which kinds of therapy are best and for which disorders these are most effective. The practical problem for researchers is that therapists have identified hundreds of psychological disorders and have developed hundreds of types of therapy. To test each form of therapy on each possible disorder would require tens of

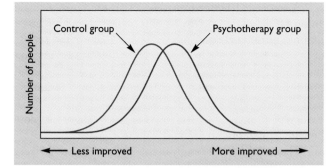

FIGURE 15.7 According to one review of 475 studies, the average person receiving psychotherapy shows more improvement than do 80% of similar, randomly assigned people who are not in therapy. Note that both groups show substantial variation; some untreated people progress better than some treated people. This comparison lumps together all kinds of therapy and all kinds of troubled people. (From Smith, Glass, & Miller, 1980.)

thousands of experiments, each using as many participants as possible. Furthermore, many clients have a mixture of several problems, not just one, and many therapists use an eclectic, trial-and-error approach instead of a single, well-defined therapy (Goldfried & Wolfe, 1996). Under these circumstances, it would be highly impractical to test every therapy for every disorder. However, the results of the studies that have been done support a stunningly simple conclusion: For the disorders that have been widely tested, all the common, mainstream forms of therapy are approximately equal in effectiveness (Lipsey & Wilson, 1993; Stiles, Shapiro, & Elliott, 1986; Wampold et al., 1997). That finding is surprising, given that psychoanalysis, behavior therapy, person-centered therapy, and the others differ so sharply in their assumptions, methods, and goals. If all treatments succeed almost equally well, they must resemble one another more than we had thought.

Research has also compared the effectiveness of thera-

pists with different kinds of training. The U.S. magazine *Consumer Reports* (1995) surveyed its readers about their mental health and their contact with psychotherapy. Of the thousands who said they had sought help for a mental health problem within the previous 3 years, most said they were satisfied with the treatment and thought it had helped them. For measuring the effectiveness of psychotherapy, this study has some obvious problems: the lack of a random sample, the lack of a control group, and reliance on clients to evaluate their own improvement (Jacobson & Christensen, 1996). Nevertheless, the results indicated that people reported about equal satisfaction and benefits from talking with a psychiatrist, a psychologist, or a social worker (Seligman, 1995). They reported somewhat less satisfaction from consulting a marriage counselor, but presumably the people who consulted marriage counselors had different, and perhaps especially difficult, problems. (See Figure 15.8.)

The same general pattern emerged in a variety of other studies that have used more traditional experimental methods, though with smaller samples of people: Therapy generally helps, but the type of therapist is not critical. In fact, studies have even compared the results for clients who were randomly assigned to talk with either an experienced therapist or a caring individual who had no formal training in psychology. Most clients gained just about as much from consulting an inexperienced as an experienced therapist. In short, we have no concrete evidence that the extensive experience or training of a therapist increases the effectiveness of psychotherapy (Christensen & Jacobson, 1994; Dawes, 1994).

Is the conclusion, then, that if you are psychologically troubled, you may as well talk to your next-door neighbor instead of a psychotherapist? No, for several reasons:

- The study just described dealt with clients who had mild problems, and we cannot assume that the same results would hold true for other clients.

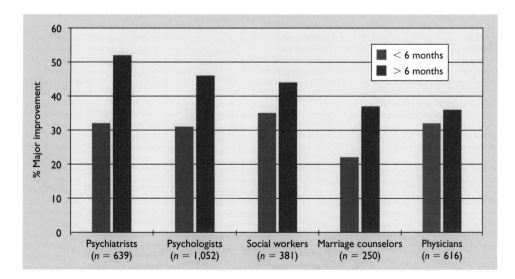

FIGURE 15.8 The percentage of *Consumer Reports* respondents who said they experienced much improvement in the problem that led them to treatment. For those who visited therapists for less than 6 months, the reported improvements were the same after visits to psychiatrists, psychologists, social workers, or family physicians. Marriage counselors, who deal with different kinds of problems, had somewhat lower ratings. (From Seligman, 1995.)

The research indicates that talking with an untrained but caring person is about as helpful as talking with an experienced therapist, at least for people with mild problems. Seeing a therapist does have advantages, however, including guaranteed privacy.

• Few of us have a friend or next-door neighbor with enough patience to listen to hours of personal ramblings and occasional outbursts of anger.
• Conversation with a professional psychotherapist is completely confidential. You cannot be sure that a friend will keep your comments secret.
• A well-trained psychotherapist can recognize symptoms of a possible brain tumor or other medical disorder and is more likely than someone else to refer you to an appropriate medical specialist.
• Clinical psychologists know enough about therapy research that they are less likely than other people to follow untested "fad" treatments (Maki & Syman, 1997).

In short, although you would probably benefit by talking to almost any sympathetic listener, there are important advantages to seeing a professional psychotherapist (Strupp, 1996).

Is More Treatment Better?

If it helps to meet with a therapist once per week for 3 months, would meeting one for 6 months help even more? Would meeting twice per week for a year help even more? How much is the right amount?

Respondents in the *Consumer Reports* (1995) study mentioned earlier were asked how much treatment they got and how much it helped them. Generally, those who received longer treatment reported that it helped them more. However, this was not an experimental study, so people were not randomly assigned to groups receiving different amounts of treatment. It may well be that the people who stayed in treatment the longest were those with the greatest problems at the start and therefore with the greatest room for improvement.

A somewhat better research design examines a single group of clients repeatedly as all progress through a given number of therapy sessions. Figure 15.9 shows the results of one such study. According to both the researchers and the clients themselves, most clients showed fairly rapid progress at first and then gradual progress that continued over 2 years (Howard, Kopta, Krause, & Orlinsky, 1986). Evidently, prolonged treatment is at least somewhat more beneficial than brief treatment, on the average.

The most elaborate study of this issue so far was a 5-year study conducted at Fort Bragg, North Carolina. A government-supported program provided free clinical services for every teenager or child needing psychological help who had a parent in the military. Each of these clients had a case manager who determined what plan of treatment was best, made sure that the client received every needed type of help, and coordinated all the service providers to make sure that each one knew what the others were doing for the client. The goal was to demonstrate that a well-planned, integrated program of treatment would be more effective than the usual forms of treatment, and that it might even be less expensive, because there would be less waste and overlap of services. Results were compared to those in a similar community that offered the usual sort of less coordinated services. The result? The integrated program at Fort Bragg provided no more benefits. It was just more expensive (Bickman, 1996). We should not draw too strong a conclusion from this study; after all, it was not a true experiment (people were not randomly assigned to groups), and the design of the integrated program at Fort Bragg may not have been as good as what someone else might design. Still, most people had expected the integrated pro-

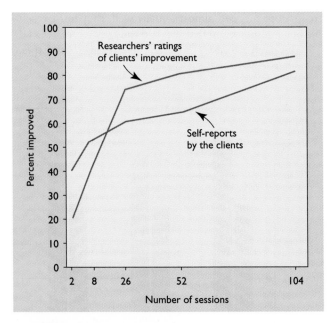

FIGURE 15.9 The relationship of the number of psychotherapy sessions and the percentage of clients who improved. (From Howard et al., 1986.)

gram to show some advantages, and the results do seem to imply that more therapy is not always better.

Similarities Among Psychotherapeutic Methods

Because all the common forms of psychotherapy have been shown to be almost equally effective, they presumably share some important features. One point in common is that all rely on the "therapeutic alliance"—a relationship between therapist and client that is characterized by acceptance, caring, respect, and attention. This relationship provides the social support that helps clients to deal with their problems and acquire social skills that they can apply to other relationships (Krupnick et al., 1994).

Moreover, in nearly all forms of therapy, clients talk openly and honestly about their beliefs and emotions, relationships with family members, and other issues that people ordinarily keep secret. They examine aspects of themselves that they usually take for granted; in so doing, they gain self-understanding. Because of the expectation of self-disclosure, psychotherapy as practiced in North America and Europe does not transplant readily into other cultures. For example, most Chinese would consider it shameful to discuss personal or family matters with a stranger (Bond, 1991).

The mere fact of entering therapy, whatever the method used, improves clients' morale. The therapist conveys the message "you are going to get better." Clients thus begin to think of themselves as people who can cope with their problems and overcome them. Just expecting improvement can lead to improvement.

Finally, every form of therapy requires clients to commit themselves to making some sort of change in their lifestyle. Simply by coming to the therapy session, they are reaffirming their commitment—to drink less, to feel less depressed, or to overcome their fears. They are also obliged to work on that change between sessions, so that they can come to the next session and report, "I've been doing a little better lately." Improvement may depend at least as much on what clients do between sessions as on what happens in the sessions themselves.

Advice for Potential Psychotherapy Clients

At some point, you or someone close to you may be interested in seeing a psychotherapist. If so, here is some advice to consider:

- Consulting a therapist does not mean that something is wrong with you. Many people who consult a therapist have no diagnosable disorder; they merely want to talk with someone.
- If you live in the United States, you can look in the white pages of your telephone directory for the Mental Health Association. Call them and ask for a recommendation of a therapist. You can specify how much you are willing to pay, what kind of problem you have, and even what kind of therapist you prefer.
- Other things being equal, you may do best with a therapist from your own cultural background (Sue, 1998). Therapists are trained to be sensitive to people from other backgrounds, but a communication barrier often remains nevertheless. For example, certain responses to grief or fear that are considered abnormal by many Western psychotherapists are considered normal in many non-Western cultures.
- If your religion is an important part of your outlook on life, you might prefer a therapist who sympathizes with your beliefs (Worthington, Kurusu, McCullough & Sandage, 1996). Conversely, of course, if you are not devoutly religious, you might want to avoid a therapist who wants to focus on religion.
- Be skeptical of any therapist who seems overconfident. Clinical experience does not give anyone quick access to your private thoughts.
- Even if your treatment is not labeled "brief therapy," expect some improvement within 6–8 weeks. If you do not seem to be making progress, there may be a good reason. But at least, ask your therapist why your progress is slow; if you do not receive a convincing answer, consider seeing a different therapist.

THE MESSAGE
Finding the Best Therapy

The research indicates that various kinds of therapy are about equally effective for the average client and that psychiatrists, psychologists, and social workers are about equally effective therapists, on the average. These results do not mean, however, that any therapist is just as good as any other.

Although no one has done the research, chances are that one could also find that, on the average, professors using a lecture approach are neither considerably more nor less effective than those using mostly discussion. And yet you know from extensive experience that some lecturers are excellent and others are poor, and that some discussion leaders are excellent and others poor. Also, a professor who meets the needs of one student may be unsatisfactory for another. The same is true for psychotherapists. No one way of doing therapy is right for every client; the challenge is to find a good match between client and therapist.

SUMMARY

✳ *Psychoanalysis.* Psychoanalysts try to uncover the unconscious reasons behind self-defeating behaviors. To bring the unconscious to consciousness, they rely on free association, dream analysis, and transference. (page 569)

✳ *Behavior therapy.* Behavior therapists set specific goals for changing a client's behavior and use a variety of learning techniques to help a client achieve those goals. (page 571)

✳ *Cognitive therapies.* Cognitive therapists try to get clients to give up their irrational beliefs and unrealistic goals and to replace defeatist thinking with more favorable views of themselves and the world. Many therapists combine features of behavior therapy and cognitive therapy, attempting to change people's behaviors by altering how they interpret the situation. (page 573)

✳ *Humanistic therapy.* Humanistic therapists, including person-centered therapists, assume that, if people accept themselves as they are, they can solve their own problems. Person-centered therapists listen with unconditional positive regard but seldom offer interpretations or advice. (page 573)

✳ *Family systems therapy.* In many cases, an individual's problem is part of an overall disorder of family communications and expectations. Family systems therapists try to work with as many family members as possible. (page 575)

✳ *Eclectic therapy.* About half of all psychotherapists today call themselves "eclectic"—that is, they use a combination of methods, depending on the circumstances. (page 575)

✳ *Brief therapy.* Many therapists set a time limit for the treatment, usually ranging from 2–6 months. Brief therapy is usually about as successful as long-term therapy, if the goals are limited. (page 575)

✳ *Group therapies and self-help groups.* Psychotherapy is sometimes provided to people in groups, often composed of people with similar problems. Self-help groups provide sessions similar to group therapy but without a therapist. (page 576)

✳ *Effectiveness of psychotherapy.* The average troubled person in therapy improves more than at least 80% of people who are not in therapy. On the average, each of the common forms of therapy provides approximately equal benefits for the disorders that have been extensively tested. Psychiatrists, psychologists, and social workers also provide approximately equal benefits, on the average. (page 577)

✳ *Similarities among therapies.* A wide variety of therapies share certain features: All rely on a caring relationship between therapist and client. All promote self-understanding. All improve clients' morale. And all require a commitment by clients to try to make changes in their lives. (page 581)

Suggestions for Further Reading

Bongar, B., & Beutler, L. E. (1995). *Comprehensive textbook of psychotherapy.* Oxford, England: Oxford University Press. Describes the theoretical assumptions and procedures of the most common forms of psychotherapy.

Dawes, R. M. (1994). *House of cards: Psychology and psychotherapy built on myth.* New York: Free Press. A harsh criticism of psychotherapists who rely on their intuition and experience instead of scientific evidence.

Seligman, M. E. P. (1993). *What you can change . . . and what you can't.* New York: Fawcett Columbine. Description of both the possibilities and the limitations of psychotherapy.

Terms

psychotherapy the treatment of psychological disorders by methods that include a personal relationship between a trained therapist and a client (page 569)

psychodynamic therapies treatments that attempt to uncover people's underlying drives and motivations (page 569)

psychoanalysis a method of psychotherapy developed by Sigmund Freud, based on identifying unconscious thoughts and emotions and bringing them to consciousness (page 569)

catharsis the release of pent-up emotions associated with unconscious thoughts and memories (page 569)

free association a procedure where a client lies on a couch, starts thinking about a particular symptom or problem and then reports everything that comes to mind (page 570)

manifest content the content that appears on the surface of a dream (page 570)

latent content the hidden content of a dream that is represented only symbolically (page 570)

transference the extension of a client's feelings toward a parent or other important figure onto the therapist (page 571)

interpretation a therapist's explanation of the underlying meaning of what a client says (page 571)

resistance according to psychoanalysts, continued repression that interferes with therapy (page 571)

behavior therapy treatment that begins with clear, well-defined behavioral goals, such as eliminating test anxiety, and then attempts to achieve those goals through learning (page 571)

cognitive therapy treatment that seeks to improve people's psychological well-being by changing their cognitions (page 573)

rational-emotive therapy treatment based on the assumption that people's emotions depend on their "internal sentences," such as "I can't be happy unless I succeed at all times" (page 573)

cognitive-behavior therapy treatment that combines important features of both behavior therapy and cognitive therapy, attempting to change people's behavior by changing their interpretation of their situation (page 573)

incongruence a mismatch between someone's self-concept and ideal self (page 574)

person-centered therapy (also known as nondirective or client-centered therapy) a procedure in which a therapist listens to the client sympathetically, provides unconditional positive regard, and offers little interpretation or advice (page 574)

family systems therapy treatment based on the assumption that a troubled individual is probably part of a troubled family (page 575)

eclectic therapy treatment that uses a combination of methods and approaches (page 575)

brief therapy (or time-limited therapy) treatment that begins with an agreement about what the therapist and the client can expect from each other and how long the treatment will last (page 575)

group therapy treatment administered to a group of people all at once (page 576)

spontaneous remission improvement of a psychological condition without therapy (page 577)

meta-analysis a method of taking the results of many experiments, weighting each one in proportion to the number of participants, and determining the overall average effect (page 578)

Answers to Concept Checks

2. Freud would disagree with the premise of this paperback. Freud believed that the symbolism of dream elements differed from one person to another. (page 570)

3. Rational-emotive therapy assumes that many thoughts lead to emotions. This assumption is the reverse of the James-Lange theory, which argues that emotion-related changes in the body give rise to thoughts. (page 573)

4. **a.** Humanistic therapy; **b.** behavior therapy; **c.** psychoanalysis and cognitive therapy. (page 574)

5. A double-blind design requires that neither the subjects nor the observers know which subjects received the experimental treatment and which ones were in the control group. It is not possible to prevent subjects from knowing whether they have received psychotherapy. (page 578)

Web Resources

The Efficacy of Psychotherapy
www.apa.org/practice/peff.html

Psychotherapy
www.psych.org/public_info/psythera.html

The American Psychological Association provides information about the efficacy of psychotherapy. The American Psychiatric Association describes the general procedures involved in psychotherapy.

Health Center: Therapy
www.health-center.com/english/brain/therapy/

This site includes definitions of therapy, descriptions of several major kinds of therapy, and suggestions on how to go about seeing a therapist.

MODULE 15.3

Social and Legal Issues in the Treatment of People with Disorders

What should our society do about psychological disorders?

A group of nearsighted people, lost in the woods, were trying to find their way home. One of the few who wore glasses said, "I think I know the way. Follow me." The others burst into laughter. "That's ridiculous," said one. "How could anybody who needs glasses be our leader?"

In 1972, the Democratic party nominated Senator Thomas Eagleton for vice president of the United States. Shortly after his nomination, he revealed that he had once received psychiatric treatment for depression. He was ridiculed mercilessly: "How could anybody who needed a psychiatrist be our leader?"

A great many people suffer from a psychological disorder at some point during their life. Unfortunately, many people in our society consider it shameful to seek help for a psychological disorder. They struggle along on their own, like a nearsighted person who refuses to wear glasses, rather than admit that they need help.

As a citizen and a voter, you will have to deal with numerous issues relating to psychological disorders and therapies: Who, if anyone, should receive psychiatric treatment against their protest? Should mental patients have the right to refuse treatment? Under what circumstances, if any, should a criminal defendant be acquitted because of "insanity"? Can society as a whole take steps to prevent certain types of psychological disorders?

Mental Hospitals and Deinstitutionalization

Until the 1950s, people with severe psychological disturbances in the United States were generally confined in large mental hospitals supported by their state or county. Most of these hospitals were understaffed, poorly funded, prisonlike institutions that kept patients alive and out of other people's way but provided little if any psychiatric care (Okin, 1983).

Hospital attendants cooked the food, did the laundry, made all the decisions, but did not try to teach patients the skills they would need if they were ever to leave the institution. After all, few patients ever did. Some hospitals were better than others, but most were pretty grim places.

With the advent of antidepressant and antischizophrenic drugs in the 1950s, advances in psychotherapy, and changes in the commitment laws, the number of long-term mental patients declined steadily. Today, the number of hospital beds reserved for psychiatric patients is one-fifth of what it was in 1955. A given patient may be admitted to a hospital repeatedly, but most stays are brief (Appleby et al., 1993).

Several alternatives to hospitalization are available. Many cities have homes staffed and organized to treat people with psychiatric problems. Another alternative is a community mental health center, where some patients reside but others just come for visits during the day. The idea behind these various forms of alternative care is that patients should receive appropriate supervision and treatment but should also have as much contact as possible with the "real world." Studies have consistently found that community mental health centers are less expensive than large mental hospitals and at least as effective in restoring people to independent living (Fenton, Mosher, Herrell, & Blyler, 1998).

Such research prompted a movement toward **deinstitutionalization,** *the removal of patients from mental hospitals,* to give them the least restrictive care possible. Hospital stays would be brief, except for people who were dangerous to themselves or others. Instead, people would live in or near their own communities and continue to receive outpatient care as needed.

Unfortunately, most states discharged great numbers of patients from their mental hospitals without planning adequate alternatives for their care and housing. Many of the

Mental hospitals of the 1950s were crowded, unpleasant warehouses of people who received minimal care. Many stayed for years, even for the rest of their lives.

Deinstitutionalization moved people out of mental hospitals, but many received little or no treatment after their release. Some became unemployed and homeless.

people who might once have been in a mental hospital are now in nursing homes or prisons; some are homeless; and many now receive no therapeutic attention (Smith, Schwebel, Dunn, & McIver, 1993).

Legal Issues in the Treatment of Disordered People

In a democratic society, we treasure both freedom and security. Sometimes these values are in conflict. For example, the right of a psychologically disordered person to be free may conflict with the right of other people to feel safe and secure. We shall consider several of these conflicts and the difficulties of resolving them.

Involuntary Commitment and Treatment

Suppose Charles mutters incoherently, cannot hold down a job, does not pay his bills or take care of his personal hygiene, and bothers his neighbors. His family wants to commit him to a mental hospital, and the psychiatrist wants to give him drugs. But Charles refuses both courses, claiming that his family is "out to get him." Should he be permitted to refuse treatment?

We can argue this question either way. On the one hand, some of the most seriously disordered people fail to recognize that there is anything wrong with them. On the

other hand, some families have been known to commit annoying relatives to mental hospitals just to get them out of the way, and some psychiatrists have given drugs to people with only minor problems, thereby doing them more harm than good.

Unfortunately, it is difficult to determine who really needs help and who doesn't. Who (if anyone) should be unwillingly confined to a mental hospital? In the United States, laws vary from state to state (Weiner & Wettstein, 1993), but in all cases, a judge holds a hearing and makes the final decision. In some states, a court can commit patients to a mental hospital only if they are suffering from a mental disorder and are dangerous to themselves or others. The American Psychiatric Association has recommended changing the laws to allow commitment of nondangerous patients also, if they have a severe but treatable disorder and "lack capacity to make an informed decision concerning treatment" (Bloom & Faulkner, 1987; Hoge, Sachs, Appelbaum, Greer, & Gordon, 1988). Even where the law does require a ruling of dangerousness, however, courts sometimes declare an apparently incompetent person to be dangerous simply because of one or two threatening statements (Durham, 1996).

After people have been committed to a mental hospital, voluntarily or involuntarily, they still have the right to refuse treatment (Appelbaum, 1988). According to their psychiatrists, most of the people who refuse treatment are hostile, emotionally withdrawn, and prone to disorganized thinking (Marder et al., 1983). According to the patients themselves, they have good reason to be hostile and withdrawn; the hospital staff is trying to force them to submit to unnecessary and dangerous treatments. Figure 15.10 compares patients with schizophrenia who refused drug treatment and patients who agreed to drug treatment. Understandably, decisions about enforced treatment can be very difficult.

SOMETHING TO THINK ABOUT

Thomas Szasz (1982) proposed that psychologically "normal" people write a "psychiatric will," specifying what treatments to give them, and what treatments to avoid, if they ever develop a severe psychological disorder. If you wrote such a will, what would you include in it? Or would you prefer to trust your judgment later, at the time of the onset of the disorder? ✳

The Duty to Protect

Suppose someone tells his psychotherapist that he is planning to kill his former girlfriend. The therapist talks with the client and, by the end of the session, believes that the client has changed his mind. However, a few days later, the client actually does kill his ex-girlfriend. Should the therapist have notified the police and warned the woman of the danger? Should the woman's family be able to sue the therapist and collect damages?

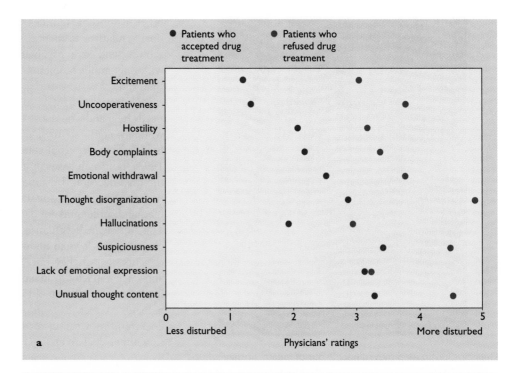

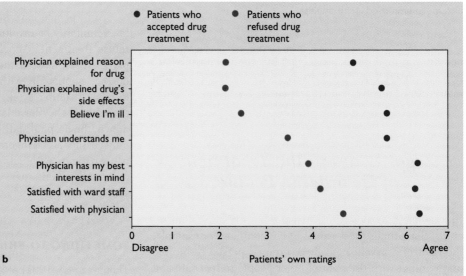

FIGURE 15.10 People with schizophrenia who refuse drug therapy impress their physicians as being seriously disturbed. The patients who refuse drugs rate themselves as dissatisfied with their physicians and their treatments. (a) Physicians' ratings of their patients. High scores indicate greater disturbance. Those refusing treatment showed greater indications of disturbance on most scales. (b) Patients' self-ratings. The higher scores of patients who agreed to drug treatment indicate their higher levels of satisfaction with their treatment. (Based on data from Marder et al., 1983.)

Before you answer "yes," consider the following: First, psychotherapy is based on a trusting relationship in which the therapist promises to keep secret anything that the client says. Second, therapists are seldom certain about which clients are really dangerous (Monahan, 1993). Suppose you are a therapist. Over the course of a day, you see eight patients, and three of them say they are so angry they could kill somebody. How do you decide which ones, if any, to take seriously?

In 1976, a California court ruled in the **Tarasoff** case that *a therapist who knew, or who should have known, that a client was dangerous is obligated to break the pledge of confidentiality and warn the endangered person* (Weiner & Wettstein, 1993). In 1991, a Canadian court made a similar ruling in the case of *Wenden v. Trikha* (Truscott & Crook, 1993). However, applying this rule in practice is difficult, because of the uncertainty in judging dangerousness. The

courts have also ruled that the duty to inform applies only to an identifiable endangered individual. If the client is, for example, an alcohol- and drug-abusing airplane pilot, countless people are endangered, but the therapist is not obligated to inform anyone. In fact, the rules on confidentiality prohibit the therapist from informing the pilot's employer (Felthous, 1993). One can sympathize with therapists who wonder what to do, short of keeping a legal consultant available. Fortunately, the courts have so far been reluctant to hold therapists legally accountable in uncertain cases.

The Insanity Defense

Suppose, in the midst of an epileptic seizure, you flail your arms about and accidentally knock someone down the stairs. If that person dies, should you be convicted of murder? Of course not. Now, suppose that, in the midst of severely disordered thinking and perception, you attack what appears to you to be a giant insect, but is in fact a human being. Should you be convicted of murder in that case?

Courts in North America and most European countries have traditionally ruled that you are "not guilty by reason of insanity." Most people agree with that principle, at least for extreme cases. The problem is where to draw the line. Under what conditions should someone be judged legally insane? *Insanity* is a legal term, not a psychological or medical one, and its definition is based at least as much on politics as it is on science.

One point of broad agreement is that the crime itself, no matter how atrocious, does not demonstrate insanity. In Chapter 5, we considered the case of the "Hillside Strangler" who committed a long series of rapes and murders but who was eventually ruled sane and sentenced to prison. The same decision was made for Jeffrey Dahmer, who was arrested in 1991 after murdering and cannibalizing several men. Theodore Kaczynski, arrested as the "Unabomber" who had mailed bombs to many people for decades, refused to plead insanity, and probably would not have been ruled insane anyway. Bizarre crimes do not, in themselves, demonstrate insanity. In fact, each of these murderers knew what he was doing and took steps to avoid getting caught.

In many cases, however, a decision about sanity or insanity is difficult; lawyers, physicians, and psychologists have long struggled to establish a clear and acceptable definition of *insanity*. Probably the most famous definition, the **M'Naghten rule,** written in Great Britain in 1843, states:

> To establish a defense on the ground of insanity, it must be clearly proved that, at the time of the committing of the act, the party accused was laboring under such a defect of reason, from disease of the mind, as not to know the nature and quality of the act he was doing; or if he did know it, that he did not know he was doing what was wrong. (Shapiro, 1985)

In other words, to be regarded as insane under the M'Naghten rule, people must be so disordered that they do not realize they are committing a criminal act. Presumably, they would continue the act even if a police officer were standing nearby. Many observers have considered that rule too narrow and would like to broaden the definition of insanity to include "irresistible impulses"—acts similar to sneezing or hiccuping, which people could not inhibit for long, no matter how hard they tried. Under the **Durham rule,** established in 1954 in the case of a man named Durham, a U.S. court held that *a defendant is not criminally responsible if the activity was "a product of mental disease or defect."* That rule confused more than it clarified and is no longer used. (Is ignorance a mental defect? What about sleepiness? grouchiness? Almost any criminal act is the product of some sort of defect, broadly defined.)

The **Model Penal Code,** written by the American Law Institute in the 1950s, offered another definition:

> A person is not responsible for criminal conduct if at the time of such conduct as a result of mental disease or defect he lacks substantial capacity either to appreciate the criminality (wrongfulness) of his conduct or to conform his conduct to the requirements of law. (Simon, 1994)

This rule is not as loose as the Durham rule but not as rigid as the M'Naghten rule. However, a jury still needs to make a difficult judgment of whether a defendant lacked "substantial capacity" to appreciate wrongfulness or to conform his or her behavior to the law. When a jury finds someone insane in a highly publicized case—as in the case of John Hinkley, who attempted to assassinate President Ronald Reagan—many people are outraged, partly because they fear that the person will be quickly released. That fear is mostly misinformed; on the average, people found not guilty by reason of insanity are confined to a mental hospital for about as long as they would have spent in prison if they had been found guilty (Silver, 1995).

Several states in the United States have experimented with allowing a verdict of "guilty but mentally ill," intended as a compromise between guilty and not guilty. However, the defendant actually receives the same sentence as if he or she had been simply found guilty and is no more likely to receive psychiatric care in prison than any other convicted

Theodore Kaczynski, once a brilliant mathematician, became a recluse who mailed bombs to people. However, merely being "strange" or committing bizarre acts of violence does not qualify a person as legally insane.

person (Tanay, 1992). In short, the guilty but mentally ill verdict is the same as a guilty verdict.

Insanity pleas are offered in less than 1% of all criminal trials—and these are generally difficult, marginal cases. If the defendant is clearly out of touch with reality, the police and district attorney ordinarily bypass the trial and allow the defendant to enter a mental hospital. If the defendant has no serious signs of mental illness, the defense attorneys seldom attempt an insanity defense.

When the defendant's sanity is in question, the jury will listen to the views of psychologists and psychiatrists who are called as "expert witnesses." Expert witnesses often disagree with one another, however, thus leaving much to the judgment of a jury untrained in either the law or psychology. A jury that sympathizes with the defendant can use the insanity defense as a way of decreasing the penalty; a jury with less sympathy can refuse to find the defendant insane. As a citizen, voter, and potential jury member, you should be concerned about how to bring more rationality to this portion of our legal system.

CONCEPT CHECK

6. Someone who has been involuntarily committed to a mental hospital escapes and commits a murder. Will this person be judged not guilty by reason of insanity? (Check your answer on page 589.)

Predicting and Preventing Mental Illness

The traditional approach of psychotherapy has been to try to relieve psychological distress after it has developed. More recently, certain psychologists, especially community psychologists, began to pay more attention to prevention. **Community psychologists** *focus on the needs of large groups rather than those of individuals.* They distinguish between **primary prevention,** *preventing a disorder from starting,* and **secondary prevention,** *identifying a disorder in its early stages and preventing it from becoming more serious.*

Just as our society puts fluoride into drinking water to prevent tooth decay and immunizes people against contagious diseases, it can take action to prevent certain types of psychological disorders (Albee, 1986; Goldston, 1986; Long, 1986; Yoshikawa, 1994). For example, we could take the following actions:

• *Banning toxins.* The sale of lead-based paint has been banned because children who eat flakes of lead-based paint sustain brain damage. Other toxins in the air and water have yet to be controlled.

• *Educating pregnant women about prenatal care.* For example, women need to be informed that the use of alcohol or other drugs during pregnancy can cause brain damage to the fetus and that certain bacterial and viral infections during pregnancy can impair fetal brain development and increase the risk of psychological disorders.

• *Jobs.* Helping people who lose their jobs to find new work enables them to regain their self-esteem.

• *Child care.* Providing better day-care facilities would contribute to the psychological health of both parents and children.

• *Improved educational opportunities.* Programs that get young people more interested in their schoolwork have made notable progress in decreasing juvenile delinquency.

These techniques are aimed at primary prevention for the entire community. Secondary prevention techniques can be targeted at specific individuals who are just beginning to show symptoms of a particular disorder. For example, psychologists identified fifth- and sixth-grade children prone to distress and then, for 12 weeks, taught them how to avoid negative beliefs about themselves. Those children showed fewer signs of depression over the next 2 years, compared to a similarly distressed group who did not receive this training (Gillham, Reivich, Jaycox, & Seligman, 1995).

Unfortunately, prevention turns out to be a difficult matter. For example, consider the problem of persuading people to change their behavior to help decrease the spread of AIDS (Helweg-Larsen & Collins, 1997).

THE MESSAGE
The Science and Politics of Mental Illness

Suppose you are a storekeeper. Someone dressed as Batman stands outside your store every day shouting gibberish at anyone who comes by. Your once-thriving business draws fewer and fewer customers each day. The disturbing man outside does not seem to be breaking any laws, but you would like to have him removed from the area. Should he be taken to a mental hospital and treated, even though he insists that he is normal? It is a difficult decision. How disordered is he? What treatment would help him, and how much is it likely to help? And if nothing is done, what happens to your rights as a storekeeper?

Similarly, the insanity defense and all the other issues in this module are complicated issues that require political decisions by society as a whole, not just the opinions of psychologists or psychiatrists. Regardless of what career you enter, you will be a voter and potential juror, and therefore you will have as much to say about these issues as anyone else. The decisions deserve serious, informed consideration.

SUMMARY

✳ *Mental hospitals and deinstitutionalization.* Today, very few patients spend a long time in mental hospitals. However, many states have released patients from mental

After screaming and stabbing himself in the throat with a screwdriver in front of the White House, this man was taken to a hospital for observation. Decisions about the treatment of such people must be based on the needs of both the individual and society.

hospitals without supplying adequate community mental health facilities. (page 584)

✳ *Involuntary commitment.* Laws on involuntary commitment to mental hospitals vary. In some states, people can be committed only if they are dangerous; in other states, people can be committed if they are judged incompetent to make decisions about their own treatment. It is difficult to frame laws that ensure treatment for those who need it while also protecting the rights of those who have good reasons for refusing it. (page 585)

✳ *Duty to warn.* The courts have ruled that a therapist who is convinced that a client is dangerous should warn the endangered person. Applying this rule in practice is difficult, however. (page 585)

✳ *The insanity defense.* Some defendants accused of a crime are acquitted for reasons of insanity, which is a legal rather than a medical or psychological concept. The criteria for establishing insanity are vague and controversial. (page 586)

✳ *Prevention of psychological disorders.* Psychologists and psychiatrists are increasingly concerned about preventing psychological disorders. Many preventive measures require the cooperation of society as a whole. (page 588)

Suggestions for Further Reading

LaFond, J. Q., & Durham, M. L. (1992). *Back to the asylum.* New York: Oxford University Press. A history of the treatment of the mentally ill in the United States since about 1960, with a discussion of important controversies.

Sheehan, S. (1982). *Is there no place on earth for me?* Boston: Houghton Mifflin. The story of a young woman with schizophrenia and her life in and out of mental hospitals.

Simon, R. I. (1994). The law and psychiatry. In R. E. Hales, S. C. Yudofsky, & J. A. Talbott (Eds.), *Textbook of psychiatry* (2nd ed.) (pp. 1297–1340). Washington, DC: American Psychiatric Press. A survey of many of the issues discussed in this module.

Terms

deinstitutionalization   the removal of patients from mental hospitals (page 584)

Tarasoff   the rule that a therapist who knew, or who should have known, that a client was dangerous is obligated to break the pledge of confidentiality and warn the endangered person (page 586)

M'Naghten rule   the rule that a defendant is not criminally responsible if, at the time of committing an unlawful act, the person was laboring under such a defect of reason, from disease of the mind, as not to know the nature and quality of the act he was doing; or if he did know it, that he did not know he was doing wrong (page 587)

Durham rule   the rule that a defendant is not criminally responsible if the activity was "a product of mental disease or defect" (page 587)

Model Penal Code   the rule that a person is not responsible for criminal conduct if, at the time of such conduct and as a result of mental disease or defect, he or she lacks substantial capacity either to appreciate the criminality (wrongfulness) of this conduct or to conform his or her conduct to the requirements of law (page 587)

community psychologist   a psychologist who focuses on the needs of large groups rather than those of individuals (page 588)

primary prevention   preventing a disorder from starting (page 588)

secondary prevention   identifying a disorder in its early stages and preventing it from becoming more serious (page 588)

Answer to Concept Check

6. Not necessarily. Having a psychological disorder, even a severe one, does not automatically qualify a person as insane in the legal sense. The judge or jury must also find that the psychological disorder prevented the person from knowing what he or she was doing or made law-abiding behavior impossible. (page 588)

Web Resources

The Insanity Defense
www.psych.org/public_info/INSANI~1.HTM
Information about the insanity defense from the American Psychiatric Association.

Landmark Cases in Forensic Psychiatry
bama.ua.edu/~jhooper/tableofc.html
In his excellent Forensic Psychiatry Resource Page, James Hooper offers brief summaries of almost 100 criminal cases that involve the insanity defense and civil cases that involve mental disorders. You can view the cases chronologically, alphabetically, or in a Java file.

Abnormalities and Therapies II: Explorations of Specific Disorders

Abnormal behavior can result from biological predisposition or stressful experience and, frequently, a combination of both influences. In Shakespeare's *Hamlet*, Ophelia became "mad" and drowned after Hamlet's behavior toward her changed from loving to cruel and he murdered her father.

16

In the 1700s and 1800s, medicine was very primitive by today's standards. Physicians would diagnose someone as being ill, but they rarely could distinguish one illness from another. Also, many of their treatments were the same for one illness as for another. They would recommend general all-purpose "tonics," suggest bed rest, sometimes apply leeches to withdraw blood, and so forth. Medical progress since then has been marked by an increasing ability to distinguish one disorder from another and to develop treatments that are useful for specific disorders.

Similarly, much of the progress in abnormal psychology has come from making appropriate distinctions between one disorder and another and developing treatments aimed at specific disorders. In this chapter, I shall concentrate on four major categories. As you read in Chapter 15, the most commonly diagnosed psychological disorders are anxiety disorders, substance abuse, and depression. The first three modules of this chapter cover those three disorders. The final module deals with schizophrenia, which is less common but in many cases extremely disabling.

MODULE 16.1

Anxiety and Avoidance Disorders

Why do some people take extreme measures to avoid something that is harmless or only slightly dangerous?

Why do some people develop strange habits and rituals?

You go to the beach, looking forward to an afternoon of swimming and surfing. Would you still go in the water if someone tells you that a shark attacked two swimmers yesterday and has just been sighted close to shore? What if the shark attack occurred a month ago and no shark has been seen in the area since then? What if no shark has attacked anyone in this area, but someone saw a small shark there a few days ago? What if no shark has ever been seen near this beach, but recently you read a magazine story about shark attacks?

How much fear and caution is normal? Staying out of the water because you see a large shark is perfectly reasonable. Staying out of the water because you read an article about sharks is, by most people's standards, unreasonable. If you refuse even to look at photographs of the ocean because they might *remind* you of sharks, you have a serious problem indeed. Excessive fear and caution are linked to some of the most common psychological disorders.

Disorders with Excessive Anxiety

Many psychological disorders are marked by a combination of fear, anxiety, and attempts to avoid anxiety. Anxiety, unlike fear, is not generally associated with a specific situation. We feel fear in the presence of a hungry tiger, but our fear passes as soon as we get away. However, we cannot escape the anxiety we experience about dying or about our personal inadequacies. Some degree of anxiety is normal; anxiety becomes a problem only when it interferes with our ability to cope with everyday life.

The people most prone to severe anxiety are those who feel helpless to control the major events of their lives (Chorpita & Barlow, 1998). Recall from Chapter 12 that shock, noise, and all sorts of other unpleasant events are more stressful for people who cannot predict or control them. Many people get a feeling of helplessness early in life and then develop a cognitive style of interpreting new events as uncontrollable. The result is vulnerability to anxiety.

Generalized Anxiety Disorder

People with **generalized anxiety disorder** are *almost constantly plagued by exaggerated worries.* They worry that "I might get sick," "My daughter might get sick," "I might lose my job," or "I might not be able to pay my bills." Although these people have no realistic reason for such worries—at least no more reason than anyone else—their worries persist and interfere with daily life. They grow tense, restless, irritable, and fatigued. About 5% of all people experience generalized anxiety disorder at some point in life, often in conjunction with depression, panic disorder, or other psychological problems (Wittchen, Zhao, Kessler, & Eaton, 1994).

Panic Disorder

People with **panic disorder** *frequently have moderate anxiety and occasionally have attacks of sudden increased heart rate, chest pains, difficulty breathing, sweating, faintness, and trembling* (see Figure 16.1). A panic attack usually lasts only a few minutes, although it can last an hour or more. During an attack, most people worry about fainting, having a heart attack, dying, or going crazy. Panic disorder occurs in 1–3% of adults at some time during their lives, in many cultures throughout the world, and it is more

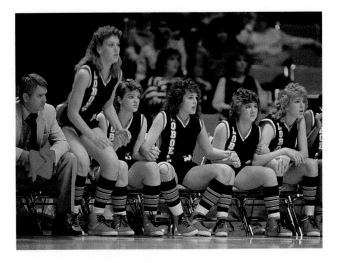

Many situations evoke temporary anxiety or tension in almost anyone. Anxiety becomes a problem only if it is frequently more intense than the situation justifies.

FIGURE 16.1 People subject to panic attacks experience moderate anxiety almost constantly, as well as occasional periods of intense anxiety. During a panic attack, the sympathetic nervous system intensely activates the heart and other organs. People are generally frightened by this experience; some believe they are having a heart attack.

common in women than men (Weissman et al., 1997). Some people with panic disorder do in fact have *mitral valve prolapse,* an abnormality of heart structure that can cause heart flutter, chest pains, and breathing problems (Katerndahl, 1993). However, most people with panic disorder have no apparent medical disorders.

One interpretation of panic disorder is that worried people **hyperventilate** *(breathe deeply and frequently)* to try to control their anxieties; in the process, they reduce their blood level of carbon dioxide. Many kinds of stressors increase the carbon dioxide level, so if the initial level is extremely low, even a small increase is a large percentage increase. The brain reacts to this sudden increase as if it were suffocating, thereby producing the full panic experience (Coplan et al., 1998; Klein, 1993). (See Figure 16.2.)

One treatment for panic disorders is to teach the person to avoid hyperventilating (Wolpe & Rowan, 1988).

Another is to teach the person to recognize sudden increases in heart rate and trembling as a sign of carbon dioxide fluctuations, and not as a sign of an impending heart attack.

Many people with panic disorder also have **social phobia,** *a severe avoidance of other people and an especially strong fear of doing anything in public,* where they might be embarrassed. Many also have **agoraphobia** (from *agora,* the Greek word for "marketplace"), *an excessive fear of open places or public places* (Magee, Eaton, Wittchen, McGonagle, & Kessler, 1996). Many relatives of people with panic disorder also have panic disorder, social phobia, or agoraphobia themselves (Goldstein et al., 1994; Kendler et al., 1995). Most psychologists believe that people with panic disorder develop their social phobia or agoraphobia because they are afraid of being incapacitated or embarrassed by a panic attack in a public place. In a sense,

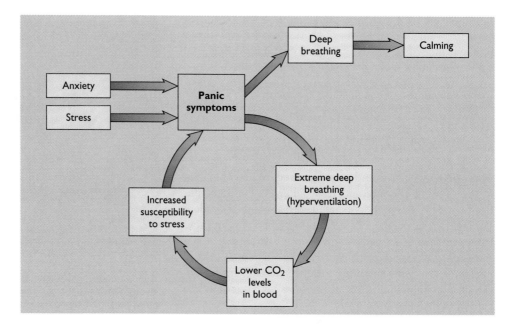

FIGURE 16.2 Deep breathing helps to calm a person, but hyperventilation increases the probability of another panic attack.

they are afraid of their own fear (McNally, 1990). To avoid the prospect of a public panic attack, they stay home as much as possible and rarely go out alone.

CONCEPT CHECK

1. Some psychologists advise people with panic attacks to stop worrying about their attacks and to adopt the attitude, "If it happens, it happens." Why would they make this recommendation? (Check your answer on page 604.)

Disorders with Exaggerated Avoidance Behaviors

People learn to avoid punishment, as we saw in Chapter 6. In some cases, their efforts to avoid punishment become so extreme and persistent that they begin to interfere with daily activities. Let's begin with some general observations on avoidance learning, which will be relevant to the later discussion of phobias (extreme fears) and compulsions (rituals designed to avoid unpleasant thoughts or events).

Avoidance Learning and Its Persistence

If you learn to do something for positive reinforcement, you will extinguish your response soon after you stop receiving reinforcements. Avoidance behaviors are different, however. Suppose you learn to press a lever to avoid electric shocks. Soon, you are responding steadily and you receive no shocks. Now, the experimenter disconnects the shock generator, without telling you. The extinction procedure has begun; you no longer need to press the lever. What will you do? You will continue pressing it, of course. As far as you can tell, nothing has changed; the response still "works." *Avoidance behaviors are highly resistant to extinction;* once

someone learns a response to avoid mishap, the response continues long after it ceases to be necessary.

You can see how this tendency would support superstitions: Suppose you believe that Friday the 13th is a dangerous day. Every Friday the 13th, you are very cautious, but occasionally a misfortune happens anyway. The misfortune only confirms your belief that Friday the 13th is dangerous. The next Friday the 13th, nothing goes wrong. You conclude, "It helps to be careful on Friday the 13th. I was cautious all day long, so I avoided bad luck." In other words, as long as you continue engaging in an avoidance behavior, you can never find out whether you are doing something useless.

CONCEPT CHECK

2. Suppose you are an experimenter, and you have trained someone to press a lever to avoid shocks. Now, you disconnect the shock generator. Other than telling the person what you have done, what procedure could you use to facilitate extinction of the lever pressing? (Check your answer on page 604.)

Phobias

Terror is the only thing that comes close to how I feel when I think of moths. Their willowy, see-through wings always seem filthy. I remember being stuck in a car with a huge moth and my date, not knowing how terrified I was of moths, thought I was kidding when I told him I was afraid. It was terrible! I can feel it right now . . . the . . . feeling trapped and the moth with its ugly body flitting around so quickly, I couldn't anticipate where it would go next. Finally that creature hit me in the arm and I screamed—it felt dirty and sleazy and then it hit me in the face and I began to scream uncontrollably. I had the terrible feeling it was going to fly into my mouth while I was screaming, but I couldn't stop. (Duke & Nowicki, 1979, p. 244)

A **phobia** is best defined as *a strong, persistent fear of a specific object, extreme enough to interfere with normal*

Many people who watched the famous shower scene in the movie *Psycho* became frightened of taking showers. Actress Janet Leigh, who portrayed the woman killed in that shower scene, was herself so terrified that she has only rarely taken a shower since then. That is, fears and phobias can be learned, either from one's own experiences or from vicarious experience.

living. It is often described as an unreasonable or irrational fear, but in most cases, the fear itself is not irrational. For example, a fear of snakes is not irrational, because snakes really can be dangerous. What is irrational is the excessive degree of the fear, which leads to avoidance behaviors— avoiding the object itself (such as a snake), places where the object might be lurking, or even anything that might remind the person of the feared object.

Confronting the object of a phobia can lead to sweating, trembling, and rapid breathing and heart rate. In most cases, people with phobias are not so much afraid of the object itself but of their own reactions (Beck & Emery, 1985). They fear that they will have a heart attack or that they will embarrass themselves by trembling or fainting. In many ways, phobias are like panic disorder, except that phobias are aroused by a specific object or event, whereas panic attacks occur at less predictable times.

Because most people with phobias are well aware that their fears are exaggerated, it does no good to tell them not to be afraid. In fact, attempts to reduce phobias by providing information sometimes backfire. One city tried to combat the phobia of elevators by posting signs on elevators throughout the city: "There is no reason to be afraid of elevators. There is almost no chance at all that the cable will break or that you will suffocate." The signs actually *increased* the phobia of elevators.

The Prevalence of Phobias

According to an extensive study of U.S. adults, about 11% of people suffer a phobia at some time in life, and 5–6% have a phobia at any given time (Magee et al., 1996). However, as with many other psychological disorders, phobias vary in degree from mild to extreme, and the apparent prevalence of phobias increases or decreases, depending on how many borderline cases one includes. Figure 16.3 shows the most frequently reported phobias. Figure 16.4 shows the prevalence of phobias by age. Note the early onset and gradual decline in prevalence with age (Burke, Burke, Regier, & Rae, 1990).

The Learning of Phobias

People seem to be born with a few fears, such as a fear of sudden loud noises, but most fears are learned, and so are most phobias. Indeed, some phobias can be traced to a specific event, such as when one child got locked in a trunk and developed a phobia of closed spaces. Another person developed a phobia of water by diving into a lake and discovering a corpse (Kendler et al., 1995).

John B. Watson, one of the founders of behaviorism, was the first to demonstrate the possibility of learning a fear (Watson & Rayner, 1920). Today, we would consider it unethical to try to create a fear, especially in humans, but in 1920, researchers felt less restraint. Watson and Rosalie Rayner studied an 11-month-old child, "Albert B.," who had previously shown no fear of white rats or other animals (Figure 16.5). They set a white rat down in front of Albert, and then, just behind him, they struck a large steel bar with a hammer. The sudden sound made Albert whimper and cover his face. After seven repetitions, the mere sight of the rat would make Albert cry and crawl away. Watson and Rayner declared that they had created a strong fear and that phobias in general might develop along similar lines.

Although Watson and Rayner's study is open to serious methodological criticisms (Harris, 1979; Samelson, 1980), it led the way for later interpretations of phobias as learned

FIGURE 16.3 The most common phobias include phobias of snakes and other animals, heights, open places and crowds, and storms. Here, people reported their severe fears. Not all severe fears qualify as phobias, however.

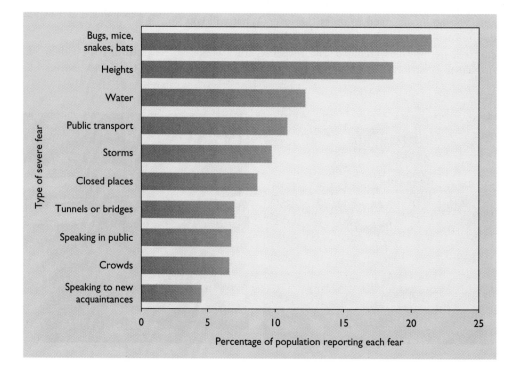

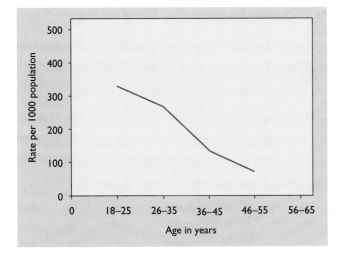

FIGURE 16.4 Most phobias are not lifelong conditions. Most young people with phobias lose their phobias by middle age, either spontaneously or because of therapy.

responses. Watson and Rayner's explanation of phobias failed to answer some important questions: Why do people develop phobias toward objects that have never injured them? Why are some phobias much more common than others? And why are phobias so persistent?

CONCEPT CHECK

3. In classical conditioning terms, what was the CS in Watson and Rayner's experiment? The UCS? The CR? The UCR? (Check your answers on page 604.)

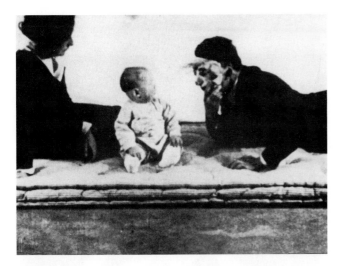

FIGURE 16.5 John B. Watson argued that most fears, including phobias, are learned. Watson first demonstrated that this child, Little Albert, showed little fear of small animals. Then Watson paired the presentation of a white rat with a loud, frightening noise. Little Albert became afraid of the white rat; he also began showing fears of other small animals, odd-looking masks, and other objects he had not previously feared. (Courtesy of Professor Benjamin Harris.)

WHAT'S THE EVIDENCE?
Learning Fear by Observation

Contrary to Watson and Rayner's explanation, almost half of all people with phobias have never had a painful experience with the object that they fear (Öst & Hugdahl, 1981). For example, many people have phobias, or at least intense fears, of snakes, spiders, or sharks, even though they have never been hurt by them. However, we have all heard about people who were injured or killed by snakes and sharks. As noted in the discussion of social learning in Chapter 6, we learn many things by watching or listening to others. Perhaps we learn our fears and phobias from other people.

That hypothesis is probably correct, but how can we demonstrate it? Susan Mineka and her colleagues demonstrated that monkeys learn fears by observing other monkeys (Mineka, 1987; Mineka, Davidson, Cook, & Keir, 1984). Her experiments show how animal studies can shed light on important human issues.

EXPERIMENT I

Hypothesis Monkeys that have seen other monkeys show fear of a snake will develop such a fear themselves.

Method Monkeys that live in the wild generally develop a strong fear of snakes; however, monkeys reared in a laboratory show no fear of snakes. Mineka put a laboratory-reared monkey together with a wild-born monkey and let them both see a snake (Figure 16.6a). The lab monkey watched the wild monkey show signs of fear. Later, Mineka tested the lab monkey by itself to see whether it had acquired a fear of snakes.

Results When the lab monkey saw how frightened its partner was of the snake, it became frightened too (Figure 16.6b). It continued to be afraid of the snake when tested by itself, even months later.

Interpretation The lab monkey may have learned a fear of snakes because it saw that its partner was afraid of snakes. But Mineka considered another possible, though less likely, interpretation: The lab-reared monkey may have become fearful simply because it observed the other monkey's fear. That is, maybe it did not matter *what* the wild-reared monkey was afraid of. To test this possibility, Mineka conducted a second experiment.

EXPERIMENT 2

Hypothesis A monkey that sees another monkey show fear but does not know what the second monkey is afraid of will not develop the same fear itself.

Method A monkey reared in a lab watched a monkey reared in the wild through a plate-glass window. The wild monkey could look through another window, where it saw a snake. Thus, when the wild monkey shrieked and ran away

Wild-reared monkey   **Lab-reared monkey**

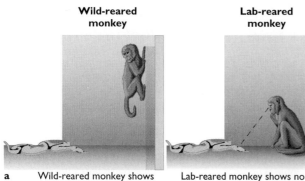

a   Wild-reared monkey shows fear of snake.

Lab-reared monkey shows no fear of snake.

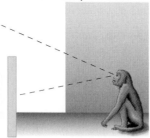

b

Lab-reared monkey learns fear of snake by observing wild-reared monkey and snake.

c

Barrier masks snake from view of lab-reared monkey.

Lab-reared monkey does not learn fear when snake is not visible.

FIGURE 16.6 A laboratory-reared monkey learns to fear snakes from the reactions of a monkey reared in the wild. But if the snake is not visible, the lab-reared monkey fails to learn any fear.

from the snake, the lab monkey saw the wild monkey's fear but did not know what it was afraid of. Later, the lab monkey was placed close to a snake to see whether it would show fear.

Results The lab monkey showed no fear of the snake.

Interpretation To develop a fear of snakes, the observer monkey needed to see that the other monkey was frightened of snakes, not just that it was frightened (Figure 16.6c).

Note that, although the observer monkey had to see *what* the other monkey was afraid of, it did not have to see *why* it was afraid. Just seeing the other monkey's fear of the snake in Experiment 1 was enough. Humans not only observe other people's fears but can also tell one another what we are afraid of and why.

✳   ✳   ✳

Why Some Phobias Are More Common Than Others

Imagine that you survey your friends. (You can actually survey them, if you like, but in this case it's pretty easy to imagine the results.) You ask them:

TRY IT YOURSELF

• Are you afraid of snakes?
• Are you afraid of cars?
• Have you ever been bitten by a snake or seen someone else get bitten by a snake?
• Have you ever been injured in a car accident or seen someone else get injured in a car accident?

I think you know what results to expect: A fair number of people will admit being afraid of snakes, some of them extremely afraid, even though very few have any firsthand experience with snakebites. Hardly anyone is afraid of cars, even though almost everyone has experienced or witnessed a car accident in which someone was injured. So, why do people develop some fears more readily than others?

The most common phobias are of open spaces, closed spaces, heights, lightning and thunder, animals, and illness. In contrast, few people have phobias of cars, guns, or tools—even though injuries from cars, guns, and tools are quite common. One explanation for this tendency is that, as Martin Seligman (1971) put it, people may be inherently "prepared" to learn certain phobias. For millions of years, people who quickly learned to avoid snakes, heights, and lightning have probably had a good chance to survive and to transmit their genes. We have not had enough time to evolve a tendency to fear cars and guns.

We have evidence to support this view from both monkey and human studies. Monkeys who watch a videotape of another monkey running away from a snake learn to fear snakes; monkeys who watch another monkey running away

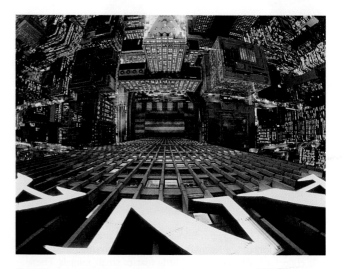

Phobias are most likely to develop for dangerous events that we can neither predict nor control. They also develop for events that give us occasional unpleasant experiences without any safe or pleasant experiences. Can you therefore explain why so many people have phobias of falling from great heights (as in this photo) and so few people have phobias of cars?

from a flower show no fear of flowers (Mineka, 1987). People who receive electric shocks paired with pictures of snakes quickly develop a strong and persistent response to snake pictures; people who receive shocks paired with pictures of houses show a much weaker response (Öhman, Eriksson, & Olofsson, 1975).

There may be other reasons why some phobias are more common than others. One is that we have many safe experiences with cars and tools to outweigh any bad experiences. Most people have few safe experiences with snakes, spiders, or falling from high places. One study found that people who had extensive experiences with tarantula spiders lost their fears and sometimes even developed an interest in tarantulas as a hobby (Kleinknecht, 1982).

Another possible explanation is that people generally develop phobias of objects they cannot predict or control. If you are afraid of spiders, for example, you must be constantly on the alert for those tiny, unpredictable critters. Because you never know where they might be or when they might strike, you can never completely relax. Lightning is also unpredictable and uncontrollable. In contrast, electric outlets can also be dangerous, but you don't have to worry that they will take you by surprise. You must be on the alert for cars when you are near a road, but not at other times.

The Persistence of Phobias

Well-established phobias can last a lifetime. Based on the discussion about avoidance learning, you can see why phobias are so difficult to extinguish: If you have learned to press a lever to avoid shock, you may not stop pressing long enough to find out that your response is no longer necessary. Similarly, if you stay away from snakes or heights or closed places because you have a phobia of them, you will never learn that your fear is exaggerated. In other words, you will not extinguish your fear.

Behavior Therapy for Phobias

Recall the concept of behavior therapy from Chapter 15: A therapist sets a specific goal and applies learning techniques to help the client achieve that goal. One type of behavior therapy is particularly effective for phobias.

Phobias persist because people try to avoid the object of the phobia. The more effectively they avoid the object, the less chance they have to learn that their avoidance is unnecessary. That is, extinction does not occur. Therefore, the best way to extinguish a phobia is to expose a person to the object that arouses the fear. When nothing bad happens, the phobia fades.

One common and usually very successful treatment for phobia is **systematic desensitization,** *a method of reducing fear by gradually exposing people to the object of their fear* (Wolpe, 1961). Someone with a phobia of snakes, for example, is first given training in methods of relaxation. Then, the client is asked to lie on a comfortable couch with relaxing music playing in the background and with the therapist nearby. The therapist asks the client to imagine a small black-and-white photo of a snake. Next, he or she is asked

to imagine a full-color photo and, then, to imagine a real snake. After the client has successfully dealt with all of those images, the same sequence is repeated with real photos and eventually with a real snake (Figure 16.7).

The process resembles Skinner's shaping procedure (see Chapter 6): The person is given time to master each step before going on to the next. The client can say "stop," if the distress becomes threatening; the therapist then goes back several steps and repeats the sequence. Some people get through the whole procedure in a single 1-hour session; others need weekly sessions for a couple of months. Systematic desensitization can easily be combined with social learning: The person with a phobia watches other people who display a fearless response to the object.

Some therapists use a high-tech approach (Rothbaum et al., 1995): The client is equipped with a helmet that displays a virtual-reality scene, as shown in Figure 16.8. Then, without even leaving the office, the therapist can expose the client to the object of his or her fears. For example, a client with a phobia of heights can go up a glass elevator in a hotel, or walk across a narrow bridge over a chasm (Rothbaum et al., 1995). This virtual-reality technology gives the therapist excellent control of the situation, including even the option of turning off the display and removing the helmet, if the client becomes too fearful.

Flooding or **implosion** is *a treatment where the person is exposed to the object of the phobia suddenly rather than gradually* (Hogan & Kirchner, 1967; Rachman, 1969). (This treatment is called "flooding" because the patient is flooded with fear.) If you had a phobia of rats, for example, you might be told to imagine that you were locked in a room full of rats crawling all over you and viciously attacking you. The image arouses your sympathetic nervous system enormously, and your heart rate and breathing rate soar to high levels (Lande, 1982).

FIGURE 16.7 One of the most effective therapies for phobia is systematic desensitization: A therapist gradually exposes a client to the object of the phobia, first in imagination and later in reality. A similar procedure is exposure therapy; the therapist demonstrates a lack of fear of the object and encourages the client to do the same.

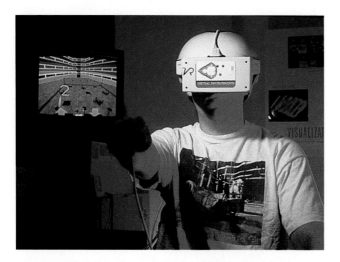

FIGURE 16.8 Some therapists provide a virtual-reality environment, so that a patient with a phobia of heights can experience heights under carefully controlled conditions.

The human sympathetic nervous system is not capable of maintaining extreme arousal for very long, however, so within a few minutes, your heart rate and breathing rate begin to decline. A little later, you report that you feel more relaxed, even though the therapist continues to suggest gory images of what rats are doing to you. Once you have reached this point, the battle is half won. The main fear of people with phobias is actually that their own fear will be overwhelming or that it will lead to a heart attack; when they learn that they can withstand even the most frightening experience, they become less afraid of their own responses.

Drug Therapies for Phobias and Other Anxieties

Tranquilizers are among the most widely prescribed drugs in the United States. The most common tranquilizers are the *benzodiazepines* (BEN-zo-die-AZ-uh-peens), including drugs with the trade names Valium, Librium, and Xanax. Benzodiazepines relieve anxiety, relax the muscles, induce sleep, and

inhibit epileptic seizures. Sometimes, they are prescribed for people with panic disorder, phobia, or other anxiety disorders; they are also frequently prescribed for people with no diagnosable disorder. These drugs can serve as a means of relieving an occasional episode of anxiety or as a sleeping pill. One disadvantage is that they can be habit-forming; another is that they suppress symptoms only temporarily. For example, someone who takes pills to combat panic disorder is likely to resume having panic attacks after discontinuing the pills (Wiborg & Dahl, 1996). In many cases, therapists treat anxiety disorders more effectively with antidepressant drugs, which we shall discuss later in this chapter.

Brain researchers now understand in reasonable detail how benzodiazepines work. The neurotransmitter GABA stimulates receptors on a neuron's membrane, as shown in Figure 16.9. On its own, GABA attaches moderately easily to this receptor, opening a channel for chloride ions (Cl^-) to enter the neuron. Benzodiazepines alter the shape of the receptor complex to enable GABA molecules to attach more readily. Thus, benzodiazepines indirectly facilitate transmission at these synapses (Macdonald, Weddle, & Gross, 1986). Facilitation of these synapses decreases anxiety and promotes sleep.

CONCEPT CHECKS

4. Alcohol facilitates transmission at GABA synapses. What effect should we expect if someone took both alcohol and a benzodiazepine tranquilizer?
5. How does systematic desensitization resemble extinction of a learned shock-avoidance response?
6. How is the flooding procedure related to the James-Lange theory of emotions that was discussed in Chapter 12? (Check your answers on page 604.)

Obsessive-Compulsive Disorder

People with **obsessive-compulsive disorder** have two kinds of problems: An **obsession** is *a repetitive, unwelcome stream of thought.* For example, such people might

FIGURE 16.9 Benzodiazepine tranquilizers attach to a site on the receptor complex for the neurotransmitter GABA. When they attach, they modify the shape of the receptor, making it easier for GABA to stimulate its receptor. Thus the benzodiazepines indirectly facilitate transmission at this synapse, thus enabling chloride molecules to enter the neuron. The effect on behavior is to relieve anxiety. (Based on Guidotti et al., 1986.)

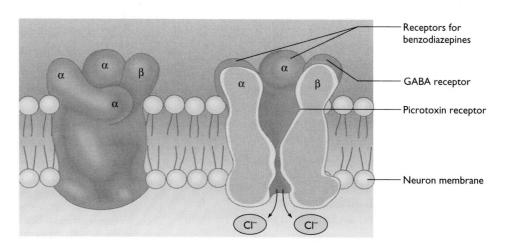

find themselves constantly imagining gruesome scenes, worrying that they are about to kill someone, dwelling on doubts about their religion, or thinking "I hate my sister, I hate my sister." The harder they try to escape such thoughts, the more repetitive they become. A **compulsion** is *a repetitive, almost irresistible action.* Obsessions generally lead to compulsions, as an itching sensation leads to scratching.

The Persistence of Obsessions People with obsessive-compulsive disorder feel a combination of guilt and anxiety over certain thoughts or impulses. They feel persistent, frightening impulses—perhaps an impulse to engage in a sexual act that they consider shameful, an impulse to hurt someone they love, or an impulse to commit suicide. They decide, "Oh, what a terrible thing to think. I don't want to think such a thing ever again." And so they resolve to shut the thought or impulse out of their consciousness. However, the harder one tries to block out a thought, the more intrusive it becomes. As a child, the Russian novelist Leo Tolstoy once organized a club with a most unusual qualification for membership: A prospective member had to stand alone in a corner *without thinking about a white bear* (Simmons, 1949).

 If you think that sounds easy, try it. Normally, you probably go months at a time between thoughts about polar bears, but when you try *not* to think about them, you can think of little else.

In one experiment, college students were asked to tape-record everything that came to mind during 5 minutes but to try *not* to think about white bears. If they did, they were to mention it and ring a bell. Subjects reported thinking about bears a mean of more than six times during the 5 minutes (Wegner, Schneider, Carter, & White, 1987). Afterward, they reported that almost everything in the room reminded them of white bears. Evidently, attempts to suppress a thought are likely to backfire, even with an emotionally trivial thought about something such as white bears; you can imagine how hard it must be with severely upsetting thoughts.

One Type of Compulsion: Cleaning People with obsessive-compulsive disorder have any of several kinds of compulsions. Some collect things. (One man collected

Most people seldom think about polar bears. But *try* to avoid thinking about them and you can think of little else but polar bears. Similarly, many attempts to block obsessive thinking backfire.

newspapers under his bed until they raised the bed so high it almost touched the ceiling.) Others have odd habits, such as touching everything they see, trying to arrange objects in a completely symmetrical manner, or walking back and forth through a doorway nine times before leaving a building. One obsessive-compulsive person could not go to sleep at night until he had counted the corners of every object in the room to make sure that the total number of corners was evenly divisible by 16. If it was not, he would add or remove objects from the room until the room had an acceptable total of corners. (The Obsessive-Compulsive Foundation produces a button that reads, "Every Member Counts"!)

The most common compulsions are cleaning and checking. Obsessive-compulsive cleaning is similar to a phobia of dirt. Here is a description of a severe cleaning compulsion (Nagera, 1976):

"R.," a 12-year-old boy, had a long-standing habit of prolonged bathing and hand washing, dating from a film about germs he had seen in the second grade. At about age 12, he started to complain about "being dirty" and having "bad thoughts," but he would not elaborate. His hand washing and bathing became longer and more frequent. When he bathed, he carefully washed himself with soap and washcloth all over, including the inside of his mouth and the inside of each nostril. He even opened his eyes in the soapy water and carefully washed his eyeballs. The only part he did not wash was his penis, which he covered with a washcloth as soon as he entered the tub.

Coupled with R.'s strange bathing habits, he developed some original superstitions. Whenever he did anything with one hand, he immediately did the same thing with the other hand. Whenever anyone mentioned a member of R.'s family, he would mention the corresponding member of the other person's family. He always walked to school by the same route, being careful never to step on any spot he had ever stepped on before. (After a while, this became a serious strain on his memory.) At school, he would wipe the palm of his hand on his pants after any "good" thought; at home, he would wipe his hand on his pants after any "bad" thought.

R.'s problems were traced to a single event. Just before the onset of his exaggerated behaviors, R. and another boy had pulled down their pants and looked at each other. Afterward, he felt guilty and full of anxiety that he might do the same thing again. The constant bathing was apparently an attempt to wash away his feelings of "dirtiness." The superstitious rituals were an attempt to impose rigid self-control. His underlying reasoning could be described as: "If I can keep myself under perfect control at all times, even following these rigid and pointless rules, I will never again lose control and do something shameful."

Another Type of Compulsion: Checking An obsessive-compulsive checker "double-checks" everything. Before going to bed at night, he or she checks to make sure that all the doors and windows are locked and that all the water faucets and gas outlets are turned off. But then the

TABLE 16.1 Obsessive-Compulsive Cleaners and Checkers

	CLEANERS	CHECKERS
Sex distribution	Mostly female	About equally male and female
Dominant emotion	Anxiety, similar to phobia	Guilt, shame
Speed of onset	Usually rapid	More often gradual
Life disruption	Dominates life	Usually does not disrupt job and family life
Ritual length	Less than one hour at a time	Some go on indefinitely
Feel better after rituals?	Yes	Usually not

SOURCE: Rachman & Hodgson, 1980.

question arises, "Did I *really* check them all, or did I only imagine it?" So everything has to be checked again. And again. "After all, I may accidentally have unlocked one of the doors when I was checking it." Obsessive-compulsive checkers can never decide when to stop checking; they may go on for hours and even then not be satisfied.

Obsessive-compulsive checkers have been known to check every door they pass to see whether anyone has been locked in, to check trash containers and bushes to see whether anyone has abandoned a baby, to call the police every day to ask whether they have committed a crime that they have forgotten, and to drive back and forth along a street to see whether they ran over any pedestrians the last time through (Pollak, 1979; Rachman & Hodgson, 1980).

Why do "checkers" go on checking? According to some reports, they do not trust their memory of what they have done (Sher, Frost, Kushner, Crews, & Alexander, 1989). In one study, the experimenters asked several people—among them some obsessive-compulsive checkers—to read a list of words and to think their opposites. (For instance, when they saw "NORTH-S . . . ," they would think *south*.) Then the experimenters combined the two sets of words—the words on the list and their opposites—and asked the subjects to identify which words they had read and which ones they had only thought. The obsessive-compulsive checkers remembered about as accurately as the control group did, but their confi-

dence in their answers was significantly lower. Compared to the control group, the checkers were less confident of their ability to distinguish between what had actually happened and what they had just imagined (Sher, Frost, & Otto, 1983).

Table 16.1 summarizes key differences between obsessive-compulsive cleaners and checkers. Table 16.2 lists some items from a questionnaire on obsessive-compulsive tendencies (Rachman & Hodgson, 1980). Try answering these questions yourself, or try guessing how an obsessive-compulsive person would answer them. (The few items listed here are not sufficient to diagnose someone as obsessive-compulsive. So don't obsess about it if you agreed with all the obsessive-compulsive answers.)

Possible Predispositions or Causes About 2–3% of all people in the United States suffer from obsessive-compulsive disorder at some time during their life (Karno, Golding, Sorenson, & Burnam, 1988). The disorder occurs most frequently among hardworking, perfectionistic people of average or above-average intelligence. It can develop either suddenly or gradually, usually beginning between the ages of 10 and 25. Nearly all people with obsessive-compulsive disorder have some insight into their own behavior and realize that their rituals are inappropriate. However, that realization does not stop the rituals.

TABLE 16.2 Obsessive-Compulsive Tendencies

1. I avoid public telephones because of possible contamination.	T	F
2. I frequently get nasty thoughts and have difficulty getting rid of them.	T	F
3. I usually have serious thoughts about the simple everyday things I do.	T	F
4. Neither of my parents was very strict during my childhood.	T	F
5. I do not take a long time to dress in the morning.	T	F
6. One of my major problems is that I pay too much attention to detail.	T	F
7. I do not stick to a very strict routine when doing ordinary things.	T	F
8. I do not usually count when doing a routine task.	T	F
9. Even when I do something very carefully, I often feel that it is not quite right.	T	F

SOURCE: Rachman & Hodgson, 1980. (Check typical answers on page 604.)

Obsessive-compulsive disorder tends to run in families, suggesting a possible genetic basis. Many of the relatives who do not have obsessive-compulsive disorder have other anxiety disorders (Black, Noyes, Goldstein, & Blum, 1992).

Therapies for Obsessive-Compulsive Disorder

Obsessive-compulsive disorder can be treated through various forms of psychotherapy, including *exposure therapy,* which resembles systematic desensitization for phobias: The obsessive-compulsive person is exposed to the situation in which he or she ordinarily performs certain rituals and is then prevented from performing them. For example, an obsessive-compulsive cleaner would be prevented from cleaning, or someone who ordinarily spends hours checking the doors and windows before going to sleep would be prevented from making the rounds. The point is to demonstrate that nothing catastrophic occurs if one leaves a little mess in the house or runs a slight risk of leaving a door unlocked.

The drug clomipramine (Anafranil) and related drugs are also helpful for at least half of obsessive-compulsive patients (Greist, Jefferson, Kobak, Katzelnick, & Serlin, 1995). Clomipramine prolongs the effects of the neurotransmitter serotonin by preventing the presynaptic neuron from reabsorbing it. That is, after an axon releases serotonin from its terminal button, clomipramine causes the serotonin to remain longer than usual in the synapse, reexciting the postsynaptic neuron. Researchers do not yet understand why prolonging serotonin activity should relieve obsessive-compulsive disorder.

THE MESSAGE
Anxieties and Avoidance

Phobia and obsessive-compulsive disorder illustrate some of the possible links between emotions and cognitions. At the risk of seriously oversimplifying, we could say that people with phobias experience emotional attacks because of their cognitions about a particular object, whereas people with obsessive-compulsive disorder experience repetitive cognitions for emotional reasons. In both conditions, most people are cognitively aware that their reactions are exaggerated, but mere awareness of the problem does not correct it. Dealing with such conditions requires attention to emotions, cognitions, and the links between them.

SUMMARY

* *Anxiety disorder and panic disorder.* People with generalized anxiety disorder or panic disorder experience extreme anxiety. Panic disorder is characterized by episodes of disabling anxiety, some of which may be triggered by hyperventilation. (page 593)

* *Persistence of avoidance behaviors.* Once an individual has learned a shock-avoidance response, the response can persist long after the possibility of shock has been removed. As with shock-avoidance responses, phobias and obsessive-compulsive disorder persist because people do not discover that their avoidance behaviors are unnecessary. (page 595)

* *Phobia.* A phobia is a fear so extreme that it interferes with normal living. Phobias are learned through observation as well as through experience. (page 595)

* *Common phobias.* People are more likely to develop phobias of certain objects than of others; for example, snake phobias are more common than car phobias. The objects of the most common phobias have menaced humans throughout evolutionary history. They pose dangers that are difficult to predict or control, and they are generally objects with which we have had few safe experiences. (page 598)

* *Systematic desensitization of phobias.* A common therapy for phobia is systematic desensitization. The patient is taught to relax and is then gradually exposed to the object of the phobia. Flooding is similar, except that the person is exposed to the object suddenly. (page 599)

* *Tranquilizers.* Drugs that facilitate activity at GABA synapses help to relieve anxiety. (page 600)

* *Obsessive-compulsive disorder.* People with obsessive-compulsive disorder try to avoid certain thoughts or impulses that cause anxiety or guilt. They also have repetitive behaviors. (page 600)

* *Types of obsessive-compulsive disorder.* Two common types of compulsion are cleaning and checking. Cleaners try to avoid any type of contamination. Checkers constantly double-check themselves and invent elaborate rituals. (page 601)

Suggestion for Further Reading

de Silva, P., & Rachman, S. (1998). *Obsessive-compulsive disorder: The facts* (2nd ed.). Oxford, England: Oxford University Press. Concise overview of the symptoms and treatments for obsessive-compulsive disorder.

Terms

generalized anxiety disorder   a disorder in which people are almost constantly plagued by exaggerated worries (page 593)

panic disorder   a disorder characterized by frequent bouts of moderate anxiety and occasional attacks of sudden increased heart rate, chest pains, difficulty breathing, sweating, faintness, and trembling (page 593)

hyperventilate   breathe deeply and frequently (page 594)

social phobia   a severe avoidance of other people and an especially strong fear of doing anything in public (page 594)

agoraphobia   an excessive fear of open places or public places (page 594)

phobia   a strong, persistent fear of a specific object, extreme enough to interfere with normal living (page 595)

systematic desensitization   a method of reducing fear by gradually exposing people to the object of their fear (page 599)

flooding or **implosion**   a treatment for phobia in which the person is suddenly exposed to the object of the phobia (page 599)

obsessive-compulsive disorder   a condition with repetitive thoughts and actions (page 600)

obsession   a repetitive, unwelcome stream of thought (page 600)

compulsion   a repetitive, almost irresistible action (page 601)

Answers to Concept Checks

1. Worrying about anything—even panic attacks themselves—often prompts these people to hyperventilate, and hyperventilation can in turn lead to another panic attack. (page 595)

2. Temporarily prevent the person from pressing the lever. Only by ceasing to press it does the person discover that pressing is not necessary. (page 595)

3. The CS was the white rat. The UCS was the loud noise. The CR and the UCR were a combination of crying and other reactions of fear. (page 597)

4. The combined effect of alcohol and a benzodiazepine tranquilizer would decrease anxiety, relax the muscles, and induce sleep more effectively than either alcohol or a benzodiazepine could by itself. In fact, the combined effect can be so strong as to be dangerous, even fatal. People given prescriptions for benzodiazepine tranquilizers are warned not to take them in conjunction with alcohol. (page 600)

5. The method of extinguishing a learned shock-avoidance response is to prevent the response so that the individual learns that the failure to respond is not followed by shock. Similarly, with systematic desensitization, the patient is prevented from fleeing the feared stimulus; he or she therefore learns that the danger is not as great as imagined. (page 600)

6. The flooding procedure is compatible with the James-Lange theory of emotions, which holds that emotions follow from perceptions of body arousal. In flooding, as arousal of the autonomic nervous system decreases, the person perceives: "I am calming down. I must not be as frightened of this situation as I thought I was." (page 600)

Answers to Other Questions in the Text

Typical answers for obsessive-compulsive people (page 602): **1.** T; **2.** T; **3.** T; **4.** F; **5.** F; **6.** T; **7.** F; **8.** F; **9.** T

Web Resources

Anxiety Disorders
www.psych.org/public_info/anxiety.html
Panic Disorder
www.psych.org/public_info/panic.html
Phobias
www.psych.org/public_info/phobias.html
Post Traumatic Stress Disorder
www.psych.org/public_info/ptsd.html
Obsessive-Compulsive Disorder
www.psych.org/public_info/PDF/ocd.pdf
Each American Psychiatric Association's *Let's Talk Facts* pamphlet describes the disorder, the major symptoms, what we know about the causes, and treatment. (OCD is available only in PDF format. You will need the free Adobe Acrobat Reader, available from www.adobe.com/prodindex/acrobat /readstep.html, to read or print it.)

Substance-Related Disorders

Why do people sometimes abuse alcohol and other drugs?

What can be done to help people quit?

How would you like to volunteer for a little experiment? I want to implant a device in your head to control your brain activity—something that will automatically lift your mood. There are still a few kinks in it, but most of the people who have tried it say that it makes them feel good at least some of the time, and some people say it makes them feel very happy.

I should tell you about the possible risks: My device will endanger your health and will reduce your life expectancy by, oh, 10 years or so. Some people believe it may cause permanent brain damage, but they haven't proved that charge, so I don't think you should worry about it. Your behavior will change a good bit, though. You may have difficulty concentrating, for example. The device affects some

Addiction is in the user, not in the drug. Some people will continue using drugs even though they know the drugs endanger their health, limit their opportunities, and provide them with little pleasure.

people more than others. If you happen to be one of those who are strongly affected, you will have difficulty completing your education, getting or keeping a job, and carrying on a satisfactory personal life. But if you are lucky, you can avoid all that. Anyway, you can quit the experiment any time you want to. You should know, though, that the longer the device remains in your brain, the harder it is to get it out.

I cannot pay you for taking part in this experiment. In fact, *you* will have to pay *me*. But I'll give you a bargain rate: only $5 for the first week and then a little more each week, as time passes. One other thing: Technically speaking, this experiment is illegal. We probably won't get caught, but if we do, we could both go to jail.

What do you say? Is it a deal? I presume you will say "no." I get very few volunteers. And yet, if I change the term *brain device* to *drug* and change *experimenter* to *drug peddler*, it is amazing how many volunteers come forward.

For some people, using alcohol or drugs is apparently a harmless pleasure. For others, it is extremely destructive. In Chapter 5, we examined the effects of several drugs on behavior. Instead of reviewing all of those drugs again here, we shall focus on substance abuse, principally of alcohol and opiates—addictions that have been familiar to humans for centuries and which continue to be major problems today.

Substance Dependence (Addiction)

Some people drink alcohol or experiment with other drugs only in moderation. Others continue until they jeopardize their health, their work or their education, and the welfare of their family. Substance abusers do not all follow the same pattern; they may use the substance daily, only on weekends, or only during sporadic binges. Those who **find it difficult or impossible to quit a self-destructive habit** are said to have a **dependence** on a substance or **addiction** to it. It is difficult to draw broad generalizations about the behavior of people who have a substance dependence. Many people with a dependence ask themselves, "am I an alcoholic?" or "am I addicted?" and manage, for a time, to convince themselves that they are not, because they do not use the substance every day or because they are able to keep a job. However, alcoholism and addiction are not simple yes-or-no matters. They vary in degree from mild to severe, and people react in different ways to drugs (Miller & Brown, 1997). It is possible to be an alcoholic or a drug addict and still keep a job; it is also possible to go days or weeks without using the substance at all. The questions to ask are, "Does the substance cause troubles in my life, and do I often take more than I had decided I would?" If the answers are "yes," then you have a problem.

Almost any substance can be addictive under certain circumstances. In one hospital ward where alcoholics were being treated, one of the patients moved his bed into the men's room (Cummings, 1979). At first, the hospital staff ignored this curious behavior. Then, one by one, other patients moved their beds into the men's room. Eventually, the staff discovered what was going on. These men, deprived of alcohol, had discovered that they could get "high" by drinking enormous amounts of water! By drinking about 30 liters (7.5 gallons) of water per day and urinating the same amount (which was why they moved into the men's room), they managed to alter the acid-to-base balance of their blood enough to produce something like drunkenness. Is water addictive? Evidently it can be, for some people.

Nevertheless, some substances are much more likely than others to be addictive. Nearly all of the commonly addictive drugs stimulate types D_2, D_3, and D_4 dopamine receptors in the brain (Koob & LeMoal, 1997). As the drugs stimulate these receptors, they produce reinforcing effects, but they also decrease the sensitivity of the receptors. Someone who quits a drug after using it extensively experiences an intense period of withdrawal when the receptors are not stimulated by the drugs and not very responsive to normal events, either. Withdrawal symptoms can be quite unpleasant. Long after the symptoms are gone, however, the person can still experience cravings for the drug (Piasecki, Kenford, Smith, Fiore, & Baker, 1997). One speculation is that the dopamine receptors are still somewhat unresponsive, so the person gets little reinforcement from everyday events (Nestler & Aghajanian, 1997; Pidoplichko, De Biasi, Williams, & Dani, 1997).

Other things being equal, the more rapidly a substance enters the brain, the more addictive it is likely to be. Cigarettes are more addictive than cigars, for example, because smokers inhale cigarette smoke more deeply, thus allowing the nicotine to enter the bloodstream and reach the brain more quickly (Bennett, 1980). For the same reason, crack cocaine is more addictive than other forms of cocaine.

You have no doubt learned that the cigarette smoking habit is based largely on nicotine addiction. One type of evidence supporting this conclusion is that people find it easier to quit smoking cigarettes if they have a replacement source of nicotine, such as a nicotine patch, nicotine chewing gum, or nicotine nasal spray (Cepeda-Benito, 1993; Schneider, 1994). "If that is so," you may have wondered, "why have so many smokers switched to low-tar, low-nicotine cigarette brands? Wouldn't those brands fail to satisfy a nicotine craving?" Yes, they would . . . *if* they delivered low nicotine! A low-tar, low-nicotine cigarette has the same kind of tobacco as other cigarettes, but a different filter. The special feature of the filter is a row of little air holes, as shown at the top of Figure 16.10. The theory is that air entering through these air holes will dilute the tobacco smoke coming through the barrel of the cigarette. People who smoke that way do indeed get lower tar and nicotine. However, many smokers wrap their fingers around the air holes, either accidentally or intentionally. Some even wrap tape over the holes. Regardless of whether people cover the holes, those who switch to low-nicotine cigarettes generally inhale more deeply than they did when smoking regular cigarettes, and they smoke more cigarettes per day. As a result

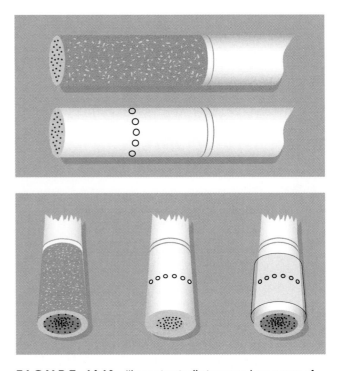

FIGURE 16.10 "Low-nicotine" cigarettes have a row of small holes in the filter; room air is supposed to enter through those holes and therefore dilute the tobacco smoke. If people smoke such cigarettes without covering the air holes, little tar and nicotine passes through the cigarette, as we see from the relatively clean filter tip. However, if people cover the holes with tape or (more commonly) with their fingers, they will receive about as much tar and nicotine as they would from any other filtered cigarette.

of all these changes in their smoking behavior, people smoking low-nicotine cigarettes inhale about as much tar and nicotine per day as do people smoking regular cigarettes (Benowitz, 1986; Kozlowski, Frecker, Khouw, & Pope, 1980).

SOMETHING TO THINK ABOUT

Are any addictive behaviors beneficial? (If a behavior is beneficial, can we call it *addictive*?) ✱

CONCEPT CHECK

7. Methadone, an opiate drug, can be taken either by injection (entering the blood rapidly) or as a pill (entering the blood slowly). Which route is more likely to lead to addiction? (Check your answer on page 613).

Predisposition to Addiction

If, when you honestly want to, you find you cannot quit entirely, or if when drinking, you have little control over the amount you take, you are probably alcoholic.

—ANONYMOUS (1955)

Why do some people become alcoholics, whereas others drink only in moderation? If we could identify the probable alcoholics early enough, we might be more effective in helping them either abstain or drink in moderation. At least, psychologists would like to try; clearly, if we wait until someone has a serious alcohol problem, fighting the problem is difficult and frustrating.

Genetics and Family Background

Alcoholism, *the habitual overuse of alcohol,* is the most common and the most costly form of drug abuse in the United States and Europe. An estimated 25–40% of all hospital patients suffer from complications caused by alcohol abuse (Holden, 1987), and a great many people who seek help for depression, anxiety, or other psychological disorders suffer from alcoholism or other substance abuse as well.

There is convincing evidence that genetics can cause a predisposition to alcoholism, although different studies give conflicting results about the importance of that role (Cadoret, Troughton, & Woodworth, 1994). Biological children of alcoholic parents have an increased risk of alcoholism, even if they are adopted by nonalcoholics (Cloninger, Bohman, & Sigvardsson, 1981; Vaillant & Milofsky, 1982). However, no one is totally safe; even people with no family history of alcoholism sometimes develop an alcohol problem. Researchers distinguish between Type I and Type II alcoholism, also known as Types A and B (Brown, Babor, Litt, & Kranzler, 1994; Devor, Abell, Hoffman, Tabakoff, & Cloninger, 1994): **Type I (or Type A) alcoholism *is generally less severe, occurs about equally in men and women, has less dependence on genetics, and develops gradually, presumably in response to the difficulties of life.* Type II** (or Type B) **alcoholism *is generally more severe, occurs mostly in men, is more often associated with aggressive behavior or antisocial personality, shows a strong genetic tendency, and usually begins early in life.*** Table 16.3 summarizes this distinction. Naturally, not every alcoholic fits neatly into one category or the other, but the distinction accounts for most cases.

The incidence of alcoholism is greater than average among people who grew up in families marked by conflict

Jewish and Italian cultures, which stress moderation, have a fair amount of alcohol use but relatively little alcohol abuse.

between parents, poor relationships between parents and children, and inadequate parental supervision of the children (Schulsinger, Knop, Goodwin, Teasdale, & Mikkelsen, 1986; Zucker & Gomberg, 1986). People who have had extremely traumatic experiences are especially likely to turn to alcohol, presumably as a means of escape (Stewart, 1996). Among college students, alcohol abuse is most common among those who are having academic troubles, although we do not know to what extent the academic frustrations led students to alcohol and to what extent the alcohol use led to the academic troubles (Wood, Sher, Erickson, & DeBord, 1997).

Culture also plays an important role. For example, most Jewish families emphasize drinking in moderation, and relatively few Jews become alcoholics (Cahalan, 1978). The same conclusion holds true for Italians as well. By contrast, the Irish tend to be more tolerant of heavy drinking, and alcoholism is indeed more prevalent among people of Irish background (Vaillant & Milofsky, 1982).

Still, individuals differ. Not all children of alcoholic parents become alcoholics themselves, and not all children who grow up in a culture that tolerates heavy drinking become alcoholics. How can we predict which people are most vulnerable to alcoholism?

TABLE 16.3 **Type I and Type II Alcoholism**				
	SEVERITY	GENDER DISTRIBUTION	GENETIC BASIS	ONSET
Type I *(or Type A)*	Generally less severe; better long-term outcome	Both males and females	Weaker genetic contribution	Gradual onset later in life
Type II *(or Type B)*	More severe, more likely to be associated with aggressive behavior and antisocial personality	Almost exclusively males	Strong evidence for genetic contribution	Rapid onset in teens or early 20s

Ways of Predicting Alcoholism

Perhaps people's early behavior might offer some indicator of who is more or less likely to become an alcoholic. One way to find such clues would be to record the presence or absence of various behaviors in hundreds of young people; 20 years later, we could find out which of them have become alcoholics and determine which early behaviors might have predicted those outcomes. But such a study would take 20 years to complete. Moreover, it might be difficult to find some of the subjects after all that time, especially the alcoholics.

A more feasible approach would be to compare children of an alcoholic parent with children of parents who are not alcoholics. From previous studies, we know that more children of alcoholics will become alcoholics. Therefore, behaviors that are significantly more prevalent among the children of alcoholics may predict vulnerability to alcoholism.

In the first of the following studies, experimenters tested whether alcohol might be more rewarding to the sons of alcoholics than to the sons of nonalcoholics (Levenson, Oyama, & Meek, 1987). (The study focused on men because alcoholism is about twice as common in men as in women.)

EXPERIMENT I

Hypothesis   When people are placed in a stressful situation, the opportunity to drink alcohol will reduce stress for almost everyone. It will have a greater effect on the adult sons of an alcoholic parent than on other men of the same age.

Method   The experiment was conducted on young men; half of them were sons of an alcoholic father, and half of them sons of nonalcoholic parents. The men were told that, at a certain time, they would receive an electric shock and, at another time, they would have to give a 3-minute speech entitled "what I like and dislike about my body." They watched a clock tick off the waiting time. Half of each group were given alcohol to drink at the start of the waiting period, and everyone who was offered alcohol drank it.

Results   All of the men showed considerable stress, as measured by heart rate, restlessness, and self-reports of emotions. All of those who drank alcohol showed a lower heart rate and reported less anxiety. The easing of stress was more pronounced in those who had an alcoholic father (Figure 16.11).

Interpretation   Men who are genetically vulnerable to alcoholism experience greater stress-reducing effects from alcohol than other men of the same age. Perhaps the degree to which alcohol relieves stress may provide a measure of vulnerability to alcoholism.

Several other studies tested and confirmed the hypothesis that young men who are vulnerable to alcoholism might have difficulty estimating their own degree of intoxication. That is, those who are most vulnerable to alcoholism may not know when to stop. The following study tested whether young drinkers who underestimate their degree of intoxication are more likely than others to become alcoholics later in life (Schuckit & Smith, 1997).

EXPERIMENT 2

Hypothesis   Men who underestimate how intoxicated they are after moderate drinking will be more likely than others to become alcoholics later.

Method   This study was limited to 18- to 25-year-old men who had a close relative who was alcoholic. All of them drank a fixed amount of alcohol and were then asked to walk and to describe how intoxicated they felt. Experimenters noted how much the men staggered or swayed when they walked. Ten years later, the experimenters located as many of these men as possible, interviewed them, and determined whether they had become alcoholics.

Results   Of those who either did not sway much when walking or stated that they did not feel intoxicated, 51 of 81 (63%) became alcoholics within 10 years. Of those who clearly swayed and reported that they felt intoxicated, only 9 of 52 (17%) became alcoholics.

FIGURE 16.11
Changes in stress over time for a typical subject: The line goes up to indicate an increase in heart rate. Note that heart rate increased as soon as the countdown began and then remained stable. It rose toward the end of the countdown and again at the time of the shock or speech. Alcohol suppressed these signs of stress, especially for the sons of alcoholics. (From Levenson, Oyama, & Meek, 1987.)

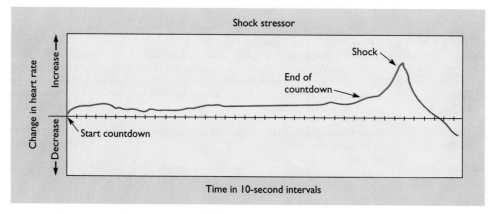

Interpretation Men who neither act nor feel intoxicated after a moderate amount of drinking are likely to continue drinking and to become alcoholics. By watching and interviewing young drinkers, psychologists may be able to identify a high-risk population.

Any research study has limitations, and one limitation of the above studies is clear: They examined only men. Considering that more men than women become alcoholics, the research strategy was reasonable; however, someone should repeat these studies with women.

✳ ✳ ✳

Treatments for Alcoholism and Drug Addiction

Of all the people who try to quit alcohol or other drugs on their own, an estimated 10–20% manage to succeed (Cohen et al., 1989), though not necessarily on the first try. Some people quit and relapse and quit and relapse many times before eventually succeeding. In many cases, however, people with a substance abuse problem find that they cannot quit on their own. Eventually, they "hit bottom," discovering that they have damaged their health, their ability to hold a job, and their relationships with friends and family. At that point, they turn to others for help—either a mental-health professional or a self-help group such as Alcoholics Anonymous.

People who seek professional help improve their likelihood of long-term abstention, although there are no guarantees. Addicts who check into a hospital for treatment can be supervised 24 hours a day to ensure full abstinence. **Detoxification** refers to *a supervised period to remove drugs from the body.* In the long run, however, most addicts respond just as well to outpatient treatment as they do to hospital treatment (Miller & Hester, 1986).

Treating Alcoholism

> *My mind is a dark place,*
> *and I should not be left alone there at night.*
> —PARTICIPANT AT ALCOHOLICS ANONYMOUS MEETING

Combatting alcoholism is difficult but not hopeless. Let's consider several approaches and controversies.

Alcoholics Anonymous The most widespread treatment for alcoholism in North America is **Alcoholics Anonymous (AA),** *a self-help group of people who are trying to abstain from alcohol use and to help others do the same.* AA meetings are held regularly in community halls, church basements, and other available spaces (Figure 16.12). The meeting format varies but often includes study of the book *Alcoholics Anonymous* (Anonymous, 1955) and discussions of participants' individual problems; some meetings feature an invited speaker. The group has a strong spiritual focus, including a reliance on "a Power greater

FIGURE 16.12 Alcoholics Anonymous (AA) is the prototypical example of a self-help group. AA meetings are held throughout the United States and in many other countries throughout the world. Members share their experiences with one another and provide help and encouragement to members in need. A member who is fighting a craving for alcohol can call a fellow member for help at any time; each understands the problems that the others are having. AA makes many recommendations, but its only requirement is that members make an effort to overcome their alcohol problems.

than ourselves," although AA has no affiliation with any particular religion. Although AA imposes no requirements on its members other than making an effort to give up drinking alcohol, new members are strongly encouraged to attend 90 meetings during the first 90 days. (Those who miss a day can compensate by attending two or more meetings another day.) From then on, members attend as often as they like.

Millions of people have participated in the AA program in the United States and elsewhere around the world. One reason for its appeal is that all its members have gone through similar experiences. If someone tries to make an excuse for drinking, saying "you just don't understand how I feel," others can retort, "oh, yes we do!" A member who feels the urge to take a drink or who has already had one, can call a fellow member day or night for support. There is no charge for attendance at meetings; members simply contribute what they can toward the cost of renting the meeting place. AA has inspired other "anonymous" self-help groups whose purpose is to help drug addicts, compulsive gamblers, compulsive eaters, and so forth.

Although AA members themselves have confidence in the value of the program, research on its effectiveness has been scarce. One reason is that the organization is serious about its members' anonymity; it does not provide a list of members, and many of its meetings are closed to nonmembers. One further problem is that people cannot be assigned randomly to an AA group and a control group; AA participants are simply those who wish to participate, and they undoubtedly differ in many ways from those who choose not to participate.

Antabuse In addition to or instead of attendance at AA meetings, some alcoholics seek medical treatment. Many years ago, investigators noticed that the workers in a certain rubber manufacturing plant drank very little alcohol. The investigators eventually linked this behavior to *disulfiram*, a chemical that was used in the manufacturing process. Ordinarily, the liver converts alcohol into a toxic substance, *acetaldehyde* (ASS-eh-TAL-de-HIDE) and then converts acetaldehyde into a harmless substance, *acetic acid*. Disulfiram, however, blocks the conversion of acetaldehyde to acetic acid. Whenever the workers drank alcohol, however, acetaldehyde accumulated in their body, and they became ill. Over time, they learned to avoid all use of alcohol.

Disulfiram, available under the trade name **Antabuse,** is now commonly used in the treatment of alcoholism (Peachey & Naranjo, 1983). *Alcoholics who take a daily Antabuse pill become very sick whenever they have a drink.* They develop a sensation of heat in the face, headache, nausea, blurred vision, and anxiety. The threat of sickness is probably more effective than the sickness itself (Fuller & Roth, 1979). By taking a daily Antabuse pill, a recovering alcoholic renews the decision not to drink. Those who actually do take a drink in spite of the threat get quite ill, at which point they may either decide not to drink again or they may decide not to take the pill again!

CONCEPT CHECK

8. About 50% of Southeast Asians have a gene that makes them unable to convert acetaldehyde to acetic acid. Would such people be more likely or less likely than others to become alcoholics? (Check your answer on page 613.)

Is Substance Abuse a "Disease"?

You have no doubt heard people say that alcoholism or drug abuse is a disease. It is hard to confirm or deny that statement, however, unless someone specifies exactly what the term *disease* means. (The medical profession gives the term no precise meaning, and the term has a wide variety of connotations.) When people call alcoholism or drug abuse a disease, they apparently mean that alcoholics and drug abusers should feel no guiltier about their condition than they would feel about having pneumonia.

Although the "disease" concept is more constructive than thinking of substance abuse as a sign of moral weakness, the concept has some implications that the data do not support. For example, it implies an all-or-none distinction between those who have the disease and those who do not. The current trend among psychologists favors a continuum from people with no problem to those with a severe problem, including every possible intermediate step (Miller & Brown, 1997; Polcin, 1997).

Also, the "disease" concept implies that alcoholism or drug abuse becomes inevitably worse over time. In fact, the long-term outcome for alcoholics and drug abusers varies enormously (Hser, Anglin, & Powers, 1993; Vaillant, 1983). As Figure 16.13 shows, some individuals deteriorate rapidly and severely, some reach a steady level of abuse, and still others show a gradual improvement in their condition over time.

Furthermore, to regard substance abuse strictly as a disease seems to imply a need for a medical intervention and downplays the importance of environmental factors.

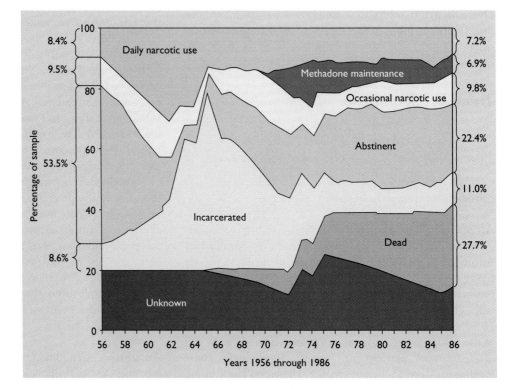

FIGURE 16.13 Researchers studied 581 young adult male narcotics addicts in 1962–1964. They asked these men about their previous drug use and located most of them again in later years to check on their progress. Over time, the results varied. Some died or went to prison; some continued using drugs as before; some decreased their use of drugs; and some abstained altogether. (From Hser, Anglin, & Powers, 1993.)

One of the most effective treatments for alcoholism or drug addiction—indeed, much research suggests it is *the* most effective treatment—is family therapy (Stanton & Shadish, 1997). By improving the person's family life, possibly improving the job situation, and helping the person to develop new interests, the therapy decreases the person's compulsion for alcohol or drug use.

The Controlled Drinking Controversy

Most physicians agree with Alcoholics Anonymous that the only hope for an alcoholic is total abstinence. Drinking in moderation, they insist, is out of the question.

A few psychologists, however, are not convinced that abstinence is the best advice for *all* alcoholics (Peele, 1998). Some alcoholics who try to abstain repeatedly fail; a few of these people do learn to reduce their drinking without eliminating it altogether. This is not to say that alcoholics can simply decide to drink in moderation; if they could, they would not have become alcoholics in the first place. Rather, the point is that a few people who fail to stick to an abstention program can learn (with difficulty) to drink less than they have been, to stay out of legal trouble, and in general to do themselves less damage. Psychologists have established several programs to try to teach alcoholics "controlled drinking," with at least occasional success (Rosenberg, 1993). Critics charge that even offering the hope of controlled drinking decreases people's motivation to abstain. Defenders of controlled drinking reply that some people still find themselves unable to abstain despite their best efforts.

One of the biggest unresolved problems in psychotherapy is matching individuals to the best treatment. A similar issue arises with regard to weight loss, depression, substance abuse, and many other fields in which therapists offer several approaches, each of which appears to be effective for some people and not for others. When treating substance abuse, the options include AA and other abstention-based programs, controlled drinking programs, family therapy, Antabuse, and psychotherapy aimed at the user's other (nondrug-related) psychological disorders. Several attempts have been made to determine each person's needs and match each to the most appropriate treatment. So far,

such procedures have produced results that are only slightly better than assigning people to therapies at random (McLellan et al., 1997). Perhaps future research will enable more effective matching.

Specific Treatments for Opiate Addiction

Before the year 1900, opiate drugs such as morphine and heroin were considered far less dangerous than alcohol (Siegel, 1987). In fact, many medical doctors used to urge their alcoholic patients to switch from alcohol to morphine. Then, around 1900, the use of opiates was made illegal in the United States, except by prescription to control pain. Since then, research on opiate use has been limited by the fact that only lawbreakers now use opiates.

Some users of heroin and other opiates try to break their habit by going "cold turkey"—abstaining altogether until the withdrawal symptoms subside, sometimes under medical supervision. Many people, however, experience a recurring urge to take the drug, even long after the withdrawal symptoms have subsided. For those who cannot quit, researchers have sought to find a nonaddictive substitute that would satisfy the craving for opiates without creating harmful effects. Heroin was originally introduced as a substitute for morphine, before physicians discovered that heroin is even more addictive and troublesome than morphine!

Today, the drug **methadone** (METH-uh-don) *is commonly offered as a less dangerous substitute for opiates.* Methadone is chemically similar to both morphine and heroin and can itself be addictive. (Table 16.4 compares methadone and morphine.) When methadone is taken in pill form, however, it enters the bloodstream gradually and also departs gradually (Dole, 1980). (If morphine or heroin is taken as a pill, much of the drug is broken down in the digestive system and never reaches the brain.) Thus, methadone does not produce the "rush" associated with intravenous injections of opiates; nor does it produce rapid withdrawal symptoms. Although methadone satisfies the craving for opiates without seriously disrupting the user's behavior, it does not eliminate the addiction itself. If the dosage is reduced, the craving returns.

TABLE 16.4 Comparison of Methadone with Morphine

	MORPHINE	METHADONE BY INJECTION	METHADONE TAKEN ORALLY
Addictive?	Yes	Yes	Weakly
Onset	Rapid	Rapid	Slow
"Rush"?	Yes	Yes	No
Relieves craving?	Yes	Yes	Yes
Rapid withdrawal symptoms?	Yes	Yes	No

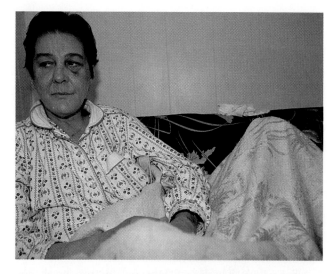

Going cold turkey: Heroin withdrawal resembles a severe bout of the flu, with aching limbs, intense chills, vomiting, and diarrhea; it lasts a week, on average. Unfortunately, even after people have suffered through withdrawal, they are likely to experience periods of craving for the drug.

Many addicts who stick to a methadone maintenance program hold down a job and commit fewer crimes than they did when they were using heroin or morphine (Woody & O'Brien, 1986). Some of them, after discovering that they can no longer get high from opiates, turn instead to a nonopiate drug such as cocaine (Kosten, Rounsaville, & Kleber, 1987). In other words, methadone maintenance programs do not eliminate addictive behaviors. At present, there is no reliable cure for opiate dependence.

THE MESSAGE
Substances, the Individual, and Society

Substance abuse is costly to society as well as to the individual. The United States and many other countries have tried to control the problem by issuing stiff prison sentences for those who use or sell certain drugs. The result? Hard to say; drug use continues to be widespread, but we do not know how much worse it might be without the legal prohibitions. However, we do know that law enforcement itself is costly; prisons are crowded with those whose only offense was drug related, and many drug users turn to theft or violence as a way of getting drugs. The Netherlands has experimented with greatly decreased penalties against the use and sale of drugs, especially marijuana. The results are in some ways favorable, in other ways unfavorable; overall, it is impossible to generalize about what might happen if other countries tried the same approach (MacCoun & Reuter, 1997). As a

voter, you will have to help our society make decisions about how to deal with substance abuse, a problem that shows no signs of becoming less difficult.

SUMMARY

✳ *Substance dependence.* People who find it difficult or impossible to stop using a substance are said to be dependent on it or addicted to it. (page 605)

✳ *Addictive substances.* Generally, the faster a substance enters the brain, the more likely it is to be addictive. Cigarette smokers inhale enough nicotine to satisfy their addiction, even if they smoke low-nicotine brands. (page 606)

✳ *Predisposition to alcoholism.* Some people may be predisposed to become alcoholics for genetic or other reasons. People at risk for alcoholism find that alcohol relieves their stress more than it does for other people. People who underestimate their level of intoxication are more likely than others to become alcoholics later. (page 606)

✳ *Alcoholics Anonymous.* The most common treatment for alcoholism in North America is provided by the self-help group called Alcoholics Anonymous. (page 609)

✳ *Antabuse.* Some alcoholics are treated with Antabuse, a prescription drug that makes them ill if they drink alcohol. (page 609)

✳ *The "disease" concept.* Whether or not substance abuse is considered a disease depends on what we mean by "disease." The long-term course varies among different alcoholics or drug abusers. One of the most effective treatments for substance abuse is family therapy, which takes a nonmedical approach. (page 610)

✳ *The "controlled drinking" controversy.* Whether certain alcoholics can be trained to drink in moderation is a controversial question. Therapists hope to improve their ability to assign each person to the most effective treatment. (page 611)

✳ *Treatments for opiate abuse.* Some opiate users quit using opiates, suffer through the withdrawal symptoms, and manage to abstain from further use. Others substitute methadone under medical supervision. Although methadone has fewer destructive effects than morphine or heroin, it does not eliminate the underlying dependence. (page 611)

Suggestion for Further Reading

Marlatt, G. A., & VandenBos, G. R. (Eds.). (1997). *Addictive behaviors: Readings on etiology, prevention, and treatment.* Washington, DC: American Psychological Association. A collection of research articles on the nature of addiction and the methods of treatment.

Terms

dependence or **addiction** a self-destructive habit that someone finds difficult or impossible to quit (page 605)

alcoholism   habitual overuse of alcohol (page 607)

Type I (or Type A) **alcoholism**   the type that is generally less severe, equally common in men and women, less dependent on genetics, and likely to develop gradually, presumably in response to the difficulties of life (page 607)

Type II (or Type B) **alcoholism**   the type that is generally more severe, more common in men, more often associated with aggressive or antisocial behavior, more dependent on genetics, and likely to begin early in life (page 607)

detoxification   a supervised period for removing drugs from the body (page 609)

Alcoholics Anonymous (AA)   a self-help group of people who are trying to abstain from alcohol use and to help others do the same (page 609)

Antabuse   the trade name for disulfiram, a drug used in the treatment of alcoholism (page 610)

methadone   a drug commonly offered as a less dangerous substitute for opiates (page 611)

Answers to Concept Checks

7. The injection route is more likely to lead to addiction. Other things being equal, the faster that a drug reaches the brain, the more likely it is to become addictive. (page 606)

8. They are less likely than others to become alcoholics. This gene is considered the probable reason that relatively few Asians become alcoholics (Harada, Agarwal, Goedde, Tagaki, & Ishikawa, 1982; Reed, 1985). (page 610)

Web Resources

Substance Abuse

www.psych.org/public_info/substance.html

In *Let's Talk Facts* pamphlets, use and abuse is examined with regard to alcohol, marijuana, cocaine, opiates, hallucinogens, inhalants, sedative hypnotics, and nicotine.

MODULE 16.3

Mood Disorders

Why do people become depressed?

What can be done to relieve depression?

Even when things are going badly, most people remain optimistic that all will be well in the end. After the hurt and disappointment we feel when a relationship breaks up, we say, "Oh, well, at least I learned something from the experience." When we lose money, we say, "It could have been worse. I still have my health."

But sometimes we feel depressed. Nothing seems as much fun as it used to be, and the future seems ominous. For some people, the depression is severe and long-lasting. Why?

Depression

When people say "I'm depressed," they often mean "I am sad; life isn't going very well for me right now." In psychology, **major depression** refers to a much more *extreme condition, persisting most of each day for a period of months, in which the person experiences little interest in* *anything, little pleasure, little reason for any productive activity.* Aaron Beck (1973) described one depressed woman who stood in front of an elevator for 15 minutes because she did not have enough desire to press the button.

Sad people are unhappy at the moment, whereas depressed people cannot even imagine anything that would make them happy. They have trouble concentrating. Their appetite and interest in sex decrease (Nofzinger et al., 1993). They feel worthless, fearful, guilty, and powerless to control what happens to them. Most severely depressed people consider suicide, and many attempt it. As with any other psychological disorder, depression varies in severity from one person to another and from one time to another (Flett, Vredenburg, & Krames, 1997).

Nearly all depressed people experience sleep abnormalities (Carroll, 1980; Healy & Williams, 1988). (See Figure 16.14.) They enter REM sleep less than 45 minutes after falling asleep (an unusually short time for most people). Most depressed people wake up too early and cannot get back to sleep. When morning comes, they feel poorly rested. In fact, they usually feel most depressed early in the morning. During most of the day, they feel a little sleepy.

Depression is common from adolescence through old age; the peak time for first diagnosis is at age 30–40. Regardless of the age at diagnosis, most people say they had been somewhat depressed for years before the condition became severe enough for them to visit a therapist (Eaton et al., 1997). Depression occurs in episodes; typically, a person might feel depressed for a few months, then recover for months or even years, and then experience the next episode of depression. In rare cases, an episode can last for years at a time. On the average, earlier episodes last a bit longer than later episodes (Solomon et al., 1997).

Bipolar disorder, previously known as *manic-depressive disorder,* is a related condition in which *a person alternates between periods of depression and periods of mania, which is the opposite extreme.* We shall return to bipolar disorder later.

FIGURE 16.14 When most people go to sleep at their usual time of day, they progress slowly to stage 4 and then back through stages 3 and 2, reaching REM sleep toward the end of their first 90-minute cycle. Depressed people, however, reach REM more rapidly, generally in less than 45 minutes. They also tend to awaken frequently during the night.

Normal sleep

1   2   3   4   3   2   REM   2

— 90 minutes —

Depressed sleep

1 2 3 4 3 2   REM   2 3   Awake

— 90 minutes —

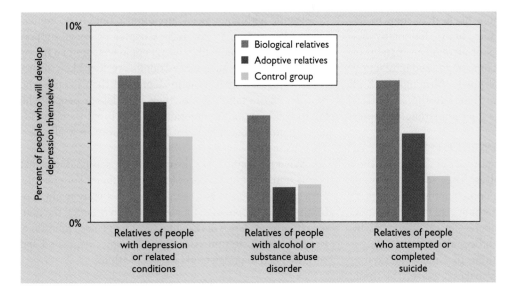

FIGURE 16.15 Blood relatives of a depressed person are more likely to suffer depression themselves, when compared with incidences of depression in the general public, which is 5–10%. The closer the genetic relationship is, the greater is the probability of experiencing depression.

Genetic Predisposition to Depression

The fact that depression tends to run in families suggests that some people have a genetic predisposition to depression (see Figure 16.15). Children and other relatives of depressed people are more likely than other people to become depressed themselves in adulthood and also somewhat more likely than others to develop phobias, panic disorder, substance abuse, and social impairments (Kendler, Heath, Neale, Kessler, & Eaves, 1993; Kendler, Neale, Kessler, Heath, & Eaves, 1992; Weissman, Warner, Wickramaratne, Moreau, & Olfson, 1997). It is likely that certain families have genes that express themselves in different ways, leading to depression in some people and to other disorders in others.

Adopted children who become depressed usually have more biological relatives than adopting relatives who are depressed (Wender et al., 1986). So far, we do not have consistent evidence to indicate whether depression depends on one gene or several (Faraone, Kremen, & Tsuang, 1990). Chances are that a disposition to depression depends on different genes or gene combinations in different families.

The Sex Difference in the Prevalence of Depression

From adolescence onward, women are about twice as likely as men to experience major depression and as much as four times as likely to experience severe depression. This ratio varies among cultures, but the tendency is in the same direction for North America, Europe, New Zealand, and Korea (Culbertson, 1997).

Why is depression more common in women than it is in men? One possibility is that hormonal changes in women's menstrual cycles or occurring as a result of pregnancy and childbirth trigger episodes of depression. For ex-

ample, *shortly after giving birth,* a time of massive hormonal changes, some women enter a **postpartum depression.** Estimates of the frequency of postpartum depression vary widely, depending on whether one counts only the severe cases (about 1 per 1,000), the moderate cases (about 1 in 10), or the mild cases (about 3 in 10). Most of the women who suffer moderate to severe postpartum depression, however, have a history of other depressive episodes; the hormonal swing after giving birth is not so much a cause of depression as a trigger for an additional depressive episode (O'Hara, Schlechte, Lewis, & Wright, 1991).

The evidence is not convincing that hormones account for the higher prevalence of depression in women than in men. Psychologists have considered several other

Depression is most common among people who have little social support.

hypotheses: that women are more likely than men to report their depression and to seek help, that many depressed men receive a diagnosis of alcoholism instead of depression, and that women become depressed in reaction to their lower status and lack of power. Although each of these possibilities probably contributes to the sex difference in depression, the evidence does not strongly support any of them.

Susan Nolen-Hoeksema (1990, 1991) has suggested another possibility: When men start to feel depressed, they generally try to distract themselves. They try not to think about whatever is making them depressed; they play basketball or watch a movie or do something else that they enjoy. Women are more likely to ruminate—to think about why they are depressed, to talk with others about their feelings, even to have a long cry. According to Nolen-Hoeksema, ruminating about depression only makes it worse. The ruminative thoughts interfere with useful problem solving and bias a person toward a pessimistic appraisal of the situation. This explanation has the advantage of suggesting ways to help women (and men) avoid or minimize their depression. It does not, however, address the question of *why* women ruminate more and distract themselves less than men do.

Events That Precipitate Depression

As a rule, people become depressed when bad things happen to them. For example, most people are clearly depressed for at least the first two months after the death of a spouse (Thompson, Gallagher-Thompson, Futterman, Gilewski, & Peterson, 1991). However, the severity of an unpleasant event is a poor predictor of how depressed a person will become following that event. Some people become depressed without any apparent stressful experience (Brown, Harris, & Hepworth, 1994), and some depressed people bring about their own stressful events (Hammen, 1991).

One study illustrated the differences among people in their responses to a stressful event by taking advantage of the fact that students in one California university had answered questionnaires about their mental health 2 weeks before a major earthquake in 1989. Psychologists asked the same students to fill out questionnaires again 10 days and 7 weeks after the earthquake. The result was that students who were already somewhat depressed before the earthquake became very depressed afterward; students who were not depressed earlier suffered some distress but in most cases recovered rapidly (Nolen-Hoeksema & Morrow, 1991). In other words, people who are vulnerable to depression are more likely to react strongly to any stressful event.

So, what makes some people more vulnerable than others? One explanation is that severe losses early in life make people more vulnerable to depression later on. For example, adolescents who lose a parent through death or divorce are likely to react strongly to other losses later in life, even to routine events such as breaking up with a boyfriend or girlfriend (Roy, 1985).

People with poor social support also tend to be vulnerable to depression. As we saw in Chapter 12, social support helps people to cope with stress. People who are in a happy marriage and who have close friends are less likely to become depressed or to remain depressed than people who have no one to talk to about their troubles, or people who fail to make use of the emotional support that their friends offer them (Rivera, Rose, Futterman, Lovett, & Gallagher-Thompson, 1991).

What most influences the onset of depression is not what events transpire but how people interpret them. For example, a trivial event such as not being invited to a party might contribute toward depression for someone who regarded the non-invitation as evidence of rejection by other people (Johnson & Roberts, 1995). To understand who becomes depressed and why, we need to understand how people think.

Cognitive Aspects of Depression

Most people believe that every cloud has a silver lining. Show depressed people a silver lining, though, and they wrap it in a cloud. Somehow, they think differently from people who are not depressed. Do their thought patterns lead to their depression?

The Learned-Helplessness Model

According to the **learned-helplessness theory,** *people become depressed if their experiences teach them that they have no control over the major events in their lives.* The learned-helplessness theory originated while testing theories about avoidance learning in animals. Steven Maier, Martin Seligman, and Richard Solomon (1969) strapped some dogs with no previous training into restraining harnesses and then repeatedly sounded a tone that was followed by a shock to the dogs' feet. The dogs soon learned that the tone predicted shock. They struggled to escape but could not. The next day, the experimenters put the same dogs into an apparatus in which a tone served as a warning signal for an escapable shock. Ordinarily, dogs quickly learn a response that enables them to escape or avoid a shock. However, the dogs that had previously received inescapable shocks were extremely slow to learn, and most never did learn the avoidance response.

Why? The dogs had learned on the first day that the tone predicted shock; they had also learned that the shock was inescapable. When they started receiving shocks on the second day, they thus made no effort to escape. They had learned that they were helpless.

These "helpless" dogs resembled depressed people in several respects. The dogs were inactive and slow to learn. Even their posture and "facial expressions" suggested sadness. The experimenters proposed that the same process might operate in humans: People who meet with only defeat and loss, despite their best efforts, may come to feel helpless and therefore fall into depression.

Explanatory Styles

The learned-helplessness hypothesis, though appealing, is no longer considered a viable explanation for depression, at least not in its original form. Experiments with humans failed to confirm that struggling with impossible tasks makes people feel depressed. It is not *failure* itself that makes people depressed, but *why people think they have failed.* For example, suppose you fail a test. Which kind of explanation would you be likely to offer?

- The test was extremely difficult. Most other students probably did badly too.
- I had a weaker background from previous courses than most other students.
- I was sick and didn't get a chance to study.
- I'm just stupid. I always do badly, no matter how hard I try.

Using any of the first three attributions for failure, you probably wouldn't feel very depressed. You would be attributing your failure to a temporary, specific, or correctable situation—a problem that has nothing to do with your abilities. But the fourth attribution applies to you at all times in all situations. If you make that attribution—and if your grades are important to you—you are likely to feel depressed about your failure (Abramson, Seligman, & Teasdale, 1978; Peterson, Bettes, & Seligman, 1985). If you continue making similar attributions in many other situations, your depression may grow.

In a given situation, such as a low grade on a test, you might have a good reason for one attribution or another. For example, perhaps you really are the only one in this French class who did not take high-school French. Still, everyone has an **explanatory style,** *a tendency to accept one kind of explanation for success or failure more often than others.* Recall from Chapter 14 that an *internal attribution* cites a cause within the person. ("I failed the French test because I did not study properly. I did well on the biology test because I spent many hours studying.") An *external attribution* identifies a causes outside the person. ("I failed the French test because it was extremely hard. I did well on the biology test because it was easy.") People are not always consistent about how they explain their successes, but they tend to be very consistent, even over decades, about how they explain their failures. That is, people who generally blame themselves for their failures today will probably still be doing so 30 or 40 years from now (Burns & Seligman, 1989).

People who consistently take the blame for their own failures are said to have a *pessimistic* explanatory style, especially if their explanations for failure are stable and global. For example, "I failed the test because I did not study hard" is an unstable explanation, because you can study harder next time. "I failed the test because I'm not good at learning foreign languages" is a stable explanation, because it implies a permanent characteristic. "I failed the test because I'm stupid" is not only stable but also global; it applies not only to foreign languages but to all kinds of learning.

Researchers can determine people's explanatory style by asking them to explain some of their successes and failures. They can also gauge the explanatory styles of famous people, even dead people, by reading their speeches and writings to find out what explanations they offered for successes and failures. Using this method, psychologists have found that pessimistic political leaders tend to be cautious, indecisive, and inactive. Leaders with an optimistic explanatory style (the opposite of a pessimistic style) tend to be bold, active, even risk-takers (Satterfield & Seligman, 1994; Zullow, Oettingen, Peterson, & Seligman, 1988). (See Figure 16.16.) Athletes with a pessimistic style tend to give up after a defeat; for them, one defeat leads to another.

FIGURE 16.16 During the Gulf War in 1991, the speeches of U.S. President George Bush and Iraqi leader Saddam Hussein varied between an optimistic and a pessimistic style from one period of time to another. Both leaders tended to make bold, risky decisions during periods when their speeches were optimistic; both were passive and cautious during periods when their speeches were pessimistic (Satterfield & Seligman, 1994).

Athletes with a more optimistic style keep on trying and even try harder after a defeat because, after all, they believe that the defeat was not their fault (Seligman, Nolen-Hoeksema, Thornton, & Thornton, 1990).

Although pessimism is hardly the same thing as depression, people with a pessimistic style are more likely than others to become depressed. Indeed, according to Aaron Beck (1973, 1987), depressed people consistently put unfavorable interpretations on the events of their lives. If someone walks by without comment, their likely response is, "See, people ignore me. They don't like me." After any kind of loss or defeat, "I'm a loser. I'm hopeless." After any kind of win, "That was just luck. I had nothing to do with it." Depressed people exaggerate their failures, minimize their successes, and give themselves a very low evaluation. Given this explanatory style, almost any event seems further grounds for feeling depressed.

CONCEPT CHECK

9. Would depressed people be more or less likely than nondepressed people to buy a lottery ticket? (Check your answers on page 625.)

Therapies for Depression

Depression is often a severe, even incapacitating disorder, but it often responds well to treatment. Both psychotherapy and drug therapy are effective.

Cognitive Therapy

According to Aaron Beck, a pioneer in cognitive therapy, depressed people are guided by certain thoughts or assumptions of which they are only dimly aware. He refers to the "negative cognitive triad of depression":

- I am deprived or defeated.
- The world is full of obstacles.
- The future is devoid of hope.

Based on these assumptions, which Beck calls "automatic thoughts," depressed people interpret ambiguous situations to their own disadvantage. When something goes wrong, they blame themselves: "I'm worthless, and I can't do anything right." When an acquaintance walks past without smiling, they think, "She doesn't like me." They do not even look for alternative interpretations of a situation (Beck, 1991). Research has confirmed that depressed people are more likely than other people to agree with such statements as "I'm a loser," or "nothing ever works out right for me, and it's all my fault," or "I never have a good time" (Hollon, Kendall, & Lumry, 1986).

The task of a cognitive therapist is to help depressed people to substitute more favorable beliefs. Unlike rational-emotive therapists, who in many cases simply tell their clients what to think, cognitive therapists try to get their clients to make discoveries for themselves. The therapist focuses on one of the client's beliefs, such as "no one likes me." The therapist points out that this is a hypothesis, not an established fact, and invites the client to test the hypothesis as a scientist would: "What evidence do you have for this hypothesis?"

"Well," a client may reply, "when I arrive at work in the morning, hardly anyone says hello."

"Is there any other way of looking at that evidence?"

"Hmm. . . . I suppose it's possible that the others are busy."

"Does anyone ever seem happy to see you?"

"Well, maybe. I'm not sure."

"Then let's find out. For the next week, keep a notebook with you and record every time that anyone smiles or seems happy to see you. The next time I see you, we'll discuss what you've discovered."

The therapist's goal is to encourage depressed clients to discover that their automatic thoughts are incorrect, that things are not nearly as bad as they seem, and that the future is not hopeless. If one of the client's thoughts does turn out to be accurate—for example, "my boyfriend is interested in someone else"—then, the therapist asks, "Even if it's true, is that the end of the world?"

Biological Therapies for Depression

Three types of drugs are currently used as antidepressants: tricyclics, monoamine oxidase inhibitors, and second-generation antidepressants. **Tricyclic drugs** (such as imipramine, trade name Tofranil) *block the reabsorption of several neurotransmitters—dopamine, norepinephrine, and serotonin—after they are released by an axon's terminal* (Figure 16.17). Thus, tricyclics prolong the effect of these neurotransmitters on the receptors of the postsynaptic cell. **Monoamine** (MAHN-oh-ah-MEEN) **oxidase inhibitors (MAOIs)** (such as phenelzine, trade name Nardil) *block the metabolic breakdown of released dopamine, norepinephrine, and serotonin* (Figure 16.17c). Thus, MAOIs also prolong the ability of released neurotransmitters to stimulate the postsynaptic cell. Tricyclic drugs are more effective than MAOIs for most patients; the MAOIs are used mainly when people fail to respond to tricyclics (Thase, Trivedi, & Rush, 1995). **Second-generation antidepressants** (such as fluoxetine, trade name Prozac) are also known as *serotonin reuptake blockers*. Like tricyclic drugs, they *act by blocking the reuptake of released neurotransmitters, but their effect is more narrowly limited to the neurotransmitter serotonin.* One advantage of the second-generation antidepressants is that they produce fewer side effects with most people; consequently, most people can take them in larger dosages and experience greater relief from depression (Burrows, McIntyre, Judd, & Norman, 1988).

The effects of antidepressant drugs build up gradually. Some depressed people report feeling better within the first

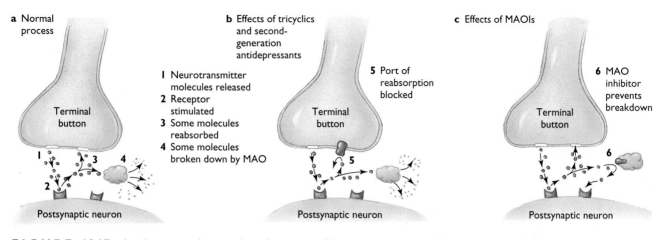

FIGURE 16.17 Antidepressant drugs prolong the activity of the neurotransmitters dopamine, norepinephrine, and serotonin. (a) Ordinarily, after the release of one of the neurotransmitters, some of the molecules are reabsorbed by the terminal button, and other molecules are broken down by the enzyme MAO (monoamine oxidase). (b) Second-generation antidepressants prevent reabsorption of serotonin. Tricyclic drugs also prevent reabsorption but are less specific, acting on dopamine, norepinephrine, and serotonin. (c) MAO inhibitors block the enzyme MAO and thereby prolong the effects of the neurotransmitters.

week or two of use. The early benefit is almost always a *placebo effect*—that is, it depends on the person's expectation of feeling better and not on the drug itself. People who report quick benefits can be switched to an inactive substance such as sugar tablets without any loss of benefit (Stewart et al., 1998). The drug itself begins to show effects after 2 to 3 weeks of use, and the effects increase over the following 4–5 weeks (Blaine, Prien, & Levine, 1983).

What causes the gradual change in response? The biochemical effects are complicated. The drugs increase the quantity of neurotransmitter molecules bombarding the receptors fairly quickly, but they also initiate a slow series of changes in both the presynaptic and postsynaptic neurons, including decreases in receptor sensitivity, increases in neurotransmitter release, and increased production of certain chemicals that promote the growth and metabolism of neurons (Duman, Heninger, & Nestler, 1997; McNeal & Cimbolic, 1986). Many of these changes develop gradually over weeks. Researchers are still far from completely understanding how all these biochemical changes combine to produce antidepressant effects.

CONCEPT CHECK

10. The drug mianserin prolongs the release of dopamine, norepinephrine, and serotonin from the terminal button. Would mianserin increase or decrease the intensity of depression? (Check your answer on page 625.)

The Advantages and Disadvantages of Antidepressant Drugs

Overall, cognitive therapy helps a slightly higher percentage of depressed patients than drug therapy does, and its benefits generally persist longer after the end of therapy (Robinson, Berman, & Neimeyer, 1990). Cognitive therapy also has the advantage of producing no side effects, whereas

about one-third of people taking tricyclic drugs report dry mouth, dizziness, sweating, or constipation (Blaine et al., 1983). Nevertheless, from the mid-1980s to the mid-1990s, the use of antidepressant drugs increased greatly, especially for second-generation antidepressants such as Prozac (Olfson et al., 1998). You might wonder why.

The reasons for this are convenience and lower cost. A client in psychotherapy will visit a therapist for at least 1 hour per week. Most therapists and clients agree that the benefits increase slowly over time, so the recommended course of treatment will last at least a couple of months, probably longer. The cost varies, depending on the therapist and the geographical region, but let's use $100 per hour as an approximation. If you are the client and you have enough available time and either have enough money yourself or have a generous insurance program that will pay for many visits, then psychotherapy is a good idea. However, if you are short of either time or money, you might be tempted by some relatively inexpensive pills. Antidepressants are often prescribed for people with anxiety disorders, obsessive-compulsive disorder, and adjustment problems, as well as depression.

Double-blind studies have consistently found that 50–70% of the adults who take tricyclic drugs experience improvements in their moods, as compared to 20–30% of those who take placebos (Blaine, Prien, & Levine, 1983; Gerson, Plotkin, & Jarvik, 1988; Morris & Beck, 1974). Similarly, talk-based psychotherapy produces benefits for most clients, but not all. Do drugs help the same people who would respond well to psychotherapy, or different people? Researchers don't know, and certainly no one knows how to identify which people might respond better to one treatment than the other.

For people with mild or moderate depression, a combination of both drugs and psychotherapy is not much more effective than either one alone—a result that suggests that drugs and psychotherapy are effective for mostly the same

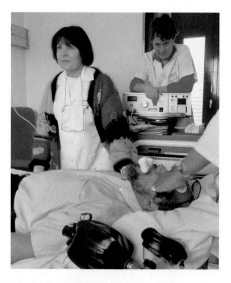

FIGURE 16.18 Electroconvulsive therapy is administered today only with the patient's informed consent. ECT is given in conjunction with muscle relaxants and anesthetics, to minimize discomfort.

people. However, for people with severe depression, a combination of drugs and psychotherapy can offer significant benefits (Thase et al., 1997).

Electroconvulsive Shock Therapy

Another well-known but controversial treatment for depression is **electroconvulsive therapy,** abbreviated **ECT** (Figure 16.18): *A brief electrical shock is administered across the patient's head to induce a convulsion similar to epilepsy.* ECT was first used in the 1930s and became popular in the 1940s and 1950s as a treatment for schizophrenia, depression, and many other psychiatric disorders. It then fell out of favor, partly because antidepressant drugs and other therapeutic methods had become available and partly because ECT had been widely abused. Some patients were subjected to ECT hundreds of times, without their consent, and in many cases, ECT was used as a threat to enforce patients' cooperation.

Beginning in the 1970s, ECT has made a comeback in modified form, mostly for severely depressed people who fail to respond to antidepressant drugs, whose thinking is seriously disordered, or who have strong suicidal tendencies (Scovern & Kilmann, 1980). For suicidal patients, ECT has the advantage of taking effect rapidly, generally within 1 week. When a life is at stake, rapid relief is important.

ECT is now used only with patients who have given their informed consent. The shock is less intense than it used to be, and the patient is given muscle relaxants and anesthetics to prevent injury and to reduce discomfort. As a rule, the procedure is applied every other day for about 2 weeks; then, the physician evaluates the progress and either stops the treatment or decides to continue a few more times.

Exactly how ECT works is uncertain. Some have sug-

gested that it relieves depression by causing people to forget certain depressing thoughts and memories. However, the data do not support that suggestion. Although ECT usually does impair memory, at least temporarily, there are ways to reduce the memory loss without lessening the antidepressant effect (McElhiney et al., 1995). ECT exerts a great many effects on the brain, including enhanced production of dopamine receptors (Smith, Lindefors, Hurd, & Sharp, 1995), decreased production of norepinephrine receptors (Kellar & Stockmeier, 1986), and increased release of both dopamine and norepinephrine (Chiodo & Antelman, 1980). At present, we do not know which of these effects is critical for the antidepressant outcome.

The use of ECT continues to be controversial. According to extensive reviews of the literature, ECT relieves depression with about 80% of the patients who receive it and generally produces fewer side effects than antidepressant drugs (Fink, 1985; Janicak et al., 1985; Weiner, 1984). However, ECT's benefits are generally temporary; about half of those who show a good response will relapse into depression within 6 months unless they receive some other therapy to prevent it (Riddle & Scott, 1995). Furthermore, the procedure's history of abuse has given it a bad reputation. Many psychiatrists therefore hesitate to recommend ECT.

Seasonal Affective Disorder

One variety of depression is known as **seasonal affective disorder,** or **depression with a seasonal pattern** (Figure 16.19). People with this disorder *become seriously depressed once per year during a particular season.* Although

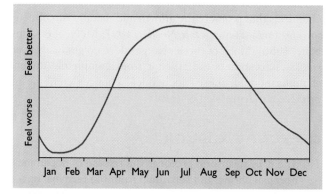

FIGURE 16.19 Most people feel slightly better during the summer (when the sun is out most of the day) than during the winter (when there are fewer hours of sunlight). People with seasonal affective disorder feel good in the summer and seriously depressed in the winter (or good in the winter and depressed in the summer). Seasonal affective disorder is commonest in far-northern locations such as Scandinavia, where the summer days are very long and bright and the winter days are very short and dark. The disorder is unheard-of in tropical locations such as Hawaii, where the amount of sunlight per day varies only slightly between summer and winter.

annual winter depressions have received the most publicity, annual summer depressions also occur (Faedda et al., 1993). Unlike most other depressed patients, people with seasonal affective disorder tend to sleep and eat excessively during their depressed periods (Jacobsen, Sack, Wehr, Rogers, & Rosenthal, 1987).

People with the winter variety of seasonal affective disorder respond to the amount of sunlight they see each day. Most of us are more cheerful when the sun is shining than we are on cloudy days, but these people are unusually sensitive to the effects of sunlight. Seasonal affective disorder can be relieved by sitting for a few hours each day in front of a bright light. Exactly how the light relieves depression is still unknown.

Bipolar Disorder

People with bipolar disorder (also known as manic-depressive disorder) alternate between the extremes of mania and depression. In most respects, **mania** is the *opposite of depression*. When people with bipolar disorder are in the depressed phase, they are slow, inactive, and inhibited. When they are in the manic phase, they are *constantly active and uninhibited*. When depressed, they feel helpless, guilt-ridden, and sad. When they are manic, they are either *happy* or *irritable*. About 1% of all adults in the United States suffer from bipolar disorder at some time during their life (Robins et al., 1984).

People in a manic phase have trouble inhibiting their impulses. Mental hospitals cannot install fire alarms in certain wards because manic patients will pull the alarm repeatedly. They make costly errors of judgment, such as investing large sums of money in highly risky or poorly considered ventures. Even after their friends warn them of the risks, they plunge on ahead.

The rambling speech of a manic person has been described as a "flight of ideas." The person starts talking about one topic, which suggests another, which in turn suggests another. Here is a quote from a manic patient:

> I like playing pool a lot, that's one of my releases, that I play pool a lot. Oh, what else? Bartend, bartend on the side, it's kind of fun to, if you're a bartender you can, you can see how people reacted, amounts of alcohol and different guys around, different chicks around, and different situations, if it's snowing outside, if it's cold outside, the weather conditions, all types of different types of environments and types of different types of people you'll usually find in a bar. (Hoffman, Stopek, & Andreasen, 1986, p. 835)

Some people experience a mild degree of mania ("hypomania") almost always. These people are productive, popular, extroverted, life-of-the-party types. Mania can become so serious, however, that it makes normal life impossible. The theatrical director Joshua Logan has described his own experiences with depression and mania. A few excerpts follow.

A Self-Report: Depressive Phase

> I had no faith in the work I was doing or the people I was working with. . . . It was a great burden to get up in the morning and I couldn't wait to go to bed at night, even though I started not sleeping well. . . . I thought I was well but feeling low because of a hidden personal discouragement of some sort—something I couldn't quite put my finger on. . . . I just forced myself to live through a dreary, hopeless existence that lasted for months on end. . . .
>
> My depressions actually began around the age of thirty-two. I remember I was working on a play, and I was forcing myself to work. . . . I can remember that I sat in some sort of aggravated agony as it was read aloud for the first time by the cast. It sounded so awful that I didn't want to direct it. I didn't even want to see it. I remember feeling so depressed that I wished that I were dead without having to go through the shame and defeat of suicide. I couldn't sleep well at all, and sleep meant, for me, oblivion, and that's what I longed for and couldn't get. I didn't know what to do and I felt very, very lost. (Fieve, 1975, pp. 42–43)

A Self-Report: Manic Phase

Here, Logan describes his manic experiences:

> Finally, as time passed, the depression gradually wore off and turned into something else, which I didn't understand either. But it was a much pleasanter thing to go through, at least at first. Instead of hating everything, I started liking things—liking them too much, perhaps. . . . I put out a thousand ideas a minute: things to do, plays to write, plots to write stories about. . . .
>
> I decided to get married on the spur of the moment. . . . I practically forced her to say yes. Suddenly we had a loveless marriage and that had to be broken up overnight. . . .
>
> I can only remember that I worked constantly, day and night, never even seeming to need more than a few hours of sleep. I always had a new idea or another conference. . . . It was an exhilarating time for me.
>
> It finally went too far. In the end I went over the bounds of reality, or law and order, so to say. I don't mean that I committed any crimes, but I could easily have done so if anyone had crossed me. I flew into rages if contradicted. I began to be irritable with everyone. Should a man, friend or foe, object to anything I did or said, it was quite possible that I could poke him in the jaw. I was eventually persuaded by the doctors that I was desperately ill and should go into the hospital. But it was not, even then, convincing to me that I was ill.
>
> There I was, on the sixth floor of a New York building that had special iron bars around it and an iron gate that had slid into place and locked me away from the rest of the world. . . . I looked about and saw that there was an open window. I leaped up on the sill and climbed out of the window on the ledge on the sixth floor and said, "Unless you open the door, I'm going to climb down the outside of this building." At the time, I remember feeling so powerful that I might actually be able to scale the building. . . . They immediately opened the steel door, and I climbed back in. That's where manic elation can take you. (Fieve, 1975, pp. 43–45)

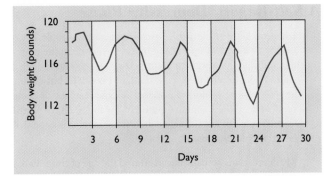

FIGURE 16.20 Records for a man who had 3-day manic periods (pink) alternating with 3-day depressed periods (blue): Note that he lost weight during the manic times because of his high activity level. (Based on Crammer, 1959.)

Bipolar Cycles

In most cases, periods of depression lasting months at a time alternate with somewhat shorter periods of mania. Less commonly, the depressed and manic phases may be very brief. Figure 16.20 shows the mood and body weight fluctuations for a manic-depressive man who had 3-day manic periods and 3-day depressed periods (Crammer, 1959).

Many artists, writers, and musical composers have suffered from either depression or bipolar disorder (Jamison, 1989). To test whether creative skills increase or decrease over various phases of the bipolar cycle, Robert Weisberg (1994) examined the works of the classical composer Robert Schumann, who is known to have had bipolar disorder. He found that Schumann produced more works during his manic phases than during his depressed phases. However, the compositions written during his depressed phases have been performed and recorded just as often as those written during his manic phases, on average. That is, the works that he composed during his depressed phases have been about as popular as those during his manic phases.

CONCEPT CHECK

11. What are the similarities and differences between seasonal affective disorder and bipolar disorder? (Check your answers on page 625.)

Lithium Therapy for Bipolar Disorder

Many years ago, researcher J. F. Cade believed that uric acid might be effective for treating mania. To get uric acid to dissolve in water, he mixed it with lithium salts. The resulting mixture proved effective, but researchers eventually discovered that the benefits depended on the lithium salts, not the uric acid.

Lithium salts were soon adopted for use in the Scandinavian countries, but they were slow to be accepted in the United States. One reason was that drug manufacturers had no interest in marketing lithium pills. (Lithium is a nat-ural substance and cannot be patented.) A second reason was that the lithium dosage must be carefully monitored. If the dosage is too low, it has no effect. If the dose is slightly higher than the recommended level, it produces nausea and blurred vision.

Properly regulated dosages of lithium are now a common and effective treatment for bipolar disorder (manic-depressive illness). Lithium reduces mania and protects the patient from relapsing into either mania or depression. It does not provide a permanent cure, so the patient must continue to take lithium pills every day. However, people can take the recommended doses of lithium for years without suffering unfavorable consequences (Schou, 1997). At this point, no one is certain how lithium relieves bipolar disorder. Many researchers believe that it works primarily on chemical pathways within the neurons, not on transmission at a particular kind of synapse (Manji, Potter, & Lenox, 1995). The other kind of medication often used for bipolar disorder is anticonvulsant drugs, such as valproate.

Suicide

Most severely depressed people consider suicide, and many attempt it. Suicides also occur for other reasons, though. Some people commit suicide because of feelings of guilt or disgrace. Some commit suicide because a cult leader assures them that death is the route to salvation (Maris, 1997). Others have a painful, terminal illness and wish to hasten the end, sometimes with a physician's assistance. The causes of a suicidal wish are often unclear; for example, someone who requests a physician's assistance in dying may be suffering from treatable depression or insufficiently controlled pain (Farberman, 1997; Muskin, 1998).

Records on suicide cannot be fully accurate, because some people disguise their suicides to look like accidents,

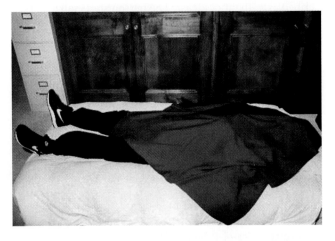

Suicide can occur for a great many reasons. The Heaven's Gate cult in San Diego committed mass suicide because their leader assured them that death was the route to being rescued from Earth by an alien spacecraft.

and because many physicians, when in doubt, record the cause of death as something other than suicide. Nevertheless, Figure 16.21 shows the best evidence available for three countries in 1988 (Lester, 1996). Note the major differences in the suicide rate as a function of age, country, and gender. In almost every country, women make more suicide attempts than men, but more men than women die by suicide (Canetto & Sakinofsky, 1998; Cross & Hirschfeld, 1986). Most men who attempt suicide use guns or other violent means. Women are more likely to try poison, drugs, or other relatively slow, nonviolent methods that are less certain to be fatal (Rich, Ricketts, Fowler, & Young, 1988). Many people,

TABLE 16.5	**People Most Likely to Attempt Suicide**

- Depressed people, especially those with feelings of hopelessness (Beck, Steer, Beck, & Newman, 1993)
- People who have made previous suicide attempts (Beck, Steer, & Brown, 1993)
- People who have untreated psychological disorders (Brent et al., 1988), especially drug or alcohol abuse (Beck & Steer, 1989)
- People who have recently suffered the death of a spouse and men who have recently been divorced or separated, especially those who have little social support from friends and family (Blumenthal & Kupfer, 1986)
- People who, during their childhood or adolescence, lost a parent through death or divorce (Adam, 1986)
- People with guns in their home, particularly those with a history of violent attacks on others (Brent et al., 1988)
- People whose relatives have committed suicide (Blumenthal & Kupfer, 1986)
- People with low activity of the neurotransmitter serotonin in the brain (Roy, DeJong, & Linnoila, 1989)

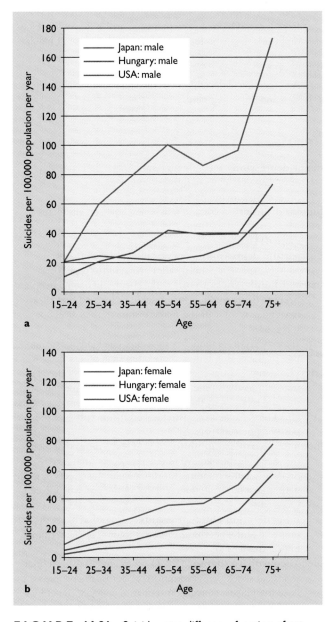

FIGURE 16.21 Suicide rates differ as a function of age, gender, and culture. The rates shown here are for 1988; the rate has dropped since then for Hungary, presumably because of economic and social changes within the country. (Based on data of Lester, 1996.)

especially women, who injure themselves in suicide attempts are believed to be crying out for help and not really intending to kill themselves. Unfortunately, some of these people actually die, and others become disabled for life.

Suicide follows no dependable pattern. Many people who attempt suicide give warning signals well in advance, but some do not. One study found that more than half of the people who made a serious suicide attempt decided on suicide less than 24 hours before making the attempt (Peterson, Peterson, O'Shanick, & Swann, 1985). However, certain factors are associated with an increased probability of attempting suicide. Anyone working with troubled people should be aware of these warning signals. Suicide attempts are most common among the types of people in Table 16.5. The same patterns have been found in the United States and China, so these are apparently not culture-specific (Cheng, 1995).

If you suspect that someone you know is thinking about suicide, what should you do? Treat the person like a normal human being. Don't assume that the person is so fragile that one wrong word will be disastrous. Don't be afraid to ask someone whether he or she has been contemplating suicide. The person may be relieved to find that you are not frightened by the thought and that you are willing to discuss it.

Most people who threaten suicide are crying out for help; they are feeling pain, either mental or physical. You may not be able to guess what kind of pain someone is feeling. Be prepared to listen.

Urge the person to get professional help. Most large cities have a suicide prevention hotline listed in the white pages of the telephone directory.

THE MESSAGE
Normal Sadness Versus Major Depression

The capacity to feel sad is important. If you never felt sad, regardless of what misfortunes befell you, you might make disastrous decisions. Major depression is much more than just sadness; a severely depressed person loses the ability to feel happy, regardless of what good events do occur. Depression can be like a monster, so we need a wide arsenal of weapons to fight it.

SUMMARY

✶ *Symptoms of depression.* A depressed person finds little interest or pleasure in life, feels worthless, powerless, and guilty, and may consider suicide. Such a person has trouble sleeping, loses interest in sex and food, and cannot concentrate. (page 614)

✶ *Predispositions.* Some people are predisposed to depression by genetic factors, by early experiences such as the loss of a parent, or by poor social support in adulthood. (page 615)

✶ *Sex differences.* Psychologists cannot convincingly explain why more women than men suffer depression. One hypothesis is that women are more likely to ruminate about their depression, and therefore aggravate and prolong it, whereas men are more likely to find some way of distracting themselves from their depression. (page 615)

✶ *Cognitive factors in depression.* People with a pessimistic explanatory style tend to blame themselves for their failures more than the evidence actually warrants. Depressed people almost invariably have an extremely pessimistic explanatory style, seeing evidence of their own failures in almost everything that happens. (page 616)

✶ *Cognitive therapy.* A frequently effective form of psychotherapy is to help depressed people reinterpret their experiences in a more favorable manner. (page 618)

✶ *Effects of antidepressant drugs.* Tricyclic drugs and MAOIs are used to treat depression. Both types of drugs prolong the stimulation of synaptic receptors by dopamine, norepinephrine, and serotonin. Second-generation antidepressants relieve depression by prolonging the action of serotonin only. With most people, second-generation antidepressants produce milder side effects. (page 618)

✶ *Advantages and disadvantages.* Psychotherapy is more likely to produce long-lasting benefits, but antidepressant drugs remain popular because of their convenience and lower cost. (page 619)

✶ *Electroconvulsive therapy.* Electroconvulsive therapy (ECT) has a long history of abuse; in modified form, ECT has made a comeback and is now helpful to some depressed people who fail to respond to antidepressant drugs. (page 620)

✶ *Seasonal affective disorder.* Seasonal affective disorder is an uncommon condition in which people become depressed during one season of the year. (page 620)

✶ *Bipolar disorder.* People with bipolar disorder alternate between periods of depression and periods of mania, when they engage in constant, driven, uninhibited activity. (page 621)

✶ *Lithium treatment.* Lithium salts are an effective treatment for bipolar disorder. (page 622)

✶ *Suicide.* Although it is difficult to know who will or will not attempt suicide, suicidal attempts are common among depressed people and people who show certain other warning signs. (page 623)

Suggestions for Further Reading

Beers, C. W. (1948). *A mind that found itself.* Garden City, NY: Doubleday. (Original work published in 1908.) An autobiography of a man who recovered from a severe case of bipolar disorder.

Whybrow, P. C. (1997). *A mood apart.* New York: HarperCollins. A nontechnical description of the various forms of depression and their treatment.

Terms

major depression   a condition lasting most of the day, day after day, with a loss of interest and pleasure and a lack of productive activity (page 614)

bipolar disorder   a condition in which a person alternates between periods of depression and periods of mania (page 614)

postpartum depression   a period of depression that some women experience shortly after giving birth (page 615)

learned-helplessness theory   the theory that some people become depressed because they have learned that they have no control over the major events in their lives (page 616)

explanatory style   a tendency to accept one kind of explanation for success or failure more often than others (page 617)

tricyclic drugs   drugs that block the reabsorption of the neurotransmitters dopamine, norepinephrine, and serotonin, after they are released by the terminal button, thus prolonging the effect of these neurotransmitters on the receptors of the postsynaptic cell (page 617)

monoamine oxidase inhibitors (MAOIs)   drugs that block the metabolic breakdown of released dopamine, norepinephrine, and serotonin, thus prolonging the effects of these neurotransmitters on the receptors of the postsynaptic cell (page 618)

second-generation antidepressants   drugs that block the reuptake of the neurotransmitter serotonin by the terminal button (page 618)

electroconvulsive therapy (ECT)   a treatment using a brief electrical shock that is administered across the patient's head to induce a convulsion similar to epilepsy, sometimes used as a treatment for certain types of depression (page 620)

seasonal affective disorder   a condition in which people become seriously depressed in one season of the year, such as winter (page 620)

mania   a condition in which people are constantly active, uninhibited, and either happy or irritable (page 621)

Answers to Concept Checks

9. Depressed people are less likely than others to buy a lottery ticket because they regard their chances of success as remote on any task. (page 618)
10. Mianserin should relieve depression and has in fact been used as an antidepressant. Although it acts by a different route from that of the tricyclics and MAOIs, it prolongs the stimulation of dopamine, norepinephrine, and serotonin receptors. (page 619)
11. Both seasonal affective disorder and bipolar disorder have repetitive cycles, sometimes with clocklike accuracy. However, people with bipolar disorder swing back and forth between two extremes, depression and mania, whereas most people with seasonal affective disorder alternate between depression and normal mood. (Some experience a slightly manic phase during the season opposite to the time of their depression.) (page 622)

Web Resources

Depression

www.psych.org/public_info/depression.html
Manic-Depressive/Bipolar Disorder
www.psych.org/public_info/manic.html
The *Let's Talk Facts* series offers information about depression and manic-depressive/bipolar disorder, describing the disorders, the major symptoms, what we know about causes, and treatment.

MODULE 16.4

Schizophrenia

What is schizophrenia?

What causes it?

What can be done about it?

How would you like to live in a world all your own? You can be the supreme ruler, and no one will ever criticize you or tell you what to do. You can tell other people—and even inanimate objects—what to do, and they will immediately obey. Each of your fantasies becomes a reality.

Perhaps that world sounds like heaven to you; I suspect it soon would be more like hell. Most of us enjoy the give and take of our interactions with other people; we enjoy struggling to achieve our fantasies more than we would enjoy their immediate fulfillment.

Some people with schizophrenia live practically in a world of their own, confusing fantasy with reality. They have trouble understanding what others say and difficulty making themselves understood. Eventually, they may retreat into a private existence and pay little attention to others.

The Symptoms of Schizophrenia

The widely misunderstood term *schizophrenia* is based on Greek roots meaning "split mind." However, the term does *not* refer to a split into two minds or personalities. Many people use the term *schizophrenia* when they really mean *dissociative identity disorder* or *multiple personality*. People with dissociative identity disorder have several personalities, any one of which might be considered normal by itself.

In contrast, people suffering from schizophrenia have just one personality, but that personality is seriously disordered. The "split" in the schizophrenic "split mind" is a split between the intellectual and emotional aspects of the personality, as if the intellect and the emotions were no longer in contact with each other (Figure 16.22). A person suffering from schizophrenia may seem happy or sad without cause, may fail to show emotion in a situation that normally

evokes them, or may even report bad news cheerfully or good news sadly.

To be diagnosed with **schizophrenia,** according to DSM-IV, *a person must exhibit a deterioration of daily activities, including work, social relations, and self-care. He or she must also exhibit at least two of the following: hallucinations, delusions, incoherent speech, grossly disorganized behavior, certain thought disorders, or a loss of normal emotional responses and social behaviors.* Exception: If someone's hallucinations or delusions are sufficiently severe, then no other symptoms are necessary. Finally, before assigning a diagnosis of schizophrenia, a psychologist or psychiatrist must rule out various other conditions that produce similar symptoms, including depression or bipolar illness, drug abuse, certain kinds of brain damage, the early stages of Huntington's disease, niacin deficiency, food allergies, and so forth.

About 1% of Americans are afflicted with schizophrenia at some point in life (Kendler, Gallagher, Abelson, & Kessler, 1996). Some sources cite somewhat higher or lower figures, depending on how many borderline cases they include. Schizophrenia occurs in all countries and in all ethnic groups, and is about equally common in men as in women.

Schizophrenia is most frequently diagnosed in young adults in their teens or 20s. Generally, men are diagnosed with schizophrenia earlier than women. A first diagnosis is rare after age 30 and unheard-of after 45. The onset can be sudden but is usually gradual. Most people with schizophrenia are described as having been "strange" children who had a short attention span, made few friends, often disrupted their classroom, and had mild thought disorders (Arboleda & Holzman, 1985; Parnas, Schulsinger, Schulsinger, Mednick, & Teasdale, 1982).

SOMETHING TO THINK ABOUT

When we ask people to recall the childhood behavior of someone who later developed schizophrenia, what kinds of memory errors are likely, and why? (Recall the issues raised in Chapters 7 and 8.) ✴

Hallucinations

Hallucinations are *sensory experiences that do not correspond to anything in the outside world.* Characteristically, people with schizophrenia hear voices and other sounds

FIGURE 16.22 Although the term *schizophrenia* is derived from Greek roots meaning "split personality," it does not refer to cases where people alternate among different personalities. Rather, the term indicates a split between the intellectual and emotional aspects of a single personality.

Intellect

Emotions

that no one else hears. Not all schizophrenic people hear voices, but most people who do are suffering from schizophrenia. The voices may speak only nonsense, or else they may tell the person to carry out certain acts. Sometimes hallucinating people think the voices are real, sometimes they know the voices are coming from within their own head, and sometimes they are not sure (Junginger & Frame, 1985). Visual hallucinations are uncommon with schizophrenia, although some people have distorted or exaggerated visual experiences (Figure 16.23). Strong visual hallucinations are usually symptoms of drug abuse.

Delusions

Delusions are *unfounded beliefs.* Three common types of delusions are delusions of persecution, grandeur, and reference: A **delusion of persecution** is *a belief that one is being persecuted,* that "people are out to get me." A **delusion of grandeur** is *a belief that one is unusually important,* perhaps a special messenger from God or a person of central importance to the future of the world. A **delusion of reference** is *a tendency to interpret all sorts of messages as if they were meant for oneself.* Someone with a delusion of reference may interpret a headline in the morning newspaper as a coded message or take a television announcer's comments as personal insults.

In some cases, it is fairly easy to identify a belief as delusional. For example, if someone who can hardly put together a complete sentence claims to be a messenger from the planet Zipton, chances are, the belief is a delusion. But what about someone who constantly sees evidence of government conspiracies in everyday events? Is that belief a delusion, or merely an unusual opinion? Members of religious and political minorities have many beliefs that other people regard as wrong, but unpopular views are not necessarily products of delusional thinking.

Furthermore, consider the following: During the Vietnam War, one U.S. Army unit massacred large numbers of unarmed women and children at My Lai. One of the soldiers, horrified at what the others were doing, refused to participate. After the war, he told a social worker about his recurring fears and nightmares stemming from that event. He also said that the other soldiers threatened to kill him if he told anyone what had happened and said that they might kill him anyway, just to prevent him from telling. When the social worker told her colleagues about this client, most of them labeled his story a delusion and suggested a diagnosis of schizophrenia. The story, however, was true (Scott, 1990).

In short: One should be cautious about labeling any belief a delusion and about diagnosing anyone as schizophrenic when the only symptom is an apparently delusional belief.

Disorders of Emotion and Movement

Many people with schizophrenia show little sign of emotion. Their faces seldom express emotion, and they speak without the inflections most people use for emphasis.

FIGURE 16.23 These portraits graphically illustrate the artist's progressive psychological deterioration. When well-known animal artist Louis Wain (1860–1939) began suffering delusions of persecution, his drawings showed a schizophrenic's disturbing distortions in perception.

When they do show emotions, the expressions are inappropriate, such as laughing without apparent reason.

Some people with schizophrenia have a movement disorder called catatonia. **Catatonia** can take the form of either *rigid inactivity or excessive activity;* in either case, the person's movement pattern seems to be unrelated to events in the outside world.

The Thought Disorder of Schizophrenia

One characteristic of schizophrenic thought is the use of loose and idiosyncratic associations, somewhat like the illogical leaps that occur in dreams. For example, one man used the words *Jesus, cigar,* and *sex* as synonyms. When he was asked to explain, he said they were all the same because Jesus has a halo around his head, a cigar has a band around it, and during sex people put their arms around each other.

Another characteristic of schizophrenic thought is difficulty using abstract concepts. For instance, many people with schizophrenia have trouble sorting objects into categories. Many also give strictly literal responses when asked to interpret the meaning of proverbs. Here are some examples (Krueger, 1978, pp. 196–197):

Proverb: People who live in glass houses shouldn't throw stones.
Interpretation: "It would break the glass."

Proverb: All that glitters is not gold.
Interpretation: "It might be brass."
Proverb: A stitch in time saves nine.
Interpretation: "If you take one stitch for a small tear now, it will save nine later."

People with schizophrenic thought disorder often misunderstand simple statements, because of their tendency to interpret everything literally. Upon being taken to the admitting office of a hospital, one person said, "Oh, is this where people go to admit their faults?"

Many schizophrenic people use vague, roundabout ways of saying something simple. For instance, one such person said, "I was born with a male sense" instead of "I'm a man." They often use many words to say nothing of importance, as in this excerpt from a letter one man wrote to his mother:

> I am writing on paper. The pen which I am using is from a factory called "Perry & Co." This factory is in England. I assume this. Behind the name of Perry Co. the city of London is inscribed; but not the city. The city of London is in England. I know this from my school-days. Then, I always liked geography. My last teacher in that subject was Professor August A. He was a man with black eyes. I also like black eyes. There are also blue and gray eyes and other sorts, too. I have heard it said that snakes have green eyes. All people have eyes. There are some, too, who are blind. These blind people are led about by a boy. It must be very terrible not to be able to see. There are people who can't see and, in addition, can't hear. I know some who hear too much. (Bleuler, 1911/1950, p. 17)

The Distinction Between Positive and Negative Symptoms

Are all the various symptoms of schizophrenia independent, or do they form clusters? Many investigators distinguish between positive symptoms and negative symptoms of schizophrenia. (In this case, *positive* means *present* and *negative* means *absent*; they do not mean *good* and *bad*.) **Positive symptoms** are *behaviors that are notable because of their presence* in schizophrenia—symptoms such as hallucinations, delusions, and thought disorder. **Negative symptoms** are *behaviors that are notable by their absence*. For example, many people with schizophrenia show a lack of emotional expression, a lack of social interaction, a deficit of speech, a lack of ability to feel pleasure, and a general inability to take care of themselves.

The research supports a further distinction between two groups of positive symptoms—"positive psychotic" symptoms (hallucinations and delusions) and "positive disorganized" symptoms (thought disorder, bizarre behavior, and inappropriate emotions). Hallucinations and delusions form a natural cluster; most people who have either hallucinations or delusions have both. Similarly, the positive disorganized symptoms correlate with one another; people who have one of them tend to have the others also

(Andreasen, Arndt, Alliger, Miller, & Flaum, 1995). The negative symptoms form a third cluster.

As a rule, both the positive psychotic and the positive disorganized symptoms fluctuate from time to time. Negative symptoms tend to be more consistent over time and more difficult to treat (Arndt, Andreasen, Flaum, Miller, & Nopoulos, 1995). People with many negative symptoms have an earlier onset of the disorder and worse performance in school and on the job (Andreasen, Flaum, Swayze, Tyrrell, & Arndt, 1990). These people are also more likely to show signs of brain abnormalities (Palmer et al., 1997).

Types of Schizophrenia

People with schizophrenia vary considerably in their symptoms; they also vary in their family histories, their results on brain scans, and their response to treatment. What we call "schizophrenia" may in fact include two or more separate conditions that produce overlapping symptoms, as if medical doctors had failed to distinguish among migraine headaches, tension headaches, and brain tumors (Heinrichs, 1993). Currently, psychologists distinguish among four types of schizophrenia, based on the behavioral symptoms. These distinctions are useful for descriptive purposes, although they do not identify the underlying causes.

Undifferentiated schizophrenia is characterized by the *basic symptoms—deterioration of daily functioning plus some combination of hallucinations, delusions, inappropriate emotions, thought disorders, and so forth*. However, none of these symptoms is unusually pronounced or bizarre.

Catatonic schizophrenia is characterized by the *basic symptoms plus prominent movement disorders*. The affected person may go through periods of extremely rapid, mostly repetitive activity alternating with periods of total inactivity. During the inactive periods, he or she may hold a given posture without moving and may resist attempts to alter that posture (Figure 16.24). Catatonic schizophrenia is rare.

Disorganized schizophrenia is characterized by *incoherent speech, extreme lack of social relationships, and "silly" or odd behavior*. For example, one man gift wrapped one of his bowel movements and proudly presented it to his therapist. Here is a conversation with someone suffering from disorganized schizophrenia (Duke & Nowicki, 1979):

Interviewer: How does it feel to have your problems?
Patient: Who can tell me the name of my song? I don't know, but it won't be long. It won't be short, tall, none at all. My head hurts, my knees hurt—my nephew, his uncle, my aunt. My God, I'm happy . . . not a care in the world. My hair's been curled, the flag's unfurled. This is my country, land that I love, this is the country, land that I love.
Interviewer: How do you feel?
Patient: Happy! Don't you hear me? Why do you talk to me? (barks like a dog). (Duke & Nowicki, 1979, p. 162)

FIGURE 16.24 A person suffering from catatonic schizophrenia can hold a bizarre posture for hours and alternate this rigid stupor with equally purposeless, excited activity. Such people may stubbornly resist attempts to change their behavior, but they need supervision to avoid hurting themselves or others. Catatonic schizophrenia is uncommon.

Paranoid schizophrenia is characterized by the *basic symptoms plus strong or elaborate hallucinations and delusions, especially delusions of persecution and delusions of grandeur.* Many people with paranoid schizophrenia are more cognitively intact than most people with other forms of schizophrenia. They can generally take care of themselves well enough to get through the activities of the day, except for their constant suspicions that "I am surrounded by spies" or that "evil forces are trying to control my mind."

Paranoid schizophrenia tends to run in different families from other types of schizophrenia (Farmer, McGuffin, & Gottesman, 1987). It usually develops gradually, somewhat later in life than other types of schizophrenia.

Many people fall on the borderline between two or more types of schizophrenia, perhaps switching back and forth between them. Switching is especially common between undifferentiated schizophrenia and one of the other types (Kendler, Gruenberg, & Tsuang, 1985).

CONCEPT CHECK

12. Why are people more likely to switch between undifferentiated schizophrenia and one of the other types than, say, between disorganized schizophrenia and one of the other types? (Check your answer on page 635.)

Causes of Schizophrenia

From all indications, schizophrenia has multiple causes. In most cases, it apparently begins with a genetic or other biological predisposition, which is then aggravated by stressful experiences. We shall examine what researchers currently understand about the causes of schizophrenia, but bear in mind that our understanding is tentative.

Brain Damage

Unlike people suffering from most other psychological disorders, people suffering from schizophrenia show minor but widespread brain damage (see Figure 16.25). The cerebral cortex is somewhat shrunken in one-fourth to one-third of all schizophrenic patients, and the cerebral ventricles (fluid-filled spaces in the brain) are enlarged, on the average (Zipursky, Lim, Sullivan, Brown, & Pfefferbaum, 1992). Enlargement of the cerebral ventricles implies decreased space for neurons; thus, it suggests mild brain damage. Most people with schizophrenia have cognitive and memory deficits similar to those of people with damage to the prefrontal cortex (Seidman et al., 1995).

At a microscopic level, researchers have found smaller than normal neurons (Selemon, Rajkowska, & Goldman-Rakic, 1995), decreased metabolic activity in the brain (Berman, Torrey, Daniel, & Weinberger, 1992), abnormal locations of certain neurons in the brain (Akbarian et al., 1993), and decreased release of neurotransmitters (Glantz & Lewis, 1997). Each of these differences is especially marked in the prefrontal cortex. Indications of brain abnormalities have been reported in patients in cultures as different as the United States and Nigeria (Ohaeri, Adeyinka, & Osuntokun, 1995).

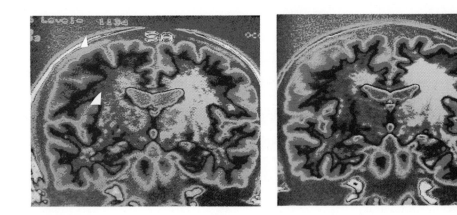

FIGURE 16.25 Many (though not all) people with schizophrenia show signs of mild loss of neurons in the brain. Here, we see views of the brains of twins. The twin on the left has schizophrenia; the twin on the right does not. Note that the ventricles (near the center of each brain) are larger in the twin with schizophrenia. The ventricles are fluid-filled cavities; an enlargement of the ventricles implies a loss of brain tissue. (Photos courtesy of E. F. Torrey & M. F. Casanova / NIMH.)

Although the causes of these brain abnormalities are uncertain, mounting evidence suggests that the abnormalities develop early in life, either before birth or early after birth. People with schizophrenia do not show signs of increasing brain abnormality in adolescence or adulthood, though (Benes, 1995).

CONCEPT CHECK

13. Following a stroke, a patient shows symptoms similar to schizophrenia. Where is the brain damage probably located? (Check your answer on page 635.)

Genetics

The evidence of a genetic basis rests primarily on studies of adopted children and comparisons of twins. With adopted children who eventually develop schizophrenia, schizophrenia is more common among their biological relatives than it is among their adoptive relatives (Kety et al., 1994). If one member of a pair of monozygotic (identical) twins develops schizophrenia, there is almost a 50% chance that the other will develop it too (Gottesman, 1991). (See Figure 16.26.) Furthermore, when one twin develops schizophrenia and the other does not, both twins run the same risk of passing schizophrenia on to their children (Gottesman & Bertelson, 1989; Kringlen & Cramer, 1989). Apparently, a gene or genes tends to increase the likelihood of schizophrenia. Even if a person with those genes does not actually develop schizophrenia, he or she still passes the genes on to the next generation.

Although nearly all researchers agree that genetic factors contribute to schizophrenia, our current research methods probably overestimate the role of genetics by underestimating the importance of the prenatal environment (Phelps, Davis, & Schartz, 1997). An adopted child shares not only the genes of his or her biological relatives, but also the prenatal environment provided by the biological mother. Most monozygotic twins share a single placenta before birth, whereas all dizygotic twins have separate placentas (Figure 16.27). Therefore, monozygotic twins have more similarities in prenatal influences than do dizygotic twins. Several types of evidence, discussed later, suggest that prenatal environment contributes to some cases of schizophrenia.

One focus of current research is to identify those people who have the presumed genes for schizophrenia but who do not show the symptoms. Identifying these people could be useful for better understanding the genetics and for understanding how genetic influences combine with environmental influences. Psychologists have examined young people who are related to people with schizophrenia. Although these young people have not yet developed schizophrenia themselves, many of them will probably develop it later. Thus, any unusual behaviors they now show are possible "markers" of vulnerability to schizophrenia—that is, people with these behaviors are more likely than others to develop schizophrenia.

Those markers include several symptoms of mild brain damage or abnormality (Cannon et al., 1994) and a failure to habituate normally to a repeated sound (Hollister, Mednick, Brennan, & Cannon, 1994). That is, many of these young people fail to filter out irrelevant information, thus responding to a repeated noise as much as they do to an unfamiliar noise.

Another possible "marker" is an impairment of pursuit eye movements, the movements necessary for keeping one's eyes focused on a moving object. Most people

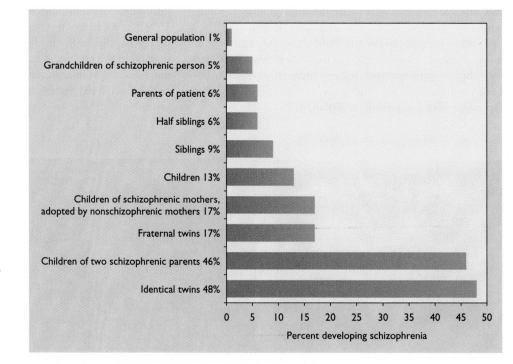

FIGURE 16.26 The relatives of a schizophrenic person have an increased probability of developing schizophrenia themselves. Note that children of a schizophrenic mother have a 17% risk of schizophrenia even if adopted by a family with no schizophrenic members. (Based on data from Gottesman, 1991.)

General population 1%
Grandchildren of schizophrenic person 5%
Parents of patient 6%
Half siblings 6%
Siblings 9%
Children 13%
Children of schizophrenic mothers, adopted by nonschizophrenic mothers 17%
Fraternal twins 17%
Children of two schizophrenic parents 46%
Identical twins 48%

Percent developing schizophrenia

with schizophrenia move their eyes in a series of rapid jerks instead of moving them smoothly (Sereno & Holzman, 1993); they show this same impairment before they develop schizophrenia, during a schizophrenic episode, and after successful therapy (Holzman, 1988). The same impairment also occurs in many of their close relatives but seldom in people who do not have a relative with schizophrenia (Keefe et al., 1997). Thus, this impaired eye movement may help us to identify people who have the genes for schizophrenia.

SOMETHING TO THINK ABOUT

People with schizophrenia, especially men, are less likely than others to have children. So, it is difficult to imagine how a gene that leads to schizophrenia could spread enough to affect 1% of the population. Can you imagine a possible explanation? ✷

The Neurodevelopmental Hypothesis

Although schizophrenia most often occurs in people who have relatives with schizophrenia, it also occurs in those who do not. Most researchers now accept the **neurodevelopmental hypothesis,** *the idea that schizophrenia originates with impaired development of the nervous system before or around the time of birth, possibly but not necessarily for genetic reasons.* For example, the probability of schizophrenia is higher than normal following these events relating to early brain development:

- The patient's mother had a very difficulty pregnancy, labor, or delivery (Hultman, Öhman, Cnattingius, Wieselgren, & Lindström, 1997).
- The mother was near starvation during the early stages of pregnancy (Susser et al., 1996).
- The mother had an Rh-negative blood type and her baby was Rh-positive. The risk of schizophrenia is especially strong for her second and later Rh-positive children, especially boys (Hollister, Laing, & Mednick, 1996).

Schizophrenia is slightly more common for children born in winter than those born at other times. However, the critical factor is probably the weather during the second trimester of pregnancy. Those born in winter were in the second trimester during fall, the main time for viral and bacterial epidemics.

Furthermore, *a person born in the winter months is slightly more likely to develop schizophrenia than a person born at any other time* (Bradbury & Miller, 1985). No other psychological disorder has this characteristic. Moreover, investigators have clearly demonstrated this **season-of-birth effect** only in the northern climates, not near the equator. Evidently, something about the weather near the time of birth contributes to some people's vulnerability to schizophrenia.

One possible explanation relates to the fact that influenza and other epidemics are most common in the fall, especially in northern climates. If a woman catches influenza or a similar disease while she happens to be in the second trimester of pregnancy, her illness can impair critical stages of brain development occurring within her fetus at that time. The virus does not cross the placenta into the fetus (Taller et al., 1996), so the problem is not the virus itself but probably the mother's fever, which can impair development of fetal neurons (Laburn, 1996). According to several studies, in years having a major influenza epidemic in the fall, the babies born 3 months later (in the winter) have an increased risk for schizophrenia, as diagnosed 20 or more years later (Kendell & Kemp, 1989; Mednick, Machon, & Huttunen, 1990; Torrey, Rawlings, & Waldman, 1988).

a   b

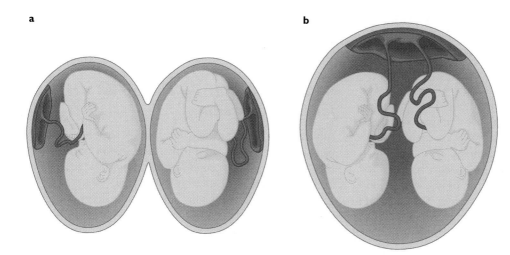

FIGURE 16.27 All dizygotic (fraternal) twins develop with separate placentas and therefore separate blood supplies. Most monozygotic (identical) twins develop with a single placenta and therefore always have the same blood supply, the same hormone levels, and so forth. Some of the similarities seen between monozygotic twins may be due to their similar prenatal environments, not just to their genetic similarity.

You might ask, if the brain damage occurs before or near the time of birth, why do the symptoms emerge so much later? One possible answer is that certain parts of the brain, especially the prefrontal cortex, go through a critical stage of development during the second trimester of pregnancy but do not become fully functional until adolescence. As the brain begins to rely more and more on those areas, the effects of the brain damage become more evident (Weinberger, 1987).

Experience

Assuming that genes or prenatal problems predispose certain people to schizophrenia, what environmental factors determine whether those genes will be expressed as schizophrenia? Decades ago, psychologists suggested that mothers who gave a confusing mixture of "come here" and "go away" signals were likely to induce schizophrenia in their children.

That theory is worth mentioning here only for the sake of explaining why it has been discarded. One reason is that it does not fit the data on adoptions. The child of a schizophrenic parent who is adopted by normal parents has a high risk of developing schizophrenia, whereas other adopted children reared in the same family generally develop normally. So, it seems unlikely that a mother's mixed signals cause schizophrenia.

Furthermore, the "bad mother" theory does not fit the course of the disorder. If the mother's behavior were the main cause of the problem, we would expect the child to improve after being separated from her. In fact, schizophrenia usually develops in early adulthood—when most people become independent of their parents.

Many researchers today attribute schizophrenia to a biological predisposition that is aggravated by stressful experiences (Walker & Diforio, 1997). As an analogy, someone with an injured foot may be able to walk normally most of the time but will start to limp when walking up a steep hill or when carrying a heavy backpack. The limp depends on both the foot injury (biological predisposition) and the hill or load (stress from the environment).

Drug Therapies for Schizophrenia

Before the discovery of effective drugs to combat schizophrenia, the outlook for people with the disorder was bleak. Usually, people underwent a gradual deterioration, interrupted by periods of partial recovery. Many spent virtually their entire adult life in mental hospitals.

During the 1950s, researchers discovered the first effective antischizophrenic drug: chlorpromazine (klor-PRAHM-uh-ZEEN; trade name: Thorazine). *Drugs that relieve schizophrenia* are known as **antipsychotic drugs** or *neuroleptic drugs.* Chlorpromazine and other antipsychotic drugs, including haloperidol (HAHL-o-PAIR-ih-dol; trade name: Haldol), have enabled many schizophrenic people to escape lifelong confinement in a mental hospital. Although these drugs do not cure the disorder, a daily dosage does help to control it, much as daily insulin shots control diabetes. Since the 1950s, a majority of people with schizophrenia have improved enough to leave mental hospitals or to avoid ever entering one (Harding, Brooks, Ashikaga, Straus, and Breier, 1987).

All antipsychotic drugs share one characteristic: They block dopamine synapses in the brain. In fact, their therapeutic effectiveness is nearly proportional to their ability to block those synapses (Seeman & Lee, 1975). Furthermore, large doses of amphetamines, cocaine, or other drugs that stimulate dopamine activity can induce a temporary state that resembles schizophrenia. These phenomena have led to the **dopamine hypothesis of schizophrenia,** which holds that *the underlying cause of schizophrenia is excessive stimulation of certain types of dopamine synapses.*

Measurements from blood and other body fluids have generally found nearly normal levels of dopamine and its metabolic breakdown products, however (Jaskiw & Weinberger, 1992). According to an alternative view, the **glutamate hypothesis of schizophrenia,** *the underlying problem causing schizophrenia is deficient stimulation of certain glutamate synapses.* In many brain areas, dopamine inhibits glutamate activity, so drugs that block dopamine synapses would increase the activity of glutamate synapses. The glutamate hypothesis is supported by the fact that prolonged use of the drug *phencyclidine* ("angel dust"), which inhibits glutamate receptors, produces symptoms that match schizophrenia even more closely than do cocaine and amphetamines, which stimulate dopamine synapses (Olney & Farger, 1995).

Antipsychotic drugs take effect gradually and produce variable degrees of recovery. As a rule, antipsychotic drugs produce their clearest effects if treatment begins shortly after a sudden onset of schizophrenia. The greater someone's deterioration before drug treatment begins, the less the recovery will be. Most of the recovery that will ever take place emerges gradually during the first month (Szymanski, Simon, & Gutterman, 1983). Beyond that point, the drugs merely maintain behavior but do not improve it. When affected people stop taking the drugs, the symptoms return and, in most cases, worsen (Figure 16.28).

Side Effects of Drug Therapies for Schizophrenia

Antipsychotic drugs produce unwelcome side effects in many people. The most serious, **tardive dyskinesia** (TAHRD-eev DIS-ki-NEE-zhuh), *a condition characterized by tremors and involuntary movements* (Chakos et al., 1996), develops gradually after years of taking antipsychotic drugs, especially with people who take large amounts of the drugs. Tardive dyskinesia is presumably related to activity at the dopamine

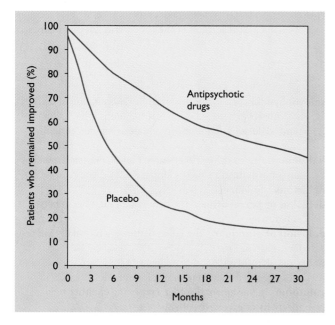

FIGURE 16.28 This graph indicates that during 2½ years following apparent recovery from schizophrenia, the percentage of schizophrenic patients who remained "improved" is higher in the group that received continuing drug treatment than in the placebo group. But the graph also shows that antipsychotic drugs do not always prevent relapse. (Based on Baldessarini, 1984.)

synapses, some of which control movement; however, the exact explanation remains uncertain (Andersson et al., 1990).

Researchers have sought new drugs that can combat schizophrenia without causing tardive dyskinesia. On the theory that the symptoms of schizophrenia depend on one type of dopamine synapse and that tardive dyskinesia reflects changes at another type of dopamine synapse, researchers have experimented with drugs that specifically antagonize one or another type of dopamine receptor. Research has also focused on the relatively new drugs *clozapine* and *risperidone,* which relieve schizophrenia by combining moderate effects on dopamine synapses with additional effects on serotonin synapses. These new drugs have shown significant promise for relieving schizophrenia with a minimum risk of tardive dyskinesia; they also tend to relieve the negative symptoms of schizophrenia (such as social withdrawal) that other antipsychotic drugs fail to address (Carpenter, 1995; Meltzer, 1995). Unfortunately, clozapine produces serious side effects of its own, including an impairment of the immune system.

CONCEPT CHECK

14. Why is early diagnosis of schizophrenia important? (Check your answer on page 635.)

Family Therapy for Schizophrenia

The degree of recovery produced by antipsychotic drugs varies. Even someone who responds well to the drugs and appears to be living fairly normally can have a sudden relapse of symptoms. Much of this fluctuation in outcome reflects stressors in the person's family environment.

If you had a brother, sister, son, or daughter with schizophrenia, how would you react? We would all like to think that we would be 100% supportive and sympathetic to this poor, troubled person. However, family members are human beings, too, and—after years of dealing with someone who says and does strange things and requires extensive attention just to get through the normal activities of the day—even the most saintly of relatives will occasionally lose patience and make *hostile or critical comments,* known as **expressed emotion.** Researchers have found that the more frequently a person is exposed to expressed emotion, the greater the probability of a relapse into severe schizophrenic symptoms (Butzlaff & Hooley, 1998). In several studies, family members were taught to reduce their expressed emotion; the result has been fewer relapses into schizophrenia, as compared to control groups where families received no such training (de Jesus Mari & Streiner, 1994).

The results regarding expressed emotion suggest one possible explanation for some cross-cultural differences: Compared to North America and western Europe, schizophrenia in India and the Arab countries tends to be less severe and marked by fewer relapses. In these cultures, troubled people are generally cared for by a large extended family including cousins, aunts and uncles, and so forth, and not just by the immediate family. By sharing care, these families decrease the amount of strain on any one individual. Relatives can thus maintain their patience and good spirits; they show much fewer expressed emotions than their U.S. counterparts (El-Islam, 1982; Leff et al., 1987; Wig et al., 1987).

THE MESSAGE
The Elusiveness of Schizophrenia

You could meet two people both diagnosed with schizophrenia who nevertheless had relatively little in common. One has hallucinations and delusions; the other has a thought disorder and a lack of emotional expression. One has relatives with schizophrenia; the other doesn't. One has evidence of brain abnormalities; the other doesn't. As you can imagine, it is difficult to draw generalizations that apply to all people with schizophrenia, so many researchers still wonder whether we are dealing with one disorder or several. We need more research to understand the disorder itself as well as its causes and treatment.

SUMMARY

* *Symptoms of schizophrenia.* A person with schizophrenia is someone whose everyday functioning has deteriorated

over a period of at least 6 months and who shows at least two of the following symptoms: hallucinations (mostly auditory), delusions, weak or inappropriate emotional expression, catatonic movements, and thought disorder. (page 626)

✱ *Thought disorder of schizophrenia.* The thought disorder of schizophrenia is characterized by loose associations, impaired use of abstract concepts, and vague, wandering speech that conveys little information. (page 627)

✱ *Positive and negative symptoms.* Positive symptoms are behaviors that attract attention by their presence, such as hallucinations and delusions. Negative symptoms are behaviors that are noteworthy by their absence, such as impaired emotional expression. (page 628)

✱ *Types of schizophrenia.* What we call *schizophrenia* may in fact consist of two or more separate conditions with overlapping symptoms. Psychologists distinguish four types of schizophrenia: undifferentiated, catatonic, disorganized, and paranoid. Some authorities believe paranoid schizophrenia resembles depression more than it does other types of schizophrenia. (page 628)

✱ *Brain abnormalities.* Many people with schizophrenia show indications of mild brain abnormalities, especially in the prefrontal cortex. The abnormalities apparently develop early in life and do not grow worse over time. (page 629)

✱ *Genetic influences.* Much evidence indicates that it is possible to inherit a predisposition toward schizophrenia, although little is known about how the genes exert their influence. (page 630)

✱ *Neurodevelopmental hypothesis.* Many researchers believe that schizophrenia originates with abnormal brain development before or around the time of birth, sometimes for genetic reasons but sometimes for other reasons, such as a fever the mother had during pregnancy. (page 631)

✱ *Antipsychotic drugs.* Drugs that alleviate schizophrenia block dopamine synapses. Results are best if treatment begins before the person has suffered serious deterioration. (page 632)

✱ *Neurotransmitters.* The effectiveness of dopamine blockers in alleviating schizophrenia has suggested that the underlying problem might be excessive dopamine activity. However, people with schizophrenia appear to have normal dopamine levels. An alternative hypothesis is that the underlying problem is a deficiency of glutamate, a neurotransmitter inhibited by dopamine. (page 632)

✱ *Family therapy.* The family's hostile comments (expressed emotion) toward someone with schizophrenia increase the risk of renewed symptoms. Reducing the family's expressed emotion improves the patient's chances for lasting recovery. (page 633)

Suggestions for Further Reading

Andreasen, N. C. (1994). *Schizophrenia: From mind to molecule.* Washington, DC: American Psychiatric Press. Review of schizophrenia by one of the leading researchers.

Heston, L. L. (1992). *Mending minds.* New York, W. H. Freeman. A nontechnical account of the use of drugs in psychiatry.

Terms

schizophrenia a condition marked by deterioration of daily activities over a period of at least 6 months, plus hallucinations, delusions, flat or inappropriate emotions, certain movement disorders, or thought disorders (page 626)

hallucinations sensory experiences that do not correspond anything in the outside world (page 626)

delusions unfounded beliefs (page 627)

delusion of persecution the belief that one is being persecuted (page 627)

delusion of grandeur the belief that one is unusually important (page 627)

delusion of reference the tendency to interpret all sorts of messages as if they were meant for oneself (page 627)

catatonia a movement disorder, consisting of either rigid inactivity or excessive activity (page 627)

positive symptoms characteristics present in people with schizophrenia and absent in others—such as hallucinations, delusions, abnormal movements, and thought disorder (page 628)

negative symptoms symptoms that are present in other people—such as the ability to take care of themselves—but absent in schizophrenic people (page 628)

undifferentiated schizophrenia a type of schizophrenia characterized by the basic symptoms but no unusual or especially prominent symptoms (page 628)

catatonic schizophrenia a type of schizophrenia characterized by the basic symptoms plus prominent movement disorders (page 628)

disorganized schizophrenia a type of schizophrenia characterized by incoherent speech, extreme lack of social relationships, and "silly" or odd behavior (page 628)

paranoid schizophrenia a type of schizophrenia characterized by the basic symptoms plus strong or elaborate hallucinations and delusions (page 629)

neurodevelopmental hypothesis the idea that schizophrenia originates with impaired development of the nervous system before or around the time of birth, possibly but not necessarily for genetic reasons (page 631)

season-of-birth effect the tendency for people born in the winter months to be slightly more likely than other people are to develop schizophrenia (page 631)

antipsychotic drugs drugs that relieve schizophrenia (page 632)

dopamine hypothesis of schizophrenia the theory that the underlying cause of schizophrenia is excessive stimulation of certain types of dopamine synapses (page 632)

glutamate hypothesis of schizophrenia the view that the underlying problem causing schizophrenia is deficient stimulation of certain glutamate synapses (page 632)

tardive dyskinesia a disorder characterized by tremors and involuntary movements (page 632)

expressed emotion hostile or critical comments directed toward a person with a psychiatric disorder such as schizophrenia (page 633)

Answers to Concept Checks

12. With any disorder, symptoms are more severe at some times than at others. Whenever any of the special symptoms of catatonic, disorganized, or paranoid schizophrenia become less severe, the person is left with undifferentiated schizophrenia. To shift between any two of the other types, a person would have to lose the symptoms of one type and gain the symptoms of the other type. (page 629)

13. The damage is probably located in the frontal or temporal lobes of the cerebral cortex, the area that is generally damaged in people with schizophrenia. (page 630)

14. Antipsychotics are more helpful to people in the early stages of schizophrenia than to those who have deteriorated severely. However, psychiatrists do not want to administer antipsychotics to people who do not need them because of the risk of tardive dyskinesia. Consequently, early and accurate diagnosis of schizophrenia is helpful. (page 633)

Web Resources

Schizophrenia

www.psych.org/public_info/schizo.html

This *Let's Talk Facts* pamphlet covers the major symptoms of schizophrenia, what we know about its causes, and treatment. The American Psychiatric Association is also conducting a Schizophrenia Awareness Project (www.degnanco.com/schizophrenia/main.html) to help patients, spouses, and siblings understand the illness and its treatment, as well as how to help the patient on the road to recovery.

Psychiatric Medication

http://www.psych.org/public_info/medication.html

Psychiatric Hospitalization

http://www.psych.org/public_info/hospital.html

The *Let's Talk Facts* series offers information about psychiatric medication and hospitalization.

Epilogue

Here we are at the end of the book. As I have been writing and revising this book, I have imagined you sitting there reading it. I have generally imagined a student somewhat like I was when I was a college student, reading about psychology for the first time and often growing excited about something I had just read. I remember periodically telling my roommate, or my family, when I was home for a vacation, "Guess what I just learned in Psychology! Isn't this interesting?" And I remember occasionally thinking, "Hmm. The book says such-and-so, but I'm not convinced. I wonder whether psychologists ever considered a different explanation. . . ." And I started thinking about possible research I might do if I ever became a psychologist.

I hope that you have had some similar experiences yourself. I hope you have occasionally become excited about something you read, so that you thought about it and talked to other people about it. In fact, I hope you told your roommate so much about psychology that you started to become annoying. And I hope you have sometimes doubted a conclusion, imagining some research project that you might like to conduct to improve and advance our knowledge.

Now, as I picture you reaching the end of the course, I'm not sure how you will react. You might be thinking, "Wow, I sure have learned a lot!" Or you might be thinking, "Is that *all?*" Maybe you are even reacting both ways: "I really have learned a lot. But it seems like there ought to be

more. I still don't understand what conscious experience is all about, and I don't understand why I react the way I do sometimes. And this book—*wonderful as it is*—hardly mentioned certain important topics. Like why do we laugh? How do we sense the passage of time? Why do people like to watch sports? How do people develop their political and religious convictions? Why do I feel like yawning whenever I see someone else yawn?"

If I didn't answer all your questions, there are two good reasons. One is that this is an introductory text; if you want to learn more, you should take other psychology courses or do some additional reading. The other reason is that psychologists do not know all the answers.

Perhaps someday you will become a psychological researcher yourself and add to the sum of our knowledge. If not, you can try to keep up to date on current developments in psychology by reading newspaper and magazine articles and an occasional book. One of the main goals of this book has been to prepare you to continue learning about psychology in that fashion. Try to read critically. If you pick up a book in the psychology section of your local bookstore, try to determine whether it is based on scientific evidence or just the author's own pronouncements. If you read an article in the newspaper, try to judge whether its conclusions follow from solid evidence. If the article reports on a survey, were the survey's questions unambiguous? If

Many fairly simple aspects of behavior remain little investigated and not well understood. For example, why do we yawn? Why do we laugh? Why are both yawning and laughter so contagious? If you decide to become a psychological researcher, you will find no shortage of topics that deserve more investigation.

the article implies a cause-and-effect relationship, was the evidence based on experiments or only correlations? No matter what the evidence, can you think of a more reasonable, more parsimonious explanation than the one the author suggests?

Above all, remember that nearly all our conclusions are tentative. Psychological researchers seldom use the work *prove*; they have many ways of indicating moderate confidence. I once suggested to my editor, half-seriously, that we should include in the index to this book the entry "*maybe*—see pages 1–677." We did not include such an entry, because our understanding of psychology is not really that bad—at least, not always. But be leery of anyone who seems a little too certain about a great new insight in psychology; the route from *maybe* to *definitely* is long and arduous.

References

Numbers in parentheses indicate the chapter in which a source is cited.

Abramson, L. Y., Seligman, M. E. P., & Teasdale, J. D. (1978). Learned helplessness in humans: Critique and reformulation. *Journal of Abnormal Psychology, 87,* 49–74. (16)

Adam, K. S. (1986). Early family influences on suicidal behavior. *Annals of the New York Academy of Sciences, 487,* 63–76. (16)

Adler, A. (1927). *Understanding human nature.* New York: Greenberg. (13)

Adler, A. (1964). Brief comments on reason, intelligence, and feeble-mindedness. In H. L. Ansbacher & R. R. Ansbacher (Eds.), *Superiority and social interest* (pp. 41–49). New York: Viking. (Original work published 1928). (13)

Adler, A. (1964). The structure of neurosis. In H. L. Ansbacher & R. R. Ansbacher (Eds.), *Superiority and social interest* (pp. 83–95). New York: Viking. (Original work published 1932). (13)

Adolphs, R., Tranel, D., Damasio, H., & Damasio, A. (1994). Impaired recognition of emotion in facial expressions following bilateral damage to the human amygdala. *Nature, 372,* 669–672. (3)

Ainsworth, M. D. S. (1979). Attachment as related to mother-infant interaction. In J. S. Rosenblatt, R. A. Hinde, C. Beer, & M. Busnel (Eds.), *Advances in the study of behavior* (Vol. 9, pp. 1–51). New York: Academic Press. (10)

Akbarian, S., Viñuela, A., Kim, J. J., Potkin, S. G., Bunney, W. E., Jr., & Jones, E. G. (1993). Distorted distribution of nicotininamide-adenine dinucleotide phosphate-diaphorase neurons in temporal lobe of schizophrenics implies anomalous cortical development. *Archives of General Psychiatry, 50,* 178–187. (16)

Albee, G. W. (1986). Toward a just society: Lessons from observations on the primary prevention of psychopathology. *American Psychologist, 41,* 891–898. (15)

Aldag, R. J., & Fuller, S. R. (1993). Beyond fiasco: A reappraisal of the groupthink phenomenon and a new model of group decision processes. *Psychological Bulletin, 113,* 533–552. (14)

Aldrich, M. S. (1993). Narcolepsy. *Neurology, 42* (Suppl. 6), 34–43. (5)

Alexander, I. E. (1982). The Freud-Jung relationship—the other side of Oedipus and countertransference. *American Psychologist, 37,* 1009–1018. (13)

Alicke, M. D., & Largo, E. (1995). The role of the self in the false consensus effect. *Journal of Experimental Social Psychology, 31,* 28–47. (14)

Alliger, G. M., Lilienfeld, S. O., & Mitchell, K. E. (1996). The susceptibility of overt and covert integrity tests to coaching and faking. *Psychological Science, 7,* 32–39. (12)

Allison, S. T., Mackie, D. M., Muller, M. M., & Worth, L. T. (1993). Sequential correspondence biases and perceptions of change: The Castro studies revisited. *Personality and Social Psychology Bulletin, 19,* 151–157. (14)

Allport, G. W. (1935). Attitudes. In C. Murchison (Ed.), *A handbook of social psychology* (pp. 798–844). Worcester, MA: Clark University. (14)

Allport, G. W. (1961). *Pattern and growth in personality.* New York: Holt, Rinehart and Winston. (13)

Allport, G. W., & Odbert, H. S. (1936). Trait-names: A psycholexical study. *Psychological Monographs, 47* (Whole No. 211). (13)

Altarriba, J., & Mathis, K. M. (1997). Conceptual and lexical development in second language acquisition. *Journal of Memory and Language, 36,* 550–568. (8)

Amato, P. R., & Keith, B. (1991). Parental divorce and the well-being of children: A meta-analysis. *Psychological Bulletin, 110,* 26–46. (10)

American Medical Association. (1986). Council Report: Scientific status of refreshing recollection by the use of hypnosis. *International Journal of Clinical and Experimental Hypnosis, 34,* 1–12. (5)

American Psychiatric Association (1994). *Diagnostic and Statistical Manual of Mental Disorders* (4th ed.). Washington, DC: Author. (12, 15)

American Psychological Association. (1982). *Ethical principles in the conduct of research with human participants.* Washington, DC: Author. (2)

Amzica, F., & Steriade, M. (1996). Progressive cortical synchronization of ponto-geniculo-occipital potentials during rapid eye movement sleep. *Neuroscience, 72,* 309–314. (5)

Anastasi, A. (1988). *Psychological testing* (6th ed.). New York: Macmillan. (9)

Andersen, B. L. (1983). Primary orgasmic dysfunction: Diagnostic considerations and review of treatment. *Psychological Bulletin, 93,* 105–136. (11)

Andersen, B. L., Kiecolt-Glaser, J. K., & Glaser, R. (1994). A biobehavioral model of cancer stress and disease course. *American Psychologist, 49,* 389–404. (12)

Anderson, C. D., Warner, J. L., & Spencer, C. C. (1984). Inflation bias in self-assessment examinations: Implications for valid employee selection. *Journal of Applied Psychology, 69,* 574–580. (13)

Anderson, J. R. (1991). The adaptive nature of human categorization. *Psychological Review, 98,* 409–429. (8)

Andersson, U., Eckernäs, S. -Å., Hartvig, P., Ulin, J., Långström, B., & Hägström, J. -E. (1990). Striatal binding of ^{11}C-NMSP studied with positron emission tomography in patients with persistent tardive dyskinesia: No evidence for altered dopamine D_2 receptor binding. *Journal of Neural Transmission, 79,* 215–226. (16)

Andreasen, N. C., Arndt, S., Alliger, R., Miller, D., & Flaum, M. (1995). Symptoms of schizophrenia: Methods, meanings, and mechanisms. *Archives of General Psychiatry, 52,* 341–351. (16)

Andreasen, N. C., Flaum, M. Swayze, V. W., II, Tyrrell, G., & Arndt, S. (1990). Positive and negative symptoms in schizophrenia. *Archives of General Psychiatry, 47,* 615–621. (16)

Anglin, D., Spears, K. L., & Hutson, H. R. (1997). Flunitrazepam and its involvement in date or acquaintance rape. *Academy of Emergency Medicine, 4,* 323–326. (5)

Anisman, H., & Zacharko, R. M. (1983). Stress and neoplasia: Speculations and caveats. *Behavioral Medicine Update, 5,* 27–35. (12)

Anonymous. (1955). *Alcoholics anonymous* (2nd ed.). New York: Alcoholics Anonymous World Services. (16)

Appelbaum, P. S. (1988). The new preventive detention: Psychiatry's problematic responsibility for the control of violence. *American Journal of Psychiatry, 145,* 779–785. (15)

Appleby, L., Desai, P. N., Luchins, D. J., Gibbons, R. D., & Hedeker, D. R. (1993). Length of stay and recidivism in schizophrenia: A study of public psychiatric hospital patients. *American Journal of Psychiatry, 150,* 72–76. (15)

Appley, M. H. (1991). Motivation, equilibration, and stress. In R. Dienstbier (Ed.), *Nebraska Symposium on Motivation 1990* (pp. 1–67). Lincoln, NE: University of Nebraska Press. (11)

Arboleda, C., & Holzman, P. S. (1985). Thought disorder in children at risk for psychosis. *Archives of General Psychiatry, 42,* 1004–1013. (16)

Arkin, A. M., & Antrobus, J. S. (1978). The effects of external stimuli applied prior to and during sleep on sleep experience. In A. M. Arkin, J. S. Antrobus, & S. J. Ellman (Eds.), *The mind in sleep* (pp. 351–391). Hillsdale, NJ: Lawrence Erlbaum. (5)

Arndt, S., Andreasen, N. C., Flaum, M., Miller, D., & Nopoulos, P. (1995). A longitudinal study of symptom dimensions in schizophrenia. *Archives of General Psychiatry, 52,* 352–360. (16)

Arnett, J. (1990). Contraceptive use, sensation seeking, and adolescent egocentrism. *Journal of Youth and Adolescence, 19,* 171–180. (10)

Arnold, H. J., & House, R. J. (1980). Methodological and substantive extensions to the job characteristics model of motivtion. *Organizational Behavior and Human Performance, 25,* 161–183. (11)

Aronow, E., Reznikoff, M., & Moreland, K. L. (1995). The Rorschach: Projective technique or psychometric test? *Journal of Personality Assessment, 64,* 213–228. (13)

Aronson, E. (1997). The theory of cognitive dissonance: The evolution and vicissitudes of an idea. In C. McGarty & S. A. Haslam (Eds.), *The message of social psychology* (pp. 20–35). Cambridge, MA: Blackwell. (14)

Aronson, E., & Carlsmith, J. M. (1963). Effect of the severity of threat on the devaluation of forbidden behavior. *Journal of Abnormal and Social Psychology, 66,* 584–588. (14)

Arvey, R. D., and 51 others. (1994, December 13). Mainstream science on intelligence. *Wall Street Journal,* page A18. (9)

Asch, S. E. (1951). Effects of group pressure upon the modification and distortion of judgments. In H. Guetzkow (Ed.), *Groups, leadership, and men* (pp. 177–190). Pittsburgh, PA: Carnegie Press. (14)

Asch, S. E. (1955, November). Opinions and social pressure. *Scientific American, 193*(5), 31–35. (14)

Asch, S. E. (1956). Studies of independence and conformity: I. A minority of one against a unanimous majority. *Psychological Monographs, 70*(9, Whole no. 416). (14)

Ash, R. (1986, August). An anecdote submitted by Ron Ash. *The Industrial-Organizational Psychologist, 23*(4), 8. (6)

Atchley, R. C. (1980). *The social forces in later life* (3rd ed.). Belmont, CA: Wadsworth. (10)

Atkinson, J. W., & Birch, D. (1978). *Introduction to motivation* (2nd ed.). New York: D. Van Nostrand. (11)

Atkinson, R. C., & Shiffrin, R. M. (1968). Human memory: A proposed system and its control. In K. W. Spence & J. T. Spence (Eds.), *The psychology of learning and motivation* (Vol. 2, pp. 89–105). New York: Academic Press. (7)

Austin, J. T., & Vancouver, J. B. (1996). Goal constructs in psychology: Structure, process, and content. *Psychological Bulletin, 120,* 338–375. (11)

Averill, J. R. (1983). Studies on anger and aggression: Implications for theories of emotion. *American Psychologist, 38,* 1145–1160. (12)

Awh, E., Jonides, J., Smith, E. E., Schumacher, E. H., Koeppe, R. A., & Katz, S. (1996). Dissociation of storage and rehearsal in verbal working memory: Evidence from positron emission tomography. *Psychological Science, 7,* 25–31. (7)

Axelrod, R., & Dion, D. (1988). The further evolution of cooperation. *Science, 242,* 1385–1390. (14)

Azrin, N. H., & Nunn, R. G. (1973). Habit-reversal: A method of eliminating nervous habits and tics. *Behaviour Research and Therapy, 11,* 619–628. (6)

Baars, B. J., Fehling, M. R., LaPolla, M., & McGovern, K. (1997). Consciousness *creates access*: Conscious goal images recruit unconscious action routines, but goal competition serves to "liberate" such routines, causing predictable slips. In J. D. Cohen & J. W. Schooler (Eds.), *Scientific approaches to consciousness* (pp. 423–444). Mahwah, NJ: Lawrence Erlbaum Associates. (13)

Babcock, R. L. & Salthouse, T. A. (1990). Effects of increased processing demands on age differences in working memory. *Psychology & Aging, 5,* 421–428. (7)

Babich, F. R., Jacobson, A. L., Bubash, S., & Jacobson, A. (1965). Transfer of a response to naive rats by injection of ribonucleic acid extracted from trained rats. *Science, 149,* 656–657. (2)

Babkoff, H., Caspy, T., Mikulincer, M., & Sing, H. C. (1991). Monotonic and rhythmic influences: A challenge for sleep deprivation research. *Psychological Bulletin, 109,* 411–428. (5)

Bachrach, A. J., Erwin, W. J., & Mohr, J. P. (1965). The control of eating behavior in an anoretic by operant conditioning techniques. In L. P. Ullmann & L. Krasner (Eds.), *Case studies in behavior modification* (pp. 153–163). New York: Holt, Rinehart, & Winston. (11, 15)

Baddeley, A. D., & Hitch, G. (1974). Working memory. In G. H. Bower (Ed.), *Psychology of Learning and Motivation* (Vol. 8, pp. 47–89). New York: Academic Press. (7)

Baddeley, A. D., & Hitch, G. (1977). Recency re-examined. In S. Dornic (Ed.), *Attention and performance VI* (pp. 647–667). Hillsdale, NJ: Lawrence Erlbaum. (7)

Baddeley, A., & Hitch, G. J. (1994). Developments in the concept of working memory. *Neuropsychology, 8,* 485–493. (7)

Bahrick, H. (1984). Semantic memory content in permastore: 50 years of memory for Spanish learned in school. *Journal of Experimental Psychology: General, 113,* 1–29. (7)

Bahrick, H. P., Bahrick, L. E., Bahrick, A. S., & Bahrick, P. E. (1993). Maintenance of foreign language vocabulary and the spacing effect. *Psychological Science, 4,* 316–321. (7)

Bahrick, H. P., Hall, L. K., & Berger, S. A. (1996). Accuracy and distortion in memory for high school grades. *Psychological Science, 7,* 265–271. (8)

Bailey, J. M., & Pillard, R. C. (1991). A genetic study of male sexual orientation. *Archives of General Psychiatry, 48,* 1089–1096. (11)

Bailey, J. M., Pillard, R. C., Neale, M. C., & Agyei, Y. (1993) Heritable factors influence sexual orientation in women. *Archives of General Psychiatry, 50,* 217–223. (11).

Baillargeon, R. (1986). Representing the existence and the location of hidden objects: Object permanence in 6- and 8-month-old infants. *Cognition, 23,* 21–41. (10)

Baillargeon, R. (1987). Object permanence in 3½- and 4½-month-old infants. *Developmental Psychology, 23,* 655–664. (10)

Baird, J. C. (1982). The moon illusion: A reference theory. *Journal of Experimental Psychology: General, 111,* 304–315. (4)

Baker, G. H. B. (1987). Invited review: Psychological factors and immunity. *Journal of Psychosomatic Research, 31,* 1–10. (12)

Baker, T. B., & Tiffany, S. T. (1985). Morphine tolerance as habituation. *Psychological Bulletin, 92,* 78–108. (5)

Baker-Ward, L., Gordon, B. N., Ornstein, P. A., Larus, D. M., & Clubb, P. A. (1993)., Young children's long-term retention of a pediatric examination. *Child Development, 64,* 1519–1533. (7)

Baldessarini, R. J. (1984). Antipsychotic drugs. In T. B. Karasu (Ed.), *The psychiatric therapies. I. The somatic therapies* (pp. 119–170). Washington, DC: American Psychiatric Press. (16)

Ballinger, B., & Yalom, I. (1995). Group therapy in practice. In B. Bongar & L. E. Beutler (Eds.), *Comprehensive textbook of psychotherapy: Theory and practice* (pp. 189–204). Oxford, England: Oxford University Press. (15)

Balloun, K. D., & Holmes, D. S. (1979). Effects of repeated examinations on the ability to detect guilt with a polygraphic examination: A laboratory experiment with a real crime. *Journal of Applied Psychology, 64,* 316–322. (12)

Banaji, M. R., & Greenwald, A. G. (1994). Implicit stereotyping and prejudice. In M. P. Zanna & J. M. Olson (Eds.), *The psychology of prejudice: The Ontario Symposium Volume 7* (pp. 55–76). Hillsdale, NJ: Lawrence Erlbaum. (16)

Bandura, A. (1977). *Social learning theory.* Englewood Cliffs, NJ: Prentice-Hall. (6)

Bandura, A. (1986). *Social foundations of thought and action.* Englewood Cliffs, NJ: Prentice-Hall. (6)

Bandura, A., Ross, D., & Ross, S. A. (1963). Imitation of film-mediated aggressive models. *Journal of Abnormal and Social Psychology, 66,* 3–11. (6)

Baptista, L. F., & Petrinovich, L. (1984). Social interaction, sensitive phases and the song template hypothesis in the white-crowned sparrow. *Animal Behaviour, 32,* 172–181. (6)

Bard, P. (1934). On emotional expression after decortication with some remarks on certain theoretical views. *Psychological Review, 41,* 309–329. (12)

Baron, J. (1997). The illusion of morality as self-interest: A reason to cooperate in social dilemmas. *Psychological Science, 8,* 330–335. (14)

Baron, J., & Norman, M. F. (1992). SATs, achievement tests, and high-school class rank as predictors of college performance. *Educational and Psychological Measurement, 52,* 1047–1055. (9)

Barrett, G. V., & Depinet, R. L. (1991). A reconsideration of testing for competence rather than intelligence. *American Psychologist, 46,* 1012–1024. (9)

Barrick, M. R., & Mount, M. K. (1991). The big five personality dimensions and job performance: A meta-analysis. *Personnel Psychology, 44,* 1–26. (13)

Bartoshuk, L. M. (1991). Taste, smell, and pleasure. In R. C. Bolles (Ed.), *The hedonics of taste* (pp. 5–28). Hillsdale, NJ: Lawrence Erlbaum. (4)

Bashore, T. R., & Rapp, P. E. (1993). Are there alternatives to traditional polygraph procedures? *Psychological Bulletin, 113,* 3–22. (12)

Bass, B. M., & Ryterband, E. C. (1979). *Organizational psychology* (2nd ed.). Boston: Allyn & Bacon. (10)

Bassetti, C., & Aldrich, M. S. (1997). Idiopathic hypersomnia: A series of 42 patients. *Brain, 120,* 1423–1435. (5)

Bauer, P. J. (1996). What do infants recall of their lives? *American Psychologist, 51,* 29–41. (7)

Baumeister, R. F., & Leary, M. R. (1995). The need to belong: Desire for interpersonal attachments as a fundamental human motivation. *Psychological Bulletin, 117,* 497–529. (14)

Baumeister, R. F., Smart, L., & Boden, J. M. (1996). Relation of threatened egotism to violence and aggression: The dark side of high self-esteem. *Psychological Review, 103,* 5–33. (12)

Baumrind, D. (1971). Current patterns of parental authority. *Developmental Psychology Monographs, 4* (1, part 2). (10)

Beck, A. T. (1973). *The diagnosis and management of depression.* Philadelphia: University of Pennsylvania Press. (16)

Beck, A. T. (1976). *Cognitive therapy and the emotional disorders.* New York: New American Library. (15)

Beck, A. T. (1987). Cognitive models of depression. *Journal of Cognitive Psychotherapy: An International Quarterly, 1,* 5–37. (16)

Beck, A. T. (1991). Cognitive therapy: A 30-year retrospective. *American Psychologist, 46,* 368–375. (16)

Beck, A. T., & Emery, G. (1985). *Anxiety disorders and phobias.* New York: Basic books. (16)

Beck, A. T., & Steer, R. A. (1989). Clinical predictors of eventual suicide: A 5- to 10-year prospective study of suicide attempters. *Journal of Affective Disorders, 17,* 203–209. (16)

Beck, A. T., Steer, R. A., Beck, J. S., & Newman, C. F. (1993). Hopelessness, depression, suicidal ideation, and clinical diagnosis of depression. *Suicide and Life-Threatening Behavior, 23,* 139–145. (16)

Beck, A. T., Steer, R. A., & Brown, G. (1993). Dysfunctional attitudes and suicidal ideation in psychiatric outpatients. *Suicide and Life-Threatening Behavior, 23,* 11–20. (16)

Bellugi, U., Poizner, H., & Klima, E. S. (1983). Brain organization for language: Clues from sign aphasia. *Human Neurobiology, 2,* 155–170. (3)

Bellugi, U., Wang, P. P., & Jernigan, T. L. (1994). Williams syndrome: An unusual neuropsychological profile. In S. H. Broman & J. Grafman (Eds.), *Atypical cognitive deficits in developmental disorders* (pp. 23–56). Hillsdale, NJ: Lawrence Erlbaum. (2, 8)

Belmore, S. M. (1987). Determinants of attention during impression formation. *Journal of Experimental Psychology: Learning, Memory, and Cognition, 13,* 480–489. (14)

Belsky, J. (1996). Parent, infant, and social-contextual antecedents of father-son attachment security. *Developmental Psychology, 32,* 905–913. (10)

Bem, D. J., & Honorton, C. (1994). Does psi exist? Replicable evidence for an anomalous process of information transfer. *Psychological Bulletin, 115,* 4–18. (2)

Bem, S. L. (1974). The measurement of psychological androgyny. *Journal of Consulting and Clinical Psychology, 42,* 155–162. (13)

Bende, M., & Nordin, S. (1997). Perceptual learning in olfaction: Professional wine tasters versus controls. *Physiology & Behavior, 62,* 1065–1070. (4)

Benes, F. M. (1995). Is there a neuroanatomic basis for schizophrenia? An old question revisited. *The Neuroscientist, 1,* 104–115. (16)

Benjamin, J., Li, L., Patterson, C., Greenberg, B. D., Murphy, D. L., & Hamer, D. H. (1996). Population and familial association between the D4 dopamine receptor gene and measures of Novelty Seeking. *Nature Genetics, 12,* 81–84. (3, 13)

Bennett, W. (1980). The cigarette century. *Science 80, 1* (6), 36–43. (16)

Benowitz, N. L. (1986). The human pharmacology of nicotine. *Research Advances in Alcohol and Drug Problems, 9,* 1–52. (16)

Benson, H. (1977). Systemic hypertension and the relaxation response. *New England Journal of Medicine, 296,* 1152–1156. (12)

Benson, H. (1985). Stress, health, and the relaxation response. In W. D. Gentry, H. Benson, & C. J. de Wolff (Eds.), *Behavioral medicine: Work, stress and health* (pp. 15–32). Dordrecht, Netherlands: Martinus Nijhoff. (12)

Berger, R. J., & Phillips, N. H. (1995). Energy conservation and sleep. *Behavioural Brain Research, 69,* 65–73. (5)

Berglas, S., & Jones, E. E. (1978). Drug choice as a self-handicapping strategy in response to noncontingent success. *Journal of Personality and Social Psychology, 36,* 405–417. (14)

Berkow, R. (Ed.) (1987). *The Merck Manual* (15th ed.). Rahway, NJ: Merck Sharp & Dohme Research Laboratories. (11)

Berkowitz, L. (1983). Aversively stimulated aggression: Some parallels and differences in research with animals and humans. *American Psychologist, 38,* 1135–1144. (12)

Berkowitz, L. (1989). Frustration-aggression hypothesis: Examination and reformulation. *Psychological Bulletin, 106,* 59–73. (12)

Berlyne, D. E. (1981). Humanistic psychology as a protest movement. In J. R. Royce & L. P. Mos (Eds.), *Humanistic psychology: Concepts and criticisms* (pp. 261–293). New York: Plenum. (13)

Berman, K. F., Torrey, E. F., Daniel, D. G., & Weinberger, D. R. (1992). Regional cerebral blood flow in monozygotic twins discordant and concordant for schizophrenia. *Archives of General Psychiatry, 49,* 927–934. (16)

Bernhardt, P. C. (1997). Influences of serotonin and testosterone in aggression and dominance: Convergence with social psychology. *Current Directions in Psychological Science, 6,* 44–48. (12)

Berntson, G. G., Cacioppo, J. T., & Quigley, K. S. (1993). Cardiac psychophysiology and autonomic space in humans: Empirical perspectives and conceptual implications. *Psychological Bulletin, 114,* 296–322. (12)

Berridge, K. C., & Robinson, T. E. (1995). The mind of an addicted brain: Neural sensitization of wanting versus liking. *Current Directions in Psychological Science, 4,* 71–76. (6)

Berry, J. W., Poortinga, Y. H., Segal, H., & Dasen, P. R. (1992). *Cross-cultural psychology.* Cambridge, England: Cambridge University Press. (15)

Berscheid, E. (1983). Emotion. In H. H. Kelley, E. Berscheid, A. Christensen, J. H. Harvey, T. L. Huston, G. Levinger, E. McClintock, L. A. Peplau, & D. R. Peterson, *Close relationships* (pp. 110–168). New York: W. H. Freeman. (14)

Bettencourt, B. A., & Miller, N. (1996). Gender differences in aggression as a function of provocation: A meta-analysis. *Psychological Bulletin, 119,* 422–447. (2)

Bickman, L. (1996). A continuum of care: More is not always better. *American Psychologist, 51,* 689–701. (15)

Bijeljac-Babic, R., Biardeau, A., & Grainger, J. (1997). Masked orthographic priming in bilingual word recognition. *Memory & Cognition, 25,* 447–457. (8)

Billy, J. O. G., Tanfer, K., Grady, W. R., & Klepinger, D. H. (1993, March/April). The sexual behavior of men in the United States. *Family Planning Perspectives, 25,* 52–60. (11)

Binet, A., & Simon, T. (1905). Méthodes nouvelles pour le diagnostic du niveau intellectuel des anormaux [New methods for the measurement of the intellectual level of the abnormal]. *L'Année Psychologique, 11,* 191–244. (9)

Birnbaum, M. H., & Sotoodeh, Y. (1991). Measurement of stress: Scaling the magnitudes of life changes. *Psychological Science, 2,* 236–243. (12)

Black, D. W., Noyes, R., Jr., Goldstein, R. B., & Blum, N. (1992). A family study of obsessive-compulsive disorder. *Archives of General Psychiatry, 49,* 362–368. (16)

Blackwell, A., & Bates, E. (1995). Inducing agrammatic profiles in normals: Evidence for the selective vulnerability of morphology under cognitive resource limitation. *Journal of Cognitive Neuroscience, 7,* 228–257. (8)

Blaine, J. D., Prien, R. F., & Levine, J. (1983). The role of antidepressants in the treatment of affective disorders. *American Journal of Psychotherapy, 37,* 502–520. (16)

Blair, I. V., & Banaji, M. R. (1996). Automatic and controlled processes in stereotype priming. *Journal of Personality and Social Psychology, 70,* 1142–1163. (14)

Blakemore, C., & Sutton, P. (1969). Size adaptation: A new aftereffect. *Science, 166,* 245–247. (4)

Bleuler, E. (1950). *Dementia praecox, or the group of schizophrenias* (J. Zinkin, Trans.). New York: International Universities Press. (Original work published 1911) (16)

Block, J. (1995). A contrarian view of the five-factor approach to personality description. *Psychological Bulletin, 117,* 187–215. (13)

Bloom, J. D., & Faulkner, L. R. (1987). Competency determinations in civil commitment. *American Journal of Psychiatry, 144,* 193–196. (15)

Blum, D. (1994). *The monkey wars.* New York: Oxford University Press. (1)

Blum, G. S., & Barbour, J. S. (1979). Selective inattention to anxiety-linked stimuli. *Journal of Experimental Psychology: General, 108,* 182–224. (4)

Blum, K., Cull, J. G., Braverman, E. R., & Comings, D. E. (1996). Reward deficiency syndrome. *American Scientist, 84,* 132–145. (3, 13)

Blumenthal, S. J., & Kupfer, D. J. (1986). Generalizable treatment strategies for suicidal behavior. *Annals of the New York Academy of Sciences, 487,* 327–340. (16)

Bond, M. H. (1991). *Beyond the Chinese face.* New York: Oxford University Press. (15)

Bond, R., & Smith, P. B. (1996). Culture and conformity: A meta-analysis of studies using Asch's (1952b, 1956) line judgment task. *Psychological Bulletin, 119,* 111–137. (14)

Bonnet, M. H., & Arand, D. L. (1996). The consequences of a week of insomnia. *Sleep, 19,* 453–461. (5)

Bonnie, R. J. (1997). Research with cognitively impaired subjects: Unfinished business in the regulation of human research. *Archives of General Psychiatry, 54,* 105–111. (2)

Bonta, J., Law, M., & Hanson, K. (1998). The prediction of criminal and violent recidivism among mentally disordered offenders: A meta-analysis. *Psychological Bulletin, 123,* 123–142. (12)

Boring, E. G. (1930). A new ambiguous figure. *American Journal of Psychology, 42,* 444–445. (4)

Bornstein, R. F. (1989). Subliminal techniques as propaganda tools: Review and critique. *Journal of Mind and Behavior, 10,* 231–262. (4)

Borum, R. (1996). Improving the clinical practice of violence risk assessment: Technology, guidelines, and training. *American Psychologist, 51,* 945–956. (12)

Boswell, J. (1990). Sexual and ethical categories in premodern Europe. In D. P. McWhirter, S. A. Sanders, & J. M. Reinisch (Eds.), *Homosexuality/heterosexuality* (pp. 15–31). New York: Oxford University Press. (11)

Bouchard, T. J., Lykken, D. T., McGue, M., Segal, N. L., & Tellegen, A. (1990). Sources of psychological differences: The Minnesota study of twins reared apart. *Science, 250,* 223–228. (10)

Bouchard, T. J., Jr., & McGue, M. (1981). Familial studies of intelligence: A review. *Science, 212,* 1055–1059. (9)

Bourne, P. G. (1971). Altered adrenal function in two combat situations in Vietnam. In B. E. Eleftheriou & J. P. Scott (Eds.), *The physiology of aggression and defeat* (pp. 265–290). New York: Plenum. (12)

Bouton, M. E. (1994). Context, ambiguity, and classical conditioning. *Current Directions in Psychological Science, 3,* 49–53. (6)

Bower, G. (1994). Temporary emotional states act like multiple personalities. In R. M. Klein & B. K. Doane (Eds.), *Psychological concepts and dissociative disorders* (pp. 207–234). Hillsdale, NJ: Lawrence Erlbaum. (7)

Bowers, K. S., Regehr, G., Balthazard, C., & Parker, K. (1990). Intuition in the context of discovery. *Cognitive Psychology, 22,* 72–110. (8)

Bowmaker, J. K., & Dartnall, H. J. A. (1980). Visual pigments of rods and cones in a human retina. *Journal of Physiology* (London), 298, 501–511. (4)

Boynton, R. M. (1988). Color vision. *Annual Review of Psychology, 39,* 69–100. (4)

Bradbury, T. N., & Miller, G. A. (1985). Season of birth in schizophrenia: A review of evidence, methodology, and etiology. *Psychological Bulletin, 98,* 569–594. (16)

Brandt, S. A., & Stark, L. W. (1997). Spontaneous eye movements during visual imagery reflect the content of the visual scene. *Journal of Cognitive Neuroscience, 9,* 27–38. (8)

Brannon, L., & Feist, J. (1992). *Health psychology* (2nd ed.). Belmont, CA: Wadsworth. (12)

Bransford, J. D., & Johnson, M. K. (1972). Contextual prerequisites for understanding: Some investigations of comprehension and recall. *Journal of Verbal Learning and Verbal Behavior, 11,* 717–726. (7)

Bransford, J. D., & Stein, B. S. (1984). *The ideal problem solver*. New York: W. H. Freeman. (8)

Bratko, D., & MarušićI. (1997). Family study of the big five personality dimensions. *Personality and Individual Differences, 23*, 365–369. (13)

Bregman, A. S. (1981). Asking the "what for" question in auditory perception. In M. Kubovy & J. R. Pomerantz (Eds.), *Perceptual organization* (pp. 99–118). Hillsdale, NJ: Lawrence Erlbaum. (4)

Brent, D. A., Perper, J. A., Goldstein, C. E., Kolko, D. J., Allan, M. J., Allman, C. J., & Zelenak, J. P. (1988). Risk factors for adolescent suicide. *Archives of General Psychiatry, 45*, 581–588. (16)

Brockner, J., & Rubin, J. Z. (1985). *Entrapment in escalating conflicts*. New York: Springer-Verlag. (14)

Brody, N. (1997). Intelligence, schooling, and society. *American Psychologist, 52*, 1046–1050. (9)

Broks, P., Young, A. W., Maratos, E. J., Coffey, P. J., Calder, A. J., Isaac, D. L., Mayes, A. R., Hodges, J. R., Montaldi, D., Cezayirli, E., Roberts, N., & Hadley, D. (1998). Face processing impairments after encephalitis: Amygdala damage and recognition of fear. *Neuropsychologia, 36*, 59–70. (12)

Brooks, J. H., & Reddon, J. R. (1996). Serum testosterone in violent and nonviolent young offenders. *Journal of Clinical Psychology, 52*, 475–483. (12)

Brooks-Gunn, J., & Furstenberg, F. F., Jr. (1989). Adolescent sexual behavior. *American Psychologist, 44*, 249–257. (10)

Brophy, J. (1987). Socializing students' motivation to learn. *Advances in Motivation and Achievement, 5*, 181–210. (11)

Brower, K. J., & Anglin, M. D. (1987). Adolescent cocaine use: Epidemiology, risk factors, and prevention. *Journal of Drug Education, 17*, 163–180. (5)

Brown, G. W., Harris, T. O., & Hepworth, C. (1994). Life events and endogenous depression. *Archives of General Psychiatry, 51*, 525–534. (16)

Brown, J. (1977). *Mind, brain, and consciousness*. New York: Academic Press. (8)

Brown, J., Babor, T. F., Litt, M. D., & Kranzler, H. R. (1994). The Type A/Type B distinction. *Annals of the New York Academy of Sciences, 708*, 23–33. (16)

Brown, R. J., & Donderi, D. C. (1986). Dream content and reported well-being among recurrent dreamers, past-recurrent dreamers, and nonrecurrent dreamers. *Journal of Personality and Social Psychology, 50*, 612–623. (5)

Brownell, K. D., & Rodin, J. (1994). The dieting maelstrom: Is it possible and advisable to lose weight? *American Psychologist, 49*, 781–791. (11)

Bruch, H. (1980). Preconditions for the development of anorexia nervosa. *American Journal of Psychoanalysis, 40*, 169–172. (11)

Bruck, M., Cavanagh, P., & Ceci, S. J. (1991). Fortysomething: Recognizing faces at one's 25th reunion. *Memory & Cognition, 19*, 221–228. (4)

Bruner, J. S., & Potter, M. C. (1964). Interference in visual recognition. *Science, 144*, 424–425. (8)

Buck, L., & Axel, R. (1991). A novel multigene family may encode odorant receptors: A molecular basis for odor recognition. *Cell, 65*, 175–187. (4)

Buck, R. (1994). Social and emotional functions in facial expression and communication: the readout hypothesis. *Biological Psychology, 38*, 95–115. (12)

Burger, J. M. (1986). Increasing compliance by improving the deal: The that's-not-all technique. *Journal of Personality and Social Psychology, 51*, 277–283. (14)

Burke, K. C., Burke, J. D., Jr., Regier, D. A., & Rae, D. S. (1990). Age at onset of selected mental disorders in five community populations. *Archives of General Psychiatry, 47*, 511–518. (16)

Burns, M. O., & Seligman, M. E. P. (1989). Explanatory style across the life span: Evidence for stability over 52 years. *Journal of Personality and Social Psychology, 56*, 471–477. (16)

Burnstein, E., & Vinokur, A. (1973). Testing two classes of theories about group-induced shifts in individual choice. *Journal of Experimental Social Psychology, 9*, 123–137. (14)

Burnstein, E., & Vinokur, A. (1977). Persuasive arguments and social comparison as determinants of attitude polarization. *Journal of Experimental Social Psychology, 13*, 315–332. (14)

Burr, D. C., Morrone, M. C., & Ross, J. (1994). Selective suppression of the magnocellular visual pathway during saccadic eye movements. *Nature, 371*, 511–513. (8)

Burrows, G. D., McIntyre, I. M., Judd, F. K., & Norman, T. R. (1988, August). Clinical effects of serotonin reuptake inhibitors in the treatment of depressive illness. *Journal of Clinical Psychiatry, 49* (Suppl. 8), 18–22. (16)

Bushman, B. J. (1993). Human aggression while under the influence of alcohol and other drugs: An integrative research review. *Current Directions in Psychological Science, 2*, 148–152. (12)

Bushman, B. J., & Cooper, H. M. (1990). Effects of alcohol on human aggression: An integrative research review. *Psychological Bulletin, 107*, 341–354. (12)

Buss, D. M. (1994). The strategies of human mating. *American Scientist, 82*, 238–249. (3, 14)

Buss, D. M., Larsen, R. J., Westen, D., & Semmelroth, J. (1992). Sex differences in jealousy: Evolution, physiology, and psychology. *Psychological Science, 3*, 251–255. (14)

Butcher, J. N., Graham, J. R., Williams, C. L., & Ben-Porath, Y. S. (1990). *Development and use of the MMPI-2 content scales*. Minneapolis: University of Minnesota Press. (13)

Butzlaff, R. L., & Hooley, J. M. (1998). Expressed emotion and psychiatric relapse. *Archives of General Psychiatry, 55*, 547–552. (16)

Buunk, B. P., Angleitner, A., Oubaid, V., & Buss, D. M. (1996). Sex differences in jealousy in evolutionary and cultural perspective: Tests from the Netherlands, Germany, and the United States. *Psychological Science, 7*, 359–363. (14)

Cadoret, R., Troughton, E., & Woodworth, G. (1994). Evidence of heterogeneity of genetic effect in Iowa adoption studies. *Annals of the New York Academy of Sciences, 708*, 59–71. (16)

Cahalan, D. (1978). Subcultural differences in drinking behavior in U.S. national surveys and selected European studies. In P. E. Nathan, G. A. Marlatt, & T. Løberg (Eds.), *Alcoholism: New directions in behavioral research and treatment* (pp. 235–253). New York: Plenum. (16)

Cahill, L., Babinsky, R., Markowitsch, H. J., & McGaugh, J. L. (1995). The amygdala and emotional memory. *Nature, 377*, 295–296. (3)

Cahill, L., Prins, B., Weber, M., & McGaugh, J. L. (1994). b-Adrenergic activation and memory for emotional events. *Nature, 371*, 702–704. (7)

Camara, W. J. (1988). Reagan signs ban of polygraph testing for job applicants. *The Industrial-Organizational Psychologist, 26*, 39–41. (12)

Camara, W. J., & Schneider, D. L. (1994). Integrity tests: Facts and unresolved issues. *American Psychologist, 49*, 112–119. (12)

Cameron, P., Proctor, K., Coburn, W., & Forde, N. (1985). Sexual orientation and sexually transmitted disease. *Nebraska Medical Journal, 70*, 292–299. (11)

Campbell, S. S., & Tobler, I. (1984). Animal sleep: A review of sleep duration across phylogeny. *Neuroscience & Biobehavioral Reviews, 8*, 269–300. (5)

Campfield, L. A., Smith, F. J., Guisez, Y., Devos, R., & Burn, P. (1995). Recombinant mouse OB protein: Evidence for a peripheral signal linking adiposity and central neural networks. *Science, 269*, 546–552. (11)

Campion, M. A., & McClelland, C. L. (1991). Interdisciplinary examination of the costs and benefits of enlarged jobs: A job design quasi-experiment. *Journal of Applied Psychology, 76*, 186–198. (11)

Campion, M. A., & Thayer, P. W. (1985). Development and field evaluation of an interdisciplinary measure of job design. *Journal of Applied Psychology, 70,* 29–43. (1, 11)

Campion, M. A., & Thayer, P. W. (1989). How do you design a job? *Personnel Journal, 68,* 43–46. (1)

Campos, J. J., Bertenthal, B. I., & Kermoian, R. (1992). Early experience and emotional development. *Psychological Science, 3,* 61–64. (10)

Canetto, S. S., & Sakinofsky, I. (1998). The gender paradox in suicide. *Suicide and Life-Threatening Behavior, 28,* 1–23. (16)

Cannon, T. D., Zorilla, L. E., Shtasel, D., Gur, R. E., Gur, R. C., Marco, E. J., Moberg, P., & Price, R. A. (1994). Neuropsychological functioning in siblings discordant for schizophrenia and healthy volunteers. *Archives of General Psychiatry, 51,* 651–661. (16)

Cannon, W. B. (1927). The James-Lange theory of emotion. *American Journal of Psychology, 39,* 106–124. (12)

Cannon, W. B. (1929). Organization for physiological homeostasis. *Physiological Reviews, 9,* 399–431. (11)

Cantor, N., & Fleeson, W. (1994). Social intelligence and intelligent goal pursuit: A cognitive slice of motivation. In W. D. Spaulding (Ed.), *Integrative views of motivation, cognition, and emotion* (pp. 125–179). Lincoln, NE: University of Nebraska Press. (11)

Capaldi, E. D. (1996). Conditioned food preferences. In E. D. Capaldi (Ed.), *Why we eat what we eat* (pp. 53–80). Washington, DC: American Psychological Association. (11)

Carey, S. (1978). The child as word learner. In M. Halle, J. Bresnan, & G. A. Miller (Eds.), *Linguistic theory and psychological reality* (pp. 264–293). Cambridge, MA: MIT Press. (8)

Carlezon, W. A., Jr., & Wise, R. A. (1996). Rewarding actions of phencyclidine and related drugs in nucleus accumbens shell and frontal cortex. *Journal of Neuroscience, 16,* 3112–3122. (5)

Carpenter, P. A., Just, M. A., & Shell, P. (1990). What one intelligence test measures: A theoretical account of the processing in the Raven Progressive Matrices test. *Psychological Review, 97,* 404–431. (9)

Carpenter, W. T. (1995). Serotonin-dopamine antagonists and treatment of negative symptoms. *Journal of Clinical Psychopharmacology, 15,* Supplement 1, S30–S35. (16)

Carroll, B. J. (1980). Implications of biological research for the diagnosis of depression. In J. Mendlewicz (Ed.), *New advances in the diagnosis and treatment of depressive illness* (pp. 85–107). Amsterdam: Excerpta medica. (16)

Catania, J. A., Coates, T. J., Stall, R., Turner, H., Peterson, J., Hearst, N., Dolcini, M. M., Hudes, E., Gagnon, J., Wiley, J., & Groves, R. (1992). Prevalence of AIDS-related risk factors and condom use in the United States. *Science, 258,* 1101–1106. (11)

Caterina, M. J., Schumacher, M. A., Tominaga, M., Rosen, T. A., Levine, J. D., & Julius, D. (1997). The capsaicin receptor: A heat-activated ion channel in the pain pathway. *Nature, 389,* 816–824. (4)

Cattell, R. B. (1965). *The scientific analysis of personality.* Chicago: Aldine. (13)

Cattell, R. B. (1987). *Intelligence: Its structure, growth and action.* Amsterdam: North-Holland. (9)

Cavell, T. A., & Woehr, D. J. (1994). Predicting introductory psychology test scores: An engaging and useful topic. *Teaching of Psychology, 21,* 108–110. (2)

Ceci, S. J. (1995). False beliefs: Some developmental and clinical considerations. In D. L. Schacter (Ed.), *Memory distortion* (pp. 91–125). Cambridge, MA: Harvard University Press. (7, 13)

Ceci, S. J., & Bruck, M. (1993). Suggestibility of the child witness: A historical review and synthesis. *Psychological Bulletin, 113,* 403–439. (7)

Ceci, S. J., & Williams, W. M. (1997). Schooling, intelligence, and income. *American Psychologist, 52,* 1046–1050. (9)

Cepeda-Benito, A. (1993). Meta-analytical review of the efficacy of nicotine chewing gum in smoking treatment programs. *Journal of Consulting and Clinical Psychology, 61,* 822–830. (16)

Chakos, M. H., Ma, J., Alvir, J., Woerner, M. G., Koreen, A., Geisler, S., Mayerhoff, D., Sobel, S., Kane, J. M., Borenstein, M., & Lieberman, J. A. (1996). Incidence and correlates of tardive dyskinesia in first episode of schizophrenia. *Archives of General Psychiatry, 53,* 313–319. (16)

Chamberlin, J. (1978). *On our own.* New York: Hawthorn. (15)

Charlton, S. G. (1983). Differential conditionability: Reinforcing grooming in golden hamsters. *Animal Learning & Behavior, 11,* 27–34. (6)

Charness, N., & Gerchak, Y. (1996). Participation rates and maximal performance: A log-linear explanation for group differences, such as Russian and male dominance in chess. *Psychological Science, 7,* 46–51. (8)

Cheetham, E. (1973). *The prophecies of Nostradamus.* New York: Putnam's. (2)

Chehab, F. F., Mounzih, K., Lu, R., & Lim, M. E. (1997). Early onset of reproductive function in normal female mice treated with leptin. *Science, 275,* 88–90. (11)

Chen, C., Lee, S., & Stevenson, H. W. (1995). Response style and cross-cultural comparisons of rating scales among East Asian and North American students. *Psychological Science, 6,* 170–175. (14)

Cheng, A. T. A. (1995). Mental illness and suicide. *Archives of General Psychiatry, 52,* 594–603. (16)

Cherlin, A. J., Furstenberg, F. F., Jr., Chase-Lansdale, P. L., Kiernan, K. E., Robins, P. K., Morrison, D. R., & Teitler, J. O. (1991). Longitudinal studies of effects of divorce on children in Great Britain and the United States. *Science, 252,* 1386–1389. (10)

Chiodo, L. A., & Antelman, S. M. (1980). Electroconvulsive shock: Progressive dopamine autoreceptor subsensitivity independent of repeated treatment. *Science, 210,* 799–801. (16)

Chomsky, N. (1980). *Rules and representations.* New York: Columbia University Press. (8)

Chorney, M. J., Chorney, K., Seese, N., Owen, M. J., Daniels, J., McGuffin, P., Thompson, L. A., Detterman, D. K., Benbow, C., Lubinski, D., Eley, T., & Plomin, R. (1998). A quantitative trait locus associated with cognitive ability in children. *Psychological Science, 9,* 159–166. (9)

Chorpita, B. F., & Barlow, D. H. (1998). The development of anxiety: The role of control in the early environment. *Psychological Bulletin, 124,* 3–21. (16)

Christensen, A., & Jacobson, N. S. (1994). Who (or what) can do psychotherapy: The status and challenge of nonprofessional therapies. *Psychological Science, 5,* 8–14. (15)

Cialdini, R. B. (1993). *Influence: The Psychology of Persuasion* (Revised ed.). New York: William Morrow. (14)

Cialdini, R. B., Vincent, J. E., Lewis, S. K., Catalan, J., Wheeler, D., & Darby, B. L. (1975). Reciprocal concessions procedure for inducing compliance: The door-in-the-face technique. *Journal of Personality and Social Psychology, 31,* 206–215. (14)

Cioffi, D. (1991). Beyond attentional strategies: A cognitive-perceptual model of somatic interpretation. *Psychological Bulletin, 109,* 25–41. (12)

Clarkin, J. F., & Carpenter, D. (1995). Family therapy in historical perspective. In B. Bongar & L. E. Beutler (Eds.), *Comprehensive textbook of psychotherapy: Theory and practice* (pp. 205–227). Oxford, England: Oxford University Press. (15)

Clausen, J. A., & Gilens, M. (1990). Personality and labor force participation across the life course: A longitudinal study of women's careers. *Sociological Forum, 5,* 595–618. (11)

"Clinicopathologic conference." (1967). *Johns Hopkins Medical Journal, 120,* 186–199. (12)

Cloninger, C. R. (1994). Temperament and personality. *Current Opinion in Neurobiology, 4,* 266–273. (13)

Cloninger, C. R., Bohman, M., & Sigvardsson, S. (1981). Inheritance of alcohol abuse: Cross-fostering analysis of adopted men. *Archives of General Psychiatry, 38,* 861–868. (16)

Coccaro, E. F., & Kavoussi, R. J. (1997). Fluoxetine and impulsive aggressive behavior in personality-disordered subjects. *Archives of General Psychiatry, 54,* 1081–1088. (12)

Cocozza, J., Melick, M., & Steadman, H. (1978). Trends in violent crime among ex-mental patients. *Criminology, 16,* 317–334. (12)

Cohen, D. J., & Bennett, S. (1997). Why can't most people draw what they see? *Journal of Experimental Psychology: Human Perception and Performance, 23,* 609–621. (4)

Cohen, J. D., Noll, D. C., & Schneider, W. (1993). Functional magnetic resonance imaging: Overview and methods for psychological research. *Behavior Research Methods, Instruments, & Computers, 25,* 101–113. (3)

Cohen, J. D., & Schooler, J. W. (1997). Science and sentience: Some questions regarding the scientific investigation of consciousness. In J. D. Cohen & J. W. Schooler (Eds.), *Scientific approaches to consciousness* (pp. 3–10). Mahwah, NJ: Lawrence Erlbaum Associates. (5)

Cohen, L. G., Celnik, P., Pascual-Leone, A., Corwell, B., Faiz, L., Dambrosia, J., Honda, M., Sadato, N., Gerloff, C., Catalá, M. D., & Hallett, M. (1997). Functional relevance of cross-modal plasticity in blind humans. *Nature, 389,* 180–183. (3)

Cohen, N. J., Eichenbaum, H., Deacedo, B. S., & Corkin, S. (1985). Different memory systems underlying acquisition of procedural and declarative knowledge. *Annals of the New York Academy of Sciences, 444,* 54–71. (7)

Cohen, N. J., & Squire, L. R. (1980). Preserved learning and retention of pattern-analyzing skill in amnesia: Dissociation of knowing how and knowing that. *Science, 210,* 207–211. (7)

Cohen, S. (1996). Psychological stress, immunity, and upper respiratory infections. *Current Directions in Psychological Science, 5,* 86–90. (12)

Cohen, S., Lichtenstein, E., Prochaska, J. O., Rossi, J. S., Gritz, E. R., Carr, C. R., Orleans, C. T., Schoenbach, V. J., Biener, L., Abrams, D., DiClemente, C., Curry, S., Marlatt, G. A., Cummings, K. M., Emont, S. L., Giovino, G., & Ossip-Klein, D. (1989). Debunking myths about self-quitting: Evidence from 10 prospective studies of persons who attempt to quit smoking by themselves. *American Psychologist, 44,* 1355–1365. (16)

Cohen, S. L., & Cohen, R. (1985). The role of activity in spatial cognition. In R. Cohen (Ed.), *The development of spatial cognition* (pp. 199–223). Hillsdale, NJ: Lawrence Erlbaum. (8)

Coie, J. D., & Dodge, K. (1983). Continuities and change in children's social status: A five-year longitudinal study. *Merrill-Palmer Quarterly, 29,* 261–282. (10)

Cole, N. S. (1981). Bias in testing. *American Psychologist, 36,* 1067–1077. (9)

Collins, A. M., & Loftus, E. F. (1975). A spreading-activation theory of semantic processing. *Psychological Review, 82,* 407–428. (8)

Collins, A. M., & Quillian, M. R. (1969). Retrieval time from semantic memory. *Journal of Verbal Learning and Verbal Behavior, 8,* 240–247. (8)

Collins, A. M., & Quillian, M. R. (1970). Does category size affect categorization time? *Journal of Verbal Learning and Verbal Behavior, 9,* 432–438. (8)

Collins, N. L., & Miller, L. C. (1994). Self-disclosure and liking: A meta-analytic review. *Psychological Bulletin, 116,* 457–475. (14)

Collins, W. A., & Gunnar, M. R. (1990). Social and personality development. *Annual Review of Psychology, 41,* 387–416. (10)

Colvin, C. R., & Block, J. (1994). Do positive illusions foster mental health? An examination of the Taylor and Brown formulation. *Psychological Bulletin, 116,* 3–20. (12)

Colwill, R. M. (1993). An associative analysis of instrumental learning. *Current Directions in Psychological Science, 2,* 111–116. (6)

Comings, D. E., & Amromin, G. D. (1974). Autosomal dominant insensitivity to pain with hyperplastic myelinopathy and autosomal dominant indifference to pain. *Neurology, 24,* 838–848. (4)

Comstock, G., & Strasburger, V. C. (1990). Deceptive appearances: Television violence and aggressive behavior. Conference: Teens and television. *Journal of Adolescent Health Care, 11,* 31–44. (2)

Connine, C. M., Blasko, D. G., & Hall, M. (1991). Effects of subsequent sentence context in auditory word recognition: Temporal and linguistic constraints. *Journal of Memory and Language, 30,* 234–250. (8)

Considine, R. V., Sinha, M. K., Heiman, M. L., Kriauciunas, A., Stephens, T. W., Nyce, M. R., Ohannesian, J. P., Maarco, C. C., McKee, L. J., Bauer, T. L., & Caro, J. F. (1996). Serum immunoreactive-leptin concentrations in normal-weight and obese humans. *New England Journal of Medicine, 334,* 292–295. (11)

Constantinides, P. (1977). Ill at ease and sick at heart: Symbolic behavior in a Sudanese healing cult. In I. Wilson (ed.), *Symbols and sentiments* (pp. 61–84). New York: Academic Press. (15)

Consumer Reports. (1995, November). Mental health: Does therapy help? pp. 734–739. (15)

Coplan, J. D., Goetz, R., Klein, D. F., Papp, L. A., Fyer, A. J., Leibowitz, M. R., Davies, S. O., & Gorman, J. M. (1998). Plasma cortisol concentrations preceding lactate-induced panic. *Archives of General Psychiatry, 55,* 130–136. (16)

Corkin, S. (1984). Lasting consequences of bilateral medial temporal lobectomy: Clinical course and experimental findings in H. M. *Seminars in Neurology, 4,* 249–259. (7)

Costa, P. T., Jr., & McCrae, R. R. (1994). Set like plaster? Evidence for the stability of adult personality. In T. F. Heatherton & J. L. Weinberger (Eds.), *Can personality change?* (pp. 21–40). Washington, DC: American Psychological Association. (13)

Costa, P. T., Jr., McCrae, R. R., & Dye, D. A. (1991). Facet scales for agreeableness and conscientiousness: A revision of the NEO personality inventory. *Personality and Individual Differences, 12,* 887–898. (13)

Cowan, C. L., Thompson, W. C., & Ellsworth, P. C. (1984). The effects of death qualification on jurors' predisposition to convict and on the quality of deliberation. *Law and Human Behavior, 8,* 53–79. (14)

Cowan, N., Wood, N. L., Nugent, L. D., Treisman, M. (1997). There are two word-length effects in verbal short-term memory: Opposed effects of duration and complexity. *Psychological Science, 8,* 290–295. (7)

Cox, M. J., Owen, M. T., Henderson, V. K., & Margand, N. A. (1992). Prediction of infant-father and infant-mother attachment. *Developmental Psychology, 28,* 474–483. (10)

Craig, A. D., Bushnell, M. C., Zhang, E. -T., & Blomqvist, A. (1994). A thalamic nucleus specific for pain and temperature sensation. *Nature, 372,* 770–773. (4)

Craik, F. I. M., & Lockhart, R. S. (1972). Levels of processing: A framework for memory research. *Journal of Verbal Learning and Verbal Behavior, 11,* 671–684. (7)

Craik, F. I. M., & Watkins, M. J. (1973). The role of rehearsal in short-term memory. *Journal of Verbal Learning and Verbal Behavior, 12,* 599–607. (7)

Cramer, P. (1996). *Storytelling, narrative, and the Thematic Apperception Test.* New York: Guilford Press. (13)

Crammer, J. L. (1959). Water and sodium in two psychotics. *Lancet, 1*(7083), 1122–1126. (16)

Crews, D. J., & Landers, D. M. (1987). A meta-analytic review of aerobic fitness and reactivity to psychosocial stressors. *Medicine & Science in Sports & Exercise, 19,* S114–S120. (12)

Crews, F. (1996). The verdict on Freud. *Psychological Science, 7,* 63–68. (13)

Crocker, J., & Major, B. (1989). Social stigma and self-esteem: The self-protective properties of stigma. *Psychological Review, 96,* 608–630. (14)

Cross, C. K., & Hirschfeld, R. M. A. (1986). Psychosocial factors and suicidal behavior. *Annals of the New York Academy of Sciences, 487,* 77–89. (16)

Croyle, R. T., & Cooper, J. (1983). Dissonance arousal: Physiological evidence. *Journal of Personality and Social Psychology, 45,* 782–791. (14)

Culbertson, F. M. (1997). Depression and gender. *American Psychologist, 52,* 25–31. (16)

Cummings, J. L. (1995). Anatomic and behavioral aspects of frontal-subcortical circuits. *Annals of the New York Academy of Sciences, 769,* 1–13. (7)

Cummings, N. A. (1979). Turning bread into stones: Our modern antimiracle. *American Psychologist, 34,* 1119–1129. (16)

Curry, S., Marlatt, A., & Gordon, J. R. (1987). Abstinence violation effect: Validation of an attributional construct with smoking cessation. *Journal of Consulting and Clinical Psychology, 55,* 145–149. (6)

Czeisler, C. A., Johnson, M. P., Duffy, J. F., Brown, E. N., Ronda, J. M., & Kronauer, R. E. (1990). Exposure to bright light and darkness to treat physiologic maladaptation to night work. *New England Journal of Medicine, 322,* 1353–1359. (5)

Czeisler, C. A., Moore-Ede, M. C., & Coleman, R. M. (1982). Rotating shift work schedules that disrupt sleep are improved by applying circadian principles. *Science, 217,* 460–463. (5)

Dabbs, J. M., Jr., Carr, T. S., Frady, R. L., & Riad, J. K. (1995). Testosterone, crime, and misbehavior among 692 male prison inmates. *Personality and Individual Differences, 18,* 627–633. (12)

Dackis, C. A., Pottash, A. L. C., Annitto, W., & Gold, M. S. (1982). Persistence of urinary marijuana levels after supervised abstinence. *American Journal of Psychiatry, 139,* 1196–1198. (5)

Dadds, M. R., Bovbjerg, D. H., Redd, W. H., & Cutmore, T. R. H. (1997). Imagery in human classical conditioning. *Psychological Bulletin, 122,* 89–103. (6)

Dallenbach, K. M. (1951). A puzzle picture with a new principle of concealment. *American Journal of Psychology, 64,* 431–433. (4)

Daly, M., Wilson, M., & Weghorst, S. J. (1982). Male sexual jealousy. *Ethology & Sociobiology, 3,* 11–27. (11, 12)

Damaser, E. C., Shor, R. E., & Orne, M. E. (1963). Physiological effects during hypnotically requested emotions. *Psychosomatic Medicine, 25,* 334–343. (5)

Damasio, A. R. (1994). *Descartes' error: Emotion, reason, and the human brain.* New York: G. P. Putnam's Sons. (12)

Damasio, H., Grabowski, T., Frank, R., Galaburda, A. M., & Damasio, A. R. (1994). The return of Phineas Gage: The skull of a famous patient yields clues about the brain. *Science, 264,* 1102–1105. (12)

Damron-Rodriguez, J. (1991). Commentary: Multicultural aspects of aging in the U.S.: Implications for health and human services. *Journal of Cross-cultural Gerontology, 6,* 135–143. (10)

Daniel, M. H. (1997). Intelligence testing: Status and trends. *American Psychologist, 52,* 1038–1045. (9)

Darling, N., & Steinberg, L. (1993). Parenting style as context: An integrative model. *Psychological Bulletin, 113,* 487–496. (10)

Darlington, R. B., Royce, J. M., Snipper, A. S., Murray, H. W., & Lazar, I. (1980). Preschool programs and later school competence of children from low-income families. *Science, 208,* 202–204. (9)

Darwin, C. (1859). *On the origin of species by means of natural selection.* New York: D. Appleton. (1, 3)

Darwin, C. (1871). *The descent of man.* New York: D. Appleton. (6)

Darwin, C. (1965). *The expression of emotions in man and animals.* Chicago: University of Chicago Press. (Original work published 1872) (12)

Das, J. P. (1992). Beyond a unidimensional scale of merit. *Intelligence, 16,* 137–149. (9)

Davenport, D., & Foley, J. M. (1979). Fringe benefits of cataract surgery. *Science, 204,* 454–457. (4)

Davenport, W. H. (1977). Sex in cross-cultural perspective. In F. A. Beach (Ed.), *Human sexuality in four perspectives* (pp. 62–86). Baltimore: Johns Hopkins University Press. (11)

Davidson, D., Jergovic, D., Imami, Z., & Theodos, V. (1997). Monolingual and bilingual children's use of the mutual exclusivity constraint. *Journal of Child Language, 24,* 3–24. (8)

Davidson, R. S. (1966). Laboratory maintenance and learning of *Alligator mississippiensis. Psychological Reports, 19,* 595–601. (6)

Dawes, R. M., & Smith, T. L. (1985). Attitude and opinion measurement. In G. Lindzey & E. Aronson (Eds.), *Handbook of social psychology* (Vol. 1, pp. 509–566). New York: Random House. (14)

Dawson, D., & Reid, K. (1997). Fatigue, alcohol, and performance impairment. *Nature, 388,* 235. (5)

Day, R. H. (1972). Visual spatial illusions: A general explanation. *Science, 175,* 1335–1340. (4)

Day, W. F., Jr., & Moore, J. (1995). On certain relations between contemporary philosophy and radical behaviorism. In J. T. Todd & E. K. Morris (Eds.), *Modern perspectives on B. F. Skinner and contemporary behaviorism* (pp. 75–84). Westport, CT: Greenwood Press. (6)

Deacon, S., & Arendt, J. (1996). Adapting to phase shifts, II. Effects of melatonin and conflicting light treatment. *Physiology & Behavior, 59,* 675–682. (5)

Deacon, T. W. (1997). *The symbolic species.* New York: W. W. Norton. (8)

Deary, I. J., & Stough, C. (1996). Intelligence and inspection time. *American Psychologist, 51,* 599–608. (9)

DeCasper, A. J., & Fifer, W. P. (1980). Of human bonding: Newborns prefer their mothers' voices. *Science, 208,* 1174–1177. (10)

Deci, E. L. (1971). Effects of externally mediated rewards on intrinsic motivation. *Journal of Personality and Social Psychology, 18,* 105–115. (11)

Deese, J. (1959). On the prediction of occurrence of particular verbal intrusions in immediate recall. *Journal of Experimental Psychology, 58,* 17–22. (7)

de Groot, A. D. (1966). Perception and memory versus thought: Some old ideas and recent findings. In B. Kleinmuntz (Ed.), *Problem solving* (pp. 19–50). New York: Wiley. (8)

de Jesus Mari, J., & Streiner, D. L. (1994). An overview of family interventions and relapse on schizophrenia: Meta-analysis of research findings. *Psychological Medicine, 24,* 565–578. (16)

DeLoache, J. S. (1989). The development of representation in young children. *Advances in Child Development and Behavior, 22,* 1–39. (10)

DeLoache, J. S., Miller, K. F., & Rosengren, K. S. (1997). The credible shrinking room: Very young children's performance with symbolic and nonsymbolic relations. *Psychological Science, 8,* 308–313. (10)

DeLuise, M., Blackburn, G. L., & Flier, J. S. (1980). Reduced activity of the red-cell sodium-potassium pump in human obesity. *New England Journal of Medicine, 303,* 1017–1022. (11)

Dement, W. (1960). The effect of dream deprivation. *Science, 131,* 1705–1707. (5)

Dement, W. C. (1972). *Some must watch while some must sleep.* Stanford, CA: Stanford Alumni Association. (5)

Dement, W., & Kleitman, N. (1957a). Cyclic variations in EEG during sleep and their relation to eye movements, body motility, and dreaming. *Electroencephalography and Clinical Neurophysiology, 9,* 673–690. (5)

Dement, W., & Kleitman, N. (1957b). The relation of eye movements during sleep to dream activity: An objective method for the study of dreaming. *Journal of Experimental Psychology, 53,* 339–346. (5)

Dement, W., & Wolpert, E. A. (1958). The relation of eye movements, body motility, and external stimuli to dream content. *Journal of Experimental Psychology, 55,* 543–553. (5)

Dennett, D. C. (1991). *Consciousness explained.* Boston: Little, Brown. (1)

Denniston, J. C., Miller, R. R., & Matute, H. (1996). Biological significance as a determinant of cue competition. *Psychological Science, 7,* 325–331. (6)

Derogatis, L. (1986). Psychology in cancer medicine: A perspective and overview. *Journal of Consulting and Clinical Psychology, 54,* 632–638. (12)

Detterman, D. K. (1979). Detterman's laws of individual differences research. In R. J. Sternberg & D. K. Detterman (Eds.), *Human intelligence* (pp. 165–175). Norwood, NJ: Ablex. (9)

Detterman, D. K., & Thompson, L. A. (1997). What is so special about special education? *American Psychologist, 52,* 1082–1090. (9)

Deutsch, J. A., & Gonzalez, M. F. (1980). Gastric nutrient content signals satiety. *Behavioral and Neural Biology, 30,* 113–116. (11)

DeValois, R. L. (1965). Behavioral and electrophysiological studies of primate vision. In W. D. Neff (Ed.), *Contributions to sensory physiology* (Vol. 1, pp. 137–178). New York: Academic. (4)

Devane, W. A., Hanuš, L., Breuer, A., Pertwee, R. G., Stevenson, L. A., Griffin, G., Gibson, D., Mandelbaum, A., Etinger, A., & Mechoulam, R. (1992). Isolation and structure of a brain constituent that binds to the cannabinoid receptor. *Science, 258,* 1946–1949. (3, 5)

Devlin, B., Daniels, M., & Roeder, K. (1997). The heritability of IQ. *Nature, 388,* 468–471. (3, 9)

Devor, E. J., Abell, C. W., Hoffman, P. L., Tabakoff, B., & Cloninger, C. R. (1994). Platelet MAO activity in Type I and Type II alcoholism. *Annals of the New York Academy of Sciences, 708,* 119–128. (16)

Devor, M. (1996). Pain mechanisms. *The Neuroscientist, 2,* 233–244. (4)

deWolff, C. J. (1985). Stress and strain in the work environment: Does it lead to illness? In W. D. Gentry, H. Benson, & C. J. deWolff (Eds.), *Behavioral medicine: Work, stress, and health* (pp. 33–43). Dordrecht, Netherlands: Martinus Nijhoff. (12)

Diamond, M., & Sigmundson, H. K. (1997). Management of intersexuality: Guidelines for dealing with persons with ambiguous genitalia. *Archives of Pediatrics and Adolescent Medicine, 151,* 1046–1050. (11)

DiClemente, C. C. (1994). If behaviors change, can personality be far behind? In T. F. Heatherton & J. L. Weinberger (Eds.), *Can personality change?* (pp. 175–198). Washington, DC: American Psychological Association. (13)

Diener, E., & Diener, C. (1996). Most people are happy. *Psychological Science, 7,* 181–185. (12)

Dion, K. E., Berscheid, E., & Walster, E. (1972). What is beautiful is good. *Journal of Personality and Social Psychology, 24,* 285–290. (14)

diTomaso, E., Beltramo, M., & Piomelli, D. (1996). Brain cannabinoids in chocolate. *Nature, 382,* 677–678. (5)

Dixon, A., Ross, D., O'Malley, S. L. C., & Burke, T. (1994). Paternal investment inversely related to degree of extrapair paternity in the reed bunting. *Nature, 371,* 698–700. (3)

Dixon, N. F. (1981). *Preconscious processing.* New York: Wiley. (4)

Dobrzecka, C., Szwejkowska, G., & Konorski, J. (1966). Qualitative versus directional cues in two forms of differentiation. *Science, 153,* 87–89. (6)

Dole, V. P. (1980). Addictive behavior. *Scientific American, 243* (6), 138–154. (16)

Dollard, J., Miller, N. E., Doob, L. W., Mowrer, O. H., & Sears, R. R. (1939). *Frustration and aggression.* New Haven, CT: Yale University Press. (12)

Domhoff, G. W. (1996). *Finding meaning in dreams: A quantitative approach.* New York: Plenum Press. (5)

Dostoyevsky, F. (1960). *Notes from underground.* New York: E. P. Dutton & Co. (Original work published 1864) (11)

Dovidio, J. F., Evans, N., & Tyler, R. B. (1986). Racial stereotypes: The contents of their cognitive representations. *Journal of Experimental Social Psychology, 22,* 22–37. (14)

Drewnowski, A. (1996). The behavioral phenotype in human obesity. In E. D. Capaldi (Ed.), *Why we eat what we eat* (pp. 291–308). Washington, DC: American Psychological Association. (11)

Dryden, W., & DiGiuseppe, R. (1990). *A primer on rational-emotive therapy.* Champaign, IL: Research Press. (15)

Duke, M., & Nowicki, S., Jr. (1979). *Abnormal psychology: Perspectives on being different.* Monterey, CA: Brooks/Cole. (16)

Duman, R. S., Heninger, G. R., & Nestler, E. J. (1997). A molecular and cellular theory of depression. *Archives of General Psychiatry, 54,* 597–606. (16)

Duncan, J., Martens, S., & Ward, R. (1997). Restricted attentional capacity within but not between sensory modalities. *Nature, 387,* 808–810. (8)

Duncan, J., Ward, R., & Shapiro, K. (1994). Direct measurement of attentional dwell time in human vision. *Nature, 369,* 313–315. (8)

Dunne, M. P., Martin, N. G., Statham, D. J., Slutske, W. S., Dinwiddie, S. H., Bucholz, K. K., Madden, P. A. F., & Heath, A. C. (1997). Genetic and environmental contributions to variance in age at first sexual intercourse. *Psychological Science, 8,* 211–216. (3)

Durham, M. L. (1996). Civil commitment of the mentally ill: Research, policy, and practice. In B. D. Sales & S. A. Shah (Eds.), *Mental health and law* (pp. 17–40). Durham, NC: Carolina Academic Press. (15)

Eagly, A. H., & Crowley, M. (1986). Gender and helping behavior: A meta-analytic review of the social psychological literature. *Psychological Bulletin, 100,* 283–308. (10)

Eagly, A. H., Karau, S. J., & Makhigani, M. G. (1995). Gender and the effectiveness of leaders: A meta-analysis. *Psychological Bulletin, 117,* 125–145. (11)

Eagly, A. H., & Warren, R. (1976). Intelligence, comprehension, and opinion change. *Journal of Personality, 44,* 226–242. (14)

Earls, C. M. (1988). Aberrant sexual arousal in sexual offenders. *Annals of the New York Academy of Sciences, 528,* 41–48. (11)

Eaton, W. O., & Saudino, K. J. (1992). Prenatal activity level as a temperament dimension? Individual differences and developmental functions in fetal movement. *Infant Behavior & Development 15,* 57–70. (10)

Eaton, W. W., Anthony, J. C., Gallo, J., Cai, G., Tien, A., Romanoski, A., Lyketsos, C., & Chen, L. -S. (1997). Natural history of diagnostic interview schedule/DSM-IV major depression. *Archives of General Psychiatry, 54,* 993–999. (16)

Ebbinghaus, H. (1913). *Memory.* New York: Teachers College. (Original work published 1885) (7)

Ebstein, R. P., Novick, O., Umansky, R., Priel, B., Osher, Y., Blaine, D., Bennett, E. R., Nemanov, L., Katz, R. M., & Belmaker, R. H. (1996). Dopamine D4 receptor (*D4DR*) exon III polymorphism associated with the personality trait of Novelty Seeking. *Nature Genetics, 12,* 78–80. (13)

Edelman, B. (1981). Binge eating in normal weight and overweight individuals. *Psychological Reports, 49,* 739–746. (11)

Edney, J. H. (1979). The nuts game: A concise commons dilemma analog. *Environmental Psychology and Nonverbal Behavior, 3,* 252–254. (14)

Educational Testing Service (1994). *GRE 1994–95 guide.* Princeton, NJ: Author. (9)

Eibl-Eibesfeldt, I. (1973). *Der vorprogrammierte Mensch* [The preprogrammed human]. Vienna: Verlag Fritz Molden. (12)

Eibl-Eibesfeldt, I. (1974). *Love and hate.* New York: Schocken. (12)

Eich, E., Macaulay, D., Loewenstein, R. J., & Dihle, P. H. (1997). Memory, amnesia, and dissociative identity disorder. *Psychological Science, 8,* 417–422. (15)

Eikelboom, R., & Stewart, J. (1982). Conditioning of drug-induced physiological responses. *Psychological Review, 89,* 507–528. (6)

Eimas, P. D., Siqueland, E. R., Jusczyk, P., & Vigorito, J. (1971). Speech perception in infants. *Science, 171,* 303–306. (10)

Einstein, G. O., & Hunt, R. R. (1980). Levels of processing and organization: Additive effects of individual item and relational processing. *Journal of Experimental Psychology: Human Learning and Memory, 6,* 588–598. (7)

Eisenberger, R., & Cameron, J. (1996). Detrimental effects of reward: Reality or myth? *American Psychologist, 51,* 1153–1166. (11)

Ekman, P. (1992). Facial expressions of emotion: New findings, new questions. *Psychological Science, 3,* 34–38. (12)

Ekman, P. (1994). Strong evidence for universals in facial expressions: A reply to Russell's mistaken critique. *Psychological Science, 3,* 34–38. (12)

Ekman, P., & Davidson, R. J. (1993). Voluntary smiling changes regional brain activity. *Psychological Science, 4,* 342–345. (12)

Ekman, P., & Friesen, W. V. (1984). *Unmasking the face* (2nd ed.). Palo Alto, CA: Consulting Psychologists Press. (12)

El-Islam, M. F. (1982). Rehabilitation of schizophrenics by the extended family. *Acta Psychiatrica Scandinavica, 65,* 112–119. (16)

Elaad, E. (1990). Detection of guilty knowledge in real life criminal investigations. *Journal of Applied Psychology, 75,* 521–529. (12)

Elbert, T., Pantev, C., Wienbruch, C., Rockstroh, B., & Taub, E. (1995). Increased cortical representation of the fingers of the left hand in string players. *Science, 270,* 305–307. (3)

Elicker, J., Englund, M., & Sroufe, L. A. (1992). Predicting peer competence and peer relationships in childhood from early parent-child relationships. In R. D. Parke & G. W. Ladd (Eds.), *Family-peer relationships* (pp. 77–106). Hillsdale, NJ: Lawrence Erlbaum. (10)

Elkind, D. (1984). *All grown up and no place to go.* Reading, MA: Addison-Wesley. (10)

Ellenberger, H. F. (1972). The story of "Anna O": A critical review with new data. *Journal of the History of the Behavioral Sciences, 8,* 267–279. (13)

Elliott, C. (1997). Caring about risks: Are severely depressed patients competent to consent to research? *Archives of General Psychiatry, 54,* 113–116. (2)

Ellis, A. (1987). The impossibility of achieving consistently good mental health. *American Psychologist, 42,* 364–375. (15)

Ellis, A., & Harper, R. A. (1961). *A guide to rational living.* Englewood Cliffs, NJ: Prentice-Hall. (15)

Ellsworth, P. C. (1994). William James and emotion: Is a century of fame worth a century of misunderstanding? *Psychological Review, 101,* 222–229. (12)

Ellsworth, P. C., & Gross, S. R. (1994). Hardening of the attitudes: Americans' views on the death penalty. *Journal of Social Issues, 50* (2), 19–52. (14)

Ellsworth, P. C., & Ross, L. (1983, January). Public opinion and capital punishment: A close examination of the views of abolitionists and retentionists. *Crime & Delinquency, 29,* 116–169. (14)

Emery, C. E., Jr. (1997, November/December). UFO survey yields conflicting conclusions. *Skeptical Inquirer, 21,* 9. (2)

Emery, R. W. (1982). Interparental conflict and the children of discord and divorce. *Psychological Bulletin, 92,* 310–330. (10)

Emmons, R. A. (1991). Personal strivings, daily life events, and psychological and physical well-being. *Journal of Personality, 59,* 453–472. (13)

Erel, O., & Burman, B. (1995). Interrelatedness of marital relations and parent-child relations: A meta-analytic review. *Psychological Bulletin, 118,* 108–132. (10)

Erev, I., Wallsten, T. S., & Budescu, D. V. (1994). Simultaneous over- and underconfidence: The role of error in judgment processes. *Psychological Review, 101,* 519–527. (8)

Ericsson, K. A., & Charness, N. (1994). Expert performance: Its structure and acquisition. *American Psychologist, 49,* 725–747. (8)

Ericsson, K. A., Chase, W. G., & Falcon, S. (1980). Acquisition of a memory skill. *Science, 208,* 1181–1182. (7)

Ericsson, K. A., Krampe, R. T., & Tesch-Römer, C. (1993). The role of deliberate practice in the acquisition of expert performance. *Psychological Review, 100,* 363–406. (8)

Erikson, E. H. (1963). *Childhood and society* (2nd ed.). New York: Norton. (10)

Ernhart, C. B., Sokol, R. J., Martier, S., Moron, P., Nadler, D., Ager, J. W., & Wolf, A. (1987). Alcohol teratogenicity in the human: A detailed assessment of specificity, critical period, and threshold. *American Journal of Obstetrics and Gynecology, 156,* 33–39. (10)

Ernst, C., & Angst, J. (1983). *Birth order: Its influence on personality.* New York: Springer-Verlag. (10)

Eronen, M., Hakola, P., & Tiihonen, J. (1996). Mental disorders and homicidal behavior in Finland. *Archives of General Psychiatry, 53,* 497–501. (12)

Esterson, A. (1998). Jeffrey Masson and Freud's seduction theory: a new fable based on old myths. *History of the Human Sciences, 11,* 1–21. (13)

Esterson, A. (1993). *Seductive mirage.* Chicago: Open Court. (13)

Evans, G. W., Bullinger, M., & Hygge, S. (1998). Chronic noise exposure and physiological response: A prospective study of children living under environmental stress. *Psychological Science, 9,* 75–77. (12)

Everson, C. A. (1995). Functional consequences of sustained sleep deprivation in the rat. *Behavioural Brain Research, 69,* 43–54. (5)

Exner, J. E., Jr. (1986). *The Rorschach: A comprehensive system* (2nd ed.). New York: Wiley. (13)

Eysenck, H. J. (1952). The effects of psychotherapy: An evaluation. *Journal of Consulting Psychology, 16,* 319–324. (15)

Eysenck, H. J. (1992). Four ways five factors are *not* basic. *Personality and Individual Differences, 13,* 667–673. (13)

Faedda, G. L., Tondo, L., Teicher, M. H., Baldessarini, R. J., Gelbard, H. A., & Floris, G. F. (1993). Seasonal mood disorders: patterns of seasonal recurrence in mania and depression. *Archives of General Psychiatry, 50,* 17–23. (16)

Fairburn, C. G., Welch, S. L., Doll, H. A., Davies, B. A., & O'Connor, M. E. (1997). Risk factors for bulimia nervosa. *Archives of General Psychiatry, 54,* 509–517. (11)

Falk, J. R., Halmi, K. A., & Tryon, W. W. (1985). Activity measures in anorexia nervosa. *Archives of General Psychiatry, 42,* 811–814. (11)

Fallon, A. E., & Rozin, P. (1985). Sex differences in perceptions of desirable body shape. *Journal of Abnormal Psychology, 94,* 102–105. (11)

Fantz, R. L. (1963). Pattern vision in newborn infants. *Science, 140,* 296–297. (10)

Farah, M. J. (1990). *Visual agnosia.* Cambridge, MA: MIT Press. (3)

Farah, M. J. (1992). Is an object an object an object? Cognitive and neuropsychological investigations of domain specificity in visual object recognition. *Current Directions in Psychological Science, 1,* 164–169. (3, 4)

Faraone, S. V., Kremen, W. S., & Tsuang, M. T. (1990). Genetic transmission of major affective disorders: Quantitative models and linkage analyses. *Psychological Bulletin, 108,* 109–127. (16)

Farber, S. L. (1981). *Identical twins reared apart: A reanalysis.* New York: Basic Books. (9)

Farberman, R. K. (1997). Terminal illness and hastened death requests: The important role of the mental health professional. *Professional Psychology: Research and Practice, 28,* 544–547. (16)

Farmer, A. E., McGuffin, P., & Gottesman, I. I. (1987). Twin concordance for DSM-III schizophrenia. *Archives of General Psychiatry, 44,* 634–641. (16)

Farmer, H. (1983). Career and homemaking plans for high school youth. *Journal of Counseling Psychology, 30,* 40–45. (11)

Farmer, H. S. (1987). Female motivation and achievement: Implications for interventions. *Advances in Motivation and Achievement, 5,* 51–97. (11)

Farmer, H., & Bohn, M. (1970). Home-career conflict reduction and the level of career interest in women. *Journal of Counseling Psychology, 17,* 228–232. (11)

Fausto-Sterling, A. (1985). *Myths of gender.* New York: Basic Books. (2, 8)

Fawzy, F. I., Fawzy, N. W., Arndt, L. A., & Pasnau, R. O. (1995). Critical review of psychosocial interventions in cancer care. *Archives of General Psychiatry, 52,* 100–113. (12)

Fay, R. E., Turner, C. F., Klassen, A. D., & Gagnon, J. H. (1989). Prevalence and patterns of same-gender sexual contact among men. *Science, 243,* 338–348. (11)

Feeney, D. M. (1987). Human rights and animal welfare. *American Psychologist, 42,* 593–599. (2)

Fehrenbach, P. A., & Thelen, M. H. (1982). Behavioral approaches to the treatment of aggressive disorders. *Behavior Modification, 6,* 465–497. (12)

Feingold, A. (1988). Cognitive gender differences are disappearing. *American Psychologist, 43,* 95–103. (9)

Feingold, A. (1992a). Good-looking people are not what we think. *Psychological Bulletin, 111,* 304–341. (14)

Feingold, A. (1992b). Gender differences in mate selection preferences: A test of the parental investment model. *Psychological Bulletin, 112,* 125–139. (14)

Feingold, A., & Mazzella, R. (1998). Gender differences in body image are increasing. *Psychological Science, 9,* 190–195. (11)

Felthous, A. R. (1993). Substance abuse and the duty to protect. *Bulletin of the American Academy of Psychiatry and the Law, 21,* 419–426. (15)

Fenton, W. S., Mosher, L. R., Herrell, J. M., & Blyler, C. R. (1998). Randomized trial of general hospital and residential alternative care for patients with severe and persistent mental illness. *American Journal of Psychiatry, 155,* 516–522. (15)

Fernández-Dols, J. M., & Ruiz-Belda, M. -A. (1997). Spontaneous facial behavior during intense emotional episodes: Artistic truth and optical truth. In J. A. Russell & J. M. Fernández-Dols (Eds.), *The psychology of facial expression* (pp. 255–274). Cambridge, England: Cambridge University Press. (12)

Fernald, D. (1984). *The Hans legacy: A story of science.* Hillsdale, NJ: Lawrence Erlbaum. (2)

Fernandez, E., & Turk, D. C. (1992). Sensory and affective components of pain: Separation and synthesis. *Psychological Bulletin, 112,* 205–217. (4)

Festinger, L. (1957). *A theory of cognitive dissonance.* Stanford, CA: Stanford University Press. (14)

Festinger, L., & Carlsmith, J. M. (1959). Cognitive consequences of forced compliance. *Journal of Abnormal and Social Psychology, 58,* 203–210. (14)

Festinger, L., Schachter, S., & Back, K. (1950). *Social pressures in informal groups: A study of human factors in housing.* New York: Harper. (14)

Fichter, M. M., & Quadflieg, N. (1997). Six-year course of bulimia nervosa. *International Journal of Eating Disorders, 22,* 361–384. (11)

Fieve, R. R. (1975). *Moodswing.* New York: William Morrow. (16)

Finch, J. F., & Cialdini, R. B. (1989). Another indirect tactic of (self-) image imagement: Boosting. *Personality and Social Psychology Bulletin, 15,* 222–232. (14)

Fine, M. A., & Schwebel, A. I. (1987). An emergent explanation of differing racial reactions to single parenthood. *Journal of Divorce, 11,* 1–15. (10)

Fink, M. (1985). Convulsive therapy: Fifty years of progress. *Convulsive Therapy, 1,* 204–216. (16)

Fischhoff, B. (1975). Hindsight ≠ foresight: The effect of outcome knowledge on judgment under uncertainty. *Journal of Experimental Psychology: Human Perception and Performance, 1,* 288–299. (7)

Fischhoff, B. (1992). Giving advice: Decision theory perspectives on sexual assault. *American Psychologist, 47,* 577–588. (12)

Fisher, S., & Greenberg, R. P. (1977). *The scientific credibility of Freud's theories and therapy.* New York: Basic Books. (13)

Fitzgerald, R., & Ellsworth, P. C. (1984). Due process vs. crime control: Death qualification and jury attitudes. *Law and Human Behavior, 8,* 31–51. (14)

Flatz, G. (1987). Genetics of lactose digestion in humans. *Advances in Human Genetics, 16,* 1–77. (3)

Flavell, J. (1986). The development of children's knowledge about the appearance-reality distinction. *American Psychologist, 41,* 418–425. (10)

Fletcher, R., & Voke, J. (1985). *Defective colour vision.* Bristol, England: Adam Hilger. (4)

Flett, G. L., Vredenburg, K., & Krames, L. (1997). The continuity of depression in clinical and nonclinical samples. *Psychological Bulletin, 121,* 395–416. (16)

Flynn, J. R. (1984). The mean IQ of Americans: Massive gains 1932 to 1978. *Psychological Bulletin, 95,* 29–51. (9)

Flynn, J. R. (1987). Massive IQ gains in 14 nations: What IQ tests really measure. *Psychological Bulletin, 101,* 171–191. (9)

Foley, V. D. (1984). Family therapy. In R. J. Corini (Ed.), *Current psychotherapies* (3rd ed.) (pp. 447–490). Itasca, IL: F. E. Peacock Publishers. (15)

Fordham, S. (1988). Racelessness as a factor in Black students' school success: Pragmatic strategy or pyrrhic victory. *Harvard Educational Review, 58,* 54–84. (10)

Forer, B. R. (1949). The fallacy of personal validation: A classroom demonstration of gullibility. *Journal of Abnormal and Social Psychology, 44,* 118–123. (13)

Forman, R. F., & McCauley, C. (1986). Validity of the positive control polygraph test using the field practice model. *Journal of Applied Psychology, 71,* 691–698. (12)

Foster, W. Z. (1968). *History of the Communist Party of the United States.* New York: Greenwood Press. (16)

Fox, B. H. (1983). Current theory of psychogenic effects on cancer incidence and prognosis. *Journal of Psychosocial Oncology, 1,* 17–31. (12)

Francis, L. J., Brown, L. B., Lester, D., & Philipchalk, R. (1998). Happiness as stable extraversion: A cross-cultural examination of the reliability and validity of the Oxford Happiness Inventory among students in the U.K., U.S.A., Australia, and Canada. *Personality and Individual Differences, 24,* 167–171. (13)

Frankenhaeuser, M. (1980). Psychoneuroendocrine approaches to the study of stressful person-environment transactions. In H. Selye (Ed.), *Selye's guide to stress research* (pp. 46–70). New York: Van Nostrand Reinhold. (12)

Freedland, R. L., & Bertenthal, B. I. (1994). Developmental changes in interlimb coordination: Transition to hands-and-knees crawling. *Psychological Science, 5,* 26–32. (10)

Freedman, J. L., & Fraser, S. C. (1966). Compliance without pressure: The foot in the door technique. *Journal of Personality and Social Psychology, 4,* 195–202. (14)

French, A. R. (1988). The patterns of mammalian hibernation. *American Scientist, 76,* 568–575. (5)

Freud, S. (1925). An autobiographical study. In J. Strachey, A. Freud, A. Strachey, & A. Tyson (Eds.), *The standard edition of the complete psychological works of Sigmund Freud* (Vol. XX, pp. 7–70). London: Hogarth Press and the Institute of Psycho-Analysis. (13)

Freud, S. (1925). *Three contributions to the theory of sex* (A. A. Brill, Trans.). New York: Nervous and Mental Disease Pub. Co. (Original work published 1905) (13)

Freud, S. (1953). *The future of an illusion* (J. Strachey, Trans.). New York: Liveright. (Original work published 1927) (13)

Freud, S. (1955). *The interpretation of dreams* (J. Strachey, Trans.). New York: Basic Books. (Original work published 1900) (15)

Freud, S. (1963). *Dora: An analysis of a case of hysteria.* New York: Collier Books. (Original work published 1905). (13)

Frick, W. B. (1983). The symbolic growth experience. *Journal of Humanistic Psychology, 23*, 108–125. (13)

Friedman, M., & Rosenman, R. H. (1974). *Type-A behavior and your heart.* New York: Knopf. (12)

Friedman, M. A., & Brownell, K. D. (1996). A comprehensive treatment manual for the management of obesity. In V. B. Van Hasselt & M. Hersen (Eds.), *Sourcebook of Psychological Treatment Manuals for Adult Disorders* (pp. 375–422). New York: Plenum. (11)

Friedman, W. J., & Huttenlocher, J. (1997). Memory for the time of "60 minutes" stories and news events. *Journal of Experimental Psychology: Learning, Memory, and Cognition, 23*, 560–569. (7)

Frijda, N. H. (1988). The laws of emotion. *American Psychologist, 45*, 349–358. (12)

Fry, A. F., & Hale, S. (1996). Processing speed, working memory, and fluid intelligence: Evidence for a developmental cascade. *Psychological Science, 7*, 237–241. (9)

Fuller, R. K., & Roth, H. P. (1979). Disulfiram for the treatment of alcoholism: An evaluation in 128 men. *Annals of Internal Medicine, 90*, 901–904. (16)

Furukawa, T. (1997). Cultural distance and its relationship to psychological adjustment of international exchange students. *Psychiatry and Clinical Neurosciences, 51*, 87–91. (11)

Gabrieli, J. D. E., Cohen, N. J., & Corkin, S. (1988). The impaired learning of semantic knowledge following bilateral medial temporal-lobe resection. *Brain and Cognition, 7*, 157–177. (7)

Gaito, J. (1976). Molecular psychobiology of memory: Its appearance, contributions, and decline. *Physiological Psychology, 4*, 476–484. (2)

Galton, F. (1978). *Hereditary genius.* New York: St. Martin's. (Original work published 1869) (1, 9)

Garcia, J. (1990). Learning without memory. *Journal of Cognitive Neuroscience, 2*, 287–305. (6)

Garcia, J., Ervin, F. R., & Koelling, R. A. (1966). Learning with prolonged delay of reinforcement. *Psychonomic Science, 5*, 121–122. (6)

Garcia, J., & Koelling, R. A. (1966). Relation of cue to consequence in avoidance learning. *Psychonomic Science, 4*, 123–124. (6)

Garcia-Andrade, C., Wall, T. L., & Ehlers, C. L. (1997)., The firewater myth and response to alcohol in Mission Indians. *American Journal of Psychiatry, 154*, 983–988. (5)

Garcia Coll, C. T. (1990). Developmental outcome of minority infants: A process-oriented look into our beginnings. *Child Development, 61*, 270–289. (10)

Gardner, H. (1985). *Frames of mind.* New York: Basic Books. (9)

Gardner, H. (1993). *Creating minds.* New York: Basic books. (8)

Gardner, H. (1995). Why would anyone become an expert? *American Psychologist, 50*, 802–803. (8)

Gardner, M. (1978). Mathematical games. *Scientific American, 239*(5), 22–32. (8)

Gardner, M. (1994). Notes of a fringe watcher: The tragedies of false memories. *Skeptical Inquirer, 18*, 464–470. (7)

Gardner, R. A., & Gardner, B. T. (1969). Teaching sign language to a chimpanzee. *Science, 165*, 664–672. (8)

Gash, D. M., Zhang, Z., Ovadia, A., Cass, W. A., Yi, A., Simmerman, L., Russell, D., Martin, D., Lapchak, P. A., Collins, F., Hoffer, B. J., & Gerhardt, G. A. (1996). Functional recovery in parkinsonian monkeys treated with GDNF. *Nature, 380*, 252–255. (3)

Gawin, F. H. (1991). Cocaine addiction: Psychology and neurophysiology. *Science, 251*, 1580–1586. (5)

Gawin, F. H., & Kleber, H. D. (1986). Abstinence symptomatology and psychiatric diagnosis in cocaine abusers. *Archives of General Psychiatry, 43*, 107–113. (5)

Geiger, G., Lettvin, J. Y., & Zegarra-Moran, O. (1992). Task-determined strategies of visual process. *Cognitive Brain Research, 1*, 39–52. (8)

Gellhorn, E. (1970). The emotions and the ergotropic and trophotropic systems. *Psychologische Forschung, 34*, 48–94. (12)

Gelman, R. (1982). Accessing one-to-one correspondence: Still another paper about conservation. *British Journal of Psychology, 73*, 209–220. (10)

Gergen, K. J., Gulerce, A., Lock, A., & Misra, G. (1996). Psychological sciences in cultural conflict. *American Psychologist, 51*, 496–503. (1)

Gernsbacher, M. A. (1993). Less skilled readers have less efficient suppression mechanisms. *Psychological Science, 4*, 294–298. (8)

Gernsbacher, M. A., & Faust, M. E. (1991). The mechanism of suppression: A component of general comprehension skill. *Journal of Experimental Psychology: Learning, Memory, and Cognition, 17*, 245–262. (8)

Gerson, S. C., Plotkin, D. A., & Jarvik, L. F. (1988). Antidepressant drug studies, 1964 to 1986: Empirical evidence for aging patients. *Journal of Clinical Pharmacology, 8*, 311–322. (16)

Geschwind, N. (1970). The organization of language and the brain. *Science, 170*, 940–944. (3)

Gibson, J. J. (1968). What gives rise to the perception of movement? *Psychological Review, 75*, 335–346. (4)

Gick, M. L., & Holyoak, K. J. (1980). Analogical problem solving. *Cognitive Psychology, 12*, 306–355. (8)

Gick, M. L., & Holyoak, K. J. (1983). Schema induction and analogical transfer. *Cognitive Psychology, 15*, 1–38. (8)

Giebel, H. D. (1958). Visuelles Lernvermögen bei Einhufern [Visual learning capacity in hoofed animals]. *Zoologische Jahrbücher Abteilung für Allgemeine Zoologie, 67*, 487–520. (6)

Gilbreth, F. B. (1911). *Motion study.* London: Constable. (1, 11)

Gillham, J. E., Reivich, K. J., Jaycox, L. H., & Seligman, M. E. P. (1995). Prevention of depressive symptoms in schoolchildren: Two year follow-up. *Psychological Science, 6*, 343–351. (15)

Gilligan, C. (1977). In a different voice: Women's conceptions of self and morality. *Harvard Educational Review, 47*, 481–517. (10)

Gilligan, C. (1979). Woman's place in man's life cycle. *Harvard Educational Review, 49*, 431–446. (10)

Gilligan, C., & Attanucci, J. (1988). Two moral orientations: Gender differences and similarities. *Merrill-Palmer Quarterly, 34*, 223–237. (10)

Glantz, L. A., & Lewis, D. A. (1997). Reduction of synaptophysin immunoreactivity in the prefrontal cortex of subjects with schizophrenia. *Archives of General Psychiatry, 54*, 660–669. (16)

Glass, D. C., Singer, J. E., & Pennebaker, J. W. (1977). Behavioral and physiological effects of uncontrollable environmental events. In D. Stokols (Ed.), *Perspectives on environment and behavior* (pp. 131–151). New York: Plenum. (12)

Gleaves, D. H. (1996). The sociocognitive model of dissociative identity disorder: A reexamination of the evidence. *Psychological Bulletin, 120*, 42–59. (15)

Gobet, F., & Simon, H. A. (1996). The roles of recognition processes and look-ahead search in time-constrained expert problem solving. *Psychological Science, 7*, 52–55. (8)

Goldfried, M. R., & Wolfe, B. E. (1996). Psychotherapy practice and research: Repairing a strained alliance. *American Psychologist, 51*, 1007–1016. (15)

Goldin-Meadow, S., Alibali, M. W., & Church, R. B. (1993). Transitions in concept acquisition: Using the hand to read the mind. *Psychological Review, 100*, 279–297. (10)

Goldin-Meadow, S., McNeill, D., & Singleton, J. (1996). Silence is liberating: Removing the handcuffs on grammatical expression in the manual modality. *Psychological Review, 103*, 34–55. (8)

Goldin-Meadow, S., & Mylander, C. (1998). Spontaneous sign systems created by deaf children in two cultures. *Nature, 391*, 279–281. (8)

Goldman-Rakic, P. S. (1994). Specification of higher cortical functions. In S. H. Broman & J. Grafman (Eds.), *Atypical cognitive deficits in developmental disorders* (pp. 3–17). Hillsdale, NJ: Lawrence Erlbaum. (3)

Goldstein, E. B. (1989). *Sensation and perception* (3rd ed.). Belmont, CA: Wadsworth. (4)

Goldstein, M. D., Hopkins, J. R., & Strube, M. J. (1994). "The eye of the beholder": A classroom demonstration of observer bias. *Teaching of Psychology, 21,* 154–157. (2)

Goldstein, M. J. (1981). Family factors associated with schizophrenia and anorexia nervosa. *Journal of Youth and Adolescence, 10,* 385–405. (11)

Goldstein, R. B., Weissman, M. M., Adams, P. B., Horwath, E., Lish, J. D., Charney, D., Woods, S. W., Sobin, C., & Wickramaratne, P. J. (1994). Psychiatric disorders in relatives of probands with panic disorder and/or major depression. *Archives of General Psychiatry, 51,* 383–394. (16)

Goldston, S. E. (1986). Primary prevention. *American Psychologist, 41,* 453–460. (15)

Goodall, J. (1971). *In the shadow of man.* Boston: Houghton Mifflin. (2)

Goodenough, O. R., & Dawkins, R. (1994). The 'St Jude' mind virus. *Nature, 371,* 23–24. (14)

Goodman, G. S., Aman, C., & Hirschman, J. (1987). Child sexual and physical abuse: Children's testimony. In S. J. Ceci, M. P. Toglia, & D. F. Ross (Eds.), *Children's eyewitness testimony* (pp. 1–23). New York: Springer-Verlag. (7)

Goodwin, C. J. (1991). Misportraying Pavlov's apparatus. *American Journal of Psychology, 104,* 135–141. (6)

Gopnik, M., & Crago, M. B. (1991). Familial aggregation of a developmental language disorder. *Cognition, 39,* 1–50. (8)

Gottesman, I. I. (1991). *Schizophrenia genesis.* New York: W. H. Freeman. (16)

Gottesman, I. I., & Bertelson, A. (1989). Confirming unexpressed genotypes for schizophrenia. *Archives of General Psychiatry, 46,* 867–872. (16)

Graf, P., & Mandler, G. (1984). Activation makes words more accessible, but not necessarily more retrievable. *Journal of Verbal Learning and Verbal Behavior, 23,* 553–568. (7)

Green, D. J., & Gillette, R. (1982). Circadian rhythm of firing rate recorded from single cells in the rat suprachiasmatic brain slice. *Brain Research, 245,* 198–200. (5)

Green, D. M., & Swets, J. A. (1966). *Signal detection theory and psychophysics.* New York: Wiley. (4)

Greenfield, M. (November 17, 1997). The way it really was. *Newsweek,* page 104. (7)

Greenfield, P. M. (1997). You can't take it with you: Why ability assessments don't cross cultures. *American Psychologist, 52,* 1115–1124. (9)

Greeno, C. G., & Wing, R. R. (1994). Stress-induced eating. *Psychological Bulletin, 115,* 444–464. (11)

Greenwald, A. G., & Banaji, M. R. (1995). Implicit social cognition: Attitudes, self-esteem, and stereotypes. *Psychological Review, 102,* 4–27. (14)

Greenwald, A. G., & Draine, S. C. (1997). Do subliminal stimuli enter the brain unnoticed? Tests with a new method. In J. D. Cohen & J. W. Schooler (Eds.), *Scientific approaches to consciousness* (pp. 83–108). Mahwah, NJ: Lawrence Erlbaum Associates. (4)

Greenwald, A. G., Spangenberg, E. R., Pratkanis, A. R., & Eskanazi, J. (1991). Double-blind tests of subliminal self-help audiotapes. *Psychological Science, 2,* 119–122. (4)

Greist, J. H., Jefferson, J. W., Kobak, K. A., Katzelnick, D. J., & Serlin, R. C. (1995). Efficacy and tolerability of serotonin transport inhibitors in obsessive-compulsive disorder. *Archives of General Psychiatry, 52,* 53–60. (16)

Griffiths, M. D. (1990). The cognitive psychology of gambling. *Journal of Gambling Studies, 6,* 31–42. (8)

Griffiths, P. E. (1997). *What emotions really are.* Chicago, IL: University of Chicago Press. (12)

Grillon, C., & Ameli, R. (1998). Effects of threat of shock, shock electrode placement, and darkness on startle. *International Journal of Psychophysiology, 28,* 223–231. (12)

Grisso, T., & Tomkins, A. J. (1996). Communicating violence risk assessments. *American Psychologist, 51,* 928–930. (12)

Grossberg, S. (1997). Cortical dynamics of three-dimensional pictures. *Psychological Review, 104,* 618–658. (4)

Grossman, K., Grossman, K. E., Spangler, S., Suess, G., & Unzner, L. (1985). Maternal sensitivity and newborn attachment orientation responses as related to quality of attachment in Northern Germany. In I. Bretherton & E. Waters (Eds.), *Growing points of attachment theory. Monographs of the Society for Research in Child Development, 50* (1–2, Serial No. 209), 233–256. (10)

Grünbaum, A. (1986). Précis of *The Foundations of Psychoanalysis:* A philosophical critique. *Behavioral and Brain Sciences, 9,* 217–284. (13)

Guidotti, A., Ferrero, P., Fujimoto, M., Santi, R. M., & Costa, E. (1986). Studies on endogenous ligands (endocoids) for the benzodiazepine/beta carboline binding sites. *Advances in Biochemical Pharmacology, 41,* 137–148. (16)

Gusterson, H. (1992, May/June). Coming of age in a weapons lab. *The Sciences, 32,* 16–22. (10)

Gynther, M. D. (1989). MMPI comparisons of blacks and whites: A review and commentary. *Journal of Clinical Psychology, 45,* 878–883. (13)

Haarmeier, T., Thier, P., Repnow, M., & Petersen, D. (1997). False perception of motion in a patient who cannot compensate for eye movements. *Nature, 389,* 849–852. (4)

Hackman, J. R., & Lawler, E. E. III (1971). Employee reactions to job characteristics. *Journal of Applied Psychology, 55,* 259–286. (11)

Halaas, J. L., Gajiwala, K. S., Maffei, M., Cohen, S. L., Chait, B. T., Rabinowitz, D., Lallone, R. L., Burley, S. K., & Friedman, J. M. (1995). Weight-reducing effects of the plasma protein encoded by the *obese* gene. *Science, 269,* 543–546. (11)

Hale, S., Myerson, J., Rhee, S. H., Weiss, C. S., & Abrams, R. A. (1996). Selective interference with the maintenance of location information in working memory. *Neuropsychology, 10,* 228–240. (7)

Hall, C. S., & Van de Castle, R. L. (1966). *The content analysis of dreams.* New York: Appleton-Century-Crofts. (5)

Halpern, D. F. (1997). Sex differences in intelligence. *American Psychologist, 52,* 1091–1102. (9)

Hamann, S. B., & Squire, L. R. (1997). Intact perceptual memory in the absence of conscious memory. *Behavioral Neuroscience, 111,* 850–854. (7)

Hammen, C. (1991). Generation of stress in the course of unipolar depression. *Journal of Abnormal Psychology, 100,* 555–561. (16)

Hammond, W. R., & Yung, B. (1993). Minority student recruitment and retention practices among schools of professional psychology: A national survey and analysis. *Professional Psychology: Research and Practice, 24,* 3–12. (1)

Hannah, B. (1976). *Jung: His life and work.* New York: Putnam's. (13)

Harada, S., Agarwal, D. P. Goedde, H. W., Tagaki, S., & Ishikawa, B. (1982). Possible protective role against alcoholism for aldehyde dehydrogenase isozyme deficiency in Japan. *Lancet, ii,* 827. (16)

Hardin, G. (1968). The tragedy of the commons. *Science, 162,* 1243–1248. (14)

Harding, C. M., Brooks, G. W., Ashikaga, T., Straus, J. S., & Breier, A. (1987). The Vermont longitudinal study of persons with severe mental illness, II: Long-term outcome of subjects who retrospectively met DSM-III criteria for schizophrenia. *American Journal of Psychiatry, 144,* 727–735. (16)

Harkins, S. G., & Jackson, J. M. (1985). The role of evaluation in eliminating social loafing. *Journal of Personality and Social Psychology, 11,* 457–465. (14)

Harlow, H. F. (1958). The nature of love. *American Psychologist, 13,* 673–685. (10)

Harlow, H. F., & Harlow, M. K. (1965). The affectional systems. In A. M. Schrier, H. F. Harlow, & F. Stollnitz (Eds.), *Behavior of nonhuman primates* (Vol. 2, pp. 287–334). New York: Academic Press. (10)

Harlow, H. F., Harlow, M. K., & Meyer, D. R. (1950). Learning motivated by a manipulative drive. *Journal of Experimental Psychology, 40,* 228–234. (11)

Harlow, H. F., Harlow, M. K., & Suomi, S. J. (1971). From thought to therapy: Lessons from a primate laboratory. *American Scientist, 59,* 538–549. (10)

Harris, B. (1979). What ever happened to Little Albert? *American Psychologist, 34,* 151–160. (14)

Harris, G. T., & Rice, M. E. (1996). The science in phallometric measurement of male sexual interest. *Current Directions in Psychological Science, 5,* 156–160. (12)

Harris, J. R. (1995). Where is the child's environment? A group socialization theory of development. *Psychological Review, 102,* 458–489. (10, 13)

Harris, J. R. (1995). Where is the child's environment? A group socialization theory of development. *Psychological Review, 102,* 458–489. (13)

Harris, R. J., Schoen, L. M., & Hensley, D. L. (1992). A cross-cultural study of story memory. *Journal of Cross-Cultural Psychology, 23,* 133–147. (7)

Harris, T. (1967). *I'm OK—You're OK.* New York: Avon. (13)

Harrison, A. O., Wilson, M. N., Pine, C. J., Chan, S. Q., & Buriel, R. (1990). Family ecologies of ethnic minority children. *Child Development, 61,* 347–362. (10)

Hathaway, S. R., & McKinley, J. C. (1940). A multiphasic personality schedule (Minnesota): I. Construction of the schedule. *Journal of Psychology, 10,* 249–254. (13)

Hauri, P. (1982). *The sleep disorders.* Kalamazoo, MI: Upjohn. (5)

Hawkins, S. A., & Hastie, R. (1990). Biased judgments of past events after the outcomes are known. *Psychological Bulletin, 107,* 311–327. (7)

Hay, D., & Oken, D. (1977). The psychological stresses of intensive care unit nursing. In A. Monat & R. S. Lazarus (Eds.), *Stress and coping* (pp. 118–140). New York: Columbia University Press. (12)

Hayes, S. C., & Helby, E. (1996). Psychology's drug problem: Do we need a fix or should we just say no? *American Psychologist, 51,* 198–206. (1)

Hays, R. B. (1985). A longitudinal study of friendship development. *Journal of Personality and Social Psychology, 48,* 909–924. (14)

He, S., Cavanagh, P., & Intiligator, J. (1996). Attentional resolution and the locus of visual awareness. *Nature, 383,* 334–337. (4)

Healy, D., & Williams, J. M. G. (1988). Dysrhythmia, dysphoria, and depression: The interaction of learned helplessness and circadian dysrhythmia in the pathogenesis of depression. *Psychological Bulletin, 103,* 163–178. (16)

Heath, A. C., Neale, M. C., Kessler, R. C., Eaves, L. J., & Kendler, K. S. (1992). Evidence for genetic influences on personality from self-reports and informant ratings. *Journal of Personality and Social Psychology, 63,* 85–96. (13)

Heatherton, T. G., & Baumeister, R. F. (1991). Binge eating as escape from self-awareness. *Psychological Bulletin, 110,* 86–108. (11)

Heckhausen, H. (1984). Emergent achievement behavior: Some early developments. *Advances in Motivation and Achievement, 3,* 1–32. (11)

Heider, F. (1958). *The psychology of interpersonal relations.* New York: Wiley. (14)

Heilman, K. M. (1979). Neglect and related disorders. In K. M. Heilman & E. Valenstein (Eds.), *Clinical neuropsychology* (pp. 268–307). New York: Oxford University Press. (3)

Heine, S. J., & Lehman, D. R. (1997). Culture, dissonance, and self-affirmation. *Personality and Social Psychology Bulletin, 23,* 389–400. (14)

Heinrichs, R. W. (1993). Schizophrenia and the brain. *American Psychologist, 48,* 221–233. (16)

Heit, E. (1993). Modeling the effects of expectations on recognition memory. *Psychological Science, 4,* 244–251. (7)

Held, R., & Hein, A. (1963). Movement-produced stimulation in the development of visually guided behavior. *Journal of Comparative and Physiological Psychology, 56,* 872–876. (10)

Heller, M. A. (1989). Picture and pattern perception in the sighted and the blind: The advantage of the late blind. *Perception, 18,* 379–389. (4)

Helmes, E., & Reddon, J. R. (1993). A perspective on developments in assessing psychopathology: A critical review of the MMPI and MMPI-2. *Psychological Bulletin, 113,* 453–471. (13)

Helweg-Larsen, M., & Collins, B. E. (1997). A social psychological perspective on the role of knowledge about AIDS in AIDS prevention. *Current Directions in Psychological Science, 6,* 23–26. (15)

Helzer, J. E., Robins, L. N., & McEnvoy, L. (1987). Post-traumatic stress disorder in the general population. *New England Journal of Medicine, 317,* 1630–1634. (12)

Hendrick, C., & Hendrick, S. (1986). A theory and method of love. *Journal of Personality and Social Psychology, 50,* 392–402. (14)

Henry, R. M. (1983). The cognitive versus psychodynamic debate about morality. *Human Development, 26,* 173–179. (10)

Hergenhahn, B. R. (1992). *An introduction to the history of psychology* (2nd ed.). Belmont, CA: Wadsworth. (1)

Herkenham, M., Lynn, A. B., deCosta, B. R., & Richfield, E. K. (1991). Neuronal localization of cannabinoid receptors in the basal ganglia of the rat. *Brain Research, 547,* 267–274. (5)

Herkenham, M., Lynn, A. B., Little, M. D., Johnson, M. R., Melvin, L. S., deCosta, B. R., & Rice, K. C. (1990). Cannabinoid receptor localization in brain. *Proceedings of the National Academy of Sciences, 87,* 1932–1936. (5)

Herman, J., Roffwarg, H., & Tauber, E. S. (1968). Color and other perceptual qualities of REM and NREM sleep. *Psychophysiology, 5,* 223. (5)

Hernandez, L., Murzi, E., Schwartz, D. H., & Hoebel, B. G. (1992). Electrophysiological and neurochemical approach to a hierarchical feeding organization. In P. Bjorntorp & B. N. Brodoff (Eds.), *Obesity* (pp. 171–183). Philadelphia, PA: J. B. Lippincott. (11)

Herrnstein, R. J., & Murray, C. (1994). *The Bell Curve.* New York: Free press. (9)

Hess, T. M., Donley, J., & Vandermaas, M. O. (1989). Aging-related changes in the processing and retention of script information. *Experimental Aging Research, 15,* 89–96. (7)

Heszen-Niejodek, I. (1997). Coping style and its role in coping with stressful encounters. *European Psychologist, 2,* 342–351. (12)

Hetherington, E. M. (1989). Coping with family transitions. Winners, losers, and survivors. *Child Development, 60,* 1–14. (10)

Hetherington, E. M., Bridges, M., & Insabella, G. M. (1998). What matters? What does not? *American Psychologist, 53,* 167–184. (10)

Hetherington, E. M., Cox, M., & Cox, R. (1982). Effects of divorce on parents and children. In M. E. Lamb (Ed.), *Nontraditional families* (pp. 233–288). Hillsdale, NJ: Lawrence Erlbaum. (10)

Hetherington, E. M., Stanley-Hagan, M., & Anderson, E. R. (1989). Marital transitions: A child's perspective. *American Psychologist, 44,* 303–312. (10)

Hilgard, E. R. (1971). Hypnotic phenomena: The struggle for scientific acceptance. *American Scientist, 59,* 567–577. (5)

Hilgard, E. R. (1973). A neodissociation interpretation of pain reduction in hypnosis. *Psychological Review, 80,* 396–411. (5)

Hinton, G. (1979). Some demonstrations of the effects of structural descriptions in mental imagery. *Cognitive Science, 3,* 231–250. (8)

Hobson, J. A. (1992). Sleep and dreaming: Induction and mediation of REM sleep by cholinergic mechanisms. *Current Opinion in Neurobiology, 2,* 759–763. (5)

Hobson, J. A., & McCarley, R. W. (1977). The brain as a dream state generator: An activation-synthesis hypothesis of the dream process. *American Journal of Psychiatry, 134,* 1335–1348. (5)

Hobson, R. P. (1993). *Autism and the development of mind.* Hove, East Sussex, UK: Lawrence Erlbaum Associates. (10)

Hodgins, S., Mednick, S. A., Brennan, P. A., Schulsinger, F., & Engberg, M. (1996). Mental disorder and crime. *Archives of General Psychiatry, 53,* 489–496. (12)

Hoebel, B. G., & Hernandez, L. (1993). Basic neural mechanisms of feeding and weight regulation. In A. J. Stunkard & T. A. Wadden (Eds.), *Obesity: Theory and therapy* (2nd ed.) (pp. 43–62). New York: Raven Press. (11)

Hoffman, J. L. (1992). Supermelons? *Science, 255,* 65. (8)

Hoffman, L. W. (1989). Effects of maternal employment in the two-parent family. *American Psychologist, 44,* 283–292. (10)

Hoffman, R. E., Stopek, S., & Andreasen, N. C. (1986). A comparative study of manic vs. schizophrenic speech disorganization. *Archives of General Psychiatry, 43,* 831–838. (16)

Hogan, J., & Quigley, A. M. (1986). Physical standards for employment and the courts. *American Psychologist, 11,* 1193–1217. (9)

Hogan, R., Hogan, J., & Roberts, B. W. (1996). Personality measurement and employment decisions. *American Psychologist, 51,* 469–477. (13)

Hogan, R. A., & Kirchner, J. H. (1967). Preliminary report of the extinction of learned fears via short-term implosive therapy. *Journal of Abnormal Psychology, 72,* 106–109. (16)

Hoge, S. K., Sachs, G., Appelbaum, P. S., Greer, A., & Gordon, C. (1988). Limitations on psychiatrists' discretionary civil commitment authority by the Stone and dangerousness criteria. *Archives of General Psychiatry, 45,* 764–769. (15)

Hohmann, G. W. (1966). Some effects of spinal cord lesions on experienced emotional feelings. *Psychophysiology, 3,* 143–156. (12)

Holden, C. (1987). Is alcoholism treatment effective? *Science, 236,* 20–22. (16)

Hollis, K. L. (1997). Contemporary research on Pavlovian conditioning. *American Psychologist, 52,* 956–965. (6)

Hollister, J. M., Laing, P., & Mednick, S. A. (1996). Rhesus incompatibility as a risk factor for schizophrenia in male adults. *Archives of General Psychiatry, 53,* 19–24. (16)

Hollister, J. M., Mednick, S. A., Brennan, P., & Cannon, T. D. (1994). Impaired autonomic nervous system habituation in those at genetic risk for schizophrenia. *Archives of General Psychiatry, 51,* 552–558. (16)

Hollon, S. D., & Beck, A. T. (1979). Cognitive therapy of depression. In P. C. Kendall & S. D. Hollon (Eds.), *Cognitive-behavioral interventions* (pp. 153–203). New York: Academic Press. (15)

Hollon, S. D., Kendall, P. C., & Lumry, A. (1986). Specificity of depressogenic cognitions in clinical depression. *Journal of Abnormal Psychology, 95,* 52–59. (16)

Holmes, D. S. (1978). Projection as a defense mechanism. *Psychological Bulletin, 85,* 677–688. (13)

Holmes, D. S. (1984). Meditation and somatic arousal reduction: A review of the experimental evidence. *American Psychologist, 39,* 1–10. (5)

Holmes, D. S. (1990). The evidence for repression: An examination of sixty years of research. In J. L. Singer (Ed.), *Repression and dissociation* (pp. 85–102). New York: Wiley. (7, 13)

Holmes, T., & Rahe, R. (1967). The social readjustment rating scale. *Journal of Psychosomatic Research, 11,* 213–218. (12)

Holzman, P. S. (1988). A single dominant gene can account for eye tracking dysfunctions and schizophrenia in offspring of discordant twins. *Archives of General Psychiatry, 45,* 641–647. (16)

Hong, C. C., Potkin, S. G., Antrobus, J. S., Dow, B. M., Callaghan, G. M., & Gillin, J. C. (1997). REM sleep eye movement counts correlate with visual imagery in dreaming: A pilot study. *Psychophysiology, 34,* 377–381. (5)

Honzik, M. P. (1974). The development of intelligence. In B. B. Wolman (Ed.), *Handbook of general psychology* (pp. 644–655). Englewood Cliffs, NJ: Prentice-Hall. (9)

Horn, J. L. (1968). Organization of abilities and the development of intelligence. *Psychological Review, 75,* 242–259. (9)

Horn, J. L., & Donaldson, G. (1976). On the myth of intellectual decline in adulthood. *American Psychologist, 31,* 701–719. (9)

Horne, J. A., Brass, C. G., & Pettitt, A. N. (1980). Circadian performance differences between morning and evening 'types.' *Ergonomics, 23,* 29–36. (5)

Horne, J. A., & Minard, A. (1985). Sleep and sleepiness following a behaviorally "active" day. *Ergonomics, 28,* 567–575. (5)

Horvath, F. (1977). The effect of selected variables on interpretation of polygraph records. *Journal of Applied Psychology, 62,* 127–136. (12)

Horwitz, W. A., Kestenbaum, C., Person, E., & Jarvik, L. (1965). Identical twin—"idiot savants"—calendar calculators. *American Journal of Psychiatry, 121,* 1075–1079. (9)

Houts, A. C., Berman, J. S., & Abramson, H. (1994). Effectiveness of psychological and pharmacological treatments for nocturnal enuresis. *Journal of Consulting & Clinical Psychology, 62,* 737–745. (15)

Hovland, C. I., & Weiss, W. (1951). The influences of source credibility on communication effectiveness. *Public Opinion Quarterly, 15,* 635–650. (14)

Howard, K. I., Cornille, T. A., Lyons, J. S., Vessey, J. T., Lueger, R. J., & Saunders, S. M. (1996). Patterns of mental health service utilization. *Archives of General Psychiatry, 53,* 696–703. (1)

Howard, K. I., Kopta, S. M., Krause, M. S., & Orlinsky, D. E. (1986). The dose-effect relationship in psychotherapy. *American Psychologist, 41,* 159–164. (15)

Howe, M. L., & Courage, M. L. (1993). On resolving the enigma of infantile amnesia. *Psychological Bulletin, 113,* 305–326. (7)

Howe, M. L., & Courage, M. L. (1997). The emergence and early development of autobiographical memory. *Psychological Review, 104,* 499–523. (7)

Hoyt, M. F., & Austad, C. S. (1992). Psychotherapy in a staff model health maintenance organization: Providing and assuring quality care in the future. *Psychotherapy, 29,* 119–129. (15)

Hser, Y. -I., Anglin, M. D., & Powers, K. (1993). A 24-year follow-up of California narcotics addicts. *Archives of General Psychiatry, 50,* 577–584. (14)

Hubel, D. H., & Wiesel, T. N. (1968). Receptive fields and functional architecture of monkey striate cortex. *Journal of Physiology* (London), *195,* 215–243. (4)

Hudson, W. (1960). Pictorial depth perception in sub-cultural groups in Africa. *Journal of Social Psychology, 52,* 183–208. (4)

Huff, D. (1954). *How to lie with statistics.* New York: Norton. (2)

Hughes, H. C., Nozawa, G., & Kitterle, F. (1996). Global precedence, spatial frequency channels, and the statistics of natural images. *Journal of Cognitive Neuroscience, 8,* 197–230. (4)

Hughes, J., Smith, T. W., Kosterlitz, H. W., Fothergill, L. A., Morgan, B. A., & Morris, H. R. (1975). Identification of two related pentapeptides from the brain with potent opiate antagonist activity. *Nature, 258,* 577–579. (5)

Hull, C. L. (1932). The goal gradient hypothesis and maze learning. *Psychological Review, 39,* 25–43. (1)

Hull, C. L. (1943). *Principles of behavior: An introduction to behavior theory.* New York: D. Appleton. (1, 11)

Hultman, C. M., Öhman, A., Cnattingius, S., Wieselgren, I. -M., & Lindström, L. H. (1997). Prenatal and neonatal risk factors for schizophrenia. *British Journal of Psychiatry, 170,* 128–133. (16)

Humphrey, P. P. A., Hartig, P., & Hoyer, D. (1993). A proposed new nomenclature for 5-HT receptors. *Trends in Pharmacological Sciences, 14,* 233–236. (3)

Hunter, J. E. (1997). Needed: A ban on the significance test. *Psychological Science, 8,* 3–7. (2)

Hyman, R. (1994). Anomaly or artifact? Comments on Bem and Honorton. *Psychological Bulletin, 115,* 19–24. (2)

Iggo, A., & Andres, K. H. (1982). Morphology of cutaneous receptors. *Annual Review of Neuroscience, 5,* 1–31. (4)

Inhoff, A. W. (1989). Lexical access during eye fixations in sentence reading: Are word access codes used to integrate lexical information across interword fixations? *Journal of Memory and Language, 28,* 444–461. (8)

Inouye, S. T., & Kawamura, H. (1979). Persistence of circadian rhythmicity in a mammalian hypothalamic "island" containing the suprachiasmatic nucleus. *Proceedings of the National Academy of Sciences, U.S.A., 76,* 5962–5966. (5)

Isaacs, E. A., & Clark, H. H. (1987). References in conversation between experts and novices. *Journal of Experimental Psychology: General, 116,* 26–37. (1)

Isenberg, D. J. (1986). Group polarization: A critical review and meta-analysis. *Journal of Personality and Social Psychology, 50,* 1141–1151. (14)

Ivry, R. B., & Diener, H. C. (1991). Impaired velocity perception in patients with lesions of the cerebellum. *Journal of Cognitive Neuroscience, 3,* 355–366. (3)

Jacobs, B. L. (1987). How hallucinogenic drugs work. *American Scientist, 75,* 386–392. (5)

Jacobs, G. H. (1981). *Comparative color vision.* New York: Academic Press. (4)

Jacobs, K. M., Mark, G. P., & Scott, T. R. (1988). Taste responses in the nucleus tractus solitarius of sodium-deprived rats. *Journal of Physiology, 406,* 393–410. (11)

Jacobsen, F. M., Sack, D. A., Wehr, T. A., Rogers, S., & Rosenthal, N. E. (1987). Neuroendocrine 5-hydroxytryptophan in seasonal affective disorder. *Archives of General Psychiatry, 44,* 1086–1091. (16)

Jacobson, N. S., & Christensen, A. (1996). Studying the effectiveness of psychotherapy: How well can clinical trials do the job? *American Psychologist, 51,* 1031–1039. (15)

James, W. (1884). What is an emotion? *Mind, 9,* 188–205. (12)

James, W. (1890). *The principles of psychology.* New York: Henry Holt. (1)

Jamison, K. R. (1989). Mood disorders and patterns of creativity in British writers and artists. *Psychiatry: Interpersonal and Biological processes, 52,* 125–134. (16)

Janicak, P. G., Davis, J. M., Gibbons, R. D., Ericksen, S., Chang, S., & Gallagher, P. (1985). Efficacy of ECT: A meta-analysis. *American Journal of Psychiatry, 142,* 297–302. (16)

Janis, I. L. (1972). *Victims of groupthink.* Boston: Houghton Mifflin. (14)

Janis, I. L. (1983). Stress inoculation in health care. In D. Meichenbaum & M. E. Jaremko (Eds.), *Stress reduction and prevention* (pp. 67–99). New York: Plenum. (12)

Janis, I. L. (1985). Sources of error in strategic decision making. In J. M. Pennings and associates (Eds.), *Organizational strategy and change* (pp. 157–197). San Francisco: Jossey-Bass. (14)

Jaremko, M. E. (1983). Stress inoculation training for social anxiety, with emphasis on dating anxiety. In D. Meichenbaum & M. E. Jaremko (Eds.), *Stress reduction and prevention* (pp. 419–450). New York: Plenum. (12)

Jaskiw, G. E., & Weinberger, D. R. (1992) Dopamine and schizophrenia—a cortically corrective perspective. *Seminars in the Neurosciences, 4,* 179–188. (16)

Jensen, A. R. (1980). *Bias in mental testing.* New York: Free Press. (10)

Jéquier, E. (1987). Energy utilization in human obesity. *Annals of the New York Academy of Sciences, 499,* 73–83. (11)

John, O. P. (1990). The "big five" factor taxonomy: Dimensions of personality in the natural language and in questionnaires. In L. A. Pervin (Ed.), *Handbook of personality* (pp. 66–100). New York: Guilford Press. (13)

Johnson, M. K., Hashtroudi, S., & Lindsay, D. S. (1993). Source monitoring. *Psychological Bulletin, 114,* 3–28. (7)

Johnson, S. L., & Roberts, J. E. (1995). Life events and bipolar disorders: Implications from biological theories. *Psychological Bulletin, 117,* 434–449. (16)

Johnston, J. C., & McClelland, J. L. (1974). Perception of letters in words: Seek not and ye shall find. *Science, 184,* 1192–1194. (8)

Johnston, J. J. (1975). Sticking with first responses on multiple-choice exams: For better or for worse? *Teaching of Psychology, 2,* 178–179. (Preface)

Jones, E. E., & Goethals, G. R. (1972). Order effects in impression formation: Attribution context and the nature of the entity. In E. Jones, D. Kanouse, H. Kelley, R. Nisbett, S. Valins, & B. Wiener (Eds.), *Attribution: Perceiving the causes of behavior* (pp. 27–46). Morristown, NJ: General Learning Press. (14)

Jones, E. E., & Harris, V. A. (1967). The attribution of attitudes. *Journal of Experimental Social Psychology, 13,* 1–24. (14)

Jones, E. E., & Nisbett, R. E. (1972). The actor and the observer: Divergent perception of the causes of behavior. In E. Jones, D. Kanouse, H. Kelley, R. Nisbett, S. Valins, & B. Wiener (Eds.), *Attribution: Perceiving the causes of behavior* (pp. 79–94). Morristown, NJ: General Learning Press. (14)

Jones, R. A. (1987). Cigarettes, respiratory rate, and the relaxation paradox. *International Journal of the Addictions, 22,* 803–809. (5)

Jones, S. S., Collins, K., & Hong, H. -W. (1991). An audience effect on smile production in 10-month-old infants. *Psychological Science, 2,* 45–49. (12)

Jouvet, M., Michel, F., & Courjon, J. (1959). Sur un stade d'activité électrique cérébrale rapide au cours du sommeil physiologique [On a state of rapid electrical cerebral activity during physiological sleep]. *Comptes Rendus des Séances de la Société de Biologie, 153,* 1024–1028. (5)

Jung, C. G. (1965). *Memories, dreams, reflections* (A. Jaffe, Ed.). New York: Random House. (13)

Junginger, J., & Frame, C. L. (1985). Self-report of the frequency and phenomenology of verbal hallucinations. *Journal of Nervous and Mental Disease, 173,* 149–155. (16)

Jurkovic, G. J. (1980). The juvenile delinquent as a moral philosopher: A structural-developmental perspective. *Psychological Bulletin, 88,* 709–727. (10)

Jusczyk, P. W. (1985). The high-amplitude sucking technique as a methodological tool in speech perception research. In G. Gottlieb & N. A. Krasnegor (Eds.), *Measurement of audition and vision in the first year of postnatal life* (pp. 195–222). Norwood, NJ: Ablex. (10)

Juslin, P., & Olsson, H. (1997). Thurstonian and Brunswikian origins of uncertainty in judgment: A sampling model of confidence in sensory discrimination. *Psychological Review, 104,* 344–366. (8)

Just, M. A., & Carpenter, P. A. (1987). *The psychology of reading and language comprehension.* Boston: Allyn & Bacon. (8)

Kagan, J. (1989). Temperamental contributions to social behavior. *American Psychologist, 44,* 668–674. (10)

Kagan, J., Reznick, J. S., & Snidman, N. (1988). Biological bases of childhood shyness. *Science, 240,* 167–171. (10)

Kagan, J., & Snidman, N. (1991). Infant predictors of inhibited and uninhibited profiles. *Psychological Science, 2,* 40–44. (10)

Kahneman, D., & Tversky, A. (1973). On the psychology of prediction. *Psychological Review, 80,* 237–251. (8)

Kaiser, M. K., Jonides, J., & Alexander, J. (1986). Intuitive reasoning about abstract and familiar physics problems. *Memory & Cognition, 14,* 308–312. (8)

Kalat, J. W. (1983). Evolutionary thinking in the history of the comparative psychology of learning. *Neuroscience & Biobehavioral Reviews, 7,* 309–314. (1, 6)

Kales, A., Scharf, M. B., & Kales, J. D. (1978). Rebound insomnia: A new clinical syndrome. *Science, 201,* 1039–1041. (5)

Kales, A., Soldatos, C. R., Bixler, E. O., & Kales, J. D. (1983). Early morning insomnia with rapidly eliminated benzodiazepines. *Science, 220,* 95–97. (5)

Kalick, S. M., Zebrowitz, L. A., Langlois, J. H., & Johnson, R. M. (1998). Does human facial attractiveness honestly advertise health? *Psychological Science, 9,* 8–13. (14)

Kamin, L. J. (1969). Predictability, surprise, attention, and conditioning. In B. A. Campbell & R. M. Church (Eds.), *Punishment and aversive behavior* (pp. 279–296). New York: Appleton-Century-Crofts. (6)

Kamin, L. J. (1974). *The science and politics of IQ.* New York: Wiley. (9)

Kanizsa, G. (1979). *Organization in vision.* New York: Praeger. (4)

Kanizsa, G. (1985). Seeing and thinking. *Acta Psychologia, 59,* 23–33. (4)

Kanner, A. D., Coyne, J. C., Schaefer, C., & Lazarus, R. S. (1981). Comparison of two modes of stress measurement: Daily hassles and uplifts versus major life events. *Journal of Behavioral Medicine, 4,* 1–39. (12)

Kaplan, E. H. (1988). Crisis? A brief critique of Masters, Johnson and Kolodny. *Journal of Sex Research, 25,* 317–322. (11)

Karau, S. J., & Williams, K. D. (1993). Social loafing: A meta-analytic review and theoretical integration. *Journal of Personality and Social Psychology, 65,* 681–706. (14)

Karau, S. J., & Williams, K. D. (1995). Social loafing: Research findings, implications, and future directions. *Current Directions in Psychological Science, 4,* 134–140. (14)

Karney, B. R., & Bradbury, T. N. (1995). The longitudinal course of marital quality and stability: A review of theory, method, and research. *Psychological Review, 118,* 3–34. (14)

Karno, M., Golding, J. M., Sorenson, S. B., & Burnam, A. (1988). The epidemiology of obsessive-compulsive disorder in five U.S. communities. *Archives of General Psychiatry, 45,* 1094–1099. (16)

Karon, B. P. (1995). Provision of psychotherapy under managed health care: A growing crisis and national nightmare. *Professional Psychology: Research and Practice, 26,* 5–9. (15)

Karon, B. P., & Widener, A. J. (1995). Psychodynamic therapies in historical perspective: "Nothing human do I consider alien to me." In B. Bongar & L. E. Beutler (Eds.), *Comprehensive textbook of psychotherapy: Theory and practice* (pp. 24–47). Oxford, England: Oxford University Press. (15)

Karpov, Y. V., & Haywood, H. C. (1998). Two ways to elaborate Vygotsky's concept of mediation. *American Psychologist, 53,* 27–36. (10)

Karrer, T., & Bartoshuk, L. (1991). Capsaicin desensitization and recovery on the human tongue. *Physiology & Behavior, 49,* 757–764. (4)

Katerndahl, D. A. (1993). Panic and prolapse: Meta-analysis. *Journal of Nervous and Mental Disease, 181,* 539–544. (16)

Kaufman, L., & Rock, I. (1989). The moon illusion thirty years later. In M. Hershenson (Ed.), *The moon illusion* (pp. 193–234). Hillsdale, NJ: Lawrence Erlbaum. (4)

Kazdin, A. E. (1995). Methods of psychotherapy research. In B. Bongar & L. E. Beutler (Eds.), *Comprehensive textbook of psychotherapy: Theory and practice* (pp. 405–433). Oxford, England: Oxford University Press. (15)

Keane, T. M., Wolfe, J., & Taylor, K. L. (1987). Post-traumatic stress disorder: Evidence for diagnostic validity and methods of psychological assessment. *Journal of Clinical Psychology, 43,* 32–43. (12)

Keefe, R. S. E., Silverman, J. M., Mohs, R. C., Siever, L. J., Harvey, P. D., Friedman, L., Roitman, S. E. L., DuPre, R. L., Smith, C. J., Schmeidler, J., & Davis, K. L. (1997). Eye tracking, attention, and schizotypal symptoms in nonpsychotic relatives of patients with schizophrenia. *Archives of General Psychiatry, 54,* 169–176. (16)

Keele, S. W., & Ivry, R. B. (1990). Does the cerebellum provide a common computation for diverse tasks? *Annals of the New York Academy of Sciences, 608,* 179–207. (3)

Kellar, K. J., & Stockmeier, C. A. (1986). Effects of electroconvulsive shock and serotonin axon lesions on beta-adrenergic and serotonin-2 receptors in rat brain. *Annals of the New York Academy of Sciences, 462,* 76–90. (16)

Kelley, H. H. (1967). Attribution theory in social psychology. In D. Levine (Ed.), *Nebraska symposium on motivation* (Vol. 15, pp. 192–238). Lincoln, NE: University of Nebraska Press. (14)

Keltner, D., & Buswell, B. N. (1997). Embarrassment: Its distinct form and appeasement functions. *Psychological Bulletin, 122,* 250–270. (12)

Keltner, D., & Robinson, R. J. (1996). Extremism, power, and the imagined basis of social conflict. *Current Directions in Psychological Science, 5,* 101–105. (14)

Kendell, R. W., & Kemp, I. W. (1989). Maternal influenza in the etiology of schizophrenia. *Archives of General Psychiatry, 46,* 878–882. (16)

Kendler, K. S., Gallagher, T. J., Abelson, J. M., & Kessler, R. C. (1996). Lifetime prevalence, demographic risk factors, and diagnostic validity of nonaffective psychosis as assessed in a U.S. community sample. *Archives of General Psychiatry, 53,* 1022–1031. (16)

Kendler, K. S., Gruenberg, A. M., & Tsuang, M. T. (1985). Subtype stability in schizophrenia. *American Journal of Psychiatry, 142,* 827–832. (16)

Kendler, K. S., Heath, A. C., Neale, M. C., Kessler, R. C., & Eaves, L. J. (1993). Alcoholism and major depression in women. *Archives of General Psychiatry, 50,* 690–698. (16)

Kendler, K. S., Neale, M. D., Kessler, R. C., Heath, A. C., & Eaves, L. J. (1992). Major depression and generalized anxiety disorder. *Archives of General Psychiatry, 49,* 716–722. (14)

Kendler, K. S., Walters, E. E., Neale, M. C., Kessler, R. C., Heath, A. C., & Eaves, L. J. (1995). The structure of the genetic and environmental risk factors for six major psychiatric disorders in women. *Archives of General Psychiatry, 52,* 374–383. (14)

Kenrick, D. T. (1994). Evolutionary social psychology: From sexual selection to social cognition. *Advances in Experimental Social Psychology, 26,* 75–121. (14)

Kenrick, D. T., & Trost, M. R. (1989). A reproductive exchange model of heterosexual relationships. In C. Hendick (Ed.), *Close relationships* (pp. 92–118). Newbury Park, CA: Sage. (14)

Keon, T. L., & McDonald, B. (1982). Job satisfaction and life satisfaction: An empirical evaluation of their interrelationship. *Human Relations, 35,* 167–180. (10)

Keppel, G., & Underwood, B. J. (1962). Proactive inhibition in short-term retention of single items. *Journal of Verbal Learning and Verbal Behavior, 1,* 153–161. (7)

Kerr, N. L., MacCoun, R. J., & Kramer, G. P. (1996). Bias in judgment: Comparing individuals and groups. *Psychological Review, 103,* 687–719. (14)

Kessler, R. C., Downey, G., Milafsky, J. R., & Stipp, H. (1988). Clustering of teenage suicides after television news stories about suicides: A reconsideration. *American Journal of Psychiatry, 145,* 1379–1383. (15)

Kessler, R. C., McGonagle, K. A., Zhao, S., Nelson, C. B., Hughes, E., Eshleman, S., Wittchen, H. -U., & Kendler, K. S. (1994). Lifetime and 12-month prevalence of *DSM-III-R* psychiatric disorders in the United States. *Archives of General Psychiatry, 51,* 8–19. (15)

Kety, S. S., Wendler, P. H., Jacobsen, B., Ingraham, L. J., Jansson, L., Faber, B., & Kinney, D. K. (1994). Mental illness in the biological and adoptive relatives of schizophrenic adoptees. *Archives of General Psychiatry, 51,* 442–455. (16)

Khalid, R. (1991). Personality and academic achievement: A thematic apperception perspective. *British Journal of Projective Psychology, 36,* 25–34. (11)

Kihlstrom, J. F. (1979). Hypnosis and psychopathology: Retrospect and prospect. *Journal of Abnormal Psychology, 88,* 459–473. (5)

Kihlstrom, J. F., Barnhardt, T. M., & Tataryn, D. J. (1992). The psychological unconscious. *American Psychologist, 47,* 788–791. (8)

Kim, K. H. S., Relkin, N. R., Lee, K. -M., & Hirsch, J. (1997). Distinct cortical areas associated with native and second language. *Nature, 388,* 171–174. (8)

Kimble, D. P. (1990). Functional effects of neural grafting in the mammalian central nervous system. *Psychological Bulletin, 108,* 462–479. (3)

Kim, S. (1989). *Inversions*. San Francisco, CA: W. H. Freeman. (4)

Kimble, G. A. (1961). *Hilgard and Marquis' Conditioning and Learning* (2nd ed.). New York: Appleton-Century-Crofts. (6)

Kimble, G. A. (1993). A modest proposal for a minor revolution in the language of psychology. *Psychological Science, 4,* 253–255. (6)

Kimble, G. A., & Garmezy, N. (1968). *Principles of general psychology* (3rd ed.). New York: Ronald. (13)

King, M. L. Jr. (1964, November 13). Speech at Duke University, Durham, NC. (10)

Kinsey, A. C., Pomeroy, W. B., & Martin, C. E. (1948). *Sexual behavior in the human male*. Philadelphia: W. B. Saunders. (11)

Kinsey, A. C., Pomeroy, W. B., Martin, C. E., & Gebhard, P. H. (1953). *Sexual behavior in the human female*. Philadelphia: W. B. Saunders. (11)

Kirsch, I., & Lynn, S. J. (1998). Dissociation theories of hypnosis. *Psychological Bulletin, 123,* 100–115. (5)

Klayman, J., & Ha, Y. -W. (1987). Confirmation, disconfirmation, and information in hypothesis testing. *Psychological Review, 94,* 211–228. (8)

Klein, D. F. (1993). False suffocation alarms, spontaneous panics, and related conditions. *Archives of General Psychiatry, 50,* 306–317. (16)

Klein, R. G., Abikoff, H., Klass, E., Ganeles, D., Seese, L. M., & Pollack, S. (1997). Clinical efficacy of methylphenidate in conduct disorder with and without attention deficit hyperactivity disorder. *Archives of General Psychiatry, 54,* 1073–1080. (12)

Kleinknecht, R. A. (1982). The origins and remission of fear in a group of tarantula enthusiasts. *Behaviour Research & Therapy, 20,* 437–443. (14)

Kleinmuntz, B., & Szucko, J. J. (1984). A field study of the fallibility of polygraphic lie detection. *Nature, 308,* 449–450. (12)

Kleitman, N. (1963). *Sleep and wakefulness* (revised and enlarged edition). Chicago: University of Chicago Press. (5)

Kline, M., Tschann, J. M., Johnston, J. R., & Wallerstein, J. S. (1989). Children's adjustment in joint and sole physical custody families. *Developmental Psychology, 25,* 430–438. (10)

Klopfer, D. S. (1996). Stroop interference and color-word similarity. *Psychological Science, 7,* 150–157. (8)

Kohlberg, L. (1969). Stage and sequence: The cognitive-developmental approach to socialization. In D. A. Goslin (Ed.), *Handbook of socialization theory and research*. Chicago: Rand McNally (10)

Kohlberg, L., & Hersh, R. H. (1977). Moral development: A review of the theory. *Theory into Practice, 16,* 53–59. (10)

Kolb, B., Cote, S., Ribeiro-da-Silva, A., & Cuello, A. C. (1997). Nerve growth factor treatment prevents dendritic atrophy and promotes recovery of function after cortical injury. *Neuroscience, 76,* 1139–1151. (3)

Koob, G. F., & LeMoal, M. (1997). Drug abuse: Hedonic homeostatic dysregulation. *Science, 278,* 52–58. (16)

Koocher, G. P., Goodman, G. S., White, C. S., Friedrich, W. N., Sivan, A. B., & Reynolds, C. R. (1995). Psychological science and the use of anatomically detailed dolls in child sexual-abuse assessments. *Psychological Bulletin, 118,* 199–222. (13)

Kopp, C. B. (1990). Risks in infancy: Appraising the research. *Merrill-Palmer Quarterly, 36,* 117–139. (10)

Koppenaal, R. J. (1963). Time changes in the strengths of A-B, A-C lists: Spontaneous recovery? *Journal of Verbal Learning and Verbal Behavior, 2,* 310–319. (7)

Korff, K. K. (1997, July/August). What *really* happened at Roswell. *Skeptical Inquirer, 21,* 24–30. (7)

Koss, M. P., & Butcher, J. N. (1986). Research on brief psychotherapy. In S. L. Garfield & A. E. Bergin (Eds.), *Handbook of psychotherapy and behavior change* (pp. 627–670). New York: Wiley. (15)

Koss, M. P., & Dinero, T. E. (1988). Predictors of sexual aggression among a national sample of male college students. *Annals of the New York Academy of Sciences, 528,* 133–147. (12)

Koss, M. P., Gidycz, C. A., & Wisniewski, N. (1987). The scope of rape: Incidence and prevalence of sexual aggression and victimization in a national sample of higher education students. *Journal of Consulting and Clinical Psychology, 55,* 162–170. (12)

Kosslyn, S. M. (1988). Aspects of a cognitive neuroscience of mental imagery. *Science, 240,* 1621–1626. (8)

Kosten, T. R., Rounsaville, B. J., & Kleber, H. D. (1987). A 2. 5-year follow-up of cocaine use among treated opioid addicts. *Archives of General Psychiatry, 44,* 281–284. (16)

Koyano, W. (1991). Japanese attitudes toward the elderly: A review of research findings. *Journal of Cross-cultural Gerontology, 4,* 335–345. (10)

Kozel, N. J., & Adams, E. H. (1986). Epidemiology of drug abuse: An overview. *Science, 234,* 970–974. (5)

Kozlowski, L. T., Frecker, R. C., Khouw, V., & Pope, M. A. (1980). The misuse of "less hazardous" cigarettes and its detection: Hole blocking of ventilated filters. *American Journal of Public Health, 70,* 1202–1203. (16)

Kraut, R. E., & Johnston, R. E. (1979). Social and emotional messages of smiling: An ethological approach. *Journal of Personality and Social Psychology, 37,* 1539–1553. (12)

Kreskin. (1991). *Secrets of the amazing Kreskin*. Buffalo, NY: Prometheus. (2)

Kringlen, E., & Cramer, G. (1989). Offspring of monozygotic twins discordant for schizophrenia. *Archives of General Psychiatry, 46,* 873–877. (16)

Krueger, B., & Neff, J. (1995, January 29). As killer dies, 2 women find diverging paths to peace. *News & Observer* (Raleigh, NC), pp. 1A, 4A. (12)

Krueger, D. W. (1978). The differential diagnosis of proverb interpretation. In W. E. Fann, I. Karacan, A. D. Pokorny, & R. L. Williams (Eds.), *Phenomenology and treatment of schizophrenia* (pp. 193–201). New York: Spectrum. (16)

Krug, S. E. (1978). Reliability and scope in personality assessment: A comparison of the Cattell and Eysenck inventories. *Multivariate Experimental Clinical Research, 3,* 195–204. (13)

Kruglanski, A. W. (1970). Attributing trustworthiness in supervisor-worker relations. *Journal of Experimental Social Psychology, 6,* 214–232. (14)

Krull, D. S., & Anderson, C. A. (1997). The process of explanation. *Current Directions in Psychological Science, 6,* 1–5. (14)

Krupnick, J. L., Elkin, I., Collins, J., Simmens, S., Sotsky, S. M., Pilkonis, P. A., & Watkins, J. T. (1994). Therapeutic alliance and clinical outcome in the NIMH Treatment of Depression Collaborative Research Program: Preliminary findings. *Psychotherapy, 31,* 28–35. (15)

Kryger, M. (Ed.). (1993). Amphetamines and narcolepsy. *Sleep, 16,* 199–206. (5)

Kübler-Ross, E. (1969). *On death and dying*. New York: Macmillan. (10)

Kuhl, P. K., Andruski, J. E., Chistovich, I. A., Chistovich, L. A., Kozhevnikova, E. V., Ryskina, V. L., Stolyarova, E. I., Sundberg, U., & Lacerda, F. (1997). Cross-language analysis of phonetic units in language addressed to infants. *Science, 277,* 684–686. (8)

Kuhn, D., & Lao, J. (1996). Effects of evidence on attitudes: Is polarization the norm? *Psychological Science, 7,* 115–120. (14)

Kulik, J. A., Bangert-Drowns, R. L., & Kulik, C. C. (1984). Effectiveness of coaching for aptitude tests. *Psychological Bulletin, 95,* 179–188. (9)

Kunda, Z., & Thagard, P. (1996). Forming impressions from stereotypes, traits, and behaviors: A parallel-constraint-satisfaction theory. *Psychological Review, 103,* 284–308. (14)

Kupsch, A., Oertel, W. H., Earl, C. D., & Sautter, J. (1995). Neuronal transplantation and neurotrophic factors in the treatment of Parkinson's disease-update February 1995. *Journal of Neural Transmission, Suppl. 46,* 193–207. (3)

Kutchins, H., & Kirk, S. A. (1997). *Making us crazy.* New York: Free Press. (15)

LaBar, K. S., LeDoux, J. E., Spencer, D. D., & Phelps, E. A. (1995). Impaired fear conditioning following unilateral temporal lobectomy in humans. *Journal of Neuroscience, 15,* 6846–6855. (3, 12)

Laburn, H. P. (1996). How does the fetus cope with thermal challenges? *News in Physiological Sciences, 11,* 96–100. (16)

Lackner, J. R. (1993). Orientation and movement in unusual force environments. *Psychological Science, 4,* 134–142. (4)

LaFromboise, T., Coleman, H. L. K., & Gerton, J. (1993). Psychological impact of biculturalism: Evidence and theory. *Psychological Bulletin, 114,* 395–412. (10)

Laing, D. G., Prescott, J., Bell, G. A., Gillmore, R., James, C., Best, D. J., Allen, S., Yoshida, M., & Yamazaki, K. (1993). A cross-cultural study of taste discrimination with Australians and Japanese. *Chemical Senses, 18,* 161–168. (4)

Laird, J. D. (1974). Self-attribution of emotion: The effects of expressive behavior on the quality of emotional experience. *Journal of Personality and Social Psychology, 29,* 475–486. (12)

Lakoff, G. (1987). *Women, fire, and dangerous things.* Chicago: University of Chicago Press. (8)

Lambert, N. M. (1981). Psychological evidence in *Larry P. v. Wilson Riles*: An evaluation by a witness for the defense. *American Psychologist, 36,* 937–952. (9)

Lamm, H., & Myers, D. G. (1978). Group-induced polarization of attitudes and behavior. *Advances in Experimental Social Psychology, 11,* 145–195. (14)

Land, E. H., Hubel, D. H., Livingstone, M. S., Perry, S. H., & Burns, M. M. (1983). Colour-generating interactions across the corpus callosum. *Nature, 303,* 616–618. (4)

Land, E. H., & McCann, J. J. (1971). Lightness and retinex theory. *Journal of the Optical Society of America, 61,* 1–11. (4)

Landauer, T. K., & Dumais, S. T. (1997). A solution to Plato's problem: The latent semantic analysis theory of acquisition, induction, and representation of knowledge. *Psychological Review, 104,* 211–240. (8)

Lande, S. D. (1982). Physiological and subjective measures of anxiety during flooding. *Behaviour Research and Therapy, 20,* 81–88. (16)

Lang, P. J. (1994). The varieties of emotional experience: A meditation on James-Lange theory. *Psychological Review, 101,* 211–221. (12)

Langer, E. J. (1975). The illusion of control. *Journal of Personality and Social Psychology, 32,* 311–328. (8)

Langlois, J. H., & Roggman, L. A. (1990). Attractive faces are only average. *Psychological Science, 1,* 115–121. (14)

Langlois, J. H., Roggman, L. A., & Musselman, L. (1994). What is average and what is not average about average faces? *Psychological Science, 5,* 214–220. (14)

Langworthy, R. A., & Jennings, J. W. (1972). Oddball, abstract olfactory learning in laboratory rats. *Psychological Record, 22,* 487–490. (1)

Larson, E. J., & Witham, L. (1997). Scientists are still keeping the faith. *Nature, 386,* 435–436. (2)

Lashley, K. S. (1951). The problem of serial order in behavior. In L. A. Jeffress (Ed.), *Cerebral mechanisms in behavior* (pp. 112–146). New York: Wiley. (8)

Latané, B., & Darley, J. M. (1968). Group inhibition of bystander intervention in emergencies. *Journal of Personality and Social Psychology, 10,* 215–221. (14)

Latané, B., & Darley, J. M. (1969). Bystander "apathy." *American Scientist, 57,* 244–268. (14)

Latané, B., Williams, K., & Harkins, S. (1979). Many hands make light the work: The causes and consequences of social loafing. *Journal of Personality and Social Psychology, 37,* 823–832. (14)

Laumann, E. O. (1969). Friends of urban men: An assessment of accuracy in reporting their socio-economic attributes, mutual choice, and attitude development. *Sociometry, 32,* 54–69. (14)

Laumann, E. O., Gagnon, J. H., Michael, R. T., & Michaels, S. (1994). *The social organization of sexuality: Sexual practices in the United States.* Chicago, IL: University of Chicago Press. (11)

Lavin, J. H., Wittert, G., Sun, W. -M., Horowitz, M., Morley, J. E., & Read, N. W. (1996). Appetite regulation by carbohydrate: Role of blood glucose and gastrointestinal hormones. *American Journal of Physiology, 271,* E209–E214. (11)

Lazarus, R. S. (1977). Cognitive and coping processes in emotion. In A. Monat & R. S. Lazarus (Eds.), *Stress and coping* (pp. 145–158). New York: Columbia University Press. (12)

Lazarus, R. S., Averill, J. R., & Opton, E. M., Jr. (1970). Towards a cognitive theory of emotion. In M. B. Arnold (Ed.), *Feelings and emotions* (pp. 207–232). New York: Academic Press. (12)

Lee, Y. -T., & Duenas, G. (1995). Stereotype accuracy in multicultural business. In Y. -T. Lee, L. J. Jussim, & C. R. McCauley (Eds.), *Stereotype accuracy* (pp. 157–186). Washington, DC: American Psychological Association. (14)

Lefcourt, H. M. (1976). *Locus of control: Current trends in theory and research.* New York: Wiley. (13)

Leff, J., Wig, N. N., Ghosh, A., Bedi, H., Menon, D. K., Kuipers, L., Korten, A., Ernberg, G., Day, R., Sartorius, N., & Jablensky, A. (1987). Expressed emotion and schizophrenia in North India. III. Influence of relatives' expressed emotion on the course of schizophrenia in Changigarh. *British Journal of Psychiatry, 151,* 166–173. (16)

Le Grange, D., Telch, C. F., & Agras, W. S. (1997). Eating and general psychopathology in a sample of Caucasian and ethnic minority subjects. *International Journal of Eating Disorders, 21,* 285–293. (11)

Leibowitz, S. F., & Alexander, J. T. (1991). Analysis of neuropeptide Y-induced feeding: Dissociation of Y_1 and Y_2 receptor effects on natural meal patterns. *Peptides, 12,* 1251–1260. (11)

Leibowitz, S. F., Hammer, N. J., & Chang, K. (1981). Hypothalamic paraventricular nucleus lesions produce overeating and obesity in the rat. *Physiology & Behavior, 27,* 1031–1040. (11)

LeMagnen, J. (1981). The metabolic basis of dual periodicity of feeding in rats. *Behavioral and Brain Sciences, 4,* 561–607. (11)

Lenneberg, E. H. (1967). *Biological foundations of language.* New York: Wiley. (10)

Lenneberg, E. H. (1969). On explaining language. *Science, 164,* 635–643. (10)

Lester, D. (1996). *Patterns of suicide and homicide in the world.* Commack, NY: Nova Science. (16)

Lester, J. T. (1983). Wrestling with the self on Mount Everest. *Journal of Humanistic Psychology, 23,* 31–41. (13)

Leuchtenburg, W. E. (1963). *Franklin D. Roosevelt and the New Deal 1932–1940.* New York: Harper & Row. (14)

LeVay, S. (1991). A difference in hypothalamic structure between heterosexual and homosexual men. *Science, 253,* 1034–1037. (11)

Levenson, R. W. (1992). Autonomic nervous system differences among emotions. *Psychological Science, 3,* 23–27. (12)

Levenson, R. W., Oyama, O. N., & Meek, P. S. (1987). Greater reinforcement from alcohol for those at risk: Parental risk, personality risk, and sex. *Journal of Abnormal Psychology, 96,* 242–253. (16)

Leventhal, H. (1970). Findings and theory in the study of fear communication. In L. Berkowitz (Ed.), *Advances in Experimental Social Psychology* (Vol. 5, pp. 119–186). New York: Academic Press. (14)

Levin, E. D., & Rose, J. E. (1995). Acute and chronic nicotine interactions with dopamine systems and working memory performance. *Annals of the New York Academy of Sciences, 757,* 245–252. (5)

Levin, M. (1994). Comment on the Minnesota transracial adoption study. *Intelligence, 19,* 13–20. (9)

Levine, L. J. (1997). Reconstructing memory for emotions. *Journal of Experimental Psychology: General, 126,* 165–177. (7)

Levine, R. V. (1990). The pace of life. *American Scientist, 78,* 450–459. (12)

Levinson, D. J. (1977). The mid-life transition: A period in adult psychosocial development. *Psychiatry, 40,* 99–112. (10)

Levinson, D. J. (1978). *The seasons of a man's life.* New York: Ballantine. (10)

Lewis, D. O., Moy, E., Jackson, L. D., Aaronson, R., Restifo, N., Serra, S., & Simos, A. (1985). Biopsychosocial characteristics of children who later murder: A prospective study. *American Journal of Psychiatry, 142,* 1161–1167. (12)

Lewis, M. (1995). Self-conscious emotions. *American Scientist, 83,* 68–78. (12)

Lewis, M., Sullivan, M. W., Stanger, C., & Weiss, M. (1991). Self development and self-conscious emotions. In S. Chess & M. E. Hertzig (Eds.), *Annual Progress in Child Psychiatry and Child Development 1990* (pp. 34–51). New York: Brunner/Mazel. (10)

Lewis, M., Thomas, D. A., & Worobey, J. (1990). Developmental organization, stress, and illness. *Psychological Science, 1,* 316–318. (10)

Lilie, J. K., & Rosenberg, R. P. (1990). Behavioral treatment of insomnia. *Progress in Behavior Modification, 25,* 152–177. (5)

Lilienfeld, S. O., Alliger, G., & Mitchell, K. (1995). Why integrity testing remains controversial. *American Psychologist, 50,* 457–458. (12)

Lillard, A. S. (1997). Other folks' theories of mind and behavior. *Psychological Science, 8,* 268–274. (1)

Lindberg, N. O., Coburn, C., & Stricker, E. M. (1984). Increased feeding by rats after subdiabetogenic streptozotocin treatment: A role for insulin in satiety. *Behavioral Neuroscience, 98,* 138–145. (11)

Lindsay, D. S., & Read, J. D. (1994). Psychotherapy and memories of childhood sexual abuse: A cognitive perspective. *Applied Cognitive Psychology, 8,* 281–338. (7)

Lindvall, O., Rehncrona, S., Brundin, P., Gustavii, B., Åstedt, B., Widner, H., Lindholm, T., Björklund, A., Leenders, K. L., Rothwell, J. C., Frackowiak, R., Marsden, D., Johnels, B., Steg, G., Freedman, R., Hoffer, B. J., Seiger, A., Bygdeman, M., Strömberg, I., & Olsen, L. (1989). Human fetal dopamine neurons grafted into the striatum in two patients wih severe Parkinson's disease. *Archives of Neurology, 46,* 615–631. (3)

Link, N. F., Sherer, S. E., & Byrne, P. N. (1977). Moral judgment and moral conduct in the psychopath. *Canadian Psychiatric Association Journal, 22,* 341–346. (10)

Linn, R., & Gilligan, C. (1990). One action, two moral orientations— The tension between justice and care voices in Israeli selective conscientious objectors. *New Ideas in Psychology, 8,* 189–203. (10)

Linton, M. (1982). Transformations of memory in everyday life. In U. Neisser (Ed.), *Memory observed* (pp. 77–91). San Francisco: W. H. Freeman. (7)

Lipsey, M. W., & Wilson, D. B. (1993). The efficacy of psychological, educational, and behavioral treatment. *American Psychologist, 48,* 1181–1209. (15)

Lisak, D., & Roth, S. (1988). Motivational factors in nonincarcerated sexually aggressive men. *Journal of Personality and Social Psychology, 55,* 795–802. (12)

Locke, E. A., & Latham, G. P. (1991). The fallacies of common sense "truths": A reply to Lamal. *Psychological Science, 2,* 131–132. (11)

Locke, E. A., Shaw, K. N., Saari, L. M., & Latham, G. P. (1981). Goal setting and task performance: 1969–1980. *Psychological Bulletin, 90,* 125–152. (11)

Locke, J. L. (1994). Phases in the child's development of language. *American Scientist, 82,* 436–445. (8)

Loeb, J. (1973). *Forced movements, tropisms, and animal conduct.* New York: Dover. (Original work published 1918.) (6)

Loehlin, J. C. (1992). *Genes and environment in personality development.* Newbury Park, CA: Sage. (13)

Loehlin, J. C., Willerman, L., & Horn, J. M. (1988). Human behavior genetics. *Annual Review of Psychology, 39,* 101–133. (3)

Loehlin, J. C., Horn, J. M., & Willerman, L. (1989). Modeling IQ change: Evidence from the Texas adoption project. *Child Development, 60,* 993–1004. (9)

Loehlin, J. C., Horn, J. M., & Willerman, L. (1994). Differential inheritance of mental abilities in the Texas Adoption Project. *Intelligence, 19,* 325–336. (9)

Loewi, O. (1960). An autobiographic sketch. *Perspectives in Biology, 4,* 3–25. (3)

Loftus, E. F. (1975). Leading questions and the eyewitness report. *Cognitive Psychology, 7,* 560–572. (7)

Loftus, E. F. (1993). The reality of repressed memories. *American Psychologist, 48,* 518–537. (7)

Loftus, E. F., Feldman, J., & Dashiell, R. (1995). The reality of illusory memories. In D. L. Schacter (Ed.) *Memory distortion* (pp. 47–68). Cambridge, MA: Harvard University Press. (7)

Loftus, G. R. (1996). Psychology will be a much better science when we change the way we analyze data. *Current Directions in Psychological Science, 5,* 161–171. (2)

Logothetis, N. K., Leopold, D. A., & Sheinberg, D. L. (1996). What is rivalling during binocular rivalry? *Nature, 380,* 621–624. (4)

London, E. D., Cascella, N. G., Wong, D. F., Phillips, R. L., Dannals, R. F., Links, J. M., Herning, R., Grayson, R., Jaffe, J. H., & Wagner, H. N. (1990). Cocaine-induced reduction of utilization in human brain. *Archives of General Psychiatry, 47,* 567–574. (5)

Long, B. B. (1986). The prevention of mental-emotional disabilities. *American Psychologist, 41,* 825–829. (15)

Longstreth, L. E. (1981). Revisiting Skeels' final study: A critique. *Developmental Psychology, 17,* 620–625. (9)

Loomis, J. M., Klatzky, R. L., Golledge, R. G., Cicinelli, J. G., Pellegrino, J. W., & Fry, P. A. (1993). Nonvisual navigation by blind and sighted: Assessment of path integration ability. *Journal of Experimental Psychology: General, 122,* 73–91. (8)

Lorenz, K. (1950). The comparative method in studying innate behaviour patterns. *Symposia of the Society for Experimental Biology, 4,* 221–268. (11)

Lourenço, O., & Machado, A. (1996). In defense of Piaget's theory: A reply to 10 common criticisms. *Psychological Review, 103,* 143–164. (10)

Lowe, M. R. (1993). The effects of dieting on eating behavior: A three-factor model. *Psychological Bulletin, 114,* 100–121. (11)

Lubinski, D., & Benbow, C. P. (1992). Gender differences in abilities and preferences among the gifted: Implications for the math-science pipeline. *Current Directions in Psychological Science, 1,* 61–66. (9)

Luck, S. J., & Vogel, E. K. (1997). The capacity of visual working memory for features and conjunctions. *Nature, 390,* 279–281. (7)

Luck, S. J., Vogel, E. K., & Shapiro, K. L. (1996). Word meanings can be accessed but not reported during the attentional blink. *Nature, 383,* 616–618. (8)

Lykken, D. T. (1979). The detection of deception. *Psychological Bulletin, 86,* 47–53. (12)

Lykken, D. T., McGue, M., Tellegen, A., & Bouchard, T. J. (1992). Emergenesis: Genetic traits that may not run in families. *American Psychologist, 47,* 1565–1577. (3)

Lykken, D. T., & Tellegen, A. (1996). Happiness is a stochastic phenomenon. *Psychological Science, 7,* 186–189. (12)

Lynam, D. R. (1996). Early identification of chronic offenders: Who is the fledgling psychopath? *Psychological Bulletin, 120,* 209–234. (12)

Lyness, S. A. (1993). Predictors of differences between Type A and B individuals in heart rate and blood pressure reactivity. *Psychological Bulletin, 114,* 266–295. (12)

Lynn, S. J., Rhue, J. W., & Weekes, J. R. (1990). Hypnotic involuntariness: A social cognitive analysis. *Psychological Review, 97,* 169–184. (5)

Lyons-Ruth, K., Alpern, L. L., & Repacholi, B. (1993). Disorganized infant attachment classification and maternal psychosocial problems as predictors of hostile-aggressive behavior in the preschool classroom. *Child Development, 64,* 572–585. (10)

Maccoby, E. E. (1990). Gender and relationships. *American Psychologist, 45,* 513–520. (10)

Maccoby, E. E., & Jacklin, C. N. (1974). *The psychology of sex differences.* Stanford, CA: Stanford University Press. (10)

MacCoun, R., & Reuter, P. (1997). Interpreting Dutch cannabis policy: Reasoning by analogy in the legalization debate. *Science, 278,* 47–52. (16)

MacDonald, M. C., Pearlmutter, N. J., & Seidenberg, M. S. (1994). Lexical nature of syntactic ambiguity resolution. *Psychological Review, 101,* 676–703. (8)

Macdonald, R. L., Weddle, M. G., & Gross, R. A. (1986). Benzodiazepine, beta-carboline, and barbiturate actions on GABA responses. *Advances in Biochemical Psychopharmacology, 41,* 67–78. (16)

Macmillan, M. (1997). *Freud evaluated.* Cambridge, MA: MIT Press. (13)

MacQuitty, J. (1996, Aug. 1). Lily the stink loses its 33-year reputation by a nose. *The Times* (London), pp. 1–2. (11)

Maehr, M. L., & Kleiber, D. A. (1981). The graying of achievement motivation. *American Psychologist, 36,* 787–793. (11)

Magee, W. J., Eaton, W. W., Wittchen, H. -U., McGonagle, K. A., & Kessler, R. C. (1996). Agoraphobia, simple phobia, and social phobia in the National Comorbidity Survey. *Archives of General Psychiatry, 53,* 159–168. (16)

Maier, S. F., Seligman, M. E. P., & Solomon, R. L. (1969). Pavlovian fear conditioning and learned helplessness: Effects on escape and avoidance behavior of (a) the CS-US contingency and (b) the independence of the US and voluntary responding. In B. A. Campbell and R. M. Church (Eds.), *Punishment and aversive behavior* (pp. 299–342). New York: Appleton-Century-Crofts. (16)

Maki, R. H. (1990). Memory for script actions: Effects of relevance and detail expectancy. *Memory & Cognition, 18,* 5–14. (7)

Maki, R. H., & Serra, M. (1992). The basis of test predictions for text material. *Journal of Experimental Psychology: Learning, Memory, and Cognition, 18,* 116–126. (7)

Maki, R. H., & Syman, E. M. (1997). Teaching of controversial and empirically validated treatments in APA-accredited clinical and counseling psychology programs. *Psychotherapy, 34,* 44–57. (15)

Malamuth, N. M., & Donnerstein, E. (1982). The effects of aggressive-pornographic mass media stimuli. In L. Berkowitz (Ed.), *Advances in experimental social psychology* (Vol. 15, pp. 103–136). New York: Academic Press. (12)

Malamuth, N. M., Sockloskie, R. J., Koss, M. P., & Tanaka, J. S. (1991). Characteristics of aggressors against women: Testing a model using a national sample of college students. *Journal of Consulting and Clinical Psychology, 59,* 670–681. (12)

Maldonado, R., Saiardi, A., Valverde, O., Samad, T. A., Roques, B. P., & Borrelli, E. (1997). Absence of opiate rewarding effects in mice lacking dopamine D$_2$ receptors. *Nature, 388,* 586–589. (5)

Malinosky-Rummell, R., & Hansen, D. J. (1993). Long-term consequences of childhood physical abuse. *Psychological Bulletin, 114,* 68–79. (12)

Malmquist, C. P. (1986). Children who witness parental murder: Posttraumatic aspects. *Journal of the American Academy of Child Psychiatry, 25,* 320–325. (7)

Mandler, J. M. (1990). A new perspective on cognitive development in infancy. *American Scientist, 78,* 236–243. (10)

Manji, H. K., Potter, W. Z., & Lenox, R. H. (1995). Signal transduction pathways. *Archives of General Psychiatry, 52,* 532–543. (16)

Mansky, P. A. (1978). Opiates: Human psychopharmacology. In L. L. Iversen, S. D. Iversen, & S. H. Snyder (Eds.), *Handbook of psychopharmacology: Vol. 12, Drugs of abuse* (pp. 95–185). New York: Plenum. (5)

Mantyh, P. W., Rogers, S. D., Honore, P., Allen, B. J., Ghilardi, J. R., Li, J., Daughters, R. S., Lappi, D. A., Wiley, R. G., & Simone, D. A. (1997). Inhibition of hyperalgesia by ablation of lamina I spinal neurons expressing the substance P receptor. *Science, 278,* 275–279. (4)

Manuck, S. B., Cohen, S., Rabin, B. S., Muldoon, M. F., & Bachen, E. A. (1991). Individual differences in cellular immune response to stress. *Psychological Science, 2,* 111–115. (12)

Maquet, P., Peters, J. -M., Aerts, J., Delfiore, G., Degueldre, C., Luxen, A., & Franck, G. (1996). Functional neuroanatomy of human rapid-eye-movement sleep and dreaming. *Nature, 383,* 163–166. (5)

Marcia, J. E. (1980). Identity in adolescence. In J. Adelson (Ed.), *Handbook of adolescent psychology* (pp. 159–187). New York: Wiley. (10)

Marder, S. R., Mebane, A., Chien, C., Winslade, W. J., Swann, E., & Van Putten, T. (1983). A comparison of patients who refuse and consent to neuroleptic treatment. *American Journal of Psychiatry, 140,* 470–472. (15)

Maris, R. W. (1997). Social suicide. *Suicide and Life-Threatening Behavior, 27,* 41–49. (16)

Markman, E. M. (1990). Constraints children place on word meanings. *Cognitive Science, 14,* 57–77. (8)

Marks, D., & Kammann, R. (1980). *The psychology of the psychic.* Buffalo, NY: Prometheus. (2, 13)

Marks, I., Lovell, K., Noshirvani, H., Livanou, M., & Thrasher, S. (1998). Treatment of posttraumatic stress disorder by exposure and/or cognitive restructuring. *Archives of General Psychiatry, 55,* 317–325. (15)

Marler, P. (1997). Three models of song learning: Evidence from behavior. *Journal of Neurobiology, 33,* 501–516. (6)

Marler, P., & Peters, S. (1981). Sparrows learn adult song and more from memory. *Science, 213,* 780–782. (6)

Marler, P., & Peters, S. (1982). Long-term storage of learned birdsongs prior to production. *Animal Behaviour, 30,* 479–482. (6)

Marler, P., & Peters, S. (1987). A sensitive period for song acquisition in the song sparrow, *Melospiza melodia:* A case of age-limited learning. *Ethology, 76,* 89–100. (6)

Marler, P., & Peters, S. (1988). Sensitive periods for song acquisition from tape recordings and live tutors in the swamp sparrow, *Melospiza georgiana. Ethology, 77,* 76–84. (6)

Marriott, F. H. C. (1976). Abnormal colour vision. In H. Davson (Ed.), *The eye* (2nd ed.) (pp. 533–547). New York: Academic Press. (4)

Marsh, R. L., Landau, J. D., & Hicks, J. L. (1997). Contributions of inadequate source monitoring to unconscious plagiarism during idea generation. *Journal of Experimental Psychology: Learning, Memory, and Cognition, 23,* 886–897. (7)

Marshall, W. L. (1988). The use of sexually explicit stimuli by rapists, child molesters, and nonoffenders. *Journal of Sex Research, 25,* 267–288. (12)

Martell, D. A., & Dietz, P. E. (1992). Mentally disordered offenders who push or attempt to push victims onto subway tracks in New York City. *Archives of General Psychiatry, 49,* 472–475. (12)

Martsh, C. T., & Miller, W. R. (1997). Extraversion predicts heavy drinking in college students. *Personality and Individual Differences, 23,* 153–155. (13)

Masling, J. M., Bornstein, R. F., Poynton, F. G., Reid, S., & Katkin, E. S. (1991). Perception without awareness and electrodermal responding: A strong test of subliminal psychodynamic activation effects. *Journal of Mind and Behavior, 12,* 33–48. (4)

Maslow, A. H. (1962). *Toward a psychology of being.* Princeton, NJ: Van Nostrand. (13)

Maslow, A. H. (1970). *Motivation and personality* (2nd ed.). New York: Harper & Row. (11)

Maslow, A. H. (1971). *The farther reaches of human nature.* New York: Viking. (13)

Masson, J. M. (1984). *The assault on truth.* New York: Farrar, Straus, and Giroux. (13)

Masson, J. M. (1985). *The complete letters of Sigmund Freud to Wilhelm Fliess 1887–1904.* Cambridge, MA: Harvard University Press. (13)

Masten, A. S., & Coatsworth, J. D. (1998). The development of competence in favorable and unfavorable environments. *American Psychologist, 53,* 205–220. (10)

Masters, W. H., & Johnson, V. E. (1966). *Human sexual response.* Boston: Little, Brown. (11)

Matheny, A. P., Jr. (1989). Children's behavioral inhibition over age and across situations: Genetic similarity for a trait to change. *Journal of Personality, 57,* 215–235. (10)

Matin, E., Clymer, A. B., & Matin, L. (1972). Metacontrast and saccadic suppression. *Science, 178,* 179–182. (8)

Matsui, T., Okada, A., & Kakuyama, T. (1982). Influence of goal setting, performance, and feedback effectiveness. *Journal of Applied Psychology, 67,* 645–648. (11)

Matthews, K. A., & Rodin, J. (1989). Women's changing work roles. *American Psychologist, 44,* 1389–1393. (11)

Matsumoto, D. (1994). *People: Psychology from a cultural perspective.* Pacific Grove, CA: Brooks/Cole. (2)

Mattson, S. N., Riley, E. P., Grambling, L., Delis, D. C., & Jones, K. L. (1998). Neuropsychological comparison of alcohol-exposed children with or without physical features of fetal alcohol syndrome. *Neuropsychology, 12,* 146–153. (10)

Matute, H. (1996). Illusion of control: Detecting response-outcome independence in analytic but not in naturalistic conditions. *Psychological Science, 7,* 289–293. (8)

May, C. P., Hasher, L., & Stoltzfus, E. R. (1993). Optimal time of day and the magnitude of age differences in memory. *Psychological Science, 4,* 326–330. (5)

Mayer, J. D., & Salovey, P. (1995). Emotional intelligence and the construction and regulation of feelings. *Applied & Preventive Psychology, 4,* 197–208. (12)

Mayer, J. D., & Salovey, P. (1997). What is emotional intelligence? In P. Salovey & D. J. Sluyter (Eds.). *Emotional development and emotional intelligence* (pp. 3–34). New York: Basic Books. (12)

McCann, U. D., Lowe, K. A., & Ricaurte, G. A. (1997). Long-lasting effects of recreational drugs of abuse on the central nervous system. *The Neuroscientist, 3,* 399–411. (5)

McCarthy, G., Puce, A., Gore, J. C., & Allison, T. (1997). Face-specific processing in the human fusiform gyrus. *Journal of Cognitive Neuroscience, 9,* 605–610. (4)

McClearn, G. E., Johansson, B., Berg, S., Pederson, N. L., Ahern, F., Petrill, S. A., & Plomin, R. (1997). Substantial genetic influence on cognitive abilities in twins 80 or more years old. *Science, 276,* 1560–1563. (9)

McClelland, D. C., Atkinson, J. W., Clark, R. A., & Lowell, E. L. (1953). *The achievement motive.* New York: Appleton-Century-Crofts. (11)

McClelland, D. C., Koestner, R., & Weinberger, J. (1989). How do self-attributed and implicit motives differ? *Psychological Review, 96,* 690–702. (11)

McClelland, J. L. (1988). Connectionist models and psychological evidence. *Journal of Memory and Language, 27,* 107–123. (8)

McClelland, J. L., & Rumelhart, D. E. (1981). An interactive activation model of context effects in letter perception: Part 1. An account of basic findings. *Psychological Review, 88,* 375–407. (8)

McClintock, M. K. (1971). Menstrual synchrony and suppression. *Nature, 229,* 244–245. (4)

McClure, J. (1998). Discounting causes of behavior: Are two reasons better than one? *Journal of Personality and Social Psychology, 74,* 7–20. (14)

McCormick, M. C. (1985). The contribution of low birth weight to infant mortality and childhood morbidity. *New England Journal of Medicine, 312,* 82–90. (10)

McCornack, R. L. (1983). Bias in the validity of predicted college grades in four ethnic minority groups. *Educational & Psychological Measurement, 43,* 517–522. (9)

McCrae, R. R. (1996). Social consequences of experiential openness. *Psychological Bulletin, 120,* 323–337. (13)

McCrae, R. R., & Costa, P. T., Jr. (1987). Validation of the five-factor model of personality across instruments and observers. *Journal of Personality and Social Psychology, 52,* 81–90. (13)

McCrae, R. R., & Costa, P. T., Jr. (1994). The stability of personality: Observations and evaluations. *Current Directions in Psychological Science, 3,* 173–175. (13)

McCrae, R. R., & Costa, P. T., Jr. (1997). Personality trait structure as a human universal. *American Psychologist, 52,* 509–516. (13)

McDaniel, M. A., Einstein, G. O., & Lollis, T. (1988). Qualitative and quantitative considerations in encoding difficulty effects. *Memory & Cognition, 16,* 8–14. (7)

McElhiney, M. C., Moody, B. J., Steif, B. L., Prudic, J., Devanand, D. P., Nobler, M. S., & Sackeim, H. A. (1995). Autobiographical memory and mood: Effects of electroconvulsive therapy. *Neuropsychology, 9,* 501–517. (16)

McGaugh, J. L. (1990). Significance and remembrance: The role of neuromodulatory systems. *Psychological Science, 1,* 15–25. (7)

McGovern, P. E., Glusker, D. L., Exner, L. J., & Voigt, M. M. (1996). Neolithic resinated wine. *Nature, 381,* 480–481. (5)

McGregor, D. M. (1960). *The human side of enterprise.* New York: McGraw-Hill. (11)

McGuire, W. J. (1985). Attitudes and attitude change. In G. Lindzey & E. Aronson (Eds.), *Handbook of social psychology* (Vol. 2, pp. 233–346). New York: Random House. (14)

McGuire, W. J., & Papageorgis, D. (1961). The relative efficacy of various types of prior belief-defense in producing immunity against persuasion. *Journal of Abnormal and Social Psychology, 62,* 327–337. (14)

McGurk, H., Caplan, M., Hennessy, E., & Moss, P. (1993). Controversy, theory, and social context in contemporary day care research. *Journal of Child Psychology, 34,* 3–23. (10)

McLellan, A. T., Grissom, G. R., Zanis, D., Randall, M., Brill, P., & O'Brien, C. P. (1997). Problem-service 'matching' in addiction treatment. *Archives of General Psychiatry, 54,* 730–735. (16)

McMahon, C. E. (1975). The wind of the cannon ball: An informative anecdote from medical history. *Psychotherapy & Psychosomatics, 26,* 125–131. (12)

McMurtry, P. L., & Mershon, D. H. (1985). Auditory distance judgments in noise, with and without hearing protection. *Proceedings of the Human Factors Society* (Baltimore, MD), pp. 811–813. (4)

McNally, R. J. (1990). Psychological approaches to panic disorder: A review. *Psychological Bulletin, 108,* 403–419. (16)

McNeal, E. T., & Cimbolic, P. (1986). Antidepressants and biochemical theories of depression. *Psychological Bulletin, 99,* 361–374. (16)

McReynolds, P. (1985). Psychological assessment and clinical practice: Problems and prospects. *Advances in Personality Assessment, 4,* 1–30. (13)

Mechner, D. A. (1998, Jan./Feb.). All systems go. *The Sciences, 38* (1), 32–37. (8)

Meddis, R., Pearson, A. J. D., & Langford, G. (1973). An extreme case of healthy insomnia. *EEG and Clinical Neurophysiology, 35,* 213–214. (5)

Mednick, S. A., Machon, R. A., & Huttunen, M. O. (1990). An update on the Helsinki influenza project. *Archives of General Psychiatry, 47,* 292. (16)

Meichenbaum, D. (1985). *Stress inoculation training.* New York: Pergamon. (12)

Meichenbaum, D., & Cameron, R. (1983). Stress inoculation training. In D. Meichenbaum & M. E. Jaremko (Eds.), *Stress reduction and prevention* (pp. 115–154). New York: Plenum. (12)

Meichenbaum, D. H. (1995). Cognitive-behavioral therapy in historical perspective. In B. Bongar & L. E. Beutler (Eds.), *Comprehensive textbook of psychotherapy: Theory and practice* (pp. 140–158). Oxford, England: Oxford University Press. (15)

Meichenbaum, D. H., & Goodman, J. (1971). Training impulsive children to talk to themselves: A means of developing self-control. *Journal of Abnormal Psychology, 77*, 115–126. (6)

Mellers, B. A., Schwartz, Ho, & Ritov, I. (1997). Decision affect theory: Emotional reactions to the outcomes of risky options. *Psychological Science, 8*, 423–429. (8)

Mello, N. K., & Mendelson, J. H. (1978). Behavioral pharmacology of human alcohol, heroin and marihuana use. In J. Fishman (Ed.), *The bases of addiction* (pp. 133–158). Berlin: Dahlem Konferenzen. (5)

Meltzer, H. Y. (1995). The role of serotonin in schizophrenia and the place of serotonin-dopamine antagonist antipsychotics. *Journal of Clinical Psychopharmacology, 15*, Supplement 1, S2–S3. (16)

Melzack, R., & Wall, P. D. (1965). Pain mechanisms: A new theory. *Science, 150*, 971–979. (4)

Melzack, R., & Wall, P. D. (1983). *The challenge of pain.* New York: Basic Books. (5)

Melzack, R., Weisz, A. Z., & Sprague, L. T. (1963). Stratagems for controlling pain: Contributions of auditory stimulation and suggestion. *Experimental Neurology, 8*, 239–247. (12)

Merikle, P. M. (1996). Memory for unconsciously perceived events: Evidence from anesthetized patients. *Consciousness and Cognition, 5*, 525–541. (5)

Mershon, D. H., Desaulniers, D. H., Kiefer, S. A., Amerson, T. L., Jr., & Mills, J. T. (1981). Perceived loudness and visually determined auditory distance. *Perception, 10*, 531–543. (4)

Mershon, D. H., & King, L. E. (1975). Intensity and reverberation as factors in the auditory perception of egocentric distance. *Perception and Psychophysics, 18*, 409–415. (4)

Mesmer, F. A. (1980). *Mesmerism: A translation of the original medical and scientific writings of F. A. Mesmer.* Los Altos, CA: William Kaufmann. (5)

Mesquita, B., & Frijda, N. H. (1992). Cultural variations in emotions: A review. *Psychological Bulletin, 112*, 179–204. (12)

Messick, S. (1995). Validity of psychological assessment. *American Psychologist, 50*, 741–749. (9)

Messick, S., & Jungeblut, A. (1981). Time and method in coaching for the SAT. *Psychological Bulletin, 89*, 191–216. (9)

Metcalfe, J., & Wiebe, D. (1987). Intuition in insight and noninsight problem solving. *Memory & Cognition, 15*, 238–246. (8)

Meyer, G. J., & Handler, L. (1997). The ability of the Rorschach to predict subsequent outcome: A meta-analysis of the Rorschach Prognostic Rating Scale. *Journal of Personality Assessment, 69*, 1–38. (13)

Meyerowitz, B. E., Richardson, J., Hudson, S., & Leedham, B. (1998). Ethnicity and cancer outcomes: Behavioral and psychosocial considerations. *Psychological Bulletin, 123*, 47–70. (12)

Mezzanotte, W. S., Tangel, D. J., & White, D. P. (1992). Waking genioglossal electromyogram in sleep apnea patients versus normal controls (a neuromuscular compensatory mechansim). *Journal of Clinical Investigation, 89*, 1571–1579. (5)

Michael, C. R. (1978). Color vision mechanisms in monkey striate cortex: Dual-opponent cells with concentric receptive fields. *Journal of Neurophysiology, 41*, 572–588. (4)

Milgram, S. (1974). *Obedience to authority.* New York: Harper & Row. (16)

Miller, D. T., & Ross, M. (1975). Self-serving biases in the attribution of causality: Fact or fiction? *Psychological Bulletin, 82*, 213–225. (14)

Miller, G. A. (1956). The magical number seven, plus or minus two: Some limits on our capacity for processing information. *Psychological Review, 63*, 81–97. (7)

Miller, L. L., & Branconnier, R. J. (1983). Cannabis: Effects on memory and the cholinergic limbic system. *Psychological Bulletin, 93*, 441–456. (5)

Miller, R. J., Hennessy, R. T., & Leibowitz, H. W. (1973). The effect of hypnotic ablation of the background on the magnitude of the Ponzo perspective illusion. *International Journal of Clinical and Experimental Hypnosis, 21*, 180–191. (5)

Miller, S. M., Shoda, Y., & Hurley, K. (1996). Applying cognitive-social theory to health-protective behavior: Breast self-examination in cancer screening. *Psychological Bulletin, 119*, 70–94. (12)

Miller, T. Q., Smith, T. W., Turner, C. W., Guijarro, M. L., & Hallet, A. J. (1996). A meta-analytic review of research on hostility and physical health. *Psychological Bulletin, 119*, 322–348. (12)

Miller, W. R., & Brown, S. A. (1997). Why psychologists should treat alcohol and drug problems. *American Psychologist, 52*, 1269–1279. (16)

Miller, W. R., & Hester, R. K. (1986). Inpatient alcohol treatment: Who benefits? *American Psychologist, 41*, 794–805. (16)

Milner, B. (1959). The memory defect in bilateral hippocampal lesions. *Psychiatric Research Reports, 11*, 43–52. (7)

Mineka, S. (1987). A primate model of phobic fears. In H. Eysenck & I. Martin (Eds.), *Theoretical foundations of behavior therapy* (pp. 81–111). New York: Plenum. (16)

Mineka, S., Davidson, M., Cook, M., & Keir, R. (1984). Observational conditioning of snake fear in rhesus monkeys. *Journal of Abnormal Psychology, 93*, 355–372. (16)

Mischel, W. (1973). Toward a cognitive social learning reconceptualization of personality. *Psychological Review, 80*, 252–283. (13)

Mischel, W. (1981). Current issues and challenges in personality. In L. T. Benjamin, Jr. (Ed.), *The G. Stanley Hall Lecture Series* (Vol. 1, pp. 81–99). Washington, DC: American Psychological Association. (13)

Mischel, W., & Shoda, Y. (1995). A cognitive-affective system theory of personality: Reconceptualizing situations, dispositions, dynamics, and invariance in personality structure. *Psychological Review, 102*, 246–268. (13)

Misrahi, M., Meduri, G., Pissard, S., Bouvattier, C. Beau, I., Loosfelt, H., Jolivet, A., Rappaport, R., Milgrom, E., & Bougneres, P. (1997). *Journal of Clinical Endocrinology and Metabolism, 82*, 2159–2165. (11)

Miyake, K., Chen, S., & Campos, J. J. (1985). Infant temperament, mother's mode of interaction, and attachment in Japan. An interim report. In I. Bretherton & E. Waters (Eds.), *Growing points of attachment theory. Monographs of the Society for Research in Child Development, 50* (1–2, Serial No. 209), 276–297. (10)

Miyake, A., Just, M. A., & Carpenter, P. A. (1994). Working memory constraints on the resolution of lexical ambiguity: Maintaining multiple interpretations in neutral contexts. *Journal of Memory and Language, 33*, 175–202. (7)

Moar, I., & Bower, G. H. (1983). Inconsistency in spatial knowledge. *Memory & Cognition, 11*, 107–113. (8)

Mobily, K. (1982). Using physical therapy activity and recreation to cope with stress and anxiety: A review. *American Corrective Therapy Journal, 36*, 77–81. (12)

Monahan, J. (1984). The prediction of violent behavior: Toward a second generation of theory and policy. *American Journal of Psychiatry, 141*, 10–15. (12)

Monahan, J. (1992). Mental disorder and violent behavior. *American Psychologist, 47*, 511–521. (12)

Monahan, J. (1993). Limiting therapist exposure to *Tarasoff* liability: Guidelines for risk containment. *American Psychologist, 48*, 242–250. (15)

Monahan, J., & Steadman, H. J. (1996). Violent storms and violent people. *American Psychologist, 51*, 931–938. (12)

Money, J., & Ehrhardt, A. A. (1972). *Man and woman, boy and girl.* Baltimore, MD: Johns Hopkins University Press. (11)

Montague, C. T., Farooqi, I. S., Whitehead, J. P., Soos, M. A., Rau, H., Wareham, N. J., Sewter, C. P. Digby, J. E., Mohammed, S. N., Hurst, J. A., Cheetham, C. H., Earley, A. R., Barnett, A. H., Prins, J. B., & O'Rahilly, S. (1997). Congenital leptin deficiency is associated with severe early-onset obesity in humans. *Nature, 387,* 903–908. (11)

Monteith, M. J., Devine, P. G., & Zuwerink, J. R. (1993). Self-directed versus other-directed affect as a consequence of prejudice-related discrepancies. *Journal of Personality and Social Psychology, 64,* 198–210. (14)

Montello, D. R. (1995). How significant are cultural differences in spatial cognition? In A. U. Frank & W. Kuhn (Eds.), *Spatial information theory* (pp. 485–500). Berlin, Germany: Springer Verlag. (4)

Monti-Bloch, L., Jennings-White, C., Dolberg, D. S., & Berliner, D. L. (1994). The human vomeronasal system. *Psychoneuroendocrinology, 19,* 673–686. (4)

Montgomery, G., & Kirsch, I. (1996). Mechanisms of placebo pain reduction: An empirical investigation. *Psychological Science, 7,* 174–176. (4)

Moorcroft, W. (1993). *Sleep, dreaming, and sleep disorders: An introduction.* (2nd ed.). Lanham, MD: University Press of America. (5)

Moore, B. C. J. (1989). *An introduction to the psychology of hearing* (3rd ed.). London: Academic Press. (4)

Moore, J. (1995). Some historical and conceptual relations among logical positivism, behaviorism, and cognitive psychology. In J. T. Todd & E. K. Morris (Eds.), *Modern perspectives on B. F. Skinner and contemporary behaviorism* (pp. 51–74). Westport, CT: Greenwood Press. (6)

Moore-Ede, M. C., Czeisler, C. A., & Richardson, G. S. (1983). Circadian timekeeping in health and disease. *New England Journal of Medicine, 309,* 469–476. (5)

Morgan, B. L. G., & Winick, M. (1989). Malnutrition, central nervous system effects. In G. Adelman (Ed.), *Neuroscience year* (pp. 97–99). Boston: Birkhäuser. (10)

Morris, J. B., & Beck, A. T. (1974). The efficacy of antidepressant drugs. *Archives of General Psychiatry, 30,* 667–674. (16)

Morrow, R. S., & Morrow, S. (1974). The measurement of intelligence. In B. B. Wolman (Ed.), *Handbook of general psychology* (pp. 656–670). Englewood Cliffs, NJ: Prentice-Hall. (9)

Moscovitch, M. (1985). Memory from infancy to old age: Implications for theories of normal and pathological memory. *Annals of the New York Academy of Sciences, 444,* 78–96. (7)

Moscovitch, M. (1989). Confabulation and the frontal systems: Strategic versus associative retrieval in neuropsychological theories of memory. In H. L. Roediger, III, & F. I. M. Craik (Eds.), *Varieties of memory and consciousness: Essays in honour of Endel Tulving* (pp. 133–160). Hillsdale, NJ: Lawrence Erlbaum. (7)

Moscovitch, M. (1992). Memory and working-with-memory: A component process model based on modules and central systems. *Journal of Cognitive Neuroscience, 4,* 257–267. (7)

Moscovitch, M. (1995). Confabulation. In D. L. Schacter (Ed.), *Memory distortion* (pp. 226–251). Cambridge, MA: Harvard University Press. (7)

Moscovitch, M., & Behrmann, M. (1994). Coding of spatial information in the somatosensory system: Evidence from patients with neglect following parietal lobe damage. *Journal of Cognitive Neuroscience, 6,* 151–155. (3)

Moscovitch, M., Winocur, G., & Behrmann, M. (1997). What is special about face recognition? Nineteen experiments on a person with visual object agnosia and dyslexia but normal face recognition. *Journal of Cognitive Neuroscience, 9,* 555–604. (4)

Moskowitz, B. A. (1978). The acquisition of language. *Scientific American, 239*(5), 92–108. (10)

Motley, M. T., & Baars, B. J. (1979). Effects of cognitive set upon laboratory induced verbal (Freudian) slips. *Journal of Speech and Hearing Research, 22,* 421–432. (13)

Mumford, M. D., & Gustafson, S. B. (1988). Creativity syndrome: Integration, application, and innovation. *Psychological Bulletin, 103,* 27–43. (8)

Munakata, Y., McClelland, J. L., Johnson, M. H., & Siegler, R. S. (1997). Rethinking infant knowledge: Toward an adaptive process account of successes and failures in object permanence tasks. *Psychological Review, 104,* 686–713. (10)

Munroe, R. (1955). *Schools of psychoanalytic thought.* New York: Dryden. (15)

Murphy, G. L., & Medin, D. L. (1985). The role of theories in conceptual coherence. *Psychological Review, 92,* 289–316. (1)

Murray, H. A. (1943). *Thematic Apperception Test manual.* Cambridge, MA: Harvard University Press. (13)

Muskin, P. R. (1998). The request to die: Role for a psychodynamic perspective on physician-assisted suicide. *JAMA, 279,* 323–328. (16)

Myers, J. K., Weissman, M. M., Tischler, G. L., Holzer, C. E., III, Leaf, P. J., Orvaschel, H., Anthony, J. C., Boyd, J. H., Burke, J. D., Jr., Kramer, M., & Stoltzman, R. (1984). Six-month prevalence of psychiatric disorders in three communities. *Archives of General Psychiatry, 41,* 959–967. (15)

Nagera, H. (1976). *Obsessional neuroses.* New York: Jason Aronson. (16)

Nash, M. (1987). What, if anything, is regressed about hypnotic age regression? A review of the empirical literature. *Psychological Bulletin, 102,* 42–52. (5)

Nash, M. R., Johnson, L. S., & Tipton, R. D. (1979). Hypnotic age regression and the occurrence of transitional object relationships. *Journal of Abnormal Psychology, 88,* 547–555. (5)

National Institute of Mental Health. (1982). *Television and behavior: Ten years of scientific progress and implications for the eighties.* Rockville, MD: Author. (2)

Nebes, R. D. (1974). Hemispheric specialization in commissurotomized man. *Psychological Bulletin, 81,* 1–14. (3)

Negy, C., Leal-Puente, L., Trainor, D. J., & Carlson, R. (1997). Mexican American adolescents' performance on the MMPI-A. *Journal of Personality Assessment, 69,* 205–214. (13)

Neher, A. (1996). Jung's theory of archetypes: A critique. *Journal of Humanistic Psychology, 36,* 61–91. (13)

Neiss, R. (1988). Reconceptualizing arousal: Psychobiological stakes in motor performance. *Psychological Bulletin, 103,* 345–366. (12)

Neisser, U. (1997). Rising scores on intelligence tests. *American Scientist, 85,* 440–447. (9)

Neisser, U. (chair), Boodoo, G., Bouchard, T. J., Jr., Boykin, A. W., Brody, N., Ceci, S. J., Halpern, D. F., Loehlin, J. C., Perloff, R., Sternberg, R. J., & Urbina, S. (1996). Intelligence: knowns and unknowns. *American Psychologist, 51,* 77–101. (9)

Nelson, K. (1981). Individual differences in language development: Implications for development and language. *Developmental Psychology, 17,* 170–187. (8)

Nelson, K. E., Baker, N. D., Denninger, M., Bonvillian, J. D., & Kaplan, B. J. (1985). Cookie versus Do-it-again: Imitative-referential and personal-social-syntactic-initiating language styles in young children. *Linguistics, 23,* 433–454. (8)

Nemeth, C. (1972). A critical analysis of research utilizing the prisoner's dilemma paradigm for the study of bargaining. In L. Berkowitz (Ed.), *Advances in Experimental Social Psychology* (Vol. 6, pp. 203–234). New York: Academic Press. (14)

Nemeth, C. J. (1986). Differential contributions of majority and minority influence. *Psychological Review, 93,* 23–32. (14)

Nestler, E. J., & Aghajanian, G. K. (1997). Molecular and cellular basis of addiction. *Science, 278,* 58–63. (16)

Newman, B. (1988, September 9). Dressing for dinner remains an issue in the naked city. *Wall Street Journal,* p. 1. (14)

Newport, E. L. (1990). Maturational constraints on language learning. *Cognitive Science, 14*, 11–28. (8)

Newstead, S. E., & Makinen, S. (1997). Psychology teaching in Europe. *European Psychologist, 2*, 3–10. (1)

Nickerson, R. S., & Adams, M. J. (1979). Long-term memory for a common object. *Cognitive Psychology, 11*, 287–307. (7)

Nietzel, M. T., & Bernstein, D. A. (1987). *Introduction to clinical psychology*. Englewood Cliffs, NJ: Prentice-Hall. (9)

Nigg, J. T., & Goldsmith, H. H. (1994). Genetics of personality disorders: Perspectives from personality and psychopathology research. *Psychological Bulletin, 115*, 346–380. (3)

Nisbett, R. E., Caputo, C., Legant, P., & Marecek, J. (1973). Behavior as seen by the actor and as seen by the observer. *Journal of Personality and Social Psychology, 27*, 154–164. (14)

Nisbett, R. E., Fong, G. T., Lehman, D. R., & Cheng, P. W. (1987). Teaching reasoning. *Science, 238*, 625–631. (8)

Noel, J. G., Wann, D. L., & Branscombe, N. R. (1995). Peripheral in-group membership status and public negativity toward outgroups. *Journal of Personality and Social Psychology, 68*, 127–137. (14)

Nofzinger, E. A., Thase, M. E., Reynolds, C. F., III, Frank, E., Jennings, J. R., Garamoni, G. L., Fasiczka, A. L., & Kupfer, D. J. (1993). Sexual function in depressed men: Assessment by self-report, behavioral, and nocturnal penile tumescence measures before and after treatment with cognitive behavior therapy. *Archives of General Psychiatry, 50*, 24–30. (16)

Nolen-Hoeksema, S. (1990). *Sex differences in depression*. Stanford, CA: Stanford University Press. (16)

Nolen-Hoeksema, S. (1991). Responses to depression and their effects on the duration of depressive episodes. *Journal of Abnormal Psychology, 100*, 569–582. (16)

Nolen-Hoeksema, S., & Morrow, J. (1991). A prospective study of depression and posttraumatic stress symptoms after a natural disaster: The Loma Prieta earthquake. *Journal of Personality and Social Psychology, 61*, 115–121. (16)

Norman, D. A. (1988). *The psychology of everyday things*. New York: Basic books. (1)

Nygard, R. (1982). Achievement motives and individual differences in situational specificity of behavior. *Journal of Personality and Social Psychology, 43*, 319–327. (11)

Oakland, T. D., & Cunningham, J. L. (1992). A survey of school psychology in developed and developing countries. *School Psychology International, 13*, 99–129. (1)

Ohaeri, J. U., Adeyinka, A. O., & Osuntokun, B. O. (1995). Computed tomographic density changes in schizophrenic and manic Nigerian subjects. *Behavioural Neurology, 8*, 31–37. (16)

O'Hara, M. W., Schlechte, J. A., Lewis, D. A., & Wright, E. J. (1991). Prospective study of postpartum blues. *Archives of General Psychiatry, 48*, 801–806. (16)

Ohayon, M. M. (1997). Prevalence of DSM-IV diagnostic criteria of insomnia: Distinguishing insomnia related to mental disorders from sleep disorders. *Journal of Psychiatric Research, 31*, 333–346. (5)

Öhman, A., Eriksson, A., & Olofsson, C. (1975). One-trial learning and superior resistance to extinction of autonomic responses conditioned to potentially phobic objects. *Journal of Comparative and Physiological Psychology, 88*, 619–627. (16)

Okin, R. L. (1983). The future of state hospitals: Should there be one? *American Journal of Psychiatry, 140*, 577–581. (15)

Olfson, M., Marcus, S. C., Pincus, H. A., Zito, J. M., Thompson, J. W., & Zarin, D. A. (1998). Antidepressant prescribing practices of outpatient psychiatrists. *Archives of General Psychiatry, 55*, 310–316. (16)

Oliver, M. B., & Hyde, J. S. (1993). Gender differences in sexuality: A meta-analysis. *Psychological Bulletin, 114*, 29–51. (11)

Olney, J. W., & Farger, N. B. (1995). Glutamate receptor dysfunction and schizophrenia. *Archives of General Psychiatry, 52*, 998–1007. (16)

Olweus, D. (1995). Bullying or peer abuse at school: Facts and intervention. *Current Directions in Psychological Science, 4*, 196–200. (12)

Ormerod, M. B., McKenzie, J., & Woods, A. (1995). Final report on research relating to the concept of five separate dimensions of personality—or six including intelligence. *Personality and Individual Differences, 18*, 451–461. (13)

Orne, M. T. (1951). The mechanisms of hypnotic age regression: An experimental study. *Journal of Abnormal and Social Psychology, 46*, 213–225. (5)

Orne, M. T. (1959). The nature of hypnosis: Artifact and essence. *Journal of Abnormal and Social Psychology, 58*, 277–299. (5)

Orne, M. T. (1969). Demand characteristics and the concept of quasi-controls. In R. Rosenthal & R. L. Rosnow (Eds.), *Artifact in behavioral research* (pp. 143–179). (2)

Orne, M. T. (1979). On the simulating subject as a quasi-control group in hypnosis research: What, why, and how. In E. Fromm & R. E. Shor (Eds.), *Hypnosis: Developments in research and new perspectives* (2nd ed.) (pp. 519–565). New York: Aldine. (5)

Orne, M. T., Dinges, D. F., & Orne, E. C. (1984). On the differential diagnosis of multiple personality in the forensic context. *International Journal of Clinical and Experimental Hypnosis, 32*, 118–169. (5)

Orne, M. T., & Evans, F. J. (1965). Social control in the psychological experiment: Antisocial behavior and hypnosis. *Journal of Personality and Social Psychology, 1*, 189–200. (5)

Orne, M. T., & Scheibe, K. E. (1964). The contribution of nondeprivation factors in the production of sensory deprivation effects: The psychology of the "panic button." *Journal of Abnormal and Social Psychology, 68*, 3–12. (2)

Orne, M. T., Whitehouse, W. G., Dinges, D. F., & Orne, E. C. (1988). Reconstructing memory through hypnosis: Forensic and clinical applications. In H. M. Pettinati (Ed.), *Hypnosis and memory* (pp. 21–63). New York: Guilford Press. (5)

Ortony, A., & Turner, T. J. (1990). What's basic about basic emotions? *Psychological Review, 97*, 315–331. (12)

Oscar-Berman, M. (1980). Neuropsychological consequences of long-term chronic alcoholism. *American Scientist, 68*, 410–419. (7)

Osofsky, J. D. (1995). The effects of exposure to violence on young children. *American Psychologist, 50*, 782–788. (12)

Öst, L. -G., & Hugdahl, K. (1981). Acquisition of phobias and anxiety response patterns in clinical patients. *Behaviour Research and Therapy, 19*, 439–447. (16)

Ottati, V., & Lee, Y. -T. (1995). Accuracy: A neglected component of stereotype research. In Y. -T. Lee, L. J. Jussim, & C. R. McCauley (Eds.), *Stereotype accuracy* (pp. 29–59). Washington, DC: American Psychological Association. (14)

Overman, W. H., Pate, B. J., Moore, K., & Peuster, A. (1996). Ontogeny of place learning in children as measured in the radial arm maze, Morris search task, and open field task. *Behavioral Neuroscience, 110*, 1205–1228. (7)

Padgham, C. A. (1975). Colours experienced in dreams. *British Journal of Psychology, 66*, 25–28. (5)

Paicheler, G. (1988). *The psychology of social influence*. Cambridge, England: Cambridge University Press. (14)

Paikoff, R. L., & Brooks-Gunn, J. (1991). Do parent-child relationships change during puberty? *Psychological Bulletin, 110*, 47–66. (10)

Palmer, B. W., Heaton, R. K., Paulsen, J. S., Kuck, J., Braff, D., Harris, M. J., Zissook, S., & Jeste, D. V. (1997). Is it possible to be schizophrenic yet neuropsychologically normal? *Neuropsychology, 11*, 437–446. (16)

Papini, M. R., & Bitterman, M. E. (1990). The role of contingency in classical conditioning. *Psychological Review, 97*, 396–403. (6)

Paradis, M. (1990). Language lateralization in bilinguals: Enough already! *Brain and Language, 39*, 576–586. (8)

Parke, R. D. (1995). Fathers and families. In M. H. Bornstein (Ed.), *Handbook of parenting* (Vol. 3, pp. 27–63). Mahwah, NJ: Lawrence Erlbaum. (10)

Parke, R. D., Berkowitz, L., Leyens, J. P., West, S. G., & Sebastian, R. J. (1977). Some effects of violent and nonviolent movies on the behavior of juvenile delinquents. In L. Berkowitz (Ed.), *Advances in experimental social psychology* (Vol. 10, pp. 135–172). New York: Academic Press. (2)

Parker, D. (1944). *The portable Dorothy Parker*. New York: Viking. (15)

Parmeggiani, P. L. (1982). Regulation of physiological functions during sleep in mammals. *Experientia, 38*, 1405–1408. (5)

Parnas, J., Schulsinger, F., Schulsinger, H., Mednick, S. A., & Teasdale, T. W. (1982). Behavioral precursors of schizophrenia spectrum. *Archives of General Psychiatry, 39*, 658–664. (16)

Parra, C., Esteves, F., Flykt, A., & Öhman, A. (1997). Pavlovian conditioning to social stimuli: Backward masking and the dissociation of implicit and explicit cognitive processes. *European Psychologist, 2*, 106–117. (6)

Pascual-Leone, A., Wasserman, E. M., Sadato, N., & Hallett, M. (1995). The role of reading activity on the modulation of motor cortical outputs to the reading hand in braille readers. *Annals of Neurology, 38*, 910–915. (3)

Pashler, H. (1994). Dual-task interference in simple tasks: Data and theory. *Psychological Bulletin, 116*, 220–244. (8)

Pate, J. L., & Rumbaugh, D. M. (1983). The language-like behavior of Lana chimpanzee: Is it merely discrimination and paired-associate learning? *Animal Learning & Behavior, 11*, 134–138. (8)

Patrick, C. J., & Iacono, W. G. (1989). Psychopathy, threat, and polygraph test accuracy. *Journal of Applied Psychology, 74*, 347–355. (12)

Patterson, C. J. (1994). Lesbian and gay families. *Current Directions in Psychological Science, 3*, 62–64. (10)

Paus, T., Marrett, S., Worsley, K. J., & Evans, A. C. (1995). Extraretinal modulation of cerebral blood flow in the human visual cortex: Implications for saccadic suppression. *Journal of Neurophysiology, 74*, 2179–2183. (8)

Pavlov, I. P. (1960). *Conditioned reflexes*. New York: Dover. (Original work published 1927) (6)

Peachey, J. E., & Naranjo, C. A. (1983). The use of disulfiram and other alcohol-sensitizing drugs in the treatment of alcoholism. *Research Advances in Alcohol and Drug Problems, 7*, 397–431. (16)

Pearce, J. M. (1994). Similarity and discrimination: A selective review and a connectionist model. *Psychological Review, 101*, 587–607. (6)

Peck, C. P. (1986). A public mental health issue: Risk-taking behavior and compulsive gambling. *American Psychologist, 41*, 461–465. (8)

Pedersen, N. L., Plomin, R., & McClearn, G. E. (1994). Is there G beyond *g*? (Is there genetic influence on specific cognitive abilities independent of genetic influence on general cognitive ability?) *Intelligence, 18*, 133–143. (9)

Peele, S. (1998 March/April). All wet. *The Sciences, 38* (2), 17–21. (16)

Pellymounter, M. A., Cullen, M. J., Baker, M. B., Hecht, R., Winters, D., Boone, T., & Collins, F. (1995). Effects of the *obese* gene product on body weight regulation in *ob/ob* mice. *Science, 269*, 540–543. (11)

Penfield, W., & Rasmussen, T. (1950). *The cerebral cortex of man*. New York: Macmillan. (3)

Pennebaker, J. W. (1990). *Opening up*. New York: William Morrow. (12)

Pennebaker, J. W. (1997). Writing about emotional experiences as a therapeutic process. *Psychological Science, 8*, 162–166. (12)

Perkins, D. N., & Grotzer, T. A. (1997). Teaching intelligence. *American Psychologist, 52*, 1125–1133. (9)

Perry, D. G., & Bussey, K. (1979). The social learning theory of sex differences: Imitation is alive and well. *Journal of Personality and Social Psychology, 37*, 1699–1712. (13)

Pert, C. B., & Snyder, S. H. (1973). The opiate receptor: Demonstration in nervous tissue. *Science, 179*, 1011–1014. (5)

Peterson, C., Bettes, B. A., & Seligman, M. E. P. (1985). Depressive symptoms and unprompted causal attributions: Content analysis. *Behaviour Research and Therapy, 23*, 379–382. (16)

Peterson, L. G., Peterson, M., O'Shanick, G. J., & Swann, A. (1985). Self-inflicted gunshot wounds: Lethality of method versus intent. *American Journal of Psychiatry, 142*, 228–231. (16)

Peterson, L. R., & Peterson, M. J. (1959). Short-term retention of individual verbal items. *Journal of Experimental Psychology, 58*, 193–198. (7)

Petrie, K. J., & Dawson, A. G. (1997). Symptoms of fatigue and coping strategies in international pilots. *International Journal of Aviation Psychology, 7*, 251–258. (5)

Petrill, S. A., Luo, D., Thompson, L. A., & Detterman, D. K. (1996). The independent prediction of general intelligence by elementary cognitive tasks: Genetic and environmental influences. *Behavior Genetics, 26*, 135–147. (9)

Petter, G. (1956). Nuove ricerche sperimentali sulla totallizzazione percettiva. *Rivista di Psicologia, 50*, 213–227. (4)

Petty, R. E., & Cacioppo, J. T. (1977). Effects of forewarning of persuasive intent and involvement on cognitive responses and persuasion. *Personality and Social Psychology Bulletin, 5*, 173–176. (14)

Petty, R. E., & Cacioppo, J. T. (1981). *Attitudes and persuasion: Classic and contemporary approaches*. Dubuque, IA: Wm. C. Brown. (14)

Petty, R. E., & Cacioppo, J. T. (1986). *Communication and persuasion: Central and peripheral routes to attitude change*. New York: Springer-Verlag. (14)

Pezdek, K., Finger, K., & Hodge, D. (1997). Planting false childhood memories: The role of event plausibility. *Psychological Science, 8*, 437–441. (7)

Pfungst, O. (1911). *Clever Hans*. New York: Holt. (2)

Phalet, K., & Claeys, W. (1993). A comparative study of Turkish and Belgian youth. *Journal of Cross-Cultural Psychology, 24*, 319–343. (11)

Phelps, J. A., Davis, J. O., & Schartz, K. M. (1997). Nature, nurture, and twin research strategies. *Current Directions in Psychological Science, 6*, 117–121. (16)

Phelps, M. E., & Mazziotta, J. C. (1985). Positron emission tomography: Human brain function and biochemistry. *Science, 228*, 799–809. (1)

Phillips, M. L., Young, A. W., Senior, C., Brammer, M., Andrew, C., Calder, A. J., Bullmore, E. T., Perrett, D. I., Rowland, D., Williams, S. C. R., Gray, J. A., & David, A. S. (1997). A spoecific neural substrate for perceiving facial expressions of disgust. *Nature, 389*, 495–498. (12)

Phillips, R. G., & LeDoux, J. E. (1992). Differential contribution of amygdala and hippocampus to cued and contextual fear conditioning. *Behavioral Neuroscience, 106*, 274–285. (12)

Phillips, R. T., & Alcebo, A. M. (1986). The effects of divorce on black children and adolescents. *American Journal of Social Psychology, 6*, 69–73. (10)

Piaget, J. (1954). *The construction of reality in the child* (M. Cook, Trans.). New York: Basic Books. (Original work published 1937) (10)

Piasecki, T. M., Kenford, S. L., Smith, S. S., Fiore, M. C., & Baker, T. B. (1997). Listening to nicotine: Negative affect and the smoking withdrawal conundrum. *Psychological Science, 8*, 184–189. (16)

Pichot, P. (1984). Centenary of the birth of Hermann Rorschach. *Journal of Personality Assessment, 48*, 591–596. (13)

Pidoplichko, V. I., De Biasi, M., Williams, J. T., & Dani, J. A. (1997). Nicotine activates and densitizes midbrain dopamine neurons. *Nature, 390*, 401–404. (16)

Pinker, S. (1994). *The language instinct*. New York: William Morrow and Company. (8)

Pion, G. M., Mednick, M. T., Astin, H. S., Hall, C. C. I., Kenkel, M. B., Keita, G. P., Kohout, J. L., & Kelleher, J. C. (1996). The shifting gender composition of psychology. *American Psychologist, 51*, 509–528. (1)

Piotrowski, C., & Keller, J. W. (1989). Psychological testing in outpatient mental health facilities: A national study. *Professional Psychology: Research and Practice, 20*, 423–425. (13)

Pitman, R. K., Orr, S. P., Forgue, D. F., deJong, J. B., & Claiborn, N. M. (1987). Psychophysiologic assessment of posttraumatic stress disorder imagery in Vietnam combat veterans. *Archives of General Psychiatry, 44*, 970–975. (12)

Pitman, R. K., van der Kolk, B. A., Orr, S. P., & Greenberg, M. S. (1990). Naloxone-reversible analgesic response to combat-related stimuli in posttraumatic stress disorder. *Archives of General Psychiatry, 47*, 541–544. (12)

Plihal, W., & Born, J. (1997). Effects of early and late nocturnal sleep on declarative and procedural memory. *Journal of Cognitive Neuroscience, 9*, 534–547. (5)

Plomin, R., Corley, R., DeFries, J. C., & Fulker, D. W. (1990). Individual differences in television viewing in early childhood: Nature as well as nurture. *Psychological Science, 1*, 371–377. (3)

Plomin, R., & DeFries, J. C. (1980). Genetics and intelligence: Recent data. *Intelligence, 4*, 15–24. (9)

Plomin, R., DeFries, J. C., & Roberts, M. K. (1977). Assortative mating by unwed biological parents of adopted children. *Science, 196*, 449–450. (14)

Plomin, R., Fulker, D. W., Corley, R., & DeFries, J. C. (1997). Nature, nurture, and cognitive development from 1 to 16 years: A parent-offspring adoption study. *Psychological Science, 8*, 442–447. (9)

Plous, S. (1996). Attitudes toward the use of animals in psychological research and education. *American Psychologist, 51*, 1167–1180. (2)

Plutchik, R. (1982). A psychoevolutionary theory of emotions. *Social Science Information, 21*, 529–553. (12)

Plutchik, R., & Ax, A. F. (1967). A critique of "determinants of emotional state" by Schachter and Singer (1962). *Psychophysiology, 4*, 79–82. (12)

Polcin, D. L. (1997). The etiology and diagnosis of alcohol dependence: Differences in the professional literature. *Psychotherapy, 34*, 297–306. (16)

Polivy, J., & Herman, C. P. (1985). Dieting and binging: A causal analysis. *American Psychologist, 40*, 193–201. (11)

Polivy, J., & Herman, C. P. (1987). Diagnosis and treatment of normal eating. *Journal of Consulting and Clinical Psychology, 55*, 635–644. (11)

Pollak, J. M. (1979). Obsessive-compulsive personality: A review. *Psychological Bulletin, 86*, 225–241. (16)

Polya, G. (1957). *How to solve it*. Garden City, NY: Doubleday Anchor. (8)

Pontieri, F. E., Tanda, G., Orzi, F., & DiChiara, G. (1996). Effects of nicotine on the nucleus accumbens and similarity to those of addictive drugs. *Nature, 382*, 255–257. (5)

Poole, A. D., Sanson-Fisher, R. W., & German, G. A. (1981). The rapid-smoking technique: Therapeutic effectiveness. *Behaviour Research and Therapy, 19*, 389–397. (15)

Poole, D. A., & White, L. T. (1995). Tell me again and again: Stability and change in the repeated testimonies of children and adults. In M. S. Zaragoza, J. R. Graham, G. C. N. Hall, R. Hirschman, & Y. S. Ben-Porath (Eds.), *Memory and testimony in the child witness* (pp. 24–43). Thousand Oaks, CA: Sage Publications (7)

Pope, K. S. (1996). Memory, abuse, and science: Questioning claims about the false memory syndrome epidemic. *American Psychologist, 51*, 957–974. (7)

Popper, K. (1986). Predicting overt behavior versus predicting hidden states. *Behavioral and Brain Sciences, 9*, 254–255. (13)

Poulos, C. X., & Cappell, H. (1991). Homeostatic theory of drug tolerance: A general model of physiological adaptation. *Psychological Review, 98*, 390–408. (6)

Poulos, C. X., Wilkinson, D. A., & Cappell, H. (1981). Homeostatic regulation and Pavlovian conditioning in tolerance to amphetamine-induced anorexia. *Journal of Comparative and Physiological Psychology, 95*, 735–746. (6)

Povinelli, D. J., & deBlois, S. (1992). Young children's (*Homo sapiens*) understanding of knowledge formation in themselves and others. *Journal of Comparative Psychology, 106*, 228–238. (10)

Powell, R. A., & Boer, D. P. (1994). Did Freud mislead patients to confabulate memories of abuse? *Psychological Reports, 74*, 1283–1298. (13)

Powlishta, K. K., & Maccoby, E. E. (1990). Resource utilization in mixed-sex dyads: The influence of adult presence and task type. *Sex Roles, 23*, 223–240. (13)

Pratkanis, A. R., Greenwald, A. G., Leippe, M. R., & Baumgardner, M. H. (1988). In search of reliable persuasion effects: III. The sleeper effect is dead. Long live the sleeper effect. *Journal of Personality and Social Psychology, 54*, 203–218. (14)

Premack, A. J., & Premack, D. (1972). Teaching language to an ape. *Scientific American, 227*(4), 92–99. (8)

Premack, D. (1965). Reinforcement theory. In D. Levine (Ed.), *Nebraska symposium on motivation* (pp. 123–188). Lincoln, NE: University of Nebraska Press. (6)

Prohaska, V. (1994). "I know I'll get an A": Confident overestimation of final course grades. *Teaching of Psychology, 21*, 141–143. (8)

Provine, R. R. (1996). Laughter. *American Scientist, 84*, 38–45. (12)

Provine, R. R. (1997). Yawns, laughs, smiles, tickles, and talking: Naturalistic and laboratory studies of facial action and social communication. In J. A. Russell & J. M. Fernandez-Dols (Eds.), *The psychology of facial expression* (pp. 158–175). Cambridge, England: Cambridge University Press. (12)

Qin, Y., & Simon, H. A. (1990). Laboratory replication of scientific discovery processes. *Cognitive Science, 14*, 281–312. (8)

Quadrel, M. J., Fischhoff, B., & Davis, W. (1993). Adolescent (in)vulnerability. *American Psychologist, 48*, 102–116. (10)

Rachlin, H. (1990). Why do people gamble and keep gambling despite heavy losses? *Psychological Science, 1*, 294–297. (8)

Rachlin, H., Siegel, E., & Cross, D. (1994). Lotteries and the time horizon. *Psychological Science, 5*, 390–393. (8)

Rachman, S. (1969). Treatment by prolonged exposure to high intensity stimulation. *Behaviour Research and Therapy, 7*, 295–302. (16)

Rachman, S. J., & Hodgson, R. J. (1980). *Obsessions and compulsions*. Englewood Cliffs, NJ: Prentice-Hall. (16)

Raine, A., Venables, P. H., & Williams, M. (1990). Relationships between central and autonomic measures of arousal at age 15 years and criminality at age 24 years. *Archives of General Psychiatry, 47*, 1003–1007. (12)

Rainville, P., Duncan, G. H., Price, D. D., Carrier, B., & Bushnell, M. C. (1997). Pain affect encoded in human anterior cingulate but not somatosensory cortex. *Science, 277*, 968–971. (5)

Raudenbush, B., & Zellner, D. A. (1997). Nobody's satisfied: Effects of abnormal eating behaviors and actual and perceived weight status on body image satisfaction in males and females. *Journal of Social and Clinical Psychology, 16*, 95–110. (11)

Ravussin, E., Lillioja, S., Knowler, W. C., Christin, L., Freymona, D., Abbott, W. G. H., Boyce, V., Howard, B. V., & Bogardus, C. (1988). Reduced rate of energy expenditure as a risk factor for body-weight gain. *New England Journal of Medicine, 318*, 467–472. (11)

Reber, A. S. (1997). How to differentiate implicit and explicit modes of acquisition. In J. D. Cohen & J. W. Schooler (Eds.), *Scientific approaches to consciousness* (pp. 137–159). Mahwah, NJ: Lawrence Erlbaum Associates. (7)

Rechtschaffen, A., & Bergmann, B. M. (1995). Sleep deprivation in the rat by the disk-over-water method. *Behavioural Brain Research, 69*, 55–63. (5)

Redican, W. K. (1982). An evolutionary perspective on human facial displays. In P. Ekman (Ed.), *Emotion in the human face* (pp. 212–280). Cambridge, England: Cambridge University Press. (12)

Reed, J. M., & Squire, L. R. (1997). Impaired recognition memory in patients with lesions limited to the hippocampal formation. *Behavioral Neuroscience, 111*, 667–675. (7)

Reed, T. E. (1985). Ethnic differences in alcohol use, abuse, and sensitivity: A review with genetic interpretation. *Social Biology, 32*, 195–209. (16)

Reed, T. E. (1997). "The genetic hypothesis": It was not tested but it could have been. *American Psychologist, 52*, 77–78. (9)

Reeves, A. G., & Plum, F. (1969). Hyperphagia, rage, and dementia accompanying a ventromedial hypothalamic neoplasm. *Archives of Neurology, 20*, 616–624. (11)

Reicher, G. M. (1969). Perceptual recognition as a function of meaningfulness of stimulus material. *Journal of Experimental Psychology, 81*, 275–280. (8)

Reichling, D. B., Kwiat, G. C., & Basbaum, A. I. (1988). Anatomy, physiology, and pharmacology of the periaqueductal gray contribution to antinociceptive controls. In H. L. Fields & J.-M. Besson (Eds.), *Progress in brain research* (Vol. 77, pp. 31–46). Amsterdam: Elsevier. (4)

Rescorla, R. A. (1968). Probability of shock in the presence and absence of CS in fear conditioning. *Journal of Comparative and Physiological Psychology, 66*, 1–5. (6)

Rescorla, R. A. (1988). Pavlovian conditioning: It's not what you think it is. *American Psychologist, 43*, 151–160. (6)

Ressler, K. J., Sullivan, S. L., & Buck, L. B. (1994). A molecular dissection of spatial patterning in the olfactory system. *Current Opinion in Neurobiology, 4*, 588–596. (4)

Rest, J. R. (1983). Morality. In P. H. Mussen (Ed.), *Handbook of child psychology* (4th ed.) (Vol. 3, pp. 556–629). New York: Wiley. (10)

Restle, F. (1970). Moon illusion explained on the basis of relative size. *Science, 167*, 1092–1096. (4)

Riccio, D. C. (1994). Memory: When less is more. *American Psychologist, 49*, 917–926. (7)

Rich, C. L., Ricketts, J. E., Fowler, R. C., & Young, D. (1988). Some differences between men and women who commit suicide. *American Journal of Psychiatry, 145*, 718–722. (16)

Richwald, G. A., Morisky, D. E., Kyle, G. R., Kristal, A. R., Gerber, M. M., & Friedland, J. M. (1988). Sexual activities in bathhouses in Los Angeles county: Implications for AIDS prevention education. *Journal of Sex Research, 25*, 169–180. (11)

Riddle, W. J. R., & Scott, A. I. F. (1995). Relapse after successful electroconvulsive therapy: The use and impact of continuation antidepressant drug treatment. *Human Psychopharmacology, 10*, 201–205. (16)

Ritz, M. C., Lamb, R. J., Goldberg, S. R., & Kuhar, M. J. (1987). Cocaine receptors on dopamine transporters are related to self-administration of cocaine. *Science, 237*, 1219–1223. (5)

Rivera, P. A., Rose, J. M., Futterman, A., Lovett, S. B., & Gallagher-Thompson, D. (1991). Dimensions of perceived social support in clinically depressed and nondepressed female caregivers. *Psychology and Aging, 6*, 232–237. (16)

Rivers, P. C. (1994). *Alcohol and human behavior*. Englewood Cliffs, NJ: Prentice-Hall. (5)

Robbins, T. W., & Everitt, B. J. (1995). Arousal systems and attention. In M. S. Gazzaniga (Ed.), *The cognitive neurosciences* (pp. 703–720). Cambridge, MA: MIT Press. (3)

Roberts, S. B., Savage, J., Coward, W. A., Chew, B., & Lucas, A. (1988). Energy expenditure and intake in infants born to lean and overweight mothers. *New England Journal of Medicine, 318*, 461–466. (11)

Robins, L. N., Helzer, J. E., Weissman, M. M., Orvaschel, H., Gruenberg, E., Burke, J. D., Jr., & Regier, D. A. (1984). Lifetime prevalence of specific psychiatric disorders in three sites. *Archives of General Psychiatry, 41*, 949–958. (15, 16)

Robinson, K. J., & Roediger, H. L., III (1997). Associative processes in false recall and false recognition. *Psychological Science, 8*, 231–237. (7)

Robinson, L. A., Berman, J. S., & Neimeyer, R. A. (1990). Psychotherapy for the treatment of depression: A comprehensive review of controlled outcome research. *Psychological Bulletin, 108*, 30–49. (16)

Robinson, R. J., & Keltner, D. (1996). Much ado about nothing? Revisionists and traditionalists choose an introductory English syllabus. *Psychological Science, 7*, 18–24. (14)

Rock, I., & Kaufman, L. (1962). The moon illusion, II. *Science, 136*, 1023–1031. (4)

Rodin, J. (1986). Aging and health: Effects of the sense of control. *Science, 233*, 1271–1276. (10)

Rogers, C. R. (1951). *Client-centered therapy*. Boston: Houghton Mifflin. (15)

Rogers, C. R. (1961). *On becoming a person*. Boston: Houghton Mifflin. (13)

Rogers, C. R. (1980). *A way of being*. Boston: Houghton Mifflin. (13)

Rogers, T. B. (1995). *The psychological testing enterprise: An introduction*. Pacific Grove, CA: Brooks/Cole. (9)

Rohrbaugh, M., Shoham, V., Spungen, C., & Steinglass, P. (1995). Family systems therapy in practice: A systemic couples therapy for problem drinking. In B. Bongar & L. E. Beutler (Eds.), *Comprehensive textbook of psychotherapy: Theory and practice* (pp. 228–253). Oxford, England: Oxford University Press. (15)

Rollman, G. B. (1991). Pain responsiveness. In M. Heller & W. Schiff (Eds.), *The psychology of touch* (pp. 91–118). Hillsdale, NJ: Lawrence Erlbaum. (4)

Rolls, E. T. (1997). Taste and olfactory processing in the brain and its relation to the control of eating. *Critical Reviews in Neurobiology, 11*, 263–287. (4)

Rosch, E. (1978). Principles of categorization. In E. Rosch & B. B. Lloyd (Eds.), *Cognition and categorization* (pp. 27–48). Hillsdale, NJ: Lawrence Erlbaum. (8)

Rosch, E., & Mervis, C. B. (1975). Family resemblances: Studies in the internal structure of categories. *Cognitive Psychology, 7*, 573–605. (8)

Roseman, I. J., Dhawan, N., Rettek, S. I., Naidu, R. K., & Thapa, K. (1995). Cultural differences and cross-cultural similarities in appraisals and emotional responses. *Journal of Cross-cultural Psychology, 26*, 23–48. (12)

Rosenbaum, M. E. (1986). The repulsion hypothesis: on the nondevelopment of relationships. *Journal of Personality and Social Psychology, 51*, 1156–1166. (14)

Rosenberg, H. (1993). Prediction of controlled drinking by alcoholics and problem drinkers. *Psychological Bulletin, 113*, 129–139. (16)

Ross, L. (1977). The intuitive psychologist and his shortcomings: Distortions in the attribution process. In L. Berkowitz (Ed.), *Advances in experimental social psychology* (Vol. 10, pp. 173–220). New York: Academic Press. (14)

Rothbaum, B. O., Hodges, L. F., Kooper, R., Opdyke, D., Williford, J. S., & North, M. (1995). Effectiveness of computer-generated (virtual reality) graded exposure in the treatment of acrophobia. *American Journal of Psychiatry, 152*, 626–628. (16)

Rothman, A. J., & Salovey, P. (1997). Shaping perceptions to motivate healthy behavior: The role of message framing. *Psychological Bulletin, 121*, 3–19. (8)

Rotter, J. B. (1966). Generalized expectancies for internal versus external control of reinforcement. *Psychological Monographs, 80* (Whole No. 603). (13)

Rotton, J., & Kelly, I. W. (1985). Much ado about the full moon: A meta-analysis of lunar-lunacy research. *Psychological Bulletin, 97*, 286–306. (2)

Rovee-Collier, C. (1984). The ontogeny of learning and memory in human infancy. In R. Kail & N. E. Spear (Eds.), *Comparative perspectives on the development of memory* (pp. 103–134). Hillsdale, NJ: Lawrence Erlbaum. (10)

Rowe, D. C., Vazsonyi, A. T., & Flannery, D. J. (1994). No more than skin deep: Ethnic and racial similarity in developmental process. *Psychological Review, 101*, 396–413. (9)

Rowe, J. W., & Kahn, R. L. (1987). Human aging: Usual and successful. *Science, 237,* 143–149. (10)

Rowland, C. V., Jr. (Ed.) (1970). *Anorexia and obesity.* Boston: Little, Brown. (11)

Roy, A. (1985). Early parental separation and adult depression. *Archives of General Psychiatry, 42,* 987–991. (16)

Roy, A., DeJong, J., & Linnoila, M. (1989). Cerebrospinal fluid monoamine metabolites and suicidal behavior in depressed patients. *Archives of General Psychiatry, 46,* 609–612. (12, 16)

Rozin, P. (1996). Sociocultural influences on human food selection. In E. D. Capaldi (Ed.), *Why we eat what we eat* (pp. 233–263). Washington, DC: American Psychological Association. (11)

Rozin, P., & Fallon, A. E. (1987). A perspective on disgust. *Psychological Review, 94,* 23–41. (11)

Rozin, P., Fallon, A., & Augustoni-Ziskind, M. L. (1986). The child's conception of food: The development of categories of acceptable and rejected substances. *Journal of Nutrition Education, 18,* 75–81. (11)

Rozin, P., & Kalat, J. W. (1971). Specific hungers and poison avoidance as adaptive specializations of learning. *Psychological Review, 78,* 459–486. (6, 11)

Rozin, P., Markwith, M., & Ross, B. (1990). The sympathetic magical law of similarity, nominal realism and neglect of negatives in response to negative labels. *Psychological Science, 1,* 383–384. (8)

Rozin, P., Markwith, M., & Stoess, C. (1997). Moralization and becoming a vegetarian: The transformation of preferences into values and the recruitment of disgust. *Psychological Science, 8,* 67–73. (11)

Rozin, P., Millman, L., & Nemeroff, C. (1986). Operation of the laws of sympathetic magic in disgust and other domains. *Journal of Personality and Social Psychology, 50,* 703–712. (11)

Rozin, P., & Pelchat, M. L. (1988). Memories of mammaries: Adaptations to weaning from milk. *Progress in Psychobiology and Physiological Psychology, 13,* 1–29. (3)

Rubenstein, R., & Newman, R. (1954). The living out of "future" experiences under hypnosis. *Science, 119,* 472–473. (5)

Rubin, D. C., & Wenzel, A. E. (1996). One hundred years of forgetting: A quantitative description of retention. *Psychological Review, 103,* 734–760. (7)

Ruch, J. (1984). *Psychology: The personal science.* Belmont, CA: Wadsworth. (3)

Ruderman, A. J. (1986). Dietary restraint: A theoretical and empirical review. *Psychological Review, 99,* 247–262. (11)

Ruderman, A. J., & Christensen, H. C. (1983). Restraint theory and its applicability to overweight individuals. *Journal of Abnormal Psychology, 92,* 210–215. (11)

Rudy, J. W., & Sutherland, R. J. (1992). Configural and elemental associations and the memory coherence problem. *Journal of Cognitive Neuroscience, 4,* 208–216. (7)

Rumelhart, D. E., & McClelland, J. L. (1982). An interactive activation model of context effects in letter perception: Part 2, The contextual enhancement effect and some tests and extensions of the model. *Psychological Review, 89,* 60–94. (8)

Rumelhart, D. E., McClelland, J. L., & the PDP Research Group. (1986). *Parallel distributed processing.* Cambridge, MA: MIT Press. (8)

Rusak, B. (1977). The role of the suprachiasmatic nuclei in the generation of circadian rhythms in the golden hamster, *Mesocricetus auratus. Journal of Comparative Physiology A, 118,* 145–164. (5)

Russell, G. F. M., Szmukler, G. I., Dare, C., & Eisler, I. (1987). An evaluation of family therapy in anorexia nervosa and bulimia nervosa. *Archives of General Psychiatry, 44,* 1047–1056. (15)

Russell, J. A. (1994). Is there universal recognition of emotion from facial expression? A review of the cross-cultural studies. *Psychological Bulletin, 115,* 102–141. (12)

Russell, J. A. (1997). Reading emotions from and into faces: Resurrecting a dimensional-contextual perspective. In J. A. Russell & J. M. Fernández-Dols (Eds.), *The psychology of facial expression* (pp. 295–320). Cambridge, England: Cambridge University Press. (12)

Russell, R. J. H., & Wells, P. A. (1991). Personality similarity and quality of marriage. *Personality and Individual Differences, 12,* 407–412. (14)

Saarinen, T. F. (1973). The use of projective techniques in geographic research. In W. H. Ittelson (Ed.), *Environment and cognition* (pp. 29–52). New York: Seminar Press. (8)

Sabo, K. T., & Kirtley, D. D. (1982). Objects and activities in the dreams of the blind. *International Journal of Rehabilitation Research, 5,* 241–242. (5)

Sadger, J. (1941). Preliminary study of the psychic life of the fetus and the primary germ. *Psychoanalytic Review, 28,* 327–358. (2)

Saegert, S., Swap, W., & Zajonc, R. B. (1973). Exposure, context, and interpersonal attraction. *Journal of Personality and Social Psychology, 25,* 234–242. (14)

Salthouse, T. A., Mitchell, D. R., Skovronek, E., & Babcock, R. L. (1989). Effects of adult age and working memory on reasoning and spatial abilities. *Journal of Experimental Psychology: Learning, Memory, and Cognition, 15,* 507–516. (7)

Salzarulo, P., & Chevalier, A. (1983). Sleep problems in children and their relationship with early disturbances of the waking-sleeping rhythms. *Sleep, 6,* 47–51. (5)

Samelson, F. (1980). J. B. Watson's Little Albert, Cyril Burt's twins, and the need for a critical science. *American Scientist, 35,* 619–625. (16)

Santrock, J. W., Warshak, R. A., & Elliott, G. L. (1982). Social development and parent-child interaction in father-custody and step-mother families. In M. E. Lamb (Ed.), *Nontraditional families* (pp. 289–314). Hillsdale, NJ: Lawrence Erlbaum. (10)

Sapolsky, R. M. (1998, March 30). Open season. *The New Yorker, 74* (6), 57–58, 71–72. (13)

Satterfield, J. M., & Seligman, M. E. P. (1994). Military aggression and risk predicted by explanatory style. *Psychological Science, 5,* 77–82. (16)

Sattler, J. M., & Gwynne, J. (1982). White examiners generally do not impede the intelligence test performance of Black children: to debunk a myth. *Journal of Consulting and Clinical Psychology, 50,* 196–208. (9)

Saudino, K. J. (1997). Moving beyond the heritability question: New directions in behavioral genetic studies of personality. *Current Directions in Psychological Science, 6,* 86–90. (13)

Savage-Rumbaugh, E. S. (1990). Language acquisition in a nonhuman species: Implications for the innateness debate. *Developmental Psychology, 23,* 599–620. (8)

Savage-Rumbaugh, E. S., Sevcik, R. A., Brakke, K. E., & Rumbaugh, D. M. (1992). Symbols: Their communicative use, communication, and combination by bonobos (*Pan paniscus*). In L. P. Lipsitt & C. Rovee-Collier (Eds.), *Advances in infancy research* (Vol. 7, pp. 221–278). Norwood, NJ: Ablex. (8)

Scarborough, E., & Furomoto, L. (1987). *Untold lives: The first generation of American women psychologists.* New York: Columbia University Press. (1)

Scarr, S. (1968). Environmental bias in twin studies. *Eugenics Quarterly, 15,* 34–40. (9)

Scarr, S. (1997). Rules of evidence: A larger context for the statistical debate. *Psychological Science, 8,* 16–17. (2)

Scarr, S. (1998). American child care today. *American Psychologist, 53,* 95–108. (10)

Scarr, S., & Carter-Saltzman, L. (1979). Twin method: Defense of a critical assumption. *Behavior Genetics, 9,* 527–542. (9)

Scarr, S., Pakstis, A. J., Katz, S. H., & Barker, W. B. (1977). The absence of a relationship between degree of white ancestry and intellectual skills within a black population. *Human Genetics, 39,* 69–86. (9)

Scarr, S., Phillips, D., & McCartney, K. (1990). Facts, fantasies and the future of child care in the United States. *Psychological Science, 1,* 26–35. (10)

Scarr, S., & Weinberg, R. A. (1976). IQ test performance of black children adopted by white families. *American Psychologist, 31,* 726–739. (9)

Schachter, D. L. (1987). Implicit memory: History and current status. *Journal of Experimental Psychology: Learning, Memory, and Cognition, 13,* 501–518. (7)

Schacter, D. L., Tharan, M., Cooper, L. A., & Rubens, A. B. (1991). Preserved priming of novel objects in patients with memory disorders. *Journal of Cognitive Neuroscience, 3,* 117–130. (7)

Schacter, D. L., Verfaellie, M., & Anes, M. D. (1997). Illusory memories in amnesic patients: Conceptual and perceptual false recognition. *Neuropsychology, 11,* 331–342. (7)

Schachter, S. (1959). *The psychology of affiliation.* Stanford, CA: Stanford University Press. (14)

Schachter, S. (1968). Obesity and eating. *Science, 161,* 751–756. (11)

Schachter, S. (1982). Recidivism and self-cure of smoking and obesity. *American Psychologist, 37,* 436–444. (11)

Schachter, S., & Singer, J. (1962). Cognitive, social, and physiological determinants of emotional state. *Psychological Review, 69,* 379–399. (12)

Schaie, K. W. (1994). The course of adult intellectual development. *American Psychologist, 49,* 304–313. (7, 10)

Schank, R., & Birnbaum, L. (1994). Enhancing intelligence., In J. Khalfa (Ed.), *What is intelligence?* (pp. 72–106). Cambridge, England: Cambridge University Press. (9)

Schatzman, M. (1992, March 21). Freud: Who seduced whom? *New Scientist,* pp. 34–37. (13)

Schenck, C. H., & Mahowald, M. W. (1996). Long-term, nightly benzodiazepine treatment of injurious parasomnias and other disorders of disrupted nocturnal sleep in 170 adults. *American Journal of Medicine, 100,* 333–337. (5)

Schiffman, S. S. (1983). Taste and smell in disease. *New England Journal of Medicine, 308,* 1275–1279, 1337–1343. (4)

Schiffman, S. S., & Erickson, R. P. (1971). A psychophysical model for gustatory quality. *Physiology & Behavior, 7,* 617–633. (4)

Schlaug, G., Jäncke, L., Huang, Y., & Steinmetz, H. (1995). In vivo evidence of structural brain asymmetry in musicians. *Science, 267,* 699–701. (3)

Schlesier-Stropp, B. (1984). Bulimia: A review of the literature. *Psychological Review, 95,* 247–257. (11)

Schmidt, F. L., & Hunter, J. E. (1981). Employment testing: Old theories and new research findings. *American Psychologist, 36,* 1128–1137. (9)

Schmidt, R. A., & Bjork, R. A. (1992). New conceptualizations of practice: Common principles in three paradigms suggest new concepts for training. *Psychological Science, 3,* 207–217. (7)

Schmitt, A. P., & Dorans, N. J. (1990). Differential item functioning for minority examinees on the SAT. *Journal of Educational Measurement, 27,* 67–81. (9)

Schneider, N. G. (1994). Nicotine nasal spray. *Health Values, 18* (3), 10–14. (16)

Schneider, W., & Shiffrin, R. M. (1977). Controlled and automatic human information processing: I. Detection, search, and attention. *Psychological Review, 84,* 1–66. (8)

Schooler, C. (1972). Birth order effects: Not here, not now! *Psychological Bulletin, 78,* 161–175. (10)

Schou, M. (1997). Forty years of lithium treatment. *Archives of General Psychiatry, 54,* 9–13. (16)

Schuckit, M. C., & Smith, T. L. (1997). Assessing the risk for alcoholism among sons of alcoholics. *Journal of Studies on Alcohol, 58,* 141–145. (16)

Schulsinger, F., Knop, J., Goodwin, D. W., Teasdale, T. W., & Mikkelsen, U. (1986). A prospective study of young men at high risk for alcoholism. *Archives of General Psychiatry, 43,* 755–760. (16)

Schwartz, G. E. (1987). Personality and health: An integrative health science approach. *The G. Stanley Hall Lecture Series, 7,* 125–157. (12)

Schwartz, M. B., & Brownell, K. D. (1995). Matching individuals to weight loss treatments: A survey of obesity experts. *Journal of Consulting and Clinical Psychology, 63,* 149–153. (11)

Schwarzwald, J., Bizman, A., & Raz, M. (1983). The foot-in-the-door paradigm: Effects of second request size on donation probability and donor generosity. *Personality and Social Psychology Bulletin, 9,* 443–450. (14)

Scott, S. K., Young, A. W., Calder, A. J., Hellawell, D. J., Aggleton, J. P., & Johnson, M. (1997). Impaired auditory recognition of fear and anger following bilateral amygdala lesions. *Nature, 385,* 254–257. (12)

Scott, W. J. (1990). PTSD in DSM-III: A case in the politics of diagnosis and disease. *Social Problems, 37,* 294–310. (16)

Scovern, A. W., & Kilmann, P. R. (1980). Status of electroconvulsive therapy: Review of the outcome literature. *Psychological Bulletin, 87,* 260–303. (16)

Scribner, S. (1974). Developmental aspects of categorized recall in a west African society. *Cognitive Psychology, 6,* 475–494. (7)

Scripture, E. W. (1907). *Thinking, feeling, doing* (2nd ed.). New York: G. P. Putnam's Sons. (1)

Seeley, R. J., Kaplan, J. M., & Grill, H. J. (1995). Effect of occluding the pylorus on intraoral intake: A test of the gastric hypothesis of meal termination. *Physiology & Behavior, 58,* 245–249. (11)

Seeman, P., & Lee, T. (1975). Antipsychotic drugs: Direct correlation between clinical potency and presynaptic action on dopamine neurons. *Science, 188,* 1217–1219. (16)

Segal, N. (1993). Twin, sibling, and adoption methods: Tests of evolutionary hypotheses. *American Psychologist, 48,* 943–956. (3)

Segall, M. H., Campbell, D. T., & Herskovits, M. J. (1966). *The influence of culture on visual perception.* Indianapolis, IN: Bobbs-Merrill. (4)

Seidenberg, M. S. (1997). Language acquisition and use: Learning and applying probabilistic constraints. *Science, 275,* 1599–1603. (8)

Seidman, L. J., Oscar-Berman, M., Kalinowski, A. G., Ajilore, O., Kremen, W. S., Faraone, S., & Tsuang, M. T. (1995). Experimental and clinical neuropsychological measures of prefrontal dysfunction in schizophrenia. *Neuropsychology, 9,* 481–490. (16)

Seife, C. (1994, May/June). Studies from life: Mathemagician. *The Sciences, 34* (3), 12–15. (7)

Selemon, L. D., Rajkowska, G., & Goldman-Rakic, P. S. (1995). Abnormally high neuronal density in the schizophrenic cortex. *Archives of General Psychiatry, 52,* 805–818. (16)

Seligman, M. E. P. (1970). On the generality of the laws of learning. *Psychological Review, 77,* 406–418. (6)

Seligman, M. E. P. (1971). Phobias and preparedness. *Behavior Therapy, 2,* 307–320. (16)

Seligman, M. E. P. (1995). The effectiveness of psychotherapy: The *Consumer Reports* study. *American Psychologist, 50,* 965–974. (15)

Seligman, M. E. P., Nolen-Hoeksema, S., Thornton, N., & Thornton, K. M. (1990). Explanatory style as a mechanism of disappointing athletic performance. *Psychological Science, 1,* 143–146. (16)

Selye, H. (1979). Stress, cancer, and the mind. In J. Taché, H. Selye, & S. B. Day (Eds.), *Cancer, stress, and death* (pp. 11–27). New York: Plenum. (12)

Sereno, A. B., & Holzman, P. S. (1993). Express saccades and smooth pursuit eye movement function in schizophrenic, affective disorder, and normal subjects. *Journal of Cognitive Neuroscience, 5,* 303–316. (16)

Sereno, S. C., Pacht, J. M., & Rayner, K. (1992). The effect of meaning frequency on processing lexically ambiguous words: Evidence from eye fixations. *Psychological Science, 3,* 296–300. (8)

Shafir, E. B., Smith, E. E., & Osheron, D. N. (1990). Typicality and reasoning fallacies. *Memory & Cognition, 18,* 229–239. (8)

Shallice, T., & Warrington, E. K. (1970). Independent functioning of verbal memory stores: A neuropsychological study. *Quarterly Journal of Experimental Psychology, 22,* 261–273. (7)

Shannon, D. A. (1955). *The Socialist Party of America.* New York: Macmillan. (14)

Shapiro, B. E., & Danly, M. (1985). The role of the right hemisphere in the control of speech prosody in propositional and affective context. *Brain and Language, 25,* 19–36. (3)

Shapiro, D. H., Jr., Schwartz, C. E., & Astin, J. A. (1996). Controlling ourselves, controlling our world. *American Psychologist, 51,* 1213–1230. (12)

Shapiro, D. L. (1985). Insanity and the assessment of criminal responsibility. In C. P. Ewing (Ed.), *Psychology, psychiatry, and the law: A clinical and forensic handbook* (pp. 67–94). Sarasota, FL: Professional Resource Exchange. (15)

Shapiro, K. L., Caldwell, J., & Sorensen, R. E. (1997). Personal names and the attentional blink: A visual "cocktail party" effect. *Journal of Experimental Psychology: Human Perception and Performance, 23,* 504–514. (8)

Shavit, Y., Terman, G. W., Martin, F. C., Lewis, J. W., Liebeskind, J. C., & Gale, R. P. (1985). Stress, opioid peptides, the immune system, and cancer. *Journal of Immunology, 135,* 834S–837S. (12)

Sheaffer, R. (1992). Psychic vibrations. *Skeptical Inquirer, 17,* 26–29. (2)

Sheaffer, R. (1993). Psychic vibrations. *Skeptical Inquirer, 17,* 138–140. (2)

Shepard, R. N., & Metzler, J. N. (1971). Mental rotation of three-dimensional objects. *Science, 171,* 701–703. (8)

Sheppard, J. A. (1995). Remedying motivation and productivity loss in social settings. *Current Directions in Psychological Science, 4,* 131–134. (14)

Sheppard, W. D., II, Staggers, F. J., Jr., & John, L. (1997). The effects of a stress management program in a high security government agency. *Anxiety, Stress, and Coping, 10,* 341–350. (12)

Shepperd, J. A. (1993). Productivity loss in performance groups: A motivation analysis. *Psychological Bulletin, 113,* 67–81. (14)

Sher, K. J., Frost, R. O., Kushner, M., Crews, T. M., & Alexander, J. E. (1989). Memory deficits in compulsive checkers: Replication and extension in a clinical sample. *Behaviour Research and Therapy, 27,* 65–69. (16)

Sher, K. J., Frost, R. O., & Otto, R. (1983). Cognitive deficits in compulsive checkers: An exploratory study. *Behaviour Research and Therapy, 21,* 357–363. (16)

Sherif, M. (1935). A study of some social factors in perception. *Archives of Psychology, 27,* 1–60. (14)

Sherif, M. (1966). *In common predicament.* Boston: Houghton Mifflin. (14)

Sherrod, D. R., Hage, J. N., Halpern, P. L., & Moore, B. S. (1977). Effects of personal causation and perceived control on responses to an aversive environment: The more control, the better. *Journal of Experimental Social Psychology, 13,* 14–27. (12)

Sherwood, G. G. (1981). Self-serving biases in person perception: A reexamination of projection as a mechanism of defense. *Psychological Bulletin, 90,* 445–459. (13)

Shiffrin, R. M., & Schneider, W. (1977). Controlled and automatic human information processing: II. Perceptual learning, automatic attending, and a general theory. *Psychological Review, 84,* 127–190. (8)

Shimamura, A. P., Berry, J. M., Mangels, J. A., Rusting, C. L., & Jurica, P. J. (1995). Memory and cognitive abilities in university professors. *Psychological Science, 6,* 271–277. (7)

Shimamura, A. P., Janowsky, J. S., & Squire, L. R. (1990). Memory for the temporal order of events in patients with frontal lobe lesions and amnesic patients. *Neuropsychologia, 28,* 803–813. (7)

Shimaya, A. (1997). Perception of complex line drawings. *Journal of Experimental Psychology: Human Perception and Performance, 23,* 25–50. (4)

Shogren, E. (1993, June 2). Survey finds 4 in 5 suffer sex harassment at school. *Los Angeles Times,* A10. (2)

Shweder, R. A., & Haidt, J. (1993). The future of moral psychology: Truth, intuition, and the pluralist way. *Psychological Science, 4,* 360–365. (10)

Shweder, R., Mahapatra, M., & Miller, J. G. (1987). Culture and moral development. In J. Kagan & S. Lamb (Eds.), *The emergence of morality in young children* (pp. 1–83). Chicago: University of Chicago Press. (10)

Siegel, S. (1977). Morphine tolerance as an associative process. *Journal of Experimental Psychology: Animal Behavior Processes, 3,* 1–13. (6)

Siegel, S. (1983). Classical conditioning, drug tolerance, and drug dependence. *Research Advances in Alcohol and Drug Problems, 7,* 207–246. (6)

Siegel, S. (1987). Alcohol and opiate dependence: Reevaluation of the Victorian perspective. *Research Advances in Alcohol and Drug Problems, 9,* 279–314. (16)

Siegelman, M. (1974). Parental background of male homosexuals and heterosexuals. *Archives of Sexual Behavior, 3,* 3–18. (11)

Siegler, R. S., & Richards, D. D. (1982). The development of intelligence. In R. J. Sternberg (Ed.), *Handbook of human intelligence* (pp. 897–971). Cambridge, England: Cambridge University Press. (10)

Silver, E. (1995). Punishment or treatment? Comparing the lengths of confinement of successful and unsuccessful insanity defendants. *Law and Human Behavior, 19,* 375–388. (15)

Simon, R. I. (1994). The law and psychiatry, In R. E. Hales, S. C. Yudofsky, & J. A. Talbott (Eds.), *Textbook of Psychiatry* (2nd ed.) (pp. 1297–1340). Washington, DC: American Psychiatric Press. (15)

Simonton, D. K. (1997). Creative productivity: A predictive and explanatory model of career trajectories and landmarks. *Psychological Review, 104,* 66–89. (8)

Simmons, E. J. (1949). *Leo Tolstoy.* London: John Lehmann. (16)

Sinha, P., & Poggio, T. (1996). I think I know that face. . . *Nature, 384,* 404. (4)

Sizemore, C. C., & Huber, R. J. (1988). The twenty-two faces of Eve. *Individual Psychology, 44,* 53–62. (15)

Sizemore, C. C., & Pittillo, E. S. (1977). *I'm Eve.* Garden City, NY: Doubleday. (15)

Skeels, H. M. (1966). Adult status of children with contrasting early life experiences. *Monographs of the Society for Research in Child Development, 31,* 1–65. (9)

Skinner, B. F. (1938). *The behavior of organisms.* New York: D. Appleton-Century. (6)

Skinner, B. F. (1960). Pigeons in a pelican. *American Psychologist, 15,* 28–37. (6)

Skinner, B. F. (1990). Can psychology be a science of mind? *American Psychologist, 45,* 1206–1210. (6)

Smith, C., & Wong, P. T. P. (1991). Paradoxical sleep increases predict successful learning in a complex operant task. *Behavioral Neuroscience, 105,* 282–288. (5)

Smith, D. E., & Cogswell, C. (1994). A cross-cultural perspective on adolescent girls' body perception. *Perceptual and Motor Skills, 78,* 744–746. (11)

Smith, G. B., Schwebel, A. I., Dunn, R. L., & McIver, S. D. (1993). The role of psychologists in the treatment, management, and prevention of chronic mental illness. *American Psychologist, 48,* 966–971. (15)

Smith, L. D. (1995). Inquiry nearer the source: Bacon, Mach, and *The Behavior of Organisms.* In J. T. Todd & E. K. Morris (Eds.), *Modern perspectives on B. F. Skinner and contemporary behaviorism* (pp. 39–50). Westport, CT: Greenwood Press. (6)

Smith, L. T. (1975). The interanimal transfer phenomenon: A review. *Psychological Bulletin, 81,* 1078–1095. (2)

Smith, M. L. (1988). Recall of spatial location by the amnesic patient H. M. *Brain and Cognition, 7,* 178–183. (7)

Smith, M. L., Glass, G. V., & Miller, T. I. (1980). *The benefits of psychotherapy.* Baltimore, MD: Johns Hopkins University Press. (15)

Smith, M. W. (1974). Alfred Binet's remarkable questions: A cross-national and cross-temporal analysis of the cultural biases built into the Stanford-Binet intelligence scale and other Binet tests. *Genetic Psychology Monographs, 89,* 307–334. (9)

Smith, S., Lindefors, N., Hurd, Y., & Sharp, T. (1995). Electroconvulsive shock increases dopamine D$_1$ and D$_2$ receptor mRNA in the nucleus accumbens of the rat. *Psychopharmacology, 120,* 333–340. (16)

Snodgrass, J. G., & Hirshman, E. (1991). Theoretical explorations of the Bruner-Potter (1964) interference effect. *Journal of Memory and Language, 30,* 273–293. (8)

Snyder, G. L., & Stricker, E. M. (1985). Effects of lateral hypothalamic lesions on food intake of rats during exposure to cold. *Behavioral Neuroscience, 99,* 310–322. (3)

Snyder, M. (1979). Self-monitoring process. *Advances in Experimental Social Psychology, 12,* 85–128. (14)

Snyder, M., Tanke, E. D., & Bersheid, E. (1977). Social perception and interpersonal behavior: On the self-fulfilling nature of social stereotypes. *Journal of Personality and Social Psychology, 35,* 656–666. (14)

Snyder, S. (1991). Movies and juvenile delinquency: An overview. *Adolescence, 26,* 121–132. (6)

Snyder, S. H. (1984). Drug and neurotransmitter receptors in the brain. *Science, 224,* 22–31. (3)

Solin, D. (1989). The systematic misrepresentation of bilingual-crossed aphasia data and its consequences. *Brain and Language, 36,* 92–116. (8)

Solomon, D. A., Keller, M. B., Leon, A. C., Mueller, T. I., Shea, T., Warshaw, M., Maser, J. D., Coryell, W., & Endicott, J. (1997). Recovery from major depression. *Archives of General Psychiatry, 54,* 1001–1006. (16)

Solomon, R. L. (1980). The opponent-process theory of acquired motivation. *American Psychologist, 35,* 691–712. (12)

Solomon, R. L., & Corbit, J. D. (1974). An opponent-process theory of motivation: I. Temporal dynamics of affect. *Psychological Review, 81,* 119–145. (12)

Solomon, Z., Mikulincer, M., & Flum, H. (1988). Negative life events, coping responses, and combat-related psychopathology: A prospective study. *Journal of Abnormal Psychology, 97,* 302–307. (12)

Spaeth, A. (1995, August). Going for the Guinness. *World Press Review,* pp. 18–20. (11)

Spangler, W. D. (1992). Validity of questionnaire and TAT measures of need for achievement: Two meta-analyses. *Psychological Bulletin, 112,* 140–154. (11)

Spanos, N. P. (1987–88). Past-life hypnotic regression: A critical view. *Skeptical Inquirer, 12,* 174–180. (5)

Spanos, N. P. (1994). Multiple identity enactments and multiple personality disorder: A sociocognitive perspective. *Psychological Bulletin, 116,* 143–165. (15)

Spearman, C. (1904). "General intelligence," objectively determined and measured. *American Journal of Psychology, 15,* 201–293. (9)

Sperling, G. (1960). The information available in brief visual presentations. *Psychological Monographs, 74*(11, Whole No. 498). (7)

Sperry, R. W. (1967). Split-brain approach to learning problems. In G. C. Quarton, T. Melnechuk, & F. O. Schmitt (Eds.), *The neurosciences: A study program* (pp. 714–722). New York: Rockefeller University Press. (3)

Spiegel, D., Frischholz, E. J., Fleiss, J. L., & Spiegel, H. (1993). Predictors of smoking abstinence following a single-session restructuring intervention with self-hypnosis. *American Journal of Psychiatry, 150,* 1090–1097. (5)

Spiegel, T. A. (1973). Caloric regulation of food intake in man. *Journal of Comparative and Physiological Psychology, 85,* 24–37. (11)

Spira, A., et al. (1993). *Les comportements sexuels en France.* Paris: La documentation Française. (11)

Sporer, S. L., Penrod, S., Read, D., & Cutler, B. (1995). Choosing, confidence, and accuracy: A meta-analysis of the confidence-accuracy relation in eyewitness identification studies. *Psychological Bulletin, 118,* 315–327. (7)

Squire, L. R., Amaral, D. G., & Press, G. A. (1990). Magnetic resonance imaging of the hippocampal formation and mammillary nuclei distinguish medial temporal lobe and diencephalic amnesia. *Journal of Neuroscience, 10,* 3106–3117. (7)

Squire, L. R., Haist, F., & Shimamura, A. P. (1989). The neurology of memory: Quantitative assessment of retrograde amnesia in two groups of amnesic patients. *Journal of Neuroscience, 9,* 828–839. (7)

Stanton, M. D., & Shadish, W. R. (1997). Outcome, attrition, and family-couples treatment for drug abuse: a meta-analysis and review of the controlled, comparative studies. *Psychological Bulletin, 122,* 170–191. (16)

Staddon, J. (1993). *Behaviorism.* London: Duckworth. (6)

Starr, C., & Taggart, R. (1992). *Biology: The unity and diversity of life* (6th ed.). Belmont, CA: Wadsworth. (3)

Staub, E. (1996). Cultural-societal roots of violence. *American Psychologist, 51,* 117–132. (12)

Staw, B. M., & Ross, J. (1989). Understanding behavior in escalation situations. *Science, 246,* 216–220. (14)

Steblay, N. M., & Bothwell, R. K. (1994). Evidence for hypnotically refreshed testimony. *Law and Human Behavior, 18,* 635–651. (5)

Steele, C. M. (1997). A threat in the air: How stereotypes shape intellectual identity and performance. *American Psychologist, 52,* 613–629. (14)

Steele, C. M., & Aronson, J. (1995). Stereotype threat and the intellectual test performance of African Americans. *Journal of Personality and Social Psychology, 69,* 797–811. (14)

Stegat, H. (1975). Die Verhaltenstherapie der Enuresis und Enkopresis [Behavior therapy for enuresis and encopresis]. *Zeitschrift für Kinder- und Jugend-psychiatrie, 3,* 149–173. (15)

Stein, M., Miller, A. H., & Trestman, R. L. (1991). Depression, the immune system, and health and illness. *Archives of General Psychiatry, 48,* 171–177. (12)

Stella, N., Schweitzer, P., & Piomelli, D. (1997). A second endogenous cannabinoid that modulates long-term potentiation. *Nature, 382,* 677–678. (5)

Sternberg, R. J. (1985). *Beyond IQ.* Cambridge, England: Cambridge University Press. (9)

Sternberg, R. J. (1991). Death, taxes, and bad intelligence tests. *Intelligence, 15,* 257–269. (9)

Sternberg, R. J. (1997). The concept of intelligence and its role in lifelong learning and success. *American Psychologist, 52,* 1030–1037. (9)

Sternberg, R. J., & Lubart, T. I. (1996). Investing in creativity. *American Psychologist, 51,* 677–688. (8)

Sternberg, R. J., Wagner, R. K., Williams, W. M., & Horvath, J. A. (1995). Testing common sense. *American Psychologist, 50,* 912–927. (9)

Stevens, A., & Coupe, P. (1978). Distortions in judged spatial relations. *Cognitive Psychology, 10,* 422–437. (8)

Stewart, I. (1987). Are mathematicians logical? *Nature, 325,* 386–387. (9)

Stewart, J. W., Quitkin, F. M., McGrath, P. J., Amsterdam, J., Fava, M., Fawcett, J., Reimherr, F., Rosenbaum, J., Beasley, C., & Roback, P. (1998). Use of pattern analysis to predict differential relapse of remitted patients with major depression during 1 year of treatment with fluoxetine or placebo. *Archives of General Psychiatry, 55,* 334–343. (16)

Stewart, S. H. (1996). Alcohol abuse in individuals exposed to trauma: A critical review. *Psychological Bulletin, 120,* 83–112. (16)

Stewart, V. M. (1973). Tests of the "carpentered world" hypothesis by race and environment in America and Zambia. *International Journal of Psychology, 8,* 83–94. (4)

Stiles, W. B., Shapiro, D. A., & Elliott, R. (1986). "Are all psychotherapies equivalent?" *American Psychologist, 41,* 165–180. (15)

Stipek, D. J. (1984). Young children's performance expectations: Logical analysis or wishful thinking? *Advances in Motivation and Achievement, 3,* 33–56. (11)

Stolerman, I. P. (1991). Behavioural pharmacology of nicotine: Multiple mechanisms. *British Journal of Addiction, 86,* 533–536. (5)

Storms, M. D. (1973). Videotape and the attribution process: Reversing actors' and observers' points of view. *Journal of Personality and Social Psychology, 27,* 165–175. (14)

Strack, F., Martin, L. L., & Stepper, S. (1988). Inhibiting and facilitating conditions of the human smile: A nonobtrusive test of the facial feedback hypothesis. *Journal of Personality and Social Psychology, 54,* 768–777. (12)

Streissguth, A. P., Sampson, P. D., & Barr, H. M. (1989). Neurobehavioral dose-response effects of prenatal alcohol exposure in humans from infancy to adulthood. *Annals of the New York Academy of Sciences, 562,* 145–158. (10)

Stroebe, M., Gergen, M. M., Gergen, K. J., & Stroebe, W. (1992). Broken hearts or broken bonds: Love and death in historical perspective. *American Psychologist, 47,* 1205–1212. (10)

Stroh, L. K., Brett, J. M., & Reilly, A. H. (1992). All the right stuff: A comparison of female and male managers' career progression. *Journal of Applied Psychology, 77,* 251–260. (11)

Strupp, H. H. (1996). The tripartite model and the *Consumer Reports* study. *American Psychologist, 51,* 1017–1024. (15)

Stunkard, A. J., Sørensen, T. I. A., Hanis, C., Teasdale, T. W., Chakraborty, R., Shull, W. J., & Schulinger, F. (1986). An adoption study of human obesity. *New England Journal of Medicine, 314,* 193–198. (11)

Stuss, D. T., Alexander, M. P., Palumbo, C. L., Buckle, L., Sayer, L., & Pogue, J. (1994). Organizational strategies of patients with unilateral or bilateral frontal lobe injury in word list learning tasks. *Neuropsychology, 8,* 355–373. (7)

Sudzak, P. D., Glowa, J. R., Crawley, J. N., Schwartz, R. D., Skolnick, P., & Paul, S. M. (1986). A selective imidazobenzodiazepine antagonist of ethanol in the rat. *Science, 234,* 1243–1247. (5)

Sue, S. (1998). In search of cultural competence in psychotherapy and counseling. *American Psychologist, 53,* 440–448. (15)

Susser, E., Neugebauer, R., Hoek, H. W., Brown, A. S., Lin, S., Labovitz, D., & Gorman, J. M. (1996). Schizophrenia after prenatal famine. *Archives of General Psychiatry, 53,* 25–31. (16)

Suzuki, L. A., & Valencia, R. R. (1997). Race-ethnicity and measured intelligence. *American Psychologist, 52,* 1103–1114. (9)

Svanum, S., & Bringle, R. G. (1982). Race, social class, and predictive bias: An evaluation using the WISC, WRAT, and teacher ratings. *Intelligence, 6,* 275–286. (9)

Swann, W. B., Jr. (1997). The trouble with change: Self-verification and allegiance to the self. *Psychological Science, 8,* 177–180. (14)

Swann, W. B., Jr., & Gill, M. J. (1997). Confidence and accuracy in person perception: Do we know what we think we know about our relationship partners? *Journal of Personality and Social Psychology, 73,* 747–757. (14)

Symons, C. S., & Johnson, B. T. (1997). The self-reference effect in memory: A meta-analysis. *Psychological Bulletin, 121,* 371–394. (7)

Szasz, T. S. (1982). The psychiatric will. *American Psychologist, 37,* 762–770. (15)

Szymanski, H. V., Simon, J. C., & Gutterman, N. (1983). Recovery from schizophrenic psychosis. *American Journal of Psychiatry, 140,* 335–338. (16)

Szymusiak, R. (1995). Magnocellular nuclei of the basal forebrain: Substrates of sleep and arousal regulation. *Sleep, 18,* 478–500. (3)

Takeuchi, A. H., & Hulse, S. H. (1993). Absolute pitch. *Psychological Bulletin, 113,* 345–361. (3)

Taller, A. M., Asher, D. M., Pomeroy, K. L., Eldadah, B. A., Godec, M. S., Falkai, P. G., Bogert, B., Kleinman, J. E., Stevens, J. R., & Torrey, E. F. (1996). Search for viral nucleic acid sequences in brain tissues of patients with schizophrenia using nested polymerase chain reaction. *Archives of General Psychiatry, 53,* 32–40. (16)

Tanay, E. (1992). The verdict with two names. *Psychiatric Annals, 22,* 571–573. (15)

Tannen, D. (1990). *You just don't understand.* New York: William Morrow. (10)

Tassinary, L. G., & Cacioppo, J. T. (1992). Unobservable facial actions and emotion. *Psychological Science, 3,* 28–33. (12)

Tassinary, L. G., & Hansen, K. A. (1998). A critical test of the waist-to-hip-ratio hypothesis of female physical attractiveness. *Psychological Science, 9,* 150–155. (14)

Taylor, F. V. (1957). Psychology and the design of machines. *American Psychologist, 12,* 249–258. (1)

Taylor, S. E. (1983). Adjustment to threatening events: A theory of cognitive adaptation. *American Psychologist, 38,* 1161–1173. (12)

Taylor, S. E., & Brown, J. D. (1988). Illusion and well-being: A social psychological perspective on mental health. *Psychological Bulletin, 103,* 193–210. (12)

Taylor, S. E., & Lobel, M. (1989). Social comparison activity under threat: Downward evaluation and upward contacts. *Psychological Review, 96,* 569–575. (14)

Teasdale, T. W., & Owen, D. R. (1984). Heredity and familial environment in intelligence and educational level: A sibling study. *Nature, 309,* 620–622. (9)

Tennen, H., & Affleck, G. (1990). Blaming others for threatening events. *Psychological Bulletin, 108,* 209–232. (12)

Teplin, L. A., Abram, K. M., & McClelland, G. M. (1996). Prevalence of psychiatric disorders among incarcerated women. *Archives of General Psychiatry, 53,* 505–512. (12)

Terman, G. W., Shavitt, Y., Lewis, J. W., Cannon, J. T., & Liebeskind, J. C. (1984). Intrinsic mechanisms of pain inhibition: Activation by stress. *Science, 226,* 1270–1277. (4)

Terr, L. (1988). What happens to early memories of trauma? A study of twenty children under age five at the time of documented traumatic events. *Journal of the American Academy of Child and Adolescent Psychiatry, 27,* 96–104. (7)

Terrace, H. S., Petitto, L. A., Sanders, R. J., & Bever, T. G. (1979). Can an ape create a sentence? *Science, 206,* 891–902. (8)

Tesser, A. (1993). The importance of heritability in psychological research: The case of attitudes. *Psychological Review, 100,* 129–142. (3)

Tetlock, P. E. (1994). Good judgment in world politics: Who gets what right, when and why? Address at the Sixth Annual Convention of the American Psychological Society, July 2, 1994. (8)

Tett, R. P., & Palmer, C. A. (1997). The validity of handwriting elements in relation to self-report personality trait measures. *Personality and Individual Differences, 22,* 11–18. (13)

Thase, M. E., Greenhouse, J. B., Frank, E., Reynolds, C. F., III, Pilkonis, P. A., Hurley, K., Grochocinski, V., & Kupfer, D. J. (1997). Treatment of major depression with psychotherapy or psychotherapy-pharmacotherapy combinations. *Archives of General Psychiatry, 54,* 1009–1015. (16)

Thase, M. E., Trivedi, M. H., & Rush, A. J. (1995). MAOIs in the contemporary treatment of depression. *Neuropsychopharmacology, 12,* 185–219. (16)

Thieman, T. J. (1984). A classroom demonstration of encoding specificity. *Teaching of Psychology, 11,* 101–102. (7)

Thigpen, C., & Cleckley, H. (1957). *The three faces of Eve.* New York: McGraw-Hill. (15)

Thomas, A., & Chess, S. (1980). *The dynamics of psychological development.* New York: Brunner/Mazel. (10)

Thomas, A., Chess, S., & Birch, H. G. (1968). *Temperament and behavior disorders in children*. New York: New York University Press. (10)

Thompson, C. R., & Church, R. M. (1980). An explanation of the language of a chimpanzee. *Science, 208,* 313–314. (8)

Thompson, D. B., Ravussin, E., Bennett, P. H., & Bogardus, C. (1997). Structure and sequence variation at the human leptin receptor gene in lean and obese Pima Indians. *Human Molecular Genetics, 6,* 675–679. (11)

Thompson, L., & Hrebec, D. (1996). Lose-lose agreements in interdependent decision making. *Psychological Bulletin, 120,* 396–409. (14)

Thompson, L. A., Detterman, D. K., & Plomin, R. (1991). Associations between cognitive abilities and scholastic achievement: Genetic overlap but environmental differences. *Psychological Science, 2,* 158–165. (9)

Thompson, L. W., Gallagher-Thompson, D., Futterman, A., Gilewski, M. J., & Peterson, J. (1991). The effects of late-life spousal bereavement over a 30-month interval. *Psychology and Aging, 6,* 434–441. (16)

Thompson, S. C. (1981). Will it hurt less if I can control it? A complex answer to a simple question. *Psychological Bulletin, 90,* 89–101. (12)

Thompson, S. C., Armstrong, W., & Thomas, C. (1998). Illusions of control, underestimations, and accuracy: A control heuristic explanation. *Psychological Bulletin, 123,* 143–161. (8)

Thorndike, E. L. (1970). *Animal intelligence*. Darien, CT: Hafner. (Original work published 1911) (6)

Thyer, B. A., & Geller, E. S. (1990). Behavior analysis in the promotion of safety belt use: A review. *Progress in Behavior Modification, 26,* 150–172. (6)

Tiffany, S. T., & Baker, T. B. (1981). Morphine tolerance in rats: Congruence with a Pavlovian paradigm. *Journal of Comparative and Physiological Psychology, 95,* 747–762. (6)

Timberlake, W., & Farmer-Dougan, V. A. (1991). Reinforcement in applied settings: Figuring out ahead of time what will work. *Psychological Bulletin, 110,* 379–391. (6)

Tinbergen, N. (1958). *Curious naturalists*. New York: Basic Books. (3)

Titchener, E. B. (1910). *A textbook of psychology*. New York: Macmillan. (1)

Todes, D. P. (1997). From the machine to the ghost within. *American Psychologist, 52,* 947–955. (6)

Tolman, E. C. (1932). *Purposive behavior in animals and men*. New York: Century. (6)

Tolman, E. C., & Honzik, C. H. (1930). Introduction and removal of reward, and maze performance in rats. *University of California Publications in Psychology, 4,* 257–275. (6)

Tolstoy, L. (1978). *Tolstoy's letters*, Vol. I: 1828–1879. New York: Charles Scribner's Sons. (Original works written 1828–1879) (10)

Tolstoy, L. (1983). *Confession*. New York: Norton. (Original work written 1882 but blocked from publication by the Russian censor) (12)

Tombaugh, C. W. (1980). *Out of the darkness, the planet Pluto*. Harrisburg, PA: Stackpole. (4)

Torrance, E. P. (1980). Growing up creatively gifted: A 22-year longitudinal study. *Creative Child and Adult Quarterly, 5,* 148–159. (8)

Torrance, E. P. (1981). Empirical validation of criterion-referenced indicators of creative ability through a longitudinal study. *Creative Child and Adult Quarterly, 6,* 136–140. (8)

Torrance, E. P. (1982). "Sounds and images" productions of elementary school pupils as predictors of the creative achievements of young adults. *Creative Child and Adult Quarterly, 7,* 8–14. (8)

Torrey, E. F., Rawlings, R., & Waldman, I. N. (1988). Schizophrenic births and viral diseases in two states. *Schizophrenia Research, 1,* 73–77. (10)

Tracy, P. E., Wolfgang, M. E., & Figlio, R. M. (1990). *Delinquency careers in two birth cohorts*. New York: Plenum. (12)

Treisman, A., & Souther, J. (1985). Search asymmetry: A diagnostic for preattentive processing of separable features. *Journal of Experimental Psychology: General, 114,* 285–310. (8)

Trivers, R. L. (1972). Parental investment and sexual selection. In B. Campbell (Ed.), *Sexual selection and the descent of man, 1871–1971* (pp. 136–179). Chicago: Aldine. (3)

Tronick, E. Z., Morelli, G. A., & Ivey, P. K. (1992). The Efe forager infant and toddler's pattern of social relationships: Multiple and simultaneous. *Developmental Psychology, 28,* 568–577. (10)

Truscott, D., & Crook, K. H. (1993). *Tarasoff* in the Canadian context: *Wenden* and the duty to protect. *Canadian Journal of Psychiatry, 38,* 84–89. (15)

Tschann, J. M., Johnston, J. R., Kline, M., & Wallerstein, J. S. (1990). Conflict, loss, change and parent-child relationships: Predicting children's adjustment during divorce. *Journal of Divorce, 13,* 1–22. (10)

Tucker, D. M. (1981). Lateral brain function, emotion, and conceptualization. *Psychological Bulletin, 89,* 19–46. (3)

Tulving, E. (1989). Remembering and knowing the past. *American Scientist, 77,* 361–367. (7)

Tulving, E., & Thomson, D. M. (1973). Encoding specificity and retrieval processes in episodic memory. *Psychological Review, 80,* 352–373. (7)

Turkheimer, E. (1991). Individual and group differences in adoption studies of IQ. *Psychological Bulletin, 110,* 392–405. (9)

Tversky, A., & Kahneman, D. (1981). The framing of decisions and the psychology of choice. *Science, 211,* 453–458. (8)

Tversky, A., & Kahneman, D. (1983). Extensional versus intuitive reasoning: The conjunctive fallacy in probability judgment. *Psychological Review, 90,* 293–315. (8)

Tversky, B. (1981). Distortions in memory for maps. *Cognitive Psychology, 13,* 407–433. (8)

Uchino, B. N., Cacioppo, J. T., & Kiecolt-Glaser, J. K. (1996). The relationship betweeen social support and physiological processes: A review with emphasis on underlying mechanisms and implications for health. *Psychological Bulletin, 119,* 488–531. (12)

U. S. Department of Labor. (1989, April). *Employment and Earnings* (Vol. 36, No. 4). Washington, DC: U. S. Government Printing Office. (10)

Udolf, R. (1981). *Handbook of hypnosis for professionals*. New York: Van Nostrand Reinhold. (5)

Ulrich, R. E., Stachnik, T. J., & Stainton, N. R. (1963). Student acceptance of generalized personality interpretations. *Psychological Reports, 13,* 831–834. (13)

Ulrich, R. S. (1984). View through a window may influence recovery from surgery. *Science, 224,* 420–421. (4)

Underwood, G. (1994). Subliminal perception on TV. *Nature, 370,* 103. (4)

Underwood, N. R., & McConkie, G. W. (1985). Perceptual span for letter distinctions during reading. *Reading Research Quarterly, 20,* 153–162. (8)

Vaillant, G. E. (1983). *The natural history of alcoholism*. Cambridge, MA: Harvard University Press. (16)

Vaillant, G. E., & Milofsky, E. S. (1982). The etiology of alcoholism: A prospective viewpoint. *American Psychologist, 37,* 494–503. (16)

Vallone, R. P., Ross, L., & Lepper, M. R. (1985). The hostile media phenomenon: Biased perception and perceptions of media bias in coverage of the "Beirut Massacre." *Journal of Personality and Social Psychology, 49,* 577–585. (14)

van der Meer, A. L. H., van der Weel, F. R., & Lee, D. N. (1995). The functional significance of arm movements in neonates. *Science, 267,* 693–695. (10)

Van Der Pligt, J., & Eiser, J. R. (1983). Actors' and observers' attributions, self-serving bias, and positivity. *European Journal of Social Psychology, 13,* 95–104. (14)

van Dyke, C., & Byck, R. (1982). Cocaine. *Scientific American, 246*(3), 128–141. (3)

van IJzendoorn, M. H., Juffer, F., & Duyvesteyn, M. G. C. (1995). Breaking the intergenerational cycle of insecure attachment: A review of the effects of attachment-based interventions on maternal sensitivity and infant security. *Journal of Child Psychology and Psychiatry, 36,* 225–248. (10)

Vargha-Khadem, F., Gadian, D. G., Watkins, K. E., Connelly, A., Paesschen, W. V., & Mishkin, M. (1997). Differential effects of early hippocampal pathology on episodic and semantic memory. *Science, 277,* 376–380. (7)

Velluti, R. A. (1997). Interactions between sleep and sensory physiology. *Journal of Sleep Research, 6,* 61–77. (5)

Vernon, M. (1967). Relationship of language to the thinking process. *Archives of General Psychiatry, 16,* 325–333. (9)

Viken, R. J., Rose, R. J., Kaprio, J., & Koskenvuo, M. (1994). A developmental genetic analysis of adult personality: Extraversion and neuroticism from 18 to 59 years of age. *Journal of Personality and Social Psychology, 66,* 722–730. (13)

Vincent, K. R., & Harman, M. J. (1991). The Exner Rorschach: An analysis of its clinical validity. *Journal of Clinical Psychology, 47,* 596–599. (13)

Virkkunen, M., Eggert, M., Rawlings, R., & Linnoila, M. (1996). A prospective follow-up study of alcoholic violent offenders and fire setters. *Archives of General Psychiatry, 53,* 523–529. (12)

Vokey, J. R., & Read, J. D. (1985). Subliminal messages: Between the devil and the media. *American Psychologist, 40,* 1231–1239. (4)

von Restorff, H. (1933). Analyse von Vorgängen im Spurenfeld. I. Über die Wirkung von Bereichsbildungen im Spurenfeld [Analysis of the events in memory. I. Concerning the effect of domain learning in the memory field]. *Psychologische Forschung, 18,* 299–342. (7)

Vygotsky, L. S. (1978). *Mind in society.* Cambridge, MA: Harvard University Press. (10)

Wadden, T. A., & Stunkard, A. J. (1987). Psychopathology and obesity. *Annals of the New York Academy of Sciences, 499,* 55–65. (11)

Wagenaar, W. A. (1986). My memory: A study of autobiographical memory over six years. *Cognitive Psychology, 18,* 225–252. (7)

Wagner, A. D., Desmond, J. E., Demb, J. B., Glover, G. H., & Gabrieli, J. D. E. (1997). Semantic repetition priming for verbal and pictorial knowledge: A functional MRI study of left inferior prefrontal cortex. *Journal of Cognitive Neuroscience, 9,* 714–726. (3)

Wagner, R. K. (1997). Intelligence, training, and employment. *American Psychologist, 52,* 1059–1069. (9)

Wahba, M. A., & Bridwell, L. G. (1976). Maslow reconsidered: A review of research on the need hierarchy theory. *Organizational Behavior & Human Performance, 15,* 212–240. (11)

Wakschlag, L. S., Lahey, B. B., Loeber, R., Green, S. M., Gordon, R. A., & Leventhal, B. L. (1997). Maternal smoking during pregnancy and the risk of conduct disorder in boys. *Archives of General Psychiatry, 54,* 670–676. (10)

Wald, G. (1968). Molecular basis of visual excitation. *Science, 162,* 230–239. (4)

Waldman, I. D., Weinberg, R. A., & Scarr, S. (1994). Racial-group differences in IQ in the Minnesota transracial adoption study: A reply to Levin and Lynn. *Intelligence, 19,* 29–44. (9)

Walker, E. F., & Diforio, D. (1997). Schizophrenia: A neural diathesis-stress model. *Psychological Review, 104,* 667–685. (16)

Waller, N. G., Kojetin, B. A., Bouchard, T. J., Jr., Lykken, D. T., & Tellegen, A. (1990). Genetic and environmental influences on religious interests, attitudes, and values: A study of twins reared apart and together. *Psychological Science, 1,* 138–142. (3)

Walster, E., Aronson, E., Abrahams, D., & Rottman, L. (1966). Importance of physical attractiveness in dating behavior. *Journal of Personality and Social Psychology, 4,* 508–516. (14)

Walters, G. C., & Grusec, J. E. (1977). *Punishment.* San Francisco: W. H. Freeman. (6)

Wampold, B. E., Mondin, G. W., Moody, M., Stich, F., Benson, K., & Ahn, H. (1997). A meta-analysis of outcome studies comparing bona fide psychotherapies: Empirically, "All must have prizes." *Psychological Bulletin, 122,* 203–215. (15)

Warren, R. M. (1970). Perceptual restoration of missing speech sounds. *Science, 167,* 392–393. (8)

Washburn, M. F. (1908). *The animal mind.* New York: Macmillan. (1)

Wason, P. C. (1960). On the failure to eliminate hypotheses in a conceptual task. *Quarterly Journal of Experimental Psychology, 12,* 129–140. (8)

Watson, D. (1982). The actor and the observer: How are their perceptions of causality divergent? *Psychological Bulletin, 92,* 682–700. (14)

Watson, J. B. (1913). Psychology as the behaviorist views it. *Psychological Review, 20,* 158–177. (1)

Watson, J. B. (1919). *Psychology from the standpoint of a behaviorist.* Philadelphia: Lippincott. (1)

Watson, J. B. (1925). *Behaviorism.* New York: Norton. (1, 6)

Watson, J. B., & Rayner, R. (1920). Conditioned emotional reactions. *Journal of Experimental Psychology, 3,* 1–14. (16)

Weaver, C. A., III, & Kelemen, W. L. (1997). Judgments of learning at delays: Shifts in response patterns or increased metamemory accuracy? *Psychological Science, 8,* 318–321. (7)

Weaver, C. N. (1980). Job satisfaction in the United States in the 1970s. *Journal of Applied Psychology, 65,* 364–367. (10)

Webb, W. B. (1979). Theories of sleep functions and some clinical implications. In R. Drucker-Colín, M. Shkurovich, & M. B. Sterman (Eds.), *The functions of sleep* (pp. 19–35). New York: Academic Press. (5)

Wechsler, D. (1991). *Wechsler intelligence scale for Children-III.* San Antonio, TX: The Psychological Corporation. (9)

Wegner, D. M., Schneider, D. J., Carter, S. R., III, & White, T. L. (1987). Paradoxical effects of thought suppression. *Journal of Personality and Social Psychology, 53,* 5–13. (16)

Wegner, D. M., Wenzlaff, R., Kerker, R. M., & Beattie, A. E. (1981). Incrimination through innuendo: Can media questions become public answers? *Journal of Personality and Social Psychology, 40,* 822–832. (8)

Weil, A. T., Zinberg, N. E., & Nelson, J. M. (1968). Clinical and psychological effects of marihuana in man. *Science, 162,* 1234–1242. (5)

Weinberg, R. A. (1989). Intelligence and IQ: Landmark issues and great debates. *American Psychologist, 44,* 98–104. (9)

Weinberg, R. A., Scarr, S., & Waldman, I. D. (1992). The Minnesota transracial adoption study: A follow-up of IQ test performances at adolescence. *Intelligence, 16,* 117–135. (9)

Weinberger, D. R. (1987). Implications of normal brain development for the pathogenesis of schizophrenia. *Archives of General Psychiatry, 44,* 660–669. (16)

Weiner, B. A., & Wettstein, R. M. (1993). *Legal issues in mental health care.* New York: Plenum. (15)

Weiner, J. (1994). *The beak of the finch.* New York: Knopf. (3)

Weiner, R. D. (1984). Does electroconvulsive therapy cause brain damage? *Behavioral and Brain Sciences, 7,* 1–53. (16)

Weinstock, C. (1984). Further evidence on psychobiological aspects of cancer. *International Journal of Psychosomatics, 31,* 20–22. (12)

Weisberg, R. W. (1994). Genius and madness: A quasi-experimental test of the hypothesis that manic-depression increases creativity. *Psychological Science, 5,* 361–367. (16)

Weissman, M. M., Bland, R. C., Canino, G. J., Faravelli, C., Greenwald, S., Hwu, H. -G., Joyce, P. R., Karan, E. G., Lee, C. -K., Lellouch, J., Lépine, J. -P., Newman, S. C., Oakley-Browne, M. A., Rubio-Stipec, M., Wells, J. E., Wickmaratne, P. J., Wittchen, H. -U., & Yeh, E. -K. (1997). The cross-national epidemiology of panic disorder. *Archives of General Psychiatry, 54,* 305–309. (16)

Weissman, M. M., Leaf, P. J., & Bruce, M. L. (1987). Single parent women: A community study. *Social Psychiatry, 22,* 29–36. (10)

Weissman, M. M., Warner, V., Wickramaratne, P., Moreau, D., & Olfson, M. (1997). Offspring of depressed parents. *Archives of General Psychiatry, 54,* 932–940. (16)

Weitzman, R. A. (1982). The prediction of college achievement by the Scholastic Aptitude Test and the high school record. *Journal of Educational Measurement, 19,* 179–191. (9)

Weller, A., & Weller, L. (1997). Menstrual synchrony under optimal conditions: Bedouin families. *Journal of Comparative Psychology, 111,* 143–151. (4)

Wellings, K., Field, J., Johnson, A., & Wadsworth, J. (1994). *Sexual behavior in Britain: The national survey of sexual attitudes and lifestyles.* New York: Penguin. (11)

Wender, P. H., Kety, S. S., Rosenthal, D., Schulsinger, F., Ortmann, J., & Lunde, I. (1986). Psychiatric disorders in the biological and adoptive families of adopted individuals with affective disorders. *Archives of General Psychiatry, 43,* 923–929. (16)

Wenger, J. R., Tiffany, T. M., Bombardier, C., Nicholls, K., & Woods, S. C. (1981). Ethanol tolerance in the rat is learned. *Science, 213,* 575–576. (5)

Werner, E. E. (1989). High-risk children in young adulthood: A longitudinal study from birth to 32 years. *American Journal of Orthopsychiatry, 59,* 72–81. (10)

Westbrook, G. L. (1994). Glutamate receptor update. *Current Opinion in Neurobiology, 4,* 337–346. (3)

Wheeler, D. D. (1970). Processes in word recognition. *Cognitive Psychology, 1,* 59–85. (8)

White, P. A. (1990). Ideas about causation in philosophy and psychology. *Psychological Bulletin, 108,* 3–18. (1)

Whitworth, R. H., & Perry, S. M. (1990). Comparison of Anglo- and Mexican-Americans on the 16-PF administered in Spanish or English. *Journal of Clinical Psychology, 46,* 857–863. (13)

Wiborg, I. M., & Dahl, A. A. (1996). Does brief dynamic psychotherapy reduce the relapse rate of panic disorder? *Archives of General Psychiatry, 53,* 689–694. (16)

Wickens, D. D. (1970). Encoding categories of words: An empirical approach to meaning. *Psychological Review, 77,* 1–15. (7)

Wicker, A. W. (1969). Attitudes vs. action: The relation of verbal and overt behavioral responses to attitude objects. *Journal of Social Issues, 25*(4), 47–78. (14)

Wicklund, R. A., & Brehm, J. W. (1976). *Perspectives on cognitive dissonance.* Hillsdale, NJ: Lawrence Erlbaum. (14)

Widom, C. S. (1989). Does violence beget violence? A critical examination of the literature. *Psychological Bulletin, 106,* 3–28. (12)

Wig, N. N., Menon, D. K., Bedi, H., Leff, J., Kuipers, L., Ghosh, A., Day, R., Koretn, A., Ernberg, G., Sartorius, N., & Jablensky, A. (1987). Expressed emotion and schizophrenia in North India. II. Distribution of expressed emotion components among relatives of schizophrenic patients in Aarhus and Chandigarh. *British Journal of Psychiatry, 151,* 160–165. (16)

Wild, H. M., Butler, S. R., Carden, D., & Kulikowski, J. J. (1985). Primate cortical area V4 important for colour constancy but not wavelength discrimination. *Nature, 313,* 133–135. (4)

Wilkins, L., & Richter, C. P. (1940). A great craving for salt by a child with corticoadrenal insufficiency. *Journal of the American Medical Association, 114,* 866–868. (11)

Willerman, L., Schultz, R., Rutledge, J. N., & Bigler, E. D. (1991). *In vivo* brain size and intelligence. *Intelligence, 15,* 223–228. (9)

Williams, J. M. G., Mathews, A., & MacLeod, C. (1996). The emotional Stroop task and psychopathology. *Psychological Bulletin, 120,* 3–24. (13)

Williams, K. D., & Karau, S. J. (1991). Social loafing and social compensation: The effects of expectations of co-worker performance. *Journal of Personality and Social Psychology, 61,* 570–581. (14)

Williams, R. W., & Herrup, K. (1988). The control of neuron number. *Annual Review of Neuroscience, 11,* 423–453. (3)

Williams, W. M., & Ceci, S. J. (1997). Are Americans becoming more or less alike? Trends in race, class, and ability differences in intelligence. *American Psychologist, 52,* 1226–1235. (9)

Wilson, D. S., Near, D., & Miller, R. R. (1996). Machiavellianism: A synthesis of the evolutionary and psychological literatures. *Psychological Bulletin, 119,* 285–299. (14)

Wilson, E. O. (1975). *Sociobiology: The new synthesis.* Cambridge, England: Belknap. (3)

Wilson, J. R., and the editors of *Life.* (1964). *The mind.* New York: Time. (4)

Wimmer, H., & Perner, J. (1983). Beliefs about beliefs: Representation and constraining function of wrong beliefs in young children's understanding of deception. *Cognition, 13,* 103–128. (10)

Winer, G. A., & Cottrell, J. E. (1996). Does anything leave the eye when we see? Extramission beliefs of children and adults. *Current Directions in Psychological Science, 5,* 137–142. (4)

Winner, E. (1986, August). *Where pelicans kiss seals.* Psychology Today, 24–35. (10)

Wiseman, R. (1995). The megalab truth test. *Nature, 373,* 391. (12)

Wiseman, R., & Lamont, P. (1996). Unravelling the Indian rope-trick. *Nature, 383,* 212–213. (7)

Wittchen, H. -U., Zhao, S., Kessler, R. C., & Eaton, W. W. (1994). DSM-III-R generalized anxiety disorder in the National Comorbidity Survey. *Archives of General Psychiatry, 51,* 355–364. (16)

Wogalter, M. S., Marwitz, D. D., & Leonard, D. C. (1992). Suggestiveness in photospread line-ups: Similarity induces distinctiveness. *Applied Cognitive Psychology, 6,* 443–453. (7)

Wolman, B. B. (1989). *Dictionary of behavioral science* (2nd ed.). San Diego, CA: Academic Press. (9)

Wolpe, J. (1961). The systematic desensitization treatment of neuroses. *Journal of Nervous and Mental Disease, 132,* 189–203. (16)

Wolpe, J., & Rowan, V. C. (1988). Panic disorder: A product of classical conditioning. *Behaviour Research and Therapy, 26,* 441–450. (16)

Wood, J. M., Nezworski, M. T., & Stejskal, W. J. (1996). The comprehensive system for the Rorschach: A critical examination. *Psychological Science, 7,* 3–10. (13)

Wood, P. K., Sher, K. J., Erickson, D. J., & DeBord, K. A. (1997). Predicting academic problems in college from freshman alcohol involvement. *Journal of Studies on Alcohol, 58,* 200–210. (16)

Wood, W., Lundgren, S., Ouellette, J. A., Busceme, S., & Blackstone, T. (1994). Minority influence: A meta-analytic review of social influence processes. *Psychological Bulletin, 115,* 323–345. (14)

Woods, J. H., & Winger, G. (1997). Abuse liability of flunitrazepam. *Journal of Clinical Psychopharmacology, 17* (Suppl. 3), S1–S57. (5)

Woods, S. C. (1991). The eating paradox: How we tolerate food. *Psychological Review, 98,* 488–505. (11)

Woodward, E. L. (1938). *The age of reform.* London: Oxford University Press. (7)

Woodworth, R. S. (1934). *Psychology* (3rd ed.). New York: Henry Holt. (1)

Woody, G. E., & O'Brien, C. P. (1986). Update on methadone maintenance. *Research Advances in Alcohol and Drug Problems, 9,* 261–277. (16)

Worthington, E. L., Jr., Kurusu, T. A., McCullough, M. E., & Sandage, S. J. (1996). Empirical research on religion and psychotherapeutic processes and outcomes: A 10-year review and research prospectus. *Psychological Bulletin, 119,* 448–487. (15)

Woychyshyn, C. A., McElheran, W. G., & Romney, D. M. (1992). MMPI validity measures: A comparative study of original with alternative indices. *Journal of Personality Assessment, 58,* 138–148. (13)

Wright, D. B. (1993). Recall of the Hillsborough disaster over time: systematic biases in 'flashbulb' memories. *Applied Cognitive Psychology, 7,* 129–138. (7)

Wright, L. (1994). *Remembering Satan*. New York: Alfred A. Knopf. (7)

Wundt, W. (1902). *Outlines of psychology* (C. H. Judd, Trans.). New York: Gustav Sechert. (Original work published 1896) (1)

Wundt, W. (1961). Contributions to the theory of sensory perception. In T. Shipley (Ed.), *Classics in psychology* (pp. 51–78). New York: Philosophical Library. (Original work published 1862) (1)

Wyatt, G. E. (1994). The sociocultural relevance of sex research. *American Psychologist, 49*, 748–754. (11)

Wynn, K. (1992). Addition and subtraction by human infants. *Nature, 358*, 749–750. (10)

Yamamoto, J., & Kubota, M. (1983). The Japanese-American family. In G. J. Powell (Ed.), *The psychosocial development of minority group children* (pp. 237–247). New York Brunner/Mazel. (10)

Yarsh, T. L., Farb, D. H., Leeman, S. E., & Jessell, T. M. (1979). Intrathecal capsaicin depletes substance P in the rat spinal cord and produces prolonged thermal analgesia. *Science, 206*, 481–483. (4)

Yates, B. (1985). *Self-management*. Belmont, CA: Wadsworth. (6)

Yoshikawa, H. (1994). Prevention as cumulative protection: Effects of early family support and education on chronic delinquency and its risks. *Psychological Bulletin, 115*, 28–54. (15)

Zahavi, A., & Zahavi, A. (1997). *The handicap principle*. New York: Oxford University Press. (14)

Zajonc, R. B. (1968). Attitudinal effects of mere exposure. *Journal of Personality and Social Psychology, 9*, Monograph Supplement 2, part 2. (14)

Zaragoza, M. S., & Mitchell, K. J. (1996). Repeated exposure to suggestions and the creation of false memories. *Psychological Science, 7*, 294–300. (7)

Zastaury, J. (1996, November/December). That old time nutrition. *Sierra*, pp. 16–17. (11)

Zeanah, C. H., Boris, N. W., & Larrieu, J. A. (1997). Infant development and developmental risk: A review of the past 10 years. *Journal of the American Academy of Child & Adolescent Psychiatry, 36*, 165–178. (10)

Zeki, S. (1980). The representation of colours in the cerebral cortex. *Nature, 284*, 412–418. (3)

Zeki, S. (1983). Colour coding in the cerebral cortex: The responses of wavelength-selective and colour-coded cells in monkey visual cortex to changes in wavelength composition. *Neuroscience, 9*, 767–781. (3)

Zeki, S. (1993). *A vision of the brain*. Oxford, England: Blackwell Scientific Publications. (4)

Zigler, E., & Hodapp, R. M. (1991). Behavioral functioning in individuals with mental retardation. *Annual Review of Psychology, 42*, 29–50. (9)

Zihl, J., von Cramon, D., & Mai, N. (1983). Selective disturbance of movement vision after bilateral brain damage. *Brain, 106*, 313–340. (3, 4)

Zipursky, R. B., Lim, K. O., Sullivan, E. V., Brown, B. W., & Pfefferbaum, A. (1992). Widespread cerebral gray matter volume deficits in schizophrenia. *Archives of General Psychiatry, 49*, 195–205. (16)

Zucker, R. A., & Gomberg, E. S. L. (1986). Etiology of alcoholism reconsidered. *American Psychologist, 41*, 783–793. (16)

Zuckerman, M. (1992). What is a basic factor and which factors are basic? Turtles all the way down. *Personality and Individual Differences, 13*, 675–681. (13)

Zuckerman, M. (1995). Good and bad humors: Biochemical bases of personality and its disorders. *Psychological Science, 6*, 325–332. (3)

Zullow, H. M., Oettingen, G., Peterson, C., & Seligman, M. E. P. (1988). Pessimistic explanatory style in the historical record. *American Psychologist, 43*, 673–682. (16)

Zuriff, G. E. (1995). Continuity over change within the experimental analysis of behavior. In J. T. Todd & E. K. Morris (Eds.), *Modern perspectives on B. F. Skinner and contemporary behaviorism* (pp. 171–178). Westport, CT: Greenwood Press. (6)

Zwislocki, J. J. (1981). Sound analysis in the ear: A history of discoveries. *American Scientist, 69*, 184–192. (4)

Credits

This page constitutes an extension of the copyright page. We have made every effort to trace the ownership of all copyrighted material and to secure permission from copyright holders. In the event of any question arising as to the use of any material, we will be pleased to make the necessary corrections in future printings. Thanks are due to the following authors, publishers, and agents for permission to use the material indicated.

Chapter 3: 76: Figure 3.15 from J. G. Brandon and R. G. Coss, *Brain Research*, 252, pp. 51-61, 1982. Used by permission of R. G. Coss. **92:** Figure 3.35 from *Clinical Neuropsychology, Third Edition*, edited by Kenneth M. Heilman and Edward Valenstein. Copyright © 1993 by Oxford University Press, Inc. Used by permission of Oxford University Press, Inc. **94:** Figure 3.38 (a) and (b) from "Specializations of the Human Brain," by Norman Geschwind, 1979, *Scientific American*. Copyright © 1979 by Scientific American, Inc. All rights reserved. Reprinted by permission of the illustrator, Carol Donner. **95:** Figure 3.40 from Wagner, A.D., Desmond, J.E., Demb, J.B., Glover, G. H., & Gabrieli, J.D.E. (1997). "Semantic repetition priming for verbal and pictorial knowledge: A functional MRI study of left inferior prefrontal cortex" in *Journal of Cognitive Neuroscience*, 9, 714–726. Reprinted by permission.

Chapter 4: 116: Figure 4.18 reproduced from *Ishihara's Test for Colour Blindness*, Kanehara & Co., Ltd., Tokyo, Japan. A test for color blindness cannot be conducted with this material. For accurate testing, the original plate should be used. Reprinted by permission. **116:** Figure 4.19 reproduced from *Ishihara's Test for Colour Blindness*, Kanehara & Co., Ltd., Tokyo, Japan. A test for color blindness cannot be conducted with this material. For accurate testing, the original plate should be used. Reprinted by permission. **125:** Figure 4.26 from "Picture and Pattern Perception in the Sighted and the Blind: The Advantage of the Late Blind," by M. A. Heller, *Perception*, 18, pp. 379–389, 1989. Reprinted by permission from Pion, London. **136:** Figure 4.36 from "Fortysomething: Recognizing Faces at One's 25th Reunion," by M. Bruck, P. Cavanagh, and S. J. Ceci, *Memory and Cognition*, 19, pp. 221–228, 1991. Reprinted by permission of M. Bruck. **137:** Figure 4.38 (b) from *Inversions*, by S. Kim. Copyright © 1989 by Scott Kim. Used with permission of W. H. Freeman and Company. **139:** Figure 4.41 from *Organization in Vision: Essays on Gestalt Perception*, by Gaetano Kanizsa, pp. 7, 8, & 9. Copyright © 1979 by Gaetano Kanizsa. Reproduced with permission of Greenwood Publishing Group, Westport, CT. **140:** Figure 4.44 (b) from "A Puzzle Picture with a New Principle of Concealment" by K. M. Dallenbach, *American Journal of Psychology*, 54, pp. 431–433, 1951. Copyright © by The Board of Trustees of the University of Illinois. **140:** Figure 4.45 (c) from *Mind Sights*, by Roger N. Shepard. Copyright © 1990 by Roger N. Shepard. Used with permission of W. H. Freeman and Company. **142:** Figure 4.48 b and c reprinted from *Acta Psychologica*, 58, G. Kanizsa, "Seeing and thinking," 23–33, with permission from Elsevier Science.

Chapter 5: 158: Figure 5.2 graphs from "Monotonic and Rhythmic Influences: A Challenge for Sleep Deprivation Research," by H. Babkoff, T. Caspy, M. Mikulincer, and H. C. Sing, 1991, *Psychological Bulletin*, 109, pp. 411–428. Copyright © 1991 American Psychological Association. Reprinted with permission. **164:** Figure 5.10 EEG recordings provided by T. E. LeVere. **167:** Cartoon Reprinted by permission of Jesse Reklaw.

Chapter 7: 232: Figure 7.5 from "Considerations of Some Problems of Comprehension," by J. D. Bransford and M. K. Johnson in *Visual Information Processing*. W. G. Chase (ed.), 1973. Copyright Academic Press. Used by permission. **237:** Figure 7.12 reprinted with permission from "Acquisition of a Memory Skill," by K. A. Ericsson, W. G. Chase, and S. Falcon, 1980, *Science*, 208, pp. 1181–1182. Copyright 1980 American Association for the Advancement of Science. Reprinted by permission of the AAAS and K. A. Ericsson. **242:** Figure 7.15 based on "Long-Term Memory for a Common Object," by R. S. Nickerson and M. J. Adams, 1979, *Cognitive Psychology*, 11, pp. 287–307. Used by permission. **244:** Figure 7.16 (left) from "Semantic Memory Content in Permastore: Fifty Years of Memory for Spanish Learned in School," by Harry P. Bahrick, 1984, *Journal of Experimental Psychology: General*, 113, pp. 1–29. Copyright 1984 by the American Psychological Association. Used by permission of the author. **264:** Lyrics From I REMEMBER IT WELL, by Alan Jay Lerner and Frederick Loewe. Reprinted by permission. © 1957, 1958 (Copyrights Renewed) Chappell & Co. All Rights Reserved. Used by Permission of WARNER BROS. PUBLICATIONS U.S. INC., Miami, FL 33014.

Chapter 8: 271: Figure 8.2 from "A Spreading-Activation Theory of Semantic Processing," by A. M. Collins and E. F. Loftus, 1975, *Psychological Review*, 82, pp. 407–428. Copyright 1975 American Psychological Association. Reprinted by permission. **273:** Figure 8.3 reprinted with permission from "Mental Rotation of Three-Dimensional Objects," by R. N. Shepard and J. N. Metzler, *Science*, 171, pp. 701–703. Copyright 1971 American Association for the Advancement of Science. **277:** Figure 8.10 reprinted with permission from "Direct Measurement of Attentional Dwell Time in Human Vision," by J. Duncan, R. Ward, and K. Shapiro, 1994, *Nature*, 369, pp. 313–315. Copyright 1994 Macmillan Magazines Ltd. **307:** Figure 8.36 from "Parallel Distributed Processing Explorations in the Microstructure of Cognition," Vol. 1: *Foundations*, by David E. Rumelhart et al., p. 8, Figure 2. (Series in Computational Models of Cognition and Perception.) Copyright 1986 by MIT Press. Used by permission of the publisher.

Chapter 9: 323: Figure 9.5 from the Wechsler Intelligence Scale for Children: Third Edition. Copyright © 1990 by The Psychological Corporation. Reproduced by permission. All rights reserved. **325:** Figure 9.9 SAT materials selected from *10 Real SATs*, College Entrance Examination Board, 1997. Reprinted by permission of

Educational Testing Service and the College Entrance Examination Board, the copyright owners. Permission to reprint SAT test materials does not constitute review or endorsement by Educational Testing Service or the College Board of this publication as a whole or of any other questions or testing information it may contain. **335:** Figure 9.13 reprinted with permission from "Familial Studies of Intelligence: A Review," by T. Bouchard et al., *Science*, 212, pp. 1055–1059, 1981. Copyright 1981 by the American Association for the Advancement of Science.

Chapter 10: 345: Figure 10.1 courtesy of Robin Kalat. **348:** Figure 10.6 modified from "Movement Produced Stimulation in the Development of Visually Guided Behavior," by R. Held and A. Hein, *Journal of Comparative Physiological Psychology*, 56, pp. 872–873. Copyright 1963 by the American Psychological Association. Adapted by permission of R. Held. **352:** Figure 10.12 From K. Wynn. (1992). "Addition and subtraction by human infants," *Nature*, 358, 749–750. Reprinted by permission.

Chapter 11: 402: Figure 11.8 reprinted by permission of Gene DeFoliart from *The Food Insects Newsletter*, March 1990.

Chapter 12: 439: Figure 12.6 based on "An Opponent-Process Theory of Motivation: I. Temporal Dynamics of Affect," by R. L. Solomon and J. D. Corbit, *Psychological Review*, 81, pp. 119–145. Copyright 1974 by the American Psychological Association. Reprinted by permission. **455:** Figure 12.20 from Tracy, P.E., Wolfgang, M.E., & Figlio, R.M. (1990). *Delinquency Careers in Two Birth Cohorts*, (12). Reprinted by permission of Plenum Publishing Corporation. **461:** Table 12.2 from "The Social Readjustment Rating Scale," by T. H. Holmes and R. H. Rahe in *Journal of Psychosomatic Research*, 11, pp. 213–218. Copyright 1967 by Pergamon Press, Ltd. Reprinted by permission of Elsevier Science Ltd., Oxford, England. **462:** Table 12.3 from "Comparison of Two Modes of Stress Measurement: Daily Hassles and Uplifts Versus Major Life Events," by A. D. Kanner, J. C. Coyne, C. Schaefer, and R. S. Lazarus, *Journal of Behavioral Medicine*, 4, p. 14. Copyright 1981 by Plenum Publishing Corporation. Adapted by permission. **464:** Figure 12.26 from *Type A Behavior and Your Heart* by Meyer Friedman and Ray H. Rosenman. Copyright © 1974 by Meyer Friedman. Reprinted by permission of Alfred A. Knopf, Inc.

Chapter 13: 506: Figure 13.20 from the Minnesota Multiphasic Personality Inventory-2. Copyright © by the Regents of the University of Minnesota 1942, 1943 (renewed 1970), 1989. This profile from 1989. All rights reserved. **507:** Figure 13.21 adapted from *Handbook for the Sixteen Personality Factors* by Raymond B. Cattell. Copyright 1970, 1988 by the Institute for Personality and Ability Testing, Inc. All rights reserved. Reproduced by permission. **508:** Figure 13.22 from *The Scientific Analysis of Personality* by Raymond B. Cattell, 1965, Penguin Library. Reprinted by permission of Raymond B. Cattell. **510:** Figure 13.24 reprinted by permission of the publisher from Henry A. Murray, *Thematic Apperception Test*, Cambridge, Mass.:

Harvard University Press, Copyright © 1943 by the President and Fellows of Harvard College, © 1971 by Henry A. Murray.

Chapter 14: 536: Figure 14.8 reprinted from *Social Pressures in Informal Groups: A Study of Human Factors in Housing* by Leon Festinger, Stanley Schachter, and Kurt Back, with the permission of the publishers, Stanford University Press. © 1950 by Leon Festinger, Stanley Schachter, and Kurt Back. **540:** Figure 14.11 from L. G. Tassinary & K. A. Hansen, "A critical test of the waist-to-hip-ratio hypotheses of female physical attractiveness," *Psychological Science*, 9, 150–155. Reprinted by permission of Blackwell Publishers. **545:** Figure 14.14 adapted from "Opinion and Social Pressure," by Solomon Asch. *Scientific American*, November 1955. Copyright © 1955 by Scientific American, Inc. All rights reserved.

Chapter 15: 569: Quote from "Observation" by Dorothy Parker, copyright 1928, renewed © 1956 by Dorothy Parker from *The Portable Dorothy Parker* by Dorothy Parker, introduction by Brendan Gill. Used by permission of Viking Penguin, a division of Penguin Books USA Inc. **579:** Figure 15.7 adapted from *The Benefits of Psychotherapy* by M. L. Smith, G. V. Glass, and T. I. Miller, The Johns Hopkins University Press, 1980. Reprinted by permission. **579:** Figure 15.8 from Seligman, M.E.P. (1995), "The effectiveness of psychotherapy: The *Consumer Reports* study," in *American Psychologist*, 50. 965–974. Copyright © 1995 by The American Psychological Association. Reprinted by permission. **580:** Figure 15.9 based on "The Dose-Effect Relationship in Psychotherapy," by Kenneth I. Howard et al., 1986, *American Psychologist*, 41, pp. 159–164. Used by permission of Kenneth I. Howard.

Chapter 16: 600: Figure 16.9 based on "Studies on Endogenous Ligands (Endacoids) for the Benzodiazepine/Beta-Carboline Binding Sites," by A. Guidotti, P. Ferrero, M. Fujimoto, R. M. Santi, and E. Costa, 1986, *Advances in Biochemical Psychopharmacology*, 41, pp. 137–148. Reprinted by permission. **602:** Table 16.1 from *Obsessions and Compulsions* by Stanley J. Rachman and Ray J. Hodgson. Copyright © 1980. Reprinted by permission of Prentice-Hall, Inc., Englewood Cliffs, NJ. **602:** Table 16.2 from *Obsession and Compulsions* by Stanley J. Rachman and Ray J. Hodgson. Copyright © 1980. Reprinted by permission of Prentice-Hall, Inc., Englewood Cliffs, NJ. **608:** Figure 16.11 adapted from Levenson et al., "Greater Reinforcement from Alcohol for Those at Risk: Parental Risk, Personality Risk, and Sex," *Journal of Abnormal Psychology*, 96, pp. 242–253, 1987. Used by permission of the author. **610:** Figure 16.13 from "A 24-Year Follow-Up of California Narcotics Addicts," by Y. I. Hser, M. D. Anglin, and K. Powers, 1993, *Archives of General Psychiatry*, 50, pp. 577–584. Copyright 1993 American Medical Association. Reprinted by permission. **621:** Excerpts from Joshua Logan in *Moodswing* by Ronald R. Fieve. Copyright © 1975 by Ronald R. Fieve. Published by William R. Morrow & Co. **622:** Figure 16.20 based on "Water and Sodium in Two Psychotics," by J. L. Crammer in *Lancet*, 1(7083), pp. 1122–1126, 1959. Used by permission of Lancet Ltd.

PHOTO CREDITS

Contents: Page iv: Thomas J. Mayberry and Catherine Archuleta. **Page xi:** Top photo © Tony Freeman/PhotoEdit. Middle photo © International Stock/Dario Perla. Bottom photo © Michael Heron/Woodfin Camp & Assoc. **Page xii:** Top photo © Jim Pickerell/Tony Stone. Middle photo © Roger Tully/Tony Stone. Bottom photo © David Madison 1995. **Page xiii:** Top photo © Michael Rosenfeld/Tony Stone Images. Bottom photo © Michael Fisher/Custom Medical Stock Photo. **Page xiv:** Top photo © Andrew Brilliant. Bottom photo © Kevin R. Morris/Corbis. **Page xv:** Top photo © AP Wide World Photo. Middle photo © Patrick Ramsey/International Stock. Bottom photo © Archive for Research in Archetypal Symbolism, San Fransisco. **Page xvi:** Top photo © Diego Lezama Orezzoli/Corbis. Middle photo © Gamma Liaison/L Marescot. Bottom photo © Neal Preston/Corbis. **Page xvii:** Top photo © The Image Works/H. Gans. Middle photo © Michael Lewis/Corbis. Bottom photo © Minden Pictures/Frans Lanting. **Page xviii:** Top photo © David Burnett/Contact Press Images. Middle photo © Owen Franken/Corbis. Bottom photo courtesy of Ann Premack. **Page xix:** Top photo © Joseph Sohm,ChromoSohm Inc./Corbis. Bottom photo © Yann Layma/Tony Stone. **Page xx:** Top photo © Stephanie Maze/Corbis. Bottom photo © Bob Daemmrich/The Image Works. **Page xxi:** Top photo © Neil Rabinowitz/Corbis. Middle photo © AP Wide World Photo. Bottom photo © Galen Rowell/Corbis. **Page xxii:** Top photo © Michel Lipchitz/AP WideWorld Photo. Middle photo © Ron Kimball Photography/Ron Kimball. Bottom photo © Nevada Wier/Corbis. **Page xxiii:** Top photo reproduction courtesy of Frederick Brown. Middle photo © Christine Garrigan. Bottom photo © Pat Berrett 1995. **Page xxiv:** Top photo © PhotoDisc. Bottom photo © Richard Hume/PhotoDisc. **Page xxv:** Top photo © Black Star/PF Bentley. Middle photo © Paul A. Souders/Corbis. Bottom photo © Bob Daemmrich/The Image Works. **Page xxvi:** Top photo © Dan Guravich/Corbis. Bottom photo © AP Wide World Photos.

Chapter 1: Page 2: Photo © Phil Schermiser/Corbis. **Page 4:** All photos © Mitchell Gerber/Corbis except. Top left photo © Galen Rowell/Corbis. Bottom left photo © Francoise deMulder/Corbis. **Page 6:** Photo © Tony Freeman/PhotoEdit. **Page 7:** Courtesy of Dr. Michael E. Phelps & Dr. John Mazziotta, UCLA School of Medicine. **Page 8:** Left photo © Tom Rosenthal/SuperStock. **Page 8:** Right photo © Bob Wickley/Super Stock. **Page 10:** Photo © Michael Heron/Woodfin Camp & Assoc. **Page 12:** Top photo © Ed Lallo/The Picture Cube. Bottom photo © Jeffery Greenberg/The Picture Cube. **Page 19:** Right photo © The Walt Disney Company. **Page 20:** Top photo © Superstock Inc./T. Rosenthal. Bottom photo © Glenn Rileyno. **Page 22:** Wellesley College Archives and Notman. **Page 23:** International Stock/Dario Perla. **Page 24:** Left photo © Bob Daemmrich/Stock Boston. Right photo © Gaye Hilsenrath/The Picture Cube.

Chapter 2: Page 26: Photo © Roger Tully/Tony Stone. **Page 32:** After Pfungst, 1911, in Fernald, 1984. **Page 33:** Photo © AP Wide World Photo. **Page 34:** Photo © Palace of Versailles, France/ET Archive,London/Superstock. **Page 35:** Photo © 1994 Center for Inquiry. **Page 39:** Left photo © Paul Chesley/Tony Stone. Right photo © Jim Pickerell/Tony Stone. **Page 40:** Photo © Gamma Liaison/Photo by Breese. **Page 44:** Photo © Deborah Davis/PhotoEdit. **Page 46:** Photo © Dave Schaefer/The Picture Cube. **Page 50:** Photo © David Madison 1995.

Chapter 3: Page 60: Photo © Michael Fisher/Custom Medical Stock Photo. **Page 62:** Photo © ZEFA. **Page 63:** Science Photo Library/CNR. **Page 65:** Photo © ZEFA/The Stock Market. **Page 68:** Photo © Arnold Zann/BlackStar. **Page 71:** Photo © Gordon Langsbury/Bruce Coleman. **Page 76:** Top photo © Custom Medical Stock Photo. Bottom photo © Manfred Kage/Peter Arnold. **Page 78:** Photo © Custom Medical Stock Photo. **Page 82:** Photo © AP Wide World Photo. **Page 83:** Photo © Herb Weitman/NFL Photos. **Page 90:** Bottom left photos © Dr. Colin Chumbley/Science Photo Library. Top right photo courtesy of Dana Copeland. **Page 95:** Left photo © Michael Rosenfeld/Tony Stone Images. Right photo © Wagner, Desmond, Demp, Glover, & Gabrieli, 1997.

Chapter 4: Page 102: © 1998 Cordon Art B.V. Baarn-Holland. **Page 107:** Photos © Glenn Rileyno. **Page 108:** Top photo E. R. Lewis, F. S. Werblin and Y. Y. Zeevi. Bottom photo © Swift Photography/Chase Swift. **Page 113:** © Musee du Louvre, Paris/SuperStock. **Page 114:** Photos © ZEFA/Klaus Benser. **Page 121:** Photo © San Francisco Chronicle/Lea Zuzukino. **Page 123:** Photo © Kevin R. Morris/Corbis. **Page 129:** Photo © Louis Psimoyos/Contacy Press Images/Colorific!. **Page 132:** Photo © Louis Psimoyos/Contact Press Images/Colorific!. **Page 135:** Photo © Neal Preston/Corbis. **Page 136:** Top photos M. Bruck, P. Cavanagh, and S. J. Ceci "Fortysomething: Recognizing Faces at One's 25th Reunion," by in Memory & Cognition, 19:221–228, 1991. Bottom photo © D. Halstead/Gamma Liaison. **Page 140:** Top courtesy of McDonnell Douglas. Upper middle photo courtesy of K. M. Dallenbach from the Amercian Journal of Psychology. Photo © 1942 by the Board of Trustees of the University of Illinios. Used with permission of the University of Illinios Press. Lower middle photo courtesy of K. M. Dallenbach from the American Journal of Psychology. Photo © 1951 by the Board of Trustees of the University of Illinios. Used with permission of the University of Illinios Press. **Page 144:** Top photo © Stock Market/Globus Bros/ZEFA. Bottom photo © Lowell Observatory Photograph/Clyde Tombaugh. **Page 145:** Photo © John Boykin. **Page 146:** Photo © Magnum Photos, Inc./Steve McGurry. **Page 148:** Top photo © Andrew Brilliant. Bottom photo The Exploratorium/S. Schwartzenberg. **Page 150:** Photo © Mark Antman/The Image Works.

Chapter 5: Page 154: Top photo © Wolfgang Kaehler/Corbis. Bottom photo © Jennie Woodcock, Reflections Photolibrary/Corbis. **Page 156:** Left photo © Roger Allyn Lee/SuperStock. Right photo © Phil Cantor/SuperStock. **Page 157:** Photo © Frank Pedrick/The Image Works. **Page 161:** San Diego Historical Society. **Page 162:** Top photo © Cliff Frith/Bruce Coleman Inc. Middle photo © Wayne Lankinen/Bruce Coleman Inc. Bottom photo © PhotoDisc. **Page 163:** Black Star/Richard Nowitz. **Page 168:** Top Slow Wave © 1996 Nick Munford and Jesse Reklaw. Bottom Slow Wave © 1997 Dana Hughes and Jesse Reklaw. Photo © Patrick Ramsey/International Stock. **Page 171:** Photo © Brian Smith/Liaison International. **Page 173:** Picture Library/Mary Evans. **Page 174:** Top photo © AP Wide World Photo. Bottom photo © John Gress/AP Photo. **Page 175:** Photo © AP Wide World Photosjk. **Page 176:** Orne, N. T. (1951). The mechanisms of hypnotic age regression; an experimental study. Journal of Abnormal and Social Psychology, 46, 213–225. **Page 177:** Left photo © John Nordell/The Image Works. Right photo © Michael A. Schwartz/The Image Works. **Page 179:** Photo © Los Angeles Times/R. L. Oliver. **Page 180:** Photo © Image Works/Tabuteau. **Page 182:** Photo © University of Pa. Museum. **Page 183:** Photo © Ted Soqui/Sygma. **Page 185:** Left photo E. D. London et al., Archives of General Psychiatry, 47:567-574, 1990. Photo © AMA. Right photo © Tannenbaum/Sygma. **Page 186:** Photo © Archive for Research in Archetypal Symbolism, San Fransisco.

Chapter 6: Page 188: Photo © Diego Lezama Orezzoli/Corbis. **Page 190:** Photo © Mary Ann McDonald/Corbis. **Page 192:** Left photo © Owen Franken/Corbis. Right photo © Liaison International/Warnher Krutein. **Page 193:** Photo © Peter Turnley/Corbis. **Page 195:** Photo © Novosti Press Agency. **Page 208:** Photo © Time Inc./Nina Leen, Life Magazine. **Page 209:** Photo © Time Inc./Robert Kelly, Life Magazine. **Page 211:** Photo © David Madison 1992. **Page 212:** Photo © Philippe Hurlin/Gamma Liasion. **Page 213:** Photo © Image Bank/Stockphotos. **Page 214:** Left photo © Miguel Gandert/Corbis. Right photo © Mark

Gibson/Corbis. **Page 215:** Photo © Gamma Liaison/L Marescot. Photo © Aurora/José Azel. **Page 220:** Photo © Stuart Ellins. **Page 221:** Photo © Joe Mcdonald/Corbis. **Page 222:** Left photo © Robb Kendrick/Aurora. Right photo © Courtesy of Dr. Albert Bandura. **Page 223:** Photo © Neal Preston/Corbis. **Page 224:** Photo © J. Berndt/Stock Boston.

Chapter 7: Page 226: Photo © Michael Lewis/Corbis. **Page 228:** Minden Pictures/Frans Lanting. **Page 229:** Courtesy of Professor John Horton Conway. **Page 230:** Wellcome Institute Library, London. **Page 232:** Courtesy of Beverly Kappler. **Page 235:** Photo © Jim Mcdonald/Corbis. **Page 236:** Ann Dowie. The Image Works/H. Gans. **Page 241:** Photo © Martin B. Withers Frank Lane Picture Agency/Corbis. **Page 243:** Left photo © Macduff Everton/Corbis. Right photo Archiv fur Kunst und Geschichte, Berlin. **Page 244:** Photo © Paul A.Souders/Corbis. **Page 250:** Top left photo © UPI/Corbis-Bettmann. Top right photo © Remi Benali/Gamma Liaison. Bottom photo © Suzanne Corkin, Psychology Dept, MIT. **Page 253:** © Walt Disney Company. **Page 254:** Photo © Network/Matrix/Anthea Sieveking. **Page 259:** Photo © John Dunn/AP Wide World Photo.

Chapter 8: Page 266: Photo © Owen Franken/Corbis. **Page 268:** Photo © Doug Menuez/PhotoDisc. **Page 274:** Photo © GPU Nuclear Corp. **Page 278:** Photo © Glenn Riley. **Page 279:** Photo © David Burnett/Contact Press Images. **Page 280:** Photo © Gamma Liaison/Chip Hires. **Page 281:** Photos © Ann Dowie. **Page 282:** Left photo © Stephen McBrady. Right photo © Jim Sugar Photography/Corbis. **Page 284:** Left photo © Steve Cole/PhotoDisc. Right Glenn Riley. **Page 285:** Photo © Bettmann. **Page 286:** Left photo © Hulton-Deutsch Collections/Corbis. Right photo © UPI/Corbis-Bettmann. **Page 289:** Photo © Susan Ashukian. **Page 291:** Photo © Susan Ashukian. **Page 292:** Photo © Dean Conger/Corbis. **Page 293:** Top photo © Susan Ashukian. Bottom photo © Brian Bohannon/AP Photo. **Page 294:** Photo © Jonathan Blair/Corbis. **Page 298:** Courtesy of Ann Premack. **Page 299:** Elizabeth Rubert, Language Reasearch Center, Georgia State University. **Page 302:** Photo © Stephen Rapley. **Page 304:** Photo © Courtesy of Gorham China. **Page 309:** Photo © Woodfin Camp & Asso./Paula Lerner.

Chapter 9: Page 312: Photo © Yann Layma/Tony Stone. **Page 314:** Photo Network/Mary Messenger. **Page 318:** Left photo © Bob Daemmrich/The Image Works. Middle left photo © Philip Gould/Corbis. Middle right photo © Richard Hamilton/Corbis. Right photo © Derick A. Thomas/Corbis. **Page 319:** Photos courtesy of Dr. Robert Sternberg, Yale University. **Page 323:** Photo © Photo Researchers, Inc./W & D McIntyre. **Page 328:** Photo © Bob Daemmrich/The Image Works. **Page 329:** Photo © Image Works/Fujifotos. **Page 332:** Photo © Lee Snider/Corbis. **Page 333:** Photo © Loren Sanlow/Tony Stone Images,Inc. **Page 334:** Left photo © Shelly Gazin/Corbis. Right photo © Liaison International. **Page 338:** Photo © Eric Furtran Photography, Chicago. **Page 339:** Photo © Joseph Sohm, ChromoSohm Inc./Corbis.

Chapter 10: Page 342: Photo © Woodfin Camp & Assoc./William Hubbell. **Page 344:** Photo © Bob Daemmrich/The Image Works. **Page 346:** Top right photo © Image Works/G. Gardner. Bottom left photo © Baldwin H. Ward/Corbis-Bettmann. **Page 347:** Photo © George Steinmetz/George Steinmetz Photography. **Page 349:** Photo © Newsweek/James Wilson. **Page 350:** Photo © Rutgers University/Dr. Carolyn Rovee-Collier, Department of Psychology, Busch Campus. Photo © Monkmeyer Press/Doug Goodman. **Page 354:** Photo © Black Star/Yves de Braine. **Page 355:** Photo © Stephen Rapley. **Page 356:** Photo © Ann Dowie. **Page 359:** Photo © Ann Dowie. **Page 362:** Photo © Elizabeth Crews/Elizabeth Crews Photography. **Page 363:** Photo © Gamma Liaison/Pugliano. **Page 365:** Photo © Rick Smolan. **Page 366:** Photo © Reuters/Str/A/Archive Photos. **Page 368:** Photo © Phil Schermeister/Corbis. **Page 370:** Top pho-

tos © UPI/Corbis-Bettmann. Bottom photo © Corbis-Bettmann. **Page 372:** Harlow Primate Laboratory, University of Wisconsin. **Page 373:** Harlow Primate Laboratory University of Wisconsin. **Page 374:** Photo © Joel Simon. **Page 375:** Photo © Doug Menuez/PhotoDisc. **Page 376:** Photo © Stock Boston/Patrick Ward. **Page 378:** Photo © Mountain Light Photography/Galen Rowell. **Page 379:** Photo © Stephane Cardinale/Sygma. **Page 382:** Photo © Sally and Richard Greenhill. **Page 383:** Photo © Anthony Bannister/Corbis. **Page 384:** Photo © C.Glassman/The Image Works. **Page 386:** Top photo © Bachmann/The Image Works. Bottom left photo © Tim Thompson/Corbis. Bottom right photo © Stephanie Maze/Corbis. **Page 387:** Photo © Sotographs/Liaison International.

Chapter 11: Page 390: Photo © Masterfile/Allan Davey. **Page 392:** Photo © Reuters/Colin Braley/Archive Photos. **Page 395:** Image Bank/Benn Mitchell. **Page 397:** Photo © AP Wide World Photo. **Page 400:** Photo © Karl Weatherly/PhotoDisc. **Page 401:** Photo © Sally and Richard Greenhill. **Page 402:** Left photo © Neil Rabinowitz/Corbis. Right photo © Stock Boston/Peter Menzel. **Page 406:** Bottom photo © Bob Daemmrich/The Image Works. **Page 407:** Left photos © Scott Vlaun Photography. Right photo © Stephen Trimble. **Page 411:** Top left photo © Museo del Prado, Madrid, Spain/Giraudon, Paris/SuperStock. **Page 411:** Bottom right photo © Photo Edit/Tony Freeman. **Page 413:** Photo © Jay Dickman. **Page 414:** Photo © Reproduced by permission of the Kinsey Institute for Research in Sex, Gender, and Reproduction, Inc. Photo by Dellenback. **Page 418:** Top left photo © Thierry Mayer/Photo Researchers,Inc. Top right photo © Douglas Peeples/Corbis. Middle left photo © Robert Holmes/Corbis. Middle right photo © Ray Scott/The Image Works. Bottom photo courtesy of the San Fransisco AIDS Foundation. **Page 421:** Left photo © Musee du Louvre, Paris/Lauros-Giraudon, Paris/SuperStock. Right photo © Neal Preston/Corbis. **Page 423:** From LeVay, S. (1991) A difference in hypothalamic structure between heterosexual and homosexual men. *Science, 253,* 1034−1037. **Page 425:** Photo © Michael Speaker. **Page 426:** Photo © Elizabeth Crews/Elizabeth Crews Photography 9734-30. **Page 427:** Photo © Galen Rowell/Corbis. **Page 428:** Photo © The Image Works/Elizabeth Crews. **Page 430:** Photo © Rose Hartman/Archive Photos.

Chapter 12: Page 432: Photo © Image Works/Bob Daemmrich. **Page 434:** Photo © Michel Lipchitz/AP WideWorld Photo. **Page 435:** American Association for the Advancement of Science. Reprinted with permission from "The return of Phineas Gage: Clues about the brain from the skull of a famous patient," by H. Damasio, T. Grabowski, R. Frank, A.M. Galabu, and A. R. Damasio in *Science, 264.* Photo © 1994. **Page 436:** Petar Kujundzic/Reuters/Bettmann. **Page 438:** Left photo © Tom Brakefield/Corbis. Right photo © Phil Schermeister/Corbis. **Page 440:** Photo © Richard Nowitz/Corbis. **Page 443:** Photo © Ann Dowie. **Page 447:** Top left photo © Ron Kimball Photography/Ron Kimball. Bottom right photos © John Boykin. **Page 448:** All photos © Eibl-Eibesfeldt. **Page 449:** All photos © P. Ekman and W. Friesen/from Unmasking the Face (2d ed.) by 1984. Used by permission of P. Ekman. **Page 454:** Left photo © Louise Gubb/The Image Works. Right photo © The Young Racers an American International Picture/Movie Still Archives. **Page 459:** Photo © Jennie Woodcock: Reflections Photolibrary/Corbis. **Page 460:** Photo © Frankee (Jim Lenoir). **Page 464:** Left photo © Stephanie Maze/Corbis. Right photo © Bill Horsman/Stock Boston. **Page 467:** Photo © Wally McNamee/Corbis. **Page 468:** Photo © Bob Winsett/Corbis. **Page 469:** Top photo © Gamma Liaison/Cindy Charles. Bottom photo © Owen Franken/Corbis. **Page 471:** Left photo © Nevada Wier/Corbis. Right photo © Skjold/The Image Works.

Chapter 13: Page 474: Reproduction courtesy of Frederick Brown. **Page 476:** Photo © Monkmeyer/Dunn. **Page 478:** Left photos © The Granger Colection, New York. Right photo © Archiv/Photo

Researchers Inc. **Page 480:** Top left photo © Paul A. Souders/ Corbis. Top right photo © Jeremy Horner/Corbis. Bottom left photo © Roger Wood/Corbis. Bottom right photo © Jeremy Horner/Corbis. **Page 481:** Top photo © Ellen Senisi/The Image Works. Bottom photo © Blair Seitz/Photo Researchers, Inc. **Page 482:** Left photo © Bettmann Archive. Right photo © Bettmann Archive. **Page 483:** Photo © Bettmann Archive. **Page 487:** Left photo © Kindra Clineff/The PictureCube. Right photo © Carol Palmer/The PictureCube. **Page 492:** Top photo © Freud Museum. Bottom photo © The Bettmann Archive. **Page 493:** Photo © Culver Pictures. **Page 494:** Top left photo © Silvio Fiore/SuperStock. Top right photo © Archive for Research in Archetypal Symbolism. Bottom left photo © Christine Garrigan. Bottom right photo © Pat Berrett 1995. **Page 495:** Photo © Bettmann Newsphotos/UPI. **Page 497:** Photo © Fujifotos/ The Image Works. **Page 498:** Courtesy of Morimura Yasumasa. **Page 503:** Glenn Riley. **Page 510:** From Thematic Apperception Test by Henry A. Murray, Harvard University Press, Cambridge, MA. Photo © 1943 by the President and Fellows of Harvard College,1971 by Henry A. Murray.

Chapter 14: Page 514: Photo © Magnum Photos, Inc./Raghu Rai. **Page 516:** Photo © AP Wide World Photo. **Page 517:** Photo © Bettmann Newsphotos/Peter Morgan. **Page 520:** Top photo © Bob Daemmrich/The Image Works. Bottom left photo © John Gillis/AP Wide World Photo. Bottom right photo © Srdjan Ilic/AP Wide World Photo. **Page 525:** Photo © Peter Turnley/Corbis. **Page 527:** Photo © AP Wide World Photo. **Page 528:** Photo © Glenn Riley. **Page 529:** Photo © Hulton-Deutsch Collection/Corbis. **Page 535:** Left photo © Peter Johnson/Corbis. Middle photo © StockTrek/ PhotoDisc. Right photo © Henry Diltz/Corbis. **Page 537:** Photo © Richard Hume/PhotoDisc. **Page 538:** Photo © CMCD/PhotoDisc. **Page 539:** Langlois, Roggman, & Musselman in *Psychological Science*, vol. 5, no. 4./"Averaging Faces." **Page 541:** Photo © PhotoDisc. **Page 544:** Photo © Bob Daemmrich/Stock Boston. **Page 545:** Photo © William Vandivert. **Page 546:** Photo © AP Wide World Photo. **Page 547:** Photo © John Boykin. **Page 548:** Photo © Chuck Nacke/Black Star. **Page 549:** Photo © PhotoDisc. **Page 551:** Photo © Superstock. **Page 555:** Photos © Stanley Milgram. From the film *Obedience*, distributed by Pennsylvania State University Audio Visual Services.

Chapter 15: Page 558: Photo © Erich Lessing/Art Resource, NY. **Page 560:** Photo © Paul A. Souders/Corbis. **Page 561:** Left photo © Rene Ritler/AP Photo/Keystone. Middle photo © AP Wide World Photo. Right photo © Mark Fallander/AP Photo. **Page 562:** Photo © Brian Bahr/Allsport. **Page 563:** Top photo © APWide World Photo. Bottom photo © Art Resource. **Page 567:** Photo © Bob Daemmrich/The Image Works. **Page 569:** Photo © Cindy Karp/NYT Pictures. **Page 571:** Photo © Express Newspapers/ Archive Photos. **Page 572:** Photo courtesy of Ideas for Living, Inc. **Page 574:** Left photo © NASA/Corbis. Right photo © Paramount Still Library. **Page 575:** Photo © Stephanie Rausser/FPG International. **Page 577:** Both photos © Richard T. Nowitz/Corbis. **Page 578:** Left photo © Tony Stone/Zigy Kaluzny. Right photo © Tony Stone Images/Ken Fisher. **Page 580:** Photo © Gary Conner/Photo Edit. **Page 584:** Photo © Jerry Cooke/Corbis. **Page 585:** Photo © Black Star/PF Bentley. **Page 587:** Left photo © Scott Manchester/ Sygma. Right photo © S. O'Sullivan/Sygma. **Page 589:** Photo © J. Scott Applewhite/AP Press.

Chapter 16: Page 590: Photo © Tate Gallery, London/ET Archives, London/SuperStock. **Page 593:** Photo © Bob Daemmrich/The Image Works. **Page 595:** Left photo © Bettmann Archive/Alfred Hitchcock. Right photo © Los Angeles Times Photo. **Page 597:** Photo courtesy of Professor Benjamin Harris. **Page 598:** Photo © Lev Nisnevith/Tony Stone. **Page 599:** Photo © Andrew Sacks Pictures/Andrew Sacks. **Page 600:** Photo © AP Wide World Photos. **Page 601:** Photo © Dan Guravich/Corbis. **Page 605:** Photo © Macduff Everton/Corbis. **Page 607:** Photo © Michael Grecco/Image Bank. **Page 609:** Photo © Hank Morgan/Science Source/Photo Researchers, Inc. **Page 612:** Photo © A. Lichtenstein/ The Image Works. **Page 615:** Photo © Art Resource. **Page 617:** Both photos © AP Wide World Photos. **Page 620:** Photo © 1994 B.S.I.P./Custom Medical Stock Photo. **Page 622:** Photo © AP Wide World Photo. **Page 627:** © Guttman-Macley Collection; The Bethlem Royal Hospital and the Maudsley Hospital. **Page 629:** Top photo © Monkmeye/Grunnitos. Bottom photos courtesy of E. F. Torrey and M. F. Casanova/NIMH. **Page 631:** Photo © Lowell Georgia/Corbis. **Page 637:** Left photo © AP Wide World Photo. Right photo © Michael S. Yamashita/Corbis.

Name Index

Myers, J. K., 564
Myerson, J., 238
Mylander, C., 302, 303

Nagera, H., 601
Naidu, R. K., 446
Naranjo, C. A., 609
Nash, M. R., 176
NcNeill, D., 302
Neale, M. C., 421, 500, 615
Near, D., 533
Nebes, R. D., 98
Negy, C., 504
Neher, A., 493
Neimeyer, R. A., 619
Neiss, R., 442
Neisser, U., 328, 331, 332
Nelson, J. M., 183
Nelson, K. E., 301
Nemeroff, C., 401, 403
Nemeth, C., 527, 553
Nester, E. J., 606
Nestler, E. J., 619
Newman, B., 544
Newman, C. F., 623
Newman, R., 176
Newport, E. L., 300
Newstead, S. E., 8
Newton, I., 23
Nezworski, M. T., 510
Nicholls, K., 186
Nickerson, R. S., 242
Nigg, J. T., 37
Nisbett, R. E., 283, 521, 523
Noel, J. G., 548
Nofzinger, E. A., 614
Nolen-Hoeksema, S., 616, 618
Noll, D. C., 95
Nopoulos, P., 628
Nordin, N., 129
Norman, D. A., 13
Norman, M. F., 330
Norman, T. R., 618
Noshirvani, H., 573
Nostradamus, 34
Nowicki, S., 595, 628
Noyes, R., 603
Nozawa, G., 138
Nugent,L. D., 238
Nygard, R., 427

Oakland, T. D., 13
O'Brien, C. P., 612
O'Connor, M. E., 411
Odbert, H. S., 498
Oertel, W. H., 82
Oettingen, G., 617
Ohaeri, J. U., 629
O'Hara, M. W., 615
Ohayon, M. M., 168
Öhman, A., 203, 599, 630
Okada, A., 427
Oken, D., 470
Okin, R. L., 584
Olfson, M., 615, 619
Oliver, M. B., 414
Olney, J. W., 632
Olofsson, C., 599

Olsson, H., 287
Olweus, D., 454
O'Malley, S. L. C., 72
Orlinsky, D. E., 575, 580
Ormerod, M. B., 499
Orne, E. C., 175, 179
Orne, M. T., 49, 175, 177, 178, 179
Ornstein, P. A., 264
Orr, S. P., 460
Ortony, A., 445
Orzi, F., 185
Oscar-Berman, M., 252
O'Shanick, G. J., 623
Osofsky, J. D., 454
Osuntokum, B. O., 629
Ottati, V., 518
Otto, R., 602
Oubaid, V., 541
Ouellette, J. A., 527
Overman, W. H., 254
Owen, D. R., 336
Owen, M. T., 373
Oyama, O. N., 608

Pacht, J. M., 310
Padgham, C. A., 163
Paicheler, G., 544
Paikoff, R. L., 375
Palmer, B. W., 628
Palmer, S. E., 510
Pantev, C., 96
Papageorgis, D., 529
Paradis, M., 303
Parke, R. D., 47, 384
Parker, K., 285
Parnas, J., 626
Parra, C., 97, 203
Pascual-Leone, A., 96
Pasnau, R. O., 465
Pate, B. J., 254
Pate, J. L., 299
Patrick, C. J., 441
Paus, T., 308
Pavlov, I. B., 195–6, 200
Peachey, J. E., 610
Pearce, J. M., 199
Pearlmutter, N. J., 310
Pearson, A. J. D., 161
Peck, C. P., 294
Pedersen, N. L., 316
Peele, S., 611
Pelchat, M. L., 68, 69
Pellymounter, M. A., 408
Penfield, W., 94
Pennebaker, J. W., 468, 469, 470
Penrod, S., 261
Perkins, D. N., 332
Perner, J., 358
Perry, D. G., 481
Perry, S. H., 114
Perry, S. M., 507
Person, E., 318
Pert, C. B., 183
Pertinovich, L., 221
Peters, S., 221
Peterson, C., 617

Peterson, D., 143
Peterson, L. G., 623
Peterson, L. R., 236, 237
Peterson, M., 623
Peterson, M. J., 236, 237
Petitto, L. A., 299
Petrie, K. J., 159
Petrill, S. A., 316
Petter, G., 142
Pettitt, A. N., 158
Petty, R. E., 524, 525, 529
Peuster, A., 254
Pfefferbaum, A., 629
Pfungst, O., 32
Phalet, K., 428
Phelps, E. A., 95, 449
Phelps, J. A., 630
Phelps, M. E., 7
Philipchalk, R., 498
Phillips, D., 383-4
Phillips, N. H., 161
Phillips, R. G., 449
Phillips, R. T., 382
Piaget, J., 350, 354, 360-2, 367
Piasecki, T. M., 606
Pichot, P., 508
Pidoplichko, V. I., 606
Pillard, R. C., 421
Pine, C. J., 388
Piomelli, D., 184
Pion G. M., 15
Piotrowski, C., 504
Pitman, R. K., 460
Pittillo, E. S., 563
Plihal, W., 166
Plomin, R., 67, 316, 335, 336, 537
Plonsky, M., 218
Plotkin, D. A., 619
Plous, S., 50
Plum, F., 405
Plutchik, R., 444
Poggio, T., 136
Poizner, H., 95
Polcin, D. L., 610
Polgar, J., 280
Polgar, L., 280
Polivy, J., 409, 411
Pollak, J. M., 602
Polya, G., 281
Pomeroy, W. B., 414
Pontieri, F. E., 185
Poole, A. D., 572
Poole, D. A., 264
Poortinga, Y. H., 562
Pope, M. A., 264, 606
Popper, K., 488
Pottash, A. L. C., 184
Potter, M. C., 288
Potter, W. Z., 622
Poulos, C. S., 200
Povinelli, D. J., 358
Powell, R. A., 486
Powers, K., 610
Powers, S., 323
Powlishta, K. K., 387, 481
Poynton, F. G., 135
Pratkanis, A. R., 135, 527

Premack, D., 212
Press, G. A., 252
Price, D. D., 174
Prien, R. F., 619
Prins, B., 241
Prohaska, V., 287
Provine, R. R., 477
Proxmire, W., 535
Puce, A., 136

Qin, Y., 285
Quadflieg, N., 411
Quadrel, M. J., 376
Quigley, A. M., 330
Quigley, K. S., 438

Rabin, B. S., 471
Rachlin, H., 293
Rachman, S. J., 599, 602
Rae, D. S., 596
Rahe, R., 461
Raine, A., 454
Rainville, P., 174
Rapp, P. E., 441
Rasmussen, T., 94
Rasputin, G., 529
Raudenbush, B., 409
Raven, J. C., 323
Ravussin, E., 407
Rawlings, R,, 455
Rawlings, R., 631
Rayner, K., 310
Rayner, R., 596–7
Raz, M., 530
Read, D., 261
Read, J. D., 134
Reber, A. S., 253
Rechtschaffen, A., 160, 162
Reddon, J. R., 455, 504
Redican, W. K., 446
Redd, W. H., 197
Reed, J. M., 251
Reed, T. E., 251
Reeves, A. G., 405
Regehr, G., 285
Regier, D. A., 596
Reichling, D. B., 125
Reid, K., 159
Reid, S., 135
Reilly, A. H., 429
Relkin, N. R., 303
Repacholi, B., 374
Repnow, M., 143
Rescorla, R. A., 202
Ressler, K. J., 128
Rest, J., 365
Restle, F., 150
Rettek, S. I., 446
Reuter, P., 612
Reznick, J. S., 383
Reznikoff, M., 509
Rhee, S. H., 238
Rhue, J. W., 178
Riad, J. K, 455
Ribeiro-da-Silva, A., 82
Ricaurte, G. A., 181
Rice, M. E., 457
Rich, C. L., 623

Subject and Glossary Index

AA. *See* Alcoholics Anonymous

absolute threshold sensory threshold at a time of maximum dark adaptation, 133

accidents, industrial, 159

accommodation Piaget's term for the modification of an established schema to fit new objects, 355

accommodation of lens adjustment of the thickness of the lens in order to focus on objects at different distances, 106

acculturation transition from feeling part of the culture of one's original country to the culture of one's adopted country, 387–88

acetaldehyde, 610

achievement, need for striving for accomplishment and excellence, 425–31
   in childhood, 428
   encouraging in jobs, 429–30
   motivation and, 425–26
   setting goals and, 426–28
   sex differences in, 428–29
   needs, hierarchy of, 397–98

acquired immune deficiency syndrome (AIDS) disease often transmitted sexually that gradually destroys the body's immune system, 417–18

acquisition process by which a conditioned response is established or strengthened, 198

ACT. *See* American College Test

action potential an excitation that travels an axon at a constant strength, no matter how far it must travel, 77–78, 79

activation-synthesis theory of dreams theory that parts of the brain are spontaneously activated during REM sleep and that a dream is the brain's attempt to synthesize that activation into a coherent pattern, 167

actor-observer effect tendency to attribute internal causes more to other people's behavior than to one's own behavior, 521

ADD. *See* attention-deficit disorder

addiction self-destructive habit that someone finds difficult or impossible to quit. *See* drug abuse/addiction

Addiction, Web of web site, 187

Adler, Alfred, Institute of San Francisco, 496

adolescence, 362–365, 375–76

adopted children
   depression and, 615
   IQ scores and, 336, 338–39
   personality studies, 500
   schizophrenia and, 630, 632
   twins, 67–68

African Americans
   alcohol use, 182–83
   death penalty, 525–27
   divorce, 384–85
   IQ testing, 334, 338–39
   in psychology, 14

stereotypes, 518
   testing abilities of, 518

afterimage. *See* negative afterimage

age and behavior. *See also* development; old age
   alcohol use, 608
   amnesia, 254–55
   brain anatomy, 96
   depression, 614
   "morning/evening people," 158
   need for achievement and, 428–29
   personality traits and, 499
   phobias, 596, 597
   schizophrenia, 626, 629
   sleep needs, 158, 165
   study group cohorts, 369
   thought processes, 354–57

age regression, 28

aggressive behavior. *See also* violence
   in children after a divorce, 384–85
   factors eliciting, 453
   imitation and, 222
   males and, 65, 453
   sex differences and, 30, 385
   television violence and, 29–20, 37–38, 47–48, 222
   web site on, 458

agoraphobia excessive fear of open places or public places, 594–95

agreeableness tendency to be compassionate toward others and not antagonistic, 499

AIDS. *See* acquired immune deficiency syndrome

alarm first stage of response to stress, a brief period of high arousal of the sympathetic nervous system, readying the body for vigorous activity, 459–60

alcohol class of molecules that includes ethanol, methanol, propyl alcohol (rubbing alcohols), and others
   effects of, 181, 182, 187
   GABA synapse and, 181
   rape and, 457
   tolerance to, 182–83, 186
   violent behavior and, 455, 457

alcohol abuse. *See* alcoholism

Alcoholics Anonymous (AA) self-help group of people who are trying to abstain from alcohol use and to help others do the same, 470, 577, 609

alcoholism habitual overuse of alcohol
   amnestic disorder, 251–52
   causes/predisposition, 182–83, 606–608
   controlled drinking and, 611
   disease concept of, 610–11
   effects of, 182–183
   fetal anomalies and, 182, 346–47
   genetics and family, 607–8
   Korsakoff's syndrome and, 251–52

Theme Index

APPLIED PSYCHOLOGY

CONTROVERSIAL TOPICS

CULTURAL AND ETHNIC INFLUENCES

EVALUATION OF EVIDENCE AND QUESTIONING ASSERTIONS

NATURE/NURTURE

SEX AND GENDER INFLUENCES

WHAT'S THE EVIDENCE

FOR STUDENTS *(continued)*

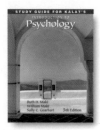

Study Guide

by Ruth H. Maki, William Maki, and Sally C. Gearhart (ISBN: 0-534-35910-8)
The Study Guide contains chapter objectives, a comprehensive check with answers and explorations, lecture material, short answer-essay questions with answers, post-test with answers, and multiple-choice questions with answers.

Electronic Study Guide

by Ruth H. Maki, William Maki, and Sally C. Gearhart
Macintosh® (ISBN: 0-534-36243-5); Windows® (ISBN: 0-534-36242-7)
Electronic version of printed Study Guide.

SUPPLEMENTAL READINGS AND SELECTIONS

NEW!
Psychology Resources on the World Wide Web

by Edward P. Kardas (ISBN: 0-534-35941-8)
This handy, concise guide to psychology-related resources available via the World Wide Web is organized by topic, and is designed to serve as a directory for students who may be conducting research via the Internet. As the use of technology in education continues to grow, instructors in all disciplines—psychology included—are looking for ways to incorporate Web resources into their classes. Ed Kardas presents an up-to-date, comprehensive book that is organized topically (similar to that of a typical introductory psychology text) and includes a chapter on how to perform research on the Web.

NEW!
College Survival Guide: Hints and References to Aid College Students

by Bruce M. Rowe (ISBN: 0-534-35569-2)
This Fourth Edition of Bruce Rowe's guide is designed to help students succeed and gives practical information that students usually have to pick up on their own. Tips include how to finance an education, how to manage time, how to study for and take exams, and more. Other sections focus on maintaining concentration, credit through examination, use of the credit/no credit option, cooperative education, and the importance of a liberal arts education.

Critical Thinking in Psychology: A Unified Skills Approach

by D. Alan Bensley (ISBN: 0-534-25620-1)
This book presents students with fascinating questions that pique interest and inspire them to think more effectively. All exercises are designed to teach a variety of skills that support inquiry in psychology using a single critical thinking model and vocabulary.

Culture and Modern Life

by David Matsumoto (ISBN: 0-534-85421-4)
David Matsumoto's book is designed to help students appreciate how cultural factors moderate psychological processes and how the viewpoint of one's own culture can distort one's interpretation of the behavior of people from other cultures. At the same time, the book stresses that behavioral phenomena are characterized by both cross-cultural similarities and differences in psychology, communication, work, and health.